THE ROAD, THE RIDE, & YOU

CONTENTS

From the seat of your Harley®, hug the shoulders along the Chief Joseph Scenic Byway in Wyoming. Pause along the bluffs in Iowa that line the Great River Road on the Mississippi River. Experience the grandeur of wind-blown waves through Nebraska's tallgrass prairie or embrace the nation's history in the White Mountain National Forest of New Hampshire.

On any of the 25 rides featured inside this first edition of the **Harley-Davidson®** *Ride Atlas of North America*, there are moments and vistas that will take your breath away.

HARLEY-DAVIDSON®
OFFICIAL LICENSED PRODUCT

We care about you. When riding your Harley-Davidson motorcycle be sure to ride safely, respectfully and within the limits of the law and your abilities. Always wear an approved helmet, proper eyewear and protective clothing and insist your passenger does too. Never ride while under the influence of alcohol or drugs. Know your Harley® and read and understand your owner's manual from cover to cover.

Sign up for a Harley-Davidson Rider's Edge® New Rider Course (call 1-800-588-2743 for a course near you) or Motorcycle Safety Foundation rider course (call 1-800-446-9227 for a course near you).

Protect your privilege to ride by joining the American Motorcyclist Association. Visit www.ama.cycle.org for more information.

RAND MCNALLY

TELL US
WHAT YOU THINK
COMMENT CARD ON THE LAST PAGE

Harley-Davidson® *Ride Atlas of North America*
1st Edition U.S./Canada/Mexico
© 2006 H-D. All rights reserved
© 2006 Rand McNally & Company. All rights reserved
Harley-Davidson, Harley, H-D, the Bar & Shield logo and others are among the trademarks of H-D Michigan, Inc. Manufactured by Rand McNally under license from Harley-Davidson Motor Company

The Harley-Davidson® dealer locations shown on the maps are accurate as of the printing date of the Ride Atlas. For additional help in locating a dealer in the United States or Canada, call the Harley-Davidson® Information Center at 1-800-443-2153 from 6 am to midnight (CST), seven days a week. Or visit our Web site at www.harley-davidson.com to find a nearby dealer.

HARLEY-DAVIDSON® RIDE ATLAS OF NORTH AMERICA

2ND FOLD LINE

BUSINESS REPLY MAIL
FIRST-CLASS MAIL   PERMIT NO. 388   CHICAGO IL

POSTAGE WILL BE PAID BY ADDRESSEE

RAND MCNALLY
CONSUMER AFFAIRS
PO BOX 7600
CHICAGO IL 60680-9915

NO POSTAGE
NECESSARY
IF MAILED
IN THE
UNITED STATES

 **RAND McNALLY**

The most trusted name on the map.

⊕ RAND MᶜNALLY

Thank you for purchasing the Harley-Davidson® *Ride Atlas of North America* from Rand McNally.

Please complete the information below so we will be able to serve you better. You can also e-mail your comments to: consumeraffairs@randmcnally.com. Please refer to the *Ride Atlas of North America* in your correspondence. (This information is for internal use ONLY and will NOT be distributed or sold to any external third party).

City/State/ZIP_____   E-mail address _____

Where did you purchase the Ride Atlas of North America? (store & location) _____

How often do you use the Ride Atlas?   ☐ Weekly   ☐ Twice a month   ☐ Monthly   ☐ Every few months   ☐ Never

For what do you use the Ride Atlas?   ☐ Planning   ☐ On-the-road navigation   ☐ Both   ☐ Coordinate group rides

☐ Other (Please explain) _____
_____

On a scale of 1 to 7, with 1 being extremely helpful and 7 being extremely unhelpful, how helpful were the 25 suggested rides?
(Please circle.)   1   2   3   4   5   6   7

On a scale of 1 to 7, with 1 being extremely clear and 7 being extremely unclear, how clear was the map page information?
(Please circle.)   1   2   3   4   5   6   7

What do you look for when planning a ride? _____
_____

What information would you add/change in the Ride Atlas to better meet your needs? _____
_____

Where else do you look for ride information? _____
_____

What motorcycle publications do you read?   ☐ American Motorcyclist   ☐ Cycle World   ☐ Enthusiast   ☐ American Iron
☐ Motorcyclist   ☐ Other _____

What is the average length of your rides?   ☐ Day trip   ☐ 1 night   ☐ 2 nights   ☐ 3+ nights

Are you likely to buy updated versions of the Ride Atlas?   ☐ Yes   ☐ No   ☐ Unsure

Would you recommend the Ride Atlas to someone else?   ☐ Yes   ☐ No   ☐ Unsure

Please provide any additional comments and suggestions you have. _____
_____

Age group   ☐ 18-27   ☐ 28-37   ☐ 38-47   ☐ 48-57   ☐ 58+
Sex: ☐ Female   ☐ Male

Total Household Income: ☐ $40,000 & below   ☐ $41,000 to $65,000   ☐ $66,000 to $80,000
☐ $80,000 to $100,000   ☐ $100,000 and above

Occupation: ☐ Full-Time   ☐ Part-Time   ☐ Retired   ☐ Unemployed

Would you like to receive information about updated editions and special offers from Rand McNally?   ☐ Yes   ☐ No

Would you be interested in participating in future Ride Atlas opinion surveys?   ☐ Yes   ☐ No

THANK YOU FOR YOUR INPUT.

$34.95
ISBN 0-528-93515-1

UPC

0 70609 93515 7

CUT ALONG DOTTED LINE

CUT ALONG DOTTED LINE

HOW TO USE THE RIDE ATLAS

The sights, sounds, and seasons of the road . . . The Ride Atlas has just the right balance of information you need for a road trip without cluttering the page. Not only can you navigate the 25 selected rides, you can create your own with the information included throughout this atlas.

❶ MOTORCYCLE LAWS
An exclusive snapshot of state laws affecting motorcycle use including helmet law, riding two abreast, eye protection, and speed limits.

❷ STATE RESOURCE INFORMATION
Road conditions, construction updates, highway emergency numbers, tourism information, and state motor vehicle information are easily accessed with this handy reference.

❸ HARLEY-DAVIDSON® DEALERSHIPS
The Harley-Davidson logo easily identifies the Harley-Davidson® dealers on the state maps. Check the map page listings for location including latitude and longitude.

❹ POINT-TO-POINT MILEAGES
Red numbers along the highways on maps represent mileage between red arrowheads.

The black numbers indicate mileage between intersections.

Only Rand McNally provides these mileages on maps. A handy mileage and driving times map is featured on page 320.

ROADS AND HIGHWAYS
Scenic routes are highlighted with light green ribbons, and construction zones are marked with orange-and-yellow stripes. For an explanation of other map symbols, see the symbols legend on each state map page or the legend on page 5.

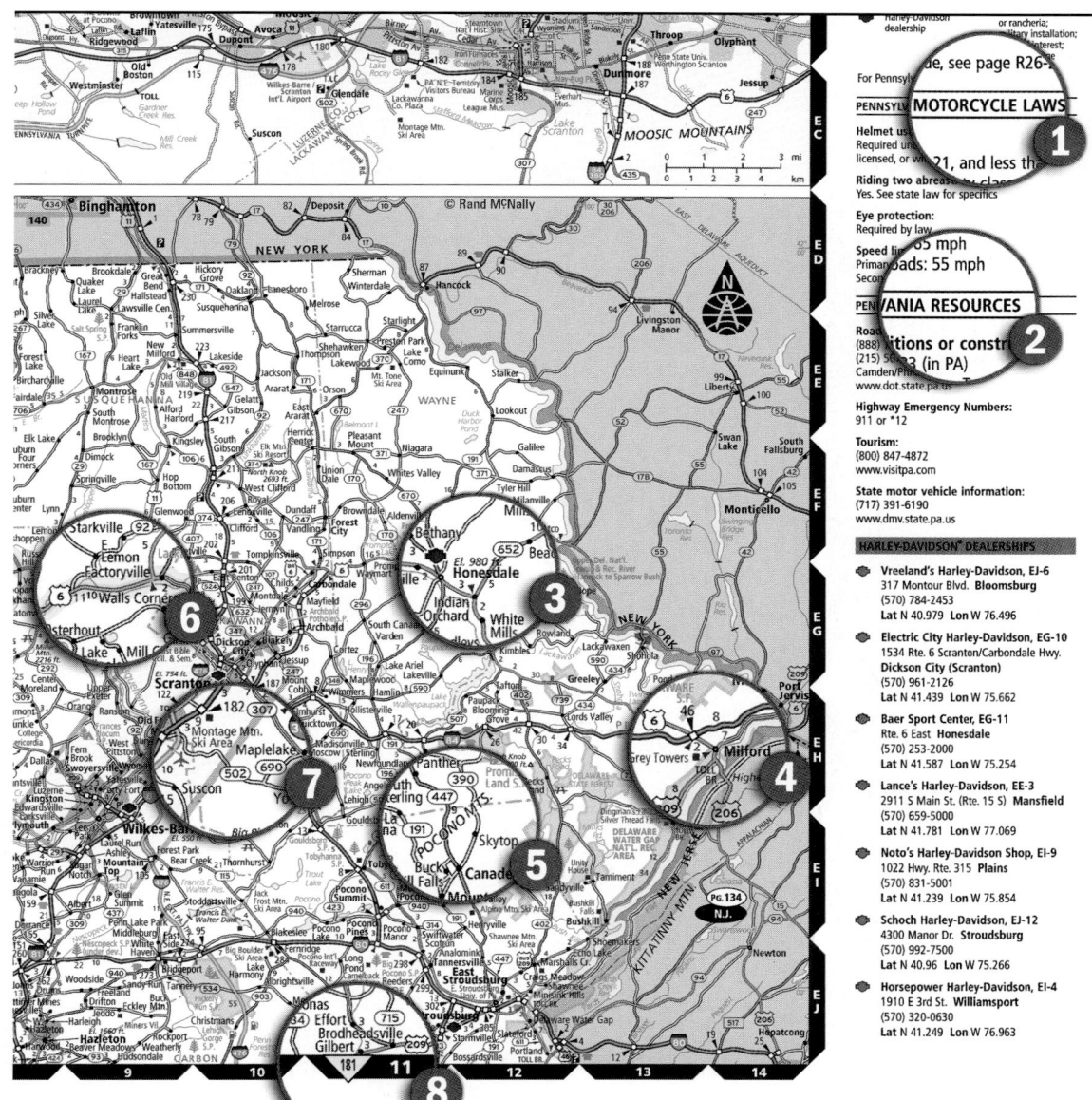

❺ UNIQUE ROAD HIERARCHY
Follow back roads more easily with prominent secondary road coloration and designated symbols. These color-cased roads stand out on backgrounds and patterns, but take a step back when you need to read the names.

❻ FEATURED RIDE
On the map pages of the states featuring rides, the route is highlighted in yellow. Detailed information on each ride is found within the "Guide to Rides and Resources" section.

❼ INSET MAP INDICATORS
Pale yellow boxes indicate that a larger scale inset map is provided. If the inset map appears on a different page, the page number is shown in a small box. **52**

❽ CONTINUATION ARROWS
The page number of the continuing map appears in a small yellow triangle at the map's edge. Use the arrow to position the page in view with the continuation page.

ARIZONA

STATE MAP AND RIDE – P. 16

ROUTE LENGTH – 190.6 miles or 5+ hours nonstop

TOURING INFORMATION

This ride starts in Ash Fork, a town that burned to the ground not once, but twice. The road that leads from this small Phoenix has been reborn even more times: Route 66. The ride takes you through former tourist stops across the northern Arizona plateau and provides a flavor of the road made famous in books, movies, television, and song.

Take a side trip east on Route 66 from Ash Fork to Winslow, where a bronze statue commemorates the lyrics in the Eagles classic "Take It Easy." The statue called "Standing on a Corner in Winslow, Arizona" is located at Kinsley and Second Streets — an ideal spot for a photo with your bike.

VISITOR INFORMATION

www.arizonaguide.com | 866-239-9712

PULL OVER

Prescott National Forest
Ranger Headquarters | 344 S. Cortez | Prescott
928-443-8000
This national forest features a wide variety of plants, from cactus to ponderosa pines. Numerous hiking trails, camping, and fishing are available. With the exception of group camp-grounds, campsites are available on a first-come, first-served basis.

Grand Canyon Caverns
Peach Springs | 928-422-3223
A privately owned development on the northern Arizona plateau includes a dry cavern 210 feet below the surface.

Hackberry General Store, Hackberry

Best season to ride:	Spring or autumn, as the heat is challenging in the summer
Gasoline availability:	Plan ahead
About the road:	This is the longest uninterrupted stretch of legendary Route 66. In some stretches, it is quite remote.
Insider tip:	Between Sitgreaves Pass (3,652 ft.) and Oatman, the route is closed to vehicles of a certain wheel length, so you won't see many RVs.

Most of Route 66 was dug up when Interstate 40 crossed Arizona, but you can find remnants of its past on the old road along with spectacular desert scenery, including canyons and caverns, gold mines, and ghost towns. The longest undisturbed stretch of Route 66 heads west out of Ash Fork . . . and so does the cool, high desert weather. Call ahead before heading out, as the weather changes quickly.

In Seligman, an oversized cutout of a bellman greets visitors at the Snow Cap Drive-In, a Mother Road landmark that still serves burgers and ice cream.

Near Peach Springs, the Grand Canyon Caverns development boasts an elevator that descends 21 stories into the earth to a series of limestone caverns formed millions of years ago. Take five or more at the nearby Hualapai Lodge, operated by the Hualapai tribe, where there is a selection of restaurants.

In Kingman, the Mohave Museum of History of Arts honors native son and former cowboy movie star Andy Devine. You can see wagon ruts left by the first pioneers at the White Cliffs historic site. Kingman also serves as a central location for the numerous ghost towns that dot the surrounding mountainsides. Some, like Mineral Park and Goldroad, offer little more than crumbling foundations, while others, like Oatman and Chloride, still maintain small populations of hardy hangers-on.

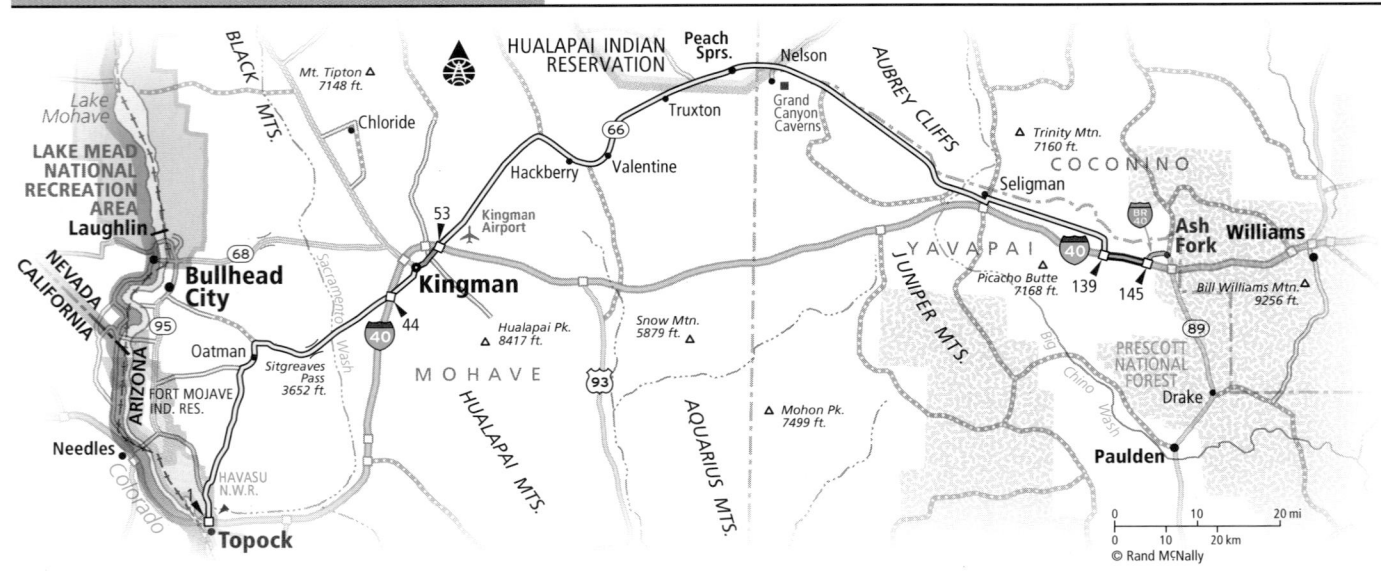

ARKANSAS

STATE MAP AND RIDE – P. 22

TOURING INFORMATION

This ride starts and ends in historic Eureka Springs. The loop twists and winds its way along state highways 23, 16, and 21 through spectacular turns on paved roads.

Take a side trip in the White Rock Wildlife Management Area. Ride southwest to White Rock Mountain for awesome views of the mixed hardwood forest, great hiking opportunities, camping, and access to the Ozark Highlands Hiking Trail.

Route 16 skirts the White Rock Wildlife Management area and connects with Route 21 in the Ozark National Forest. Be vigilant for deer, elk, and even bear sightings.

VISITOR INFORMATION

www.arkansas.com | 800-628-8725

PULL OVER

Two Dumb Dames Fudge Factory
33 S. Main St. | Eureka Springs | 479-253-7268
This small confectionary offers an exclusive selection of sweets, including what locals call the best fudge in town. From smooth marble to nutty pecan, the recipes are based on family favorites. The shop is located in the historic district; parking in one of the town's public lots is recommended.

Buffalo National River
Pruitt Ranger Station | Hwy. 7 | Jasper | 870-446-5373
The Buffalo National River winds 135 miles through ancient Ozark mountains in the upper Ponca wilderness. Home to elk, black bears, whitetail deer, and numerous songbirds, the area attracts people watching for wildlife as they canoe or float the meandering river. A number of outfitters rent canoes in Ponca. Hikers can tackle the challenging switchbacks of the Boxley River Trail as it zigzags 37 miles past former homesteads and scenic river overlooks.

Onyx Cave
Route 4 | near Eureka Springs | 479-253-9321
Go underground for an afternoon on a self-guided tour through formations of stalactites and stalagmites that form silhouettes called Witches' Fireplace, the Lion's Head, and the Friendly Dragon. Visitors on the self-guided tour are issued headsets and helmets with headlights. The cave opened in 1893 and is considered the oldest in Arkansas.

ROUTE LENGTH – 141.8 Miles or 4+ hours nonstop

Thorncrown Chapel is an architectural gem nestled in the dense woods near Eureka Springs.

Best season to ride: Fall, when the verdant mountain tops of summer turn crimson
Gasoline availability: Plentiful
About the road: Twisting, climbing two-lane road riddled with switchbacks
Insider tip: Take your time and enjoy the ride. Watch for slower vehicles.

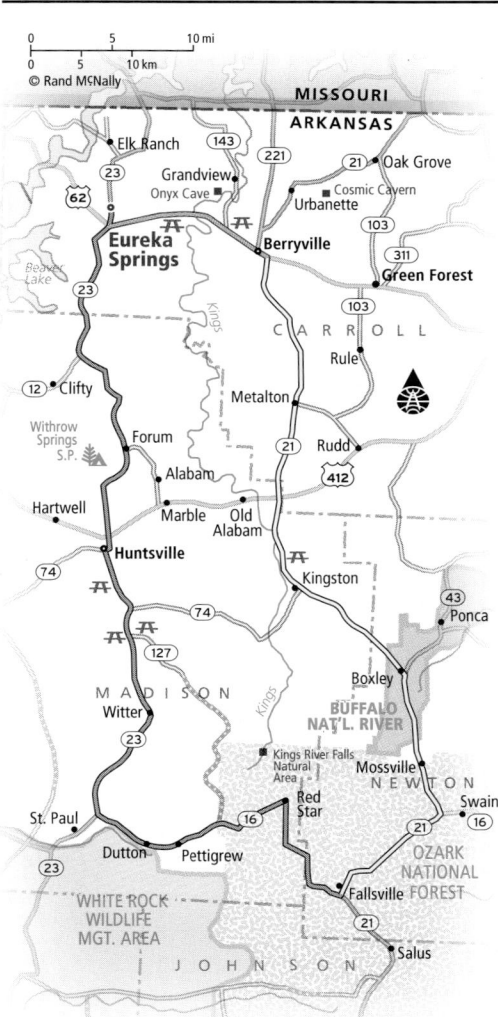

In northwestern Arkansas, there are switchbacks so sharp you'll be able to see your own taillights when you lean into a turn. Stop for a while in one of the hamlets to share a few tales with the locals, or try your hand at fishing in any of the major lakes that anchor the area. The Ozark National Forest, more than 1 million acres big, has springs so clear you can count the whiskers on a catfish.

At any time of the year, the Eureka Springs area probably has a festival going on. It might be the annual Ozark UFO Conference in April, the Native American Pow Wow or Blues Eureka Springs Festival in June, or the acclaimed Ozark Opera Festival in late summer. If you go in September, you'll have to share the road with other legendary vehicles during the annual Corvette Weekend.

Looking more like turn-of-the-century San Francisco with its painted lady residences, Eureka Springs offers a variety of lodging including many bed-and-breakfasts.

CALIFORNIA

STATE MAP AND RIDE – P. 24

TOURING INFORMATION

The alpine landscape on either side of CA 44 and 89 doesn't disappoint. Both roads meander from one national forest to another.

Stay a while in the Lassen Volcanic National Park, near Mineral. Besides the access trails leading to various thermal areas such as Devils Kitchen and Boiling Springs Lake and the unique volcanic and geological features of the park, there are flora and fauna to see. Activities such as stargazing, backcountry hiking, camping, and wildlife watching provide a peek into the dynamics of this living volcanic laboratory. You can see examples of almost every volcanic feature here at Lassen, including cinder cones, sulfur vents, lava flows and pinnacles, hot springs, fumaroles, and mud pots. Stop by park headquarters in Mineral or one of the two visitor contact stations inside the park to acquaint yourself with its terrain and check out the daily activity schedule in the summer. Pick up a guide for the main park road. Along the way, take time to stop and wander through the thermal features of Bumpass Hell, or view the "Devastated Area" from one of the many turnouts.

Along this route there is always moderate traffic, including commercial traffic.

VISITOR INFORMATION

www.visitcalifornia.com | 916-444-4429

PULL OVER

Shasta Trinity National Forest
3644 Avtech Parkway | Redding | 530-226-2500
Drive the Trinity Heritage Scenic Byway to see beautiful vistas and pristine mountain lakes in the largest national forest in California. The immense Mt. Shasta, at 14,162 feet, is the second-highest slumbering volcano in the United States. Fish in 6,278 miles of streams, hike the many trails, and enjoy the scenery at this outdoor gem.

McArthur Burney Falls Memorial State Park
Near Burney | 916-653-6995
One hundred million gallons of strikingly clear water flow over the spectacular 129-foot falls at this park every day. A hurried visitor can get an inspiring glimpse of the falls in a few minutes. The park's other claim to fame? Appearing in movies including *Willow* and *Stand by Me*.

ROUTE LENGTH – 210 miles or 4+ hours nonstop

Bumpass Hell, Lassen Volcanic National Park, near Highway 44

Best season to ride:	Summer recommended (due to seasonal road closures)
Gasoline availability:	Adequate
About the road:	Two-lane road with moderate traffic
Insider tip:	Watch for logging trucks

This journey through the Cascade Range is all about the ride. The road curves and twists before gradually ascending to reveal a panorama of trees, emerald lakes, clear streams, and wildlife. It is a place of dense virgin forest, clear lakes, swift streams, and open spaces, all comprising rich wildlife habitat. Mule and black-tail deer are abundant in the foothills and mountains. The forests, streams, and meadows surrounding McCloud offer excellent opportunities for summer bird watching.

Hiking, fishing, and camping abound within the Caribou Wilderness Area of Lassen National Forest. It occupies a 20,000-acre, gently rolling plateau where more than 20 forest-fringed lakes support brook, brown, and rainbow trout.

Find sailing and water skiing on Big Lake and mountain biking on a network of logging trails. Tour Hat Creek Observatory and the Crystal Lake Fish Hatchery. Explore Subway Cave, formed 20,000 years ago from flowing lava.

Local outfitters can arrange white-water rafting trips, horseback riding, and fly-fishing expeditions. Find photo ops at McArthur-Burney waterfalls and the 1886 Glenburn Church near Fall River Mills.

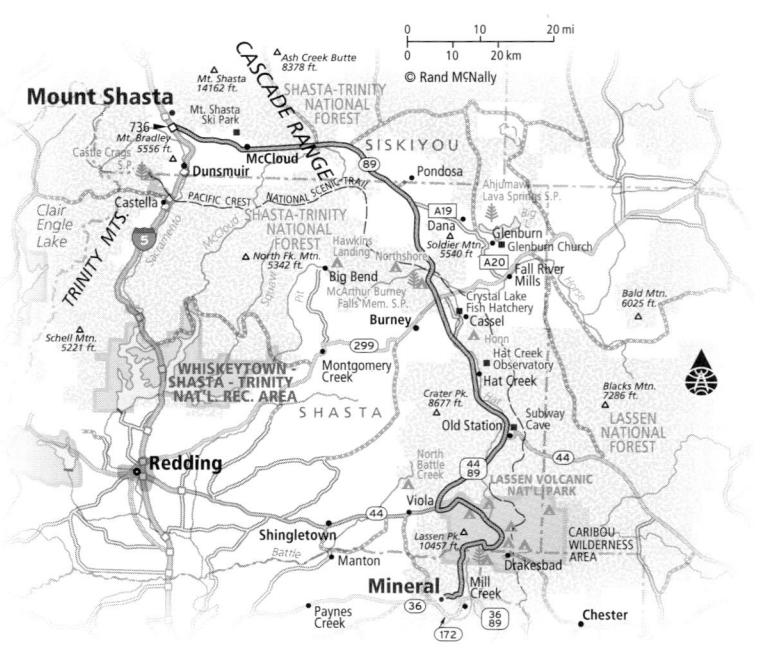

COLORADO

STATE MAP – P. 40, RIDE – P. 41

TOURING INFORMATION

Start in Durango and ride toward the only place in the United States where four states meet. Here the state lines of Colorado, New Mexico, Arizona, and Utah converge at a common point called the Four Corners. There are plenty of whispering pines and aspens along the way. In the spring, wildflowers, many from the sunflower family, dance along the roadway.

Take a side trip through the San Juan National Forest to Ridgway for an overnight at Ridgway State Park. It offers a full experience of Colorado's great outdoors and has a sandy swim beach, beach house, and full-service marina, making it a top choice for water-sports enthusiasts. In nearby Ouray, the Ouray Hot Springs provide a great way to unwind and relax after a day's ride.

When you ride at this high elevation, weather is always a factor. Watch for temperature changes and sudden summer thunderstorms. Pack accordingly.

VISITOR INFORMATION

www.colorado.com | 800-265-6723

PULL OVER

Mesa Verde National Park
Near Cortez | 970-529-4465
These cliff dwellings were once occupied by 24 Indian tribes of the Pueblo Indians of New Mexico, the Hopi Tribe of Arizona, and the Ute and Navajo peoples. Mesa Verde Park rangers lead memorable tours of several dwellings. Cliff Palace, Balcony House, and Spruce Tree are among the most popular.

Anasazi Heritage Center
27501 Highway 184 | Three miles west of Dolores
970-882-4811
The center houses a museum dedicated exclusively to the study and interpretation of prehistoric Native American culture. The museum features a variety of learning experiences designed to give visitors a look at how the Ancestral Puebloan lived. Some examples: hands-on exhibits for weaving and grinding corn, as well as lectures, films, cultural activities, demonstrations, and special exhibits. Walk around the Escalante Pueblo. Twenty rooms and a kiva (a underground ceremonial room) have been partially excavated.

ROUTE LENGTH – 105 miles or 2+ hours nonstop

Point Lookout in the winter, Mesa Verde National Park

Best season to ride:	Summer to autumn
Gasoline availability:	Adequate
About the road:	Two-lane highway
Insider tip:	Watch the weather and the traffic near Mesa Verde National Park

Colorado has a reputation for laid-back friendliness. Everyone is on the move, but no one hurries. Biking, skiing, hiking, and boating are only a few of the things to do in this Rocky Mountain paradise, where grassy meadows build up to stubbly mesas before dropping into deep stone canyons.

If you've ever seen a Hollywood western, you've seen bits and pieces of Durango. This town on Route 160 relishes its Wild West roots. Take in an old-fashioned play at the Diamond Circle Melodrama & Vaudeville, or go for a ride on the Durango & Silverton Narrow Gauge Railroad featuring steam-powered iron horses. The views are spectacular.

Leaving Durango, you'll head toward the town of Mancos. In Mancos, you can ride on a real stagecoach. At Bartel's Mancos Valley Stage Line, you can sign up for a lunch or dinner excursion. Ask to ride on top with the driver.

Further on is Cortez, home of the Crow Canyon Archaeological Center. At the Center you can join a dig and learn about the civilizations that flourished in this area as early as A.D. 700. Leaving Cortez, you'll ride through the Ute Mountain Ute Indian Reservation on your way to Four Corners.

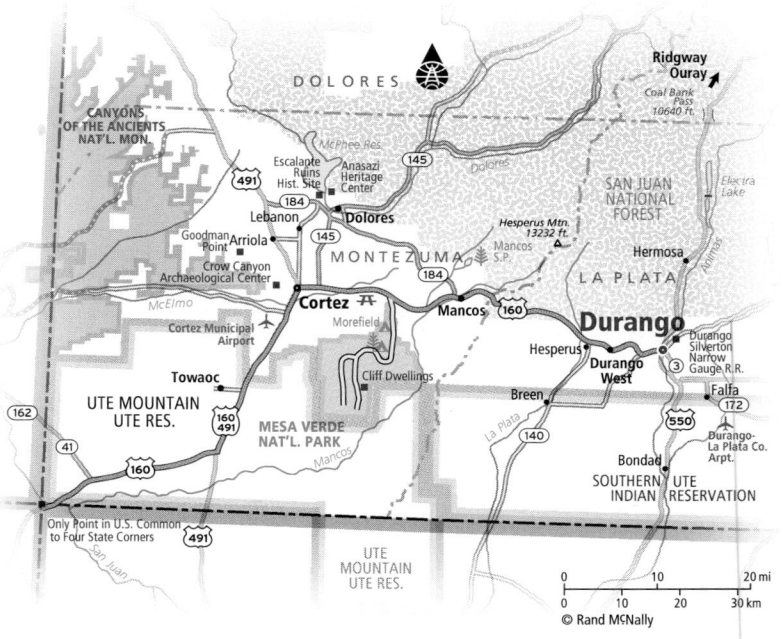
© Rand McNally

GEORGIA

STATE MAP AND RIDE – P. 58

TOURING INFORMATION

Take GA 60 into Dahlonega. Continue on US 19/GA 60 to Suches. Turn onto GA 180 to Vogel State Park — a great curvy road. Stay on 180 until it connects with GA 348, which will take you toward Helen. From there, use GA 75 (not the alternate) to Cleveland and then take GA 115/52 to Long Branch Road. Long Branch Road puts you at the beginning of GA 400.

Take a side trip to Brasstown Bald. At 4,784 feet, it is the highest point in Georgia. Located between Robertstown and Blairsville off Georgia Spur 180, the Chattahoochee National Forest offers spectacular views. If the day is clear, you may see beyond Georgia to Tennessee, North Carolina, and even South Carolina.

For a rugged rollercoaster ride, this roundtrip from Dahlonega through the foothills of the Blue Ridge Mountains is sure to challenge the best you've got to offer. Some of the descents are technically challenging, and the ascents are breathtaking. The ingredients for a perfect ride are here — steep twisting mountain roads, lots of tight curves, well-maintained roadways, little commercial traffic, great scenery, amenities along the way, friendly folks, and interesting places to stop.

VISITOR INFORMATION

www.georgiaonmymind.org | 800-847-4842

PULL OVER

Dahlonega Gold Museum Historic Site
#1 Public Square | Dahlonega | 706-864-2257
At the Dahlonega Gold Museum Historic Site, learn that the first gold rush wasn't in 1849 in California but 20 years earlier in Georgia. Thousands of gold seekers came to Dahlonega and Auraria between 1828 and 1861 after hearing gold had been discovered on Cherokee Nation land. More than $6 million in gold from this area was coined by the U.S. mint. Visitors can learn about the life of a prospector and how to pan for gold. A five-ounce gold nugget is on display.

Smithgall Woods Conservation Area and Lodge
61 Tsalaki Trail | Helen | 706-878-3087
In 1994, noted conservationist and businessman Charles A. Smithgall Jr. donated this beautiful mountain retreat lodge and five cottages so visitors could enjoy a nature experience. Dukes Creek runs through the property, where the park offers catch-and-release trout fishing. Enjoy a hike or unpack the camera to capture the views.

ROUTE LENGTH – 105 miles or 2+ hours nonstop

Dawn, Chattahoochee National Forest

Best season to ride: Spring through fall
Gasoline availability: Adequate
About the road: Two-lane, twisty road
Insider tip: This ride in north Georgia is peppered with small towns.

This 105-mile ride through the North Georgia mountains is exhilarating and relaxing at the same time. The rural two-lane roads pass through the Chattahoochee National Forest with miles of thick woods, many waterfalls, and cascading mountain streams. There are also warm-water lakes and fishing ponds. South of Suches, the road crosses the historic Appalachian Trail, where you can park and walk for a bit. Suches also has the intriguing nickname of "The Valley above the Clouds." Stop for a look and you'll see why.

The ride covers big peaks and small towns such as Dahlonega, site of the famous gold rush, and Helen, an Alpine village with cobblestone streets and plenty of oom-pah music venues.

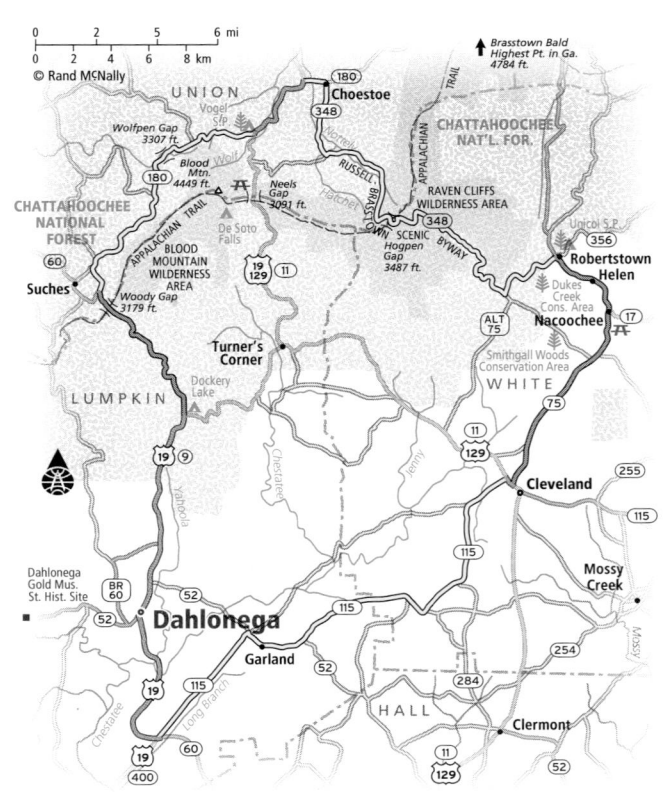

IDAHO/MONTANA

STATE MAP AND RIDE – P. 64

TOURING INFORMATION

From Kooskia, Idaho, to the Montana state line, Hwy. 12 parallels the largest wilderness area in the lower 48 states.

Be cognizant of fuel — services are extremely limited. Partial services are available in a few towns between Spalding and Powell. According to Idaho Scenic Byways, only limited services are available for approximately 85 miles on this route.

Enjoy the pull-outs along this route, as the jaw-dropping scenery in the panhandle of Idaho will make every moment worth it. Alpine forests, bubbling mountain streams, high canyon walls, and imposing rock faces await. Be aware that parts of this road look like a child's doodling — with many squiggles and twists.

VISITOR INFORMATION

www.visitid.org | 800-847-4843

PULL OVER

Lochsa Historic Ranger Station
Route One | Kooskia | 208-926-4274
Built from native materials with simple tools, this 1920s Forest Service Ranger Station is a fine example of construction in a remote area. The station is listed on the National Register of Historic Places.

Nez Perce National Historical Park
39063 US 95 | Spalding | 208-843-2261
Learn about the history of the Nez Perce Indians and their sacred land in Idaho, Montana, Oregon, and Washington. For more information about this fascinating group, view the artifacts and a 20-minute film at the visitor center.

ROUTE LENGTH – 217.8 miles or 4+ hours nonstop

The Clearwater River winds along U.S. 12, east of Orofino

Best season to ride:	Summer
Gasoline availability:	Plan ahead
About the road:	Two-lane road skirts over river and through canyon
Insider tip:	This area is home to melodious songbirds, elk herds, and roaming mountain lions.

Follow the route of Lewis and Clark across northern Idaho as history unfolds with help from roadside markers and interpretive displays. Running parallel is the Lolo Motorway, a winding, one-lane dirt road built by the Civilian Conservation Corps in the 1930s. It follows the ridge tops, tracing the route of the expedition more closely.

Keep an eye out for wildlife: Deer, moose, mountain goats, and bear are plentiful, as are pheasant and grouse.

Friendly communities all along the route offer chuckwagon breakfasts, barbecues, and rodeos. Activities range from white-water rafting and jet boating to visiting small historical museums that chronicle the Lewis and Clark expedition and the history of the Nez Perce tribe. Visit the 1862 courthouse at Pierce, oldest city in Idaho; photograph the large Winchester rifle replica that hangs above Main Street in its namesake town, Winchester.

Beautiful foothills surround Kamiah, nestled in a valley of the Clearwater River. The Nez Perce wintered here and fished for steelhead trout. Today, anglers cast for steelhead that can reach 45 inches in length and for hard-fighting Chinook salmon. Lewis and Clark, returning east, camped in the canyon for several weeks in 1806 while awaiting the spring thaw.

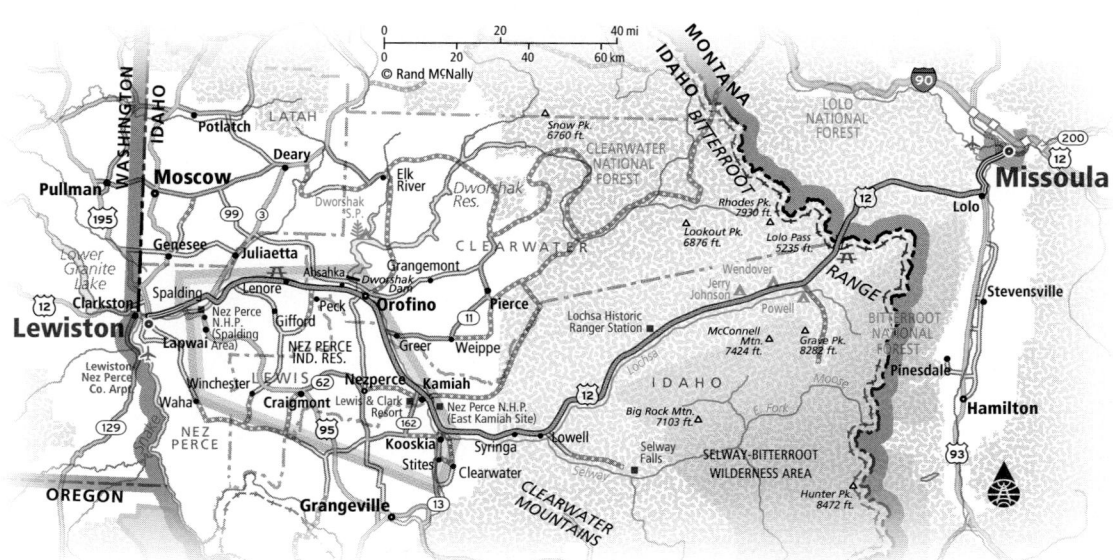

IOWA

STATE MAP – P. 78, RIDE – PP. 80-81

TOURING INFORMATION

The numbers change from US 61 to 67, then 52 to Iowa Hwy. 26, but the road remains the same. It is the Great River Road, identified from Minnesota to Louisiana with a road marker represented by a river pilot's wheel.

Take a side trip to Luxembourger Village in St. Donatus, located about 12 miles from Dubuque. Settled by Luxembourg immigrants, the village has 34 sites on the National Register of Historic Places.

The Great River Road stretches along the Mississippi River and follows the eastern edge of Iowa. The slow-moving Mississippi River meanders along with you as you ride its curves and bends. The rolling hills peak along bluff lines as you ride from one end of the state to the other.

Historians often refer to the Mississippi as America's first interstate. For commerce, it certainly filled that role as one of the great waterways along the western frontier. In the 19th century, its ships and barges carried raw materials and finished goods as well as passengers between the vast forests of the north and the wetlands along the Gulf of Mexico.

To merchants, manufacturers, and consumers alike, this great river still provides an avenue for business, expansion, and transportation. Following its route through Iowa, the Great River Road invites riders to share in that great journey.

VISITOR INFORMATION
www.traveliowa.com | 800-345-4692

ROUTE LENGTH – 325 miles – 2 to 3 days

View of Hanging Rock near Redfield

Best season to ride:	Autumn
Gasoline availability:	Plentiful
About this road:	One word for this primarily two-lane road? Slalom
Insider tip:	This is farm country. Be aware of slow-moving vehicles, and heed signage for deer.

Migrating eagles, ducks, and geese fly over limestone bluffs while commercial barges maneuver through the lock-and-dam system of the Mississippi River. All along the Great River Road that follows it you can enjoy the beauty of nature, learn a bit of history, and see commerce at work.

The 500-foot-high limestone bluff known as Pike's Peak, located near McGregor in a state park of the same name, is one of the highest points along the Mississippi River. Park your bike and take the hike; the view is worth it.

When the Great River Road curves away from the river, you'll pass pastures and farmland that stretch to the horizon. You are so close to the land that you can smell the alfalfa or freshly mowed hay. The landscape is replete with rolling countryside and dense wetlands. Along parts of the shoreline, water lilies may bloom; along inland areas, the scenery quickly changes as you roll through hills and bends. Many quaint villages and charming river towns dot this route. Be sure to build in time to enjoy one or two.

Just south of Burlington, for example, ride the double-decker swing bridge — motorcycles go up top — to Fort Madison, and you'll land next to an old state prison.

View from Fire Point at Effigy Mounds National Monument

PULL OVER

Effigy Mounds National Monument
151 Hwy. 76 | Harpers Ferry | 563-873-3491
Prehistoric mounds shaped to represent mammals, birds, and reptiles were created by ancient Native American cultures beginning around 500 B.C. The park has 11 miles of hiking trails. Park and walk — no roads exist in the park. Rangers give guided hikes and prehistoric tool demonstrations throughout the summer.

National Mississippi River Museum and Aquarium
350 E. Third St. | Dubuque | 563-557-9545
At this riverside complex, aquariums and exhibits re-create habitats of the Mississippi River. One is home to deep-channel denizens such as five-foot-long catfish or sturgeon. A virtual pilothouse allows you to guide the towboat and even blow a warning whistle. Parking is plentiful.

Port Louisa National Wildlife Refuge
10728 County Road X61 | Wapello | 319-523-6982
Part of the larger Mark Twain National Wildlife Refuge complex, Port Louisa was established for the protection of migratory birds including waterfowl, shorebirds, and song-birds. Located along the Mississippi Flyway, it lies on one of the major routes for migrating waterfowl.

George M. Verity Riverboat Museum
Johnson and Victory Park | 415 Blondeau | Keokuk
319-524-4765
This retired steam sternwheeler, now a museum, was one of the earliest paddlewheel barges on the Upper Mississippi.

KENTUCKY/TENNESSEE

STATE MAP – P. 86, RIDE – P. 87

ROUTE LENGTH – 50 miles or 2 hours with stops

TOURING INFORMATION

Be sure to fill the tank before leaving Grand Rivers for KY 253 to the Trace. Gasoline is available only at either side of the recreation area. KY 253 crosses the Kentucky Dam as it makes its way past old cemeteries and an abundance of trees, hills, and nature centers. The rolling hills, sweeping curves, and several twisties require varied speeds.

Take a side trip on I-24 to Paducah (about 25 miles from Grand Rivers), a major inland port that was named for the Padouca Indian tribe. The city is home to the Museum of the American Quilter's Society, where both antique and contemporary examples of the quilter's art are on display. The city's historic downtown is anchored by the Market House (1905), a cultural center containing a museum, theater, and art gallery. In the Market House Museum, you'll find the interior of an 1877 drugstore among other artifacts. Nearby, you can trace the city's evolution through murals painted on the riverfront floodwall. Native son Alben Barkley, who served as vice president under Harry Truman, is remembered at the museum bearing his name. If you have time, stop by the River Heritage Center, the Paducah Railroad Museum, and the trendy Lower Town Artists Studios and Galleries section of Paducah's Lower Town district.

During the summer months, be aware of increased traffic in the area, especially on weekends. Also, watch for wildlife, especially deer.

VISITOR INFORMATION
www.kentuckytourism.com | 800-225-8747

PULL OVER
Kentucky Dam Village State Resort Park
Gilbertsville | 800-325-0146
The combination of water and woods makes Kentucky Dam Village State Resort Park a wonderful destination for fishing, swimming, and boating. One of three state resort parks in the National Recreation Area, the dam was crucial to forming Lake Barkley and Kentucky Lake. Lodging and restaurants are available in the park.

Fort Donelson National Battlefield
120 Fort Donelson Rd | TN | 931-232-5706
Fort Donelson National Battlefield is located on the Cumberland River, close to the Kentucky border. The battlefield is the site of the first major Union victory during the Civil War. The centerpiece of Fort Donelson National Battlefield is a 15-acre earthen fort, now covered with grass.

Land Between the Lakes

Best season to ride:	Spring, summer, or autumn
Gasoline availability:	Plan ahead
About the road:	Speeds clearly identified, good pavement markings
Insider tip:	Due to free-range animals, motorcycles are not allowed in the Elk and Bison Prairie.

Ride through history as you follow "The Trace," named for ancient buffalo trails. It passes through prairieland where vast herds of elk and bison once grazed and hills that buckskin-clad frontiersman Daniel Boone trekked in 1795.

Explore the Land Between the Lakes, a sprawling peninsula created by damming the Tennessee and Cumberland rivers. It contains a 170,000-acre national recreation area, where Kentucky Lake and Lake Barkley offer 300 miles of undeveloped shoreline for fishing and boating. You'll find fiddle festivals, horseback riding, and virtually unlimited camping and canoeing.

Visit a re-created pioneer farmstead, home to rare Cotswold sheep (a breed that dates back to the Roman occupation of England), and admire gardens planted with heirloom vegetables. Catch a state-of-the-art sky show at Golden Pond Planetarium.

Park and hike a trail at the South Buffalo Range, home to a herd of up to 100 bison. Seasonal wildflowers including black-eyed Susans, brilliant orange butterfly weed, and red-blooming Indian paintbrush brighten the roadside. You'll see deer, wild turkey, and migratory songbirds such as ruby-throated warblers.

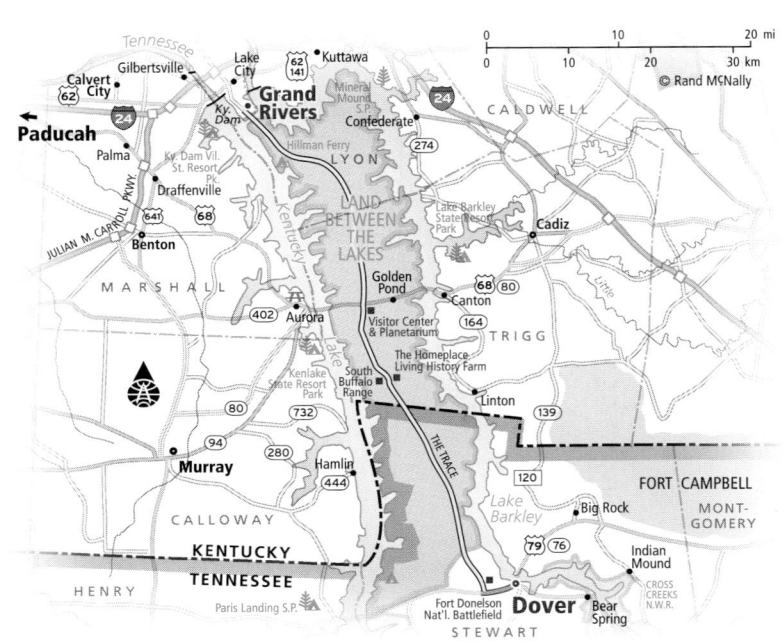

Fort Donelson National Battlefield, Dover, Tennessee

MASSACHUSETTS

STATE MAP – P. 98, RIDE - PP. 98 & 100

ROUTE LENGTH – 142.6 miles or 3+ hours nonstop

Pumping Station Covered Bridge, Greenfield

TOURING INFORMATION

This circuitous ride uses interstate highways, state highways, and roads to loop around the charming counties of Worcester, Franklin, and Hampshire in north central Massachusetts. Terrific scenery, small towns, and scenic farmlands flourish along this route.

Take a side trip to Amherst College in Amherst, where poets Emily Dickinson, Robert Frost, and Eugene Field lived. The town of Amherst is also the site of the University of Massachusetts and Hampshire College. At Amherst College, also take in the Mead Art Museum, which houses some 14,000 works acquired since 1839. It includes one of the nation's finest collegiate collections of American art and several virtual exhibitions.

This ride takes about half of a day, but stretch it out. There's so much to see and do. Stop, shop, and enjoy the journey. The Mohawk Trail offers a sense of history.

VISITOR INFORMATION

www.massvacation.com | 800-227-6277

PULL OVER

Higgins Armory Museum
100 Barber Ave. | Worcester | 508-853-6015
To view the largest collection of medieval and Renaissance armor on display in the Western Hemisphere, all in a Gothic castle setting, stop here. The founder, John Woodman Higgins, was a Worcester industrialist who spent a lifetime building his collection.

Quabbin Reservoir
485 Ware Rd. | Belchertown | 413-323-7221
The 412-billion gallon reservoir, one of the largest man-made reservoirs in the world, covers 39 square miles. Eighteen miles long with 181 miles of shoreline, it provides water for more than two million people. The visitor's center and the New Salem and Enfield lookouts offer great views of the reservoir.

Historic Deerfield
Off Rts. 5 & 10 | Deerfield | 413-775-7214
Considered one of the most beautiful streets in America, "The Street" is lined with 14 original homes preserved as museums displaying Deerfield history and culture and more than 25,000 objects made or used in America between 1650 and 1850.

Best season to ride:	Autumn
Gasoline availability:	Plentiful
Road conditions:	Two-lane roads, some winding, some hilly
Insider tip:	Be aware of wildlife, especially deer

Riding in Massachusetts is like traveling through history. You can touch the places where Pilgrims created a new life, hear the cannons of Old Ironsides, and get a hint of what it was like living in a 17th-century village. The Mohawk Trail and Pioneer Valley Loop take you through mostly rural areas with expansive valleys and thick forests. Seeing the leaves ignite each year in autumn, you'll understand why for centuries travelers have visited this beautiful region.

On this route you can stop in Jump Town USA near Orange, where a skydiving company makes its headquarters. You can make reservations to jump, but "walk-ons" are always welcomed. Jump Town also hosts an annual River Rat Race each April for canoe and kayak enthusiasts.

Try out another means of transportation in Worcester. The Bella Via Balloon Company takes riders up in hot-air balloons, but call ahead for reservations and atmospheric conditions. South Deerfield is headquarters of the Yankee Candle Company. Stop in and see how these popular, fragrant candles are produced. Nearby Deerfield and its meticulously preserved New England village depicts life between 1650 and 1850.

French King Bridge, Erving

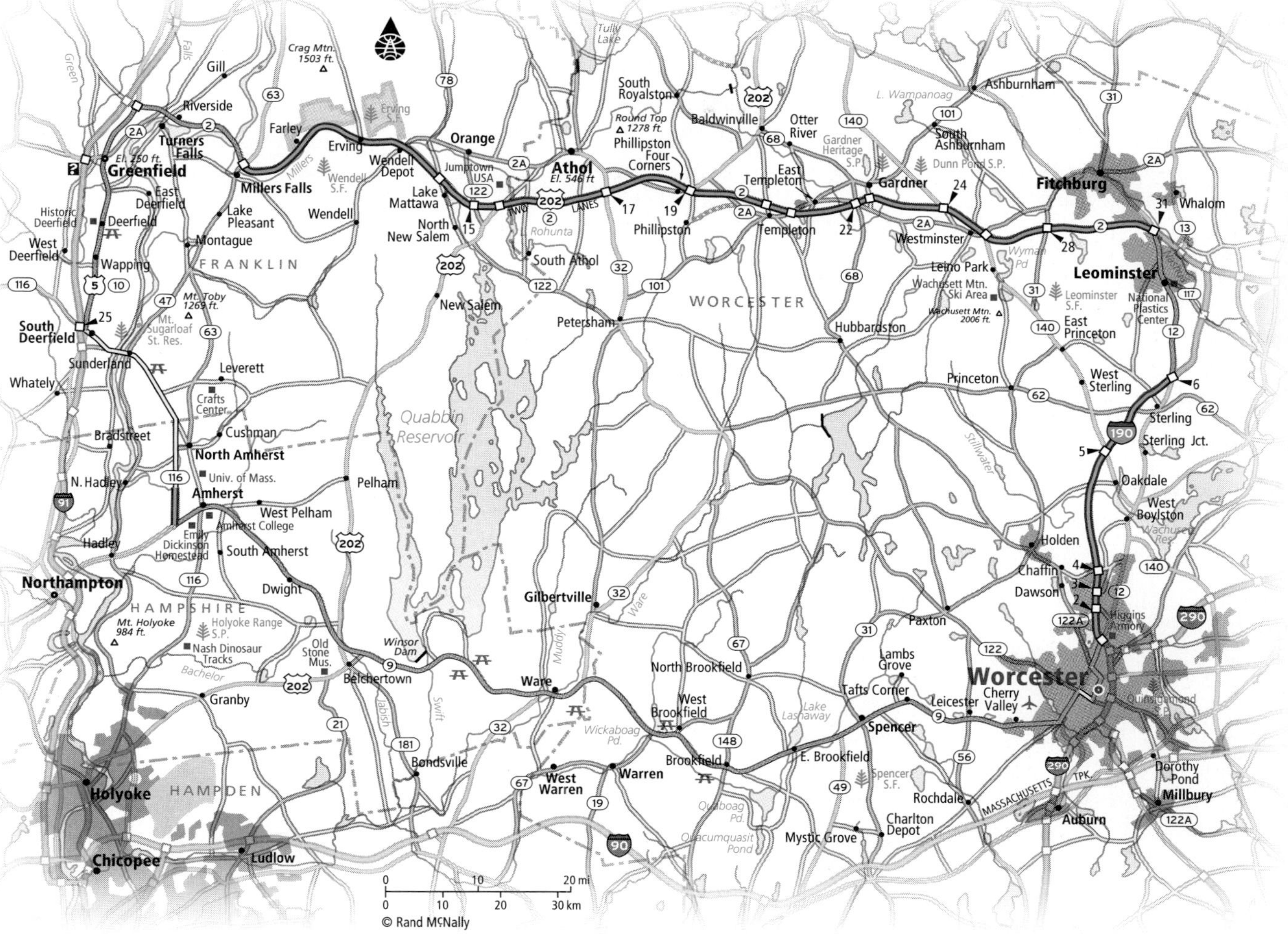

Gill
Crag Mtn. 1503 ft.
78
Tully Lake
63
Riverside
L. Wampanoag
Ashburnham
31
2A
Turners Falls
2
Farley
Erving
Erving
Orange
South Royalston
Baldwinville
Otter River
140
101
South Ashburnham
Dunn Pond S.P.
Fitchburg
2A
Whalom
Greenfield
East Deerfield
Millers Falls
Wendell Depot
Lake Mattawa
Jumptown USA
122
Athol El. 546 ft.
Round Top 1278 ft.
Phillipston Four Corners
East Templeton
68
Gardner Heritage S.P.
Gardner
24
31
13
Historic Deerfield
Deerfield
Lake Pleasant
Wendell
North New Salem
15
202
Phillipston
Templeton
2A
22
Westminster
28
Leominster
117
West Deerfield
Montague
FRANKLIN
2
South Athol
32
101
68
Leino Park
Wachusett Mtn. Ski Area
31
Leominster S.F.
National Plastics Center
Wapping
5
10
New Salem
122
WORCESTER
Hubbardston
Wachusett Mtn. 2006 ft.
140
East Princeton
12
116
47
Mt. Toby 1269 ft.
Mt. Sugarloaf St. Res.
63
South Deerfield
25
Petersham
West Sterling
6
Whately
Sunderland
Leverett
Crafts Center
Cushman
Princeton
62
Sterling
62
Bradstreet
North Amherst
Pelham
Sterling Jct.
190
5
N. Hadley
116
Univ. of Mass.
West Pelham
Oakdale
West Boylston
Wachusett Res.
Amherst
Amherst College
Holden
140
Hadley
Emily Dickinson Homestead
South Amherst
Chaffin
4
Dwight
202
Gilbertville
32
Dawson
2
12
Northampton
116
Higgins Armory
290
HAMPSHIRE
Mt. Holyoke 984 ft.
Holyoke Range S.P.
Old Stone Mus.
Ware
Paxton
122A
Worcester
Quinsigamond
Nash Dinosaur Tracks
Bachelor
Winsor Dam
9
Belchertown
Swift
North Brookfield
67
Lambs Grove
Tafts Corner
Leicester
Cherry Valley
9
Granby
202
Ware
West Brookfield
Lake Lashaway
Spencer
56
Dorothy Pond
21
181
32
Wickaboag Pd.
Brookfield
148
E. Brookfield
Spencer S.F.
Rochdale
MASSACHUSETTS TPK.
290
Millbury
Holyoke
HAMPDEN
Bondsville
67
West Warren
Warren
19
Quaboag Pd.
49
Charlton Depot
Mystic Grove
Auburn
122A
Chicopee
Ludlow
90
Quacumquasit Pond
0 10 20 mi
0 10 20 30 km
© Rand McNally

MINNESOTA

STATE MAP – P. 108, RIDE – P. 109

TOURING INFORMATION

With the glistening harbor of Duluth in your rearview mirror, ride through Canal Park one more time as you take I-35 N to MN 61 . . . then keep on going. At Knife River you'll pick up Scenic MN 61 AKA the North Shore Scenic Byway.

If you've packed your passport, don't stop at Grand Portage – cross into Canada. The road remains 61 but is now called Provincial Highway 61. Thunder Bay, a metropolis of 80,000+, is less than an hour into the country. Fort William Historical Park is on this side of the city and well worth a visit. In the early 19th century, Fort William replaced Grand Portage as the meeting place for fur traders. The reconstructed fort is staffed with talented reenactors. Both scheduled and self-guided tours are available.

This ride is not very winding or twisty, but it is lofty. With the Great Lake on one side of the road and the Sawtooth Mountains on the other, the views are simply grand.

VISITOR INFORMATION
www.exploreminnesota.com | 651-296-5029

PULL OVER

Split Rock Lighthouse State Park and Historic Site
MN 61 | Two Harbors | 218-226-6377
Tour the light station that was built atop a 130-foot cliff in 1910 and blast the fog signal by the keeper's home. Split Rock was the last lighthouse that the SS *Edmund Fitzgerald* passed on its fatal trip across Lake Superior toward Detroit. The state park that surrounds the lighthouse offers wonderful hiking trails, cart-in campsites, cobblestone beaches, and fishing.

Lutsen Mountains Ski Area
371 Ski Hill Road off MN 61 | Lutsen | 218-663-7214
Nestled in the Sawtooth Mountains, this premier four-season destination resort offers a multitude of activities from spring river fishing to golfing to the fall color tours. Take the enclosed tram to the top of the mountain for a spectacular view of the forest and Lake Superior.

Grand Portage National Monument
211 Mile Creek Road off MN 61 | Grand Portage
218-475-2202
All 710 acres of the monument lie within the Grand Portage Ojibwe Indian Reservation. The reconstructed depot celebrates the 18th-century fur trade and Ojibwe life. There are open displays of trade goods and a staff of reenactors help make the fort and trade depot of 200 years ago come to life. The Ojibwe Grand Portage Lodge and Casino is adjacent to the monument.

ROUTE LENGTH – 145 miles or 3 hours nonstop

Moose in Superior National Forest

Best season to ride:	Early autumn
Gasoline availability:	Plentiful
Road conditions:	Two-lane with sweeping curves
Insider tip:	Watch for wildlife, especially moose

As the road climbs from Duluth at the southern tip of Lake Superior toward the Canadian border, you will be glad your bike has a motor. There are no descents on this trip. This road only rises as it grips the bluffs that form the rocky shoreline of the largest Great Lake.

Most communities along the north shore have no downtowns, just homes and services along the sides of the road. The views of the boreal forest are interrupted only by roadside stops and state and national parks.

At Van Hoven Park in Two Harbors, you can watch as ore carriers are loaded or visit the permanently docked Edna G, a tugboat that serves as a museum. The natural beauty of Gooseberry Falls State Park offers a peaceful respite with its labyrinth of creeks and five waterfalls.

Grand Marais is a haven for artists. You can buy original works at the local five-and-dime or at any of the galleries that line the streets. There are many spots for gourmet coffee and a shore lunch. In Minnesota, you can never tire of walleye.

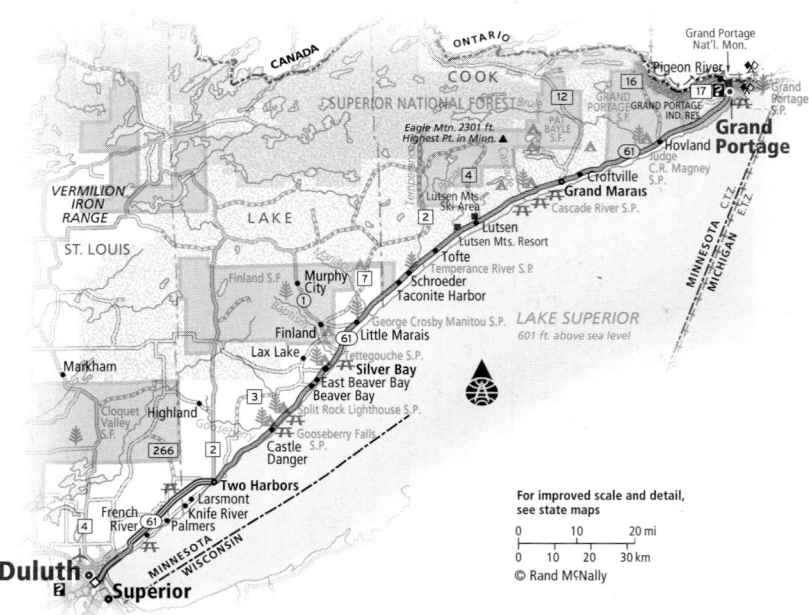

MISSISSIPPI

STATE MAP – P. 114, RIDE – PP. 114-115

ROUTE LENGTH – 315 miles or 6+ hours nonstop

Country road, Natchez Trace, near Jackson

TOURING INFORMATION

Take a couple of days to enjoy this ride. There's plenty to see and explore along this picturesque route between Natchez and Tishomingo.

Spend some time in Tupelo to savor the unassuming surroundings of Elvis Presley's boyhood. Drop by the Tupelo Convention and Visitors Bureau (399 E. Main St.) to pick up a map of a four-mile tour. It begins at the King's birthplace and includes the church where the Presley family worshipped; the schools that Elvis attended and where he began his career in music; Tupelo Hardware, where Elvis bought his first guitar; and the city's fairgrounds, the site of Elvis concerts in both 1956 and 1957, when the King was at the height of his popularity as a teen idol.

Each June for the past eight years Tupelo has hosted the Elvis Presley Festival to commemorate Presley's homecoming in June of 1956, when he performed for the hometown folks. The festival draws quite a crowd so be wary of busy thoroughfares as you make your way to the carnival midway or catch one of the live entertainers including the best of Elvis tribute artists. You can walk on to the Running with the King marathon or just watch the "Elvis Look Alike Pet Parade."

Riding the Natchez Trace is most popular in the spring when wildflowers bloom in colorful carpets and again in the fall when autumn leaves glow. Keep an eye out for deer and wild turkey darting across the roadway, especially at dusk and dawn. The posted speed limit is 50 mph.

VISITOR INFORMATION
www.visitmississippi.org | 601-359-3297

Winding road, Natchez Trace

Best season to ride:	Any time of the year, though summers can be hot
Gasoline availability:	Plan ahead, as you must exit the parkway for gasoline
About this road:	Sweeping curves on a two-lane road with no commercial traffic
Insider tip:	Plan your overnights, as you have to leave the Trace for lodging

No traffic lights. No stop signs. No commercial vehicles. The Natchez Trace Parkway was made for leisurely riding through one of the most beautiful parts of the country. Starting off in Natchez, the Mississippi segment of the three-state parkway includes sweeping curves, winding roads, cypress swamps, and trees dripping with Spanish moss. Very few buildings are visible on the ride — just southern pastoral scenery.

This scenic road was built to commemorate the legendary footpath of the Old Natchez Trace. Featuring historic signposts and trails, the parkway took 67 years to construct, starting in 1938 and finishing in Mississippi in 2005. Good places to learn the fascinating history of the Natchez Trace are at the visitor center in Tupelo and at Mount Locust in Natchez. It's worth scheduling a trip to see the annual Natchez Trace Festival, always held the last Saturday in April in Kosciusko.

The ride could take a couple of days if you allow time to explore the Indian mounds, battlefields, scenic overlooks, and friendly towns along the way. There are no motels or restaurants on the parkway, but plenty can be found nearby.

Four National Park Service campgrounds provide rustic campsites along the way.

PULL OVER
Under the Hill
Section of downtown Natchez | 800-647-6724
Hard by the Mississippi River, Silver Street snakes its way through Natchez Under the Hill, once the city's commercial center. Now it's chock-a-block with antique shops, gift boutiques, saloons, and an eclectic array of restaurants.

Brices Cross Roads National Battlefield Site
Off US 45 and MS 370 | Baldwyn | 800-305-7417
This one-acre battlefield is always open, but has no facilities or scheduled programs. Informative folders are available on site and at the Natchez Trace Parkway Visitor Center, located at milepost 266 on the Natchez Trace north of Tupelo. Markers and interpretive signs are placed around the field.

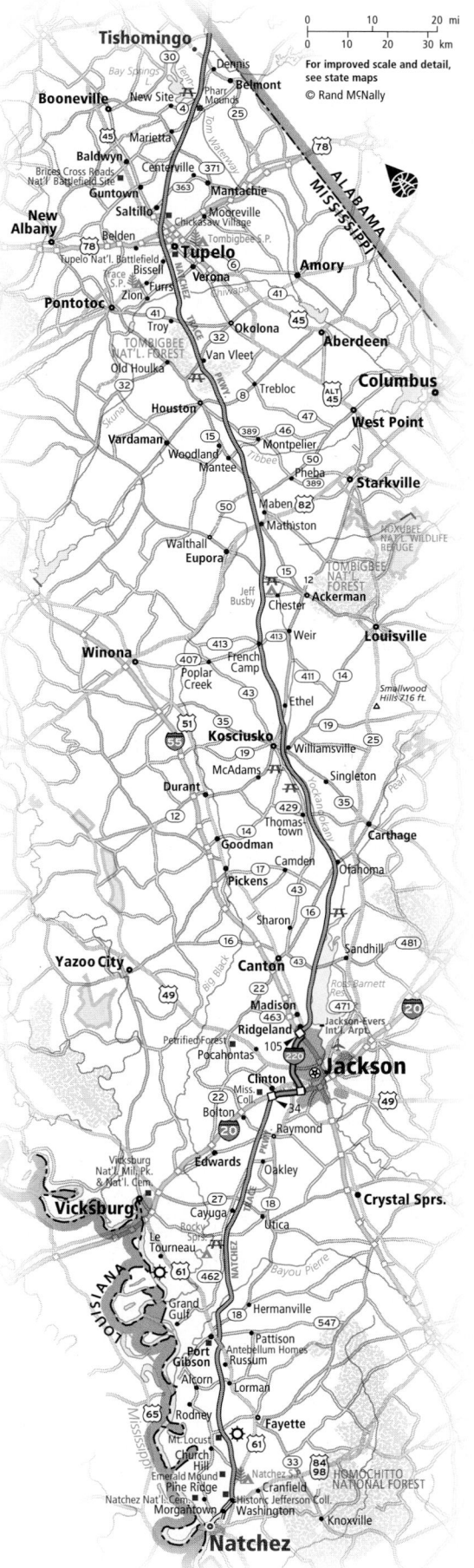

MONTANA

STATE MAP AND RIDE – P. 122

TOURING INFORMATION

Early mornings may be overcast in Kalispell, as it is high in the Rocky Mountains and nestled between a number of lakes. Head toward US 93 and meander your way to MT 35, which encircles Flathead Lake. To complete the loop, follow it around to US 2, which will connect with US 93 for your return to Kalispell.

Plan a stop at Polson, where the state's largest fiddling contest is held each summer. Contestants from ages 6 to 90 compete. Be sure to visit the University of Montana Biological Station, too. People come from all over the world to this peninsula in Flathead Lake to study at this natural laboratory. Self-guided tours of the grounds include a beach walk and a one-mile nature trail loop through old-growth forest.

Along this ride there's plenty of water as you curve your way around Flathead Lake. Roadside stands pop up in the warm weather, especially around the summer vacation towns of Elmo and Rollins. There are sweeping curves, tight turns, and steep hills along this route. Take your time and enjoy the ride.

VISITOR INFORMATION

www.visitmt.com | 800-847-4868

PULL OVER

Lone Pine State Park
Montana Department of Fish Wildlife and Parks
Lone Pine Rd. | Kalispell | 406-755-2706
The day-use park offers a self-guided nature trail tour and several informal hiking trails, horse trails, and an archery range. The visitor center provides grills and picnic tables.

Flathead Lake State Park
490 North Meridian Rd. | Kalispell | 406-752-5501
Flathead Lake has two parks within its organization, Yellow Bay and West Shore. Yellow Bay is near the center of Montana's sweet cherry orchards, which provide a colorful bloom each spring. The park offers walk-in tent camping spots and a sandy beach for swimming. Located in a mature fir, pine, and larch forest, West Shore State Park offers overlooks with spectacular views of the lake and the mountains. The beach is rocky, but swimming is permitted.

Pablo National Wildlife Refuge
National Bison Range | 132 Bison Range Rd. | Moiese
406-644-2211
Pablo National Wildlife Refuge is located on tribal trust lands of the Confederated Salish and Kootenai Tribes. It contains 2,500 acres of water, marsh, and upland grassland. The refuge provides nesting and resting areas for migratory birds and other wildlife. If you packed your camera, this is a place to use it.

ROUTE LENGTH – 108+ miles or 2+ hours nonstop

Flathead Lake shoreline

Best season to ride: Summer to early autumn
Gasoline availability: Adequate
About the road: Two-lane road with pavement markings and some guard rails
Insider tip: Be alert for animals, as this area is rich in wildlife. Remember: You are riding in the Rockies, so be prepared for temperature changes.

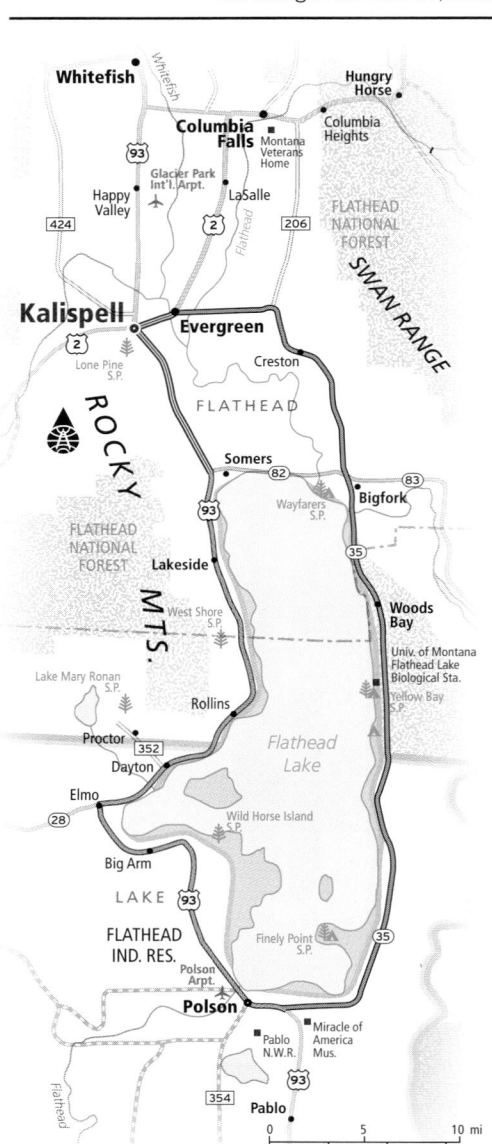

With the Rocky Mountains on one side and Flathead Lake on the other, the view from your bike is a joy to behold. Tucked into the northwest corner of Montana, the valley lies next to the rugged grandeur of Glacier National Park. The centerpiece is Flathead Lake, the largest natural freshwater lake west of the Mississippi. The product of Ice Age glaciers, the lake is fed by mountain snow, making it refreshingly cool on the hottest summer days.

The roads that hug Flathead Lake pass through tall pine and evergreen forests followed by miles of cherry orchards. Stop by roadside stands in August for deliciously fresh, sweet cherries. The contrast of the valley floor to the surrounding mountains is humbling. These are not gentle inclines but sudden towering slopes that provide a beautiful backdrop for villages below.

Rocky shores and beaches beckon with water activities — boat cruises, fishing, sailing, swimming, parasailing, recreational boating, and white-water rafting. A fun way to get a great view is to take the gondola to the top of the mountain at Big Mountain Ski Resort, just north of Whitefish.

NEBRASKA

STATE MAP – P. 126, RIDE – PP. 126-129

TOURING INFORMATION

Scenic Route 2 stretches from Grand Island through Broken Bow and beyond to the Wyoming state line. It is a long, lean route that cuts through the wide open spaces of the tall grass prairie. Look to the sky, as there are usually hawks overhead. Near Scottsbluff, there are sandstone formations that have been carved by the wind.

Take a side trip to the Bridgeport State Recreational Area on Hwys. 26 and 92 near the town of Bridgeport. Comprising of 190 or so acres of sand pit lakes on the North Platte River, it is open year-round.

Nebraska is carnivore country, where hefty steaks are grilled to your liking, then washed down with "red beer," an improbable blend of beer and tomato juice.

VISITOR INFORMATION

www.visitnebraska.org | 877-632-7275

PULL OVER

Chimney Rock National Historic Site
Bayard | 308-586-2581
Chimney Rock National Historic Site commemorates the massive migration of settlers moving west across the country. This landmark was so striking it remained a vivid memory for many of the pioneers. Practice "packing your wagon" at the visitor center exhibit.

Scotts Bluff National Monument
Gering | 308-436-4340
Set in a 3,000-acre national monument, this site preserves the memory of the Oregon, California, and Mormon Trails. The Summit Road allows visitors to ride to the top of Scotts Bluff for a spectacular view of the valley.

ROUTE LENGTH – 350 miles or 7+ hours nonstop (a weekend trip)

Cranes pause on the Platte River, near Grand Island

Best season to ride:	Spring and summer
Gasoline availability:	Plan ahead
About the road:	Flat with a big, wide view; desolate
Insider tip:	Be aware of sudden summer storms

While seashore and mountains shout at you, "the prairie only whispers." So noted the Rev. Val Peters, former director of Nebraska's Girls and Boys Town. "You must listen closely," he urged, "and not miss the message."

There's plenty of prairie whispering along the Sandhills Journey Scenic Byway. This enormously diverse landscape — much of it remote — ranges from waving cornfields and the rolling hills of cattle country to marshes, wetlands, and dramatic grass-covered sand hills. More than 500,000 migrating sandhill cranes stop here annually.

At Grand Island, the Stuhr Museum of the Prairie Pioneer re-creates a railway town like those that sprung up along the Union Pacific right-of-way in the 1880s. The Nebraska National Forest near Halsey is the largest man-made, hand-planted forest in the world. At the bustling railroad town of Alliance, Carhenge whimsically recreates Britain's ancient Stonehenge using a circle of automobiles.

Near Bridgeport and Scottsbluff, look for wagon wheel ruts left by westward-bound "prairie schooners" on the famed Oregon Trail. Landmarks include the monumental geologic formations known as Courthouse and Jail Rocks. Scotts Bluff National Monument displays a collection of watercolor paintings by frontier photographer and artist William Henry Jackson.

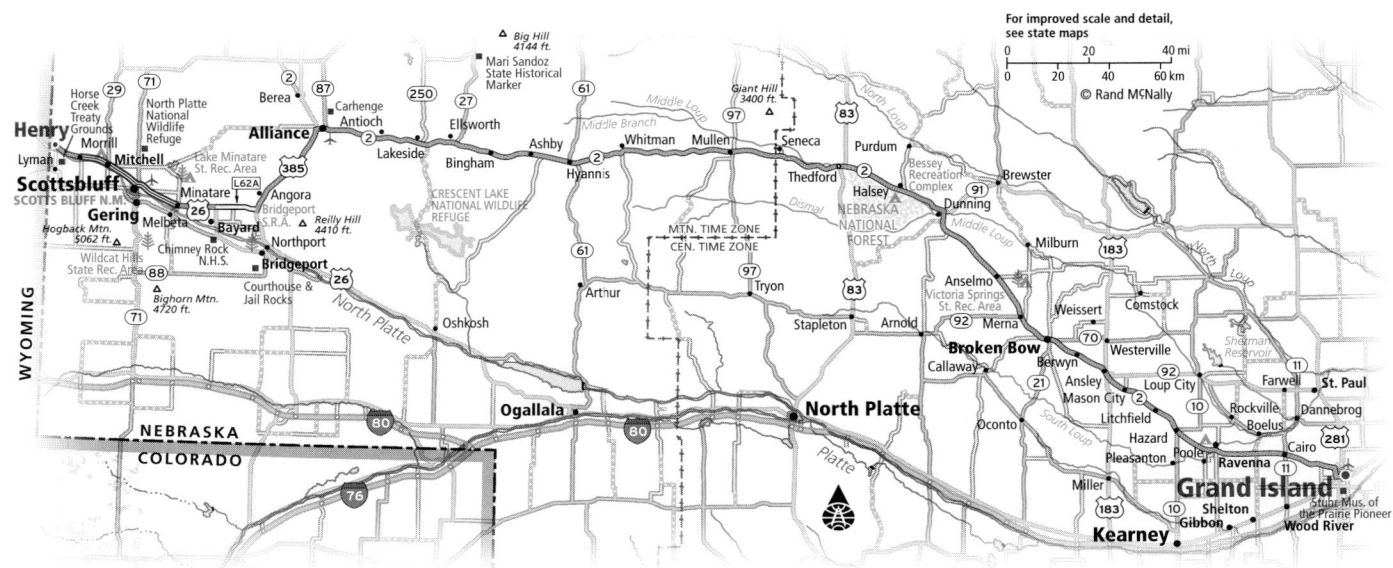

NEW HAMPSHIRE

STATE MAP AND RIDE – P. 132

TOURING INFORMATION

This road winds and has some sharp curves. The view from the road is primarily tree-covered, round-topped mountains — some with slide areas and bare patches of exposed stone.

Spend some time in Lincoln to enjoy the ambience of a resort area and pick up some of the best fudge in the Northeast. At White Mountain Crafters on Main Street you'll find lots of area crafts, collectibles, and confections.

This ride twists and turns as the highway climbs to nearly 3,000 feet at the peak of Mount Kancamagus. Twilight is a dramatic time of day to travel the Kanc, as the setting sun casts shadows and patterns along the drive. Be watchful: Dusk is also a favorite time for moose to cross the highway.

VISITOR INFORMATION
www.visitnh.gov | 603-271-2665

PULL OVER
Franconia Notch State Parkway
North of North Woodstock | 603-745-8391
The deep valley known as Franconia Notch covers almost 6,500 acres in the White Mountains between the Franconia and Kinsman ranges. Franconia Notch State Park preserves the natural beauty of the area, but also offers visitors a banquet of outdoor activity. Mountain flowers bloom beside the tumbling waters of the Flume Gorge, a mountain stream falling through a gorge surrounded by tall cliffs and mountains. Other scenic highlights include the site of the Old Man of the Mountain. Discovered in 1805, the rocks that made up the famous profile of the Old Man of the Mountain collapsed in 2003.

Loon Mountain Ski Area
Kancamagus Hwy. | Lincoln | 603-745-8111
This ski area offers a variety of activities throughout the year including BBQs, fine dining restaurants, music festivals, horseback riding, and events like "Blue Grass and Barbeque" in the summer and Oktoberfest in the fall.

Jigger Johnson Campground
White Mountain National Forest | 33 Kancamagus Hwy. near Conway | 603-447-5448
Not only fun to say, this campground is great for any type of camper. Carroll County has many outdoor activities. Fishing opportunities abound along the Swift River, Rob Brook, and Douglas Brook. The dominant feature in this area is the Ossipee Mountains, excellent for some exercise if you're in the mood to climb.

ROUTE LENGTH – 115+ miles or 3 hours nonstop

Fall scene at Swift River, near Kancamagus Highway, Albany

Best season to ride:	Summer and early autumn
Gasoline availability:	Adequate, except along the 32-mile stretch of the Kanc where there are no services.
About the road:	Two-lane winding road
Insider tip:	Weather changes quickly; watch for wildlife

With its tongue-twister name, the Kancamagus Highway between Lincoln and Conway is often called "the Kanc" for short. Named for an Indian chief known as "The Fearless One," the New Hampshire National Scenic Byway along Route 112 is one of New England's most scenic drives. The 34-mile thickly treed road cuts an east-west channel through the 800,000-acre White Mountain National Forest.

Dense stands of deciduous trees and evergreens provide a dramatic backdrop with their beautiful spring and summer greens and dazzling autumn shades. Scenic overlooks are strategically placed along the rugged terrain on the curvy two-lane road. Meander through lush forests, follow old logging roads, and cross Indian hunting paths. Hike to waterfalls, rocky swimming holes, and peaceful sites such as the Rocky Gorge Scenic Area where the Swift River has, over time, worn a narrow cleft through solid stone.

If you have time for only one hike, the Boulder Loop Trail is it. At about three miles round trip, the hike offers outstanding views of Mt. Chocorua and the Swift River Valley. You may need a recreation pass from the White Mountain National Forest if you leave your bike at some sites.

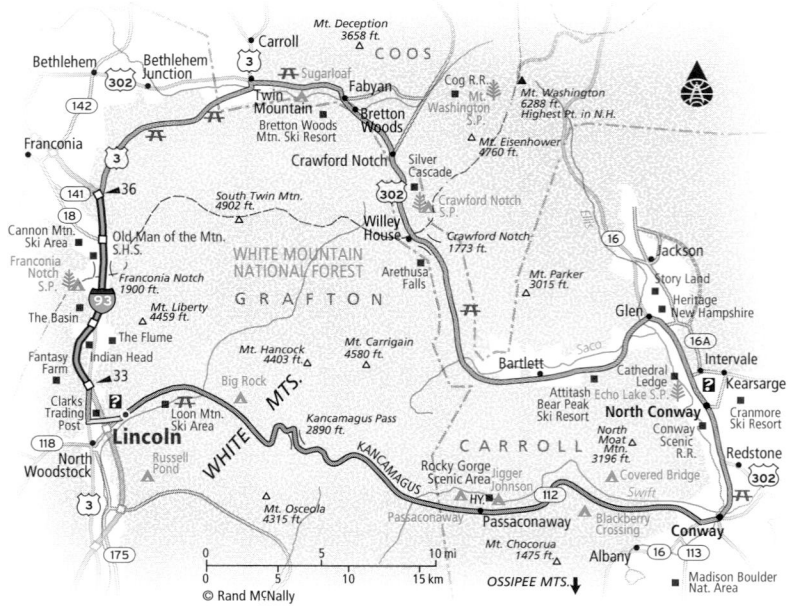

© Rand McNally

NEW YORK

STATE MAP – P. 140, RIDE – P. 143

TOURING INFORMATION:

Near Canandaigua, take NY 332 to NY 21 and on to NY 53 and ride to Corning and then Elmira/Horseheads. Stay on NY 14 into Seneca Falls and back toward Geneva.

Take a step back in history in Seneca Falls, where the women's movement began in 1848. Your first stop should be the Women's Rights National Historical Park, which includes a Visitor Center/Museum, the Elizabeth Cady Stanton House, the M'Clintock House where the Declaration of Sentiments was written, and the remains of the chapel where the resolutions were debated. A charming town, Seneca Falls is considered the inspiration for the small town of Bedford Falls in the classic holiday movie *It's a Wonderful Life*.

This ride through part of New York's Finger Lakes region takes you through rolling rural hills blanketed with vineyards. There are many glimpses of the lakes from the road. This region is peppered with small, quaint towns.

VISITOR INFORMATION
www.iloveny.com | 800-225-5697

PULL OVER

Glenn H. Curtiss Museum
8419 State Route 54 | Hammondsport | 607-569-2160
Glenn Curtiss loved building bicycles and, later, motorcycles and airplanes. A reproduction of the 1907 motorcycle that he rode at the astounding speed of 136 MPH is on display. This feat afforded him the title "fastest man on earth." A year later he took to the skies and was awarded pilot's license #1 when he flew over 5,000 feet to win the first pre-announced, public flight in America. This museum celebrates the genius of Glenn Curtiss and his many inventions—many of which are on display.

Corning Museum of Glass

One Museum Way | Corning | 800-732-6845
The Corning Museum of Glass offers a live, narrated glassblowing demonstration enabling guests to see every step of the glassblowing process. Walk-in Workshops are another favorite, as guests can try hot glassblowing. The Innovation Center highlights include a submarine periscope, a flight simulator mirror, and a glass floor that visitors can walk on.

ROUTE LENGTH – 160 miles or 4+ hours nonstop

Watkins Glen State Park, Finger Lakes region

Best season to ride: Late spring, summer, autumn
Gasoline availability: Plentiful
About the road: Two-lane, winding roads with roller-coaster-like hills
Insider tip: Watch out for wildlife; increased traffic in some areas during tourist season

Along the shoreline of the five major lakes in the Finger Lakes region of New York, the autumns are stunners, the villages always postcard-perfect, and the climate ideal for growing grapes. More than 75 wineries operate in the Finger Lakes, many with tours and wine trails. There's plenty to see and do along this route.

North of Ithaca, enjoy the cool and the green within the gorge made possible by Taughannock Falls, the highest free-falling waterfall in the eastern United States. At 215 feet, its drop is longer than any at Niagara. With a stop at Watkins Glen, you can sign up for a sail on a vintage schooner named *Malabar X* or experience stock car racing at Watkins Glen International Race Track.

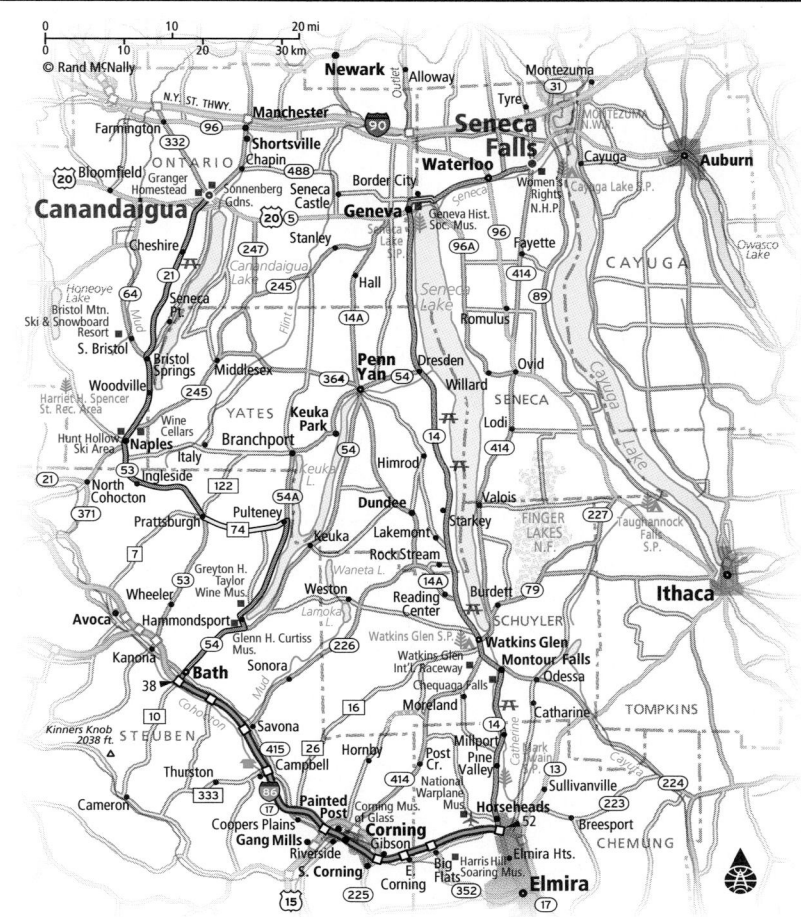

NORTH CAROLINA

STATE MAP AND RIDE – P. 150

TOURING INFORMATION

This ride wanders around the Pisgah National Forest. Starting in Marion, you link up with US 221 and then turn and twist along state roads. Enjoy a stretch along the Blue Ridge Parkway before returning along more meandering roads to Morganton.

The Blue Ridge Parkway passes the lovely and historic town of Asheville. It is well worth the short ride over from Marion, about 36 miles. Nearby Biltmore Estate features the 250-room George W. Vanderbilt Mansion. Tour the house and its on-site winery. At Pack Place Education Arts and Science Center, see the Asheville Art and Colburn Mineral museums. Novelist Thomas Wolfe's boyhood home at 52 N. Market St. is now a state historic site.

This ride is all about the road! It is twisty and winding.

VISITOR INFORMATION
www.visitnc.com | 800-847-4862

PULL OVER
Linville Caverns
U.S. 221 north, between Linville and Marion
828-756-4171
Explore the limestone rock formations found deep within Humpback Mountain. Watch for the Frozen Waterfall. Short guided tours of the caverns are available.

Linville Falls
Blue Ridge Pkwy, milepost 316.3 near Linville
828-765-1045
View famous Linville Falls as it cascades into Linville Gorge or, for the serious outdoor adventurer, walk down to the base of the falls. Visitors will find an information center, camping, and picnic grounds.

ROUTE LENGTH – 125 miles or about 3 hours

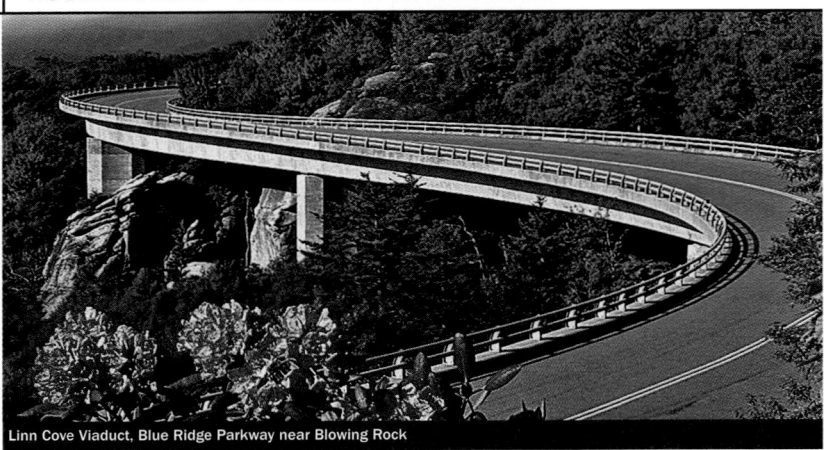

Linn Cove Viaduct, Blue Ridge Parkway near Blowing Rock

Best season to ride:	Spring, summer, and autumn
Gasoline availability:	Adequate
Road conditions:	Mostly two-lane roads, although there are some four-lane areas
Insider tip:	During tourist season, plan your ride for the middle of the week

Sometimes called "America's Favorite Drive," the Blue Ridge Parkway is one of the most visited units of America's National Park Service. One ride and you'll see why. Stunning, long-range panoramas and up-close looks at the natural and cultural history of the southern Appalachian Mountains create a wealth of reasons to choose this path.

The two-lane modern road with wide bends and moderate gradients meanders for 252 miles through North Carolina. Traveling through five mountain ranges, the parkway varies in elevation from just under 2,000 feet to over 6,000 feet and dips into coves, hollows, and water gaps. Part of the beauty and enjoyment of the parkway is its lack of commercial signs and vehicles. This is a route to ramble along slowly with frequent stops. New vistas open up at every turn, and there are numerous fascinating attractions along the way, from pioneer farms and cabins to small museums and scenic overlooks.

OKLAHOMA

STATE MAP – P. 166, RIDE – P. 168

TOURING INFORMATION

A bounty of scenic beauty, historic sites, outdoor recreation, and unusual festivals make this route through northeastern Oklahoma a pure delight.

Take a side trip to Tulsa (about 28 miles from Claremore), where jazz rivals country music. The Oklahoma Jazz Hall of Fame is located in Tulsa, which is also home to the Greenwood District, where you can relive the days when the likes of Louis Armstrong and Dizzy Gillespie stopped in Tulsa to perform with local artists. Riverside Drive follows a scenic route along the Arkansas River past flowering trees that were blooming before the city was built. The drive also passes Zink Lake, where area crew teams practice and fishermen test their luck.

During the week, you may have these rolling country roads all to yourself. When you can look around, try to spot mistletoe in the trees of the mixed hardwood forests.

VISITOR INFORMATION
www.travelok.com | 800-652-6552

PULL OVER
Will Rogers Memorial
1720 West Will Rogers Blvd. | Claremore
918-341-0719
Dedicated to arguably the most famous Oklahoman, this memorial complex includes a permanent exhibit of Roger's work as a humorist, author, and film star and a selection of his personal belongings including a collection of saddles and cowboy memorabilia. One of his most famous quotations appears on the base of an oversized statue of him in the rotunda. It reads "I never met a man I didn't like."

Pensacola Dam
Langley | 918-782-9594
Built between the years 1938 and 1940, this dam was the first hydroelectric facility constructed in Oklahoma. It spans a mile across the Grand River Valley and holds back the 43,500 acres of water that forms Grand Lake O' the Cherokees. Free tours are offered five days a week during the summer months. The tour lasts about an hour.

Disney/Little Blue State Park
OK 28 E | Disney | 918-435-8066
This popular park is located by the flood gates of the Pensacola Dam and is close to Cherokee State Park. A favorite for bass fishing, boating, and water skiing, it also offers fine picnic areas and many tent camping sites.

ROUTE LENGTH – 135+ miles or 4 hours nonstop

Will Rogers Memorial, Claremore

Best season to ride:	Any season
Gasoline availability:	Plentiful
Road conditions:	Lightly traveled, two-lane and back roads
Insider tip:	Watch for wildlife around OK 20/82 near the lakes

Winding roads, wooded trails, overhanging bluffs, glistening streams, and top-notch state parks add to the reasons to travel this road. Flowering dogwoods and redbuds in the spring and spectacular hardwood foliage in the fall provide a feast for the eyes in these foothills of the Ozarks.

The road skirts the Grand Lake O' The Cherokees leaving Grove and climbs to an elevation of 1,032 feet outside Jay. The hills on OK 28 past Disney will make the ride seem like a rollercoaster. At some points you may not see the bottom of the hills.

Keep an eye on the sky for migrating pelicans in April and September. The gawky birds are celebrated the fourth weekend in September with the annual Pelican Festival in Grove.

Five state parks provide plenty of camping and cabins, along with a wealth of treasures from Mother Nature.

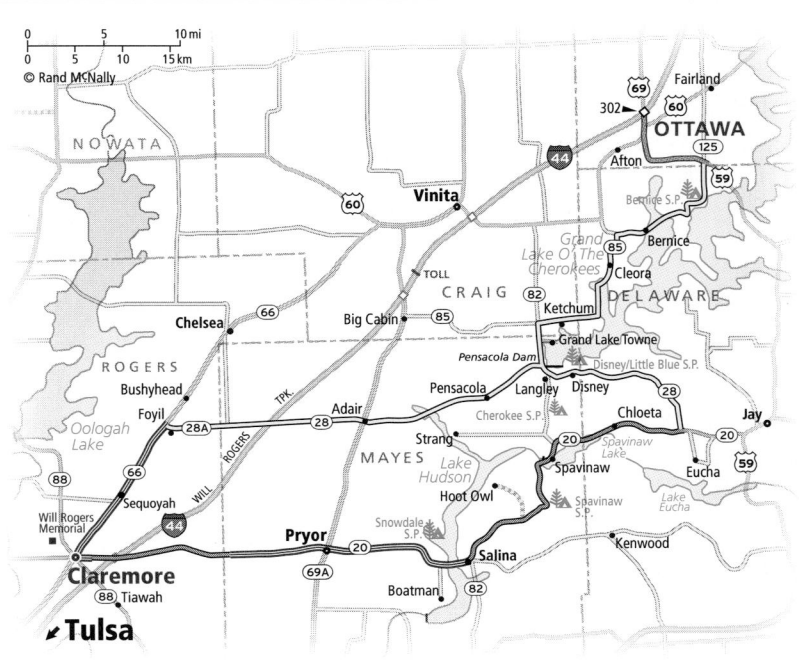

PENNSYLVANIA

STATE MAP – PP. 174 - 175, RIDE PP. 174 - 175, 178 - 179 | **ROUTE LENGTH – 372+ miles or 7+ hours nonstop**

TOURING INFORMATION

The name of the road is US 6. Start near Scranton and chase the sun all the way to the state line.

Try to stay a night at Cherry Springs State Park, located about 25 miles from Wellsboro. Cherry Springs has been designated an Official Dark Sky Park for its outstanding stargazing. It is a glorious place to camp and be amazed by the starry, starry sky.

Along the way there are tree-covered hills and river scenery to be savored in the Allegheny National Forest. The wildflowers that bloom provide a carpet of pink, violet, and green. Make time to stop in any of the small towns, swap stories over coffee, and visit the local memorials to veterans.

VISITOR INFORMATION

www.visitpa.com | 800-847-4872

PULL OVER

French Azilum

RR 2 | Towanda | 570-265-3376

When the exiled French royalists arrived in the fall of 1793, they renamed this bucolic, meadow-strewn area Azilum (asylum), for its beauty and for what their flight from the French Revolution meant to them. Today the site contains more than 20 acres of the original settlement.

Tioga State Forest

1 Nessmuk Lane | Wellsboro | 570-724-2868

The 160,000-acre forest is surrounded by timber-producing land. Named after the tribe of Seneca Indians that once lived in the area, Tioga translates as "the meeting of two rivers." In the 1940s birch stills were in operation within the forest. These stills processed the bark from the trees to produce birch oil, which is used topically to relieve muscle and joint aches.

Pennsylvania Lumber Museum

5660 US Route 6 West | Galeton | 814-435-2652

Activities at the Lumber Museum include tours, educational workshops, and classes. Experience the Bark Peelers' convention in July, where Pennsylvania's early lumberjacks' skills are re-created and demonstrated. The museum is set in the heart of Susquehannock State Forest, where state parks, campgrounds, and rental cabins are available.

Hills Creek near Stokesdale

Best season to ride:	Spring, summer, and autumn
Gasoline availability:	Plentiful
About the road:	Pavement on this two-lane road is well-marked with light to moderate traffic
Insider tip:	To explore the area in addition to riding it, plan on two to three days

With picture-perfect panoramas, US 6 delivers mile after pleasurable mile across the northern tier of the state. The drive showcases historic towns, rushing streams, scenic mountains, and deep forests — a multitude of nature's gifts. The area was smoothed centuries ago by glacial ice. Today the highway trades large differences in elevation for a road that gently rises, falls, and turns in long flowing sweeps — a delight to ride.

The road begins a long, winding climb out of the Delaware River Valley near Scranton. Its two lanes course along the first of many hills and ridges with a series of sweeps and curves. Heading west, the road is known as the Grand Army of the Republic Highway. It cuts through hardwood forests and past small lakes in the area west of the Poconos called the Endless Mountains. For 40 miles, US 6 stays with the Susquehanna River, rising and falling as it follows the hillsides to the north. At times, the highway leaves the river to climb a series of five long grades — each, fortunately, has a passing lane.

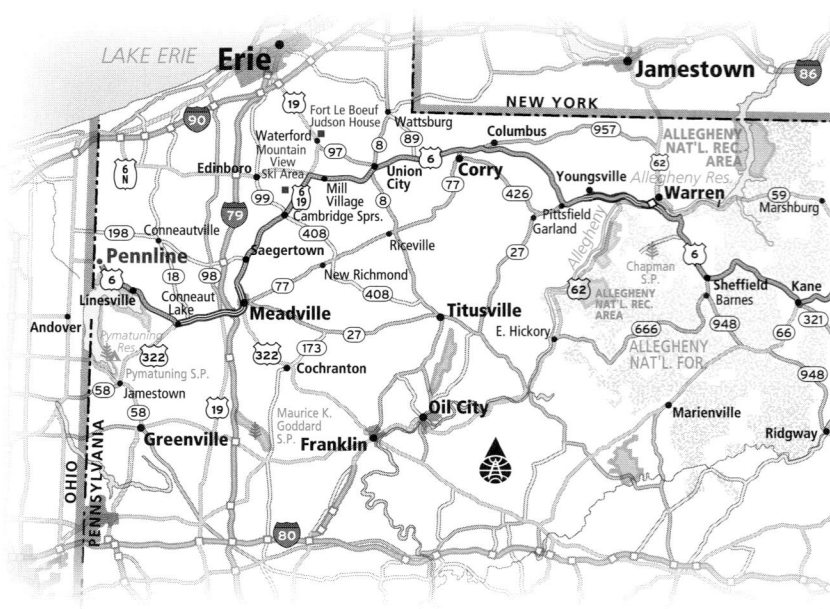

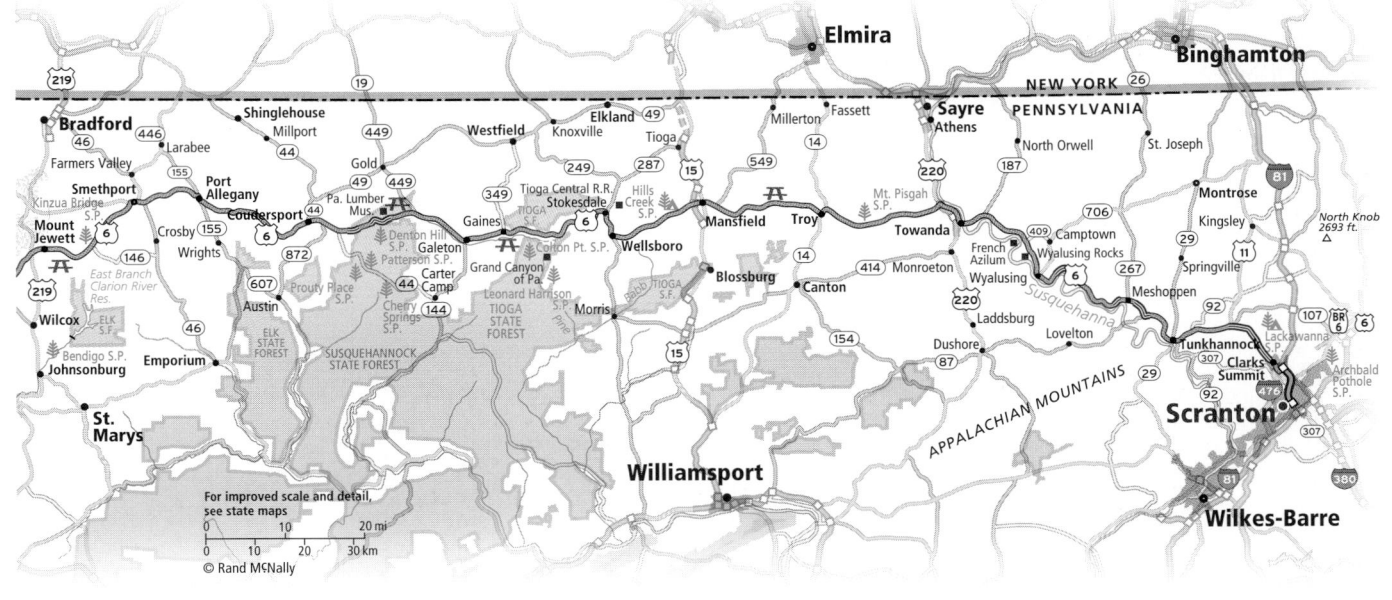

Pine Creek Gorge, also known as Pennsylvania Grand Canyon, in Tioga State forest near Wellsboro

SOUTH DAKOTA

STATE MAP AND RIDE – PP. 188 - 189

TOURING INFORMATION

This route starts in Chamberlain on SD 50 north to BIA 4 to SD Hwy. 47. Cross the Big Bend Dam and follow BIA 10 west to the junction with SD 1806. Follow SD 1806 into Fort Pierre.

Take a side trip to the site of Fort Pierre Chouteau near Pierre, known as the "Fur Capital of the West." Between 1817 and 1868 traders dealt with Sioux, offering guns, tobacco, blankets, beads, and other supplies for furs and buffalo robes. Today, movie buffs can find their way to a nearby buffalo ranch that was a major filming location for *Dances with Wolves*. Lt. Dunbar's fort and swimming hole remain.

This ride between Chamberlain and Fort Pierre is part of the Native American Scenic Highway. It crosses the Big Bend Dam and skirts Fort Pierre National Grassland. Along the way, it passes several U.S. Cavalry outposts, including Fort Defiance, which was built in 1842.

VISITOR INFORMATION

www.travelsd.com | 800-732-5682

PULL OVER

Akta Lakota Museum
N. Main St. | Chamberlain | 800-798-3452
Located on the campus of St. Joseph's Indian School, this museum features a large collection of Sioux artifacts and handcrafts as well as several dioramas that depict life on the prairie.

Farm Island State Recreation Area
1301 Farm Island Rd. | Pierre | 605-773-2885
With easy access to Lake Sharpe and popular beaches and trails, this park stays busy throughout the year. Anglers can fish for walleye, smallmouth bass, and northern pike on this Missouri River reservoir. Additionally, the park has ties to the Lewis and Clark expedition.

Verendrye Monument
900 Governors Dr. | Pierre | 605-773-3458
This is one of South Dakota's most historic landmarks. The history of the site began in 1743 when two explorers buried a lead plate atop a bluff overlooking what would become the city of Fort Pierre. The plate was discovered in 1913 and is now housed in the Cultural Heritage Center.

ROUTE LENGTH – 110 miles or 3+ hours nonstop

Highway 16 Bridge, Chamberlain/Oacoma

Best season to ride:	Spring, summer, autumn
Gasoline availability:	Plan ahead
About the road:	Lightly traveled two-lane road through rolling prairie
Insider tip:	Watch out for farm equipment and errant livestock

Wild mustangs and bison roam the high plains alongside the nation's only designated Native American Scenic Byway. It alternates between two tribal reservations and past historic sites such as the ruins of the Great Diamond A Cattle Company.

Absorb Sioux culture at Akta Lakota Museum, located on the beautiful campus of St. Joseph's Indian School in Chamberlain. Discover local artisans skilled in jewelry-making, bead- and quilt-work, and crafting decorative pipestones from locally quarried red stone. In Pierre, the South Dakota Cultural Heritage Center offers glimpses of what life on the plains was like for Native Americans before the arrival of the settlers.

In September 1804, Lewis and Clark and their Corps of Discovery stopped at the mouth of the Bad River during their heroic quest for the elusive Northwest Passage. A tension-filled meeting with the Teton Lakota Sioux almost led to armed confrontation. Today that site is in Fischers Lilly Park.

The beauty of Lake Francis Case and Lake Sharpe may encourage you to pull over and stay awhile. Both were created by dams along the Missouri River. Scenic camping spots include Farm Island Recreation Area and Big Bend Dam, a fishing hot spot.

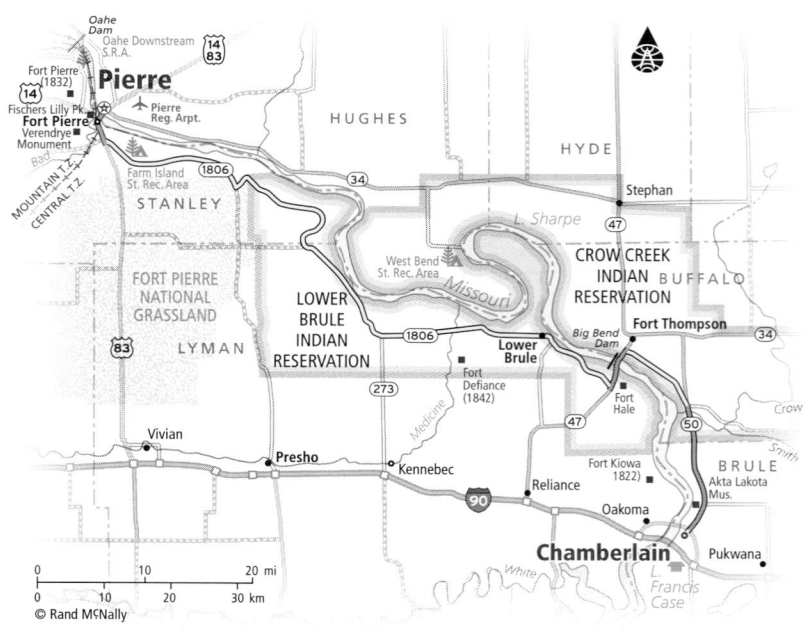

© Rand McNally

TENNESSEE

STATE MAP AND RIDE – P. 190

TOURING INFORMATION

This ride curves and twists through the lightly traveled back roads of Tennessee. From Dover take TN 49 to Erin. Take TN 13 to Linden to connect with 128 into and through Savannah, then on to TN 57 in the Pickwick area. There is more traffic around the Pickwick Dam, and this small stretch of TN 57 is much straighter than the rest of the route.

Take a side trip to visit Shiloh National Military Park, southwest of Savanna near Hurley. Spread over 4,000 acres adjacent to the Tennessee River, this park is notable not only for the battlefield and Shiloh National Cemetery, but also for numerous prehistoric Indian mounds.

For fans of country music, American history, and great natural beauty, Tennessee is the place to see. The area that follows the Tennessee River is the state's heartland. It is filled with towns small in size but big in hospitality. There are hundreds of back roads that will carry you through hills, hollers, and forests. This route explores some of them.

VISITOR INFORMATION

www.tnvacation.com | 800-462-8366

PULL OVER

Fort Donelson National Battlefield
120 Fort Donelson Rd. | 931-232-5706
Fort Donelson National Battlefield is located on the Cumberland River, close to the Kentucky border. The centerpiece of Fort Donelson National Battlefield is a 15-acre earthen fort, now covered with grass.

Pickwick Landing State Park
Hwy. 57 | Pickwick Dam | 731-689-3129
The park lies in wooded rolling hills on a 48,000-acre lake created by a dam across the Tennessee River. Large boats use the park's waterway on their way from the Ohio River to the Gulf of Mexico. Visitors enjoy bass fishing (including tournaments), boating, golf, sailing, sand beaches and hiking. Check with the park for required permits. A large private marina offers boat rentals. Accommodations include cabins, tent and RV camping, and a 78-room, full-service inn with restaurant.

ROUTE LENGTH – 150 miles or 4 to 8 hours, depending on stops

Bluff at Quarry Park, Hwy. 49, Erin

Best season to ride:	Spring or autumn
Gasoline availability:	Plenty
About the road:	Well-marked winding roads
Insider tip:	Be aware of logging trucks and wildlife, such as deer

Round-topped mountains covered in trees compete with the meadows and the serenity of the tree-lined route that curves and twists from Tennessee's northern border to Mississippi. The ride follows the back roads of Tennessee and offers plenty of places to stop and see.

You don't have to be Irish to visit Erin, but on the third Saturday in March, everyone wears green for the town's Irish festival.

Loretta Lynn bought a 6,500-acre ranch in Hurricane Mills, which is now home to the Loretta Lynn Dude Ranch. Visitors can tour the Coal Miner's Daughter Museum.

Author Alex Haley's ancestors are buried in a Savannah cemetery, and the Trail of Tears crossed nearby. A few miles away in Adamsville, the Sheriff Buford Pusser Home and Museum pays tribute to the hero of *Walking Tall*.

TEXAS

STATE MAP – P. 198, RIDE – PP. 202 & 204

ROUTE LENGTH – 140 miles or 2+ hours nonstop

TOURING INFORMATION

Leave Kerrville westbound to follow a winding loop through the towering oaks and cedars of Texas Hill Country. Along the way you'll discover rugged terrain, rolling hills, and real cowboys.

Ride over to Fredericksburg, which was founded by a colony of German settlers in 1846. German influence survives to this day in the steep-roofed stone houses. Kammlah House, a restored old home, is now a museum; octagon-shaped Vereins Kirche, the town's first church and meeting hall, has been faithfully reproduced. Many old houses are still in use. The town's most famous native son is the late Fleet Admiral Chester Nimitz, head of naval operations in the Pacific during World War II.

This ride takes you through the Guadalupe River Valley, a popular spot for tubing, rafting, or canoeing. In heavy rainy seasons some low-lying roads may have washed-out areas.

VISITOR INFORMATION

www.traveltex.com | 800-888-8839

PULL OVER

Museum of Western Art
1550 Bandera Highway | Kerrville | 830-896-2553
Rough riding cowboys may not seem like the artsy type, but this intimate gallery shows the creative side of some of the most influential Texas cowboy artists. Western inspired paintings, bronze and stone sculptures, and other pieces are displayed in a bright and inviting environment.

Kerrville-Schreiner Park
2385 Bandera Highway | Kerrville | 830-257-5392
Camp, hike, and watch for deer as well as armadillos at this 500-acre park near the Guadalupe River.

Garner State Park
Park Road 29 | Concan | 830-232-6132
Located on the Frio River in the Texas Hill Country, this park is busiest in summer, when campers rent inner tubes for a river float, play miniature golf, or dance nightly at the pavilion. There are about five miles of hiking trails, and lake fishing enthusiasts can land bass, catfish, or perch.

Lost Maples State Natural Area
Farm Road 187 | 5 miles north of Vanderpool
830-966-3413
The stand of rare uvalde bigtooth maple trees greets visitors with a spectacular show of color in the fall at this state natural area. Continue the visual delights with views of limestone canyons and scenic woods. This area draws huge weekend crowds.

Lost Maples State Natural Area near Vanderpool

Best season to ride:	Spring
Gasoline availability:	Adequate
About the road:	Two-lane paved roads bordered by ranches, primarily dirt shoulders
Insider tip:	Some open grazing areas; watch for animals

Leave Kerrville for Ingram and stroll the Old Ingram Loop to wander by studios and galleries of an artists' colony. Ride by Stonehenge II, a quirky replica of England's Druid megaliths and experience cattle country via the Y.O. Ranch.

The Y.O. Ranch sprawls over 40,000 acres. Established in 1880 by Texas Ranger Captain Charles Schreiner, the working ranch maintains a large herd of Texas longhorns. You can sign up for a trail drive or join a photo safari. Guided tours focus on 58 species of exotic animals, including zebras and giraffes. Introduced to this region in the 1930s, their numbers are estimated at more than 100,000. Many of the species are endangered or extinct in their countries of origin.

Enjoy scenic lookouts over Frio River Canyon; watch for whitetail deer, wild turkey, and javelinas (wild boar). You may spot rare species of birds, too, such as green kingfisher and golden-cheeked warbler. You may want to stop and swap stories at the Lone Star Motorcycle Museum on your way to Medina's famous u-pick farms.

Back in Kerrville, you can two-step to country and western music, attend a rodeo or Texas cookout, or sample down-home barbecue, chicken-fried steaks, and grilled prime beef.

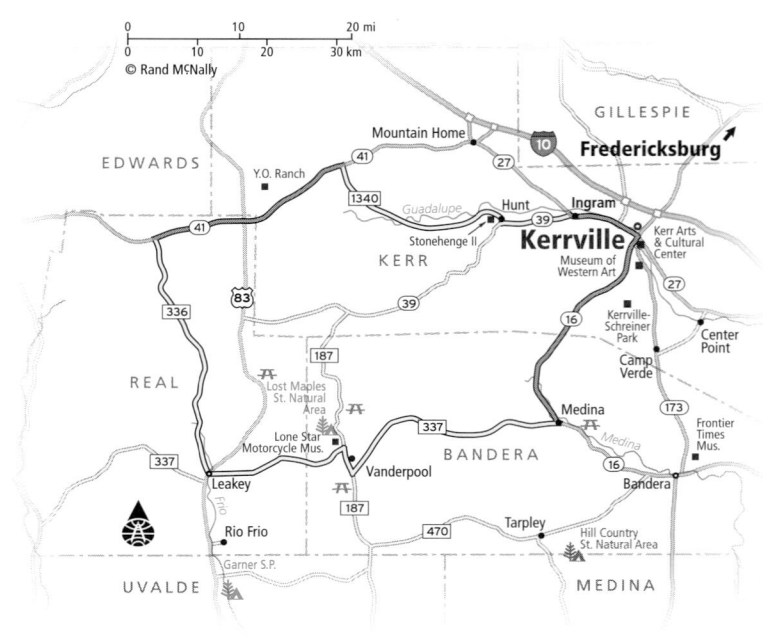

UTAH/WYOMING

STATE MAP AND RIDE – P. 206

ROUTE LENGTH – 87.7 miles or 2+ hours nonstop

TOURING INFORMATION

In distance the Ogden River Scenic Byway (SR 39) is relatively short, but in beauty, it soars to Olympian heights. The ride climbs up to and through the Wasatch Range including the Wasatch-Cache National Forest of spruce and Douglas fir all the way to Woodruff, ending just over the state line in Wyoming.

Take a side trip from Ogden to Brigham City for a stop at the Bear River Migratory Bird Refuge. Most of the 74,000 acres at the northern end of the Great Salt Lake consist of marsh, open water, and mudflats; the rest is upland, wet meadows, and ponds. The refuge is a respite for shorebirds and waterfowl and people as well, with many finding the sunset over the Promontory Mountains reason enough to visit.

Due to heavy snowfall The eastern stretch of Route 39 toward Woodruff is closed in the winter. Call ahead regarding road conditions.

VISITOR INFORMATION

www.utah.com | 800-200-1160 or 801-538-1030

PULL OVER

Pineview Reservoir
Route 39 | 8 miles east of Ogden | 801-625-5112
Built in 1937 with the Pineview Dam Project, the reservoir has a surface area of 2,870 feet and is situated at an elevation of 4,900 feet. No camping is allowed, but there's plenty of fishing for record muskie and plump panfish. Water enthusiasts also windsurf on the sparkling water.

Abbey of Our Lady of the Holy Trinity
1250 South 9500 | Huntsville | 801-745-3784
Only the gift shop is open to the public at this Trappist-Cistercian monastery. But the creamed honey and two-grain cereal mix sold there are worth the short drive from town. The honey is available in 14 flavors. Another food product produced and sold at the monastery is freshly ground peanut butter. The Abbey is located on 1,800 acres of land; only 700 acres are farmed.

Pastoral landscape fills Ogden Valley near the Pineview Reservoir

Best season to ride:	Summer is cool and green, but the colors in the fall are awesome.
Gasoline availability:	Adequate
About the road:	Tight and winding
Insider tip:	The weather cools as you climb pass the Snowbasin Ski Area; pack appropriately.

Begin in the city of Ogden on historic 25th Street. The urban surroundings soon succumb to alpine landscapes as the road climbs the rugged peaks of the Wasatch Mountain Range. The byway slips through a narrow quartzite canyon carved by the Ogden River, where layers of white, pink, red, and cream limestone and shale paint steep cliff walls. Hiking and climbing are popular pursuits in the Wasatch-Cache National Forest, and this canyon accesses numerous trailheads. Wildlife includes elk, moose, deer, sure-footed mountain goats, and, albeit rarely, mountain lions.

Water-skiers and windsurfers as well as folks with fishing poles head for Pineview Reservoir, which is stocked with tiger muskie. The vast reservoir also tempts anglers with bass, catfish, and a variety of panfish.

This byway passes through high valley and mountain meadows, where Monte Cristo rises to 11,121 feet. Near Huntsville, the monks at a Trappist monastery produce honey and other foodstuffs for sale. The bucolic setting, a tranquil stop, invites reflection.

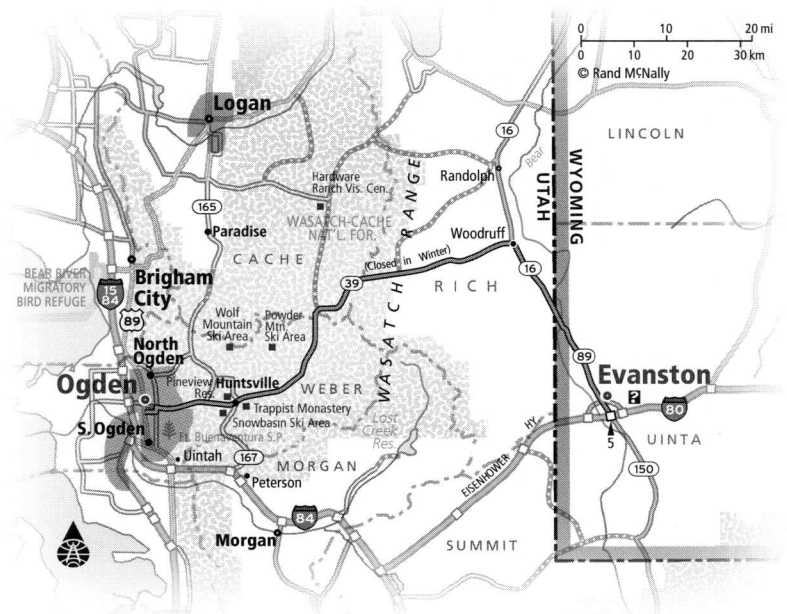

WASHINGTON

STATE MAP – P. 218, RIDE – PP. 219 & 221

TOURING INFORMATION

The Lewis & Clark Highway (WA 14) meanders out of Vancouver and follows the Columbia River to Plymouth, Washington.

Take a side trip to Fort Vancouver National Historic Site, the western headquarters of the Hudson's Bay Company, which was established in 1825. Located near Vancouver on the Columbia River, several reconstructed buildings are housed within the 20-foot-high palisade and have been furnished with period pieces. Park staff lead hourly guided tours throughout the year.

The road simply follows the river, where views of the mountains, the water, gorges, and trees look much the same as when they were seen by Lewis and Clark on their quest to explore the northwest. The road leads by mountainous terrain to plains and pastures.

VISITOR INFORMATION

www.experiencewashington.com | 800-544-1800

PULL OVER
Maryhill Museum of Art

35 Maryhill Museum Dr. | Goldendale | 509-773-3733
This museum serves as the major cultural resource in the Columbia River Gorge region. Its collections are housed in a castle-like chateau on 6,000 acres of ranch land. The museum is open 9-5 daily, March through November. Visit the Stonehenge memorial, a full-scale replica of England's Stonehenge. The memorial includes monuments to soldiers of Klickitat County who died in WWII, the Korean War, and the Vietnam War.

ROUTE LENGTH – About 175 miles or 1 day's ride

Mount Hood in Oregon towers in the distance behind Lacamas Lake near Camas, Washington

Best season to ride: Spring, summer, or autumn
Gasoline availability: Adequate; watch fuel toward eastern side of ride
About the road: Two-lane, some curves and hills, gently winds and climbs
Insider tip: Watch for wildlife

Retrace the steps of Lewis and Clark along the Columbia River Gorge on Washington's southern border. Highway 14 offers 170 miles of two-lane motoring with curves, out-of-the-way places, and the haunting beauty of nature's handiwork.

The surreal landscape of the Columbia River Gorge is the result of cataclysmic floods that carved out the gorge about 13,000 years ago. Be prepared to stop frequently to absorb the gorgeous sights in the nation's first National Scenic Area. The Columbia Gorge Interpretive Center in Stevenson is a good resource for everything about the gorge.

Next to the Columbia River itself, the effect of the wind is a sight to behold. One moment the river can be as peaceful as a sheltered lake, and the next moment the wind can churn up huge swells and white-capped waves. The result is the windsurfing capital of the world. Watch Hood River to see windsurfers skimming across the water like vividly colored butterflies. Doug's Beach State Park is adjacent to Highway 14 and named after Hood River windsurfing legend Doug Campbell.

Oregon's Mount Hood is the visual anchor for the Columbia River Gorge from either side of the river. Rising out of the river, 848-foot-high Beacon Rock is the core of an ancient volcano. Beacon Rock was named by Lewis and Clark in 1805. The mile-long trail to its summit provides outstanding views of the Columbia River Gorge.

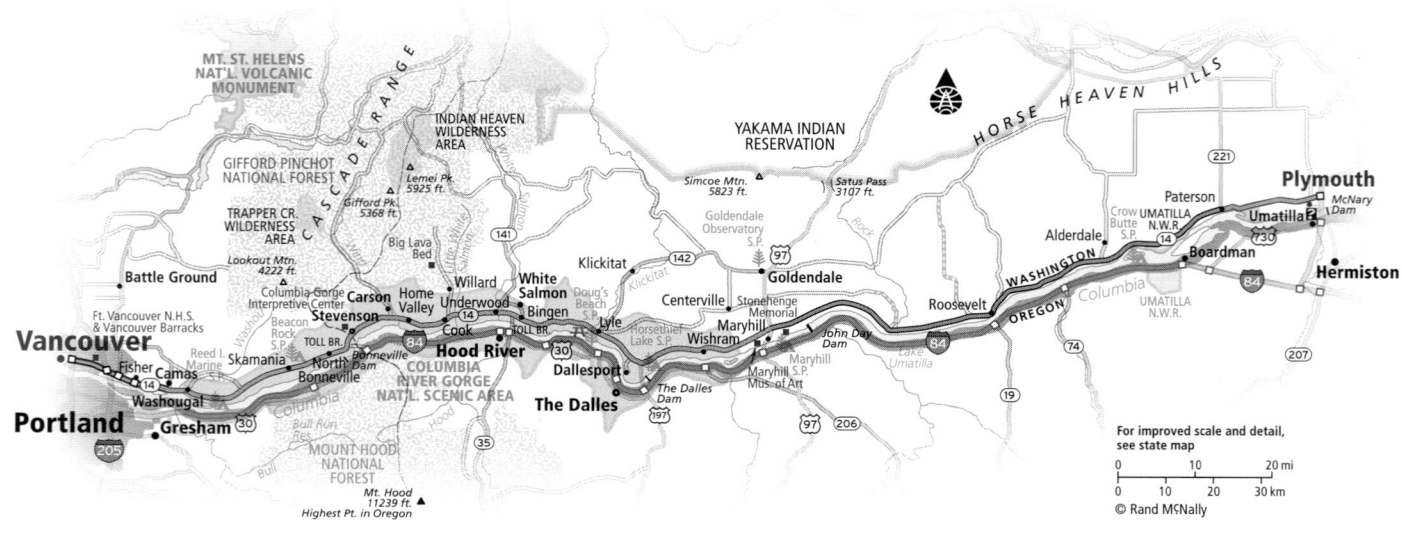

WISCONSIN

STATE MAP – P. 228, RIDE – P. 231

ROUTE LENGTH – 24 miles – An afternoon with stops

TOURING INFORMATION

A posted speed of 35 mph holds for most of this ride, which explores county roads and streets with names like Loos and Branch, Hogs Back, and Holy Hill. Although it curves and gently climbs as it slices through residential and wooded areas, it is a comfortable ride.

Take a side trip into Milwaukee and sign up for The Great American Factory Tour at Harley-Davidson. See page R36 for details. Be sure to ride over to the magnificent lakefront along Lake Michigan, especially the Milwaukee Art Museum. Even if you don't have time to go inside, the Santiago Calatrava-designed Quadracci Pavilion is a sight to behold. Three times a day you have the opportunity to see the "wings" in motion. When the sun rises high enough to touch the museum, the wings open to shade the collection inside. At noon, they close and open (or "flap") for the benefit of visitors. And at dusk they close to maintain the required interior temperature. The Milwaukee County War Memorial Center, including the Vietnam Veteran's Memorial, is adjacent to the museum. Its outdoor plaza offers great views of the lake and the city's skyline.

This run is considered one of "the" motorcycle roads in the area. Hogs Back Road offers the most curves as it gently climbs toward Holy Hill. For most of the route, the shoulders are narrow.

VISITOR INFORMATION

www.travelwisconsin.com | 800-432-8747

PULL OVER

Holy Hill National Shrine of Mary
1525 Carmel Rd | Hubertus | 262-628-1838
This shrine, 1,350 ft. above sea level, provides spectacular views of the surrounding woodlands and pastoral landscape.

Kettle Moraine State Forest – Pike Lake Unit
Washington County | 262-670-3400
Some 20,000 years ago, vast ice sheets plowed across much of Wisconsin and created the landscape that we know today. Two lobes of the ice sheet met along a line that stretches from Walworth County in the south to Kewaunee County in the north, and when they melted away they left behind the Kettle Moraine, a wonderland of unusual topographical features. The five units of Kettle Moraine State Forest encompass steep-sided ridges, cone-shaded hills, and glacial outwash plains dotted with lakes.

Holy Hill area

Best season to ride: Fall color is beautiful
Gasoline availability: Plentiful
Road conditions: Narrow, two-lane roads with pavement markings
Insider tip: Watch for turning vehicles, as this ride passes through residential areas and increased traffic when colors change in fall.

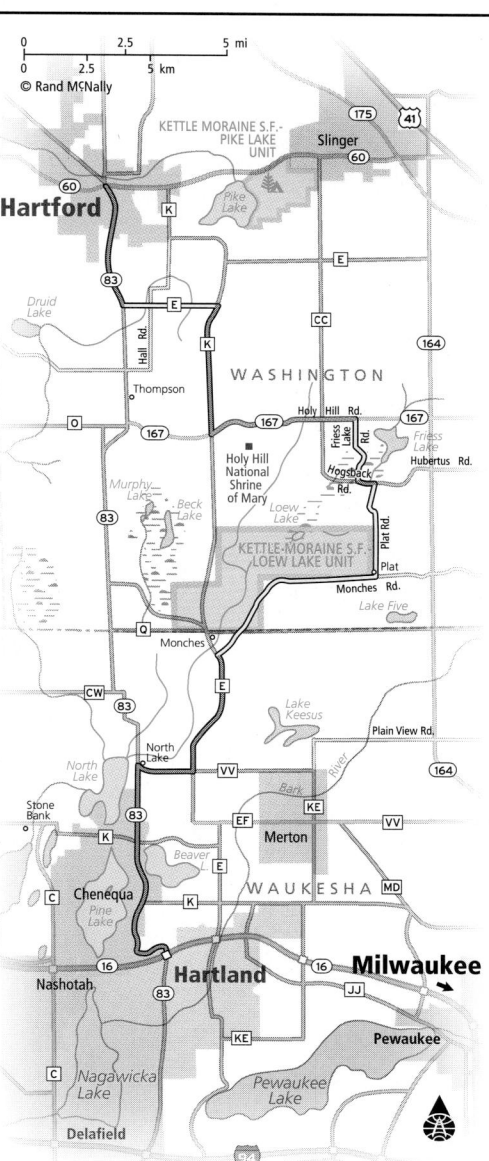

The heart of America's heartland beats in Wisconsin. The home of Harley-Davidson Motor Company, world-class cheese, and the Green Bay Packers also boasts stunning scenery, abundant lakes, and miles of scenic back roads.

Hartford offers "gemuetlichkeit" – the good feeling – as only Wisconsin can. Raise a couple of steins or try the polka at the town's annual Oktoberfest/Polkafest. Or do your holiday shopping early at the Great Hartford Craft Exposition, which is held along with the Lion's Club Pancake Dinner. Hop on scenic WI 83 and explore some of the back roads as you wind your way to Holy Hill. From this elevated vantage, gaze down upon the charming rural scenery for which Wisconsin is acclaimed. If you take this ride in August, watch out for traffic; the shrine is the focus of an annual pilgrimage and there are plenty of cars on the road.

Rustic WI 83, a winding, hilly route, offers spectacular views of the church's spire and nearby Lowe Lake.

WYOMING

STATE MAP AND RIDE – P. 234

TOURING INFORMATION

WY 296 leads from Cody through the Shoshone National forest.

Take a side trip to Mammoth Hot Springs in Yellowstone National Park (about 30 miles west of Cody) — the overlook of the Clarks Fork of the Yellowstone River and Mammoth Hot Springs is worth the short ride. At this location, fissures create about 50 hot springs. There are hundreds of campgrounds in the nearby state park, national forest, and Yellowstone National Park, so you can kick back and stay a while.

Fur trappers refer to WY 296 as the "Sunlight Basin Road" because light in the valley is brilliant year-round. From the road in the Shoshone National Forest you'll be able to spot glaciers among the mountain peaks that soar more than 10,000 feet high.

VISITOR INFORMATION

www.wyomingtourism.org | 800-225-5996

PULL OVER

Shoshone National Forest

808 Meadow Lane | Cody | 307-527-6241
This 2.4-million-acre forest includes terrain ranging from sagebrush flats to rugged mountain peaks. Often climbing to elevations over 12,000 feet, the area boasts 156 glaciers. Visitors enjoy hiking, fishing, hunting, boating on the numerous lakes, canoeing (no rentals), and rafting. More than half the forest is designated as a wilderness area. There are more than 1,500 miles of scenic roadways. Keep your eyes open for resident big-horn sheep, grizzly bear, and elk. When heading out onto the hiking trails, check trailhead bulletin boards for closings due to grizzly bears. Theodore Roosevelt, an early champion of wilderness preservation, insisted that Hwy. 14/16/20 between Cody and Yellowstone was the most scenic 52 miles in the United States.

Buffalo Bill Historical Center

720 Sheridan Ave. | Cody | 307-587-4771
The Wild West era comes to life at the Buffalo Bill Historical Center. It comprises five museum galleries, and a variety of permanent and traveling exhibitions. The Buffalo Bill Museum contains memorabilia of Col. William F. Cody, in his day one of the most famous people in the world. It interprets the history of the cowboy and offers attractions. The Whitney Gallery of Western Art has in its collection works by the likes of George Catlin, Alfred Jacob Miller, and Thomas Moran. The Plains Indian Museum promotes public recognition of Plains art and culture. The Cody Firearms Museum houses the Winchester collection. The Draper Museum of Natural History is where visitors can take a virtual tour as they discover the natural forces that shape Yellowstone National Park and the surrounding region.

ROUTE LENGTH – 60+ miles or 1 day with stops

The Old Trail Town, Cody

Best season to ride:	Summer
Gasoline availability:	Adequate
About the road:	Twists and curves plus inclines and declines
Insider tip:	Elevations change; pack and dress accordingly

You'll likely spot mountain goats along this route, since this is the habitat of the largest herd in Wyoming. Keep an eye out for bears, wolves, and coyote that range through this region graced by mountains, meadows, and the magnificent Shoshone National Forest. It is a beautiful wilderness.

WY 296 is known as "Chief Joseph Scenic Highway" after the Nez Perce chief who valiantly fought the U.S. Cavalry to defend tribal lands and then led 1,000 of his people on a 1,800-mile trek toward Canada. They were forced to surrender just 30 miles from freedom. It heads out of Cody up to the 8,048-foot-high Dead Indian Pass and continues through a series of switchbacks that provide beautiful views of the basin and Clarks Fork Canyon.

Activities include wildlife safaris, horseback riding, wagon rides, cookouts, white-water rafting, and fishing fresh-running brooks for brown, rainbow, and cutthroat trout.

Cody, eastern gateway to Yellowstone National Park, stages seasonal nightly rodeos and houses the Buffalo Bill Historical Center.

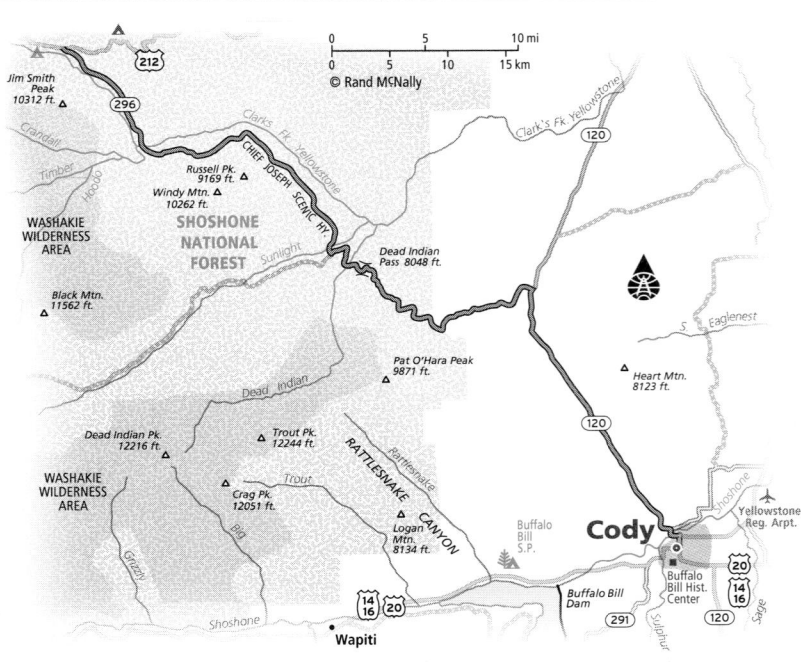

RIDING NORTH & SOUTH OF THE BORDER

National Palace, Mexico City, D.F.

Citizenship Documents

A U.S. passport or proof of citizenship, such as an original or certified birth certificate and photo identification (such as a driver's license), is required for entry into Mexico or Canada. Naturalized U.S. citizens should carry citizenship papers; permanent residents of the United States must bring proof of residency and photo identification.

Re-entry to the U.S.

Proof of both citizenship and identity is required for entry into the United States. Be able to provide proof of U.S. citizenship via a U.S. passport or a certified copy of your birth certificate, a Certificate of Naturalization, a Certificate of Citizenship, or a Report of Birth Abroad of a U.S. citizen. To prove your identity, present either a valid driver's license or a government identification card that includes a photo or physical description.

Border Crossing Waits

Allow plenty of time. The average time for customs clearance is 30 minutes, but this varies greatly depending on traffic flow and security issues.

Traveling with Kids

For children under the age of 18, parents should be prepared to provide evidence, such as a birth certificate or adoption decree, to prove they are indeed the parents. Divorced parents sharing custody should carry copies of the legal custody documents. If children are traveling with only one parent, a written letter of permission from the other parent must be presented. The same evidence is required for children traveling with grandparents, legal guardians, or any other adults who are not the parents.

BORDER CROSSING INFORMATION

RIDING IN MEXICO

According to U.S. Customs and Border Protection, visitors intending to ride a motorcycle in Mexico must obtain a vehicle permit (valid for six months) from the Mexican Customs Office at the border. The permit must be held and then surrendered when leaving Mexico.

A processing fee (about $25) is also mandatory, along with the posting of a bond to guarantee the departure of the vehicle within the dates stated on the permit. To recover the bond, you must return to the same Mexican Customs office when you leave Mexico.

Carry proof of vehicle ownership (the current registration card or a letter of authorization from the finance or leasing company). Vehicle insurance policies, other than Mexican, are not valid in Mexico. A short-term liability policy is obtainable at the border.

Tourist Cards

Tourist cards are valid for any period up to six months, are free of charge, and are required for all persons, regardless of age, to visit the interior of Mexico. Cards may be obtained from Mexican border authorities, Consuls of Mexico, or from Federal Delegates in major cities. Cards are also distributed to passengers en route to Mexico by air.

More Information

Mexican Embassy in Washington, D.C.: 202-736-1000; www.embassyofmexico.org

RIDING IN CANADA

Drivers need proof of ownership of the vehicle or documentation of its rental, a valid U.S. motorcycle driver's license, and vehicle insurance. Most motorcycle laws in Canada mirror those in the United States. There are some that differ. Remember, when riding in Canada:

- Safety helmets are required.
- There are no passenger age restrictions in Canada.
- See motorcycle laws on province page maps.
- Use of turn signals is required in all provinces except Northwest Territories, New Brunswick, and Ontario.
- Eye protection is required in Newfoundland & Labrador and Saskatchewan, unless the bike is equipped with a windscreen.

More Information

Canadian Embassy in Washington, D.C.: 202-682-1740; www.canadianembassy.org

HARLEY-DAVIDSON® SERVICES

THE GREAT AMERICAN FACTORY TOUR

FACTORY TOURS

Behind every great machine are people with a passion. Since 1903, Harley-Davidson has built the most coveted motorcycles on the planet. And now you can see first-hand how these machines come to life. Through exclusive exhibits and stops on the factory floor, Harley-Davidson Factory Tours give you a behind-the-scenes look at what it takes to create an American legend. They're guided and unlike anything you've ever experienced. Because you won't just watch motorcycles being built, you'll watch history being made.

For more information and specific site guidelines and safety requirements, call 1-877-883-1450 (toll free) or 414-343-7850 or visit www.harley-davidson.com.

RIDER'S EDGE® - THE HARLEY-DAVIDSON ACADEMY OF MOTORCYCLING

Learn to Ride

No matter what path takes you into the saddle of a Harley-Davidson® motorcycle, you should feel confident there. That's the mission of Rider's Edge®, the Harley-Davidson Academy of Motorcycling.

The New Rider Course uses the proven curriculum of the Motorcycle Safety Foundation's® Basic RiderCourseSM, with a twist provided by the enthusiasts at Harley-Davidson and Buell. It includes about 25 hours of instruction, both in the classroom, where you'll learn the basics of riding, and on a controlled practice range, where you'll hone the skills that will make you ready for the road. The Rider's Edge New Rider Course won't just teach you how to operate a motorcycle. It will show you a whole new world.

Learn to Ride Better

Whether you're a recent graduate of the Rider's Edge® New Rider Course or a seasoned road veteran, the Rider's Edge® Skilled Rider Course is the perfect place to brush up on your riding technique and to challenge your current skill level.

Hook up with a Rider's Edge course at a participating Harley-Davidson dealer or visit www.ridersedge.com.

LIFE STARTS AT THE EDGE. ®

HARLEY-DAVIDSON® AUTHORIZED RENTALS

Whether vacationing or traveling on business, you can turn any trip into a thundering adventure with a Harley-Davidson Authorized Rental.

Harley-Davidson Authorized Rentals locations always offer the latest model Harley-Davidson motorcycles, strictly serviced and maintained to Motor Company standards.

Each Harley-Davidson Authorized Rentals experience includes the use of a Harley-Davidson country-approved helmet and raingear, short-term luggage storage, and 24-hour emergency roadside assistance.

Choose from over 260 worldwide locations – and discover our latest additions – at www.hdrentals.com.

THE HARLEY OWNERS GROUP® - OR H.O.G.® - is the largest factory-sponsored motorcycle club
in the world. Its stated mission is a simple one: "To Ride and Have Fun." With so many benefits, programs, and activities available, members can spend a lifetime fulfilling their motorcycling dreams. And with world-wide membership approaching 1,000,000, there is no shortage of fellow riders to share in your journey.

For more information, contact our United States office at 1-800-CLUBHOG (1-800-258-2464) or 414-343-4896 (outside U.S. and Canada) • www.hog.com
Contact our Canadian office at 800-668-4836 or 905-660-3500 (outside Canada and U.S.) • www.hog.com

MOTORCYCLE SHIPPING

Harley-Davidson has partnered with the largest and most trusted vehicle transport company in America to ship your motorcycle anywhere within the continental U.S. and into and out of Canada and Hawaii. Harley-Davidson® Shipping offers convenient locations for shipping, including door-to-door pick-up and delivery from a business or personal residence. The new service goes beyond other shipping services by offering honored real-time quotes and multi-bike group discounts – perfect for your next chapter trip. Harley-Davidson Shipping is open for any enthusiast to use, while additional discounts on shipments are offered to all full Harley Owners Group (H.O.G.) and Buell Riders Adventure Group™ (BRAG®) members. Contact us for your next vacation or rally, or when buying or selling your motorcycle – we can help make shipping your motorcycle worry-free!

For more information about Harley-Davidson Shipping rates, locations, transit schedules and other services available, call 1-888-224-BIKE. Shipping quotes and vehicle tracking can be done online at www.harley-davidson.com/shipping.

STATE PARK INFORMATION

Mount Katahdin, Baxter State Park, Millinocket, Maine

Check out these numbers and websites for general information and camping availability in each state.

Alabama
800-252-7275 | www.alapark.com

Alaska
907-269-8400 | www.alaskastateparks.org

Arizona
602-542-4174 | www.pr.state.az.us/

Arkansas
888-287-2757 | www.arkansasstateparks.com

California
916-653-6995 | 800-777-0369
www.parks.ca.gov

Colorado
303-866-3437 | parks.state.co.us/

Connecticut
860-424-3200 | www.dep.state.ct.us/stateparks

Delaware
302-739-9220 | www.destateparks.com

Florida
850-245-2157 | www.floridastateparks.org

Georgia
404-656-3530 | www.gastateparks.org

Hawaii
808-587-0400
www.hawaii.gov/dlnr/dsp/hawaii.html

Idaho
208-334-4199 | www.idahoparks.org

Illinois
217-782-6302
www.dnr.state.il.us/lands/landmgt/parks

Indiana
317-232-4124 | www.in.gov/dnr/parklake

Iowa
515-281-5918 | www.exploreiowaparks.com

Kansas
620-672-5911 | www.kdwp.state.ks.us

Kentucky
800-255-7275 | www.parks.ky.gov

Louisiana
888-677-1400 | www.lastateparks.com

Maine
207-287-3821 | www.maine.gov/doc/parks

Maryland
800-830-3974 | www.dnr.state.md.us/publiclands

Massachusetts
617-626-1250 | www.massparks.org

Michigan
517-373-9900 | www.michigan.gov/dnr

Minnesota
888-646-6367 | www.dnr.state.mn.us

Mississippi
800-467-2757 | www.mdwfp.com/parks.asp

Missouri
800-334-6946 | www.mostateparks.com

Montana
406-444-3750 | www.fwp.state.mt.us

Nebraska
800-826-7275
www.ngpc.state.ne.us/parks/parks.asp

Nevada
775-687-4384 | parks.nv.gov

New Hampshire
603-271-3556 | www.nhstateparks.org

New Jersey
800-843-6420
www.state.nj.us/dep/parksandforests/parks/
index.html

New Mexico
888-667-2757 | www.emnrd.state.nm.us/nmparks/

New York
518-474-0456 | nysparks.state.ny.us

North Carolina
919-733-7275
www.ils.unc.edu/parkproject/ncparks.html

North Dakota
701-328-5357 | www.parkrec.nd.gov

Ohio
866-644-6727 | www.dnr.state.oh.us/parks

Oklahoma
800-654-8240 | www.oklahomaparks.com

Oregon
800-551-6949 | www.oregonstateparks.org

Pennsylvania
888-727-3757
www.dcnr.state.pa.us/stateparks/index.asp

Rhode Island
401-222-2632 | www.riparks.com

South Carolina
803-734-1700 | www.southcarolinaparks.com

South Dakota
605-773-3391 | www.sdgfp.info/parks

Tennessee
888-867-2757
www.state.tn.us/environment/parks

Texas
800-792-1112 | www.tpwd.state.tx.us

Utah
801-538-7220 | www.stateparks.utah.gov

Vermont
802-241-3655
www.vtstateparks.com/htm/info.cfm

Virginia
800-933-7275 | www.dcr.state.va.us/parks

Washington
360-902-8844 | www.parks.wa.gov

West Virginia
800-225-5982 | www.wvstateparks.com

Wisconsin
608-266-2181 | www.wiparks.net

Wyoming
307-777-6303 | www.wyoparks.state.wy.us

10 MOST POPULAR NATIONAL PARKS

Yosemite National Park in the Sierra Nevada, California

1. Great Smoky Mountains National Park

Eastern Tennessee and western North Carolina
(P. 154, H-4)

Established: 1934
Visitors in 2004: 9,167,046
Website: www.nps.gov/grsm
Visitor Information: 865-436-1200

Ride: Watch for black bears and other critters roadside as the main road (US 441) bisects the park, climbing through the Appalachians from Tennessee to North Carolina.

Stretching 800 square miles over ancient mountains, with the Appalachian Trail threading through the middle, Great Smoky Mountains National Park preserves one of the largest wilderness sanctuaries in the east. Mist-filled clouds produce the haze that resulted in the park's name.

Don't miss: The Roaring Fork Motor Nature Trail (closed in winter), which leads to Grotto Falls, the park's only waterfall that you can walk behind; Cades Cove, a valley with preserved log cabins, barns, and other structures built by mountain folk; Clingman's Dome, the park's highest point.

2. Grand Canyon National Park

Grand Canyon, Arizona
(P. 16, C-4)

Established: 1919
Visitors in 2004: 4,326,234
Website: www.nps.gov/grca
Visitor Information: 928-638-7888

Ride: Arizona Highway 64 loops into the park at the edge of the Kaibab National Forest, with magnificent views of the canyon at Mather and Yavapai Points.

A geologic wonder, the Grand Canyon spans 277 miles, where the Colorado River and other water has eroded the Colorado Plateau as deep as 6,000 feet and up to 15 miles across at some points. The river still runs through the bottom of the canyon in this national park of 1.2 million acres.

Don't miss: Sunrise at Mather Point or anywhere along the South Rim Trail; mule rides down the Bright Angel Trail (reservations are taken up to 23 months in advance, so plan ahead); train ride into the heart of the park from nearby Williams, Arizona; hiking through forests of the North Rim trails; wild-life viewing in the mountain meadows.

3. Cuyahoga Valley National Park

Between Cleveland and Akron, Ohio
(P. 160, NG-15)

Established: 2000
Visitors in 2004: 3,306,175
Website: www.nps.gov/cuva
Visitor Information: 216-524-1497

Ride: Riverview Road runs right through the center of the park, providing easy access to the ski resort, Hunt Farm Visitor Information Center, and the park headquarters.

Encompassing a swath of 33,000 acres between Cleveland and Akron along the crooked path of the Cuyahoga River, the Cuyahoga Valley National Park has steep ravines and wooded uplands, historical tours and hiking along the Ohio & Erie Canal towpath, plus a winter sports center for sledding and tobogganing.

Don't miss: A scenic rail ride through the heart of the park on a circa-1940 rail coach of the Cuyahoga Valley Scenic Railroad; Brandywine Falls, a 67-foot high waterfall; hiking or biking the 20-mile Ohio & Erie Canal Towpath Trail; winter sledding on the Kendall Hills.

4. Yosemite National Park

In the Sierra Nevada, California
(P. 27, NL-11)

Established: 1890
Visitors in 2004: 3,280,911
Website: www.nps.gov/yose
Visitor Information: 209-372-0200

Ride: In summer, take the scenic Tioga Road, which bisects the park, to Tuolumne Meadows, crossing Yosemite Creek and passing by Porcupine Flat.

Championed by 19th-century environmentalist John Muir, Yosemite National Park epitomizes the splendor of the western Sierra Nevada range filled with granite cliffs, magnificent waterfalls, and ancient giant sequoias. Elevations range from 2,000 to more than 13,000 feet over its 761,000 acres.

Don't miss: Hiking on the John Muir Trail through Lyell Canyon; views from the bridge at the base of Lower Yosemite Fall; the stunning scene in summer and early fall from Glacier Point; the Mariposa Grove of giant sequoias.

MAP LEGEND

Roads and related symbols

Free limited-access highway

Toll limited-access highway

New road (under construction as of press time)

Other multilane highway

Principal highway

Other through highway

Other road (conditions vary — local inquiry suggested)

Unpaved road (conditions vary — local inquiry suggested)

Ramp; one way route

Ferry

Interstate highway; Interstate highway business route

U.S. highway; U.S. highway business route

Trans-Canada highway; Autoroute

Mexican or Central American highway

State or provincial highway

Secondary state, secondary provincial, or county highway

County trunk highway

Construction site or construction zone

Scenic route; **Featured ride**

Service area; toll booth or fee booth

Tunnel; mountain pass

Interchanges and exit numbers (For most states, the mileage between interchanges may be determined by subtracting one number from the other.)

Highway mileages (segments of one mile or less not shown): Cumulative miles (red): the distance between arrows Intermediate miles (black): the distance between intersections

Cities & towns
(size of type on map indicates relative population)

National capital; state or provincial capital

County seat or independent city

City, town, or recognized place; neighborhood

Urbanized area

Separate cities within metropolitan area

Parks, recreation areas, & points of interest

U.S. or Canadian national park

U.S. or Canadian national monument, other National Park Service facility, state/provincial park or recreation area

Park with camping facilities; park without camping facilities

Campsite; wayside or roadside park

City park

National forest, national grassland

Wilderness area; wildlife refuge

Point of interest, historic site or monument

Airport

Building

Foot trail

Hospital or medical center

Indian reservation

Information center or Tourist Information Center (T.I.C.)

Military or governmental installation

Rest area with toilets; rest area without toilets

Harley-Davidson® Dealer

Physical Features

Dam

Mountain peak; highest point in state/province

Lake; intermittent lake; dry lake

River; intermittent river

Desert

Glacier

Swamp or mangrove swamp

Other symbols

Area shown in greater detail on inset map

52 Inset map page indicator (if not on same page)

Great River Road

Port of entry

Intracoastal waterway

Railroad

COOK County or parish boundary and name

State or provincial boundary

National boundary

Continental divide

Time zone boundary

33° 00' 95° 00' Latitude; longitude

Comparative distances

1 mile = 1.609 kilometers

1 kilometer = .621 miles

Population figures are from the latest available census or are Census Bureau or Rand McNally estimates.

For a complete list of abbreviations that appear on the maps, go to **www.randmcnally.com** and key in the Express Access Code **ABBR**.

©2006 by Rand McNally & Company

For licensing and copyright permissions, contact us at licensing@randmcnally.com

If you have a comment or suggestion, please call (800) 777- MAPS (-6277) **or e-mail us at:** consumeraffairs@randmcnally.com **or write to:** Rand McNally Consumer Affairs P.O. Box 7600 Chicago, Illinois 60680-9915

Made in U.S.A.

10 9 8 7 6 5 4 3 2 1

EXPRESS ACCESS CODES

randmcnally.com/eac

Express Access Code: **WA**

Each map and editorial feature in this atlas has its own unique Express Access Code. These codes give you quick and easy access to tons of useful trip-planning information at randmcnally.com/eac.

Seattle **WA**

Here's how to use them:

1. Look for the red Express Access Code box **WA** located in the top corner of state and province map pages, or next to the city name on inset maps. You'll also find Express Access Codes on the mileage chart, mileage and riding times map, and editorial feature pages.

2. Go to www.randmcnally.com/eac.

3. Type in a code from the atlas, and click "go."

4. Begin exploring! Road construction updates, riding directions, fun things to see and do, mileages, and expanded editorial features are all right at your fingertips.

RAND MCNALLY. THE ROAD CONTINUES ONLINE.

GASOLINE AVAILABILITY

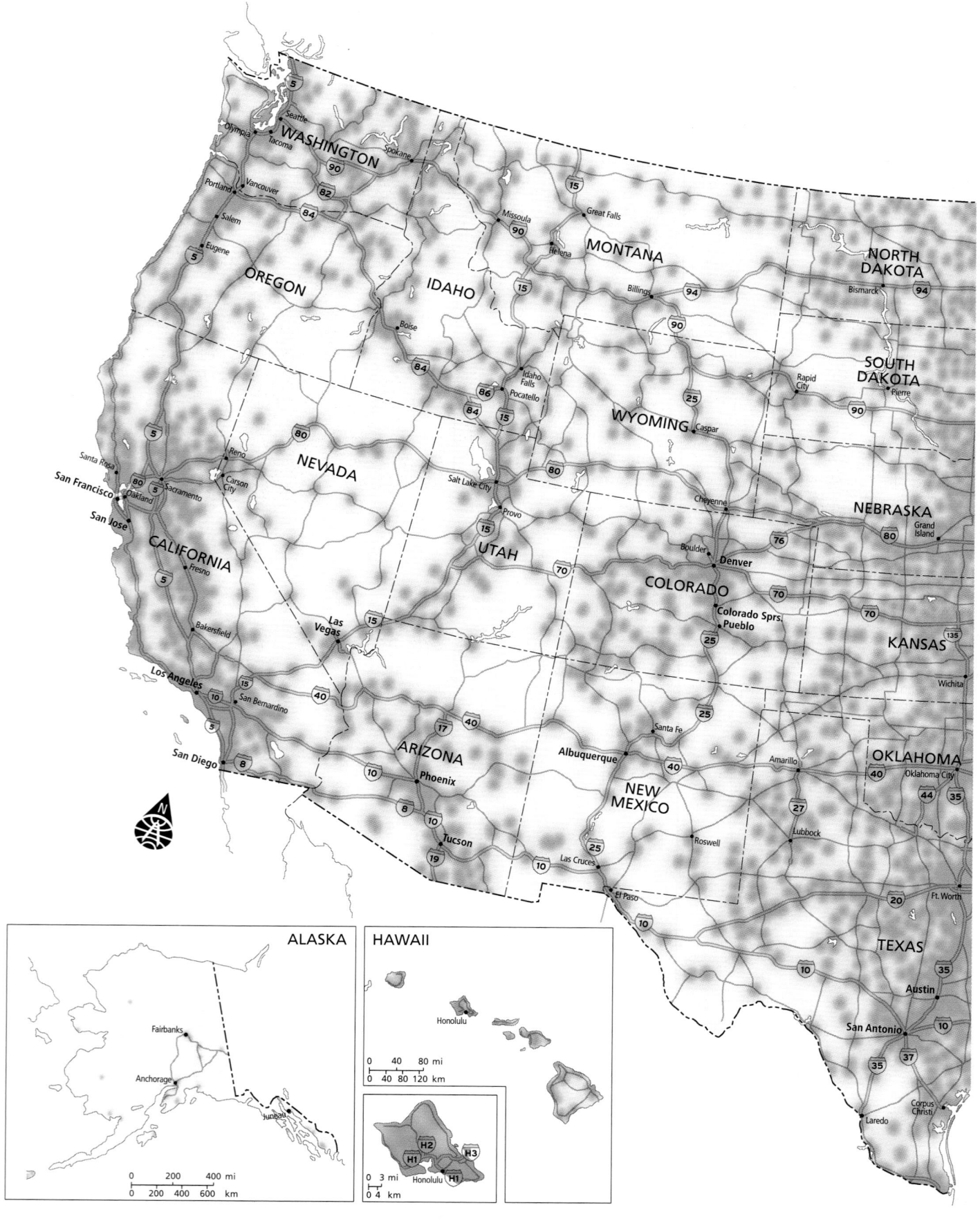

Readily available

Plan ahead

On the road one resource you can't be without is fuel. This exclusive map of the United States was created as a reference to use when planning your rides. The colors tell you where access to fuel is plentiful, adequate or limited. See above scale for detail.

© Rand McNally

Data by
infoUSA

Distance scale
One inch represents about 202 miles

0 50 100 150 200 mi
0 100 200 300 km

BRITISH COLUMBIA
SASKATCHEWAN
Saskatoon
Kamloops
Vancouver
Victoria
Calgary
ALBERTA
Regina
Seattle
Tacoma
Spokane
WASHINGTON
Olympia
Astoria
CANADA
Brandon
Portland
Salem
Vancouver
Eugene
OREGON
Bend
Missoula
Great Falls
MONTANA
Helena
Lewiston
Billings
NORTH DAKOTA
Bismarck
Boise
IDAHO
WYOMING
SOUTH DAKOTA
Rapid City
Pierre
Idaho Falls
Pocatello
Casper
Reno
Carson City
NEVADA
Salt Lake City
Ogden
Provo
Cheyenne
Denver
NEBRASKA
Grand Island
San Francisco
Oakland
San Jose
Sacramento
Fresno
UTAH
COLORADO
Colorado Sprs.
Pueblo
KANSAS
Las Vegas
CALIFORNIA
Bakersfield
Los Angeles
San Bernardino
San Diego
ARIZONA
Phoenix
Tucson
Albuquerque
NEW MEXICO
Santa Fe
Amarillo
Roswell
Lubbock
OKLAHOMA
Oklahoma City
TEXAS
Ft. Worth
El Paso
Ciudad Juárez
Las Cruces
MEXICO
PACIFIC OCEAN
BAJA CALIF.
Mexicali
SONORA
Nogales
CHIHUAHUA
San Antonio
Austin
Corpus Christi
Laredo
COAHUILA
NUEVO LEÓN
Monterrey
DURANGO
Brownsville
McAllen
TAMP.

© Rand McNally

ALASKA
RUSSIA
NUNAVUT
NORTHWEST TERRITORIES
YUKON TERR.
Nome
Fairbanks
Anchorage
Juneau
BRITISH COLUMBIA
MT. McKINLEY 20,320 FT. HIGHEST PT. IN NORTH AMERICA
Kodiak

HAWAII
HAWAII-ALEUTIAN TIME ZONE
KAUA'I
NI'IHAU
O'AHU
Honolulu
MOLOKA'I
LĀNA'I
MAUI
KAHO'OLAWE
HAWAI'I
Hilo
PACIFIC OCEAN

How to determine distance

Mileages in red between red arrowheads;
in black, between intersections.

CENTRAL TIME ZONE

EASTERN TIME ZONE

National Monuments and Memorials

1M	Agate Fossil Beds	E-6
2M	Alibates Flint Quarries	G-7
3M	Admiralty Island	J-3
4M	Agua Fria	G-4
5M	Aniakchak	J-1
6M	Aztec Ruins	F-5
7M	Cabrillo	G-2
8M	Canyon de Chelly	F-4
9M	Cape Krusenstern	I-1
10M	Capulin Volcano	F-6
11M	Casa Grande Ruins	G-4
12M	Castillo de San Marcos	H-12
13M	Cedar Breaks	F-4
14M	Chiricahua	H-4
15M	Colorado	E-5
16M	Craters of the Moon	D-4
17M	Devils Tower	D-6
18M	Dinosaur	E-5
19M	Effigy Mounds	D-9
20M	El Malpais	G-5
21M	El Morro	G-5
22M	Florissant Fossil Beds	F-6
23M	Fort Clatsop	B-2
24M	Fort Frederica	H-12
25M	Fort Matanzas	H-12
26M	Fort Pulaski	G-12
27M	Fort Sumter	G-12
28M	Fort Union	G-6
29M	Fossil Butte	D-5
30M	George Washington Carver	F-8
31M	Giant Sequoia	F-2
32M	Gila Cliff Dwellings	G-5
33M	Grand Canyon-Parashant	F-3
34M	Grand Portage	C-9
35M	Grand Staircase-Escalante	F-4
36M	Hagerman Fossil Beds	D-4
37M	Homestead	E-8
38M	Hovenweep	F-5
39M	Jewel Cave	D-6
40M	Lava Beds	D-2
41M	Montezuma Castle	G-4
42M	Mount Rushmore	D-6
43M	Mount St. Helens	B-2
44M	Natural Bridges	F-4
45M	Navajo	F-4
46M	Newberry Volcanic	C-2
47M	Ocmulgee	H-11
48M	Organ Pipe Cactus	G-3
49M	Petroglyph	G-5
50M	Pinnacles	E-1
51M	Pipe Spring	F-4
52M	Pipestone	D-8
53M	Rainbow Bridge	F-4
54M	Russell Cave	G-10
55M	Salinas Pueblo Missions	G-5
56M	Scotts Bluff	E-6
57M	Sunset Crater Volcano	F-4
58M	Timpanogos Cave	E-4
59M	Tonto	G-4
60M	Tuzigoot	G-4
61M	Vermillion Cliffs	F-4
62M	White Sands	H-5
63M	Wright Brothers	F-13
64M	Wupatki	F-4

National Parks

1P	Acadia	C-14	19P	Gates of the Arctic	I-1	39P	Mammoth Cave	F-10
2P	Arches	E-5	20P	Glacier Bay	J-2	40P	Mesa Verde	F-5
3P	Badlands	D-7	21P	Glacier	B-4	41P	Mt. Rainier	B-3
4P	Big Bend	I-6	22P	Grand Canyon	F-4	42P	North Cascades	B-3
5P	Biscayne	J-13	23P	Grand Teton	D-5	43P	Olympic	B-2
6P	Black Canyon	F-5	24P	Great Basin	E-3	44P	Petrified Forest	G-4
7P	Bryce Canyon	F-4	25P	Great Sand Dunes	F-6	45P	Redwood	C-1
8P	Canyonlands	F-4	26P	Great Smoky Mts.	G-11	46P	Rocky Mountain	E-6
9P	Capitol Reef	E-4	27P	Guadalupe Mts.	H-5	47P	Saguaro	H-4
10P	Carlsbad Caverns	H-6	28P	Haleakalā	I-4	48P	Sequoia	F-2
11P	Channel Islands	F-1	29P	Hawai'i Volcanoes	J-5	49P	Shenandoah	E-12
12P	Congaree	G-12	30P	Hot Springs	G-8	50P	Theodore Roosevelt	C-6
13P	Crater Lake	C-2	31P	Isle Royale	C-9	51P	Voyageurs	C-8
14P	Cuyahoga Valley	E-11	32P	Joshua Tree	G-3	52P	Wind Cave	D-6
15P	Death Valley	F-2	33P	Katmai	J-1	53P	Wrangell-St. Elias	I-2
16P	Denali	I-2	34P	Kenai Fjords	J-1	54P	Yellowstone	C-5
17P	Dry Tortugas	J-12	35P	Kings Canyon	F-2	55P	Yosemite	E-2
18P	Everglades	J-12	36P	Kobuk Valley	I-1	56P	Zion	F-4
			37P	Lake Clark	J-1			
			38P	Lassen Volcanic	D-2			

06-1

How to determine distance

Mileages in red between red arrowheads;
in black, between intersections.

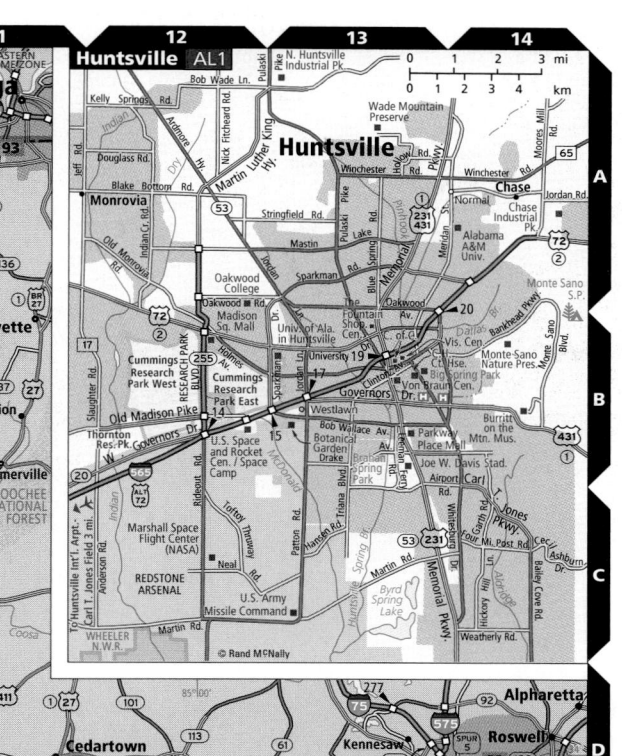

Huntsville AL1

© Rand McNally

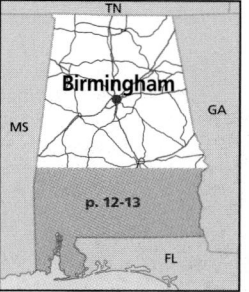

Birmingham

p. 12-13

SYMBOLS

- Featured ride
- Scenic route
- Long-term construction
- Historic site or monument; Indian reservation or rancheria; military installation; point of interest; wildlife refuge
- Harley-Davidson dealership

ALABAMA MOTORCYCLE LAWS

Helmet use:
Required

Riding two abreast:
Yes. See state law for specifics

Eye protection:
Not required

Speed limit
Primary roads: 70 mph
Secondary roads: 65 mph

ALABAMA RESOURCES

Road conditions or construction:
www.dot.state.al.us

Highway Emergency Numbers:
(334) 242-4378 or *HP

Tourism:
(800) 252-2262
www.800alabama.com
Tourism information and road construction updates also available at randmcnally.com

State motor vehicle information:
(334) 242-4371
www.dps.state.al.us

HARLEY-DAVIDSON DEALERSHIPS

Rocket Harley-Davidson Rocket Buell, B-7
15100 AL Hwy. 20 West **Madison**
(256) 340-7333; (888) 414-7316
Lat N 34.631 **Lon** W 86.876

Harley-Davidson of Montgomery, J-8
655 N. Eastern Blvd. **Montgomery**
(334) 277-2540
Lat N 32.402 **Lon** W 86.213

Big Swamp Harley-Davidson Shop, I-11
1201 Fox Run Pkwy. **Opelika**
(334) 364-0400
Lat N 32.656 **Lon** W 85.357

Mt. Cheaha Harley-Davidson, F-10
231 Davis Loop Rd. **Oxford**
(256) 832-8888
Lat N 33.595 **Lon** W 85.842

Heart of Dixie Harley-Davidson, G-7
333 Cahaba Valley Pkwy. **Pelham**
(205) 560-1234
Lat N 33.336 **Lon** W 86.784

Riders Harley-Davidson, F-7
4750 Norrell Dr. **Trussville**
(205) 655-1234
Lat N 33.641 **Lon** W 86.614

Foster Harley-Davidson, B-4
595 Hwy. 72 West **Tuscumbia**
(256) 383-5814
Lat N 34.714 **Lon** W 87.706

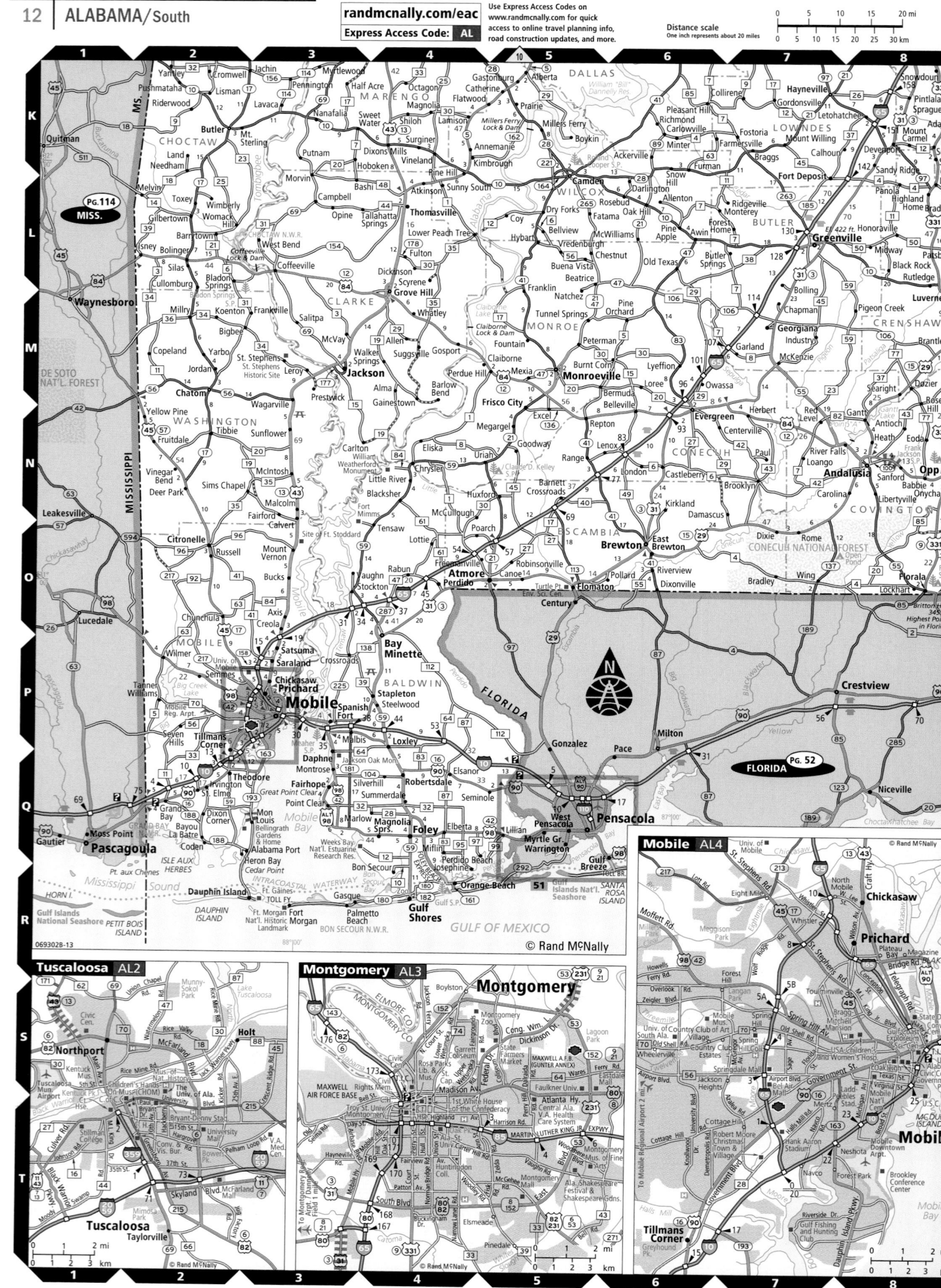

How to determine distance

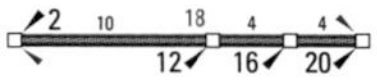

Mileages in red between red arrowheads;
in black, between intersections.

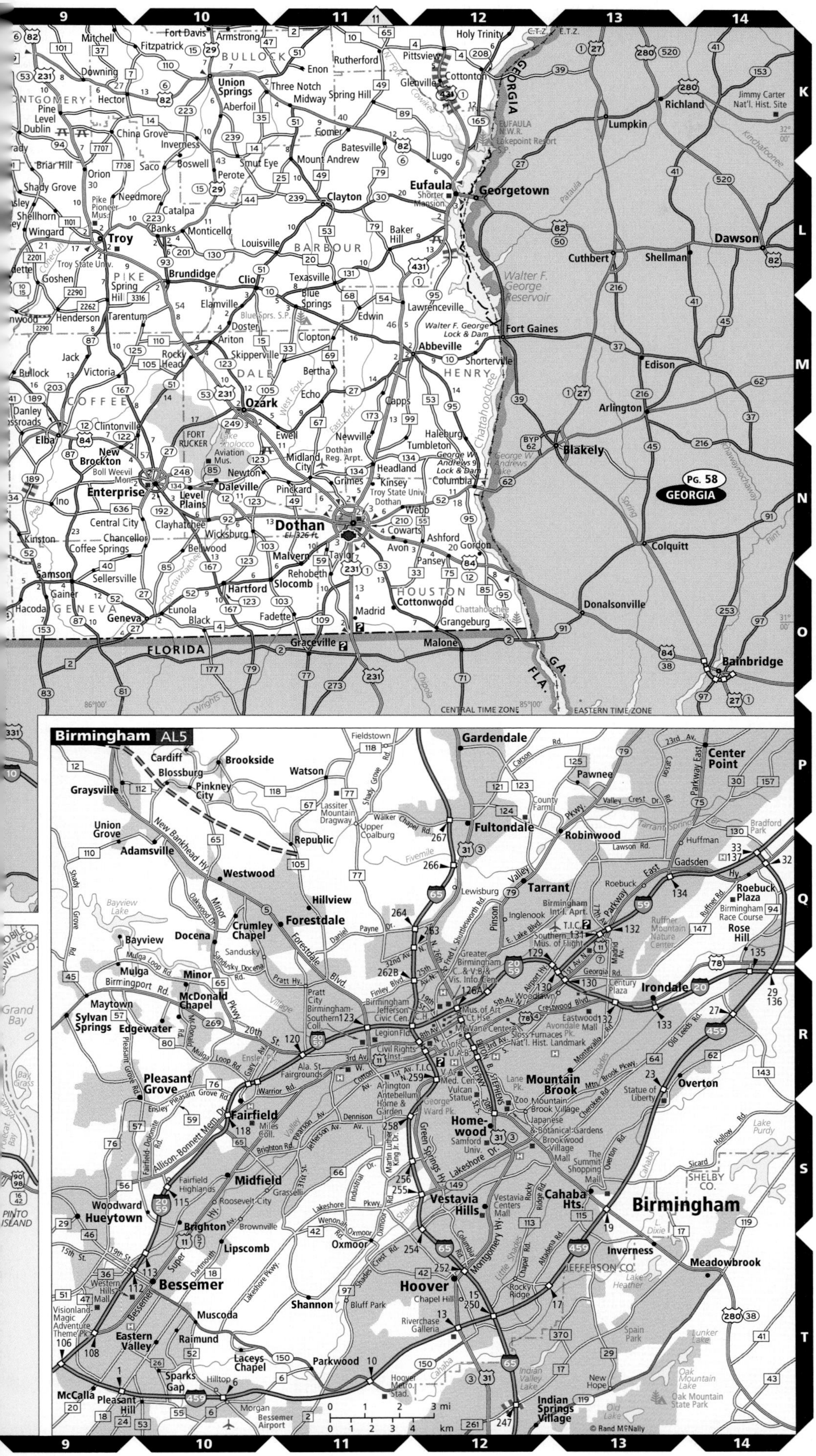

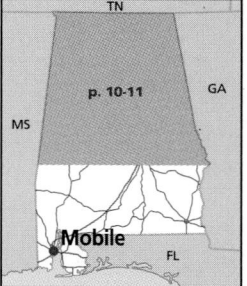

p. 10-11

TN
MS GA
Mobile
FL

SYMBOLS

Featured ride   Scenic route

Long-term construction   ■ Historic site or monument; Indian reservation or rancheria; military installation; point of interest; wildlife refuge

Harley-Davidson dealership

CITY-TO-CITY MILEAGE

	ATLANTA, GA	BIRMINGHAM	CHATTANOOGA, TN	DOTHAN	HUNTSVILLE	MOBILE	MONTGOMERY	TUSCALOOSA
Andalusia	249	181	319	75	277	125	89	194
Anniston	90	66	116	210	103	282	113	121
Atlanta, GA		148	115	202	193	329	160	203
Auburn	106	111	218	124	244	225	56	161
Birmingham	148		143	199	98	261	92	59
Chattanooga, TN	115	143		314	105	399	230	202
Decatur	227	80	130	277	26	339	170	135
Dothan	202	199	314		295	201	107	212
Eufaula	151	182	263	51	278	255	90	195
Florence	275	128	172	325	67	387	218	122
Gadsden	120	61	86	255	73	317	148	120
Huntsville	193	98	105	295		357	188	153
Jasper	188	41	183	238	90	300	131	56
Meridian, MS	290	146	289	253	240	134	152	93
Mobile	329	261	399	201	357		169	206
Montgomery	160	92	230	107	188	169		95
Pensacola, FL	319	251	389	156	347	55	159	261
Phenix City	105	141	217	97	276	257	88	193
Selma	210	94	232	151	190	193	50	75
Troy	193	142	280	57	238	173	50	155
Tuscaloosa	203	59	202	212	153	206	105	

HARLEY-DAVIDSON DEALERSHIPS

Harley-Davidson of Dothan
Buell of Dothan, N-11
2418 Ross Clark Circle S.W. **Dothan**
(334) 792-0063
Lat N 31.198 **Lon** W 85.413

Mobile Bay Harley-Davidson, P-3
3260 Pleasant Valley Rd. **Mobile**
(251) 471-2174
Lat N 30.662 **Lon** W 88.124

Birmingham AL5

© Rand McNally

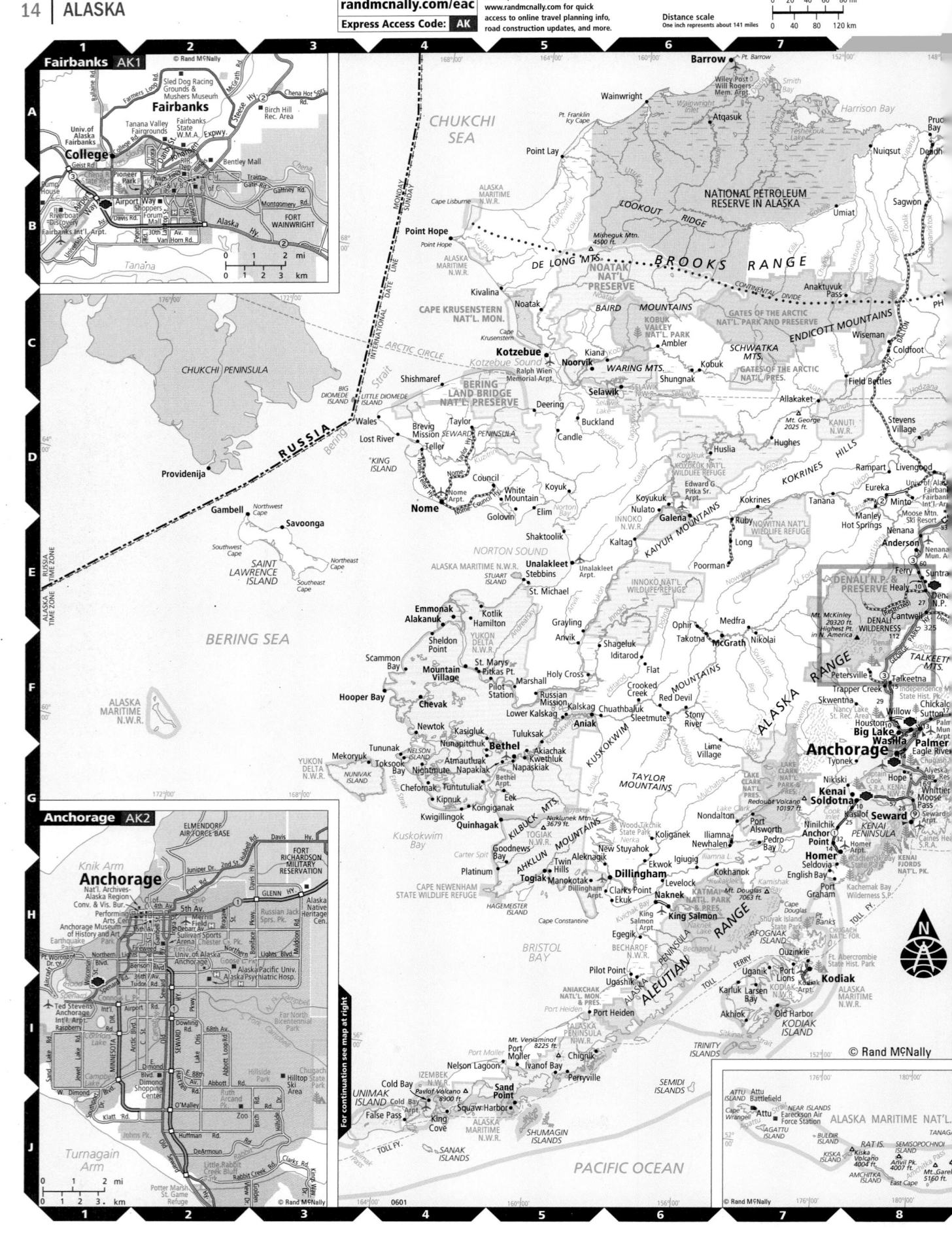

randmcnally.com/eac

Express Access Code: AK

Use Express Access Codes on www.randmcnally.com for quick access to online travel planning info, road construction updates, and more.

Distance scale
One inch represents about 141 miles

0 20 40 60 80 mi
0 40 80 120 km

Fairbanks AK1

© Rand McNally

Sled Dog Racing Grounds & Mushers Museum

Fairbanks

Univ. of Alaska Fairbanks

Tanana Valley Fairgrounds
Fairbanks State W.M.A.

College

Birch Hill Rec. Area

Pioneer Park

Riverboat Discovery
Fairbanks Int'l. Arpt.

FORT WAINWRIGHT

Tanana

0 1 2 mi
0 1 2 3 km

CHUKCHI SEA

CHUKCHI PENINSULA

RUSSIA

Providenija

Gambell

Savoonga

Northwest Cape
Southwest Cape

SAINT LAWRENCE ISLAND

Northeast Cape
Southeast Cape

BERING SEA

ALASKA MARITIME N.W.R.

Anchorage AK2

Knik Arm

ELMENDORF AIR FORCE BASE

FORT RICHARDSON MILITARY RESERVATION

Anchorage

Nat'l. Archives–Alaska Region
Conv. & Vis. Bur.

Performing Arts Center
Anchorage Museum of History and Art
Earthquake Park

Alaska Native Heritage Cen.

Univ. of Alaska Anchorage
Alaska Pacific Univ.

Ted Stevens Anchorage Int'l. Arpt.

Far North Bicentennial Park

Chugach State Park

Hilltop Ski Area

Dimond Shopping Center

Zoo

Turnagain Arm

Potter Marsh St. Game Refuge

0 1 2 mi
0 1 2 3 km

© Rand McNally

Barrow
Pt. Barrow

Wainwright

Atqasuk

Smith Bay

Harrison Bay

Prudhoe Bay

Nuiqsut

Deadh

Point Lay

NATIONAL PETROLEUM RESERVE IN ALASKA

Umiat

Sagwon

Cape Lisburne

LOOKOUT RIDGE

Mishiguk Mtn. 4500 ft.

BROOKS RANGE

Point Hope

DE LONG MTS.

NOATAK NAT'L. PRESERVE

Anaktuvuk Pass

CONTINENTAL DIVIDE

PH

Kivalina

Noatak

BAIRD MOUNTAINS

KOBUK VALLEY NAT'L. PARK

Ambler

SCHWATKA MTS.

GATES OF THE ARCTIC NAT'L PARK AND PRESERVE

ENDICOTT MOUNTAINS

Wiseman

Coldfoot

CAPE KRUSENSTERN NAT'L. MON.

Shishmaref

Kotzebue
Kotzebue Sound

Noorvik

Kiana

Kobuk

Shungnak

GATES OF THE ARCTIC NATL. PRES.

Allakaket

Field Bettles

Cape Krusenstern

Ralph Wien Memorial Arpt.

WARING MTS.

SELAWIK N.W.R.

Mt. George 2025 ft.

KANUTI N.W.R.

Stevens Village

Wales

Deering

Selawik

Buckland

Huslia

Hughes

KOKRINES HILLS

Rampart

Livengood

Brevig Mission
Teller

SEWARD PENINSULA

Candle

Koyukuk

KOYUKUK N.W.R.

Eureka

Univ. of Alaska Fairbanks Int'l. Ar.

Minto

Lost River

"KING ISLAND"

Nome Arpt.

White Mountain

Council

Koyuk

Nulato

Edward G. Pitka Sr. Arpt.

Kokrines

Tanana

Manley Hot Springs

Moose Mtn. Ski Resort

Nenana

Nome

Golovin

Elim

INNOKO N.W.R.

Galena

KAIYUH MOUNTAINS

Ruby

NOWITNA NAT'L. WILDLIFE REFUGE

Anderson

Nenana Mun. Arpt.

Shaktoolik

NORTON SOUND

Kaltag

Long

Poorman

Ferry

DENALI N.P. & PRESERVE

Suntra

Healy

Denali N.P.

Unalakleet
Unalakleet Arpt.

Stebbins

ALASKA MARITIME N.W.R.

STUART ISLAND

St. Michael

Grayling

Anvik

Ophir

Medfra

Mt. McKinley 20320 ft. Highest Pt. in N. America

DENALI WILDERNESS

Cantwell

Emmonak
Alakanuk

Kotlik
Hamilton

YUKON DELTA N.W.R.

Shageluk
Iditarod

Takotna

McGrath

Nikolai

TALKEETNA MTS.

Sheldon Point

St. Marys
Pitkas Pt.

Marshall

Holy Cross

Flat

ALASKA RANGE

Petersville

George Parks

Mountain Village

Pilot Station

Russian Mission

Crooked Creek

Red Devil

MOUNTAINS

Trapper Creek

Talkeetna

Hooper Bay

Chevak

Newtok

Kasigluk

Nunapitchuk

Bethel

Tuluksak

Lower Kalskag

Kalskag

Chuathbaluk

Sleetmute

Stony River

Lime Village

Skwentna

Nancy Lake St. Rec. Area

Houston

Willow

Chickalo

Sutton

Independence Mine State Hist. Pk.

Tununak

Mekoryak

Toksook Bay

NELSON ISLAND

Atmautluak
Nightmute

Napakiak

Akiachak
Kwethluk

Napaskiak

Aniak

KUSKOKWIM MTS.

TAYLOR MOUNTAINS

Big Lake
Wasilla

Anchorage
Palmer

Eagle River

NUNIVAK ISLAND

Chefornak

Kipnuk

Tuntutuliak

Eek

Kwigillingok

Kongiganak

KILBUCK MTS.

Nuklunek Mtn. 3679 ft.

TOGIAK MOUNTAINS

Wood-Tikchik State Park

LAKE CLARK NAT'L. PARK & PRES.

Nikiski

Typnek

Kenai
Soldotna

Hope

Whittier

Alyeska Res.

Moose Pass

Quinhagak

Goodnews Bay

Carter Spit

AHKLUN MOUNTAINS

Lake Nerka

New Stuyahok

Koliganek

Nondalton

Port Alsworth

Iliamna

Kasilof

KENAI PENINSULA

Seward

KENAI FJORDS NAT'L. PK.

Kuskokwim Bay

Platinum

Twin Hills

Aleknagik

Newhalen

Pedro Bay

Iliamna L.

Ninilchik

Anchor Point

Seward Arpt.

CAPE NEWENHAM STATE WILDLIFE REFUGE

HAGEMEISTER ISLAND

Togiak
Manokotak

Dillingham
Dillingham Arpt.

Ekwok

Igiugig

Kokhanok

Homer

Seldovia

English Bay

Port Graham

Clarks Point

KATMAI NAT'L. PARK & PRES.

Mt. Douglas 7063 ft.

Cape Douglas

Kachemak Bay Wilderness S.P.

Cape Constantine

BRISTOL BAY

Naknek

Ekuk

Egegik

King Salmon
King Salmon Arpt.

Naknek L.

BECHAROF N.W.R.

PENINSULA

ALEUTIAN

RANGE

AFOGNAK ISLAND

Shuyak Island State Park

Ft. Abercrombie State Hist. Park

CHUGACH NAT'L. FOR.

Ouzinkie

Port Lions

Uganik

Kodiak
Kodiak Arpt.

Pilot Point
Ugashik

ANIAKCHAK NAT'L. MON. & PRES.

Karluk
Larsen Bay

Port Heiden

Akhiok

Old Harbor

KODIAK ISLAND

ALASKA MARITIME N.W.R.

TRINITY ISLANDS

Mt. Veniaminof 8225 ft.

Port Moller

Nelson Lagoon

IZEMBEK N.W.R.

Chignik

Ivanof Bay

Perryville

Sitka

SEMIDI ISLANDS

Cold Bay

UNIMAK ISLAND

Pavlof Volcano 8900 ft.

Cold Bay Arpt.

Sand Point

Squaw Harbor

False Pass

King Cove

ALASKA MARITIME N.W.R.

SHUMAGIN ISLANDS

SANAK ISLANDS

PACIFIC OCEAN

ALASKA MARITIME NAT'L.

ATTU ISLAND
Attu Battlefield

NEAR ISLANDS
Attu
Eareckson Air Force Station

AGATTU ISLAND

BULDIR ISLAND

RAT IS.
KISKA ISLAND
Kiska Volcano 4004 ft.

SEMISOPOCHNOI ISLAND

Anvil Pk. 4007 ft.

AMCHITKA ISLAND

Mt. Gareloi 5160 ft.

East Cape

© Rand McNally

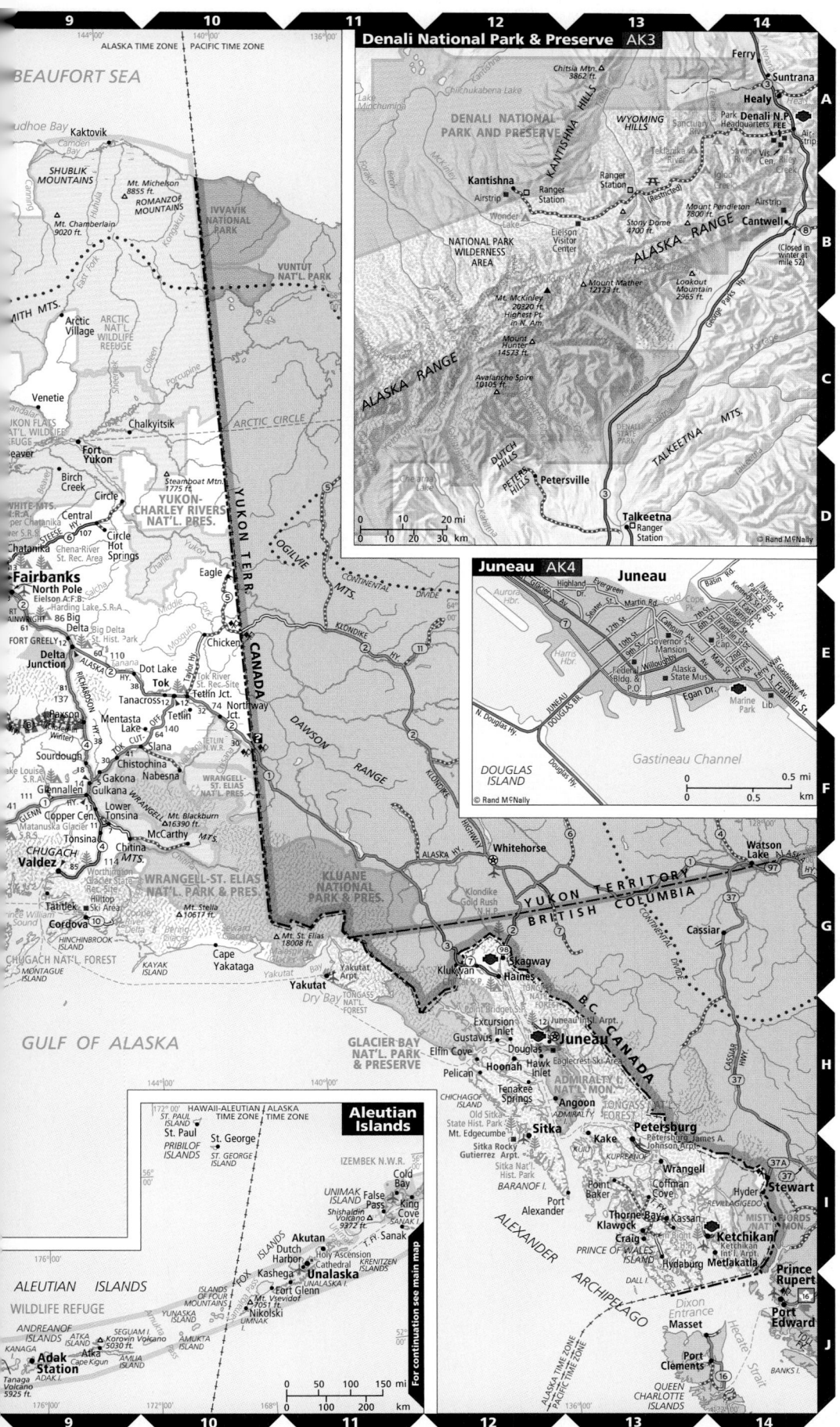

How to determine distance

Mileages in red between red arrowheads; in black, between intersections.

SYMBOLS

- Featured ride
- Scenic route
- Long-term construction
- Harley-Davidson dealership
- Historic site or monument; Indian reservation or rancheria; military installation; point of interest; wildlife refuge

ALASKA MOTORCYCLE LAWS

Helmet use:
Required under age 18

Riding two abreast:
Yes. See state law for specifics

Eye protection:
Required unless equipped with windscreen which is 15 inches or higher above handlebars

Speed limit:
Primary roads: 65 mph
Secondary roads: 55 mph

ALASKA RESOURCES

Road conditions or construction:
511
(866) 282-7577
(800) 478-7675 (in AK)
(907) 456-7623
(907) 269-0450
www.dot.state.ak.us

Highway Emergency Numbers:
911 or *273

Tourism:
(907) 929-2200
www.travelalaska.com

State motor vehicle information:
(907) 269-5551
www.state.ak.us/dmv

HARLEY-DAVIDSON DEALERSHIPS

House of Harley-Davidson, G-8
4334 Spenard Rd. **Anchorage**
(907) 248-5300
Lat N 61.182 Lon W 149.934

Mt. McKinley Harley-Davidson, E-8
Mile 238.6 Parks Hwy. **Denali Nat'l Park**
(907) 683-4275
Lat N 63.624 Lon W 150.140

Harley-Davidson Farthest North Outpost, E-9
1450 Karen Way **Fairbanks**
(907) 456-3265
Lat N 64.835 Lon W 147.830

Taku Harley-Davidson Shop, H-12
263 Marine Way **Juneau**
(907) 586-4100
Lat N 58.298 Lon W 134.404

Inside Passage Harley-Davidson, I-14
34 Front St. Ste. 204 **Ketchikan**
(907) 225-4625
Lat N 55.343 Lon W 131.653

Chilkoot Pass Harley-Davidson, G-12
750 Broadway St. **Skagway**
(907) 983-3620
Lat N 59.460 Lon W 135.307

Kenai Peninsula Harley-Davidson Shop, G-8
41605 Sterling Hwy. **Soldotna**
(907) 260-6777
Lat N 60.498 Lon W 151.021

Denali Harley-Davidson Shop, F-8
1497 S Hyer Rd. **Wasilla**
(907) FREEDOM
Lat N 61.592 Lon W 149.458

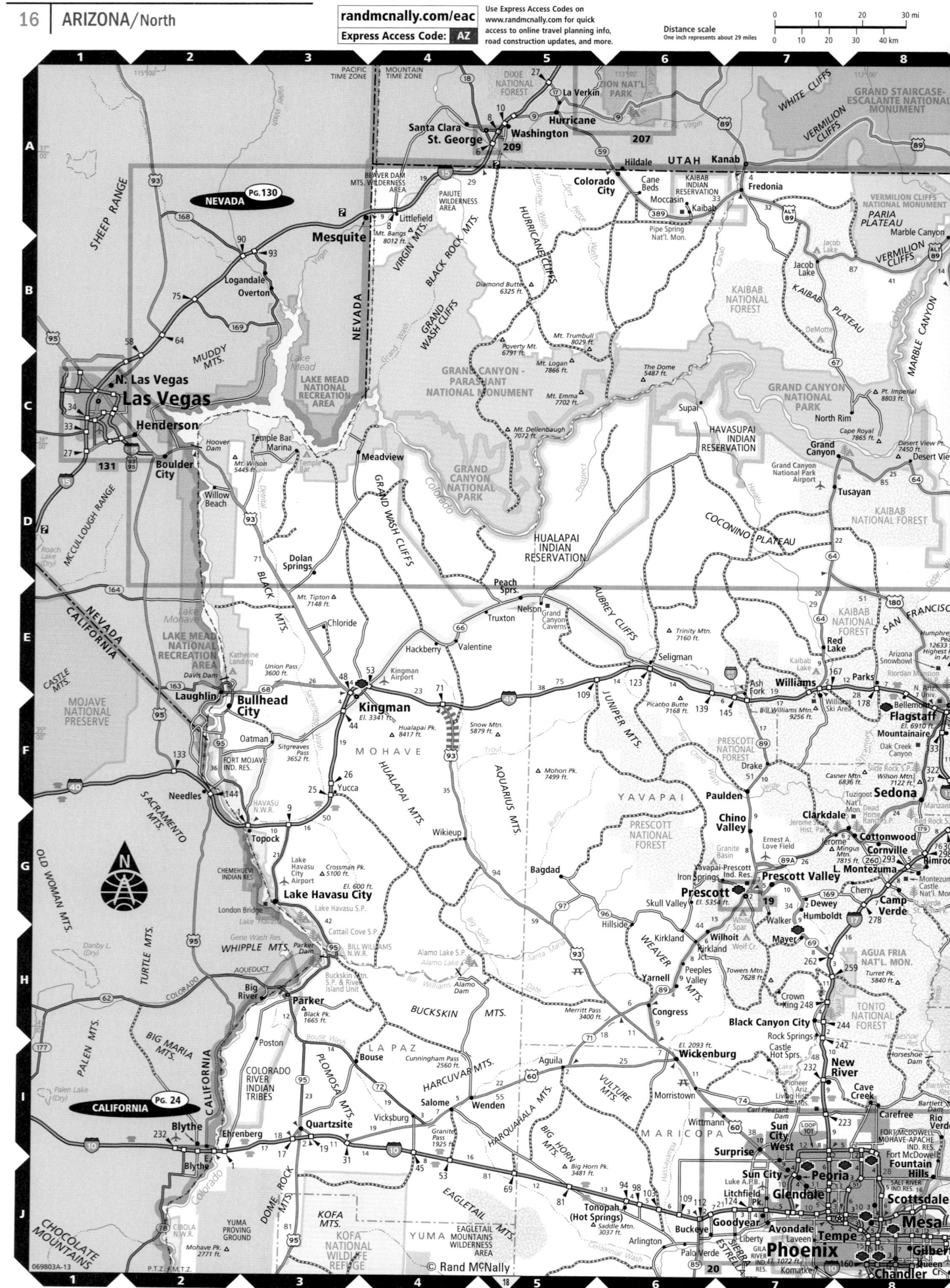

Distance scale
One inch represents about 29 miles

PG.130

NEVADA

UTAH

CALIFORNIA

PG. 24

© Rand McNally

How to determine distance

Mileages in red between red arrowheads; in black, between intersections.

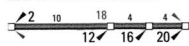

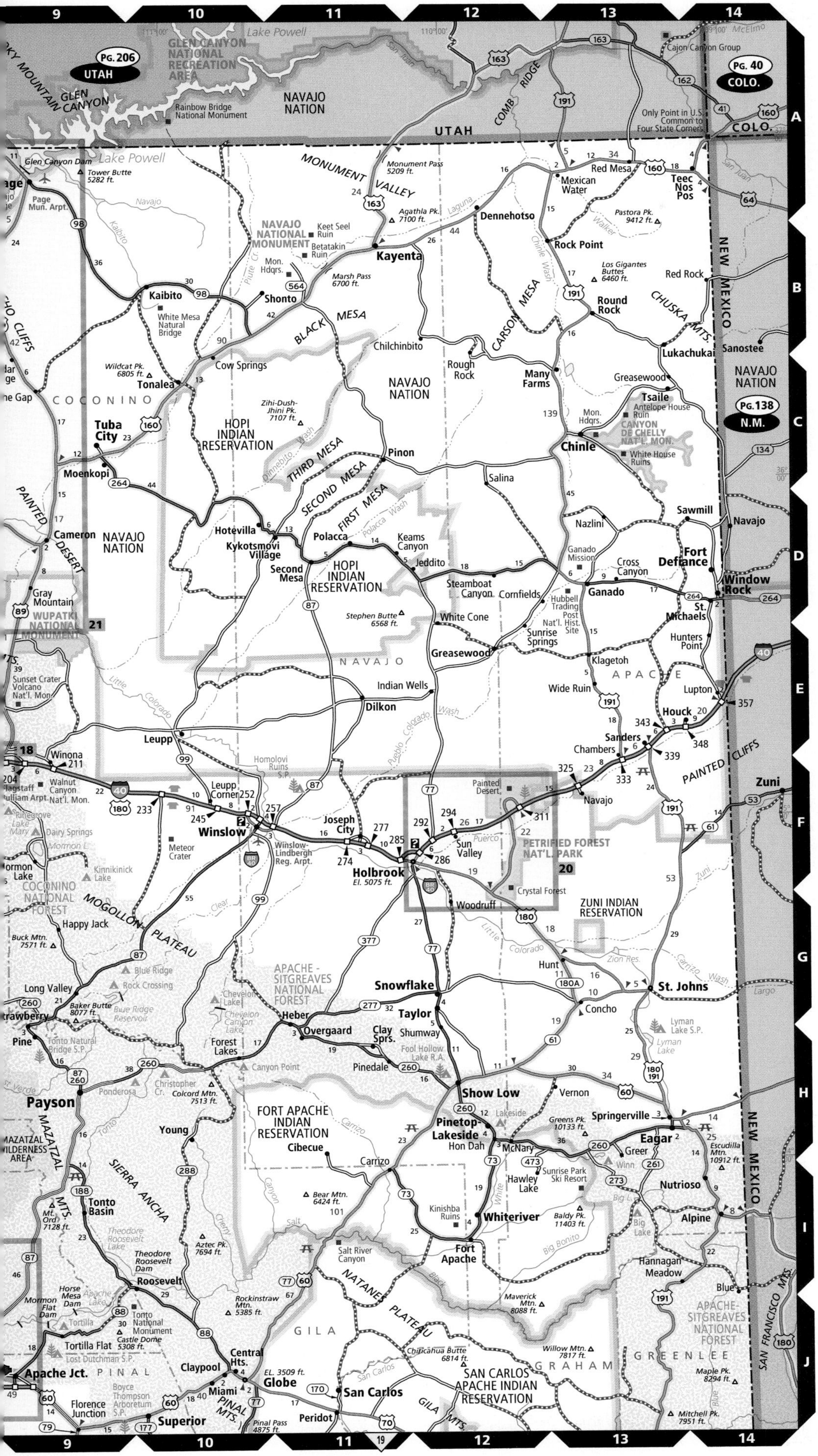

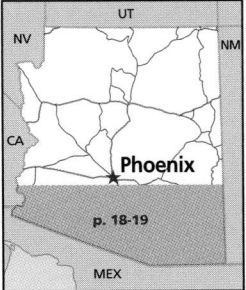

Phoenix

p. 18-19

SYMBOLS

- ═══ Featured ride
- ▦ Long-term construction
- 🏍 Harley-Davidson dealership
- ═══ Scenic route
- ■ Historic site or monument; Indian reservation or rancheria; military installation; point of interest; wildlife refuge

For Arizona ride, see page R4.

ARIZONA MOTORCYCLE LAWS

Helmet use:
Required under age 18

Riding two abreast:
Yes. See state law for specifics

Eye protection:
Required unless equipped with windscreen

Speed limit:
Primary roads: 75 mph
Secondary roads: 55 mph

ARIZONA RESOURCES

Road conditions or construction:
511
(888) 411-7623
www.az511.com

Highway Emergency Numbers:
911

Tourism:
(866) 239-9712
www.arizonaguide.com

State motor vehicle information:
(602) 712-7090
www.dot.state.az.us/mvd

HARLEY-DAVIDSON DEALERSHIPS

For the Phoenix metro area, please see dealer listings on page 21.

🏍 **Grand Canyon Harley-Davidson, F-8**
I-40 Exit 185 **Bellemont**
(928) 774-3896
Lat N 35.174 **Lon** W 111.894

🏍 **Mother Road Harley-Davidson, E-3**
2501 Beverly Ave. **Kingman**
(928) 757-1166
Lat N 35.218 **Lon** W 114.020

🏍 **Grand Canyon Harley-Davidson Shop, H-7**
10434 S Hwy. 69 **Mayer**
(928) 632-4009
Lat N 34.392 **Lon** W 112.222

🏍 **Grand Canyon Harley-Davidson, G-7**
138 S Montezuma **Prescott**
(928) 778-2241
Lat N 34.541 **Lon** W 112.470

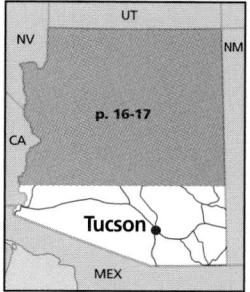

p. 16-17

Tucson

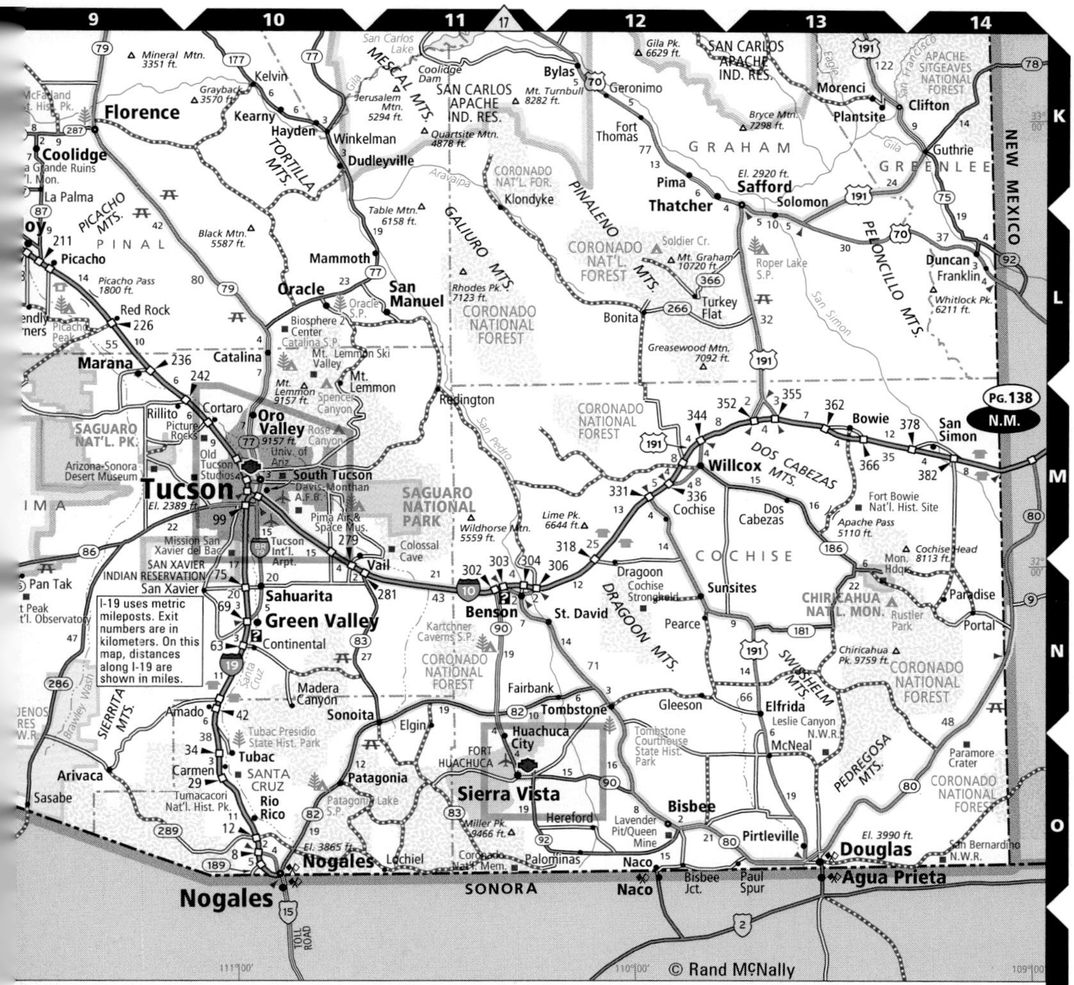

SYMBOLS

- Featured ride
- Scenic route
- Long-term construction
- Historic site or monument; Indian reservation or rancheria; military installation; point of interest; wildlife refuge
- Harley-Davidson dealership

CITY-TO-CITY MILEAGE

	CASA GRANDE	FLAGSTAFF	HOLBROOK	KINGMAN	PHOENIX	PRESCOTT	TUCSON	YUMA
Blythe, CA	197	282	374	157	146	155	263	103
Casa Grande		187	221	236	51	145	67	172
Eagar	221	179	87	323	225	272	241	397
Flagstaff	187		92	144	136	93	253	318
Gallup, NM	318	188	97	332	324	281	338	506
Grand Canyon	268	81	169	167	217	123	334	373
Holbrook	221	92		236	228	185	241	410
Kingman	236	144	236		185	146	302	215
Lake Havasu City	249	204	296	60	198	206	315	155
Las Vegas, NV	341	249	341	105	290	251	407	296
Lordsburg, NM	224	410	265	459	274	368	157	394
Nogales	131	317	305	366	181	275	64	301
Page	324	137	217	279	273	230	390	455
Phoenix	51	136	228	185		94	117	182
Prescott	145	93	185	146	94		211	214
Shiprock, NM	411	281	190	425	417	374	431	599
Tucson	67	253	241	302	117	211		237
Yuma	172	318	410	215	182	214	237	

HARLEY-DAVIDSON DEALERSHIPS

- **Sierra Vista Harley-Davidson Shop, O-11**
  176 W Fry Blvd. **Sierra Vista**
  (520) 458-9500
  Lat N 31.555 Lon W 110.301

- **Harley-Davidson of Tucson, M-10**
  250 E Grant Rd. **Tucson**
  (520) 792-0111
  Lat N 32.250 Lon W 110.968

- **Bobby's Territorial Harley-Davidson, L-2**
  2550 E Gila Ridge Rd. **Yuma**
  (928) 782-1931
  Lat N 32.688 Lon W 114.589

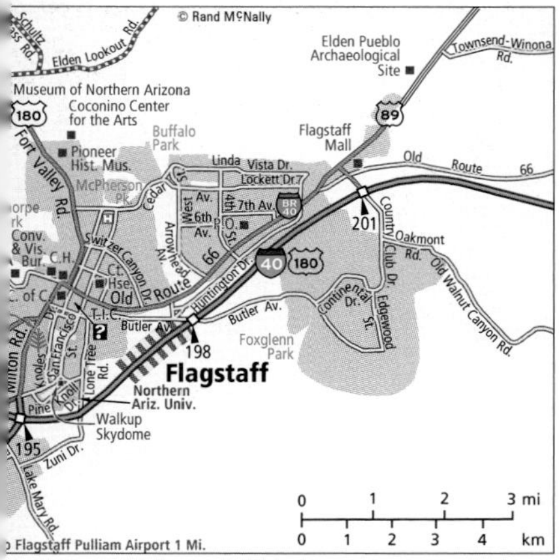

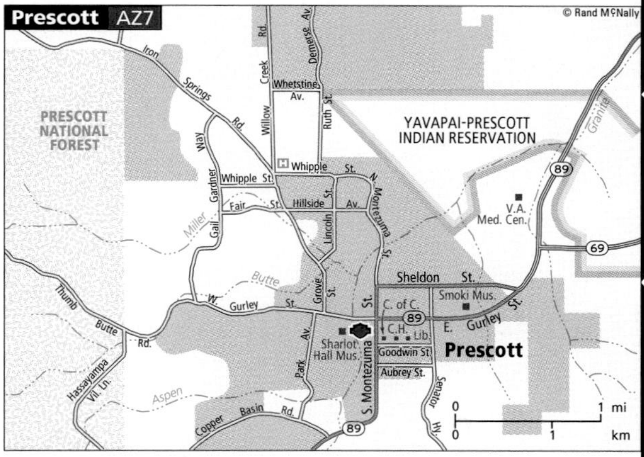

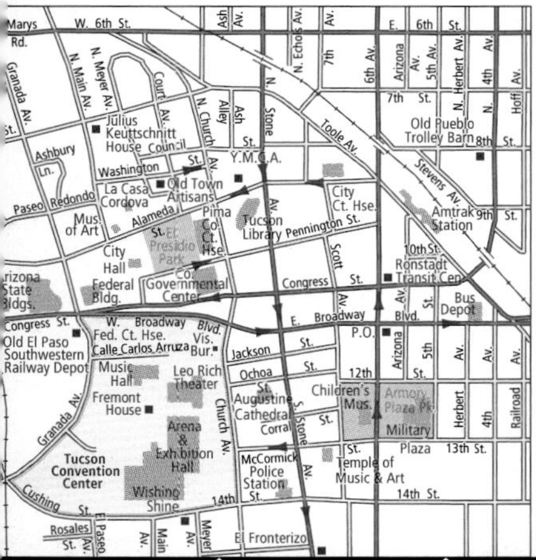

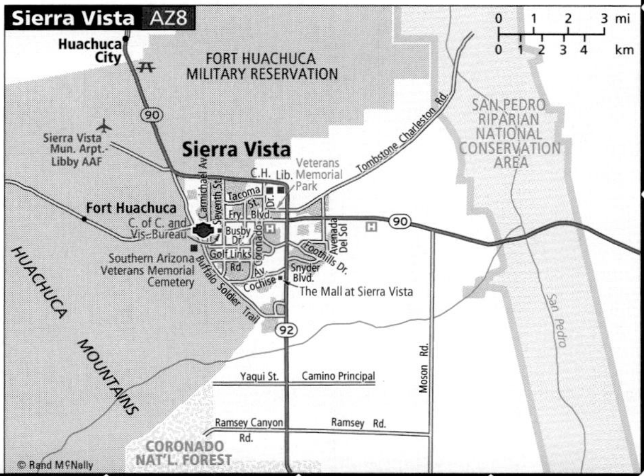

How to determine distance

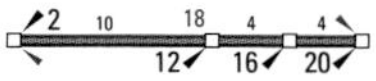

Mileages in red between red arrowheads; in black, between intersections.

© Rand McNally

Prescott AZ7

Sierra Vista AZ8

Flagstaff

How to determine distance

Mileages in red between red arrowheads; in black, between intersections.

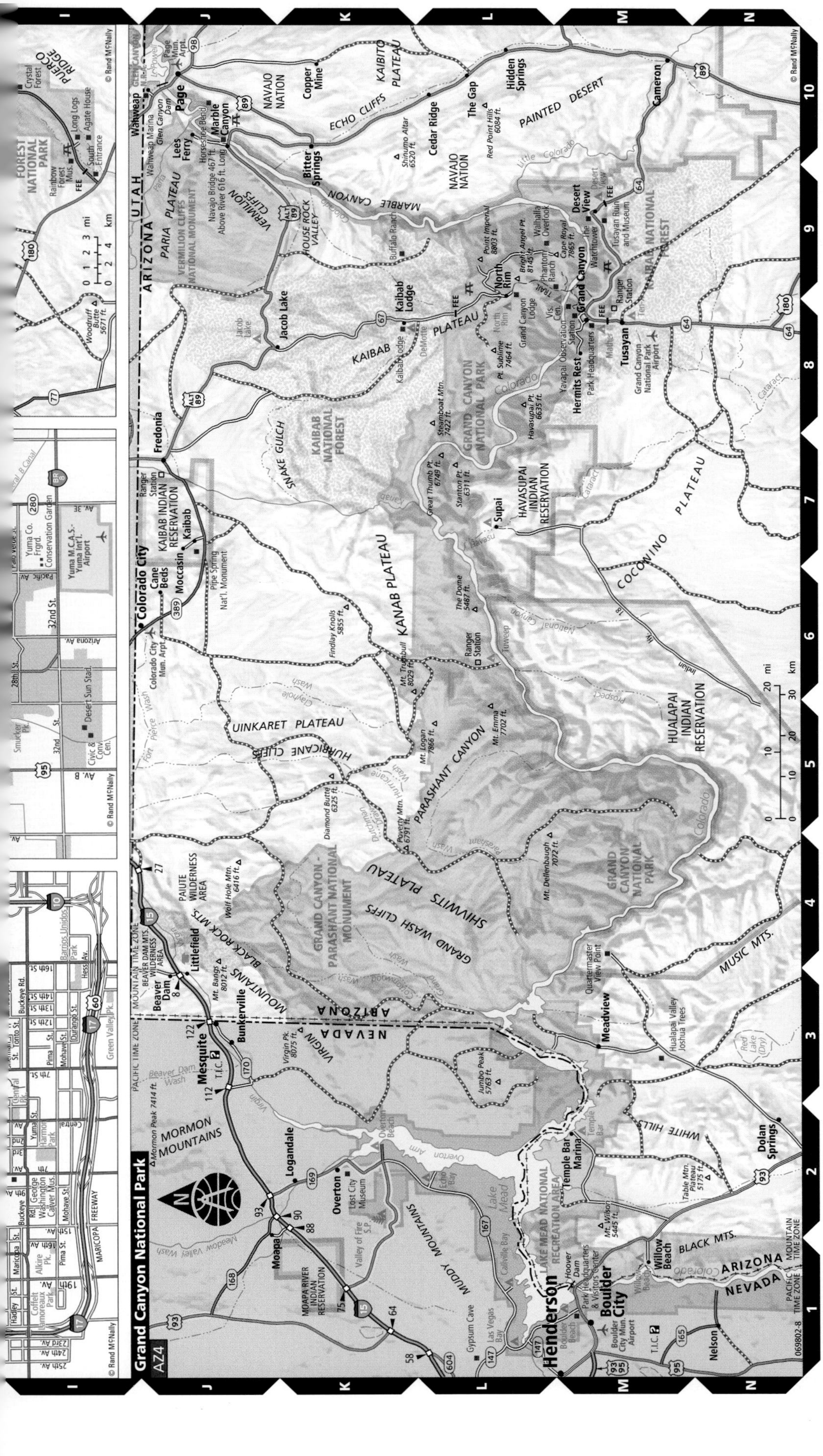

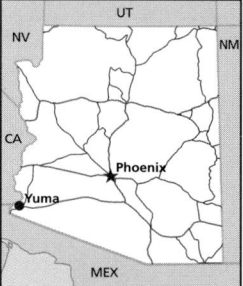

SYMBOLS

- Featured ride
- Scenic route
- Long-term construction
- Harley-Davidson dealership
- Historic site or monument; Indian reservation or rancheria; military installation; point of interest; wildlife refuge

ARIZONA MOTORCYCLE LAWS

Helmet use:
Required under age 18

Riding two abreast:
Yes. See state law for specifics

Eye protection:
Required unless equipped with windscreen

Speed limit:
Primary roads: 75 mph
Secondary roads: 55 mph

ARIZONA RESOURCES

Road conditions or construction:
511
(888) 411-7623
www.az511.com

Highway Emergency Numbers:
911

Tourism:
(866) 239-9712
www.arizonaguide.com

State motor vehicle information:
(602) 712-7090
www.dot.state.az.us/mvd

HARLEY-DAVIDSON DEALERSHIPS

Superstition Harley-Davidson, E-10
2910 W Apache Trail Apache Junction
(480) 346-0600
Lat N 33.415 Lon W 111.578

Chandler Harley-Davidson, F-6
6895 W Chandler Blvd. Chandler
(480) 496-6800
Lat N 33.305 Lon W 111.961

Harley-Davidson of Chandler, F-7
3155 W Chandler Blvd. Chandler
(480) 917-2300
Lat N 33.306 Lon W 111.897

Chester's Harley-Davidson, E-7
922 S Country Club Dr. Mesa
(480) 894-0404
Lat N 33.398 Lon W 111.840

Arrowhead Harley-Davidson, C-4
16130 N Arrowhead Fountain Center Dr. Peoria
(623) 247-5542
Lat N 33.634 Lon W 112.237

Buddy Stubbs Harley-Davidson, C-6
13850 N Cave Creek Rd. Phoenix
(602) 971-3400
Lat N 33.613 Lon W 112.035

Hacienda Harley-Davidson, C-7
15600 N Hayden Rd. Scottsdale
(480) 905-1903
Lat N 33.627 Lon W 111.896

Chester's Harley-Davidson, E-6
690 S Mill Ave. Tempe
(480) 355-6160
Lat N 33.423 Lon W 111.940

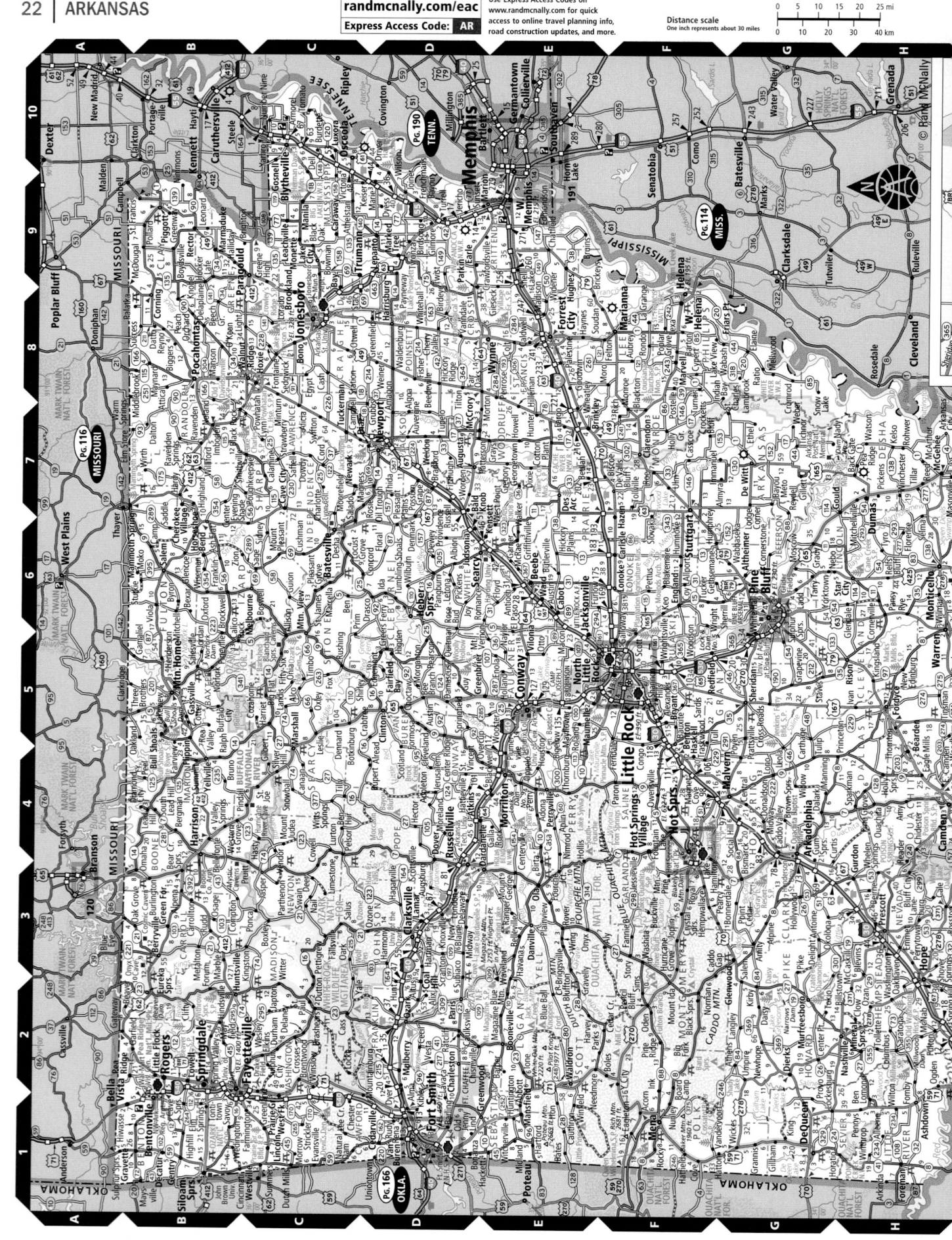

How to determine distance

Mileages in red between red arrowheads; in black, between intersections.

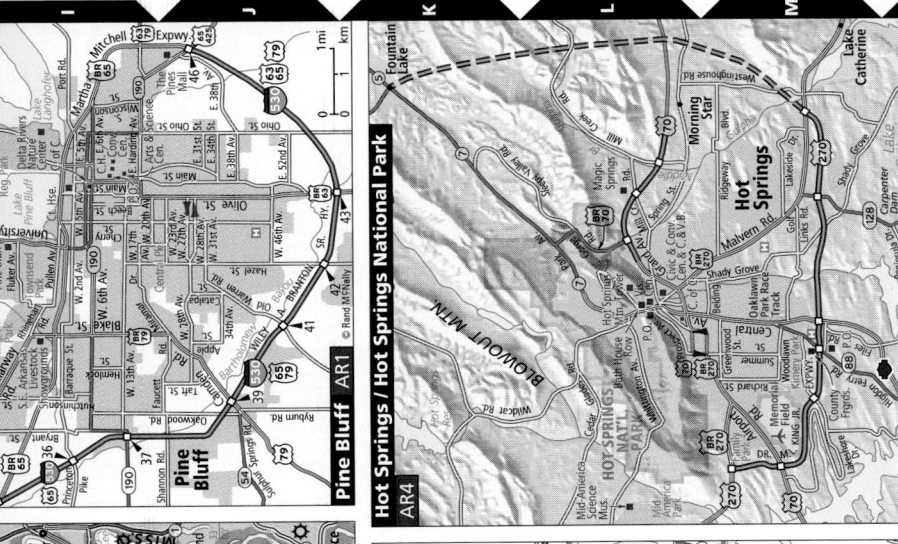

Pine Bluff **AR1**

Hot Springs / Hot Springs National Park **AR4**

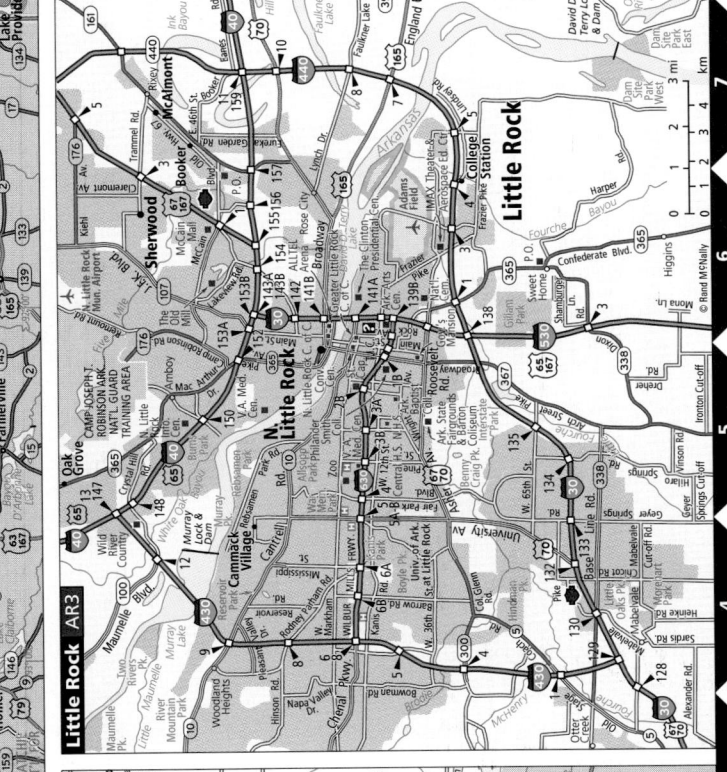

Little Rock **AR3**

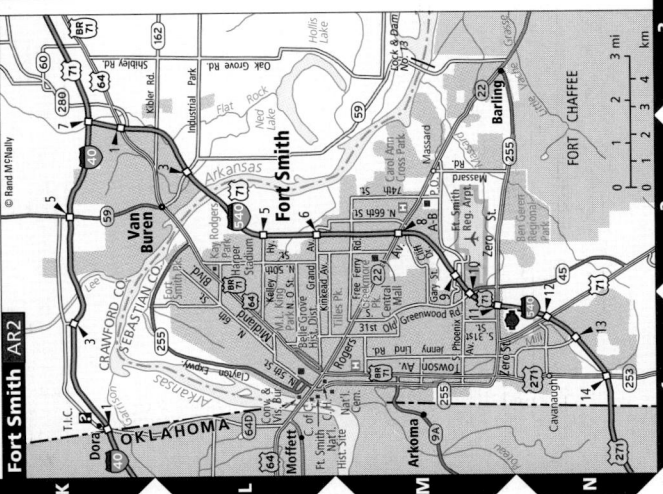

Fort Smith **AR2**

SYMBOLS

- Featured ride
- Long-term construction
- Harley-Davidson dealership
- Scenic route
- Historic site or monument; Indian reservation or rancheria; military installation; point of interest; wildlife refuge

For Arkansas ride, see page R5.

ARKANSAS MOTORCYCLE LAWS

Helmet use:
Required under age 21

Riding two abreast:
No reference in administrative code or statutes

Eye protection:
Required by law

Speed limit:
Primary roads: 70 mph
Secondary roads: 55 mph

ARKANSAS RESOURCES

Road conditions or construction:
(800) 245-1672
(501) 569-2374
(501) 569-2227
www.arkansashighways.com
www.arkansasinterstates.com

Highway Emergency Numbers:
911

Tourism:
(800) 828-8974
(800) 628-8725 (to request travel materials only)
www.arkansas.com

State motor vehicle information:
(501) 618-8810
www.asp.state.ar.us

CITY-TO-CITY MILEAGE

	El Dorado	Fayetteville	Fort Smith	Harrison	Jonesboro	Little Rock	Texarkana	West Memphis
El Dorado		310	275	255	248	117	90	244
Fayetteville	310		61	88	294	195	239	316
Fort Smith	275	61		150	259	160	180	281
Harrison	255	88	150		170	140	272	261
Jonesboro	248	294	259	170		133	273	63
Little Rock	117	195	160	140	133		140	129
Pine Bluff	91	235	200	180	173	42	151	135
Texarkana	90	239	180	272	273	140		269
West Memphis	244	316	281	261	63	129	269	

HARLEY-DAVIDSON DEALERSHIPS

Old Ft. Harley-Davidson of Ft. Smith, D-1
6304 S 36th St. **Fort Smith**
(479) 648-1666
Lat N 35.322 Lon W 94.396

Jones Harley-Davidson Shop of Hot Springs, F-4
4446 Central Ave. **Hot Springs**
(501) 520-4442
Lat N 34.452 Lon W 93.077

Harley-Davidson of Jonesboro, C-8
4500 Oliver St. **Jonesboro**
(870) 932-0780
Lat N 35.811 Lon W 90.643

Jones Harley-Davidson, F-5
10210 I-30 **Little Rock**
(501) 568-3160
Lat N 34.675 Lon W 92.351

Jones Harley-Davidson Shop of North Little Rock, F-5
4300 Landers Rd. **North Little Rock**
(501) 945-4206
Lat N 34.794 Lon W 92.221

Razorback Harley-Davidson, B-2
2409 W Hudson Rd. **Rogers**
OPENING IN 2006
Lat N 36.356 Lon W 94.152

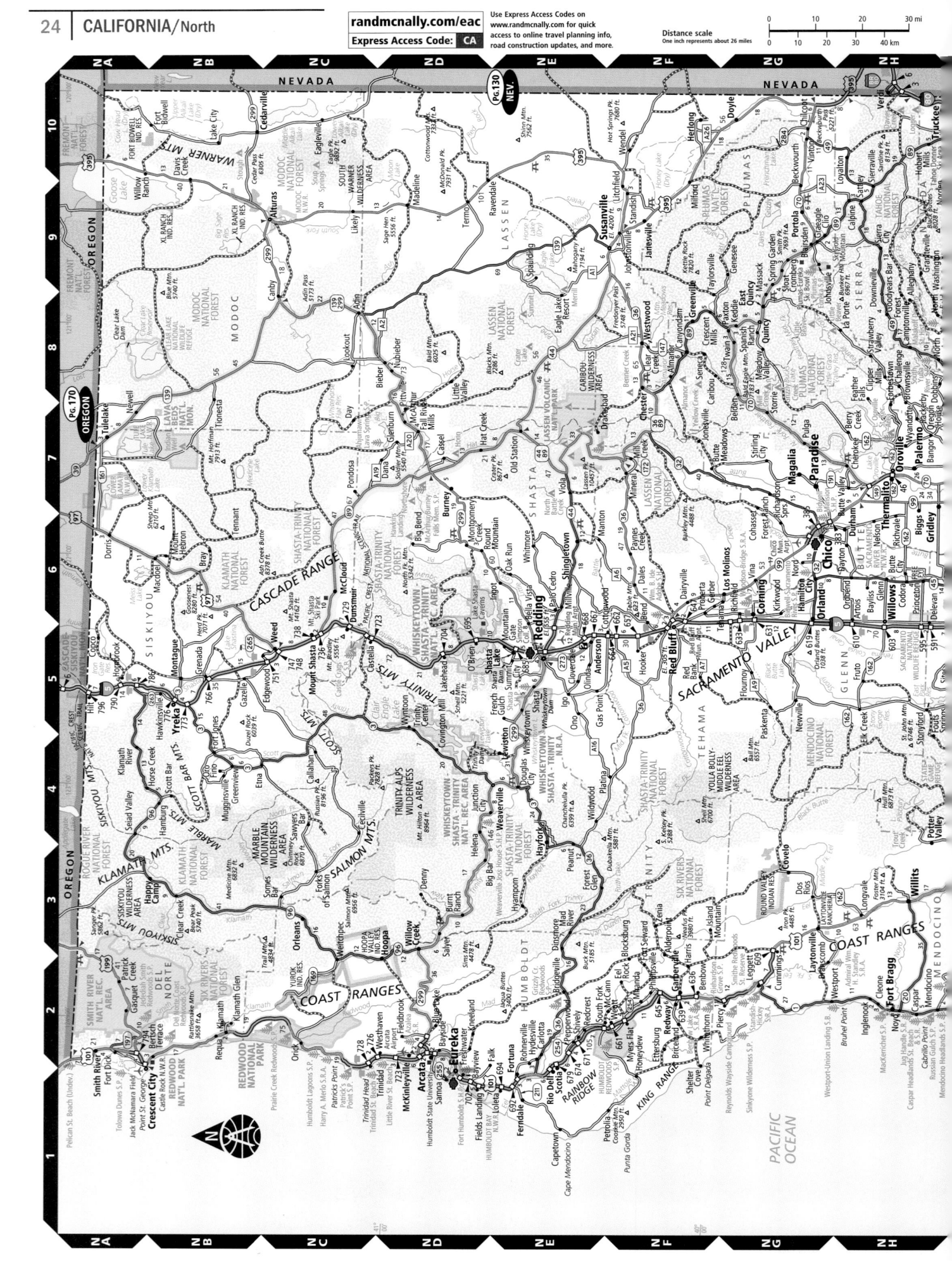

How to determine distance

Mileages in red between red arrowheads; in black, between intersections.

San Francisco
Sacramento
Oakland
San Jose
Stockton
Modesto
Merced
Yosemite National Park
CA8
© Rand McNally

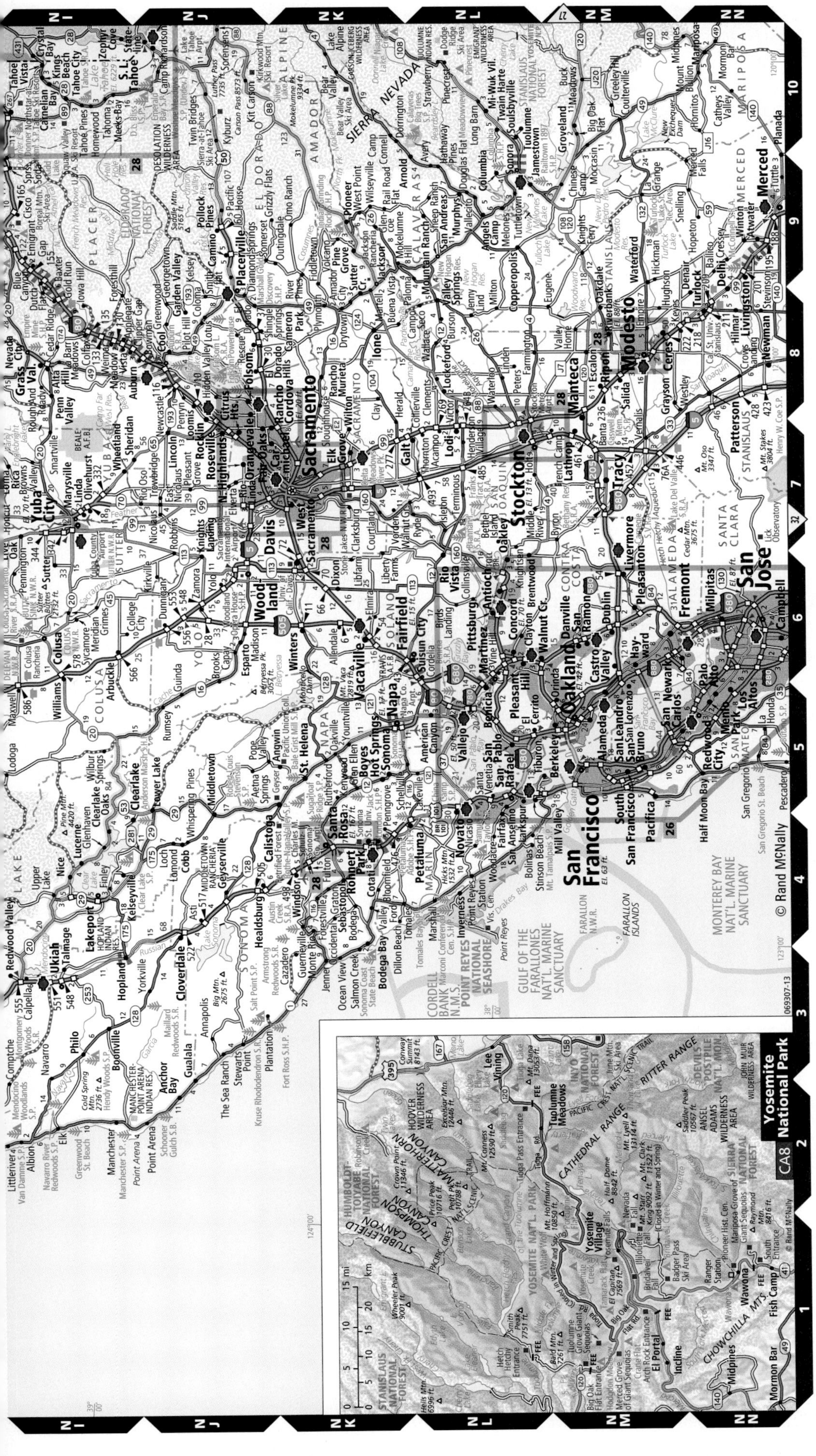

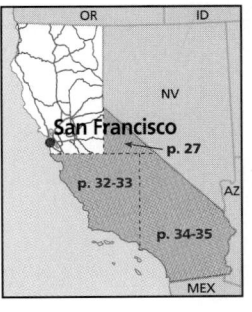

OR
ID
NV
San Francisco
p. 27
p. 32-33
p. 34-35
AZ
MEX

SYMBOLS

- Featured ride
- Scenic route
- Long-term construction
- Harley-Davidson dealership

For California ride, see page R6.

HARLEY-DAVIDSON DEALERSHIPS

For the Bay Area, please see dealer listings on page 27; for northern cities, please see dealer listings on page 29.

Auburn Harley-Davidson, NJ-8
12075 Locksley Ln. **Auburn**
(530) 885-7161
Lat N 38.950 **Lon** W 121.099

Hall's Harley-Davidson, NG-6
1501 Mangrove Ave. **Chico**
(530) 893-1918
Lat N 39.746 **Lon** W 121.841

Michael's Harley-Davidson, NK-4
7601 Redwood Dr. **Cotati**
(707) 793-9180
Lat N 38.334 **Lon** W 122.713

Harley-Davidson of Elk Grove Shop, NK-7
10291 E Stockton Blvd. **Elk Grove**
(916) 714-6952
Lat N 38.380 **Lon** W 121.366

Redwood Harley-Davidson, ND-1
21 W 4th St. **Eureka**
(707) 444-0111
Lat N 40.802 **Lon** W 124.172

Harley-Davidson of Folsom, NJ-8
115 Woodmere Rd. **Folsom**
(916) 608-9922
Lat N 38.656 **Lon** W 121.185

Jamestown Harley-Davidson, NL-9
18275 Hwy. 108 **Jamestown**
(209) 984-4888
Lat N 37.963 **Lon** W 120.408

Hangtown Harley-Davidson Shop, NJ-8
629 Main St. **Placerville**
(530) 344-0401
Lat N 38.730 **Lon** W 120.793

Redding Harley-Davidson, NE-5
1268 Twin View Blvd. **Redding**
(530) 241-7117
Lat N 40.624 **Lon** W 122.365

Harley-Davidson of Rocklin, NJ-8
4425 Granite Dr. **Rocklin**
(916) 624-9211
Lat N 38.798 **Lon** W 121.215

Harley-Davidson of Ukiah, NI-3
2501 N State St. **Ukiah**
(707) 462-1672
Lat N 39.183 **Lon** W 123.209

Vacaville Harley-Davidson, NK-6
100 Auto Center Dr. **Vacaville**
(707) 455-7000
Lat N 38.380 **Lon** W 121.942

Guideras Harley-Davidson, NI-7
720 W Onstott Rd. **Yuba City**
(530) 673-3548
Lat N 39.134 **Lon** W 121.635

randmcnally.com/eac

Express Access Code: CA

Use Express Access Codes on www.randmcnally.com for quick access to online travel planning info, road construction updates, and more.

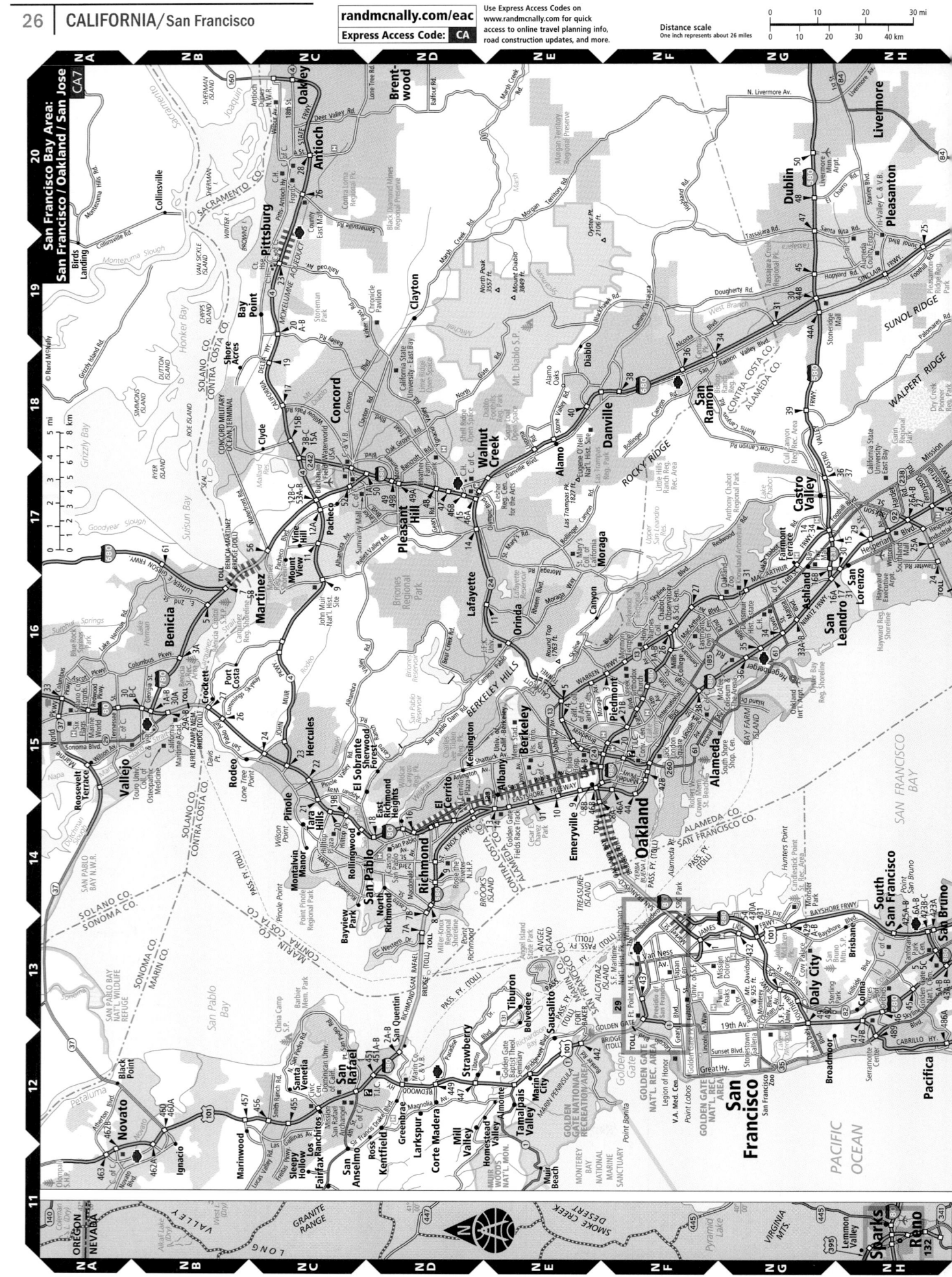

San Francisco Bay Area: San Francisco / Oakland / San Jose

CA7

How to determine distance

Mileages in red between red arrowheads;
in black, between intersections.

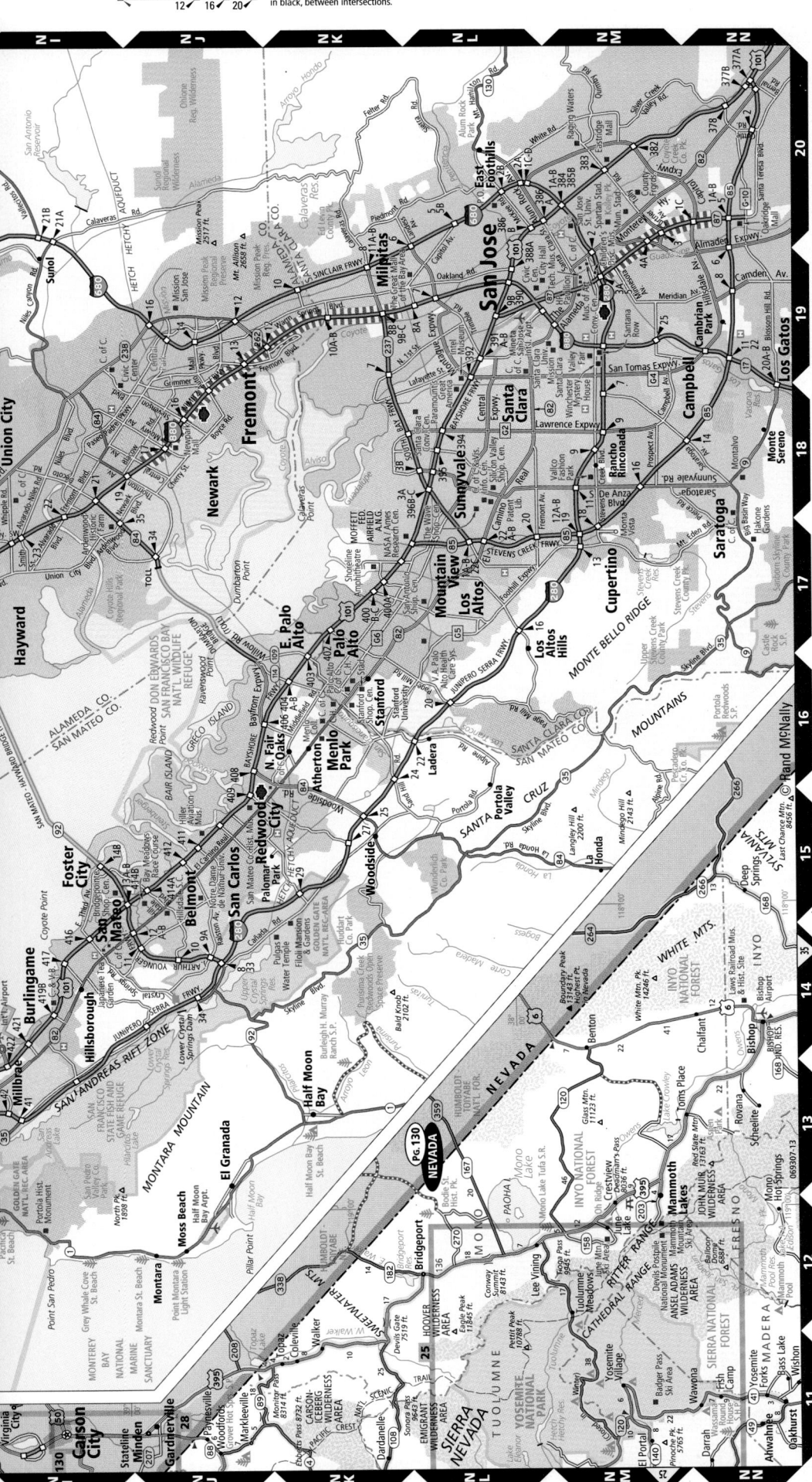

SYMBOLS

	Featured ride		Scenic route
	Long-term construction	■	Historic site or monument; Indian reservation or rancheria; military installation; point of interest; wildlife refuge
	Harley-Davidson dealership		

HARLEY-DAVIDSON DEALERSHIPS

Golden Gate Harley-Davidson, ND-12
13 San Clemente Dr. **Corte Madera**
(415) 927-4464
Lat N 37.922 Lon W 122.510

Harley-Davidson of Fremont, NJ-18
41315 Albrae St. **Fremont**
(510) 657-7200
Lat N 37.517 Lon W 121.980

Livermore Harley-Davidson, NM-6
7576 Southfront Rd. **Livermore**
(925) 606-0100
Lat N 37.715 Lon W 121.704

Golden Gate Harley-Davidson Shop, NB-11
7077 Redwood Blvd. **Novato**
(415) 878-4988
Lat N 38.100 Lon W 122.568

Bob Dron Harley-Davidson, NG-16
200 Hegenberger Rd. **Oakland**
(510) 635-0100
Lat N 37.731 Lon W 122.199

Devil Mountain Harley-Davidson Shop, NC-20
2240 Loveridge Rd. **Pittsburg**
(925) 427-2700
Lat N 38.009 Lon W 121.871

Peninsula Harley-Davidson, NJ-15
380 Convention Way **Redwood City**
(650) 568-0800
Lat N 37.495 Lon W 122.231

Dudley Perkins Co. Harley-Davidson, NF-13
2595 Taylor St. **San Francisco**
(415) 776-7781
Lat N 37.806 Lon W 122.415

San Jose Harley-Davidson, NM-19
1551 Parkmoor Ave. **San Jose**
(408) 998-1464
Lat N 37.317 Lon W 121.917

McGuire Harley-Davidson Shop, NF-18
2000 San Ramon Valley Blvd. **San Ramon**
(925) 838-4647
Lat N 37.785 Lon W 121.980

Dudley Perkins Co. Harley-Davidson, NH-13
333 Corey Way **South San Francisco**
OPENING IN 2006
Lat N 37.645 Lon W 122.402

Harley-Davidson of Vallejo, NB-15
1600 Sonoma Blvd. (Hwy. 29) **Vallejo**
(707) 643-1413
Lat N 38.100 Lon W 122.255

McGuire Harley-Davidson, ND-17
1425 Parkside Dr. **Walnut Creek**
(925) 945-6500
Lat N 37.912 Lon W 122.064

Central Sacramento CA2

Stockton CA6

Santa Rosa CA5

Salinas

Monterey / Salinas CA4

Sacramento CA2

Lake Tahoe Region CA1

Modesto CA3

How to determine distance

Mileages in red between red arrowheads;
in black, between intersections.

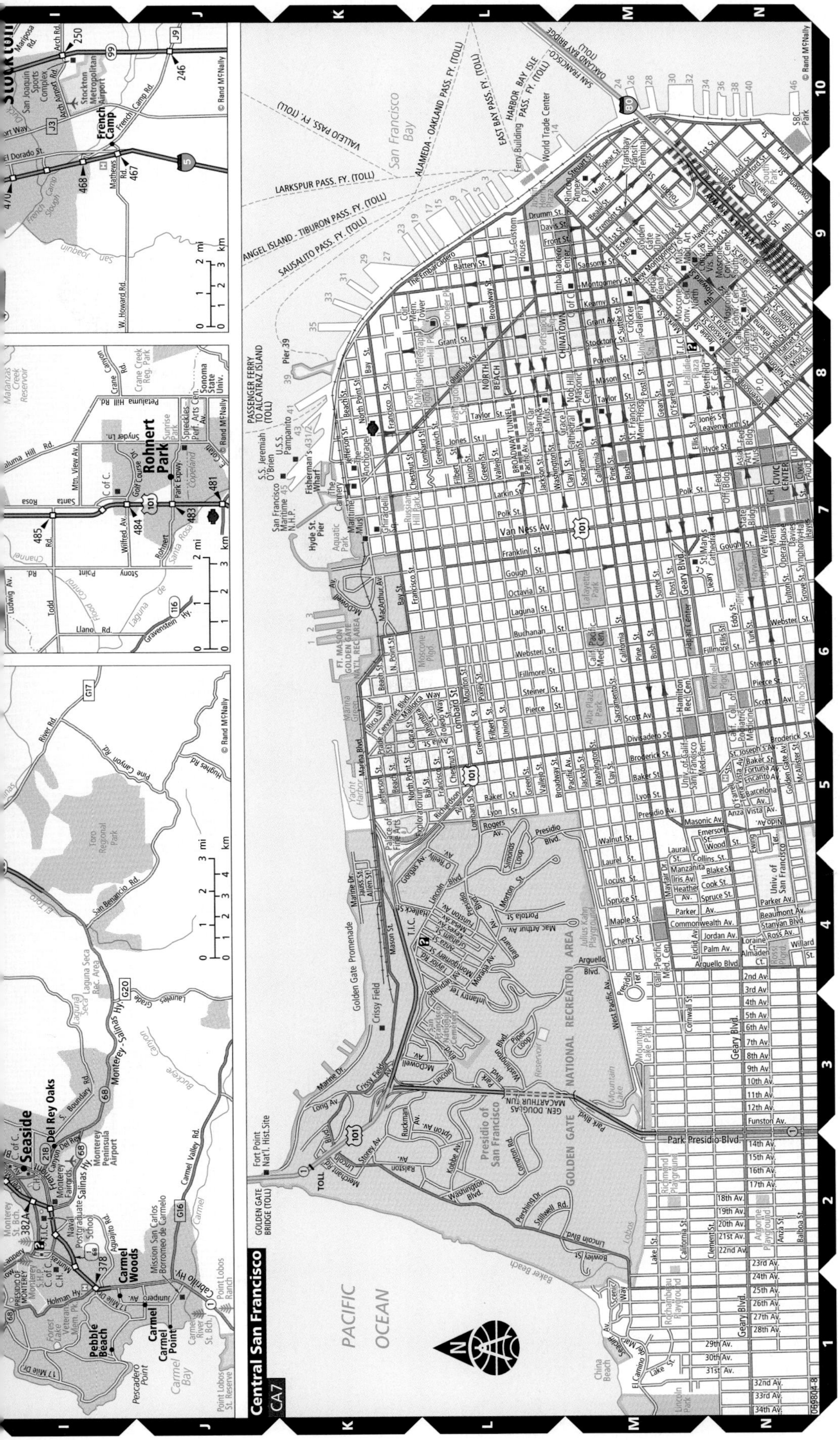

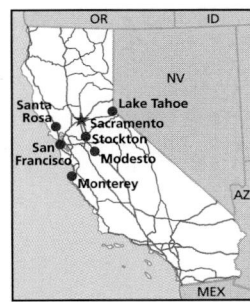

SYMBOLS

— Featured ride
||||| Long-term construction
Harley-Davidson dealership

═══ Scenic route
■ Historic site or monument; Indian reservation or rancheria; military installation; point of interest; wildlife refuge

CALIFORNIA MOTORCYCLE LAWS

Helmet use:
Required

Riding two abreast:
No reference in administrative code or statutes

Eye protection:
Not required

Speed limit:
Primary roads: 70 mph
Secondary roads: 65 mph

CALIFORNIA RESOURCES

Road conditions or construction:
511 (San Francisco Bay and Sacramento areas)
(800) 427-7623 (in CA)
(916) 445-7623
www.dot.ca.gov
www.511.org

Highway Emergency Numbers:
911

Tourism:
(916) 444-4429
(800) 862-2543 (to request travel materials only)
www.visitcalifornia.com

State motor vehicle information:
(800) 777-0133
www.dmv.ca.gov

HARLEY-DAVIDSON DEALERSHIPS

Carson City Harley-Davidson, B-3
2749 N Carson St. **Carson City, NV**
(775) 882-7433
Lat N 39.185 Lon W 119.77

Mitchell's Modesto Harley-Davidson, E-2
500 N Carpenter Rd. **Modesto**
(209) 522-1061
Lat N 37.643 Lon W 121.030

Harley-Davidson of Sacramento, C-6
1000 Arden Way **Sacramento**
(916) 929-4680
Lat N 38.606 Lon W 121.444

Carson City Harley-Davidson at Lake Tahoe, C-2
3930 Lake Tahoe Blvd. **South Lake Tahoe**
(530) 544-8393
Lat N 38.953 Lon W 119.947

Valley Harley-Davidson, H-9
711 E Miner Ave. **Stockton**
(209) 941-0420
Lat N 37.957 Lon W 121.283

Central San Francisco
CA7

PACIFIC OCEAN

randmcnally.com/eac
Express Access Code: **CA**
Use Express Access Codes on www.randmcnally.com for quick access to online travel planning info, road construction updates, and more.

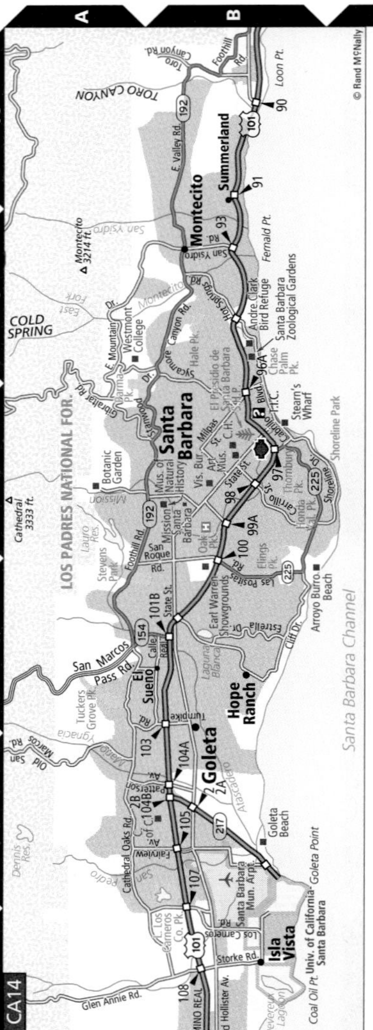

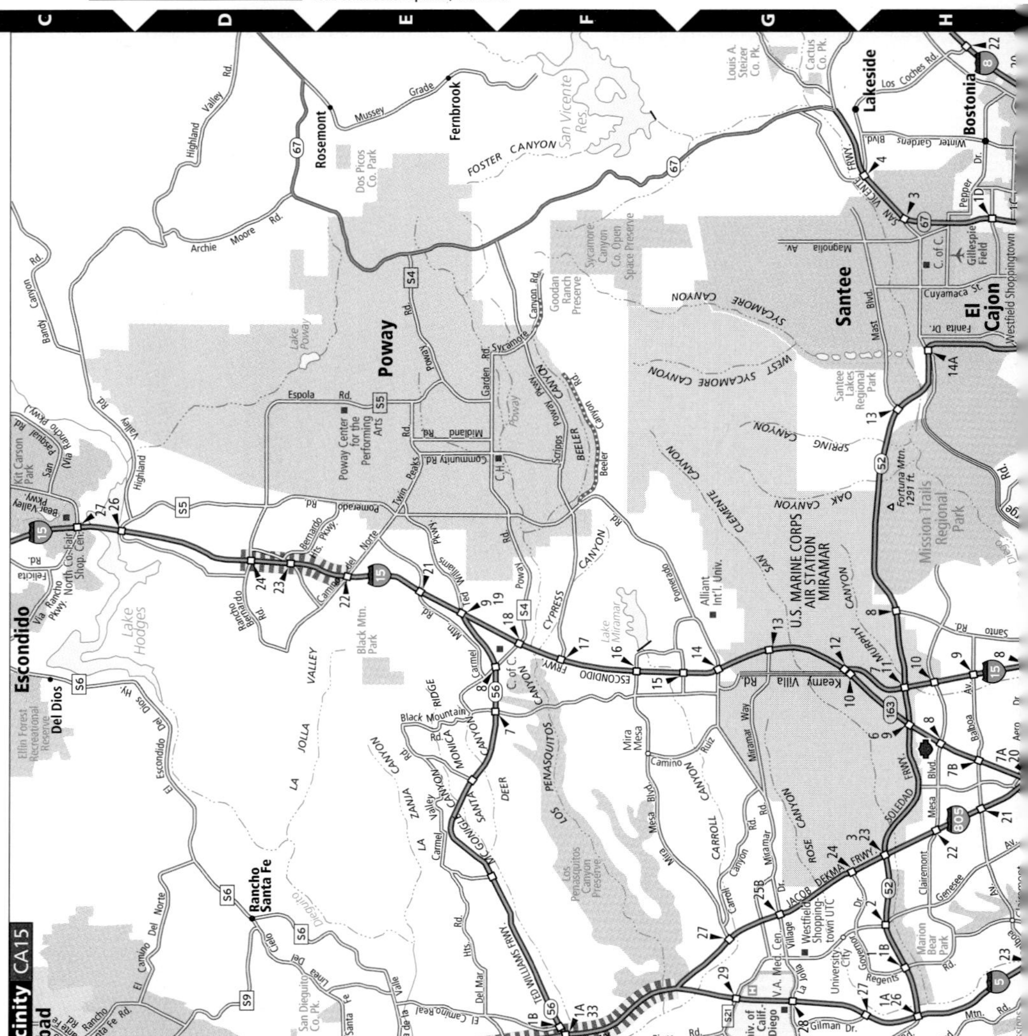

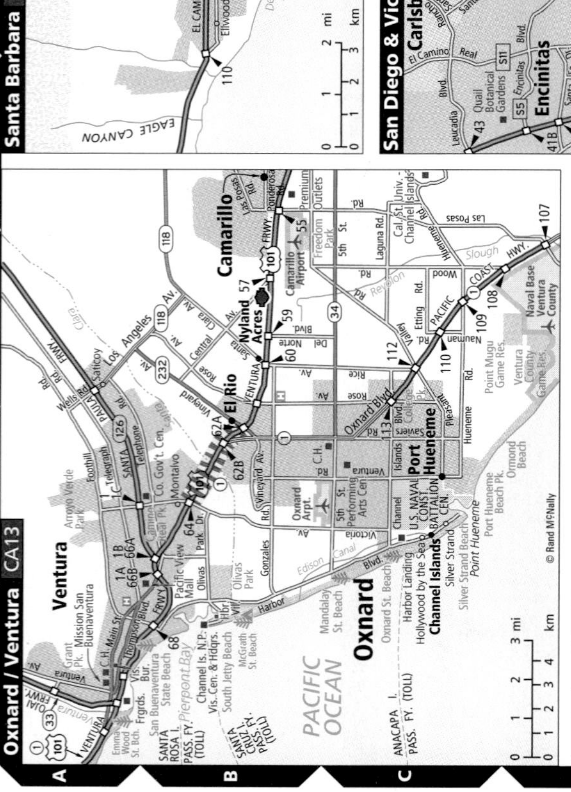

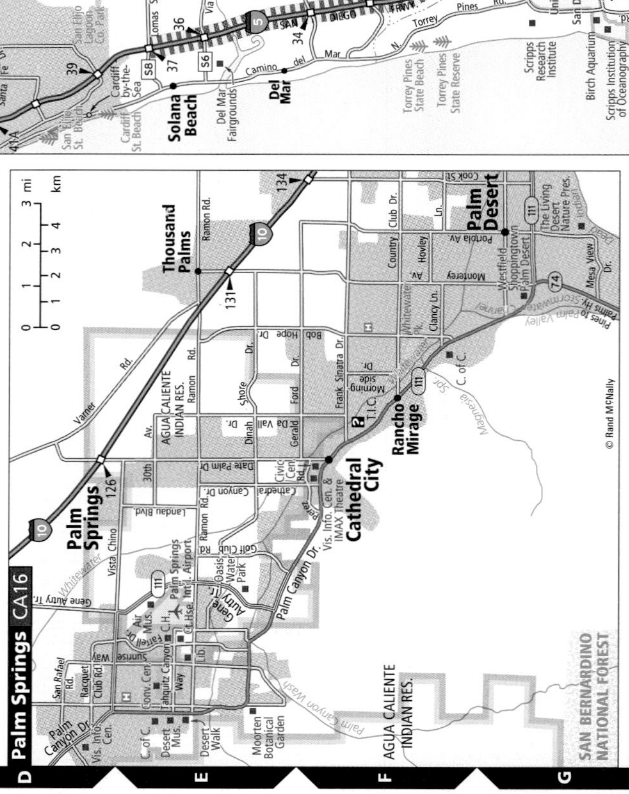

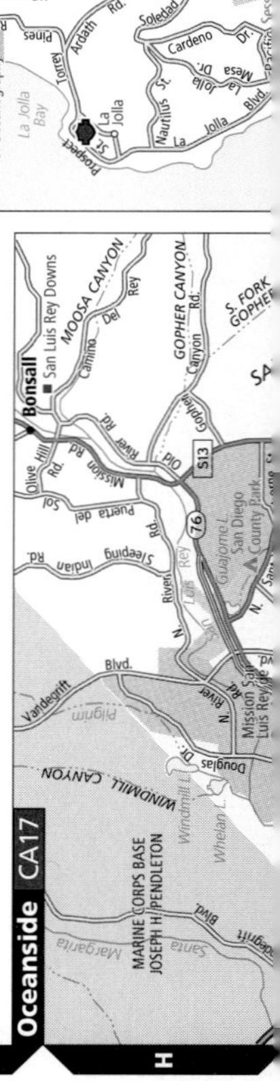

Santa Barbara CA14

Summerland
Montecito
Santa Barbara
Goleta
Hope Ranch
Isla Vista
San Marcos
El Sueno

LOS PADRES NATIONAL FOR.
COLD SPRING
Santa Barbara Channel

San Diego & Vicinity CA15

Escondido
Del Dios
Rancho Santa Fe
Carlsbad
Encinitas
Solana Beach
Del Mar
Poway
Santee
Lakeside
El Cajon
Bostonia
Fernbrook
Rosemont

U.S. MARINE CORPS AIR STATION MIRAMAR
FOSTER CANYON
WEST SYCAMORE CANYON
LA JOLLA
PACIFIC OCEAN

Oxnard / Ventura CA13

Camarillo
Nyland Acres
El Rio
Ventura
Oxnard
Port Hueneme

PACIFIC OCEAN
Channel Islands N.P. Vis. Cen. & Hdqrs.

Palm Springs CA16

Thousand Palms
Palm Desert
Rancho Mirage
Cathedral City
Palm Springs

AGUA CALIENTE INDIAN RES.
SAN BERNARDINO NATIONAL FOREST

Oceanside CA17

Bonsall

MARINE CORPS BASE CAMP JOSEPH H. PENDLETON
© Rand McNally

How to determine distance

Mileages in red between red arrowheads; in black, between intersections.

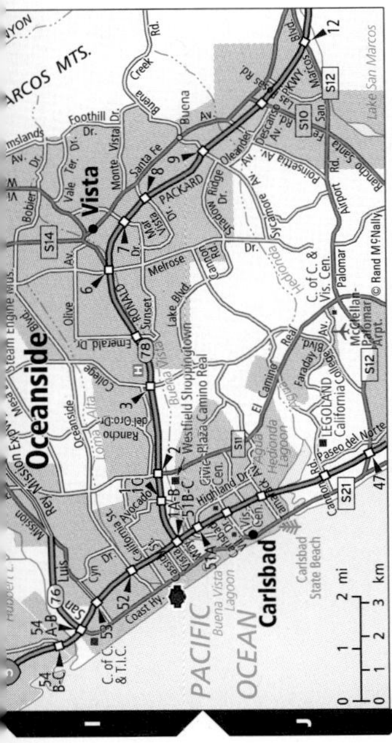

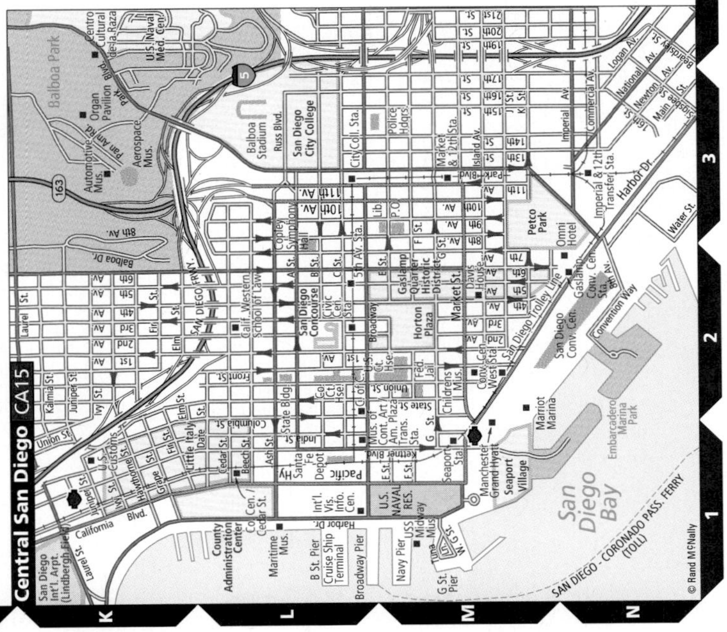

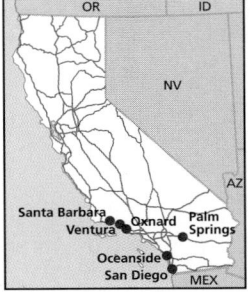

SYMBOLS

- Featured ride
- Long-term construction
- Harley-Davidson dealership
- Scenic route
- ■ Historic site or monument; Indian reservation or rancheria; military installation; point of interest; wildlife refuge

CITY-TO-CITY MILEAGE

	BISHOP	EUREKA	REDDING	SACRAMENTO	SAN FRANCISCO	SAN JOSE	SOUTH LAKE TAHOE	VALLEJO
Alturas	385	300	146	307	359	388	239	331
Bishop		556	402	273	297	286	180	298
Crescent City	623	82	217	378	363	406	477	346
Eureka	556		154	296	281	324	398	264
Oakland	289	281	209	83	8	43	185	24
Oroville	333	233	98	72	149	178	155	121
Redding	402	154		165	217	246	267	189
Sacramento	273	296	165		91	116	102	63
San Francisco	297	281	217	91		44	193	32
San Jose	286	324	246	116	44		218	63
Santa Rosa	347	223	226	100	58	101	202	52
South Lake Tahoe	180	398	267	102	193	218		165
Stockton	237	342	211	47	80	69	149	68
Susanville	288	268	114	197	269	298	142	241
Ukiah	421	162	189	148	119	162	250	102
Vallejo	298	264	189	63	32	63	165	
Yosemite N.P.	139	463	336	171	190	179	187	191
Yreka	458	214	97	260	312	341	312	284

HARLEY-DAVIDSON DEALERSHIPS

Ventura Harley-Davidson, B-4
1326 Del Norte Rd. **Camarillo**
(805) 981-9904
Lat N 34.224 Lon W 119.104

El Cajon Harley-Davidson, I-9
621 El Cajon Blvd. **El Cajon**
(619) 444-1123
Lat N 32.789 Lon W 116.973

San Diego Harley-Davidson La Jolla, H-4
1145 Prospect St. **La Jolla**
(858) 551-6800
Lat N 32.849 Lon W 117.273

Sweetwater Harley-Davidson, K-7
3201 Hoover Ave. **National City**
(619) 477-4477
Lat N 32.654 Lon W 117.102

San Diego Harley-Davidson Co., H-6
5600 Kearny Mesa Rd. **San Diego**
(858) 616-6999
Lat N 32.835 Lon W 117.139

San Diego Harley-Davidson Shop, K-1
2400 Kettner Blvd. Ste. 101 **San Diego**
(619) 233-6677
Lat N 32.729 Lon W 117.172

San Diego Harley-Davidson, M-1
861 W Harbor Dr. **San Diego**
(619) 234-5780
Lat N 32.711 Lon W 117.169

Santa Barbara Harley-Davidson Shop, B-8
506 Chapala St. **Santa Barbara**
(805) 966-5605
Lat N 34.416 Lon W 119.697

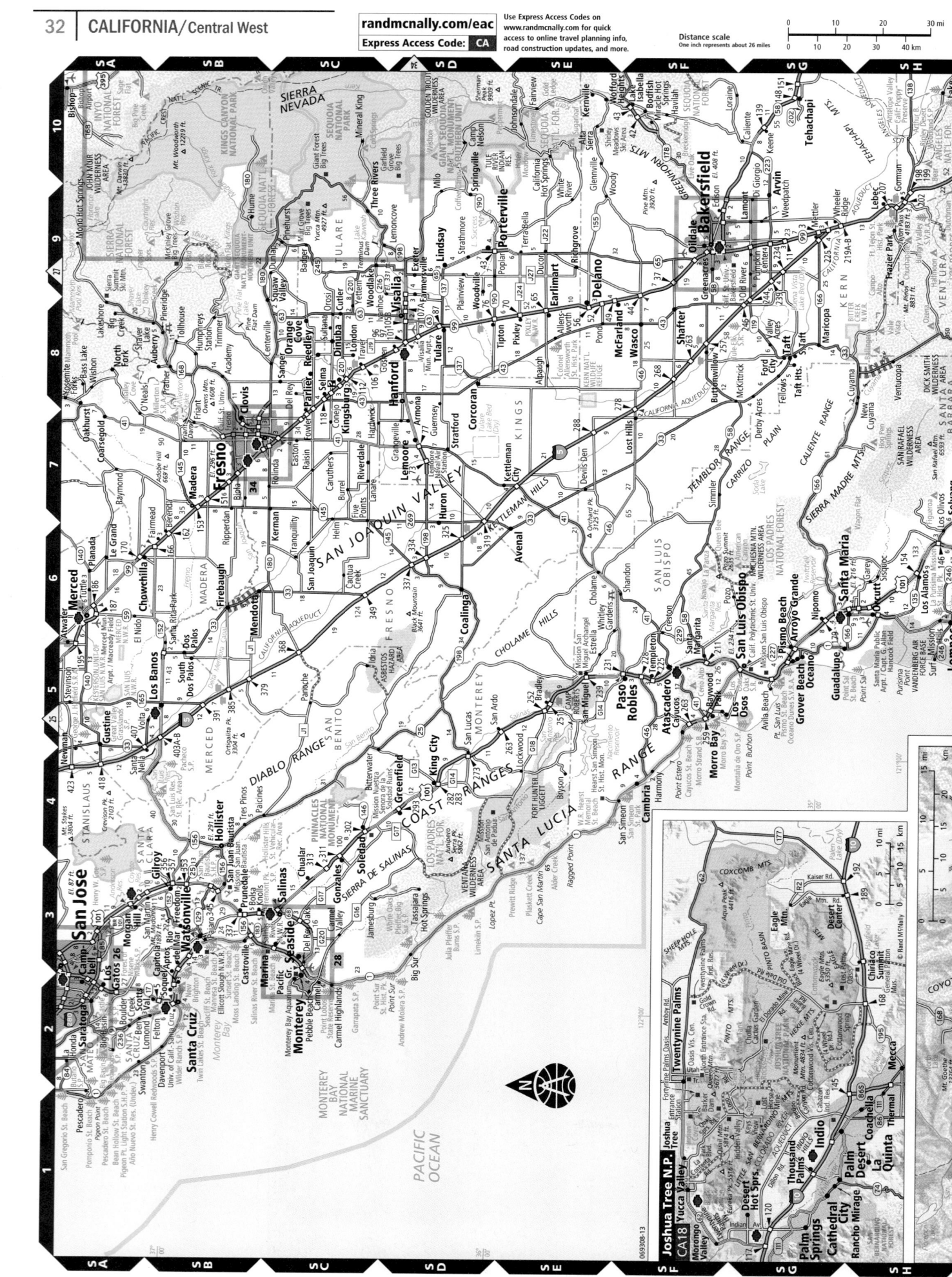

randmcnally.com/eac

Express Access Code: CA

Use Express Access Codes on
www.randmcnally.com for quick
access to online travel planning info,
road construction updates, and more.

Distance scale
One inch represents about 26 miles

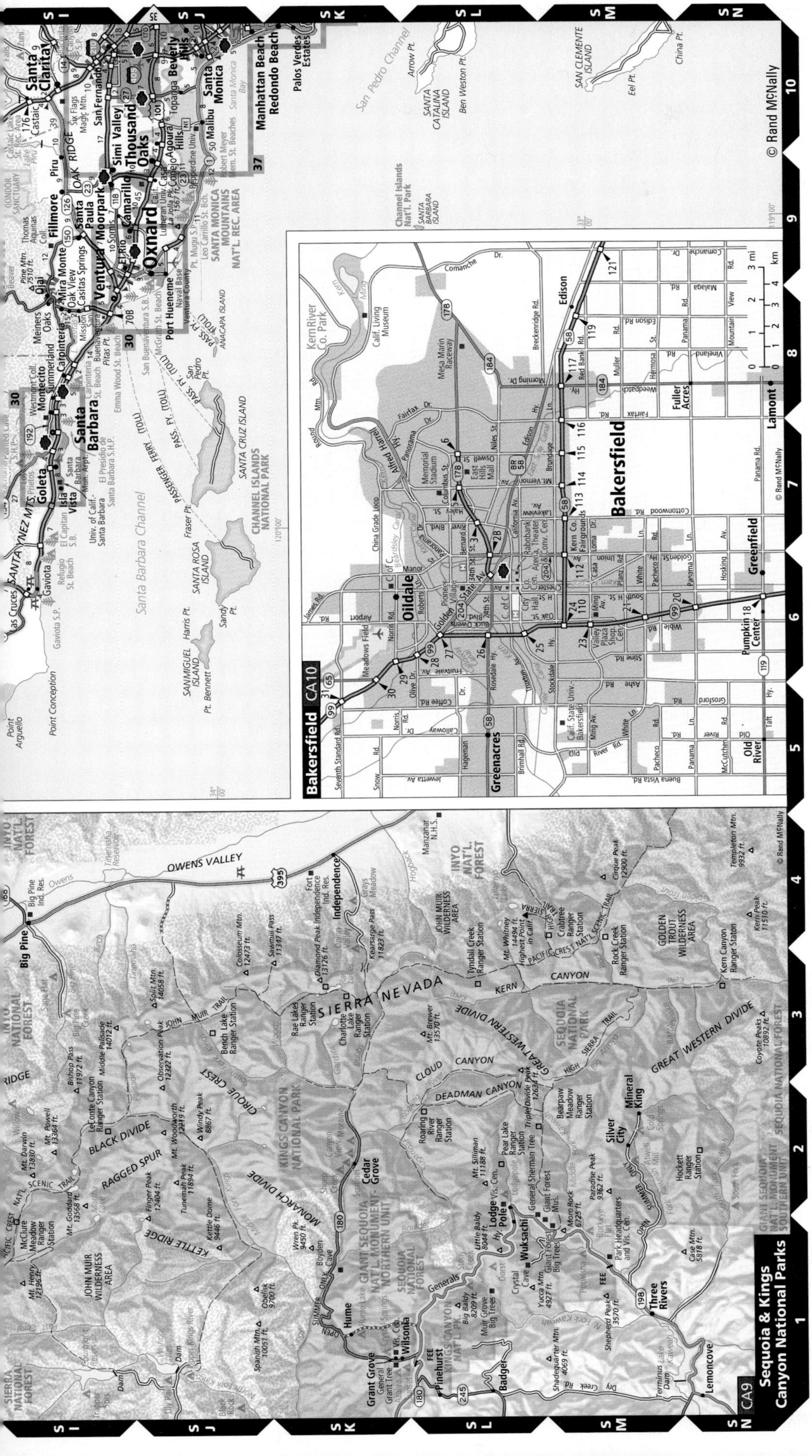

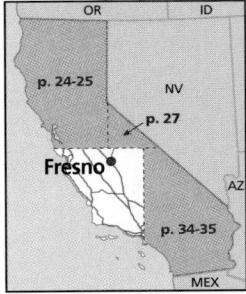

HARLEY-DAVIDSON DEALERSHIPS

For the Bay Area, please see dealer listings on page 27; for the Los Angeles Vicinity/West, please see page 37.

Gary Bang Harley-Davidson, SF-5
7935 San Luis Ave. **Atascadero**
(805) 461-1818
Lat N 35.479 Lon W 120.670

Bakersfield Harley-Davidson, SF-9
MOVING IN 2006: 824 18th St. **Bakersfield**
(661) 325-3644
Lat N 35.381 Lon W 119.020

Santa Barbara Harley-Davidson, SI-8
3501 Via Real **Carpinteria (Santa Barbara)**
(805) 745-1911
Lat N 34.414 Lon W 119.556

Harley-Davidson of Fresno, SB-7
4345 W Shaw Ave. **Fresno**
(559) 275-8586
Lat N 36.808 Lon W 119.870

Mathews Harley-Davidson, SB-7
548 N Blackstone Ave. **Fresno**
(559) 233-5279
Lat N 36.751 Lon W 119.790

Golden Valley Harley-Davidson Shop, SB-5
1415 Badger Flat Rd. **Los Banos**
(209) 827-5900
Lat N 37.075 Lon W 120.876

Yosemite Harley-Davidson of Merced, SA-6
1645 W Hwy. 140 **Merced**
(209) 723-9702
Lat N 37.303 Lon W 120.503

Simi Valley Harley-Davidson, SI-9
6190 Condor Dr. **Moorpark**
(805) 552-9555
Lat N 34.291 Lon W 118.857

House of Thunder Harley-Davidson, SA-3
16175 Condit Rd. **Morgan Hill**
(408) 776-1900
Lat N 37.121 Lon W 121.625

Warren's Harley-Davidson, SC-3
333 N Main St. **Salinas**
(831) 424-1909
Lat N 36.683 Lon W 121.653

Santa Cruz Harley-Davidson, SB-2
1148 Soquel Ave. **Santa Cruz**
(831) 421-9600
Lat N 36.979 Lon W 122.011

Santa Maria Harley-Davidson, SG-6
2022 N Preisker Ln. **Santa Maria**
(805) 928-3668
Lat N 34.977 Lon W 120.430

Visalia Harley-Davidson, SD-8
30681 Hwy. 99 **Visalia**
(559) 733-4647
Lat N 36.350 Lon W 119.427

Green Valley Harley-Davidson Shop, SB-3
1059 S Green Valley Rd. **Watsonville**
(831) 768-9500
Lat N 36.918 Lon W 121.784

randmcnally.com/eac

Express Access Code: CA

Use Express Access Codes on
www.randmcnally.com for quick
access to online travel planning info,
road construction updates, and more.

Distance scale
One inch represents about 26 miles

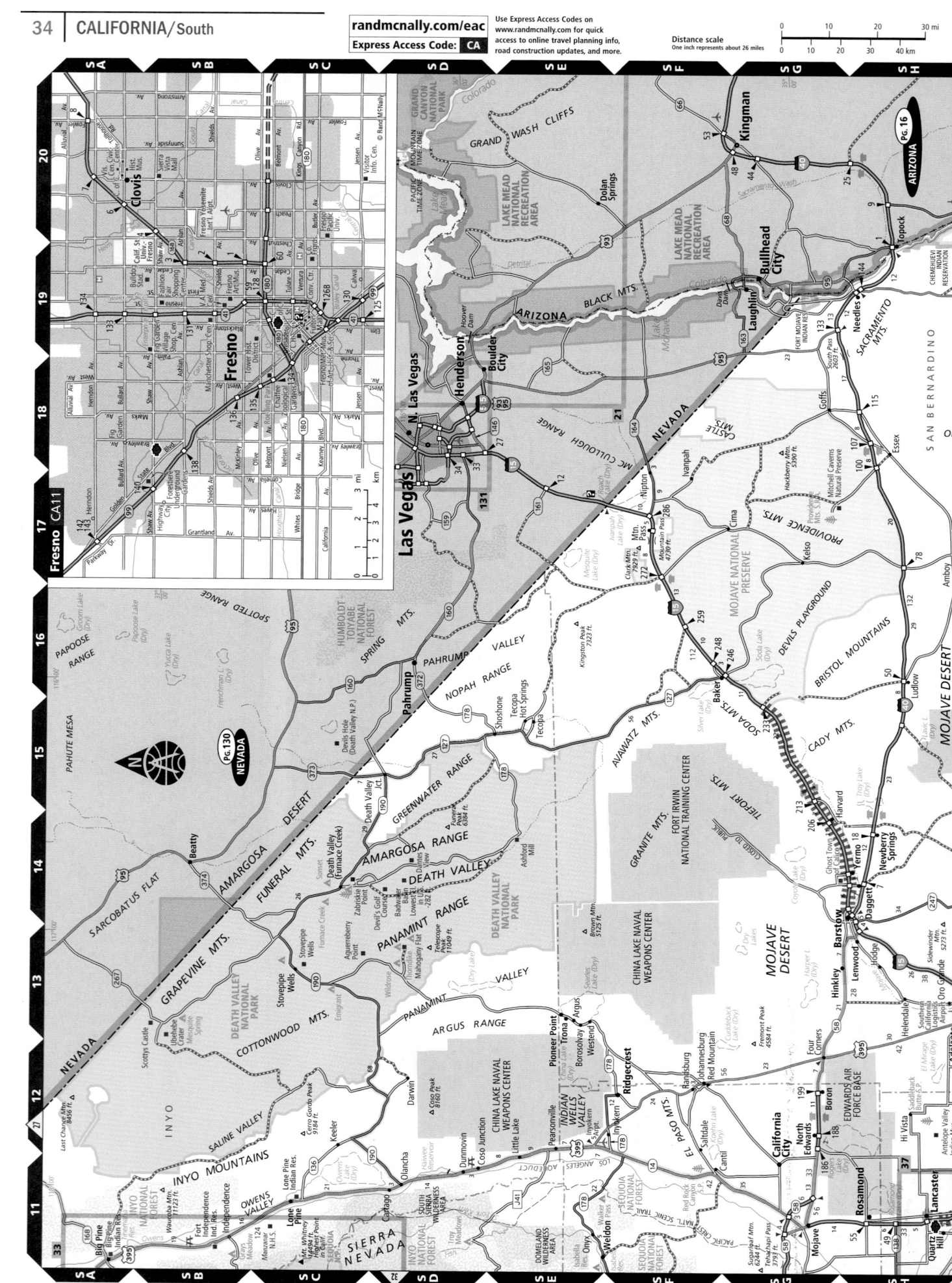

How to determine distance

Mileages in red between red arrowheads;
in black, between intersections.

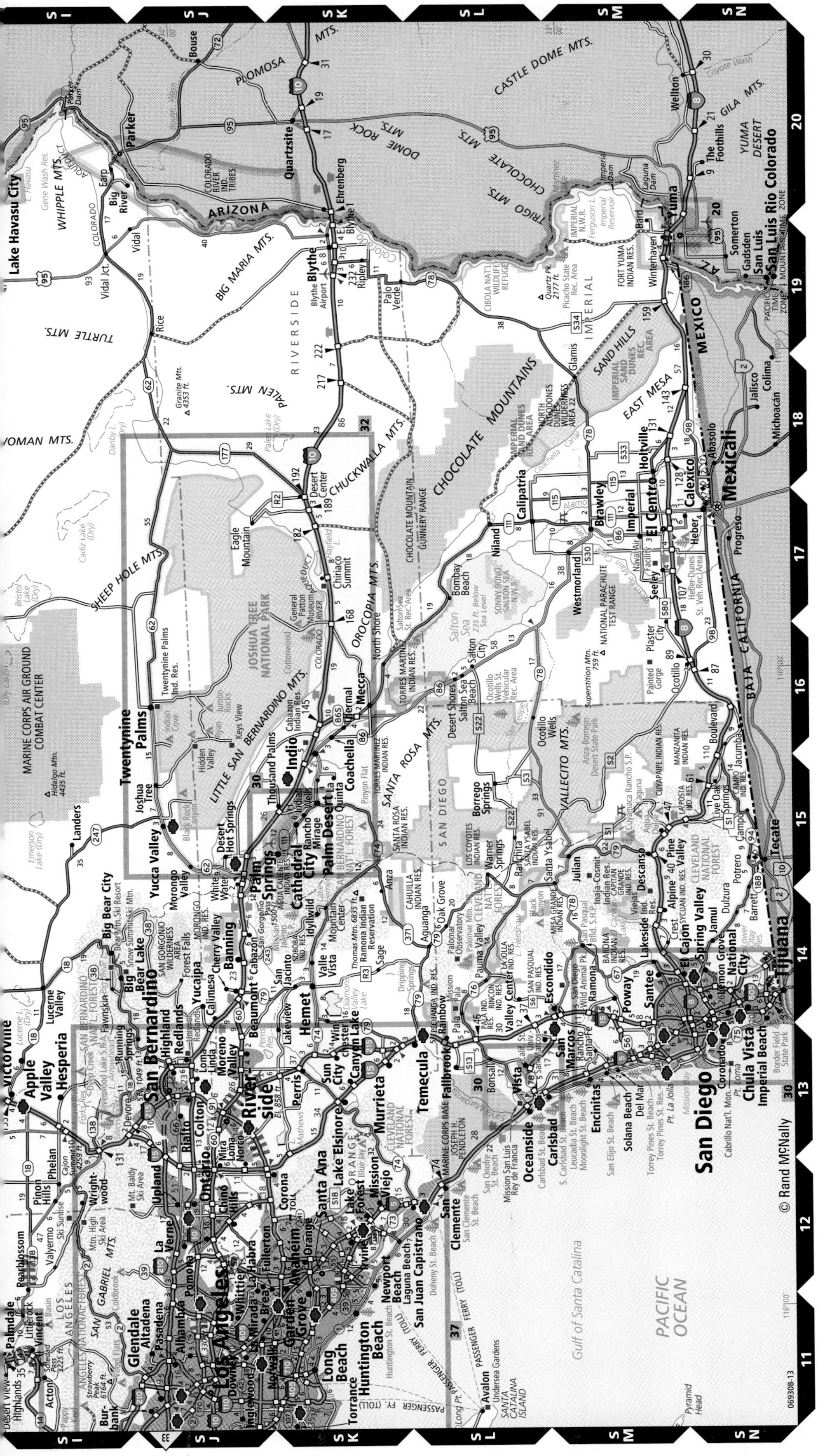

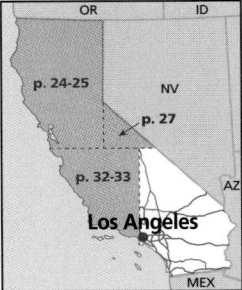

SYMBOLS

Featured ride	Scenic route
Long-term construction	■ Historic site or monument; Indian reservation or rancheria; military installation; point of interest; wildlife refuge
Harley-Davidson dealership	

HARLEY-DAVIDSON DEALERSHIPS

For southern cities, please see dealer listings on page 31; for the Los Angeles Vicinity/West, please see page 37; for L.A. Vicinity/East, please see page 39.

Antelope Valley Harley-Davidson, SH-11
1759 W Ave. J-12 **Lancaster**
(661) 948-5959
Lat N 34.694 Lon W 118.150

Palm Springs Harley-Davidson, SJ-15
19465 N Indian Ave. **North Palm Springs**
(760) 329-1448
Lat N 33.914 Lon W 116.549

Biggs Harley-Davidson Shop, SL-13
1555 S Coast Hwy. **Oceanside**
(760) 433-2060
Lat N 33.179 Lon W 117.366

Palm Springs Harley-Davidson Shop, SK-15
39101 Leopard St. **Palm Desert**
(760) 200-1775
Lat N 33.765 Lon W 116.307

Capistrano Harley-Davidson, SL-12
32421 Calle Perfecto **San Juan Capistrano**
(949) 388-3000
Lat N 33.484 Lon W 117.672

Biggs Harley-Davidson, SM-13
717 Center Dr. **San Marcos**
(760) 481-7300
Lat N 33.134 Lon W 117.124

Quaid Temecula Harley-Davidson, SL-13
28964 Old Town Front St. **Temecula**
(951) 506-6903
Lat N 33.489 Lon W 117.145

Victor Valley Harley-Davidson, SI-13
14522 Valley Center Dr. **Victorville**
(760) 951-1119
Lat N 34.515 Lon W 117.320

Hutchins Harley-Davidson, SJ-15
55405 29 Palms Hwy. **Yucca Valley**
(760) 365-6311
Lat N 34.111 Lon W 116.475

© Rand McNally

069308-13

Los Angeles & Vicinity / West

CA12

Central Los Angeles CA12

Mileages in red between red arrowheads;
in black, between intersections.

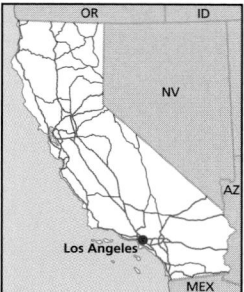

CALIFORNIA MOTORCYCLE LAWS

Helmet use: Required

Riding two abreast:
No reference in administrative code or statutes

Eye protection: Not required

Speed limit:
Primary roads: 70 mph
Secondary roads: 65 mph

CALIFORNIA RESOURCES

Road conditions or construction:
511 (San Francisco Bay and Sacramento areas)
(800) 427-7623 (in CA)
(916) 445-7623
www.dot.ca.gov
www.511.org

Highway Emergency Numbers: 911

Tourism:
(916) 444-4429
www.visitcalifornia.com

State motor vehicle information:
(800) 777-0133
www.dmv.ca.gov

HARLEY-DAVIDSON DEALERSHIPS

Laidlaw's Harley-Davidson Sales, E-10
1919 Puente Ave. **Baldwin Park**
(626) 851-0412
Lat N 34.069 Lon W 117.963

Barger Harley-Davidson, C-2
22107 Sherman Way **Canoga Park**
(818) 999-3355
Lat N 34.201 Lon W 118.608

Harley-Davidson of Anaheim-Fullerton, H-10
2635 W Orangethorpe Ave. **Fullerton**
(714) 871-6563
Lat N 33.859 Lon W 117.974

Harley-Davidson of Glendale, D-7
3717 San Fernando Rd. **Glendale**
(818) 246-5618
Lat N 34.125 Lon W 118.256

California Harley-Davidson, I-6
1517 W Pacific Coast Hwy. **Harbor City**
(310) 539-3366
Lat N 33.789 Lon W 118.303

Bartels' Harley-Davidson, F-4
4141 Lincoln Blvd. (Rte. 1) **Marina Del Ray**
(310) 823-1112
Lat N 33.988 Lon W 118.446

Los Angeles Harley-Davidson, G-8
13300 Paramount Blvd. **South Gate**
(562) 408-6088
Lat N 33.915 Lon W 118.159

Hollywood Harley-Davidson, D-5
1000 Universal Studios Blvd. Ste. V112
Universal City
(818) 754-6200
Lat N 34.136 Lon W 118.351

Van Nuys Harley-Davidson, C-4
7630 Van Nuys Blvd. **Van Nuys**
(818) 989-2230
Lat N 34.209 Lon W 118.449

Harley-Davidson of Westminster, I-10
13031 Golden West St. **Westminster**
(714) 893-6274
Lat N 33.773 Lon W 118.007

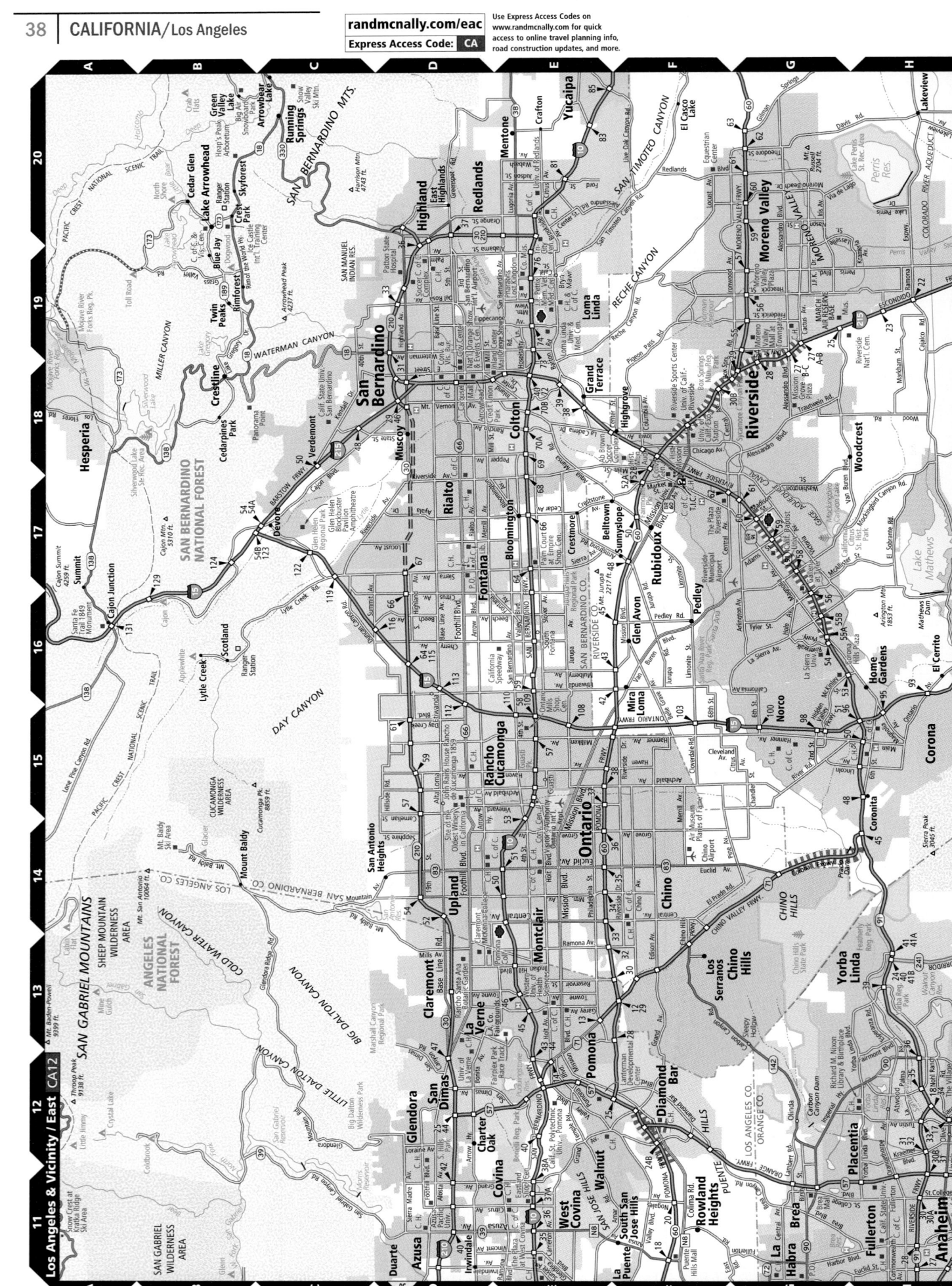

How to determine distance

Mileages in red between red arrowheads;
in black, between intersections.

SYMBOLS

- Featured ride
- Long-term construction
- Harley-Davidson dealership
- Scenic route
- Historic site or monument; Indian reservation or rancheria; military installation; point of interest; wildlife refuge

CITY-TO-CITY MILEAGE

	BAKERSFIELD	FRESNO	LOS ANGELES	MONTEREY	PALM SPRINGS	RIVERSIDE	SAN DIEGO	SANTA BARBARA
Bakersfield		107	112	226	226	168	236	148
Barstow	136	243	120	362	128	81	180	212
Blythe	335	438	223	548	116	165	223	315
El Centro	331	434	219	544	110	161	114	311
Fresno	107		215	158	329	271	339	251
Las Vegas, NV	287	394	275	513	283	236	335	367
Los Angeles	112	215		325	114	56	124	92
Monterey	226	158	325		439	381	449	246
Needles	280	387	264	506	187	225	324	356
Palm Springs	226	329	114	439		56	131	206
Riverside	168	271	56	381	56		99	148
Sacramento	271	164	379	186	493	435	503	383
San Bernardino	161	268	63	388	57	10	109	155
San Diego	236	339	124	449	131	99		216
San Francisco	282	183	381	111	495	437	505	332
San Luis Obispo	125	127	195	143	309	251	319	103
Santa Barbara	148	251	92	246	206	148	216	
Sequoia N.P.	125	94	233	252	347	289	357	269

HARLEY-DAVIDSON DEALERSHIPS

Orange County Harley-Davidson, K-13
8677 Research Dr. **Irvine**
(949) 727-4464
Lat N 33.645 **Lon** W 117.741

Quaid Harley-Davidson, E-19
25160 Redlands Blvd. **Loma Linda**
(909) 796-8399
Lat N 34.063 **Lon** W 117.257

Pomona Valley Harley-Davidson, E-13
8710 Central Ave. **Montclair**
(909) 981-9500
Lat N 34.095 **Lon** W 117.690

Skip Fordyce Harley-Davidson Sales, G-17
7688 Indiana Ave. **Riverside**
(951) 785-0100
Lat N 33.933 **Lon** W 117.407

randmcnally.com/eac

Express Access Code: CO

Use Express Access Codes on
www.randmcnally.com for quick
access to online travel planning info,
road construction updates, and more.

Distance scale
One inch represents about 23 miles

0 5 10 15 20 25 mi

0 10 20 30 40 km

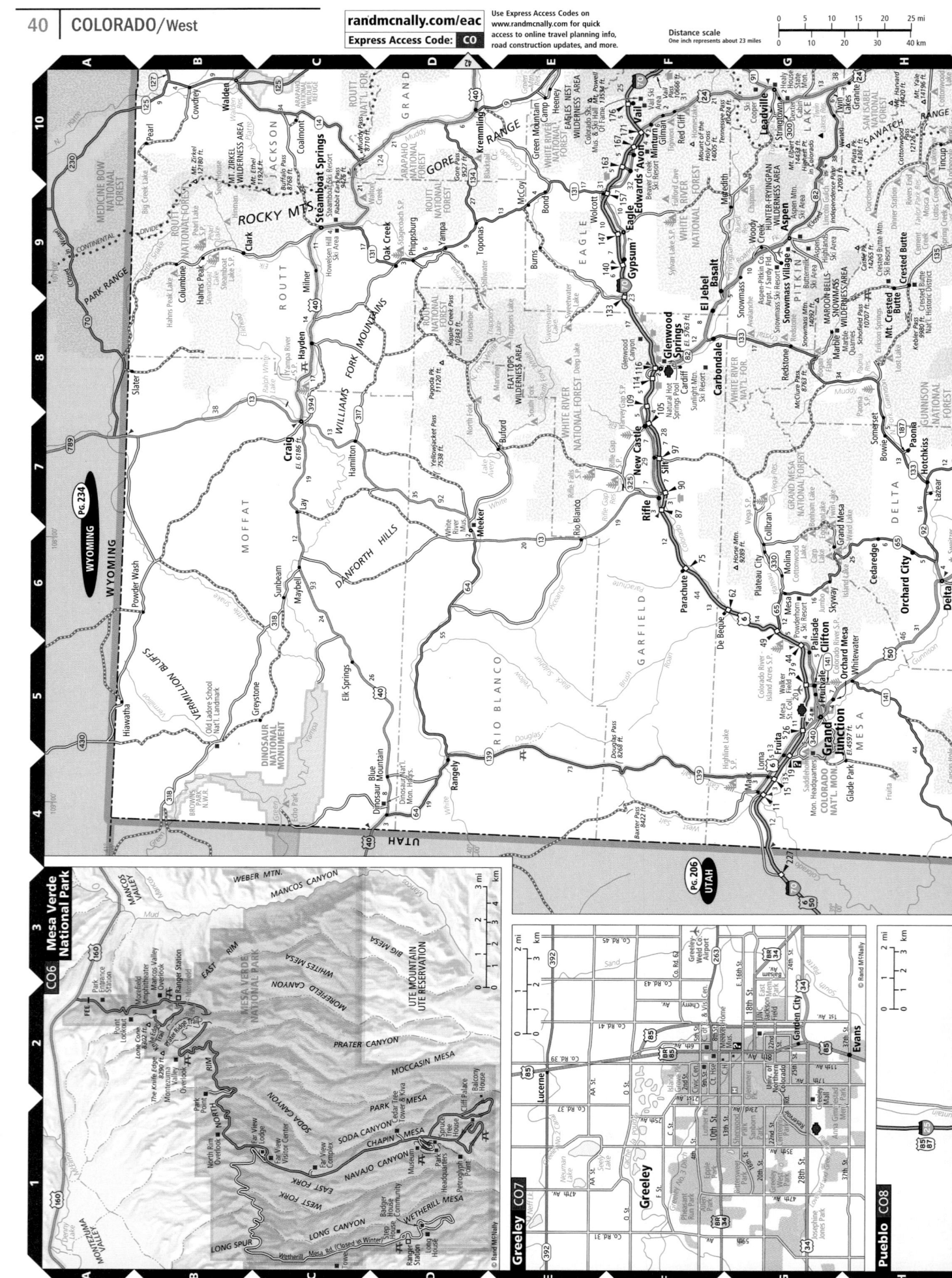

Mesa Verde National Park — CO6

Greeley — CO7

Pueblo — CO8

© Rand McNally

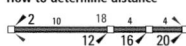

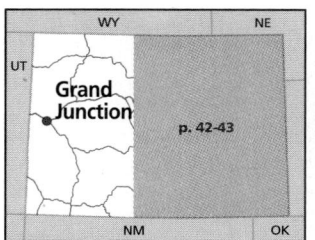

How to determine distance

Mileages in red between red arrowheads; in black, between intersections.

SYMBOLS

	Featured ride		Scenic route
++++	Long-term construction	■	Historic site or monument; Indian reservation or rancheria; military installation; point of interest; wildlife refuge
	Harley-Davidson dealership		

For Colorado ride, see page R7.

COLORADO MOTORCYCLE LAWS

Helmet use:
Not required

Riding two abreast:
Yes. See state law for specifics

Eye protection:
Required by law

Speed limit:
Primary roads: 75 mph
Secondary roads: 65 mph

COLORADO RESOURCES

Road conditions or construction:
511
(877) 315-7623 (in CO)
(303) 639-1111
www.cotrip.org

Highway Emergency Numbers:
911 or *CSP or *DUI

Tourism:
(800) 265-6723
www.colorado.com

State motor vehicle information:
(303) 205-5600
www.revenue.state.co.us/mv_dir/home.asp

HARLEY-DAVIDSON DEALERSHIPS

Durango Harley-Davidson, M-6
750 S Camino Del Rio (US 550) **Durango**
(970) 259-0778
Lat N 37.246 **Lon** W 107.874

Aspen Valley Harley-Davidson, F-8
2922 S Glen Ave. **Glenwood Springs**
(970) 928-7493
Lat N 39.522 **Lon** W 107.321

Grand Junction Harley-Davidson, G-5
2747 Crossroads Blvd. **Grand Junction**
(970) 245-0812
Lat N 39.116 **Lon** W 108.545

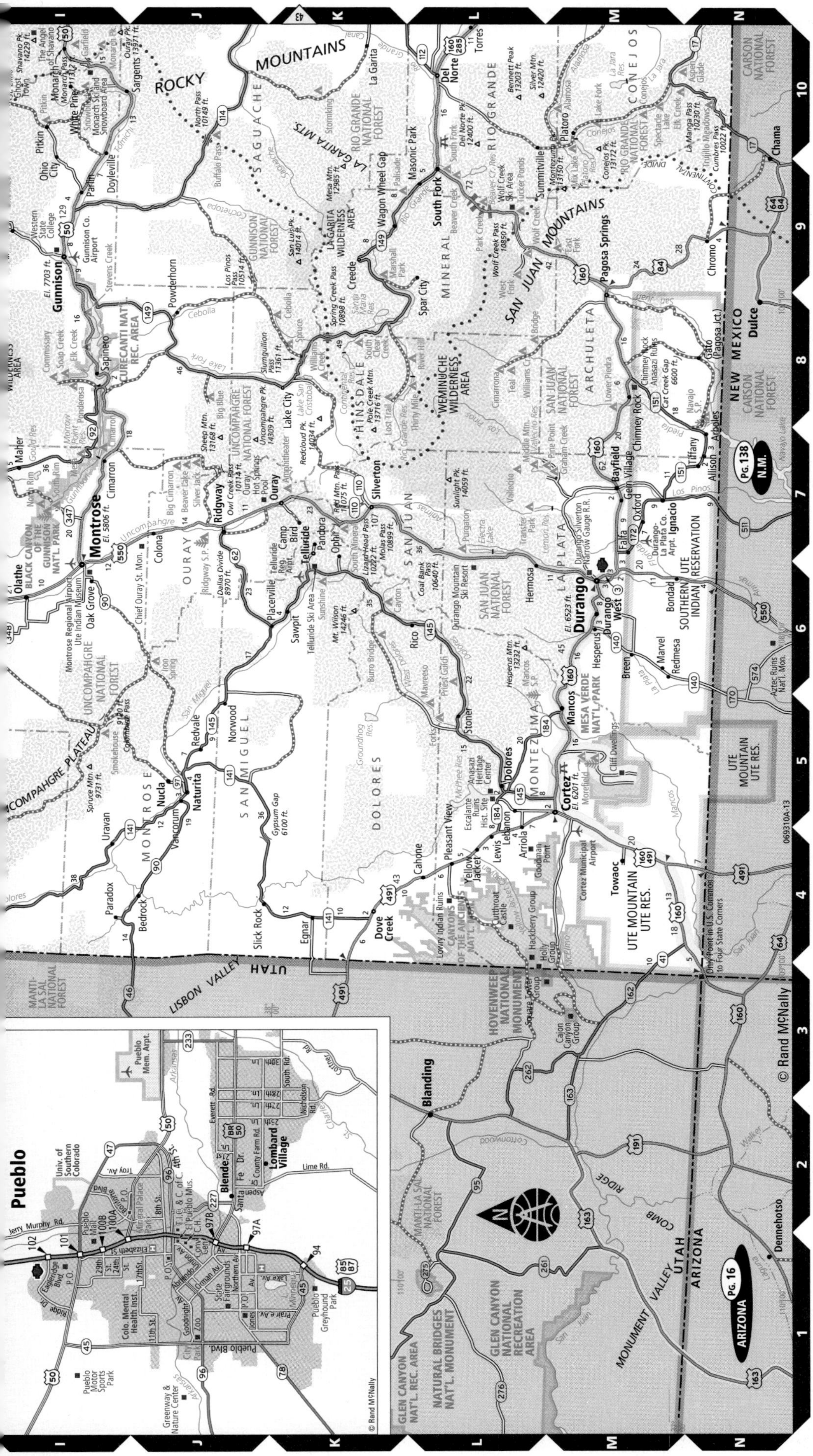

© Rand McNally

Distance scale
One inch represents about 23 miles

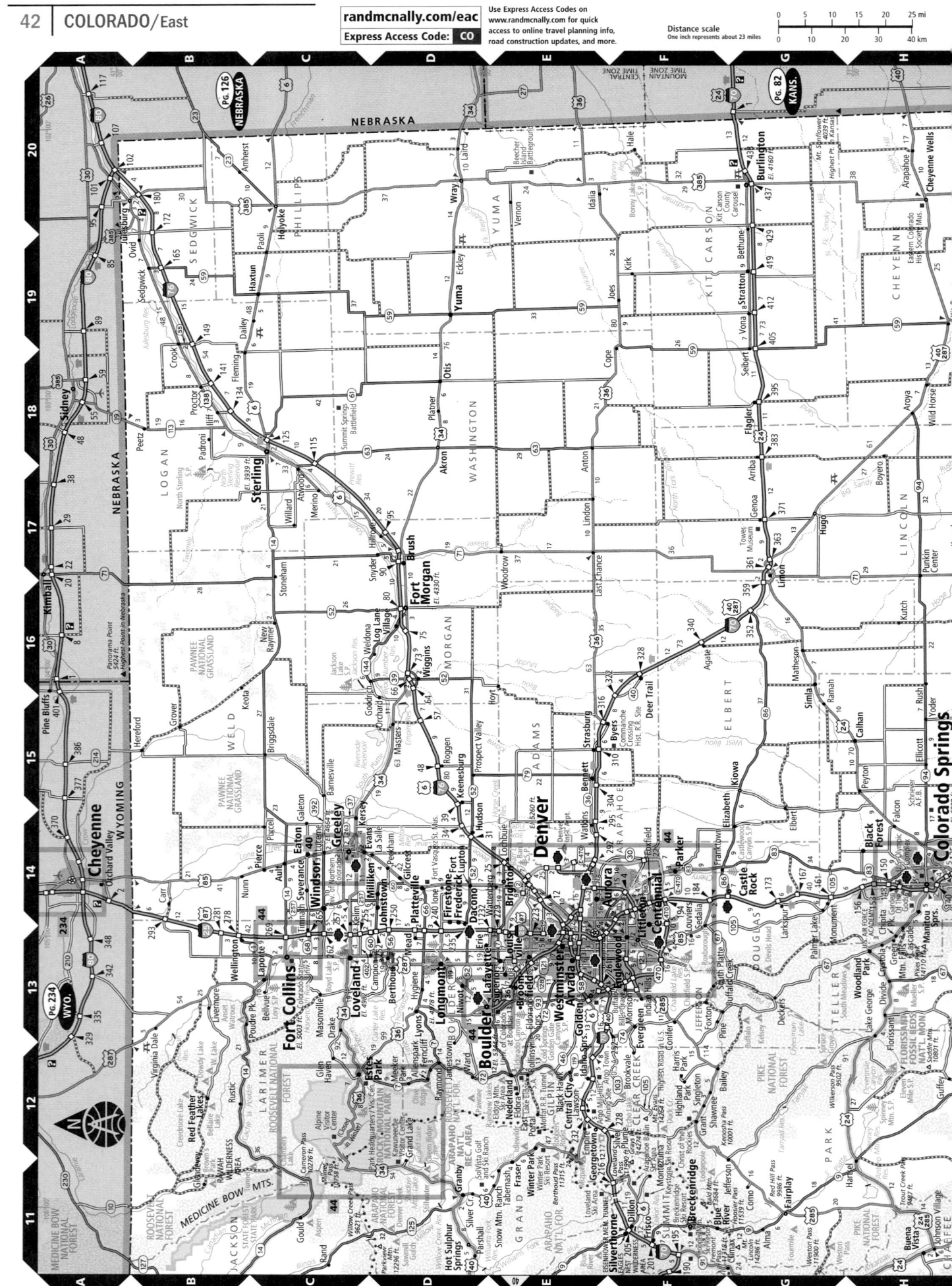

How to determine distance

Mileages in red between red arrowheads; in black, between intersections.

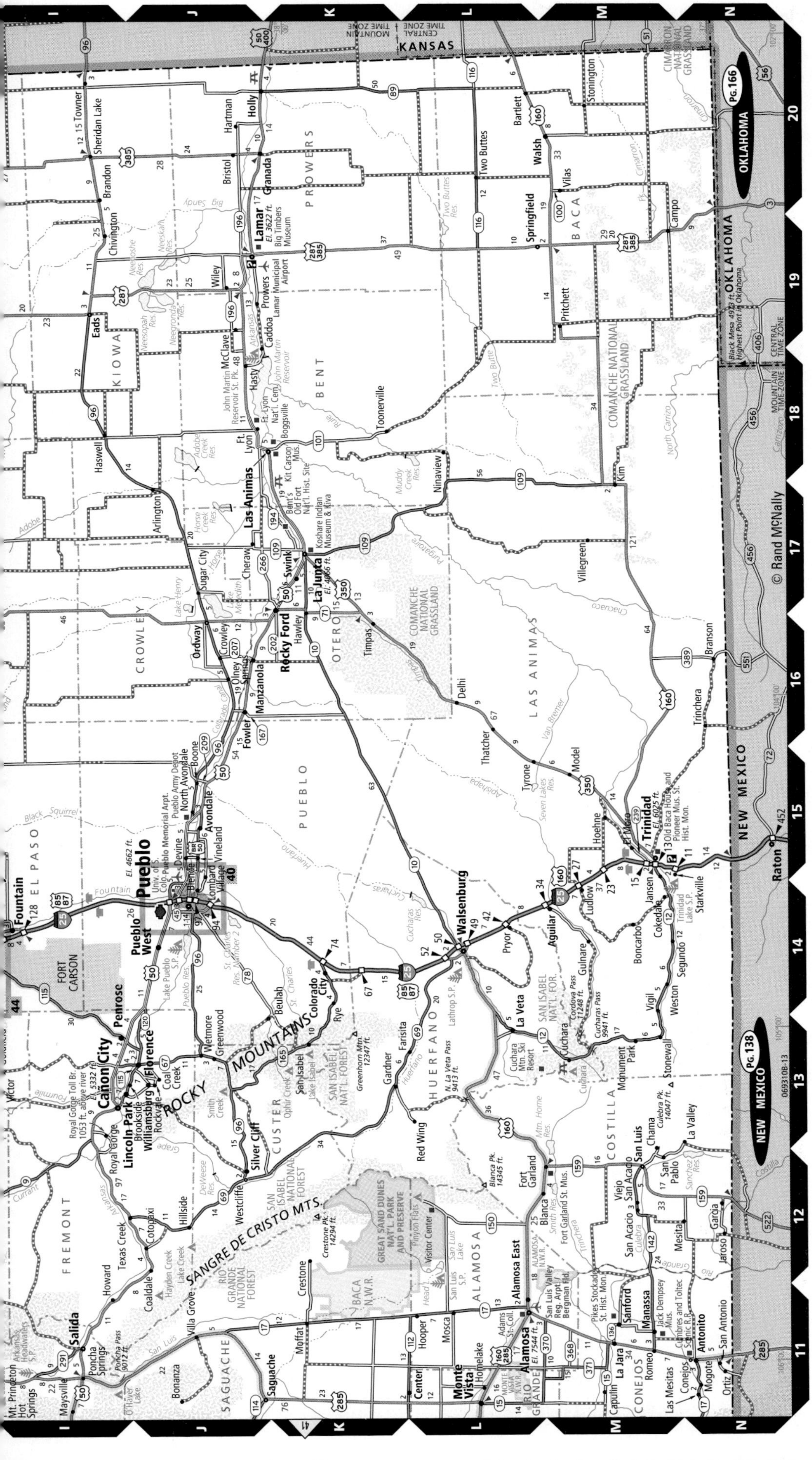

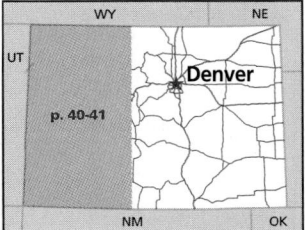

SYMBOLS

- Featured ride
- Long-term construction
- Harley-Davidson dealership
- Scenic route
- Historic site or monument; Indian reservation or rancheria; military installation; point of interest; wildlife refuge

HARLEY-DAVIDSON DEALERSHIPS

Mile High Harley-Davidson, E-14
16565 E 33rd Dr. **Aurora**
(303) 343-3300
Lat N 39.765 **Lon** W 104.795

Boulder Harley-Davidson Shop, D-13
2901 55th St. **Boulder**
(303) 545-6777
Lat N 40.028 **Lon** W 105.225

Rocky Mountain Harley-Davidson Shop, F-14
970 Park St. **Castle Rock**
(303) 327-7799
Lat N 39.380 **Lon** W 104.866

Pike's Peak Harley-Davidson, H-14
5867 N Nevada Ave. at I-25 **Colorado Springs**
(719) 278-2300
Lat N 38.916 **Lon** W 104.766

Pike's Peak Harley-Davidson Shop, H-14
2180 Victor Place **Colorado Springs**
(719) 591-7594
Lat N 38.863 **Lon** W 104.721

Freedom Harley-Davidson, E-13
8020 W Colfax Ave. **Denver**
(303) 238-0425
Lat N 39.740 **Lon** W 105.086

Mile High Harley-Davidson, E-14
8900 Peña Blvd. **Denver**
(303) 342-9021
Lat N 39.852 **Lon** W 104.677

Pike's Peak Harley-Davidson at Ft. Carson, H-14
6110 Martinez St. **Ft. Carson**
(719) 576-0278
Lat N 38.740 **Lon** W 104.797

High Country Harley-Davidson, D-14
3761 Monarch St. **Frederick**
(303) 833-6777
Lat N 40.081 **Lon** W 104.982

Greeley Harley-Davidson, C-14
3010 W 29th St. **Greeley**
(970) 351-8150
Lat N 40.390 **Lon** W 104.727

Rocky Mountain Harley-Davidson, F-13
2885 W County Line Rd. **Littleton**
(303) 703-2885
Lat N 39.566 **Lon** W 105.021

Thunder Mountain Harley-Davidson, C-13
4250 Byrd Dr. **Loveland**
(970) 292-0400
Lat N 40.437 **Lon** W 104.996

Outpost Harley-Davidson, J-14
5001 N Elizabeth St. **Pueblo**
(719) 542-6032
Lat N 38.324 **Lon** W 104.616

Sun Harley-Davidson, E-13
8858 N Pearl St. **Thornton**
(303) 287-7567
Lat N 39.857 **Lon** W 104.979

randmcnally.com/eac
Express Access Code: **CO**

Use Express Access Codes on www.randmcnally.com for quick access to online travel planning info, road construction updates, and more.

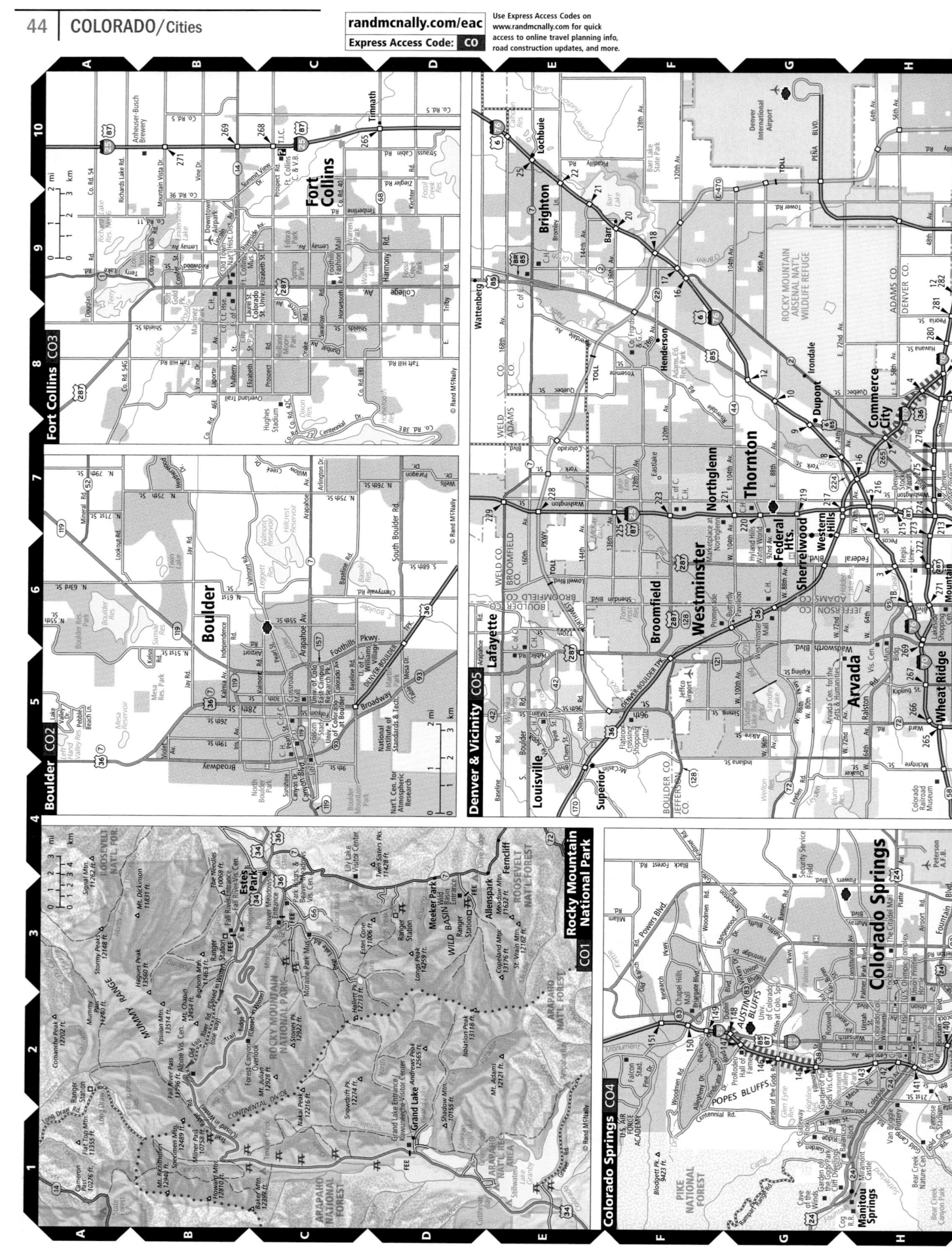

Fort Collins **CO3**

Boulder **CO2**

Denver & Vicinity **CO5**

Rocky Mountain National Park **CO1**

Colorado Springs **CO4**

How to determine distance

Mileages in red between red arrowheads;
in black, between intersections.

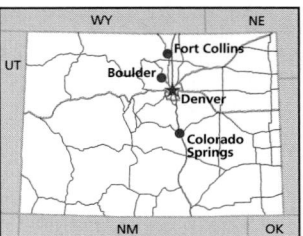

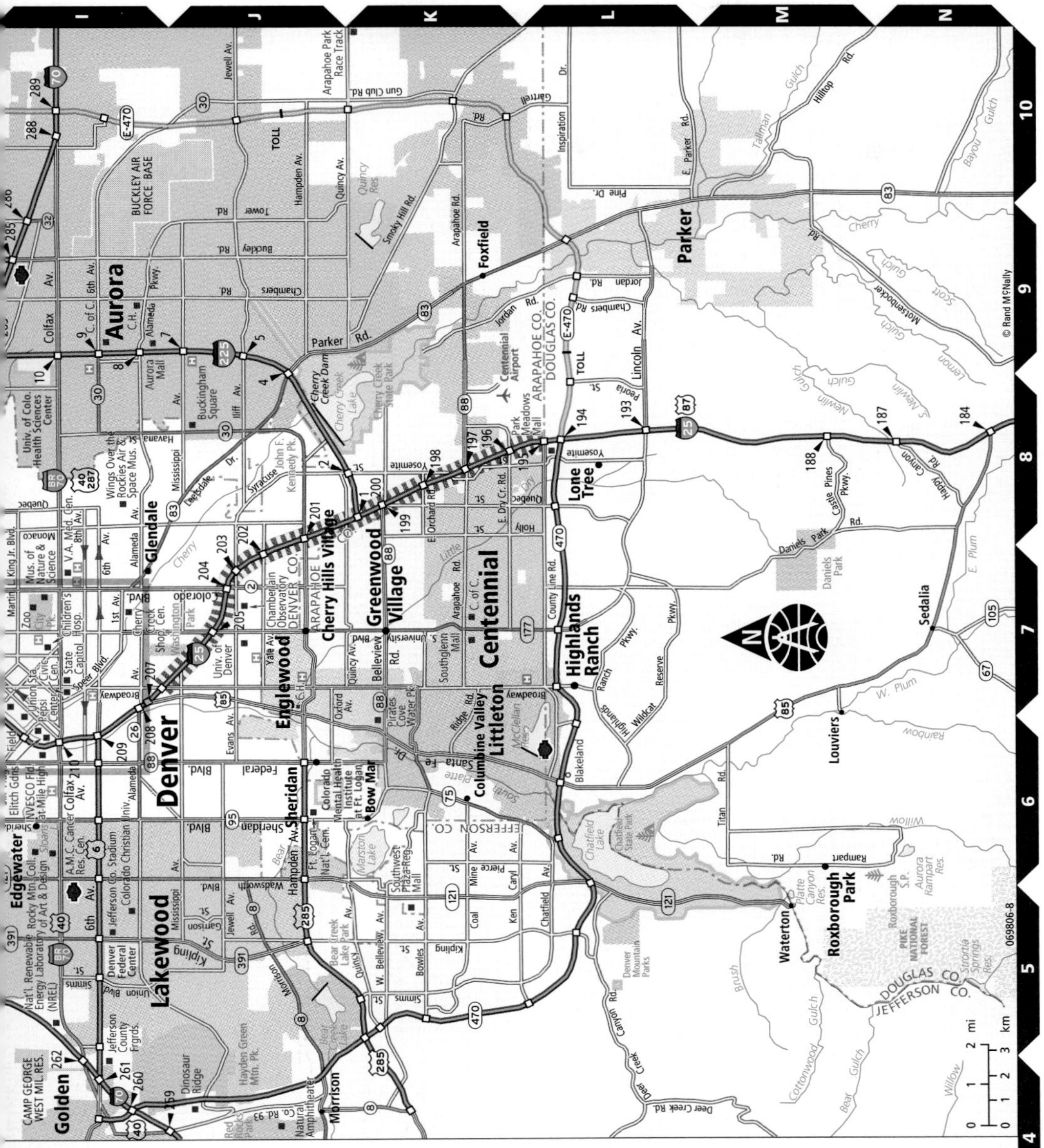

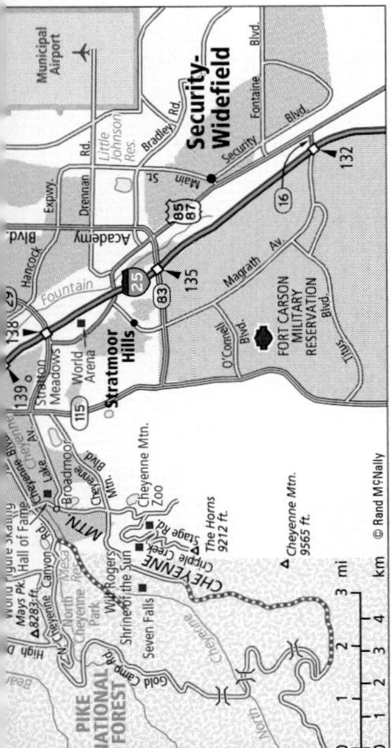

SYMBOLS

- Featured ride
- Long-term construction
- Harley-Davidson dealership
- Scenic route
- Historic site or monument; Indian reservation or rancheria; military installation; point of interest; wildlife refuge

COLORADO MOTORCYCLE LAWS

Helmet use:
Not required

Riding two abreast:
Yes. See state law for specifics

Eye protection:
Required by law

Speed limit:
Primary roads: 75 mph
Secondary roads: 65 mph

COLORADO RESOURCES

Road conditions or construction:
511
(877) 315-7623 (in CO)
(303) 639-1111
www.cotrip.org

Highway Emergency Numbers:
911 or *CSP or *DUI

Tourism:
(800) 265-6723
www.colorado.com

State motor vehicle information:
(303) 205-5600
www.revenue.state.co.us/mv_dir/home.asp

Central Denver CO5

© Rand McNally

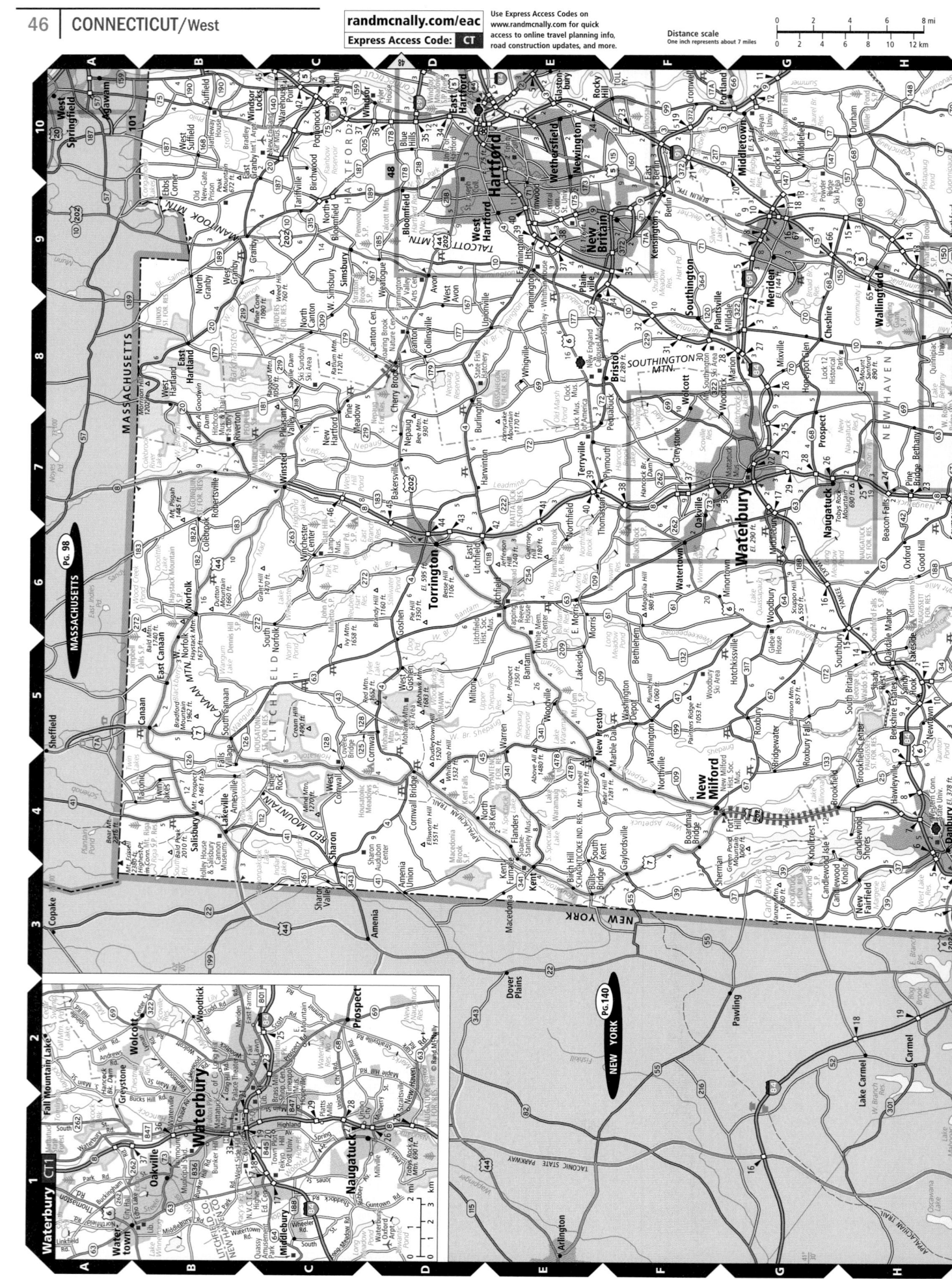

How to determine distance

Mileages in red between red arrowheads; in black, between intersections.

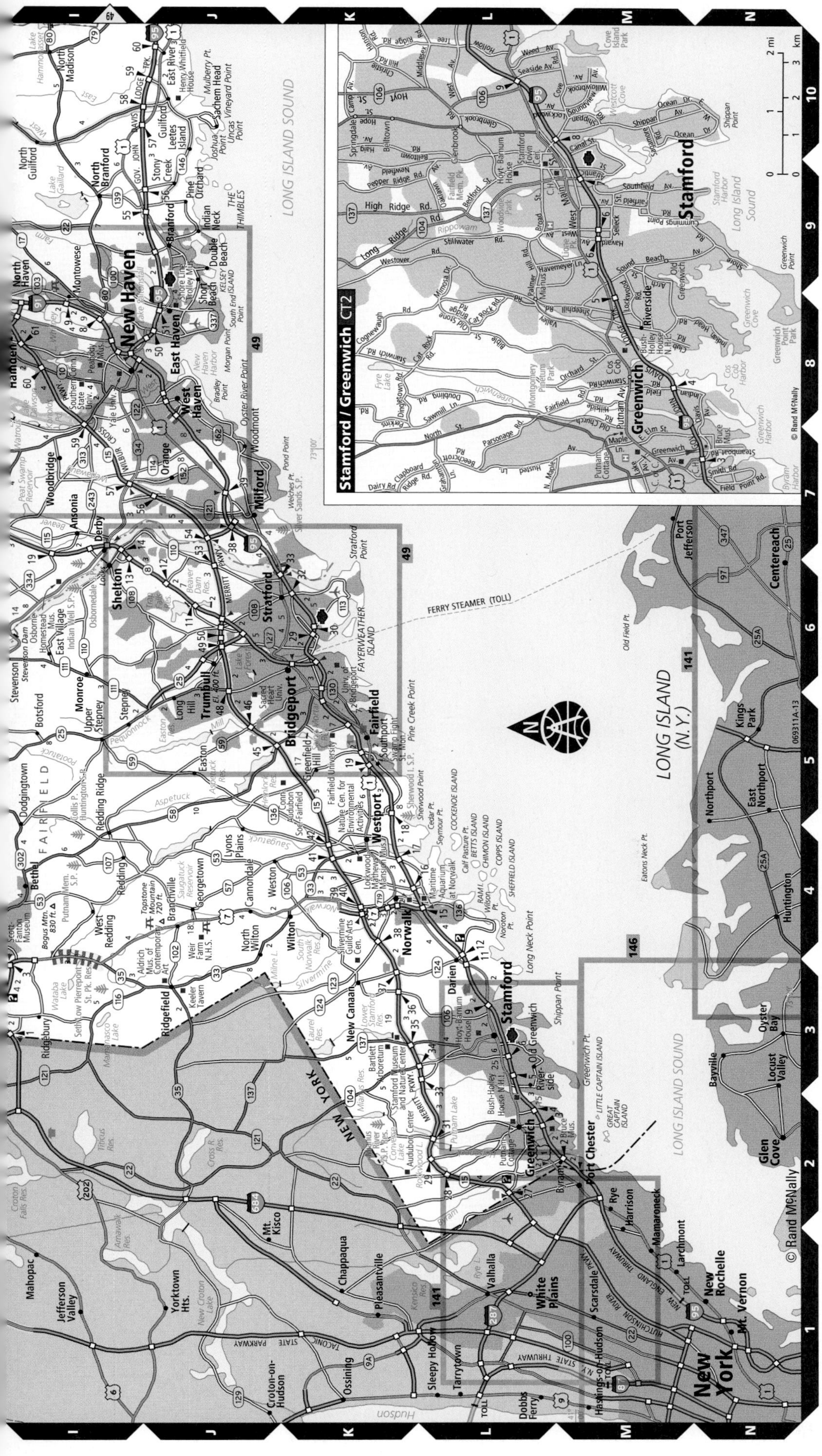

SYMBOLS

- Featured ride
- Long-term construction
- Harley-Davidson dealership
- Scenic route
- ■ Historic site or monument; Indian reservation or rancheria; military installation; point of interest; wildlife refuge

CONNECTICUT MOTORCYCLE LAWS

Helmet use:
Required under age 18, and for instructional permit holders

Riding two abreast:
Yes. See state law for specifics

Eye protection:
Required unless equipped with windscreen

Speed limit:
Primary roads: 65 mph
Secondary roads: 55 mph

CONNECTICUT RESOURCES

Road conditions or construction:
(800) 443-6817 (in CT)
(860) 594-2650
www.ct.gov/dot

Highway Emergency Numbers:
911

Tourism:
(800) 282-6863
www.ctbound.org

State motor vehicle information:
(860) 263-5700
www.ct.gov/dmv

HARLEY-DAVIDSON DEALERSHIPS

Brothers' Harley-Davidson, J-9
557 W Main St. **Branford**
(203) 315-4759
Lat N 41.279 Lon W 72.845

Yankee Harley-Davidson, E-8
488 Farmington Ave. (Rte. 6) **Bristol**
(860) 583-8484
Lat N 41.690 Lon W 72.927

Harley-Davidson of Danbury, H-4
51 Federal Rd. **Danbury**
(203) 730-2453
Lat N 41.406 Lon W 73.430

Gengras Harley-Davidson, D-10
221 Governor St. **East Hartford**
(860) 528-7200
Lat N 41.771 Lon W 72.653

Fritz's Harley-Davidson of Stamford, L-3
575-579 Pacific St. **Stamford**
(203) 975-1985
Lat N 41.046 Lon W 73.537

Bridgeport Harley-Davidson, K-6
155 Research Dr. **Stratford**
(203) 380-2600
Lat N 41.173 Lon W 73.154

© Rand McNally

Distance scale
One inch represents about 7 miles

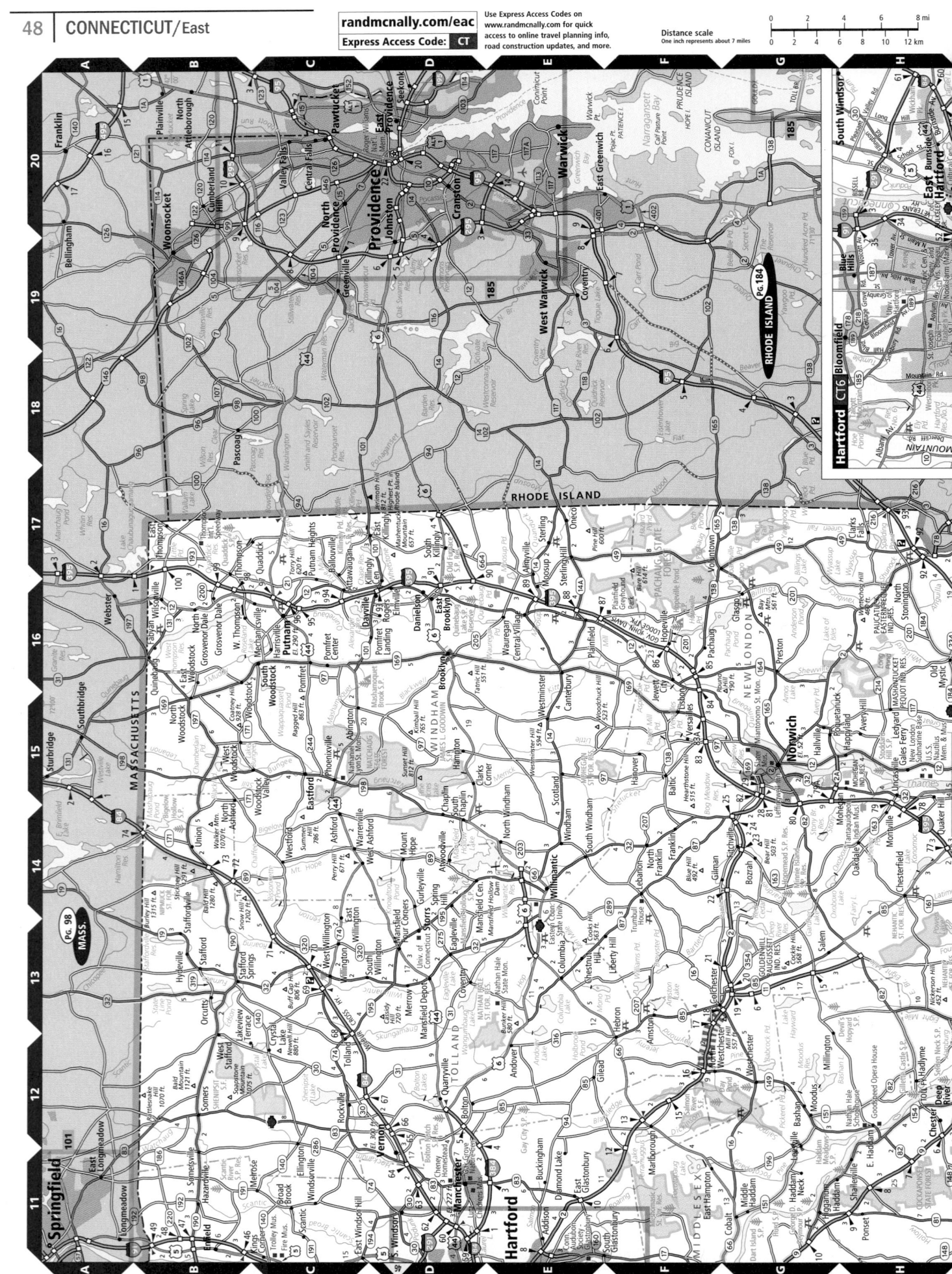

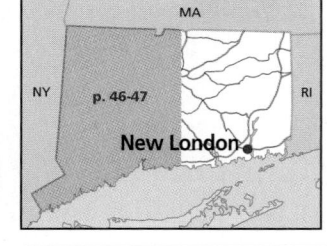

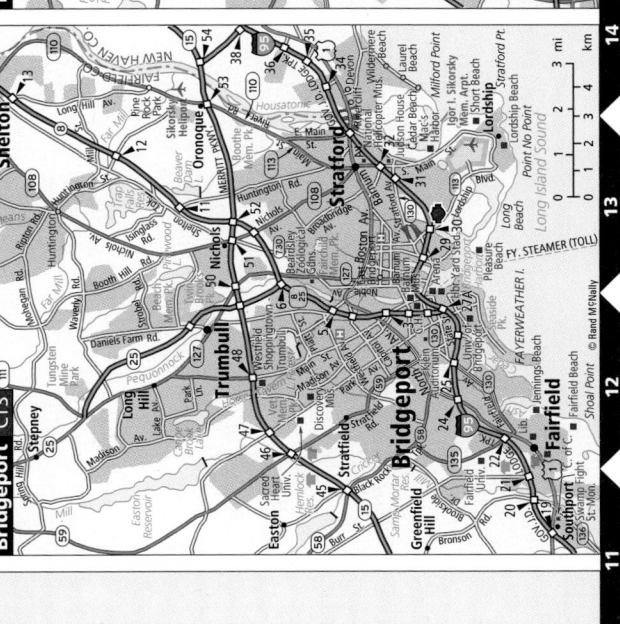

SYMBOLS

- Featured ride
- Long-term construction
- Harley-Davidson dealership
- Scenic route
- Historic site or monument; Indian reservation or rancheria; military installation; point of interest; wildlife refuge

CITY-TO-CITY MILEAGE

	Bridgeport	Danbury	Hartford	New Haven	New London	Putnam	Torrington	Waterbury
Bridgeport		29	57	19	69	112	51	31
Canaan	75	53	43	69	89	122	26	44
Clinton	41	57	40	22	30	73	67	47
Danbury	29		61	35	85	107	49	29
Hartford	57	61		40	46	46	36	32
Meriden	42	44	24	25	56	68	35	15
Middletown	45	54	17	28	44	70	45	25
New Haven	19	35	40		50	93	45	25
New London	69	85	46	50		49	89	69
New York, NY	54	61	111	73	123	166	105	85
Norwich	76	100	47	53	13	39	77	71
Providence, RI	125	146	87	106	56	33	123	117
Putnam	112	107	46	93	49		82	78
Springfield, MA	83	87	26	66	72	63	51	58
Stamford	22	31	79	41	91	134	73	53
Torrington	51	49	36	45	89	82		20
Waterbury	31	29	32	25	69	78	20	
Willimantic	83	91	30	66	28	31	66	62

HARLEY-DAVIDSON DEALERSHIPS

T.S.I. Columbia Harley-Davidson, E-13
8 Commerce Dr. **Columbia**
(860) 423-3116
Lat N 41.717 Lon W 72.247

T.S.I. Harley-Davidson Sales & Service, C-12
398 Somers Rd. (Rte. 83) **Ellington**
(860) 875-6663
Lat N 41.929 Lon W 72.456

Mike's Famous Harley-Davidson of Groton, I-15
1416 Gold Star Hwy. (Rte. 184) **Groton**
(860) 445-9745
Lat N 41.352 Lon W 72.051

How to determine distance

Mileages in red between red arrowheads; in black, between intersections.

Distance scale
One inch represents about 10 miles

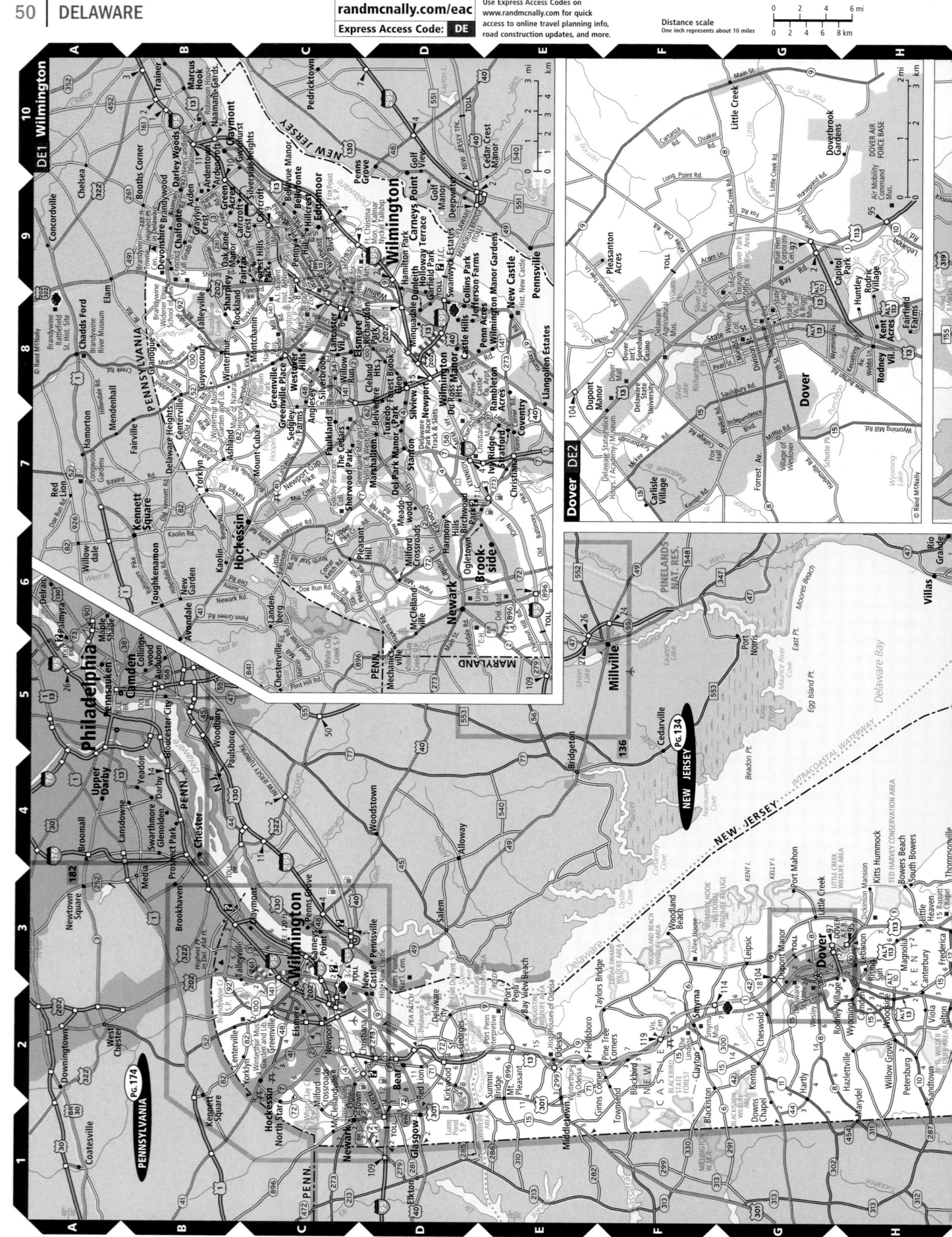

How to determine distance

Mileages in red between red arrowheads; in black, between intersections.

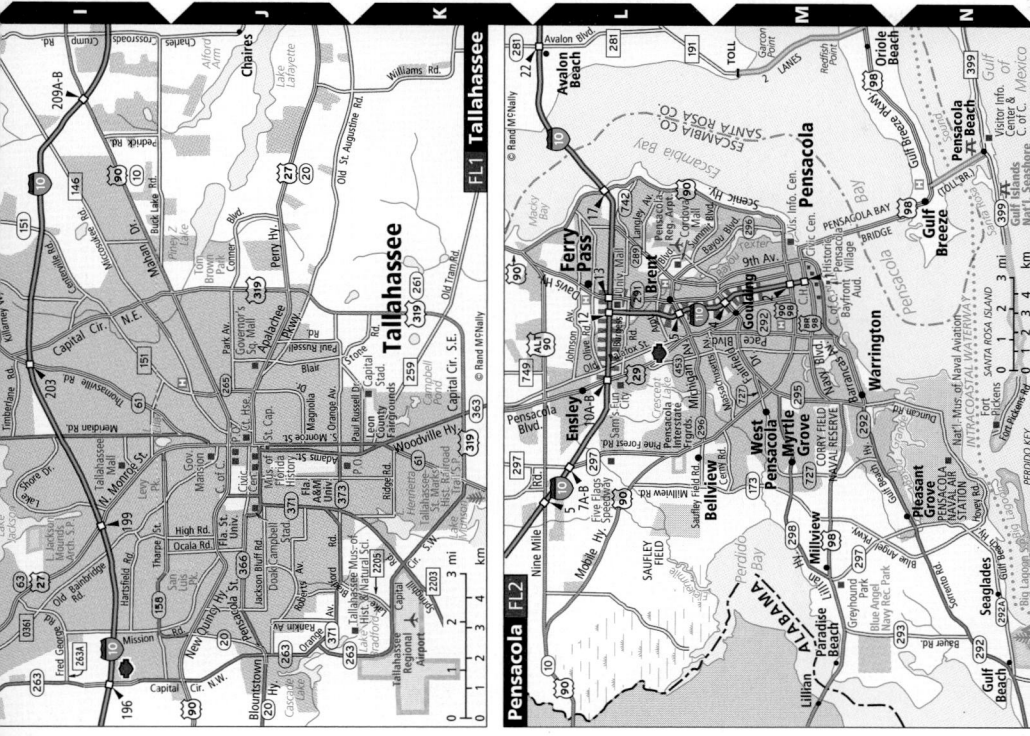

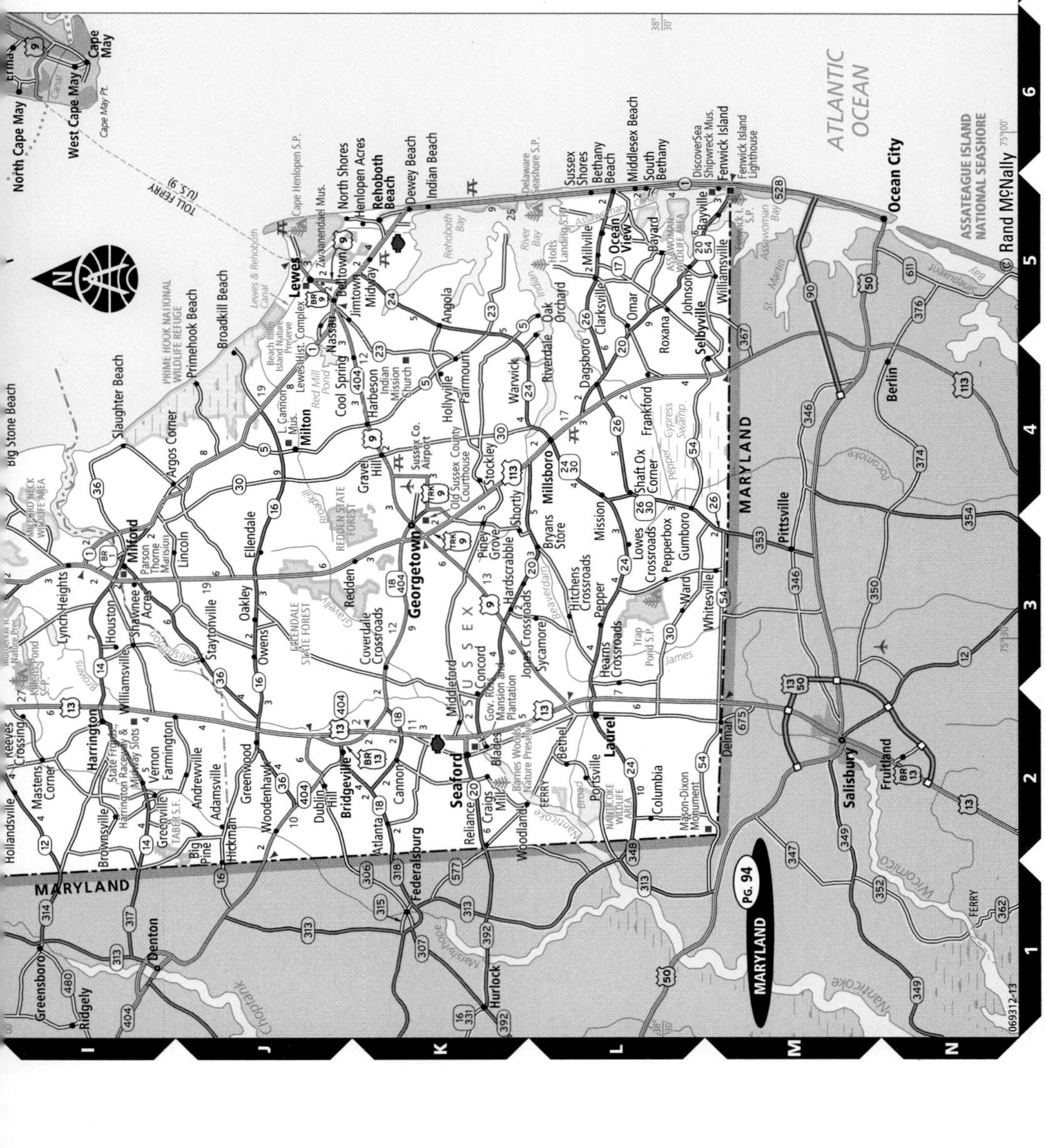

SYMBOLS

Featured ride

Scenic route

Long-term construction

Harley-Davidson dealership

■ Historic site or monument; Indian reservation or rancheria; military installation; point of interest; wildlife refuge

DELAWARE MOTORCYCLE LAWS

Helmet use:
Required under age 19, and required for instructional permit holders, and reflectorization required

Riding two abreast:
No reference in administrative code or statutes

Eye protection:
Required by law

Speed limit:
Primary roads: 65 mph
Secondary roads: 55 mph

DELAWARE RESOURCES

Road conditions or construction:
(800) 652-5600 (in DE)
(302) 760-2080
www.deldot.net

Highway Emergency Numbers:
911

Tourism:
(866) 284-7483
(302) 739-4271
www.visitdelaware.com

State motor vehicle information:
(302) 434-3200
www.dmv.de.gov

CITY-TO-CITY MILEAGE

	DOVER	GEORGETOWN	LEWES	MILFORD	NEWARK	SALISBURY, MD	SELBYVILLE	WILMINGTON
Dover		35	38	19	46	56	55	47
Georgetown	35		14	16	83	27	21	84
Lewes	38	14		20	86	41	33	87
Milford	19	16	20		67	42	36	68
Newark	46	83	86	67		104	103	13
Salisbury, MD	56	27	41	42	104		24	105
Selbyville	55	21	33	36	103	24		104
Wilmington	47	84	87	68	13	105	104	

HARLEY-DAVIDSON DEALERSHIPS - DE

Mike's Famous Harley-Davidson, D-2
2160 New Castle Ave. **New Castle**
(302) 658-8800
Lat N 39.692 Lon W 75.555

Harley-Davidson of Rehoboth Beach, K-5
36726 Bayside Outlet Ste. 810 **Rehoboth Beach**
(302) 226-8894
Lat N 38.712 Lon W 75.103

Harley-Davidson of Seaford, Del., K-2
22586 Sussex Hwy. **Seaford**
(302) 629-6161
Lat N 38.671 Lon W 75.593

Mike's Famous Harley-Davidson Shop of Smyrna, F-2
450 Stadium St. **Smyrna**
(302) 659-6400
Lat N 39.249 Lon W 75.593

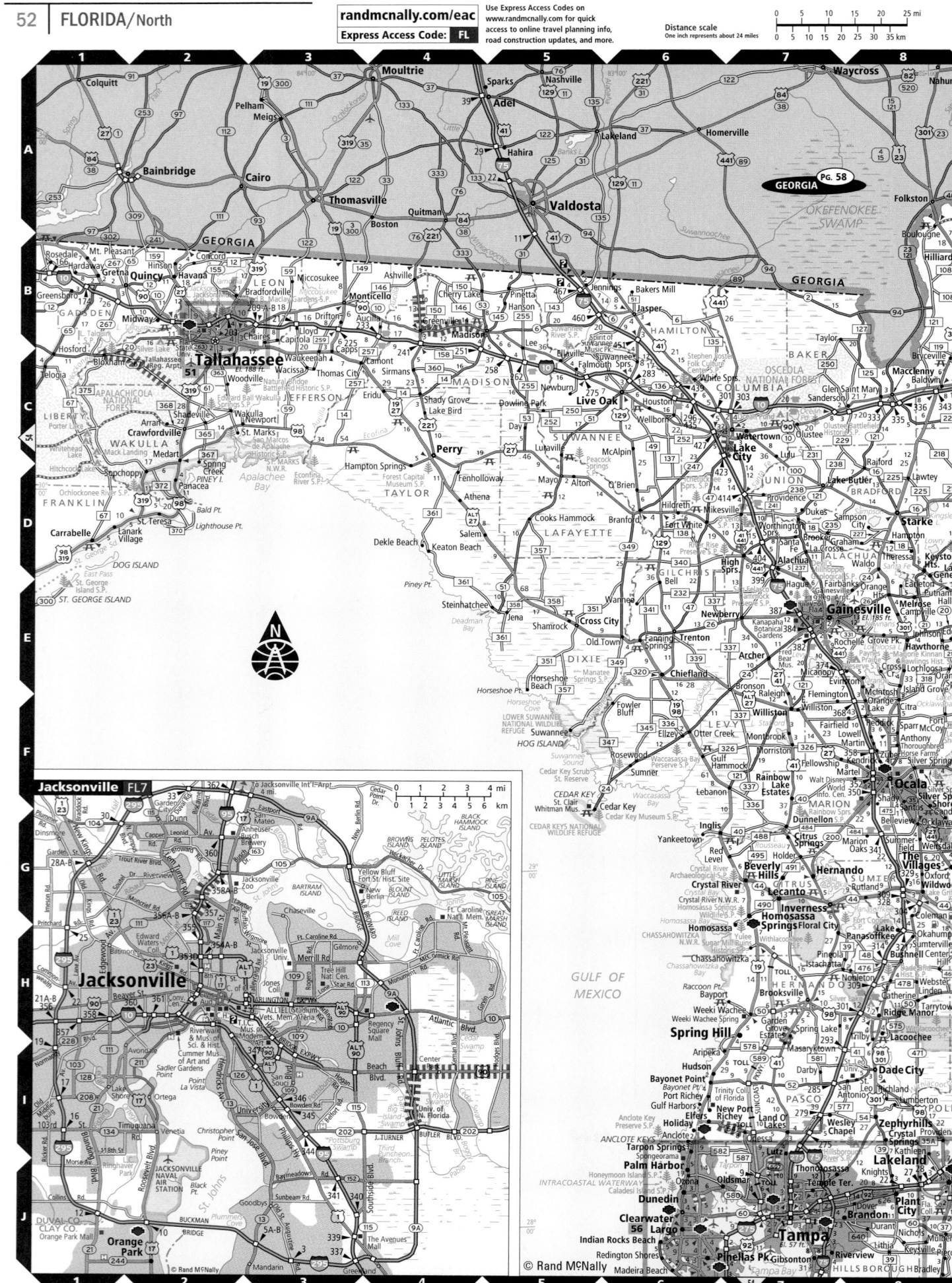

How to determine distance

Mileages in red between red arrowheads; in black, between intersections.

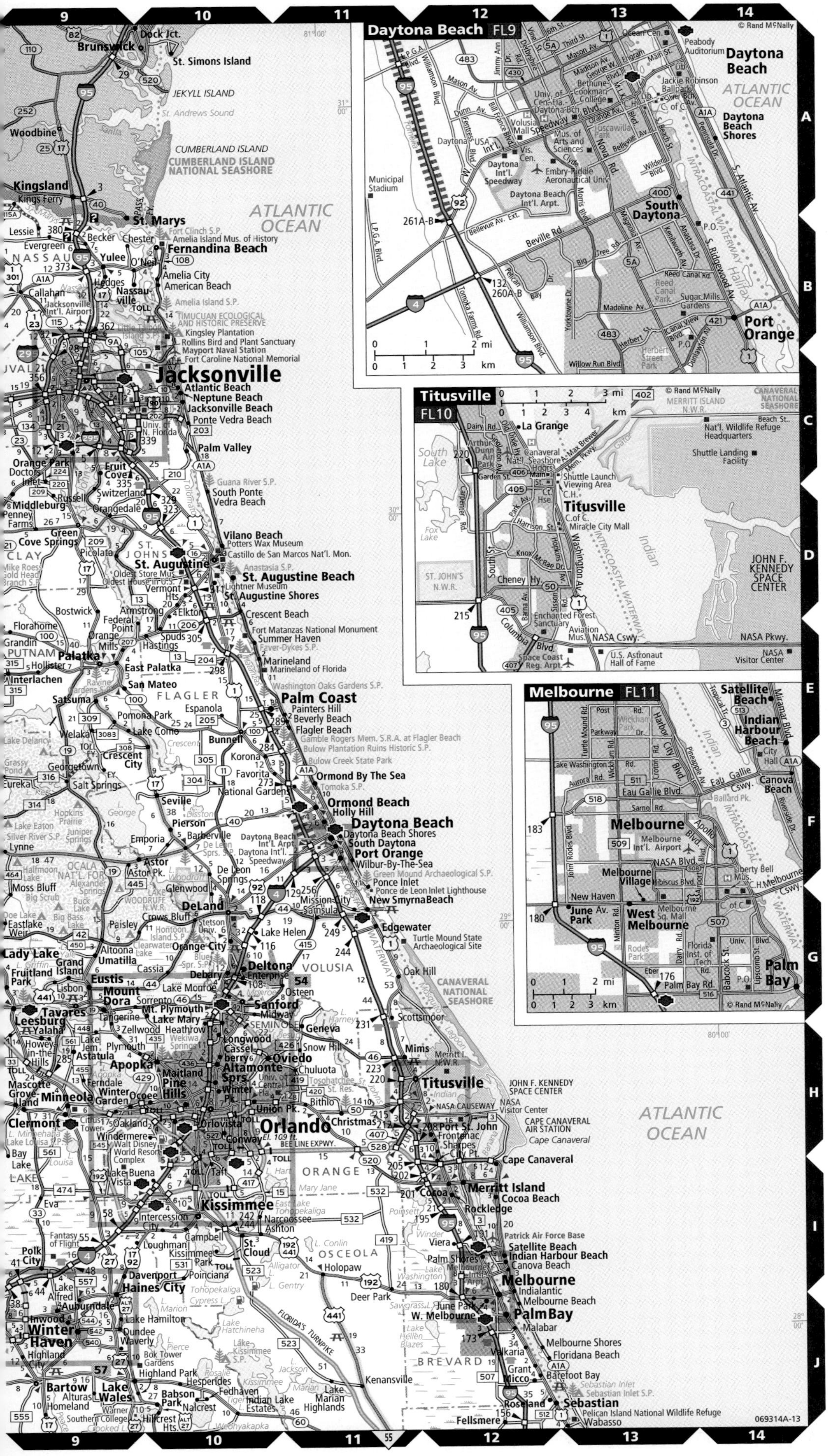

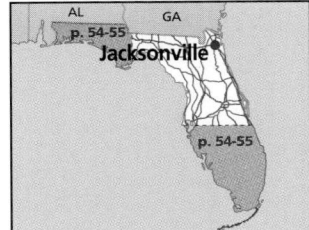

HARLEY-DAVIDSON DEALERSHIPS

For the Orlando area, please see dealer listings on page 55; for the Tampa/St. Petersburg/Lakeland area, see page 57.

- **Harley-Davidson Shop of Clermont, H-9**
  2480 S Hwy. 27 **Clermont**
  (352) 243-7111
  Lat N 28.534 **Lon** W 81.743
- **Bruce Rossmeyers Harley-Davidson Shop, F-11**
  290 N Beach St. **Daytona Beach**
  (386) 253-2453
  Lat N 29.217 **Lon** W 81.022
- **Daytona Harley-Davidson, F-11**
  250 N Atlantic Ave. Ste. 111 **Daytona Beach**
  (386) 271-2400
  Lat N 29.231 **Lon** W 81.010
- **Gainesville Harley-Davidson, E-7**
  4125 NW 97th Blvd. **Gainesville**
  (352) 331-6363
  Lat N 29.690 **Lon** W 82.451
- **Harley-Davidson of Crystal River, G-7**
  1785 SE Hwy. 19 **Homosassa**
  (352) 563-9900
  Lat N 28.800 **Lon** W 82.579
- **Adamec Harley-Davidson at Regency, C-9**
  10399 Atlantic Blvd. **Jacksonville**
  (904) 641-3735
  Lat N 30.348 **Lon** W 81.499
- **Gator Harley-Davidson, G-9**
  1745 E Main St. **Leesburg**
  (352) 787-8050
  Lat N 28.817 **Lon** W 81.847
- **Pineda Harley-Davidson Shop, I-12**
  6030 N US Hwy. 1 **Melbourne**
  (321) 259-1311
  Lat N 28.209 **Lon** W 80.664
- **Gulf Coast Harley-Davidson, I-6**
  5817 State Rd. 54 **New Port Richey**
  (727) 842-4547
  Lat N 28.217 **Lon** W 82.718
- **Bruce Rossmeyers Harley-Davidson, G-11**
  1899 State Rd. 44 **New Smyrna Beach**
  (386) 409-3034
  Lat N 29.014 **Lon** W 80.945
- **Harley-Davidson of Ocala, F-8**
  5331 N Hwy. 44 **Ocala**
  (352) 732-2488
  Lat N 29.226 **Lon** W 82.156
- **Adamec Harley-Davidson of Orange Park, C-9**
  1520 Wells Rd. **Orange Park**
  (904) 215-1931
  Lat N 30.190 **Lon** W 81.712
- **Bruce Rossmeyers Harley-Davidson, F-11**
  1637 N US Hwy. 1 **Ormond Beach**
  (386) 671-7100
  Lat N 29.288 **Lon** W 81.105
- **Space Coast Harley-Davidson, J-12**
  1440 Executive Circle NE **Palm Bay**
  (321) 259-1311
  Lat N 28.033 **Lon** W 80.652
- **Harley-Davidson of St. Augustine, D-10**
  2575 State Rte. 16 **St. Augustine**
  (904) 829-8782
  Lat N 29.920 **Lon** W 81.416
- **Capital City Harley-Davidson, B-2**
  1745 Capital Circle NW **Tallahassee**
  (850) 205-4294
  Lat N 30.477 **Lon** W 84.363

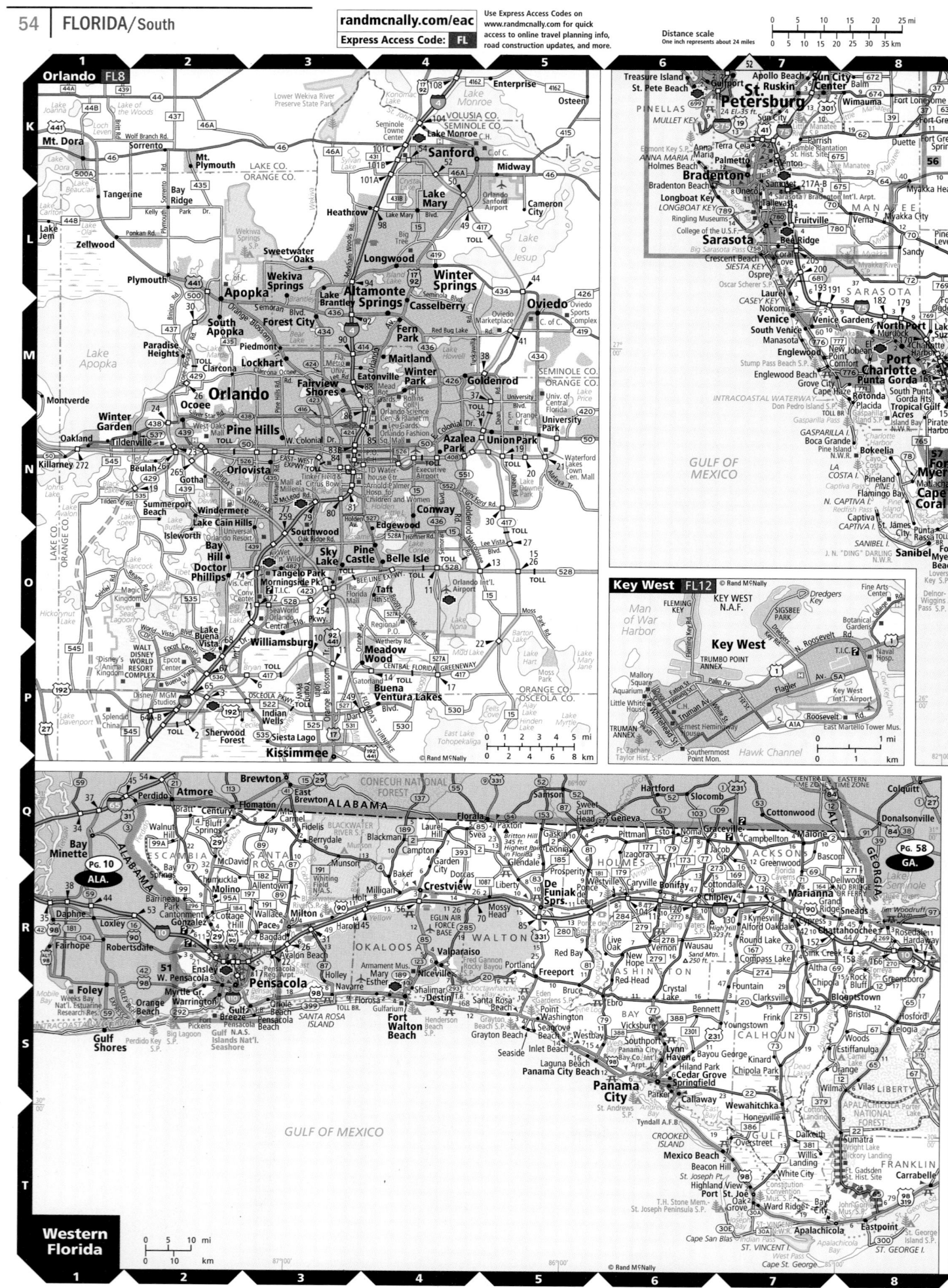

randmcnally.com/eac
Express Access Code: FL

Use Express Access Codes on www.randmcnally.com for quick access to online travel planning info, road construction updates, and more.

Distance scale
One inch represents about 24 miles

Orlando FL8

Key West FL12

Western Florida

© Rand McNally

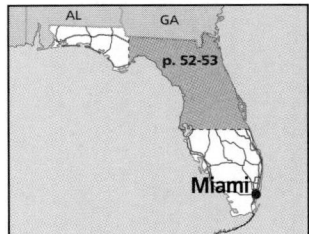

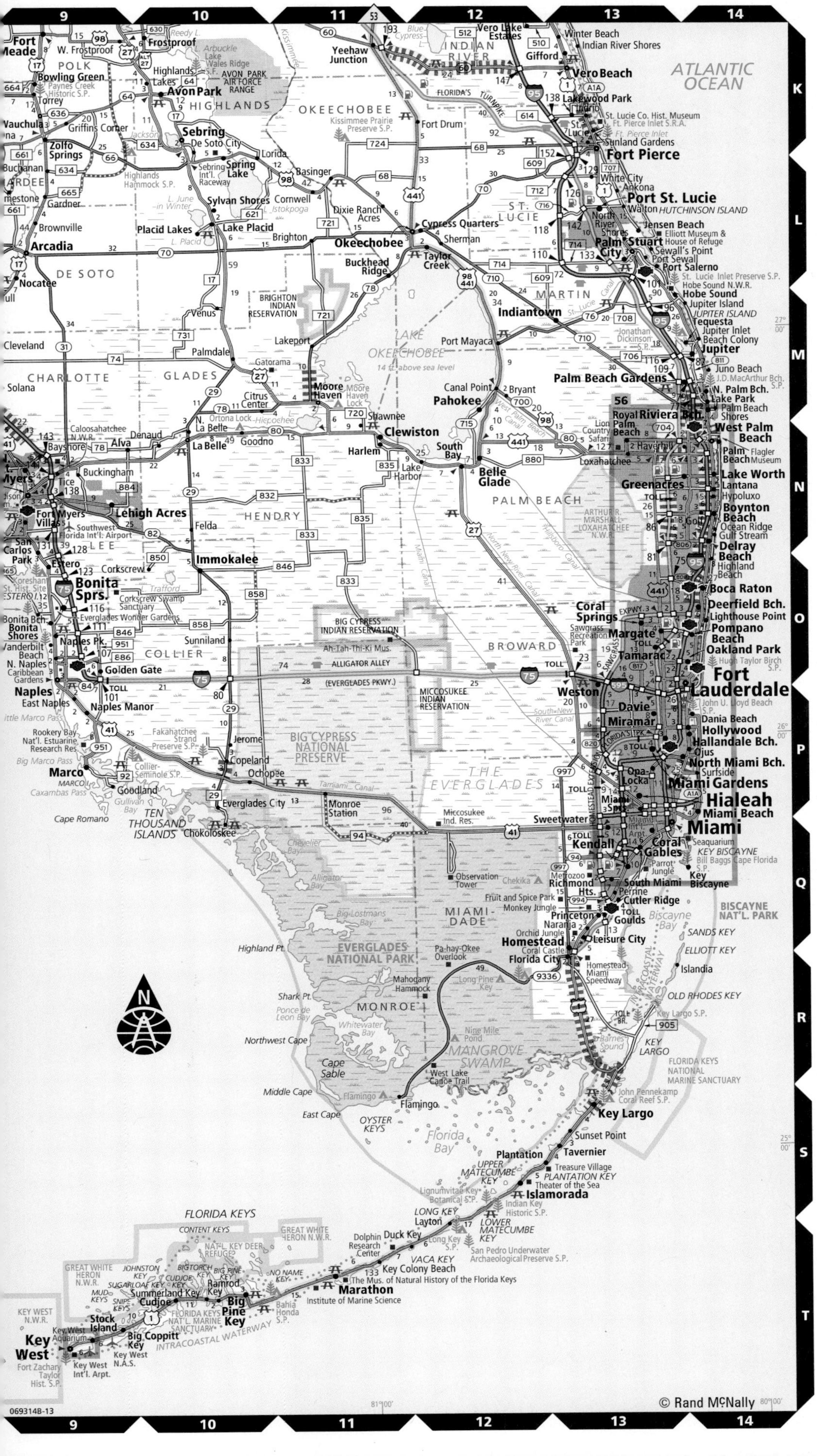

FLORIDA MOTORCYCLE LAWS

Helmet use:
Required under 21 with a minimum of $10,000 medical insurance

Riding two abreast:
Yes. See state law for specifics

Eye protection: Required by law

Speed limit:
Primary roads: 70 mph; Secondary roads: 65 mph

FLORIDA RESOURCES

Road conditions or construction: 511
www.dot.state.fl.us; www.511tampabay.com

Highway Emergency Numbers: *FHP

State motor vehicle information:
(850) 922-9000; www.hsmv.state.fl.us

HARLEY-DAVIDSON DEALERSHIPS

For the Miami, Tampa/St. Petersburg, and Ft. Myers areas, please see dealer listings on page 57.

Harley-Davidson of Ft. Walton Beach, S-4
788 N Beal Pkwy. **Ft. Walton Beach**
(850) 862-4706
Lat N 30.446 Lon W 86.639

Orlando Harley-Davidson South Shop, P-3
5881 W Irlo Bronson Hwy. **Kissimmee**
(407) 944-3700
Lat N 28.333 Lon W 81.520

Orlando Harley-Davidson, P-2
1590 E Buena Vista Dr. Bldg One **Lake Buena Vista**
(407) 938-0522
Lat N 28.371 Lon W 81.513

Peterson's Harley-Davidson South, Q-13
19825 S Dixie Hwy. **Miami**
(305) 235-4023
Lat N 25.584 Lon W 80.365

Harley-Davidson of Naples, O-9
3645 Gateway Ln. **Naples**
(239) 594-5504
Lat N 26.212 Lon W 81.745

Orlando Harley-Davidson, M-3
3770 37th St. **Orlando**
(407) 423-0346
Lat N 28.505 Lon W 81.425

Orlando Harley Gear Store, M-3
8000 International Dr. at Sand Lake Rd. **Orlando**
(407) 351-3302
Lat N 28.461 Lon W 81.477

Orlando Harley-Davidson Airport Stores, M-3
9331-9347 Airport Blvd. **Orlando**
(407) 825-3470
Lat N 28.429 Lon W 81.302

Harley-Davidson of Pensacola, R-2
6385 Pensacola Blvd. (Hwy. 29) **Pensacola**
(850) 494-1224
Lat N 30.481 Lon W 87.255

Harley-Davidson of Port Charlotte, M-8
2224 El Jobean Rd. **Port Charlotte**
(941) 883-8000
Lat N 27.001 Lon W 82.181

Seminole Harley-Davidson, K-4
620 Hickman Circle **Sanford**
(407) 831-7888
Lat N 28.816 Lon W 80.213

Treasure Coast Harley-Davidson of Stuart, L-13
4967 SE Federal Hwy. **Stuart**
(772) 287-3871
Lat N 27.143 Lon W 80.213

© Rand McNally

069314B-13

randmcnally.com/eac
Express Access Code: FL
Use Express Access Codes on www.randmcnally.com for quick access to online travel planning info, road construction updates, and more.

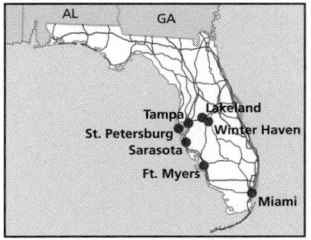

How to determine distance

Mileages in red between red arrowheads; in black, between intersections.

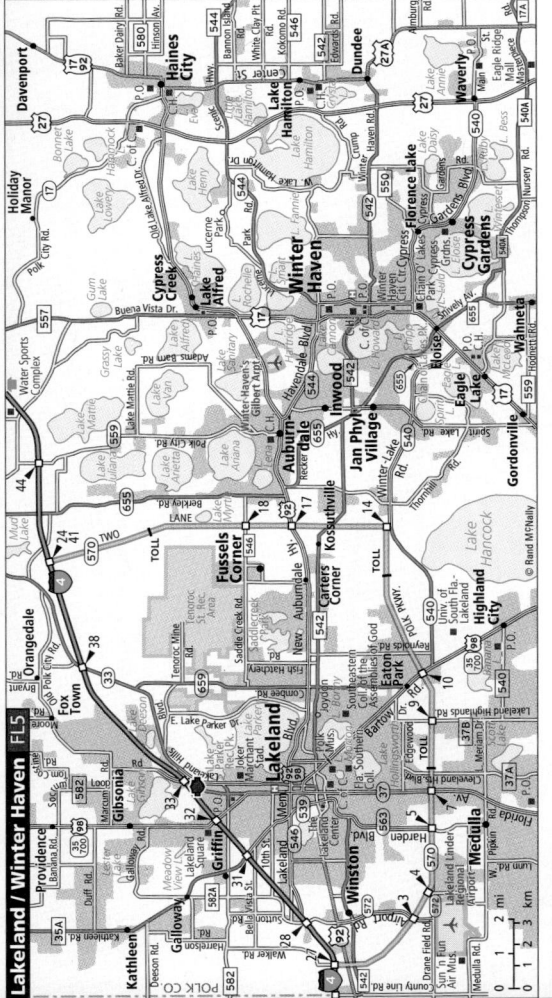

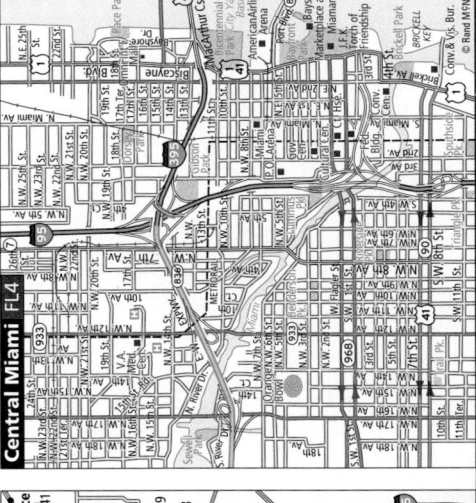

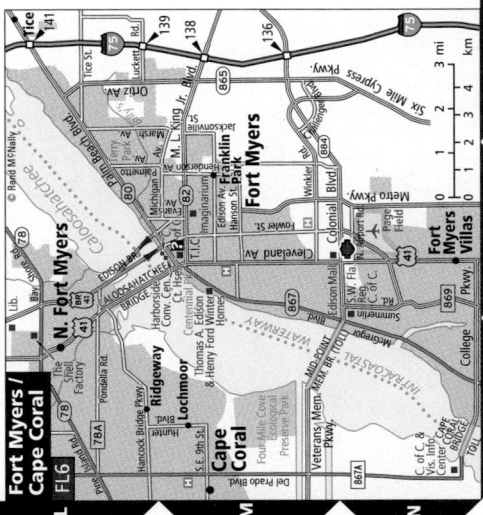

SYMBOLS

- Featured ride
- Long-term construction
- Scenic route
- Harley-Davidson dealership

HARLEY-DAVIDSON DEALERSHIPS

Bruce Rossmeyers Harley-Davidson, F-9
5100 Town Center Circle Ste. 223 **Boca Raton**
Lat N 26.362 Lon W 80.122

Manatee River Harley-Davidson, F-3
624 67th St. Circle East **Bradenton**
(941) 745-2429
Lat N 27.494 Lon W 82.475

Fletcher's Harley-Davidson Sales, B-1
17129 US Hwy. 19 N **Clearwater**
(727) 535-1844
Lat N 27.928 Lon W 82.730

Fletcher's Clearwater Beach Harley-Davidson, B-1
389 Mandalay Ave. **Clearwater Beach**
(727) 446-1844
Lat N 27.979 Lon W 82.827

Bruce Rossmeyers Harley-Davidson, H-9
2871 N Federal Hwy. **Ft. Lauderdale**
(954) 491-0300
Lat N 26.164 Lon W 80.116

Harley-Davidson of Ft. Myers, M-2
2160 Colonial Blvd. **Ft. Meyers**
(239) 275-4647
Lat N 26.597 Lon W 81.868

Harley-Davidson of Lakeland, J-2
4202 Lakeland Hills Blvd. **Lakeland**
(863) 802-1971
Lat N 28.095 Lon W 81.952

Peterson's Harley-Davidson of Miami, J-8
19400 NW 2nd Ave. **Miami**
(305) 651-4811
Lat N 25.952 Lon W 80.206

Bruce Rossmeyers Harley-Davidson Shop, G-9
2900 Center Point Circle **Pompano Beach**
(954) 545-3200
Lat N 26.265 Lon W 80.132

Jim's On the Beach, D-2
6600 Gulf Blvd. **St. Pete Beach**
(727) 363-1333
Lat N 27.737 Lon W 82.748

Jim's Harley-Davidson of St. Petersburg, D-3
2805 54th Ave. N **St. Petersburg**
(727) 527-9672
Lat N 27.821 Lon W 82.671

Rossiter's Harley-Davidson, H-3
330 Cattlemen Rd. **Sarasota**
(941) 951-6103
Lat N 27.334 Lon W 82.449

Harley-Davidson of Tampa, C-3
6920 N Dale Mabry Hwy. **Tampa**
(813) 886-7433
Lat N 28.011 Lon W 82.505

Brandon Harley-Davidson Shop, C-3
9839 E Adamo Dr. **Tampa**
(813) 740-9898
Lat N 27.948 Lon W 82.344

Harley-Davidson of Palm Beach, A-9
2955 45th St. **West Palm Beach**
(561) 659-4131
Lat N 26.759 Lon W 80.098

randmcnally.com/eac

Express Access Code: GA

Use Express Access Codes on www.randmcnally.com for quick access to online travel planning info, road construction updates, and more.

Distance scale
One inch represents about 23 miles

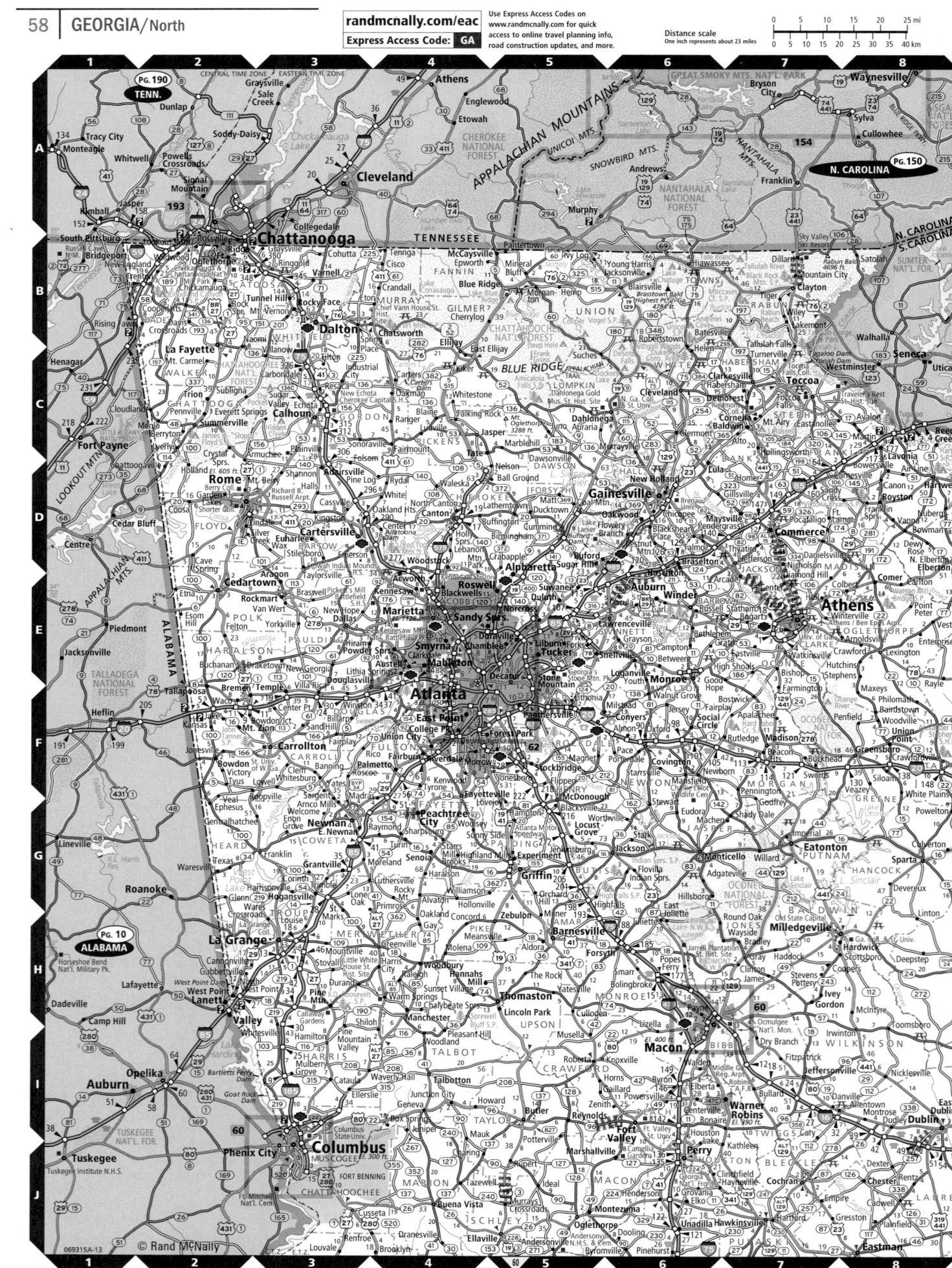

© Rand McNally

069315A-13

How to determine distance

Mileages in red between red arrowheads; in black, between intersections.

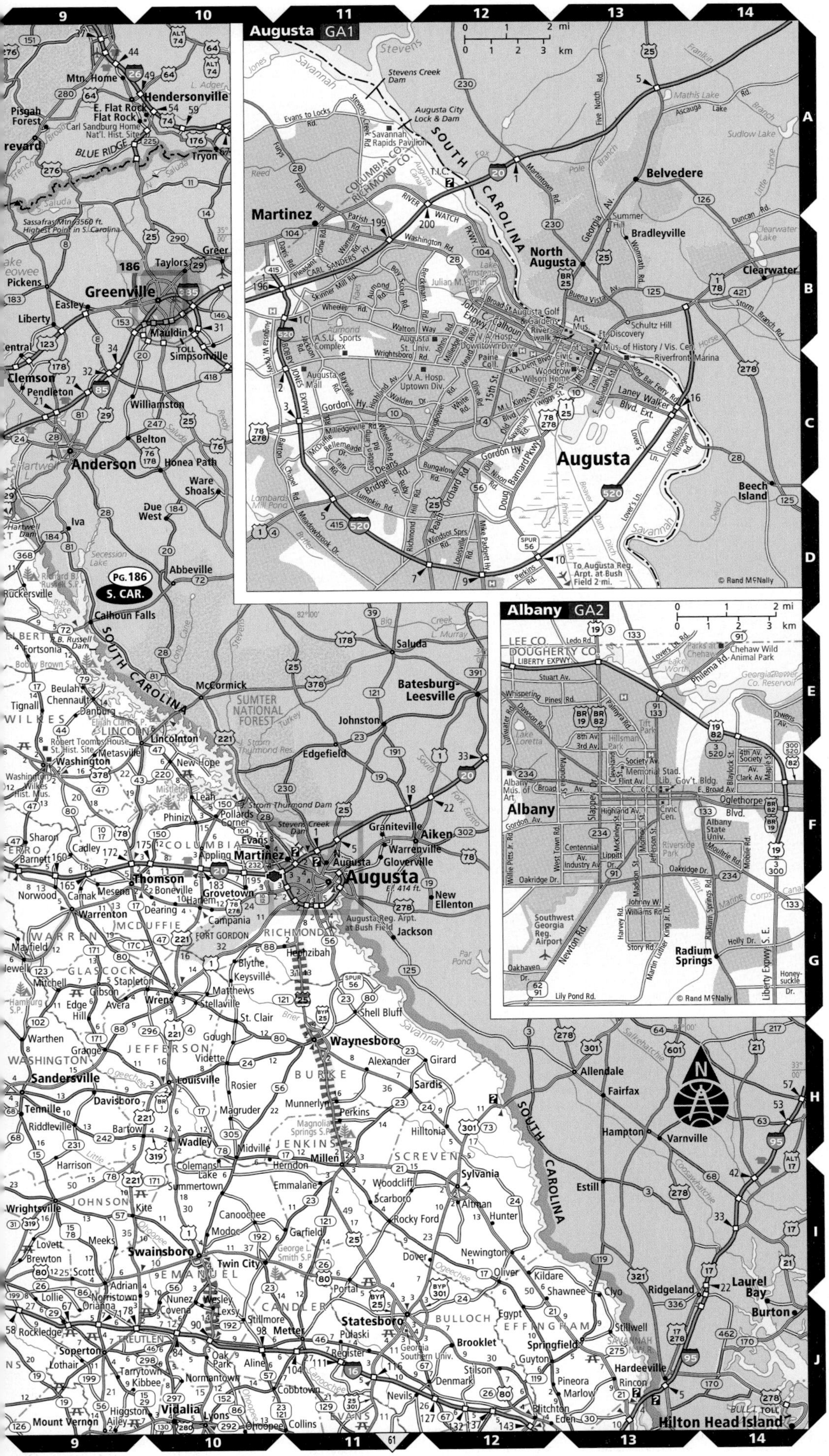

Augusta GA1

Albany GA2

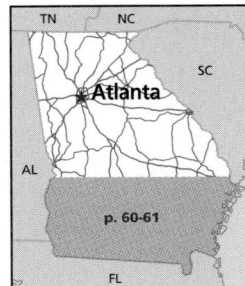

SYMBOLS

— Featured ride
— Scenic route
Long-term construction
■ Historic site or monument; Indian reservation or rancheria; military installation; point of interest; wildlife refuge
🏍 Harley-Davidson dealership

For Georgia ride, see page R8.

HARLEY-DAVIDSON DEALERSHIPS

Augusta Harley-Davidson, F-11
4200 Belair Frontage Rd. **Augusta**
(706) 651-0444
Lat N 33.484 Lon W 82.108

Harley-Davidson of Athens, E-7
4225 Atlanta Hwy. **Bogart**
(706) 549-6890
Lat N 33.941 Lon W 83.481

Frazier's Harley-Davidson, D-6
4699 Friendship Rd. **Buford**
(770) 945-6011
Lat N 34.140 Lon W 83.949

Harley-Davidson of Cartersville, D-3
422 N Tennessee St. **Cartersville**
(678) 721-0203
Lat N 34.175 Lon W 84.793

Chattahoochee Harley-Davidson, I-3
7373 Fortson Rd. **Columbus**
(706) 324-4294
Lat N 32.554 Lon W 84.948

Granite Mountain Harley-Davidson, F-5
900 Dogwood Dr. SE **Conyers**
(770) 785-3999
Lat N 33.658 Lon W 84.018

Mountain Creek Harley-Davidson Shop, B-3
1001 Market St. Ste. 37 **Dalton**
(706) 370-7433
Lat N 34.759 Lon W 85.000

Stone Mountain Harley-Davidson, E-5
2060 Ross Rd. **Lilburn**
(770) 979-7999
Lat N 33.835 Lon W 84.080

Harley-Davidson of Atlanta, E-4
501 Thornton Rd. **Lithia Springs**
(770) 944-1340
Lat N 33.791 Lon W 84.628

Harley-Davidson of Macon, H-6
5000 Mercer University Dr. **Macon**
(478) 474-3344
Lat N 32.831 Lon W 83.725

Earl Small's Harley-Davidson, E-4
993 S Cobb Dr. **Marietta**
(770) 919-0000
Lat N 33.929 Lon W 84.551

Harley-Davidson of Clayton County, F-5
1384 Southlake Pkwy. **Morrow**
(770) 960-6000
Lat N 33.575 Lon W 84.345

Killer Creek Harley-Davidson, E-5
11480 Alpharetta Hwy. **Roswell**
(770) 777-1000
Lat N 34.060 Lon W 84.325

© Rand McNally

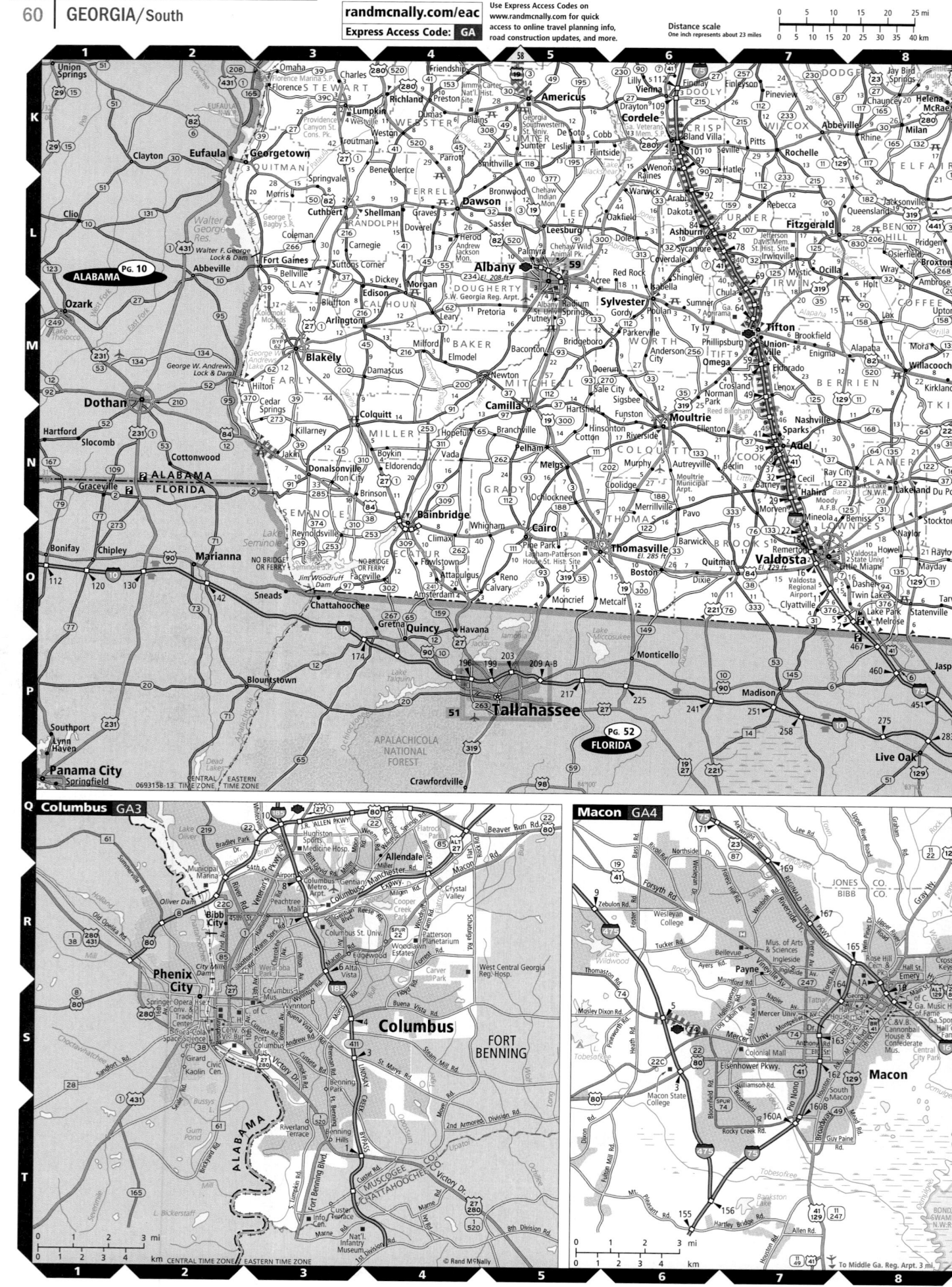

How to determine distance

Mileages in red between red arrowheads; in black, between intersections.

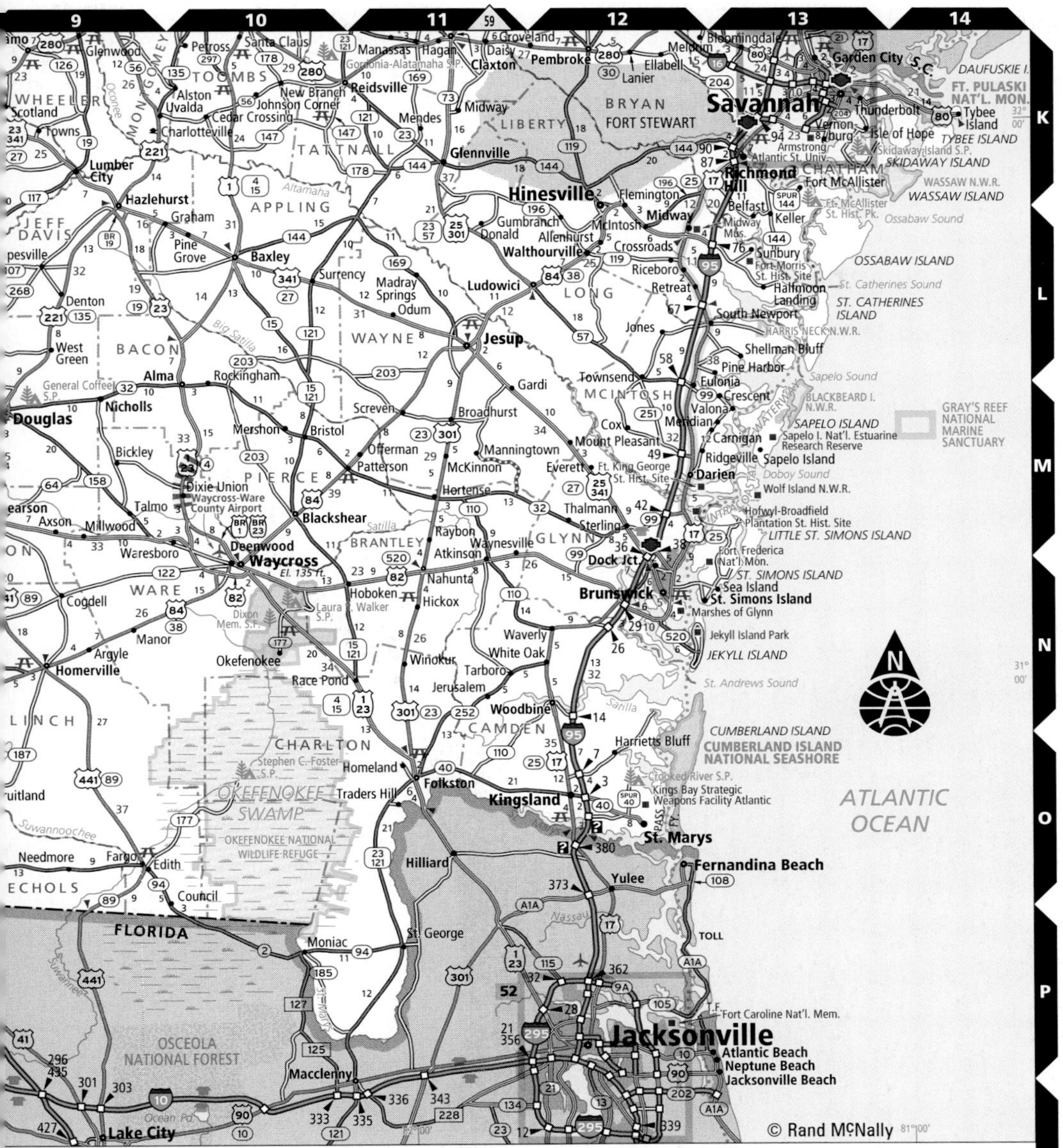

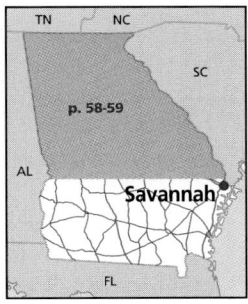

Savannah

SYMBOLS

— Featured ride
═ Scenic route
▦ Long-term construction
■ Historic site or monument; Indian reservation or rancheria; military installation; point of interest; wildlife refuge
Harley-Davidson dealership

GEORGIA MOTORCYCLE LAWS

Helmet use:
Required

Riding two abreast:
Yes. See state law for specifics

Eye protection:
Required unless equipped with windscreen

Speed limit:
Primary roads: 70 mph
Secondary roads: 65 mph

GEORGIA RESOURCES

Road conditions or construction:
(404) 635-8000
www.dot.state.ga.us

Highway Emergency Numbers:
911 or *GSP

Tourism:
(800) 847-4842
www.georgiaonmymind.org

State motor vehicle information:
(404) 657-9300
www.dds.ga.gov/

HARLEY-DAVIDSON DEALERSHIPS

Flint River Harley-Davidson, L-5
2815 Old Dawson Rd. **Albany**
(229) 639-0035
Lat N 31.614 Lon W 84.223

Golden Isles Harley-Davidson Shop, N-12
153 Venture Dr. **Brunswick**
(912) 280-0448
Lat N 31.245 Lon W 81.506

Savannah Harley-Davidson, K-13
6 Gateway Blvd. W **Savannah**
(912) 925-0005
Lat N 32.006 Lon W 81.286

Savannah Harley-Davidson on River St., K-13
503 River St. **Savannah**
(912) 231-8000
Lat N 32.069 Lon W 81.093

Little River Harley-Davidson Shop, M-7
49 Casseta Dr. **Tifton**
(877) 387-8855
Lat N 31.439 Lon W 83.527

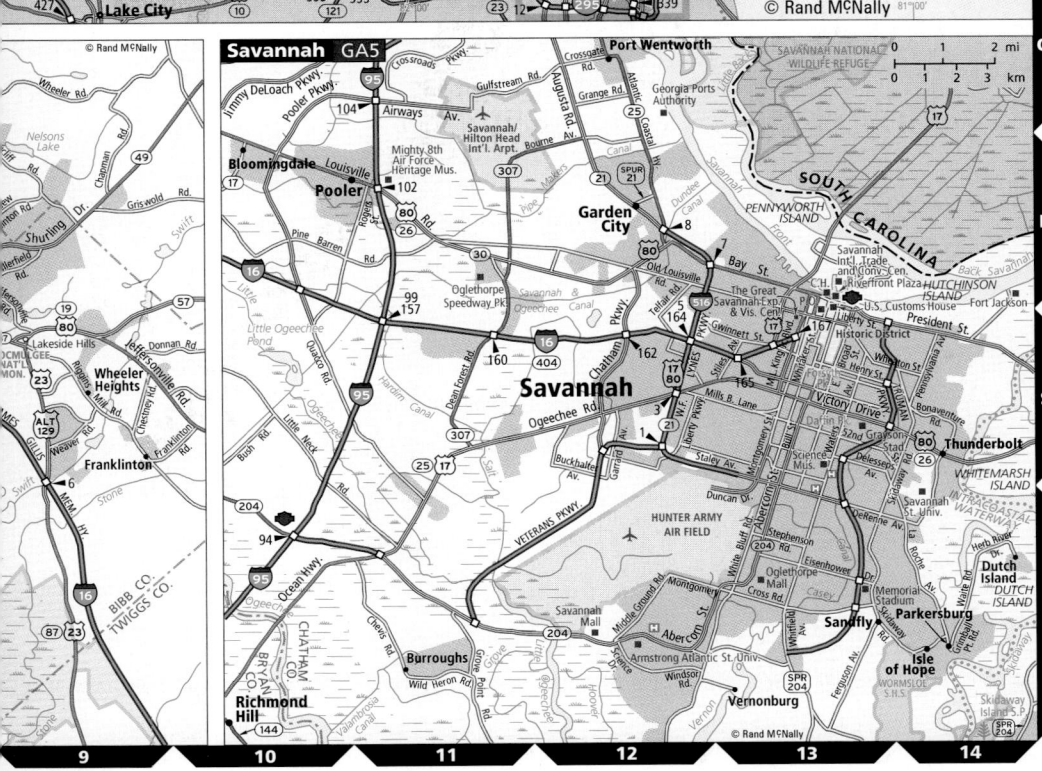

© Rand McNally

Savannah GA5

randmcnally.com/eac

Express Access Codes: Georgia **GA** Hawaii **HI**

Use Express Access Codes on
www.randmcnally.com for quick
access to online travel planning info,
road construction updates, and more.

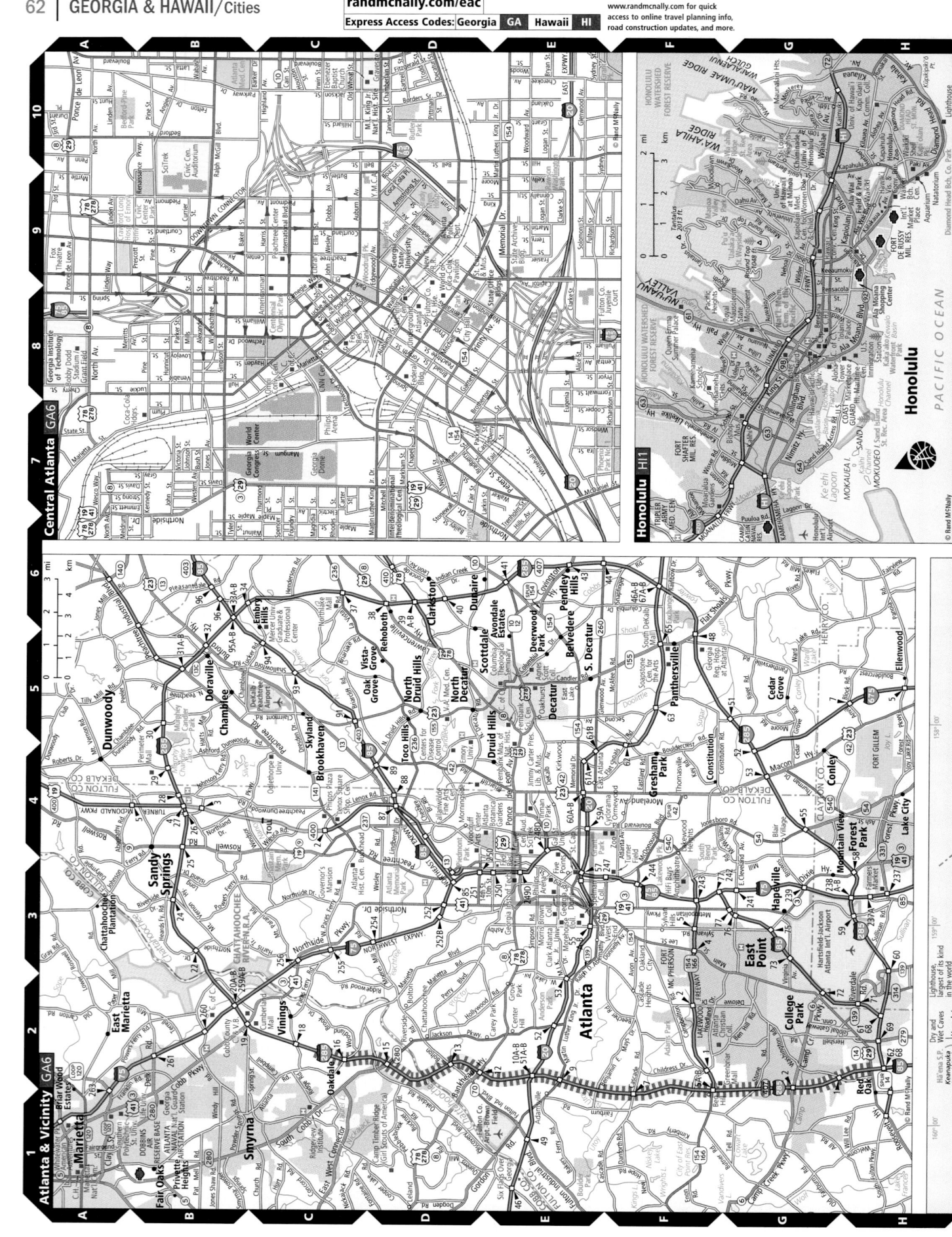

Central Atlanta **GA6**

Honolulu **HI1**

Atlanta & Vicinity **GA6**

Distance scale
One inch represents about 41 miles

How to determine distance

Mileages in red between red arrowheads;
in black, between intersections.

SYMBOLS

- Featured ride
- Long-term construction
- Harley-Davidson dealership
- Scenic route
- Historic site or monument; Indian reservation or rancheria; military installation; point of interest; wildlife refuge

HAWAII MOTORCYCLE LAWS

Helmet use:
Required under age 18, and reflectorization required

Riding two abreast:
Yes. See state law for specifics

Eye protection:
Required unless equipped with windscreen

Speed limit:
Primary roads: 60 mph
Secondary roads: 50 mph

HAWAII RESOURCES

Road conditions or construction:
(808) 536-6566
www.hawaii.gov/dot

Highway Emergency Numbers:
911

Tourism:
(800) 464-2924
www.gohawaii.com

State motor vehicle information:
(808) 587-2220
www.state.hi.us/dot/highways/hwy-v/mvso.htm

HARLEY-DAVIDSON DEALERSHIPS

Hilo Harley-Davidson, M-10
200 Kanoe Lehua Ave. **Hilo**
(808) 934-9090
Lat N 19.720 **Lon** W 155.065

Cycle City Ltd., N-4
600 Puuloa Rd. **Honolulu**
(808) 831-2600
Lat N 21.336 **Lon** W 157.901

Pacific Harley-Davidson Motorclothes & Collectibles, N-4
2333 Kalakaua Ave. **Honolulu**
(808) 971-3500
Lat N 21.278 **Lon** W 157.827

Pacific Harley-Davidson Motorclothes & Collectibles, N-4
2005 Kalia Rd. **Honolulu**
(808) 973-4630
Lat N 21.285 **Lon** W 157.836

Pacific Harley-Davidson Motorclothes & Collectibles, N-4
1450 Ala Moana Blvd. #303 **Honolulu**
(808) 973-2300
Lat N 21.289 **Lon** W 157.843

Maui Harley-Davidson, I-8
150 Dairy Rd. **Kahului**
(808) 877-RIDE
Lat N 20.879 **Lon** W 156.458

Kona Harley-Davidson, M-8
74-5615 E Luhia St. **Kailua Kona**
(808) 326-9887
Lat N 19.685 **Lon** W 155.978

Domenicos Motorcycles, M-5
46-162 Kahuhipa St. **Kāne'ohe**
(808) 235-8711
Lat N 21.41676 **Lon** W 157.805

Two Wheels, I-2
4555 Pouli Rd. **Kapaa**
(808) 822-7283
Lat N 22.061 **Lon** W 159.323

South Seas Cycle Exchange, M-3
94-896 Moloalo St. **Waipahu**
(808) 671-6711
Lat N 21.385 **Lon** W 158.002

© Rand McNally

Distance scale
One inch represents about 41 miles

0   10   20   30 mi
0 10 20 30 40 km

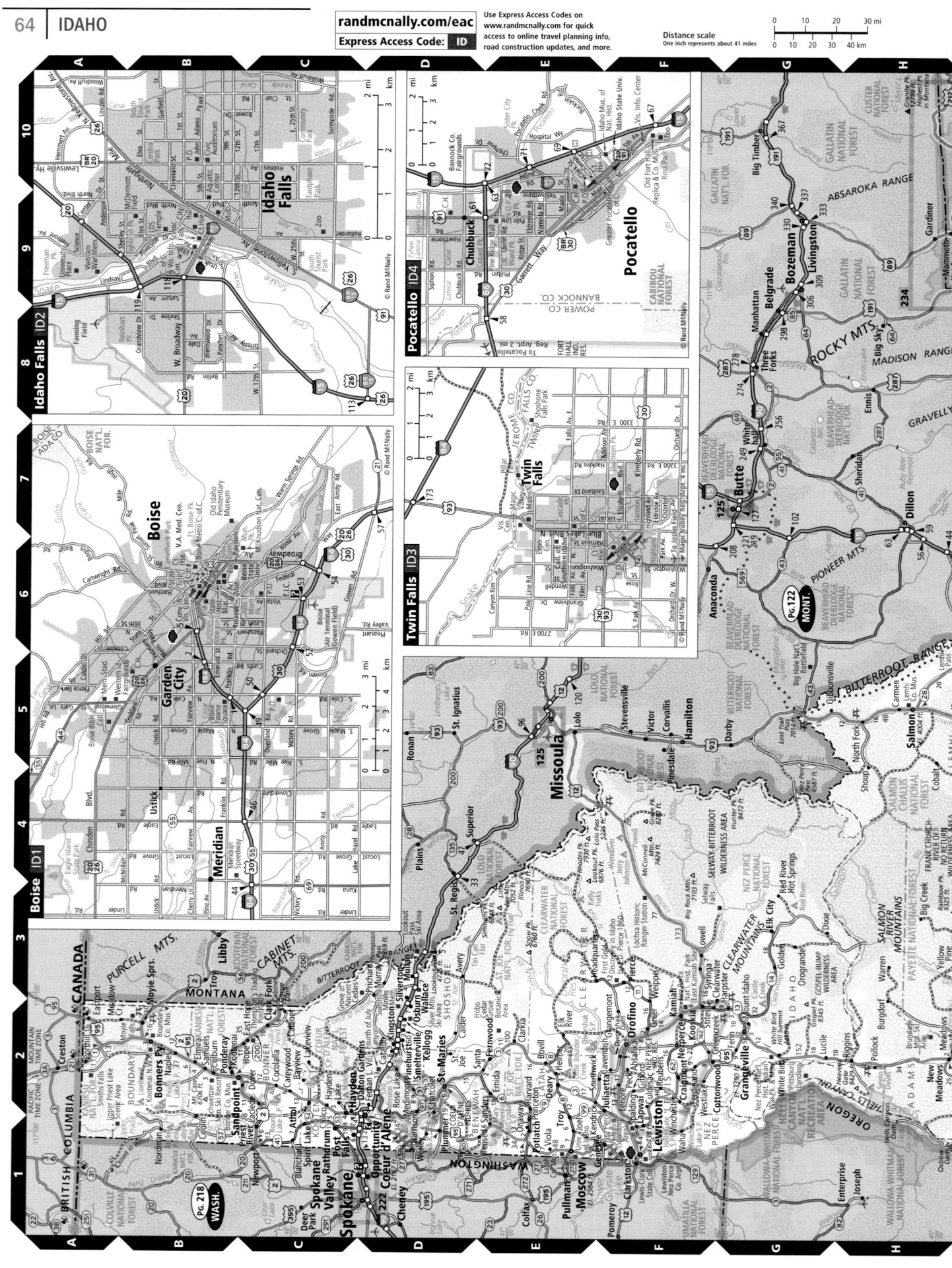

© Rand McNally

How to determine distance

Mileages in red between red arrowheads;
in black, between intersections.

SYMBOLS

≡≡≡	Featured ride	═══	Scenic route
┼┼┼┼	Long-term construction	■	Historic site or monument; Indian reservation or rancheria; military installation; point of interest; wildlife refuge
🏍	Harley-Davidson dealership		

For Idaho/Montana ride, see page R9.

IDAHO MOTORCYCLE LAWS

Helmet use:
Required under age 18

Riding two abreast:
No reference in administrative code or statutes

Eye protection:
Not required

Speed limit:
Primary roads: 75 mph
Secondary roads: 75 mph

IDAHO RESOURCES

Road conditions or construction:
(888) 432-7623
www.state.id.us/itd/

Highway Emergency Numbers:
911 or *ISP or (800) 233-1212

Tourism:
(800) 847-4843
www.visitid.org

State motor vehicle information:
(208) 334-8000
www.itd.idaho.gov/dmv

CITY-TO-CITY MILEAGE

	BOISE	COEUR D'ALENE	LEWISTON	MISSOULA, MT	MOUNTAIN HOME	POCATELLO	SALMON	TWIN FALLS
Boise		454	276	371	45	237	255	130
Coeur d'Alene	454		119	168	494	528	308	579
Lewiston	276	119		218	325	517	337	410
Missoula, MT	371	168	218		420	360	143	471
Mountain Home	45	494	325	420		193	294	86
Pocatello	237	528	517	360	193		212	115
Salmon	255	308	337	143	294	212		247
Twin Falls	130	579	410	471	86	115	247	

HARLEY-DAVIDSON DEALERSHIPS

🏍 **High Desert Harley-Davidson, K-2**
3602 Chinden Blvd. **Boise**
(208) 338-5599
Lat N 43.625 **Lon** W 116.242

🏍 **Birds of Prey Harley-Davidson Shop, K-1**
721 Hannibal **Caldwell**
(208) 455-8049
Lat N 43.673 **Lon** W 116.680

🏍 **Grand Teton Harley-Davidson, K-7**
848 Houston Ave. **Idaho Falls**
(208) 523-1464
Lat N 43.497 **Lon** W 112.071

🏍 **Shumate Harley-Davidson Shop, F-1**
2408 North & South Hwy. **Lewiston**
(208) 746-7735
Lat N 46.428 **Lon** W 116.998

🏍 **Eagle Rock Harley-Davidson Shop, L-7**
1444 Yellowstone Ave. **Pocatello**
(208) 237-7433
Lat N 42.901 **Lon** W 112.451

🏍 **Snake Harley-Davidson, M-4**
2404 Addison Ave. E **Twin Falls**
(208) 734-8400
Lat N 42.563 **Lon** W 114.436

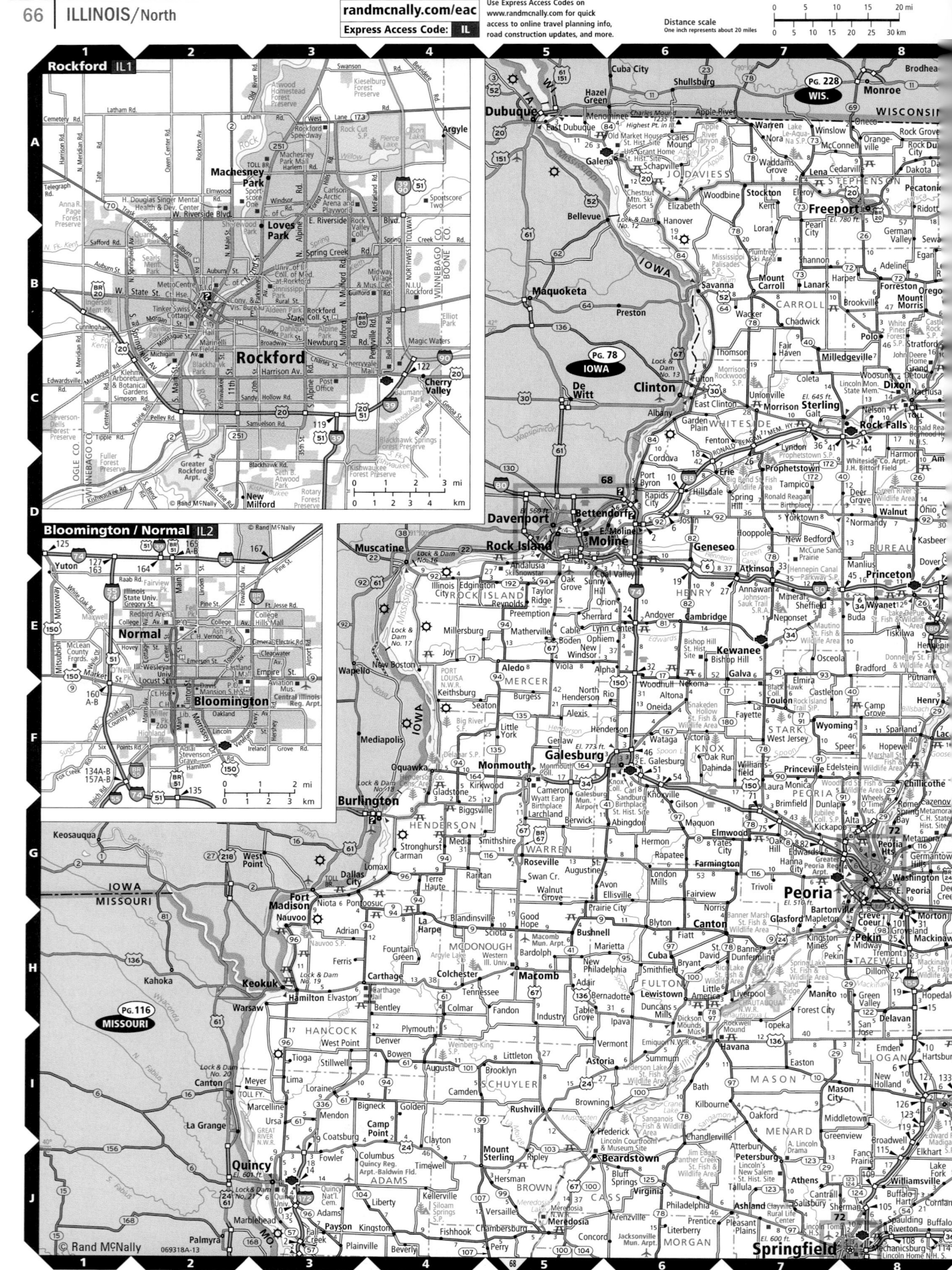

How to determine distance

Mileages in red between red arrowheads;
in black, between intersections.

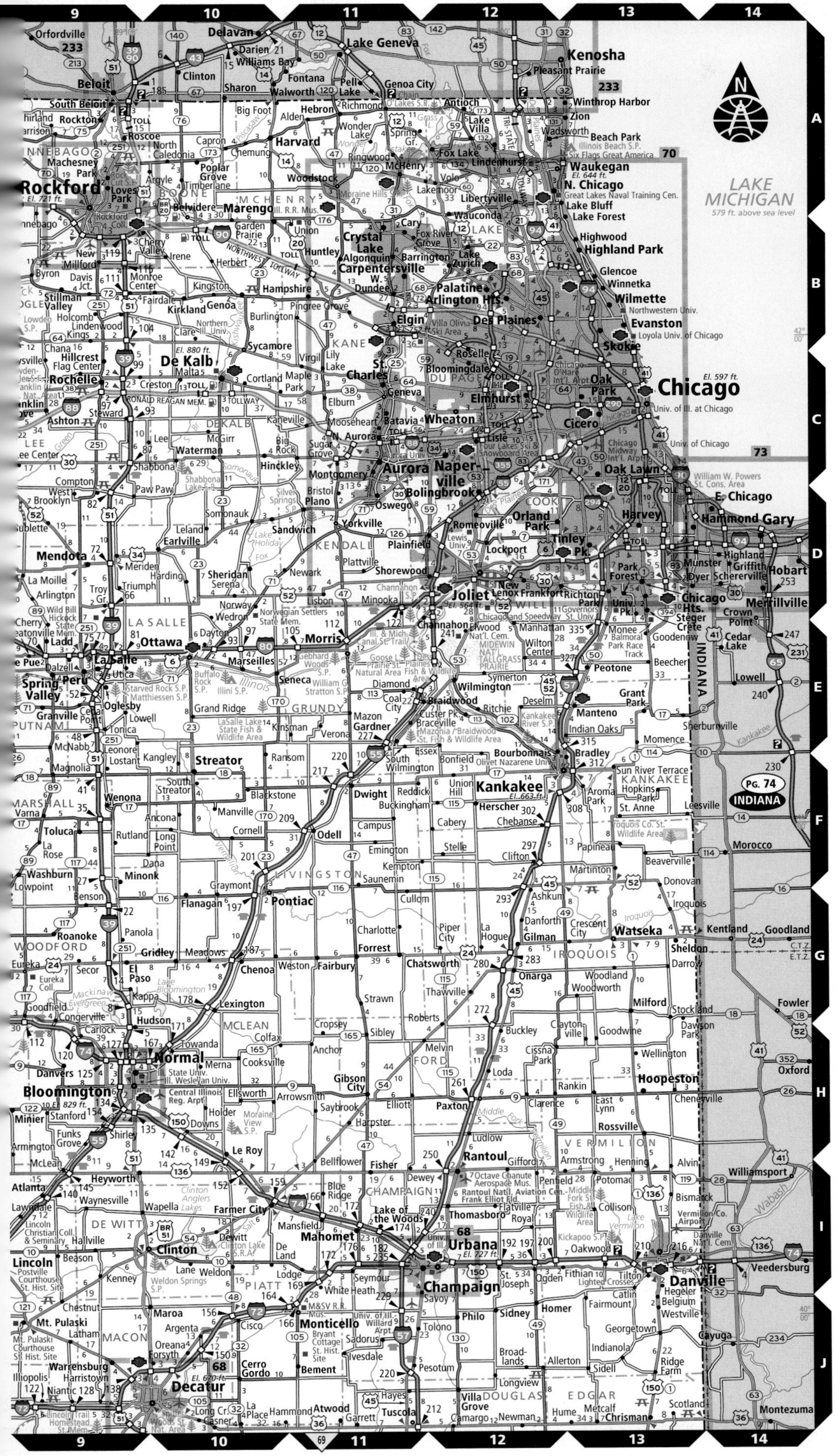

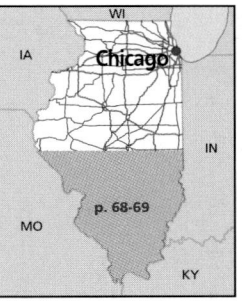

SYMBOLS

— Featured ride
▦ Long-term construction
⬗ Harley-Davidson dealership
┅ Scenic route
■ Historic site or monument; Indian reservation or rancheria; military installation; point of interest; wildlife refuge

HARLEY-DAVIDSON DEALERSHIPS

For Chicagoland, please see dealer listings on page 71; for Peoria and Springfield, see page 73.

Chuck's Harley-Davidson, H-9
2027 Ireland Grove Rd. **Bloomington**
(309) 662-1648
Lat N 40.459 Lon W 88.968

Harley-Davidson of Crete, D-13
3445 Eagle Nest Dr. **Crete**
(708) 672-6601
Lat N 41.467 Lon W 87.578

Gutterridge Harley-Davidson, I-13
1606 Georgetown Rd. **Danville**
(217) 446-4555
Lat N 40.097 Lon W 87.636

Pierce Harley-Davidson Sales, C-10
969 Peace Rd. **DeKalb**
(815) 756-4558
Lat N 41.944 Lon W 88.716

Coziahr Harley-Davidson, J-9
150 W Marion Ave. **Forsyth**
(217) 877-7115
Lat N 39.922 Lon W 88.959

Harley-Davidson Shop of Galena, A-5
939 Galena Square Dr. **Galena**
(815) 777-9800
Lat N 42.424 Lon W 90.443

Nees Harley-Davidson, F-6
2365 Grand Ave. **Galesburg**
(309) 342-3910
Lat N 40.934 Lon W 90.334

Reiman's Harley-Davidson, E-7
623 N Main St. **Kewanee**
(309) 854-6661
Lat N 41.249 Lon W 89.925

Shreffler's Land of Lincoln Harley-Davidson, E-13
291 N Cypress St. **Manteno**
(815) 468-8673
Lat N 41.253 Lon W 87.849

Starved Rock Harley-Davidson, E-10
750 Centennial Dr. **Ottawa**
(815) 431-1900
Lat N 41.375 Lon W 88.825

Dant's Harley-Davidson, E-8
230 Backbone Rd. E **Princeton**
(815) 875-8350
Lat N 41.393 Lon W 89.464

TNT Harley-Davidson, J-3
5101 Oak St. (off I-72) **Quincy**
(217) 224-1004
Lat N 39.937 Lon W 91.336

Workman Harley-Davidson, C-8
1903 Harley-Davidson Dr. (Rte. 40) **Rock Falls**
(815) 626-1213
Lat N 41.763 Lon W 89.689

Kegel Harley-Davidson, A-9
7125 Harrison Ave. **Rockford**
(815) 332-7125
Lat N 42.241 Lon W 88.977

Andrae's Harley-Davidson, I-12
2010 N Lincoln Ave. **Urbana**
(217) 328-2092
Lat N 40.132 Lon W 88.22

randmcnally.com/eac

Express Access Code: IL

Use Express Access Codes on
www.randmcnally.com for quick
access to online travel planning info,
road construction updates, and more.

Distance scale
One inch represents about 20 miles

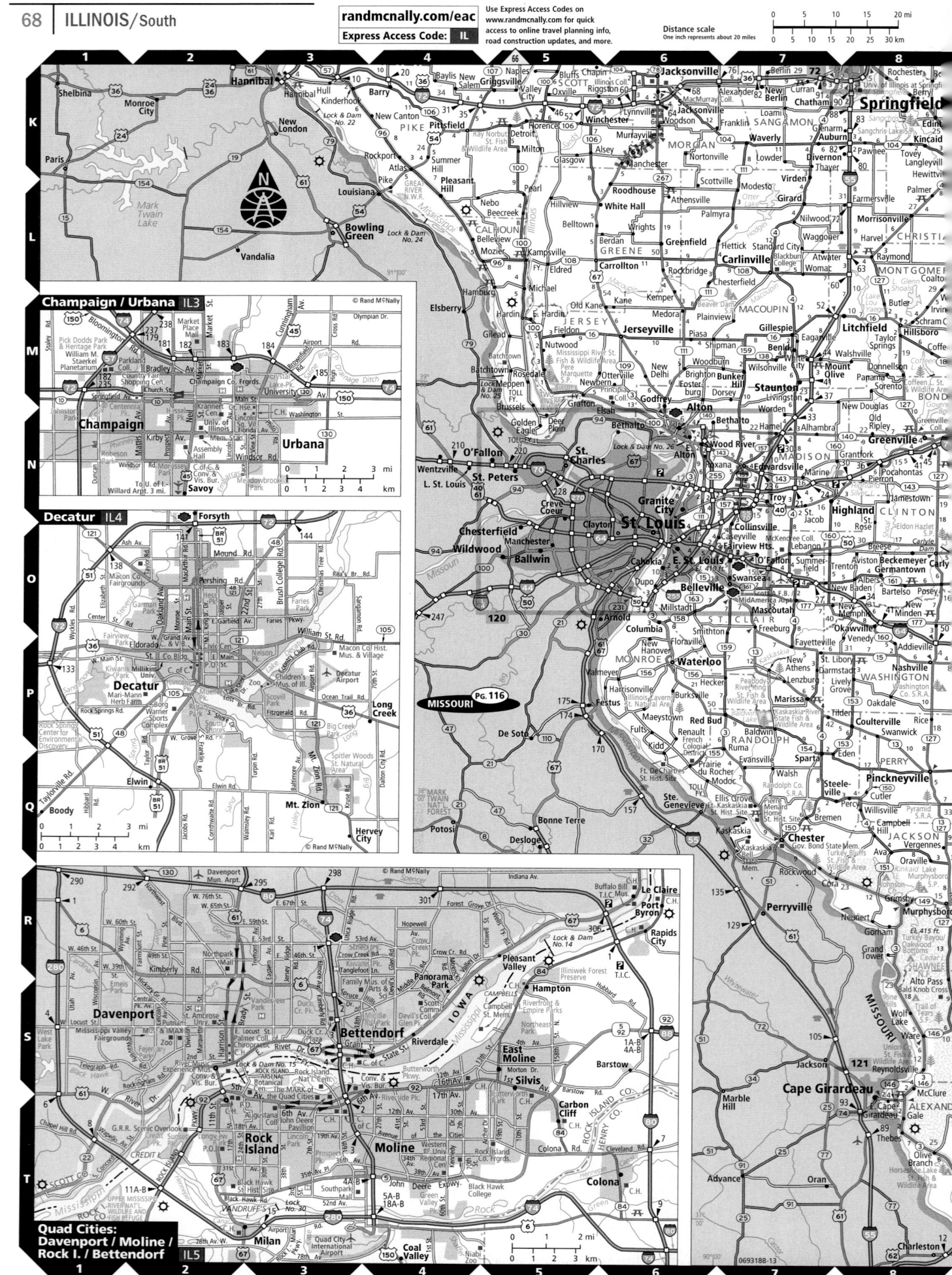

Champaign / Urbana IL3

Decatur IL4

MISSOURI PG. 116

**Quad Cities:
Davenport / Moline /
Rock I. / Bettendorf** IL5

How to determine distance

Mileages in red between red arrowheads; in black, between intersections.

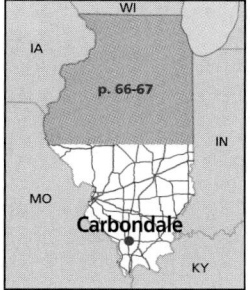

Carbondale

SYMBOLS

- Featured ride
- Long-term construction
- Harley-Davidson dealership
- Scenic route
- Historic site or monument; Indian reservation or rancheria; military installation; point of interest; wildlife refuge

CITY-TO-CITY MILEAGE

	CARBONDALE	CHAMPAIGN	CHICAGO	MOLINE	PEORIA	ROCKFORD	ST. LOUIS, MO	SPRINGFIELD
Bloomington	249	51	136	132	40	136	164	64
Cairo	59	244	375	410	318	426	169	248
Carbondale		202	333	340	248	384	108	178
Champaign	202		135	182	90	186	182	85
Chicago	333	135		165	170	84	300	200
Decatur	185	47	178	169	77	179	118	38
De Kalb	370	172	66	103	129	44	282	182
Dubuque, IA	415	257	175	74	167	91	337	237
Effingham	124	78	209	256	164	260	104	89
Elgin	369	171	38	152	153	48	307	207
Galesburg	297	139	198	48	49	150	219	119
Kankakee	274	76	56	153	121	138	254	157
Lawrenceville	149	127	250	305	213	309	147	154
Moline	340	182	165		92	117	262	162
Mt. Vernon	58	148	279	314	222	330	82	152
Peoria	248	90	170	92		143	170	70
Quincy	231	195	310	147	130	267	133	110
Rockford	384	186	84	117	143		296	196
St. Louis, MO	108	182	300	162	70	196		100
Springfield	178	85	200	162	70	196	100	
Waukegan	377	179	40	189	198	71	328	228

HARLEY-DAVIDSON DEALERSHIPS

Ted's Harley-Davidson of Alton, N-6
4103 Humbert Rd. **Alton**
(618) 462-3030
Lat N 38.936 Lon W 90.156

Frieze Harley-Davidson Sales, O-7
517 S Illinois St. **Belleville**
(618) 277-8864
Lat N 38.509 Lon W 89.984

Legacy Harley-Davidson, M-11
1315 Althoff Ave. **Effingham**
(217) 342-3494
Lat N 39.118 Lon W 88.568

Campbell's Harley-Davidson, R-10
2400 Williamson County Pkwy. **Marion**
(618) 997-4577
Lat N 37.743 Lon W 88.97

Dale's Harley-Davidson, P-10
205 N 44th St. **Mt. Vernon**
(618) 244-4116
Lat N 38.313 Lon W 88.949

Frieze Harley-Davidson of O'Fallon, O-7
1607 W Hwy. 50 **O'Fallon**
(618) 622-0045
Lat N 38.593 Lon W 89.955

© Rand McNally

How to determine distance

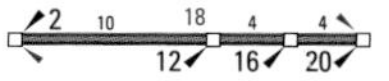

Mileages in red between red arrowheads; in black, between intersections.

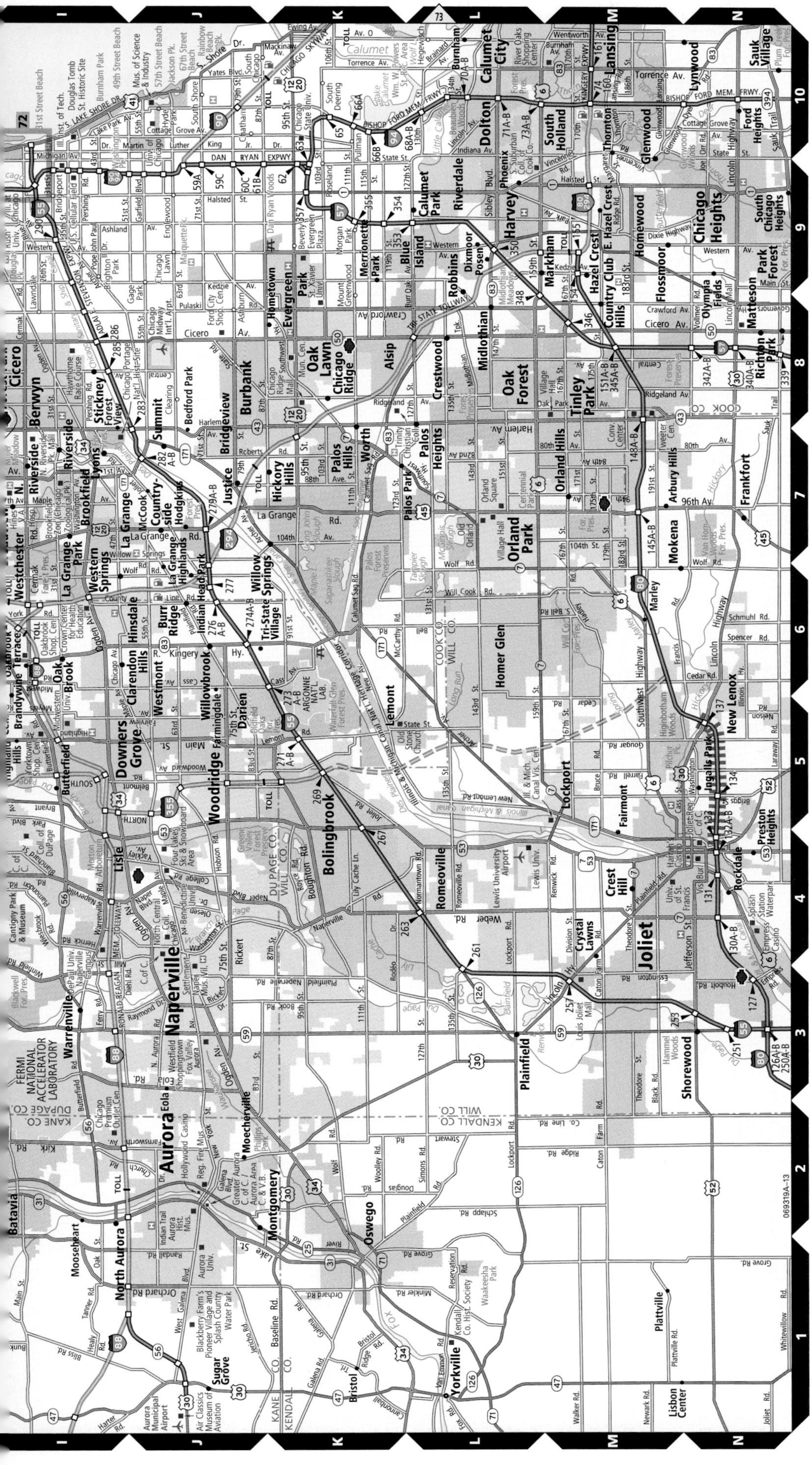

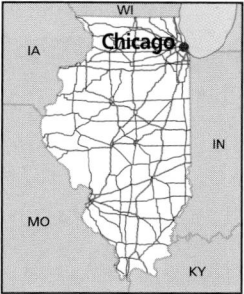

SYMBOLS

Featured ride		Scenic route	
Long-term construction		Harley-Davidson dealership	

HARLEY-DAVIDSON DEALERSHIPS

Illinois Harley-Davidson, I-8
1301 S Harlem Ave. **Berwyn**
(708) 788-1300
Lat N 41.863 Lon W 87.804

Chicago Harley-Davidson, F-9
6868 N Western Ave. **Chicago**
(773) 338-6868
Lat N 42.006 Lon W 87.69

Chicago Harley-Davidson Downtown, H-10
66 E Ohio St. **Chicago**
(312) 274-9666
Lat N 41.893 Lon W 87.626

Zylstra Harley-Davidson, F-2
920 S McLean Blvd. **Elgin**
(847) 742-4455
Lat N 42.035 Lon W 88.328

Chicago Harley-Davidson Shop of Glenview, E-7
2929 Patriot Blvd. **Glenview**
(847) 679-2929
Lat N 42.107 Lon W 87.822

Conrad's Harley-Davidson, N-3
1541 Riverboat Center Dr. **Joliet**
(815) 725-2000
Lat N 41.495 Lon W 88.166

Lake Shore Harley-Davidson, B-6
14000 Rockland Rd. (Rte. 176) **Libertyville**
(847) 662-4500
Lat N 42.28 Lon W 87.905

Heritage Harley-Davidson, J-4
2595 Ogden Ave. **Lisle**
(630) 420-1942
Lat N 41.797 Lon W 88.104

McHenry Harley-Davidson Shop, A-3
2103 Rte. 120 **McHenry**
(815) 344-9300
Lat N 42.331 Lon W 88.218

Oak Lawn Harley-Davidson, K-8
11040 S Cicero Ave. **Oak Lawn**
(708) 423-9005
Lat N 41.692 Lon W 87.74

Suburban Harley-Davidson, D-5
2200 N Rand Rd. **Palatine**
(847) 358-2112
Lat N 42.15 Lon W 88.034

Chi-Town Harley-Davidson, M-7
17801 S La Grange Rd. **Tinley Park**
(708) 623-6000
Lat N 41.565 Lon W 87.852

Wild Fire Harley-Davidson, H-6
120 W North Ave. **Villa Park**
(800) 400-RIDE
Lat N 41.905 Lon W 87.981

Woodstock Harley-Davidson, B-1
2050 S Eastwood Dr. **Woodstock**
(815) 337-3511
Lat N 42.293 Lon W 88.433

randmcnally.com/eac

Express Access Codes: Illinois **IL** Indiana **IN**

Use Express Access Codes on www.randmcnally.com for quick access to online travel planning info, road construction updates, and more.

How to determine distance

Mileages in red between red arrowheads; in black, between intersections.

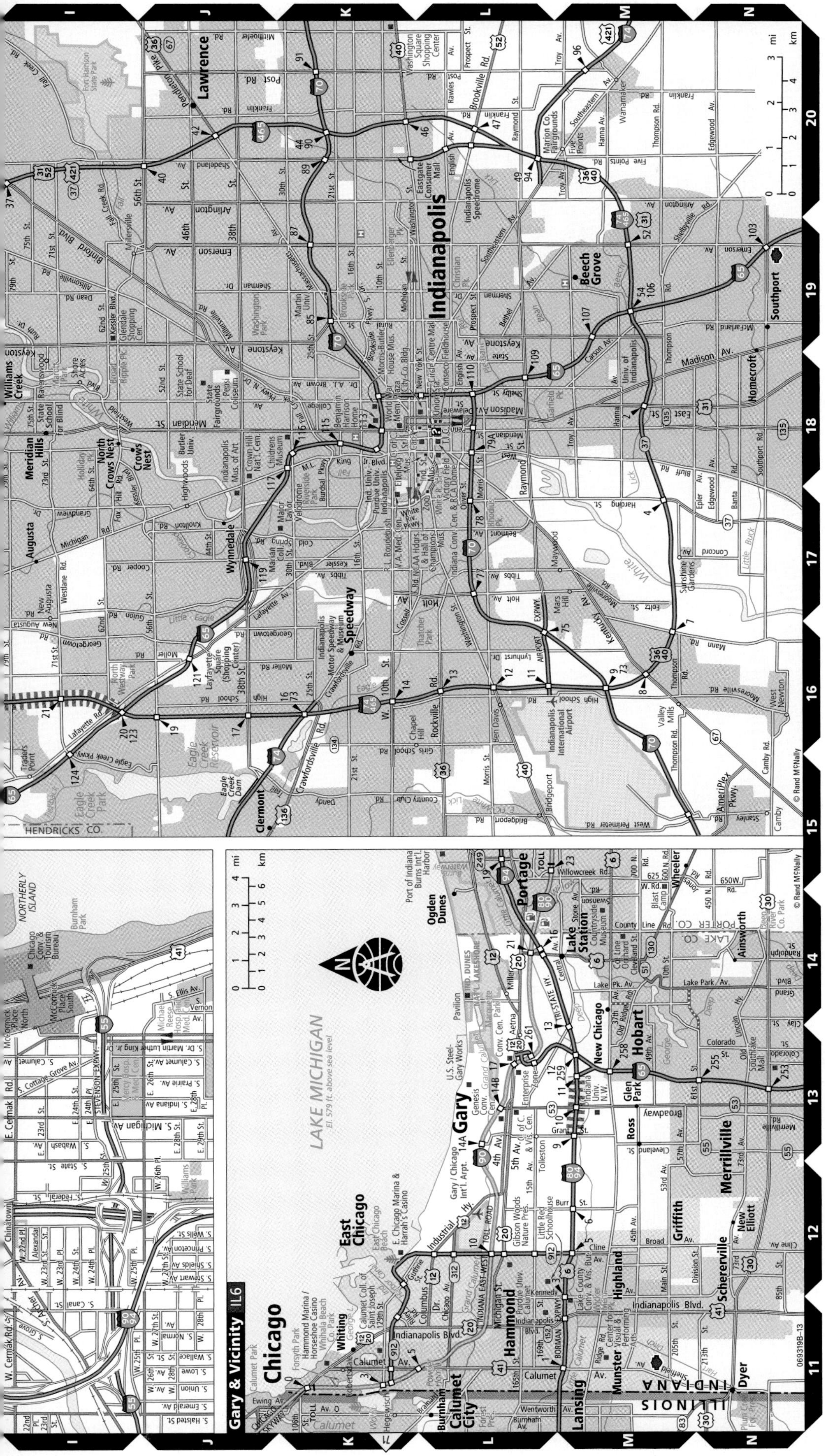

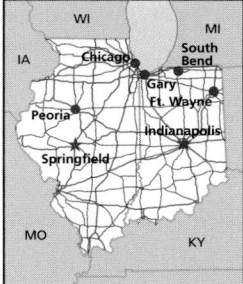

SYMBOLS

- Featured ride
- Long-term construction
- Harley-Davidson dealership
- Scenic route
- Historic site or monument; Indian reservation or rancheria; military installation; point of interest; wildlife refuge

ILLINOIS MOTORCYCLE LAWS

Helmet use: Not Required

Riding two abreast:
No reference in administrative code or statutes

Eye protection:
Required unless equipped with windscreen

Speed limit:
Primary roads: 65 mph; Secondary roads: 55 mph

ILLINOIS RESOURCES

Road conditions or construction:
(800) 452-4368; (312) 368-4636
www.dot.state.il.us
www.illinoisroads.info

Highway Emergency Numbers: 911 or *999

Tourism:
(800) 226-6632; www.enjoyillinois.com

State motor vehicle information:
(217) 782-6212; (312) 814-2975 (Chicago Metro)
www.sos.state.il.us/departments/drivers

INDIANA MOTORCYCLE LAWS

Helmet use:
Required under age 18 and for instructional permit holders

Riding two abreast:
Yes. See state law for specifics

Eye protection: Required under age 18

Speed limit:
Primary roads: 65 mph; Secondary roads: 55 mph

INDIANA RESOURCES

Road conditions or construction:
(800) 261-7623
www.in.gov/dot

Highway Emergency Numbers: 911

Tourism:
(888) 365-6946
www.enjoyindiana.com

State motor vehicle information:
(317) 233-6000
www.in.gov/bmv

HARLEY-DAVIDSON DEALERSHIPS

Walters Bros. Harley-Davidson, G-8
615 S Maxwell Rd. **Peoria**
(309) 697-1917
Lat N 40.688 Lon W 89.693

Hall's Harley-Davidson, J-8
2301 N Dirksen Pkwy. **Springfield**
(217) 528-8356
Lat N 39.833 Lon W 89.605

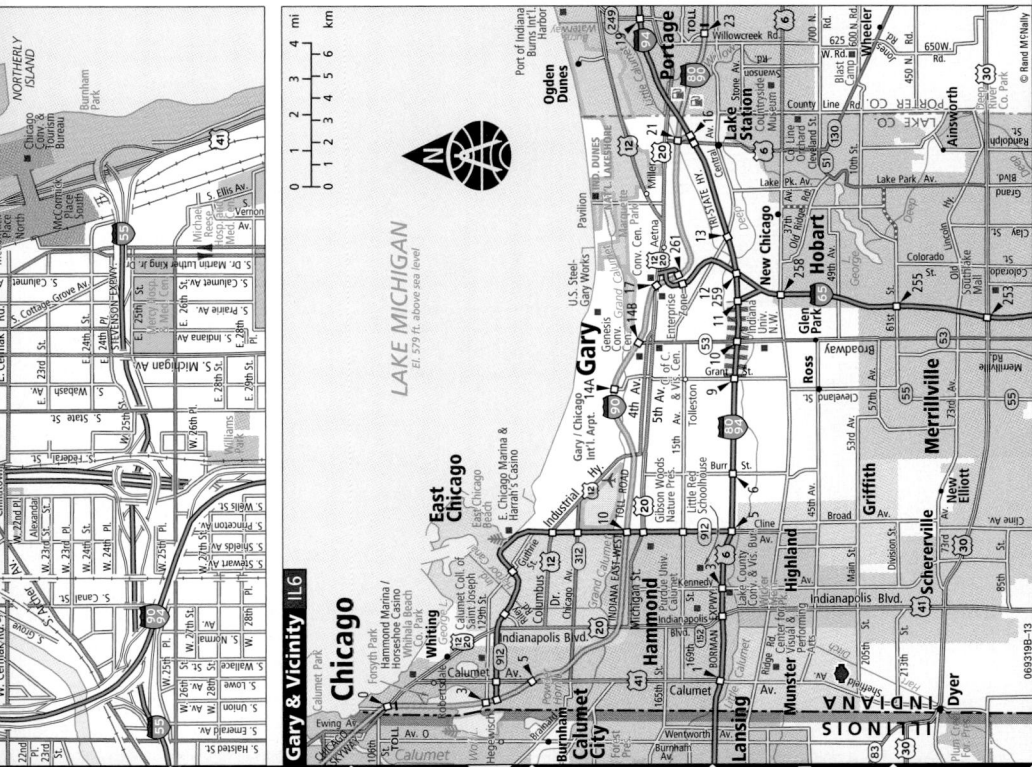

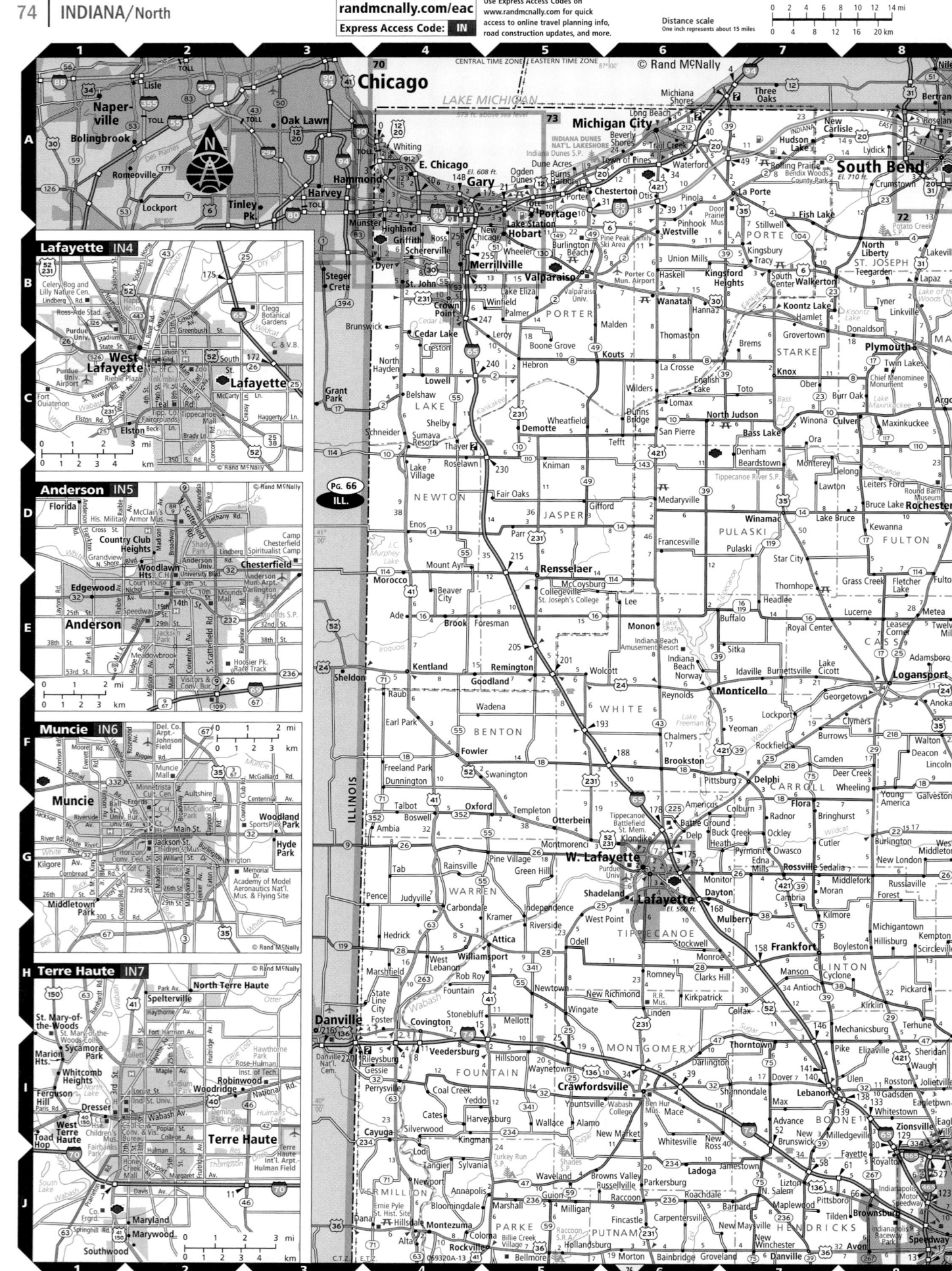

randmcnally.com/eac

Express Access Code: IN

Use Express Access Codes on www.randmcnally.com for quick access to online travel planning info, road construction updates, and more.

Distance scale
One inch represents about 15 miles

© Rand McNally

How to determine distance

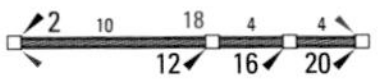

Mileages in red between red arrowheads; in black, between intersections.

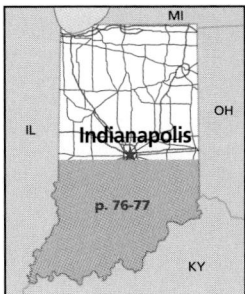

MI
IL
Indianapolis
OH
p. 76-77
KY

SYMBOLS

▬▬▬ Featured ride ▬▬▬ Scenic route

╫╫╫ Long-term construction ⬡ Harley-Davidson dealership

HARLEY-DAVIDSON DEALERSHIPS

Gerencer's Harley-Davidson, A-9
720 W Bristol St. **Elkhart**
(574) 262-2735
Lat N 41.703 **Lon** W 85.986

Jim Bailey's Harley-Davidson, D-12
6315 Illinois Rd. **Fort Wayne**
(260) 489-2464
Lat N 41.075 **Lon** W 85.222

River City Harley-Davidson, D-13
5525 Hwy. 930 E **Fort Wayne**
(260) 493-9900
Lat N 41.07 **Lon** W 85.106

Harley-Davidson of Indianapolis, J-9
4146 E 96th St. **Indianapolis**
(317) 815-1800
Lat N 39.927 **Lon** W 86.1

Harley-Davidson of Kokomo, G-9
335 S County Rd. OOE/W **Kokomo**
(765) 864-9999
Lat N 40.449 **Lon** W 86.129

Eagle Harley-Davidson, G-6
702 Navco Dr. **Lafayette**
(765) 448-9132
Lat N 40.41 **Lon** W 86.853

Stone's Harley-Davidson, G-11
6333 E Steltzer Dr. **Marion**
(765) 664-1331
Lat N 40.53 **Lon** W 85.655

The Harley-Davidson Shop of Michigan City, A-6
2968 N US Hwy. 421 **Michigan City**
(219) 878-8885
Lat N 41.615 **Lon** W 86.894

Benson Motorcyles, H-12
6410 W McGalliard (Rte. 332) **Muncie**
(765) 288-1817
Lat N 40.219 **Lon** W 85.461

Calumet Harley-Davidson, B-4
10350 Calumet Ave. **Munster**
(219) 934-6366
Lat N 41.526 **Lon** W 87.509

Harley-Davidson Center, J-13
2240 Chester Blvd. **Richmond**
(765) 962-0596
Lat N 39.864 **Lon** W 84.889

McDaniel's Harley-Davidson, A-8
1910 Lincoln Way E **South Bend**
(574) 289-6650
Lat N 41.658 **Lon** W 86.218

Harley-Davidson of Valparaiso, B-5
1151 US 30 **Valparaiso**
(219) 462-2223
Lat N 41.481 **Lon** W 87.111

Brandt's Harley-Davidson, E-10
1400 N Cass St. **Wabash**
(260) 563-6443
Lat N 40.815 **Lon** W 85.838

Kersting's Harley-Davidson Sales, C-6
8774 W 700 N **Winamac**
(574) 896-2974
Lat N 41.157 **Lon** W 86.772

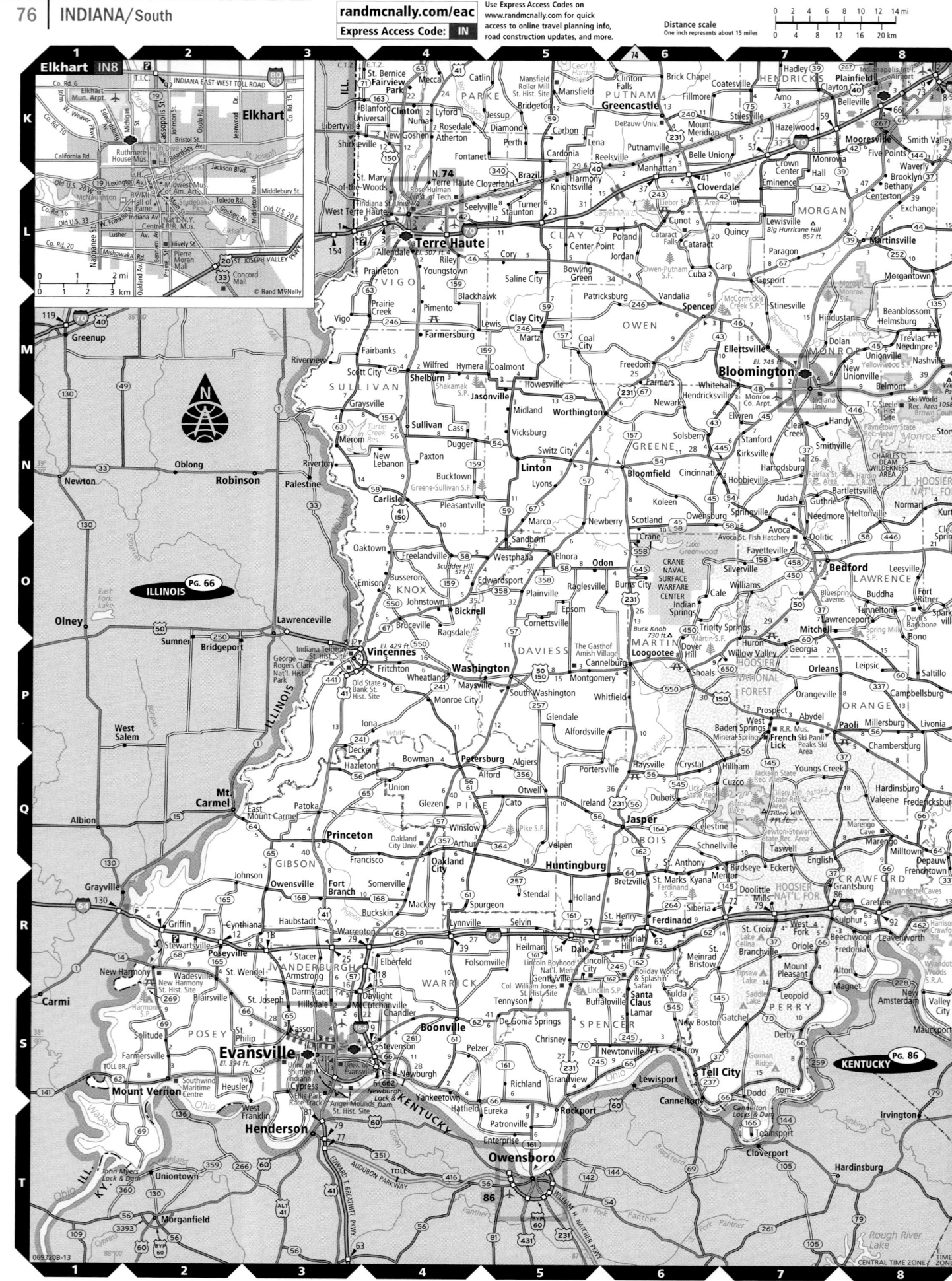

randmcnally.com/eac
Express Access Code: IN

Use Express Access Codes on
www.randmcnally.com for quick
access to online travel planning info,
road construction updates, and more.

How to determine distance

Mileages in red between red arrowheads; in black, between intersections.

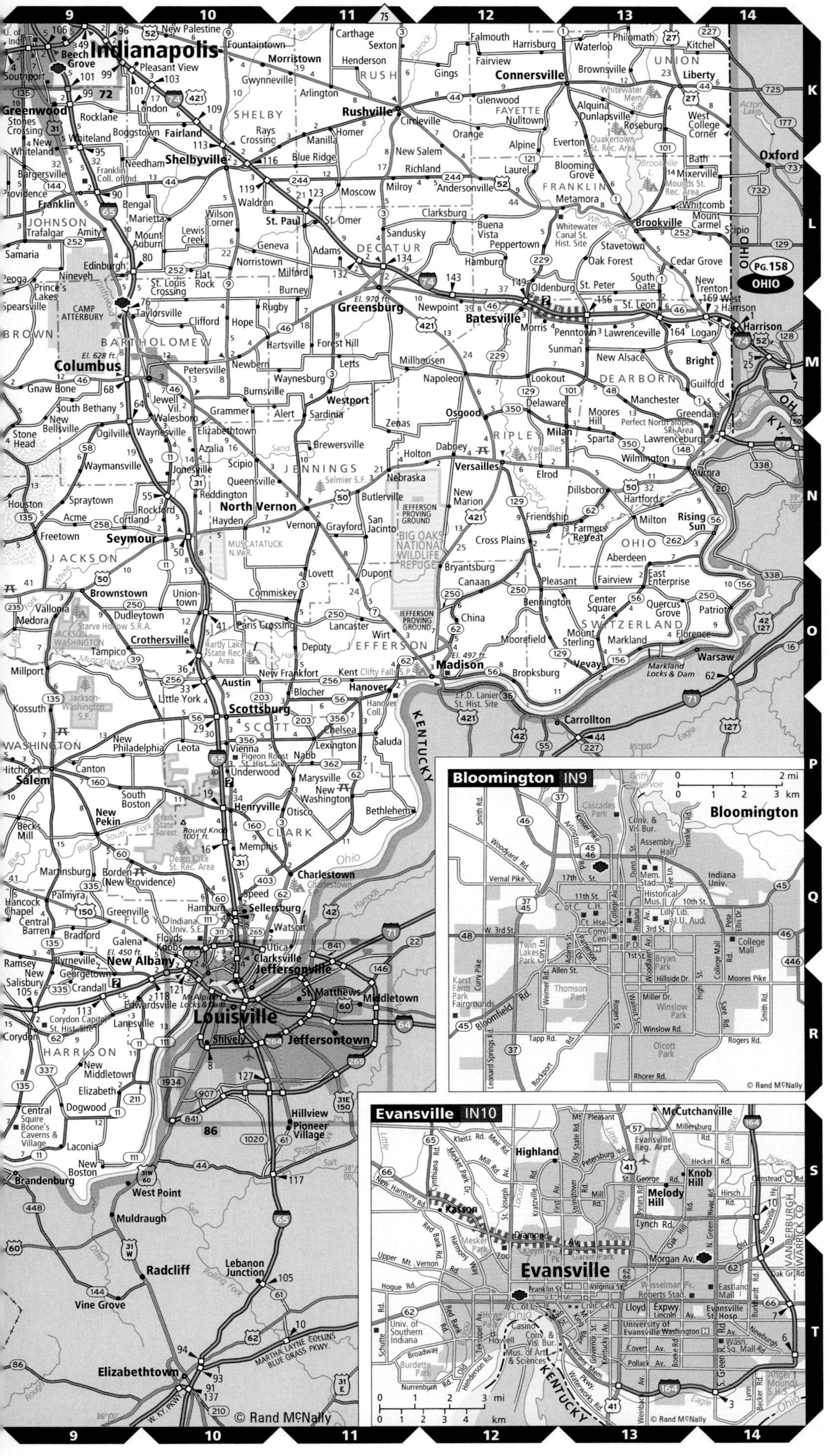

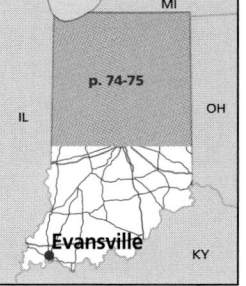

SYMBOLS

- Featured ride
- Long-term construction
- Harley-Davidson dealership
- Scenic route
- Historic site or monument; Indian reservation or rancheria; military installation; point of interest; wildlife refuge

CITY-TO-CITY MILEAGE

	Evansville	Fort Wayne	Gary	Indianapolis	New Albany	Richmond	South Bend	Terre Haute
Anderson	234	89	182	48	157	59	142	126
Angola	353	42	135	167	276	140	76	245
Bloomington	134	180	199	50	89	120	198	57
Chicago, IL	294	164	28	179	298	250	87	182
Columbus	179	175	202	48	71	195	192	121
Crawfordsville	178	168	150	56	166	129	133	57
Danville, IL	169	208	130	96	206	169	173	57
Evansville		319	278	186	111	259	326	112
Fort Wayne	319		135	133	242	95	92	211
Gary	278	135		150	269	221	58	166
Greensburg	198	152	202	50	90	67	186	123
Indianapolis	186	133	150		115	73	140	78
Kokomo	239	90	136	53	172	104	91	131
Lafayette	203	120	92	62	181	133	107	92
Michigan City	298	138	26	170	289	241	34	186
Muncie	248	85	196	62	171	43	141	140
New Albany	111	242	269	115		182	259	188
Richmond	259	95	221	73	182		191	151
South Bend	326	92	58	140	259	191		218
Terre Haute	112	211	166	78	188	151	218	
Vincennes	54	265	224	132	137	205	272	58

HARLEY-DAVIDSON DEALERSHIPS

- **Harley-Davidson of Bloomington, M-7**
  522 W Gourley Pike **Bloomington**
  (800) 667-7939
  Lat N 39.185 Lon W 86.538

- **Mann's Harley-Davidson, M-9**
  3250 W Market Place Dr. **Edinburgh**
  (812) 526-3485
  Lat N 39.312 Lon W 85.965

- **Bud's Harley-Davidson Sales, S-3**
  4700 E Morgan Ave. **Evansville**
  (812) 473-2837
  Lat N 37.991 Lon W 87.496

- **Bud's Harley-Davidson Shop, S-3**
  2124 W Franklin St. **Evansville**
  (812) 425-7687
  Lat N 37.981 Lon W 87.596

- **Indianapolis Southside Harley-Davidson, K-9**
  4930 Southport Crossing Pl. **Indianapolis**
  (317) 885-5180
  Lat N 39.665 Lon W 86.084

- **Indy West Harley-Davidson, K-8**
  6201 Cambridge Way **Plainfield**
  (317) 279-0062
  Lat N 39.673 Lon W 86.369

- **Wabash Valley Harley-Davidson, L-4**
  3912 S US Hwy. 41 **Terre Haute**
  (812) 232-7821
  Lat N 39.419 Lon W 87.416

Bloomington IN9

Evansville IN10

© Rand McNally

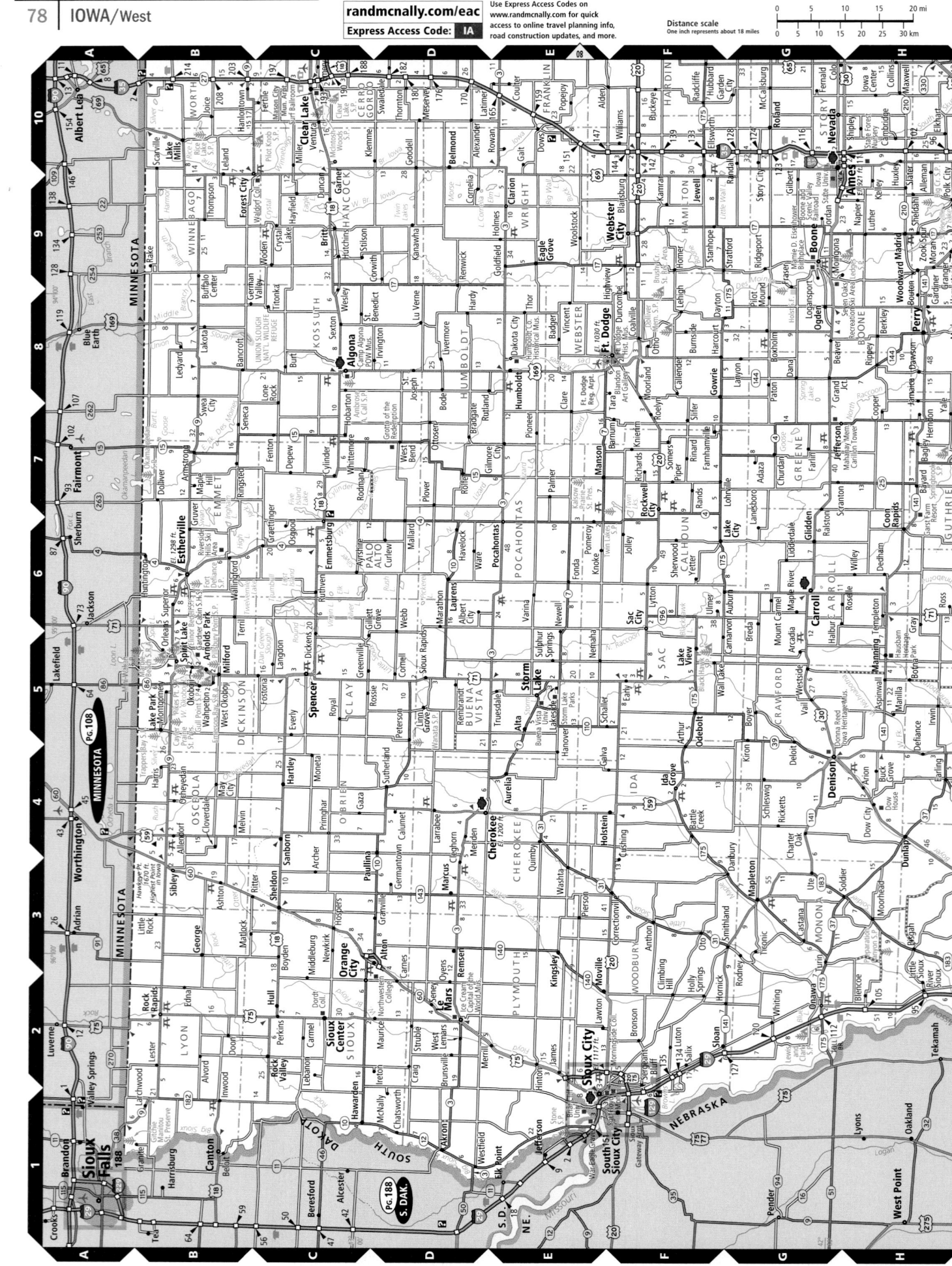

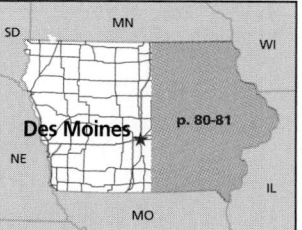

Des Moines — p. 80-81

SYMBOLS

- Featured ride
- Long-term construction
- Harley-Davidson dealership
- Scenic route
- Historic site or monument; Indian reservation or rancheria; military installation; point of interest; wildlife refuge

IOWA MOTORCYCLE LAWS

Helmet use: Not Required

Riding two abreast:
Yes. See state law for specifics

Eye protection: Not required

Speed limit:
Primary roads: 65 mph
Secondary roads: 55 mph

IOWA RESOURCES

Road conditions or construction:
511
(800) 288-1047
www.511ia.org

Highway Emergency Numbers: 911

Tourism:
(800) 345-4692 (to request travel materials only)
(888) 472-6035
(515) 242-4705
www.traveliowa.com

State motor vehicle information:
(800) 532-1121
www.dot.state.ia.us/mvd/ods

HARLEY-DAVIDSON DEALERSHIPS

Ernie's Harley-Davidson, C-8
2613 Hwy. 18 E **Algona**
(515) 295-7951
Lat N 43.083 Lon W 94.202

Zylstra Harley-Davidson, G-10
1930 E 13th St. **Ames**
(515) 232-6223
Lat N 42.035 Lon W 93.587

Harley-Davidson of Carroll, G-6
1327 Plaza Dr. (Hwy. 30 E) **Carroll**
(712) 792-1610
Lat N 42.064 Lon W 94.848

Zylstra Harley-Davidson, D-4
1450 N 2nd St. **Cherokee**
(712) 225-6104
Lat N 42.766 Lon W 95.553

Zook's Harley-Davidson, I-10
81 NW 49th Pl. **Des Moines**
(515) 265-4444
Lat N 41.65 Lon W 93.619

Route 65 Harley-Davidson Shop, J-10
404 E Euclid **Indianola**
(515) 962-2160
Lat N 41.366 Lon W 93.557

Chipps Harley-Davidson Shop, K-9
1301 Southwest Blvd. **Osceola**
(641) 342-7494
Lat N 41.025 Lon W 93.798

Walker's Harley-Davidson, K-3
57408 190th St. Exit 35 **Pacific Junction**
(712) 622-4000
Lat N 41.031 Lon W 95.807

Rooster's Harley-Davidson, E-1
1930 N Lewis Blvd. **Sioux City**
(712) 252-2750
Lat N 42.51 Lon W 96.374

How to determine distance

Mileages in red between red arrowheads; in black, between intersections.

© Rand McNally

randmcnally.com/eac

Express Access Code: IA

Use Express Access Codes on www.randmcnally.com for quick access to online travel planning info, road construction updates, and more.

Distance scale
One inch represents about 18 miles

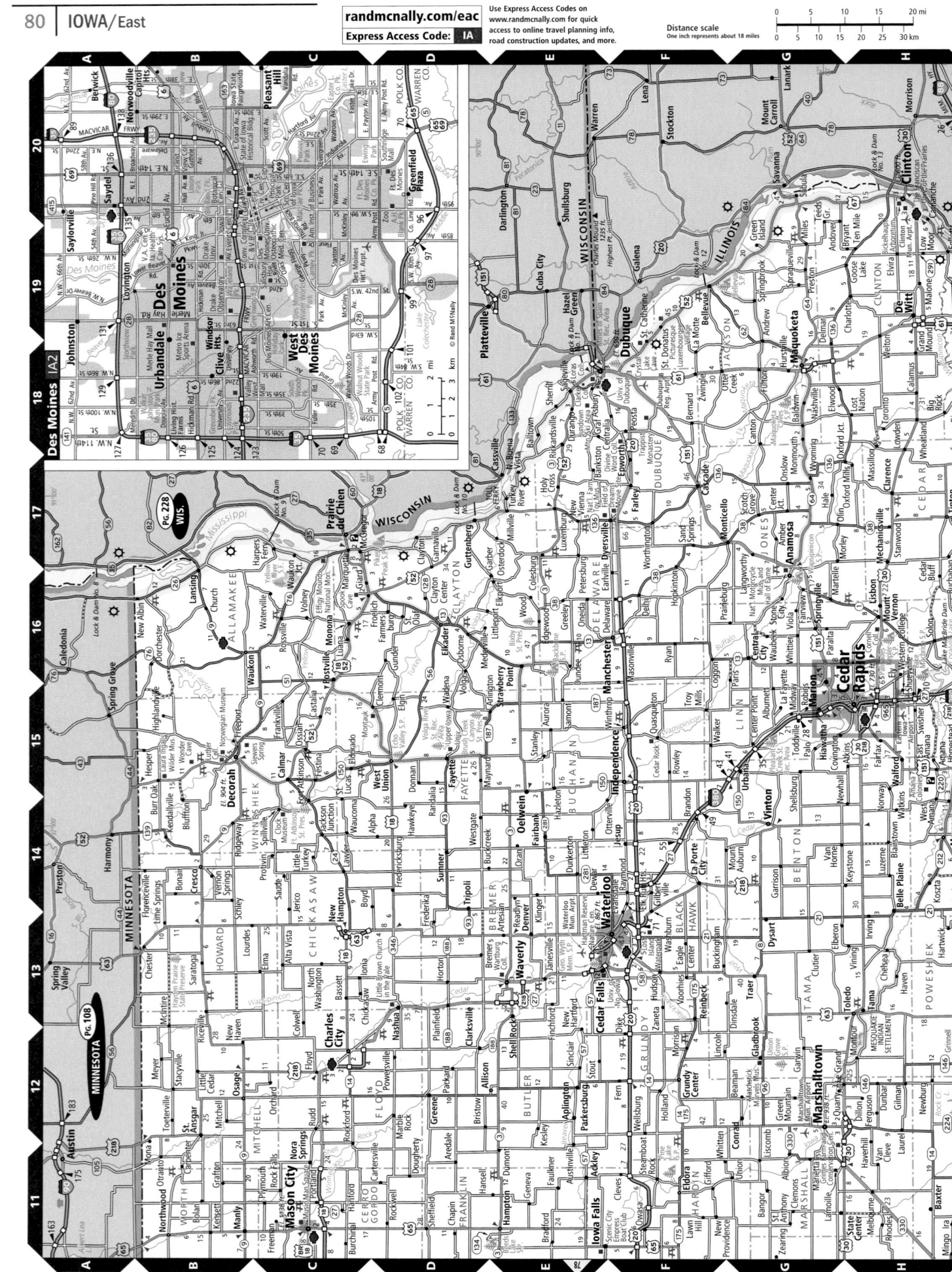

How to determine distance

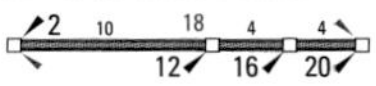

Mileages in red between red arrowheads; in black, between intersections.

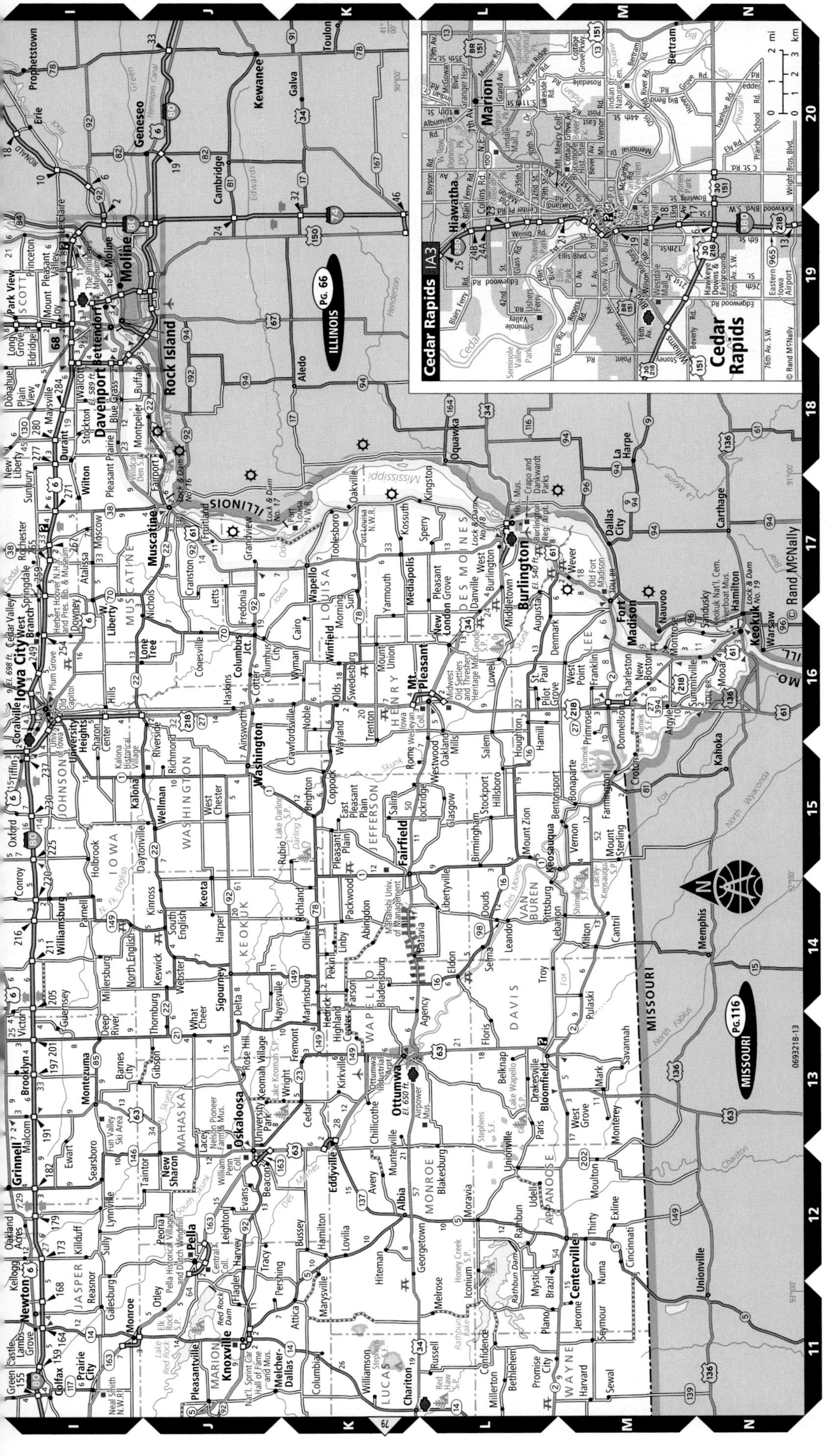

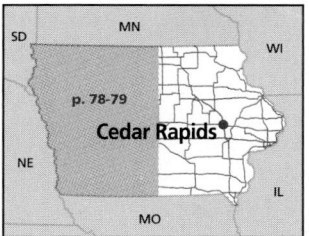

Cedar Rapids

SYMBOLS

Featured ride — Scenic route
Long-term construction — Harley-Davidson dealership

For Iowa ride, see page R10-11.

CITY-TO-CITY MILEAGE

	BURLINGTON	CEDAR RAPIDS	COUNCIL BLUFFS	DAVENPORT	DES MOINES	DUBUQUE	SIOUX CITY	WATERLOO
Ames	208	106	162	190	33	187	176	99
Burlington		100	314	79	185	151	386	158
Cedar Rapids	100		256	82	127	72	328	58
Council Bluffs	314	256		296	127	329	95	237
Davenport	79	82	296		167	70	368	140
Decorah	210	110	337	175	208	105	309	79
Des Moines	185	127	127	167		200	199	108
Dubuque	151	72	329	70	200		325	93
Fort Dodge	273	174	158	255	98	209	123	114
Iowa City	77	26	240	57	111	85	312	84
Keokuk	42	118	332	121	203	191	404	176
Mason City	239	139	250	221	121	174	213	81
Ottumwa	77	113	217	129	90	186	289	131

HARLEY-DAVIDSON DEALERSHIPS

Heartland Harley-Davidson, L-17
155 S Roosevelt Ave. **Burlington**
(319) 754-1100
Lat N 40.809 Lon W 91.141

Metro Harley-Davidson, H-15
2415 Westdale Dr. SW **Cedar Rapids**
(319) 362-9496
Lat N 41.955 Lon W 91.723

C & C Harley-Davidson, K-11
130 E Lincoln Ave. **Chariton**
(641) 774-7400
Lat N 41.004 Lon W 93.292

Cedar River Harley-Davidson Shop, C-12
1750 Cedar View Rd. **Charles City**
(641) 228-2192
Lat N 43.097 Lon W 92.719

Clinton Harley-Davidson, H-20
2519 Lincolnway **Clinton**
(563) 242-1901
Lat N 41.816 Lon W 90.247

Hawkeye Harley-Davidson, I-15
2812 Commerce Dr. **Coralville**
(319) 545-7495
Lat N 41.696 Lon W 91.614

Wiebler's Quad Cities Harley-Davidson, I-19
5320 Corporate Park Dr. **Davenport**
(563) 355-6437
Lat N 41.575 Lon W 90.517

Wilwert's Harley-Davidson Sales, E-18
145 N Crescent Ridge **Dubuque**
(563) 557-8040
Lat N 42.488 Lon W 90.718

Harley-Davidson of Mason City, C-11
706 S Federal Ave. **Mason City**
(641) 423-6007
Lat N 43.145 Lon W 93.201

Lentner Cycle Company, K-13
2021 Albia Rd. **Ottumwa**
(641) 682-0493
Lat N 41.009 Lon W 92.459

Silver Eagle Harley-Davidson, F-13
4022 Sergeant Rd. **Waterloo**
(319) 235-6505
Lat N 42.469 Lon W 92.395

Waukon Harley-Davidson, B-16
208 Hwy. 9 SW **Waukon**
(563) 568-3471
Lat N 43.315 Lon W 91.454

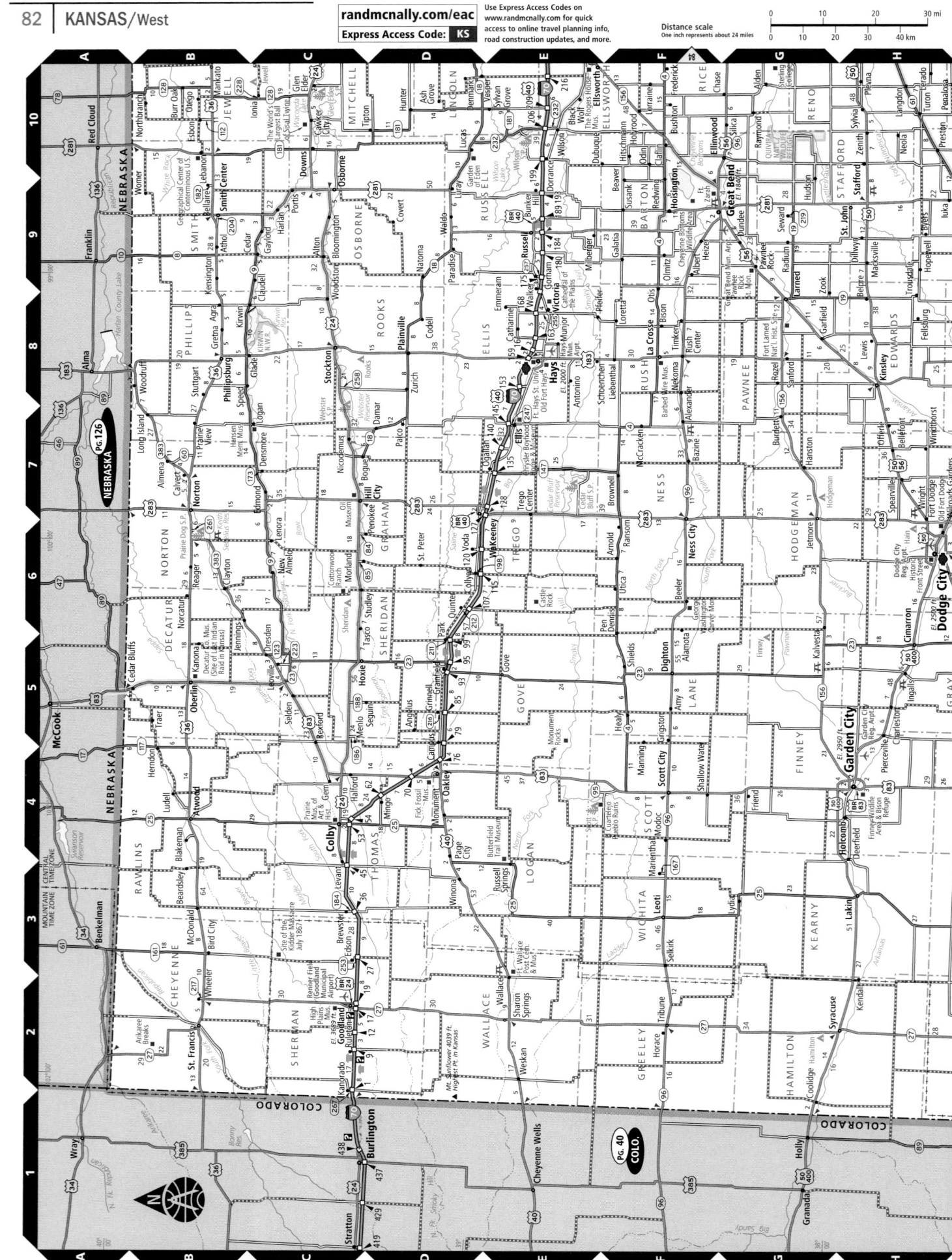

How to determine distance

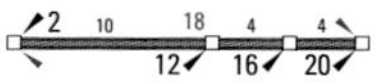

Mileages in red between red arrowheads;
in black, between intersections.

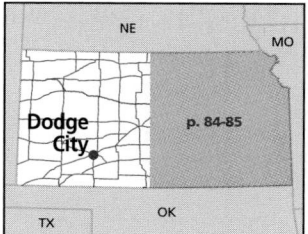

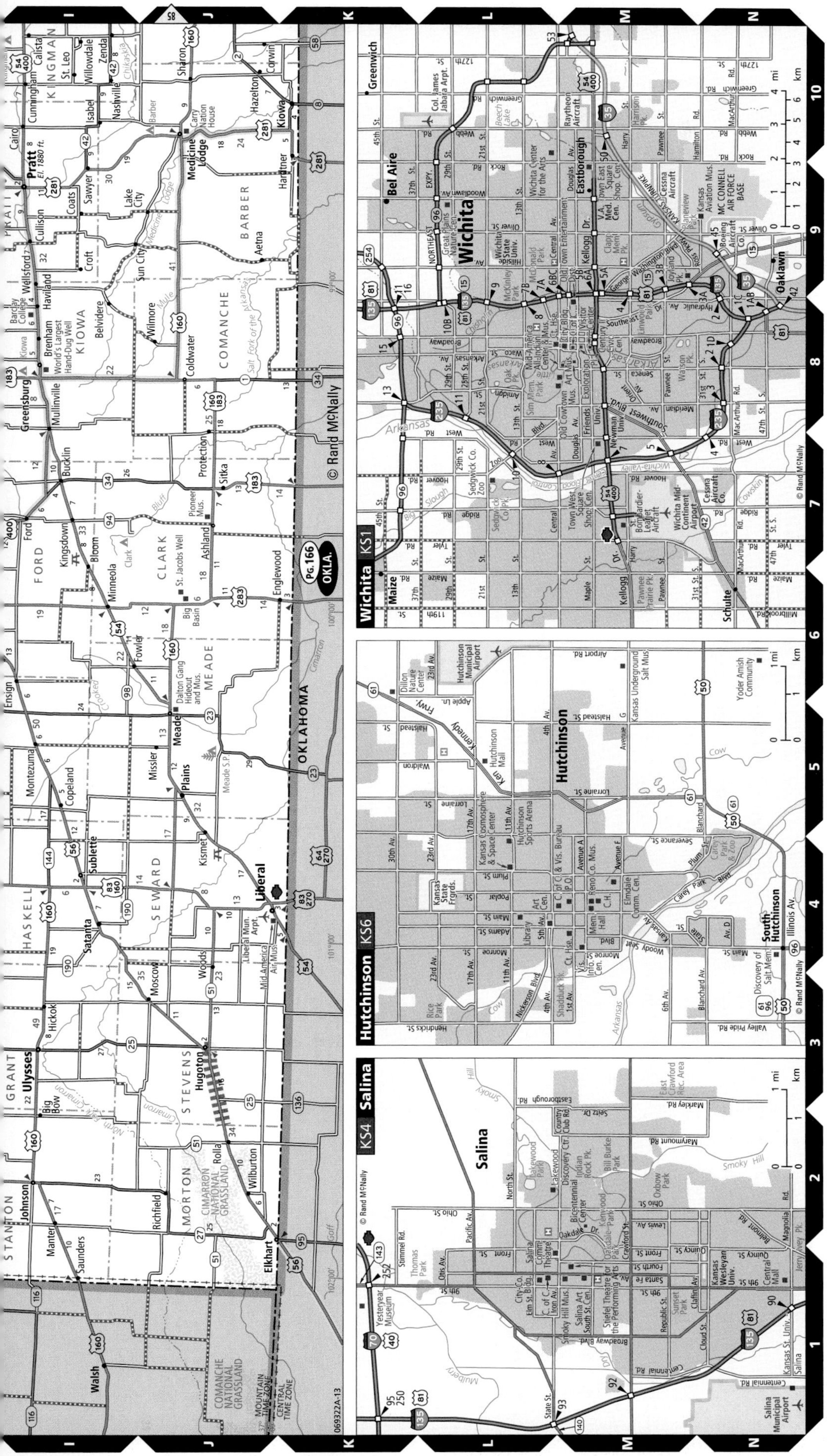

Pg. 166
OKLA.

© Rand McNally

SYMBOLS

— Featured ride
╫╫╫ Long-term construction
🏍 Harley-Davidson dealership

▤ Scenic route
■ Historic site or monument; Indian reservation or rancheria; military installation; point of interest; wildlife refuge

KANSAS MOTORCYCLE LAWS

Helmet use:
Required under age 18

Riding two abreast:
Yes. See state law for specifics

Eye protection:
Required unless equipped with windscreen

Speed limit:
Primary roads: 70 mph
Secondary roads: 70 mph

KANSAS RESOURCES

Road conditions or construction:
511
(800) 585-7623
www.511.ky.gov

Highway Emergency Numbers:
911 or *HP or *KTA

Tourism:
(800) 252-6727 (to request travel materials only)
(785) 296-2009
www.travelks.com

State motor vehicle information:
(785) 296-3963
www.ksrevenue.org/vehicle.htm

HARLEY-DAVIDSON DEALERSHIPS

🏍 **Dodge City Harley-Davidson, H-6**
1312 S Second Ave. **Dodge City**
(620) 227-6351
Lat N 37.73 **Lon** W 100.019

🏍 **Doerfler's Harley-Davidson, E-8**
1100 E 43rd St. **Hays**
(785) 625-2022
Lat N 38.901 **Lon** W 99.342

🏍 **Liberal Harley-Davidson, J-4**
1009 S Kansas Ave. **Liberal**
(620) 624-5588
Lat N 37.024 **Lon** W 100.922

Wichita KS1

Maize

Schulte

Hutchinson KS6

South Hutchinson

Salina KS4

Bel Aire

Wichita

Eastborough

Oaklawn

Greenwich

069322A-13

randmcnally.com/eac
Express Access Code: KS

Use Express Access Codes on www.randmcnally.com for quick access to online travel planning info, road construction updates, and more.

Distance scale
One inch represents about 24 miles

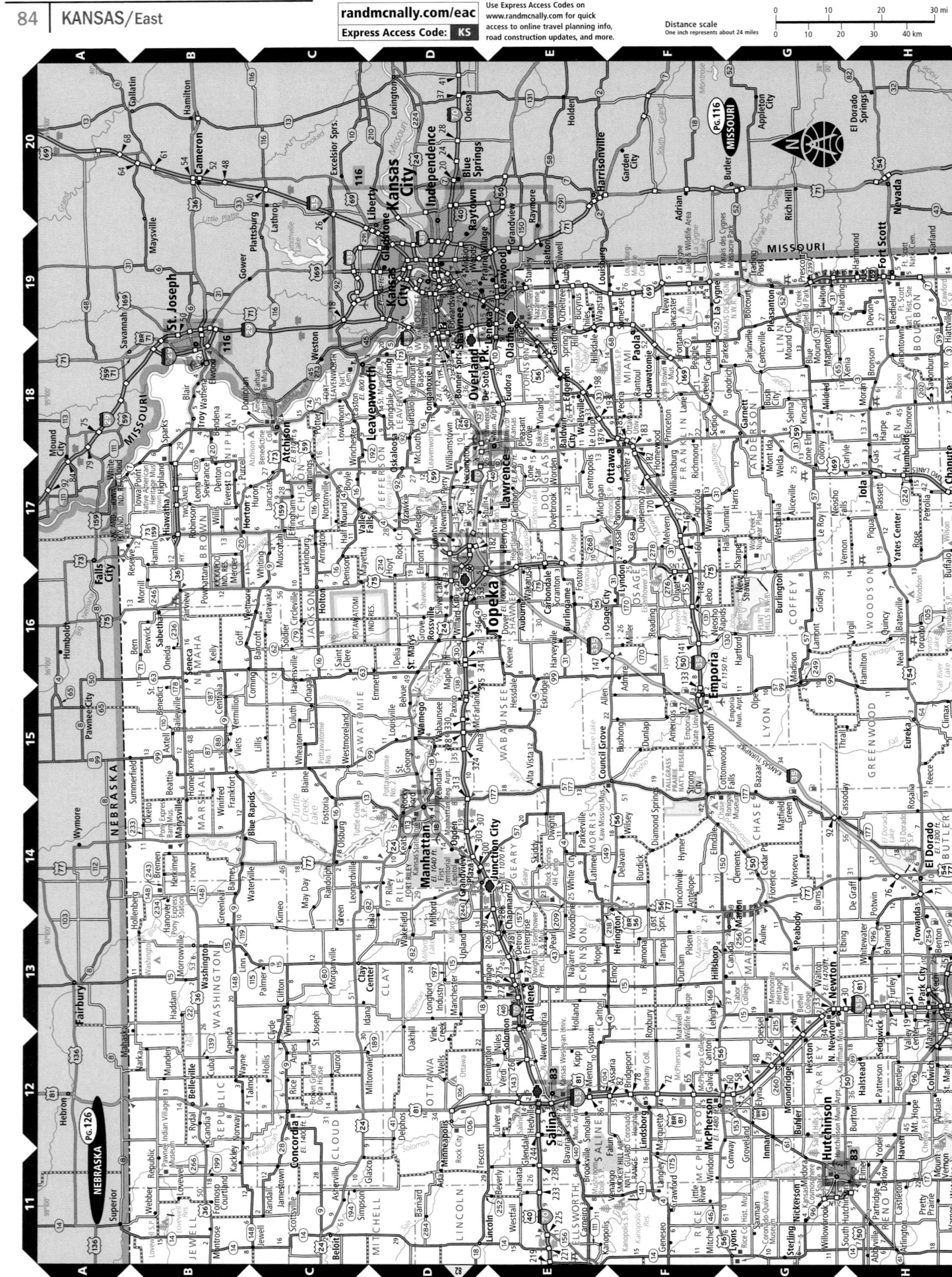

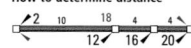

How to determine distance

Mileages in red between red arrowheads; in black, between intersections.

p. 82-83

Wichita

SYMBOLS

- Featured ride
- Long-term construction
- Harley-Davidson dealership
- Scenic route
- Historic site or monument; Indian reservation or rancheria; military installation; point of interest; wildlife refuge

CITY-TO-CITY MILEAGE

	DODGE CITY	GOODLAND	HUTCHINSON	JOPLIN, MO	KANSAS CITY	SALINA	TOPEKA	WICHITA
Arkansas City	211	385	120	157	225	153	177	61
Atchison	328	398	235	196	54	162	52	192
Coffeyville	300	459	194	68	171	227	158	138
Dodge City		193	125	345	338	166	277	154
Emporia	239	349	109	175	103	117	61	85
Fort Scott	306	481	205	59	89	245	134	152
Goodland	193		268	512	408	236	347	324
Great Bend	85	207	63	307	253	81	192	119
Hays	104	145	127	371	267	95	206	183
Hutchinson	125	268		247	212	73	184	59
Joplin, MO	345	512	247		148	280	193	191
Kansas City	338	408	212	148		172	61	188
Liberal	83	208	192	434	401	250	353	213
Manhattan	231	301	138	251	119	65	58	129
Oakley	134	59	211	455	351	179	290	267
Salina	166	236	73	280	172		111	92
Topeka	277	347	184	193	61	111		140
Wichita	154	324	59	191	188	92	140	

HARLEY-DAVIDSON DEALERSHIPS

- **City Cycle Sales, E-14**
  1021 Golden Belt Blvd. **Junction City**
  (785) 238-3411
  Lat N 39.002 Lon W 96.85

- **Central Harley-Davidson South, E-19**
  725 N Rawhide Rd. **Olathe**
  (913) 764-7433
  Lat N 38.891 Lon W 94.79

- **Harley-Davidson of Salina, E-12**
  2200 N Ohio St. **Salina**
  (785) 823-3767
  Lat N 38.878 Lon W 97.594

- **Central Harley-Davidson Shop, D-19**
  6801 Hedge Lane Terrace **Shawnee**
  (913) 422-3400
  Lat N 39.007 Lon W 94.859

- **Topeka Harley-Davidson, D-17**
  2047 SW Topeka Blvd. **Topeka**
  (785) 234-6174
  Lat N 39.031 Lon W 95.683

- **Alef's Harley-Davidson, I-13**
  MOVING IN 2006: 7800 W Kellogg Dr. **Wichita**
  (316) 721-3500
  Lat N 37.67 Lon W 97.443

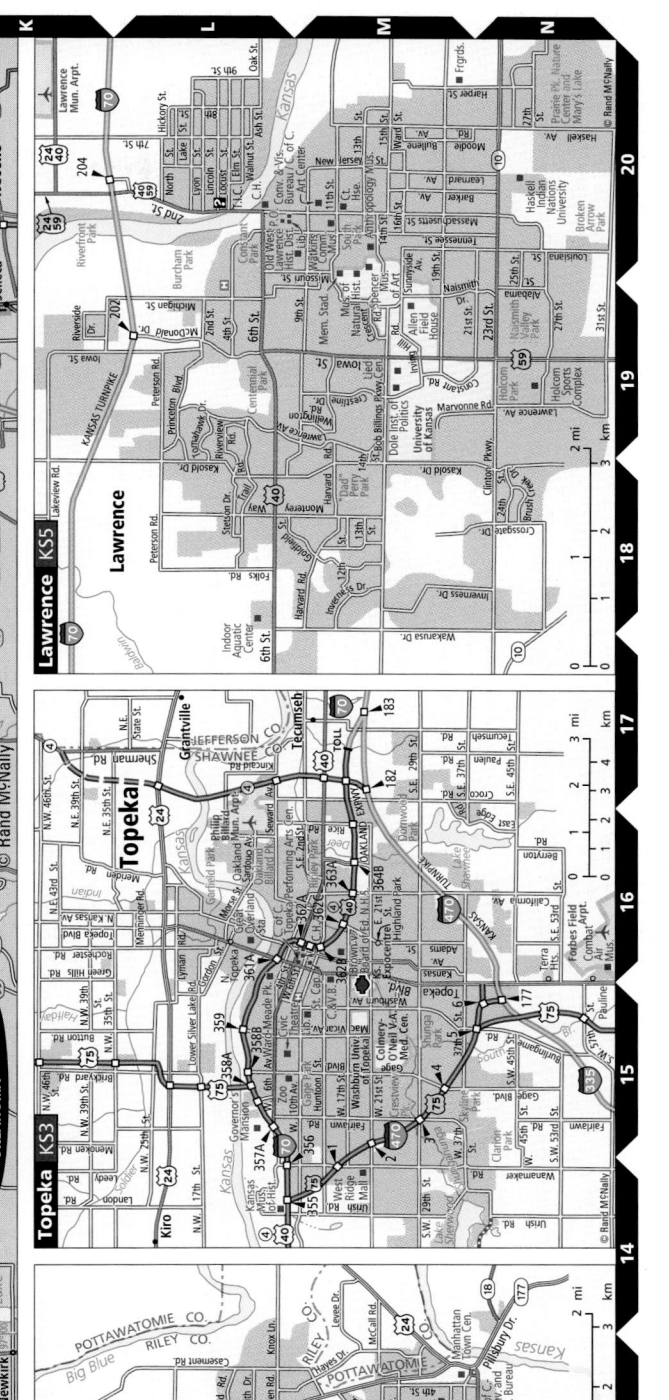

Lawrence KS5

Topeka KS3

Manhattan KS2

© Rand McNally

randmcnally.com/eac
Express Access Code: KY

Use Express Access Codes on
www.randmcnally.com for quick
access to online travel planning info,
road construction updates, and more.

Distance scale
One inch represents about 18 miles

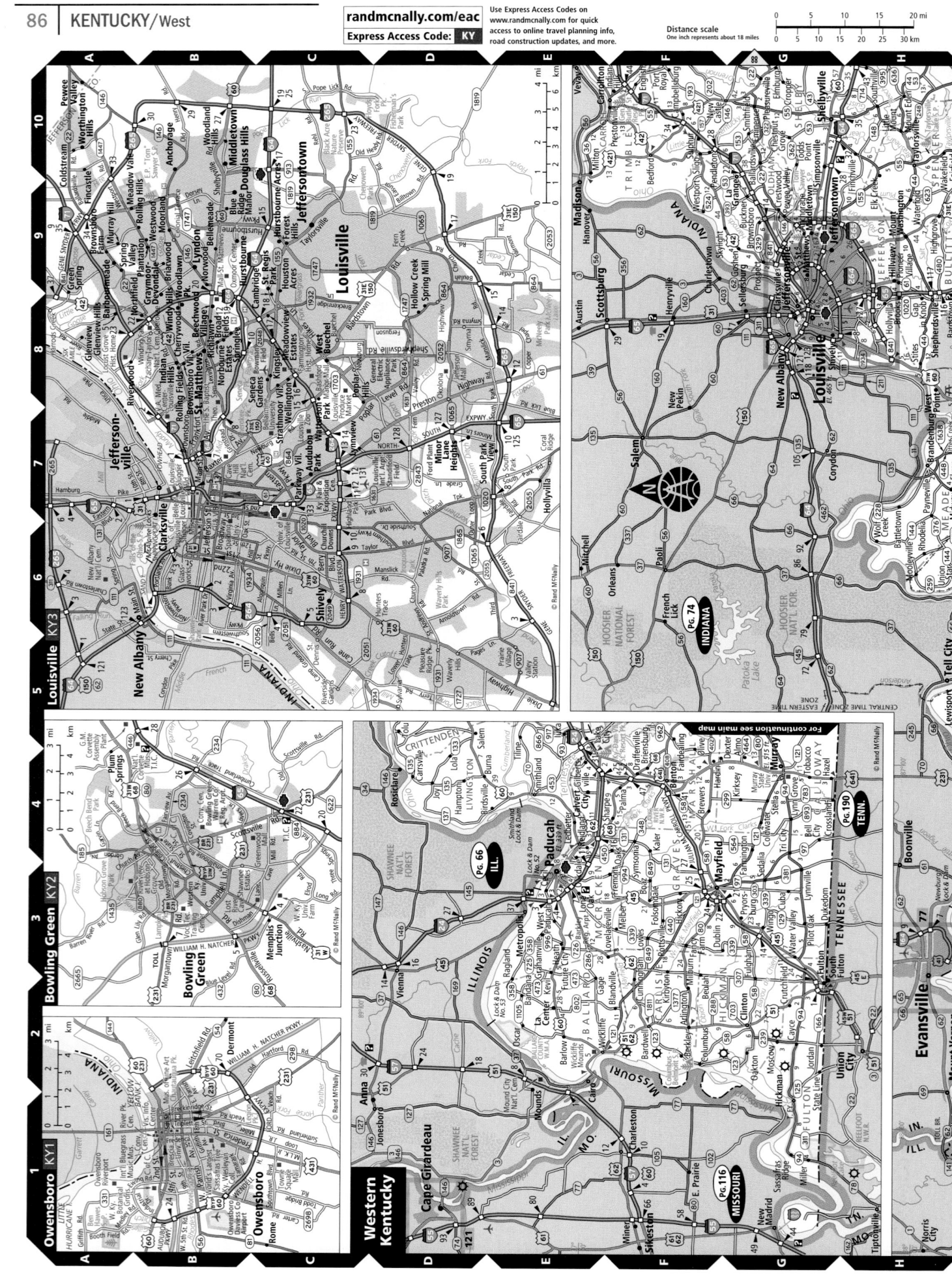

How to determine distance

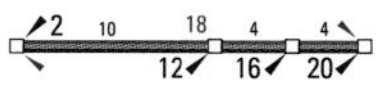

Mileages in red between red arrowheads; in black, between intersections.

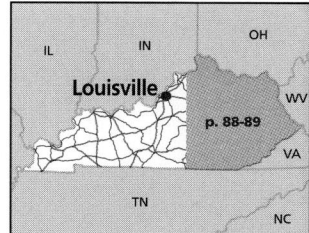

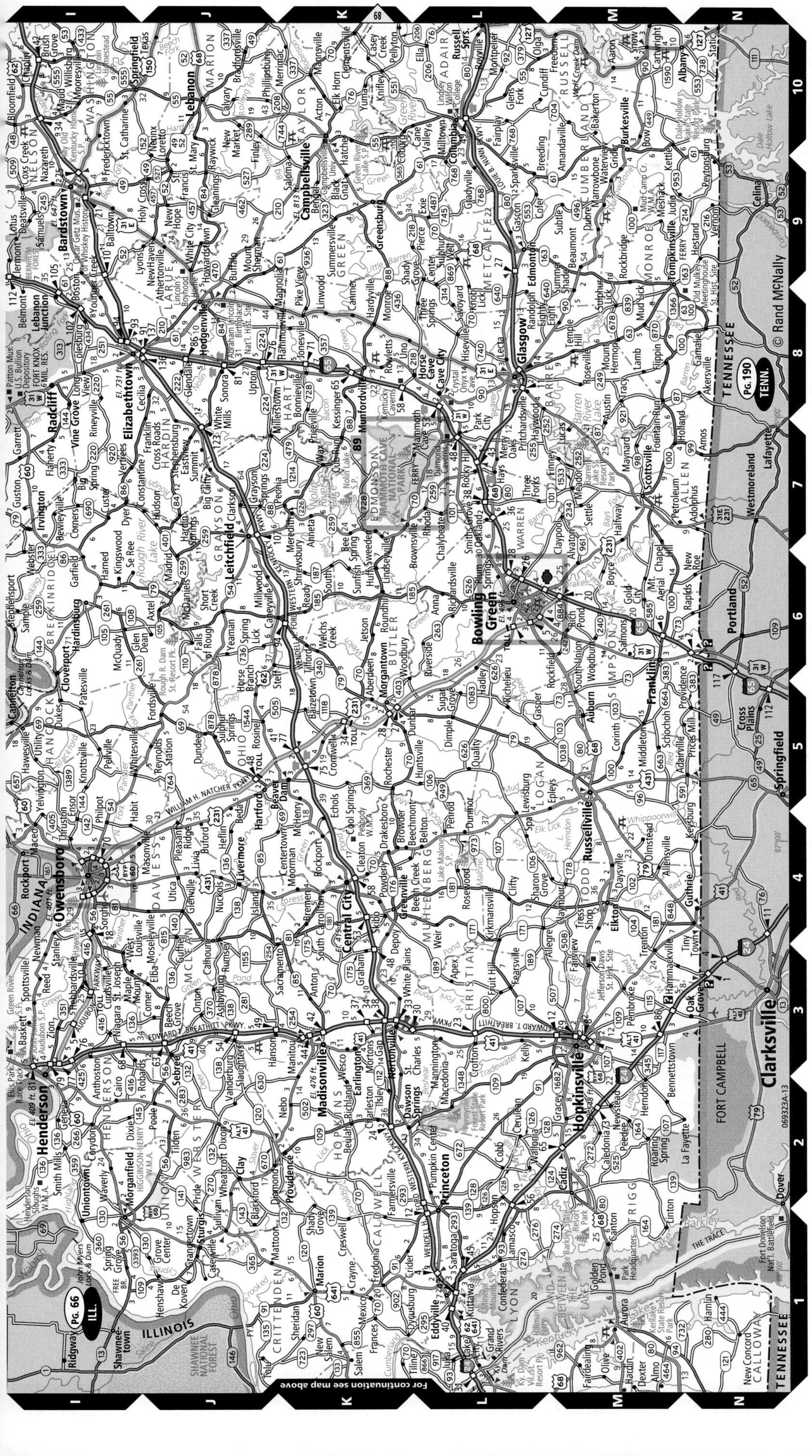

© Rand McNally

SYMBOLS

- ▦ Featured ride
- ▦ Long-term construction
- 🏍 Harley-Davidson dealership
- ▨ Scenic route
- ■ Historic site or monument; Indian reservation or rancheria; military installation; point of interest; wildlife refuge

For Kentucky/Tennessee ride, see page R12.

KENTUCKY MOTORCYCLE LAWS

Helmet use:
Required for novice riders, those under age 21, and for instructional permit holders

Riding two abreast:
No reference in administrative code or statutes

Eye protection:
Required by law

Speed limit:
Primary roads: 65 mph
Secondary roads: 65 mph

KENTUCKY RESOURCES

Road conditions or construction:
511 (Cincinnati/northern Kentucky area)
(866) 737-3767
www.ksdot.org

Highway Emergency Numbers:
911 or (800) 222-5555

Tourism:
(800) 225-8747
(502) 564-4930
www.kentuckytourism.com

State motor vehicle information
(502) 564-6800
www.kytc.state.ky.us/drlic

HARLEY-DAVIDSON DEALERSHIPS

🏍 **Harley-Davidson Bowling Green, L-6**
251 Cumberland Trace Rd. **Bowling Green**
(270) 846-4488
Lat N 36.933 Lon W 86.415

🏍 **Louisville Harley-Davidson, G-8**
1700 Arthur St. **Louisville**
(502) 634-1340
Lat N 38.222 Lon W 85.751

🏍 **Bluegrass Harley-Davidson, G-9**
11701 Gateworth Way **Louisville**
(502) 244-8095
Lat N 38.225 Lon W 85.542

🏍 **Sills Harley-Davidson, E-3**
1212 Brown St. **Paducah**
(270) 443-5636
Lat N 37.065 Lon W 88.597

randmcnally.com/eac

Express Access Code: KY

Use Express Access Codes on www.randmcnally.com for quick access to online travel planning info, road construction updates, and more.

Distance scale
One inch represents about 18 miles

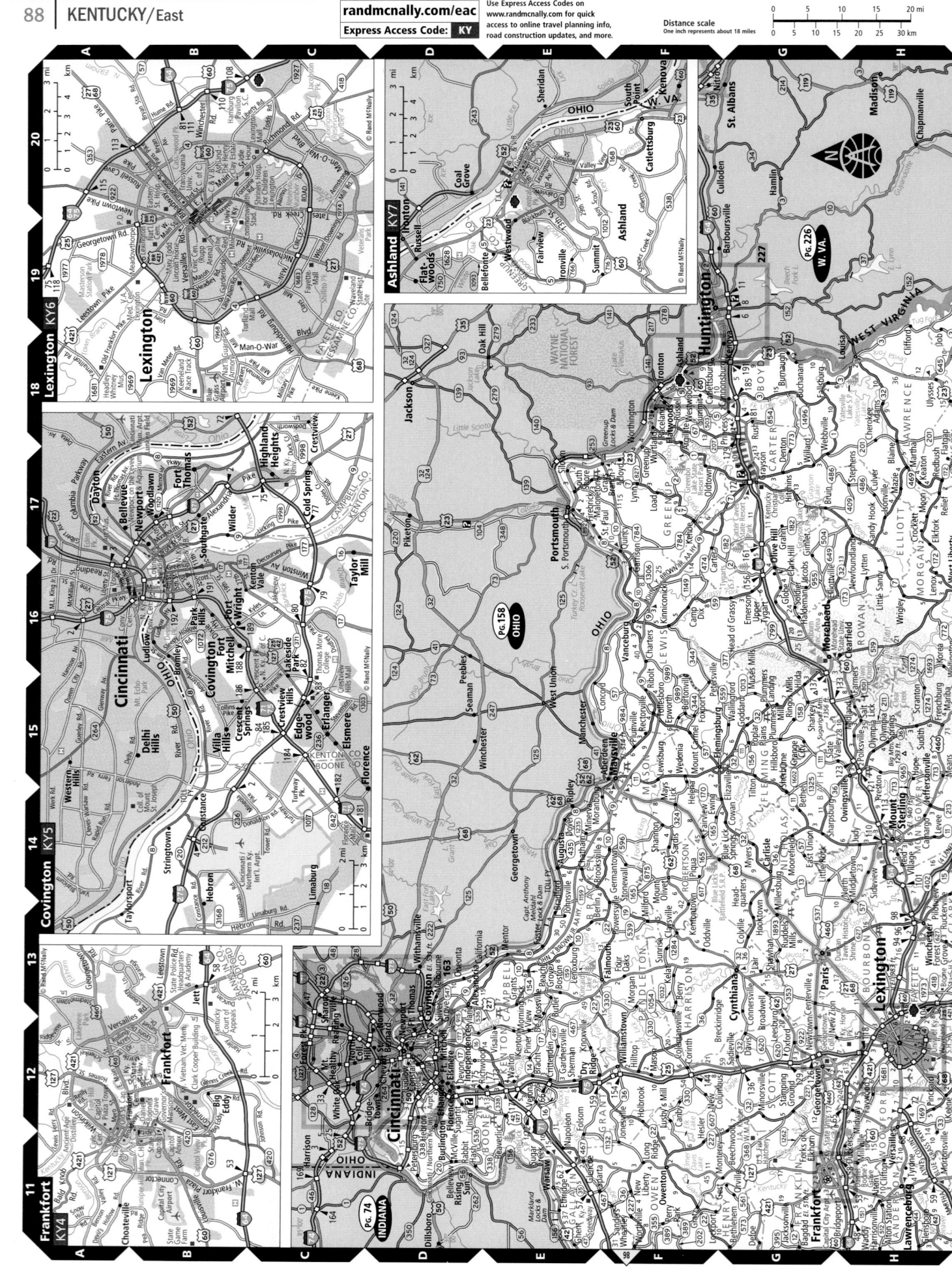

Lexington KY6

Ashland KY7

Covington KY5

Frankfort KY4

How to determine distance

Mileages in red between red arrowheads;
in black, between intersections.

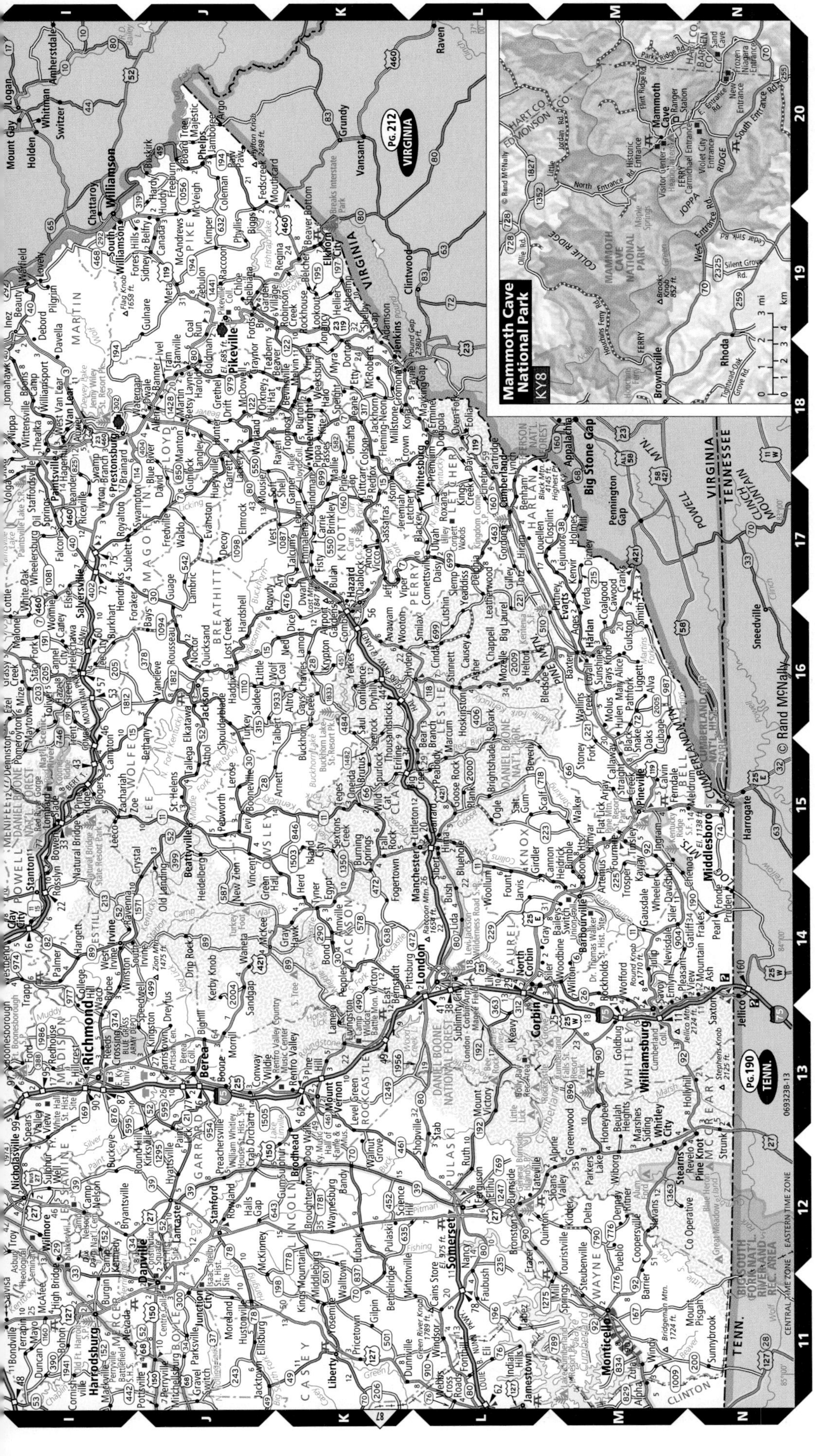

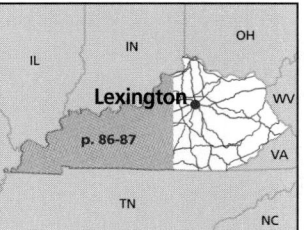

SYMBOLS

- Featured ride
- Long-term construction
- Harley-Davidson dealership
- Scenic route
- Historic site or monument; Indian reservation or rancheria; military installation; point of interest; wildlife refuge

CITY-TO-CITY MILEAGE

	Ashland	Bowling Green	Covington	Hopkinsville	Lexington	Louisville	Owensboro	Paducah
Ashland		278	135	334	123	197	303	385
Bardstown	183	95	137	151	60	40	120	202
Bowling Green	278		218	63	155	116	71	153
Cave City	250	30	190	97	127	88	108	190
Covington	135	218		274	82	102	208	325
Elizabethtown	209	71	147	127	86	45	96	178
Frankfort	146	145	89	201	23	52	170	252
Hopkinsville	334	63	274		211	172	99	76
Huntington, WV	18	282	159	338	127	201	307	389
Lexington	123	155	82	211		74	180	262
London	176	145	154	212	78	152	223	305
Louisville	197	116	102	172	74		106	223
Mayfield	394	162	334	85	271	232	159	24
Maysville	80	225	153	266	75	135	252	334
Owensboro	303	71	208	99	180	106		150
Paducah	385	153	325	76	262	223	150	
Pikeville	100	263	218	353	142	216	322	404
Somerset	179	111	157	178	81	134	189	271

HARLEY-DAVIDSON DEALERSHIPS

Benjy's Harley-Davidson, F-18
500 Winchester Ave. **Ashland**
(606) 326-9074
Lat N 38.485 Lon W 82.652

Harley-Davidson of Lexington, H-13
2073 Bryant Rd. **Lexington**
(859) 253-2461
Lat N 38.016 Lon W 84.41

Harley-Davidson of Pikeville, J-19
114 Harley Dr. **Pikeville**
(606) 433-0911
Lat N 37.487 Lon W 82.543

Prestonsburg Harley-Davidson, I-18
631 S Lake Dr. **Prestonsburg**
(606) 886-6076
Lat N 37.669 Lon W 82.758

Mammoth Cave National Park KY8

© Rand McNally

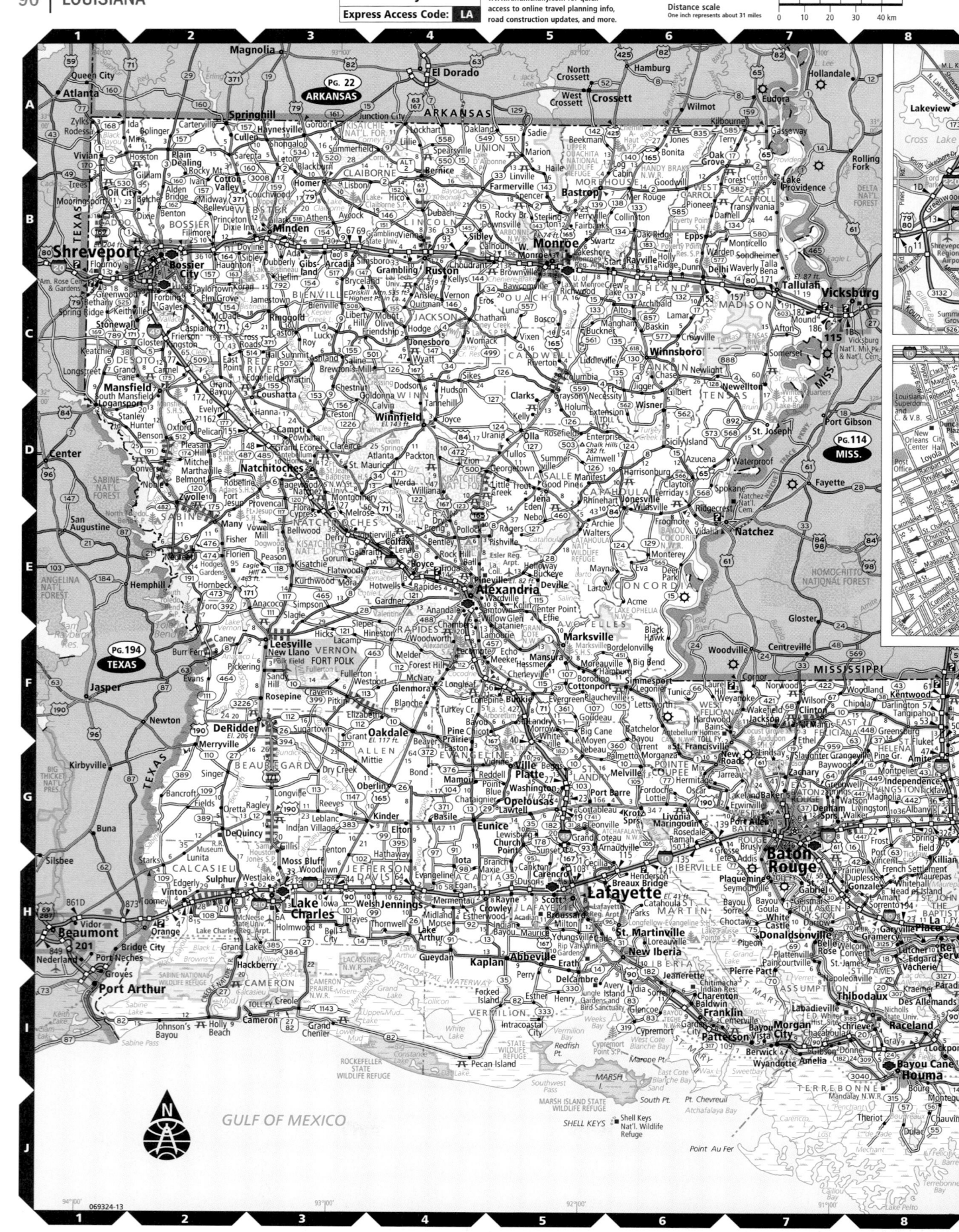

randmcnally.com/eac
Express Access Code: LA

Use Express Access Codes on www.randmcnally.com for quick access to online travel planning info, road construction updates, and more.

Distance scale
One inch represents about 31 miles

GULF OF MEXICO

How to determine distance

Mileages in red between red arrowheads; in black, between intersections.

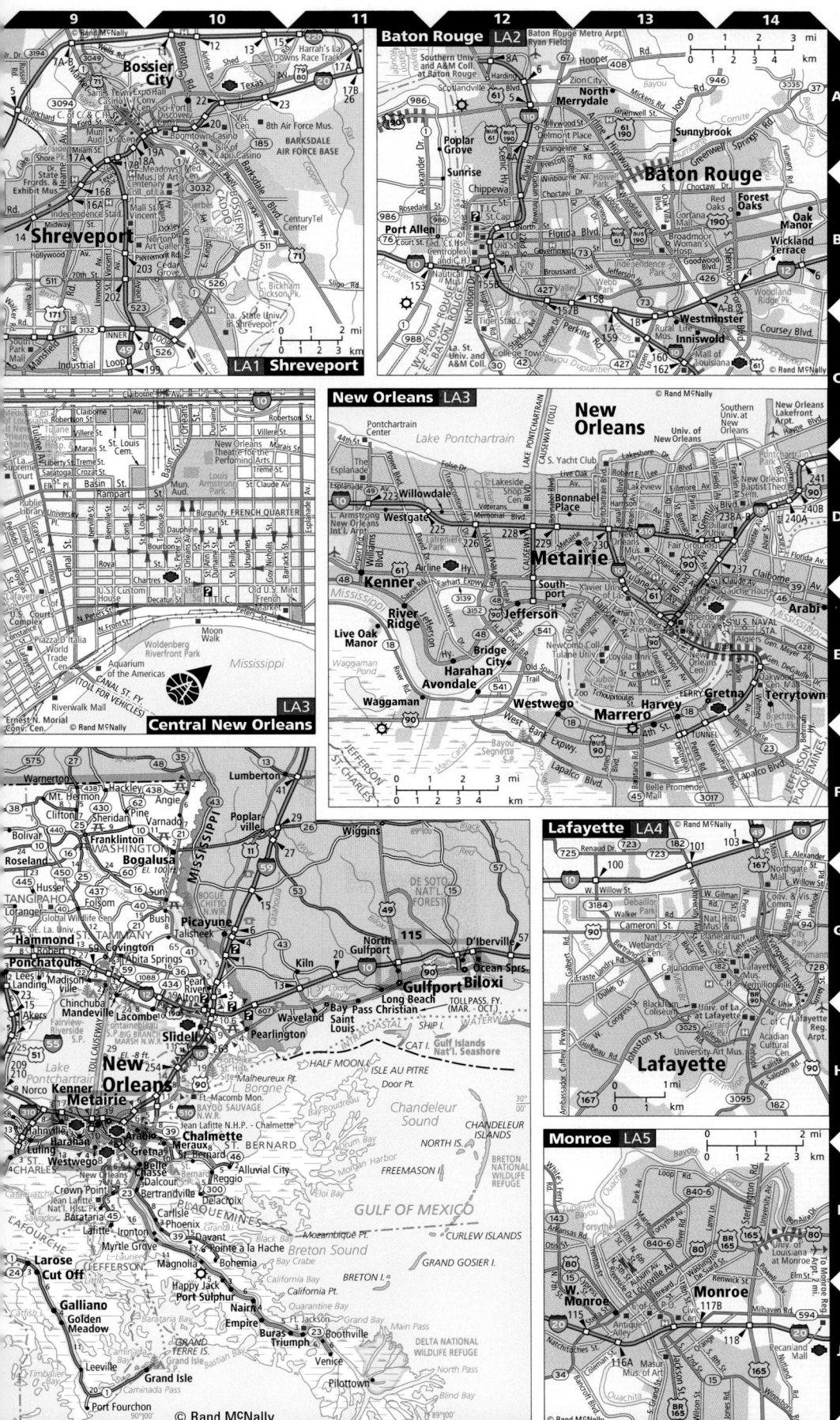

SYMBOLS

- Featured ride
- Long-term construction
- Scenic route
- Harley-Davidson dealership

LOUISIANA MOTORCYCLE LAWS

Helmet use: Required

Riding two abreast:
Yes. See state law for specifics

Eye protection:
Required unless equipped with windscreen

Speed limit:
Primary roads: 70 mph; Secondary roads: 70 mph

LOUISIANA RESOURCES

Road conditions or construction:
www.dotd.state.la.us

Highway Emergency Numbers:
911 or *LSP

Tourism:
(800) 334-8626
www.louisianatravel.com

State motor vehicle information:
(877) DMV-LINE
www.dps.state.la.us/

HARLEY-DAVIDSON DEALERSHIPS

Renegade Harley-Davidson, E-4
2030 N Mall Dr. Alexandria
(318) 448-1509
Lat N 31.277 Lon W 92.456

Harley-Davidson of Baton Rouge, G-7
5853 Siegen Ln. Baton Rouge
(225) 292-9632
Lat N 30.397 Lon W 91.057

Bossier City Harley-Davidson Shop, B-2
3333 E Texas Bossier City
(318) 549-1571
Lat N 32.529 Lon W 93.695

The Harley-Davidson Shop of New Orleans, I-9
1208 Lafayette St. Gretna
(504) 362-4004
Lat N 29.911 Lon W 90.057

Mike Bruno's Bayou Country Harley-Davidson, I-8
1740 Martin Luther King Blvd. Houma
(985) 872-4380
Lat N 29.612 Lon W 90.754

Harley-Davidson of Lake Charles, H-3
2120 Broad St. Lake Charles
(337) 436-0022
Lat N 30.228 Lon W 93.19

Harley-Davidson of New Orleans, H-9
6015 Airline Dr. Metarie
(504) 736-9600
Lat N 29.977 Lon W 90.201

Bleu Bayou Harley-Davidson, B-5
6200 Frontage Rd. Monroe
(318) 343-1650
Lat N 32.493 Lon W 92.047

VooDoo Harley-Davidson, H-9
633 Toulouse St. New Orleans
(504) 561-0263
Lat N 29.957 Lon W 90.065

Cajun Harley-Davidson, H-5
724 I-10 S Frontage Rd. Scott
(337) 289-3030
Lat N 30.249 Lon W 92.098

Shreveport Harley-Davidson, B-2
805 Brook Hollow Dr. Shreveport
(318) 798-1064
Lat N 32.418 Lon W 93.725

NorthShore Harley-Davidson, H-10
791 W I-10 Service Rd. Slidell
(985) 641-5100
Lat N 30.252 Lon W 89.762

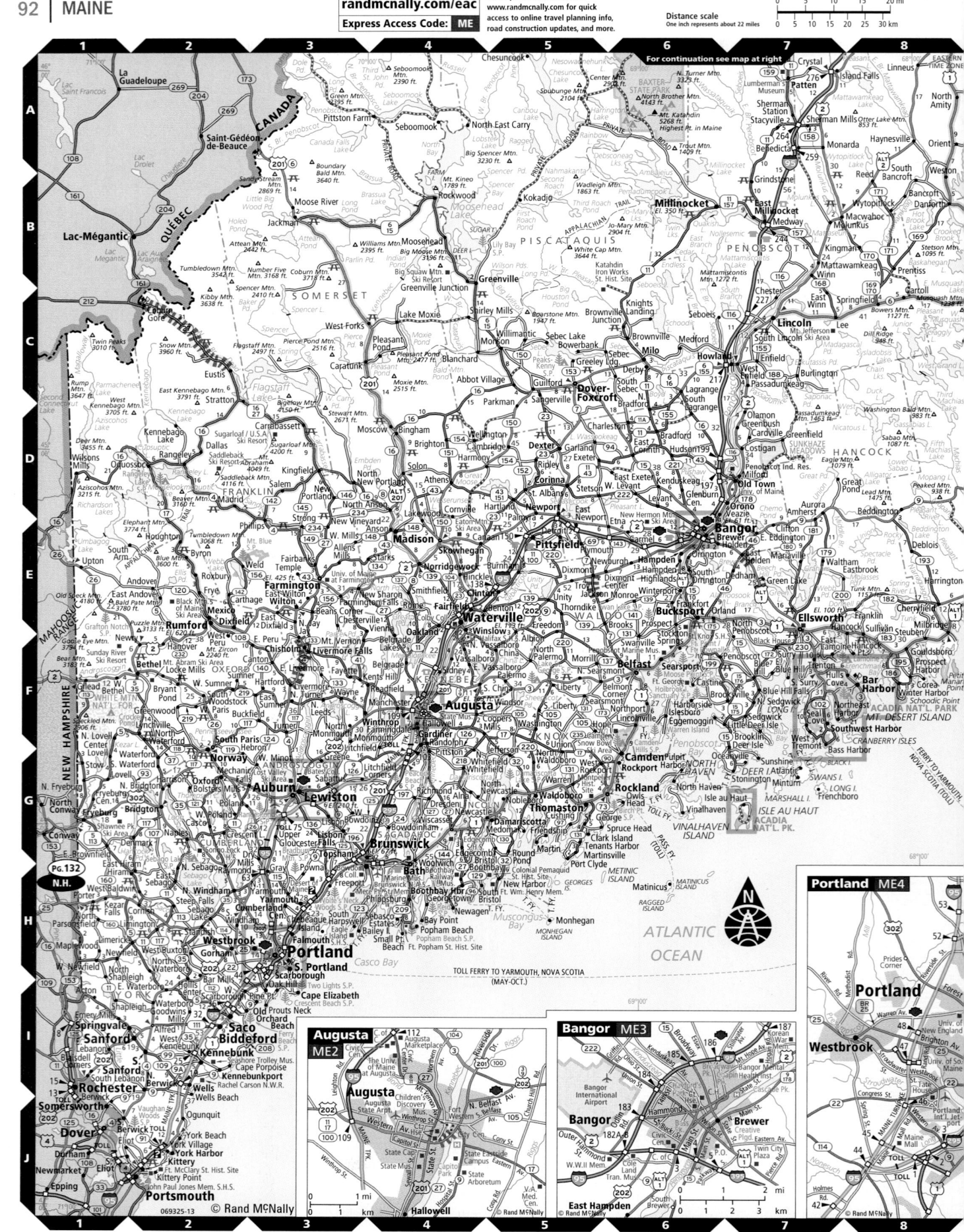

randmcnally.com/eac
Express Access Code: ME

Use Express Access Codes on www.randmcnally.com for quick access to online travel planning info, road construction updates, and more.

Distance scale
One inch represents about 22 miles

For continuation see map at right

ATLANTIC OCEAN

TOLL FERRY TO YARMOUTH, NOVA SCOTIA (MAY-OCT.)

Portland ME4

Augusta ME2

Bangor ME3

© Rand McNally

069325-13

SYMBOLS

- ═══ Featured ride
- ═══ Scenic route
- ╫╫╫ Long-term construction
- ⬛ Historic site or monument; Indian reservation or rancheria; military installation; point of interest; wildlife refuge
- Harley-Davidson dealership

MAINE MOTORCYCLE LAWS

Helmet use:
Required under age 15 with learner's permit, or for 1 year after obtaining license, and for passenger when operator is required to wear helmet

Riding two abreast:
Yes. See state law for specifics

Eye protection:
Not required

Speed limit:
Primary roads: 65 mph
Secondary roads: 65 mph

MAINE RESOURCES

Road conditions or construction:
511
(207) 624-3595
www.state.me.us/mdot/

Highway Emergency Numbers:
911 or *77

Tourism:
(888) 624-6345
www.visitmaine.com

State motor vehicle information:
(207) 624-9000
www.state.me.us/sos/bmv

CITY-TO-CITY MILEAGE

	BANGOR	EAST MILLINOCKET	EASTPORT	HOULTON	PORTLAND	PORTSMOUTH, NH	RANGELEY	WATERVILLE
Bangor		63	130	121	132	182	122	57
East Millinocket	63		119	60	193	243	183	118
Eastport	130	119		119	261	311	251	186
Houlton	121	60	119		251	301	241	176
Portland	132	193	261	251		50	120	75
Portsmouth, NH	182	243	311	301	50		168	125
Rangeley	122	183	251	241	120	168		77
Waterville	57	118	186	176	75	125	77	

HARLEY-DAVIDSON DEALERSHIPS

North Country Harley-Davidson, F-4
3099 N Belfast Ave. **Augusta**
(207) 622-7994
Lat N 44.327 Lon W 69.745

Central Maine Harley-Davidson Shop, E-6
570 Stillwater Ave. **Bangor**
(207) 947-6456
Lat N 44.83 Lon W 68.754

Plourdes Harley-Davidson, B-14
11 Laurette St. **Caribou**
(207) 496-3211
Lat N 46.868 Lon W 68.005

Central Maine Harley-Davidson, E-6
2387 Rte. 2 **Hermon (Bangor)**
(207) 848-5709
Lat N 44.803 Lon W 68.927

L-A Harley-Davidson, G-3
839 Main St. **Lewiston**
(207) 786-2822
Lat N 44.131 Lon W 70.198

Big Moose Harley-Davidson, H-3
375 Riverside St. **Portland**
(207) 797-6061
Lat N 43.688 Lon W 70.328

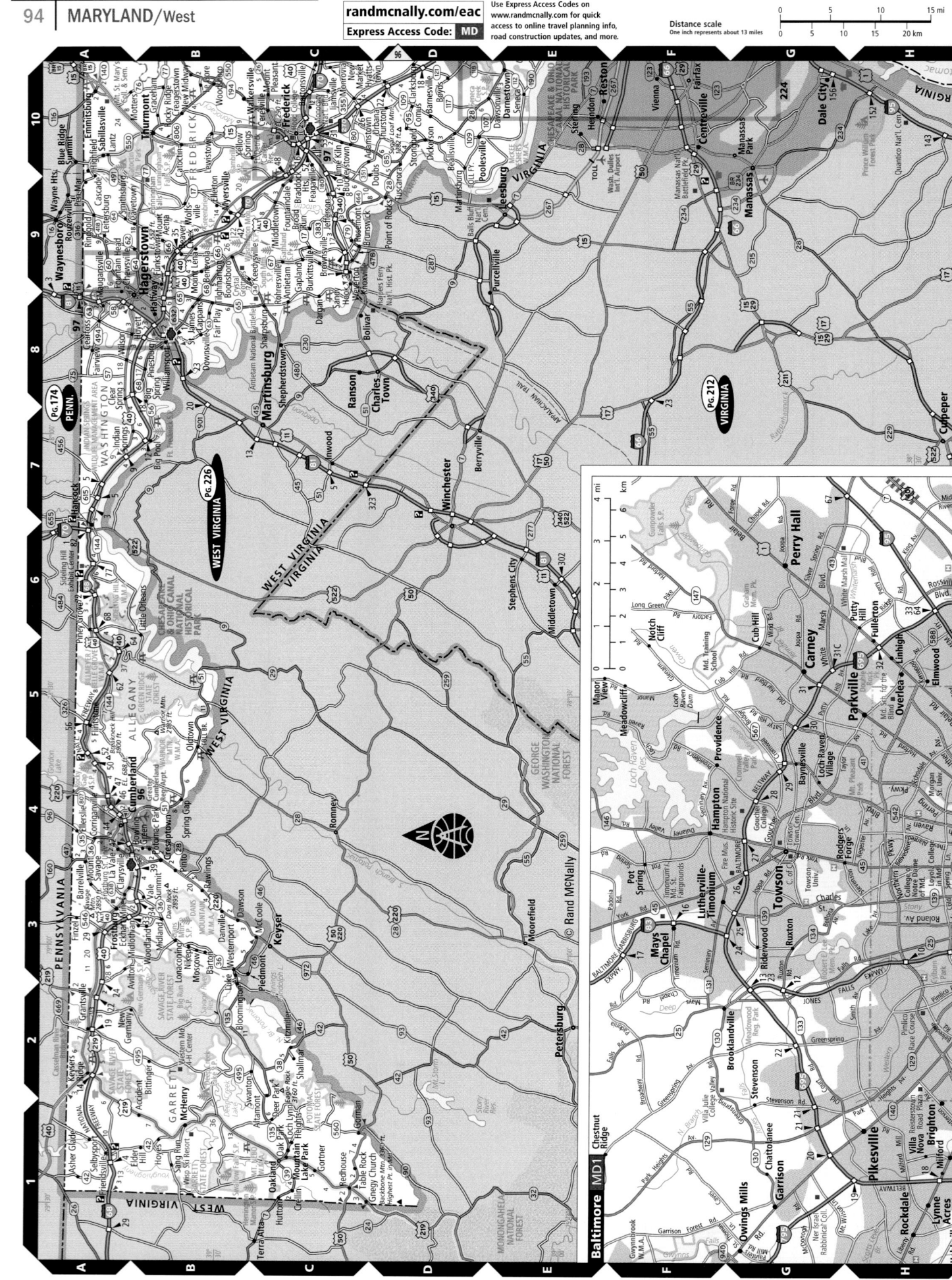

Distance scale
One inch represents about 13 miles

0   5   10   15 mi
0   5   10   15   20 km

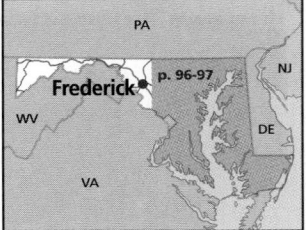

How to determine distance

Mileages in red between red arrowheads; in black, between intersections.

Central Baltimore MD1

SYMBOLS

- Featured ride
- Scenic route
- Long-term construction
- Historic site or monument; Indian reservation or rancheria; military installation; point of interest; wildlife refuge
- Harley-Davidson dealership

MARYLAND MOTORCYCLE LAWS

Helmet use:
Required and reflectorization required

Riding two abreast:
Yes. See state law for specifics

Eye protection:
Required unless equipped with windscreen

Speed limit:
Primary roads: 65 mph
Secondary roads: 65 mph

MARYLAND RESOURCES

Road conditions or construction:
(800) 327-3125
(800) 541-9595
www.chart.state.md.us

Highway Emergency Numbers:
#77

Tourism:
(800) 634-7386
www.mdisfun.org

State motor vehicle information:
(301) 729-4550
www.mva.state.md.us

HARLEY-DAVIDSON DEALERSHIPS

Harley-Davidson of Frederick, C-10
5722 Urbana Pike **Frederick**
(301) 694-8177
Lat N 39.389 Lon W 77.404

Highland Harley-Davidson Shop, A-4
1285 National Hwy. **La Vale**
(240) 362-0200
Lat N 39.637 Lon W 78.843

Harley-Davidson Shop of Williamsport, B-8
10210 Governor Lane Blvd. Ste. 2004
Williamsport
(301) 223-1800
Lat N 39.593 Lon W 77.807

Distance scale
One inch represents about 13 miles

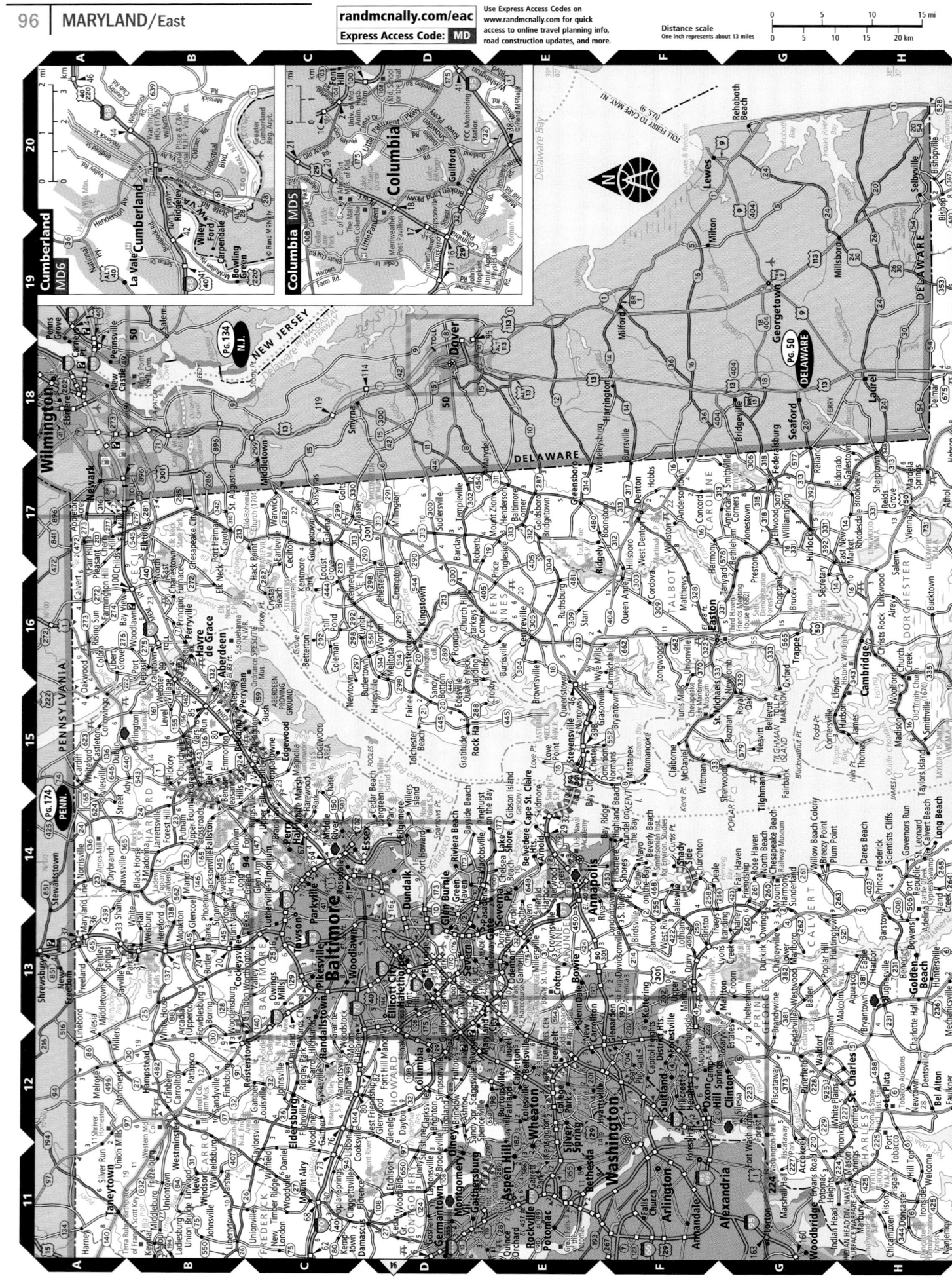

How to determine distance

Mileages in red between red arrowheads; in black, between intersections.

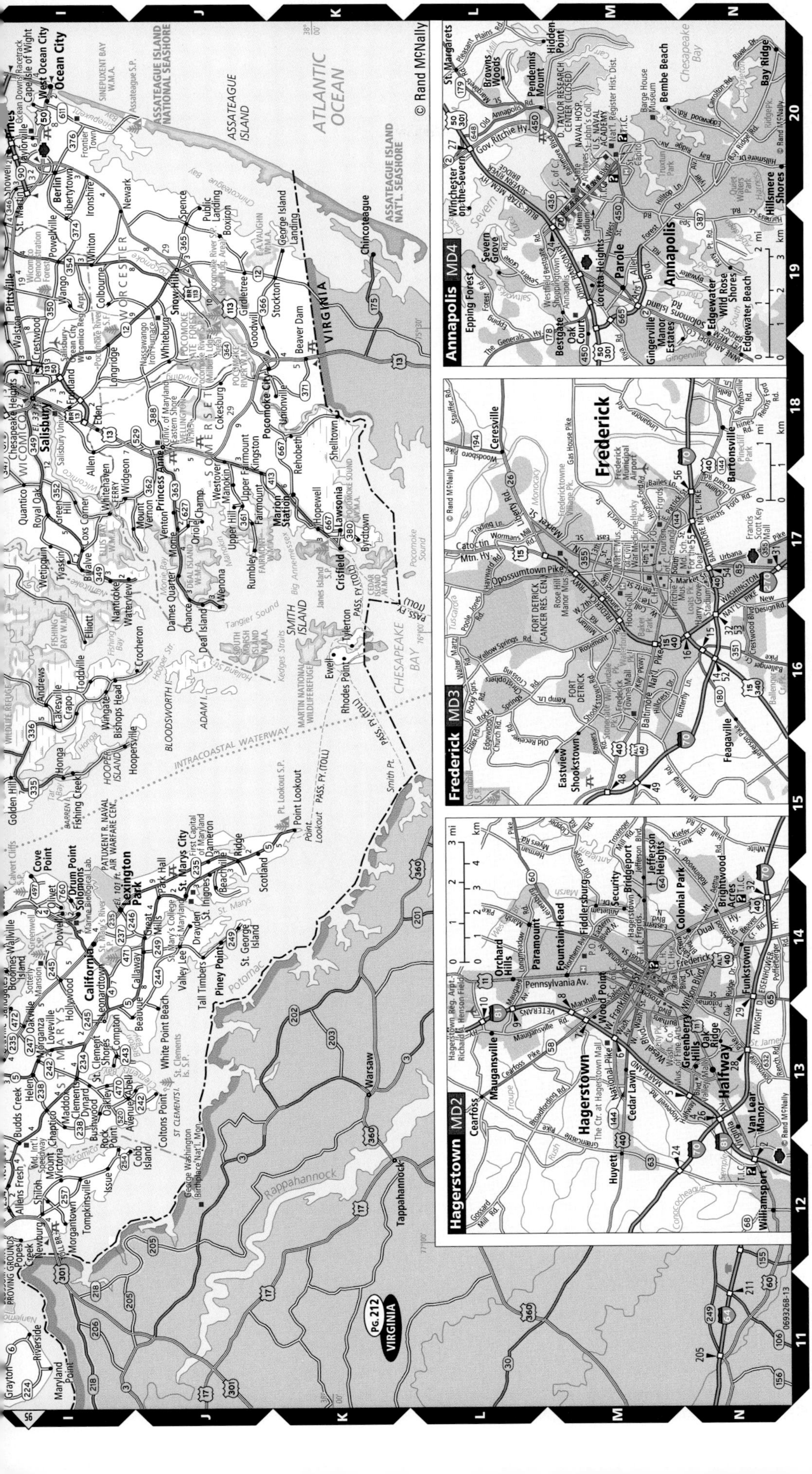

© Rand McNally

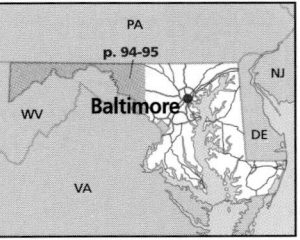

SYMBOLS

- ▭ Featured ride
- ▭ Scenic route
- ▤ Long-term construction
- ■ Historic site or monument; Indian reservation or rancheria; military installation; point of interest; wildlife refuge
- Harley-Davidson dealership

CITY-TO-CITY MILEAGE

	ABERDEEN	ANNAPOLIS	BALTIMORE	CUMBERLAND	HAGERSTOWN	LEXINGTON PARK	WASHINGTON, DC
Aberdeen		56	30	175	107	113	121	64
Annapolis	56		28	163	95	72	89	28
Baltimore	30	28		142	74	85	116	38
Cambridge	113	58	85	210	152	33	85
Chestertown	65	48	75	210	142	119	85	75
Cumberland	175	163	142		70	210	251	143
Edgewood	11	48	22	167	99	105	141	56
Frederick	83	71	50	93	25	118	159	51
Hagerstown	107	95	74	70		142	183	75
Harrisburg, PA	107	122	88	143	75	179	212	126
Lexington Park	113	72	85	210	142		160	67
Ocean City	134	111	138	273	205	182	29	138
Pocomoke City	149	115	142	277	209	186	26	138
Rockville	73	39	43	121	53	86	127	22
St. Charles	86	43	60	176	108	42	131	33
Salisbury	121	89	116	251	183	160		116
Washington, DC	64	28	38	143	75	67	116	
Wilmington, DE	41	95	69	214	146	152	105	103

HARLEY-DAVIDSON DEALERSHIPS

Harley-Davidson of Annapolis, E-14
30 Hudson St. **Annapolis**
(410) 263-3345
Lat N 38.985 Lon W 76.532

The Harley-Davidson Store of Baltimore, C-14
8845 Pulaski Hwy. **Baltimore**
(410) 238-2003
Lat N 39.338 Lon W 76.48

Harley-Davidson Shop of Ocean City, I-20
10716 Ocean Gateway **Berlin**
(410) 629-1599
Lat N 38.344 Lon W 75.189

Ramsey's Chesapeake Harley-Davidson, A-15
3938 Conowingo Rd. **Darlington**
(410) 457-4541
Lat N 39.647 Lon W 76.248

Harley-Davidson of Maryland, D-13
7010 Troy Hill Dr. **Elkridge**
(410) 796-1044
Lat N 39.197 Lon W 76.748

Harley-Davidson of Washington, G-12
9407 Livingston Rd. **Ft. Washington**
(301) 248-1200
Lat N 38.761 Lon W 76.995

Rockville Harley-Davidson, D-11
7830 Airpark Rd. **Gaithersburg**
(301) 948-4581
Lat N 39.17 Lon W 77.16

All American Harley-Davidson, H-13
8126 Leonardtown Rd. **Hughesville**
(301) 884-2800
Lat N 38.54 Lon W 76.788

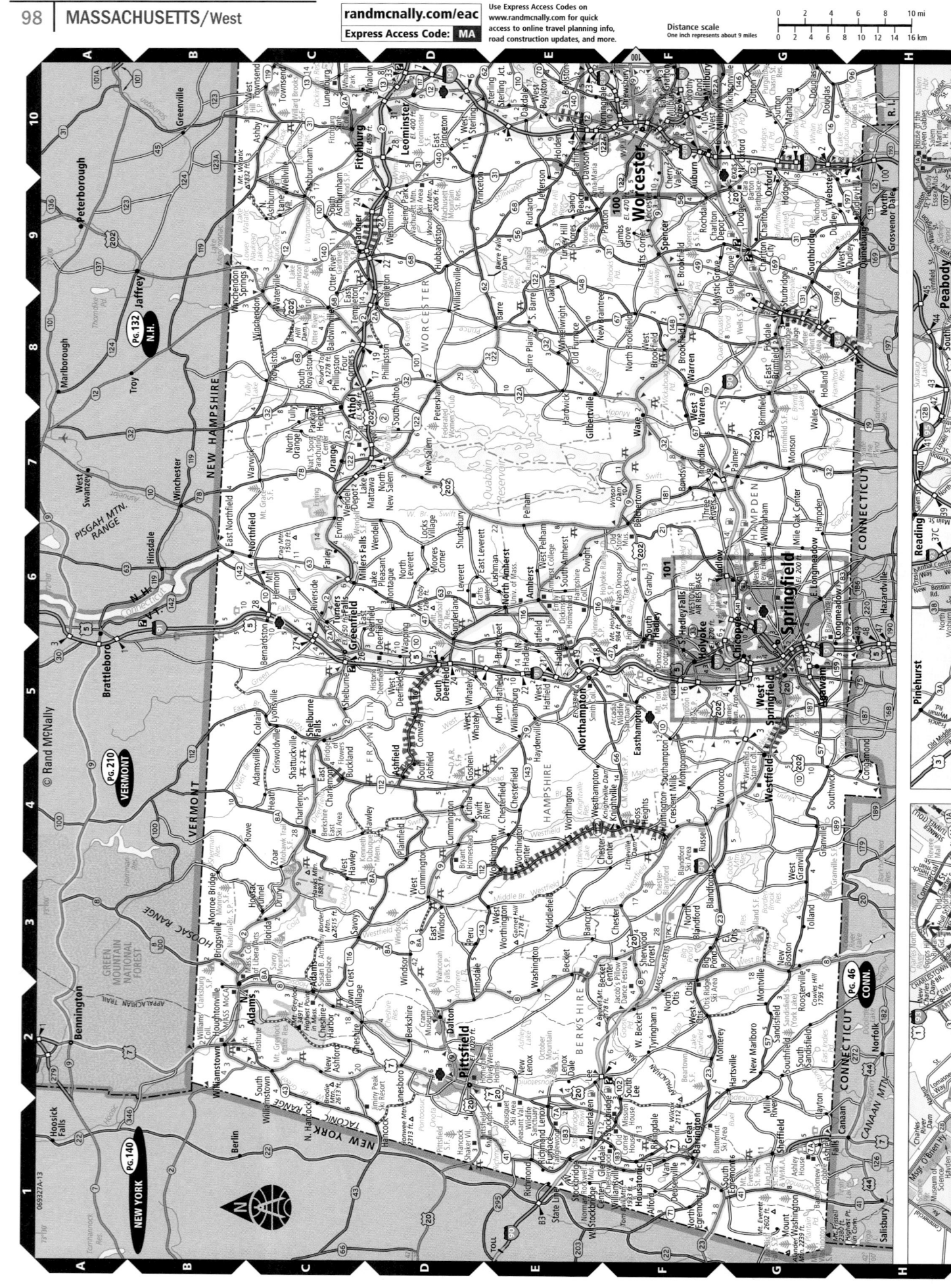

randmcnally.com/eac

Express Access Code: MA

Use Express Access Codes on
www.randmcnally.com for quick
access to online travel planning info,
road construction updates, and more.

How to determine distance

Mileages in red between red arrowheads; in black, between intersections.

SYMBOLS

- ━━━ Featured ride
- ━━━ Scenic route
- ▦ Long-term construction
- ▪ Historic site or monument; Indian reservation or rancheria; military installation; point of interest; wildlife refuge
- ⛟ Harley-Davidson dealership

For Massachusetts ride, see page R14-15.

MASSACHUSETTS MOTORCYCLE LAWS

Helmet use:
Required

Riding two abreast:
Yes. See state law for specifics

Eye protection:
Required for instructional permit holders
Required unless equipped with windscreen

Speed limit:
Primary roads: 65 mph
Secondary roads: 65 mph

MASSACHUSETTS RESOURCES

Road conditions or construction:
(617) 374-1234 (SmarTraveler, Greater Boston only)
www.state.ma.us/eotc/

Highway Emergency Numbers:
911

Tourism:
(800) 227-6277
(617) 973-8500
www.massvacation.com
State motor vehicle information:
(617) 351-4500
www.mass.gov/rmv

HARLEY-DAVIDSON DEALERSHIPS

⛟ **Sheldon's Harley-Davidson, F-10**
914 Southbridge St. **Auburn**
(508) 721-9876
Lat N 42.175 Lon W 71.875

⛟ **Aldo's Harley-Davidson, C-6**
203 South St. **Bernardston**
(413) 648-9302
Lat N 42.658 Lon W 72.561

⛟ **American Harley-Davidson, D-10**
1437 Central St. **Leominster**
(978) 537-6919
Lat N 42.482 Lon W 71.75

⛟ **Ronnie's Harley-Davidson, D-2**
501 Wahconah St. **Pittsfield**
(413) 443-0638
Lat N 42.474 Lon W 73.246

⛟ **Easthampton Harley-Davidson, F-5**
17 College Hwy. **Southampton**
(413) 527-1556
Lat N 42.252 Lon W 72.7

⛟ **Tibby's Harley-Davidson Sales, G-6**
227 Berkshire Ave. **Springfield**
(413) 781-0785
Lat N 42.129 Lon W 72.536

randmcnally.com/eac
Express Access Code: **MA**

Use Express Access Codes on www.randmcnally.com for quick access to online travel planning info, road construction updates, and more.

Distance scale
One inch represents about 9 miles

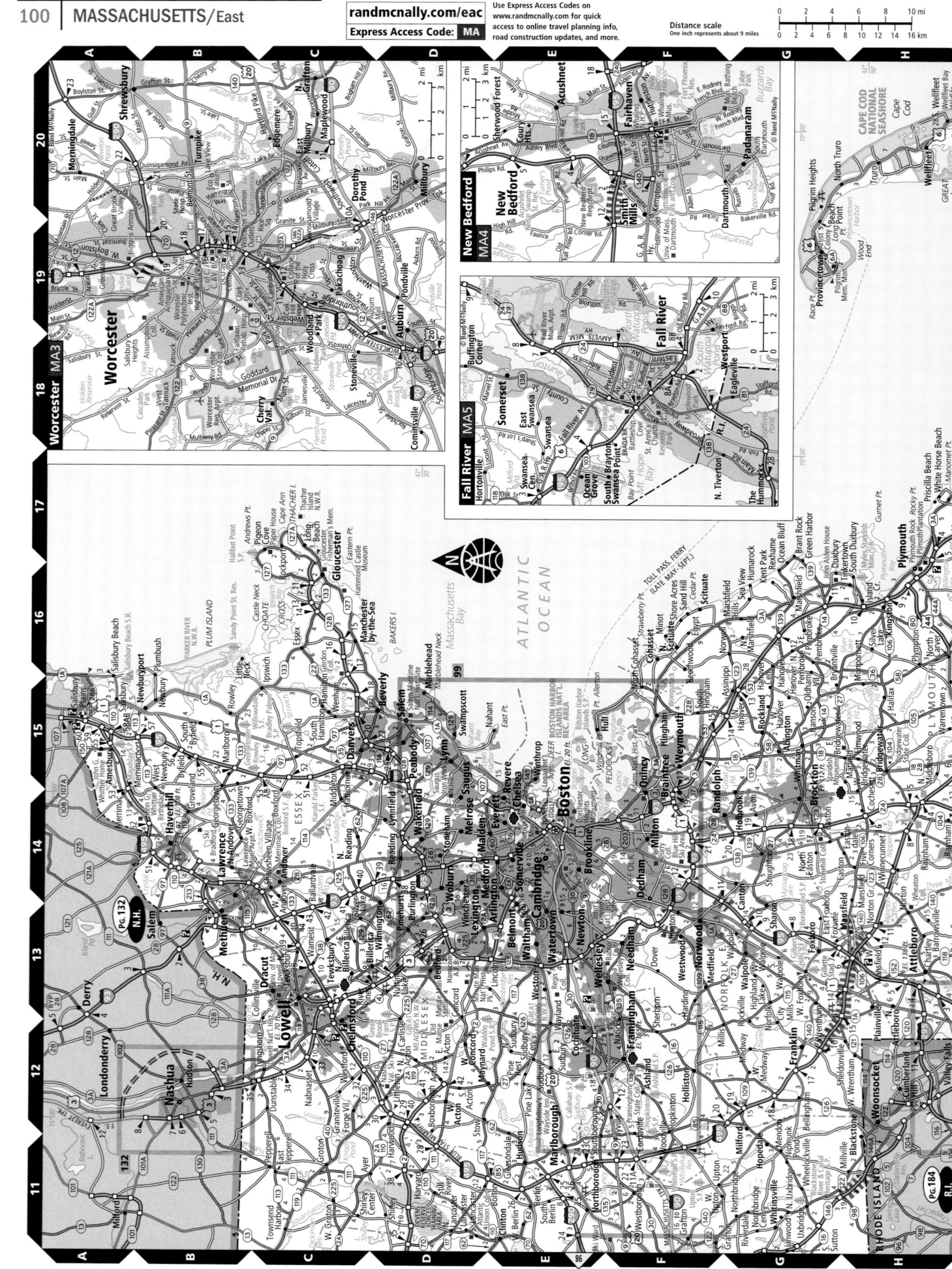

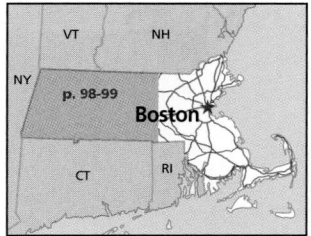

How to determine distance

Mileages in red between red arrowheads; in black, between intersections.

SYMBOLS

- ———— Featured ride
- ⫴⫴⫴ Long-term construction
- 🏍 Harley-Davidson dealership
- ≡≡≡ Scenic route
- ■ Historic site or monument; Indian reservation or rancheria; military installation; point of interest; wildlife refuge

CITY-TO-CITY MILEAGE

	BOSTON	GLOUCESTER	LOWELL	NEW BEDFORD	PITTSFIELD	PLYMOUTH	SPRINGFIELD	WORCESTER
Albany, NY	166	201	168	199	36	197	83	127
Boston		43	32	58	134	40	90	48
Brockton	24	67	51	37	149	24	105	63
Falmouth	71	114	104	40	186	35	142	103
Fitchburg	51	77	33	93	122	89	78	27
Gloucester	43		49	101	169	83	125	85
Greenfield	99	125	81	154	75	137	38	82
Hartford, CT	102	137	104	119	77	133	26	63
Lowell	32	49		85	136	72	92	51
New Bedford	58	101	85		167	45	123	84
North Adams	163	164	120	196	29	194	80	124
Northampton	102	137	104	135	56	133	19	63
Pittsfield	134	169	136	167		165	51	95
Plymouth	40	83	72	45	165		121	82
Providence, RI	50	93	71	32	131	53	87	43
Provincetown	117	160	149	92	238	81	194	155
Springfield	90	125	92	123	51	121		51
Worcester	48	85	41	84	95	82	51	

HARLEY-DAVIDSON DEALERSHIPS

🏍 **Boston Harley-Davidson, E-14**
1760 Revere Beach Pkwy. (Rte. 16) **Everett**
(617) 389-8888
Lat N 42.402 Lon W 71.046

🏍 **Paramount Harley-Davidson, F-12**
266-300 Waverly St. **Framingham**
(508) 879-6666
Lat N 42.278 Lon W 71.411

🏍 **Kelly's House of Harley-Davidson, C-13**
1 Chelmsford Rd. **North Billerica**
(978) 663-6298
Lat N 42.584 Lon W 71.292

🏍 **Harley-Davidson Cycle Center, J-17**
750 MacArthur Blvd. **Pocasset**
(508) 563-7387
Lat N 41.692 Lon W 70.588

🏍 **Monty's Cycle Shop, G-14**
751 N Main St. (Rte. 28) **West Bridgewater**
(508) 583-1172
Lat N 42.041 Lon W 71.009

🏍 **Big Boar Harley-Davidson, J-14**
1030 State Rd. (Rte. 6) **Westport**
(508) 674-5780
Lat N 41.647 Lon W 71.06

© Rand McNally

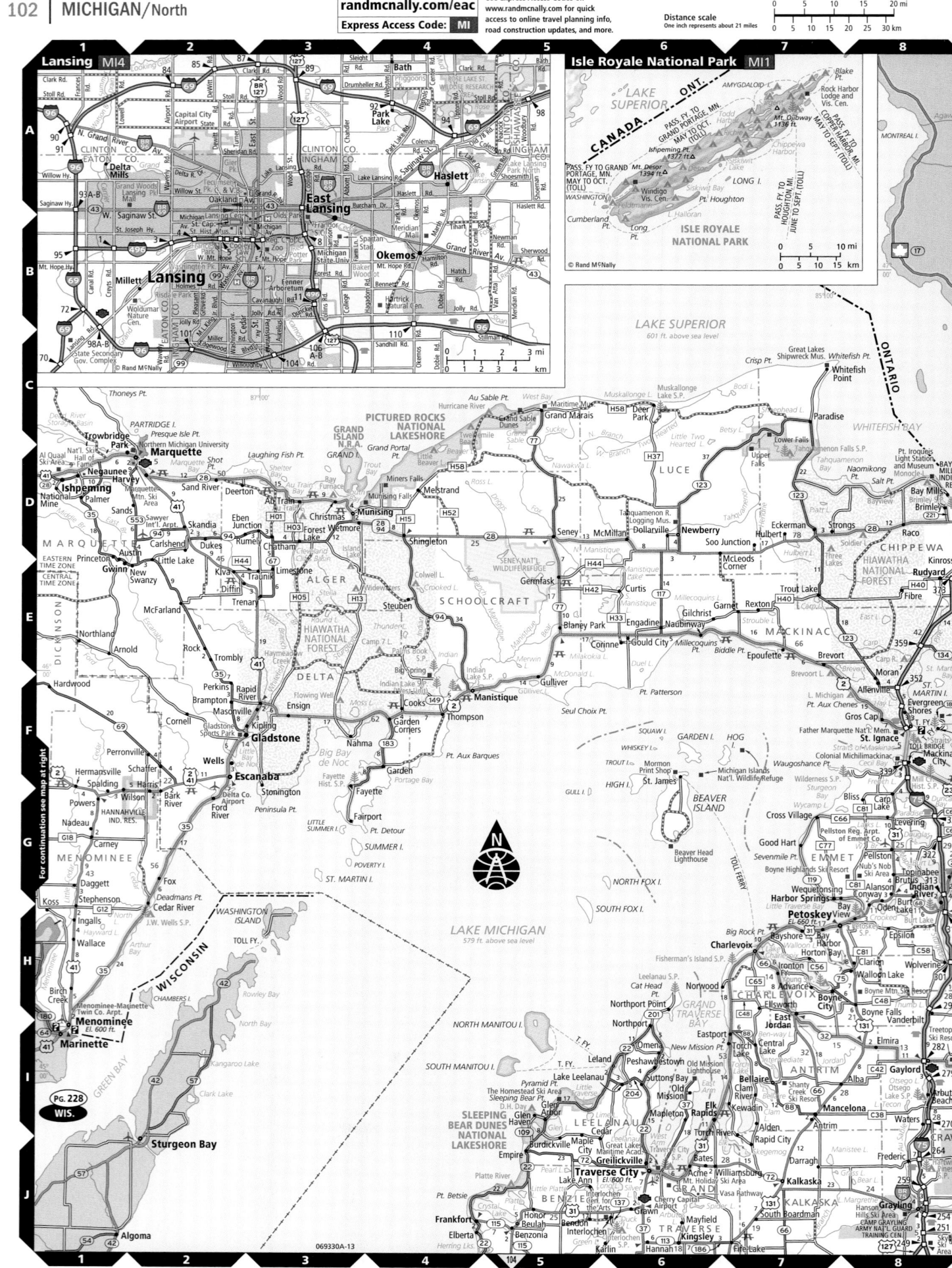

Use Express Access Codes on www.randmcnally.com for quick access to online travel planning info, road construction updates, and more.

Distance scale
One inch represents about 21 miles

Lansing MI4

Isle Royale National Park MI1

How to determine distance
Mileages in red between red arrowheads; in black, between intersections.
2 10 18 4 4
12 16 20

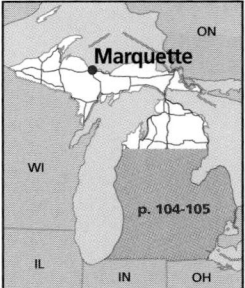

Marquette
ON
WI
p. 104-105
IL IN OH

SYMBOLS

Featured ride — Scenic route

Long-term construction

Harley-Davidson dealership

■ Historic site or monument; Indian reservation or rancheria; military installation; point of interest; wildlife refuge

MICHIGAN MOTORCYCLE LAWS

Helmet use:
Required

Riding two abreast:
Yes. See state law for specifics

Eye protection:
Required unless equipped with windscreen
Required at speeds over 35 mph

Speed limit:
Primary roads: 70 mph
Secondary roads: 65 mph

MICHIGAN RESOURCES

Road conditions or construction:
(800) 381-8477
(888) 305-7283 (for west and southwest Michigan)
(800) 641-6368 (Metro Detroit)
www.michigan.gov/mdot/

Highway Emergency Numbers:
911

Tourism:
(888) 784-7328
www.michigan.org

State motor vehicle information:
(517) 322-1460
www.michigan.gov/sos

HARLEY-DAVIDSON DEALERSHIPS

Northwoods Harley-Davidson, I-8
980 S Wisconsin Ave. **Gaylord**
(989) 732-8000
Lat N 45.018 **Lon** W 84.682

Northwoods Harley-Davidson, F-8
276 S Huron Ave. **Mackinaw City**
(231) 436-5331
Lat N 45.779 **Lon** W 84.726

Bald Eagle Harley-Davidson, D-2
2080 US 41 W **Marquette**
(906) 228-5330
Lat N 46.53 **Lon** W 87.397

Classic Motor Sports Harley-Davidson, J-6
3939 S Blue Star Dr. **Traverse City**
(231) 943-9344
Lat N 44.694 **Lon** W 85.656

Western Upper Peninsula

Saginaw MI2

© Rand McNally

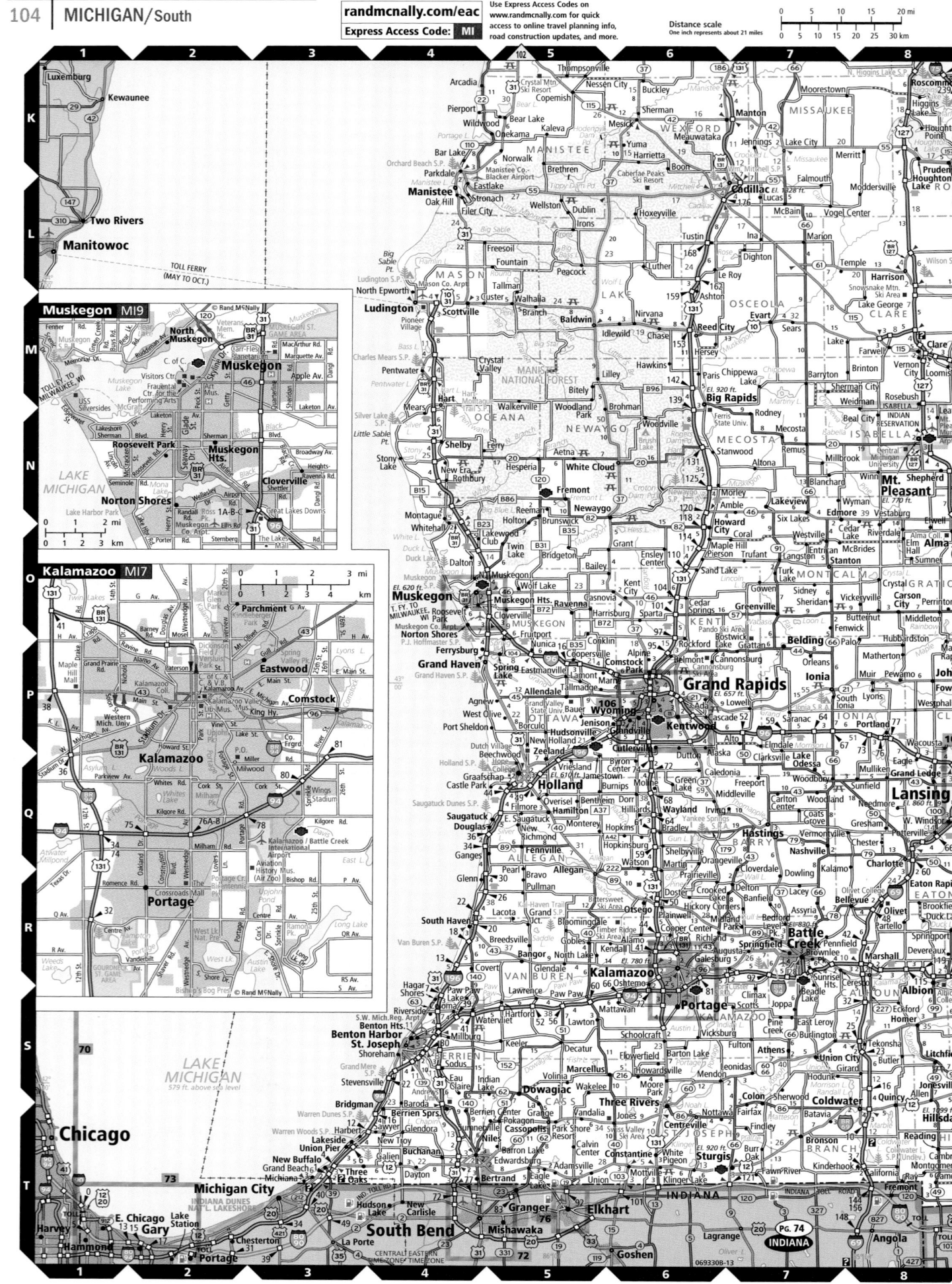

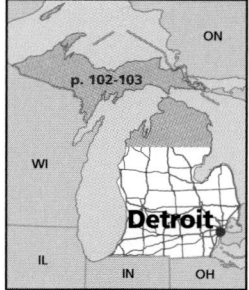

Detroit

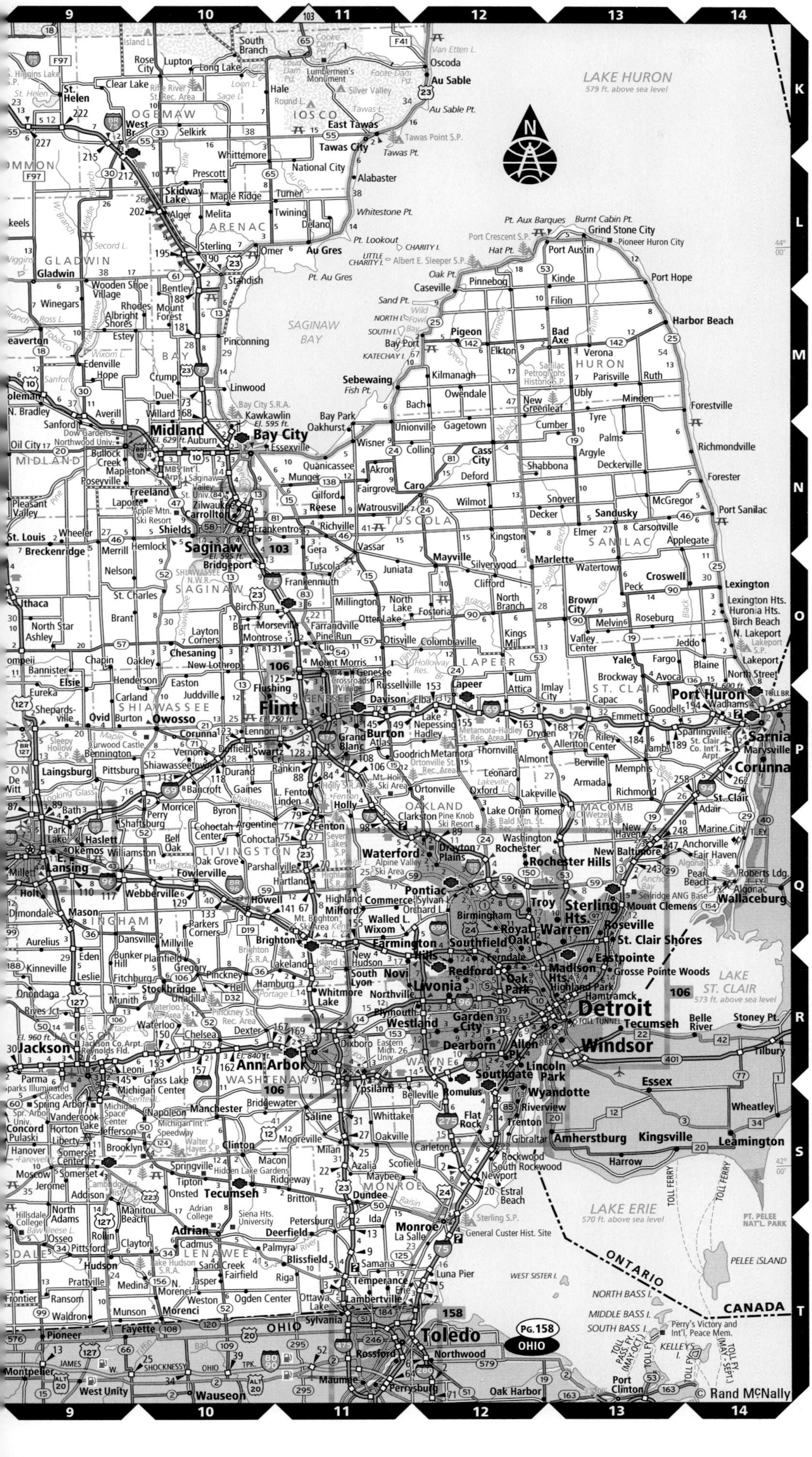

HARLEY-DAVIDSON DEALERSHIPS

For Ann Arbor, Detroit metro, Flint, and Grand Rapids areas, please see dealer listings on page 107.

- **Mahrle's Harley-Davidson, R-7**
  5738 Beckley Rd. **Battle Creek**
  (269) 979-2233
  Lat N 42.261 Lon W 85.183

- **Saginaw Valley Harley-Davidson, N-10**
  3850 S Huron Rd. **Bay City**
  (989) 686-0400
  Lat N 43.629 Lon W 83.915

- **Shiawassee Harley-Davidson, O-11**
  11901 N Beyer Rd. **Birch Run**
  (989) 624-4400
  Lat N 43.267 Lon W 83.794

- **Brighton Harley-Davidson, Q-11**
  5942 Whitmore Lake Rd. **Brighton**
  (810) 225-2915
  Lat N 42.517 Lon W 83.759

- **Town & Country Sports Harley-Davidson, S-9**
  US 12 & US 127 **Cement City**
  (517) 547-3333
  Lat N 42.061 Lon W 84.354

- **Capitol Harley-Davidson, Inc., Q-8**
  9550 Woodlane Dr. **Dimondale**
  (517) 646-2345
  Lat N 42.681 Lon W 84.650

- **Harley-Davidson at Birchwood Mall, P-14**
  4350 24th Ave. Unit 102 **Fort Gratiot**
  (810) 385-3763
  Lat N 43.036 Lon W 82.456

- **Sandy's Harley-Davidson Sport Center, N-5**
  11940 N Maple Island Rd. **Fremont**
  (231) 924-3020
  Lat N 43.466 Lon W 86.039

- **Wild Boar Harley-Davidson, P-5**
  2977 Corporate Grove Dr. **Hudsonville**
  (616) 896-0111
  Lat N 42.848 Lon W 85.857

- **Perry Harley-Davidson, R-6**
  5331 S Sprinkle Rd. **Kalamazoo**
  (269) 324-3400
  Lat N 42.24 Lon W 85.537

- **Ray C's Harley-Davidson of Lapeer, P-12**
  1422 Imlay City Rd. **Lapeer**
  (810) 664-9261
  Lat N 43.048 Lon W 83.288

- **C & S Harley-Davidson, N-8**
  4741 E Pickard St. (M-20) **Mt. Pleasant**
  (989) 772-5513
  Lat N 43.612 Lon W 84.753

- **Hot Rod Harley-Davidson, O-4**
  590 Ottawa St. **Muskegon**
  (231) 722-3653
  Lat N 43.242 Lon W 86.241

- **Gilbert's Harley-Davidson, P-14**
  3350 Lapeer Rd. **Port Huron**
  (810) 982-4351 (24 hours)
  Lat N 42.979 Lon W 82.466

- **Hamlin's Harley-Davidson, T-6**
  68951 White School Rd. **Sturgis**
  (269) 651-3424
  Lat N 41.797 Lon W 85.448

- **Biker Bob's Harley-Davidson Motown, S-12**
  14100 Telegraph Rd. **Taylor**
  (734) 947-4647
  Lat N 42.204 Lon W 83.269

- **Tecumseh Harley-Davidson Shop, S-10**
  8080 Matthews Hwy. **Tecumseh**
  (517) 423-3333
  Lat N 42.008 Lon W 83.985

- **Gildner's Harley-Davidson, K-9**
  2723 S M-76 **West Branch**
  (989) 345-1330
  Lat N 44.254 Lon W 84.21

randmcnally.com/eac
Express Access Code: MI

Use Express Access Codes on
www.randmcnally.com for quick
access to online travel planning info,
road construction updates, and more.

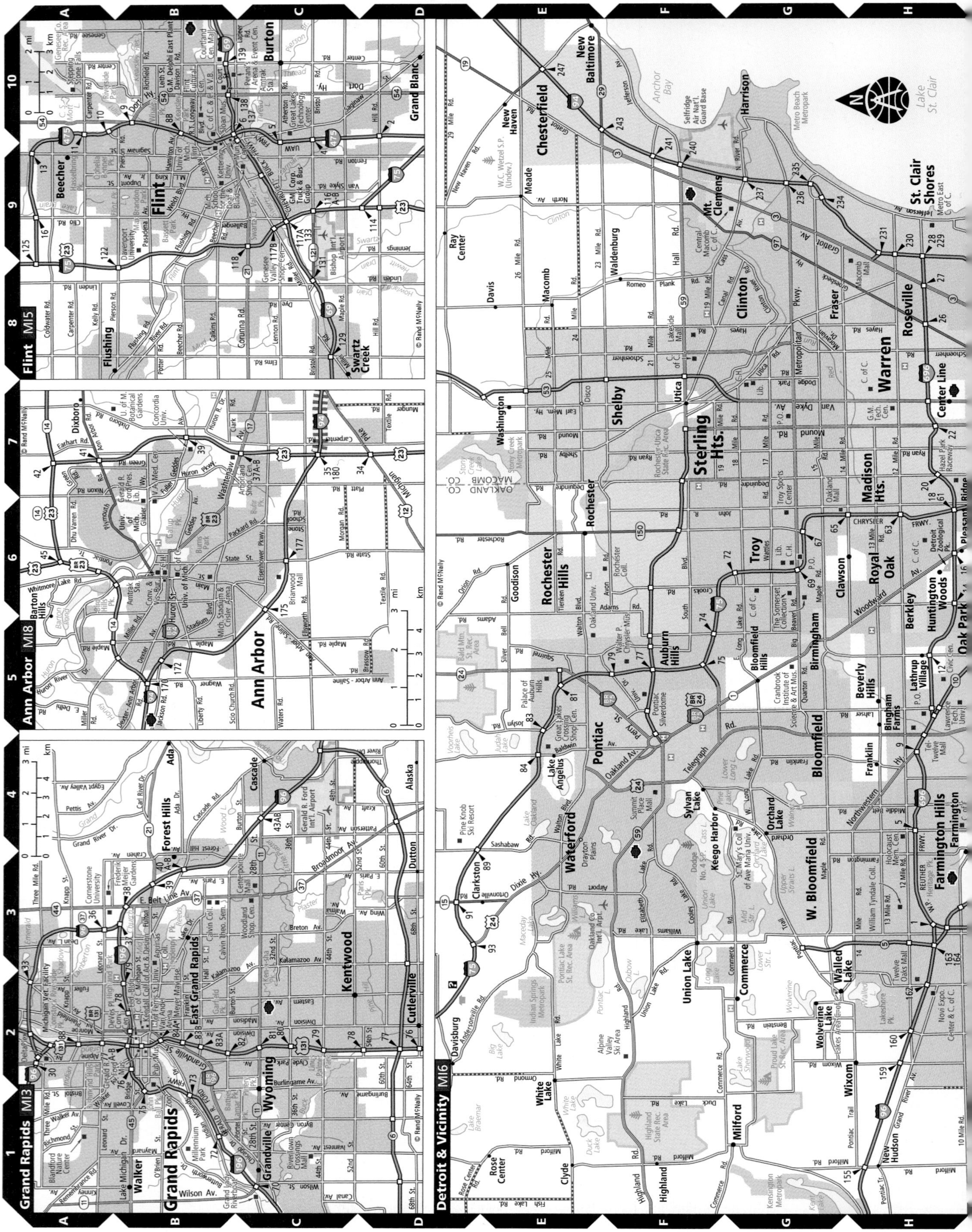

Flint MI5

Ann Arbor MI8

Grand Rapids MI3

Detroit & Vicinity MI6

Major cities and areas labeled on the maps include:

Beecher, Flushing, Flint, Swartz Creek, Burton, Grand Blanc

Dixboro, Barton Hills, Ann Arbor

Forest Hills, Cascade, Ada, Alaska, Dutton, Cutlerville, Kentwood, Wyoming, Grandville, Grand Rapids, East Grand Rapids, Walker

Washington, Ray Center, Meade, New Haven, New Baltimore, Chesterfield, Harrison, St. Clair Shores, Roseville, Center Line, Warren, Fraser, Clinton, Mt. Clemens, Waldenburg, Macomb

Shelby, Sterling Hts., Madison Hts., Utica, Rochester, Rochester Hills, Goodison, Troy, Clawson, Royal Oak, Berkley, Huntington Woods, Oak Park, Pleasant Ridge, Birmingham, Beverly Hills, Bingham Farms, Franklin, Bloomfield, Bloomfield Hills, Auburn Hills, Pontiac, Lake Angelus, Sylvan Lake, Keego Harbor, Orchard Lake, W. Bloomfield, Farmington Hills, Farmington, Walled Lake, Wixom, Commerce, Union Lake, Waterford, Drayton Plains, Clarkston, Davisburg, White Lake, Highland, Milford, New Hudson, Wolverine Lake, Rose Center, Clyde

© Rand McNally

How to determine distance

Mileages in red between red arrowheads; in black, between intersections.

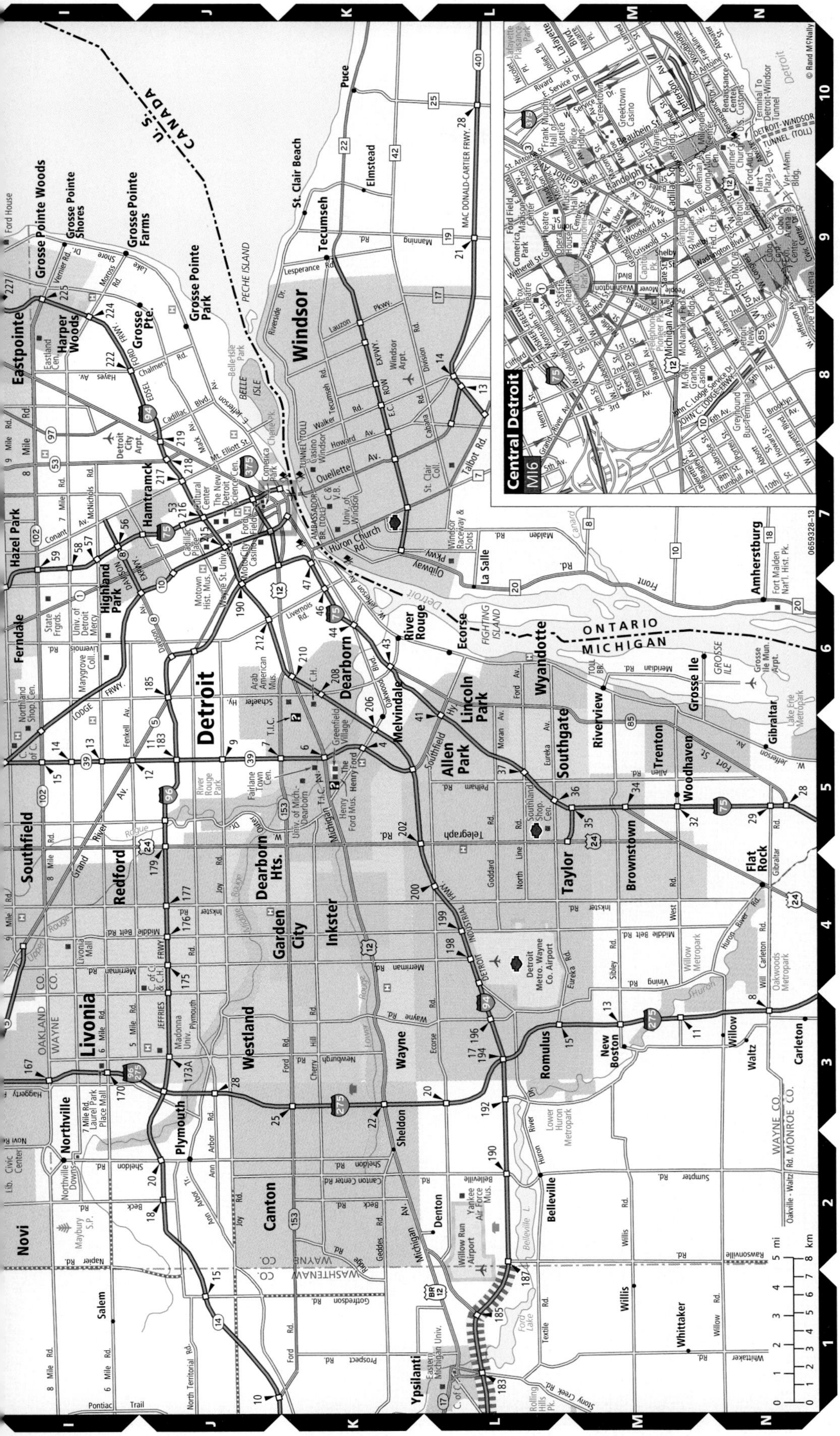

2 10 18 4 4
12 16 20

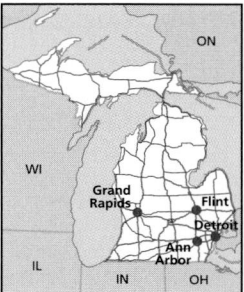

SYMBOLS

— Featured ride
▤ Scenic route
⊞ Long-term construction
■ Historic site or monument; Indian reservation or rancheria; military installation; point of interest; wildlife refuge
Harley-Davidson dealership

HARLEY-DAVIDSON DEALERSHIPS

American Harley-Davidson, B-5
5436 Jackson Rd. **Ann Arbor**
(734) 747-8008
Lat N 42.288 Lon W 83.836

Cummings Harley-Davidson Sales, B-10
5350 Davison Rd. **Burton**
(810) 234-6646
Lat N 43.033 Lon W 83.602

Detroit Harley-Davidson, H-7
25152 Van Dyke Rd. **Center Line**
(586) 756-1284
Lat N 42.479 Lon W 83.027

Wolverine Harley-Davidson, F-9
44660 N Gratiot Ave. **Clinton Township**
(586) 463-7700
Lat N 42.626 Lon W 82.863

Motown Harley-Davidson, L-4
830 Metro Airport 6-2B **Detroit**
(734) 229-5755
Lat N 42.22 Lon W 83.347

Motor City Harley-Davidson, H-3
34900 Grand River Ave. **Farmington Hills**
(248) 473-7433
Lat N 42.469 Lon W 83.391

Wild Boar Harley-Davidson Shop, C-2
624 28th St. SE **Grand Rapids**
(616) 243-1111
Lat N 42.913 Lon W 85.651

A.B.C. Harley-Davidson, F-3
4405 Highland Rd. (M-59) **Waterford**
(248) 674-3175
Lat N 42.644 Lon W 83.354

Distance scale
One inch represents about 23 miles

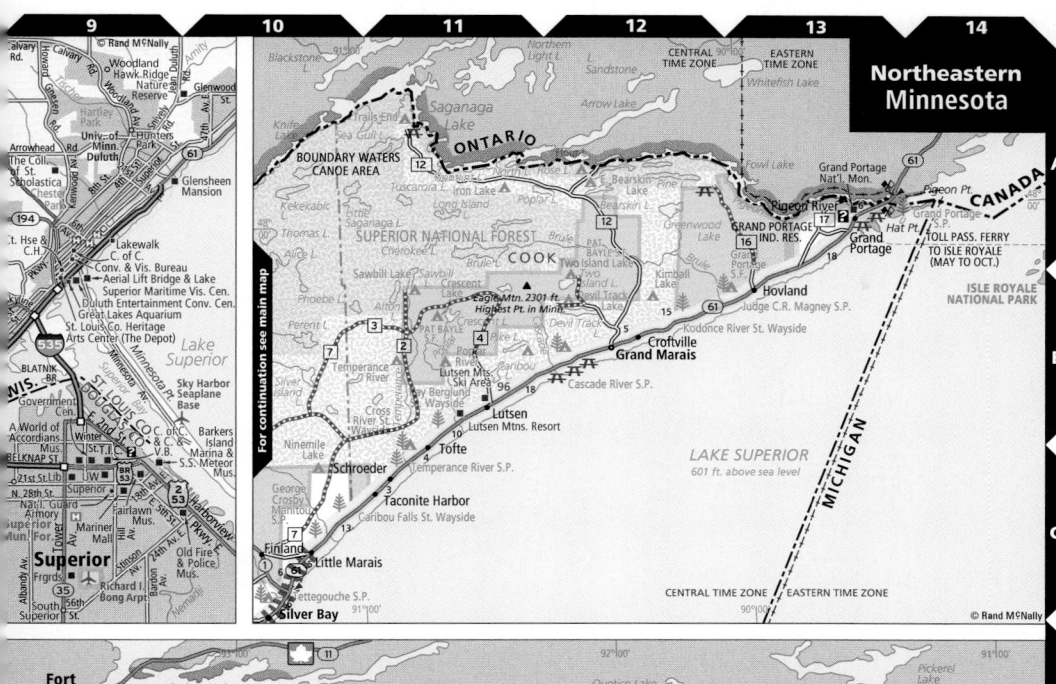

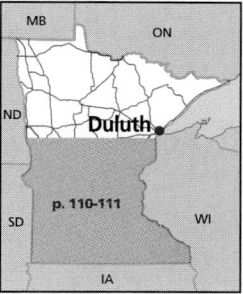

Northeastern Minnesota

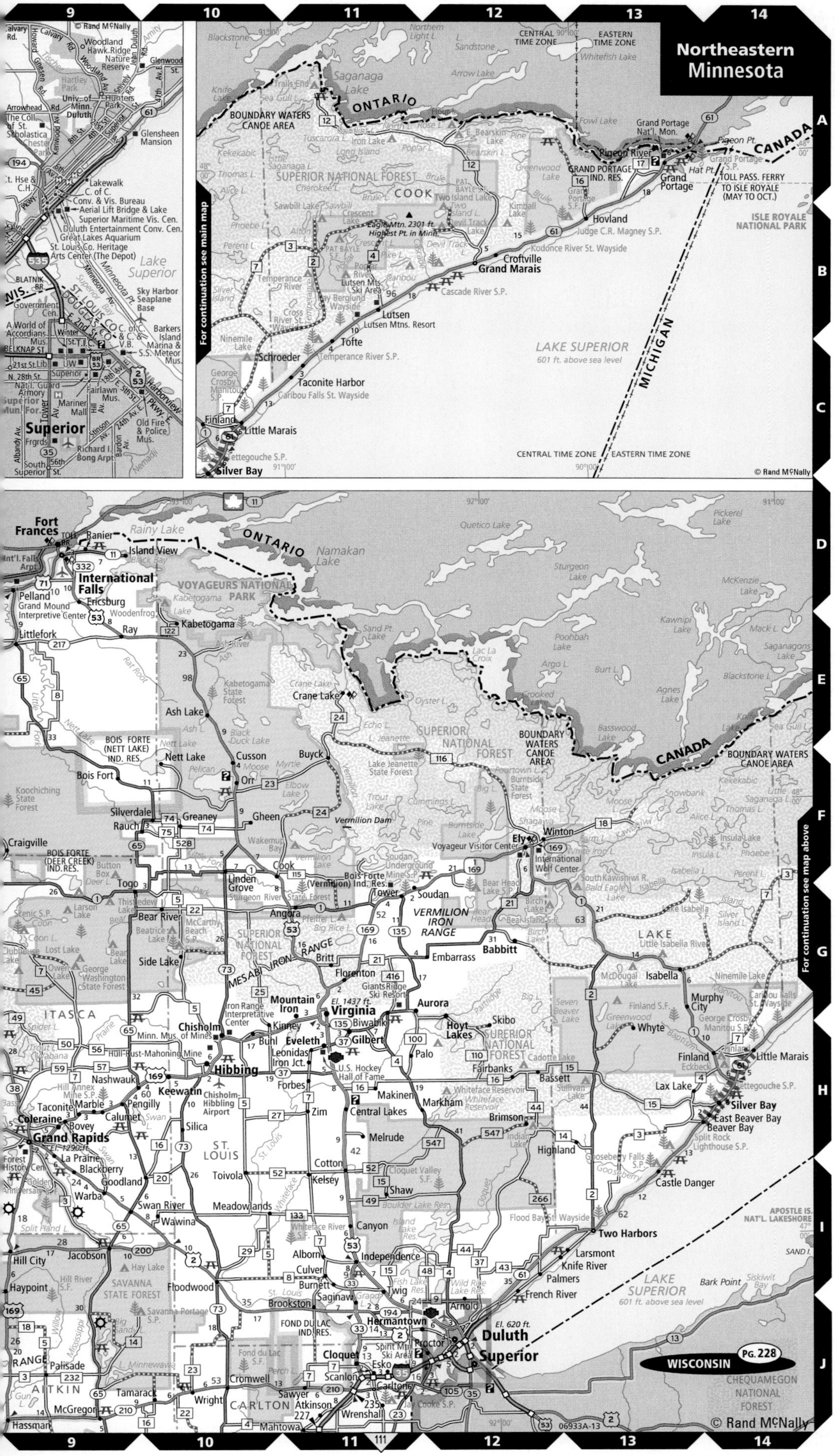

SYMBOLS

═══ Featured ride	═══ Scenic route
╫╫╫ Long-term construction	■ Historic site or monument; Indian reservation or rancheria; military installation; point of interest; wildlife refuge
Harley-Davidson dealership	

For Minnesota ride, see page R16.

MINNESOTA MOTORCYCLE LAWS

Helmet use:
Required under age 18 and for instructional permit holders

Riding two abreast:
Yes. See state law for specifics

Eye protection:
Required by law

Speed limit:
Primary roads: 70 mph
Secondary roads: 65 mph

MINNESOTA RESOURCES

Road conditions or construction:
511
(800) 542-0220
www.dot.state.mn.us

Highway Emergency Numbers:
911

Tourism:
(800) 657-3700
(651) 296-5029
www.exploreminnesota.com

State motor vehicle information:
(651) 296-6911
www.dps.state.mn.us/dvs

HARLEY-DAVIDSON DEALERSHIPS

🏍 **Harley-Davidson Sport Center, J-12**
4355 Stebner Rd. **Duluth**
(218) 729-9600
Lat N 46.827 **Lon** W 92.196

🏍 **Five Seasons Sports Center, H-11**
Box 360 Hwy. 53 **Eveleth**
(218) 744-5871
Lat N 47.428 **Lon** W 92.517

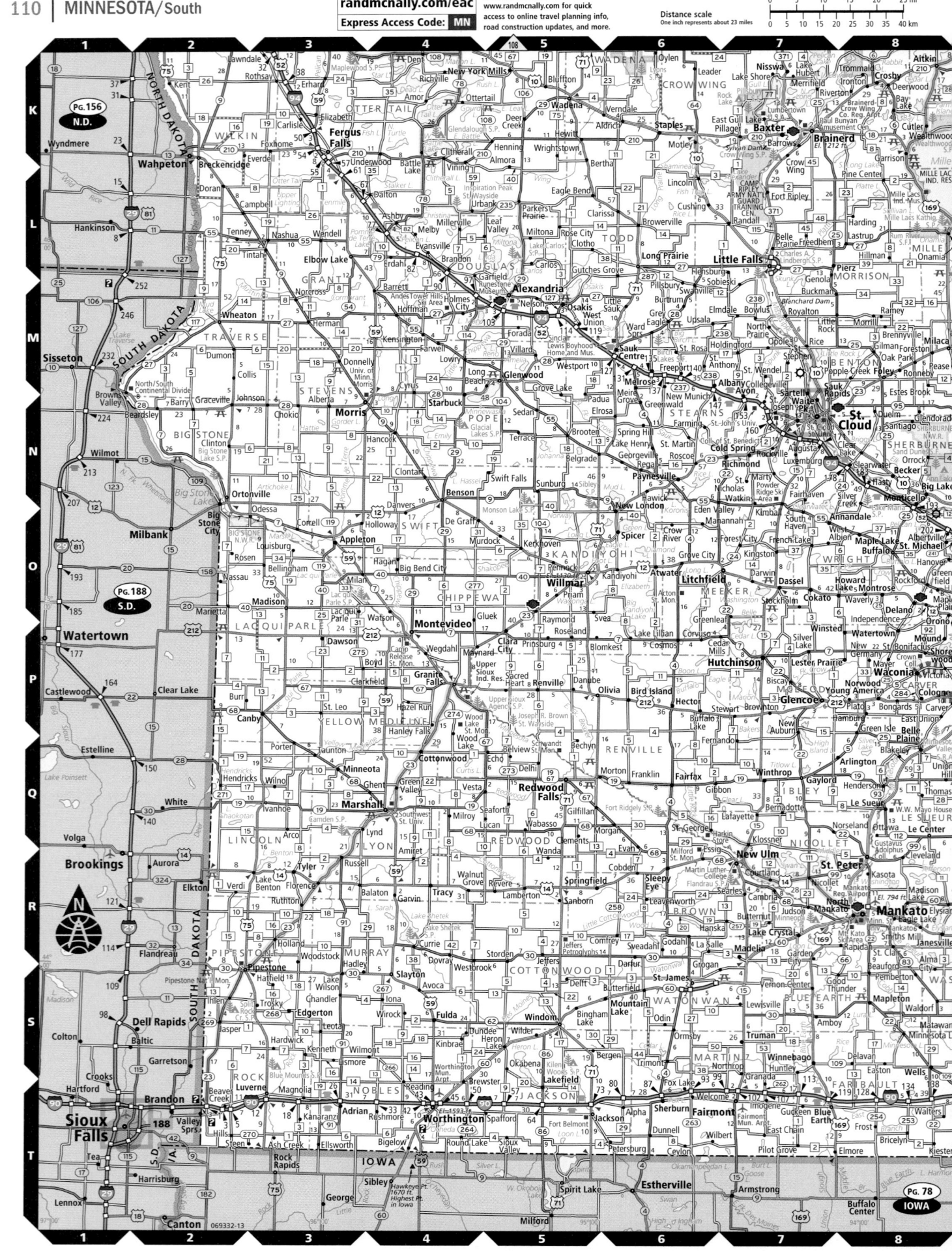

How to determine distance

Mileages in red between red arrowheads; in black, between intersections.

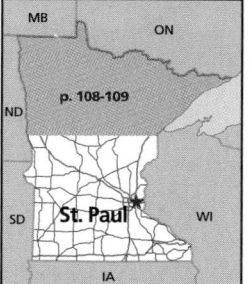

SYMBOLS

- —— Featured ride
- ▦ Long-term construction
- ● Harley-Davidson dealership
- ▨ Scenic route
- ■ Historic site or monument; Indian reservation or rancheria; military installation; point of interest; wildlife refuge

HARLEY-DAVIDSON DEALERSHIPS

For the Minneapolis/St. Paul metro area, please see dealer listings on page 113.

Bergdale Harley-Davidson, T-9
905 Plaza St. **Albert Lea**
(507) 373-5236
Lat N 43.661 **Lon** W 93.372

Apol's Harley-Davidson, M-5
1515 42nd Ave. West **Alexandria**
(888) 544-1791
Lat N 45.890 **Lon** W 95.366

Donahue Harley-Davidson Shop of Brainerd, K-7
15808 Edgewood **Baxter**
(218) 822-4434
Lat N 46.356 **Lon** W 94.244

Donahue Harley-Davidson, O-8
4354 US Hwy. 12 SE **Delano**
(763) 972-2677
Lat N 45.04 **Lon** W 93.796

Zylstra Harley-Davidson, N-9
19600 Evans St. NW **Elk River**
(763) 241-2000
Lat N 45.329 **Lon** W 93.56

Faribault Harley-Davidson, R-9
2704 W Airport Dr. **Faribault**
(507) 334-5130
Lat N 44.299 **Lon** W 93.29

Twin Cities Harley-Davidson, P-9
10770 165th St. W **Lakeville**
(952) 898-4515
Lat N 44.71 **Lon** W 93.283

Mankato Harley-Davidson, R-8
1200 N River Dr. **Mankato**
(507) 345-6077
Lat N 44.183 **Lon** W 94.008

Apol's Harley-Davidson Shop, O-5
Hwy. 23 **Raymond**
(320) 967-4511
Lat N 45.018 **Lon** W 95.209

Rochester Harley-Davidson, S-11
7180 Hwy. 14 E **Rochester**
(507) 288-9050
Lat N 44.003 **Lon** W 92.336

Donahue Harley-Davidson, N-7
3555 Shadowwood Dr. NE **Sauk Rapids**
(320) 251-6980
Lat N 45.582 **Lon** W 94.09

Harley-Davidson Shop of Winona, R-13
1845 Mobile Dr. **Winona**
(507) 454-4578
Lat N 44.026 **Lon** W 91.606

© Rand McNally

How to determine distance

Mileages in red between red arrowheads;
in black, between intersections.

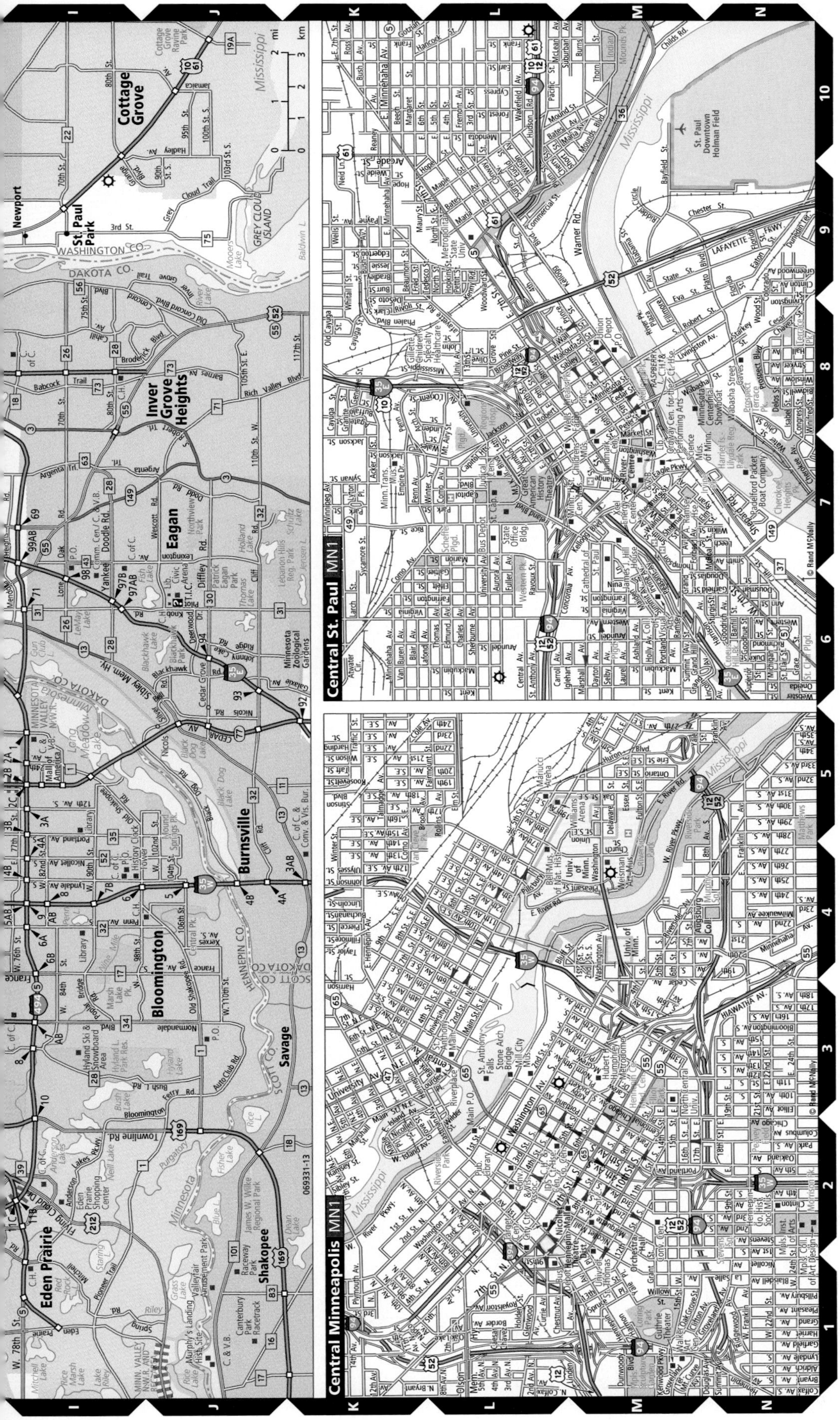

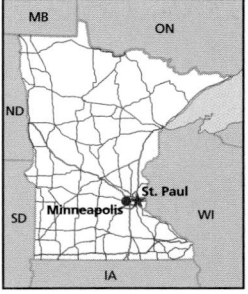

SYMBOLS

Featured ride	Scenic route
Long-term construction	■ Historic site or monument; Indian reservation or rancheria; military installation; point of interest; wildlife refuge
Harley-Davidson dealership	

CITY-TO-CITY MILEAGE

	BEMIDJI	DULUTH	MINNEAPOLIS	MOORHEAD	ROCHESTER	ST. CLOUD	SIOUX FALLS SD	ST. PAUL
Albert Lea	315	251	97	330	64	165	100	175
Austin	319	255	101	334	39	169	104	197
Bemidji		153	222	142	315	150	231	384
Brainerd	99	114	133	140	226	61	142	274
Duluth	153		157	254	235	143	151	423
Fairmont	296	306	152	357	119	146	155	121
Fergus Falls	141	211	184	55	277	120	193	236
Grand Forks, ND	113	264	318	80	411	254	327	318
Hibbing	108	76	196	216	274	178	190	462
International Falls	116	164	299	256	377	250	293	498
La Crosse, WI	389	239	164	400	72	235	154	297
Mankato	272	237	80	283	82	122	86	155
Marshall	261	276	155	202	193	133	161	90
Minneapolis	222	157		237	94	72	10	269
Moorhead	142	254	237		330	173	246	244
Red Wing	280	198	60	295	49	130	50	283
Rochester	315	235	94	330		165	84	236
St. Cloud	150	143	72	173	165		81	221
St. Paul	231	151	10	246	84	81		72
Sioux Falls, SD	384	423	269	244	236	221	272	
Willmar	194	209	96	174	186	66	106	156

HARLEY-DAVIDSON DEALERSHIPS

Twin Cities Harley-Davidson North, C-5
1441 85th Ave. NE **Blaine**
(763) 786-9079
Lat N 45.125 **Lon** W 93.234

St. Paul Harley-Davidson, G-9
2899 Hudson Blvd. **St. Paul**
(651) 738-2168
Lat N 44.949 **Lon** W 92.978

Twin Cities Harley-Davidson / Minneapolis-St. Paul International Airport, H-6
4300 Glumack Dr. **St. Paul**
(407) 447-3178
Lat N 44.883 **Lon** W 93.206

Central St. Paul MN1

Central Minneapolis MN1

randmcnally.com/eac

Express Access Code: MS

Use Express Access Codes on www.randmcnally.com for quick access to online travel planning info, road construction updates, and more.

Distance scale
One inch represents about 29 miles

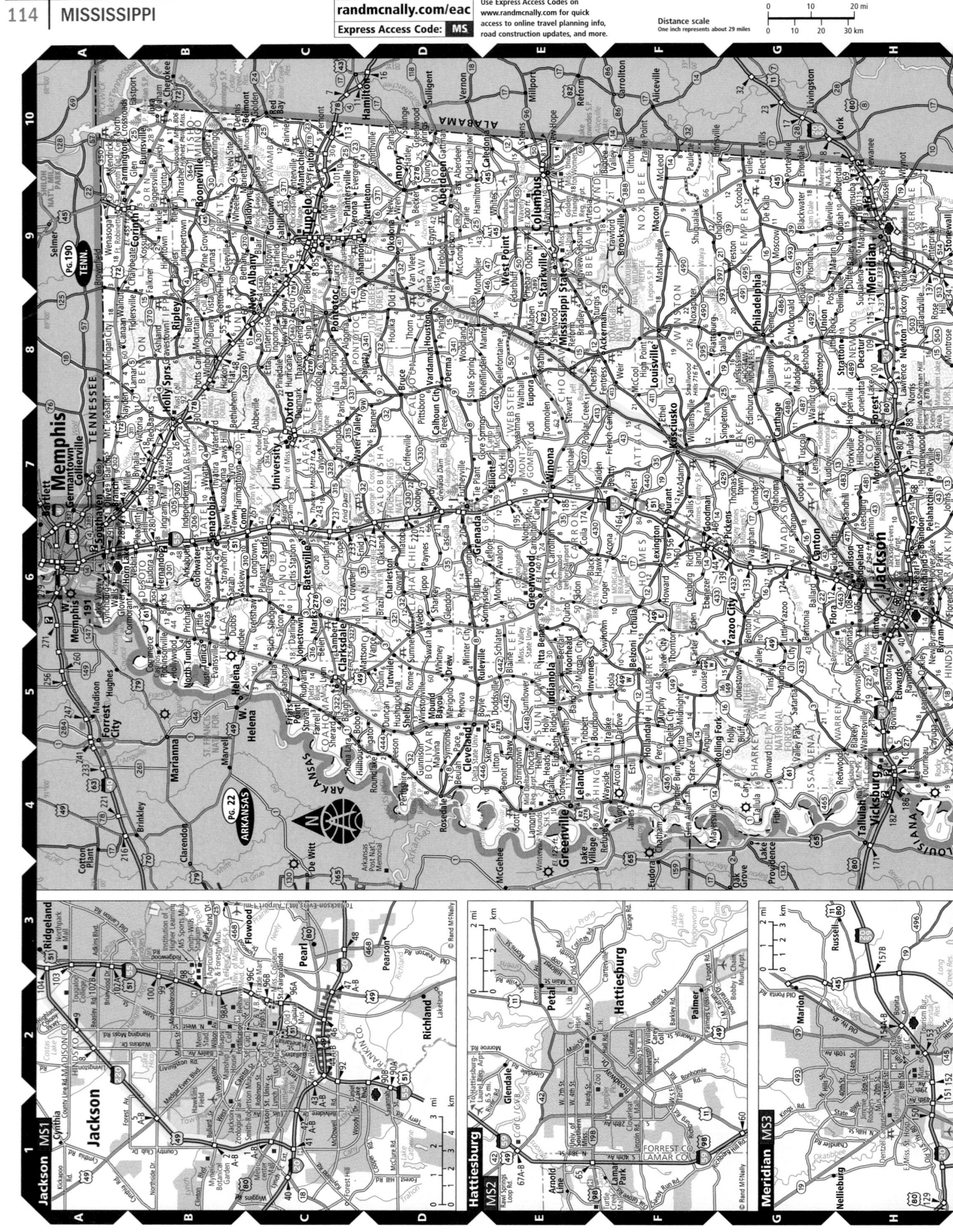

How to determine distance

Mileages in red between red arrowheads;
in black, between intersections.

© Rand McNally

SYMBOLS

- Featured ride
- Long-term construction
- Harley-Davidson dealership
- Scenic route
- Historic site or monument; Indian reservation or rancheria; military installation; point of interest; wildlife refuge

For Mississippi ride, see page R18-19.

MISSISSIPPI MOTORCYCLE LAWS

Helmet use:
Required

Riding two abreast:
No reference in administrative code or statutes

Eye protection:
Not required

Speed limit:
Primary roads: 70 mph
Secondary roads: 70 mph

MISSISSIPPI RESOURCES

Road conditions or construction:
(601) 987-1211
(601) 359-7301
www.mdot.state.ms.us

Highway Emergency Numbers:
911 or *HP

Tourism:
(800) 927-6378
(601) 359-3297
www.visitmississippi.org

State motor vehicle information:
(601) 987-1200
www.dps.state.ms.us

CITY-TO-CITY MILEAGE

	BILOXI	GREENVILLE	JACKSON	MEMPHIS, TN	MERIDIAN	NEW ORLEANS, LA	TUPELO	VICKSBURG
Biloxi		290	170	378	168	87	312	215
Greenville	290		120	147	192	300	193	101
Jackson	170	120		212	93	180	225	45
Memphis, TN	378	147	212		230	392	107	254
Meridian	168	192	93	230		196	144	138
Natchez	223	153	114	326	207	175	339	74
New Orleans, LA	87	300	180	392	196		340	225
Tupelo	312	193	225	107	144	340		267
Vicksburg	215	101	45	254	138	225	267	

HARLEY-DAVIDSON DEALERSHIPS

Mississippi Coast Harley-Davidson, M-9
941 Cedar Lake Rd. **Biloxi**
(228) 388-8700
Lat N 30.445 **Lon** W 88.934

Harley-Davidson of De Soto County, A-6
6935 Windchase Dr. **Horn Lake**
(662) 349-1099
Lat N 34.955 **Lon** W 90.049

Harley-Davidson of Jackson, H-6
3509 I-55 S **Jackson**
(601) 372-5770
Lat N 32.252 **Lon** W 90.214

Chunky River Harley-Davidson, H-9
584 Bonita Lakes Dr. **Meridian**
(601) 482-4131
Lat N 32.36 **Lon** W 88.672

randmcnally.com/eac
Express Access Code: MO

Use Express Access Codes on www.randmcnally.com for quick access to online travel planning info, road construction updates, and more.

Distance scale
One inch represents about 26 miles

How to determine distance

Mileages in red between red arrowheads; in black, between intersections.

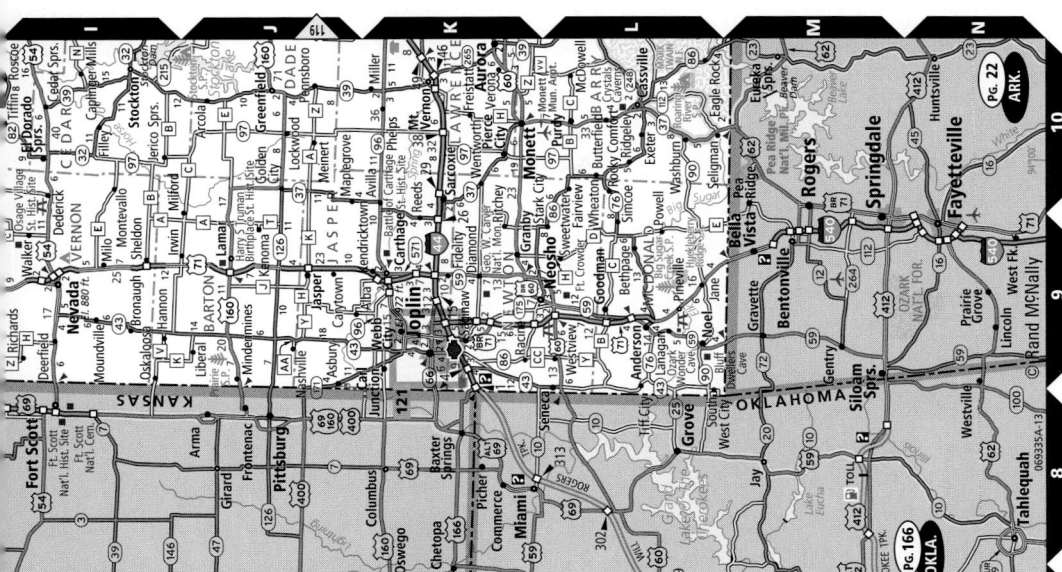

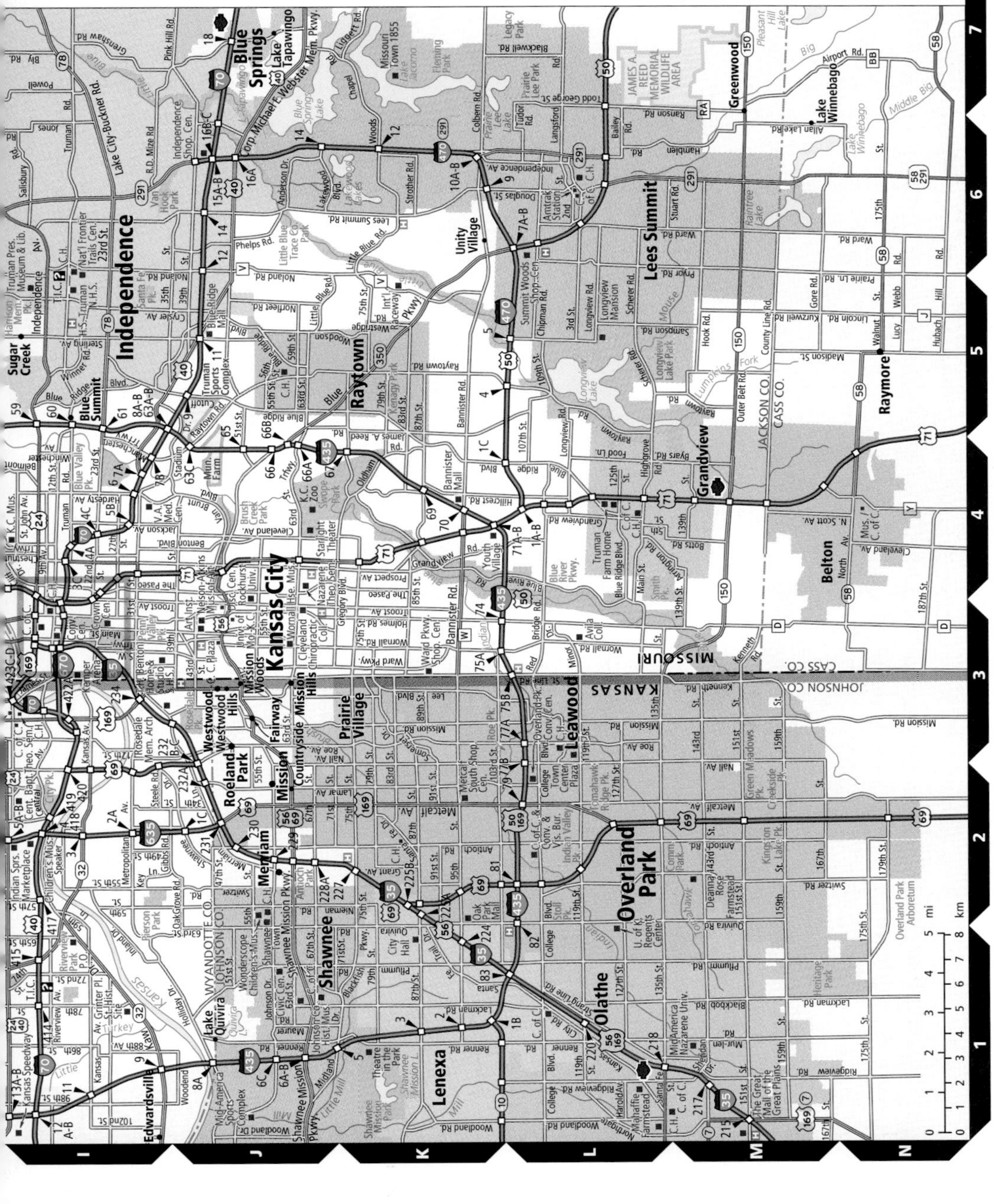

Kansas City
p. 118-119

SYMBOLS

- Featured ride
- Long-term construction
- Harley-Davidson dealership
- Scenic route
- Historic site or monument; Indian reservation or rancheria; military installation; point of interest; wildlife refuge

MISSOURI MOTORCYCLE LAWS

Helmet use:
Required

Riding two abreast:
No reference in administrative code or statutes

Eye protection:
Not required

Speed limit:
Primary roads: 70 mph
Secondary roads: 60 mph

MISSOURI RESOURCES

Road conditions or construction:
(800) 222-6400 (in MO)
www.modot.state.mo.us

Highway Emergency Numbers:
911 or *55

Tourism:
(800) 810-5500 (to request travel materials only)
(573) 751-4133
www.visitmo.com

State motor vehicle information:
(573) 751-4600
www.dor.state.mo.us/mvdl/drivers

HARLEY-DAVIDSON DEALERSHIPS

Blue Springs Harley-Davidson, F-9
3100 NW Jefferson St. **Blue Springs**
(816) 224-5005
Lat N 39.035 **Lon** W 94.3

Worth Harley-Davidson North, E-9
6609 N Oak Traffic Way **Gladstone**
(816) 420-9000
Lat N 39.214 **Lon** W 94.576

Gail's Harley-Davidson, F-9
5900 E Hwy. 150 **Grandview**
(816) 966-2222
Lat N 38.882 **Lon** W 94.521

Cycle Connection Harley-Davidson, K-9
I-44 (Exit 6) **Joplin**
(417) 623-1054
Lat N 37.044 **Lon** W 94.512

St. Joe Harley-Davidson, D-8
4020 S 169 Hwy. **St. Joseph**
(816) 233-9061
Lat N 39.733 **Lon** W 94.821

randmcnally.com/eac
Express Access Code: MO

Use Express Access Codes on www.randmcnally.com for quick access to online travel planning info, road construction updates, and more.

Distance scale
One inch represents about 26 miles

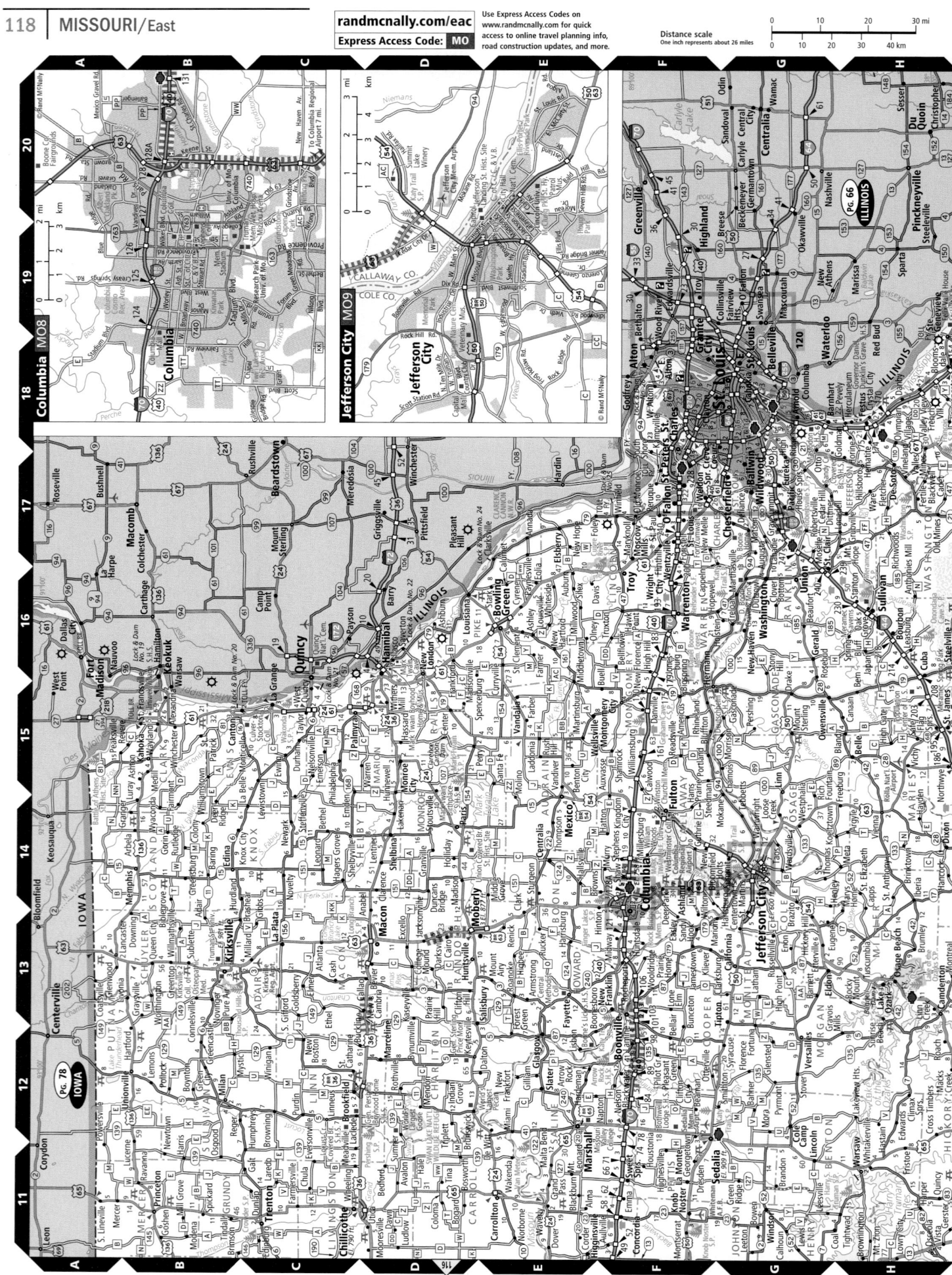

Columbia MO8

Jefferson City MO9

How to determine distance

Mileages in red between red arrowheads; in black, between intersections.

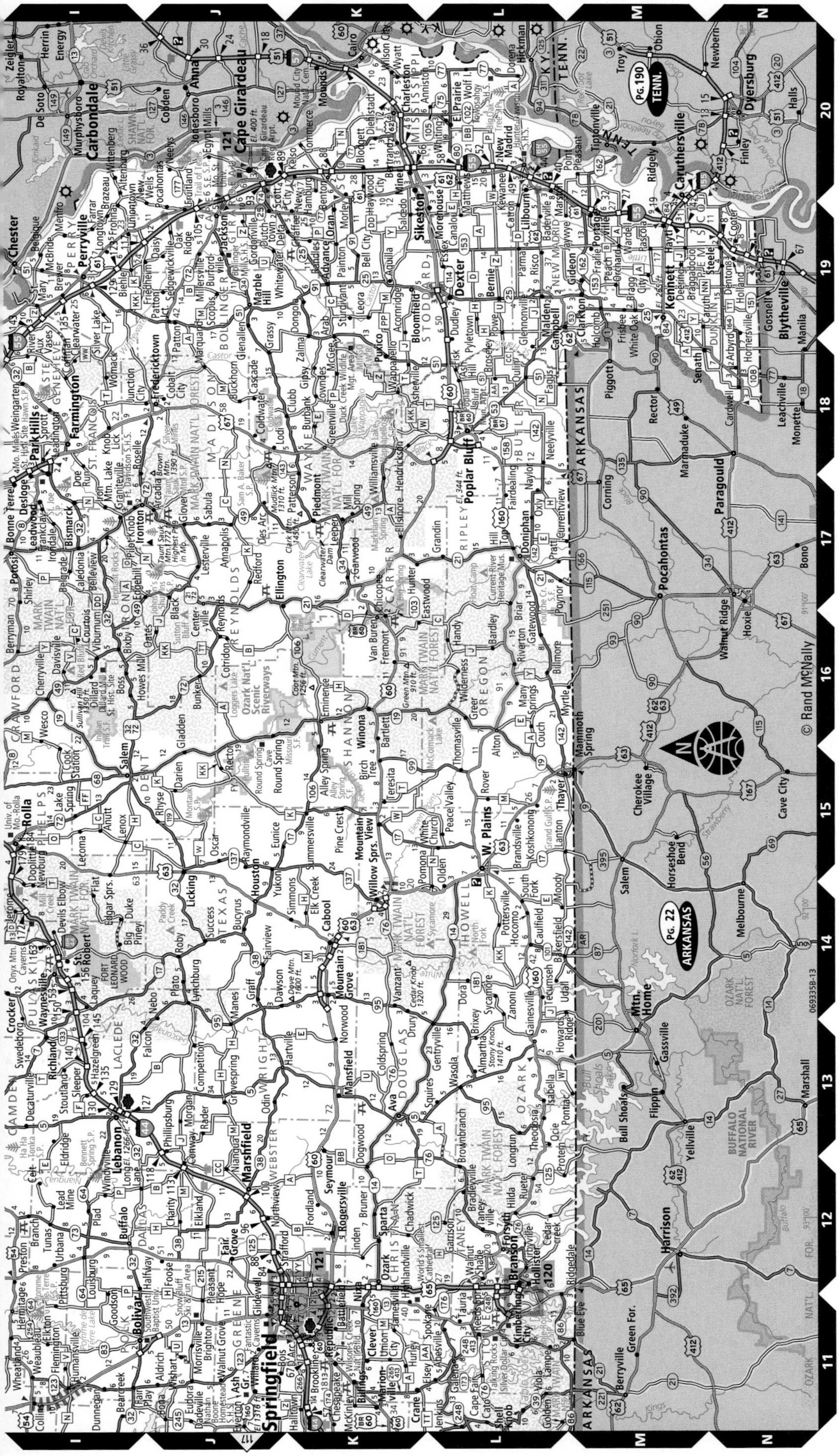

p. 116–117
St. Louis

SYMBOLS

Featured ride	Scenic route
Long-term construction	▪ Historic site or monument; Indian reservation or rancheria; military installation; point of interest; wildlife refuge
Harley-Davidson dealership	

CITY-TO-CITY MILEAGE

	CAPE GIRARDEAU	COLUMBIA	JOPLIN	KANSAS CITY	POPLAR BLUFF	ST. JOSEPH	ST. LOUIS	SPRINGFIELD
Branson	342	205	112	211	219	265	250	42
Brookfield	320	97	274	117	357	100	217	200
Cape Girardeau		227	374	356	84	412	114	304
Columbia	227		237	129	264	185	124	167
Hannibal	219	97	312	213	256	196	116	242
Hayti	81	304	326	433	63	489	191	256
Jefferson City	236	31	206	160	222	216	133	136
Joplin	374	237		150	263	202	282	72
Kansas City	356	129	150		393	54	253	169
Kirksville	320	97	315	158	377	141	217	260
Maryville	452	225	242	94	489	42	349	263
Osage Beach	257	76	161	173	230	229	165	91
Poplar Bluff	84	264	263	393		449	151	193
Rolla	197	93	178	222	170	278	105	108
St. Joseph	412	185	202	54	449		309	223
St. Louis	114	124	282	253	151	309		212
Springfield	304	167	72	169	193	223	212	
West Plains	186	192	180	279	102	333	204	110

HARLEY-DAVIDSON DEALERSHIPS

For the St. Louis metro area, please see dealer listings on page 121.

Mid America Harley-Davidson, F-14
5704 Freedom Dr. **Columbia**
(573) 875-4444
Lat N 38.962 Lon W 92.252

Gary Surdyke Harley-Davidson, H-18
2435 Hwy. 67 S **Festus**
(636) 931-8700
Lat N 38.178 Lon W 90.446

Ozark Harley-Davidson, I-13
2300 Evergreen Pkwy. **Lebanon**
(417) 532-2900
Lat N 37.636 Lon W 92.48

Lake of the Ozarks Harley-Davidson Shop, H-13
6482 Hwy. 54 **Osage Beach**
(573) 302-7600
Lat N 38.099 Lon W 92.685

Minor's Harley-Davidson Sales, J-20
2100 E Outer Rd. N (Exit 91) **Scott City**
(800) 474-0516
Lat N 37.227 Lon W 89.559

Yeager Cycle Sales, G-12
3001 S Limit (Hwy. 65) **Sedalia**
(660) 826-2925
Lat N 38.686 Lon W 93.251

Denney's Harley-Davidson of Springfield, K-11
3980 W Sunshine St. **Springfield**
(417) 882-0100
Lat N 37.181 Lon W 93.361

Bourbeuse Valley Harley-Davidson, G-17
1418 Hwy. AT **Villa Ridge**
(636) 742-2707
Lat N 38.459 Lon W 90.879

© Rand McNally

randmcnally.com/eac
Use Express Access Codes on
www.randmcnally.com for quick
access to online travel planning info,
road construction updates, and more.
Express Access Code: **MO**

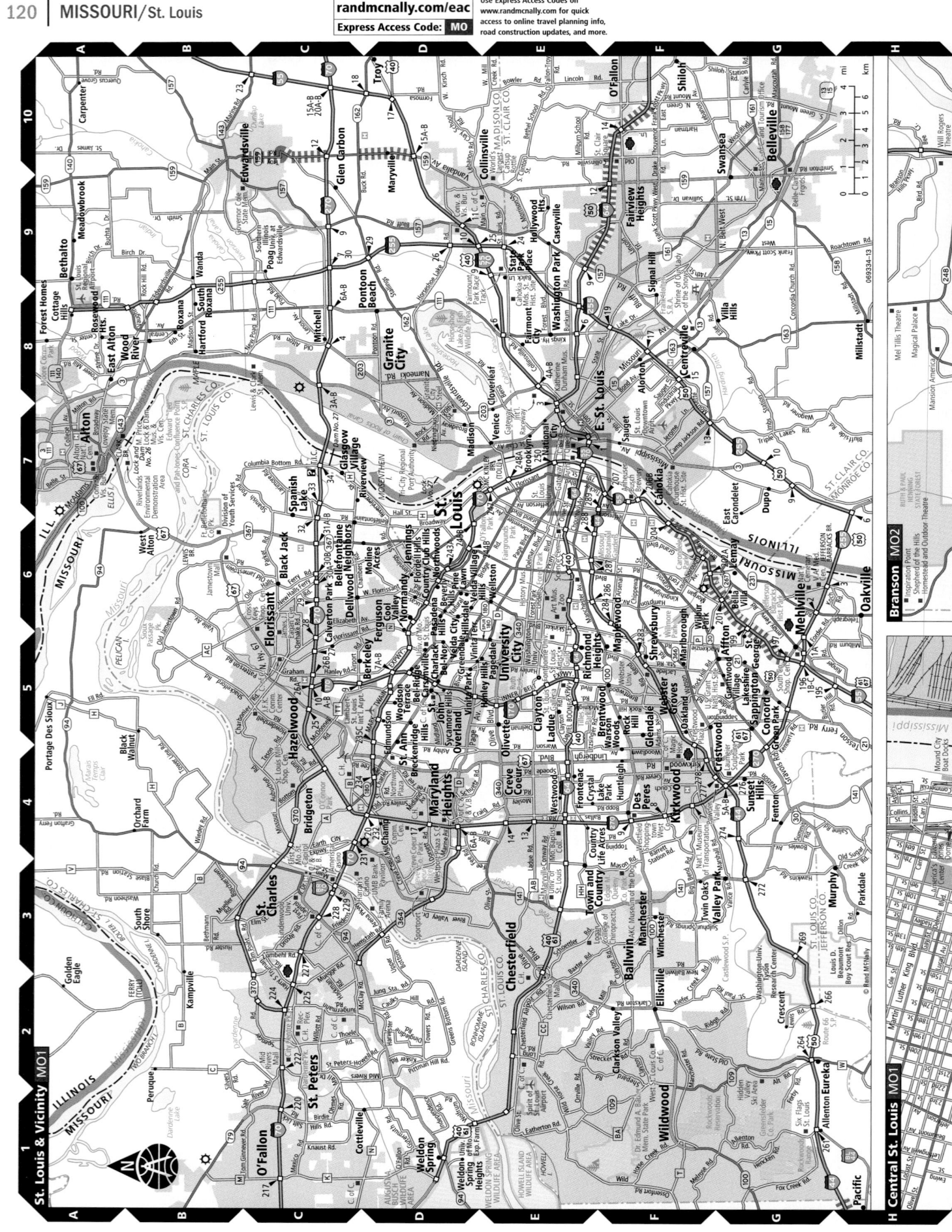

How to determine distance

2
10
18
4
4
12
16
20

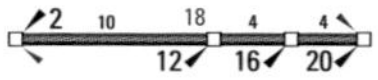

Mileages in red between red arrowheads; in black, between intersections.

Branson
Hollister
Point Lookout
East St. Louis
Cape Girardeau MO5
Cape Girardeau
East Cape Girardeau
Springfield MO4
Springfield
Joplin MO3
Joplin
Webb City
Carterville
Prosperity
Duquesne
Airport Drive
Tuckahoe
Lone Elm
Silver Creek
Leawood
Dennis Acres
Shoal Creek Drive
© Rand McNally

IA
IL
KS
St. Louis
Joplin
Springfield
Cape Girardeau
Branson
OK
AR
TN

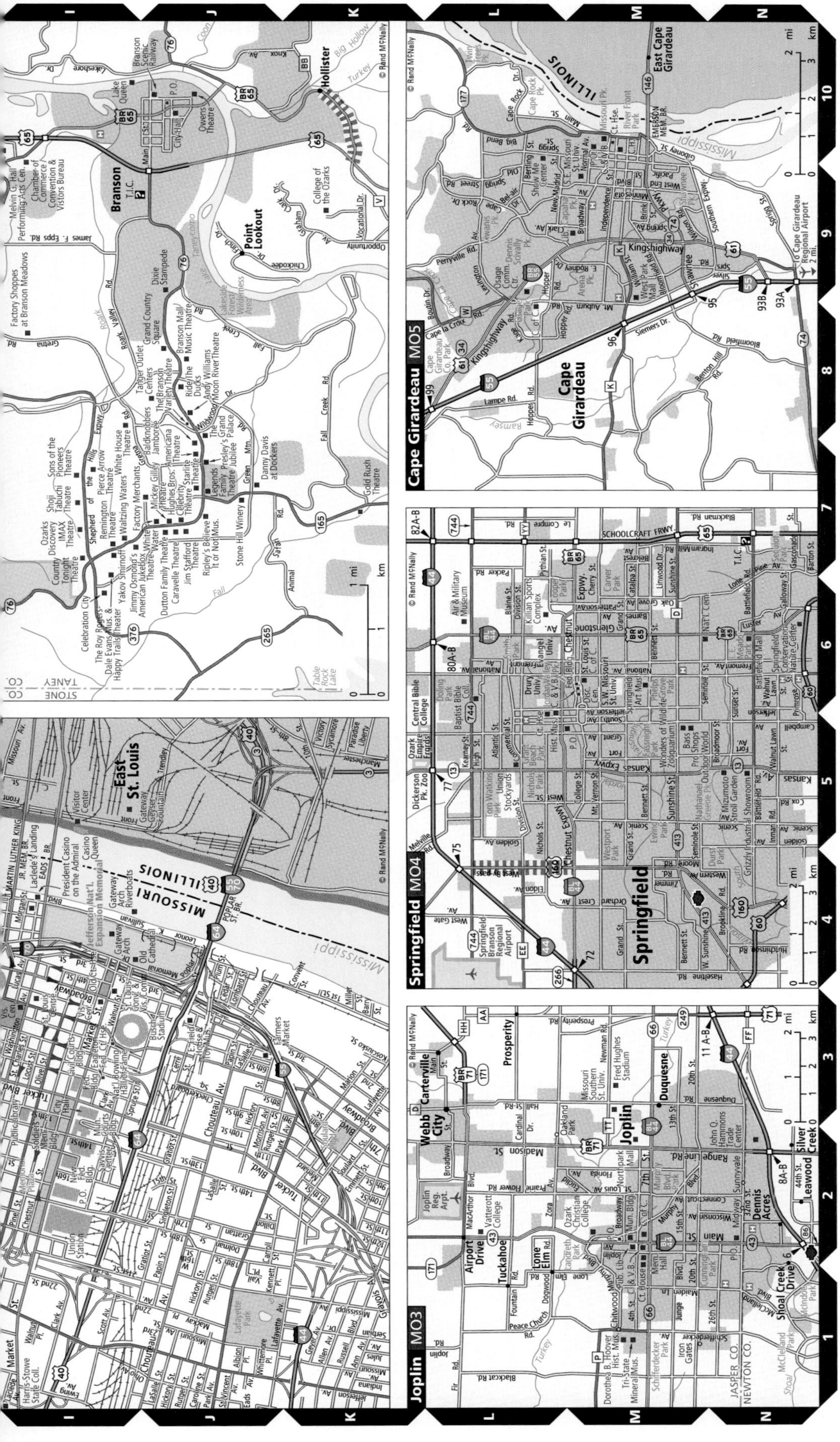

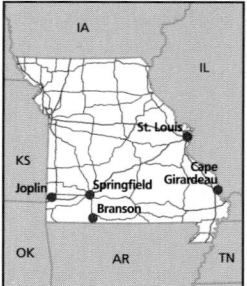

SYMBOLS

- Featured ride
- Scenic route
- Long-term construction
- Historic site or monument; Indian reservation or rancheria; military installation; point of interest; wildlife refuge
- Harley-Davidson dealership

MISSOURI MOTORCYCLE LAWS

Helmet use:
Required

Riding two abreast:
No reference in administrative code or statutes

Eye protection:
Not required

Speed limit:
Primary roads: 70 mph
Secondary roads: 60 mph

MISSOURI RESOURCES

Road conditions or construction:
(800) 222-6400 (in MO)
www.modot.state.mo.us

Highway Emergency Numbers:
911 or *55

Tourism:
(573) 751-4133
www.visitmo.com

State motor vehicle information:
(573) 751-4600
www.dor.state.mo.us/mvdl/drivers

HARLEY-DAVIDSON DEALERSHIPS

Doc's Harley-Davidson Motorcycle Sales & Service, F-4
930 S Kirkwood Rd. **Kirkwood**
(314) 965-0166
Lat N 38.568 **Lon** W 90.407

Bob Schultz Harley-Davidson, C-3
3830 W Clay St. **St. Charles**
(636) 946-6487
Lat N 38.792 **Lon** W 90.56

Gateway to the West Harley-Davidson, G-6
3600 LeMay Ferry Rd. **St. Louis**
(314) 845-9900
Lat N 38.511 **Lon** W 90.32

randmcnally.com/eac
Express Access Code: MT
Use Express Access Codes on
www.randmcnally.com for quick
access to online travel planning info,
road construction updates, and more.

Distance scale
One inch represents about 31 miles

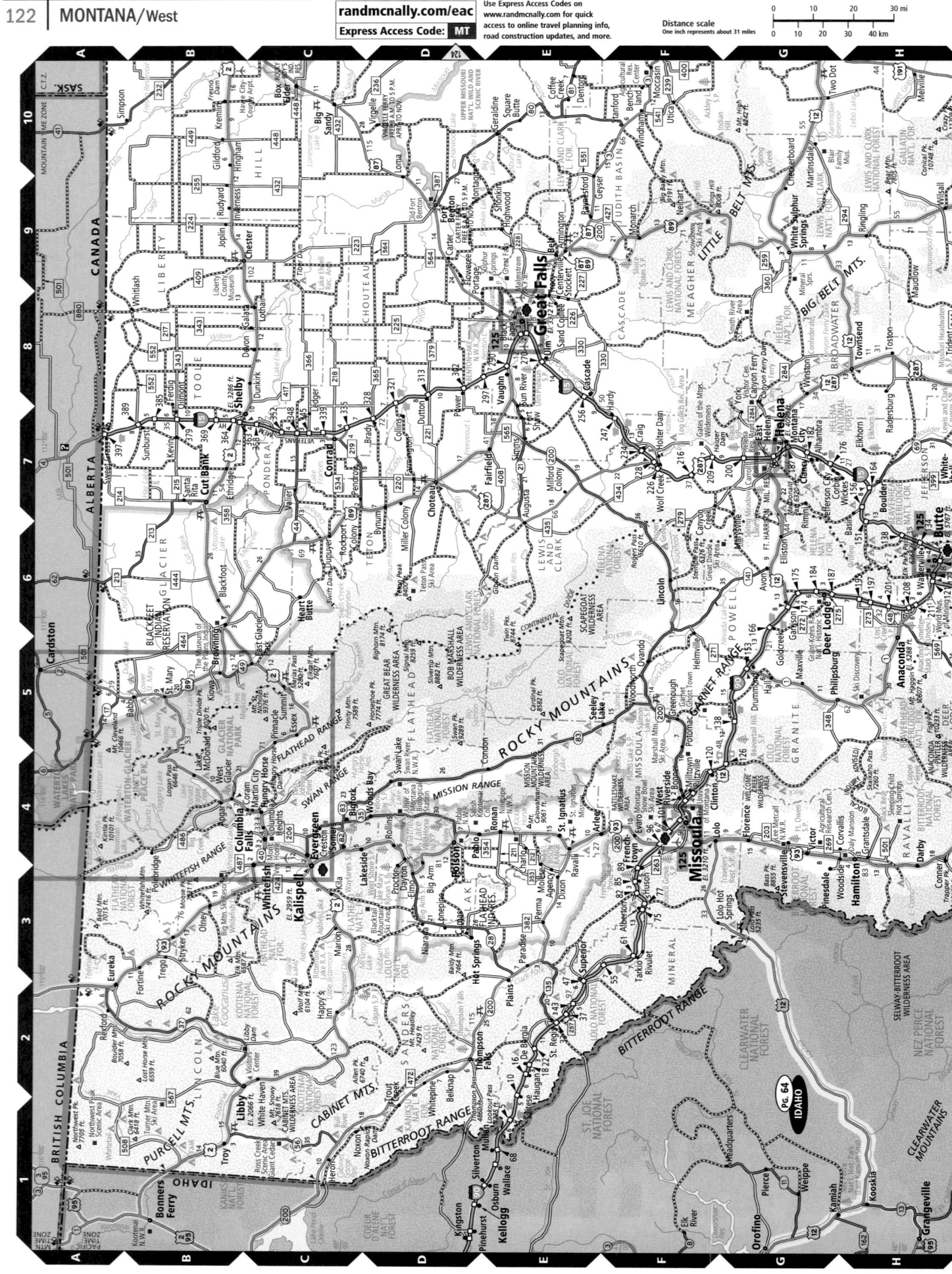

How to determine distance

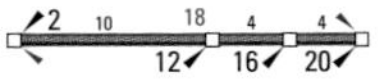

Mileages in red between red arrowheads; in black, between intersections.

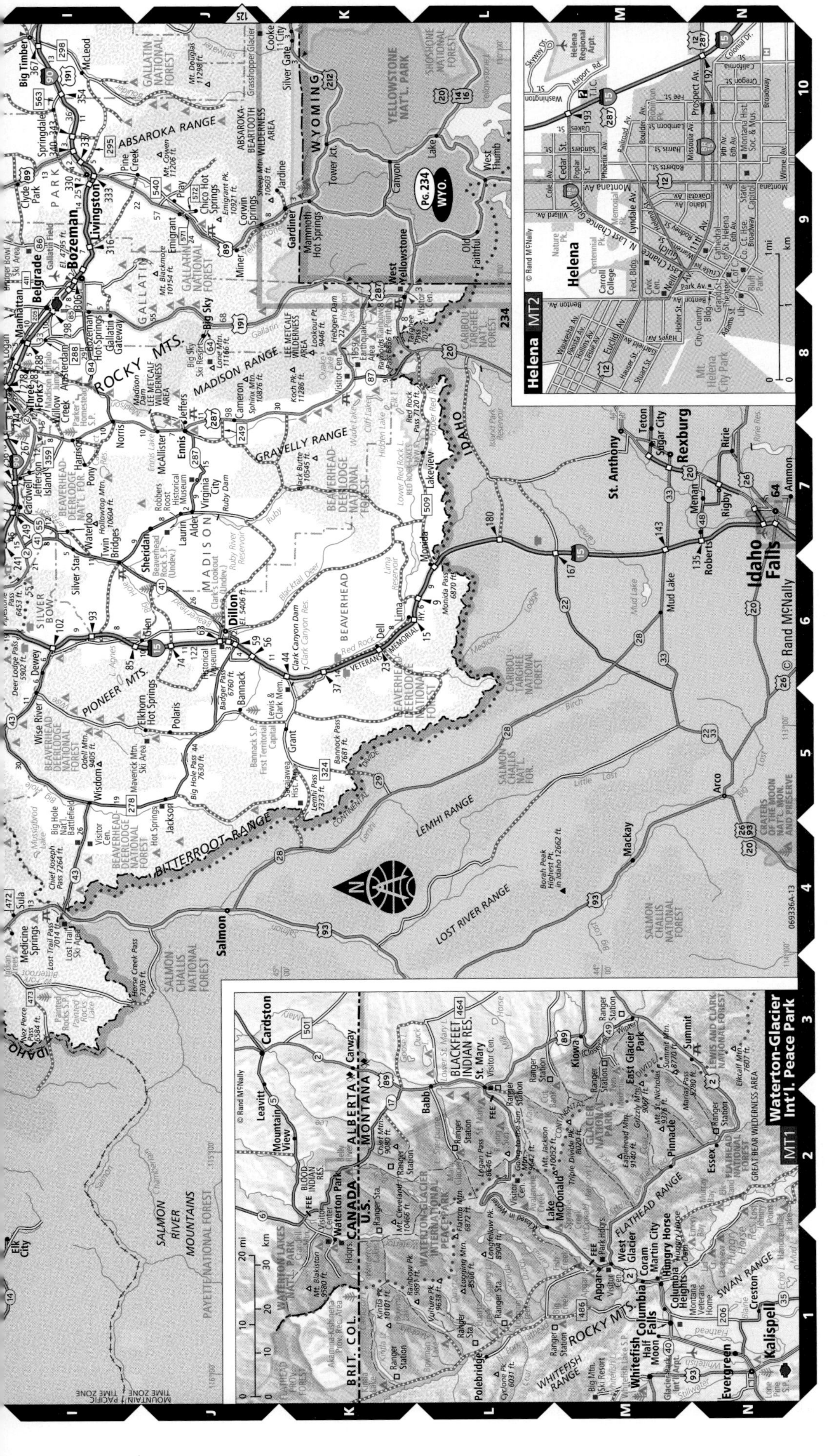

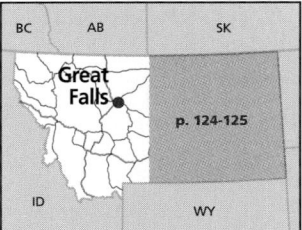

Great Falls

p. 124-125

SYMBOLS

Featured ride

Long-term construction

Harley-Davidson dealership

Scenic route

Historic site or monument; Indian reservation or rancheria; military installation; point of interest; wildlife refuge

For Montana ride, see page R20.
For Idaho/Montana ride, see page R9.

MONTANA MOTORCYCLE LAWS

Helmet use:
Required under age 18

Riding two abreast:
Yes. See state law for specifics

Eye protection:
Not required

Speed limit:
Primary roads: 75 mph
Secondary roads: 65 mph

MONTANA RESOURCES

Road conditions or construction:
511
(800) 226-7623
www.mdt.state.mt.us/travelinfo/

Highway Emergency Numbers:
911 or (800) 525-5555

Tourism:
(800) 847-4868
(406) 841-2870
www.visitmt.com

State motor vehicle information:
(406) 444-3288
www.doj.state.mt.us/driving

HARLEY-DAVIDSON DEALERSHIPS

Yellowstone Harley-Davidson of Belgrade, I-8
540 Alaska Frontage Rd. **Belgrade**
(406) 388-7684
Lat N 45.761 Lon W 111.166

Thunderbolt Harley-Davidson, H-6
34 Olympic Way **Butte**
(406) 782-5601
Lat N 45.962 Lon W 112.477

Big Sky Harley-Davidson, E-8
4258 10th Ave. S **Great Falls**
(406) 727-2161
Lat N 47.494 Lon W 111.234

Montana Harley-Davidson Shop, C-4
2480 Hwy. 93 S **Kalispell**
(406) 752-6843
Lat N 48.221 Lon W 114.235

Montana Harley-Davidson, F-4
5106 E Harrier Blvd. **Missoula**
(406) 721-2154
Lat N 46.934 Lon W 114.087

randmcnally.com/eac

Express Access Code: **MT**

Use Express Access Codes on
www.randmcnally.com for quick
access to online travel planning info,
road construction updates, and more.

Distance scale
One inch represents about 31 miles

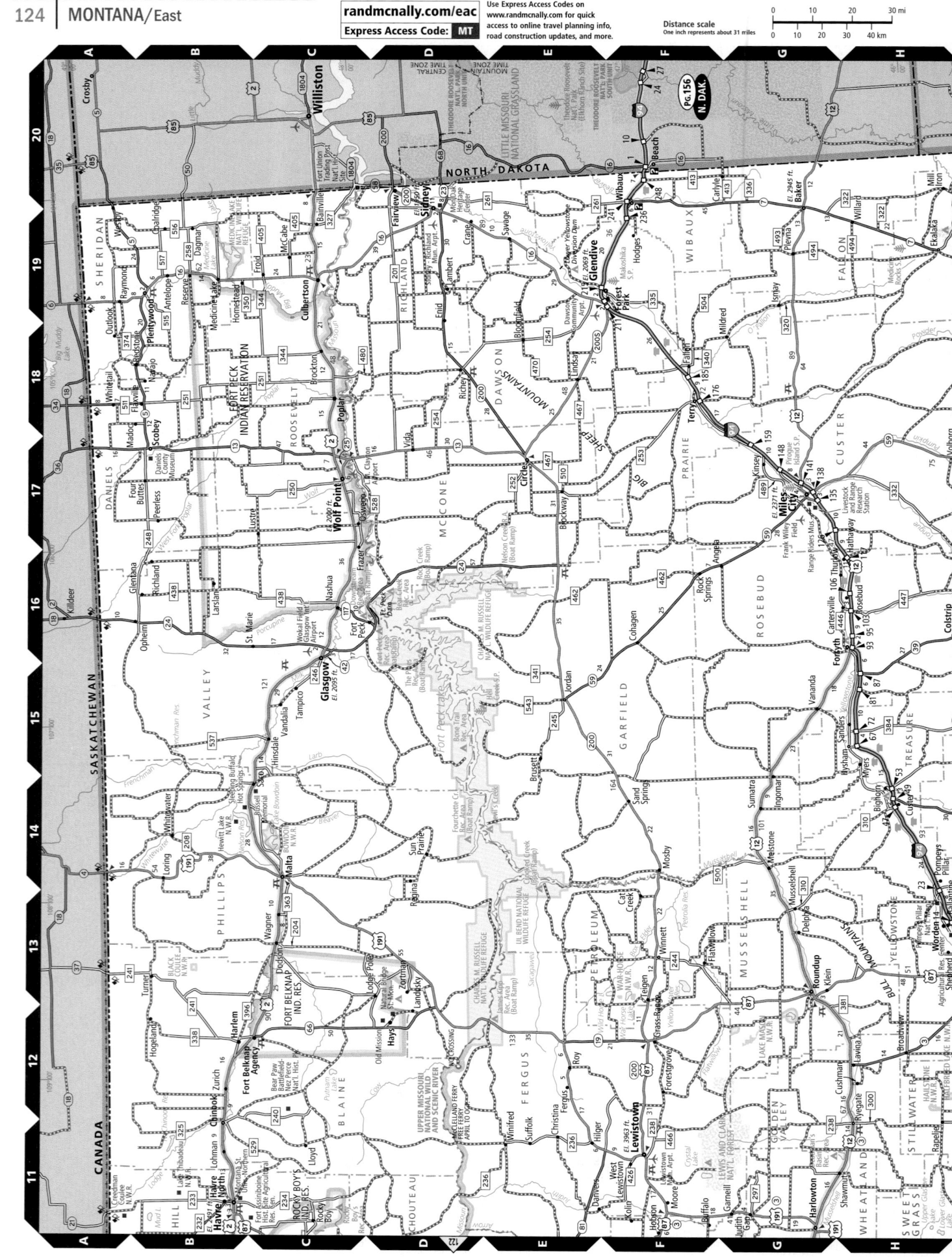

How to determine distance

Mileages in red between red arrowheads; in black, between intersections.

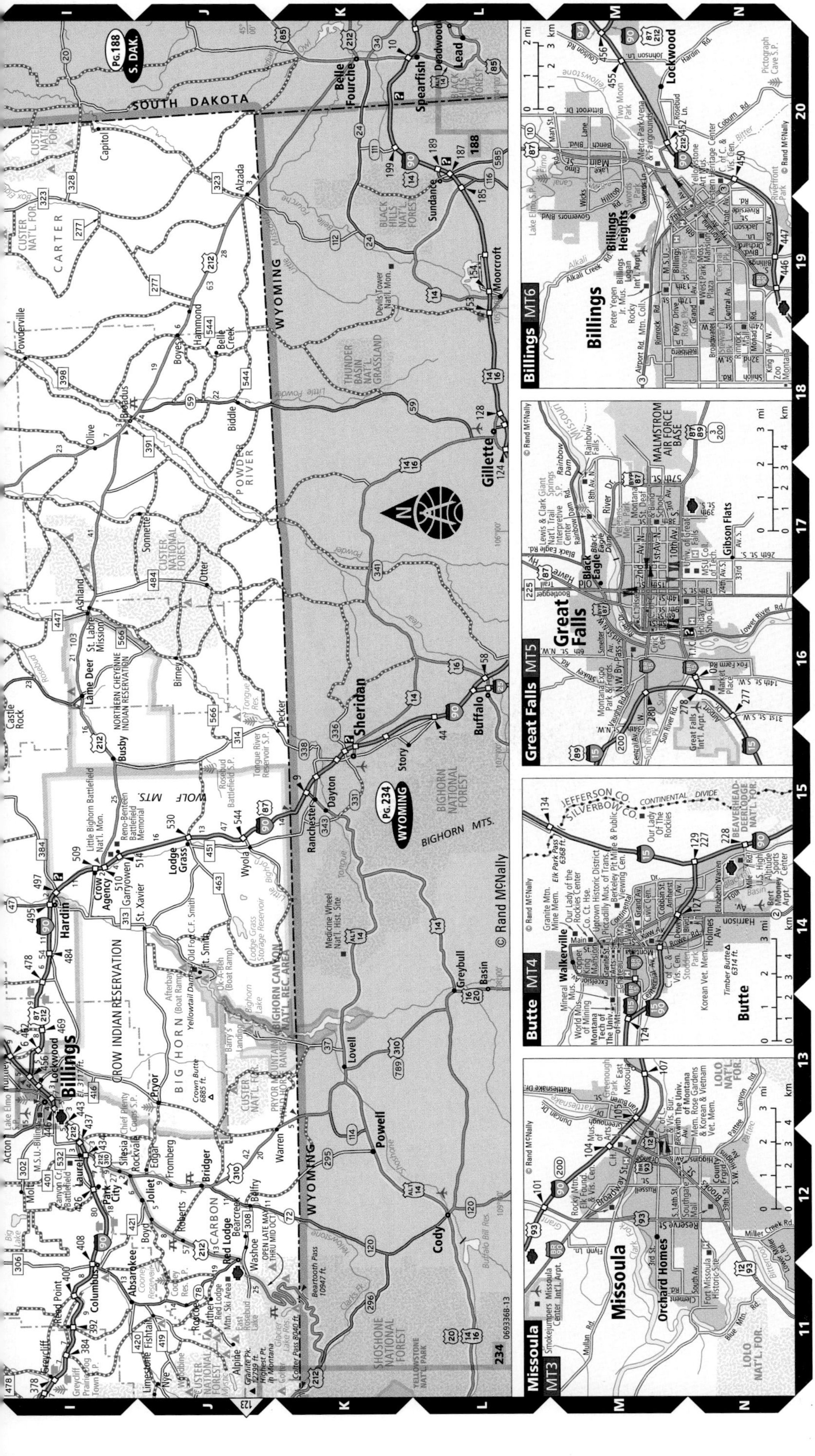

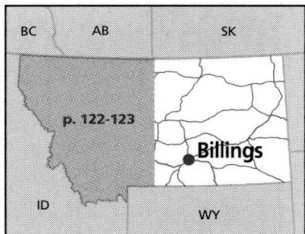

SYMBOLS

- Featured ride
- Scenic route
- Long-term construction
- Harley-Davidson dealership
- ▪ Historic site or monument; Indian reservation or rancheria; military installation; point of interest; wildlife refuge

CITY-TO-CITY MILEAGE

	BILLINGS	BOZEMAN	BUTTE	GREAT FALLS	HELENA	KALISPELL	MILES CITY	MISSOULA
Billings		140	221	222	239	463	144	340
Bozeman	140		82	190	100	324	286	201
Butte	221	82		155	65	242	367	119
Dillon	254	115	67	222	132	295	400	172
Glasgow	278	367	431	276	367	425	222	443
Great Falls	222	190	155		91	233	327	167
Havre	249	305	270	115	206	264	344	282
Helena	239	100	65	91		198	385	111
Kalispell	463	324	242	233	198		609	123
Lewistown	126	162	243	106	195	340	221	274
Libby	532	393	311	324	289	91	678	192
Miles City	144	286	367	327	385	609		486
Missoula	340	201	119	167	111	123	486	
St. Mary	387	306	271	164	207	86	492	209
Shelby	309	271	236	86	172	160	414	227
Sheridan, WY	127	269	350	349	368	592	201	469
Sidney	271	413	494	379	512	565	129	613
West Yellowstone	229	89	148	269	179	390	375	267

HARLEY-DAVIDSON DEALERSHIPS

Beartooth Harley-Davidson, I-13
6900 S Frontage Rd. **Billings**
(406) 252-2888
Lat N 45.739 Lon W 108.589

Beartooth Harley-Davidson of Red Lodge, J-11
213 N Broadway **Red Lodge**
(406) 446-9856
Lat N 45.195 Lon W 109.309

Distance scale
One inch represents about 24 miles

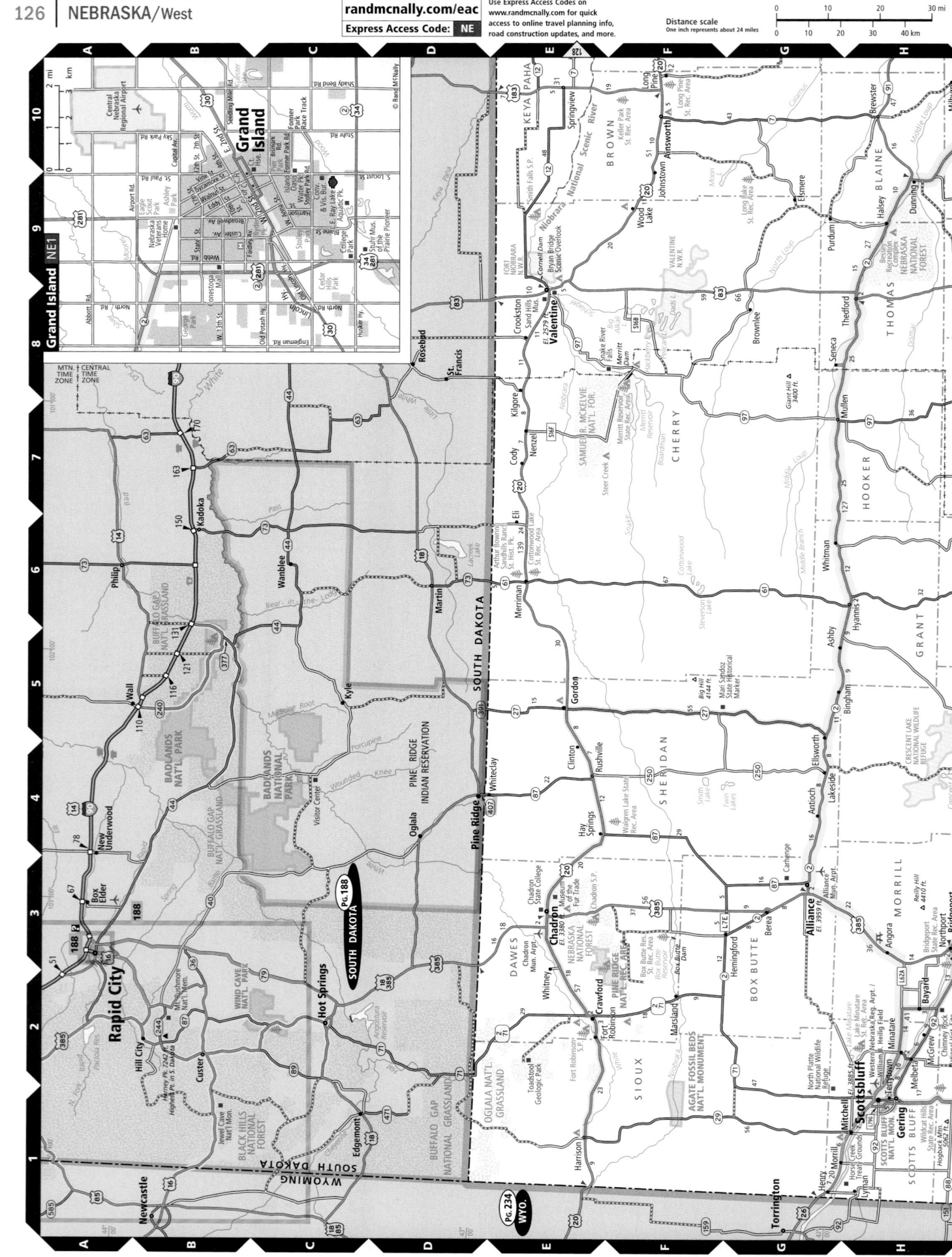

Grand Island NE1

How to determine distance

Mileages in red between red arrowheads; in black, between intersections.

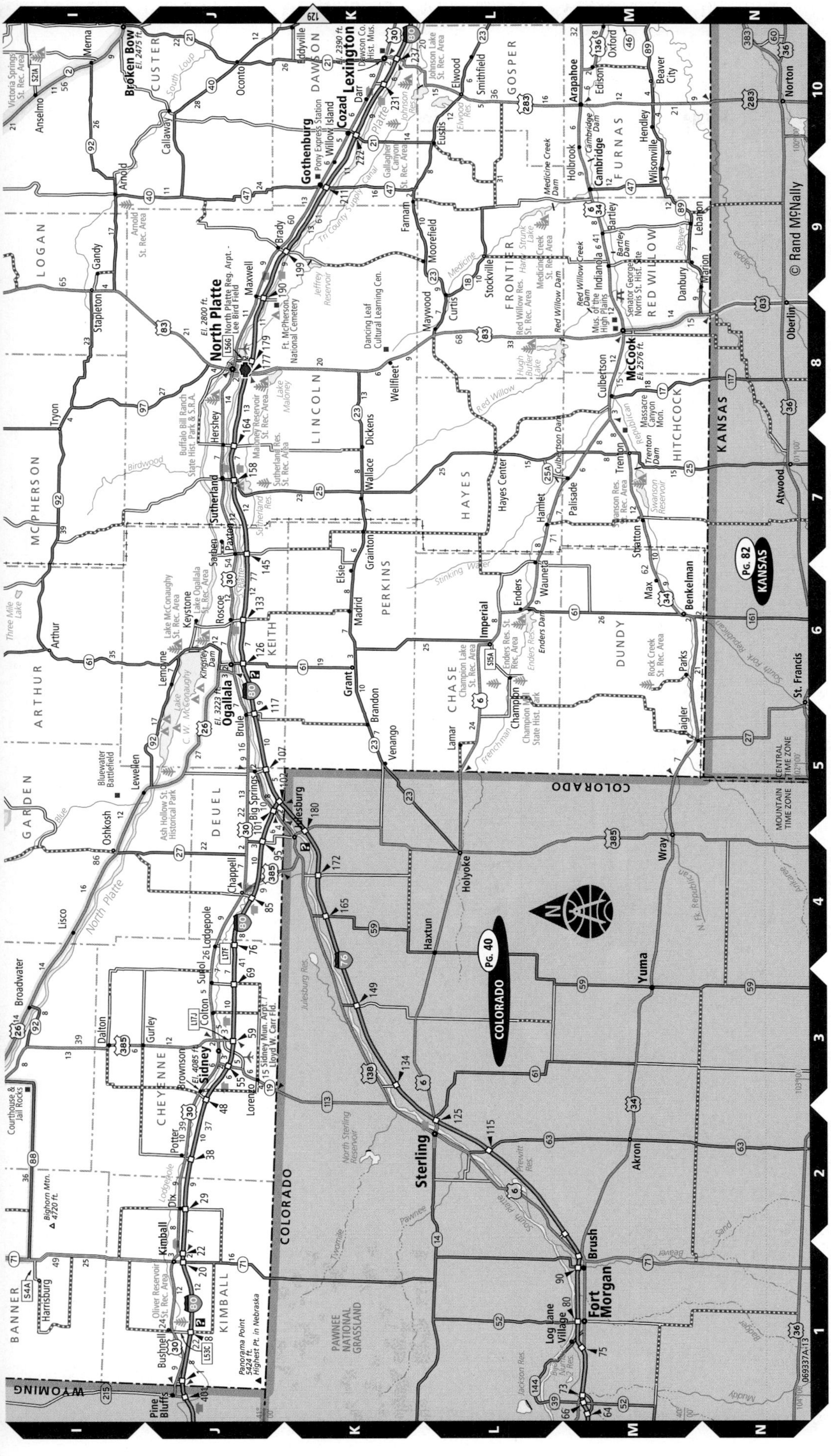

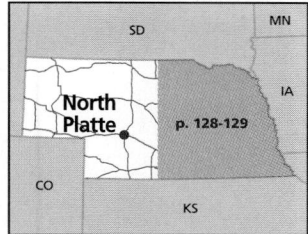

© Rand McNally

SYMBOLS

- Featured ride
- Scenic route
- Long-term construction
- Harley-Davidson dealership
- Historic site or monument; Indian reservation or rancheria; military installation; point of interest; wildlife refuge

For Nebraska ride, see page R21.

NEBRASKA MOTORCYCLE LAWS

Helmet use:
Required

Riding two abreast:
Yes. See state law for specifics

Eye protection:
Not required

Speed limit:
Primary roads: 75 mph
Secondary roads: 65 mph

NEBRASKA RESOURCES

Road conditions or construction:
511
(800) 906-9069
(402) 471-4533
www.dor.state.ne.us

Highway Emergency Numbers:
911 or (800) 525-5555

Tourism:
(877) 632-7275 (to request travel materials only)
(800) 228-4307 (to request travel materials only)
(402) 471-3796
www.visitnebraska.org

State motor vehicle information:
(402) 471-2281
www.dmv.state.ne.us

HARLEY-DAVIDSON DEALERSHIPS

Budke's Harley-Davidson, J-8
695 E Halligan Dr. **North Platte**
(308) 532-4339
Lat N 41.111 **Lon** W 100.756

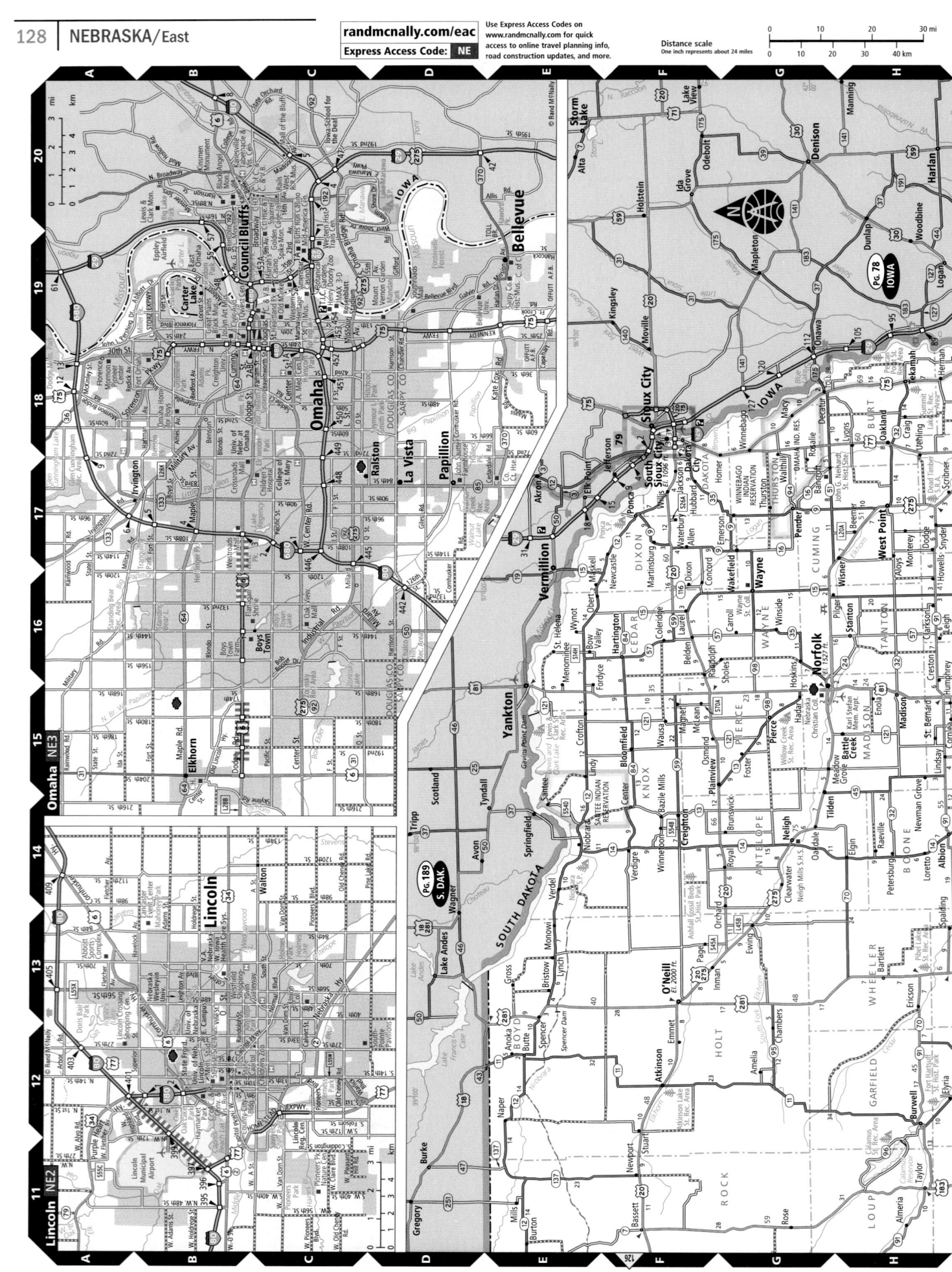

How to determine distance

Mileages in red between red arrowheads; in black, between intersections.

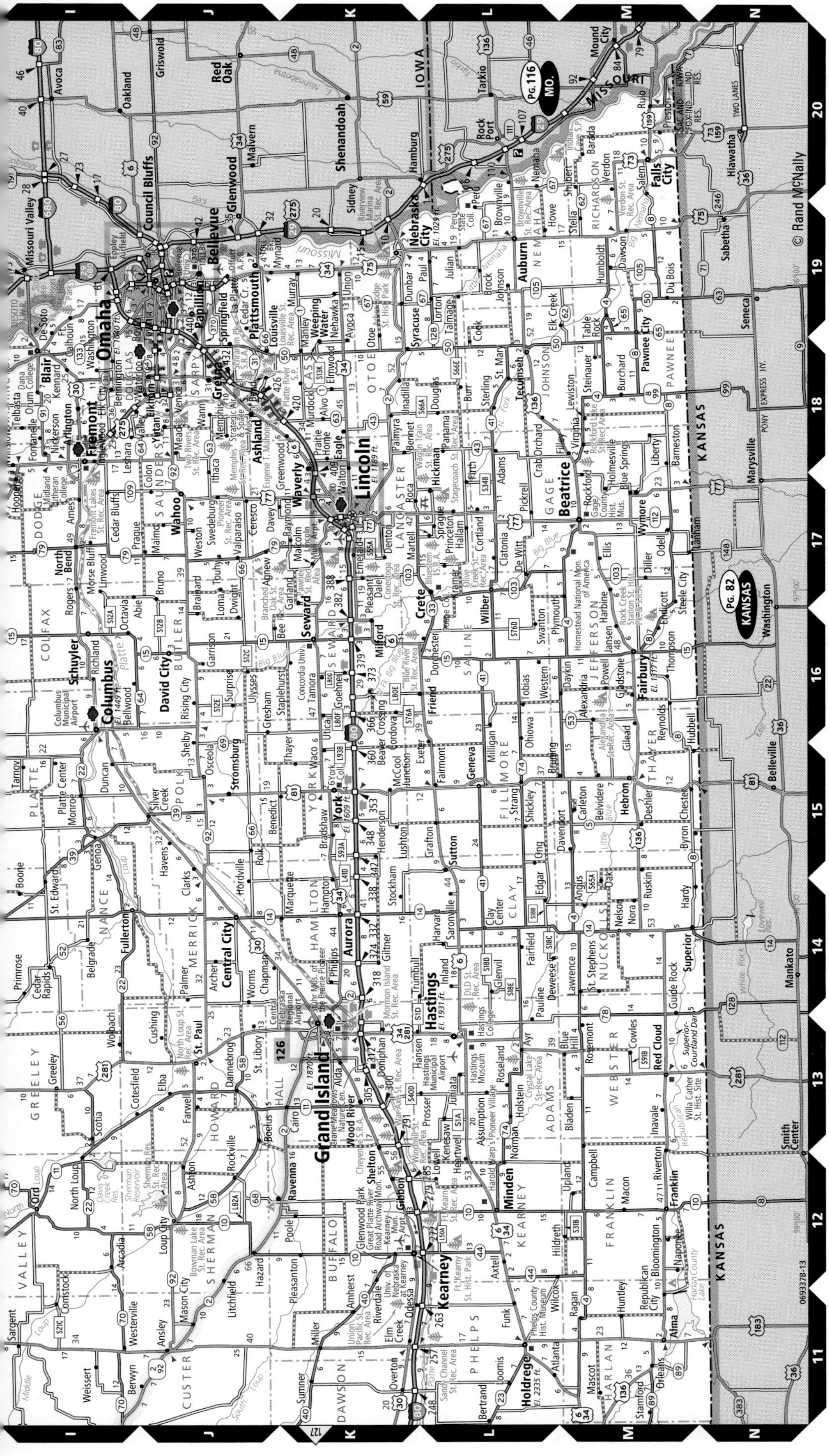

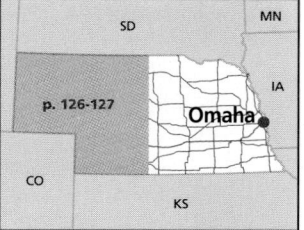

SYMBOLS

Featured ride | Scenic route

Long-term construction | ■ Historic site or monument; Indian reservation or rancheria; military installation; point of interest; wildlife refuge

Harley-Davidson dealership

For Nebraska ride, see page R21.

© Rand McNally

CITY-TO-CITY MILEAGE

	GRAND ISLAND	LINCOLN	NORFOLK	NORTH PLATTE	OGALLALA	OMAHA	SCOTTSBLUFF	VALENTINE
Alliance	321	400	329	177	123	455	57	164
Beatrice	134	40	161	263	314	98	436	343
Chadron	379	458	324	235	181	513	99	138
Cheyenne, WY	365	444	474	221	169	499	109	352
Columbus	63	78	46	210	261	88	383	232
Grand Island		97	109	147	198	152	320	211
Kearney	51	130	160	100	151	185	273	195
Lincoln	97		124	226	277	58	399	306
McCook	155	234	264	68	118	289	240	199
Nebraska City	145	49	154	274	325	44	447	354
Norfolk	109	124		256	307	112	429	186
North Platte	147	226	256		54	281	176	131
Ogallala	198	277	307	54		332	122	185
Omaha	152	58	112	281	332		454	299
O'Neill	111	207	75	194	248	188	329	123
Scottsbluff	320	399	429	176	122	454		218
Sioux City, IA	179	155	74	378	429	98	453	235
Valentine	211	306	186	131	185	299	218	

HARLEY-DAVIDSON DEALERSHIPS

Harley-Davidson Sales, I-16
410 23rd St. **Columbus**
(402) 564-8733
Lat N 41.439 Lon W 97.331

Dillon Brothers Harley-Davidson Shop, I-18
2440 E 23rd St. (Hwy. 30) **Fremont**
(402) 721-2007
Lat N 41.451 Lon W 96.468

Harley-Davidson Central, K-13
2719 S Locust St. **Grand Island**
(308) 382-7020
Lat N 40.896 Lon W 98.34

Frontier Harley-Davidson, K-17
2801 N 27th St. **Lincoln**
(402) 466-9100
Lat N 40.856 Lon W 96.71

Elworth's Harley-Davidson Sales & Service, G-15
2311 Riverside Blvd. **Norfolk**
(402) 371-6210
Lat N 42.059 Lon W 97.425

Dillon Brothers Harley-Davidson, I-18
3838 N HWS Cleveland Blvd. **Omaha**
(402) 289-5556
Lat N 41.296 Lon W 96.159

Harley-Davidson of Omaha, J-19
7337 L St. **Omaha**
(402) 331-0022
Lat N 41.212 Lon W 96.026

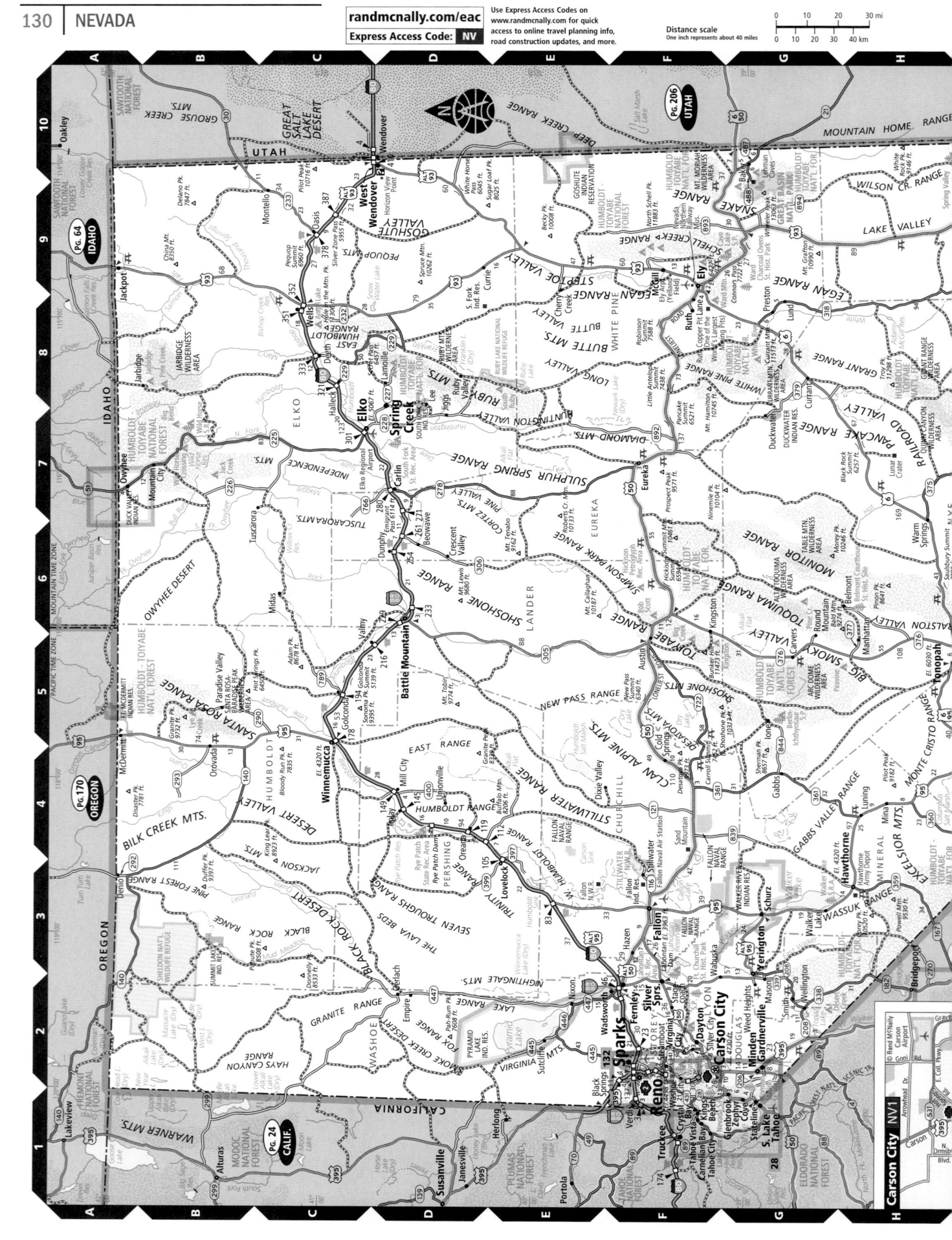

How to determine distance

Mileages in red between red arrowheads; in black, between intersections.

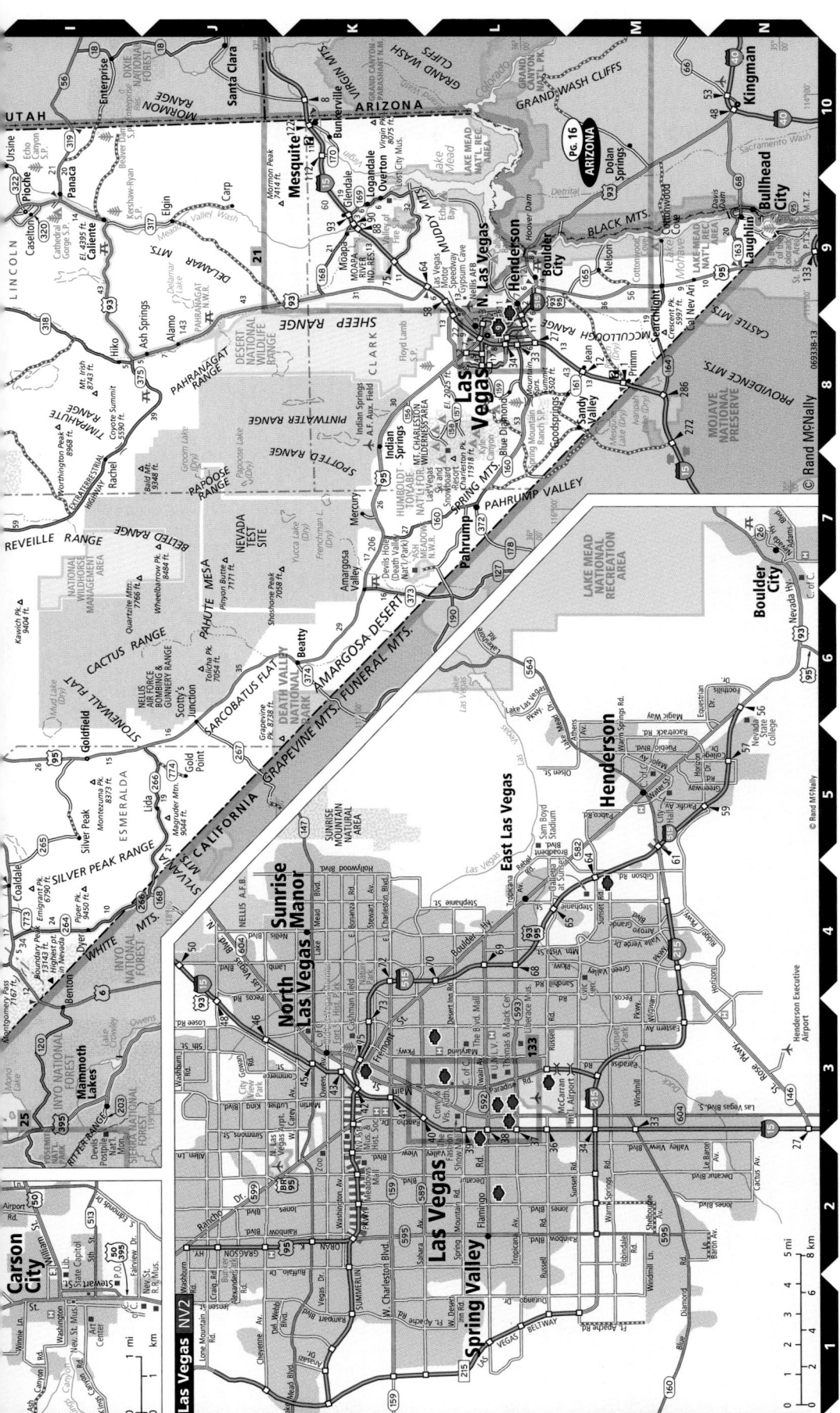

SYMBOLS

— Featured ride

━━━ Scenic route

▦ Long-term construction

■ Historic site or monument; Indian reservation or rancheria; military installation; point of interest; wildlife refuge

⬡ Harley-Davidson dealership

NEVADA MOTORCYCLE LAWS

Helmet use: Required

Riding two abreast:
Yes. See state law for specifics

Eye protection:
Required unless equipped with windscreen

Speed limit:
Primary roads: 75 mph; Secondary roads: 65 mph

NEVADA RESOURCES

Road conditions or construction:
(877) 687-6237
www.nevadadot.com

Highway Emergency Numbers:
911 or *NHP

Tourism:
(800) 638-2328
www.travelnevada.com

State motor vehicle information:
(877) 368-7828
www.dmvnv.com

HARLEY-DAVIDSON DEALERSHIPS

⬡ **Carson City Harley-Davidson, F-2**
2749 N Carson St. **Carson City**
(775) 882-7433
Lat N 39.185 **Lon** W 119.77

⬡ **Henderson Harley-Davidson, L-9**
1010 W Warm Springs Rd. **Henderson**
(702) 456-1666
Lat N 36.056 **Lon** W 115.029

⬡ **Las Vegas Harley-Davidson, L-8**
2605 S Eastern Ave. **Las Vegas**
(702) 431-8500
Lat N 36.142 **Lon** W 115.119

⬡ **Las Vegas Harley-Davidson, L-8**
5835 W Flamingo Rd. **Las Vegas**
(702) 876-2884
Lat N 36.115 **Lon** W 115.221

⬡ **Las Vegas Harley-Davidson, L-8**
3799 Las Vegas Blvd. S **Las Vegas**
(702) 795-7073
Lat N 36.101 **Lon** W 115.17

⬡ **Las Vegas Harley-Davidson, L-8**
5757 Wayne Newton Blvd. **Las Vegas**
(702) 736-9493
Lat N 36.084 **Lon** W 115.149

⬡ **Las Vegas Harley-Davidson, L-8**
328 E Fremont St. **Las Vegas**
(702) 383-1010
Lat N 36.17 **Lon** W 115.143

⬡ **Las Vegas Harley-Davidson, L-8**
3645 S Las Vegas Blvd. **Las Vegas**
(702) 893-7773
Lat N 36.112 **Lon** W 115.173

⬡ **Las Vegas Harley-Davidson, L-8**
3700 W Flamingo Rd. **Las Vegas**
(702) 252-5130
Lat N 36.115 **Lon** W 115.187

⬡ **Las Vegas Harley-Davidson, L-8**
3790 Las Vegas Blvd. S **Las Vegas**
(702) 891-0530
Lat N 36.102 **Lon** W 115.173

⬡ **Las Vegas Harley-Davidson, L-8**
3150 Paradise Rd. **Las Vegas**
(702) 943-6822
Lat N 36.132 **Lon** W 115.155

⬡ **Reno Harley-Davidson, F-2**
2295 Market St. **Reno**
(775) 329-2913
Lat N 39.516 **Lon** W 119.783

⬡ **Reno Harley-Davidson at Silver Legacy, F-2**
407 N Virginia St. **Reno**
(775) 329-2913
Lat N 39.530 **Lon** W 119.814

© Rand McNally

randmcnally.com/eac

Express Access Code: NH

Use Express Access Codes on www.randmcnally.com for quick access to online travel planning info, road construction updates, and more.

Distance scale
One inch represents about 15 miles

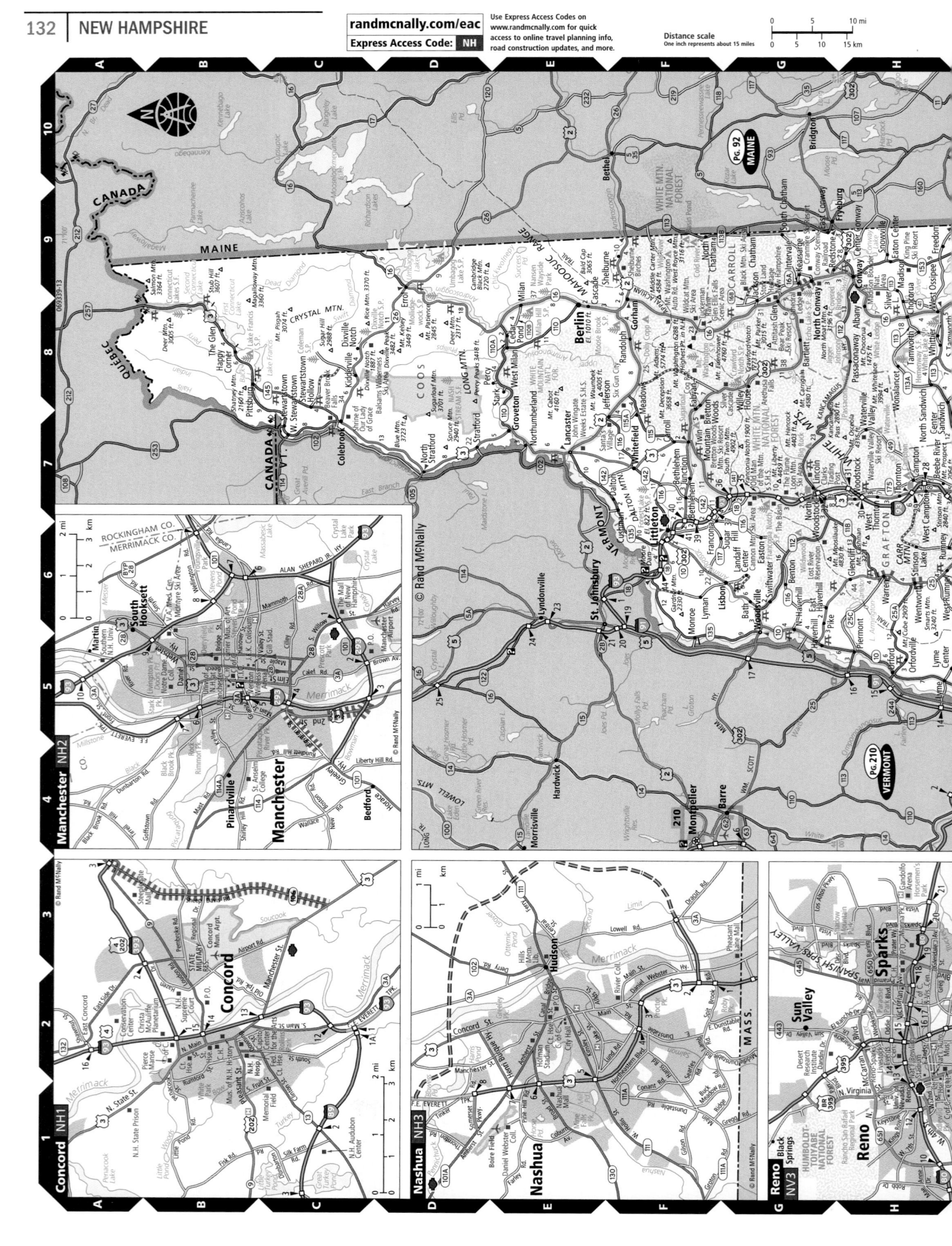

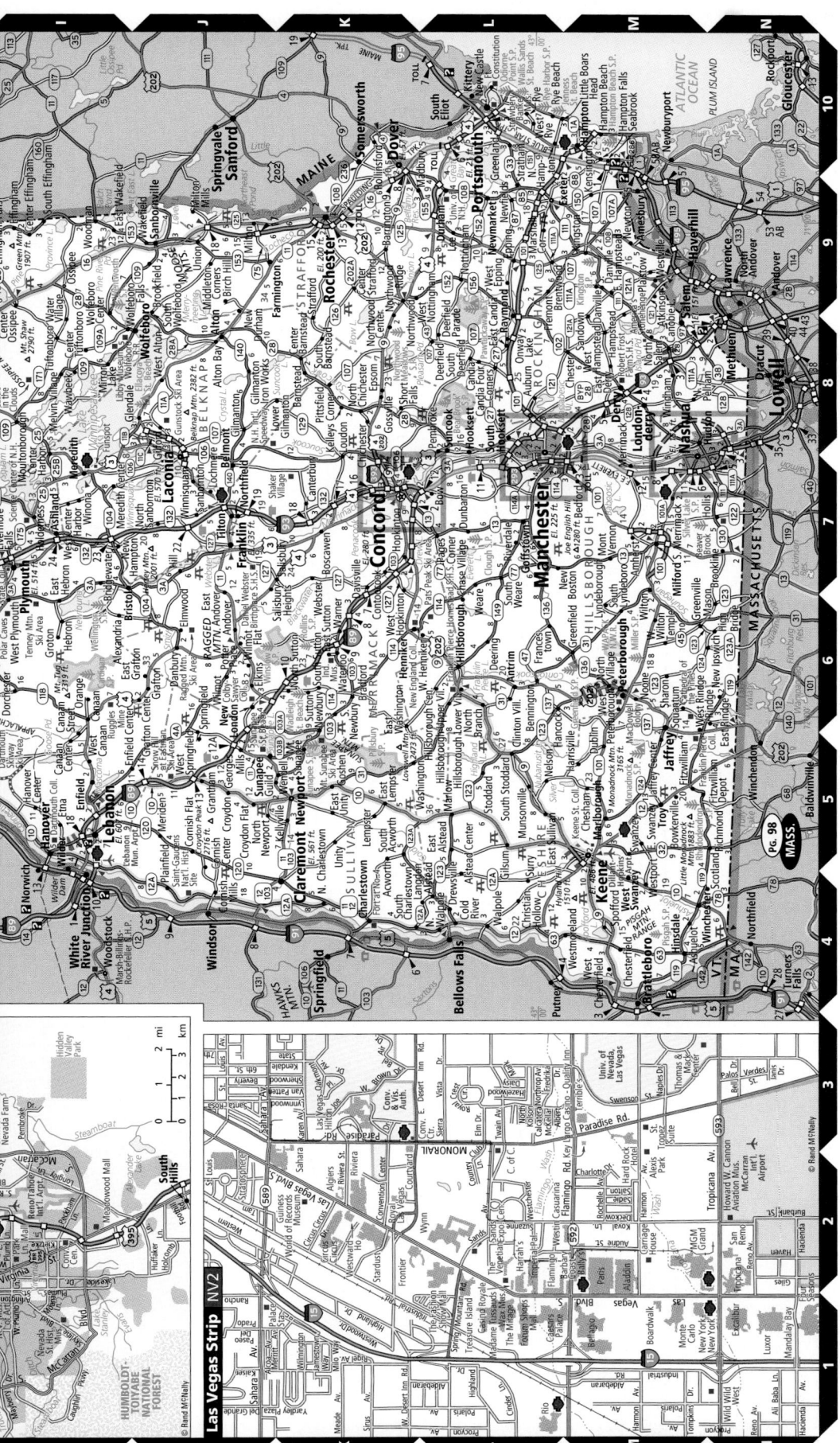

SYMBOLS

- Featured ride
- Long-term construction
- Harley-Davidson dealership
- Scenic route
- Historic site or monument; Indian reservation or rancheria; military installation; point of interest; wildlife refuge

For New Hampshire ride, see page R22.

NEW HAMPSHIRE MOTORCYCLE LAWS

Helmet use:
Required under age 18

Riding two abreast:
Yes. See state law for specifics

Eye protection:
Required unless equipped with windscreen

Speed limit:
Primary roads: 65 mph
Secondary roads: 65 mph

NEW HAMPSHIRE RESOURCES

Road conditions or construction:
511
(866) 282-7579
www.511nh.com

Highway Emergency Numbers:
911 or *64

Tourism:
(800) 386-4664 (to request travel materials only)
(603) 271-2665
www.visitnh.gov

State motor vehicle information:
(603) 271-7000
www.state.nh.us/safety/dmv

HARLEY-DAVIDSON DEALERSHIPS

Littleton Harley-Davidson, F-6
1341 Whitefield Rd. **Bethlehem**
(603) 444-1300
Lat N 44.313 Lon W 71.792

Heritage Harley-Davidson, K-7
142 Manchester St. **Concord**
(603) 224-3268
Lat N 43.188 Lon W 71.503

Meredith Harley-Davidson Shop of Conway, H-9
1275 White Mountain Hwy. (Rte. 16) **Conway**
(603) 356-7775
Lat N 43.974 Lon W 71.174

Monadnock Harley-Davidson, M-5
588 Monadnock Hwy. **East Swanzey**
(603) 352-1472
Lat N 42.875 Lon W 72.231

Twin States Harley-Davidson, I-5
351 Miracle Mile **Lebanon**
(603) 448-4664
Lat N 43.637 Lon W 72.286

Manchester Harley-Davidson, L-8
115 John E Devine Dr. **Manchester**
(603) 622-2461
Lat N 42.959 Lon W 71.444

Meredith Harley-Davidson, I-7
239 Daniel Webster Hwy. (Rte. 3) **Meredith**
(603) 279-4526
Lat N 43.655 Lon W 71.497

Nashua Harley-Davidson, M-7
717 Rte. 101A **Merrimack**
(603) 578-9400
Lat N 42.805 Lon W 71.547

Seacoast Harley-Davidson, M-10
17 Lafayette Rd. (US Rte. 1) **North Hampton**
(603) 964-9959
Lat N 42.961 Lon W 70.834

Meredith Harley-Davidson of Tilton, J-7
120 Laconia Rd. #217 **Tilton**
(603) 286-7028
Lat N 43.459 Lon W 71.558

How to determine distance

Mileages in red between red arrowheads; in black, between intersections.

randmcnally.com/eac
Express Access Code: NJ

Use Express Access Codes on www.randmcnally.com for quick access to online travel planning info, road construction updates, and more.

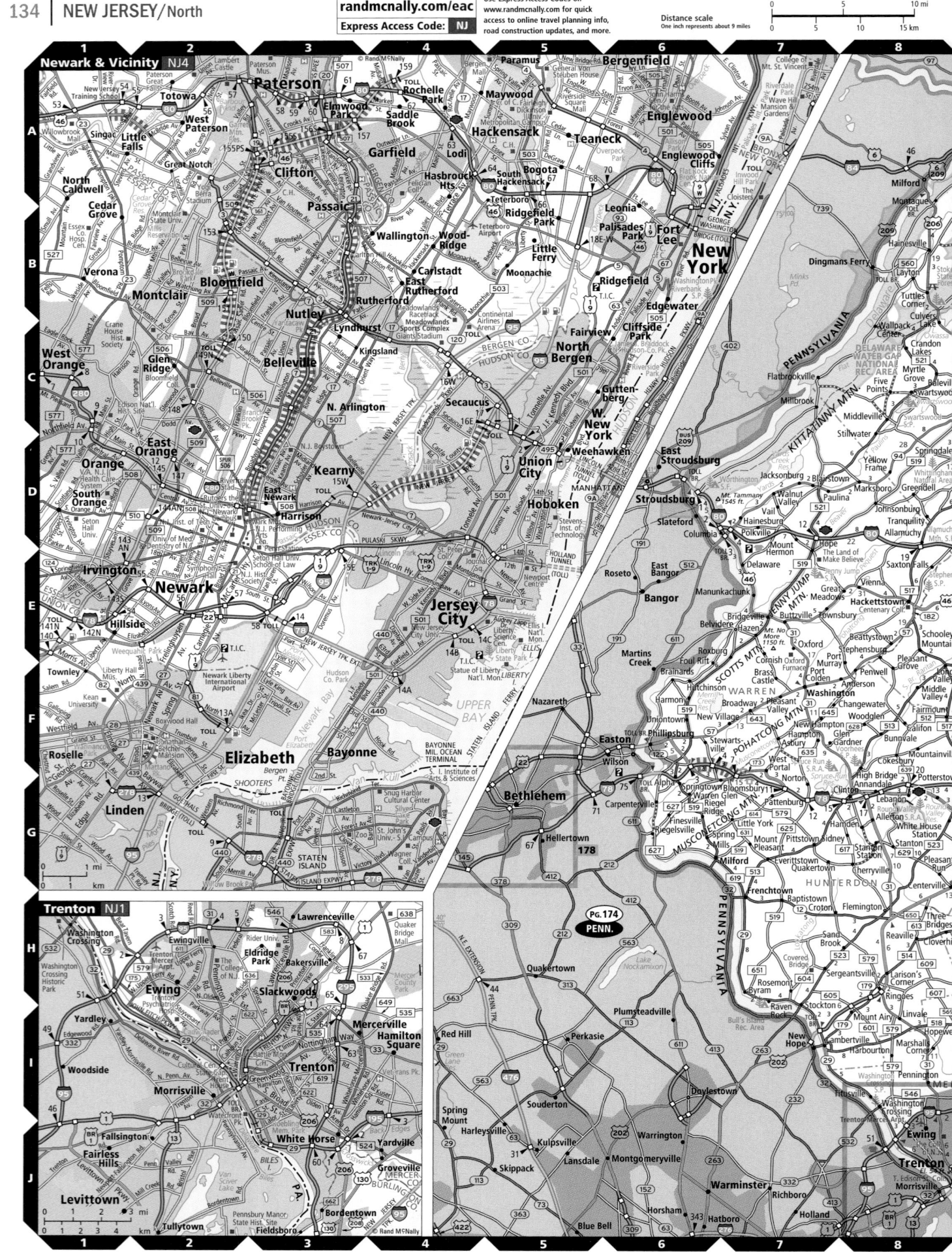

How to determine distance

Mileages in red between red arrowheads; in black, between intersections.

© Rand McNally

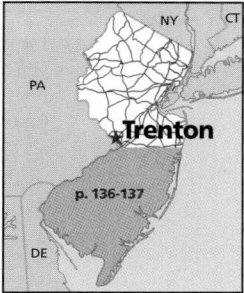

p. 136-137

NEW JERSEY MOTORCYCLE LAWS

Helmet use:
Required and reflectorization required

Riding two abreast:
No reference in administrative code or statutes

Eye protection:
Required for instructional permit holders
Required unless equipped with windscreen

Speed limit:
Primary roads: 65 mph; Secondary roads: 55 mph

NEW JERSEY RESOURCES

Road conditions or construction:
(732) 247-0900, then 2 (turnpike)
(800) 336-5875 (turnpike)
(732) 727-5929 (Garden State Parkway)
www.state.nj.us/njcommuter/
www.state.nj.us/turnpike/

Highway Emergency Numbers: 911 or #77

Tourism:
(800) 847-4865 (to request travel materials only)
(609) 292-2470
www.visitnj.org

State motor vehicle information:
(609) 292-6500
www.state.nj.us/mvc

HARLEY-DAVIDSON DEALERSHIPS

Harley-Davidson of Essex, F-12
168 Bloomfield Ave. **Bloomfield**
(973) 748-2500
Lat N 40.78 Lon W 74.19

Trenton World-Class Harley-Davidson, J-9
960 US Rte. 130 & I-195 **Hamilton**
(609) 689-0200
Lat N 40.214 Lon W 74.614

Harley-Davidson of Edison, H-11
211 Woodbridge Ave. **Highland Park**
(732) 985-7546
Lat N 40.501 Lon W 74.413

Tramontin Harley-Davidson, E-7
Rte. 80 W Exit 12 **Hope**
(908) 459-4101
Lat N 40.911 Lon W 74.968

Kosco Harley-Davidson, D-11
1149 Rte. 23 S **Kinnelon**
(973) 838-8800
Lat N 40.993 Lon W 74.366

Williams Harley-Davidson, G-8
1100 US Hwy. 22 W **Lebanon**
(908) 236-0767
Lat N 40.645 Lon W 74.812

Legends Harley-Davidson, E-9
1895 Rte. 46 W **Ledgewood**
(973) 347-0258
Lat N 40.883 Lon W 74.659

Harley-Davidson of Long Branch, I-13
671 Broadway **Long Branch**
(732) 229-8518
Lat N 40.299 Lon W 74.006

Liberty Harley-Davidson, G-11
12 W Milton Ave. **Rahway**
(732) 381-2400
Lat N 40.606 Lon W 74.278

Harley-Davidson of Bergen County, E-13
124 Essex St. **Rochelle Park**
(201) 843-6930
Lat N 40.893 Lon W 74.074

How to determine distance

Mileages in red between red arrowheads; in black, between intersections.

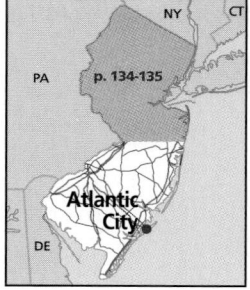

Atlantic City

SYMBOLS

- Featured ride
- Long-term construction
- Harley-Davidson dealership
- Scenic route
- Historic site or monument; Indian reservation or rancheria; military installation; point of interest; wildlife refuge

CITY-TO-CITY MILEAGE

	ATLANTIC CITY	CAMDEN	NEWARK	NEW BRUNSWICK	PATERSON	PHILLIPSBURG	TRENTON	WILMINGTON DE
Atlantic City		60	117	95	129	145	81	86
Camden	60		82	63	94	85	37	36
Cape May	49	93	151	129	163	178	114	93
Cherry Hill	55	6	78	59	90	91	33	43
Elizabeth	114	79	5	22	22	63	52	114
Jersey City	122	87	5	30	15	68	60	122
Long Branch	81	77	46	33	58	86	50	112
Newark	117	82		25	19	63	55	117
New Brunswick	95	63	25		37	52	36	98
New York, NY	140	107	25	50	31	88	80	142
Paterson	129	94	19	37		66	67	129
Phillipsburg	145	85	63	52	66		57	100
Point Pleasant	64	71	56	38	68	96	44	106
Port Jervis, NY	182	147	75	90	54	76	107	162
Princeton	93	48	41	18	58	56	12	79
Somerville	119	70	34	14	41	39	31	101
Toms River	51	55	66	44	78	106	46	88
Trenton	81	37	55	36	67	57		68
Vineland	37	38	115	96	127	123	70	44
Willingboro	70	14	68	49	80	70	20	51
Wilmington, DE	86	36	117	98	100	68		

HARLEY-DAVIDSON DEALERSHIPS

- **Atlantic County Harley-Davidson, P-10**
  219 E White Horse Pike (Rte. 30) **Absecon** (Galloway)
  (609) 652-5555
  Lat N 39.448 Lon W 74.531

- **Atlantic City Harley-Davidson, Q-10**
  101 N Michigan Ave. **Atlantic City**
  (609) 344-6464
  Lat N 39.361 Lon W 74.437

- **Mills Harley-Davidson Sales, K-8**
  612 Tyler St. **Burlington**
  (609) 386-1871
  Lat N 40.073 Lon W 74.852

- **Salem County Harley-Davidson Sales, O-6**
  354 Rte. 77 **Elmer**
  (856) 358-8188
  Lat N 39.608 Lon W 75.235

- **Harley-Davidson of Ocean County, K-12**
  300 Rte. 70 **Lakewood**
  (732) 367-7000
  Lat N 40.049 Lon W 74.209

- **Harley-Davidson of Millville, Q-7**
  1131 S 2nd St. **Millville**
  (856) 327-0266
  Lat N 39.379 Lon W 75.028

- **Barb's Harley-Davidson, M-6**
  926 Black Horse Pike **West Collingswood Heights**
  (856) 456-4141
  Lat N 39.89 Lon W 75.09

- **The Harley Shop of Wildwood, T-8**
  127 W Rio Grande Ave. **Wildwood**
  (609) 522-7151
  Lat N 38.984 Lon W 74.825

© Rand McNally

060213-4

Distance scale
One inch represents about 40 miles

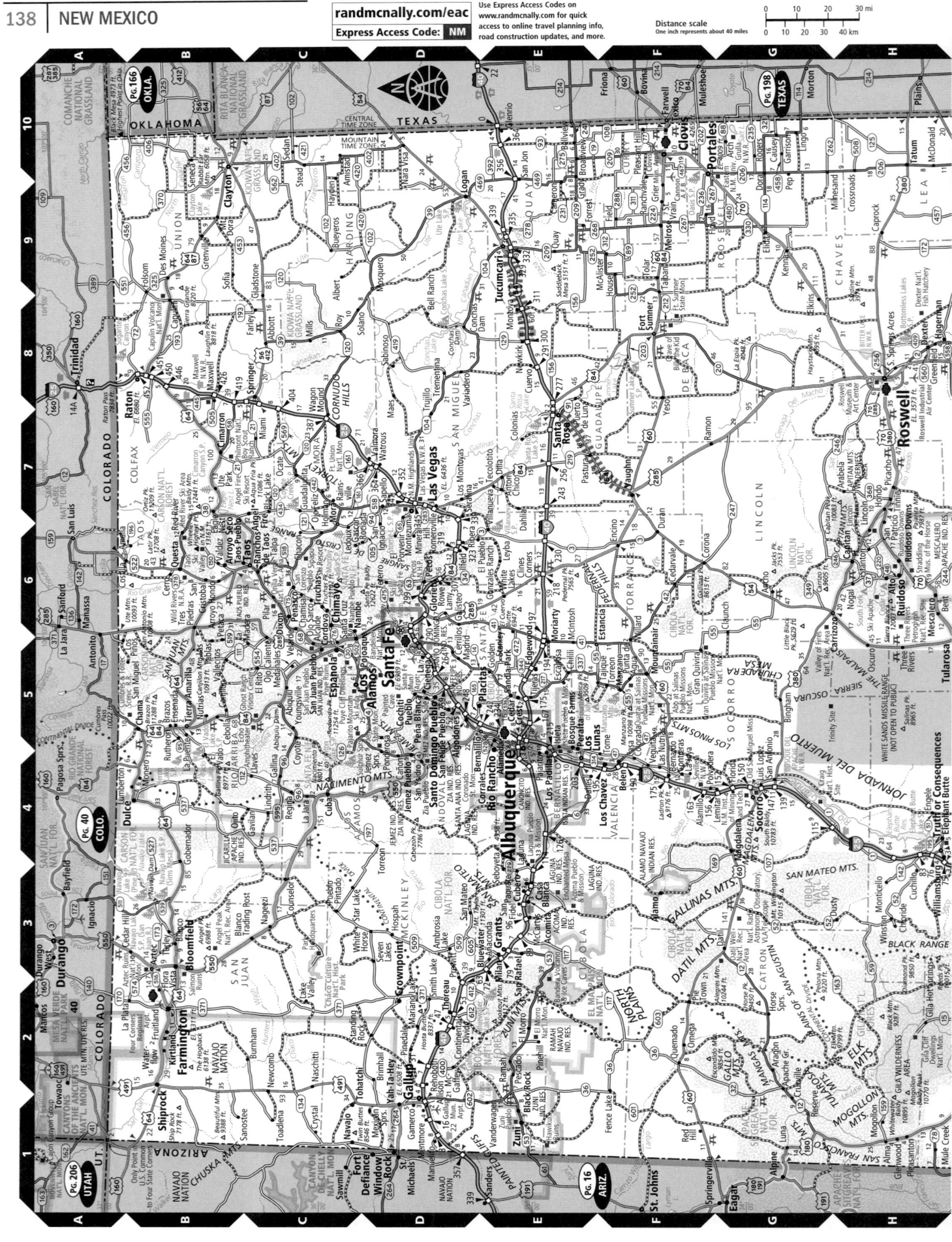

SYMBOLS

- ▬▬ Featured ride
- ▦▦ Long-term construction
- 🏍 Harley-Davidson dealership
- ▬▬ Scenic route
- ■ Historic site or monument; Indian reservation or rancheria; military installation; point of interest; wildlife refuge

NEW MEXICO MOTORCYCLE LAWS

Helmet use:
Required under age 18 and reflectorization required

Riding two abreast:
No reference in administrative code or statutes

Eye protection:
Required unless equipped with windscreen

Speed limit:
Primary roads: 75 mph; Secondary roads: 75 mph

NEW MEXICO RESOURCES

Road conditions or construction:
(800) 432-4269
www.nmshtd.state.nm.us

Highway Emergency Numbers:
(505) 827-9301

Tourism:
(800) 733-6396
www.newmexico.org

State motor vehicle information:
(888) 683-4636
www.state.nm.us/tax/mvd

CITY-TO-CITY MILEAGE

	ALBUQUERQUE	CARLSBAD	CLOVIS	LAS CRUCES	SANTA FE	TRINIDAD, CO	TUCUMCARI
Alamogordo	210	146	229	324	69	217	345	236
Albuquerque		275	217	139	224	58	246	174
Carlsbad	275		179	414	208	381	242
Clovis	217	179		356	298	209	255	82
El Paso, TX	267	165	314	381	46	325	430	321
Farmington	182	447	389	122	406	208	298	346
Gallup	139	414	356	61	378	197	385	313
Grants	79	354	296	61	278	137	325	253
Hobbs	315	70	127	454	257	307	382	200
Las Cruces	224	208	298	338		282	470	305
Las Vegas	118	253	165	257	342	63	128	147
Lordsburg	294	324	416	303	118	352	540	468
Raton	224	359	233	363	448	169	22	177
Roswell	198	77	111	337	187	190	304	165
Santa Fe	58	267	209	197	282		191	166
Silver City	240	317	408	270	111	298	486	414
Socorro	78	240	246	192	146	136	324	252
Taos	126	328	240	265	350	69	118	197
Truth or Consequences	150	280	318	264	75	208	396	324
Tucumcari	174	242	82	313	305	166	199	

HARLEY-DAVIDSON DEALERSHIPS

🏍 **Thunderbird Harley-Davidson, E-5**
5000 Alameda Blvd. NE **Albuquerque**
(505) 856-1600
Lat N 35.184 Lon W 106.59

🏍 **High Plains Harley-Davidson, F-10**
4400 Mabry Dr. **Clovis**
(505) 769-1000
Lat N 34.394 Lon W 103.149

🏍 **Four Corners Harley-Davidson, B-2**
6520 E Main St. **Farmington**
(505) 325-6710
Lat N 36.778 Lon W 108.126

🏍 **Barnetts Las Cruces Harley-Davidson, J-4**
2600 Lakeside Dr. **Las Cruces**
(505) 541-1440
Lat N 32.291 Lon W 106.806

🏍 **Champion Harley-Davidson, H-8**
2801 W 2nd St. **Roswell**
(505) 624-0151
Lat N 33.394 Lon W 104.563

🏍 **Santa Fe Harley-Davidson, D-5**
3501 Cerrillos Rd. **Santa Fe**
(505) 471-3808
Lat N 35.646 Lon W 106.006

How to determine distance

Mileages in red between red arrowheads; in black, between intersections.

Distance scale
One inch represents about 15 miles

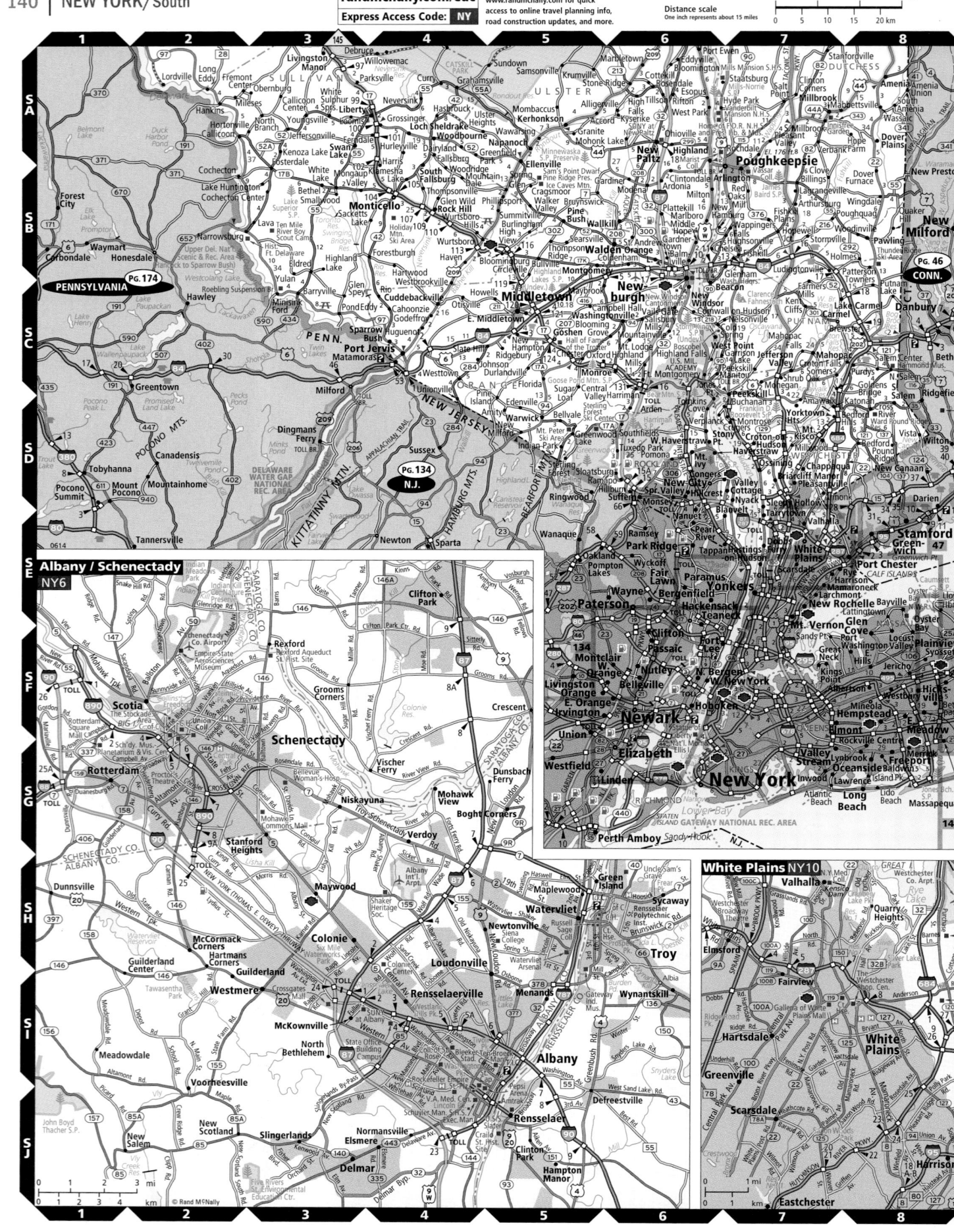

Albany / Schenectady
NY6

White Plains NY10

© Rand McNally

How to determine distance

Mileages in red between red arrowheads; in black, between intersections.

New York

SYMBOLS

Featured ride	Scenic route
Long-term construction	Historic site or monument; Indian reservation or rancheria; military installation; point of interest; wildlife refuge
Harley-Davidson dealership	

HARLEY-DAVIDSON DEALERSHIPS

Harley-Davidson of Nassau County, SF-8
2428 Sunrise Hwy. **Bellmore**
(516) 409-9200
Lat N 40.666 Lon W 73.537

Brooklyn Harley-Davidson, SG-6
3449 Fort Hamilton Pkwy. **Brooklyn**
(718) 851-6666
Lat N 40.646 Lon W 73.986

Prestige Harley-Davidson, SD-7
MOVING IN 2006: 205 Rte. 9 W **Congers**
(845) 268-6651
Lat N 41.151 Lon W 73.941

Harley-Davidson of Hempstead, SF-8
4 Laurel Ave. **Hempstead**
(516) 481-7100
Lat N 40.701 Lon W 73.627

Lighthouse Harley-Davidson, SF-9
670 E Jericho Turnpike **Huntington Station**
(631) 427-0382
Lat N 40.834 Lon W 73.386

Harley-Davidson of New York, SF-7
42-11 Northern Blvd. **Long Island City**
(718) 707-9300
Lat N 40.753 Lon W 73.921

Newroc Harley-Davidson, SE-7
8 Industrial Ln. **New Rochelle**
(914) 632-6743
Lat N 40.898 Lon W 73.794

Moroney's Harley-Davidson Sales, SC-6
833 Union Ave. **New Windsor**
(845) 564-5400
Lat N 41.492 Lon W 74.076

Harley-Davidson of New York, SF-6
686 Lexington Ave. **New York**
(212) 355-3003
Lat N 40.761 Lon W 73.969

Suffolk County Harley-Davidson, SI-13
4020 Sunrise Hwy. **Oakdale**
(631) 244-9000
Lat N 40.748 Lon W 73.141

Eastern Harley-Davidson, SE-11
1570 Old Country Rd. **Riverhead**
(631) 727-4700
Lat N 40.925 Lon W 72.696

Lombardi's Staten Island Harley-Davidson, SG-6
440-442 Bay St. **Staten Island**
(718) 447-4009
Lat N 40.632 Lon W 74.076

Reggie Pink, SE-7
295 Central Ave. **White Plains**
(914) 946-6622
Lat N 41.035 Lon W 73.784

H-D Military Sales, SF-8
100 Crossways Park West **Woodbury**
(516) 921-2800
Lat N 40.809 Lon W 73.489

O'Tooles Harley-Davidson, SB-5
4 Sullivan St. P.O. Box 837 **Wurtsboro**
(845) 888-2426
Lat N 41.572 Lon W 74.476

Binghamton NY7

Utica NY5

Central Long Island NY9

LONG ISLAND

LONG ISLAND SOUND

ATLANTIC OCEAN

© Rand McNally

randmcnally.com/eac

Express Access Code: NY

Use Express Access Codes on www.randmcnally.com for quick access to online travel planning info, road construction updates, and more.

Distance scale
One inch represents about 18 miles

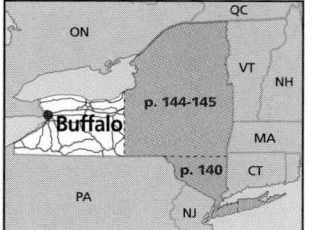

How to determine distance

Mileages in red between red arrowheads; in black, between intersections.

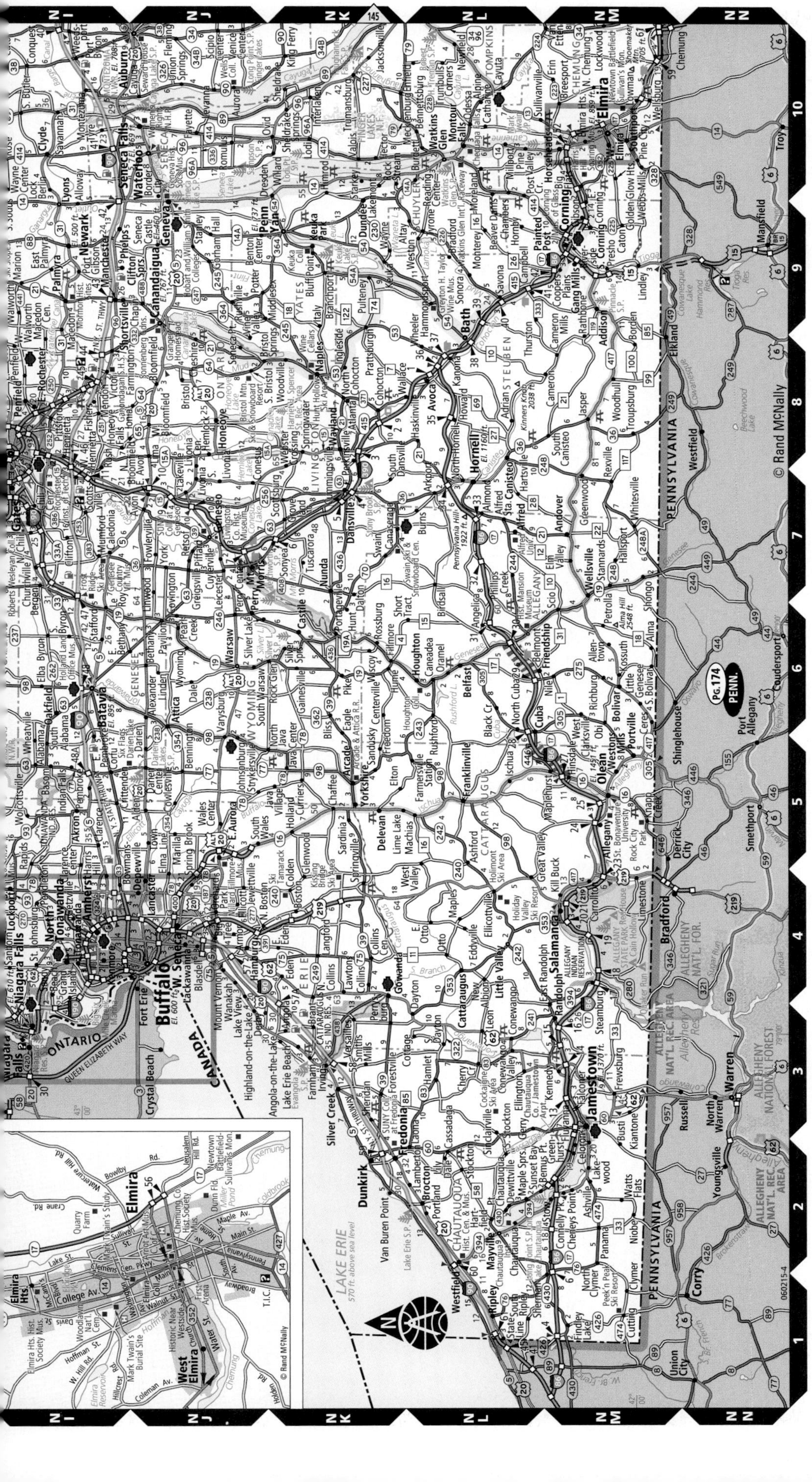

SYMBOLS

- Featured ride
- Long-term construction
- Harley-Davidson dealership
- Scenic route
- Historic site or monument; Indian reservation or rancheria; military installation; point of interest; wildlife refuge

For New York ride, see page R23.

HARLEY-DAVIDSON DEALERSHIPS

Buffalo Harley-Davidson, NI-4
4220 Bailey Ave. **Amherst**
(716) 832-7159
Lat N 42.97 Lon W 78.814

Arkport Harley-Davidson, NK-7
1 Main St. **Arkport**
(607) 295-7426
Lat N 42.462 Lon W 77.772

Stan's Harley-Davidson, NI-6
4425 W Saile Dr. **Batavia**
(585) 343-9598
Lat N 43.029 Lon W 78.191

Ithaca Harley-Davidson, NL-10
6033 Rte. 13 (at jct. of Rte. 224) **Cayuta**
(607) 594-3536
Lat N 42.294 Lon W 76.713

Harding Harley-Davidson, NM-9
26 Bridge St. **Corning**
(607) 937-8351
Lat N 42.148 Lon W 77.061

Geneva Harley-Davidson Sales & Service, NJ-9
1103 Rtes. 5 & 20 **Geneva**
(315) 789-7976
Lat N 42.859 Lon W 77.03

Gowanda Harley-Davidson, NK-3
2535 Gowanda Zoar Rd. **Gowanda**
(716) 532-4584
Lat N 42.461 Lon W 78.908

Harley-Davidson of Jamestown, NM-2
2950 N Main St. Ext. (Exit 12 I-86) **Jamestown**
(716) 484-0113
Lat N 42.094 Lon W 79.245

Harv's Harley-Davidson, NI-8
3120 Kittering Rd. **Macedon**
(585) 377-0711
Lat N 43.119 Lon W 77.369

American Harley-Davidson, NI-3
1940 Military Rd. **Niagara Falls**
(716) 298-4849
Lat N 43.097 Lon W 78.974

American Harley-Davidson, NI-4
1149 Erie Ave. **North Tonawanda**
(716) 692-7200
Lat N 43.05 Lon W 78.848

Harley-Davidson of Rochester, NI-7
2600 W Henrietta Rd. (Rte. 15) **Rochester**
(585) 424-2120
Lat N 43.101 Lon W 77.629

Wyoming County Harley-Davidson, NJ-5
Rtes. 20A & 98 **Varysburg**
(585) 535-7900
Lat N 42.745 Lon W 78.321

© Rand McNally

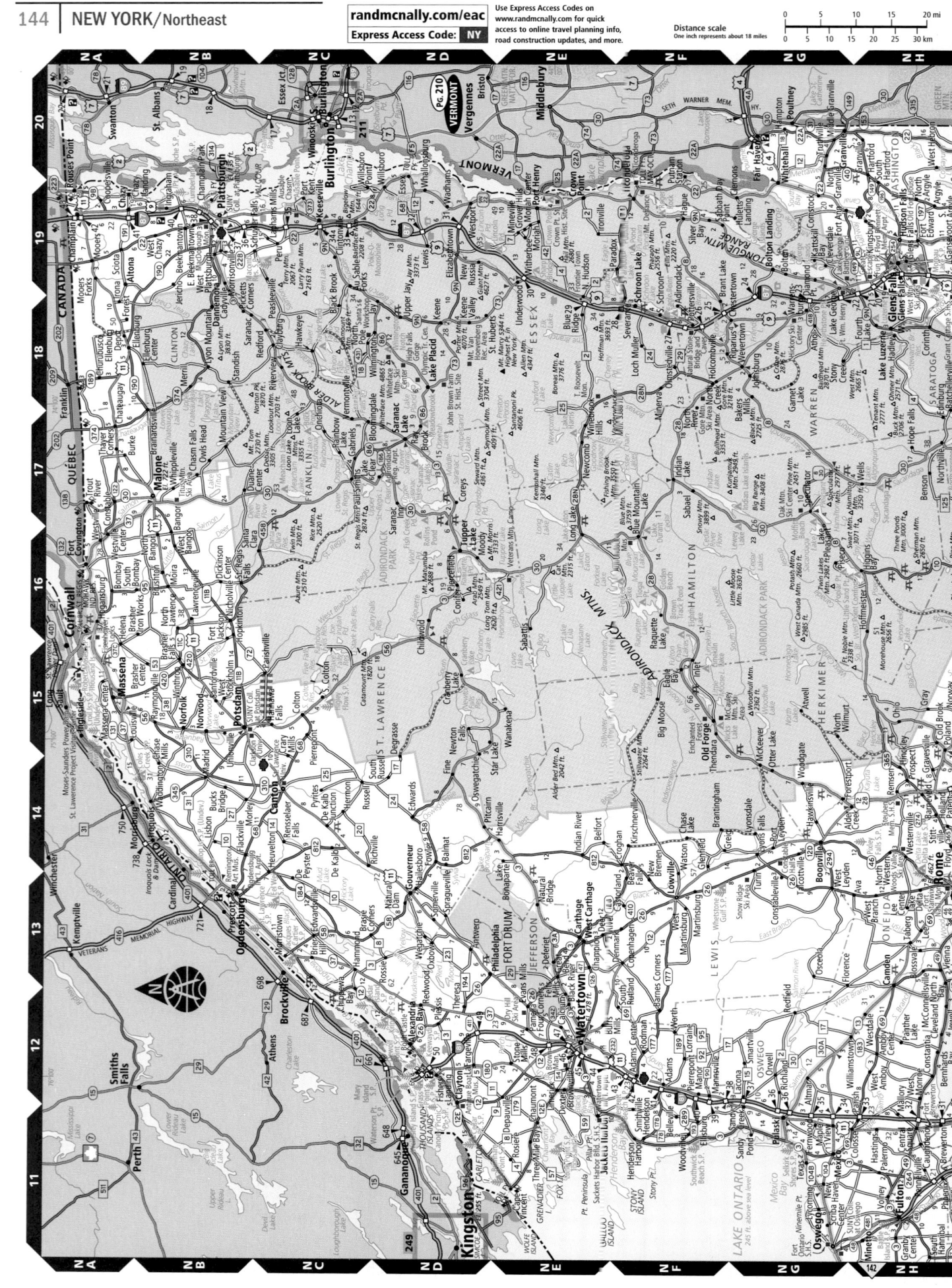

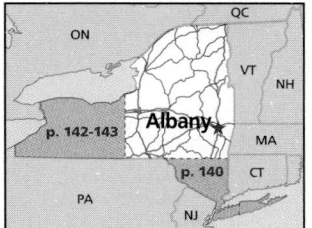

How to determine distance

Mileages in red between red arrowheads; in black, between intersections.

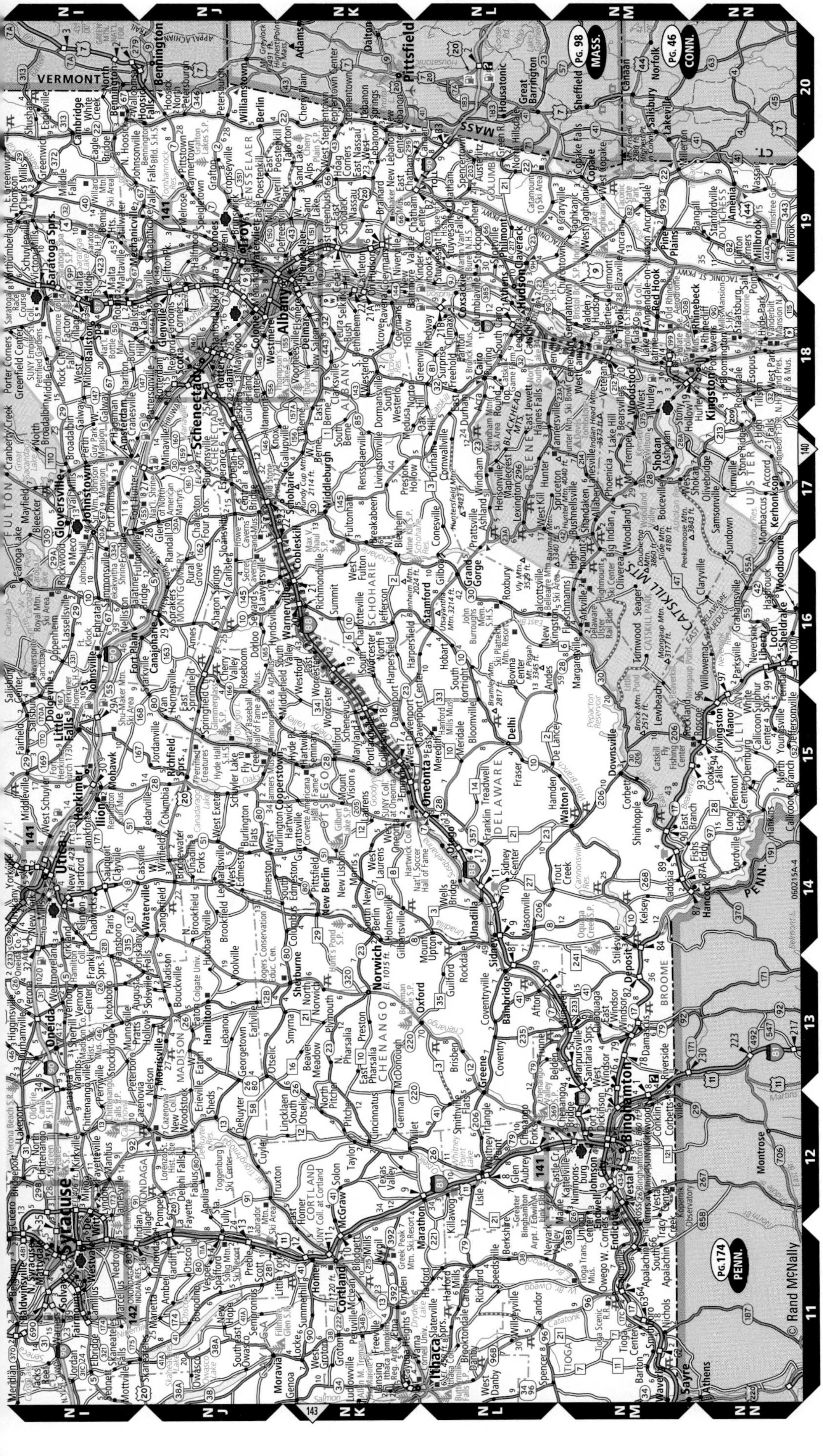

SYMBOLS

▓▓▓ Featured ride

╫╫╫ Long-term construction

🏍 Harley-Davidson dealership

▓▓▓ Scenic route

■ Historic site or monument; Indian reservation or rancheria; military installation; point of interest; wildlife refuge

HARLEY-DAVIDSON DEALERSHIPS

🏍 **Iron Block Harley-Davidson, NF-12**
17890 Goodnough St. **Adams Center**
(315) 583-6177
Lat N 43.865 **Lon** W 76.015

🏍 **Spitzie's Motorcycle Center, NJ-18**
1970 Central Ave. **Albany**
(518) 456-RIDE (7433)
Lat N 42.741 **Lon** W 73.86

🏍 **Southern Tier Harley-Davidson, NM-12**
1152 Front St. **Binghamton**
(607) 773-0264
Lat N 42.15 **Lon** W 75.899

🏍 **Tom McDermott Motorcycle Sales, NH-20**
4294 State Rte. 4 **Fort Ann**
(518) 746-9303
Lat N 43.384 **Lon** W 73.503

🏍 **Van's Harley-Davidson, NI-17**
432 S Main St. **Gloversville**
(518) 725-3698
Lat N 43.035 **Lon** W 74.356

🏍 **Woodstock Harley-Davidson, NM-18**
949 Rte. 28 **Kingston**
(845) 338-2800
Lat N 41.98 **Lon** W 74.086

🏍 **Harley-Davidson of Utica, NI-14**
4870 Commercial Dr. **New York Mills**
(315) 797-5570
Lat N 43.1 **Lon** W 75.301

🏍 **North End Harley-Davidson, NB-19**
594 Rte. 3 **Plattsburgh**
(518) 563-4360
Lat N 44.696 **Lon** W 73.506

🏍 **Sovie's Harley-Davidson, NC-15**
590 Ames Rd. **Potsdam**
(315) 265-4297
Lat N 44.631 **Lon** W 75.084

🏍 **Dick's Harley-Davidson, NH-14**
725 Erie Blvd. **Rome**
(315) 337-9160
Lat N 43.216 **Lon** W 75.473

🏍 **Spitzie's Harley-Davidson of Saratoga Springs, NI-18**
514 Broadway **Saratoga Springs**
(518) 581-8777
Lat N 43.085 **Lon** W 73.784

🏍 **Performance Harley-Davidson, NI-11**
807 N Geddes St. **Syracuse**
(315) 471-1157
Lat N 43.056 **Lon** W 76.17

🏍 **Brunswick Harley-Davidson, NJ-19**
1130 Hoosick Rd. (NY-7) **Troy**
(518) 279-1145
Lat N 42.759 **Lon** W 73.602

© Rand McNally

randmcnally.com/eac

Express Access Code: NY

Use Express Access Codes on
www.randmcnally.com for quick
access to online travel planning info,
road construction updates, and more.

How to determine distance

Mileages in red between red arrowheads; in black, between intersections.

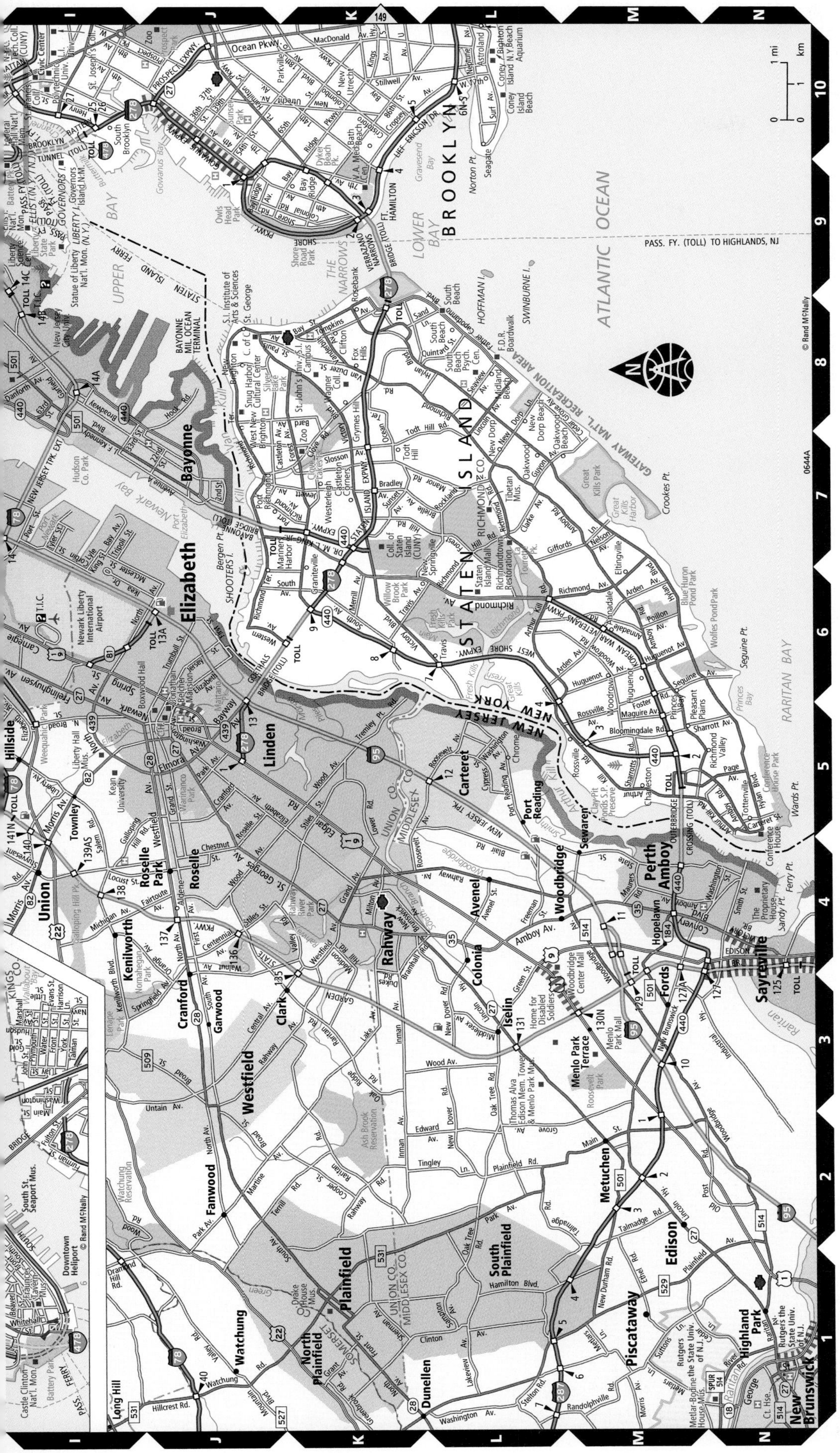

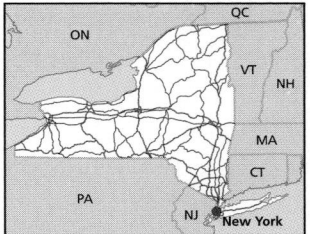

© Rand McNally

PASS. FY. (TOLL) TO HIGHLANDS, NJ

SYMBOLS

Featured ride

Long-term construction

Harley-Davidson dealership

Scenic route

Historic site or monument; Indian reservation or rancheria; military installation; point of interest; wildlife refuge

NEW YORK MOTORCYCLE LAWS

Helmet use:
Required and reflectorization required

Riding two abreast:
Yes. See state law for specifics

Eye protection:
Required by law

Speed limit:
Primary roads: 65 mph
Secondary roads: 65 mph

NEW YORK RESOURCES

Road conditions or construction:
(800) 847-8929 (thruway)
www.thruway.state.ny.us (thruway)
www.dot.state.ny.us (all other roads)

Highway Emergency Numbers:
911

Tourism:
(800) 225-5697
(518) 474-4116
www.iloveny.com

State motor vehicle information:
(518) 473-5595
www.nydmv.state.ny.us

randmcnally.com/eac
Express Access Code: **NY**

Use Express Access Codes on
www.randmcnally.com for quick
access to online travel planning info,
road construction updates, and more.

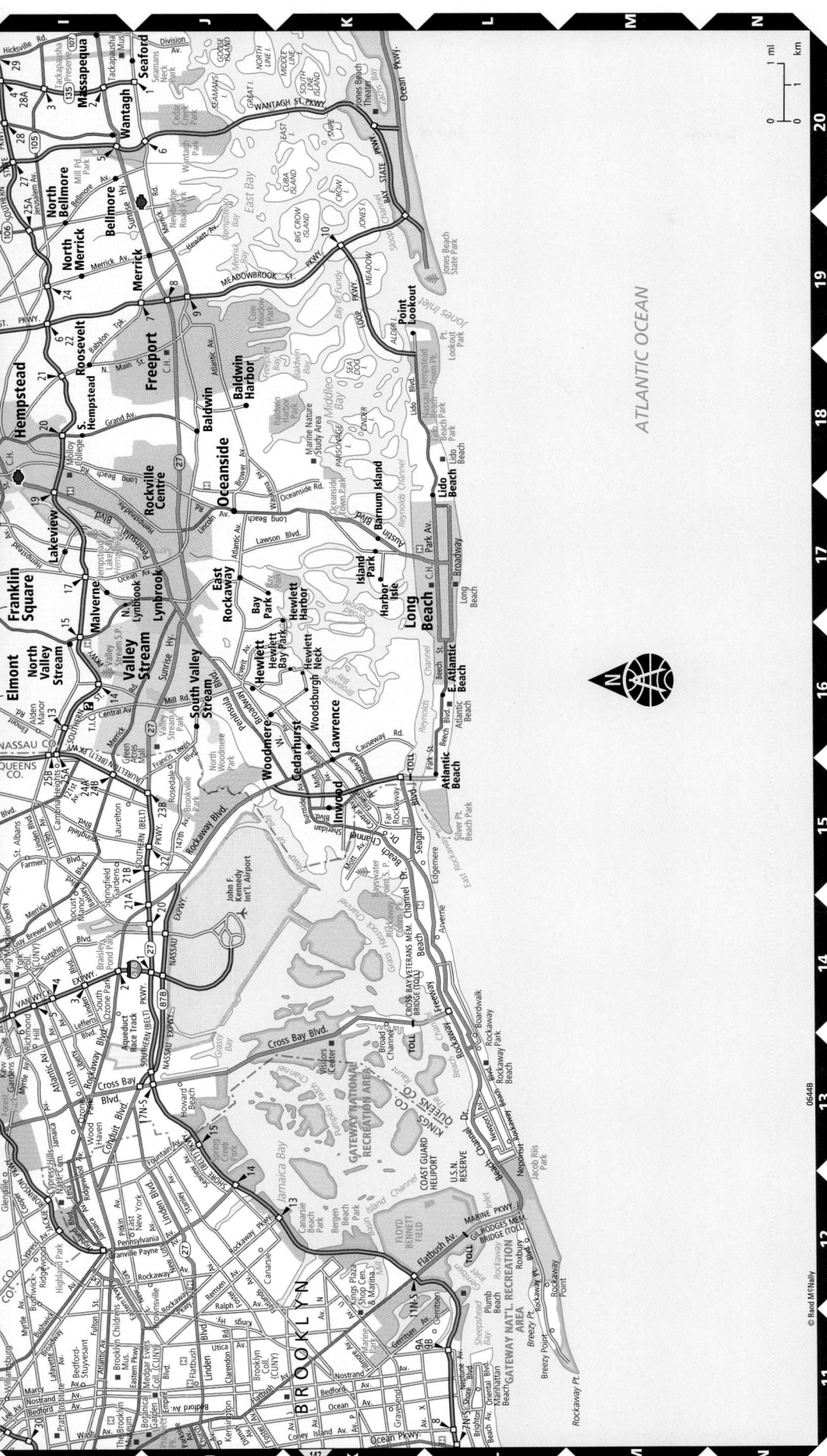

How to determine distance

Mileages in red between red arrowheads;
in black, between intersections.

SYMBOLS

Featured ride	Scenic route
Long-term construction	■ Historic site or monument; Indian reservation or rancheria; military installation; point of interest; wildlife refuge
Harley-Davidson dealership	

CITY-TO-CITY MILEAGE

	ALBANY	BINGHAMTON	BUFFALO	JAMESTOWN	PLATTSBURGH	ROCHESTER	SYRACUSE	UTICA
Albany		134	295	357	161	231	147	95
Auburn	176	90	128	193	259	64	27	85
Binghamton	134		230	224	282	166	76	93
Buffalo	295	230		71	378	78	154	204
Elmira	192	59	148	166	340	121	92	147
Glens Falls	58	179	313	402	110	249	165	113
Ithaca	176	51	154	191	287	90	58	113
Jamestown	357	224	71		505	143	219	269
Kingston	54	134	345	356	214	281	197	145
Lake Placid	142	263	347	412	49	283	201	164
Massena	221	242	312	377	87	248	166	161
New York	159	195	417	417	319	359	269	250
Niagara Falls	309	244	22	93	392	92	168	218
Olean	304	171	77	56	452	118	191	241
Oneonta	80	56	277	279	228	213	123	62
Oswego	176	116	159	224	259	77	40	85
Plattsburgh	161	282	378	505		314	230	188
Rochester	231	166	78	143	314		90	140
Syracuse	147	76	154	219	230	90		56
Utica	95	93	204	269	188	140	56	
Watertown	208	148	218	283	170	154	72	84

Use Express Access Codes on www.randmcnally.com for quick access to online travel planning info, road construction updates, and more.

Distance scale
One inch represents about 21 miles

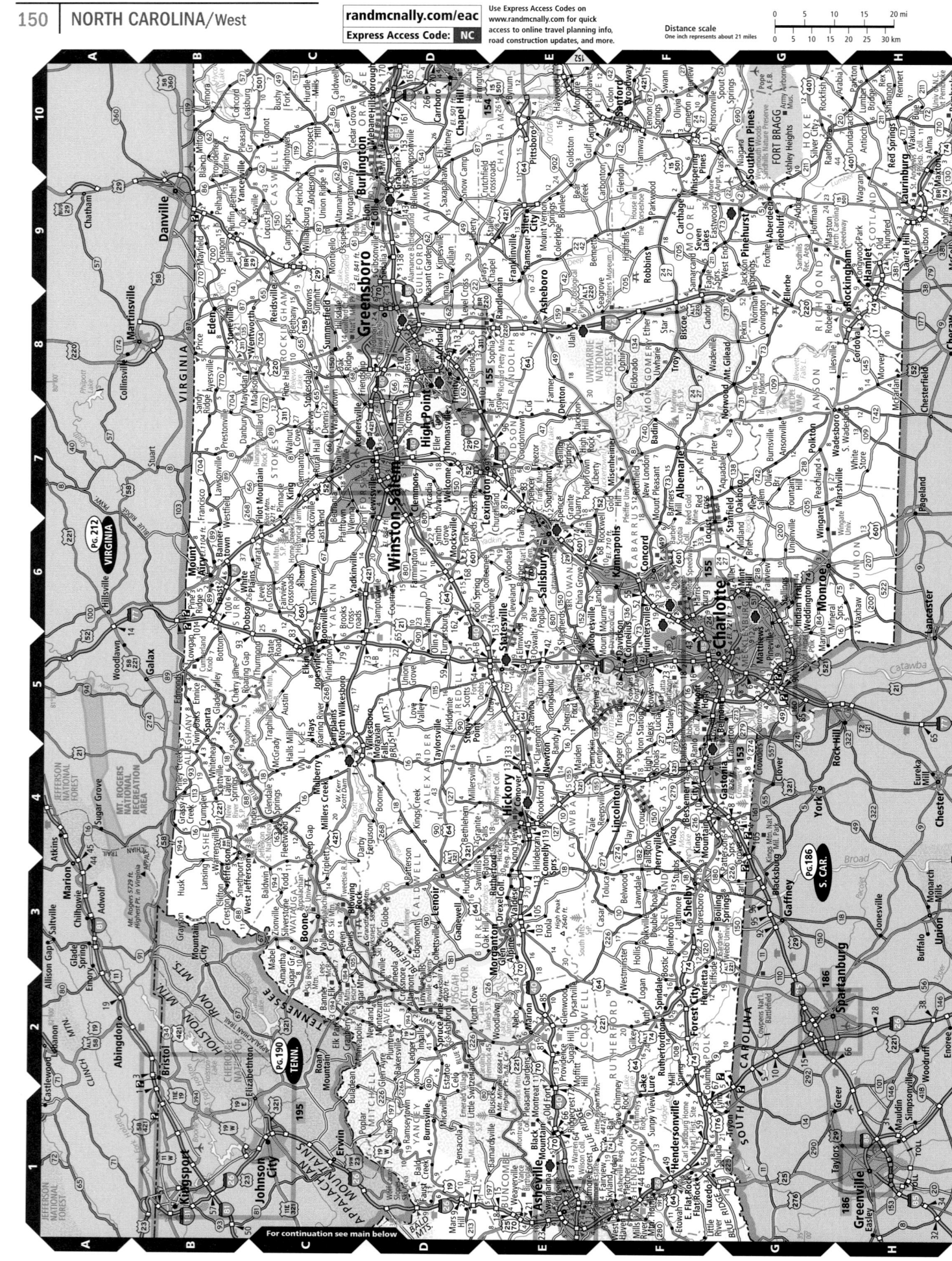

For continuation see main below

For North Carolina ride, see page R24.

NORTH CAROLINA MOTORCYCLE LAWS

Helmet use: Required

Riding two abreast:
Yes. See state law for specifics

Eye protection: Not required

Speed limit:
Primary roads: 70 mph; Secondary roads: 70 mph

NORTH CAROLINA RESOURCES

Road conditions or construction:
511
(877) 368-4968
www.ncsmartlink.org

Highway Emergency Numbers: 911 or *HP

Tourism:
(800) 847-4862; (919) 733-8372
www.visitnc.com

State motor vehicle information:
(919) 715-7000
www.ncdot.org/dmv/driver_services

HARLEY-DAVIDSON DEALERSHIPS

For Charlotte and Winston-Salem/Greensboro areas,
please see dealer listings on page 155.

Cox's Harley-Davidson, E-8
2795 NC Hwy. 134 **Asheboro**
(336) 629-2415
Lat N 35.615 **Lon** W 79.823

Davis' Harley-Davidson, D-9
2215 Hanford Rd. **Burlington**
(336) 227-1261
Lat N 36.062 **Lon** W 79.434

Pat Rogers Speedway Harley-Davidson, F-6
10049 Weddington Rd. **Concord**
(704) 979-7433
Lat N 35.363 **Lon** W 80.713

Pat Rogers Speedway Harley-Davidson, F-6
8111 Concord Mills Blvd. **Concord**
(704) 456-1024
Lat N 35.371 **Lon** W 80.718

Carolina Harley-Davidson, F-4
2830 E Franklin Blvd. **Gastonia**
(704) 867-2855
Lat N 35.26 **Lon** W 81.128

Blue Ridge Harley-Davidson, E-4
2002 13th Ave. Dr. SE **Hickory**
(828) 327-3030
Lat N 35.711 **Lon** W 81.305

Sandhill Harley-Davidson, G-9
7540 NC Hwy. 15-501 S **Pinehurst**
(910) 295-9033
Lat N 35.195 **Lon** W 79.464

Tilley's Harley-Davidson Shop, E-6
1509 E Innes St. **Salisbury**
(704) 638-6044
Lat N 35.653 **Lon** W 80.456

Tilley Harley-Davidson, E-5
1226 Morland Dr. **Statesville**
(704) 872-3883
Lat N 35.77 **Lon** W 80.86

Gene Lummus Harley-Davidson, E-1
20 Patton Cove Rd. **Swannanoa**
(828) 298-1683
Lat N 35.6 **Lon** W 82.403

Ghost Town Harley-Davidson, L-4
82 Locust Rd. **Waynesville**
(828) 454-0066
Lat N 35.476 **Lon** W 83.011

Crossroads Harley-Davidson, C-4
1921 US Hwy. 421 **Wilkesboro**
(336) 667-1003
Lat N 36.15 **Lon** W 81.185

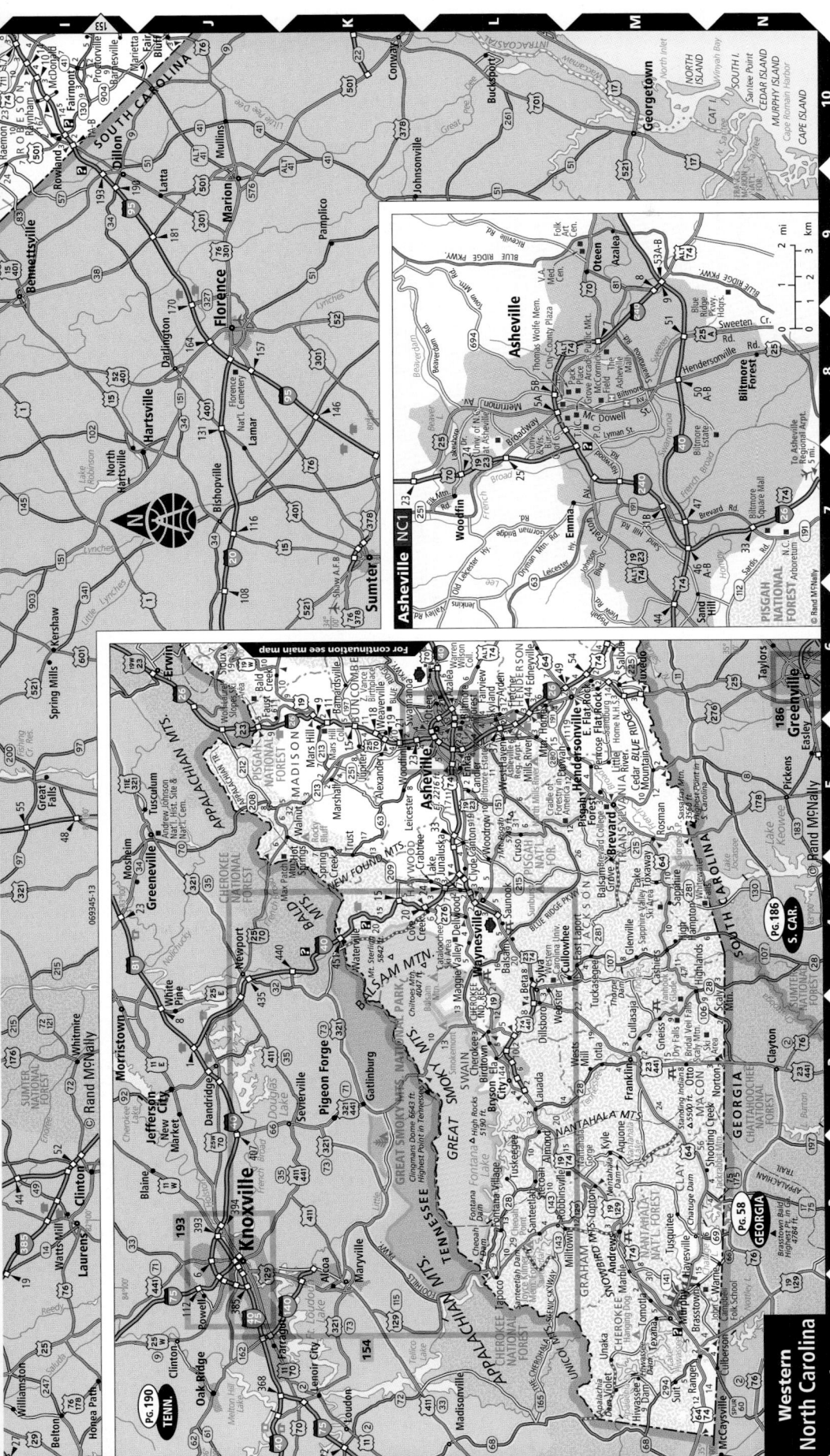

How to determine distance

Mileages in red between red arrowheads;
in black, between intersections.

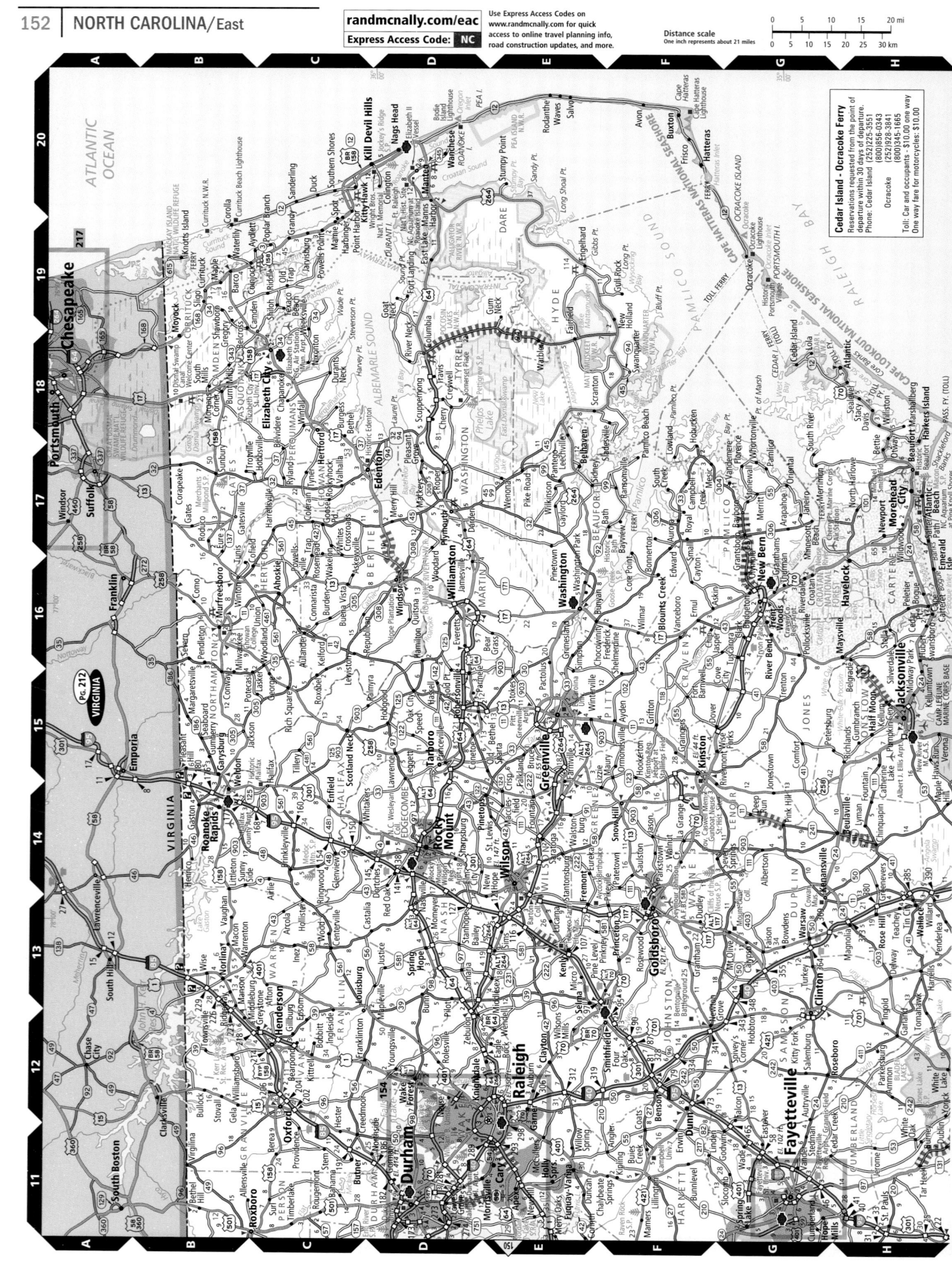

How to determine distance

Mileages in red between red arrowheads; in black, between intersections.

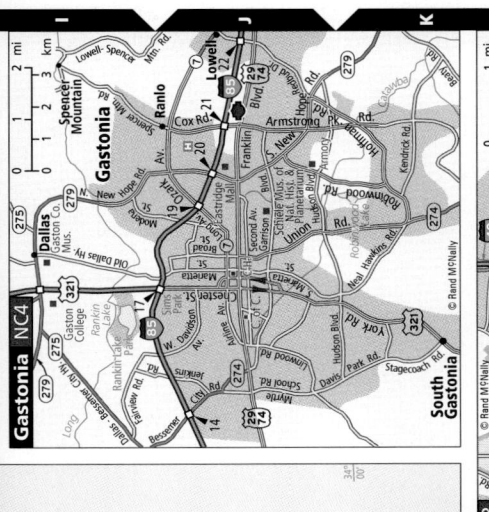

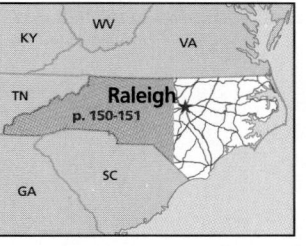

SYMBOLS

- Featured ride
- Long-term construction
- Harley-Davidson dealership
- Scenic route
- Historic site or monument; Indian reservation or rancheria; military installation; point of interest; wildlife refuge

HARLEY-DAVIDSON DEALERSHIPS

For the Raleigh/Durham area, please see dealer listings on page 155.

Outer Banks Harley-Davidson, C-18
1223 US Hwy. 17 **Elizabeth City**
(252) 338-8866
Lat N 36.296 Lon W 76.246

Cape Fear Harley-Davidson, G-11
3950 Sycamore Dairy Rd. **Fayetteville**
(910) 864-1200
Lat N 35.077 Lon W 78.951

Shelton's Harley-Davidson, F-13
606 Corporate Dr. **Goldsboro**
(919) 731-2776
Lat N 35.4 Lon W 77.984

New River Harley-Davidson Shop, H-15
2394 Wilmington Hwy. **Jacksonville**
(910) 346-9997
Lat N 34.739 Lon W 77.482

Nags Head Harley-Davidson, D-20
4104 S Virginia Dare Trail #22 **Nags Head**
(252) 255-5922
Lat N 35.954 Lon W 75.622

Harley-Davidson of New Bern, G-16
1613 Hwy. 70 E **New Bern**
(252) 633-4060
Lat N 35.075 Lon W 77.028

Collier Harley-Davidson, B-14
316 Premier Blvd. **Roanoke Rapids**
(252) 537-6493
Lat N 36.43 Lon W 77.641

Rocky Mount Harley-Davidson, D-14
928 N Winstead Ave. **Rocky Mount**
(252) 446-7292
Lat N 35.979 Lon W 77.844

Shelton's Harley-Davidson Mall Shop, F-12
1043 Industrial Park Dr. **Smithfield**
(919) 938-1592
Lat N 35.509 Lon W 78.313

J & E Harley-Davidson @ River City Shop, E-16
985 Carolina Ave. **Washington**
(252) 974-1345
Lat N 35.555 Lon W 77.059

Carolina Coast Harley-Davidson, J-14
6620 Market St. **Wilmington**
(910) 791-9997
Lat N 34.257 Lon W 77.84

J & E Harley-Davidson, E-15
2300 Elaines' Way **Winterville**
(252) 439-1345
Lat N 35.536 Lon W 77.408

© Rand McNally

randmcnally.com/eac
Express Access Code: NC

Use Express Access Codes on www.randmcnally.com for quick access to online travel planning info, road construction updates, and more.

© Rand McNally

Raleigh / Durham / Chapel Hill NC5

Durham
Chapel Hill
Carrboro
Parkwood
Farrington
Fearrington
Wilsonville
Apex
Morrisville
Carpenter
Green Level
Cary
Macedonia
Garner
Raleigh
New Hope
Wake Forest
Forestville
Falls
Bayleaf
McAdenville
Belmont
Neuse
S. CAR.
Lake Wylie

Knoxville
Marbledale
Kodak
Clevenger
Newport
Bridgeport
Del Rio
Stanleyvi
Kimberlin Heights
Boyds Creek
Chestnut Hill
Seymour
Oak City
Trundel Crossroad
Sevierville
Harrisburg
ENGLISH MOUNTAIN
SNOW MOUNTAIN
CHEROKEE NATIONAL FOREST
Nough
Louisville
Rockford
Wildwood
Knob Creek
Du Pont
Cherokee Hills
East Fork
Jones Cove
Cosby
Hartford
Alcoa
Maryville
Miser Station
Binfield
Walden Creek
Pigeon Forge
Cove Creek Cascades
Dollywood
Great Smoky Arts & Crafts Community
Pittman Center
Waterville
CHILHOWEE MOUNTAIN
Wear Valley
Gatlinburg
Ranger Station
TENNESSEE
BALSAM MOUNTAIN
PISGAH NAT'L FOR.
Walland
Townsend
Elkmont
Mt. Le Conte 6593 ft.
APPALACHIAN MOUNTAINS
Mt. Sterling 5842 ft.
Cove Creek
Tuckaleechee Cavern
Newfound Gap 5048 ft.
Cades Cove
Clingmans Dome 6643 ft.
GREAT SMOKY MOUNTAINS NAT'L PK.
Chiltoes Mtn. 4047 ft.
Maggie Valley
Dellwood
Tallassee
NORTH CAROLINA
Thunderhead Mtn. 5527 ft.
Andrews Bald 5920 ft.
GREAT SMOKY MOUNTAINS
Oconaluftee Visitor Center
Cherokee Indian Reservation
Waynesville
Arcadia
Tapoco
Fontana Village
WELCH RIDGE
High Rocks 5190 ft.
Birdtown
Cherokee
PLOTT BALSAMS
Yellow Creek
Tuskeegee
Bryson City
Ela
Whittier
Saunook
Balsam
CHEROKEE NATIONAL FOREST
UNICOI MOUNTAINS
Stecoah
Almond
Lauada
COWEE MOUNTAINS
Barkers Creek
Beta
Sylva
Welcome
CHEOAH MOUNTAINS
Santeetlah
Robbinsville
NANTAHALA NATIONAL FOREST
Dillsboro
Webster
Western Carolina Univ.
Arnold

Great Smoky Mountains National Park NC7

© Rand McNally

How to determine distance

Mileages in red between red arrowheads;
in black, between intersections.

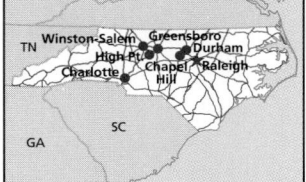

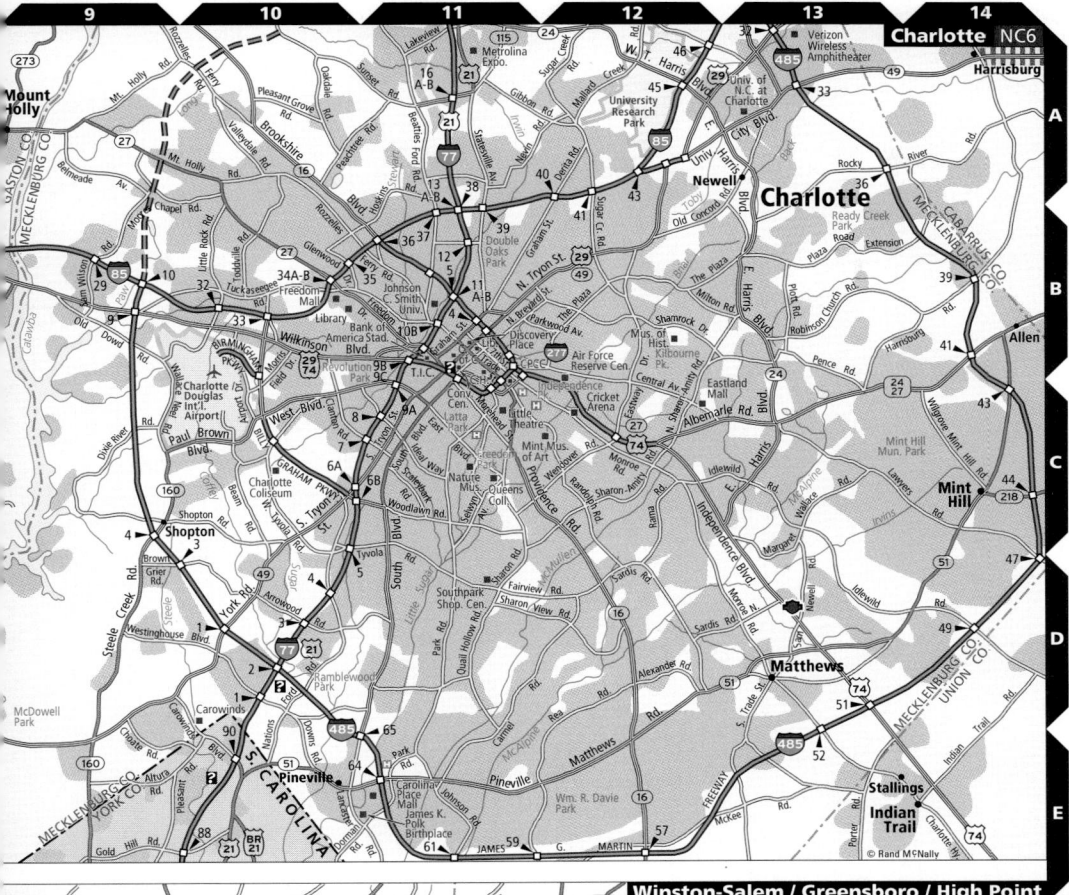

Charlotte NC6

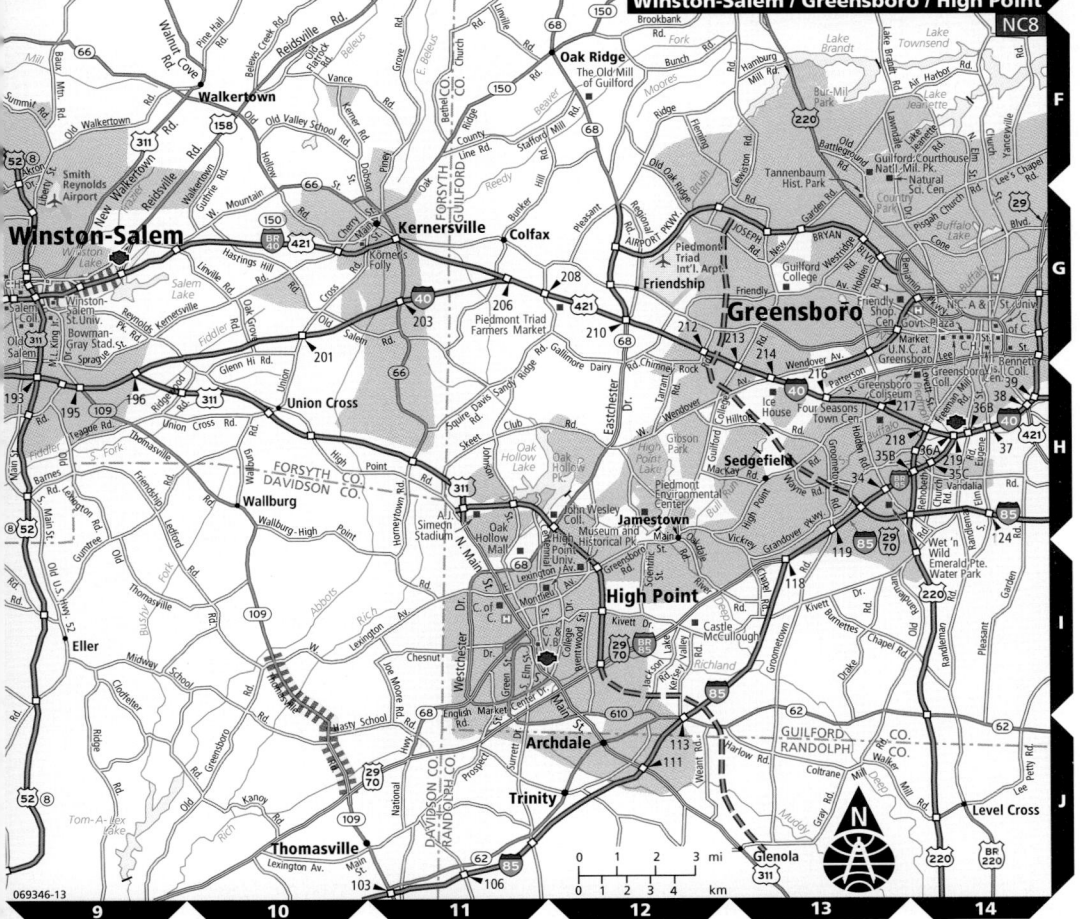

Winston-Salem / Greensboro / High Point NC8

SYMBOLS

- Featured ride
- Long-term construction
- Harley-Davidson dealership
- Scenic route
- ■ Historic site or monument; Indian reservation or rancheria; military installation; point of interest; wildlife refuge

CITY-TO-CITY MILEAGE

	ASHEVILLE	CHARLOTTE	FAYETTEVILLE	GREENSBORO	GREENVILLE	RALEIGH	WILMINGTON	WINSTON-SALEM
Asheville		126	261	168	325	247	328	144
Boone	85	118	206	113	270	192	321	89
Charlotte	126		139	97	247	169	204	83
Durham	221	143	92	53	105	27	156	81
Elizabeth City	409	331	206	241	96	164	213	269
Fayetteville	261	139		98	109	66	118	121
Greensboro	168	97	98		157	79	208	28
Greenville	325	247	109	157		80	137	185
Hickory	73	63	192	99	256	178	307	75
Knoxville, TN	115	229	373	280	437	359	431	256
Nags Head	444	366	241	276	131	199	239	304
New Bern	358	280	130	190	46	112	90	218
Raleigh	247	169	66	79	80		130	107
Roanoke Rapids	306	228	128	138	80	86	192	166
Rockingham	199	75	64	90	174	97	129	109
Rocky Mt.	299	221	96	131	38	54	160	159
Wilmington	328	204	118	208	137	130		236
Winston-Salem	144	83	121	28	185	107	236	

HARLEY-DAVIDSON DEALERSHIPS

- **Shelton's Harley-Davidson of Durham, A-3**
  300 Muldee St. **Durham**
  (919) 682-6695
  Lat N 35.994 Lon W 78.863

- **Harley-Davidson of Greensboro, H-14**
  538 Farragut St. **Greensboro**
  (336) 273-1101
  Lat N 36.033 Lon W 79.806

- **Harley-Davidson Shop of High Point, I-12**
  1033 S Main St. **High Point**
  (336) 883-1105
  Lat N 35.945 Lon W 80.003

- **Harley-Davidson of Charlotte, D-13**
  9205 E Independence Blvd. **Matthews**
  (704) 847-4647
  Lat N 35.141 Lon W 80.719

- **Ray Price Harley-Davidson, D-6**
  1126 S Saunders St. **Raleigh**
  (919) 832-2261
  Lat N 35.766 Lon W 78.649

- **Curly's Harley-Davidson, G-9**
  3825 Reidsville Rd. **Winston-Salem**
  (336) 722-3106
  Lat N 36.108 Lon W 80.19

069346-13

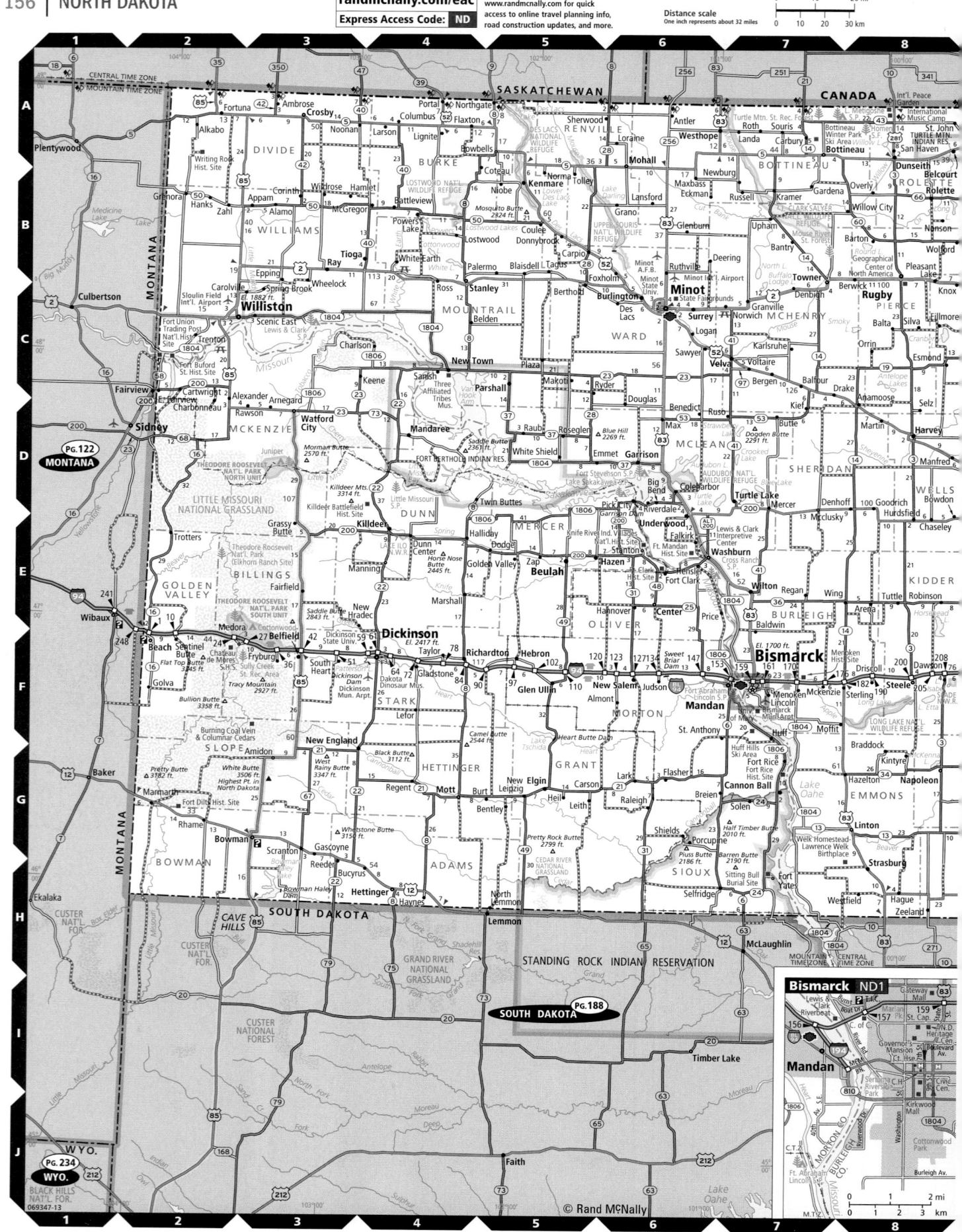

Distance scale
One inch represents about 32 miles

© Rand McNally

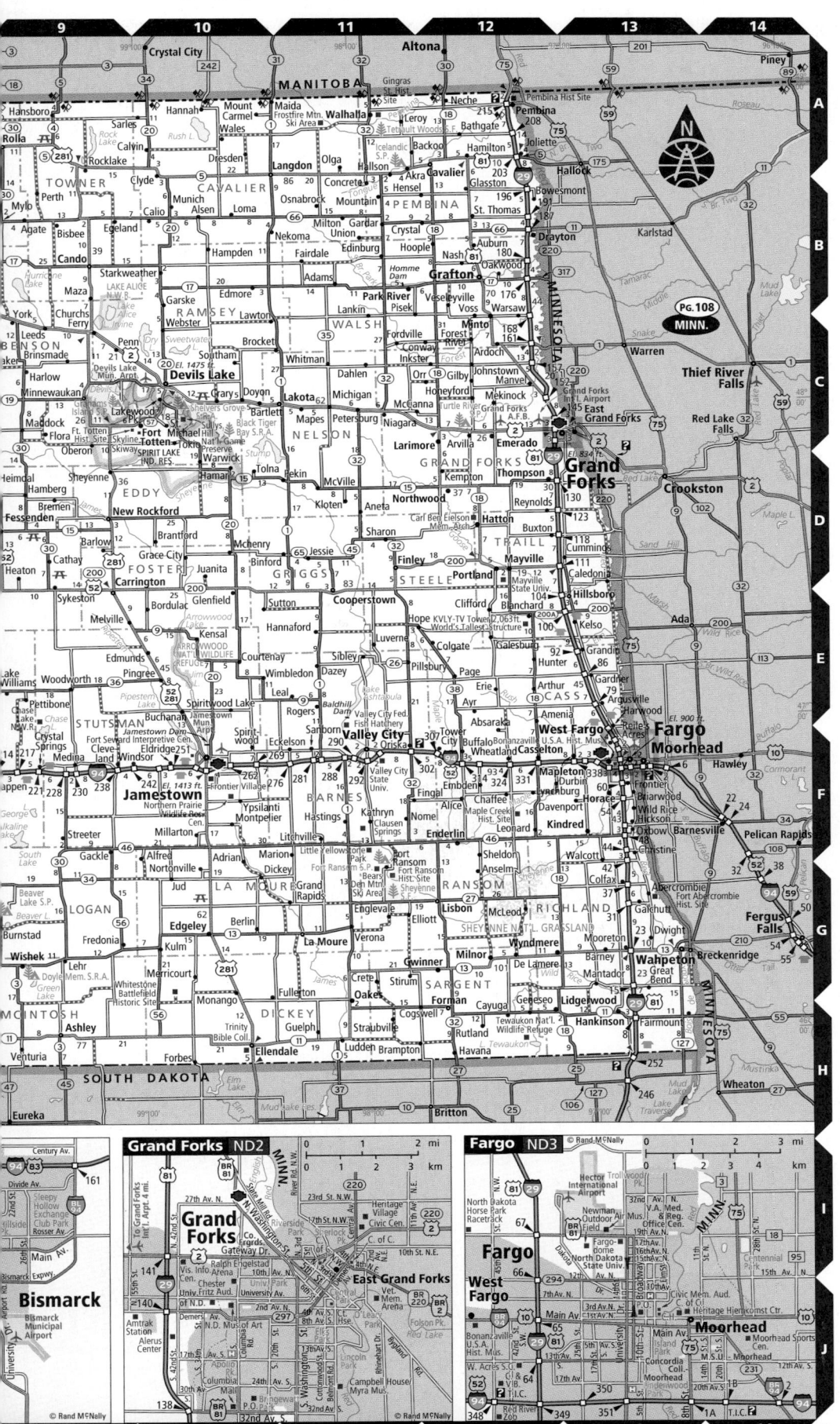

How to determine distance

Mileages in red between red arrowheads;
in black, between intersections.

SYMBOLS

Featured ride	Scenic route
Long-term construction	Historic site or monument; Indian reservation or rancheria; military installation; point of interest; wildlife refuge
Harley-Davidson dealership	

NORTH DAKOTA MOTORCYCLE LAWS

Helmet use:
Required under age 18, and reflectorization required

Riding two abreast:
Yes. See state law for specifics

Eye protection:
Not required

Speed limit:
Primary roads: 75 mph
Secondary roads: 75 mph

NORTH DAKOTA RESOURCES

Road conditions or construction:
511
(866) 696-3511
www.state.nd.us/dot/

Highway Emergency Numbers:
911 or (800) 472-2121

Tourism:
(800) 435-5663
(701) 328-2525
www.ndtourism.com

State motor vehicle information:
(701) 328-2500
www.state.nd.us/dot/dlts.html

CITY-TO-CITY MILEAGE

	BISMARCK	DEVILS LAKE	DICKINSON	FARGO	GARRISON	GRAND FORKS	MINOT	WILLISTON
Bismarck		179	99	193	76	269	111	230
Devils Lake	179		275	163	168	89	121	249
Dickinson	99	275		289	148	365	183	131
Fargo	193	163	289		266	78	263	420
Garrison	76	168	148	266		257	47	141
Grand Forks	269	89	365	78	257		210	338
Minot	111	121	183	263	47	210		126
Williston	230	249	131	420	141	338	126	

HARLEY-DAVIDSON DEALERSHIPS

Andy's Harley-Davidson, C-13
2756 N Washington St. **Grand Forks**
(701) 775-6098
Lat N 47.948 Lon W 97.068

Stutsman Harley-Davidson, F-10
1202 12th Ave. SE **Jamestown**
(701) 252-5271
Lat N 46.897 Lon W 98.692

Roughrider Harley-Davidson, F-7
3708 Memorial Hwy. (I-94) **Mandan**
(701) 663-2220
Lat N 46.816 Lon W 100.845

Rough Rider Harley-Davidson Minot, C-6
515 20th Ave. SE **Minot**
(701) 839-6330
Lat N 48.211 Lon W 101.286

Fargo Harley-Davidson Sales & Service, F-13
600 W Main Ave. **West Fargo**
(701) 277-1000
Lat N 46.877 Lon W 96.909

randmcnally.com/eac

Express Access Code: OH

Use Express Access Codes on
www.randmcnally.com for quick
access to online travel planning info,
road construction updates, and more.

Distance scale
One inch represents about 12 miles

0   5   10   15 mi

0   5   10   15   20 km

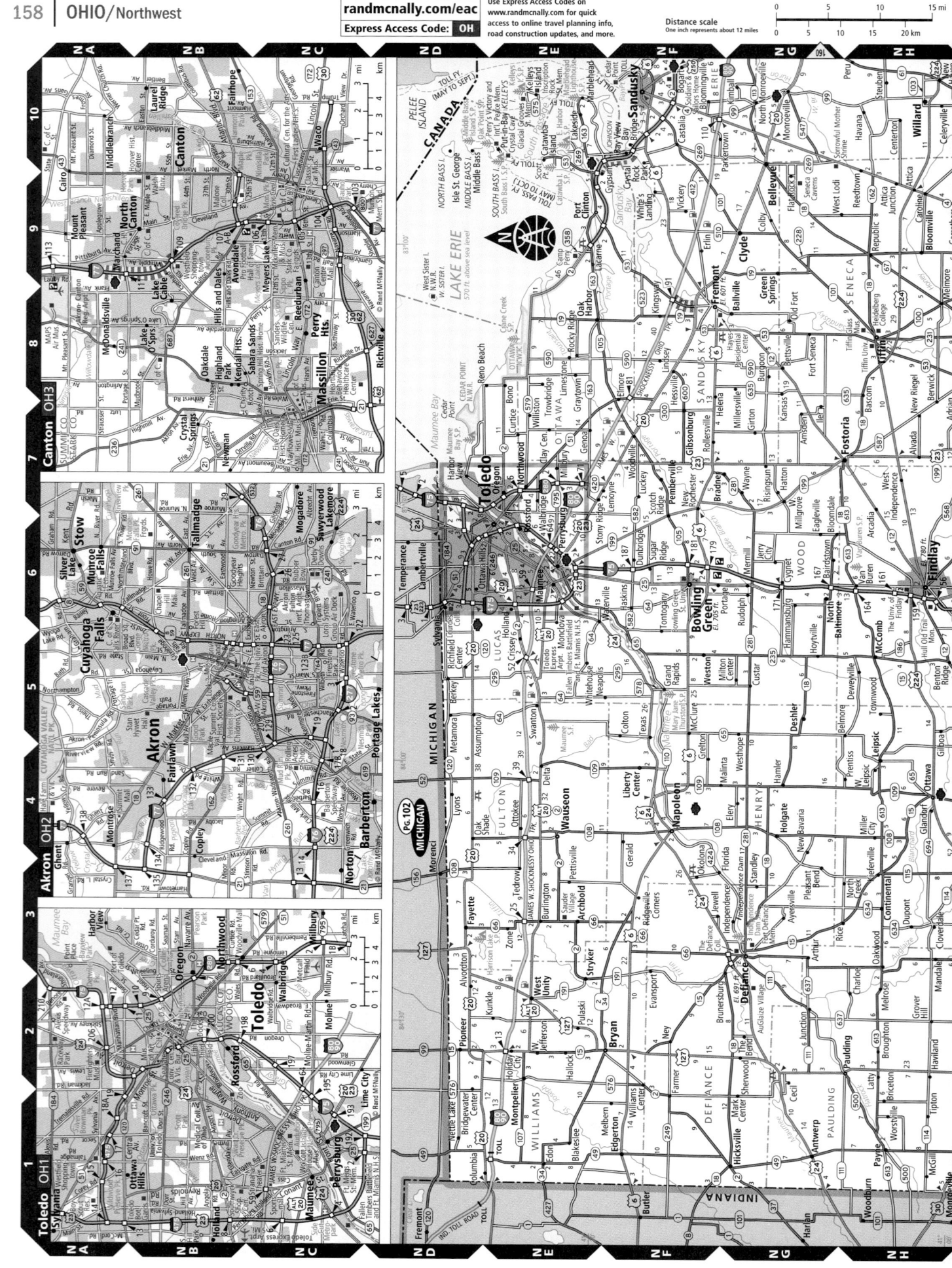

How to determine distance

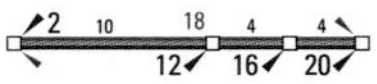

Mileages in red between red arrowheads; in black, between intersections.

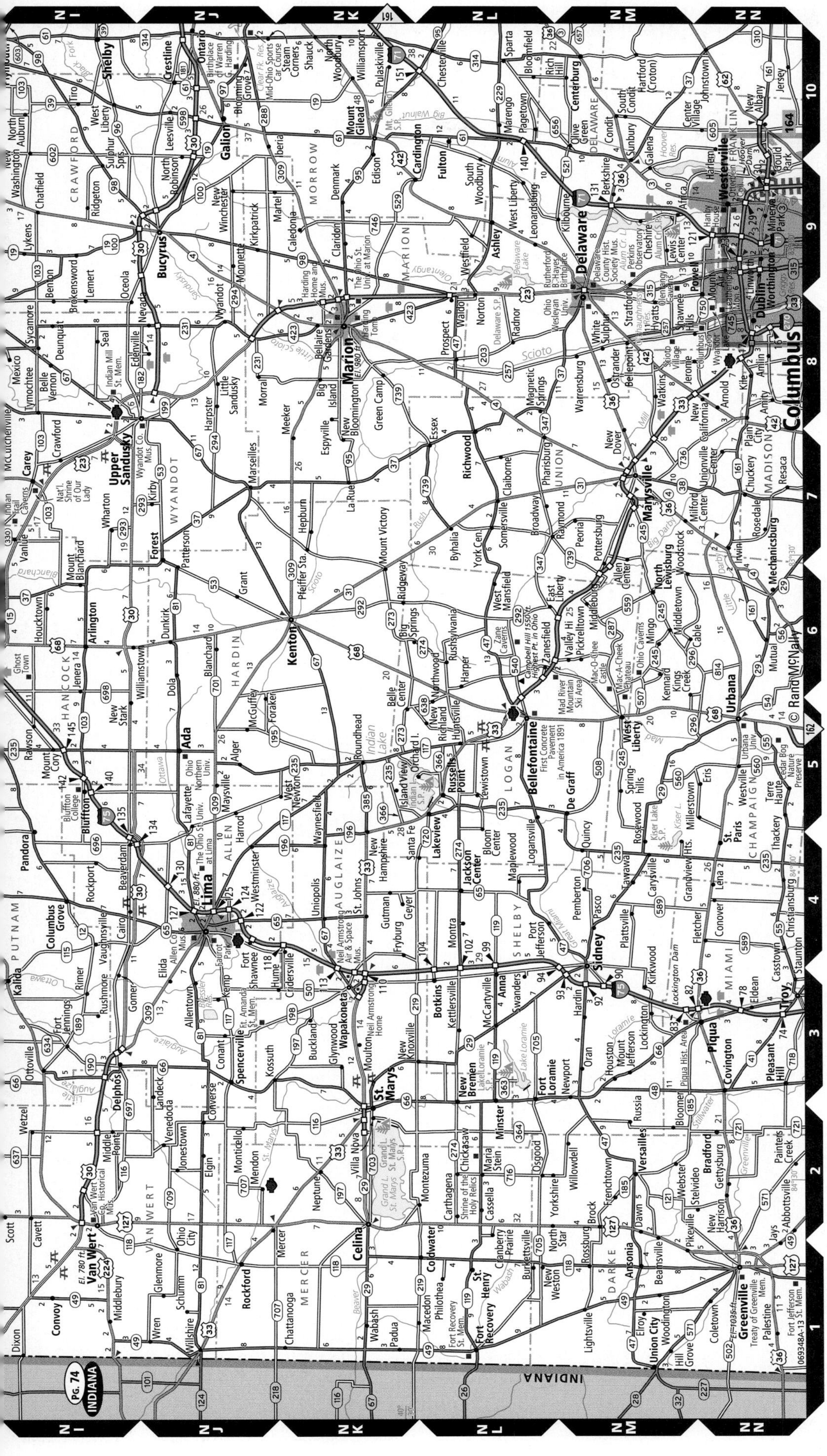

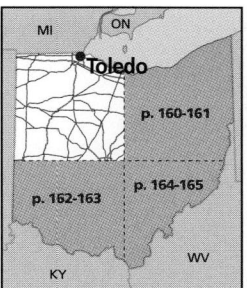

MI | ON
Toledo
p. 160-161
p. 162-163 | p. 164-165
KY | WV

SYMBOLS

—— Featured ride
Long-term construction
Harley-Davidson dealership
——— Scenic route
■ Historic site or monument; Indian reservation or rancheria; military installation; point of interest; wildlife refuge

HARLEY-DAVIDSON DEALERSHIPS

High Point Harley-Davidson, NL-5
288 Stockyard Rd. (TR-217) **Bellefontaine**
(937) 599-4550
Lat N 40.382 **Lon** W 83.76

Harley-Davidson of Lima, NJ-4
3255 Fort Shawnee Industrial Dr. **Lima**
(419) 331-3027
Lat N 40.688 **Lon** W 84.124

Jim's Harley-Davidson Sales, NJ-2
7172 Rte. 707 **Mendon**
(419) 795-4185
Lat N 40.671 **Lon** W 84.524

Roeder Harley-Davidson Shop, NG-10
3684 US 20 W **Monroeville**
(419) 465-2546
Lat N 41.239 **Lon** W 82.703

Harley-Davidson Sales & Service, NF-4
862 American Rd. **Napoleon**
(419) 592-7123
Lat N 41.363 **Lon** W 84.084

Ben Breece Harley-Davidson, NH-4
242 W 4th St. **Ottawa**
(419) 523-4274
Lat N 41.021 **Lon** W 84.05

Signature Harley-Davidson, NE-6
1176 Professional Dr. **Perrysburg**
(419) 873-2453
Lat N 41.55 **Lon** W 83.607

Gover Harley-Davidson, NN-3
1501 E Ash St. (US Rte. 36) **Piqua**
(937) 773-8733
Lat N 40.154 **Lon** W 84.243

C & A Harley-Davidson, NN-8
7610 Commerce Place **Plain City**
(614) 873-4604
Lat N 40.124 **Lon** W 83.189

Roeder Harley-Davidson, NE-10
3976 Harbor Light Landing Dr. **Port Clinton**
(419) 732-6282
Lat N 41.503 **Lon** W 82.835

Roeder Harley-Davidson, NF-10
5316 Milan Rd. **Sandusky**
(419) 621-1046
Lat N 41.397 **Lon** W 82.653

Toledo Harley-Davidson, ND-6
7960 W Central Ave. **Toledo**
(419) 843-7892
Lat N 41.674 **Lon** W 83.734

Thiel's Wheels Harley-Davidson, NI-8
350 Tarhe Trail **Upper Sandusky**
(419) 294-4951
Lat N 40.856 **Lon** W 83.274

Cleveland
p. 158-159
p. 162-163   p. 164-165

MI   ON
KY   WV

SYMBOLS

— Featured ride
⫴ Long-term construction
🏍 Harley-Davidson dealership
▨ Scenic route
■ Historic site or monument; Indian reservation or rancheria; military installation; point of interest; wildlife refuge

HARLEY-DAVIDSON DEALERSHIPS

🏍 **Liberty Harley-Davidson of Akron, NH-16**
32 E Cuyahoga Falls **Akron**
(330) 535-9900
Lat N 41.105 **Lon** W 81.514

🏍 **Lake Erie Harley-Davidson Shop, NF-13**
38401 Chester Rd. **Avon**
(440) 934-5000
Lat N 41.467 **Lon** W 82.051

🏍 **South East Harley-Davidson Sales, NF-16**
23105 Aurora Rd. **Bedford Heights**
(440) 439-5300
Lat N 41.417 **Lon** W 81.514

🏍 **Liberty Harley-Davidson North Shop, NG-16**
334 E Hines Hill Rd. **Boston Heights**
(330) 650-2799
Lat N 41.263 **Lon** W 81.502

🏍 **Harley-Davidson of Youngstown, NH-19**
4478 Boardman-Canfield Rd. **Canfield**
(330) 702-1010
Lat N 41.025 **Lon** W 80.733

🏍 **Harley-Davidson Sales, NF-14**
14550 Lorain Ave. **Cleveland**
(216) 252-3111
Lat N 41.454 **Lon** W 81.796

🏍 **Warren Harley-Davidson Sales, NF-19**
2102 Elm Rd. **Cortland**
(330) 395-4700
Lat N 41.316 **Lon** W 80.733

🏍 **Adventure Harley-Davidson, NK-16**
1465 Rte. 39 NW **Dover**
(330) 364-6519
Lat N 40.536 **Lon** W 81.478

🏍 **Elyria Harley-Davidson Sales, NF-13**
561 Cleveland St. **Elyria**
(440) 365-7354
Lat N 41.376 **Lon** W 82.08

🏍 **Hale's Harley-Davidson, NJ-11**
1400 Harrington Memorial Rd. **Mansfield**
(419) 522-8602
Lat N 40.794 **Lon** W 82.513

🏍 **Carlton Harley-Davidson, NG-17**
11771 State Rte. 44 **Mantua**
(330) 274-3141
Lat N 41.309 **Lon** W 81.222

🏍 **Century Harley-Davidson, NH-14**
3053 Eastpointe Circle **Medina**
(330) 721-1702
Lat N 41.137 **Lon** W 81.797

🏍 **Western Reserve Harley-Davidson, ND-16**
8567 Tyler Blvd. **Mentor**
(440) 974-6900
Lat N 41.686 **Lon** W 81.333

🏍 **Freedom Harley-Davidson, NI-16**
7233 Sunset Strip Ave. NW **North Canton**
(330) 494-2453
Lat N 40.887 **Lon** W 81.433

🏍 **Neidengard's Harley-Davidson, NL-19**
284 Canton Rd. (Rte. 43) **Wintersville**
(740) 266-6188
Lat N 40.381 **Lon** W 80.708

How to determine distance
Mileages in red between red arrowheads; in black, between intersections.

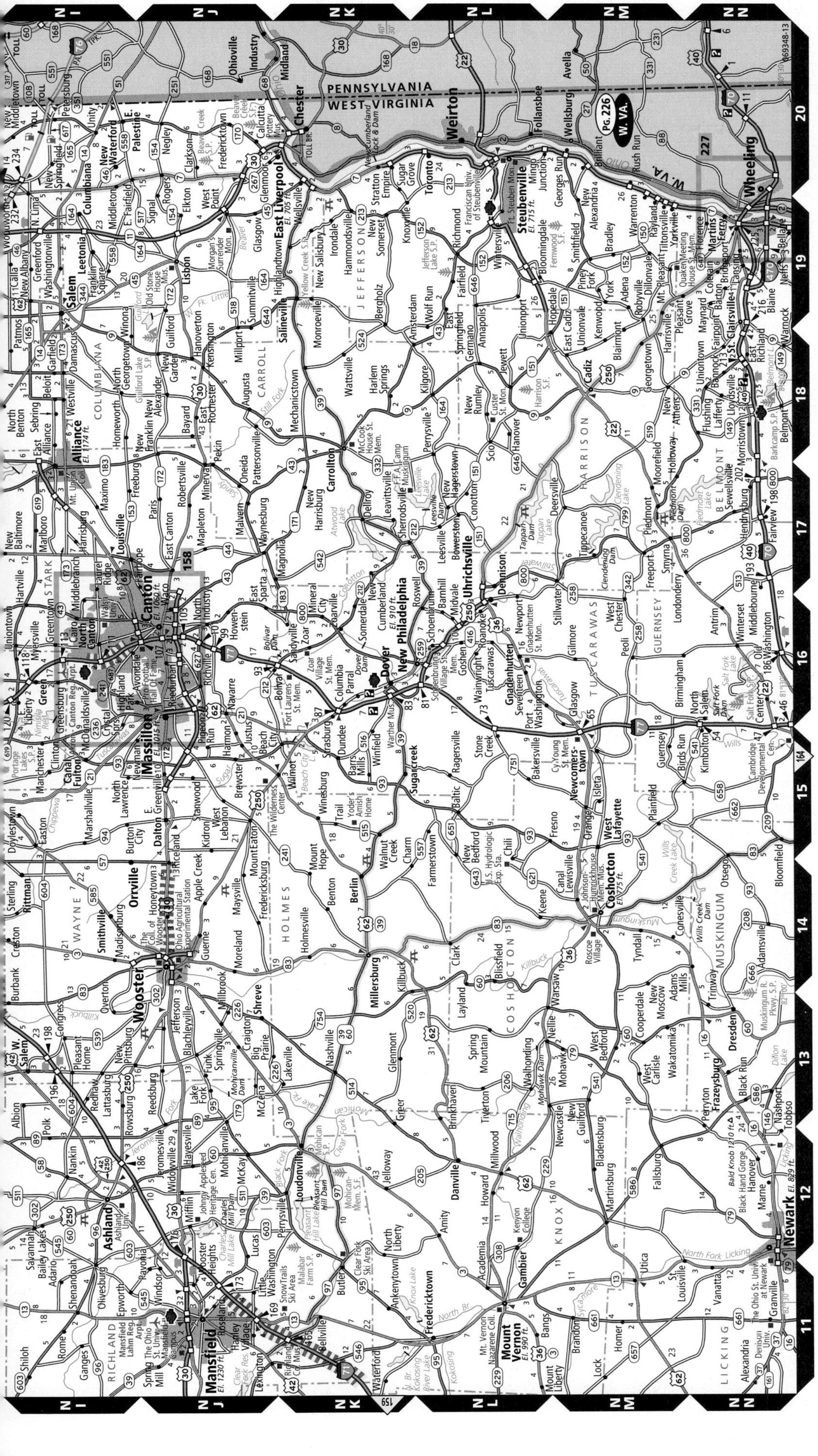

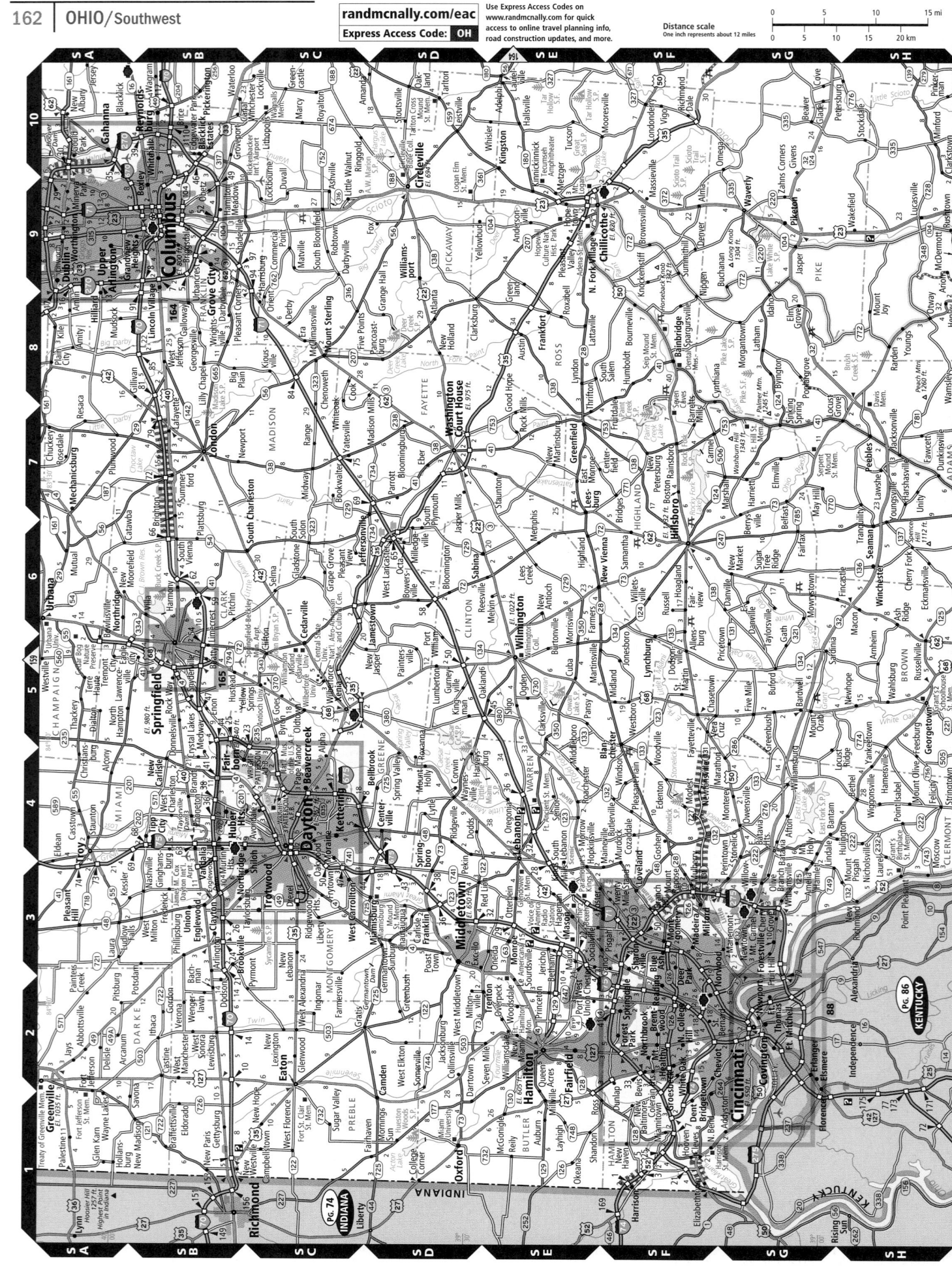

How to determine distance

Mileages in red between red arrowheads; in black, between intersections.

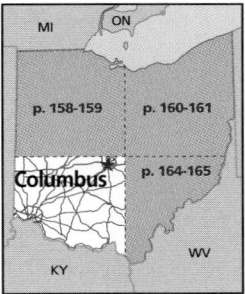

HARLEY-DAVIDSON DEALERSHIPS

Harley-Davidson of Chillicothe, SE-9
818 Eastern Ave. **Chillicothe**
(740) 773-8826
Lat N 39.324 Lon W 82.957

Harley-Davidson of Cincinnati-Eastgate, SG-3
699 Old SR 74 **Cincinnati (Eastgate)**
(513) 528-1400
Lat N 39.071 Lon W 84.277

Harley-Davidson of Cincinnati-Eastgate, SG-3
4601 Eastgate Blvd. Ste. 816 **Cincinnati**
(513) 752-7890
Lat N 39.104 Lon W 84.279

Fargo Harley-Davidson Sales & Service, SF-2
1799 Tennessee Ave. **Cincinnati**
(513) 641-1188
Lat N 39.167 Lon W 84.466

A.D. Farrow Harley-Davidson, SB-9
491 W Broad St. **Columbus**
(614) 228-6353
Lat N 39.961 Lon W 83.013

F & S Harley-Davidson, SC-4
7220 N Dixie Dr. **Dayton**
(937) 898-8084
Lat N 39.835 Lon W 84.199

Tri-County Harley-Davidson, SE-2
5960 Dixie Hwy. **Fairfield**
(513) 874-4343
Lat N 39.328 Lon W 84.514

Aces & Eights Harley-Davidson, SE-3
2383 Kings Center Ct. **Mason**
(513) 459-1777
Lat N 39.356 Lon W 84.26

Centennial Park Harley-Davidson, SA-10
12477 Broad St. SW **Pataskala**
(740) 964-2205
Lat N 39.995 Lon W 82.724

Mid-Ohio Harley-Davidson, SB-6
2100 Quality Ln. **Springfield**
(937) 322-3590
Lat N 39.894 Lon W 83.734

Buckminn's Harley-Davidson, SC-5
1213 Cincinnati Ave. **Xenia**
(937) 376-3344
Lat N 39.67 Lon W 83.944

© Rand McNally

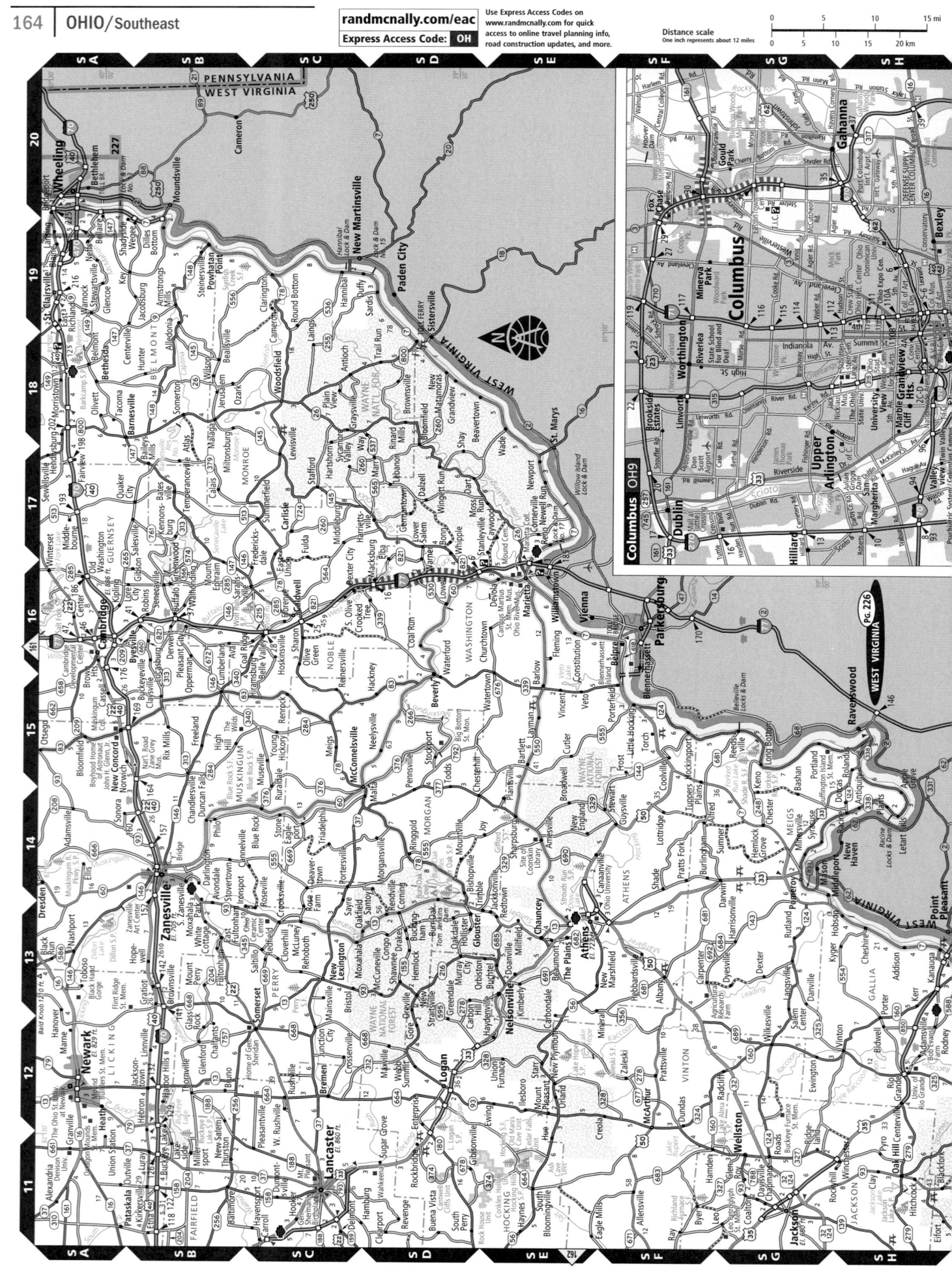

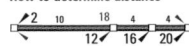

How to determine distance

Mileages in red between red arrowheads; in black, between intersections.

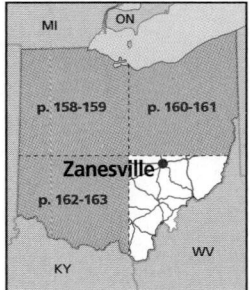

MI ON

p. 158-159   p. 160-161

Zanesville

p. 162-163

KY   WV

SYMBOLS

▬ Featured ride	▬ Scenic route
╫╫╫ Long-term construction	■ Historic site or monument; Indian reservation or rancheria; military installation; point of interest; wildlife refuge
🏍 Harley-Davidson dealership	

OHIO MOTORCYCLE LAWS

Helmet use:
Required under age 18, and required for novice riders

Riding two abreast:
Yes. See state law for specifics

Eye protection:
Required unless equipped with windscreen

Speed limit:
Primary roads: 65 mph
Secondary roads: 65 mph

OHIO RESOURCES

Road conditions or construction:
511 (Cincinnati/northern Kentucky area)
(888) 264-7623 (in OH)
(614) 644-7013
(440) 234-2030 (turnpike)
(888) 876-7453 (turnpike)
www.buckeyetraffic.org
www.ohioturnpike.org

Highway Emergency Numbers:
911 or (877) 7PATROL

Tourism:
(800) 282-5393
www.ohiotourism.com

State motor vehicle information:
(614) 752-7500
www.ohiobmv.com

HARLEY-DAVIDSON DEALERSHIPS

🏍 **Athens Harley-Davidson, SE-13**
165 Columbus Rd. **Athens**
(740) 592-1692
Lat N 39.353 **Lon** W 82.099

🏍 **Valley Harley-Davidson Shop, SA-18**
41255 Reco Rd. **Belmont**
(740) 695-9591
Lat N 40.058 **Lon** W 81.052

🏍 **Baxter Harley-Davidson, SH-13**
1900 Jackson Pike **Bidwell**
(740) 446-6336
Lat N 38.843 **Lon** W 82.271

🏍 **Joe Carson Harley-Davidson, SC-11**
2930 Helena Dr. **Carroll**
(740) 756-1900
Lat N 39.77 **Lon** W 82.684

🏍 **Marietta Cycle Center, SE-17**
1100 Pike St. **Marietta**
(740) 374-7070
Lat N 39.403 **Lon** W 81.411

🏍 **Fink's Harley-Davidson, SB-14**
2650 Maysville Pike **Zanesville**
(740) 454-0010
Lat N 39.898 **Lon** W 82.036

Cleveland & Vicinity OH8

Springfield OH7

LAKE ERIE
570 ft. above sea level

© Rand McNally

Distance scale
One inch represents about 26 miles

Tulsa OK1

How to determine distance

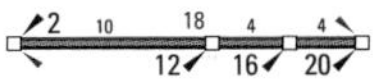

Mileages in red between red arrowheads; in black, between intersections.

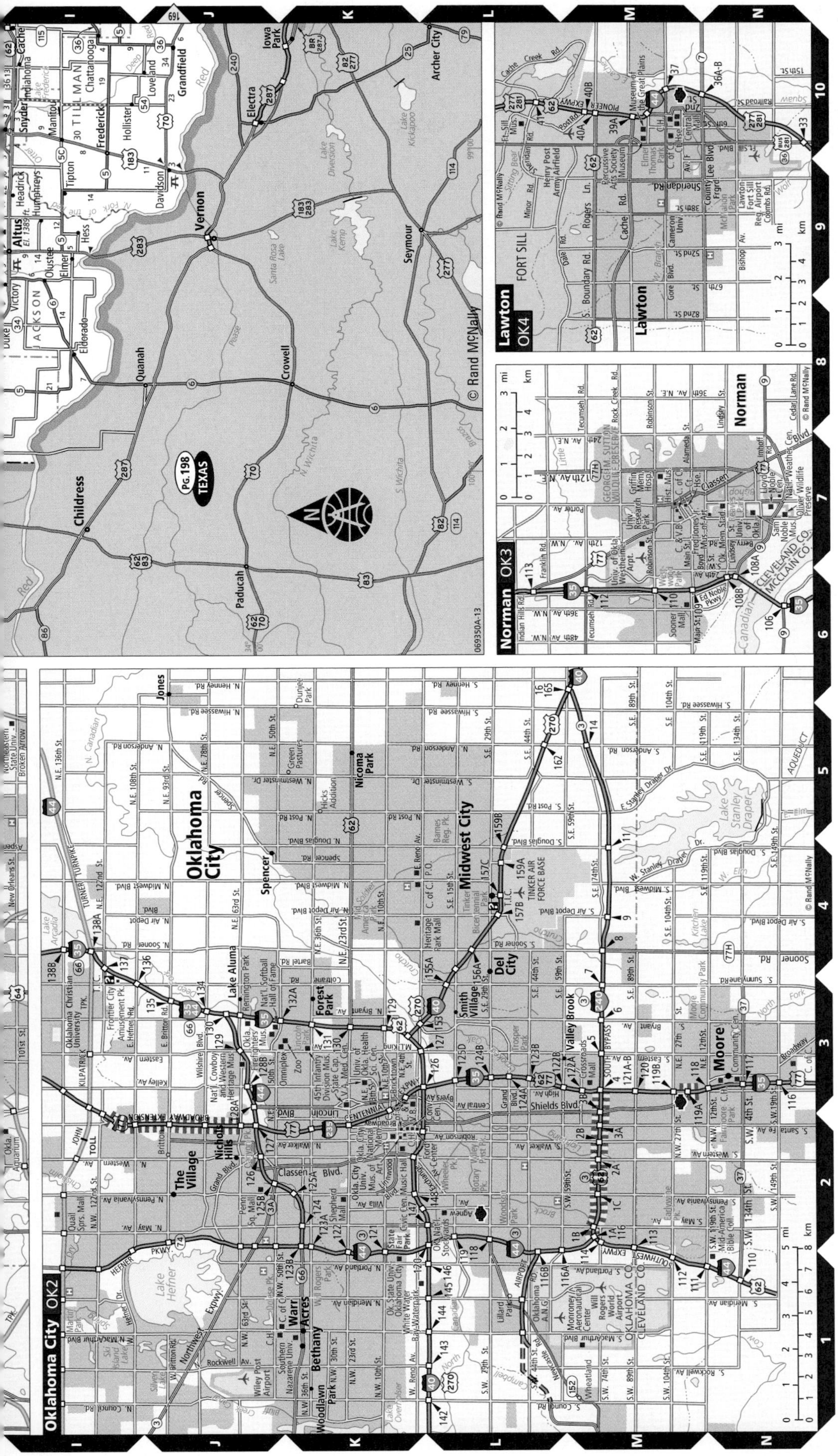

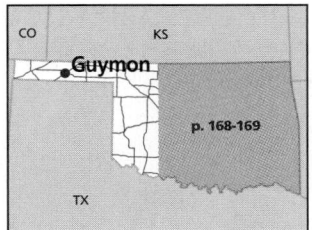

Guymon

CO KS

p. 168-169

TX

SYMBOLS

Featured ride	Scenic route
Long-term construction	■ Historic site or monument; Indian reservation or rancheria; military installation; point of interest; wildlife refuge
Harley-Davidson dealership	

OKLAHOMA MOTORCYCLE LAWS

Helmet use:
Required under age 18

Riding two abreast:
No reference in administrative code or statutes

Eye protection:
Required unless equipped with windscreen

Speed limit:
Primary roads: 75 mph
Secondary roads: 70 mph

OKLAHOMA RESOURCES

Road conditions or construction:
(405) 425-2385
www.okladot.state.ok.us

Highway Emergency Numbers:
911 or *55

Tourism:
(800) 652-6552
www.travelok.com

State motor vehicle information:
(405) 425-2026
www.dps.state.ok.us/

Lawton OK4

Norman OK3

Oklahoma City OK2

© Rand McNally

randmcnally.com/eac

Use Express Access Codes on www.randmcnally.com for quick access to online travel planning info, road construction updates, and more.

Express Access Code: OK

Distance scale
One inch represents about 26 miles

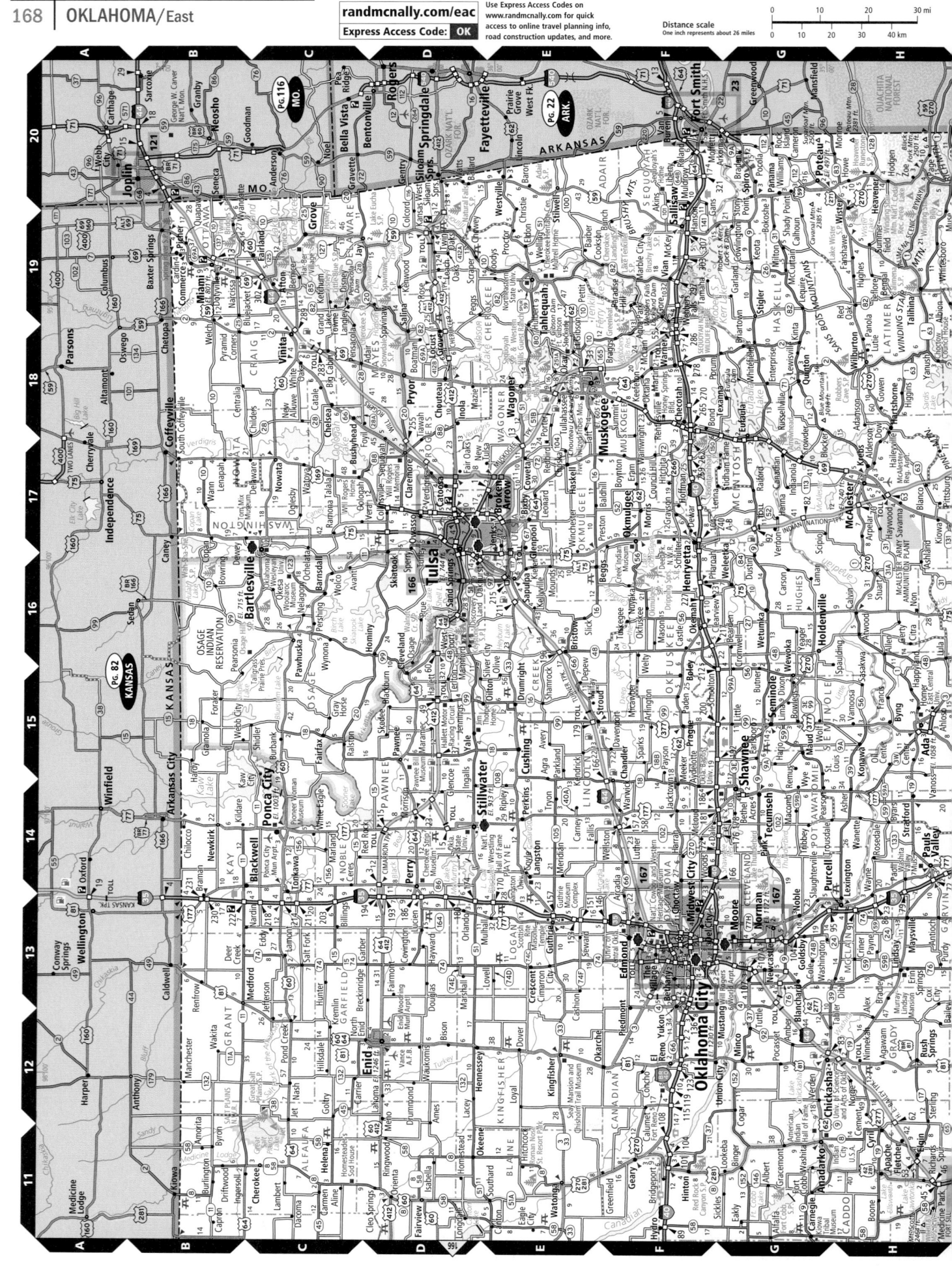

How to determine distance

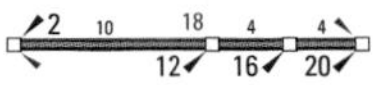

Mileages in red between red arrowheads; in black, between intersections.

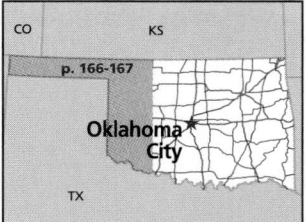

SYMBOLS

- Featured ride
- Scenic route
- Long-term construction
- Harley-Davidson dealership
- Historic site or monument; Indian reservation or rancheria; military installation; point of interest; wildlife refuge

For Oklahoma ride, see page R25.

CITY-TO-CITY MILEAGE

	ARDMORE	ELK CITY	ENID	LAWTON	MUSKOGEE	OKLAHOMA CITY	TULSA	WICHITA FALLS TX
Altus	160	59	195	55	274	140	246	85
Ardmore		210	196	106	191	98	203	91
Bartlesville	248	263	132	238	91	150	45	291
Dallas, TX	112	320	306	187	238	208	262	134
Elk City	210		151	108	250	112	218	144
Enid	196	151		145	164	98	115	198
Ft. Smith, AR	233	292	231	263	71	180	116	316
Guymon	362	185	213	297	377	264	328	317
Joplin, MO	315	330	229	305	119	217	114	358
Lawton	106	108	145		221	87	193	53
McAlester	120	240	204	211	67	128	93	264
Muskogee	191	250	164	221		138	49	274
Oklahoma City	98	112	98	87	138		105	140
Ponca City	203	218	69	193	141	105	92	246
Stillwater	163	178	65	153	120	65	71	206
Tulsa	203	218	115	193	49	105		246
Wichita Falls, TX	91	144	198	53	274	140	246	
Woodward	236	79	87	171	251	138	202	224

HARLEY-DAVIDSON DEALERSHIPS

Bartlesville Cycle Sports, C-17
1400 Tuxedo Blvd. **Bartlesville**
(918) 336-3800
Lat N 36.757 Lon W 95.956

Harley-Davidson World Shop, F-13
3433 S Broadway **Edmond**
(405) 478-4024
Lat N 35.622 Lon W 97.488

ProTeam Harley-Davidson, I-11
301 SE Interstate Dr. **Lawton**
(580) 353-5088
Lat N 34.603 Lon W 98.378

Bryan Harley-Davidson, G-13
MOVING IN 2006: 2624 N Moore Ave. **Moore**
(405) 793-8877
Lat N 35.338 Lon W 97.485

Harley-Davidson World, F-13
2823 S Agnew Ave. **Oklahoma City**
(405) 631-8680
Lat N 35.448 Lon W 97.563

Forman Harley-Davidson, E-14
3512 S Boomer Rd. **Stillwater**
(405) 377-0045
Lat N 36.085 Lon W 97.053

Route 66 Harley-Davidson, D-17
3637 S Memorial Dr. **Tulsa**
(918) 622-1340
Lat N 36.111 Lon W 95.886

Myers-Duren Harley-Davidson, D-17
4848 S Peoria Ave. **Tulsa**
(918) 743-4440
Lat N 36.094 Lon W 95.976

© Rand McNally

Use Express Access Codes on
www.randmcnally.com for quick
access to online travel planning info,
road construction updates, and more.

Distance scale
One inch represents about 25 miles

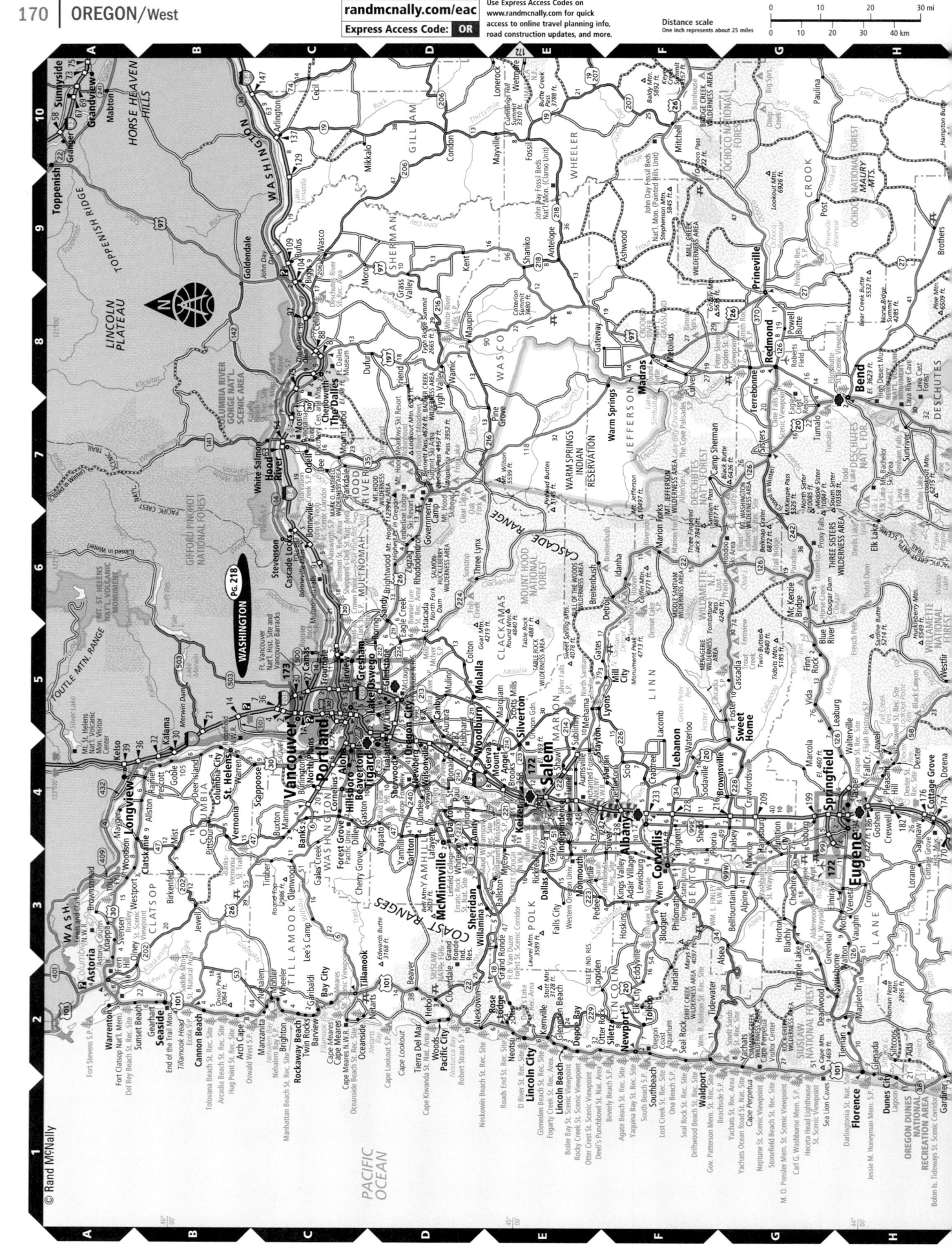

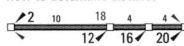

How to determine distance

Mileages in red between red arrowheads; in black, between intersections.

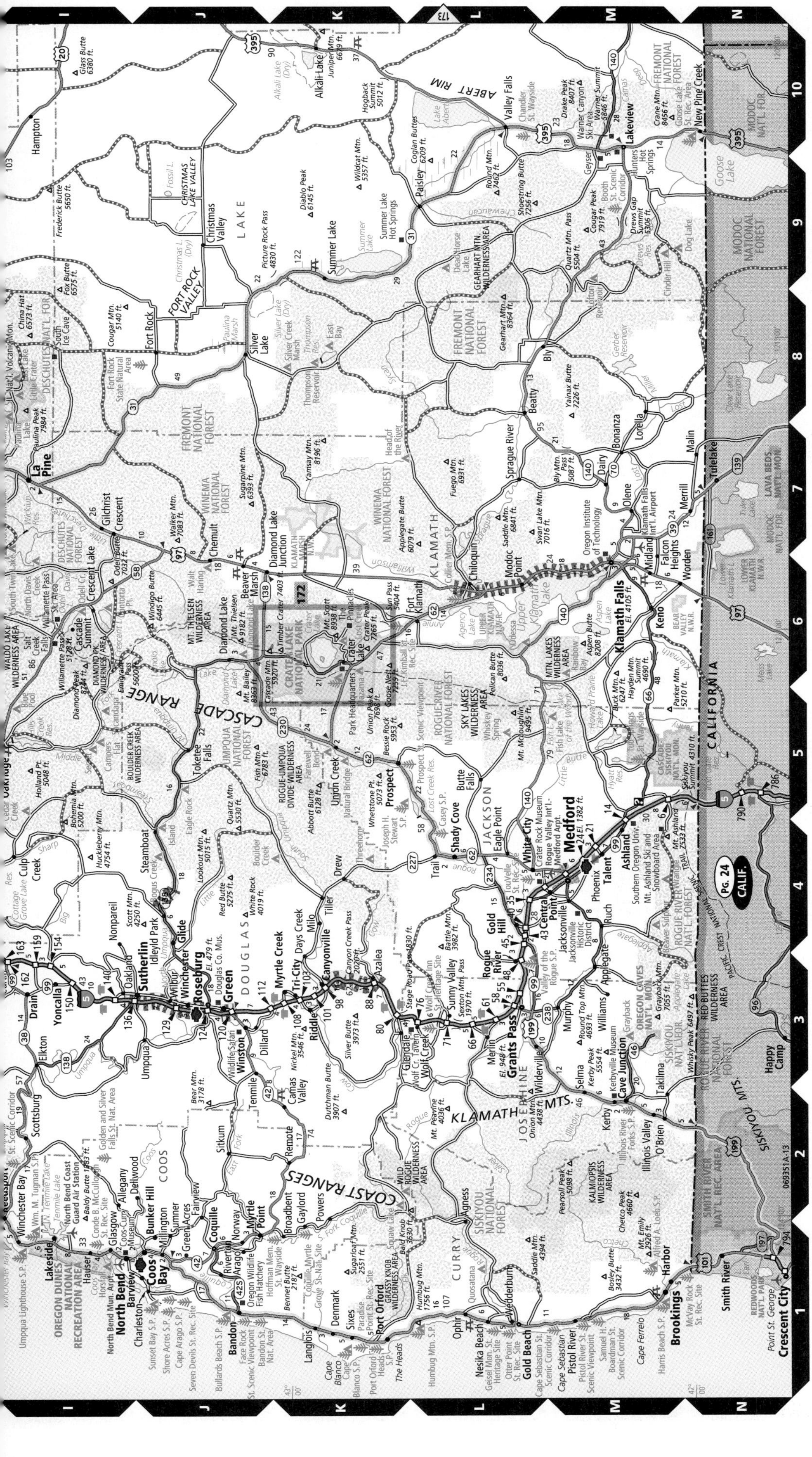

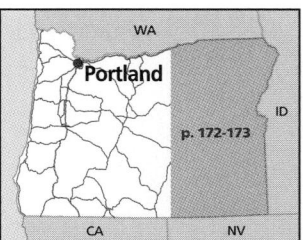

p. 172-173

SYMBOLS

- Featured ride
- Long-term construction
- Harley-Davidson dealership
- Scenic route
- Historic site or monument; Indian reservation or rancheria; military installation; point of interest; wildlife refuge

OREGON MOTORCYCLE LAWS

Helmet use: Required

Riding two abreast:
Yes. See state law for specifics

Eye protection: Not required

Speed limit:
Primary roads: 65 mph
Secondary roads: 55 mph

OREGON RESOURCES

Road conditions or construction:
511
(800) 977-6368
(503) 588-2941
www.tripcheck.com

Highway Emergency Numbers: 911

Tourism:
(800) 547-7842
www.traveloregon.com

State motor vehicle information:
(503) 945-5000
www.odot.state.or.us/dmv

HARLEY-DAVIDSON DEALERSHIPS

American Motorcycle Classics Harley-Davidson, F-4
1600 Century Dr. NE **Albany**
(541) 928-6234
Lat N 44.656 Lon W 123.06

Bears & Roses Harley-Davidson, H-7
63028 Sherman Rd. **Bend**
(541) 330-6228
Lat N 44.088 Lon W 121.303

Highway 101 Harley-Davidson of Coos Bay, J-1
536 S 2nd St. **Coos Bay**
(541) 266-7051
Lat N 43.364 Lon W 124.215

Doyle's Harley-Davidson, H-4
86441 College View Rd. **Eugene**
(541) 747-1033
Lat N 44.011 Lon W 123.022

Latus Motors Harley-Davidson, D-5
870 E Berkeley St. **Gladstone**
(503) 249-8653
Lat N 45.383 Lon W 122.581

D & S Harley-Davidson, M-4
3846 S Pacific Hwy. **Medford**
(541) 535-5515
Lat N 42.284 Lon W 122.828

Doyle's Harley-Davidson Shop, J-3
2675 NW Edenbower Blvd. **Roseburg**
(541) 440-1088
Lat N 43.242 Lon W 123.361

Salem Harley-Davidson, E-4
3601 Silverton Rd. NE **Salem**
(503) 363-0634
Lat N 44.969 Lon W 122.989

Paradise Harley-Davidson, C-4
10770 SW Cascade Ave. **Tigard**
(503) 924-3700
Lat N 45.442 Lon W 122.78

randmcnally.com/eac

Express Access Code: OR

Use Express Access Codes on
www.randmcnally.com for quick
access to online travel planning info,
road construction updates, and more.

Distance scale
One inch represents about 25 miles

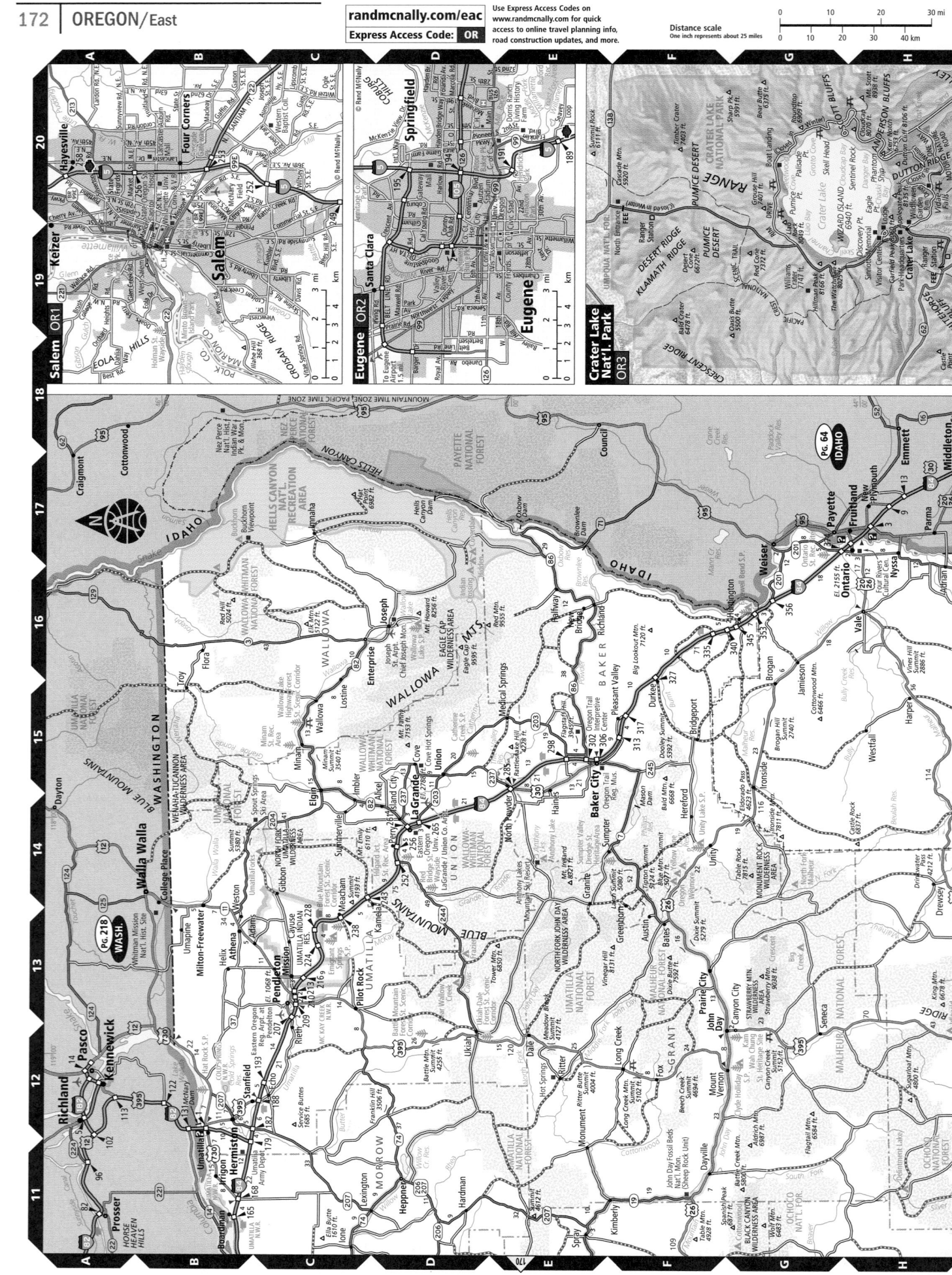

How to determine distance

Mileages in red between red arrowheads; in black, between intersections.

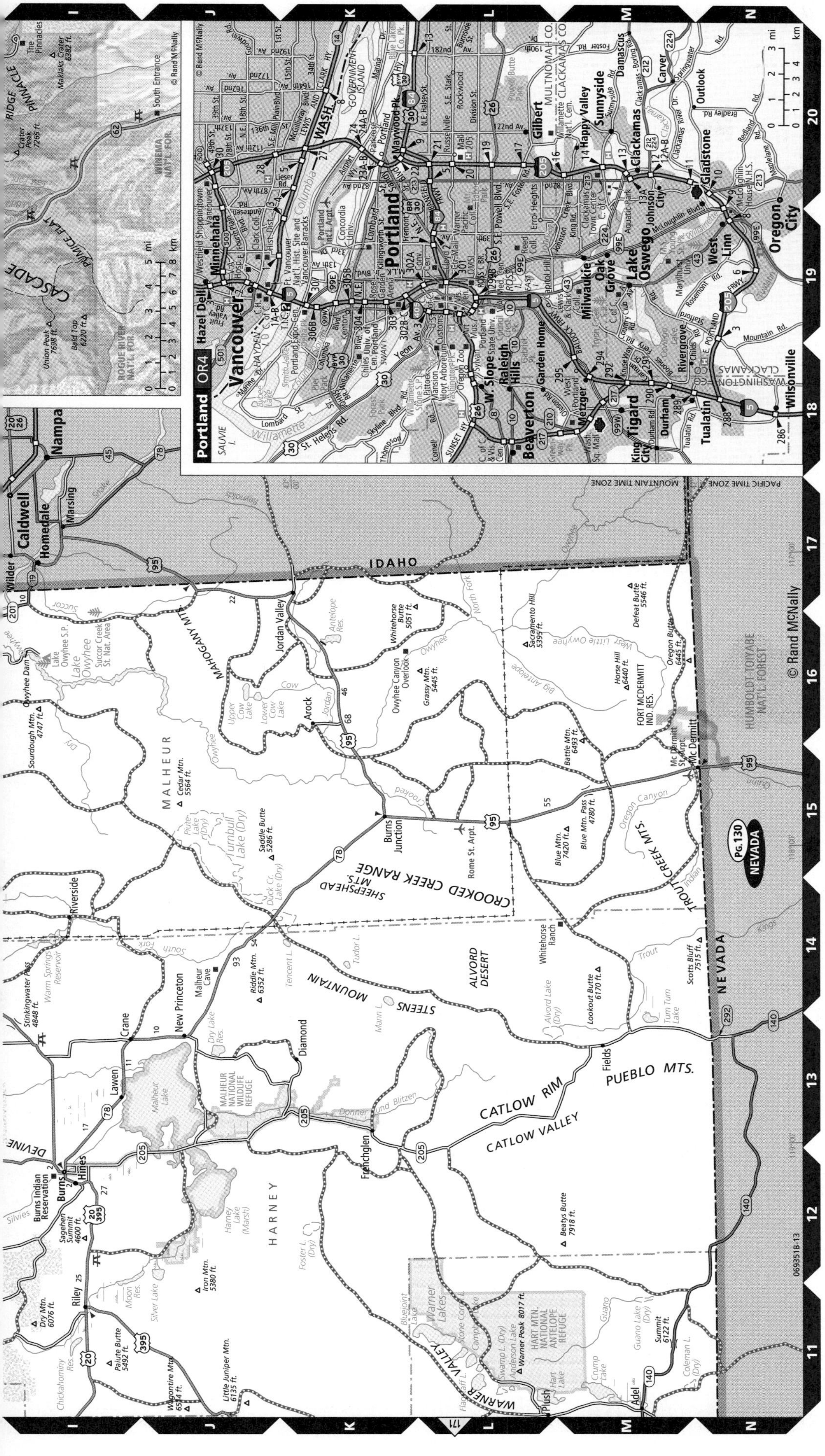

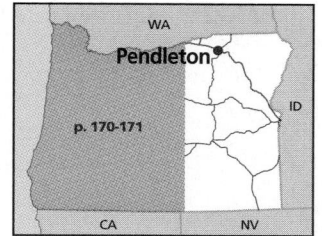

Pendleton

p. 170-171

SYMBOLS

- Featured ride
- Long-term construction
- Harley-Davidson dealership
- Scenic route
- Historic site or monument; Indian reservation or rancheria; military installation; point of interest; wildlife refuge

CITY-TO-CITY MILEAGE

	BEND	BURNS	CORVALLIS	EUGENE	MEDFORD	ONTARIO	PENDLETON	PORTLAND
Astoria	257	387	177	205	368	466	302	100
Bend		130	128	115	175	261	243	161
Brookings	296	426	227	214	129	557	515	308
Burns	130		258	245	305	131	199	291
Coos Bay	222	352	120	107	170	483	408	201
Corvallis	128	258		45	208	389	288	81
Crater Lake NP	106	236	183	142	79	367	349	247
Eugene	115	245	45		167	376	316	109
Grants Pass	194	324	182	141	27	455	453	246
John Day	153	70	263	250	328	133	129	265
Klamath Falls	139	236	216	175	78	367	382	280
Lakeview	175	140	303	263	172	271	339	336
Medford	175	305	208	167		436	418	272
Ontario	261	131	389	376	436		164	371
Pendleton	243	199	288	316	418	164		207
Portland	161	291	81	109	272	371	207	
Salem	132	262	36	64	227	418	254	47
The Dalles	133	263	165	193	356	287	123	84

© Rand McNally

0693518-13

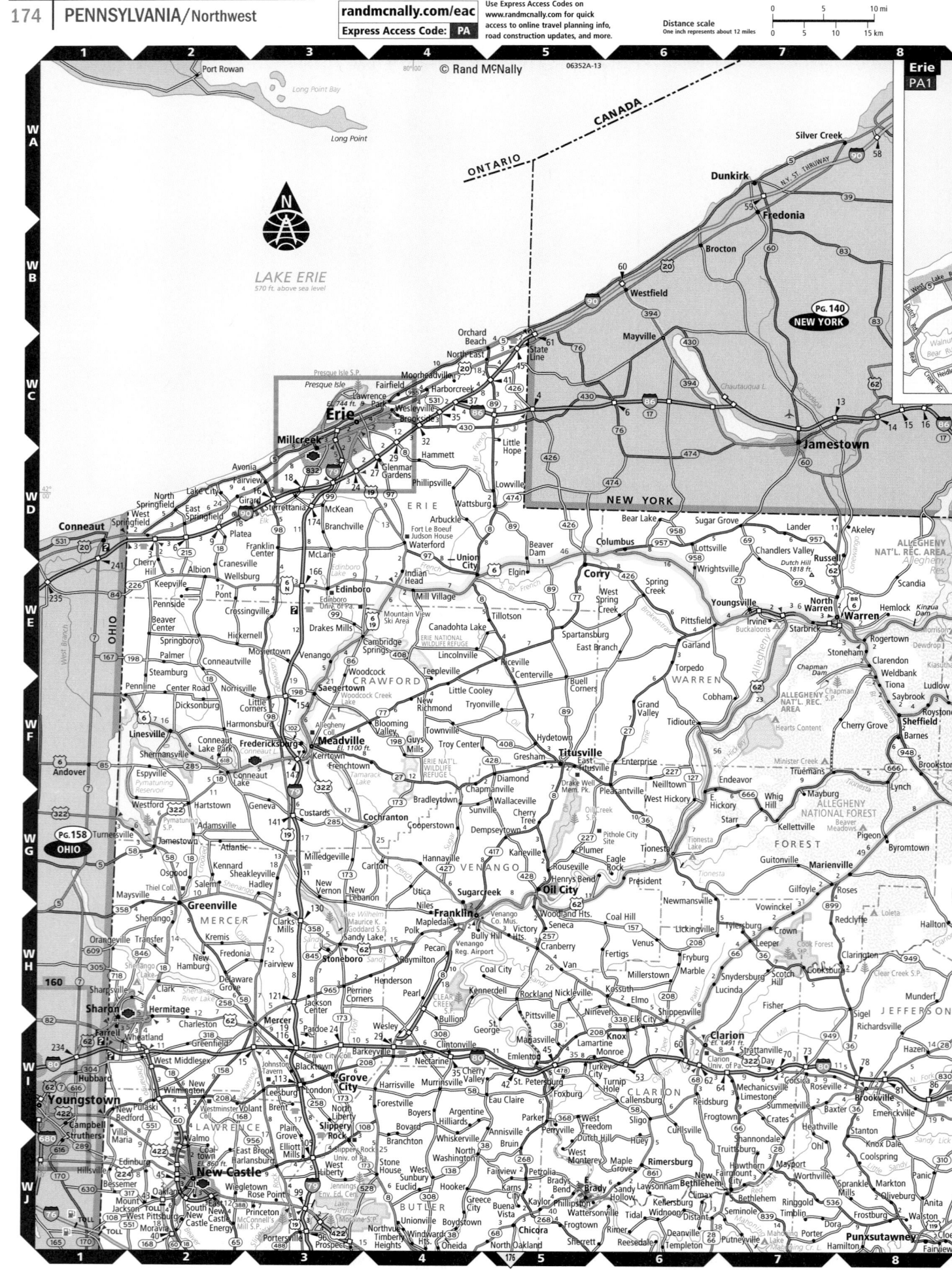

© Rand McNally

06352A-13

Distance scale
One inch represents about 12 miles

Erie
PA1

How to determine distance

Mileages in red between red arrowheads; in black, between intersections.

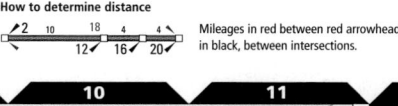

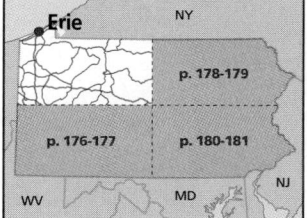

SYMBOLS

- Featured ride
- Scenic route
- Long-term construction
- Historic site or monument; Indian reservation or rancheria; military installation; point of interest; wildlife refuge
- Harley-Davidson dealership

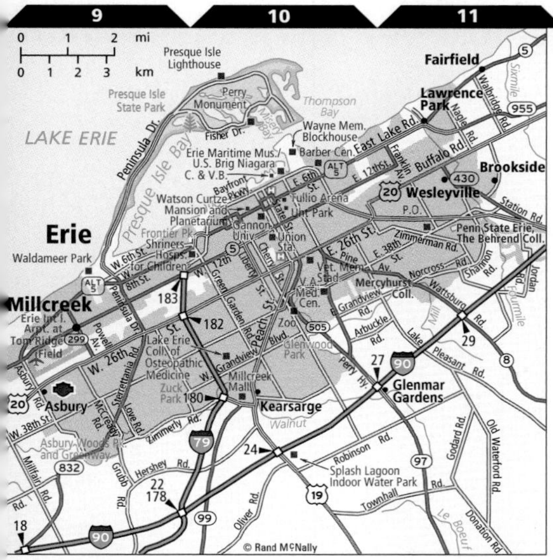

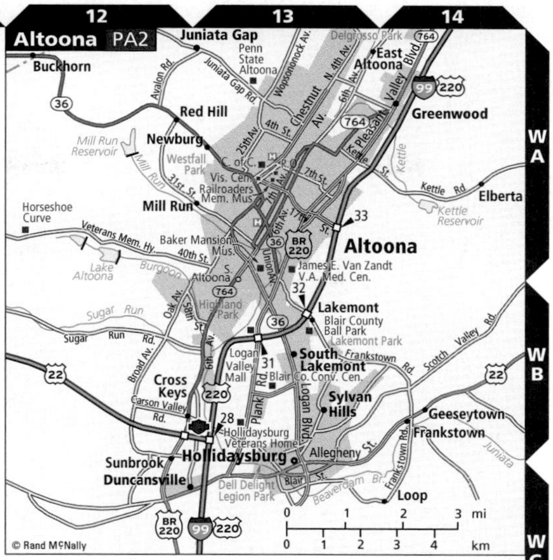

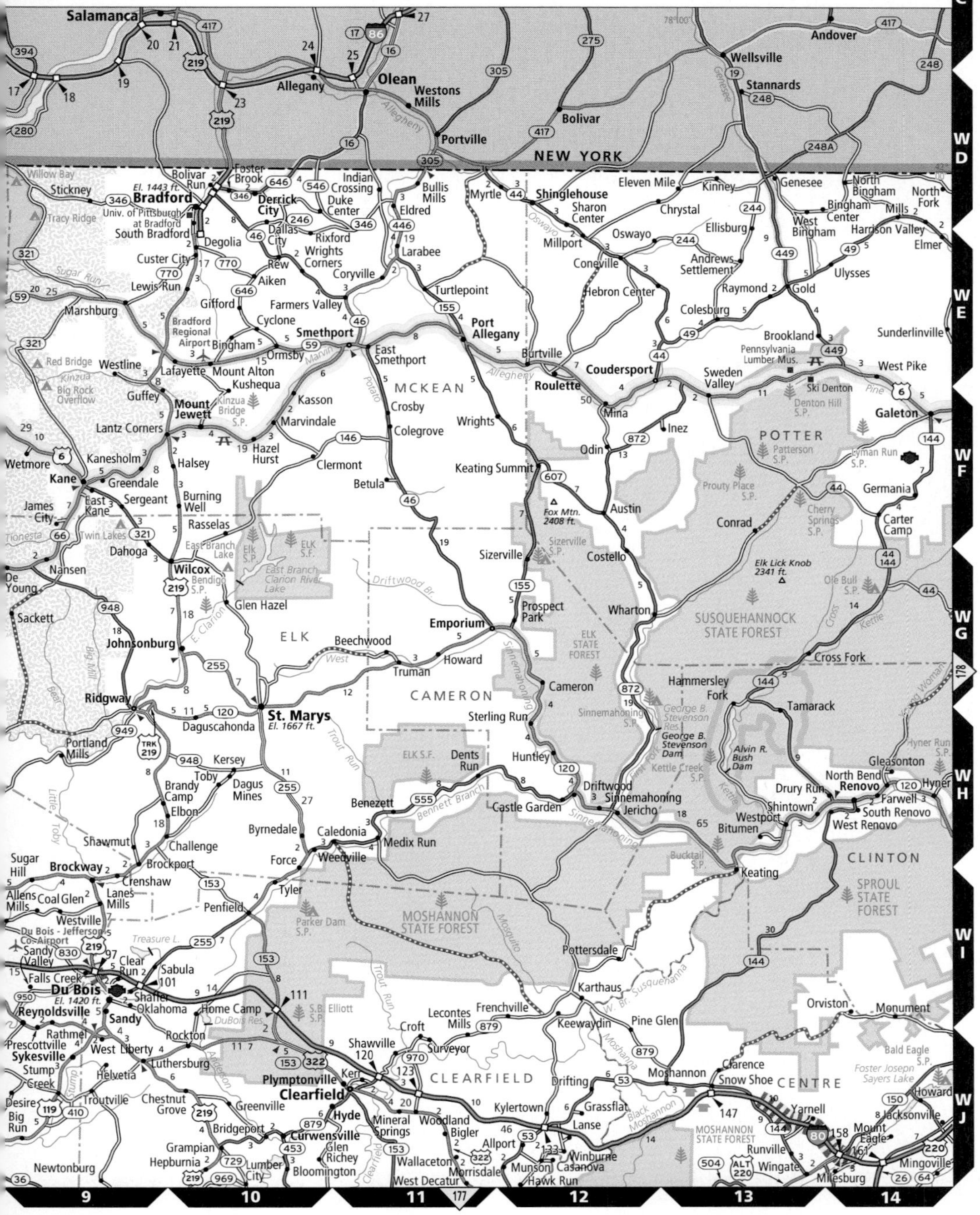

For Pennsylvania ride, see page R26-27.

PENNSYLVANIA MOTORCYCLE LAWS

Helmet use:
Required under age 21, and less than 2 years licensed, or without safety class

Riding two abreast:
Yes. See state law for specifics

Eye protection:
Required by law

Speed limit:
Primary roads: 65 mph
Secondary roads: 55 mph

PENNSYLVANIA RESOURCES

Road conditions or construction:
(888) 783-6783 (in PA)
(215) 567-5678 (SmarTraveler, Camden/Philadelphia area)
www.dot.state.pa.us

Highway Emergency Numbers:
911 or *12

Tourism:
(800) 847-4872
www.visitpa.com

State motor vehicle information:
(717) 391-6190
www.dmv.state.pa.us

HARLEY-DAVIDSON DEALERSHIPS

Street Track N Trail Harley-Davidson, WF-3
13723 Conneaut Lake Rd. **Conneaut Lake**
(814) 382-4821
Lat N 41.614 **Lon** W 80.259

Du Bois Harley-Davidson, WI-9
101 W Du Bois Ave. (Rte. 219) **Du Bois**
(814) 371-5750
Lat N 41.128 **Lon** W 78.759

Harley-Davidson of Erie, WD-3
4575 W Ridge Rd. **Erie**
(814) 838-1356
Lat N 42.075 **Lon** W 80.177

Larry's Harley-Davidson, WF-14
US 6 West Pike **Galeton**
(814) 435-6548
Lat N 41.695 **Lon** W 77.678

New Castle Harley-Davidson, WJ-2
4655 US Rte. 422 **New Castle**
(724) 924-2310
Lat N 40.992 **Lon** W 80.33

Thunder Harley-Davidson, WH-1
1344 E State St. **Sharon**
(724) 981-7282
Lat N 41.233 **Lon** W 80.484

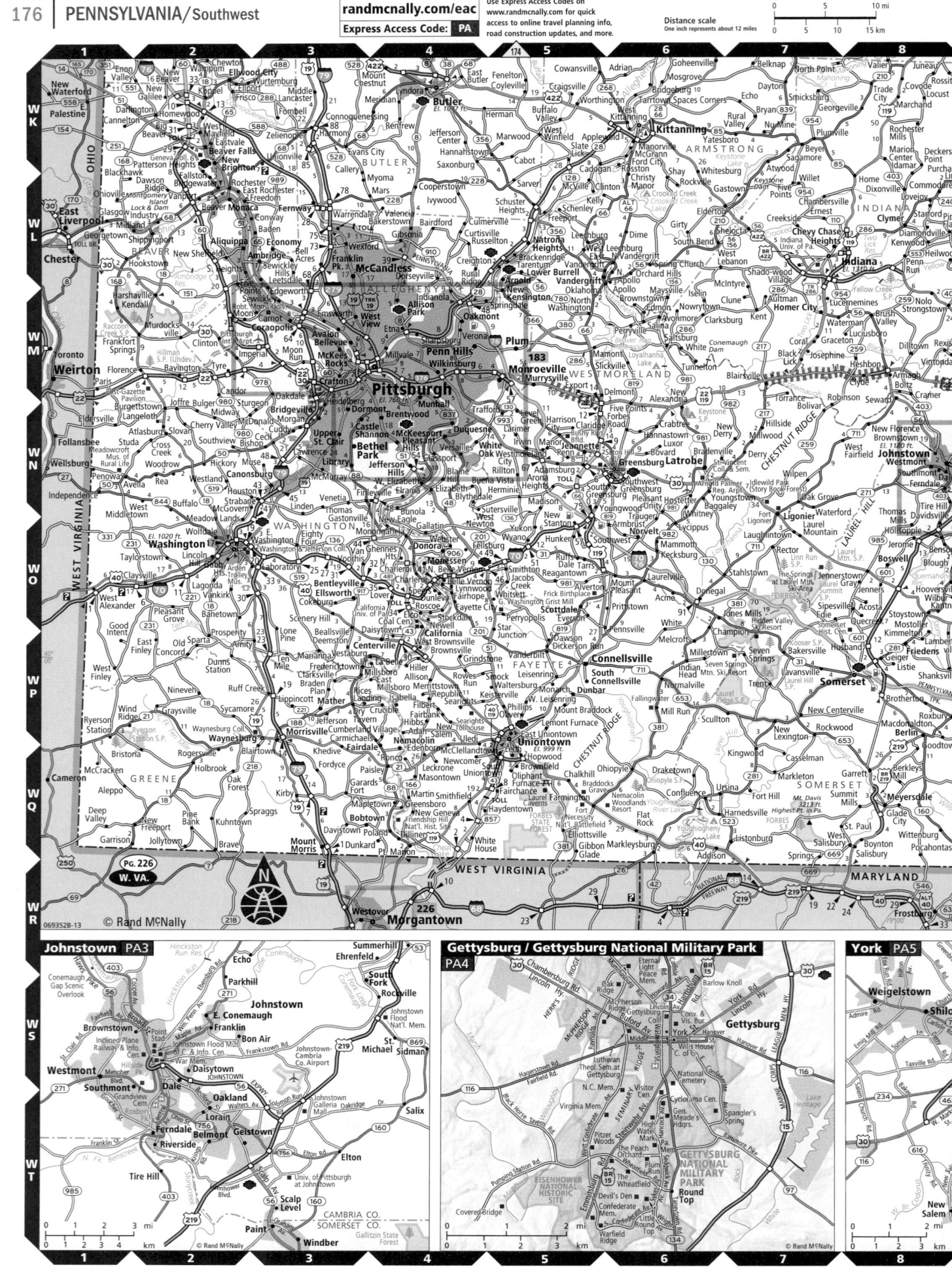

randmcnally.com/eac
Express Access Code: PA

Use Express Access Codes on www.randmcnally.com for quick access to online travel planning info, road construction updates, and more.

Distance scale
One inch represents about 12 miles

© Rand McNally
069352B-13

Johnstown PA3

Gettysburg / Gettysburg National Military Park PA4

York PA5

How to determine distance

Mileages in red between red arrowheads; in black, between intersections.

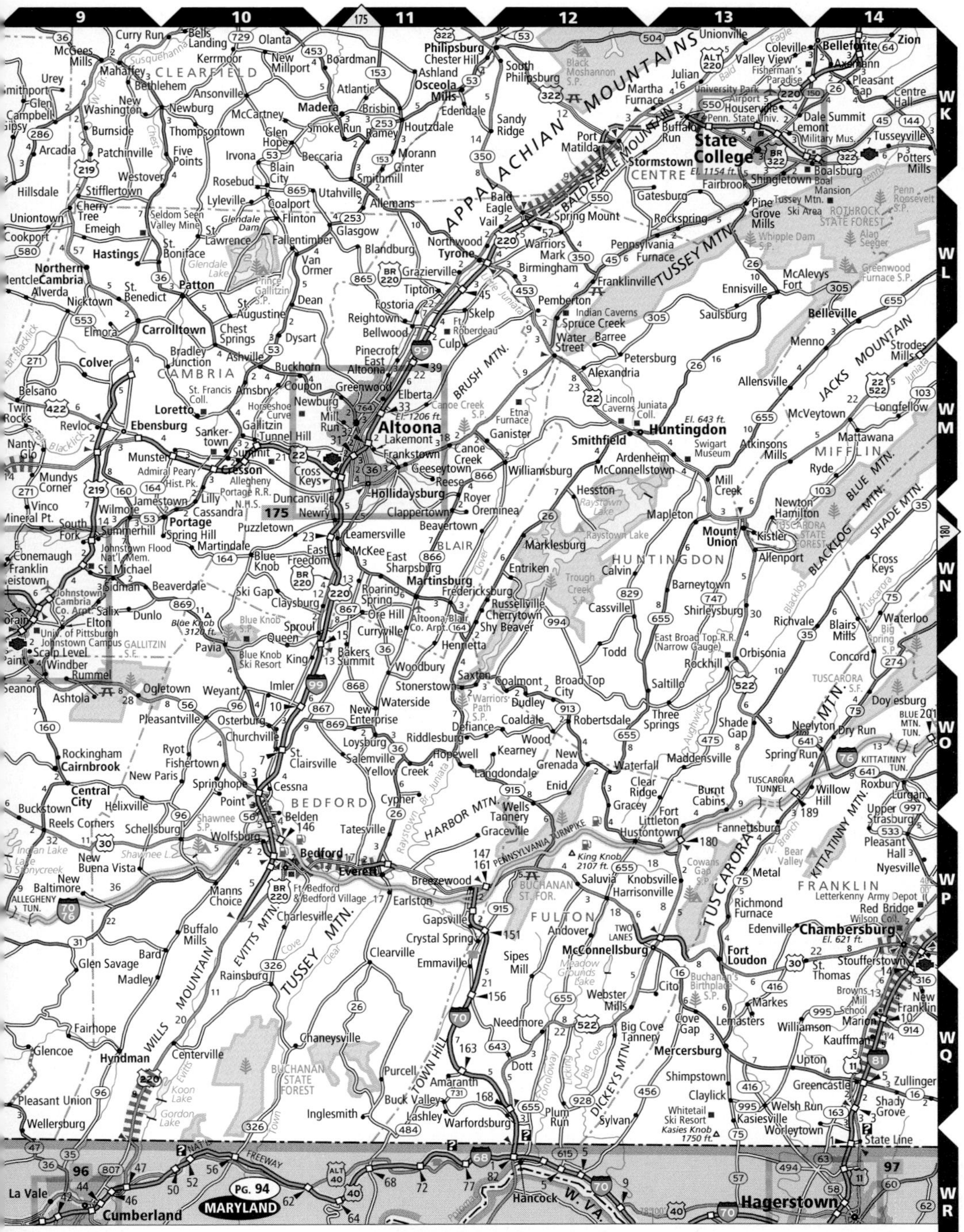

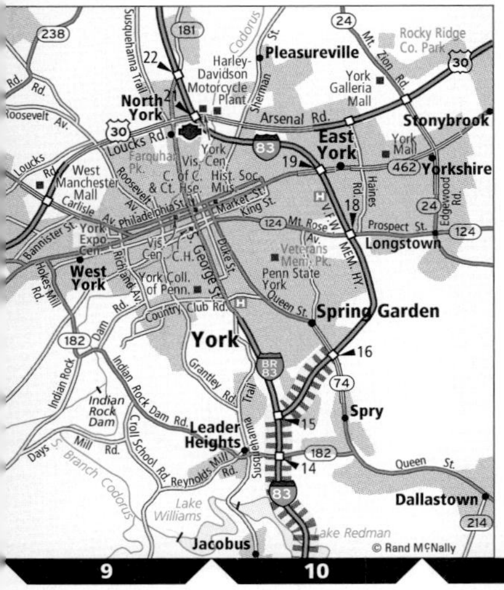

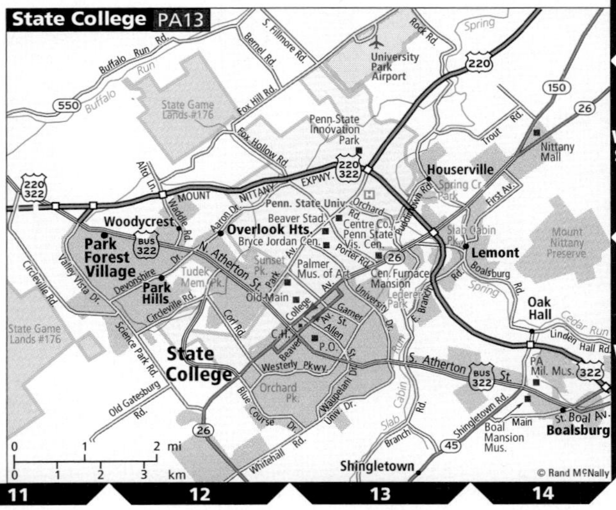

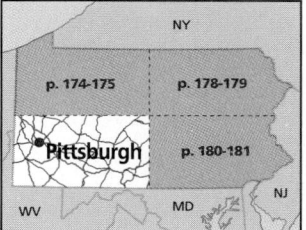

SYMBOLS

- Featured ride
- Long-term construction
- Harley-Davidson dealership
- Scenic route
- Historic site or monument; Indian reservation or rancheria; military installation; point of interest; wildlife refuge

HARLEY-DAVIDSON DEALERSHIPS

For the Pittsburgh metro area, please see dealer listings on page 183.

Apple Harley-Davidson, WM-11
495 Municipal Dr. Altoona (Duncansville)
(814) 696-7433
Lat N 40.446 **Lon** W 78.433

McMahon's Harley-Davidson, WK-2
613 7th Ave. Beaver Falls
(724) 846-6251
Lat N 40.739 **Lon** W 80.329

Cerini Harley-Davidson, WO-4
4325 State Rte. 51 N Belle Vernon
(724) 930-8443
Lat N 40.16 **Lon** W 79.78

Zanotti Motor Co., WK-4
170 Pittsburgh Rd. (Rte. 8) Butler
(724) 283-2777
Lat N 40.837 **Lon** W 79.92

No. 1 Cycle Center Harley-Davidson, WK-14
107 Yearicks Blvd. Centre Hall
(814) 364-1340
Lat N 40.789 **Lon** W 77.71

M & S Harley-Davidson, WP-14
160 Falling Spring Rd. Chambersburg
(717) 709-9650
Lat N 39.926 **Lon** W 77.635

Z & M Harley-Davidson Sales, WN-6
Rural Rte. 6 Box 224 (Rte. 30) Greensburg
(724) 837-9404
Lat N 40.294 **Lon** W 79.501

Zepka Harley-Davidson, WN-9
960 Eisenhower Blvd. Johnstown
(814) 262-7777
Lat N 40.268 **Lon** W 78.861

Highland Harley-Davidson, WP-8
802 N Center Ave. Somerset
(814) 444-1903
Lat N 40.016 **Lon** W 79.078

Gatto Harley-Davidson, WL-5
139 E 6th Ave. Tarentum
(724) 224-0500
Lat N 40.602 **Lon** W 79.756

Gatto Cycle Shop, WL-5
562 Pittsburg Mills Circle Tarentum
(724) 274-4474
Lat N 40.616 **Lon** W 79.784

Cerini's National Road Harley-Davidson, WP-5
69 Romeo Ln. Uniontown
(724) 439-8888
Lat N 39.915 **Lon** W 79.724

Steel City Harley-Davidson, WO-3
1375 Washington Rd. Washington
(724) 225-7020
Lat N 40.211 **Lon** W 80.197

© Rand McNally

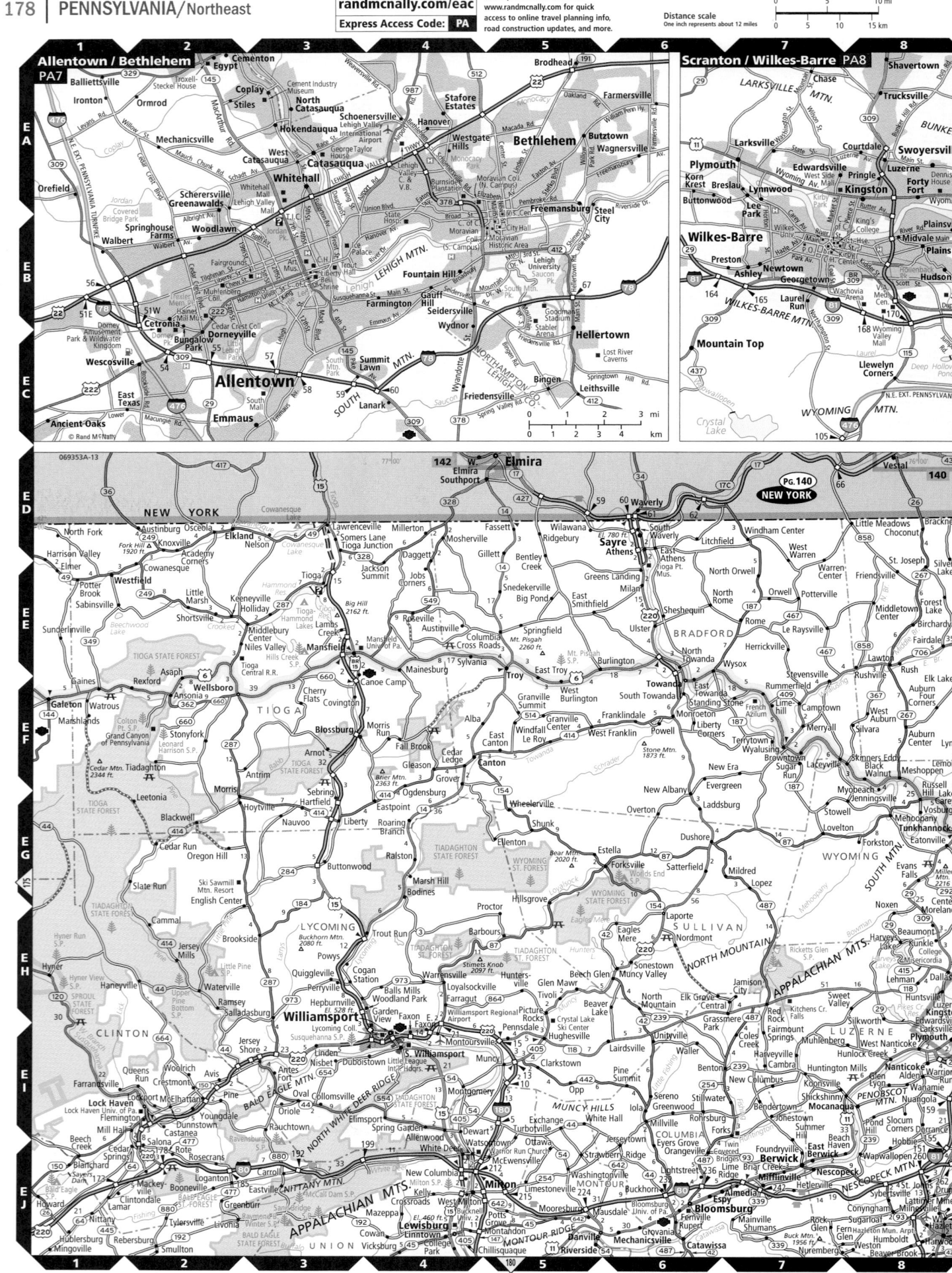

randmcnally.com/eac
Express Access Code: PA

Use Express Access Codes on
www.randmcnally.com for quick
access to online travel planning info,
road construction updates, and more.

Distance scale
One inch represents about 12 miles

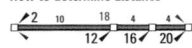

How to determine distance

Mileages in red between red arrowheads; in black, between intersections.

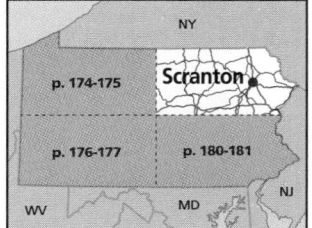

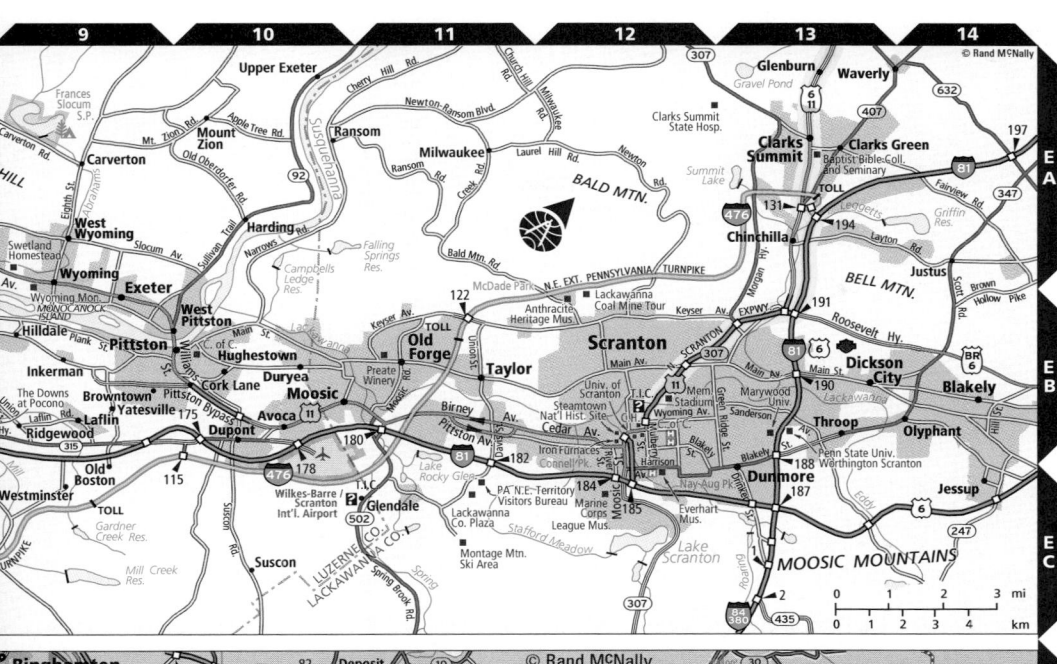

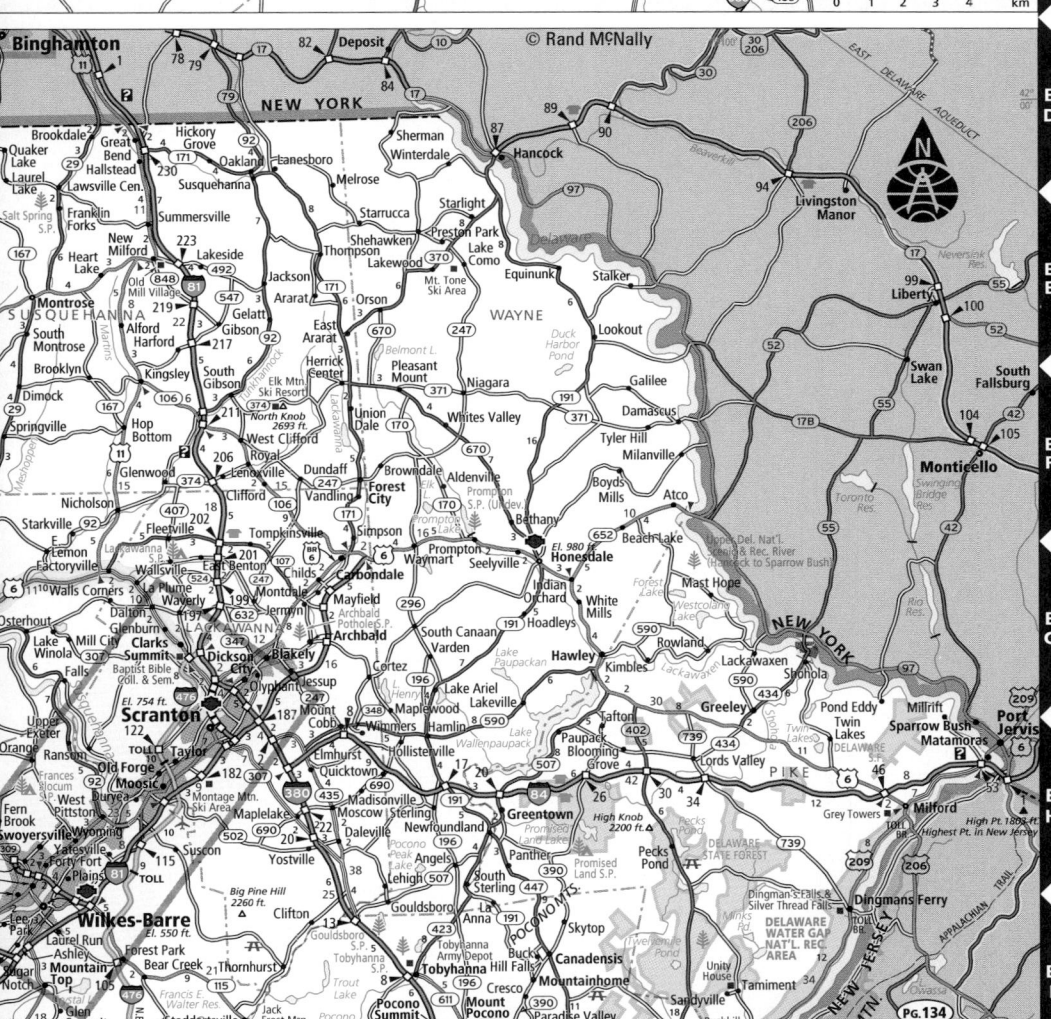

© Rand McNally

SYMBOLS

- Featured ride
- Scenic route
- Long-term construction
- Historic site or monument; Indian reservation or rancheria; military installation; point of interest; wildlife refuge
- Harley-Davidson dealership

For Pennsylvania ride, see page R26-27.

PENNSYLVANIA MOTORCYCLE LAWS

Helmet use:
Required under age 21, and less than 2 years licensed, or without safety class

Riding two abreast:
Yes. See state law for specifics

Eye protection:
Required by law

Speed limit:
Primary roads: 65 mph
Secondary roads: 55 mph

PENNSYLVANIA RESOURCES

Road conditions or construction:
(888) 783-6783 (in PA)
(215) 567-5678 (SmarTraveler, Camden/Philadelphia area)
www.dot.state.pa.us

Highway Emergency Numbers:
911 or *12

Tourism:
(800) 847-4872
www.visitpa.com

State motor vehicle information:
(717) 391-6190
www.dmv.state.pa.us

HARLEY-DAVIDSON DEALERSHIPS

- **Vreeland's Harley-Davidson, EJ-6**
  317 Montour Blvd. **Bloomsburg**
  (570) 784-2453
  Lat N 40.979 Lon W 76.496

- **Electric City Harley-Davidson, EG-10**
  1534 Rte. 6 Scranton/Carbondale Hwy.
  Dickson City (Scranton)
  (570) 483-0883
  Lat N 41.439 Lon W 75.662

- **Baer Sport Center, EG-11**
  Rte. 6 East **Honesdale**
  (570) 253-2000
  Lat N 41.587 Lon W 75.254

- **Lance's Harley-Davidson, EE-3**
  2911 S Main St. (Rte. 15 S) **Mansfield**
  (570) 659-5000
  Lat N 41.781 Lon W 77.069

- **Noto's Harley-Davidson Shop, EI-9**
  1022 Hwy. Rte. 315 **Plains**
  (570) 831-5001
  Lat N 41.239 Lon W 75.854

- **Schoch Harley-Davidson, EJ-12**
  4300 Manor Dr. **Stroudsburg**
  (570) 992-7500
  Lat N 40.96 Lon W 75.266

- **Horsepower Harley-Davidson, EI-4**
  1910 E 3rd St. **Williamsport**
  (570) 320-0630
  Lat N 41.249 Lon W 76.963

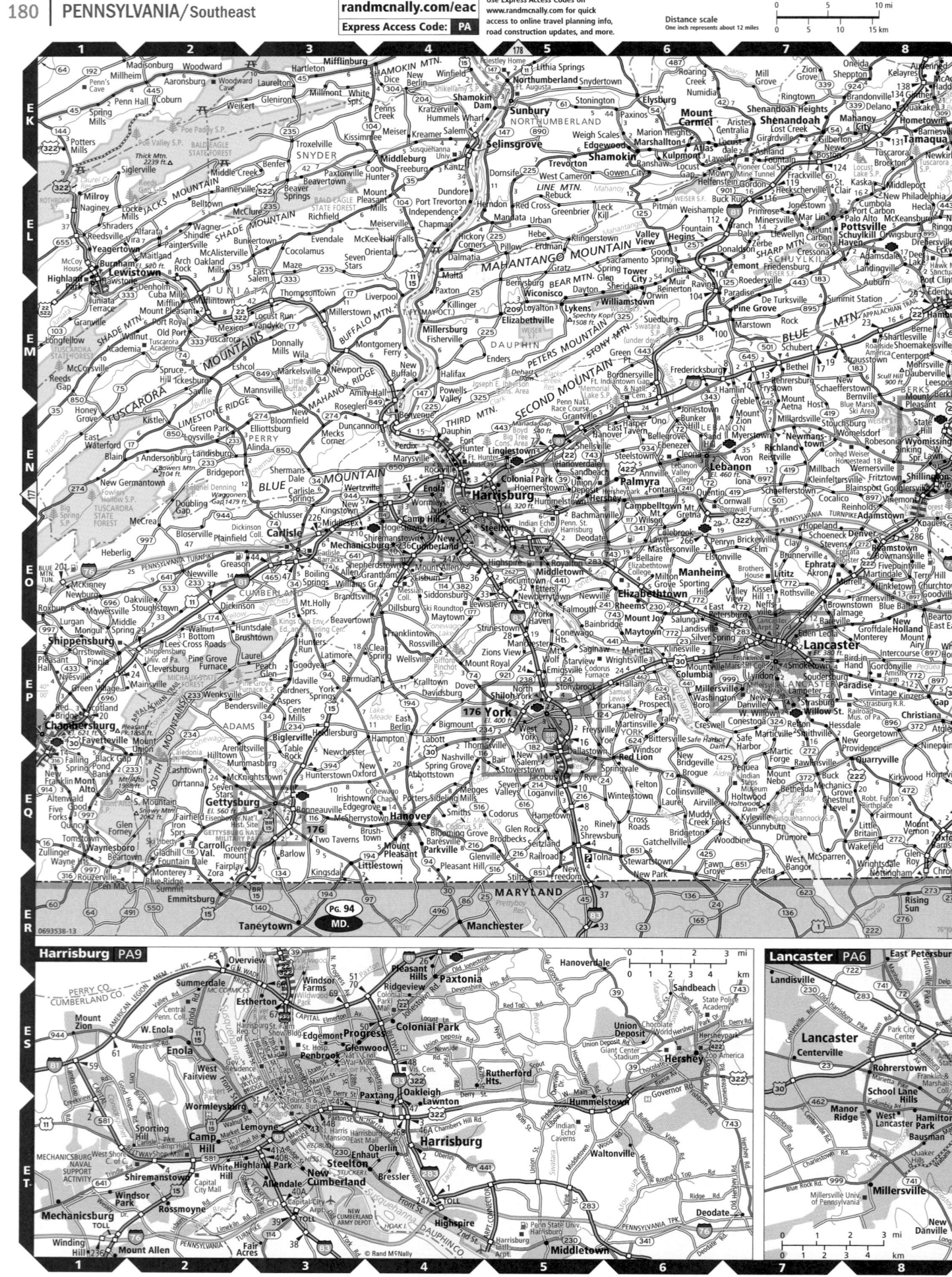

randmcnally.com/eac
Express Access Code: PA
Use Express Access Codes on www.randmcnally.com for quick access to online travel planning info, road construction updates, and more.

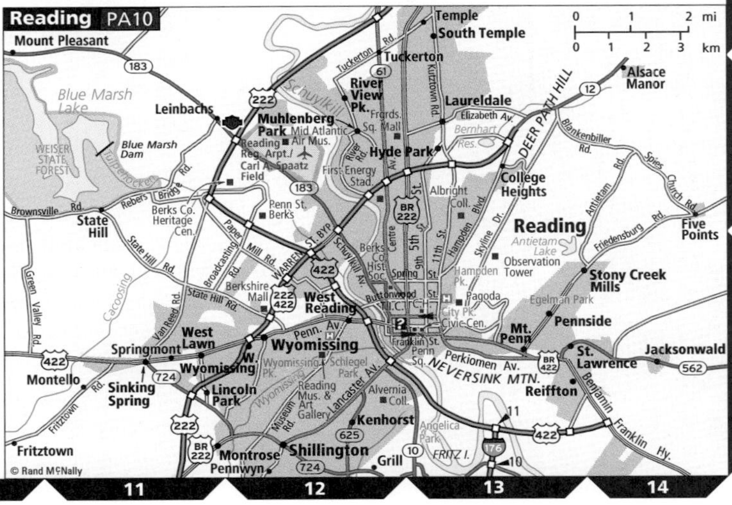

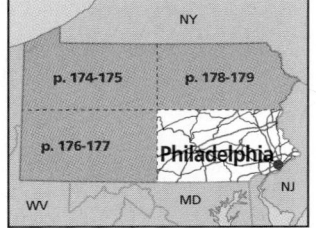

SYMBOLS

Featured ride | Scenic route

Long-term construction | Harley-Davidson dealership

HARLEY-DAVIDSON DEALERSHIPS

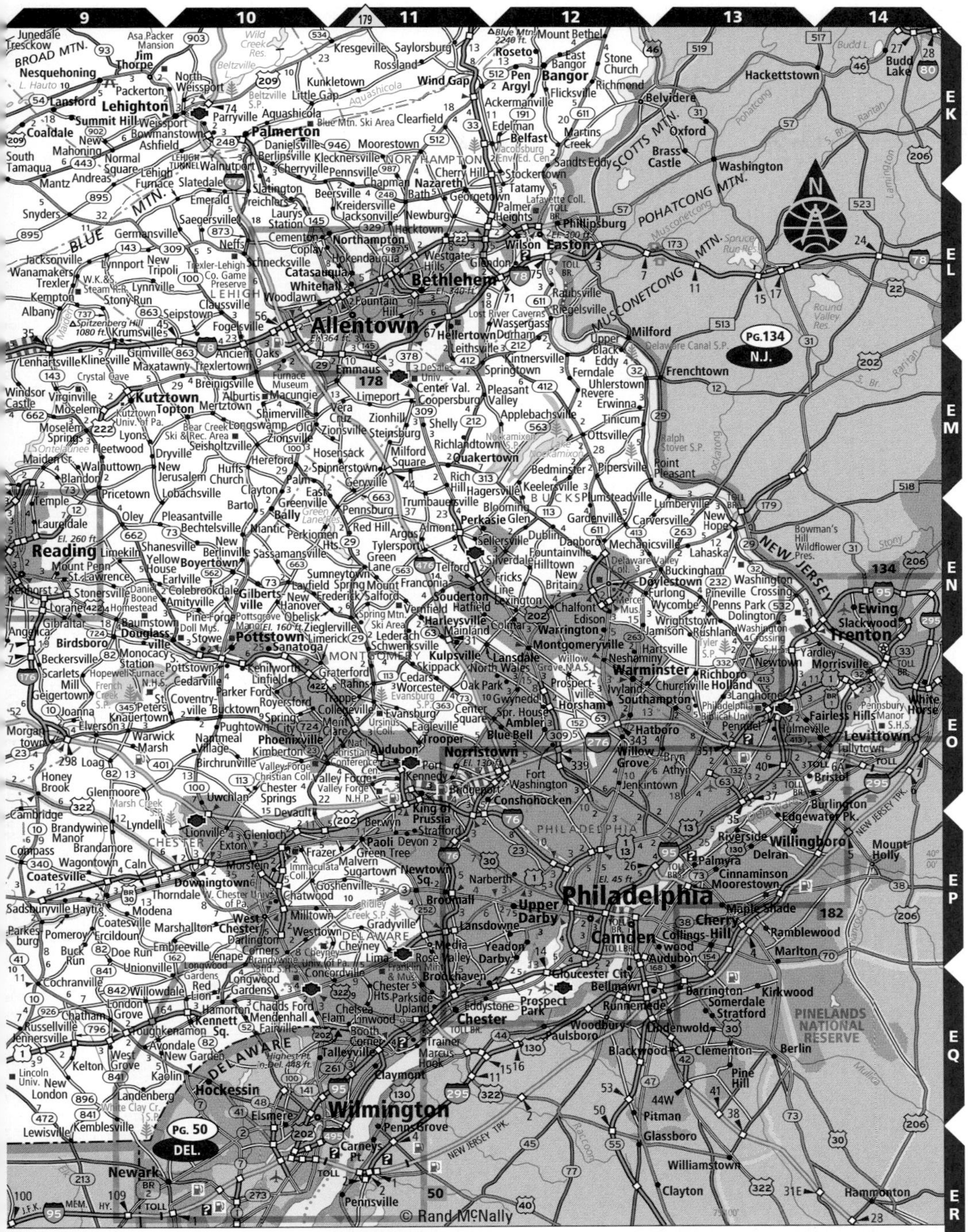

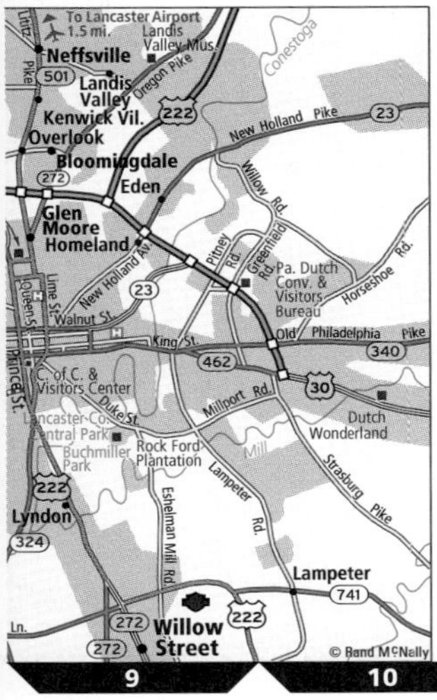

For the Philadelphia metro area, please see dealer listings on page 183.

Crossroads Harley-Davidson, EM-11
5118 Rte. 309 S **Center Valley**
(610) 797-7979
Lat N 40.538 Lon W 75.411

Harley-Davidson Shop of Chadds Ford, EQ-10
1241 Baltimore Pike **Chadds Ford**
(610) 558-3331
Lat N 39.879 Lon W 75.552

Smaltz's Harley-Davidson, EO-10
12 Pottstown Pike (Rte. 100) **Eagle**
(610) 458-9004
Lat N 40.077 Lon W 75.688

Battlefield Harley-Davidson, EQ-3
21 Cavalry Field Rd. **Gettysburg**
(717) 337-9005
Lat N 39.847 Lon W 77.182

Susquehanna Valley Harley-Davidson, EN-5
6300 Allentown Blvd. (Rte. 22) **Harrisburg**
(717) 810-1993
Lat N 40.338 Lon W 76.784

Brian's Harley-Davidson, EO-13
600 S Flowers Mill Rd. **Langhorne**
(215) 752-9400
Lat N 40.169 Lon W 74.899

White's Harley-Davidson, EN-7
1515 E Cumberland St. **Lebanon**
(717) 272-4986
Lat N 40.349 Lon W 76.386

Classic Harley-Davidson, EN-8
983 James Dr. (Rte. 183) **Leesport**
(610) 916-7777
Lat N 40.392 Lon W 75.996

Iron Valley Harley-Davidson Shop, EO-6
3091 Lebanon Rd. **Manheim**
(717) 664-0888
Lat N 40.237 Lon W 76.436

Appalachian Harley-Davidson, EO-4
6695 Carlisle Pike **Mechanicsburg**
(800) 369-7743
Lat N 40.241 Lon W 77.05

Hannum's Harley-Davidson Sales, EP-11
1011 W Baltimore Pike **Media**
(610) 566-5562
Lat N 39.915 Lon W 75.426

Valley Forge Harley-Davidson, EO-11
1217-19 S Trooper Rd. **Norristown**
(610) 666-5122
Lat N 40.114 Lon W 75.419

Schaeffer's Harley-Davidson Sales & Service, EL-8
1123 Brick Hill Rd. **Orwigsburg**
(570) 366-0143
Lat N 40.645 Lon W 76.083

Blocker Harley-Davidson, EK-10
Rte. 248 Box 204 **Parryville**
(610) 377-0440
Lat N 40.818 Lon W 75.673

Dean's Harley-Davidson, EN-11
3255 State Rd. (Rte. 152) **Sellersville**
(215) 257-6112
Lat N 40.345 Lon W 75.306

Lancaster Harley-Davidson, EP-7
Rtes. 222 & 741 **Willow Street**
(717) 464-2703
Lat N 39.964 Lon W 76.271

Laugerman's Harley-Davidson Sales, EP-5
Rte. 30 & I-83 **York**
(717) 854-3214
Lat N 39.968 Lon W 76.769

© Rand McNally

randmcnally.com/eac

Express Access Code: PA

Use Express Access Codes on
www.randmcnally.com for quick
access to online travel planning info,
road construction updates, and more.

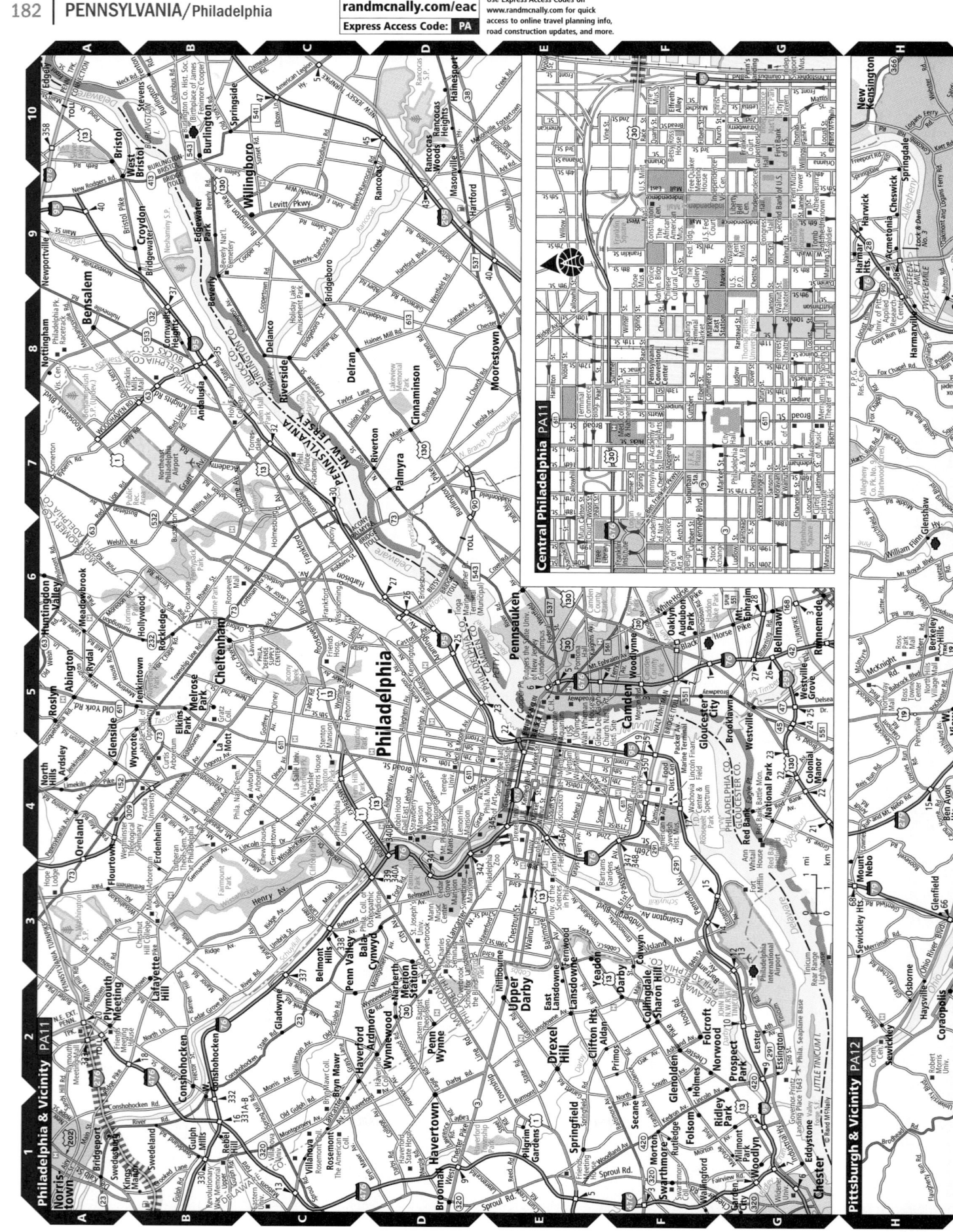

How to determine distance

2 10 18 4 4 / 12 16 20 — Mileages in red between red arrowheads; in black, between intersections.

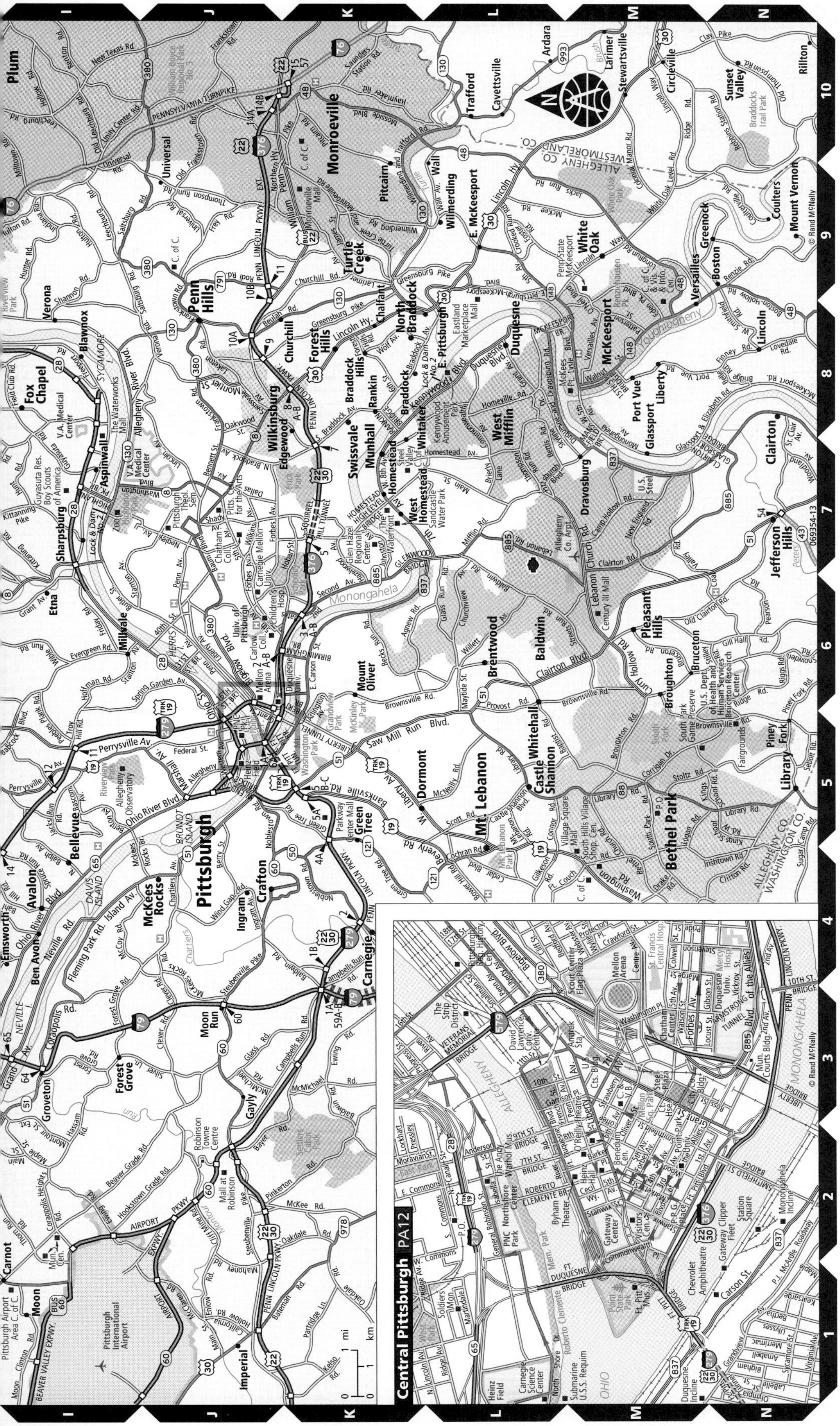

Central Pittsburgh PA12
Pittsburgh
Monroeville
McKeesport
Bethel Park
Mt. Lebanon
© Rand McNally

NY
Pittsburgh
Philadelphia
WV
MD
NJ

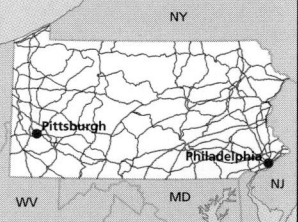

SYMBOLS

- Featured ride
- Scenic route
- Long-term construction
- Historic site or monument; Indian reservation or rancheria; military installation; point of interest; wildlife refuge
- Harley-Davidson dealership

PENNSYLVANIA MOTORCYCLE LAWS

Helmet use:
Required under age 21, and less than 2 years licensed, or without safety class

Riding two abreast:
Yes. See state law for specifics

Eye protection:
Required by law

Speed limit:
Primary roads: 65 mph
Secondary roads: 55 mph

PENNSYLVANIA RESOURCES

Road conditions or construction:
(888) 783-6783 (in PA)
(215) 567-5678 (SmarTraveler, Camden/Philadelphia area)
www.dot.state.pa.us

Highway Emergency Numbers:
911 or *12

Tourism:
(800) 847-4872
www.visitpa.com

State motor vehicle information:
(717) 391-6190
www.dmv.state.pa.us

HARLEY-DAVIDSON DEALERSHIPS

Spirit Harley-Davidson, H-6
1463 Glenn Ave. **Glenshaw**
(412) 487-3377
Lat N 40.529 **Lon** W 79.953

Barb's Harley-Davidson, G-2
8800 Essington Ave. **Philadelphia**
(856) 456-4141
Lat N 40.06 **Lon** W 75.048

Heritage Harley-Davidson, L-7
1122 Lebanon Rd. (Rte. 885) **West Mifflin**
(412) HOG-WILD
Lat N 40.36 **Lon** W 79.933

randmcnally.com/eac

Express Access Code: RI

Use Express Access Codes on
www.randmcnally.com for quick
access to online travel planning info,
road construction updates, and more.

Distance scale
One inch represents about 6 miles

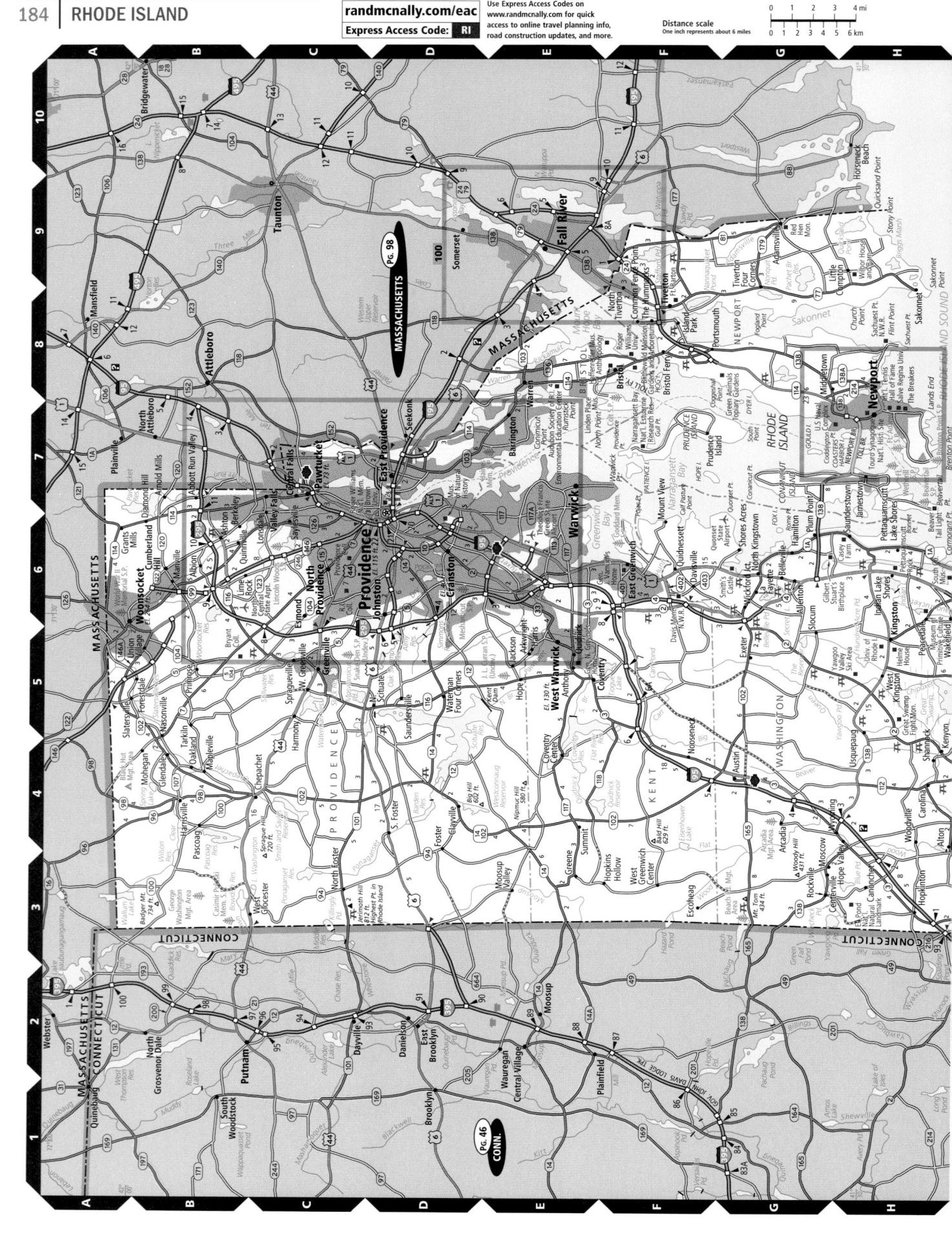

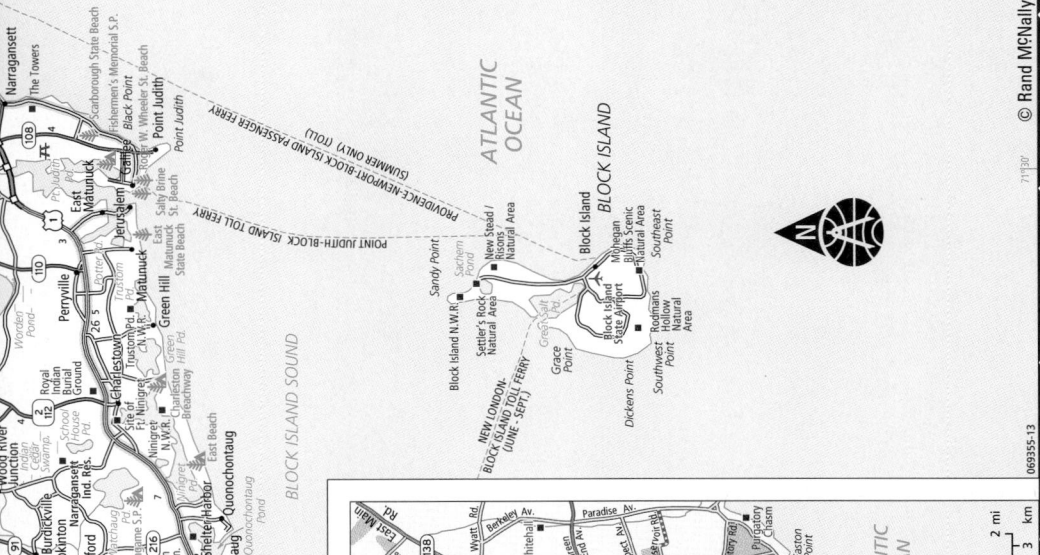

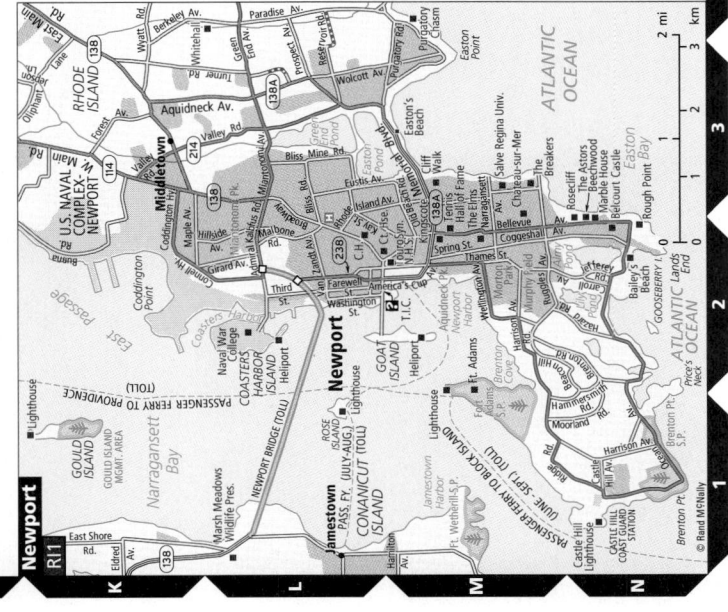

SYMBOLS

- Featured ride
- Long-term construction
- Harley-Davidson dealership
- Scenic route
- Historic site or monument; Indian reservation or rancheria; military installation; point of interest; wildlife refuge

RHODE ISLAND MOTORCYCLE LAWS

Helmet use:
Required under age 21, and for novice riders, and for passengers

Riding two abreast:
Yes. See state law for specifics

Eye protection:
Required by law

Speed limit:
Primary roads: 65 mph
Secondary roads: 55 mph

RHODE ISLAND RESOURCES

Road conditions or construction:
511
www.dot.state.ri.us

Highway Emergency Numbers:
911 or *77

Tourism:
(888) 886-9463
(800) 556-2484
(401) 222-2601
www.visitrhodeisland.com

State motor vehicle information:
(401) 588-3020
www.dmv.state.ri.us

CITY-TO-CITY MILEAGE

	FALL RIVER, MA	KINGSTON	NEWPORT	PROVIDENCE	WARWICK	WESTERLY	WOONSOCKET	WORCESTER, MA
Chepachet	36	44	46	20	27	56	17	37
Fall River, MA		37	23	16	26	58	32	59
Kingston	37		16	30	25	24	47	74
Newport	23	16		30	37	49	76	
Providence	16	30	32		10	42	16	43
Warwick	26	25	27	10		37	26	53
Westerly	58	24	37	42	37		59	70
Woonsocket	32	47	49	16	26	59		32
Worcester, MA	59	74	76	43	53	70	32	

HARLEY-DAVIDSON DEALERSHIPS

Ocean State Harley-Davidson Shop, G-4
435 Nooseneck Hill Rd. (Rte 3) **Exeter**
(401) 392-1162
Lat N 41.572 Lon W 71.656

Precision Harley-Davidson, C-7
269 Armistice Blvd. **Pawtucket**
(401) 724-0010
Lat N 41.881 Lon W 71.366

Ocean State Harley-Davidson, E-6
5 Albany Rd. **Warwick**
(401) 781-6866
Lat N 41.75 Lon W 71.437

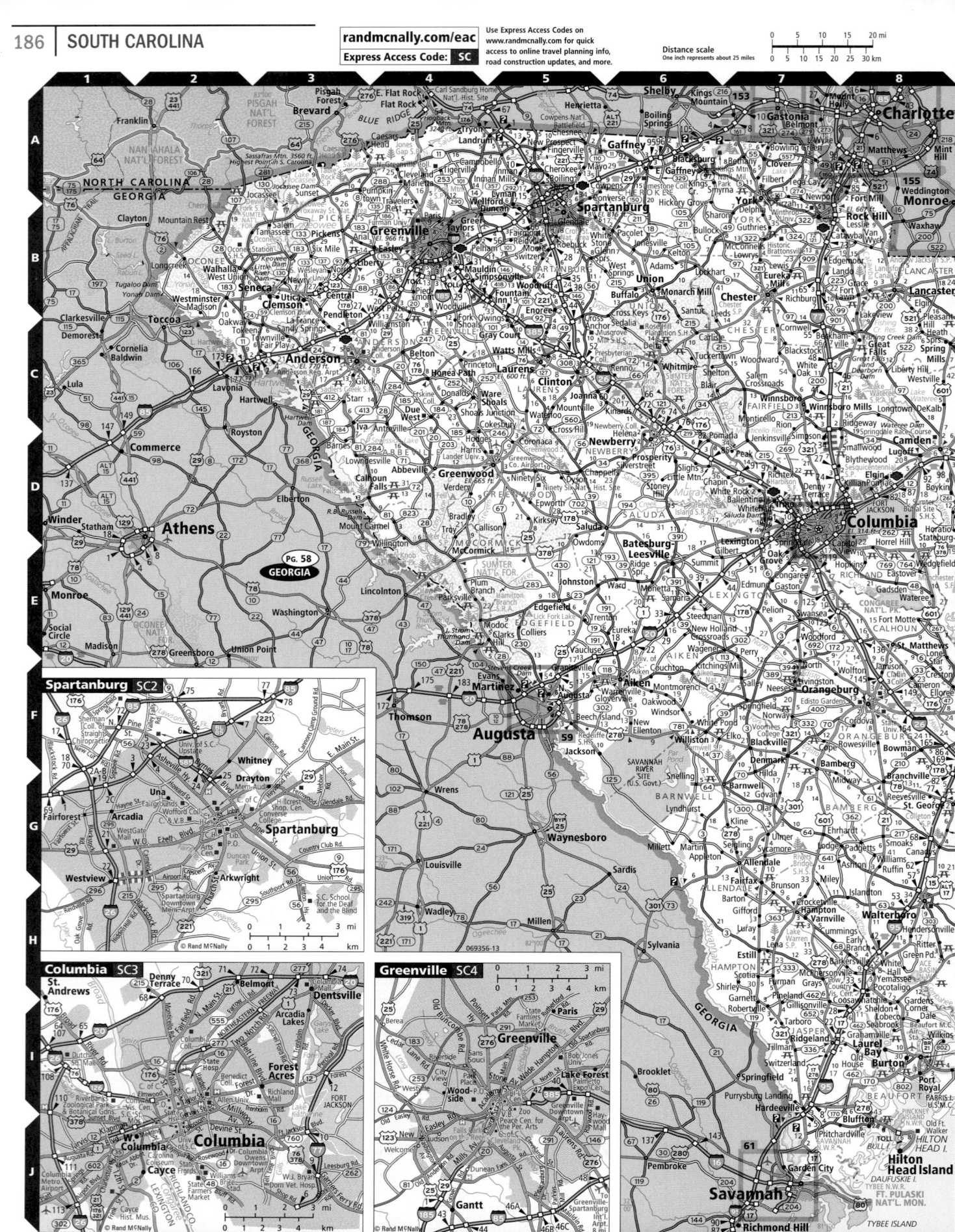

How to determine distance

Mileages in red between red arrowheads; in black, between intersections.

SYMBOLS

- ═══ Featured ride
- ╫╫╫ Long-term construction
- Harley-Davidson dealership
- ═══ Scenic route
- ■ Historic site or monument; Indian reservation or rancheria; military installation; point of interest; wildlife refuge

SOUTH CAROLINA MOTORCYCLE LAWS

Helmet use:
Required under age 21, and reflectorization required

Riding two abreast:
Yes. See state law for specifics

Eye protection:
Required under age 21
Required unless equipped with windscreen

Speed limit:
Primary roads: 70 mph
Secondary roads: 70 mph

SOUTH CAROLINA RESOURCES

Road conditions or construction:
www.dot.state.sc.us

Highway Emergency Numbers: 911 or *HP

Tourism:
(888) 727-6453 (to request travel materials only)
(803) 734-1700
www.discoversouthcarolina.com

State motor vehicle information:
(803) 896-5000
www.scdmvonline.com

HARLEY-DAVIDSON DEALERSHIPS

- **Timms Harley-Davidson, C-3**
  4110 Clemson Blvd. **Anderson**
  (864) 224-1531
  Lat N 34.56 Lon W 82.692

- **Low Country Harley-Davidson, H-10**
  4707 Dorchester Rd. **Charleston**
  (843) 554-1847
  Lat N 32.854 Lon W 80.02

- **The Harley Shop, H-10**
  57 S Market St. **Charleston**
  (843) 722-9472
  Lat N 32.781 Lon W 79.929

- **Thunder Tower Harley-Davidson, D-8**
  190 Pontiac Business Center Dr. **Elgin**
  (803) 988-0004
  Lat N 34.106 Lon W 80.837

- **Doug's Harley-Davidson, D-10**
  2207 T.V. Rd. **Florence**
  (843) 669-9961
  Lat N 34.239 Lon W 79.749

- **Harley-Davidson of Greenville, B-4**
  30 Chrome Dr. **Greenville**
  (864) 234-1340
  Lat N 34.836 Lon W 82.296

- **Harley Haven, D-7**
  941 Western Ln. **Irmo**
  (803) 794-4887
  Lat N 34.12 Lon W 81.195

- **Myrtle Beach Harley-Davidson, E-12**
  4710 S Kings Hwy. **Myrtle Beach**
  (843) 369-5555
  Lat N 33.647 Lon W 78.942

- **Myrtle Beach Harley-Davidson, E-13**
  913A N Ocean Blvd. **Myrtle Beach**
  (843) 946-9499
  Lat N 33.692 Lon W 78.88

- **Myrtle Beach Harley-Davidson at Broadway at the Beach, E-13**
  1316 Celebrity Circle **Myrtle Beach**
  (843) 293-5555
  Lat N 33.719 Lon W 78.882

- **The Harley-Davidson Shop at the Beach, E-13**
  4002 Hwy. 17 S **North Myrtle Beach**
  (843) 663-5555
  Lat N 33.802 Lon W 78.729

- **Cox's Harley-Davidson of Rock Hill, B-7**
  1093 Albright Rd. **Rock Hill**
  (803) 327-1183
  Lat N 34.906 Lon W 81.024

- **Spartanburg Harley-Davidson, A-5**
  365 Sha Ln. **Spartanburg**
  (864) 583-8840
  Lat N 35.028 Lon W 81.871

© Rand McNally

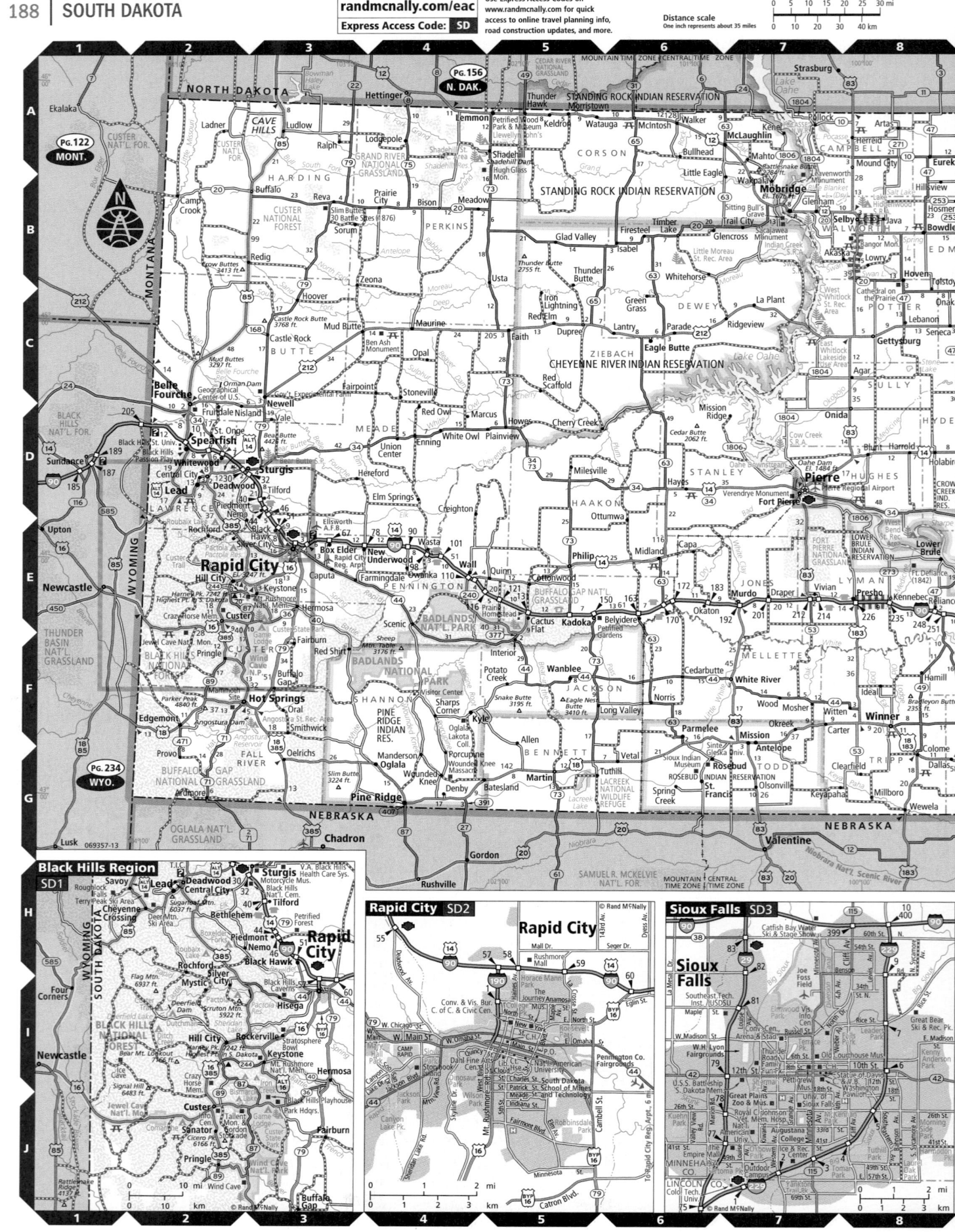

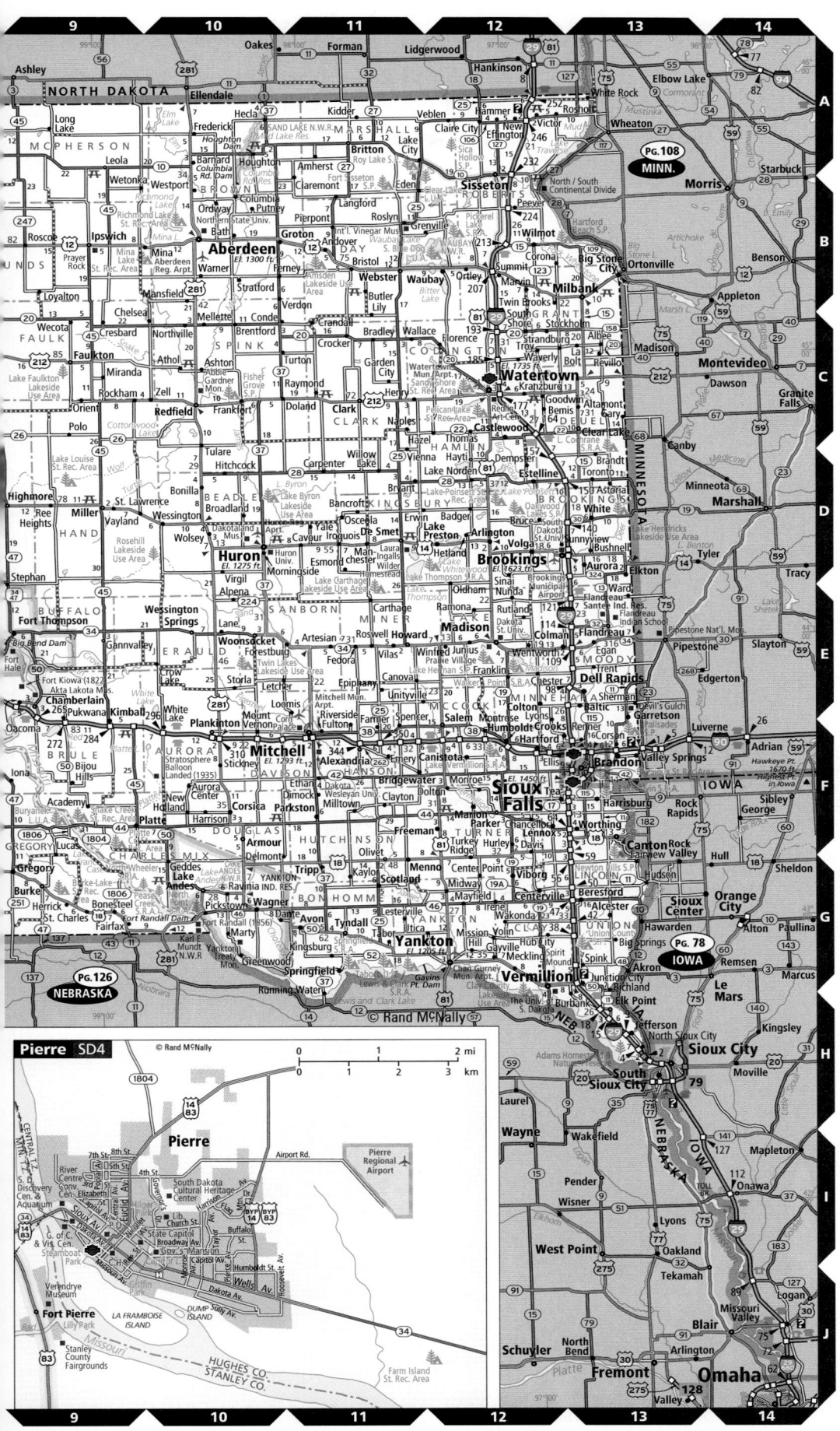

How to determine distance

Mileages in red between red arrowheads; in black, between intersections.

SYMBOLS

- Featured ride
- Scenic route
- Long-term construction
- Historic site or monument; Indian reservation or rancheria; military installation; point of interest; wildlife refuge
- Harley-Davidson dealership

For South Dakota ride, see page R28.

SOUTH DAKOTA MOTORCYCLE LAWS

Helmet use:
Required under age 18

Riding two abreast:
Yes. See state law for specifics

Eye protection:
Required unless equipped with windscreen

Speed limit:
Primary roads: 75 mph
Secondary roads: 75 mph

SOUTH DAKOTA RESOURCES

Road conditions or construction:
511
(866) 697-3511
www.sddot.com

Highway Emergency Numbers:
911

Tourism:
(800) 732-5682
(605) 773-3301
www.travelsd.com

State motor vehicle information:
(800) 952-3696
www.state.sd.us/dcr/dl

CITY-TO-CITY MILEAGE

	Aberdeen	Belle Fourche	Mobridge	Pierre	Rapid City	Sioux City, IA	Sioux Falls	Watertown
Aberdeen		312	100	159	350	285	204	105
Belle Fourche	312		213	247	60	485	404	365
Mobridge	100	213		109	241	385	304	205
Pierre	159	247	109		191	306	225	190
Rapid City	350	60	241	191		429	348	406
Sioux City, IA	285	485	385	306	429		85	185
Sioux Falls	204	404	304	225	348	85		104
Watertown	105	365	205	190	406	185	104	

HARLEY-DAVIDSON DEALERSHIPS

Petersen Motors Harley-Davidson, D-7
422 S Fort St. **Pierre**
(605) 224-4242
Lat N 44.366 Lon W 100.357

Black Hills Harley-Davidson, E-3
2820 Harley Dr. **Rapid City**
(605) 342-9362
Lat N 44.124 Lon W 103.296

J & L Harley-Davidson, F-13
2601 W 60th St. N **Sioux Falls**
(605) 334-2721
Lat N 43.602 Lon W 96.762

J & L Harley-Davidson, F-13
5019 S Louise Ave. **Sioux Falls**
No Phone Found
Lat N 43.5 Lon W 96.771

Sturgis Harley-Davidson, D-2
1040 Junction Ave. **Sturgis**
(605) 347-2056
Lat N 44.414 Lon W 103.509

Glacial Lakes Harley-Davidson Shop, C-12
1000 19th St. SE **Watertown**
(605) 886-3448
Lat N 44.912 Lon W 97.118

randmcnally.com/eac
Express Access Code: TN

Use Express Access Codes on
www.randmcnally.com for quick
access to online travel planning info,
road construction updates, and more.

Distance scale
One inch represents about 20 miles

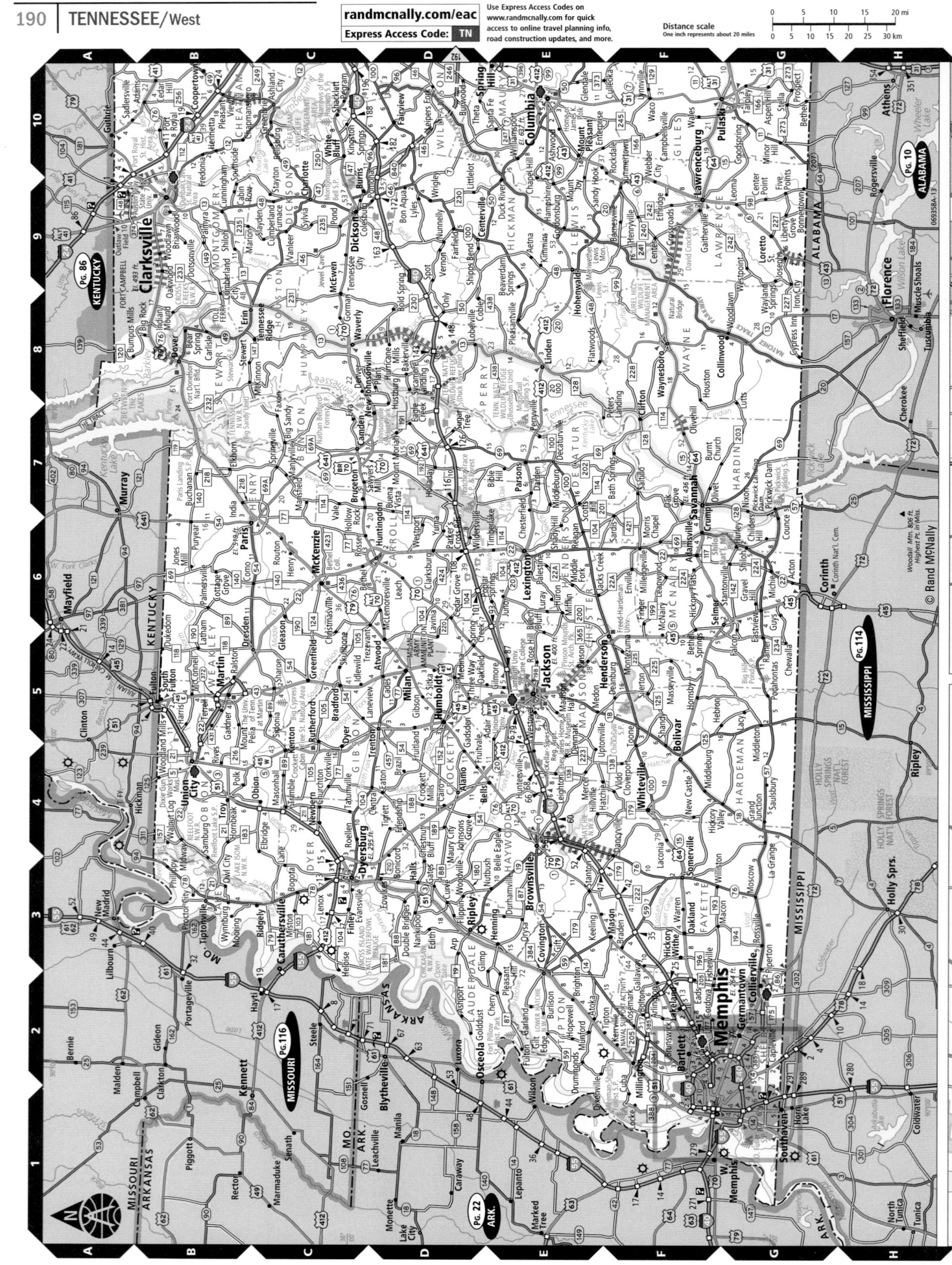

© Rand McNally

How to determine distance

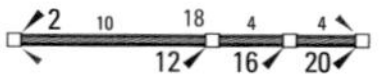

Mileages in red between red arrowheads;
in black, between intersections.

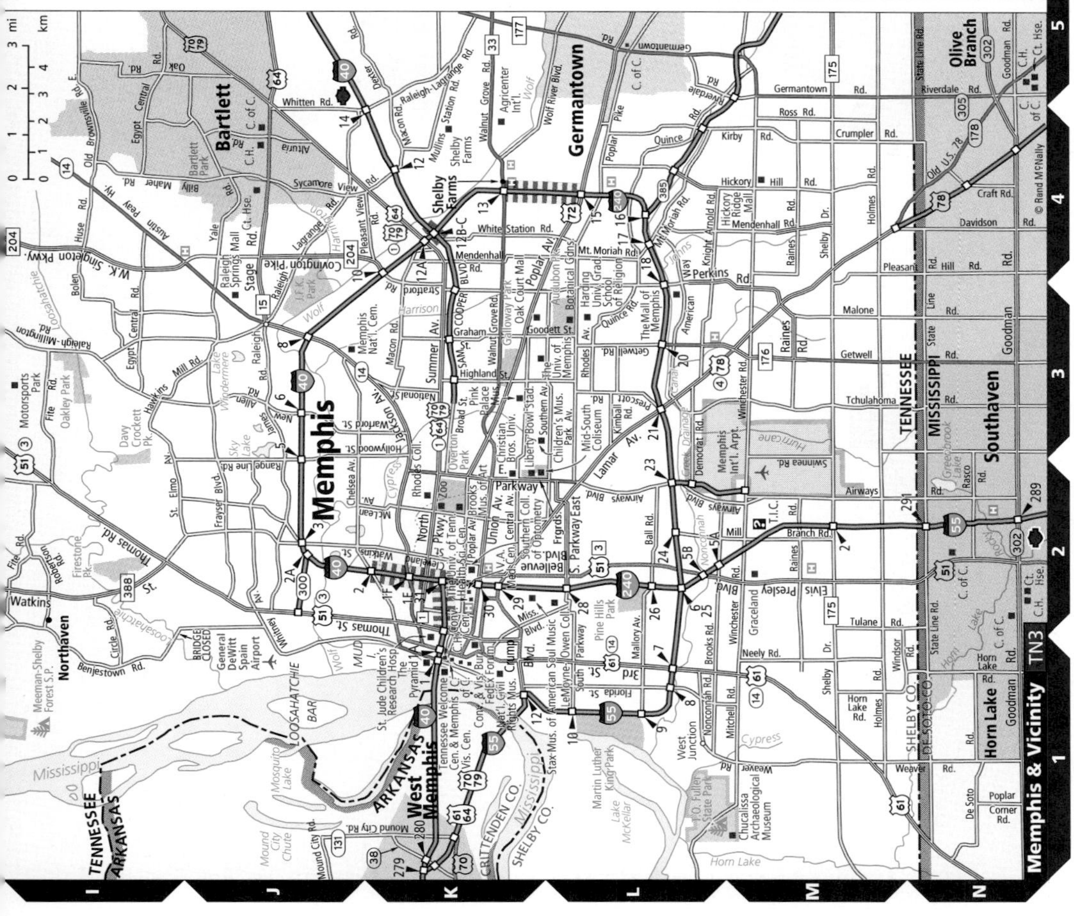

p. 192-193

Memphis

SYMBOLS

Featured ride — Scenic route

Long-term construction

Harley-Davidson dealership

■ Historic site or monument; Indian reservation or rancheria; military installation; point of interest; wildlife refuge

For Tennessee ride, see page R29.

TENNESSEE MOTORCYCLE LAWS

Helmet use:
Required

Riding two abreast:
Yes. See state law for specifics

Eye protection:
Required unless equipped with windscreen

Speed limit:
Primary roads: 70 mph
Secondary roads: 70 mph

TENNESSEE RESOURCES

Road conditions or construction:
(800) 342-3258
(800) 858-6349
www.tdot.state.tn.us/travel.htm

Highway Emergency Numbers:
911 or (615) 741-2060 or *THP

Tourism:
(800) 462-8366
(615) 741-2159
www.tnvacation.com

State motor vehicle information:
(615) 741-3954
www.tennessee.gov/safety

HARLEY-DAVIDSON DEALERSHIPS

Appleton's Harley-Davidson, B-9
2501 Hwy. 41A Bypass Clarksville
(931) 648-1607
Lat N 36.502 Lon W 87.286

Bumpus Harley-Davidson Shop of Collierville, G-2
325 S Byhalia Rd. Collierville
(901) 316-1121
Lat N 35.037 Lon W 89.689

Harley-Davidson Shop of Columbia, E-10
1028 Nashville Hwy. Columbia
(931) 540-0099
Lat N 35.635 Lon W 87.018

Bumpus Harley-Davidson of Jackson, E-5
326 Carriage House Dr. Jackson
(731) 422-5508
Lat N 35.667 Lon W 88.842

Bumpus Harley-Davidson of Memphis, F-2
2160 Whitten Rd. Memphis
(901) 372-1121
Lat N 35.185 Lon W 89.836

Abernathy's Motorcycle Sales, B-4
1704 W Main St. Union City
(731) 885-1792
Lat N 36.428 Lon W 89.077

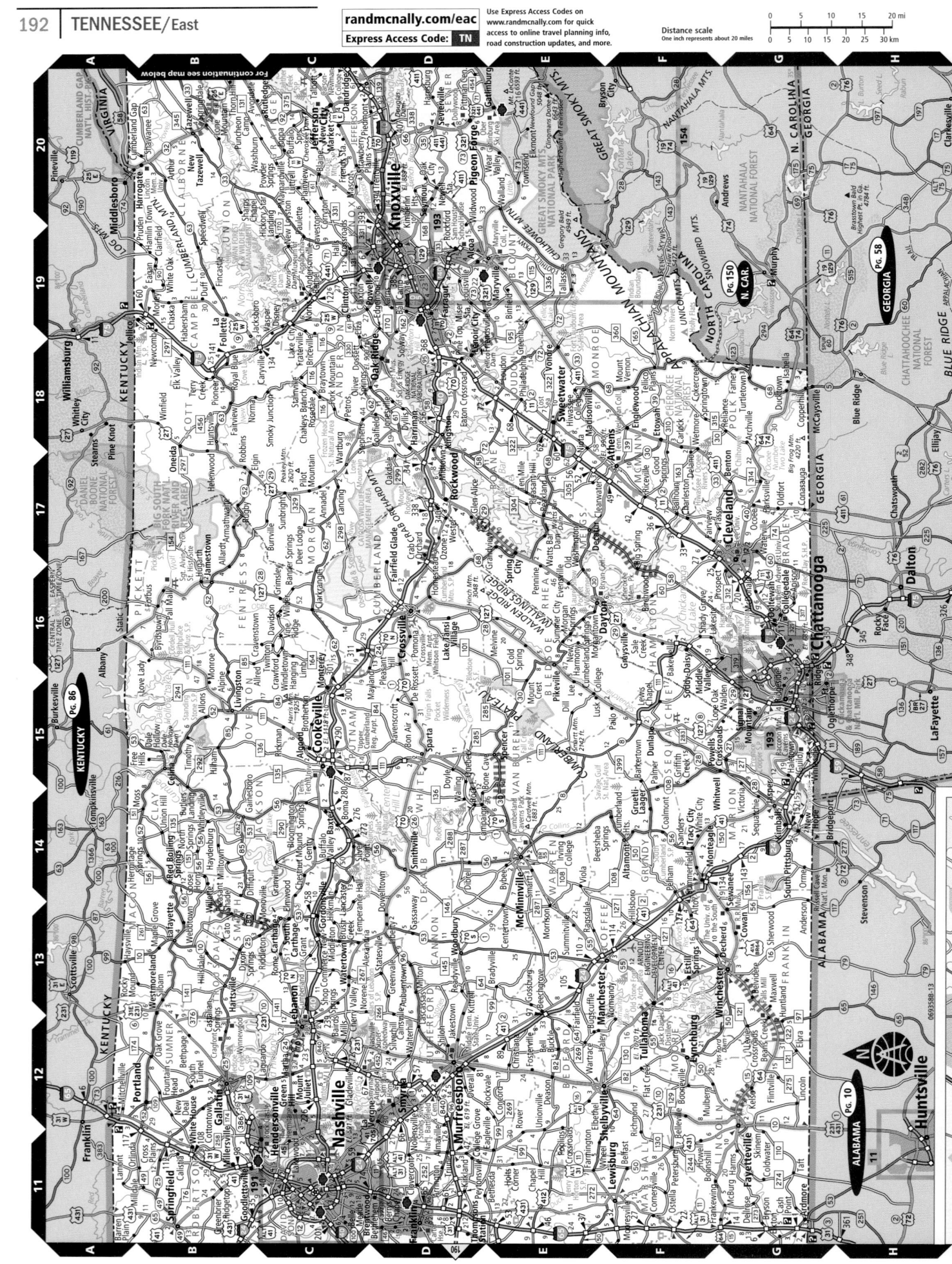

How to determine distance

Mileages in red between red arrowheads; in black, between intersections.

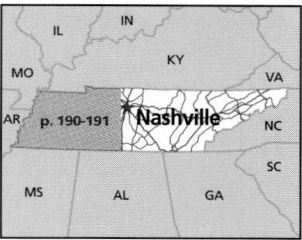

Eastern Tennessee

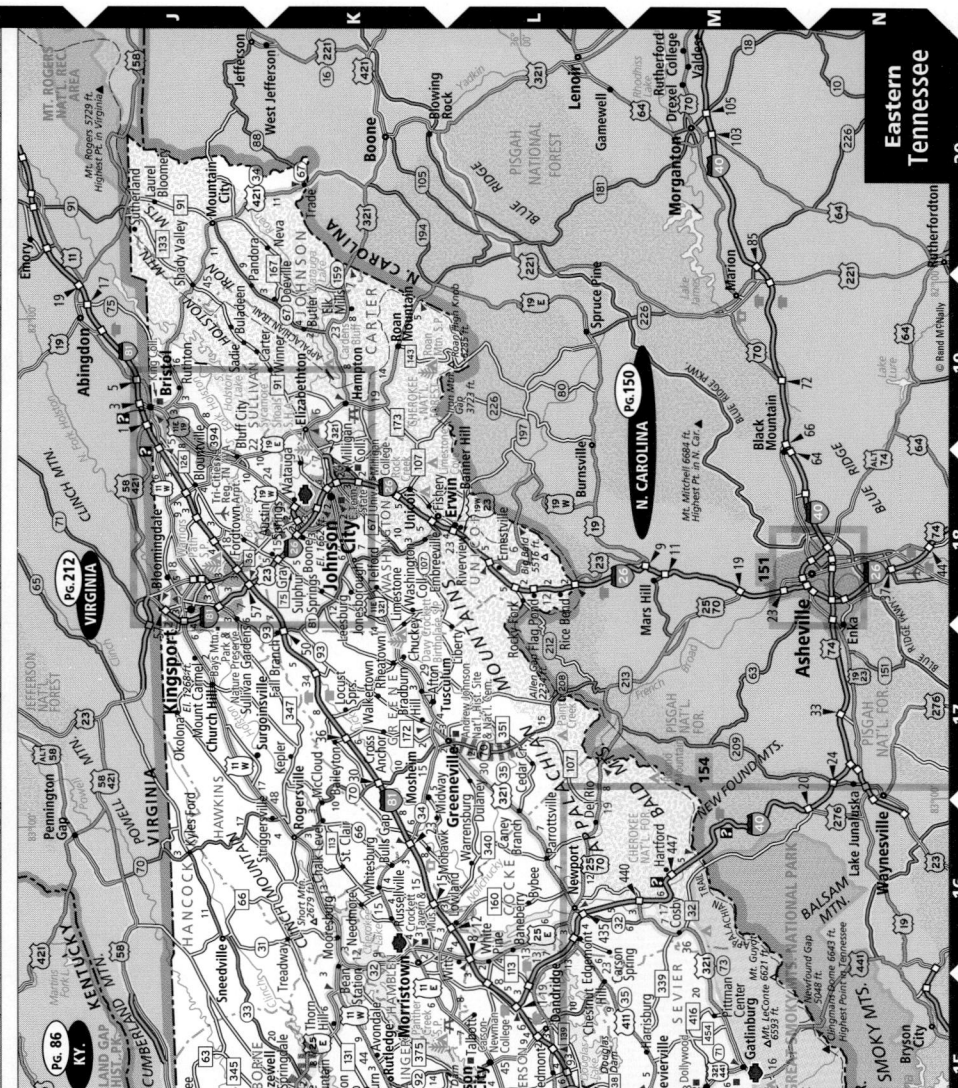

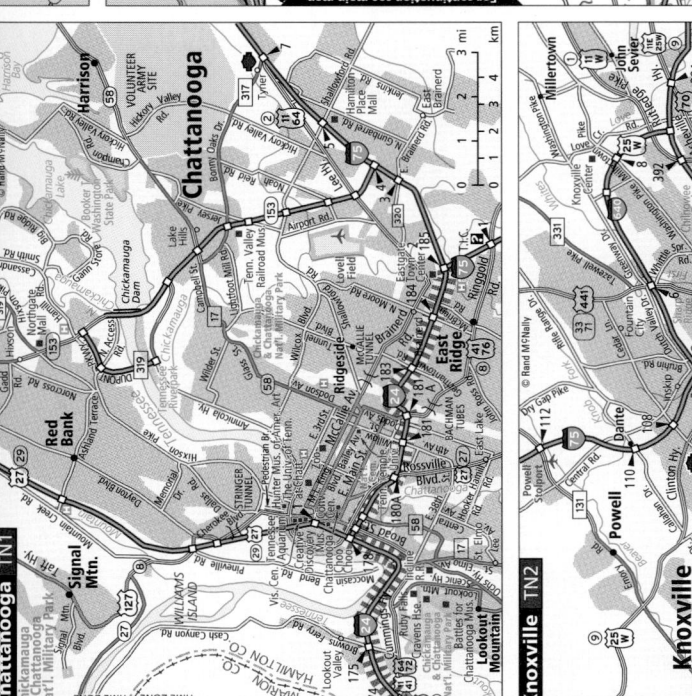

Chattanooga TN1

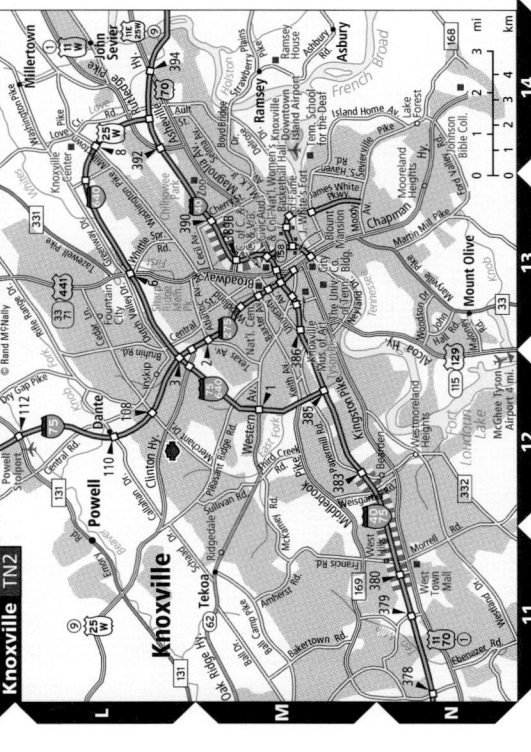

Knoxville TN2

SYMBOLS

Featured ride

Scenic route

Long-term construction

Historic site or monument; Indian reservation or rancheria; military installation; point of interest; wildlife refuge

Harley-Davidson dealership

HARLEY-DAVIDSON DEALERSHIPS

Thunder Creek Harley-Davidson, G-16
7720 Lee Hwy. **Chattanooga**
(423) 892-4888
Lat N 35.061 Lon W 85.133

Boswell's Harley-Davidson Shop of Cookeville, C-15
1424 Interstate Dr. **Cookeville**
(931) 526-3139
Lat N 36.138 Lon W 85.513

Harley-Davidson of Cool Springs, D-11
7128 S Springs Dr. **Franklin**
(615) 771-7775
Lat N 35.952 Lon W 86.816

Smoky Mountain Harley-Davidson, E-20
530 Parkway **Gatlinburg**
(865) 430-1602
Lat N 35.714 Lon W 83.511

Smith Brothers Harley-Davidson Sales, K-18
3518 Bristol Hwy. **Johnson City**
(423) 283-0422
Lat N 36.373 Lon W 82.374

Knoxville Harley-Davidson, D-19
5800 Clinton Hwy. **Knoxville**
(865) 689-2454
Lat N 36.007 Lon W 83.989

Knoxville Harley-Davidson West Shop, D-19
605 Lovell Rd. **Knoxville**
(865) 671-2454
Lat N 35.909 Lon W 84.149

Boswell's Harley-Davidson Shop, C-11
2200 Gallatin Pike N **Madison**
(615) 855-1001
Lat N 36.305 Lon W 86.689

Smoky Mountain Harley-Davidson, D-19
1820 W Lamar Alexander Pkwy. **Maryville**
(865) 977-1669
Lat N 35.755 Lon W 84.02

Colboch Harley-Davidson Sales, K-16
1830 N Davy Crockett Pkwy. **Morristown**
(423) 586-5343
Lat N 36.243 Lon W 83.266

Bumpus Harley-Davidson of Murfreesboro, D-12
2250 NW Broad St. **Murfreesboro**
(615) 849-8025
Lat N 35.883 Lon W 86.431

Boswell's Harley-Davidson, C-11
401 Fesslers Ln. **Nashville**
(615) 242-6067
Lat N 36.149 Lon W 86.743

C & S Harley-Davidson of Nashville, C-11
4600 Delaware Ave. **Nashville**
(615) 297-7500
Lat N 36.154 Lon W 86.842

randmcnally.com/eac

Express Access Codes: Tennessee TN Texas TX

Use Express Access Codes on
www.randmcnally.com for quick
access to online travel planning info,
road construction updates, and more.

Central Houston TX15
Tri-Cities: Johnson City / Kingsport / Bristol TN5
© Rand McNally

MO
KY
VA
Bristol
Kingsport
Johnson City
AR
NC
MS
AL
GA
SC

CA
AZ
NM
OK
AR
TN
MS
AL
GA
LA
Houston
MEX

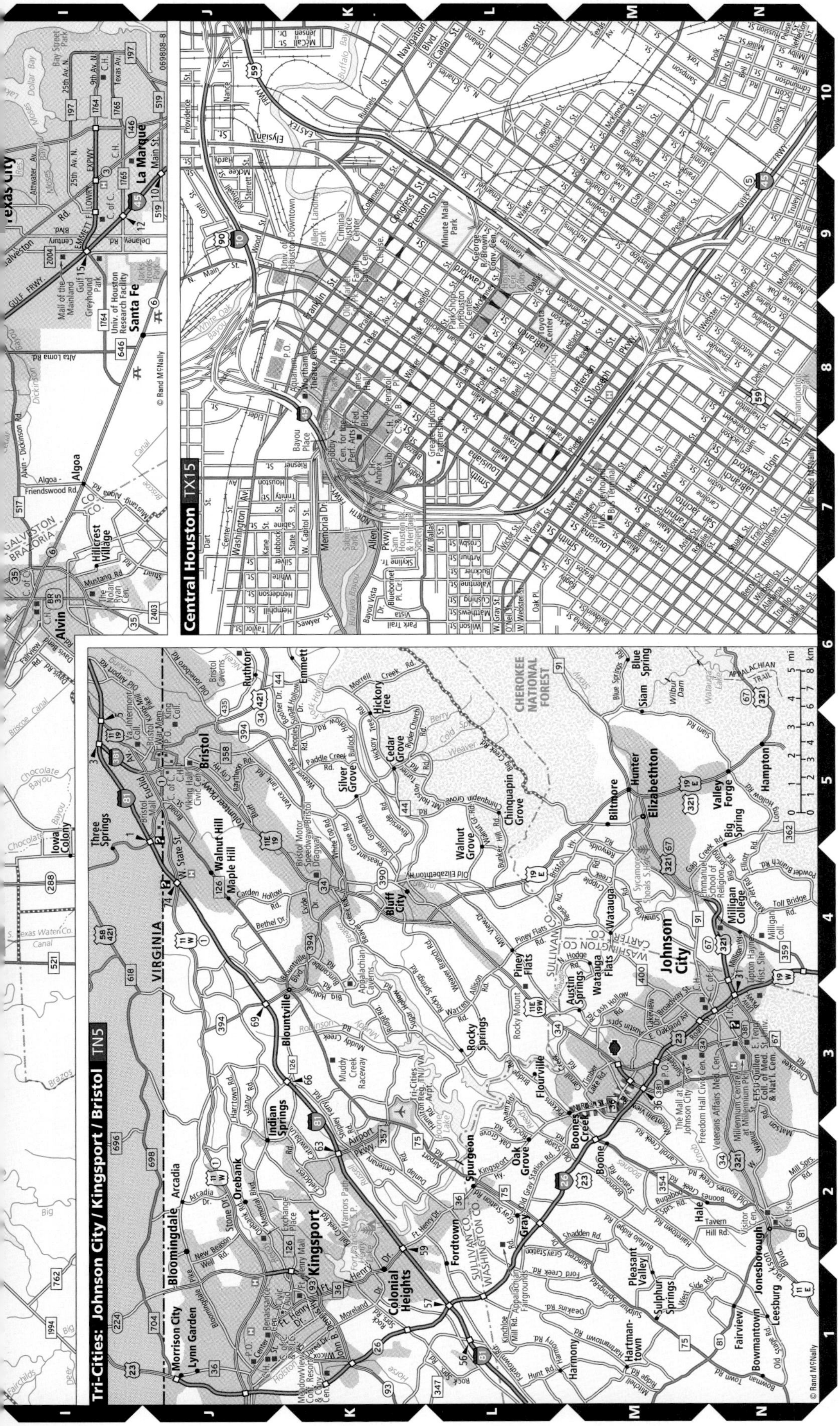

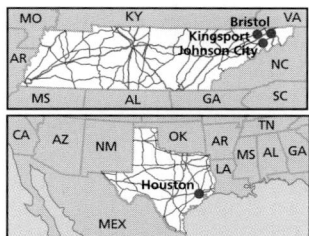

SYMBOLS

Featured ride	Scenic route
Long-term construction	Historic site or monument; Indian reservation or rancheria; military installation; point of interest; wildlife refuge
Harley-Davidson dealership	

HARLEY-DAVIDSON DEALERSHIPS

Mancuso Harley-Davidson Central, D-5
535 North Loop **Houston**
(713) 880-5666
Lat N 29.814 **Lon** W 95.393

Mancuso Harley-Davidson, B-2
12710 Crossroads Park Dr. **Houston**
(281) 970-9700
Lat N 29.915 **Lon** W 95.609

Stubbs Harley-Davidson, E-6
4400 Telephone Rd. **Houston**
(713) 644-7535
Lat N 29.7 **Lon** W 95.303

San Jacinto Harley-Davidson, F-7
3636 East Sam Houston Parkway South **Pasadena**
OPENING IN 2006
Lat N 29.657 **Lon** W 95.157

Republic Harley-Davidson, F-2
12707 Southwest Frwy. **Stafford**
(281) 295-1000
Lat N 29.637 **Lon** W 95.583

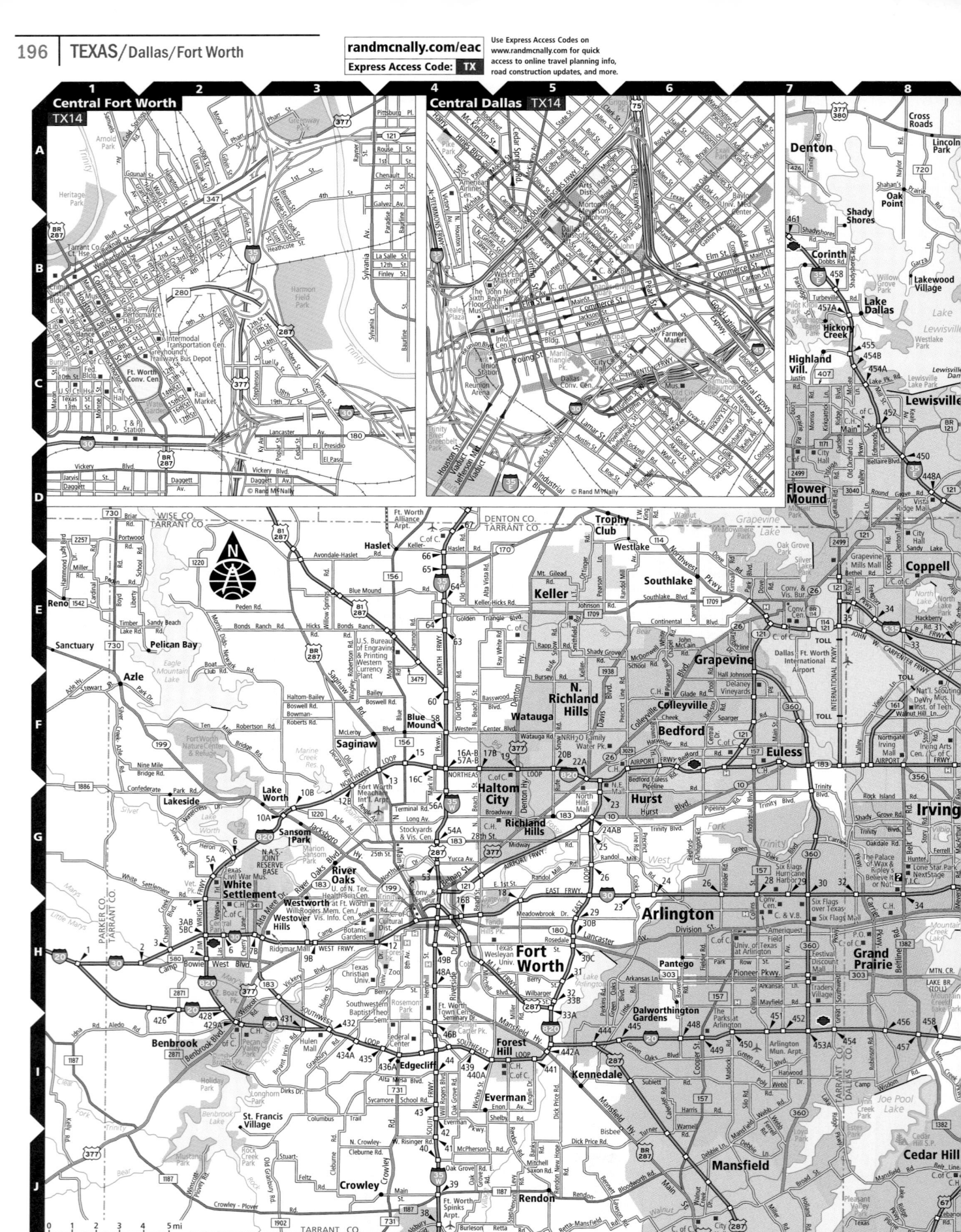

Central Fort Worth TX14

Central Dallas TX14

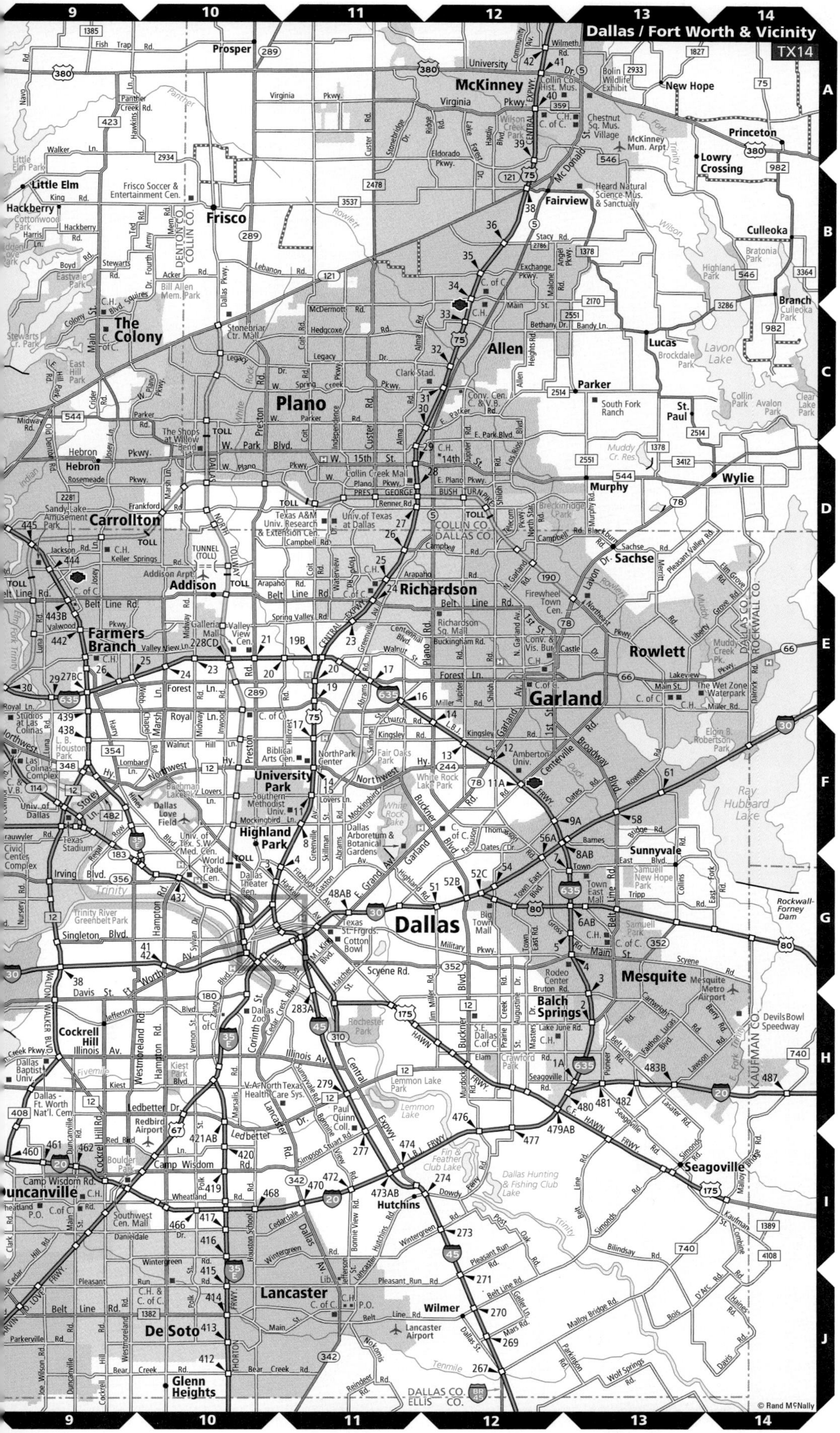

Dallas / Fort Worth & Vicinity

TX14

SYMBOLS

- 〜〜〜 Featured ride
- ⊬⊬⊬ Long-term construction
- ⬤ Harley-Davidson dealership
- 〰〰 Scenic route
- ■ Historic site or monument; Indian reservation or rancheria; military installation; point of interest; wildlife refuge

HARLEY-DAVIDSON DEALERSHIPS

⬤ **Harley-Davidson of Dallas, B-12**
304 Central Expy. S (US 75) **Allen**
(214) 495-0259
Lat N 33.099 **Lon** W 96.679

⬤ **Texas Harley-Davidson, F-6**
1839 Airport Frwy. **Bedford**
(817) 267-2646
Lat N 32.837 **Lon** W 97.137

⬤ **Harley-Davidson of North Texas, D-9**
1910 Old Denton Rd. **Carrollton**
(972) 245-1492
Lat N 32.965 **Lon** W 96.913

⬤ **American Eagle Harley-Davidson, B-7**
5920 S I-35 E **Corinth**
(940) 498-5000
Lat N 33.153 **Lon** W 97.062

⬤ **Ft. Worth Harley-Davidson, H-2**
3025 W Loop 820 S **Fort Worth**
(817) 696-9090
Lat N 32.73 **Lon** W 97.481

⬤ **Dallas Harley-Davidson, F-12**
1334 W Centerville Rd. **Garland**
(972) 270-3962
Lat N 32.857 **Lon** W 96.648

⬤ **Longhorn Harley-Davidson, H-7**
2618 W I-20 **Grand Prairie**
(972) 988-1903
Lat N 32.673 **Lon** W 97.024

© Rand McNally

Distance scale
One inch represents about 33 miles

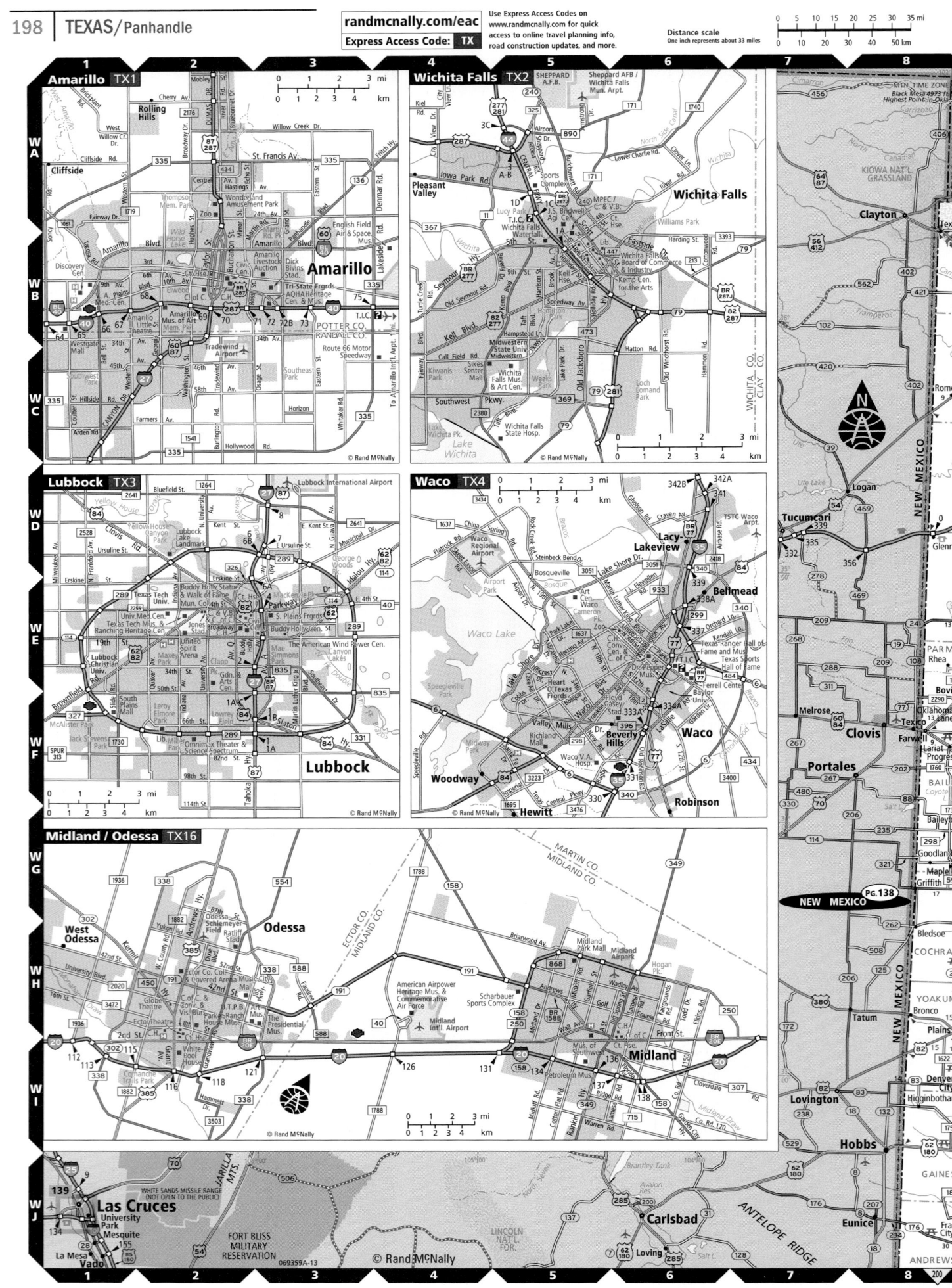

Amarillo TX1

Wichita Falls TX2

Lubbock TX3

Waco TX4

Midland / Odessa TX16

© Rand McNally

069359A-13

How to determine distance

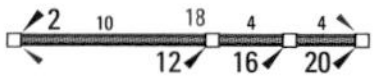

Mileages in red between red arrowheads; in black, between intersections.

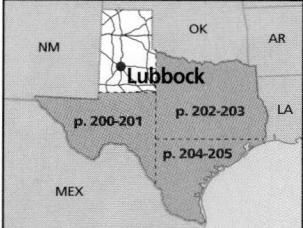

SYMBOLS

- Featured ride
- Scenic route
- Long-term construction
- Harley-Davidson dealership
- Historic site or monument; Indian reservation or rancheria; military installation; point of interest; wildlife refuge

TEXAS MOTORCYCLE LAWS

Helmet use:
Required under age 21; not required over 21 with successful completion of rider training or $10,000 medical insurance

Riding two abreast:
No reference in administrative code or statutes

Eye protection:
Not required

Speed limit:
Primary roads: 75 mph
Secondary roads: 70 mph

TEXAS RESOURCES

Road conditions or construction:
(800) 452-9292
www.dot.state.tx.us

Highway Emergency Numbers:
911

Tourism:
(800) 888-8839 (to request travel materials only)
www.traveltex.com

State motor vehicle information:
(512) 424-2000
www.txdps.state.tx.us

HARLEY-DAVIDSON DEALERSHIPS

Kent's Harley-Davidson Sales, WJ-14
3106 S Clack Abilene
(325) 673-7103
Lat N 32.415 **Lon** W 99.778

Tripp's Harley-Davidson, WD-10
6040 I-40 W Amarillo
(806) 352-2021
Lat N 35.19 **Lon** W 101.905

Wild West Harley-Davidson, WH-10
5702 58th St. Lubbock
(866) 791-4597
Lat N 33.541 **Lon** W 101.937

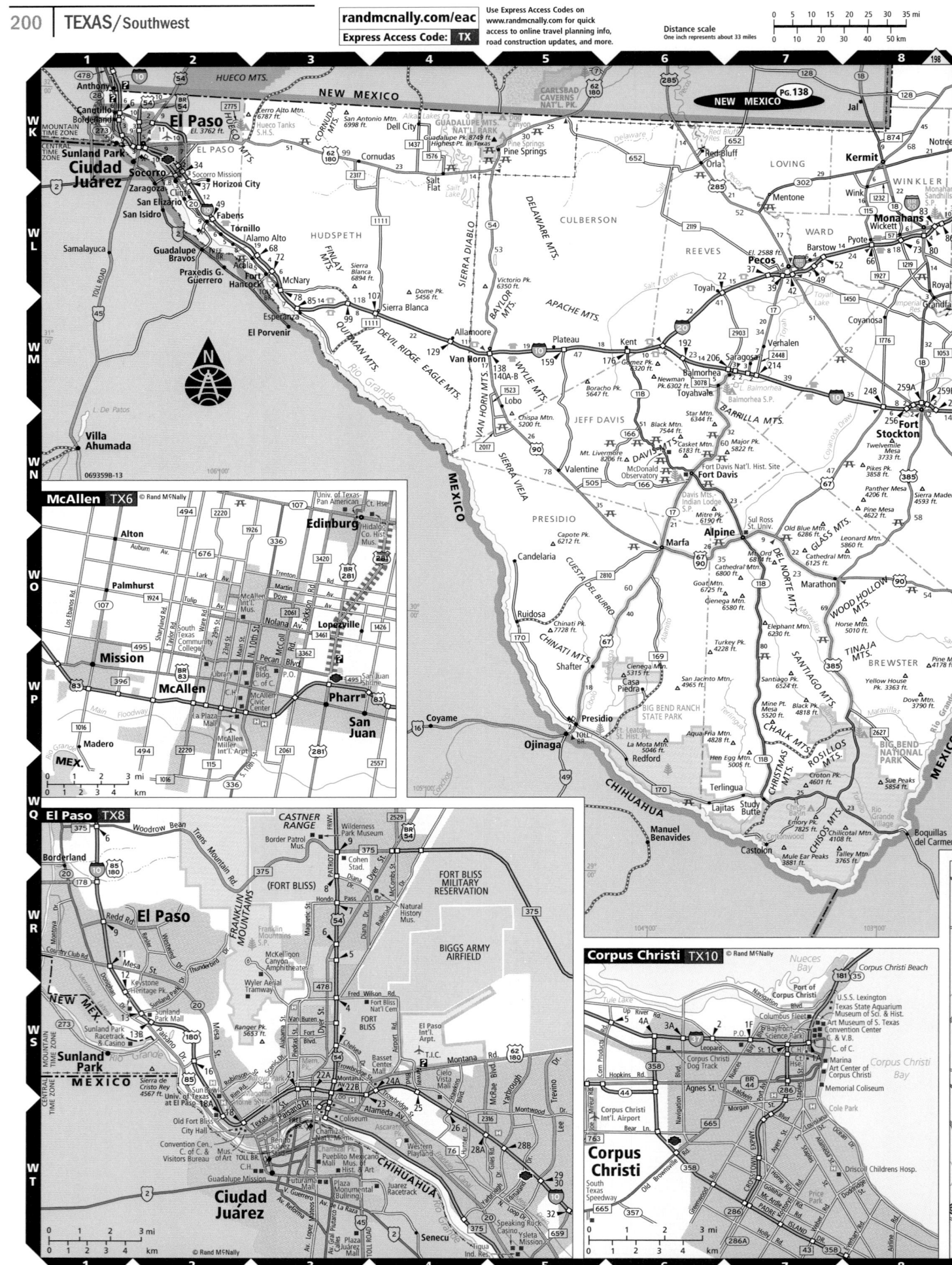

PG. 138

randmcnally.com/eac
Express Access Code: TX

Use Express Access Codes on www.randmcnally.com for quick access to online travel planning info, road construction updates, and more.

Distance scale
One inch represents about 33 miles

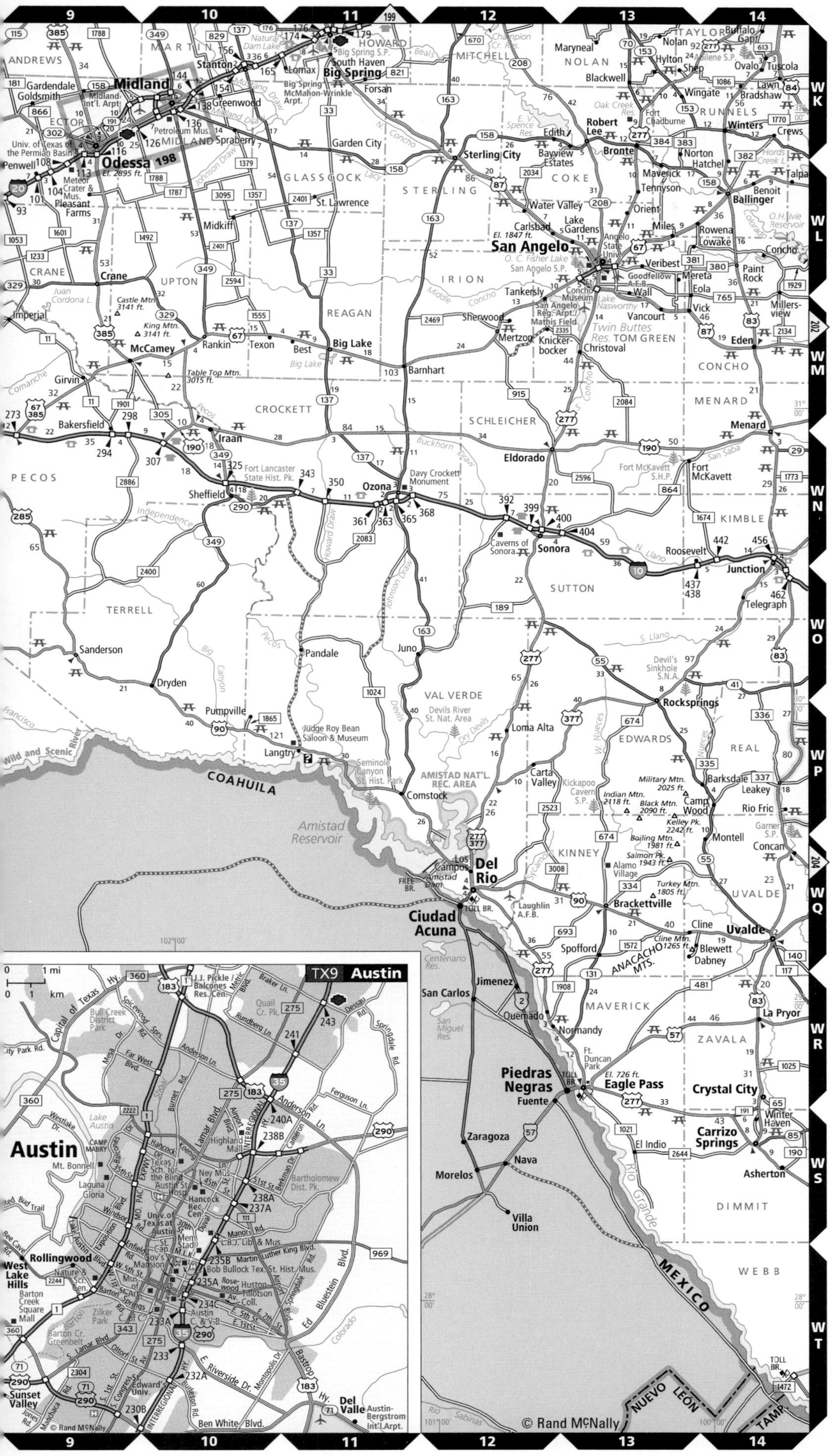

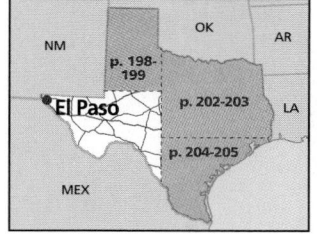

SYMBOLS

Featured ride	Scenic route
Long-term construction	■ Historic site or monument; Indian reservation or rancheria; military installation; point of interest; wildlife refuge
Harley-Davidson dealership	

CITY-TO-CITY MILEAGE

	ABILENE	AMARILLO	DALLAS	EL PASO	LUBBOCK	ODESSA	SAN ANGELO	SAN ANTONIO
Abilene		283	185	447	165	168	92	261
Amarillo	283		359	432	118	258	300	512
Big Bend NP	379	469	565	324	351	213	290	446
Big Spring	108	225	294	340	107	61	86	299
Carlsbad, NM	276	296	462	165	179	139	255	458
Childress	155	117	242	556	147	277	226	417
Clovis, NM	269	103	455	314	104	203	286	498
Dallas	185	359		633	351	354	262	277
Del Rio	247	449	425	424	331	250	155	151
Eagle Pass	302	504	416	479	386	305	210	139
El Paso	447	432	633		344	281	402	558
Fort Stockton	252	342	438	238	224	86	163	319
Houston	347	605	247	753	519	546	363	199
Lubbock	165	118	351	344		140	182	394
Midland	147	235	333	301	117	22	111	331
Odessa	168	258	354	281	140		131	351
Pecos	242	332	428	207	214	76	205	374
Perryton	307	121	396	524	239	379	378	569
San Angelo	92	300	262	402	182	131		213
San Antonio	261	512	277	558	394	351	213	
Van Horn	328	418	514	119	300	162	283	439

HARLEY-DAVIDSON DEALERSHIPS

The Harley-Davidson Shop, WK-11
908 W 3rd St. **Big Spring**
(432) 263-2322
Lat N 32.249 Lon W 101.486

Barnett Harley-Davidson, WK-2
8272 Gateway Blvd. E **El Paso**
(915) 592-5804
Lat N 31.742 Lon W 106.329

Legacy Harley-Davidson, WK-9
12100 W Hwy. 80 E **Odessa**
(432) 561-8991
Lat N 31.907 Lon W 102.247

© Rand McNally

How to determine distance

Mileages in red between red arrowheads; in black, between intersections.

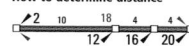

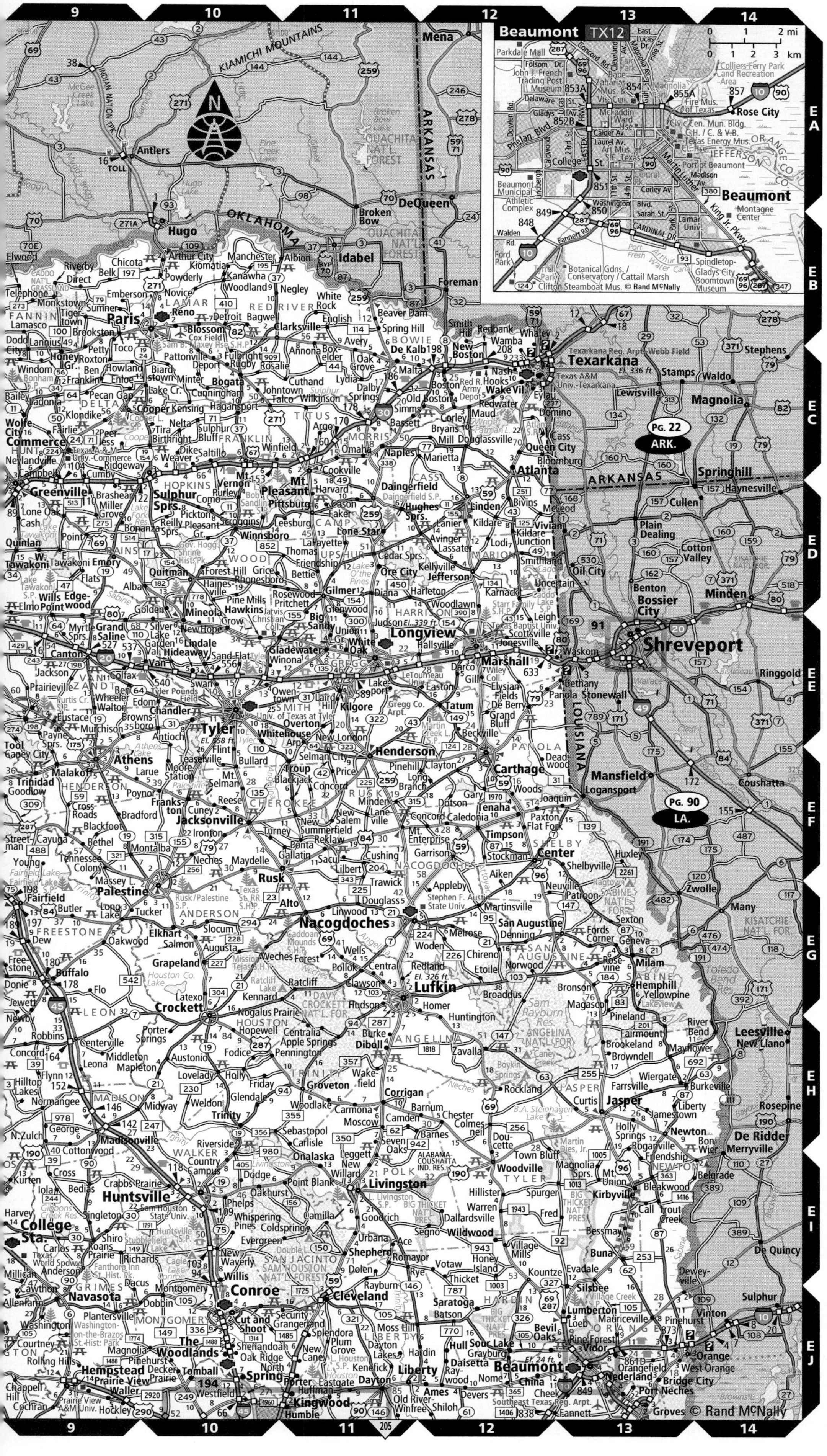

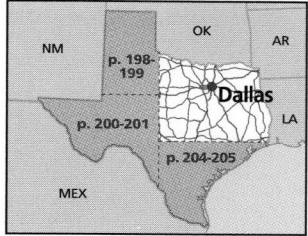

For Texas ride, see page R30.

HARLEY-DAVIDSON DEALERSHIPS

For the Dallas/Fort Worth metro area, please see dealer listings on page 197.

Central Texas Harley-Davidson, EJ-6
804 E Braker Ln. (Exit 243) **Austin**
(512) 973-8521
Lat N 30.377 **Lon** W 97.675

Austin Harley-Davidson, EJ-6
10917 S I-35 (Exit 225) **Austin**
(512) 448-4294
Lat N 30.14 **Lon** W 97.765

Cowboy Harley-Davidson of Beaumont, EJ-13
1150 I-10 S **Beaumont**
(409) 840-6969
Lat N 30.065 **Lon** W 94.175

Independence Harley-Davidson, EI-9
4101 State Hwy. 6 S **College Station**
(979) 690-1669
Lat N 30.576 **Lon** W 96.278

Texan Harley-Davidson, EJ-10
2111 N Frazier St. **Conroe**
(936) 539-1726
Lat N 30.334 **Lon** W 95.467

Bell County Harley-Davidson, EH-6
875 W Central Texas Expy. **Harker Heights**
(254) 680-4747
Lat N 31.075 **Lon** W 97.684

Red River Harley-Davidson, EB-4
MOVING IN 2006: US 287 N & Bell Rd. PO Box 86
Iowa Park
(940) 592-5642
Lat N 33.954 **Lon** W 98.681

The Harley Shop, EE-11
3400 N 4th St. **Longview**
(903) 663-3838
Lat N 32.544 **Lon** W 94.731

Texas Thunder Harley-Davidson Shop, EG-11
2518 NW Stallings Dr. **Nacogdoches**
(936) 715-0100
Lat N 31.624 **Lon** W 94.684

Paris Harley-Davidson, EB-10
2875 NE Loop 286 **Paris**
(903) 784-6392
Lat N 33.675 **Lon** W 95.523

Texoma Harley-Davidson, EB-8
MOVING IN 2006: 1908 Texoma Pkwy. **Sherman**
(903) 893-7971
Lat N 33.632 **Lon** W 96.589

Bell County Harley-Davidson of Temple, EH-6
720 N Gen Bruce Dr. **Temple**
(254) 773-2243
Lat N 31.109 **Lon** W 97.357

Doolins Harley-Davidson, EC-12
4810 W 7th **Texarkana**
(903) 832-4366
Lat N 33.418 **Lon** W 94.105

Harley-Davidson of the Woodlands, EJ-10
25545 I-45 N **The Woodlands**
(281) 681-0099
Lat N 30.141 **Lon** W 95.468

Lone Star Harley-Davidson, EE-10
1211 SSE Loop 323 **Tyler**
(903) 597-1488
Lat N 32.335 **Lon** W 95.266

Harley-Davidson of Waco, EG-7
4201 S Jack Kultgen Fwy. **Waco**
(254) 753-0393
Lat N 31.506 **Lon** W 97.144

Use Express Access Codes on www.randmcnally.com for quick access to online travel planning info, road construction updates, and more.

Distance scale
One inch represents about 33 miles

© Rand McNally

How to determine distance

Mileages in red between red arrowheads; in black, between intersections.

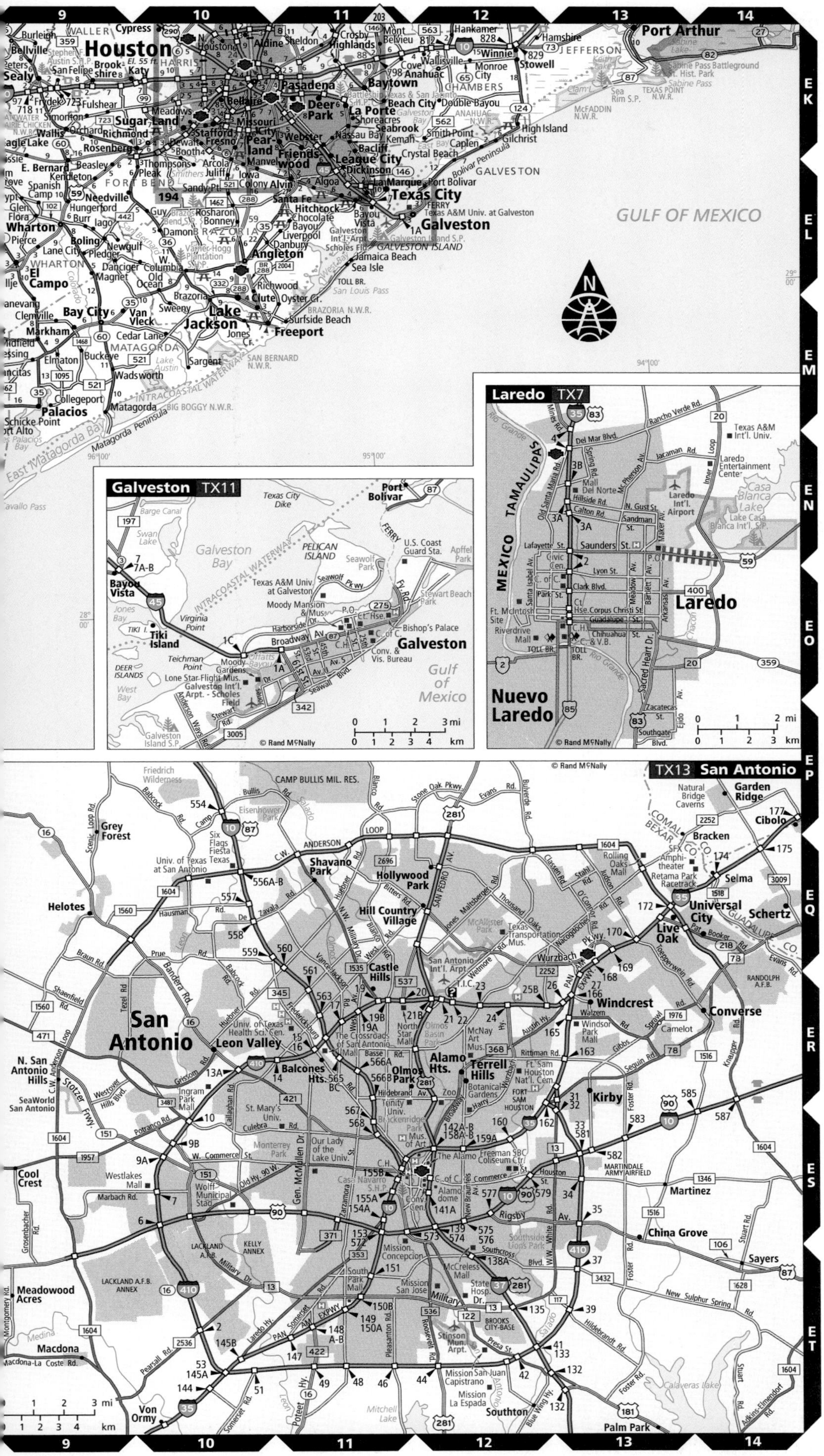

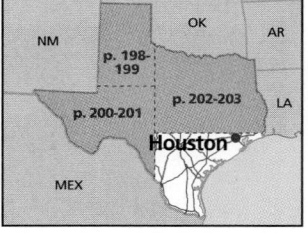

SYMBOLS

- Featured ride
- Scenic route
- Long-term construction
- Harley-Davidson dealership

For Texas ride, see page R30.

CITY-TO-CITY MILEAGE

	ABILENE	AUSTIN	BROWNSVILLE	CORPUS CHRISTI	DALLAS	HOUSTON	SAN ANTONIO	SHREVEPORT, LA
Abilene		230	539	405	185	347	261	373
Austin	230		352	218	195	162	82	327
Beaumont	467	246	443	303	294	88	283	195
Brownsville	539	352		159	547	355	278	593
Corpus Christi	405	218	159		413	215	144	453
Dallas	185	195	547	413		247	277	186
Fort Worth	155	190	542	408	30	267	272	216
Galveston	394	209	386	232	294	47	246	286
Houston	347	162	355	215	247		199	239
Laredo	409	232	203	141	427	349	150	559
Lufkin	359	222	473	333	182	119	313	119
McAllen	497	310	60	152	505	348	236	586
Paris	294	304	656	522	109	310	386	150
San Angelo	92	206	491	357	262	363	213	450
San Antonio	261	82	278	144	277	199		409
Shreveport, LA	373	327	593	453	186	239	409	
Texarkana	362	372	646	506	177	292	454	71
Tyler	285	228	580	446	98	206	310	99
Waco	191	99	451	317	96	188	181	228

HARLEY-DAVIDSON DEALERSHIPS

For the Houston metro area, please see dealer listings on page 195.

Goe Harley-Davidson, EL-10
1350 S Hwy. 288-B **Angleton**
(979) 849-3681
Lat N 29.17 **Lon** W 95.452

Javelina Harley-Davidson, EK-4
29078 W I-10 **Boerne**
(800) 860-9696
Lat N 29.818 **Lon** W 98.72

Corpus Christi Harley-Davidson, EP-6
502 S Padre Island Dr. **Corpus Christi**
(361) 854-3146
Lat N 27.758 **Lon** W 97.462

Laredo Harley-Davidson, EP-2
7080 San Bernardo **Laredo**
(956) 717-8763
Lat N 27.57 **Lon** W 99.504

RGV Harley-Davidson, ES-5
1007 E Expy. 83 **Pharr**
(956) 782-4243
Lat N 26.206 **Lon** W 98.17

Alamo City Harley-Davidson, EL-5
11005 I-35 N **San Antonio**
(210) 646-0499
Lat N 29.539 **Lon** W 98.381

Alamo City Harley-Davidson, EL-4
111 W Crockett St. Ste. 206 **San Antonio**
(210) 212-4461
Lat N 29.425 **Lon** W 98.489

Roadrunner Harley-Davidson Shop, ES-6
3515 W Expy. 83 **San Benito**
(956) 399-4244
Lat N 26.123 **Lon** W 97.634

Victoria Harley-Davidson, EM-7
608 N Moody St. **Victoria**
(361) 575-7881
Lat N 28.804 **Lon** W 97.007

Laredo TX7

Galveston TX11

© Rand McNally

TX13 San Antonio

© Rand McNally

GULF OF MEXICO

randmcnally.com/eac

Express Access Code: UT

Use Express Access Codes on
www.randmcnally.com for quick
access to online travel planning info,
road construction updates, and more.

Distance scale
One inch represents about 28 miles

How to determine distance

Mileages in red between red arrowheads;
in black, between intersections.

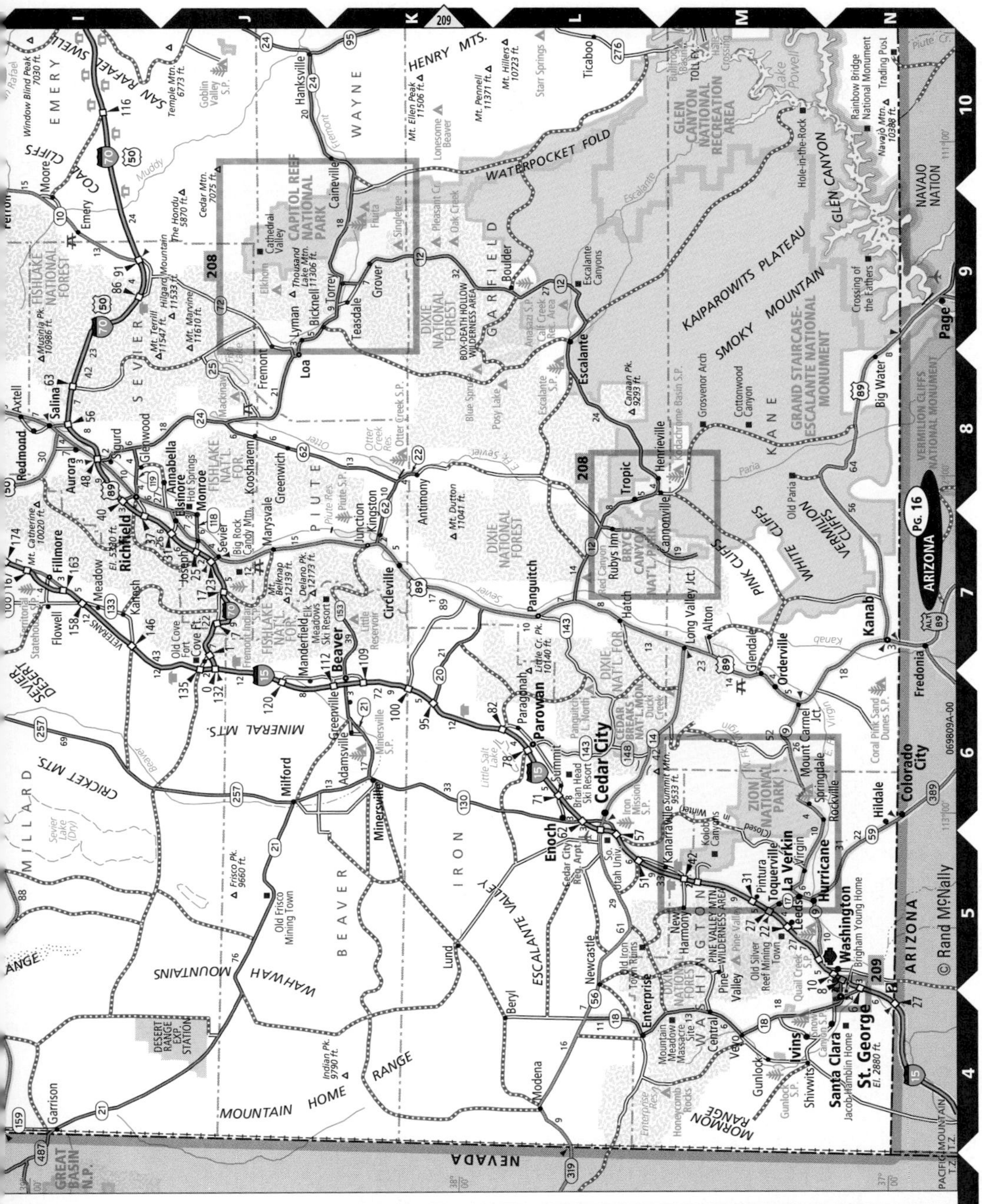

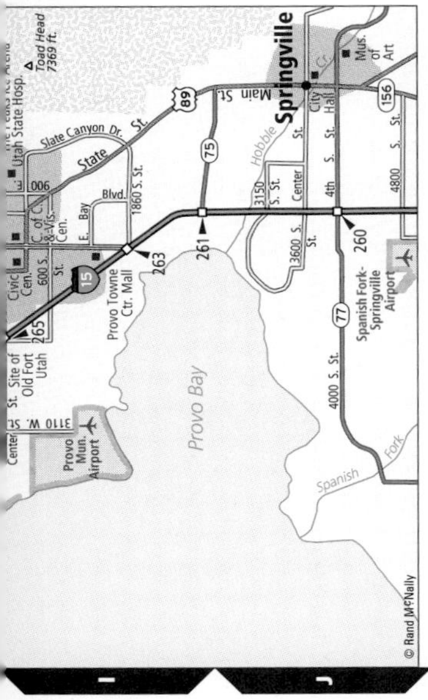

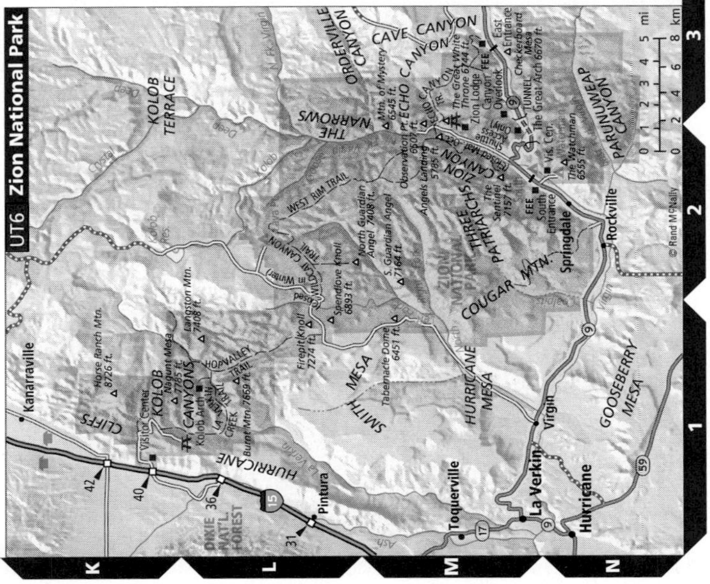

SYMBOLS

- Featured ride
- Scenic route
- |||| Long-term construction
- Harley-Davidson dealership
- ■ Historic site or monument; Indian reservation or rancheria; military installation; point of interest; wildlife refuge

For Utah/Wyoming ride, see page R31.

UTAH MOTORCYCLE LAWS

Helmet use:
Required under age 18

Riding two abreast:
Yes. See state law for specifics

Eye protection:
Not required

Speed limit:
Primary roads: 75 mph
Secondary roads: 65 mph

UTAH RESOURCES

Road conditions or construction:
511
(800) 492-2400
www.dot.state.ut.us

Highway Emergency Numbers:
911

Tourism:
(800) 200-1160
(801) 538-1030
www.utah.com

State motor vehicle information:
(801) 965-4437
www.driverlicense.utah.gov

HARLEY-DAVIDSON DEALERSHIPS

Saddleback Harley-Davidson Shop, B-8
2359 N Main St. **Logan**
(435) 787-8100
Lat N 41.775 Lon W 111.834

Harley-Davidson of Northern Utah, C-8
892 W Riverdale Rd. **Ogden**
(801) 394-4464
Lat N 41.178 Lon W 112

Monarch Harley-Davidson, E-8
350 W 800 North **Orem**
(801) 224-4070
Lat N 40.312 Lon W 111.704

Harley-Davidson of Salt Lake City, D-8
2928 S State St. **Salt Lake City**
(801) 487-4647
Lat N 40.707 Lon W 111.888

South Valley Harley-Davidson Shop, E-8
8886 S Sandy Pkwy.. Dr. **Sandy**
(801) 563-1100
Lat N 40.58 Lon W 111.886

Zion Harley-Davidson Shop, N-5
2345 N Coral Canyon Blvd. **Washington**
(435) 673-5100
Lat N 37.153 Lon W 113.46

© Rand McNally

randmcnally.com/eac
Express Access Code: UT

Use Express Access Codes on www.randmcnally.com for quick access to online travel planning info, road construction updates, and more.

Distance scale
One inch represents about 28 miles

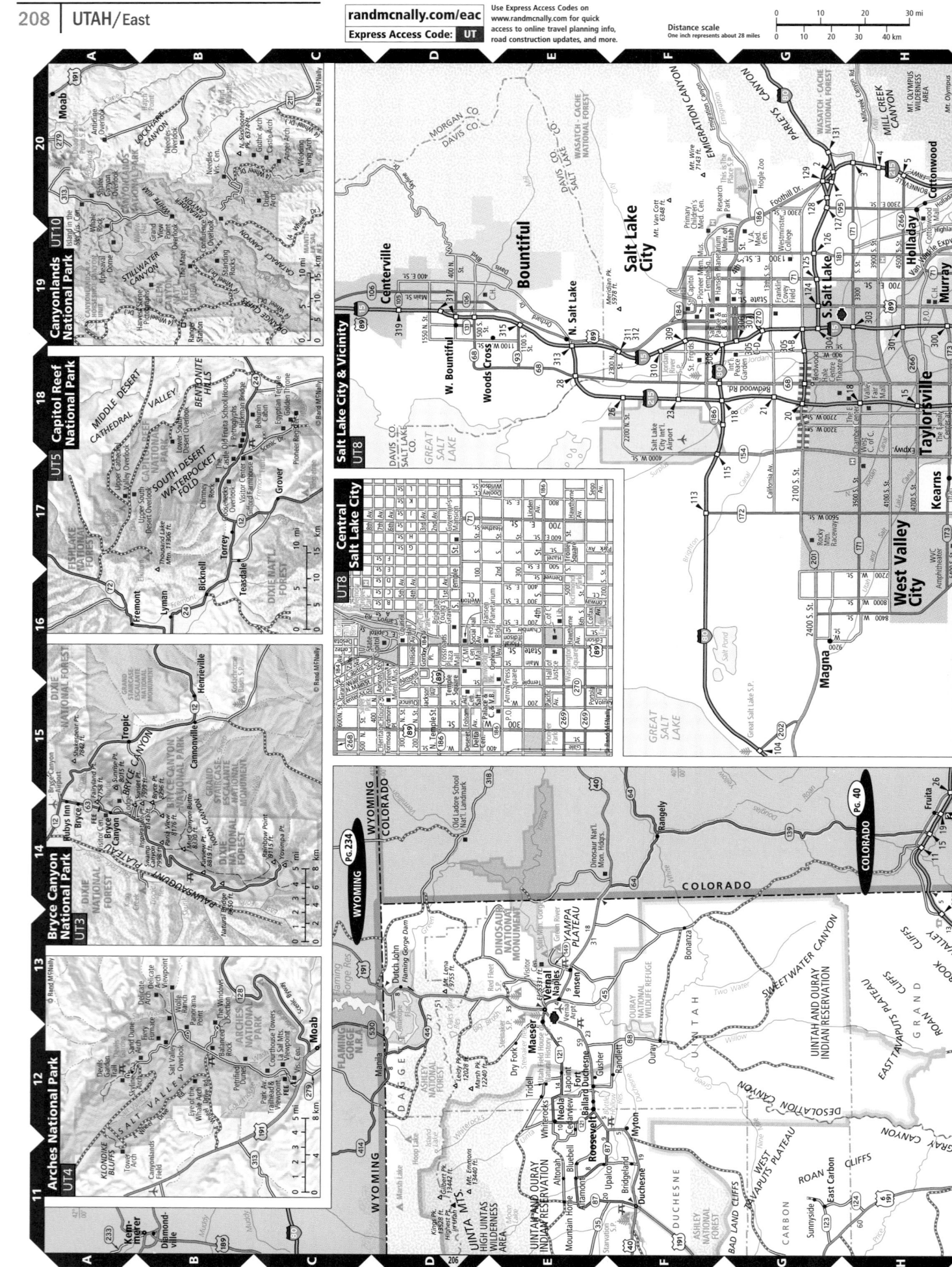

How to determine distance

Mileages in red between red arrowheads; in black, between intersections.

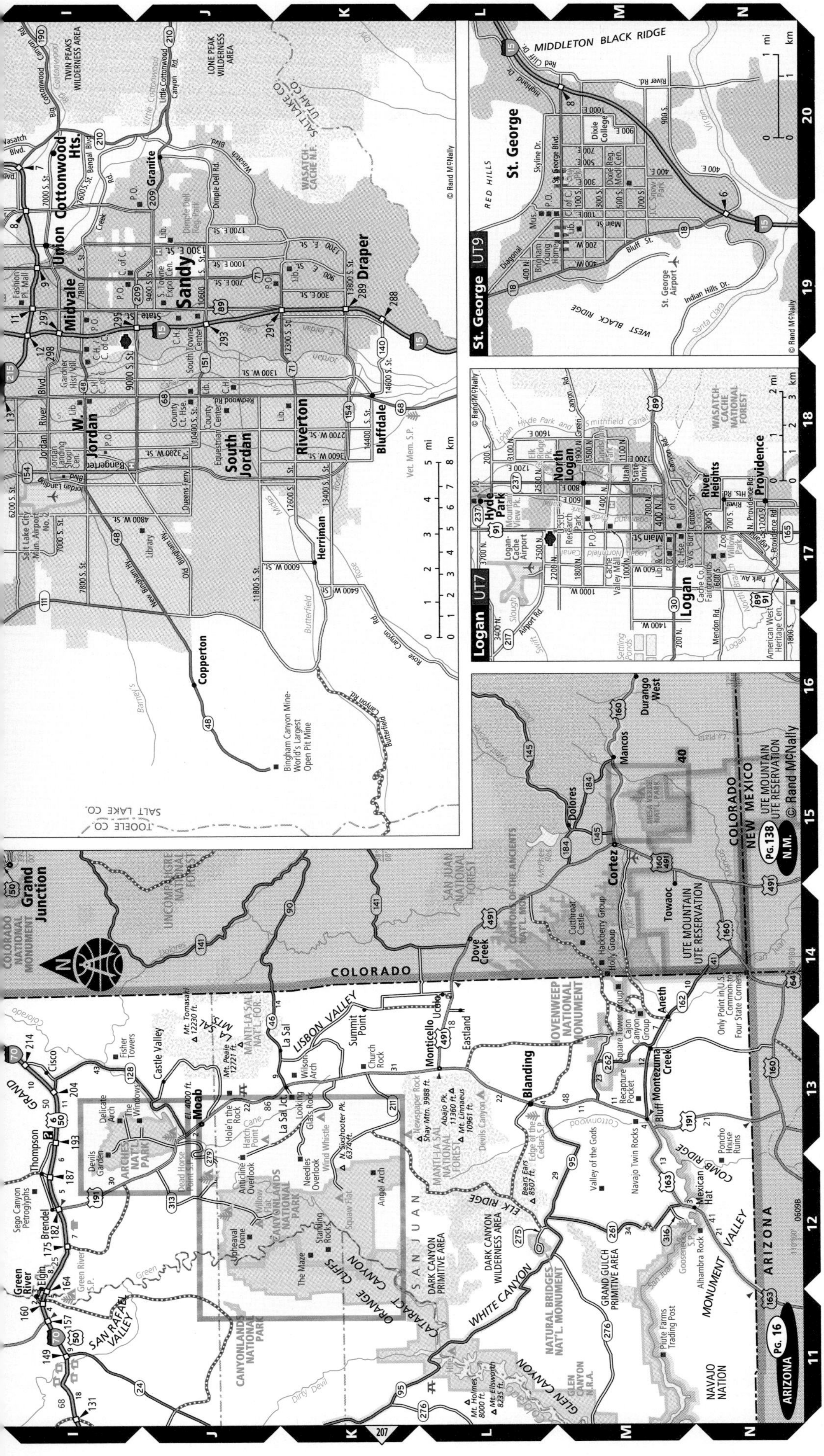

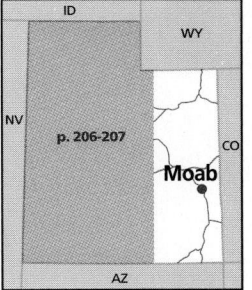

p. 206-207

Moab

SYMBOLS

- Featured ride
- Long-term construction
- Harley-Davidson dealership
- Scenic route
- Historic site or monument; Indian reservation or rancheria; military installation; point of interest; wildlife refuge

CITY-TO-CITY MILEAGE

	GRAND JCT., CO	LOGAN	MOAB	OGDEN	PROVO	SALT LAKE CITY	ST. GEORGE	VERNAL
Bicknell	217	274	169	234	156	199	199	199
Blanding	186	387	74	347	269	345	312	297
Cedar City	332	318	284	278	200	54	243	356
Evanston, WY	287	115	295	75	101	353	78	146
Grand Jct., CO		361	112	321	243	385	286	141
Las Vegas, NV	505	491	457	451	373	121	416	529
Logan	361		313	42	118	371	74	249
Moab	112	313		273	195	337	238	223
Ogden	321	42	273		78	331	34	209
Page, AZ	375	458	263	418	340	156	383	453
Park City	288	110	240	70	46	298	28	147
Price	165	197	117	157	79	280	122	115
Provo	243	118	195	78		253	43	157
Richfield	224	232	176	192	114	162	157	233
St. George	385	371	337	331	253	296		409
Salt Lake City	286	74	238	34	43		296	170
Vernal	141	249	223	209	157	409	170	
Wendover	403	192	355	152	160	413	122	293

HARLEY-DAVIDSON DEALERSHIPS

Beers Harley-Davidson, E-13
2029 W Hwy. 40 **Vernal**
(435) 789-5196
Lat N 40.438 **Lon** W 109.567

© Rand McNally

0609B

randmcnally.com/eac

Express Access Code: VT

Use Express Access Codes on www.randmcnally.com for quick access to online travel planning info, road construction updates, and more.

Distance scale
One inch represents about 14 miles

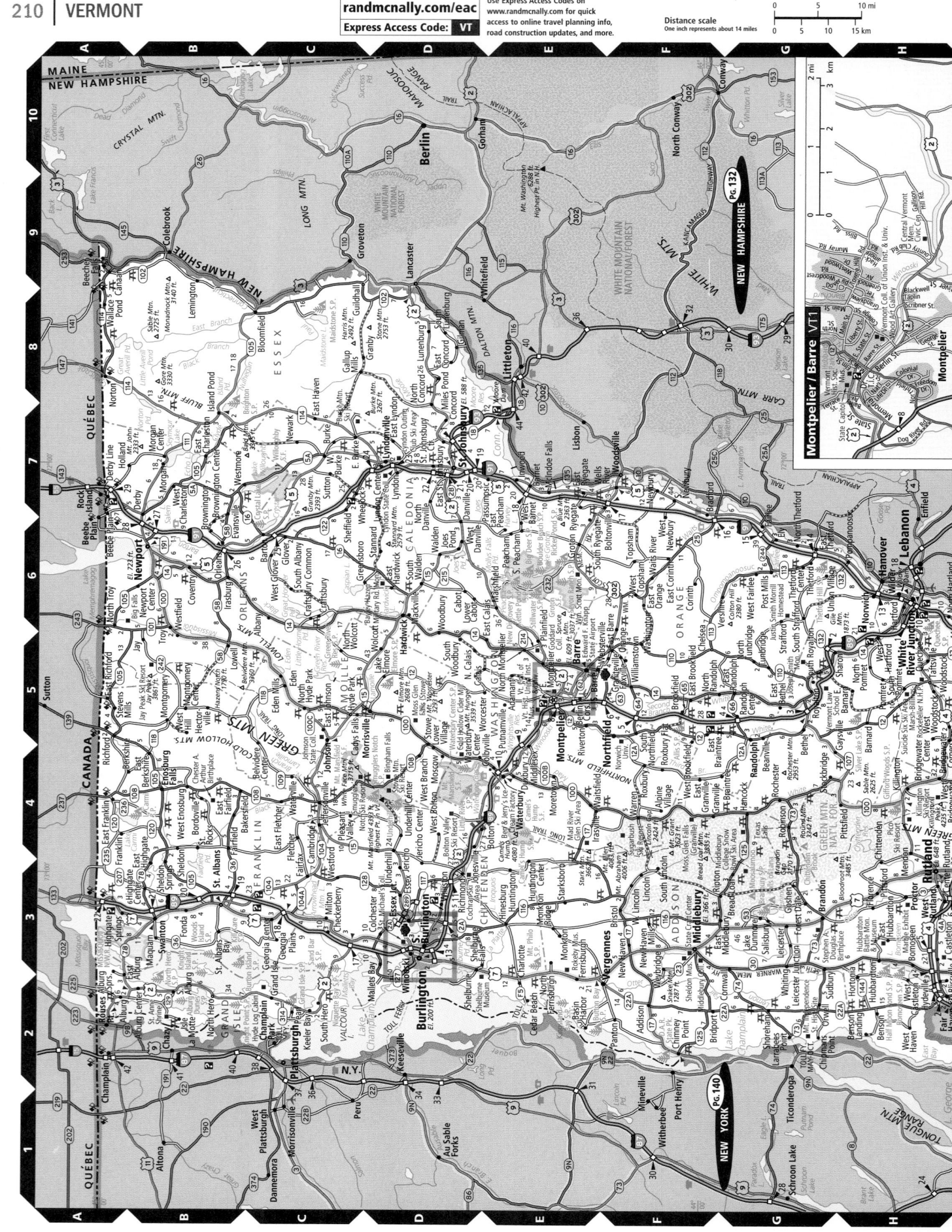

Montpelier / Barre VT1

How to determine distance

Mileages in red between red arrowheads;
in black, between intersections.

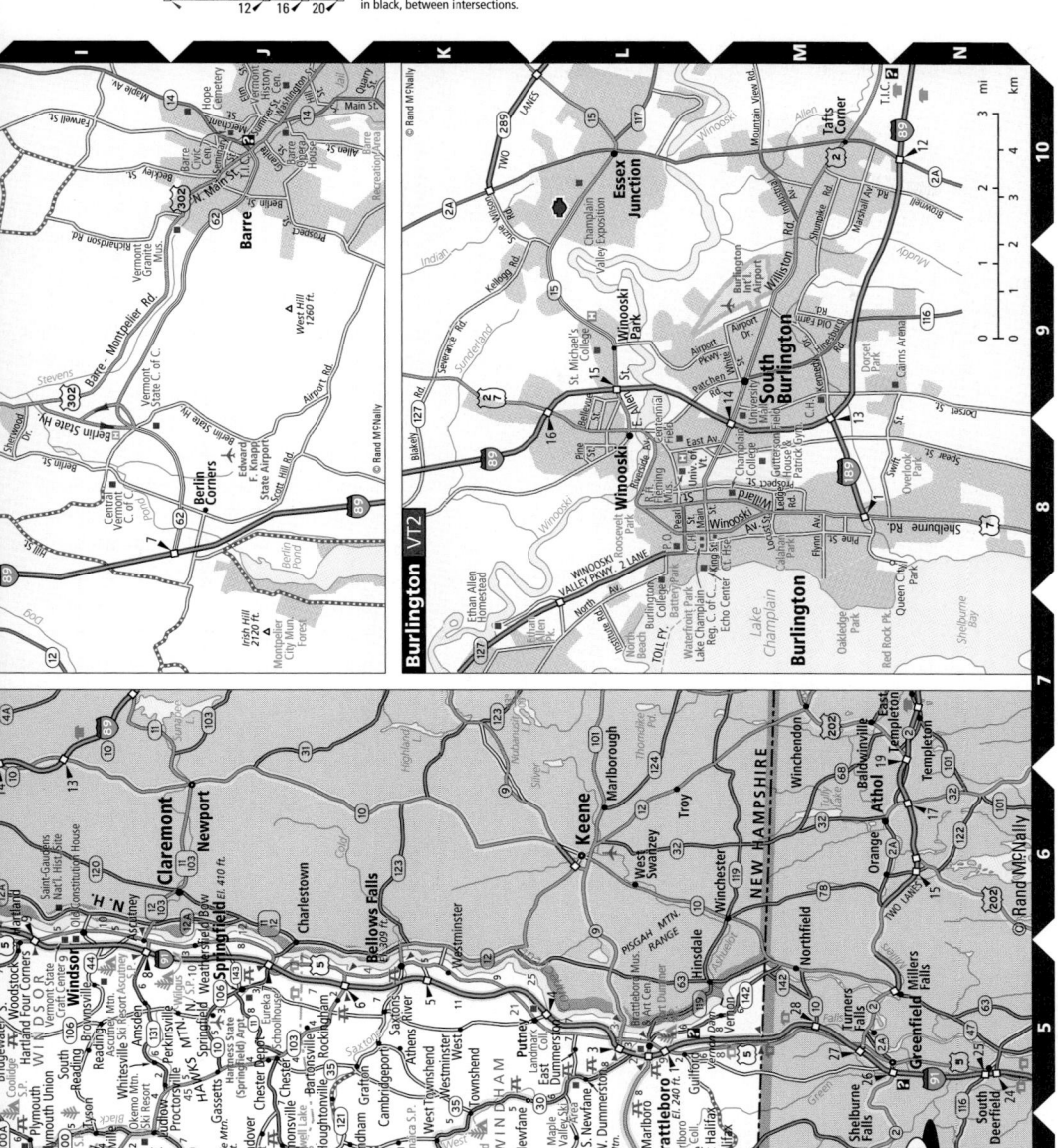

SYMBOLS

Featured ride	Scenic route
Long-term construction	Historic site or monument; Indian reservation or rancheria; military installation; point of interest; wildlife refuge
Harley-Davidson dealership	

VERMONT MOTORCYCLE LAWS

Helmet use:
Reflectorization required

Riding two abreast:
No reference in administrative code or statutes

Eye protection:
Required unless equipped with windscreen

Speed limit:
Primary roads: 65 mph
Secondary roads: 55 mph

VERMONT RESOURCES

Road conditions or construction:
511
(800) 429-7623
www.aot.state.vt.us/travelinfo.htm
www.511vt.org

Highway Emergency Numbers:
911

Tourism:
(800) 837-6668
www.vermontvacation.com

State motor vehicle information:
(802) 828-2000
www.dmv.state.vt.us

CITY-TO-CITY MILEAGE

	ALBANY, NY	BRATTLEBORO	BURLINGTON	MONTPELIER	NEWPORT	RUTLAND	ST. JOHNSBURY	WHITE RIVER JUNCTION
Albany, NY		81	152	162	246	96	202	145
Brattleboro	81		154	117	166	77	122	65
Burlington	152	154		39	75	67	77	91
Montpelier	162	117	39		80	66	38	54
Newport	246	166	75	80		146	44	101
Rutland	96	77	67	66	146		102	45
St. Johnsbury	202	122	77	38	44	102		57
White River Junction	145	65	91	54	101	45	57	

HARLEY-DAVIDSON DEALERSHIPS

Wilkins Harley-Davidson, F-5
663 S Barre Rd. **Barre**
(802) 476-6104
Lat N 44.168 Lon W 72.51

Green Mountain Harley-Davidson, D-3
157 Pearl St. **Essex Junction**
(802) 878-4778
Lat N 44.498 Lon W 73.128

Distance scale
One inch represents about 18 miles

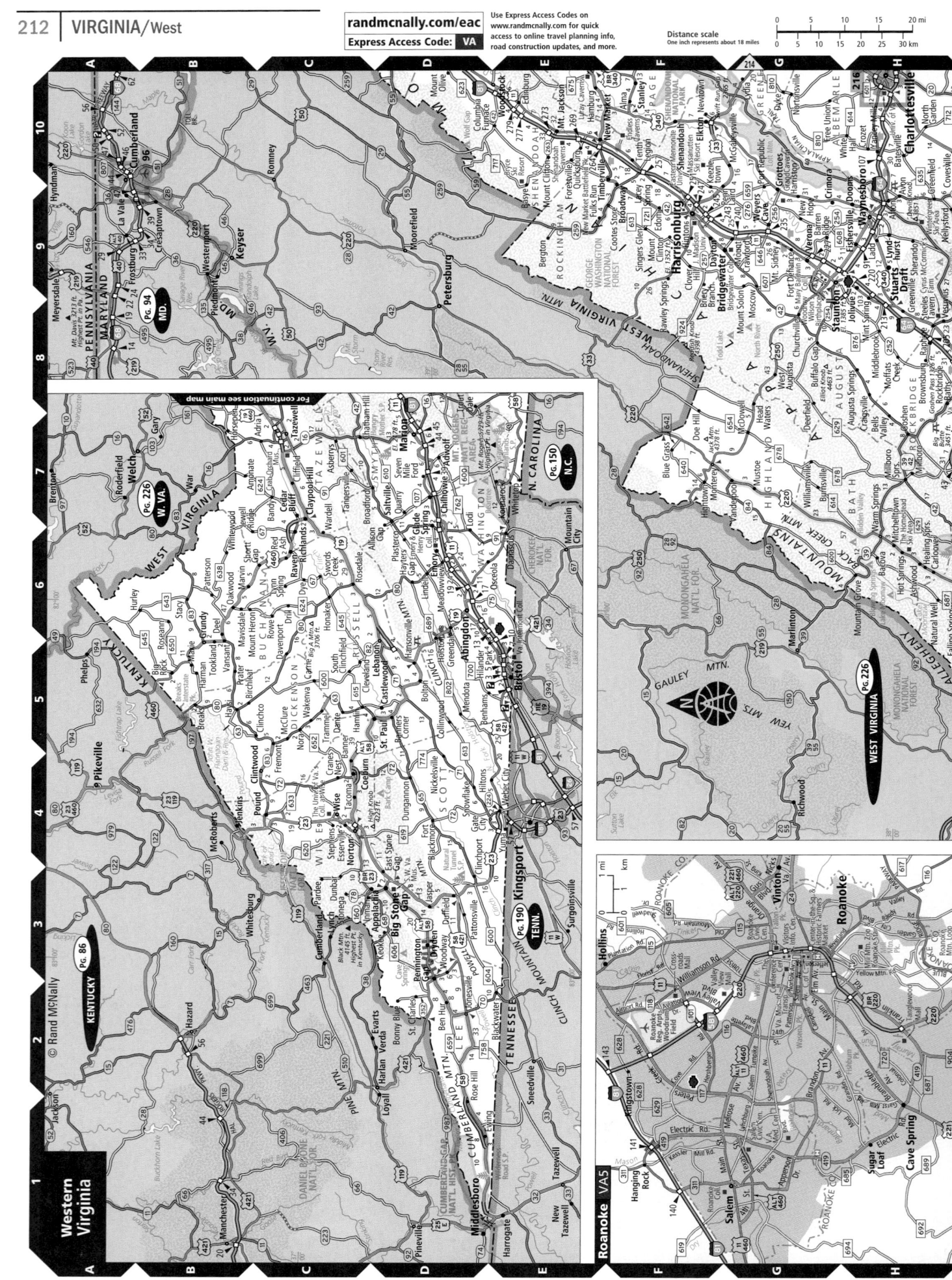

Western Virginia

Roanoke VA5

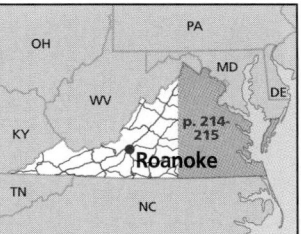

How to determine distance

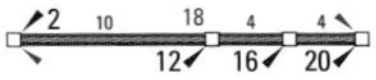

Mileages in red between red arrowheads;
in black, between intersections.

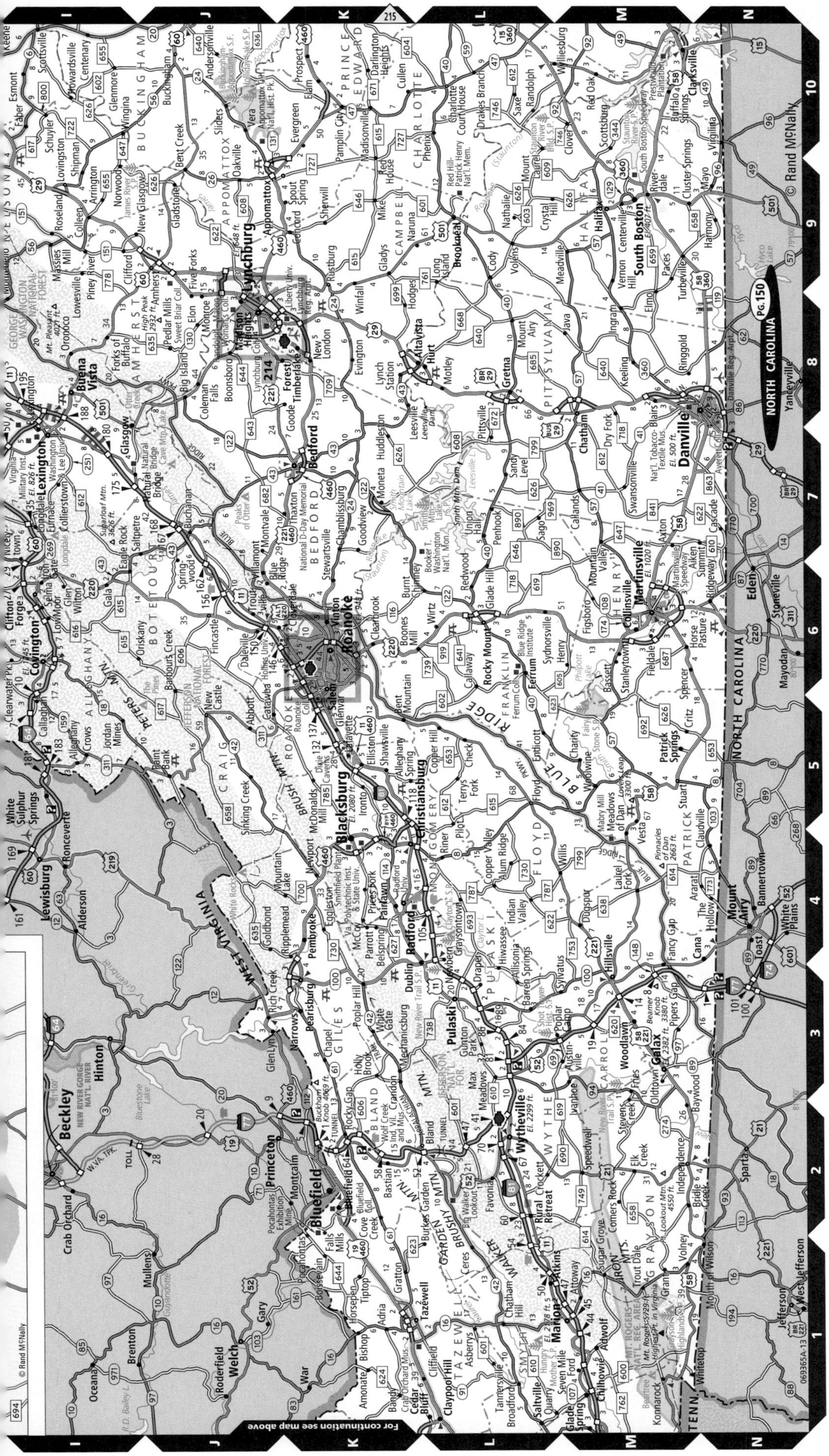

SYMBOLS

Featured ride
Long-term construction
Harley-Davidson dealership
Scenic route
Historic site or monument; Indian reservation or rancheria; military installation; point of interest; wildlife refuge

© Rand McNally

VIRGINIA MOTORCYCLE LAWS

Helmet use:
Required

Riding two abreast:
No. See state law for specifics

Eye protection:
Required unless equipped with windscreen

Speed limit:
Primary roads: 65 mph
Secondary roads: 65 mph

VIRGINIA RESOURCES

Road conditions or construction:
511
(800) 367-7623
(800) 578-4111
www.511virginia.org
www.virginiadot.org

Highway Emergency Numbers:
911 or #77

Tourism:
(800) 321-3244 (to request travel materials only)
(800) 847-4882 (to request travel materials only)
(804) 786-4484 (to request travel materials only)
(804) 786-4485
www.virginia.org

State motor vehicle information:
(866) 368-5463 or (800) 435-5137
www.dmvnow.com

HARLEY-DAVIDSON DEALERSHIPS

Black Wolf Harley-Davidson, D-6
18100 Black Wolf Dr. **Abingdon**
(276) 628-5822
Lat N 36.655 **Lon** W 81.893

Harley-Davidson of Lynchburg, K-8
20452 Timberlake Rd. **Lynchburg**
(434) 237-2381
Lat N 37.342 **Lon** W 79.236

Roanoke Valley Harley-Davidson, K-6
1925 Peters Creek Rd. **Roanoke**
(540) 562-5424
Lat N 37.3 **Lon** W 80.007

Shenandoah Harley-Davidson, H-9
213 Rolling Thunder Ln. **Staunton**
(540) 213-RIDE
Lat N 38.105 **Lon** W 79.073

Harley-Davidson Shop of Wytheville, L-2
430 Lithia Rd. **Wytheville**
(276) 228-9000
Lat N 36.951 **Lon** W 81.055

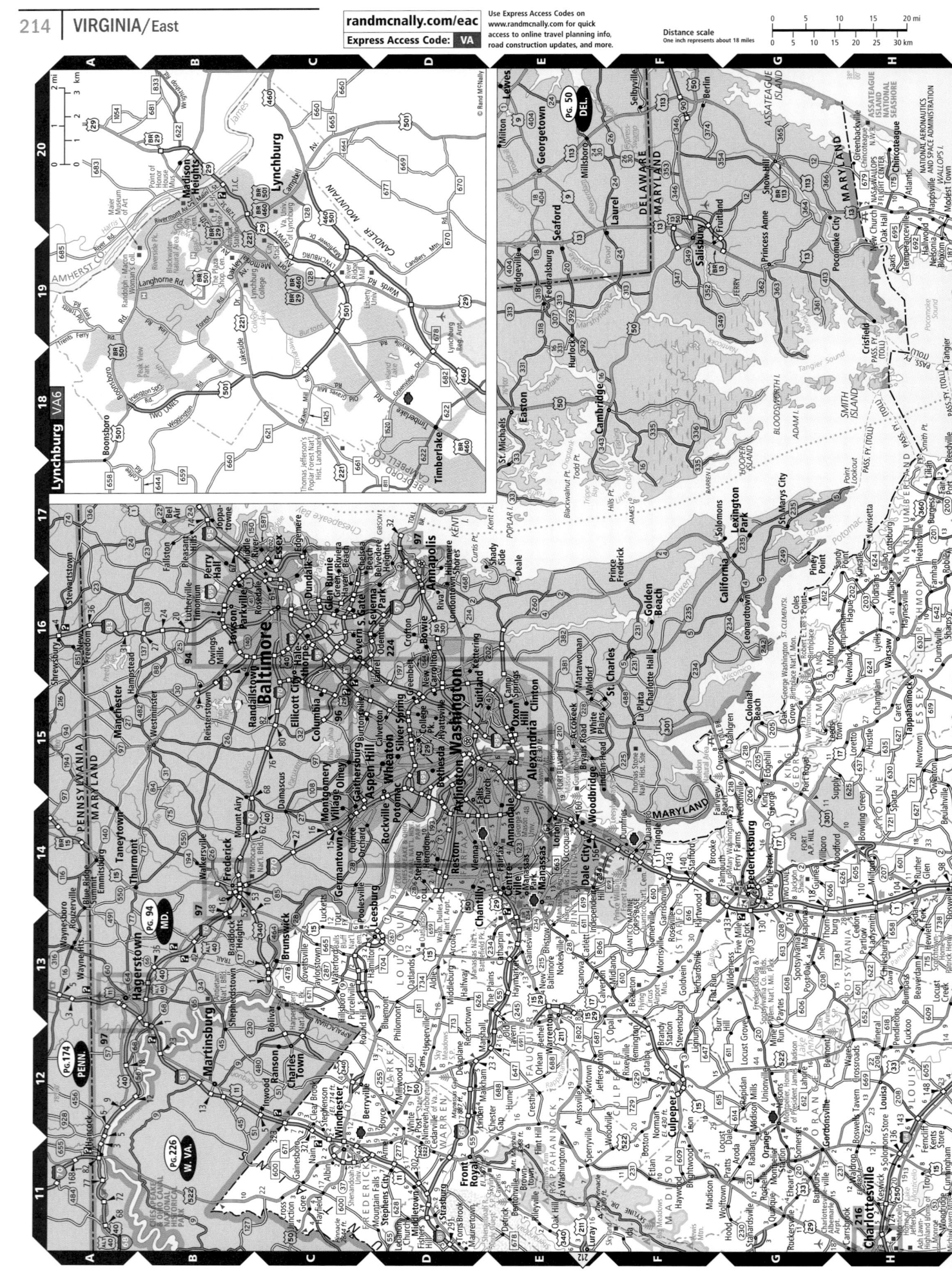

Use Express Access Codes on www.randmcnally.com for quick access to online travel planning info, road construction updates, and more.

Distance scale
One inch represents about 18 miles

How to determine distance

Mileages in red between red arrowheads; in black, between intersections.

© Rand McNally

SYMBOLS

- Featured ride
- Long-term construction
- Scenic route
- Harley-Davidson dealership

CITY-TO-CITY MILEAGE

	CHARLOTTESVILLE	EMPORIA	NORFOLK	RICHMOND	ROANOKE	WASHINGTON, DC	WINCHESTER	WYTHEVILLE
Bristol	252	341	418	324	146	374	313	69
Charlottesville		138	168	74	114	122	125	182
Chincoteague	261	180	105	186	373	161	242	441
Danville	126	113	186	149	82	250	220	120
Emporia	138		74	64	178	170	198	271
Fredericksburg	80	119	145	55	194	54	82	262
Hagerstown, MD	167	235	261	171	217	75	42	285
Harrisonburg	59	195	225	131	109	129	68	177
Lynchburg	63	127	194	118	54	185	157	132
Manassas	95	156	182	92	209	37	53	277
Norfolk	168	74		93	280	196	224	348
Richmond	74	64	93		186	106	134	254
Roanoke	114	178	280	186		236	175	76
Virginia Beach	180	88	17	105	292	208	236	360
Washington, DC	122	170	196	106	236		77	304
Williamsburg	126	106	46	51	238	154	182	306
Winchester	125	198	224	134	175	77		243
Wytheville	182	271	348	254	76	304	243	

HARLEY-DAVIDSON DEALERSHIPS

For the Richmond and Williamsburg areas, please see dealer listings on page 217.

East Coast Harley-Davidson, F-14
17975 Main St. (US 1) **Dumfries**
(703) 221-3757
Lat N 38.563 Lon W 77.331

Patriot Harley-Davidson, D-14
9739 Lee Hwy. **Fairfax**
(703) 352-5400
Lat N 38.864 Lon W 77.281

Richmond Harley-Davidson, I-14
10441 Washington Hwy. **Glen Allen**
(804) 550-9280
Lat N 37.695 Lon W 77.463

Whitt's Harley-Davidson Sales, E-14
9321 Center St. **Manassas**
(703) 631-3750
Lat N 38.751 Lon W 77.480

Waugh Enterprises Harley-Davidson, G-12
385 Waugh Blvd. **Orange**
(540) 672-5550
Lat N 38.243 Lon W 78.097

Bayside Harley-Davidson, L-17
3403 High St. **Portsmouth**
(757) 397-5550
Lat N 36.834 Lon W 76.344

Southside Harley-Davidson, L-18
385 N Witchduck Rd. **Virginia Beach**
(757) 499-8964
Lat N 36.849 Lon W 76.155

Harley Haven, L-19
1920 Atlantic Ave. **Virginia Beach**
(757) 425-2458
Lat N 36.847 Lon W 75.975

Grove's Winchester Harley-Davidson, C-12
140 Independence Dr. **Winchester**
(540) 662-4468
Lat N 39.14 Lon W 78.125

Hampton Roads Harley-Davidson, K-17
6450 George Washington Hwy. (Rte. 17) **Yorktown**
(757) 872-7223
Lat N 37.17 Lon W 76.473

randmcnally.com/eac

Express Access Code: VA

Use Express Access Codes on www.randmcnally.com for quick access to online travel planning info, road construction updates, and more.

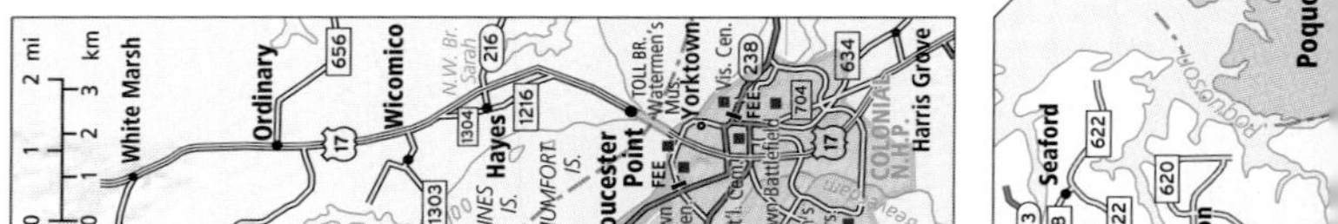

Richmond / Petersburg VA2

Charlottesville VA1

Williamsburg / Colonial National Historic Park VA3

© Rand McNally

Richmond / Petersburg (VA2)

Mechanicsville, Highland Springs, Sandston, Montrose, Varina, Atlee, Glen Allen, Laurel, Lakeside, Greendale, Bon Air, Short Pump, Richmond, Hopewell, Colonial Heights, Ettrick, Matoaca, Chester, Chesterfield, Centralia, Kingsland, Bensley, Hopkins, Beach

Henrico Co., Hanover Co., Chesterfield Co., Charles City Co., Prince George Co., Petersburg

Charlottesville (VA1)

Charlottesville, Key West, Northfields, Montvue, Canterbury Hills, Colthurst, Farmington, Bellair, Ednam Forest

Univ. of Virginia, Monticello–Home of T. Jefferson, Michie Tavern Museum

Williamsburg / Colonial National Historic Park (VA3)

White Marsh, Ordinary, Wicomico, Hayes, Gloucester Point, Yorktown, Harris Grove, Clay Bank, Lackey, Grove, York Terrace, Carter Gardens, Queens Lake, Williamsburg, Kings Point, Five Forks, Centerville, Lightfoot, Ewell, Scotland, Seaford, Grafton, Harris Grove, Newport News

Gloucester Co., York Co., James City Co., Surry Co., James City Co.

Jamestown Island, Jamestown N.H.P., Colonial N.H.P., Hog Island Game Refuge

VA4
Hampton Roads: Norfolk / Virginia Beach / Newport News
Norfolk
Virginia Beach
Chesapeake
Portsmouth
Hampton
Newport News
Suffolk
Petersburg
Smithfield
ATLANTIC OCEAN
CHESAPEAKE BAY
© Rand McNally
069364-13

PA
OH
MD
WV
DE
Charlottesville
Richmond
KY
Norfolk
Virginia Beach
TN
NC

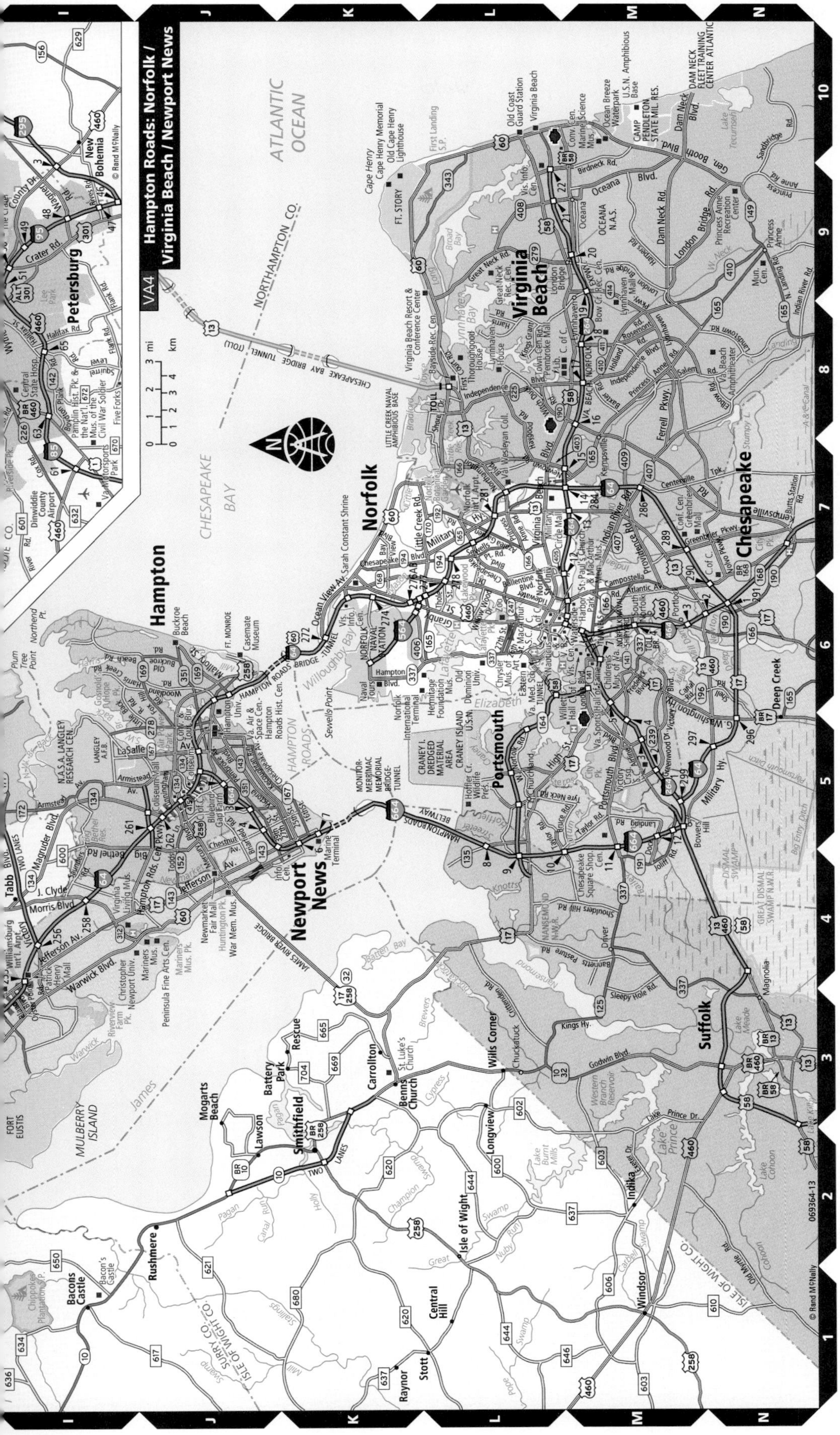

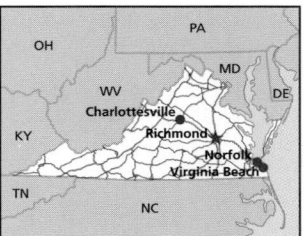

SYMBOLS

- Featured ride
- Scenic route
- Long-term construction
- Historic site or monument; Indian reservation or rancheria; military installation; point of interest; wildlife refuge
- Harley-Davidson dealership

VIRGINIA MOTORCYCLE LAWS

Helmet use:
Required

Riding two abreast:
No. See state law for specifics

Eye protection:
Required unless equipped with windscreen

Speed limit:
Primary roads: 65 mph
Secondary roads: 65 mph

VIRGINIA RESOURCES

Road conditions or construction:
511
(800) 367-7623
(800) 578-4111
www.511virginia.org
www.virginiadot.org

Highway Emergency Numbers:
911 or #77

Tourism:
(800) 321-3244 (to request travel materials only)
(800) 847-4882 (to request travel materials only)
(804) 786-4484 (to request travel materials only)
(804) 786-4485
www.virginia.org

State motor vehicle information:
(866) 368-5463 or (800) 435-5137
www.dmvnow.com

HARLEY-DAVIDSON DEALERSHIPS

Revolutionary Harley-Davidson, F-2
6401 Richmond Rd. Store 71 **Lightfoot**
(757) 565-5122
Lat N 37.269 **Lon** W 76.755

Colonial Harley-Davidson, H-8
1701 Temple Pkwy. **Prince George**
(804) 861-4700
Lat N 37.251 **Lon** W 77.372

South Richmond Harley-Davidson Shop, E-6
10011 Hull St. Rd. **Richmond**
(804) 745-3445
Lat N 37.444 **Lon** W 77.579

randmcnally.com/eac
Express Access Code: WA
Use Express Access Codes on www.randmcnally.com for quick access to online travel planning info, road construction updates, and more.

Distance scale
One inch represents about 21 miles

How to determine distance

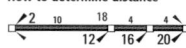

Mileages in red between red arrowheads;
in black, between intersections.

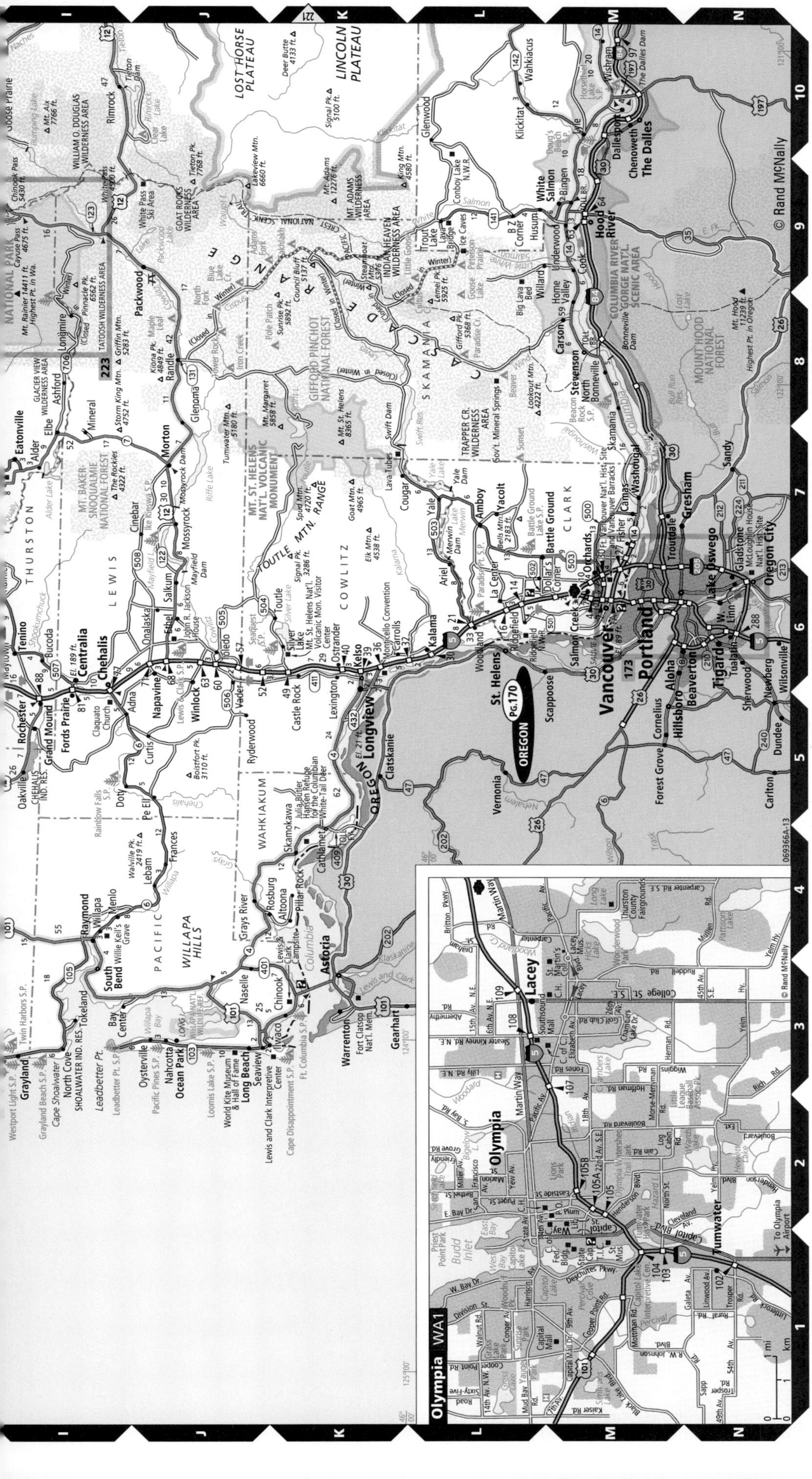

© Rand McNally

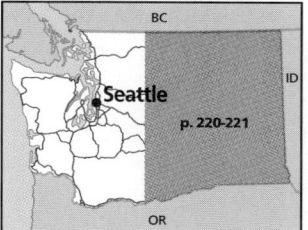

Seattle p. 220–221

SYMBOLS

- Featured ride
- Long-term construction
- Harley-Davidson dealership
- Scenic route
- ■ Historic site or monument; Indian reservation or rancheria; military installation; point of interest; wildlife refuge

For Washington ride, see page R32.

WASHINGTON MOTORCYCLE LAWS

Helmet use:
Required

Riding two abreast:
Yes. See state law for specifics

Eye protection:
Required unless equipped with windscreen

Speed limit:
Primary roads: 70 mph
Secondary roads: 60 mph

WASHINGTON RESOURCES

Road conditions or construction:
511
(800) 695-7623
www.wsdot.wa.gov/traffic/

Highway Emergency Numbers:
911

Tourism:
(800) 544-1800
www.experiencewashington.com

State motor vehicle information:
(360) 902-3600
www.dol.wa.gov/drivers.htm

HARLEY-DAVIDSON DEALERSHIPS

For the Seattle/Tacoma metro area, please see dealer listings on page 223.

Harley-Davidson of Bellingham, B-7
1419 N State St. **Bellingham**
(360) 671-7575
Lat N 48.75 Lon W 122.475

Harley-Davidson of Bellingham, B-7
Bellis Fair Mall Unit 324 **Bellingham**
(360) 527-9418
Lat N 48.784 Lon W 122.482

Skagit Harley-Davidson, C-7
1337 Goldenrod Rd. **Burlington**
(360) 757-1515
Lat N 48.463 Lon W 122.343

Northwest Harley-Davidson, H-6
8000 Freedom Ln. NE **Lacey**
(360) 705-8515
Lat N 47.062 Lon W 122.769

Harley-Davidson of Seattle, E-7
5711 188th St. SE **Lynnwood**
(425) 921-1100
Lat N 47.828 Lon W 122.31

Destination Harley-Davidson Shop, H-7
18810 Meridian Ave. E (Hwy. 161) **Puyallup**
OPENING IN 2006
Lat N 47.085 Lon W 122.294

Legend Harley-Davidson, F-6
9625 Provost Rd. NW **Silverdale**
(360) 698-3700
Lat N 47.653 Lon W 122.707

Columbia Motorcycle Harley-Davidson, M-6
1314 NE 102nd St. **Vancouver**
(360) 695-8831
Lat N 45.713 Lon W 122.631

Olympia WA1

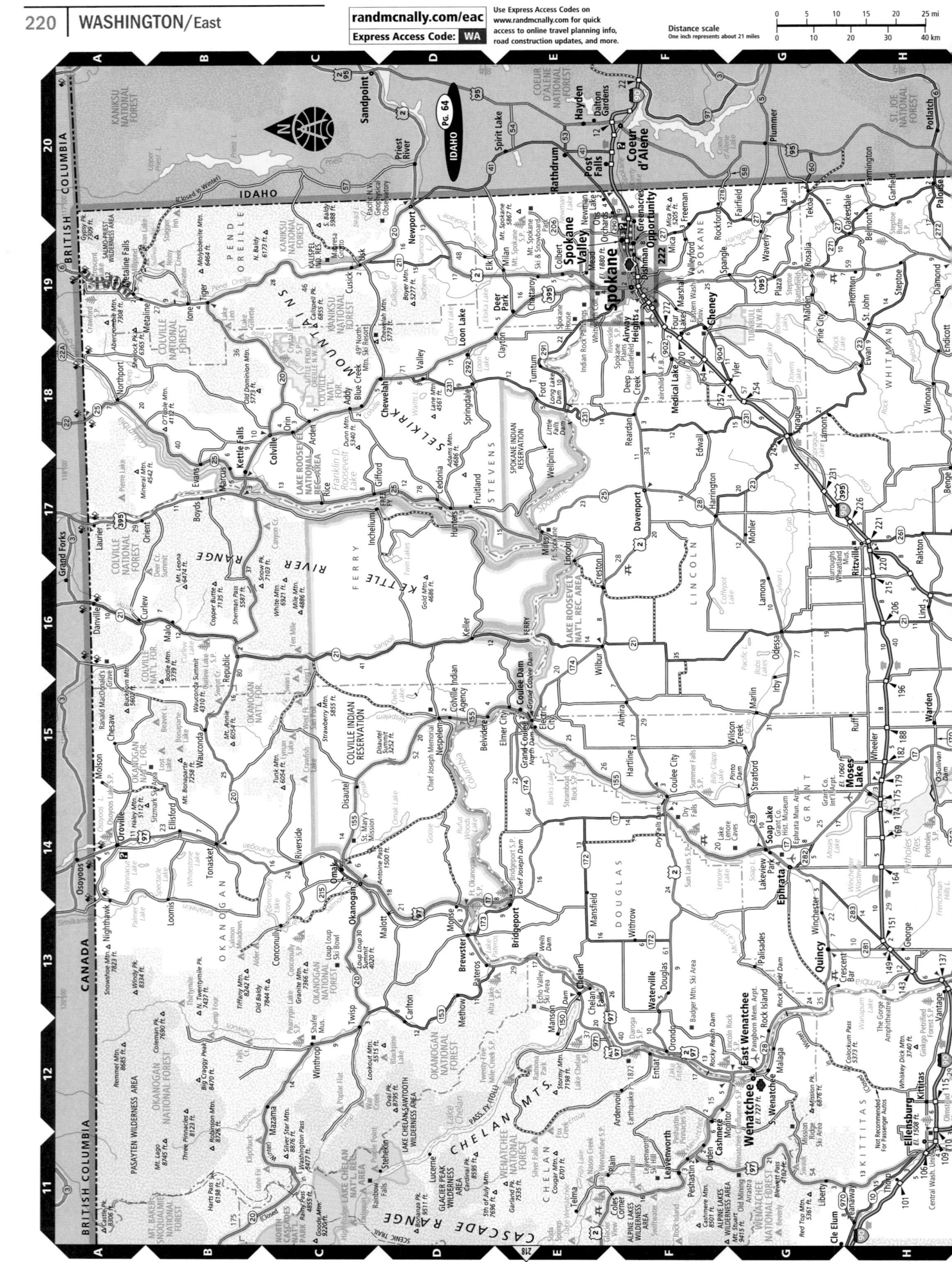

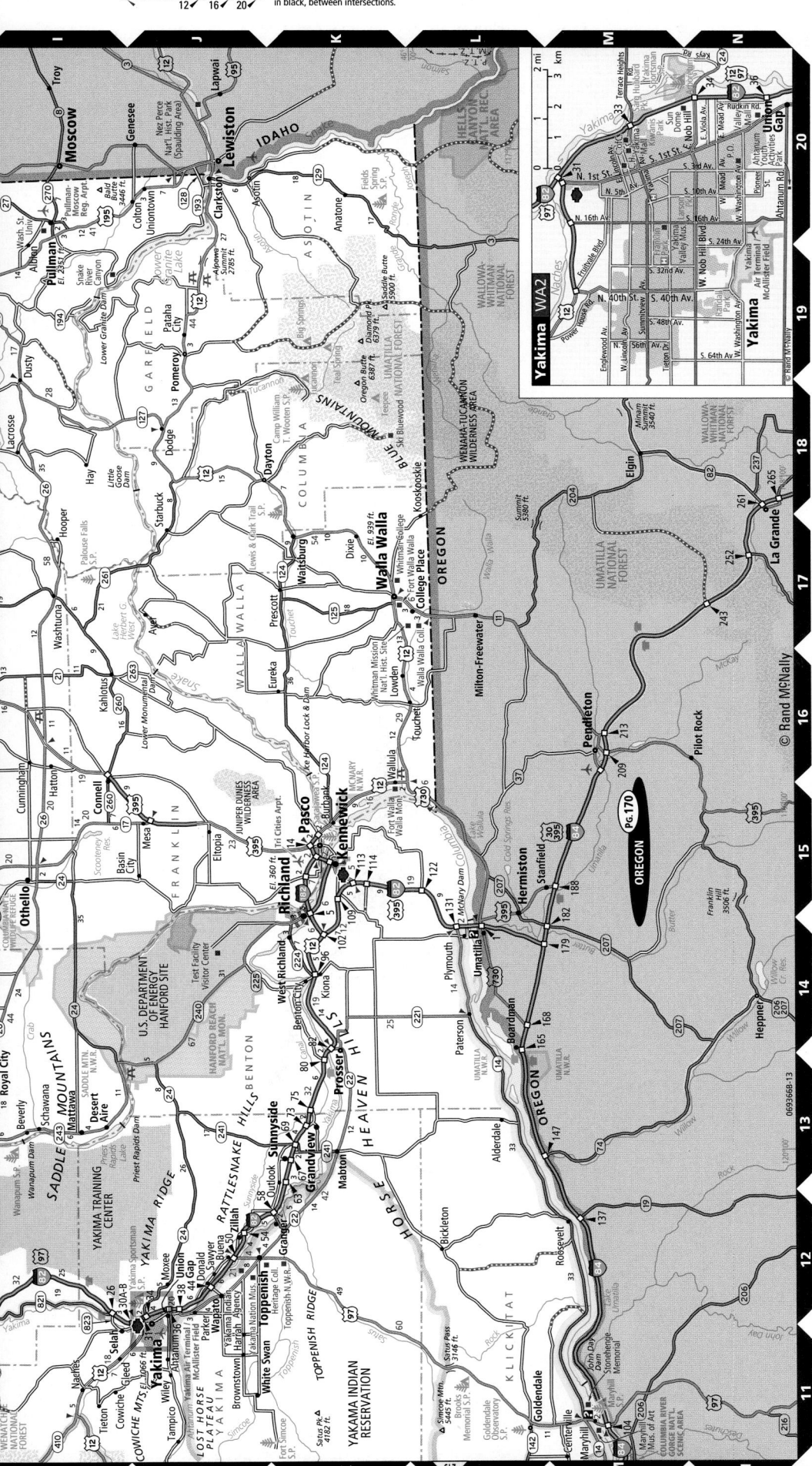

How to determine distance

Mileages in red between red arrowheads;
in black, between intersections.

SYMBOLS

Featured ride	Scenic route
Long-term construction	■ Historic site or monument; Indian reservation or rancheria; military installation; point of interest; wildlife refuge
Harley-Davidson dealership	

For Washington ride, see page R32.

CITY-TO-CITY MILEAGE

	BELLINGHAM	KENNEWICK	PORTLAND OR SEATTLE	SPOKANE	THE DALLES OR TACOMA	YAKIMA
Aberdeen	197	286	145	109	373	78	222	207
Bellingham		302	262	88	365	119	324	223
Bremerton	152†	265†	174	64†	328†	33	251	186†
Colville	326	210	423	353	71	366	339	273
Kennewick	302		213	219	139	232	129	79
Lewiston, ID	397	122	334	314	109	327	250	200
Longview	217	255	49	129	371	98	126	169
Olympia	147	260	115	59	323	28	192	181
Omak	208	189	377	241	138	254	293	192
Port Angeles	124†	338	232	82†	401†	106†	309	259†
Portland, OR	262	213		174	352	143	84	185
Seattle	88	219	174		282	31	241	140
Spokane	365	139	352	282		295	268	202
Tacoma	119	232	143	31	295		220	153
The Dalles, OR	324	129	84	241	268	220		101
Vancouver, BC	55	357	317	143	420	174	379	278
Wenatchee	185	140	291	153	172	166	207	106
Yakima	223	79	185	140	202	153	101	

† Via ferry

HARLEY-DAVIDSON DEALERSHIPS

Shumate Harley-Davidson, K-15
3305 W 19th Ave. **Kennewick**
(509) 735-9775
Lat N 46.192 **Lon** W 119.167

Shumate Harley-Davidson Spokane, F-19
6815 E Trent Ave. **Spokane Valley**
(509) 928-6811
Lat N 47.675 **Lon** W 117.313

Wenatchee Harley-Davidson, G-12
708 S Wenatchee Ave. **Wenatchee**
(509) 662-3434
Lat N 47.415 **Lon** W 120.304

Owens Harley-Davidson, J-12
1707 N 1st St. **Yakima**
(509) 575-1916
Lat N 46.622 **Lon** W 120.512

randmcnally.com/eac
Express Access Code: **WA**
Use Express Access Codes on www.randmcnally.com for quick access to online travel planning info, road construction updates, and more.

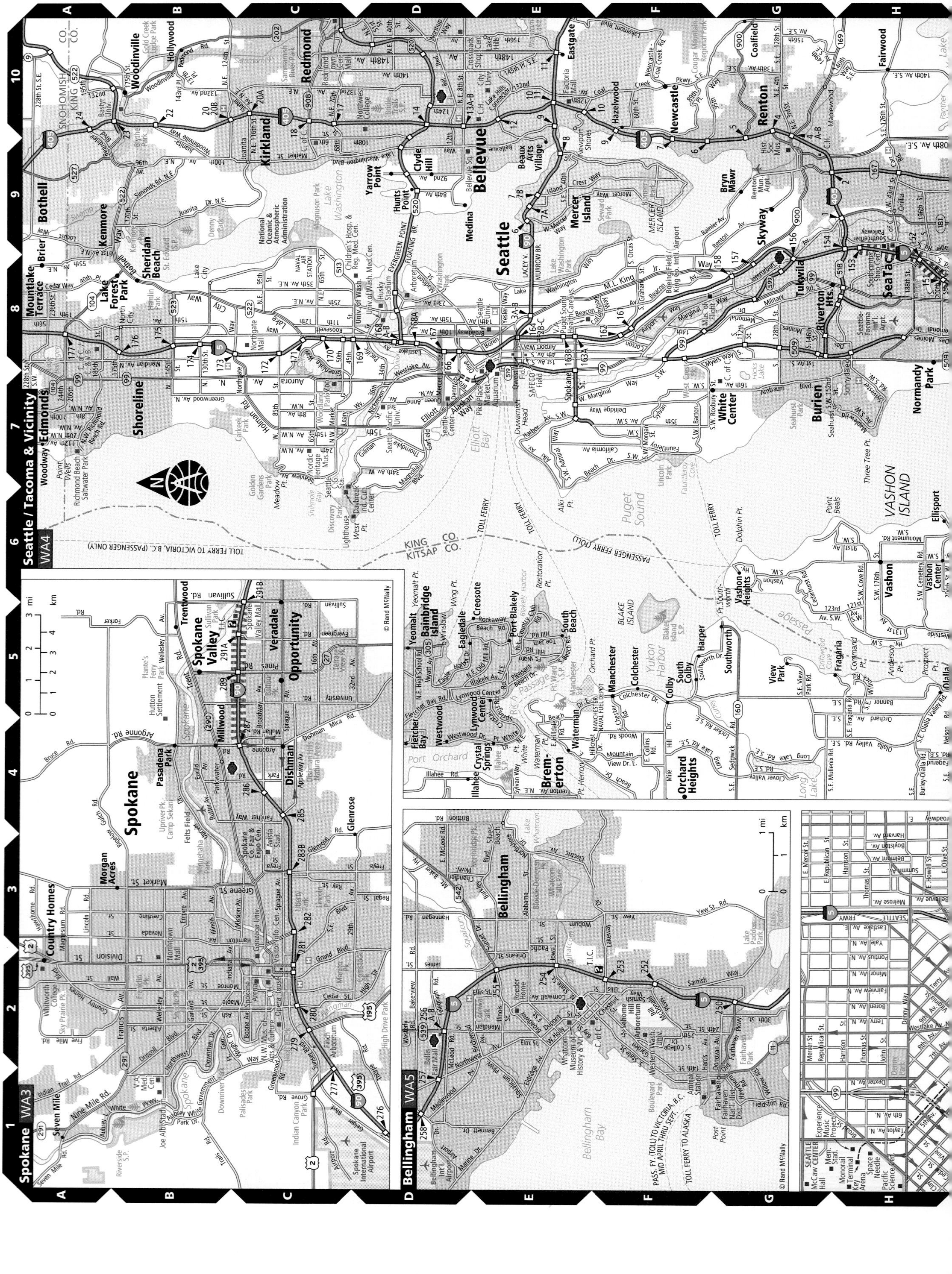

Seattle / Tacoma & Vicinity WA4

Woodinville, Hollywood, Redmond, Bothell, Kenmore, Brier, Kirkland, Yarrow Point, Hunts Point, Clyde Hill, Medina, Bellevue, Eastgate, Newcastle, Coalfield, Fairwood, Renton, Hazelwood, Mountlake Terrace, Lake Forest Park, Sheridan Beach, Shoreline, Edmonds, Woodway, Seattle, Mercer Island, Bryn Mawr, Skyway, Tukwila, Riverton Hts., SeaTac, White Center, Burien, Normandy Park

Lake Washington, Puget Sound, Elliott Bay, Vashon Island, Blake Island, Bainbridge Island

SNOHOMISH CO. / KING CO.
KING CO. / KITSAP CO.

TOLL FERRY TO VICTORIA, B.C. (PASSENGER ONLY)
TOLL FERRY — PASSENGER FERRY (TOLL)

Bainbridge Island, Winslow, Eagledale, Creosote, Port Blakely, South Beach, Rockaway Beach, Yeomalt, Manchester, Colchester, South Colby, Colby, Harper, Southworth, Yukon Harbor, Fragaria, Olalla, Bremerton, Port Orchard, Orchard Heights, Illahee, Crystal Springs, Westwood, Fletcher Bay, Waterman, View Park, Vashon, Vashon Heights, Vashon Center, Ellisport, Burton

Spokane WA3

Spokane, Spokane Valley, Opportunity, Veradale, Trentwood, Millwood, Dishman, Pasadena Park, Morgan Acres, Country Homes, Seven Mile, Glenrose

Bellingham WA5

Bellingham

SEATTLE CENTER
McCaw Hall, Mem. Stadium, Key Arena, Space Needle, Pacific Science Center, Monorail, Experience Music Project

© Rand McNally

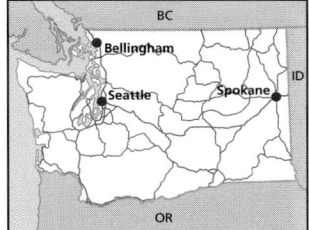

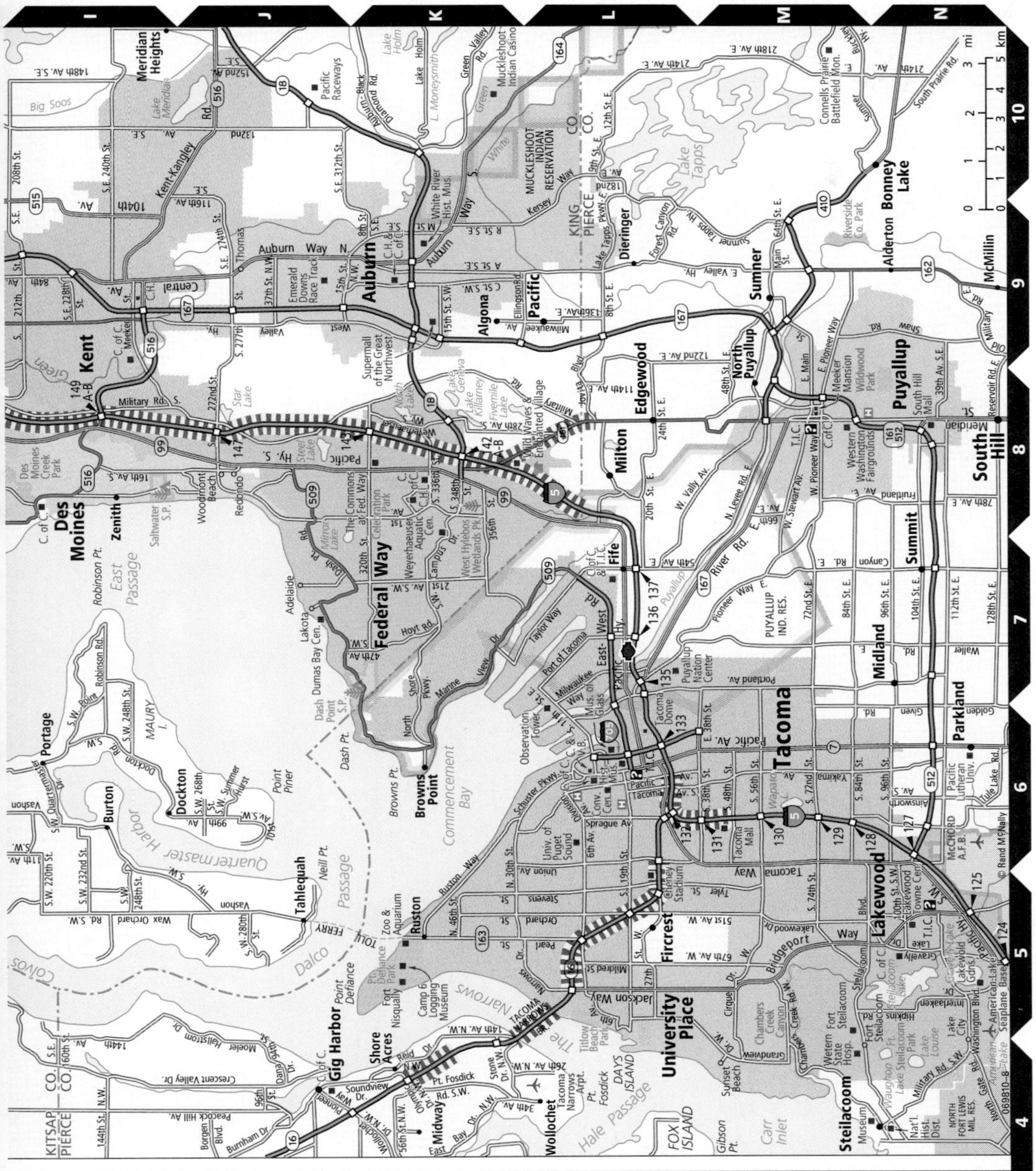

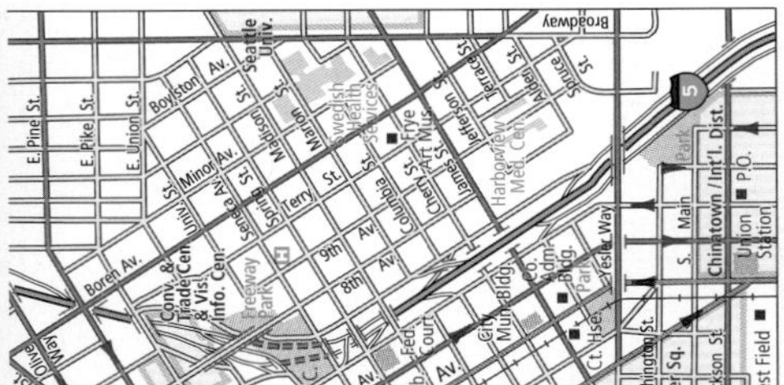

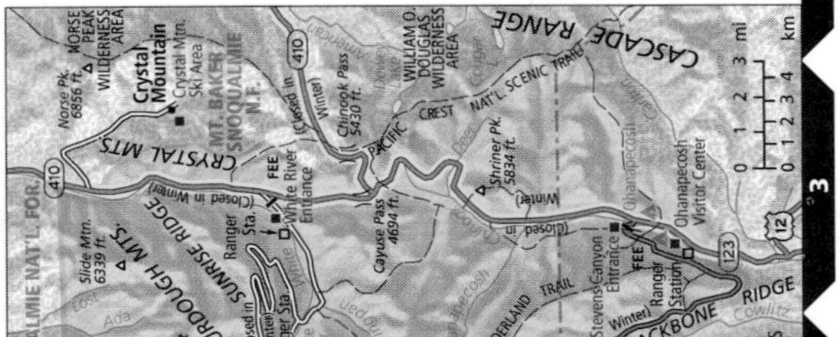

SYMBOLS

- Featured ride
- Long-term construction
- Harley-Davidson dealership
- Scenic route
- ■ Historic site or monument; Indian reservation or rancheria; military installation; point of interest; wildlife refuge

WASHINGTON MOTORCYCLE LAWS

Helmet use:
Required

Riding two abreast:
Yes. See state law for specifics

Eye protection:
Required unless equipped with windscreen

Speed limit:
Primary roads: 70 mph
Secondary roads: 60 mph

WASHINGTON RESOURCES

Road conditions or construction:
511
(800) 695-7623
www.wsdot.wa.gov/traffic/

Highway Emergency Numbers:
911

Tourism:
(800) 544-1800
www.experiencewashington.com

State motor vehicle information:
(360) 902-3600
www.dol.wa.gov/drivers.htm

HARLEY-DAVIDSON DEALERSHIPS

Eastside Harley-Davidson, D-10
13131 NE 20th St. **Bellevue**
(425) 702-2000
Lat N 47.628 **Lon** W 122.165

Destination Harley-Davidson, L-7
2302 Pacific Hwy. E **Fife (Tacoma)**
(253) 922-3700
Lat N 47.243 **Lon** W 122.397

Downtown Harley-Davidson, E-8
1305 1st Ave. **Seattle**
(206) 448-5661
Lat N 47.607 **Lon** W 122.338

Downtown Harley-Davidson, G-8
13001 48th Ave. S **Tukwila**
(206) 243-5000
Lat N 47.486 **Lon** W 122.269

randmcnally.com/eac

Express Access Code: **DC**

Use Express Access Codes on www.randmcnally.com for quick access to online travel planning info, road construction updates, and more.

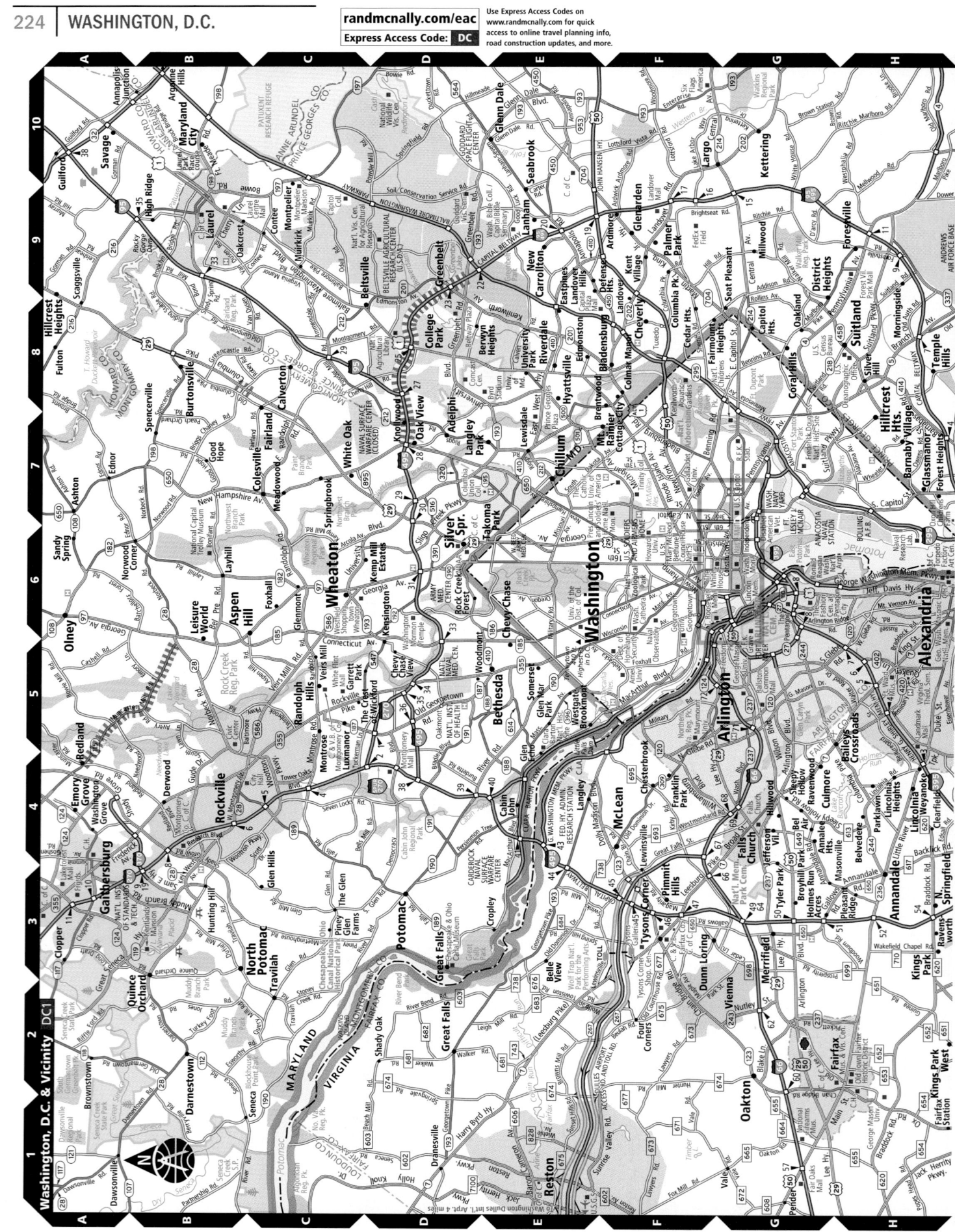

SYMBOLS

Featured ride
Long-term construction
Harley-Davidson dealership
Scenic route
Historic site or monument; Indian reservation or rancheria; military installation; point of interest; wildlife refuge

WASHINGTON, D.C. MOTORCYCLE LAWS

Helmet use:
Required

Riding two abreast:
No reference in administrative code or statutes

Eye protection:
Required unless equipped with windscreen

Speed limit:
Primary roads: 55 mph
Secondary roads: N/A

WASHINGTON, D.C. RESOURCES

Road conditions or construction:
www.ddot.dc.gov

Highway Emergency Numbers:
N/A

Tourism:
(800) 422-8644 (to request travel materials only)
(202) 789-7000
www.washington.org

State motor vehicle information:
(202) 727-5000
http://dmv.washingtondc.gov

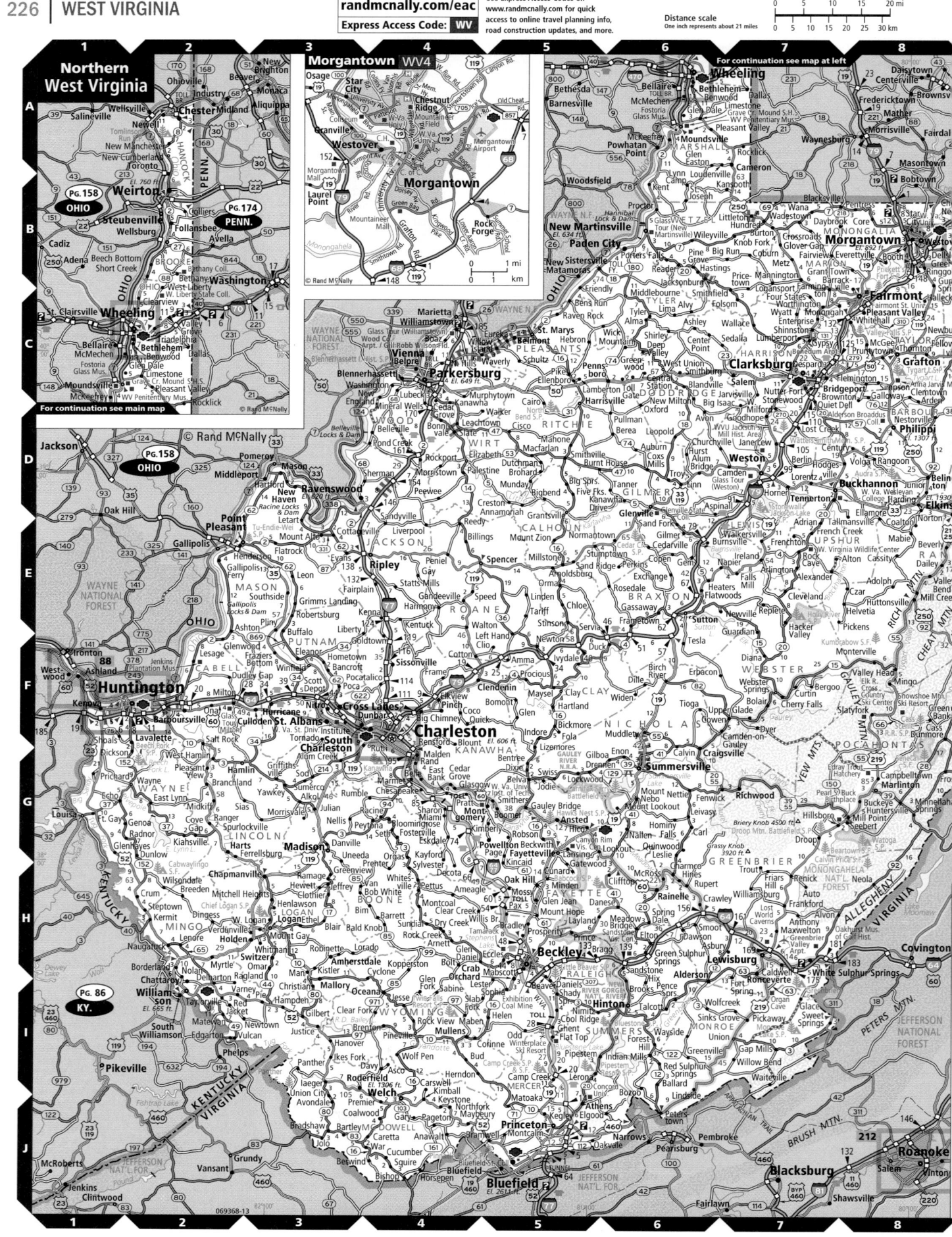

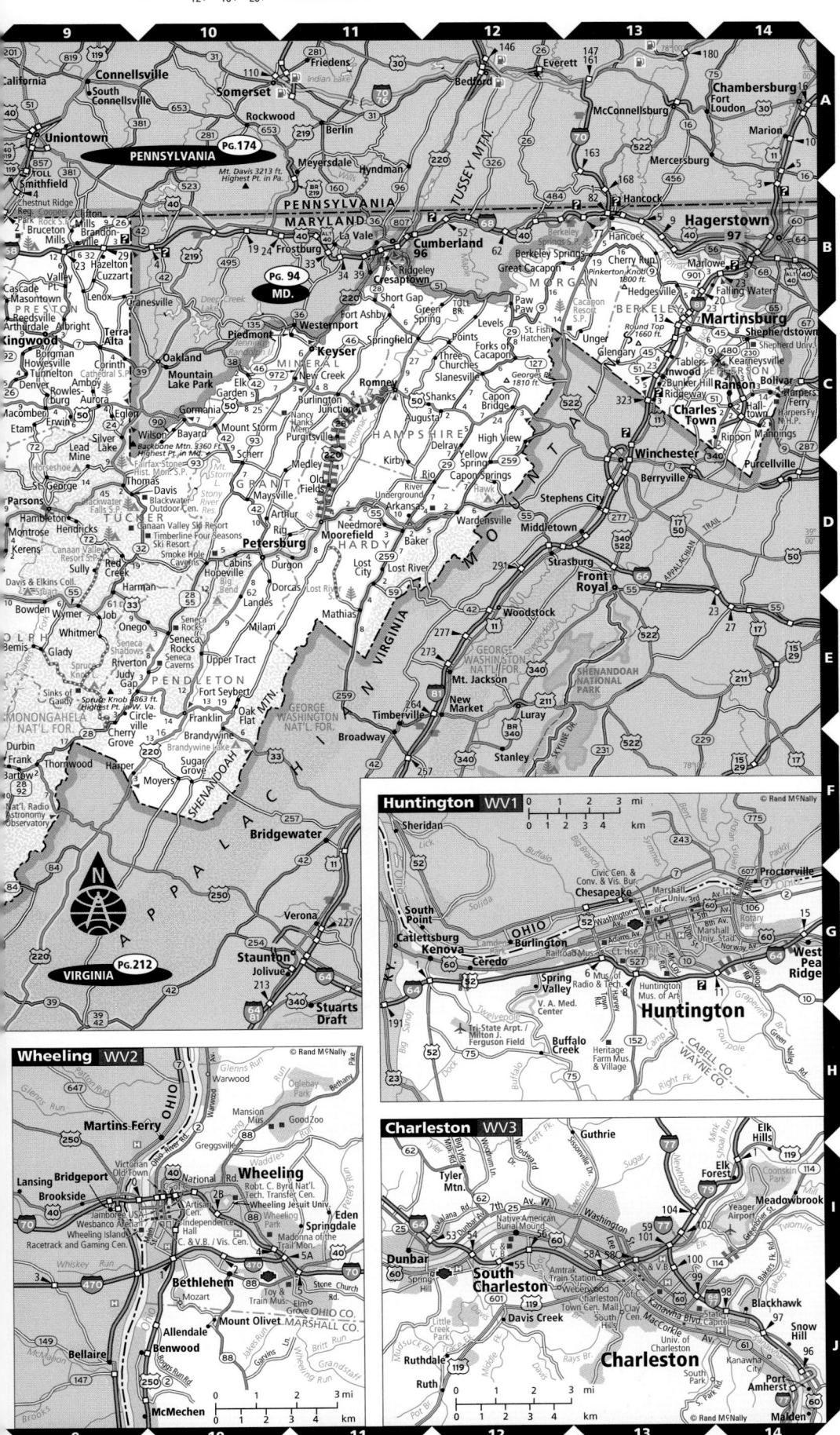

How to determine distance

Mileages in red between red arrowheads; in black, between intersections.

SYMBOLS

- Featured ride
- Long-term construction
- Harley-Davidson dealership
- Scenic route
- Historic site or monument; Indian reservation or rancheria; military installation; point of interest; wildlife refuge

WEST VIRGINIA MOTORCYCLE LAWS

Helmet use:
Reflectorization required

Riding two abreast:
No reference in administrative code or statutes

Eye protection:
Required by law

Speed limit:
Primary roads: 70 mph
Secondary roads: 55 mph

WEST VIRGINIA RESOURCES

Road conditions or construction:
(877) 982-7623
www.wvdot.com

Highway Emergency Numbers:
911 or *SP

Tourism:
(800) 225-5982
www.callwva.com

State motor vehicle information:
(304) 558-3900
www.wvdot.com

CITY-TO-CITY MILEAGE

	Beckley	Charleston	Cumberland, MD	Huntington	Morgantown	Parkersburg	Wheeling	White Sulphur Springs
Beckley		60	241	111	169	135	236	60
Charleston	60		227	51	155	75	176	125
Cumberland, MD	241	227		278	72	181	146	193
Huntington	111	51	278		206	126	227	176
Morgantown	169	155	72	206		109	74	201
Parkersburg	135	75	181	126	109		105	200
Wheeling	236	176	146	227	74	105		301
White Sulphur Sprs.	60	125	193	176	201	200	301	

HARLEY-DAVIDSON DEALERSHIPS

Cole Harley-Davidson, J-5
1804 Bland St. (Rte. 52 N) **Bluefield**
(304) 324-8116
Lat N 37.276 Lon W 81.219

Mike's Harley-Davidson Sales, I-2
Rte. 2 Box 102 **Delbarton**
(304) 426-4241
Lat N 37.642 Lon W 82.031

New River Gorge Harley-Davidson Shop, G-6
52489 Midland Trail **Hico**
(304) 658-3300
Lat N 38.106 Lon W 80.958

Benjy's Harley-Davidson, F-2
408 4th St. **Huntington**
(304) 523-1340
Lat N 38.419 Lon W 82.452

Triple S Harley-Davidson, B-8
308 Cheat Rd. **Morgantown**
(304) 284-8244
Lat N 39.651 Lon W 79.909

B & B Harley-Davidson Cycle Sales, C-7
100 Alexander Ave. **Nutter Fort (Clarksburg)**
(304) 623-0484
Lat N 39.275 Lon W 80.359

Harley-Davidson of West Virginia, F-3
4924 MacCorkle Ave. SW **South Charleston**
(304) 768-1600
Lat N 38.355 Lon W 81.732

Valley Harley-Davidson, A-6
1034 E Bethlehem **Wheeling**
(304) 243-9300
Lat N 40.039 Lon W 80.677

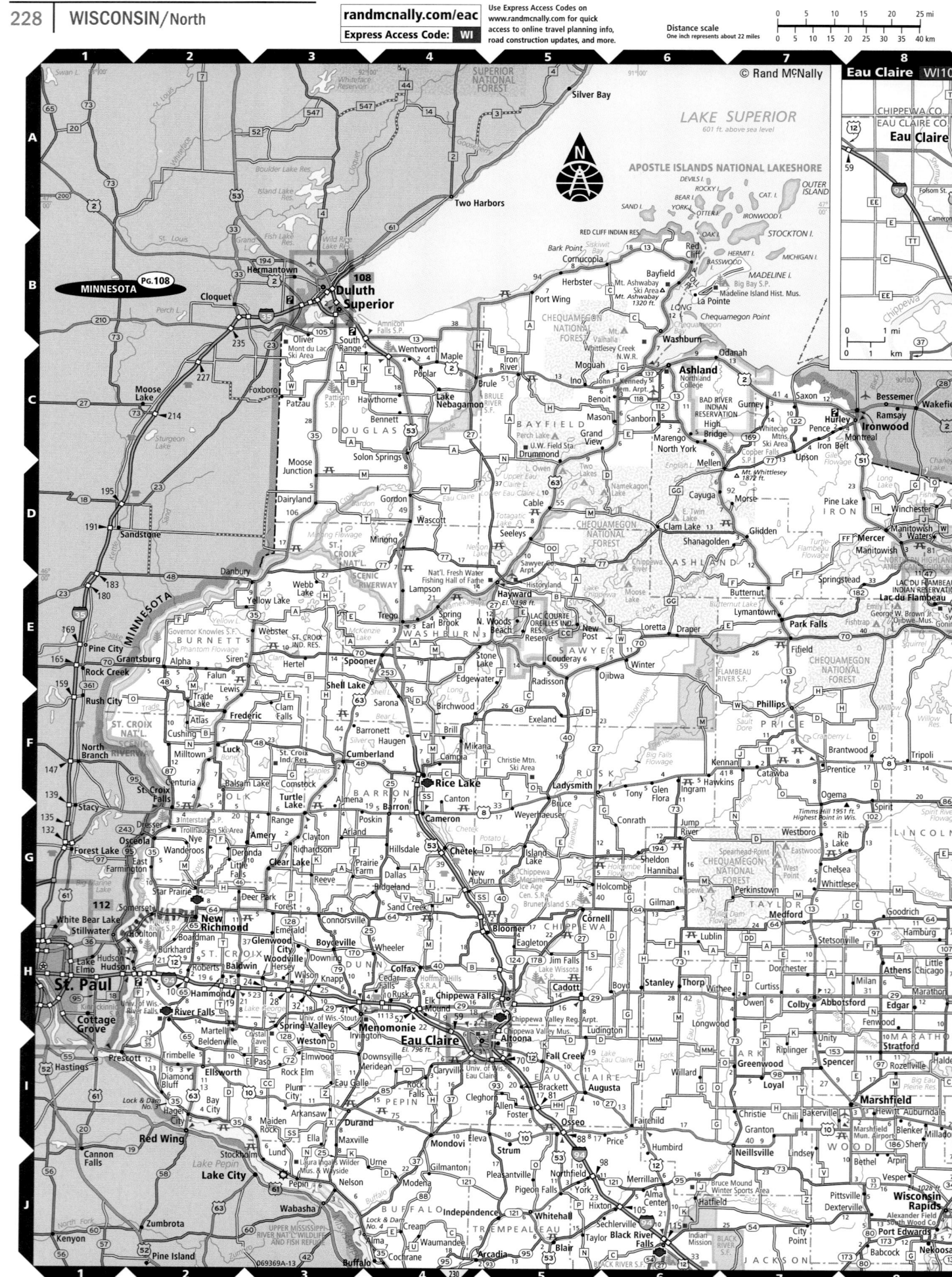

randmcnally.com/eac

Express Access Code: WI

Use Express Access Codes on www.randmcnally.com for quick access to online travel planning info, road construction updates, and more.

© Rand McNally

Eau Claire WI10

How to determine distance

Mileages in red between red arrowheads; in black, between intersections.

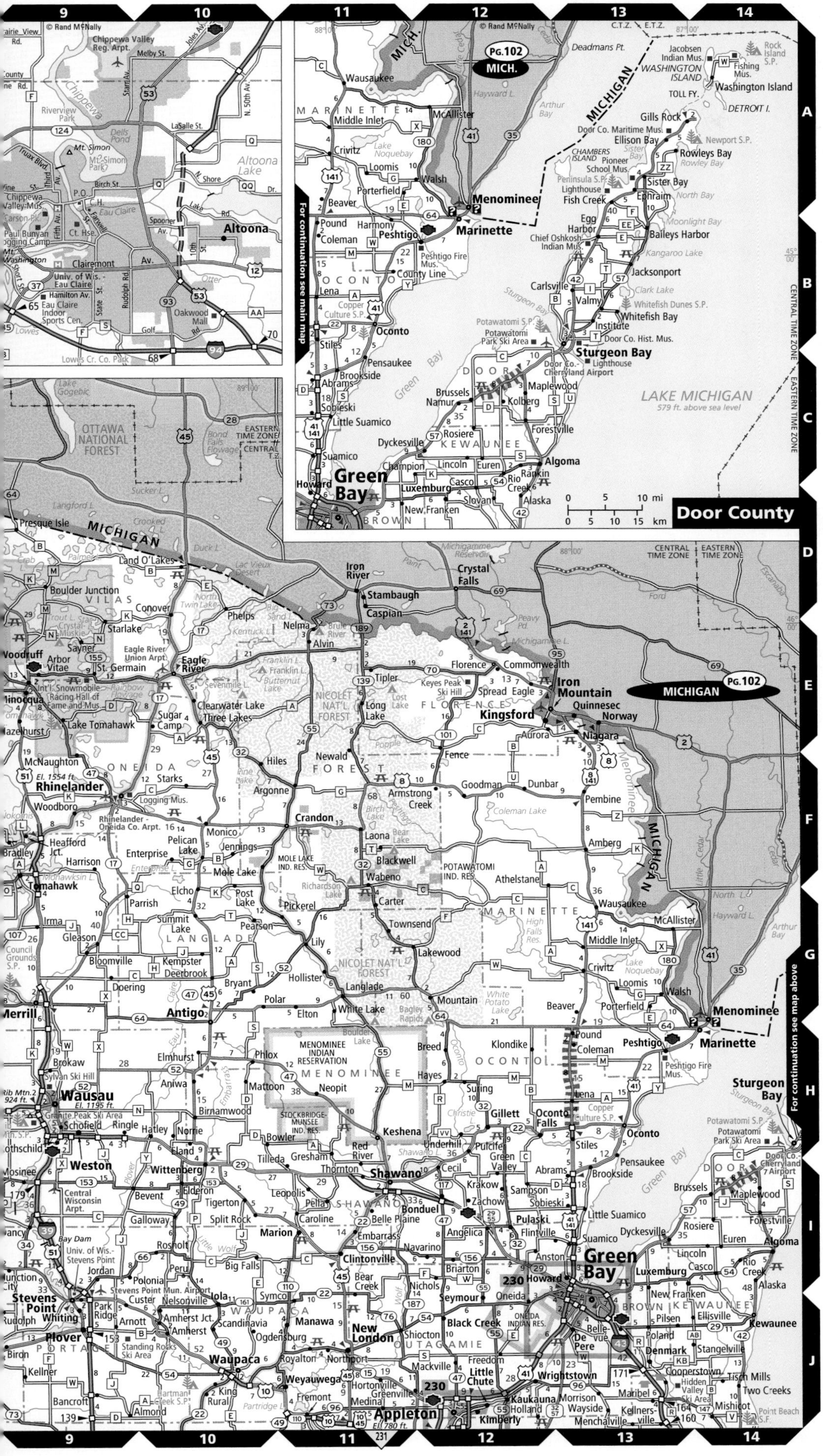

Green Bay

p. 230-231

SYMBOLS

- Featured ride
- Scenic route
- Long-term construction
- Historic site or monument; Indian reservation or rancheria; military installation; point of interest; wildlife refuge
- Harley-Davidson dealership

WISCONSIN MOTORCYCLE LAWS

Helmet use:
Required under age 18, and for instructional permit holders

Riding two abreast:
Yes. See state law for specifics

Eye protection:
Required for instructional permit holders
Required unless equipped with windscreen which is 15" or higher above handlebars

Speed limit:
Primary roads: 65 mph
Secondary roads: 65 mph

HARLEY-DAVIDSON DEALERSHIPS

Harley-Davidson Appleton, J-12
5322 Clairemont Dr. **Appleton**
(920) 757-1651
Lat N 44.285 **Lon** W 88.487

Northern Lights Harley-Davidson, E-9
1700 Hwy. 51 **Arbor Vitae**
(715) 358-5054
Lat N 45.922 **Lon** W 89.683

Al Muth Harley-Davidson Sales, J-6
N6630 Cty. Hwy. A **Black River Falls**
(715) 284-4725
Lat N 44.283 **Lon** W 90.822

Doc's Harley-Davidson of Shawano, I-12
W2709 State Hwy. 29 **Bondeul**
(715) 758-9080
Lat N 44.703 **Lon** W 88.369

Sport Motors Harley-Davidson, H-5
2452 Hallie Rd. (US Hwy. 53) **Chippewa Falls**
(715) 723-7433
Lat N 44.875 **Lon** W 91.433

McCoy's Harley-Davidson Green Bay, J-13
2728 Manitowoc Rd. **Green Bay**
(920) 406-3900
Lat N 44.465 **Lon** W 87.947

Wausau Harley-Davidson, H-9
1570 County Rd. XX **Mosinee**
(715) 355-4464
Lat N 44.858 **Lon** W 89.635

St. Croix Harley-Davidson, G-2
2060 Hwy. 65 N **New Richmond**
(715) 246-2959
Lat N 45.160 **Lon** W 92.529

Vandervest Harley-Davidson, H-13
810 Frontage Rd. **Peshtigo**
(715) 582-8843
Lat N 45.053 **Lon** W 87.733

Rice Lake Harley-Davidson, F-4
2801 S Wisconsin Ave. **Rice Lake**
(715) 234-5400
Lat N 45.495 **Lon** W 91.745

St. Croix Harley-Davidson Shop, H-2
883 Hwy. 65 **River Falls**
(715) 426-0199
Lat N 44.859 **Lon** W 92.629

Door County

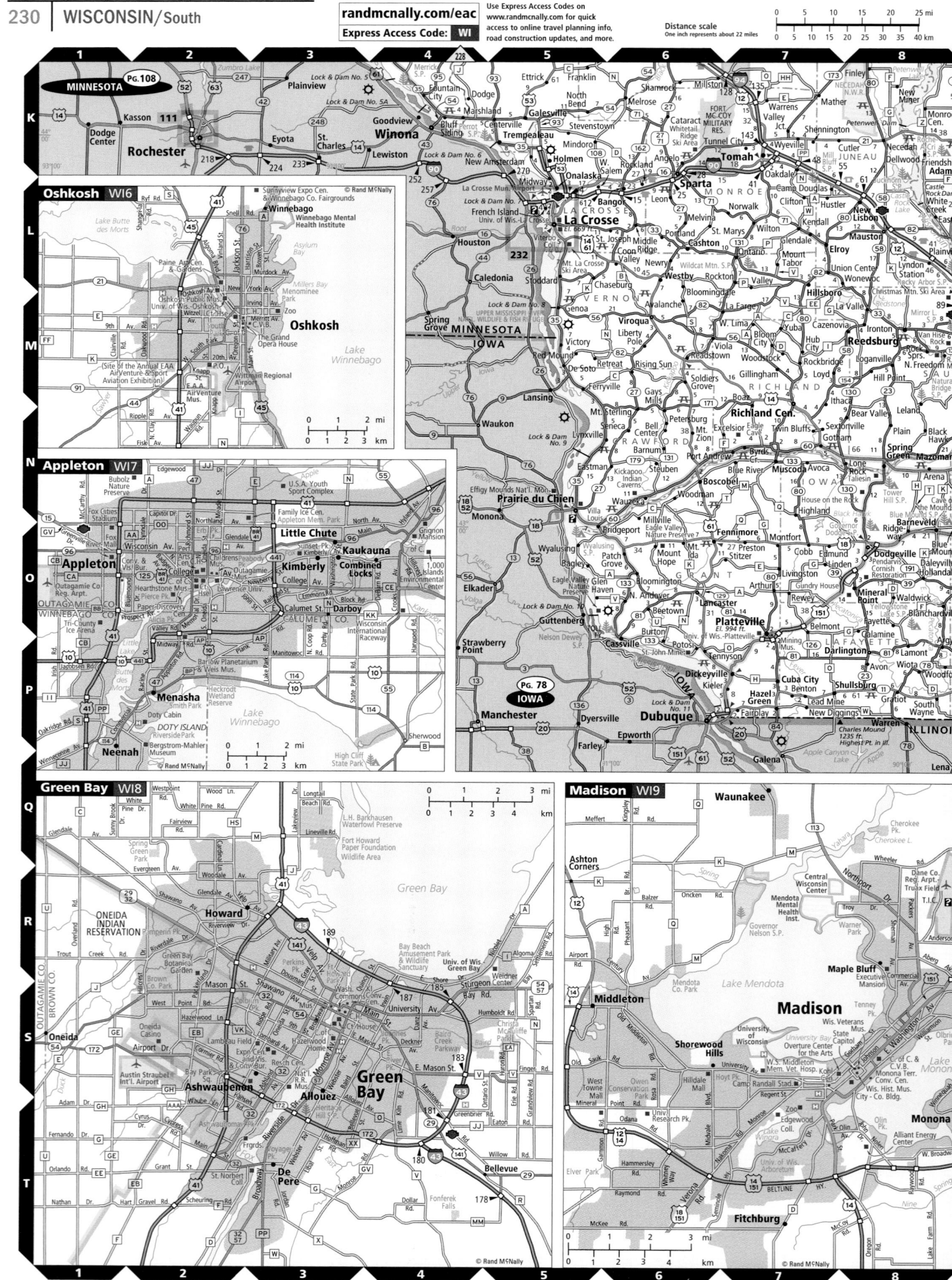

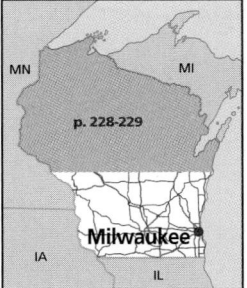

Milwaukee

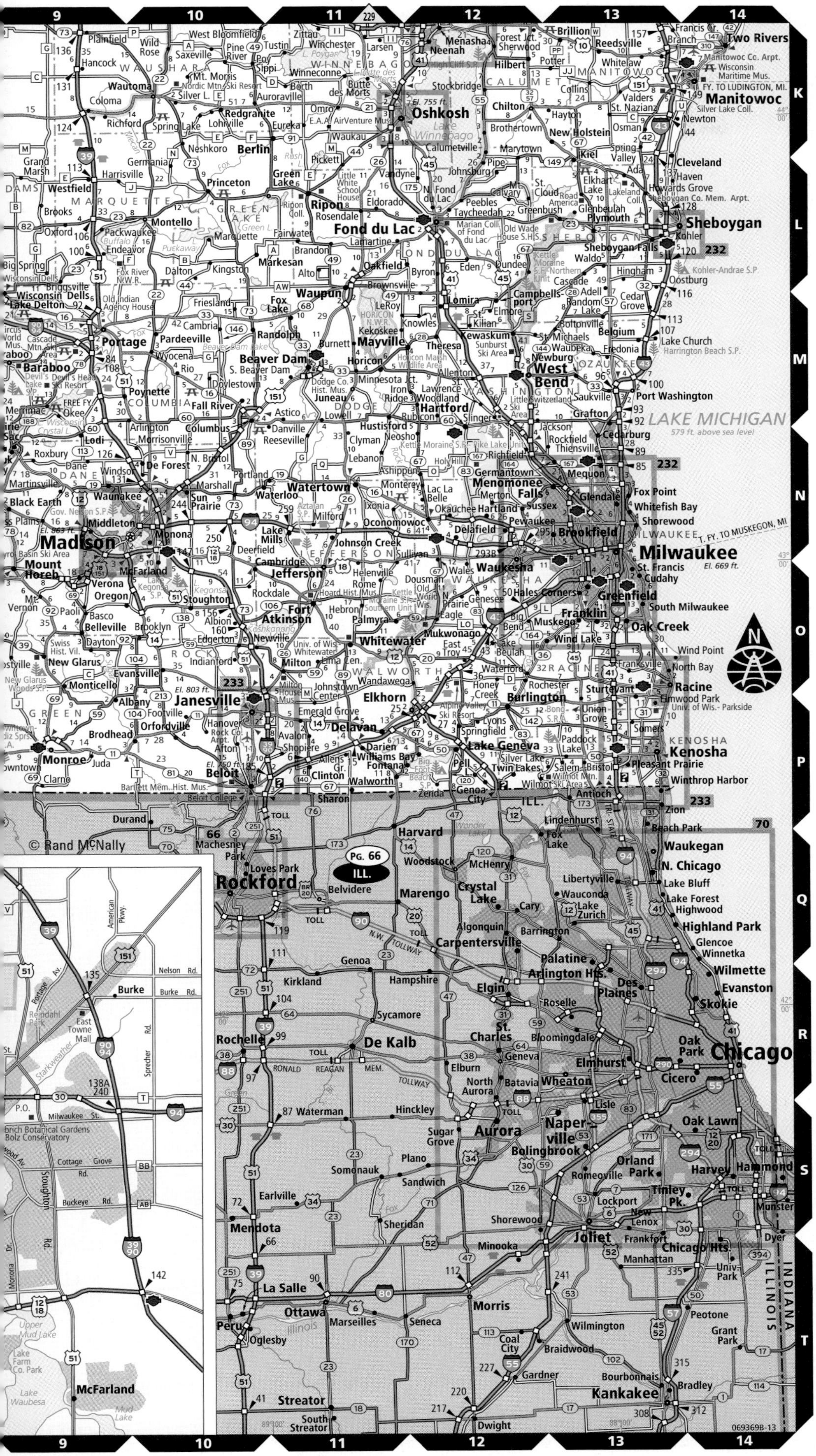

SYMBOLS

	Featured ride		Scenic route
	Long-term construction	■	Historic site or monument; Indian reservation or rancheria; military installation; point of interest; wildlife refuge
	Harley-Davidson dealership		

For Wisconsin ride, see page R33.

HARLEY-DAVIDSON DEALERSHIPS

For Milwaukee and Racine/Kenosha area dealers, please see listings on page 233.

Mischler's Harley-Davidson, M-11
N8131 Kellom Rd. **Beaver Dam**
(920) 887-8425
Lat N 43.481 **Lon** W 88.820

Bob's Harley-Davidson, L-12
24 S Rolling Meadows Dr. **Fond du Lac**
(920) 921-2344
Lat N 43.776 **Lon** W 88.483

Hartford Harley-Davidson Shop, M-12
427 Sumner St. (Hwy. 60 W) **Hartford**
(262) 670-1000
Lat N 43.317 **Lon** W 88.369

Kutter Harley-Davidson, P-10
3223 N Pontiac Dr. **Janesville**
(608) 757-0880
Lat N 42.721 **Lon** W 88.989

Capital City Harley-Davidson, N-10
6200 Millpond Rd. **Madison**
(608) 221-2761
Lat N 43.044 **Lon** W 89.273

Stock's Harley-Davidson, K-14
3206 Menasha Ave. **Manitowoc**
(920) 684-0237
Lat N 44.119 **Lon** W 87.688

Bala's Harley-Davidson, L-8
N 4833 Hwy. 58 **Mauston**
(608) 847-7702
Lat N 43.801 **Lon** W 90.049

Kutter Harley-Davidson Shop, P-9
129 W 6th St. **Monroe**
(608) 329-4884
Lat N 42.607 **Lon** W 89.658

Wisconsin Harley-Davidson, N-12
1280 Blue Ribbon Dr. **Oconomowoc**
(262) 569-8500
Lat N 43.064 **Lon** W 88.472

La Crosse Area Harley-Davidson, L-5
1116 Oak Forest Dr. **Onalaska**
(608) 783-6112
Lat N 43.871 **Lon** W 91.220

Sauk Prairie Harley-Davidson, N-9
836 Phillips Blvd. **Sauk City**
(608) 643-3735
Lat N 43.271 **Lon** W 89.737

Route 43 Harley-Davidson, L-13
3736 S Taylor Dr. **Sheboygan**
(920) 458-0777
Lat N 43.716 **Lon** W 87.759

West Bend Harley-Davidson, M-12
2910 W Washington St. **West Bend**
(262) 338-8761
Lat N 43.427 **Lon** W 88.223

Bala's Harley-Davidson of Wisconsin Dells, M-8
524 Wisconsin Dells Pkwy. **Wisconsin Dells**
(608) 253-2252
Lat N 43.595 **Lon** W 89.794

Mileages in red between red arrowheads; in black, between intersections.

© Rand McNally

How to determine distance

Mileages in red between red arrowheads; in black, between intersections.

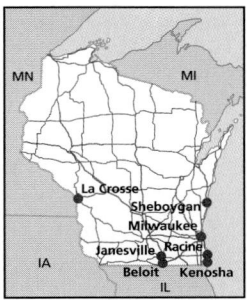

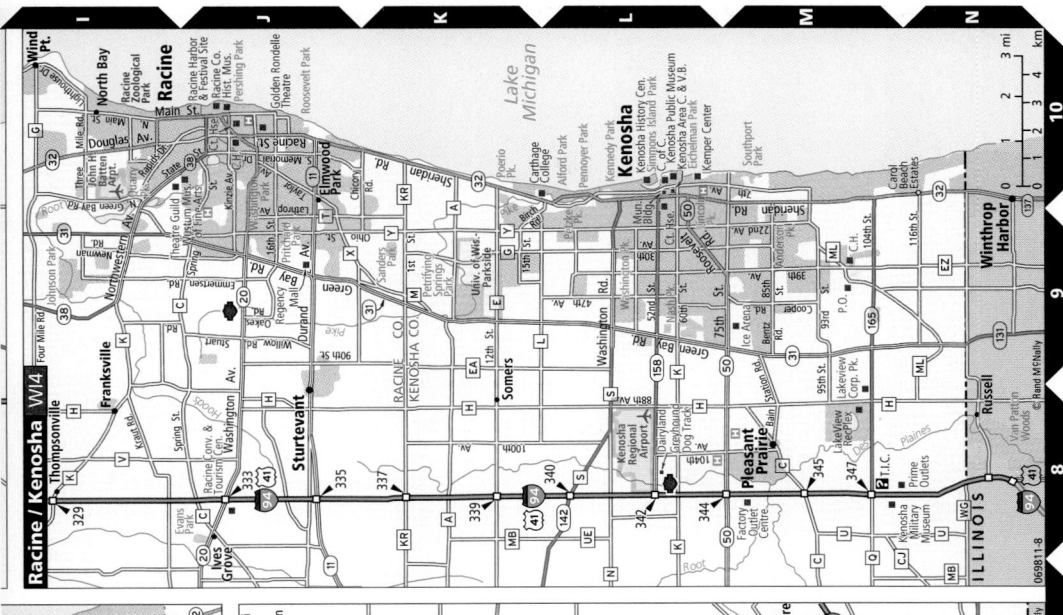

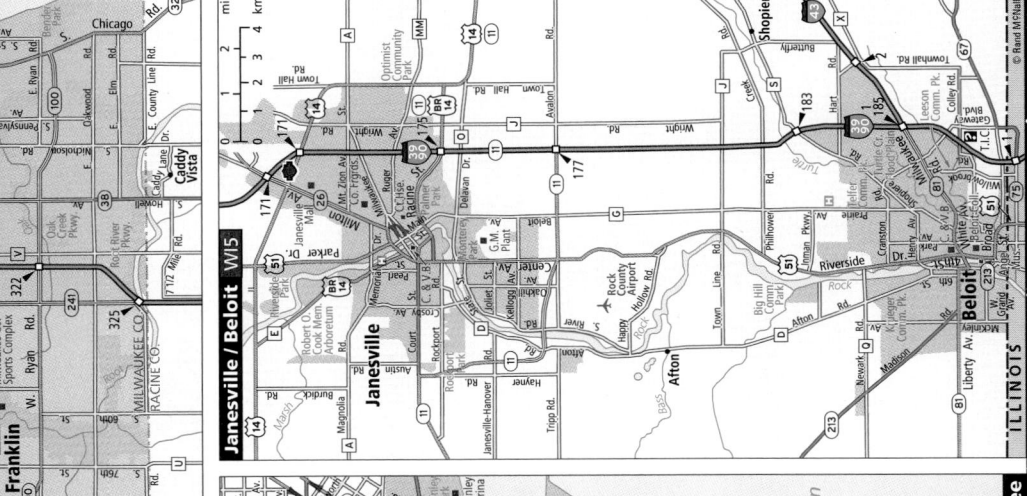

SYMBOLS

━━━ Featured ride

━━━ Scenic route

╫╫╫ Long-term construction

■ Historic site or monument; Indian reservation or rancheria; military installation; point of interest; wildlife refuge

⬥ Harley-Davidson dealership

WISCONSIN MOTORCYCLE LAWS

Helmet use:
Required under age 18, and for instructional permit holders

Riding two abreast:
Yes. See state law for specifics

Eye protection:
Required for instructional permit holders
Required unless equipped with windscreen which is 15" or higher above handlebars

Speed limit:
Primary roads: 65 mph
Secondary roads: 65 mph

WISCONSIN RESOURCES

Road conditions or construction:
(800) 762-3947
www.dot.state.wi.us

Highway Emergency Numbers:
911

Tourism:
(800) 432-8747
www.travelwisconsin.com

State motor vehicle information:
(608) 266-2353
www.dot.state.wi.us

HARLEY-DAVIDSON DEALERSHIPS

⬥ **Uke's Harley-Davidson, L-8**
5995 120th Ave. **Kenosha**
(262) 857-UKES
Lat N 42.582 Lon W 87.952

⬥ **House of Harley-Davidson, G-5**
6221 W Layton Ave. **Milwaukee**
(414) 282-2211
Lat N 42.959 Lon W 87.992

⬥ **House of Harley-Davidson Airport, G-6**
5300 S Howell Ave. **Milwaukee**
(414) 747-5384
Lat N 42.948 Lon W 87.910

⬥ **Milwaukee Harley-Davidson, D-4**
11310 W Silver Spring Rd. **Milwaukee**
(414) 461-4444
Lat N 43.119 Lon W 88.052

⬥ **Hal's Harley-Davidson, F-3**
1925 S Moorland Rd. **New Berlin**
(262) 860-2060
Lat N 43.009 Lon W 88.108

⬥ **Racine Harley-Davidson, J-9**
1155 Oakes Rd. **Racine**
(262) 884-0123
Lat N 42.720 Lon W 87.870

⬥ **Suburban Motors Harley-Davidson, A-5**
139 N Main St. **Thiensville**
(262) 242-2464
Lat N 43.232 Lon W 87.984

randmcnally.com/eac

Express Access Code: WY

Use Express Access Codes on www.randmcnally.com for quick access to online travel planning info, road construction updates, and more.

Distance scale
One inch represents about 40 miles

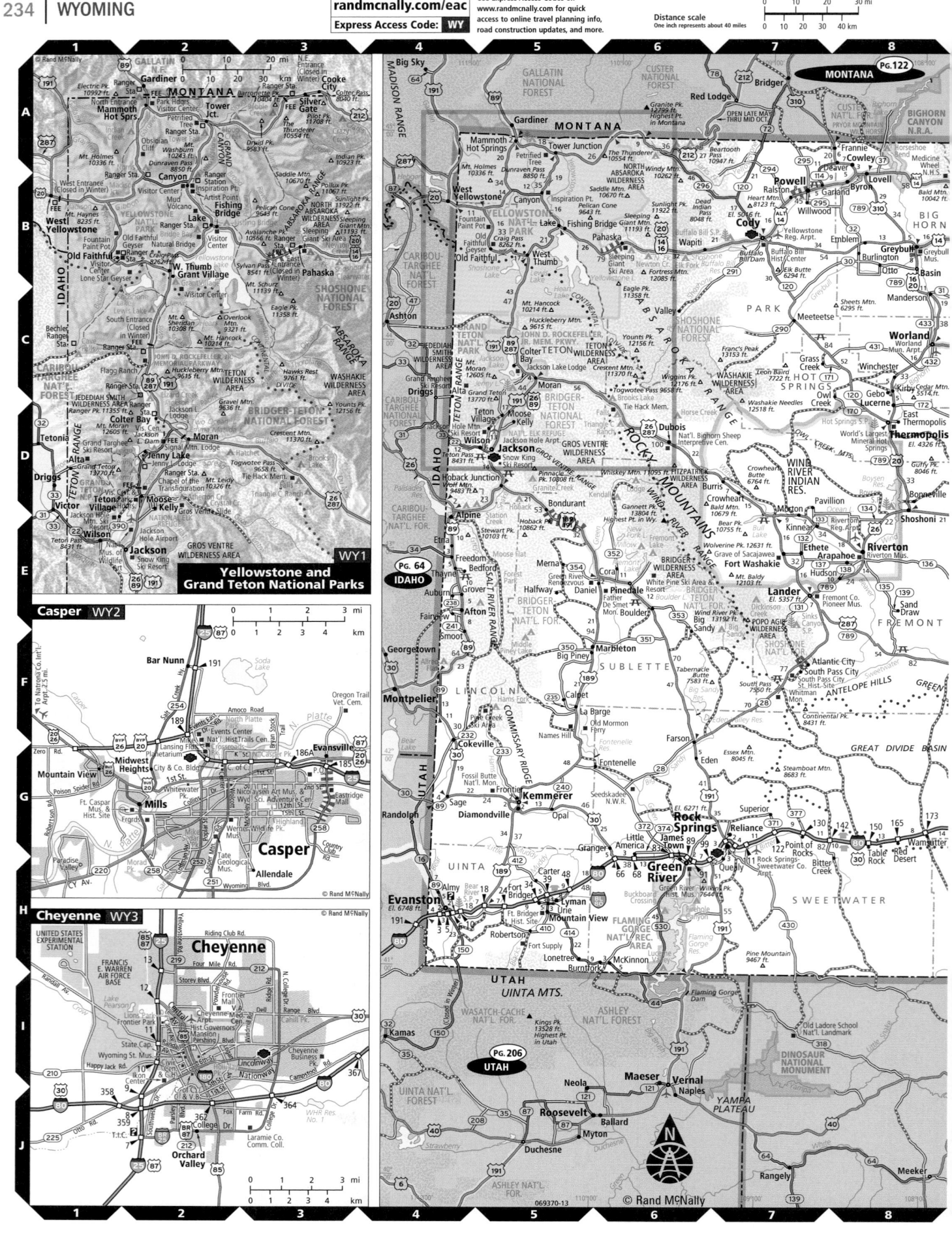

Yellowstone and Grand Teton National Parks

WY1

Casper WY2

Cheyenne WY3

© Rand McNally

069370-13

How to determine distance

Mileages in red between red arrowheads;
in black, between intersections.

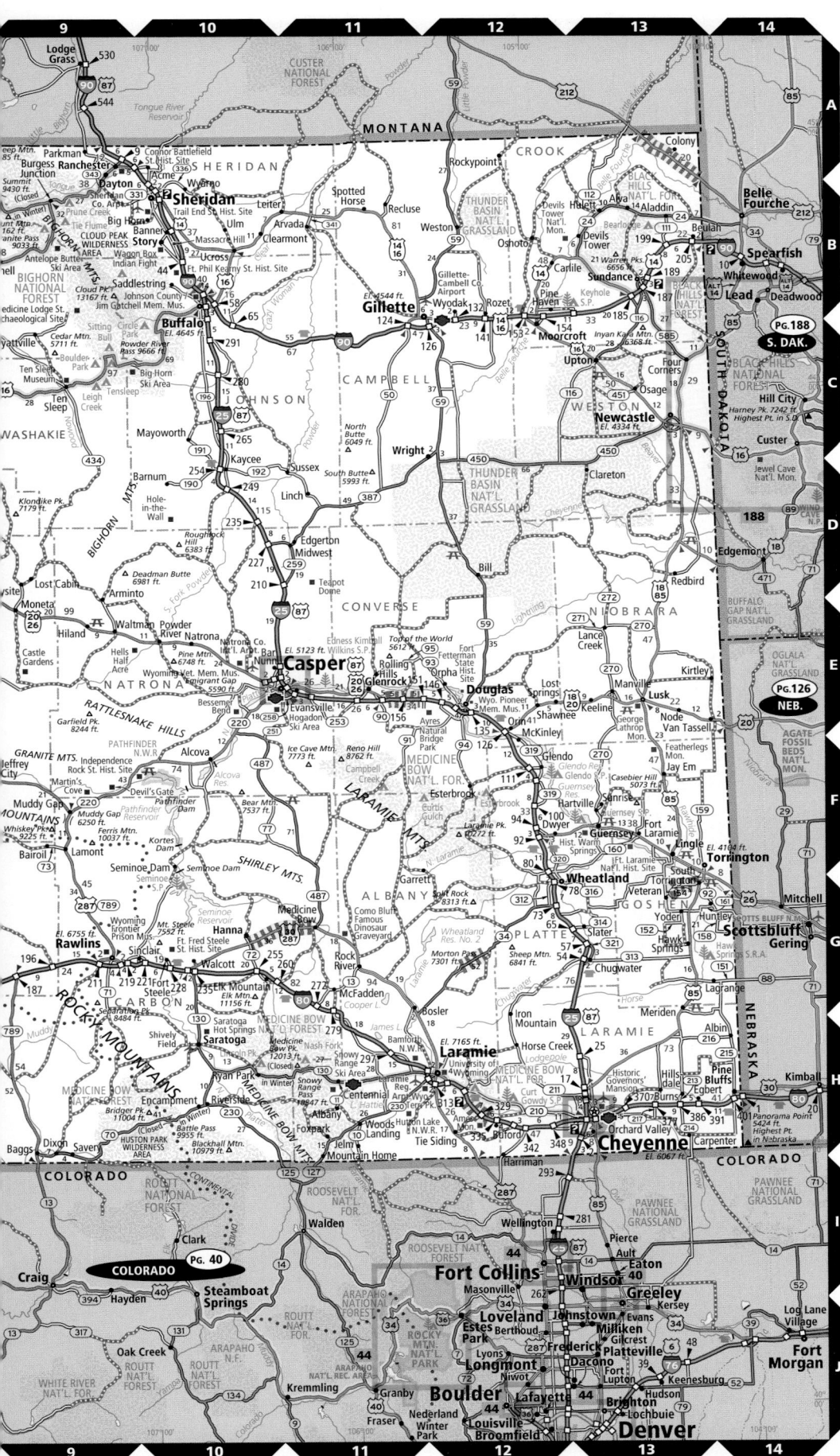

For Wyoming ride, see page R34.
For Utah/Wyoming ride, see page R31.

SYMBOLS

- Featured ride
- Scenic route
- Long-term construction
- Harley-Davidson dealership
- ■ Historic site or monument; Indian reservation or rancheria; military installation; point of interest; wildlife refuge

WYOMING MOTORCYCLE LAWS

Helmet use:
Required
Required under age 18

Riding two abreast:
Yes. See state law for specifics

Eye protection:
Not required

Speed limit:
Primary roads: 75 mph
Secondary roads: 60 mph

WYOMING RESOURCES

Road conditions or construction:
(888) 996-7623 (in WY)
(307) 772-0824
www.dot.state.wy.us

Highway Emergency Numbers:
(800) 442-9090 or #HELP

Tourism:
(800) 225-5996
www.wyomingtourism.org

State motor vehicle information:
(307) 777-4800
www.dot.state.wy.us/Index.jsp

CITY-TO-CITY MILEAGE

	CASPER	CHEYENNE	CODY	JACKSON	RIVERTON	ROCK SPRINGS	SHERIDAN	SPEARFISH SD
Casper		180	214	282	119	226	152	223
Cheyenne	180		395	436	275	258	329	295
Cody	214	395		178	139	282	148	346
Jackson	282	436	178		166	178	326	509
Riverton	119	275	139	166		143	217	346
Rock Springs	226	258	282	178	143		378	449
Sheridan	152	329	148	326	217	378		199
Spearfish, SD	223	295	346	509	346	449	199	

HARLEY-DAVIDSON DEALERSHIPS

Deluxe Harley-Davidson, E-11
831 N Glenn Rd. **Casper**
(307) 265-3211
Lat N 42.859 Lon W 106.339

Cheyenne Harley-Davidson, H-13
3320 E Lincoln Way **Cheyenne**
(307) 638-8307
Lat N 41.138 Lon W 104.776

Beartooth Harley-Davidson, B-7
1137 Sheridan Ave. **Cody**
(307) 527-7776
Lat N 44.526 Lon W 109.065

Deluxe Harley-Davidson Shop, C-12
3300 Conestoga Dr. **Gillette**
(307) 687-2001
Lat N 44.295 Lon W 105.454

Jackson Hole Harley-Davidson, D-5
40 S Millward **Jackson**
(307) 739-1500
Lat N 43.479 Lon W 110.765

Laramie Harley-Davidson Shop, H-11
2061 Snowy Range Rd. **Laramie**
(307) 721-1024
Lat N 41.294 Lon W 106.016

Flaming Gorge Harley-Davidson, G-7
2401 Foothill Blvd. **Rock Springs**
(307) 382-9099
Lat N 41.579 Lon W 109.264

Distance scale
One inch represents about 265 miles

0 100 200 mi
0 100 200 300 km

BEAUFORT SEA

YUKON TERRITORY

MACKENZIE MOUNTAINS

NORTHWEST TERRITORIES

VICTORIA ISLAND

NUN...

ALASKA

ALASKA RANGE

Denali Natl. Park & Pres.
Mt. McKinley 20,320 ft. Highest in North America

Anchorage
Cordova
Fairbanks

WRANGELL-ST. ELIAS NATL. PARK AND PRES.

GLACIER BAY NATL. PARK & PRES.

GULF OF ALASKA

UNITED STATES

Dawson
Haines Junction
Whitehorse
Haines
Juneau
Ross River
Watson Lake
Fort Nelson

PELLY MOUNTAINS
SELWYN MOUNTAINS
CONTINENTAL DIVIDE

Tuktoyaktuk
Inuvik
Fort McPherson
ARCTIC CIRCLE

Cape Dalhousie
Cape Bathurst
Holman
BANKS ISLAND
AULAVIK N.P.
Sachs Harbour
Cape Kellett
Cape Lambton

Amundsen Gulf
Prince of Wales Strait
Dolphin and Union Strait
Prince Albert Sound

TUKTUT NOGAIT NAT'L. PK.

MELVILLE ISLAND
Viscount Melville Sound
PRINCE OF WALES ISLAND
SOMERSET ISLAND
BATHURST ISLAND
CORNWALLIS ISLAND
Qausuittuq (Resolute)
Barrow Strait

Kugluktuk
Ikaluktutiak (Cambridge Bay)
Coronation Gulf
Queen Maud Gulf
Talurjuak (Taloyoak)
KING WILLIAM ISLAND
Oqsuqtooq (Gjoa Haven)
QUEEN MAUD GULF MIGRATORY BIRD SANCTUARY
Boothia Peninsula
Gulf of Boothia
Tununirus (Arctic Bay)

Great Bear Lake
Port Radium
Wrigley
FY. Fort Simpson
Yellowknife
Great Slave Lake
Enterprise
Hay River
Ft. Providence
Fort Smith
Fitzgerald
Uranium City
THELON WILDLIFE SANCTUARY
Aylmer L.
Dubawnt L.
Baker L.
Aberdeen L.
Nueltin Lake
Igluligaarjuk (Chesterfield Inlet)

WOOD BUFFALO N.P.
NAHANNI N.P.
STONE MTN. PROV. PARK
MUNCHO LAKE PROV. PARK

ALBERTA

SASKATCHEWAN

MANITOBA

BRITISH COLUMBIA

ROCKY MOUNTAINS
COAST MOUNTAINS

Stewart
Prince Rupert
QUEEN CHARLOTTE ISLANDS
GWAII HAANAS NAT'L. PK. RESERVE
Cape St. James

Chetwynd
Dawson Creek
Grande Prairie
Peace River
Valleyview
Whitecourt
Hinton
Jasper
JASPER N.P.
MT. ROBSON PROV. PK.
BANFF N.P.
Rocky Mountain House
Red Deer
Banff
Calgary
Edmonton
St. Paul
Lloydminster
Lesser Slave Lake
Ft. McMurray
La Loche
Fort MacKay
GREGOIRE LAKE PROV. PARK
MEADOW LAKE PROV. PARK
CLEARWATER RIVER PROV. PARK
ATHABASCA SAND DUNES
Lake Athabasca
Wollaston Lake
Reindeer Lake
Cree Lake
LAC LA RONGE PROV. PARK
PRINCE ALBERT N.P.
North Battleford
Prince Albert
Saskatoon
Melfort
Hudson Bay
Rosetown
Moose Jaw
Regina
Swift Current
Weyburn
Estevan
Melville
Yorkton
Swan River
Dauphin
RIDING MTN. N.P.
DUCK MTN. PROV. PK.
Lake Winnipegosis
Lake Manitoba
Lake Winnipeg
Grand Rapids
Flin Flon
Lynn Lake
Thompson
GRASS RIVER PROV. PARK
CLEARWATER PROV. PARK
GRAND RAPIDS
NUMAYKOOS LAKE PROV. PARK
CARIBOU RIVER PROV. PARK
SAND LAKES PROV. PARK
Cape Churchill
WAPUSK NATIONAL PARK
Cape Tatnam
Northern Indian Lake

Bella Coola
Williams Lake
Quesnel
Prince George
WELLS GRAY PROV. PARK
MT. REVELSTOKE N.P.
GLACIER N.P.
Kamloops
Vancouver
Victoria
VANCOUVER ISLAND
PACIFIC RIM N.P. RESERVE
GARIBALDI PROV. PK.
SELKIRK MTS.
KOOTENAY N.P.
Penticton
Cranbrook
Kimberley
Brooks
Medicine Hat
Lethbridge
Cypress Hills Interprov. Park
GRASSLANDS N.P.
WATERTON LAKES N.P.
WATERTON-GLACIER INT'L. PEACE PARK

PACIFIC OCEAN

Seattle
Tacoma
Olympia
OLYMPIC N.P.
NORTH CASCADES N.P.
MT. RAINIER N.P.
WASH.
Spokane
Portland
Salem
Eugene
CRATER LAKE N.P.
NEWBERRY NAT'L. VOLCANIC MON.
OREGON
CASCADE RANGE
Lewiston
Missoula
Great Falls
Helena
Butte
BITTERROOT RANGE
LEWIS RANGE
MONTANA
Billings
Boise
IDAHO
CRATERS OF THE MOON NAT'L. MON.
LAVA BEDS NAT'L. MON.
LASSEN VOLCANIC N.P.
CALIF.
Sacramento
Carson City
Reno
YOSEMITE N.P.
NEVADA
Great Salt Lake
Ogden
Salt Lake City
UTAH
Pocatello
YELLOWSTONE N.P.
GRAND TETON N.P.
WYOMING
Casper
Pathfinder Reservoir
CONTINENTAL DIVIDE
DINOSAUR NAT'L. MON.
COLO.
Cheyenne

UNITED STATES

NORTH DAKOTA
Minot
Bismarck
THEODORE ROOSEVELT N.P.
Oahe Res.
SOUTH DAKOTA
Pierre
Rapid City
BADLANDS NAT'L. PARK
Fort Peck Lake
Grand Forks
Fargo
Duluth
MINNESOTA
Minneapolis
St. Paul
Rochester
Sioux Falls
Sioux City
NEBRASKA
IOWA
WISCO...
Madison
ILL.

Winnipeg
Kenora
Portage la Prairie
Brandon
Fort Frances
LAKE OF THE WOODS
VOYAGEURS N.P.
QUETICO PROV. PARK
Red Lake
Pickle Lake
TURTLE MTN. PROV. PK.
SPRUCE WOODS PROV. PK.
NOPIMING PROV. PARK
WHITESHELL PROV. PARK

PACIFIC TIME ZONE
MOUNTAIN TIME ZONE
CENTRAL TIME ZONE
ALASKA TIME ZONE

How to determine distance

Kilometers in blue and mileages in red between red arrowheads; mileages in black between intersections.

NORTHWEST TERRITORIES AND YUKON TERRITORY MOTORCYCLE LAWS

Helmet use: Required

Eye protection: Not Required

Speed limit: As posted

Riding two abreast in one lane: Illegal

NORTHWEST TERRITORIES RESOURCES

Road conditions or construction:
(800) 661-0750
www.hwy.dot.gov.nt.ca/highways/

Highway Emergency Numbers: 911

Tourism:
(800) 661-0788
www.explorenwt.com/

Provincial motor vehicle information:
(867) 873-7406
www.gov.nt.ca

YUKON TERRITORY RESOURCES

Road conditions or construction:
(867) 456-7623
www.gov.yk.ca/roadreport/

Highway Emergency Numbers: 911

Tourism:
(800) 789-8566
www.touryukon.com

Provincial motor vehicle information:
(867) 667-5315
www.community.gov.yk.ca/

HARLEY-DAVIDSON DEALERSHIPS

Harley-Davidson of Ft. McMurray, F-4
284 MacDonald Crescent
Ft. McMurray, AB
(780) 715-9402
Lat N 56.669 **Lon** W 111.341

Yukon Harley-Davidson, C-2
21 Waterfront Place **Whitehorse, YT**
(867) 633-1903
Lat N 60.743 **Lon** W 135.075

© Rand McNally

06-1

randmcnally.com/eac

Express Access Codes: British Columbia **BC** Alberta **AB**

Use Express Access Codes on www.randmcnally.com for quick access to online travel planning info, road construction updates, and more.

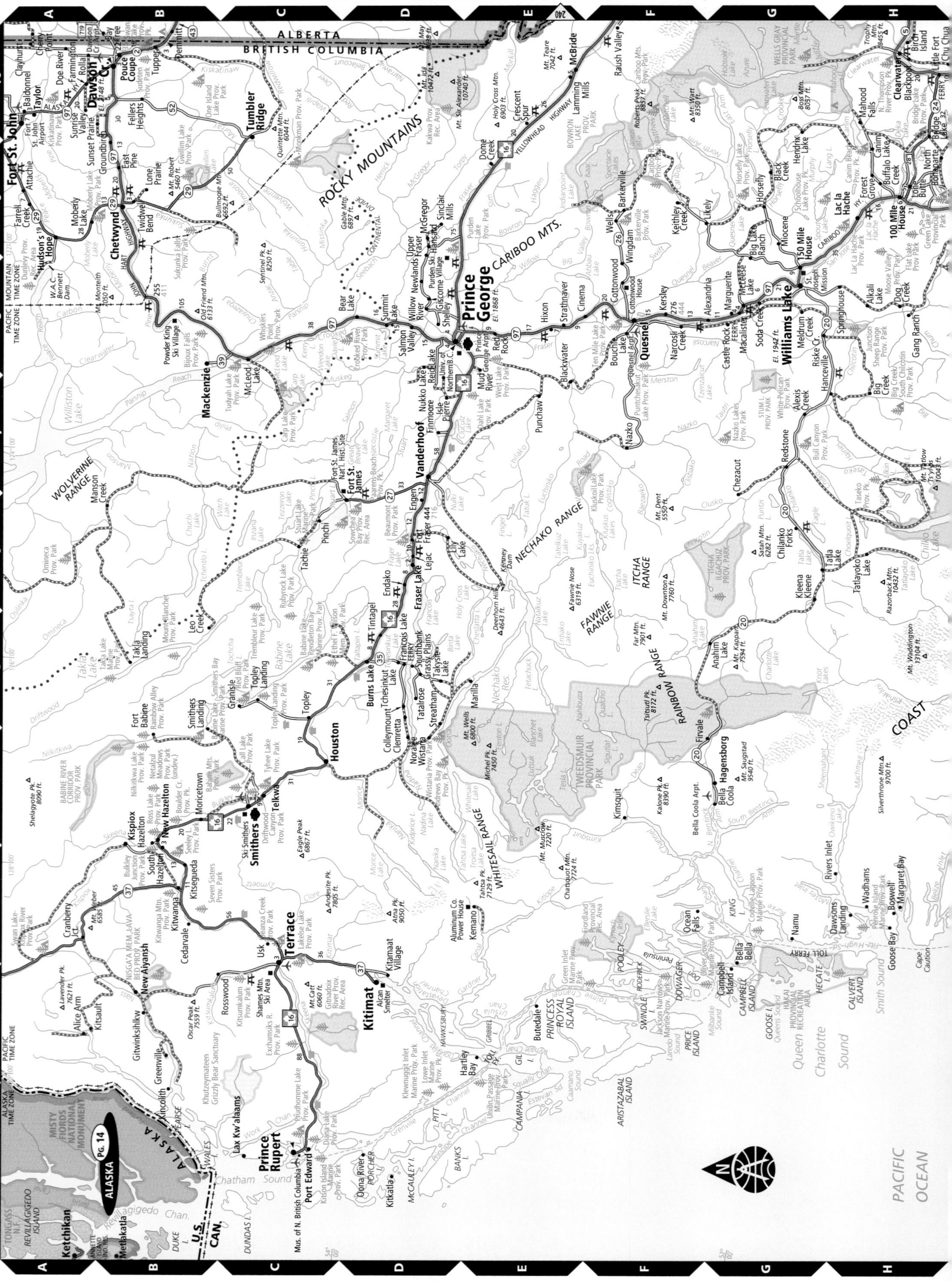

ALBERTA
BRITISH COLUMBIA

ROCKY MOUNTAINS

CARIBOO MTS.

WOLVERINE RANGE

NECHAKO RANGE

ITCHA RANGE

FAWNIE RANGE

RAINBOW RANGE

WHITESAIL RANGE

COAST

TWEEDSMUIR PROVINCIAL PARK

MISTY FIORDS NATIONAL MONUMENT

ALASKA Pg. 14

PACIFIC OCEAN

Queen Charlotte Sound

Hecate Strait

Fort St. John
Dawson Creek
Tumbler Ridge
Chetwynd
Hudson's Hope
Mackenzie
Prince George
Quesnel
Williams Lake
100 Mile House
150 Mile House
Vanderhoof
Fort St. James
Houston
Burns Lake
Smithers
Telkwa
New Hazelton
Kispiox
Moricetown
Terrace
Kitimat
Kitamaat Village
Prince Rupert
Port Edward
New Aiyansh
Ketchikan
Metlakatla

McBride
Crescent Spur
Dome Creek
Barkerville
Wells
Hixon
Strathnaver
Cinema
Cottonwood
Kersley
Alexandria
Marguerite
Soda Creek
Hanceville
Alexis Creek
Redstone
Tatla Lake
Kleena Kleene
Anahim Lake
Firvale
Hagensborg
Bella Coola
Ocean Falls
Bella Bella
Namu
Wadhams
Rivers Inlet
Goose Bay

PRINCESS ROYAL ISLAND
CAMPBELL ISLAND
PRICE ISLAND
ARISTAZABAL ISLAND
POOLEY ISLAND
SWINDLE ISLAND

U.S.
CAN.

N

Distance scale
One inch represents about 47 miles
0 10 20 30 40 mi
0 10 20 30 40 50 60 km

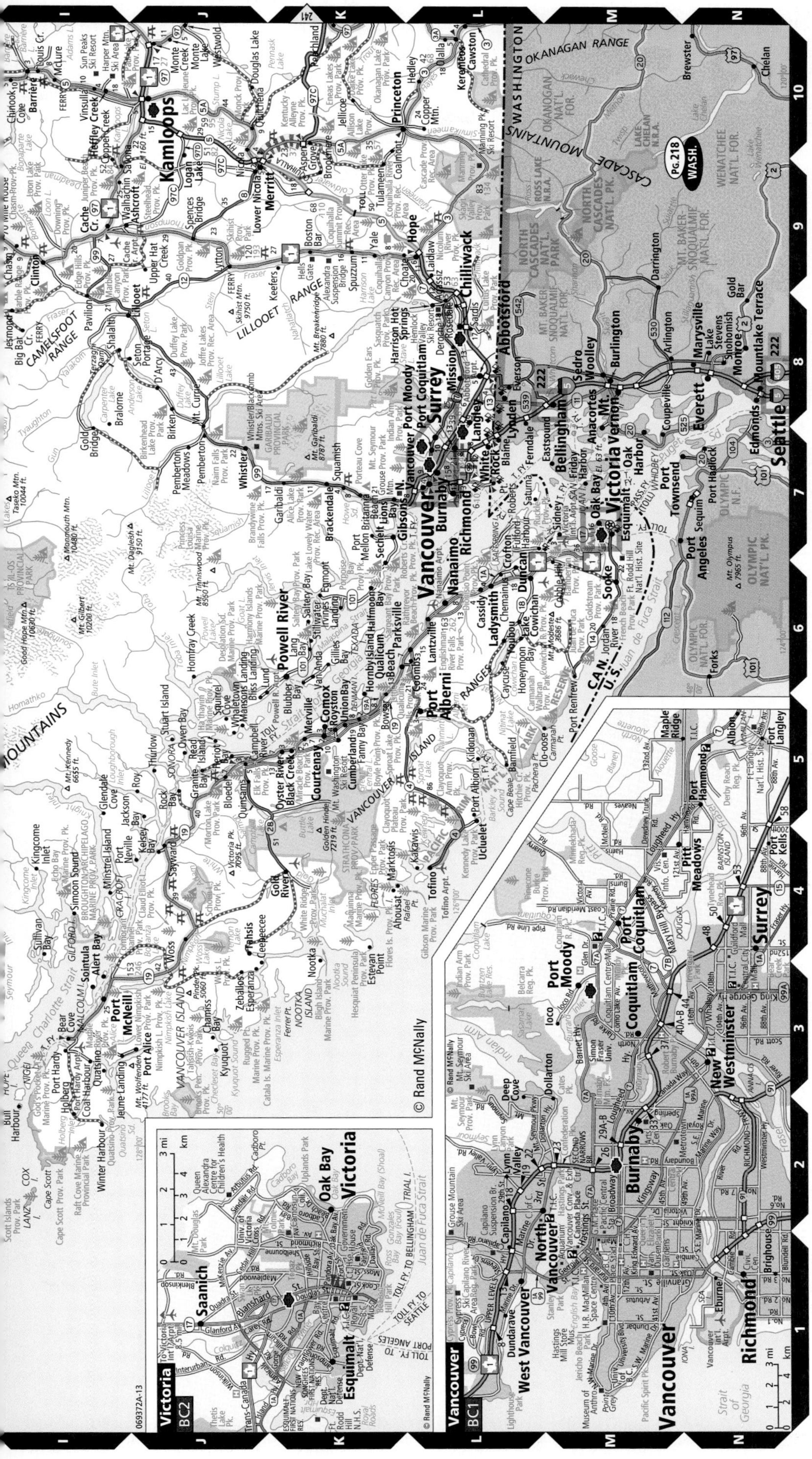

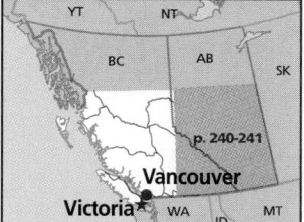

SYMBOLS

- Featured ride
- Scenic route
- Long-term construction
- Historic site or monument; Indian reservation or rancheria; military installation; point of interest; wildlife refuge
- Harley-Davidson dealership

BRITISH COLUMBIA MOTORCYCLE LAWS

Helmet use: Required

Eye protection: Not Required

Speed limit: As posted

Riding two abreast in one lane: Legal

BRITISH COLUMBIA RESOURCES

Road conditions or construction:
(800) 550-4997 (in BC only)
www.drivebc.ca

Highway Emergency Numbers: 911

Tourism:
(800) 435-5622
www.hellobc.com

Provincial motor vehicle information:
(604) 661-2800
www.icbc.com

HARLEY-DAVIDSON DEALERSHIPS

Harley-Davidson of Chilliwack, L-8
44768 Yale Rd. West **Chilliwack, BC**
(604) 792-7820
Lat N 49.145 **Lon** W 121.987

Kamloops Harley-Davidson, J-10
1465 Iron Mask Rd., Exit 366 **Kamloops, BC**
(250) 828-0622
Lat N 50.660 **Lon** W 120.403

Barnes Harley-Davidson, L-7
20091 Logan Ave. **Langley, BC**
(604) 534-6044
Lat N 49.111 **Lon** W 122.666

Cariboo Motorcycles, L-7
3066 St. Johns St. **Port Moody, BC**
(604) 461-3458
Lat N 49.277 **Lon** W 122.844

Harley-Davidson of Prince George, E-8
2626 Vance Rd. **Prince George, BC**
(250) 564-6667
Lat N 53.881 **Lon** W 122.774

Harley-Davidson of Smithers, C-4
Hwy. 16 West, Box 1086 **Smithers, BC**
(250) 847-5473
Lat N 54.780 **Lon** W 127.169

Trev Deeley Motorcycles, L-7
2375 Boundary Rd. **Vancouver, BC**
(604) 291-2453
Lat N 49.263 **Lon** W 123.024

Steve Drane Harley-Davidson, M-7
735 Cloverdale Ave. **Victoria, BC**
(250) 475-1345
Lat N 48.450 **Lon** W 123.372

randmcnally.com/eac

Express Access Codes: British Columbia BC   Alberta AB

Use Express Access Codes on
www.randmcnally.com for quick
access to online travel planning info,
road construction updates, and more.

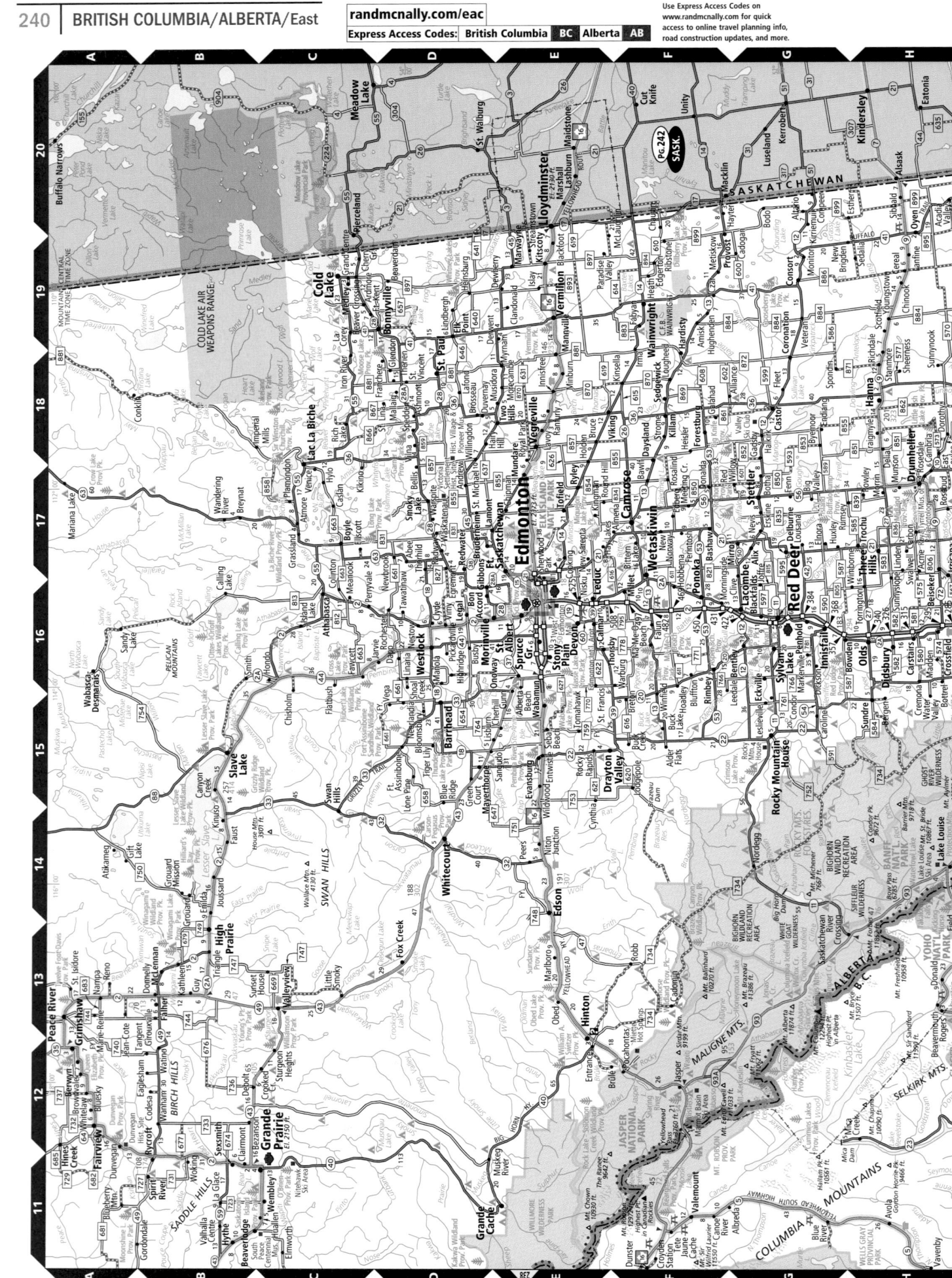

Distance scale
One inch represents about 47 miles

0 10 20 40 mi
0 10 20 30 40 50 60 km

© Rand McNally

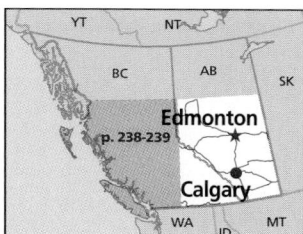

SYMBOLS

Featured ride

Long-term construction

Scenic route

Harley-Davidson dealership

ALBERTA MOTORCYCLE LAWS

Helmet use: Required

Eye protection: Not Required

Speed limit: As posted

Riding two abreast in one lane: Illegal

ALBERTA RESOURCES

Road conditions or construction:
(403) 246-5853
www.trans.gov.ab.ca

Highway Emergency Numbers: 911

Tourism:
1-800-252-3782
www.travelalberta.com

Provincial motor vehicle information:
(780) 427-2731
www.trans.gov.ab.ca

HARLEY-DAVIDSON DEALERSHIPS

Calgary Harley-Davidson, I-16
2245 Pegasus Rd. N.E. **Calgary, AB**
(403) 250-3141
Lat N 51.094 Lon W 114.010

Calgary Harley-Davidson, I-16
2000 Airport Trail N.E. **Calgary, AB**
(403) 398-3637
Lat N 51.131 Lon W 114.009

Kane's Motor Cycle Shop, I-16
914 11th St. S.E. **Calgary, AB**
(403) 269-8577
Lat N 51.042 Lon W 114.037

Harley-Davidson of Cranbrook, K-15
1817 Cranbrook St. North **Cranbrook, BC**
(250) 426-6606
Lat N 49.529 Lon W 115.748

Harley-Davidson of Medicine Hat, J-20
Hwy. 1, Box 150 1923 2nd Ave. **Dunmore, AB**
(403) 527-9235
Lat N 49.968 Lon W 110.587

Harley-Davidson Motorcycles of Edmonton, E-16
12506 124th St. **Edmonton, AB**
(780) 451-7857
Lat N 53.582 Lon W 113.536

Heritage Harley-Davidson, E-16
9743 51st Ave. **Edmonton, AB**
(780) 430-7200
Lat N 53.488 Lon W 113.476

Harley-Davidson Grande Prairie, C-11
12401 99 St. **Grande Prairie, AB**
(780) 814-5771
Lat N 55.193 Lon W 118.791

Kane's Harley-Davidson, K-11
1075 McCurdy Rd. **Kelowna, BC**
(250) 765-6666
Lat N 49.901 Lon W 119.405

Lethbridge Harley-Davidson, K-17
1505 2nd Ave. South **Lethbridge, AB**
(403) 320-1903
Lat N 49.698 Lon W 112.82

Gasoline Alley Harley-Davidson, G-16
37423 Hwy. 2 South **Red Deer, AB**
(403) 341-3040
Lat N 52.223 Lon W 113.814

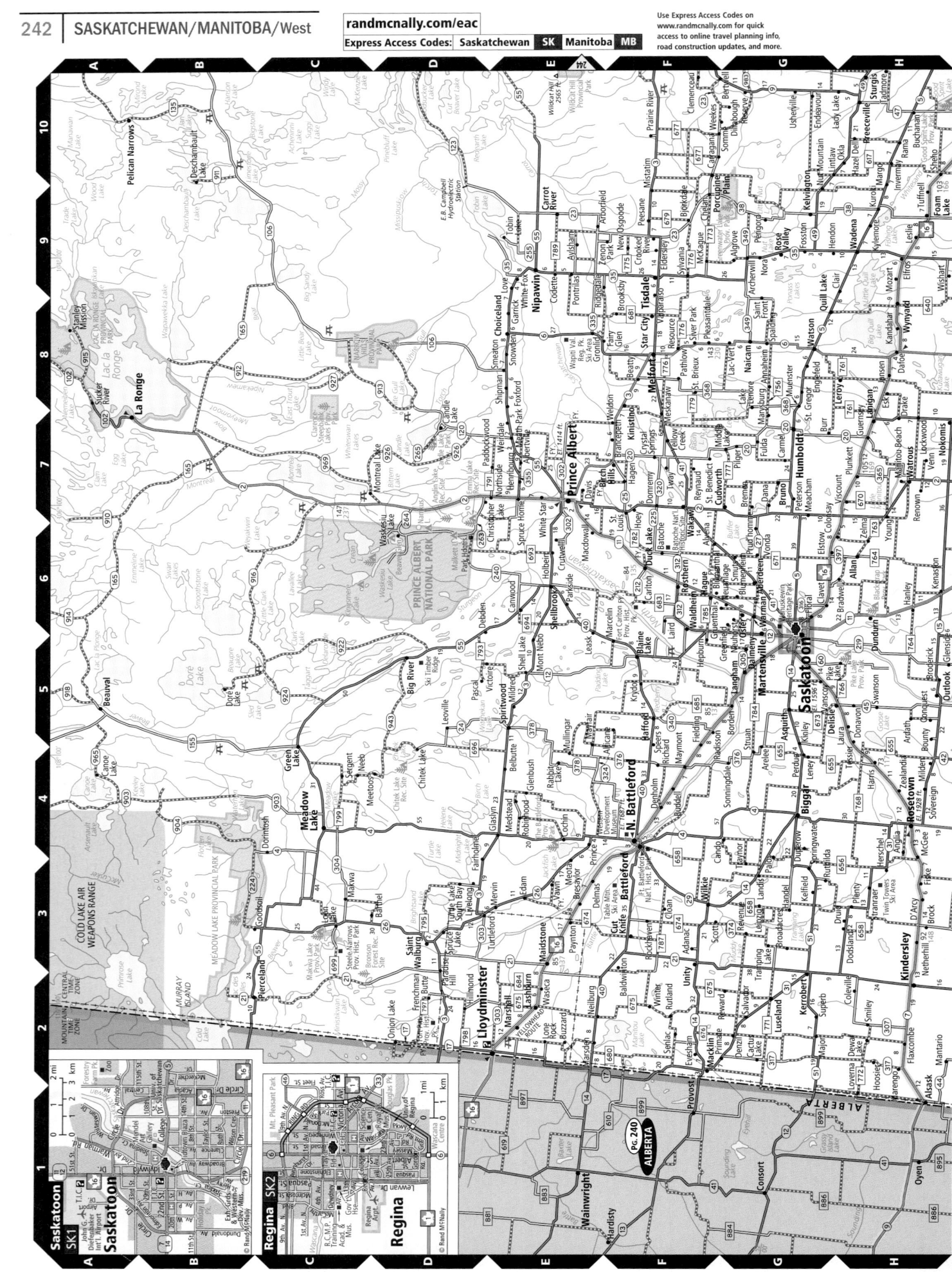

randmcnally.com/eac

Express Access Codes: Saskatchewan **SK** Manitoba **MB**

Use Express Access Codes on
www.randmcnally.com for quick
access to online travel planning info,
road construction updates, and more.

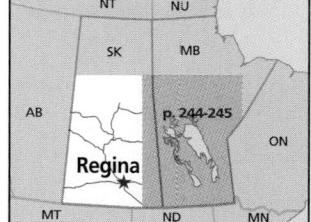

SYMBOLS

~~	Featured ride	═══	Scenic route
┼┼┼	Long-term construction	■	Historic site or monument; Indian reservation or rancheria; military installation; point of interest; wildlife refuge
⬤	Harley-Davidson dealership		

SASKATCHEWAN MOTORCYCLE LAWS

Helmet use: Required

Eye protection:
Required unless equipped with windscreen

Speed limit: As posted

Riding two abreast in one lane: Illegal

SASKATCHEWAN RESOURCES

Road conditions or construction:
(306) 787-7623 (Regina and surrounding areas; areas outside of province)
(306) 933-8333 (Saskatoon and surrounding areas)
(888) 335-7623 (All other areas)
www.highways.gov.sk.ca

Highway Emergency Numbers: 911

Tourism:
(877) 237-2273
www.sasktourism.com/

Provincial motor vehicle information:
(306) 751-1200
www.sgi.sk.ca/sgi_internet/index.html

SASKATCHEWAN CITY-TO-CITY MILEAGE

	ESTEVAN	LLOYDMINSTER	MEADOW LAKE	PRINCE ALBERT	REGINA	SASKATOON	SWIFT CURRENT	YORKTON
Flin Flon, MB	471	458	393	243	438	330	498	317
Hudson Bay	283	371	317	156	239	204	389	129
Kindersley	354	147	214	212	244	125	135	307
La Loche	662	335	220	319	539	379	510	554
La Ronge	508	350	235	148	379	235	404	383
Medicine Hat, AB	395	286	365	396	293	309	141	408
Melfort	299	275	221	60	173	108	276	175
Melville	135	383	394	246	91	210	241	26
Moose Jaw	149	311	322	223	47	138	109	162
North Battleford	368	88	99	127	245	85	191	288
Prince Albert	355	208	161		231	87	255	235
Regina	127	333	344	231		160	152	117
Saskatoon	283	173	184	87	160		168	203
Yorkton	161	376	387	235	117	203	267	

HARLEY-DAVIDSON DEALERSHIPS

⬤ **Prairie Motorcycle, K-8**
1355 McIntyre St. **Regina, SK**
(306) 522-1747
Lat N 50.458 **Lon** W 104.616

⬤ **Redline Harley-Davidson, G-5**
102 23rd St. East **Saskatoon, SK**
(306) 934-2750
Lat N 52.131 **Lon** W 106.664

⬤ **Harley-Davidson of Yorkton, I-10**
86 7th Ave. South **Yorkton, SK**
(306) 783-1999
Lat N 51.207 **Lon** W 102.453

Distance scale
One inch represents about 37 miles
0 10 20 30 mi
0 10 20 30 40 km

randmcnally.com/eac

Express Access Codes: Saskatchewan **SK** Manitoba **MB**

Use Express Access Codes on
www.randmcnally.com for quick
access to online travel planning info,
road construction updates, and more.

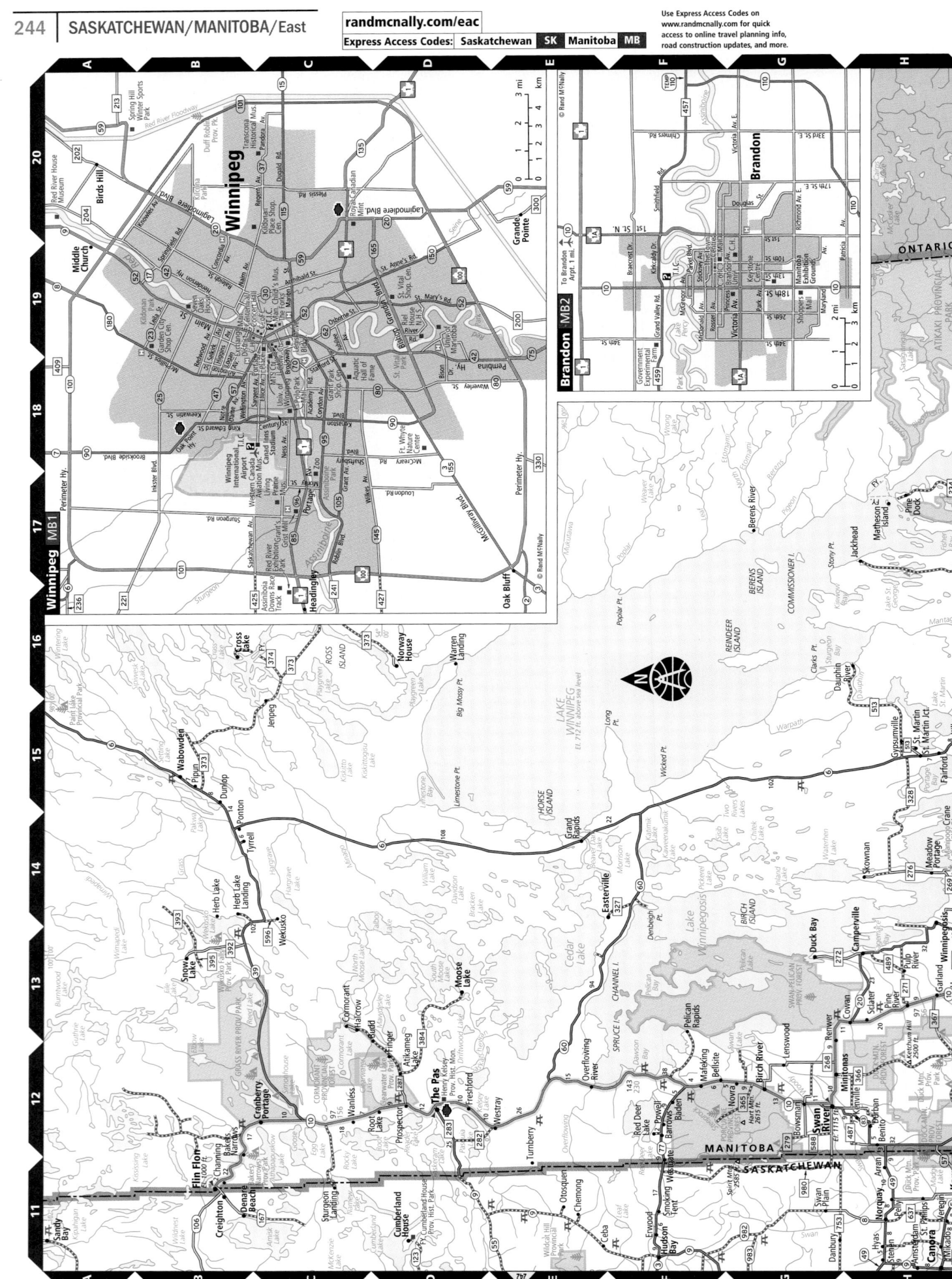

Winnipeg **MB1**

Brandon **MB2**

To Brandon
Arpt. 1 mi.

ONTARIO

MANITOBA

SASKATCHEWAN

© Rand McNally

Distance scale
One inch represents about 37 miles

© Rand McNally

SYMBOLS

- Featured ride
- Long-term construction
- Harley-Davidson dealership
- Scenic route
- Historic site or monument; Indian reservation or rancheria; military installation; point of interest; wildlife refuge

MANITOBA MOTORCYCLE LAWS

Helmet use: Required

Eye protection: Not Required

Speed limit: As posted

Riding two abreast in one lane: Illegal

MANITOBA RESOURCES

Road conditions or construction:
(877) 627-6237 (in MB)
(204) 945-3704
www.gov.mb.ca/roadinfo

Highway Emergency Numbers: 911

Tourism:
(800) 665-0040
www.travelmanitoba.com

Provincial motor vehicle information:
(204) 985-1100
www.gov.mb.ca/tgs

MANITOBA CITY-TO-CITY MILEAGE

	BRANDON	DAUPHIN	FLIN FLON	MORDEN	PORTAGE LA PRAIRIE	SWAN RIVER	VIRDEN	WINNIPEG
Ashern	199	125	366	180	117	232	246	111
Brandon		104	445	133	80	209	50	134
Dauphin	104		343	209	138	107	151	192
Grand Rapids	354	280	255	335	272	213	401	266
Killarney	62	166	507	86	120	271	105	147
Minnedosa	34	75	416	152	81	180	81	135
Pine Falls	214	266	543	163	132	369	259	80
Portage la Prairie	80	138	483	69		245	127	52
Riverton	203	170	449	153	121	277	250	75
Russell	113	91	344	236	164	108	73	218
Selkirk	157	209	488	101	75	314	204	23
The Pas	353	251	92	454	391	144	325	385
Thompson	557	483	241	538	475	385	566	469
Winnipeg	134	192	477	75	52	52	181	

HARLEY-DAVIDSON DEALERSHIPS

Gaslight Harley-Davidson, M-16
999 Thornhill St. **Morden, MB**
(204) 822-5877
Lat N 49.192 **Lon** W 98.128

Northland Leisure Products, D-12
17th St. Settee **The Pas, MB**
(204) 623-3504
Lat N 53.826 **Lon** W 101.256

Harley-Davidson Winnipeg, L-17
1377 Niakwa Rd. East **Winnipeg, MB**
(204) 254-3974
Lat N 49.857 **Lon** W 97.039

Lone Star Motorcycles, K-17
231 Oak Point Hwy. **Winnipeg, MB**
(204) 633-2453
Lat N 49.933 **Lon** W 97.215

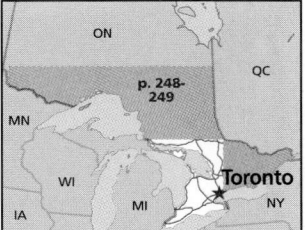

ONTARIO MOTORCYCLE LAWS

Helmet use: Required

Eye protection: Not Required

Speed limit: As posted

Riding two abreast in one lane: Not illegal

ONTARIO RESOURCES

Road conditions or construction:
(800) 268-4686 (in ON)
(416) 235-4686 (in area codes 416 and 905)
www.mto.gov.on.ca

Highway Emergency Numbers: 911

Tourism:
(800) 668-2746
www.ontariotravel.net

Provincial motor vehicle information:
(416) 235-4686
www.mto.gov.on.ca

HARLEY-DAVIDSON DEALERSHIPS

Barrie Harley-Davidson, H-10
311 Byrne Dr. **Barrie**
(705) 728-5322
Lat N 44.337 Lon W 79.688

Dukes Harley-Davidson, M-5
Five Classic Car Dr. **Blenheim**
(519) 354-0650
Lat N 42.327 Lon W 81.999

Clare's Cycle & Sports, K-10
799 Hwy. 20 West **Fenwick**
(905) 892-2664
Lat N 43.084 Lon W 79.352

Poole's Cycle, K-9
215 Parkdale Ave. North **Hamilton**
(905) 545-0687
Lat N 43.243 Lon W 79.789

Kitchener Harley-Davidson, J-8
2255 Kingsway Dr. **Kitchener**
(519) 893-0493
Lat N 43.434 Lon W 80.451

The Shop, B-7
112 Fielding Rd. **Lively**
(705) 682-4463
Lat N 46.441 Lon W 81.098

Rocky's Harley-Davidson of London, K-7
900 Wilton Grove Rd. **London**
(519) 438-1450
Lat N 42.928 Lon W 81.195

Jacox Harley-Davidson, J-9
2815 Argentia Rd. **Mississauga**
(905) 858-0966
Lat N 43.600 Lon W 79.774

Fox Harley-Davidson, G-7
123003 Story Book Park Rd. **Owen Sound**
(519) 371-6666
Lat N 44.564 Lon W 80.857

Davies Harley-Davidson, I-10
8779 Yonge St. **Richmond Hill**
(905) 709-1340
Lat N 43.843 Lon W 79.430

Motorsport Custom Accessories, K-5
1375 Confederation St. **Sarnia**
(519) 337-5601
Lat N 42.960 Lon W 82.355

Harley-Davidson of Toronto, I-10
578 Front St. West **Toronto**
(416) 703-HOGS
Lat N 43.641 Lon W 79.401

Thunder Road Harley-Davidson, M-3
2139 Huron Church Rd. **Windsor**
(519) 966-1520
Lat N 42.276 Lon W 83.051

randmcnally.com/eac

Express Access Code: ON

Use Express Access Codes on
www.randmcnally.com for quick
access to online travel planning info,
road construction updates, and more.

Distance scale
One inch represents about 28 miles

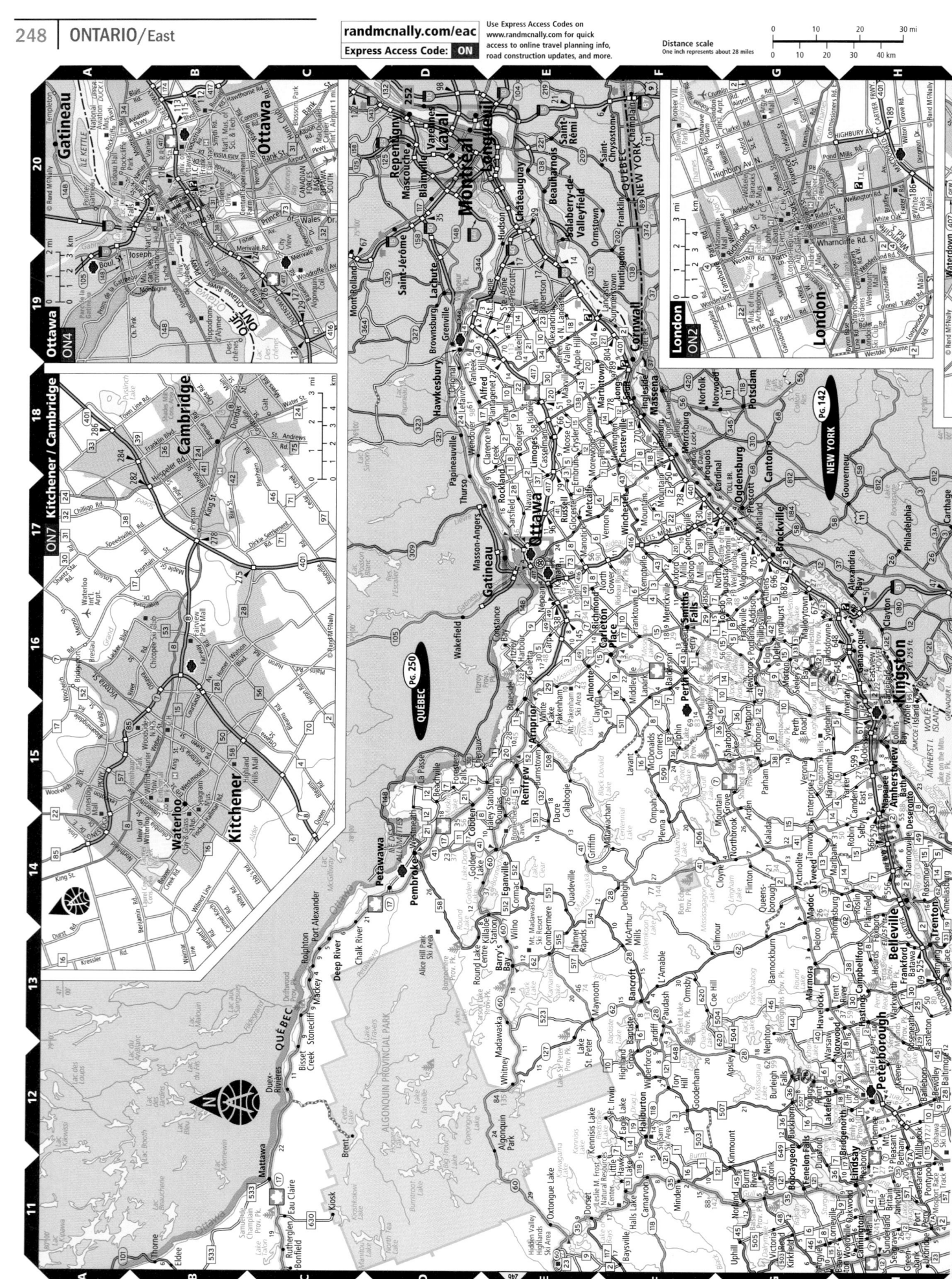

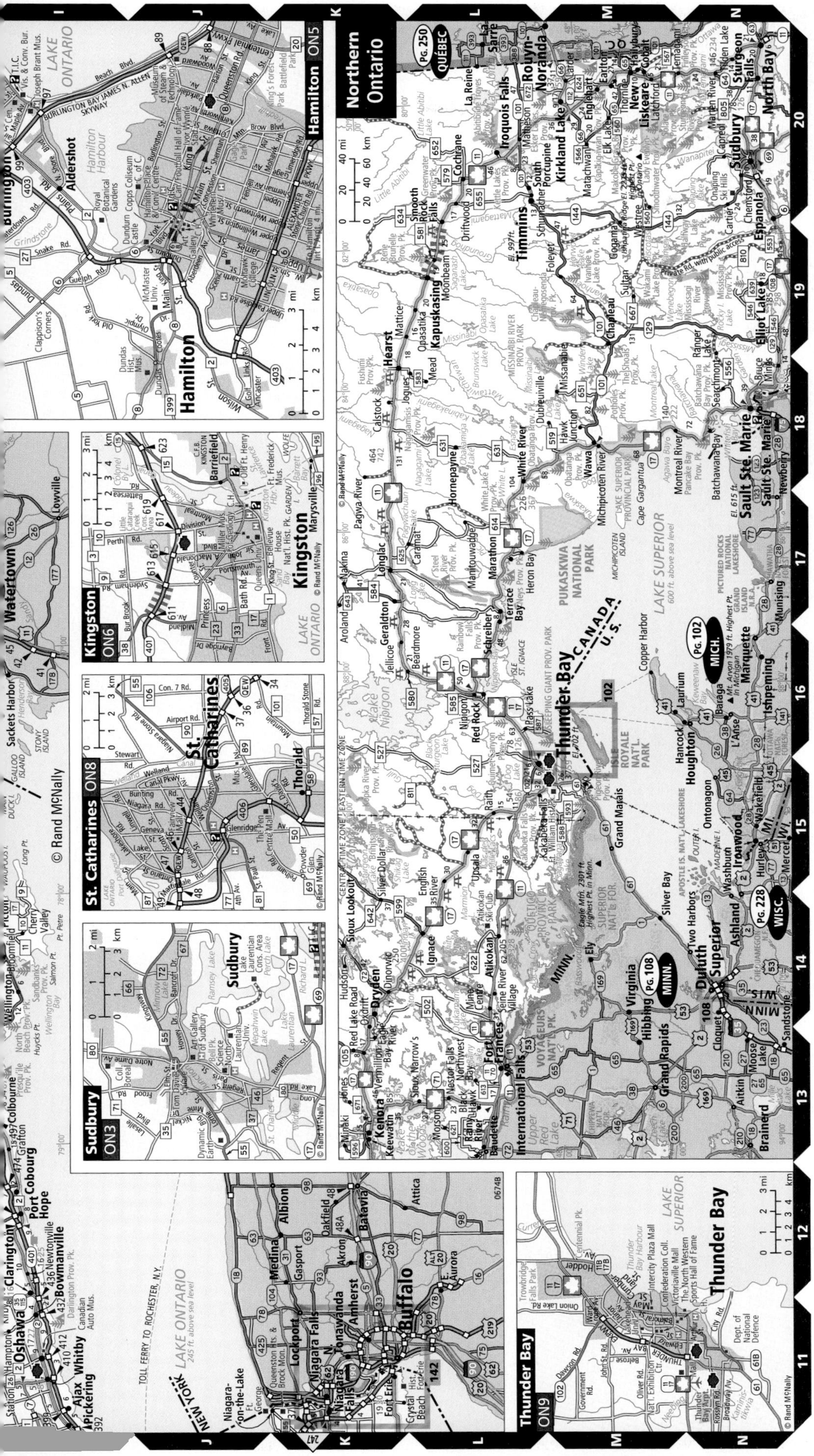

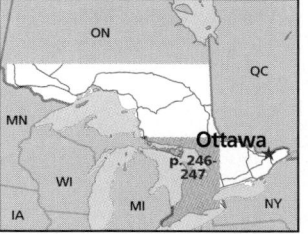

Ottawa p. 246-247

SYMBOLS

- ▬▬▬ Featured ride
- ▬▬▬ Scenic route
- ┼┼┼ Long-term construction
- ⬢ Harley-Davidson dealership

CITY-TO-CITY MILEAGE

	KINGSTON	LONDON	NIAGARA FALLS	OTTAWA	SUDBURY	THUNDER BAY	TORONTO	WINDSOR
Barrie	210	160	132	269	189	806	62	272
Hamilton	206	85	48	294	281	898	47	197
Kenora	1304	1274	1246	1225	930	307	1176	1386
Kingston		275	247	117	380	997	161	387
London	275		138	363	350	967	125	120
Montréal, QC	187	456	428	133	441	1002	342	568
Niagara Falls	247	138		335	322	939	88	250
Ottawa	117	363	335		308	918	249	475
Owen Sound	285	144	163	343	253	870	121	275
Pembroke	156	361	333	95	208	818	247	473
Peterborough	122	196	168	171	258	875	82	308
Sarnia	341	71	204	429	416	1033	191	99
Sault Ste. Marie	557	527	499	494	183	440	429	639
Sudbury	380	350	322	308		623	252	462
Thunder Bay	997	967	939	918	623		869	1079
Timmins	516	533	505	455	181	519	435	645
Toronto	161	125	88	249	252	869		237
Windsor	387	120	250	475	462	1079	237	

HARLEY-DAVIDSON DEALERSHIPS

Goulet Motosports, D-19
189 John St. **Hawkesbury**
(613) 632-3462
Lat N 45.611 Lon W 74.605

MotoSport Plus Kingston, H-15
295 Dalton Ave. **Kingston**
(613) 544-4600
Lat N 44.268 Lon W 76.511

Freedom Harley-Davidson, E-16
1450 Merivale Rd. **Nepean (Ottawa)**
(613) 228-9449
Lat N 45.363 Lon W 75.733

Mackie Harley-Davidson, I-11
880 Champlain Ave. **Oshawa**
(905) 434-6550
Lat N 43.874 Lon W 78.887

Harley-Davidson of Ottawa, E-17
505 Industrial Ave. **Ottawa**
(613) 736-8899
Lat N 45.412 Lon W 75.645

Pete's Sales & Service, D-14
2107 Petawawa Blvd. **Pembroke**
(613) 735-3711
Lat N 45.829 Lon W 77.109

Cameron Motorcycle Sales, F-15
R.R. 7, 6 mi. west of Perth **Perth**
(613) 267-3873
Lat N 44.916 Lon W 76.352

Longley Harley-Davidson of Peterborough, H-12
1097 Hwy. 7 East **Peterborough**
(705) 745-0421
Lat N 44.322 Lon W 78.264

Thunder Bay Harley-Davidson, M-15
636 Arthur St. West **Thunder Bay**
(807) 577-6221
Lat N 48.381 Lon W 89.297

Thunder Bay Harley-Davidson, M-15
1330 Rosslyn Rd. **Thunder Bay**
(807) 577-6221
Lat N 48.363 Lon W 89.323

© Rand McNally

randmcnally.com/eac

Express Access Code: QC

Use Express Access Codes on www.randmcnally.com for quick access to online travel planning info, road construction updates, and more.

Distance scale
One inch represents about 38 miles

0   10   20   30 mi
0   10   20   30   40 km

Central Montréal QC1

Trois-Rivières QC5

Québec QC3

ONTARIO

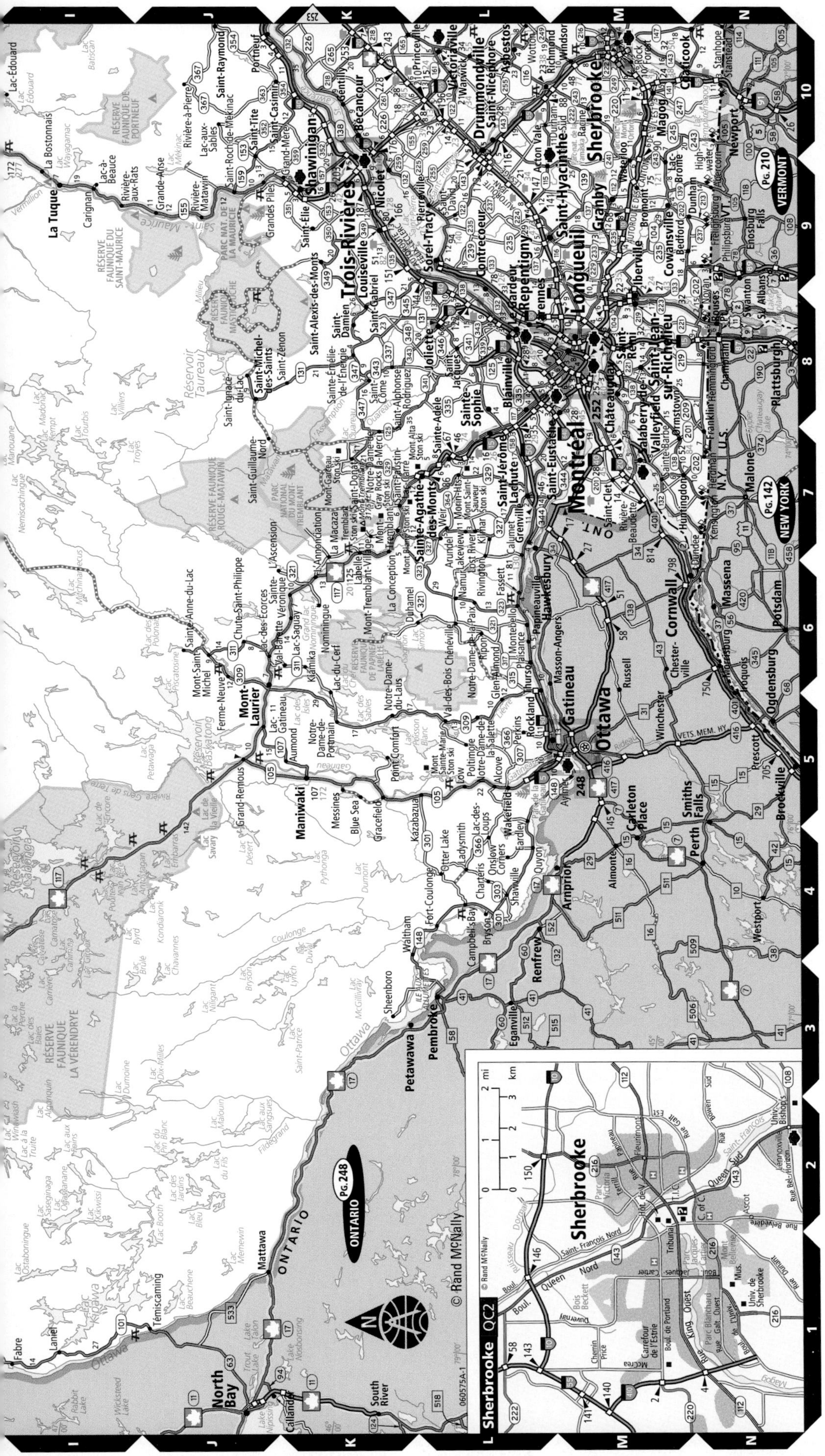

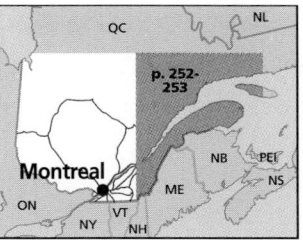

SYMBOLS

- Featured ride
- Long-term construction
- Harley-Davidson dealership
- Scenic route
- Historic site or monument; Indian reservation or rancheria; military installation; point of interest; wildlife refuge

HARLEY-DAVIDSON DEALERSHIPS

Boileau Moto Service Enrg., L-10
888 Route 116 Ouest **Acton Vale**
(450) 549-4341
Lat N 45.579 Lon W 72.468

Centre de Moto Harley-Davidson, M-8
8705 Boul. Taschereau **Brossard**
(450) 674-3986
Lat N 45.440 Lon W 73.473

Harley-Davidson de L'Outaouais, M-5
22 Boul. Mont-Bleu **Gatineau**
(819) 772-8008
Lat N 45.462 Lon W 75.745

L'Ami Denis, M-10
2 Rue Queen **Lennoxville**
(819) 565-1376
Lat N 45.363 Lon W 71.856

Harley-Davidson Montréal, L-8
6695 St.-Jacques West **Montréal**
(514) 483-6686
Lat N 45.459 Lon W 73.628

Blanchette (The Shop), L-8
515 Rue Leclerc **Repentigny**
(450) 582-2442
Lat N 45.748 Lon W 73.451

N.J.N. Motosport, G-10
450 Rue Principal **Saint-Prime**
(418) 251-4830
Lat N 48.588 Lon W 72.330

Shawinigan Harley-Davidson, K-9
6033 Boul. de Hêtre **Shawinigan**
(819) 539-1450
Lat N 46.571 Lon W 72.724

Bibeau Moto Sport, G-3
372 Rue Gareau **Val d'Or (Jacola)**
(819) 824-2541
Lat N 48.108 Lon W 77.815

Sport Boutin, M-7
2000 Boul. Hébert **Valleyfield**
(450) 373-6565
Lat N 45.269 Lon W 74.097

G.P. Motosports, L-10
12 Bl. Arthabaska (Route 116) **Victoriaville**
(819) 758-8830
Lat N 46.088 Lon W 71.980

Moto Sport Blanchette, K-9
4350 Arsenault **Ville de Becancourt**
(819) 233-3303
Lat N 46.269 Lon W 72.488

© Rand McNally

randmcnally.com/eac
Express Access Code: QC

Use Express Access Codes on
www.randmcnally.com for quick
access to online travel planning info,
road construction updates, and more.

Distance scale
One inch represents about 38 miles

0   10   20   30 mi
0 10 20 30 40 km

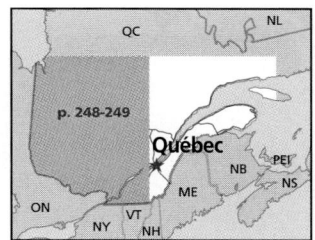

SYMBOLS

⟋ Featured ride		⟋ Scenic route	
┼┼┼┼ Long-term construction		■ Historic site or monument; Indian reservation or rancheria; military installation; point of interest; wildlife refuge	
Harley-Davidson dealership			

QUÉBEC MOTORCYCLE LAWS

Helmet use: Required

Eye protection: Not Required

Speed limit: As posted

Riding two abreast in one lane: Legal only in a zig-zag formation

QUÉBEC RESOURCES

Road conditions or construction:
(888) 355-0511
(877) 393-2363 (in Québec)
(418) 684-2363 (in Québec City)
(514) 284-2363 (in Montréal)
www.mtq.gouv.qc.ca/fr/index.asp (French)
www.mtq.gouv.qc.ca/en/index.asp (English)

Highway Emergency Numbers: 911

Tourism:
(877) 266-5687
www.bonjourquebec.com

Provincial motor vehicle information:
(418) 643-7620
www.saaq.gouv.qc.ca/en/index.html

HARLEY-DAVIDSON DEALERSHIPS

Hamilton & Bourassa, F-15
324 Boul. Lasalle **Baie Comeau**
(418) 296-9191
Lat N 49.214 **Lon** W 68.194

RPM Moto Plus, G-12
2510 Rue Dubose **Jonquière**
(418) 699-7766
Lat N 48.402 **Lon** W 71.159

Harley-Davidson Laval, L-14
4501 Autoroute Laval West **Laval**
(450) 973-4501
Lat N 45.560 **Lon** W 73.791

New Richmond Mcanique Sport, G-18
162 Route 132 East **New Richmond**
(418) 392-5281
Lat N 48.256 **Lon** W 65.719

Atelier de Mcanique Prmont, J-11
2495 Boul. Hamel Ouest **Québec**
(418) 683-1340
Lat N 46.806 **Lon** W 71.300

Harley-Davidson of Rimouski, G-15
424 Montée Industrielle **Rimouski**
(418) 724-0883
Lat N 48.449 **Lon** W 68.495

randmcnally.com/eac **New Brunswick** NB **Nova Scotia** NS

Express Access Codes: **Newfoundland & Lab.** NL **Prince Edward Island** PE

Use Express Access Codes on www.randmcnally.com for quick access to online travel planning info, road construction updates, and more.

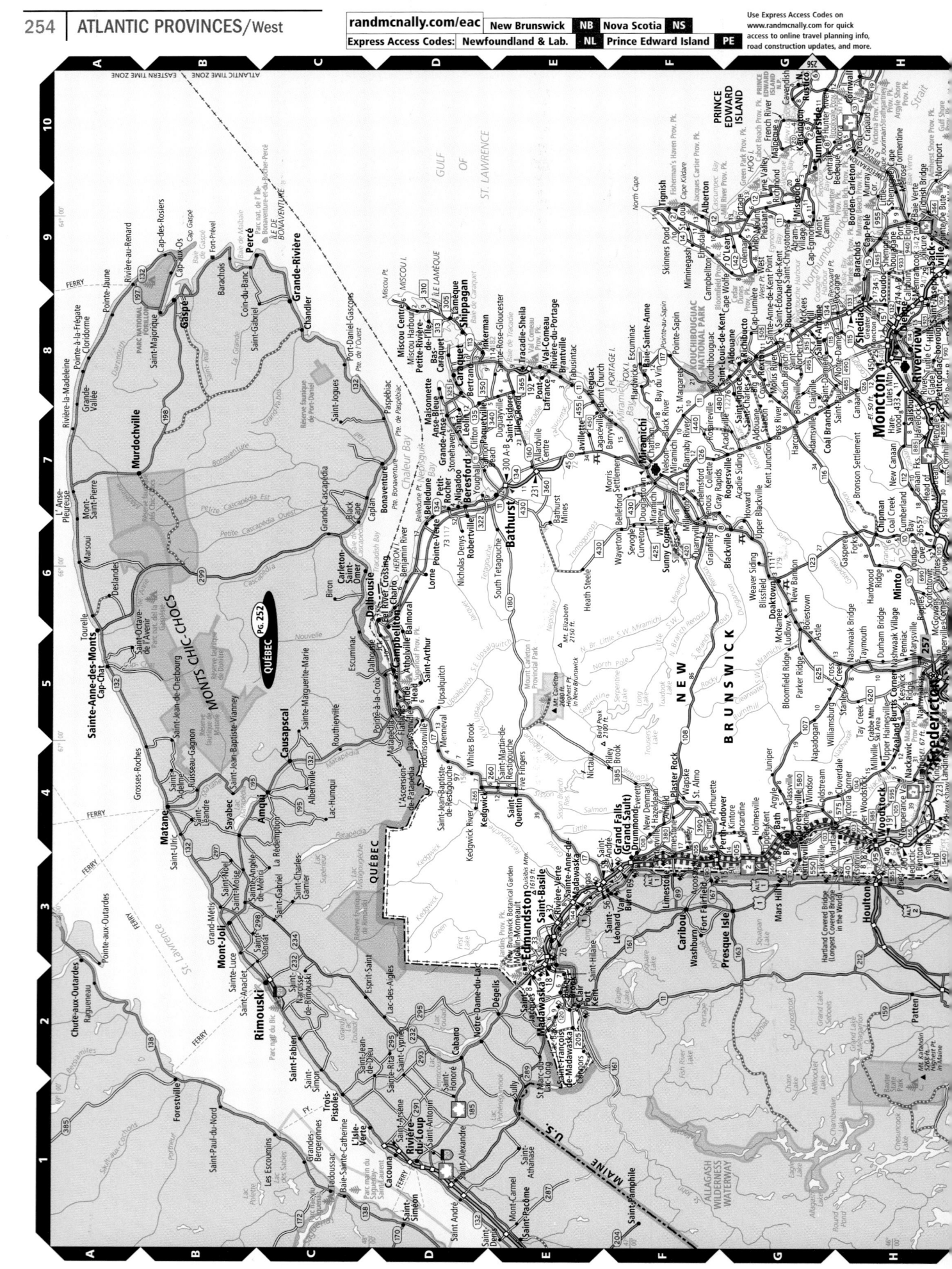

Distance scale
One inch represents about 33 miles

0 10 20 30 mi
0 10 20 30 40 km

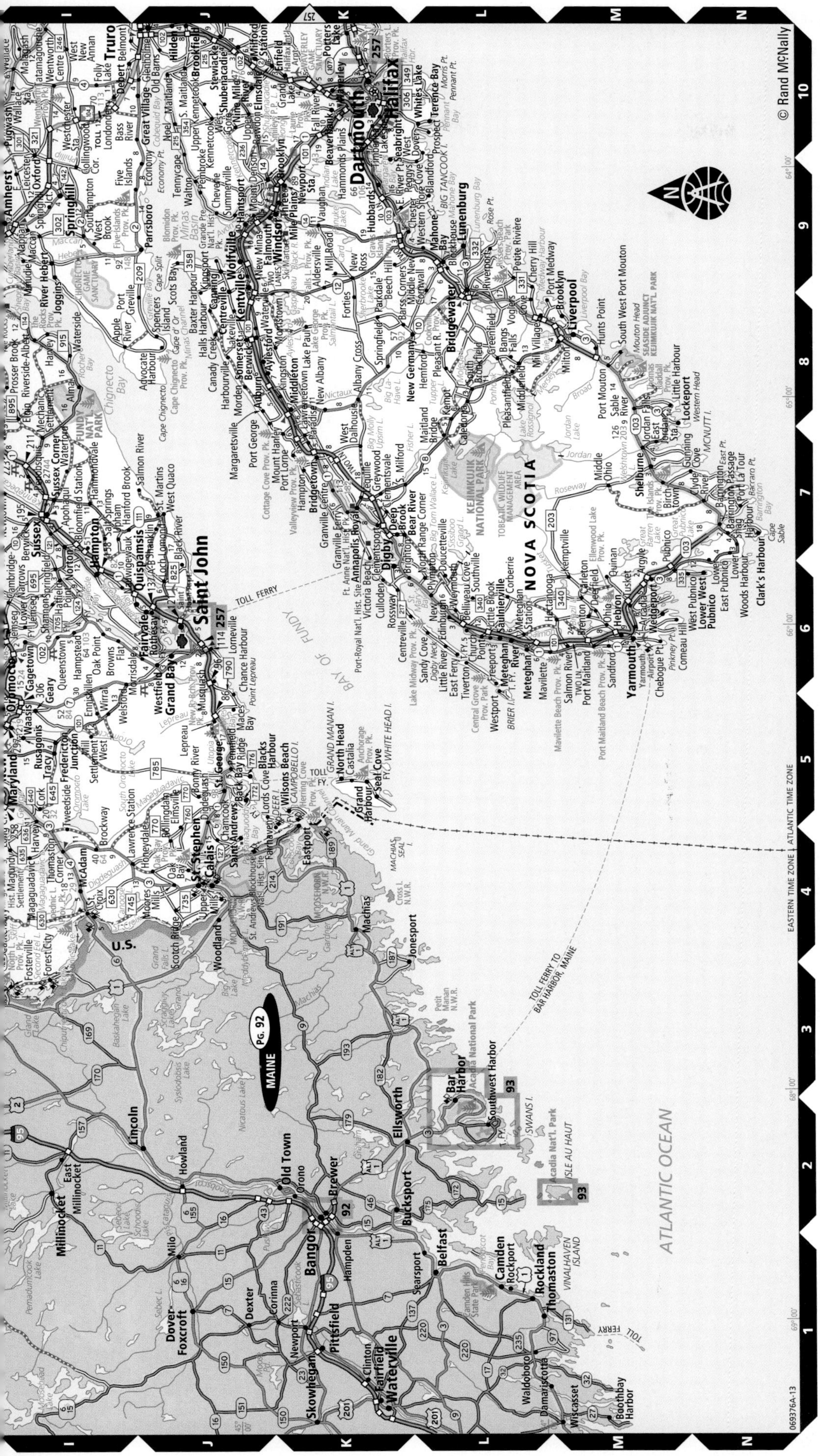

© Rand McNally

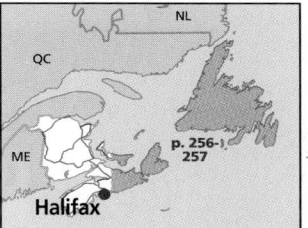

Halifax

SYMBOLS

- ▨ Featured ride
- ▥ Scenic route
- ▦ Long-term construction
- Harley-Davidson dealership
- ■ Historic site or monument; Indian reservation or rancheria; military installation; point of interest; wildlife refuge

NEW BRUNSWICK, NOVA SCOTIA, AND PRINCE EDWARD ISLAND MOTORCYCLE LAWS

Helmet use: Required

Eye protection: Not Required

Speed limit: As posted

Riding two abreast in one lane:
New Brunswick: Illegal
Nova Scotia and Prince Edward Island: Legal

NEW BRUNSWICK RESOURCES

Road conditions or construction:
(800) 561-4063 (in NB)
www.gnb.ca/0113

Highway Emergency Numbers: 911

Tourism:
(800) 561-0123
www.tourismnbcanada.com

Provincial motor vehicle information:
(506) 453-2410
www.snb.ca

NOVA SCOTIA RESOURCES

Road conditions or construction:
(800) 307-7669 (in NS)
(902) 424 3933
www.gov.ns.ca

Highway Emergency Numbers: 911

Tourism:
(800) 565-0000
novascotia.com

Provincial motor vehicle information:
(902) 424-5851
www.gov.ns.ca/snsmr/rmv

PRINCE EDWARD ISLAND RESOURCES

Road conditions or construction:
(902) 368-4770
www.gov.pe.ca/roadconditions

Highway Emergency Numbers: 911

Tourism:
(888) 734-7529
www.peiplay.com

Provincial motor vehicle information:
(902) 368-5100
www.gov.pe.ca/tpw/

HARLEY-DAVIDSON DEALERSHIPS

- **Privateers Harley-Davidson, K-10**
  100 Susie Lake Crescent, Unit 10 Halifax, NS
  (902) 444-HOGS
  Lat N 44.651 Lon W 63.677

- **J.H. Stewart, F-7**
  564 Water St. Miramichi, NB
  (506) 622-3405
  Lat N 47.002 Lon W 65.546

- **Toys for Big Boys, H-8**
  633 Salisbury Rd. Moncton, NB
  (506) 858-8088
  Lat N 46.070 Lon W 64.831

- **Eldridge's Harley-Davidson, J-6**
  1230 Fairville Blvd. Saint John, NB
  (506) 635-1223
  Lat N 45.253 Lon W 66.098

069376A-13

randmcnally.com/eac
New Brunswick NB Nova Scotia NS
Express Access Codes: Newfoundland & Lab. NL Prince Edward Island PE

Use Express Access Codes on
www.randmcnally.com for quick
access to online travel planning info,
road construction updates, and more.

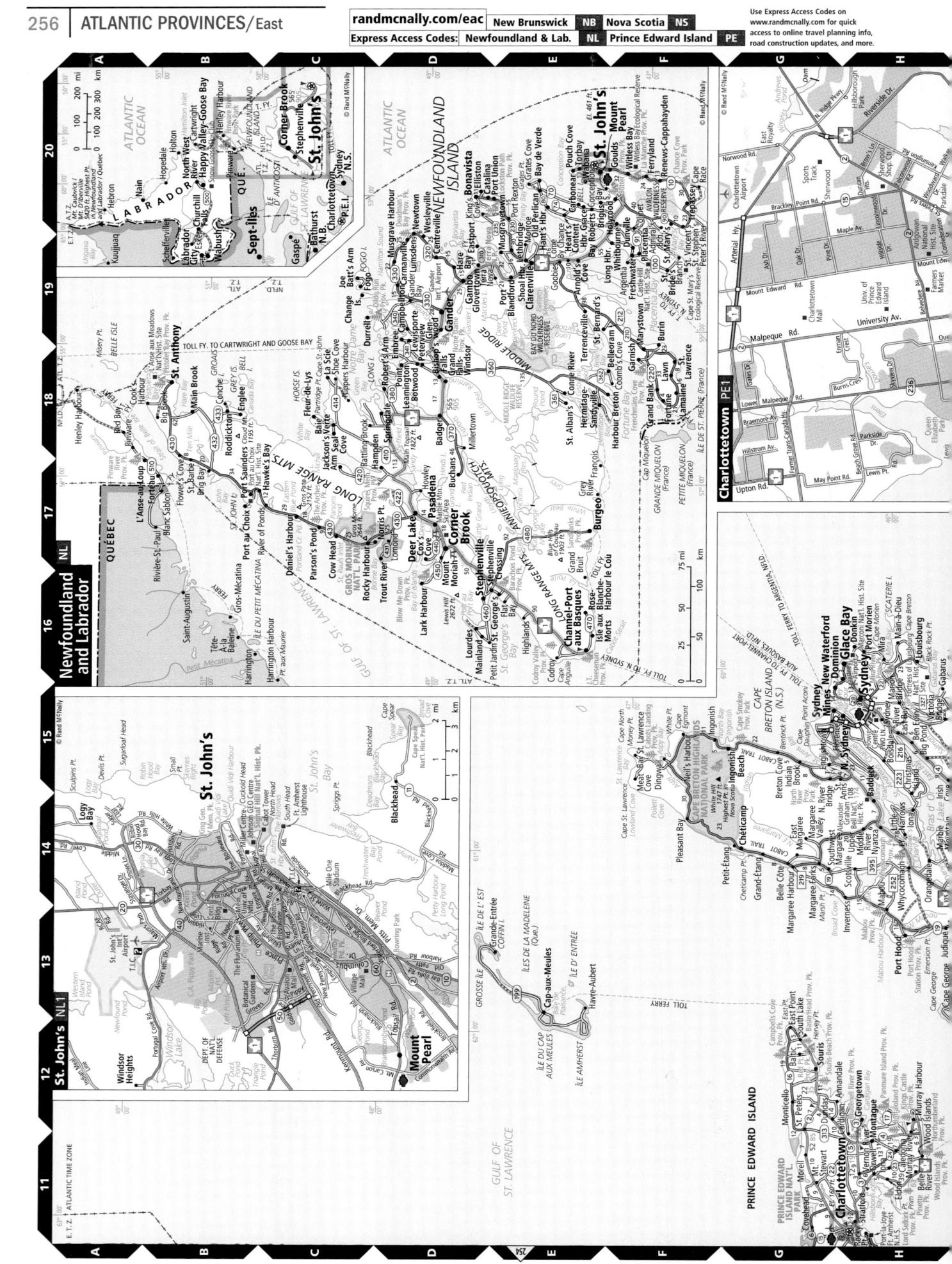

Distance scale
One inch represents about 33 miles
0 10 20 30 mi
0 10 20 30 40 km

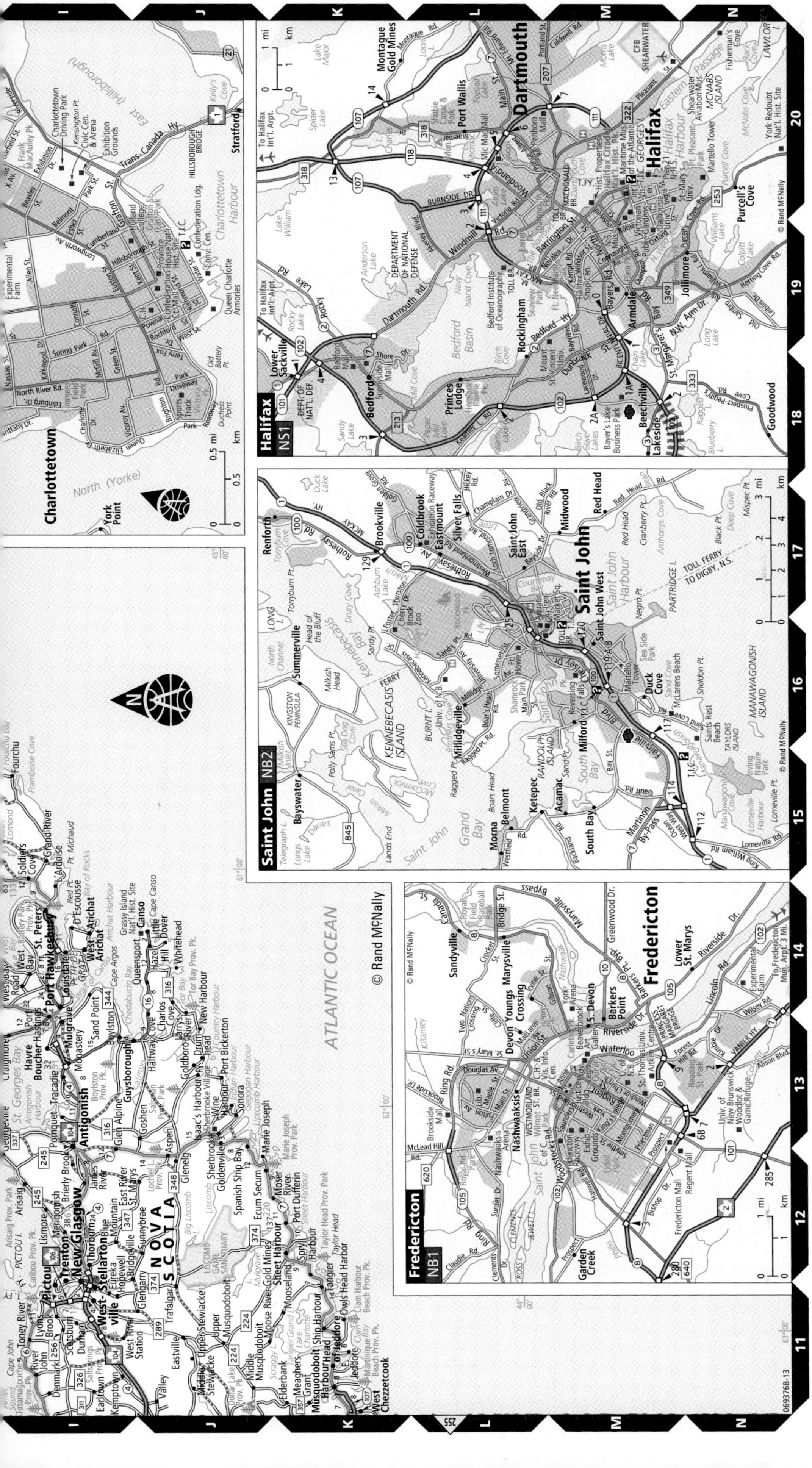

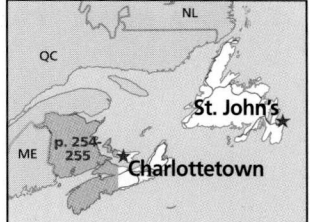

SYMBOLS

- Featured ride
- Scenic route
- Long-term construction
- Historic site or monument; Indian reservation or rancheria; military installation; point of interest; wildlife refuge
- Harley-Davidson dealership

NEWFOUNDLAND & LABRADOR MOTORCYCLE LAWS

Helmet use: Required

Eye protection:
Required unless equipped with windscreen

Speed limit: As posted

Riding two abreast in one lane: Illegal

NEWFOUNDLAND & LABRADOR RESOURCES

Road conditions or construction:
www.roads.gov.nf.ca
www.roads.gov.nl.ca

Highway Emergency Numbers: 911

Tourism:
(800) 563-6353
(709) 729-2830
www.gov.nf.ca/tourism

Provincial motor vehicle information:
(709) 729-2519
www.gov.nl.ca/services/transport.stm

CITY-TO-CITY MILEAGE

	CHARLOTTETOWN, PE	EDMUNDSTON, NB	FREDERICTON, NB	HALIFAX, NS	MONCTON, NB	SAINT JOHN, NB	ST. JOHN'S, NL	SYDNEY, NS
Amherst, NS	93	336	158	135	38	136	945†	263
Bathurst, NB	249	193	158	306	131	229	1116†	434
Campbellton, NB	319	129	238	386	211	309	1196†	514
Charlottetown, PE		417†	239†	157†	119	218	597	247
Corner Brook, NL	482	860†	682	519†	562†	660†	427	267†
Edmundston, NB	422		177	471	294	246	1281†	599
Fredericton, NB	241	177		293	116	70	1103†	421
Gander, NL	688	1080†	902	739†	782†	880†	201	487†
Grand Falls, NB	384	37	139	433	256	208	1243	561
Halifax, NS	164	471	293		173	271	940†	258
Moncton, NB	119	294	116	173		94	983†	301
New Glasgow, NS	67	446	268	105	148	246	837†	155
Saint John, NB	218	246	70	271	94		1081†	399
St. John's, NL	597	1281†	1103†	940†	983†	1081†		688†
St. Stephen, NB	321	220	79	341	164	70	1151†	469
Sydney, NS	247	599	421	258	301	399	688†	
Truro, NS	104	409	231	64	111	209	878†	196
Yarmouth, NS	326	356	180	186	365	110	1132	450

† Via ferry

HARLEY-DAVIDSON DEALERSHIPS

Cycle City and Recreation, E-20
1073 Topsail Rd. **Mount Pearl, NL**
(709) 364-9051
Lat N 47.525 **Lon** W 52.808

Ramsay's Harley-Davidson, H-15
616 Keltic Dr. **Sydney, NS**
(902) 539-1730 or 7644
Lat N 46.127 **Lon** W 60.252

Red Rock Harley-Davidson, G-11
5 Campbell Rd. **Winsloe (Charlottetown), PEI**
(902) 368-8324
Lat N 46.295 **Lon** W 63.179

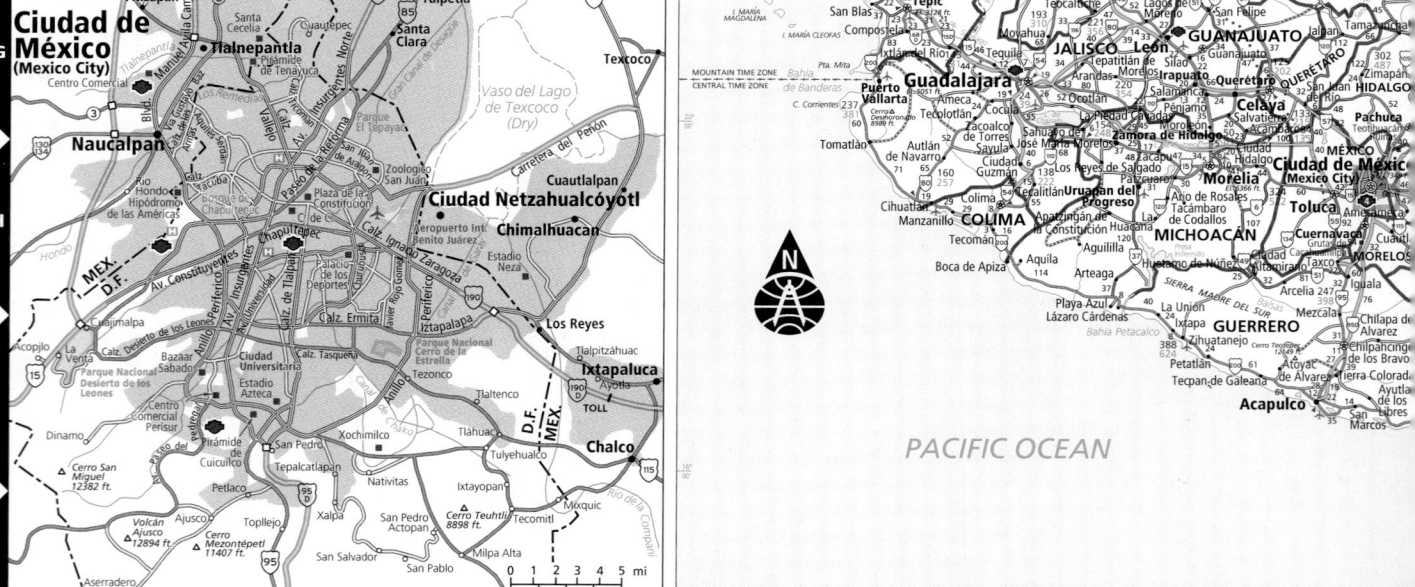

United States Citizens Visiting Mexico

To visit Mexico, tourists need proof of U.S. citizenship. Native-born citizens will need either a U.S. passport or a certified birth certificate plus a photo ID. Naturalized citizens should carry their naturalization certificate to ensure entry into Mexico and re-entry into the United States.

Tourist cards are valid for any period up to six months, are free of charge, and are required for all persons, regardless of age, to visit the interior of Mexico. Cards may be obtained from Mexican border authorities, from Consuls of Mexico, or from Federal Delegates in major cities.

Obtain $27 automobile permit (pay with Master Card or Visa credit card only) good for six months, from the Mexican Customs Office at the border, hold and surrender when leaving Mexico. Carry proof of car ownership (the current registration card or a letter of authorization from the finance or leasing company). Permits must also be obtained for trailers and boats. Auto insurance policies, other than Mexican, are not valid in Mexico. A short-term liability policy is obtainable at the border.

Each returning U.S. resident may bring back articles for personal use valued at up to $800.00 free of duty; plant and animal products are carefully regulated whether entering or leaving Mexico. For further information obtain a copy of the booklet, *Know Before You Go* from any U.S. Customs and Border Protection office.

Mileage between principal cities
Miles in red; kilometers in blue

		Acapulco	Chihuahua	Ciudad Juárez	Guadalajara	Hermosillo	León	Matamoros	Mazatlán	Mérida	Mexico City	Monterrey	Nogales	Nuevo Laredo	Oaxaca	San Luis Potosí	Tampico	Tijuana	Torreón	Tuxtla Gutiérrez	Veracruz
CIUDAD JUÁREZ	mi	1322	234		924	444	891	959	851	1977	1103	747	355	892	1407	854	1095	786	519	1674	1321
	km	2128	377		1487	715	1434	1543	1370	3182	1775	1202	571	1436	2264	1374	1762	1265	835	2694	2126
GUADALAJARA	mi	509	690	924		869	136	628	306	1218	358	448	1042	603	688	211	452	1423	433	915	562
	km	819	1110	1487		1399	219	1011	492	1960	554	737	1677	970	1043	340	727	2290	697	1473	904
MÉRIDA	mi	1093	1743	1977	1218	2087	1115	1292	1524		874	1315	2231	1460	783	1123	982	2641	1486	568	693
	km	1759	2805	3182	1960	3359	1794	2079	2453		1407	2116	3590	2350	1260	1807	1580	4250	2391	914	1115
MEXICO CITY	mi	219	869	1103	344	1213	241	607	650	874		578	1357	723	304	249	297	1767	612	571	218
	km	352	1399	1775	554	1952	388	977	1046	1407		930	2184	1164	489	401	478	2844	985	919	351
MONTERREY	mi	797	513	747	458	887	430	212	588	1315	578		1001	145	882	335	333	1432	228	1052	622
	km	1283	826	1202	737	1427	692	341	946	2116	930		1611	233	1419	539	536	2305	367	1693	1001
TIJUANA	mi	1926	919	786	1423	554	1559	1644	1117	2641	1767	1432	515	1577	2071	1539	1780		1204	2338	1985
	km	3100	1479	1265	2290	892	2509	2646	1798	4250	2844	2305	829	2538	3333	2477	2865		1938	3763	3195

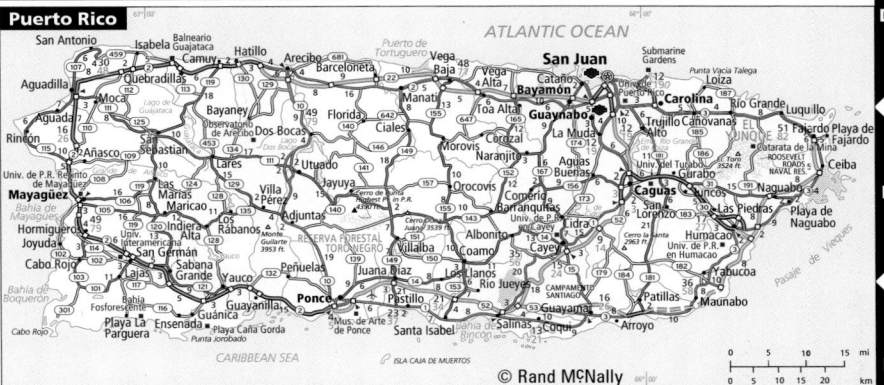

© Rand McNally

SYMBOLS

- Featured ride
- Long-term construction
- Harley-Davidson dealership
- Scenic route
- Historic site or monument; Indian reservation or rancheria; military installation; point of interest; wildlife refuge

MEXICO HARLEY-DAVIDSON DEALERSHIPS

Harley-Davidson Veracruz
Avenida Viveros Lote 1, Colonia Jardines de Virginia **Boca Del Rio, VE**
(52) 229-927-2560

Harley-Davidson Los Cabos
Av. Lazaro Cardenas, Plaza Puerto Paraiso, Local 40 **Cabo San Lucas, BCS**
(52) 624-143-3337

Harley-Davidson Motorclothes
Kukulkan Plaza, Blvd. Kukulkan Km 13.5, Local 119–125, Zona Hotelera **Cancun, QR**
(52) 555-520-3390

Harley-Davidson Motorclothes
Forum Plaza, Blvd. Kukulkan Km 9, Local A-19, Zona Hotelera **Cancun, QR**
(52) 998-883-4850

Harley-Davidson Satelite
Blvd. Manuel Avila Camacho 2170, Ciudad Satelite Poniente **Naucalpan, DF**
(52) 555-374-2302

Harley-Davidson Leon
Av. Cerro Gordo No. 111, Col. Valle del Campestre **Leon, GT**
(52) 477-781-1400

Harley-Davidson Mexico
Bolivar No. 482, Col. Algarin **Mexico City, DF**
(52) 55-5519-6389

Harley-Davidson Mexico
Carretera Picacho Ajusco No. 486, Col. Heroes De Padierna **Mexico City, DF**
(52) 55-5644-4421

Harley-Davidson Santa Fe
Prol. Paseo de la Reforma No. 71, Manzana 4 Lote 6, Col. Paseo de las Lomas, Santa Fe **Mexico City, DF**
(52) 555-292-4733

Motocicletas de Milwaukee
Rio Tamazunchale 404 Norte, Col. Del Valle, San Pedro Garza Garcia **Monterrey, NL**
(52) 818-356-5680

Harley-Davidson Motorclothes
Paseo del Carmen, Calle 10 Av. Sur, Local 44 **Playa del Carmen, QR**
(52) 9984-803-3956

Harley-Davidson Puebla, S.A.
31 Pte. No. 1707, Col. Volcanes **Puebla, PU**
(52) 222-211-2249

Harley-Davidson Jalisco
Av. Patria 1848-A, Col. Santa Isabel **Zapopan, JA**
(52) 33-3642-1560

PUERTO RICO HARLEY-DAVIDSON DEALERSHIPS

Motor Sport, Inc.
Acuarela St. #92 **Guaynabo**
(787) 790-4900

Harley-Davidson Boutique
Plaza del Sheraton Hotel, Waterfront **San Juan**
(787) 721-4202

2000 Census populations or latest available estimate.
Index to Canada and Mexico cities and towns, pages 274-275.

Forestville, 2370 ....NK-4
Ft. Bragg, 6867 ....NH-2
Fortuna, 10868 ....NE-1
Foster City, 28866 ....NI-15
Fountain Valley, 55747 ....‡J-10
Fowler, 4398 ....SC-7
Frazier Park, 2348 ....SH-9
Freedom, 6000 ....SB-3
Fremont, 204525 ....NM-6
French Camp, 4109 ....NM-7
FRESNO CO., 850325 ....SD-6
Fresno, 451455 ....SB-7
Fullerton, 131249 ....SJ-12
Fulton, 1300 ....NK-4
Galt, 22578 ....NL-7
Garberville, 800 ....NF-2
Gardena, 59941 ....‡H-6
Garden Acres, 9747 ....*H-10
Garden Grove, 167029 ....SK-12
Garden Valley, 700 ....NJ-8
Georgetown, 962 ....NJ-8
Gerber, 950 ....NF-6
Geyserville, 1300 ....NJ-4
Gilroy, 43817 ....SB-3
Glen Avon, 14853 ....‡F-16
Glendale, 200499 ....SJ-11
Glendora, 50853 ....‡D-12
Glen Ellen, 992 ....NK-5
GLENN CO., 27256 ....NH-5
Goleta, 28522 ....SI-7
Gonzales, 8510 ....SC-3
Goshen, 2394 ....SD-8
Grand Ter., 12205 ....‡E-18
Grant Grove SK-1
Grass Valley, 11629 ....NI-8
Graton, 1815 ....NK-4
Greeley Hill, 250 ....NM-10
Greenacres, 7379 ....SF-9
Greenbrae, 3400 ....ND-12
Greenfield, 12953 ....SD-4
Greenville, 1160 ....NF-8
Gridley, 5670 ....NH-7
Grover Beach, 13030 ....SG-5
Guadalupe, 5869 ....SG-5
Gualala, 1500 ....NJ-3
Guerneville, 2441 ....NK-4
Gustine, 5346 ....SA-5
Hacienda Hts., 53122 ....‡F-10
Half Moon Bay, 12143 ....NN-5
Hamilton City, 1903 ....NG-6
Hanford, 45368 ....SD-8
Happy Camp, 1200 ....NB-3
Hathaway Pines, 350 ....NL-9
Hawaiian Gardens, 15357 ....‡H-9
Hawthorne, 86173 ....‡G-6
Hayfork, 2315 ....NE-4
Hayward, 141336 ....NM-6
Healdsburg, 11187 ....NJ-4
Heber, 2988 ....SN-17
Hemet, 65044 ....SK-14
Hercules, 21602 ....NC-15
Herlong, 1000 ....NF-10
Hermosa Beach, 19429 ....‡H-5
Hesperia, 69179 ....SI-13
Hidden Hills, 1986 ....‡D-2
Hidden Valley, 950 ....NJ-8
Highgrove, 3445 ....‡F-18
Highland, 48516 ....SJ-13
Hillsborough, 10578 ....NI-14
Hilmar, 4807 ....NN-8
Hinkley, 1000 ....SG-13
Hollister, 36555 ....SB-4
Holtville, 5536 ....SM-18
Home Gardens, 9461 ....‡H-16
Homeland, 3710 ....‡I-20
Homestead Valley, 3500 ....NE-12
Hoopa, 1200 ....ND-2
Hope Ranch, 9000 ....†B-7
Hopland, 630 ....NI-3
Hughson, 5498 ....NM-8
HUMBOLDT CO., 127915 ....NE-2
Huntington Beach, 194248 ....SK-11
Huntington Park, 63139 ....‡F-7
Huron, 6991 ....SD-7
Hydesville, 1209 ....NE-2
Idyllwild, 2320 ....SK-14
Ignacio NB-12
IMPERIAL CO., 149232 ....SM-19
Imperial, 8885 ....SM-17
Imperial Beach, 27151 ....SN-14
Independence, 574 ....SB-11
Indian Wells, 4481 ....SK-15
Indio, 58241 ....SK-16
Inglewood, 115208 ....SJ-11
Inverness, 1421 ....NL-4
INYO CO., 18326 ....SB-12
Inyokern, 984 ....SF-12
Ione, 7514 ....NK-8
Irvine, 170561 ....SK-12
Irwindale, 1480 ....‡D-11
Isla Vista, 21069 ....SI-7
Isleton, 846 ....NL-7
Ivanhoe, 4474 ....SC-9
Jackson, 4102 ....NK-9
Jamestown, 3017 ....NL-9
Jamul, 5920 ....SN-14
Janesville, 1000 ....NF-9
Joshua Tree, 4207 ....SJ-15
Julian, 1621 ....SM-15
June Lake, 600 ....NM-12
Kelseyville, 2928 ....NI-4
Kensington, 4936 ....ND-15
Kentfield, 6351 ....ND-12
Kenwood, 1500 ....NK-5
Kerman, 9765 ....SC-7
KERN CO., 713087 ....SG-9
Kernville, 1736 ....SE-10
Kettleman City, 1499 ....SE-7
Keyes, 4575 ....NN-8
King City, 11323 ....SD-4
KINGS CO., 138564 ....SE-7
Kings Beach, 4037 ....NI-10
Kingsburg, 10504 ....SC-8
Klamath, 651 ....NB-2
Knights Ldg., 1250 ....NJ-6
La Cañada Flintridge, 20980 ....‡C-7
La Crescenta, 13000 ....‡C-7
Ladera, 1900 ....NL-16
Ladera Hts., 6568 ....‡F-5
Lafayette, 24574 ....ND-16
Laguna Beach, 24126 ....SK-12
Laguna Hills, 32181 ....‡L-14
Laguna Niguel, 64326 ....‡M-14
Laguna Woods, 17962 ....‡L-13
La Habra, 59703 ....SJ-12
La Habra Hts., 5963 ....‡F-10
La Honda, 850 ....NN-5
LAKE CO., 63369 ....NI-4
Lake Arrowhead, 8934 ....‡B-20
Lake Elsinore, 34914 ....SK-13
Lake Forest, 76738 ....SK-12
Lake Forest, 700 ....*B-2
Lake Hughes, 300 ....SH-10
Lake Isabella, 3315 ....SF-10
Lakeland Village, 5626 ....‡K-18
Lakeport, 5186 ....NI-4
Lakeside, 19560 ....SM-14
Lakeview, 1619 ....SK-13
Lakewood, 81300 ....‡H-8
La Mesa, 54571 ....†I-8
La Mirada, 48887 ....SJ-11
Lamont, 13296 ....SG-9
Lancaster, 125896 ....SH-11
Landers, 2300 ....SI-15
La Palma, 15903 ....‡H-10
La Puente, 42143 ....‡E-10
La Quinta, 32139 ....SK-15
Larkspur, 11827 ....NL-5
LASSEN CO., 33926 ....NE-9
Lathrop, 12181 ....NM-7
La Verne, 33005 ....SJ-12
Lawndale, 32490 ....‡H-5
Laytonville, 1301 ....NG-3
Lebec, 1285 ....SH-9
Lee Vining, 300 ....NL-12
Leggett, 100 ....NG-2
Le Grand, 1760 ....SA-6
Lemon Gr., 24935 ....SN-14
Lemon Hts., 2800 ....‡I-13
Lemoore, 21584 ....SD-7
Lennox, 22950 ....‡G-6
Lenwood, 3222 ....SH-13
Lewiston, 1305 ....NE-4
Lincoln, 23080 ....NJ-7
Lincoln Acres, 1800 ....†K-8
Linda, 13474 ....NI-7
Linden, 1103 ....NL-8
Lindsay, 10611 ....SD-9
Littlerock, 1402 ....SI-11
Live Oak, 6487 ....NI-7
Livermore, 77744 ....NM-6
Livingston, 11484 ....NN-9
Lockeford, 3179 ....NL-8
Lodi, 61027 ....NL-7
Loleta, 600 ....NE-1
Loma Linda, 20089 ....SJ-13
Loma Rica, 2075 ....NI-7
Lomita, 20548 ....‡I-6
Lompoc, 41167 ....SH-6
London, 1848 ....SC-8
Lone Pine, 1655 ....SC-11
Long Beach, 475460 ....SK-11
Loomis, 6312 ....NJ-8
Los Alamitos, 11697 ....‡I-9
Los Alamos, 1372 ....SH-6
Los Altos, 27173 ....NN-5
Los Altos Hills, 8097 ....NL-17
LOS ANGELES CO., 9871506 ....SH-10
Los Angeles, 3819951 ....SJ-11
Los Banos, 30538 ....SB-5
Los Gatos, 27976 ....SA-2
Los Molinos, 1952 ....NG-6
Los Nietos, 8200 ....‡F-9
Los Osos, 10500 ....SF-5
Los Ranchitos, 425 ....NC-12
Lost Hills, 1938 ....SF-7
Lower Lake, 1755 ....NJ-5
Loyalton, 847 ....NH-10
Lucerne, 2870 ....NI-4
Lucerne Valley, 2100 ....SI-14
Lynwood, 71619 ....‡G-7
Lytle Creek, 700 ....‡B-16
MADERA CO., 133463 ....SB-6
Madera, 47952 ....SB-7
Magalia, 10569 ....NG-7
Malibu, 13223 ....SJ-10
Mammoth Lakes, 7304 ....NM-13
Manhattan Beach, 36007 ....SJ-10
Manteca, 59500 ....NM-8
Maricopa, 1154 ....SG-8
MARIN CO., 246073 ....NL-5
Marina, 18919 ....SC-3
Marina Del Rey, 8176 ....‡G-4
Marin City, 2500 ....NE-12
Marinwood, 2300 ....NB-12
MARIPOSA CO., 17803 ....NN-10
Mariposa, 1373 ....NN-10
Martinez, 36595 ....NL-6
Marysville, 12498 ....NI-7
Maxwell, 850 ....NI-5
Maywood, 28751 ....‡F-7
McCloud, 1343 ....NC-6
McFarland, 10125 ....SE-8
McKinleyville, 13599 ....ND-2
Meadow Vista, 3096 ....NI-8
Mecca, 5402 ....SK-16
Meiners Oaks, 3750 ....SI-8
MENDOCINO CO., 88358 ....NH-3
Mendocino, 824 ....NH-2
Mendota, 8473 ....SB-6
Menlo Park, 29811 ....NN-5
Mentone, 7803 ....‡E-20
MERCED CO., 231574 ....SB-4
Merced, 69512 ....NN-9
Middletown, 1020 ....NJ-5
Midway City, 4400 ....‡J-10
Millbrae, 20040 ....NI-13
Mill Valley, 13418 ....NL-5
Milpitas, 63081 ....NN-6
Mira Loma, 17617 ....SJ-12
Mira Monte, 7177 ....SI-8
Mission Hills, 3142 ....SH-6
Mission Viejo, 95831 ....SK-12
Mi-Wuk Village, 1485 ....NL-10
Modesto, 206872 ....NM-8
MODOC CO., 9417 ....NB-8
Mojave, 3836 ....SG-11
MONO CO., 12988 ....NL-12
Monrovia, 37996 ....‡D-10
Montague, 1447 ....NB-5
Montalvin Manor, 2000 ....NC-14
Montara, 2950 ....NJ-12
Montclair, 34776 ....‡E-13
Montebello, 63747 ....‡F-8
Montecito, 10000 ....SI-8
MONTEREY CO., 414449 ....SD-5
Monterey, 29960 ....SC-2
Monterey Park, 62213 ....‡E-8
Monte Rio, 1104 ....NK-4
Monte Sereno, 3446 ....NN-18
Montgomery Creek, 96 ....ND-6
Montrose, 4100 ....‡C-7
Moorpark, 35168 ....SI-9
Morada, 3726 ....*G-10
Moraga, 16701 ....NE-17
Moreno Valley, 157063 ....SJ-13
Morgan Hill, 34128 ....SA-3
Morongo Valley, 1929 ....SJ-15
Morro Bay, 10372 ....SF-5
Moss Beach, 1953 ....NJ-12
Mtn. Pass, 200 ....SF-17
Mtn. View, 69366 ....NL-17
Mt. Shasta, 3614 ....NC-5
Mount View, 1500 ....NC-17
Murphys, 2061 ....NL-9
Murrieta, 66729 ....SK-13
Muscoy, 8919 ....‡D-18
NAPA CO., 131607 ....NK-5
Napa, 75560 ....NK-5
National City, 58292 ....SN-14
Needles, 5276 ....SH-19
NEVADA CO., 96099 ....NH-9
Nevada City, 3009 ....NI-8
Newark, 43042 ....NM-6
Newberry Sprs., 1500 ....SH-14
Newcastle, 2200 ....NJ-8
Newman, 7874 ....NN-8
Newport Beach, 78043 ....SK-12
Nice, 2509 ....NI-4
Niland, 1143 ....SL-17
Nipomo, 12626 ....SG-6
Norco, 26265 ....SJ-12
N. Edwards, 1227 ....SG-12
N. Fair Oaks, 15440 ....NK-16
N. Fork, 500 ....SA-8
N. Highlands, 44187 ....NJ-7
N. Richmond, 2200 ....ND-14
Norwalk, 107155 ....SJ-11
Novato, 48383 ....NL-5
Noyo NH-2
Nuevo, 4135 ....‡I-20
Nyland Acres, 2300 ....†B-3
Oakdale, 17440 ....NM-8
Oakhurst, 2868 ....NN-11
Oakland, 398844 ....NM-5
Oakley, 26349 ....NL-6
Oak View, 4199 ....SI-8
Oceano, 7260 ....SG-5
Oceanside, 167082 ....SL-13
Oildale, 27885 ....SF-9
Ojai, 8006 ....SI-8
Olivehurst, 11061 ....NI-7
Olympic Valley, 1000 ....*B-1
Ontario, 167402 ....SJ-12
ORANGE CO., 2957766 ....SK-12
Orange, 132197 ....SK-12
Orange Cove, 8993 ....SC-8
Orange Park Acres, 1800 ....‡I-13
Orangevale, 26705 ....NJ-8
Orcutt, 28830 ....SH-6
Orinda, 18091 ....NM-5
Orland, 6412 ....NG-6
Orleans, 375 ....NC-3
Oro Grande, 1000 ....SH-13
Orosi, 7318 ....SC-8
Oroville, 13137 ....NH-7
Oxnard, 180872 ....SJ-9
Pacheco, 3562 ....NC-17
Pacifica, 37291 ....NM-5
Pacific Gr., 15444 ....SC-2
Pajaro, 3420 ....SB-3
Palermo, 5720 ....NH-7
Palmdale, 127759 ....SI-11
Palm Desert, 45624 ....SK-15
Palm Sprs., 45228 ....SK-15
Palo Alto, 57233 ....NN-5
Palo Cedro, 1247 ....NE-6
Palomar Park, 700 ....NK-15
Palos Verdes Estates, 13827 ....SK-10
Paradise, 26796 ....NG-7
Paramount, 56660 ....‡H-8
Parkway, 14280 ....*E-6
Parlier, 12358 ....SC-8
Pasadena, 141114 ....SJ-11
Paso Robles, 26413 ....SF-5
Patterson, 14239 ....NN-8
Pearblossom, 700 ....SI-12
Pebble Beach, 3600 ....SC-2
Pedley, 11207 ....‡F-16
Penn Valley, 1387 ....NI-8
Perris, 41208 ....SK-13
Petaluma, 55175 ....NK-4
Philo, 250 ....NI-3
Pico Rivera, 65317 ....‡F-9
Piedmont, 10846 ....NF-15
Pine Gr., 1000 ....NK-9
Pine Valley, 1501 ....SM-15
Pinole, 19433 ....NC-14
Pioneer, 700 ....NK-9
Pioneer Pt., 1000 ....SE-13
Piru, 1196 ....SI-9
Pismo Beach, 8560 ....SG-5
Pittsburg, 61004 ....NL-6
Pixley, 2586 ....SE-8
Placentia, 48210 ....‡H-12
PLACER CO., 292235 ....NI-9
Placerville, 10123 ....NJ-8
Planada, 4369 ....NN-9
Pleasant Hill, 33859 ....NL-6
Pleasanton, 65982 ....NM-6
PLUMAS CO., 21148 ....NG-10
Plymouth, 1049 ....NK-8
Point Reyes Station, 818 ....NL-4
Pollock Pines, 4728 ....NJ-9
Pomona, 154147 ....SJ-12
Poplar, 1496 ....SD-9
Porterville, 42484 ....SD-9
Port Hueneme, 21837 ....SJ-9
Portola, 2219 ....NG-9
Portola Valley, 4418 ....NL-16
Potter Valley, 1025 ....NH-4
Poway, 49201 ....SM-14
Prunedale, 16514 ....SB-3
Pumpkin Cen., 520 ....SG-9
Quail Valley, 1639 ....‡J-19
Quartz Hill, 9890 ....SH-11
Quincy, 1879 ....NG-8
Ramona, 15691 ....SM-14
Rancho Cordova, 55060 ....NJ-7
Rancho Cucamonga, 151640 ....‡D-15
Rancho Mirage, 15297 ....SK-15
Rancho Palos Verdes, 42265 ....‡J-5
Rancho Rinconada, 4206 ....NM-18
Rancho Santa Fe, 3252 ....SM-13
Rancho Santa Margarita, 49142 ....‡K-15
Red Bluff, 13690 ....NF-5
Redding, 87579 ....NE-5
Red Hill, 2800 ....‡J-12
Redlands, 67859 ....SJ-13
Redondo Beach, 66337 ....SK-10
Redway, 1188 ....NF-2
Redwood City, 73472 ....NN-5
Redwood Valley, 1900 ....NI-3
Reedley, 21549 ....SC-8
Rialto, 98091 ....SJ-13
Richgrove, 2723 ....SE-9
Richmond, 102327 ....ND-14
Ridgecrest, 25635 ....SF-12
Rio Dell, 3148 ....NE-1
Rio Del Mar, 9198 ....SB-3
Rio Linda, 10466 ....NJ-7
Rio Vista, 6142 ....NL-6
Ripon, 12150 ....NM-8
Riverbank, 17847 ....NM-8
Riverdale, 2416 ....SC-7
RIVERSIDE CO., 1782650 ....SK-19
Riverside, 281514 ....SJ-13
Rocklin, 46937 ....NJ-8
Rodeo, 8717 ....NB-15
Rohnert Park, 41871 ....NK-4
Rolling Hills, 1931 ....‡I-6
Rolling Hills Estates, 7982 ....‡I-6
Rollingwood, 2900 ....NC-14
Romoland, 2764 ....‡I-20
Roosevelt Terrace, 2500 ....NA-15
Rosamond, 14349 ....SH-11
Roseland, 6369 ....*H-7
Rosemead, 55262 ....‡E-9
Rosemont, 22904 ....*D-8
Rosemont ....†E-10
Roseville, 98359 ....NJ-7
Ross, 2298 ....ND-12
Rossmoor, 10298 ....‡I-9
Rough and Ready, 140 ....NI-8
Round Mtn., 122 ....ND-6
Rowland Hts., 48553 ....‡F-11
Rubidoux, 29180 ....‡F-17
Running Springs, 5125 ....SJ-13
Rutherford, 700 ....NK-5
SACRAMENTO CO., 1330711 ....NK-8
Sacramento, 445335 ....NK-7
St. Helena, 6028 ....NK-5
Salida, 12560 ....NM-8
Salinas, 147840 ....SC-3
Salton City, 978 ....SL-16
Salyer, 800 ....ND-3
San Andreas, 2615 ....NL-9
San Anselmo, 12132 ....NL-5
San Antonio Hts., 3122 ....‡D-14
SAN BENITO CO., 56300 ....SC-5
SAN BERNARDINO CO., 1859678 ....SH-18
San Bernardino, 195357 ....SJ-13
San Bruno, 39602 ....NM-5
San Carlos, 27004 ....NM-5
San Clemente, 57768 ....SL-12
SAN DIEGO CO., 2930886 ....SL-15
San Diego, 1266753 ....SN-13
San Dimas, 36000 ....‡D-12
San Fernando, 24253 ....SI-10
SAN FRANCISCO CO., 751682 ....NM-5
San Francisco, 751682 ....NM-5
San Gabriel, 40987 ....‡E-9
Sanger, 20113 ....SC-8
San Jacinto, 26929 ....SK-14
SAN JOAQUIN CO., 632760 ....NL-7
San Joaquin, 3530 ....SC-6
San Jose, 898349 ....NN-6
San Juan Bautista, 1675 ....SB-3
San Juan Capistrano, 34796 ....SL-12
San Leandro, 80139 ....NM-5
San Lorenzo, 21898 ....NM-5
SAN LUIS OBISPO CO., 253118 ....SF-6
San Luis Obispo, 44202 ....SG-5
San Marcos, 64242 ....SL-13
San Marino, 13230 ....‡D-9
San Martin, 4230 ....SA-3
SAN MATEO CO., 697456 ....SA-2
San Mateo, 91157 ....NI-14
San Miguel, 1427 ....SE-5
San Pablo, 31041 ....NL-5
San Rafael, 55805 ....NL-5
San Ramon, 45907 ....NM-6
Santa Ana, 342510 ....SK-12
SANTA BARBARA CO., 403134 ....SH-7
Santa Barbara, 88251 ....SI-7
SANTA CLARA CO., 1678421 ....NN-7
Santa Clara, 102095 ....NL-18
Santa Clarita, 162742 ....SI-10
SANTA CRUZ CO., 251584 ....SA-2
Santa Cruz, 54262 ....SB-2
Santa Fe Sprs., 17032 ....‡G-9
Santa Margarita, 1500 ....SF-5
Santa Maria, 81944 ....SG-6
Santa Monica, 87162 ....SJ-10
Santa Paula, 28879 ....SI-9
Santa Rosa, 153386 ....NK-4
Santa Venetia, 4298 ....NL-5
Santa Ynez, 4584 ....SH-7
Santee, 52942 ....SM-14
Saratoga, 29309 ....SA-2
Sausalito, 7223 ....NE-12
Scotia, 850 ....NE-2
Scotts Valley, 11284 ....SB-2
Seal Beach, 24441 ....‡J-9
Seaside, 33897 ....SC-3
Sebastopol, 7732 ....NK-4
Sedco Hills, 3078 ....‡K-19
Seeley, 1624 ....SM-17
Selma, 21176 ....SC-8
Shafter, 13720 ....SF-8
SHASTA CO., 175650 ....NE-7
Shasta, 950 ....NE-5
Shasta Lake, 9979 ....NE-5
Sheridan, 1100 ....NI-7
Sherwood Forest, 2600 ....ND-15
Shingle Springs, 2643 ....NJ-8
Shore Acres, 4000 ....NB-18
SIERRA CO., 3502 ....NH-9
Sierra City, 680 ....NH-9
Sierra Madre, 10936 ....‡D-9
Signal Hill, 10159 ....‡I-8
Silverado, 1100 ....‡J-14
Simi Valley, 117115 ....SI-9
SISKIYOU CO., 44626 ....NB-6
Skyforest, 680 ....‡B-20
Sleepy Hollow, 2400 ....NC-11
Smith River, 950 ....NA-2
Solana Beach, 12993 ....SM-13
SOLANO CO., 412336 ....NK-6
Soledad, 25248 ....SC-4
Solvang, 5286 ....SH-6
Somis, 2500 ....SI-9
SONOMA CO., 466725 ....NJ-4
Sonoma, 9521 ....NK-5
Sonora, 4632 ....NL-9
Soquel, 5081 ....SB-2
Soulsbyville, 1729 ....NL-10
S. Dos Palos, 1385 ....SB-5
S. El Monte, 21776 ....‡E-9
S. Gate, 98966 ....‡G-7
S. Lake Tahoe, 23912 ....NJ-10
S. Pasadena, 24847 ....‡D-8
S. San Francisco, 59415 ....NM-5
S. San Gabriel, 7595 ....‡E-9
S. San Jose Hills, 20218 ....‡F-11
S. Taft, 1898 ....SG-8
Spr. Valley, 26663 ....SN-14
Springville, 1109 ....SD-9
Squaw Valley, 2691 ....SB-8
Stanford, 13315 ....NK-16
STANISLAUS CO., 492233 ....SA-4
Stanton, 37853 ....‡I-10
Stinson Beach, 751 ....NL-4
Stockton, 271466 ....NL-7
Stratford, 1264 ....SD-7
Strathmore, 2584 ....SD-9
Strawberry, 5302 ....ND-12
Suisun City, 26968 ....NL-6
Sultana, 700 ....SC-8
Summerland, 1545 ....SI-8
Summit City, 1300 ....NE-5
Sun City, 17773 ....SK-13
Sunnyside, 950 ....†K-8
Sunnyslope, 4437 ....‡F-17
Sunnyvale, 128549 ....NL-18
Sunol, 1332 ....NI-19
Sunset Beach, 2500 ....‡J-9
Susanville, 17584 ....NF-9
SUTTER CO., 84703 ....NI-7
Sutter, 2885 ....NI-6
Sutter Cr., 2402 ....NK-8
Taft, 9047 ....SG-8
Taft Hts., 1865 ....SG-8
Tahoe City, 1100 ....NI-10
Tahoe Vista, 1668 ....NI-10
Talmage, 1141 ....NI-3
Tamalpais Valley, 7000 ....NE-12
Tara Hills, 5332 ....NC-14
Tehachapi, 11434 ....SG-10
TEHAMA CO., 58582 ....NF-5
Temecula, 76836 ....SL-13
Temple City, 36325 ....‡E-9
Templeton, 4687 ....SF-5
Terra Bella, 3466 ....SE-9
Thermal, 1400 ....SK-16
Thermalito, 6045 ....NH-7
Thornton, 800 ....NL-7
Thousand Oaks, 124192 ....SJ-9
Thousand Palms, 5120 ....SK-15
Three Rivers, 2248 ....SC-9
Tiburon, 8688 ....NL-5
Tipton, 1790 ....SD-8
Topanga, 700 ....SJ-10
Torrance, 142621 ....‡H-5
Tracy, 72456 ....NM-7
Tranquillity, 813 ....SC-6
TRINITY CO., 13476 ....NF-3
Trinity Center, 500 ....ND-5
Trona, 1100 ....SE-13
Truckee, 14930 ....NI-10
TULARE CO., 390791 ....SC-9
Tulare, 47421 ....SD-8
Tulelake, 1019 ....NA-7
TUOLUMNE CO., 56755 ....NL-11
Tuolumne, 1865 ....NL-10
Turlock, 63467 ....NN-8
Tustin, 68478 ....‡J-12
Twain Harte, 2586 ....NL-10
Twentynine Palms, 25971 ....SJ-16
Twin Peaks, 2400 ....‡B-19
Ukiah, 15661 ....NI-3
Union City, 69309 ....NI-18
Upland, 72040 ....SJ-12
Upper Lake, 989 ....NI-4
Vacaville, 94129 ....NK-6
Valinda, 21776 ....‡E-10
Vallecito, 427 ....NL-9
Vallejo, 119708 ....NL-5
Valle Vista, 10488 ....SK-14
Valley Center, 7323 ....SL-14
Venice ....‡F-4
VENTURA CO., 791130 ....SH-9
Ventura, 104140 ....SI-8
Victorville, 74987 ....SI-13
View Park, 5500 ....‡F-6
Villa Park, 6039 ....‡I-12
Vine Hill, 3260 ....NL-6
Visalia, 100612 ....SD-8
Vista, 91813 ....SL-13
Walnut, 31089 ....‡E-11
Walnut Cr., 65151 ....NL-6
Walnut Gr., 669 ....NL-7
Walnut Park, 16180 ....‡F-7
Wasco, 22476 ....SF-8
Waterford, 8038 ....NM-9
Watsonville, 46159 ....SB-3
Weaverville, 3554 ....NE-4
Weed, 2977 ....NC-5
Weedpatch, 2726 ....SG-9
Weimar, 1300 ....NI-8
W. Covina, 108251 ....‡E-11
Westhaven, 370 ....ND-2
W. Hollywood, 36731 ....‡E-5
Westlake Vil., 8575 ....‡D-1
Westley, 747 ....NM-8
Westminster, 89493 ....‡J-10
Westmont, 31623 ....‡G-6
Westmorland, 2100 ....SM-17
W. Point, 746 ....NK-9
W. Sacramento, 37897 ....NK-7
Westwood, 1998 ....NF-8
Wheatland, 2840 ....NI-7
Whittier, 85368 ....SJ-11
Wildomar, 14064 ....‡L-19
Williams, 3925 ....NI-6
Willits, 5139 ....NH-3
Willowbrook, 34138 ....‡G-7
Willow Cr., 1743 ....ND-3
Willows, 6320 ....NH-6
Winchester, 2155 ....SK-14
Windsor, 24412 ....NK-4
Windsor Hills, 5000 ....‡F-5
Winterhaven, 529 ....SM-19
Winters, 6658 ....NK-6
Winton, 8832 ....NN-9
Wofford Hts., 2276 ....SE-10
Woodacre, 1393 ....NL-4
Woodcrest, 8342 ....‡H-18
Woodlake, 6938 ....SC-9
Woodland, 50988 ....NJ-6
Woodside, 5256 ....NK-15
Woodville, 1678 ....SD-9
Wrightwood, 3837 ....SI-12
Yermo, 1600 ....SH-14
YOLO CO., 183042 ....NJ-6
Yolo, 400 ....NJ-6
Yorba Linda, 62358 ....‡G-13
Yountville, 3337 ....NK-5
Yreka, 7204 ....NB-5
YUBA CO., 63432 ....NI-7
Yuba City, 48998 ....NI-7
Yucaipa, 46171 ....SJ-14
Yucca Valley, 18301 ....SJ-15

Colorado

Map pp. 40-45

* City keyed to pp. 44-45

ADAMS CO., 380273 ....E-15
Aguilar, 582 ....M-14
Akron, 1649 ....D-18
ALAMOSA CO., 15126 ....L-12
Alamosa, 8570 ....L-11
Alamosa E., 1528 ....L-11
Allenspark, 496 ....D-12
Almont, 70 ....I-9
Antonito, 839 ....M-11
ARAPAHOE CO., 516060 ....F-14
ARCHULETA CO., 11313 ....M-18
Arriba, 232 ....G-18
Arvada, 101972 ....E-13
Aspen, 5850 ....G-9
Ault, 1411 ....C-14
Aurora, 290418 ....E-14
Avon, 6393 ....F-10
Avondale, 754 ....J-15
BACA CO., 4223 ....M-19
Basalt, 2969 ....F-9
Bayfield, 1625 ....M-7
Bellvue, 400 ....C-13
Bennett, 2271 ....E-15
BENT CO., 5613 ....K-18
Berthoud, 5098 ....D-13
Beulah, 280 ....J-13
Black Forest, 13247 ....H-14
Black Hawk, 110 ....E-12
Blanca, 386 ....L-12
Blende, 1500 ....J-14
Boone, 337 ....J-15
BOULDER CO., 278231 ....D-13
Boulder, 93051 ....D-13
Bow Mar, 815 ....*K-6
Breckenridge, 2670 ....F-11
Brighton, 25459 ....E-14
Bristol, 130 ....J-20
BROOMFIELD CO., 42169 ....E-13
Broomfield, 42169 ....E-13
Brush, 5173 ....D-17
Buena Vista, 2189 ....H-11
Burlington, 3640 ....G-20
Byers, 1233 ....E-15
Calhan, 910 ....H-15
Campion, 1832 ....D-13
Cañon City, 15780 ....I-13
Carbondale, 5625 ....F-8
Cascade, 500 ....H-13
Castle Rock, 29869 ....G-14
Cedaredge, 2042 ....H-6
Centennial, 98586 ....F-14
Center, 2491 ....L-11
Central City, 483 ....E-12
CHAFFEE CO., 16841 ....H-11
Chama, 245 ....M-13
Cheraw, 210 ....J-17
Cherry Hills Vil., 6090 ....*J-7
CHEYENNE CO., 2052 ....H-19
Cheyenne Wells, 926 ....H-20
Clark B-9
CLEAR CREEK CO., 9538 ....F-12
Clifton, 17345 ....G-5
Collbran, 402 ....G-6
Colorado Sprs., 370448 ....H-14
Columbine Valley, 1141 ....*K-6
Commerce City, 26228 ....*H-8
CONEJOS CO., 8403 ....M-10
Conifer, 200 ....F-13
Cortez, 8181 ....M-5
COSTILLA CO., 3563 ....M-13
Craig, 9282 ....C-7
Crawford, 376 ....I-7
Creede, 397 ....K-9
Crested Butte, 1505 ....H-9
Cripple Cr., 1084 ....H-13
CROWLEY CO., 5449 ....J-16
Crowley, 182 ....J-16
CUSTER CO., 3784 ....K-13
Dacono, 3272 ....D-14
De Beque, 469 ....F-6
Deer Trail, 589 ....F-16
Del Norte, 1625 ....L-10
DELTA CO., 29409 ....H-7
Delta, 7788 ....H-6
DENVER CO., 557478 ....E-14
Denver, 557478 ....E-13
Dillon, 796 ....F-11
Dinosaur, 345 ....D-4
Divide, 50 ....H-13
DOLORES CO., 1825 ....K-5
Dolores, 848 ....L-5
DOUGLAS CO., 223471 ....G-13
Dove Cr., 693 ....K-4
Dupont, 3650 ....*G-8
Durango, 14741 ....M-6
Eads, 664 ....I-19
EAGLE CO., 46020 ....E-9
Eagle, 3508 ....F-9
Eastlake *F-7
Eaton, 3652 ....C-14
Eckley, 279 ....D-19
Edgewater, 5356 ....*I-6
ELBERT CO., 22254 ....F-15
Eldorado Sprs., 557 ....E-13
Elizabeth, 1520 ....G-14
El Jebel, 4488 ....F-8
EL PASO CO., 550478 ....I-15
Empire, 357 ....E-12
Englewood, 32762 ....F-13
Erie, 8904 ....D-13
Estes Park, 5655 ....C-12
Evans, 15175 ....C-14
Evergreen, 9216 ....F-13
Fairplay, 674 ....G-11
Federal Hts., 11850 ....*G-6
Flagler, 612 ....G-18
Fleming, 451 ....B-18
Florence, 3705 ....J-13
Ft. Collins, 125740 ....C-13
Ft. Garland, 432 ....M-12
Ft. Lupton, 7071 ....D-14
Ft. Morgan, 10995 ....D-16
Fountain, 15709 ....I-14
Fowler, 1156 ....J-16
Foxfield, 858 ....F-14
Fraser, 913 ....E-11
Frederick, 5273 ....D-14
FREMONT CO., 47556 ....I-12
Frisco, 2490 ....F-11
Fruita, 6751 ....G-4
Fruitvale, 6936 ....G-5
Garden City, 344 ....G-2
GARFIELD CO., 47611 ....F-6
Gateway H-4
Genoa, 200 ....G-17
Georgetown, 1102 ....E-12
Gilcrest, 1159 ....D-14
GILPIN CO., 4845 ....E-12
Glendale, 4816 ....*I-7
Glenwood Sprs., 8333 ....F-8
Golden, 17550 ....E-13
Granada, 626 ....J-20
Granby, 1546 ....D-11
GRAND CO., 13173 ....D-10
Grand Jct., 44382 ....G-5
Grand Lake, 444 ....D-11
Greeley, 83414 ....C-14
Green Mtn. Falls, 782 ....H-13
Greenwood Vil., 12731 ....*K-7
GUNNISON CO., 14046 ....H-9
Gunnison, 5313 ....I-9
Gypsum, 4553 ....F-9
Haxtun, 984 ....C-19
Hayden, 1585 ....C-8
Henderson, 600 ....*F-8
Highlands Ranch, 70931 ....*L-7
HINSDALE CO., 759 ....K-8
Hoehne, 85 ....M-15
Holly, 1024 ....J-20
Holyoke, 2266 ....C-20
Hotchkiss, 1024 ....H-7
Hot Sulphur Sprs., 529 ....D-11
Hudson, 1583 ....D-14
HUERFANO CO., 7827 ....L-13
Hugo, 837 ....G-17
Hygiene, 400 ....D-13
Idaho Sprs., 1884 ....E-12
Ignacio, 671 ....M-7
Indian Hills, 1197 ....F-13
Irondale, 440 ....*G-8
JACKSON CO., 1507 ....C-10
Jamestown, 198 ....D-12
Jansen, 210 ....M-15
JEFFERSON CO., 528563 ....F-13
Johnson Vil., 270 ....H-11
Johnstown, 5595 ....D-14
Julesburg, 1426 ....A-20
Keenesburg, 1117 ....D-15
Kersey, 1371 ....C-14
KIOWA CO., 1444 ....I-18
Kiowa, 612 ....G-15
KIT CARSON CO., 7911 ....F-19
Kit Carson, 235 ....H-19
Kremmling, 1610 ....D-10
Lafayette, 23654 ....E-13
La Jara, 838 ....M-11
La Junta, 7379 ....K-17
LAKE CO., 7731 ....G-10
Lake City, 360 ....K-8
Lake George, 120 ....H-13
Lakewood, 142474 ....*I-5
Lamar, 8630 ....J-19
LA PLATA CO., 46229 ....M-7
Laporte, 2691 ....C-13
LARIMER CO., 266610 ....C-12
La Salle, 1786 ....D-14
LAS ANIMAS CO., 15499 ....L-16
Las Animas, 2575 ....K-18
La Veta, 905 ....L-13
Lawson, 320 ....E-12
Leadville, 2712 ....G-10
Limon, 2014 ....G-17
LINCOLN CO., 5881 ....H-17
Lincoln Park, 3904 ....I-13
Littleton, 40599 ....F-13
Lochbuie, 3209 ....E-14
LOGAN CO., 20928 ....B-17
Log Lane Vil., 1055 ....D-16
Loma, 400 ....G-4
Lombard Vil., 600 ....J-15
Longmont, 79556 ....D-13
Louisville, 18387 ....E-13
Louviers, 237 ....F-13
Loveland, 56436 ....C-13
Lucerne, 160 ....C-14
Lyons, 1606 ....D-13
Manassa, 1015 ....M-11
Mancos, 1140 ....M-5
Manitou Sprs., 5036 ....H-14
Manzanola, 506 ....J-16
Masonville, 140 ....C-13
Meeker, 2210 ....D-6
Meeker Park, 120 ....D-12
Merino, 277 ....C-17
MESA CO., 124676 ....H-5
Milliken, 4635 ....D-14
MINERAL CO., 881 ....L-9
Minturn, 1131 ....F-10
MOFFAT CO., 13527 ....B-7
Monte Vista, 4370 ....L-11
MONTEZUMA CO., 24335 ....L-5
MONTROSE CO., 35984 ....J-5
Montrose, 14195 ....I-7
Monument, 2500 ....G-14
MORGAN CO., 27922 ....D-16
Morrison, 418 ....F-13
Mtn. View, 544 ....*H-6
Naturita, 673 ....J-5
Nederland, 1355 ....E-12
New Castle, 2675 ....F-7
Niwot, 4160 ....D-13
Northglenn, 32943 ....*F-7
Norwood, 471 ....J-5
Nucla, 743 ....J-5
Nunn, 510 ....B-14
Oak Cr., 819 ....D-9
Olathe, 1648 ....I-6
Olney Sprs., 382 ....J-16
Orchard City, 3029 ....H-6
Orchard Mesa, 6456 ....G-5
Ordway, 1194 ....J-16
OTERO CO., 19754 ....K-16
Otis, 524 ....D-18
OURAY CO., 4021 ....J-7
Ouray, 832 ....K-7
Ovid, 327 ....B-19
Pagosa Sprs., 1528 ....M-8
Palisade, 2650 ....G-5
Palmer Lake, 2262 ....G-14
Paonia, 1586 ....H-7
Parachute, 1055 ....F-6
PARK CO., 16465 ....G-12
Parker, 34527 ....F-14
Penrose, 4070 ....I-13
PHILLIPS CO., 4511 ....C-20
Pierce, 877 ....C-14
Pine, 150 ....F-13
PITKIN CO., 15002 ....G-9
Platteville, 2547 ....D-14
Poncha Sprs., 469 ....I-11
PROWERS CO., 14164 ....K-20
PUEBLO CO., 148751 ....K-15
Pueblo, 103648 ....J-14
Pueblo W., 16899 ....J-14
Rangely, 2065 ....D-4
Red Cliff, 303 ....F-10
Ridgway, 737 ....J-7
Rifle, 7483 ....F-7
RIO BLANCO CO., 5938 ....E-5
RIO GRANDE CO., 12346 ....L-10
Rockvale, 416 ....J-13
Rocky Ford, 4137 ....K-17
Rollinsville, 150 ....E-12
Romeo, 372 ....M-11
ROUTT CO., 20788 ....C-9
Roxborough Park, 4446 ....*M-6
SAGUACHE CO., 6708 ....J-10
Saguache, 600 ....J-11
Salida, 5494 ....I-11
Sanford, 795 ....M-11
SAN JUAN CO., 572 ....L-7
San Luis, 720 ....M-12
SAN MIGUEL CO., 7154 ....J-5
Security, 4400 ....H-14
Sedalia, 211 ....F-14
SEDGWICK CO., 2683 ....B-20
Sheridan, 5577 ....*J-6
Sherrelwood, 17657 ....*G-7
Silt, 2094 ....F-7
Silver Cliff, 574 ....J-12
Silverthorne, 3623 ....F-11
Silverton, 545 ....K-7
Simla, 715 ....G-16
Snowmass Village, 1791 ....G-9
South Fork, 578 ....L-9
Springfield, 1439 ....L-19
Steamboat Sprs., 9390 ....C-9
Sterling, 12785 ....C-18
Strasburg, 1402 ....E-15
Stratmoor Hills, 2350 ....*I-2
Stratton, 657 ....G-19
Sugar City, 269 ....J-17
SUMMIT CO., 25143 ....F-11
Superior, 10287 ....E-13
Swink, 691 ....K-17
Tabernash, 165 ....E-11
TELLER CO., 21786 ....G-13
Telluride, 2321 ....K-7
Thornton, 96584 ....*G-7
Timnath, 217 ....C-13
Towaoc, 1097 ....M-4
Trinidad, 9152 ....M-15
Uravan I-4
Vail, 4603 ....F-10
Victor, 422 ....I-13
Walden, 690 ....B-10
Walsenburg, 4017 ....L-14
Walsh, 697 ....M-20
WASHINGTON CO., 4813 ....D-18
Watkins, 300 ....E-14
Wattenberg, 330 ....E-14
WELD CO., 211272 ....B-15
Wellington, 2632 ....B-13
Westcliffe, 460 ....J-12
Western Hills, 2600 ....*G-6
Westminster, 103391 ....E-13
Wheat Ridge, 31782 ....*H-5
Widefield, 4200 ....H-14
Wiggins, 922 ....D-16
Wiley, 475 ....J-19
Windsor, 13086 ....C-14
Winter Park, 715 ....E-12
Woodland Park, 6751 ....H-13
Woody Cr., 260 ....G-9
Wray, 2165 ....D-20
Yampa, 426 ....D-9
YUMA CO., 9799 ....E-20
Yuma, 3269 ....D-19

Connecticut

Map pp. 46-49

Addison, 800 ....E-11
Ansonia, 18818 ....I-7
Avon, 1800 ....D-9
Baltic, 2000 ....F-15
Beacon Falls, 1650 ....H-7
Berlin, 1230 ....F-9
Bethany, 1280 ....H-7
Bethel, 9137 ....I-4
Bethlehem, 2022 ....F-6
Bloomfield, 7500 ....D-9
Blue Hills, 3020 ....D-10
Branford, 5735 ....J-9
Bridgeport, 139664 ....K-6
Bristol, 60722 ....E-8
Broad Brook, 3469 ....C-11
Brookfield, 1650 ....G-4
Brookfield Cen., 1550 ....H-4
Brooklyn, 1650 ....D-16
Canaan, 1288 ....B-5
Candlewood Shores, 1800 ....H-4
Cannondale, 1500 ....J-4
Canton, 1565 ....D-8
Centerbrook, 1000 ....I-12
Central Vil., 1800 ....E-16
Cheshire, 5789 ....G-8
Chester, 1546 ....H-12
Clinton, 3516 ....J-11
Colchester, 4500 ....F-13
Collinsville, 2686 ....D-8
Coventry, 2914 ....D-13
Cromwell, 2500 ....F-10
Danbury, 77353 ....H-4
Danielson, 4273 ....D-16
Darien, 19607 ....L-3
Dayville, 1650 ....D-16
Deep River, 2470 ....H-12
Derby, 12593 ....I-7
Durham, 2773 ....H-10
E. Berlin, 1100 ....F-10
E. Brooklyn, 1473 ....D-16
E. Canaan, 1000 ....B-5
E. Granby, 1300 ....C-10
E. Hampton, 2254 ....F-11
E. Hartford, 49575 ....D-10
E. Haven, 28189 ....J-8
E. Lyme, 1330 ....I-14
E. River, 3800 ....J-10
E. Village, 100 ....I-6
E. Windsor, 2100 ....C-10
Ellington, 1700 ....C-12
Enfield, 45539 ....B-11
Essex, 2573 ....I-12
FAIRFIELD CO., 899152 ....I-4
Fairfield, 57300 ....K-5
Farmington, 3100 ....E-9
Gales Ferry, 1200 ....H-15
Georgetown, 1650 ....J-4
Giants Neck, 1330 ....I-14
Glastonbury, 7157 ....E-10
Granby, 2453 ....B-9
Greenwich, 61100 ....L-2
Groton, 10237 ....I-15
Groton Long Pt., 680 ....I-15
Guilford, 2603 ....J-10
Haddam, 1300 ....G-11
Hamden, 56900 ....H-8
HARTFORD CO., 871457 ....C-9
Hartford, 124387 ....D-10
Harwinton, 3242 ....D-7
Hazardville, 4900 ....B-11
Higganum, 1671 ....G-11
Honeypot Glen, 1200 ....G-8
Indian Neck, 2500 ....J-9
Ivoryton, 2600 ....I-12
Jewett City, 3037 ....F-16
Kensington, 8541 ....F-9
Lakeside, 1340 ....H-5
Lakeville, 1900 ....B-4
LITCHFIELD CO., 187801 ....C-5
Litchfield, 1331 ....E-6
Madison, 2222 ....J-11
Manchester, 54700 ....D-11
Mansfield Cen., 973 ....D-14
Marion, 850 ....G-8
Marlborough, 1048 ....F-12
Meriden, 58962 ....G-9
Middlebury, 4200 ....G-6
MIDDLESEX CO., 161439 ....F-11
Middletown, 46918 ....G-10
Milford, 52122 ....J-7
Milldale, 900 ....G-8
Mixville, 1400 ....G-8
Montville, 610 ....H-14
Moodus, 1263 ....G-12
Moosup, 3237 ....E-16
Mystic, 4001 ....I-16
Naugatuck, 31700 ....G-7
New Britain, 71572 ....F-9
New Canaan, 17864 ....K-3
New Fairfield, 5200 ....H-3
New Hartford, 1049 ....C-7
NEW HAVEN CO., 841873 ....H-7
New Haven, 124512 ....I-8
Newington, 29306 ....E-10
NEW LONDON CO., 263989 ....G-16
New London, 26201 ....I-15
New Milford, 6633 ....F-4
New Preston, 1120 ....E-4
Newtown, 1847 ....H-5
Niantic, 3085 ....I-14
Noank, 1830 ....I-16
Norfolk, 1430 ....B-6
N. Branford, 7400 ....I-9
Northford, 3600 ....H-9
N. Grosvenor Dale, 1424 ....B-16
N. Haven, 23035 ....H-8
Norwalk, 84170 ....K-4
Norwich, 36227 ....G-15
Oakdale, 910 ....H-14
Oakville, 8618 ....F-7
Old Saybrook, 1962 ....J-12
Orange, 13233 ....J-7
Oxford, 2100 ....H-6
Pawcatuck, 5474 ....I-17
Pine Bridge, 1000 ....H-7
Pine Orchard, 950 ....J-9
Plainfield, 2638 ....E-16
Plainville, 17392 ....E-9
Plantsville, 6000 ....F-8
Pleasure Beach, 1450 ....I-14
Plymouth, 1200 ....E-7
Poquonock, 1100 ....C-10
Poquonock Bridge, 1592 ....I-15
Portland, 5534 ....G-10
Prospect, 7775 ....G-7
Putnam, 6746 ....C-16
Quaker Hill, 1700 ....H-15
Quinebaug, 1122 ....B-16
Ridgefield, 7212 ....J-3
Rocky Hill, 16554 ....F-10
Salisbury, 1700 ....B-4
Sandy Hook, 1200 ....H-5
Seymour, 14288 ....H-7
Sharon, 1200 ....C-4
Shelton, 39121 ....I-6
Short Beach, 200 ....J-9
Simsbury, 5603 ....C-9
Somers, 1626 ....B-12
Somersville, 1300 ....B-11
Southbury, 3400 ....H-6
S. Glastonbury, 2000 ....E-11
Southington, 41397 ....F-8
S. Windham, 1278 ....E-14
S. Windsor, 14000 ....D-11
S. Woodstock, 1211 ....C-16
Stafford Sprs., 4900 ....B-13
Stamford, 120107 ....L-3
Stepney, 750 ....K-12
Stonington, 1022 ....I-16
Storrs, 11106 ....D-13
Stratford, 49976 ....K-6
Suffield, 1244 ....B-10
Tariffville, 1371 ....C-9
Terryville, 5360 ....E-7
Thomaston, 4000 ....E-7
TOLLAND CO., 145039 ....D-12
Tolland, 1350 ....C-12
Torrington, 35756 ....D-6
Trumbull, 34243 ....J-6
Uncasville, 1420 ....H-15
Unionville, 4400 ....E-8
Upper Stepney, 1000 ....I-5
Vernon, 28100 ....D-11
Wallingford, 17509 ....H-9
Waterbury, 108130 ....G-7
Waterford, 2935 ....I-14
Watertown, 6300 ....F-6
Wauregan, 1085 ....E-16
Weatogue, 2805 ....D-9
Wequetequock, 850 ....I-16
Westbrook, 2238 ....J-12
W. Hartford, 61046 ....E-9
W. Haven, 53004 ....J-8
W. Mystic, 3595 ....I-16
Weston, 1460 ....J-4
Westport, 25749 ....K-4
W. Simsbury, 2395 ....C-8
Wethersfield, 26271 ....E-10
Willimantic, 15823 ....E-14
Wilton, 7500 ....K-4
WINDHAM CO., 112622 ....D-15
Windsor, 18800 ....D-10
Windsor Locks, 12043 ....C-10
Winsted, 7321 ....C-7
Wolcott, 6400 ....F-8
Woodbridge, 7860 ....I-7
Woodbury, 1298 ....G-6
Woodmont, 1747 ....J-7

Delaware

Map pp. 50-51

Bear, 17593 ....D-2
Bellefonte, 1264 ....C-9
Bellevue Manor, 200 ....C-9
Belvedere, 800 ....D-8
Birchwood Park, 400 ....D-7
Blades, 985 ....K-2
Brandywood, 800 ....B-9
Bridgeville, 1518 ....J-2
Brookside, 14806 ....E-6
Camden, 2152 ....H-2
Carrcroft, 500 ....C-9
Carrcroft Crest, 900 ....B-9
Castle Hills, 2000 ....D-8
Chalfonte, 1400 ....B-9
Claymont, 9220 ....C-3
Clayton, 1306 ....F-2
Cleland Hts., 900 ....D-8
Collins Park, 1500 ....D-8
Coventry, 1500 ....E-7
Darley Woods, 1300 ....B-9
Delaware City, 1482 ....D-2
Delmar, 1453 ....M-2
Del Park Manor, 1100 ....D-7
Devonshire, 2200 ....B-9
Dover, 32808 ....G-3
Dunleith, 2400 ....D-8
Dupont Manor, 300 ....G-3
Du Ross Hts., 900 ....D-8
Edgemoor, 5992 ....C-9
Elsmere, 5764 ....C-2
Fairfax, 1600 ....C-9
Faulkland, 1300 ....C-7
Felton, 798 ....H-2
Forest Brook Glen, 400 ....D-8
Forest Hills Park, 650 ....C-9
Fox Hall F-7
Frankford, 733 ....L-4
Frederica, 661 ....H-3
Garfield Park, 400 ....D-8
Georgetown, 4811 ....K-3
Graylyn Crest, 450 ....B-9
Green Acres, 1100 ....B-9
Greenville, 2332 ....C-2
Greenville Place, 1000 ....C-8
Greenwood, 860 ....J-2
Gwinhurst, 400 ....B-10
Harmony Hills, 800 ....D-7
Harrington, 3161 ....I-2
Hockessin, 12902 ....C-2
Holloway Ter., 1200 ....D-9
Ivy Ridge, 1800 ....E-7
Jefferson Farms, 2000 ....D-8
KENT CO., 134390 ....H-3
Lancaster Vil., 1100 ....C-8
Laurel, 3752 ....L-2
Lewes, 3006 ....J-5
Llangollen Estates, 1400 ....E-8
Marshallton, 1800 ....D-7
Meadowood, 600 ....D-7
Middletown, 6496 ....E-2
Milford, 6991 ....I-3
Millsboro, 2467 ....L-4
Milton, 1750 ....J-4
Minquadale, 650 ....D-8
Naamans Gardens, 600 ....B-10
Newark, 29821 ....C-1
NEW CASTLE CO., 515074 ....F-2
New Castle, 4787 ....D-2
Newport, 1115 ....C-2
North Star, 8277 ....C-1
Oak Lane Manor, 950 ....B-9
Penn Acres, 2000 ....D-8
Penny Hill, 600 ....C-9
Rambleton Acres, 1500 ....E-8
Rehoboth Beach, 1501 ....K-5
Richardson Park, 500 ....D-8
Rising Sun, 250 ....H-3
Rodney Vil., 1606 ....H-3
Seaford, 6948 ....K-2
Selbyville, 1711 ....M-4
Sharpley, 1400 ....B-8
Sherwood Park, 2000 ....C-7
Silview, 1500 ....D-8
Smyrna, 6207 ....F-2
Stanton, 2000 ....D-7
Stratford, 1100 ....E-7
SUSSEX CO., 168027 ....K-3
Swanwyck Estates, 800 ....D-8
Talleyville, 800 ....B-3
Tuxedo Park, 1300 ....D-7
Westover Hills, 1200 ....C-8
Willow Run, 500 ....C-8
Wilmington, 72051 ....C-3
Wilmington Manor, 8262 ....D-8
Wilmington Manor Gardens, 1800 ....E-8
Wyoming, 1134 ....H-2
Yorklyn, 300 ....C-2

District of Columbia

Map pp. 224-225

Washington, 563384 ....E-6

Florida

Map pp. 52-57

* City keyed to pp. 56-57
† City keyed to p. 51

ALACHUA CO., 223578 ....D-8
Alachua, 6759 ....D-7
Altamonte Sprs., 40942 ....H-10
Andover Lake Estates, 1500 ....*J-8
Anna Maria, 1824 ....K-6
Anthony, 1150 ....F-8
Apalachicola, 2310 ....T-8
Apollo Beach, 7444 ....K-7
Apopka, 30703 ....H-10
Arcadia, 6902 ....L-9
Archer, 1293 ....E-7
Atlantic Beach, 13565 ....C-10
Auburndale, 11956 ....J-4
Aventura, 26882 ....*J-9
Avon Park, 8684 ....K-10
Azalea Park, 11073 ....N-4
Babson Park, 1182 ....J-10
Bagdad, 1490 ....R-3
BAKER CO., 23424 ....C-7
Baldwin, 1616 ....C-8
Bal Harbour, 3256 ....*K-9
Bartow, 15574 ....J-9
BAY CO., 155193 ....S-6
Bay Hbr. Islands, 5181 ....*K-9
Bay Hill, 5177 ....O-2
Bayonet Pt., 23577 ....I-6
Bay Pines, 3065 ....*D-1
Bay Ridge, 155 ....L-2
Baywood Village *A-1
Bee Ridge, 8744 ....L-7
Belleair, 4097 ....*C-1
Belleair Beach, 1628 ....*C-1
Belleair Bluffs, 2242 ....*C-1
Belle Glade, 15206 ....N-12
Belle Isle, 6242 ....O-4
Belleview, 3654 ....G-8
Bellview, 21201 ....†L-8
Belvedere Homes, 4000 ....*B-10
Beverly Hills, 8317 ....G-7
Big Coppitt Key, 2595 ....T-9
Big Pine Key, 5032 ....T-10
Biscayne Gardens, 1150 ....*K-8
Biscayne Park, 3219 ....*K-9
Bithlo, 4626 ....H-11
Blountstown, 2387 ....S-7
Boca Pointe, 3302 ....*F-9
Boca Raton, 78449 ....O-14
Boca West, 2100 ....*F-9
Bonifay, 2669 ....R-6
Bonita Shores, 2000 ....O-9
Bonita Sprs., 36230 ....O-9
Bowling Green, 2908 ....K-9
Boynton Beach, 64384 ....N-14
Bradenton, 52498 ....K-7
Bradenton Beach, 1513 ....L-6
BRADFORD CO., 26928 ....D-8
Bradley, 600 ....J-8
Brandon, 77871 ....J-8
Brent, 22257 ....†L-9
BREVARD CO., 505711 ....J-12
Brooksville, 7436 ....H-7
BROWARD CO., 1731347 ....O-12
Brownsville, 14393 ....*L-8
Buccaneer Estates, 1000 ....*J-8
Buckhead Ridge, 1390 ....L-11
Buena Venture Lakes, 14000 ....P-4
Bunche Park, 3972 ....*K-8
Bunnell, 2258 ....E-10
Bushnell, 2056 ....H-8
CALHOUN CO., 12921 ....S-7
Callahan, 963 ....B-9
Callaway, 14639 ....S-6
Campbell, 2677 ....I-10
Canal Pt., 525 ....M-12
Canova Beach, 150 ....I-12
Cantonment, 2800 ....R-2
Cape Canaveral, 9509 ....I-12
Cape Coral, 118737 ....N-8
Carrabelle, 1292 ....D-1
Carrollwood, 3100 ....*B-3
Casselberry, 23707 ....H-10
Century, 1783 ....Q-2
Century Village, 7616 ....*B-9
Chaires, 100 ....B-3
CHARLOTTE CO., 153392 ....M-9
Chattahoochee, 3299 ....R-8
Chiefland, 2038 ....E-6
Chipley, 3600 ....R-6
Chuluota, 1921 ....H-11
CITRUS CO., 126458 ....G-7
Citrus Sprs., 4157 ....G-7
Clair-Mel City, 7500 ....*C-4
Clarcona, 800 ....M-2
CLAY CO., 157502 ....D-9
Clearwater, 108272 ....J-6

262 | FLORIDA – ILLINOIS

*, †, ‡, See explanation under state title in this index.
County names are listed in capital letters and in boldface type.

Clermont, 10577 H-9
Clewiston, 6770 N-11
Cocoa, 16429 I-12
Cocoa Beach, 12432 I-12
Coconut Cr., 48198 *G-9
COLLIER CO., 286634 O-10
COLUMBIA CO., 60244 C-7
Conway, 14394 H-10
Cooper City, 28853 *I-8
Coral Cove, 1160 L-7
Coral Gables, 42539 Q-13
Coral Sprs., 127005 O-13
Coral Way Vil., 3200 *M-7
Cottondale, 852 R-7
Crawfordville, 1400 C-2
Crescent City, 1780 E-10
Crestview, 15826 R-4
Cross City, 1801 E-5
Crystal Beach, 1350 *A-1
Crystal River, 3565 G-7
Cudjoe T-10
Cutler Ridge, 24781 Q-13
Cypress Creek *J-4
Cypress Gardens, 8844 *K-5
Cypress Quarters, 1150 L-12
Dade City, 6476 I-8
Dania Beach, 28202 P-14
Davenport, 1986 I-9
Davie, 80364 P-13
Daytona Beach, 64581 F-11
Daytona Beach Shores, 4429 F-11
Debary, 16127 G-10
Deerfield Beach, 65694 O-14
De Funiak Sprs., 5250 R-5
DeLand, 21902 G-10
De Leon Sprs., 2358 F-10
Delray Beach, 63321 N-14
Deltona, 76597 G-10
DESOTO CO., 33879 L-9
Desoto Lakes, 3198 *G-4
Destin, 11769 S-4
DIXIE CO., 13982 E-5
Doctor Phillips, 9548 O-2
Dover, 2798 J-8
Dundee, 2986 J-9
Dunedin, 36715 J-6
Dunnellon, 1954 G-7
DUVAL CO., 817480 C-9
Eagle Lake, 2493 *K-4
E. Naples, 2050 P-9
E. Palatka, 1707 E-9
Eastpoint, 2158 T-8
Eatonville, 2411 M-3
Edgewater, 20211 G-11
Edgewood, 2052 N-4
Egypt Lake, 3500 *B-3
Elfers, 13161 I-6
Ellenton, 3142 K-7
El Portal, 2470 *L-9
Englewood, 16196 M-7
Ensley, 18752 R-2
ESCAMBIA CO., 295886 Q-2
Eustis, 16316 G-9
Fairview Shores, 13898 M-3
Fellsmere, 4029 J-12
Fernandina Beach, 11059 B-10
Fern Park, 8318 M-4
Ferry Pass, 27176 †L-9
FLAGLER CO., 62206 E-10
Flagler Beach, 5317 E-11
Floral City, 4989 H-7
Florida City, 7902 R-13
Forest City, 12612 M-3
Ft. Lauderdale, 162917 O-14
Ft. McCoy, 300 F-8
Ft. Meade, 5724 K-9
Ft. Myers, 51028 N-9
Ft. Myers Beach, 6768 O-8
Ft. Myers Villas, 5600 N-9
Ft. Pierce, 37841 K-13
Ft. Walton Beach, 19936 S-4
FRANKLIN CO., 10003 D-1
Frostproof, 2940 K-10
Fruitland Park, 3393 G-9
Fruitville, 12741 L-7
GADSDEN CO., 45134 B-1
Gainesville, 109146 E-7
Gibsonia, 4507 *I-1
Gibsonton, 8752 J-7
Gifford, 7599 K-13
GILCHRIST CO., 15633 D-6
GLADES CO., 11165 M-10
Glenvar Heights, 16243 *M-7
Golden Gate, 20951 O-9
Golden Lakes, 6694 *B-9
Goldenrod, 12871 M-4
Goodland, 320 P-9
Goulding, 4484 †M-9
Goulds, 7453 Q-13
Graceville, 2357 Q-6
Greenacres, 31111 N-14
Green Cove Sprs., 5671 D-9
Greenville, 824 B-4
Gretna, 1697 B-1
Grove City, 2092 M-7
Groveland, 3951 H-9
GULF CO., 15247 T-7
Gulf Breeze, 6199 S-3
Gulf City, 550 *E-4
Gulf Gate Estates, 11647 *H-3
Gulf Harbors, 3300 I-6
Gulfport, 12586 K-6
Gulf Stream, 737 N-14
Haines City, 13956 I-9
Hallandale Beach, 35369 P-14
HAMILTON CO., 13917 B-6
HARDEE CO., 27659 L-8
Harlem, 2730 N-11
Havana, 1685 B-2
Haverhill, 1621 N-14
Hawthorne, 1454 E-8
Heathrow, 4068 G-10
HENDRY CO., 37064 N-10
HERNANDO CO., 143449 H-7
Hernando, 8253 G-7
Hialeah, 226401 P-13
Highland City, 2051 J-9
Highland Lakes *A-2
HIGHLANDS CO., 91051 K-10
Highpoint, 2300 *C-2
High Sprs., 4167 D-7
Hiland Park, 999 S-6
Hilliard, 2812 B-8
Hillsboro Beach, 2264 *G-10
HILLSBOROUGH CO., 1073407 J-8
Hobe Sound, 11376 M-13
Holiday, 21904 I-6
Holly Hill, 12586 F-11
Hollywood, 143408 P-14
HOLMES CO., 18986 Q-6
Holmes Beach, 4983 K-6
Homestead, 34182 Q-13
Homosassa, 2294 G-7
Homosassa Sprs., 12458 G-7
Hudson, 12765 I-6
Immokalee, 19763 O-10
Indialantic, 2958 I-12
Indian Harbour Beach, 8462 I-12
INDIAN RIVER CO., 120463 K-12
Indian Rocks Beach, 5152 J-6
Indian Shores, 1759 *C-1
Indiantown, 5588 M-13
Indian Wells P-3
Inverness, 7184 G-7
Inwood, 6925 J-4
Islamorada, 6812 S-12
Ives Estates, 17586 *J-9
JACKSON CO., 46508 Q-7
Jacksonville, 773781 C-9
Jacksonville Beach, 21339 C-10
Jan Phyl Village, 5633 *K-4
Jasper, 1825 B-6
JEFFERSON CO., 14037 C-3
Jensen Beach, 11100 L-13
June Park, 4367 J-12
Juno Beach, 3347 M-14
Jupiter, 45100 M-14
Kathleen, 3280 I-8
Kendall, 75226 Q-13
Kenneth City, 4421 *D-2
Kensington Park, 3720 *G-3
Key Biscayne, 10319 Q-14
Key Largo, 11886 S-13
Keystone Hts., 1384 D-8
Key West, 25031 T-9
Kissimmee, 54598 I-10
La Belle, 4383 N-10
Lacoochee, 1345 H-8
Lady Lake, 12740 G-8
LAFAYETTE CO., 7333 D-5
LAKE CO., 245877 I-9
Lake Alfred, 3924 J-9
Lake Brantley, 3000 L-3
Lake Butler, 1986 D-7
Lake Cain Hills, 1600 N-3
Lake City, 10471 C-7
Lake Clarke Shores, 3501 *B-10
Lake Hamilton, 1366 J-9
Lake Helen, 2787 G-10
Lakeland, 87860 J-8
Lake Magdalene, 28873 *B-4
Lake Mary, 13260 G-10
Lake Panasoffkee, 3413 H-8
Lake Park, 9158 M-14
Lake Placid, 1714 L-10
Lakeside Green, 3311 *A-9
Lake Suzy, 1040 M-8
Lake Wales, 11194 J-9
Lakewood Park, 10458 K-13
Lake Worth, 35612 N-14
Land O Lakes, 20971 I-7
Lantana, 9665 N-14
Largo, 71166 J-6
Lauderdale-by-the-Sea, 5895 *H-10
Lauderdale Lakes, 31571 *H-8
Lauderhill, 59096 *H-8
Laurel, 8393 L-7
Lealman, 4200 *D-2
LEE CO., 492210 N-9
Leesburg, 17216 G-9
Lehigh Acres, 33430 N-9
Leisure City, 22152 Q-13
LEON CO., 242577 B-3
LEVY CO., 36270 F-7
LIBERTY CO., 7315 C-1
Lighthouse Pt., 11112 O-14
Live Oak, 6670 C-6
Lockhart, 12944 M-3
Longboat Key, 7478 L-6
Longwood, 13674 H-10
Loughman, 1385 I-9
Loxahatchee, 120 N-13
Lutz, 17081 I-7
Lynn Haven, 14238 S-6
Macclenny, 4838 C-8
Madeira Beach, 4459 J-6
MADISON CO., 18766 C-4
Madison, 3140 B-5
Maitland, 11857 H-10
MANATEE CO., 286804 L-8
Mangonia Park, 1302 *A-10
Marathon, 10143 T-11
Marco, 15410 P-9
Margate, 54954 O-13
Marianna, 6112 R-7
MARION CO., 280288 F-7
MARTIN CO., 135122 M-13
Mary Esther, 4090 S-4
Mascotte, 3673 H-9
Matlacha, 735 N-8
Mayo, 1013 D-5
Meadow Wood, 11286 P-3
Medulla, 6637 *K-4
Melbourne, 74545 J-12
Melbourne Beach, 3341 J-12
Melrose, 1100 E-8
Melrose Park, 7114 *I-8
Memphis, 7264 *F-3
Merritt Island, 36090 I-12
Mexico Beach, 1020 T-7
Miami, 376815 Q-13
Miami Beach, 89312 P-14
MIAMI-DADE CO., 2341167 Q-12
Miami Gardens, 100809 P-13
Miami Lakes, 22666 *K-7
Miami Shores, 10234 *K-9
Miami Sprs., 13585 P-13
Middleburg, 10338 D-9
Midway, 1714 G-10
Midway, 1440 B-2
Millview, 1100 †M-7
Milton, 7740 R-3
Mims, 9147 H-11
Minneola, 6151 H-9
Miramar, 96646 P-13
Mission City, 1700 G-11
Molino, 1312 R-2
MONROE CO., 78940 R-11
Monticello, 2546 B-3
Moore Haven, 1734 M-11
Morningside Park, 500 O-3
Mt. Dora, 10284 G-9
Mulberry, 3233 J-8
Myrtle Gr., 17211 R-2
Nalcrest, 500 J-10
Naples, 21284 O-9
Naples Park, 6741 O-9
Naranja, 4034 Q-13
Narcoossee, 200 I-10
NASSAU CO., 61625 B-9
Neptune Beach, 7179 C-10
Newberry, 3505 E-7
New Port Richey, 16711 I-6
New Smyrna Beach, 20742 G-11
Niceville, 12235 R-4
Nocatee, 1600 L-9
Nokomis, 3334 M-7
Norland, 22995 *K-8
N. Bay Village, 6798 *L-9
Northdale *A-3
N. Fort Myers, 40214 N-9
N. Lauderdale, 33534 *G-8
N. Miami, 59310 *K-9
N. Miami Beach, 40345 P-13
N. Naples, 400 O-9
N. Palm Beach, 12612 M-14
N. Port, 30945 M-8
N. Redington Beach, 1519 *D-1
North River Shores, 3101 L-13
Oak Hill, 1423 G-11
Oakland Park, 31462 O-14
Ocala, 47921 F-8
Ocean Ridge, 1682 N-14
Ocklawaha, 860 G-8
Ocoee, 27133 H-9
Ojus, 16642 P-14
OKALOOSA CO., 178104 R-4
OKEECHOBEE CO., 37481 K-11
Okeechobee, 5563 L-12
Oldsmar, 13609 J-7
Oneco, 3200 L-7
Opa Locka, 14794 P-13
ORANGE CO., 964865 I-11
Orange City, 6702 G-10
Orange Park, 9210 C-9
Orlando, 199336 H-10
Orlovista, 6047 H-10
Ormond Beach, 37617 F-11
Ormond By The Sea, 8430 F-11
OSCEOLA CO., 205870 I-11
Osprey, 4143 L-7
Osteen, 550 G-11
Oviedo, 27940 H-10
Ozona, 1900 J-6
Pace, 7393 R-3
Pahokee, 6263 M-12
Palatka, 10462 E-9
Palma Sola, 3100 *F-2
Palm Bay, 85076 J-12
PALM BEACH CO., 1216282 N-12
Palm Beach, 9759 N-14
Palm Beach Gardens, 41834 M-14
Palm Beach Shores, 1443 M-14
Palm City, 20097 L-13
Palm Coast, 37266 E-10
Palmetto, 12767 K-7
Palm Hbr., 59248 J-6
Palm Sprs., 13673 *B-10
Palm Springs North, 5460 *K-7
Panacea, 900 D-2
Panama City, 37085 S-6
Panama City Beach, 8290 S-6
Parker, 4713 S-6
PASCO CO., 388906 I-7
Pembroke Park, 5651 *J-9
Pembroke Pines, 148927 *J-7
Pensacola, 54897 R-2
Pensacola Beach, 1200 S-3
Perrine, 1370 Q-13
Perry, 6749 C-4
Pierson, 2602 F-10
Pine Castle, 8803 O-4
Pine Hills, 41764 H-10
Pine Island Ridge, 5199 *I-8
PINELLAS CO., 926146 K-6
Pinellas Park, 46449 J-6
Pinewood Park, 3400 *K-8
Placid Lakes, 3054 L-10
Plantation, 84929 *I-8
Plantation, 1900 S-12
Plant City, 31117 J-8
Playland Isles, 1000 *I-8
Pleasant Grove, 1000 †N-8
Plymouth, 1250 H-9
POLK CO., 510458 I-8
Pompano Beach, 88064 O-14
Ponte Vedra Beach, 3000 C-10
Port Charlotte, 46451 M-8
Port Orange, 50930 F-11
Port Richey, 3221 I-6
Port St. Joe, 3627 T-7
Port St. John, 12112 H-12
Port St. Lucie, 105507 L-13
Port Salerno, 10141 L-13
Princeton, 10090 Q-13
Progress Vil., 2482 *C-4
Punta Gorda, 16720 M-8
PUTNAM CO., 71841 E-9
Quincy, 6915 B-1
Rainbow Lakes, 1550 *C-9
Redington Beach, 1531 *D-1
Redington Shores, 2009 J-6
Richmond Hts., 8479 Q-13
Ridge Manor, 4108 H-8
Riverview, 12040 J-7
Riviera Beach, 31733 M-14
Rockledge, 22239 I-12
Royal Palm Beach, 28506 N-13
Ruskin, 8321 K-7
Safety Hbr., 17424 *B-2
St. Augustine, 11915 D-10
St. Augustine Beach, 5413 D-10
St. Augustine Shores, 4922 D-10
St. Cloud, 21480 I-10
St. James City, 4105 N-8
ST. JOHNS CO., 142869 D-10
St. Leo, 782 I-8
ST. LUCIE CO., 213447 L-12
St. Pete Beach, 10014 K-6
St. Petersburg, 247610 K-7
Salt Sprs., 600 F-9
Samoset, 3440 K-7
San Carlos Park, 16317 N-9
Sanford, 43556 G-10
Sanibel, 6043 O-8
San Mateo, 1100 E-9
SANTA ROSA CO., 133092 Q-3
Santa Rosa Beach, 600 S-5
SARASOTA CO., 346793 L-8
Sarasota, 53259 L-7
Sarasota Springs, 15875 *H-4
Satellite Beach, 9752 I-12
Sebastian, 17744 J-12
Sebring, 9878 K-10
Seffner, 5467 *B-5
SEMINOLE CO., 386374 H-11
Seminole, 16628 *DC
Seminole Manor, 2546 *C-9
Seville, 530 F-10
Sharpes, 3415 H-12
Siesta Key, 7150 *H-3
Silver Sprs., 1050 F-8
Silver Springs Shores, 6690 F-8
Sky Lake, 5651 O-3
Sneads, 1899 R-8
Solana, 1011 M-8
S. Apopka, 5800 M-2
S. Bay, 4080 N-12
S. Bradenton, 21587 *G-3
S. Daytona, 13799 F-11
Southgate, 7455 *H-3
S. Miami, 11355 Q-13
S. Pasadena, 5740 *D-2
Southport, 1500 S-6
S. Venice, 13539 M-7
Southwest Ranches, 7280 *I-7
Southwood, 1700 O-3
Springfield, 9035 S-6
Spring Hill, 69078 H-7
Starke, 5665 D-8
Stock Island, 4410 T-9
Stuart, 14891 L-13
Sugar Mill *B-3
SUMTER CO., 58875 G-8
Sun City Cen., 9000 K-7
Sunny Isles, 15327 *K-9
Sunrise, 89136 *H-8
Sun Valley, 1300 *D-9
Surfside, 4832 P-14
SUWANNEE CO., 36695 C-5
Sweetwater, 14137 Q-13
Sweetwater Oaks, 1100 L-3
Sylvan Shores, 2424 L-10
Taft, 1938 I-10
Taft, 1938 I-10
Tallahassee, 153938 B-2
Tamarac, 57967 O-13
Tampa, 317647 J-7
Tangelo Park, 2430 O-3
Tangerine, 826 G-9
Tarpon Lake Village *A-2
Tarpon Sprs., 22240 I-6
Tavares, 10831 G-9
Tavernier, 2173 S-13
TAYLOR CO., 19415 D-4
Taylor Creek, 4289 L-12
Temple Ter., 21860 J-7
Tequesta, 5644 M-14
The Hamptons *E-9
The Meadows, 4423 *G-4
The Villages, 8333 G-8
Thonotosassa, 6091 J-7
Tice, 4538 N-9
Titusville, 41752 H-11
Treasure Island, 7487 K-6
Trenton, 1720 E-6
Uleta, 2300 *K-9
Umatilla, 2416 G-9
UNION CO., 14002 D-7
Union Park, 10191 H-10
University West *B-4
Valparaiso, 6358 R-4
Venice, 19351 M-7
Venice Gardens, 7466 M-7
Vero Beach, 17357 K-13
Viera, 200 J-12
Villages of Oriole, 4758 *E-9
Virginia Gardens, 2326 *L-7
VOLUSIA CO., 468663 G-11
WAKULLA CO., 26131 C-2
Waldo, 797 D-8
WALTON CO., 46373 R-5
Warrington, 15207 S-2
WASHINGTON CO., 21604 R-6
Wauchula, 4406 K-9
Waverly, 1927 J-9
Weirsdale, 840 G-8
Wekiva Springs, 23169 L-3
Wellington, 46604 *B-8
West Bradenton, 4444 *F-2
Westchester, 30271 *M-7
W. Melbourne, 12334 J-12
W. Miami, 6009 *M-7
Weston, 62243 O-13
W. Palm Beach, 88932 N-14
W. Pensacola, 21939 R-2
Westwood Lakes, 12005 *M-7
Wewahitchka, 1700 S-7
White City, 4221 L-13
Wildwood, 3625 G-8
Williamsburg, 6736 O-3
Williston, 2395 F-7
Wilton Manors, 12861 *H-9
Wimauma, 4246 K-8
Windermere, 1924 H-10
Winter Garden, 20307 H-9
Winter Haven, 27137 J-9
Winter Park, 26755 H-10
Winter Springs, 31808 L-4
Woodville, 3006 C-2
Yalaha, 1175 H-9
Zellwood, 2540 H-9
Zephyrhills, 11554 I-8
Zolfo Sprs., 1653 K-9

Georgia

Map pp. 58-62

* City keyed to p. 62

Abbeville, 2407 K-7
Acworth, 17434 E-4
Adairsville, 2979 D-3
Adel, 5295 N-7
Adrian, 570 I-9
Ailey, 534 J-9
Alamo, 2420 K-9
Alapaha, 688 M-8
Albany, 76202 L-5
Allenhurst, 734 L-12
Alma, 3187 M-10
Alpharetta, 35139 D-5
Alto, 893 C-7
Americus, 16886 K-5
APPLING CO., 17797 L-10
Aragon, 1051 E-3
Arlington, 1559 M-3
Ashburn, 4435 L-6
Athens, 102498 E-7
ATKINSON CO., 7891 M-8
Atlanta, 423019 E-4
Auburn, 6843 E-6
Augusta, 193316 F-11
Austell, 6430 E-4
Avondale Estates, 2630 *E-5
BACON CO., 10135 L-9
Baconton, 916 M-5
Bainbridge, 11823 O-4
BAKER CO., 4307 M-4
BALDWIN CO., 44953 G-7
Baldwin, 2649 C-7
Ball Ground, 774 D-5
BANKS CO., 15483 D-7
Barnesville, 5890 H-5
BARROW CO., 53479 E-6
BARTOW CO., 84730 D-3
Baxley, 4379 L-10
Belvedere, 6000 *E-5
BEN HILL CO., 17235 L-8
Berlin, 612 N-6
BERRIEN CO., 16484 M-7
BIBB CO., 154287 I-6
Bibb City, 510 R-2
Blackshear, 3302 M-10
Blacksville, 4 G-5
Blackwells, 5000 E-4
Blairsville, 696 B-6
Blakely, 5588 M-3
BLECKLEY CO., 11842 J-7
Bloomingdale, 2642 K-13
Blue Ridge, 1191 B-5
Bogart, 1101 E-7
Bonaire, 900 I-7
Boston, 1432 O-6
Bowdon, 1958 F-2
Bowdon Jct., 400 F-2
Bowman, 970 D-8
BRANTLEY CO., 15279 M-11
Bremen, 5057 F-2
Brookhaven, 7000 *C-4
Brooklet, 1100 J-12
BROOKS CO., 16242 O-7
Broxton, 1460 L-8
Brunswick, 15984 N-12
BRYAN CO., 26340 K-12
Buchanan, 977 E-2
Buena Vista, 1657 J-4
Buford, 10820 D-5
BULLOCH CO., 58360 J-11
BURKE CO., 22949 H-11
Butler, 1928 I-5
BUTTS CO., 22099 G-5
Byromville, 412 J-6
Byron, 3062 I-6
Cairo, 9342 O-5
CALHOUN CO., 6122 M-4
Calhoun, 12342 C-3
CAMDEN CO., 45470 N-11
Camilla, 5609 N-5
CANDLER CO., 10023 J-11
Canon, 787 D-8
Canton, 13195 D-4
Carnesville, 586 D-8
CARROLL CO., 98525 F-3
Carrollton, 20615 F-3
Cartersville, 17221 D-3
Cataula, 550 I-3
CATOOSA CO., 58085 B-2
Cave Spr., 992 D-2
Cedar Gr., 2000 *G-5
Cedartown, 9583 E-2
Centerville, 5268 I-6
Chamblee, 9228 E-5
CHARLTON CO., 10707 O-10
CHATHAM CO., 235270 K-13
Chatsworth, 3768 B-3
CHATTAHOOCHEE CO., 19333 J-3
CHATTOOGA CO., 26422 C-2
CHEROKEE CO., 166639 D-4
Chickamauga, 2392 B-2
Chicopee, 750 D-6
Clarkdale, 500 E-4
CLARKE CO., 103691 E-7
Clarkesville, 1347 C-7
Clarkston, 7122 *D-6
Claxton, 2394 K-11
CLAY CO., 3358 L-3
CLAYTON CO., 259736 F-4
Clayton, 2065 B-7
Cleveland, 2225 C-6
CLINCH CO., 6967 N-9
COBB CO., 651027 E-4
Cochran, 4501 J-7
COFFEE CO., 38994 L-9
Colbert, 497 E-8
College Park, 18940 F-4
Collins, 528 J-11
COLQUITT CO., 43203 N-6
Colquitt, 1909 N-3
COLUMBIA CO., 97505 F-10
Columbus, 185702 J-3
Comer, 1110 E-8
Commerce, 5333 D-7
Conley, 6188 *G-4
Constitution, 600 *F-4
Conyers, 12034 F-5
COOK CO., 15951 N-7
Coolidge, 558 N-6
Cordele, 11500 K-6
Cornelia, 3730 C-7
Covington, 13152 F-6
COWETA CO., 101395 G-3
CRAWFORD CO., 12553 I-5
Crawford, 829 E-8
Crawfordville, 536 F-8
CRISP CO., 21994 K-6
Cumming, 5034 D-5
Cusseta, 1258 J-3
Cuthbert, 3592 L-3
Dacula, 4397 E-6
DADE CO., 15910 B-2
Dahlonega, 4158 C-6
Dallas, 6847 E-3
Dalton, 30341 B-3
Danville, 361 I-7
Darien, 1670 M-12
Dasher, 829 O-8
DAWSON CO., 18575 D-5
Dawson, 5035 L-4
Dearing, 439 G-10
DECATUR CO., 28212 O-4
Decatur, 17859 E-5
Deenwood, 1836 N-10
Deerwood Park, 3000 *E-5
DE KALB CO., 674334 F-5
Demorest, 1611 C-7
Dexter, 527 J-8
Dock Jct., 6951 N-12
DODGE CO., 19374 J-7
Doerun, 831 M-6
Donalsonville, 2743 N-3
DOOLY CO., 11552 K-6
Doraville, 10029 E-5
DOUGHERTY CO., 95684 L-4
DOUGLAS CO., 102015 F-3
Douglas, 10753 M-9
Douglasville, 25307 F-3
Druid Hills, 12741 *E-4
Dublin, 15976 I-8
Duluth, 23697 E-5
Dunaire, 8000 *D-6
Dunwoody, 32808 *A-4
EARLY CO., 12224 M-3
E. Dublin, 2550 I-9
Eastman, 5422 J-8
East Marietta, 12000 *A-2
E. Newnan, 1305 G-3
E. Point, 37220 F-4
Eatonton, 6917 G-7
ECHOLS CO., 3999 O-8
Echota, 650 C-3
Eden, 750 J-12
Edison, 1269 L-3
EFFINGHAM CO., 42715 J-12
ELBERT CO., 20636 E-8
Elberta, 950 I-6
Elberton, 4612 D-8
Ellaville, 1662 J-5
Ellijay, 1556 C-4
EMANUEL CO., 21885 I-10
Embry Hills, 1600 *C-6
Emerson, 1130 D-3
Enigma, 887 M-7
Euharlee, 3653 D-3
EVANS CO., 11365 J-11
Evans, 17727 F-10
Experiment, 3233 G-5
Fairburn, 6771 F-4
Fairmount, 761 C-4
Fair Oaks, 8443 *B-1
FANNIN CO., 21234 B-4
Fargo, 382 O-9
FAYETTE CO., 98914 G-4
Fayetteville, 13455 F-4
Fitzgerald, 8752 L-7
Five Forks, 3200 E-5
Flowery Branch, 1958 D-6
FLOYD CO., 93368 D-2
Folkston, 3263 O-11
Forest Park, 21247 F-4
FORSYTH CO., 123811 D-5
Forsyth, 4354 H-6
Ft. Gaines, 1088 L-3
Ft. Oglethorpe, 7854 B-2
Ft. Valley, 8040 I-6
FRANKLIN CO., 21164 C-7
Franklin, 886 G-3
Franklin Sprs., 750 D-8
FULTON CO., 818322 F-4
Gainesville, 29806 D-6
Garden City, 10942 K-13
Garden Lakes, 4000 D-2
Georgetown, 915 K-2
Gibson, 713 G-9
GILMER CO., 25973 B-4
GLASCOCK CO., 2636 G-9
Glennville, 4859 K-11
Glenwood, 826 K-9
GLYNN CO., 70131 M-12
GORDON CO., 47777 C-3
Gordon, 2131 H-7
GRADY CO., 24185 N-5
Grantville, 1903 G-3
Gray, 2053 H-7
GREENE CO., 15263 F-8
Greensboro, 3318 F-8
Greenville, 893 H-4
Gresham Park, 9215 *F-4
Griffin, 23460 G-5
Grovetown, 6675 F-10
Guyton, 1133 J-12
GWINNETT CO., 673345 E-6
HABERSHAM CO., 38446 C-7
Haddock, 750 H-7
Hagan, 1003 K-11
Hahira, 1756 N-7
HALL CO., 156101 D-6
Hamilton, 502 I-3
Hampton, 4458 G-5
HANCOCK CO., 9977 G-8
Hapeville, 5705 *G-3
HARALSON CO., 27460 E-2
Hardwick, 4800 H-7
Harlem, 1804 G-10
HARRIS CO., 25891 I-3
HART CO., 23432 D-8
Hartwell, 4273 D-8
Hawkinsville, 4194 J-7
Hazlehurst, 3757 K-9
HEARD CO., 11152 G-2
Helena, 2297 K-8
HENRY CO., 150003 F-5
Hephzibah, 4084 G-11
Hiawassee, 806 B-6
Highland Mills, 700 G-5
Hinesville, 29396 K-12
Hiram, 1480 E-3
Hoboken, 487 N-10
Hogansville, 2751 G-3
Holly Sprs., 4420 D-4
Homeland, 796 O-11
Homer, 1011 D-7
Homerville, 2813 N-9
Hoschton, 1393 D-6
HOUSTON CO., 120434 J-6
Ideal, 513 J-5
IRWIN CO., 10060 L-7
Irwinton, 587 I-8
Isle of Hope, 2605 K-13
JACKSON CO., 46998 D-7
Jackson, 4338 G-6
JASPER CO., 12547 G-6
Jasper, 2381 C-4
JEFF DAVIS CO., 12888 L-9
JEFFERSON CO., 17001 H-9
Jefferson, 4182 D-7
Jeffersonville, 1242 I-7
JENKINS CO., 8765 H-11
Jesup, 9424 L-11
JOHNSON CO., 9421 I-9
JONES CO., 25472 H-7
Jonesboro, 3818 F-5
Kennesaw, 25816 E-4
Kingsland, 11064 O-12
Kingston, 665 D-3
La Fayette, 6774 B-2
La Grange, 26576 H-3
Lake City, 2844 *H-4
Lakeland, 2743 N-8
LAMAR CO., 16234 H-5
LANIER CO., 7361 N-8
LAURENS CO., 46108 J-8
Lavonia, 1879 C-8
Lawrenceville, 26698 E-6
Leary, 642 M-4
LEE CO., 28410 L-5
Leesburg, 2609 L-5
Lenox, 888 M-7
Leslie, 449 K-5
LIBERTY CO., 58925 K-11
Lilburn, 11363 E-5
LINCOLN CO., 8536 E-9
Lincoln Park, 1122 H-5
Lincolnton, 1621 E-10
Lindale, 4088 D-2
Lithia Sprs., 2072 E-4
Lithonia, 2194 F-5
Lizella, 600 I-6
Locust Gr., 2755 G-5
Loganville, 7880 E-6
LONG CO., 10780 L-12
Lookout Mtn., 1577 B-2
Louisville, 2653 H-10
LOWNDES CO., 94579 N-7
Ludowici, 1500 L-12
Lula, 1609 D-6
Lumber City, 1215 K-9
LUMPKIN CO., 23185 C-5
Lumpkin, 1293 K-3
Luthersville, 839 G-3
Lyerly, 505 C-2
Lyons, 4269 J-10
Mableton, 29733 E-4
MACON CO., 14025 J-5
Macon, 95267 H-6
MADISON CO., 27075 D-7
Madison, 3779 F-7
Manchester, 3792 H-4
Marietta, 61282 E-4
MARION CO., 7170 J-4
Marshallville, 1303 J-6
Martinez, 27749 F-11
Maysville, 1459 D-7
McCaysville, 1042 B-5
McDonough, 11721 F-5
McDUFFIE CO., 21445 G-9
McINTOSH CO., 10885 M-12
McRae, 2664 K-8
Meigs, 1103 N-5
Menlo, 500 C-2
MERIWETHER CO., 22786 H-3
Metter, 4000 J-11
Midville, 466 H-10
Midway, 1047 L-12
Milan, 915 K-8
Milledgeville, 19159 H-8
Millen, 3547 I-11
MILLER CO., 6328 N-4
Milstead, 1500 F-5
MITCHELL CO., 23832 M-5
MONROE CO., 23244 H-5
Monroe, 11892 E-6
Montezuma, 4017 J-5
MONTGOMERY CO., 8691 K-9
Monticello, 2517 G-6
MORGAN CO., 16775 F-7
Morrow, 5034 F-5
Morven, 628 N-7
Moultrie, 14500 N-6
Mtn. City, 806 B-7
Mtn. View, 1100 *G-3
Mt. Airy, 669 C-7
Mt. Berry, 500 D-2
Mt. Vernon, 2126 J-9
Mt. Zion, 1407 F-2
MURRAY CO., 39446 B-4
Murrayville, 800 C-6
MUSCOGEE CO., 185702 J-3
Nahunta, 1013 N-11
Nashville, 4760 N-7
Nelson, 693 D-5
New Holland, 1200 D-6
Newnan, 20551 G-3
NEWTON CO., 76144 F-6
Newton, 897 M-4
Nicholls, 2538 M-9
Norcross, 9294 E-5
Norman Park, 862 M-6
N. Decatur, 15270 *D-5
N. Druid Hills, 18852 *D-5
N. West Point, 700 H-2
Oakdale, 1100 *C-2
Oak Gr., 2850 *D-5
Oakwood, 3100 D-6
Ochlocknee, 612 N-5
Ocilla, 3255 L-7
OCONEE CO., 28087 E-7
OGLETHORPE CO., 13379 E-8
Oglethorpe, 1172 J-5
Omega, 1353 M-7
Oxford, 2040 F-6
Palmetto, 3614 F-4
Panthersville, 11791 F-5
Patterson, 637 M-10
PAULDING CO., 100071 E-3
Pavo, 713 N-6
PEACH CO., 24320 I-6
Peachtree City, 33010 G-4
Pearson, 1860 M-9
Pelham, 3981 N-5
Pembroke, 2414 K-12
Pendley Hills, 5000 *E-6
Perry, 10566 J-6
Phillipsburg, 887 M-7
PICKENS CO., 26905 C-4
PIERCE CO., 16327 M-10
PIKE CO., 14979 H-4
Pine Mtn., 1184 H-3
Pine Mtn. Valley, 950 H-3
Pineview, 536 K-7
Plains, 624 K-4
POLK CO., 39800 E-2
Pooler, 8344 R-11
Portal, 584 I-11
Porterdale, 1420 F-6
Port Wentworth, 3148 Q-12
Poulan, 925 M-6
Powder Sprs., 13760 E-4
PULASKI CO., 9724 J-7
PUTNAM CO., 19575 G-7
Putney, 2998 M-5
QUITMAN CO., 2480 K-3
Quitman, 4488 O-7
RABUN CO., 15757 B-7
Radium Sprs., 1400 M-5
RANDOLPH CO., 7465 L-3
Ray City, 758 N-8
Red Oak, 2800 *H-2
Rehoboth, 1300 *D-6
Reidsville, 2291 K-10
Remerton, 826 O-7
Reynolds, 1029 I-5
Rhine, 421 K-8
Richland, 1707 K-4
RICHMOND CO., 198149 G-10
Richmond Hill, 8266 K-13
Rincon, 5598 J-13
Ringgold, 2591 B-3
Riverdale, 14880 F-4
Roberta, 771 I-5
Rochelle, 1430 K-7
ROCKDALE CO., 74941 F-5
Rockmart, 3977 E-3
Rocky Face, 1000 B-3
Rome, 35303 D-2
Rossville, 3406 B-2
Roswell, 78229 E-5
Royston, 2619 D-8
Rutledge, 736 F-7
St. Marys, 15811 O-12
St. Simons Island, 13381 N-12
Sandersville, 5981 H-9
Sandy Sprs., 85781 E-4
Sardis, 1211 H-11
Sargent, 900 F-3
Savannah, 127573 K-13
SCHLEY CO., 3935 J-4
Scottdale, 9803 *D-6
SCREVEN CO., 15407 H-11
Screven, 723 M-11
Sea Island, 700 N-13
SEMINOLE CO., 9270 N-3
Senoia, 2297 G-4
Shannon, 1682 D-3
Shellman, 1094 L-4
Skyland, 2500 *C-5
Smithville, 863 K-5
Smyrna, 45610 E-4
Snellville, 17961 E-5
Social Circle, 3722 F-6
Soperton, 2769 J-9
S. Decatur, 19400 *E-5
SPALDING CO., 60483 G-5
Sparks, 1756 N-7
Sparta, 1432 G-8
Springfield, 1971 J-13
Statenville, 650 O-8
Statesboro, 23744 J-11
Statham, 2310 E-7
STEPHENS CO., 25264 C-7
STEWART CO., 5001 K-3
Stillmore, 740 J-10
Stockbridge, 11256 F-5
Stone Mtn., 7097 E-5
Sugar Hill, 13820 D-5
Sugar Valley, 300 C-3
Summerville, 4705 C-2
SUMTER CO., 33217 K-5
Suwanee, 10562 E-5
Swainsboro, 7063 I-10
Sylvania, 2611 I-12
Sylvester, 5903 M-6
TALBOT CO., 6562 I-4
Talbotton, 1003 I-4
TALIAFERRO CO., 1957 F-8
Tallapoosa, 2956 F-2
Tate, 1000 C-4
TATTNALL CO., 22385 K-10
TAYLOR CO., 8901 I-4
TELFAIR CO., 11523 K-8
Temple, 3531 F-3
Tennille, 1442 H-9
TERRELL CO., 10854 L-4
THOMAS CO., 43667 N-6
Thomaston, 9295 H-5
Thomasville, 18233 O-5
Thomson, 6782 F-9
Thunderbolt, 2319 K-13
TIFT CO., 39523 M-7
Tifton, 15862 M-7
Tignall, 652 E-9
Toccoa, 9324 C-7
Toco Hills, 3200 *D-5
TOOMBS CO., 26469 K-10
Toomsboro, 620 H-8
TOWNS CO., 9901 B-6
Trenton, 2122 B-2
TREUTLEN CO., 6952 J-9
Trion, 2001 C-2
TROUP CO., 60218 G-3
Tucker, 26532 E-5
Tunnel Hill, 1220 B-3
TURNER CO., 9570 L-7
TWIGGS CO., 10466 I-7
Twin City, 1760 I-10
Twin Lakes, 950 O-8
Tybee Island, 3474 K-14
Tyrone, 4783 F-4
Ty Ty, 741 M-6
Unadilla, 2736 J-6
UNION CO., 19119 B-5
Union City, 13054 F-4
Union Pt., 1650 F-8
Unionville, 2074 M-7
UPSON CO., 27978 H-5
Uvalda, 546 K-9
Valdosta, 45059 O-7
Vidalia, 10625 J-10
Vienna, 2935 K-6
Villa Rica, 8087 F-3
Vinings, 9677 *C-2
Vista-Grove, 3000 *D-5
Waco, 489 F-2
Wadley, 2040 H-10
Waleska, 718 D-4
WALKER CO., 62584 C-2
Walthourville, 3785 L-12
WALTON CO., 69381 E-6
WARE CO., 35503 N-9
Warner Robins, 54264 I-7
WARREN CO., 6129 G-9
Warrenton, 2016 G-9
Warwick, 417 L-6
WASHINGTON CO., 20780 H-9
Washington, 4233 F-9
Watkinsville, 2252 E-7
Waverly Hall, 739 I-3
Waycross, 15156 N-10
WAYNE CO., 27509 L-11
Waynesboro, 5865 H-11
WEBSTER CO., 2295 K-4
W. Point, 3305 H-2
WHEELER CO., 6593 K-9
Whigham, 624 O-5
WHITE CO., 22815 C-6
White, 722 D-4
Whitesburg, 591 F-3
WHITFIELD CO., 87833 B-3
WILCOX CO., 8764 K-7
WILKES CO., 10653 E-9
WILKINSON CO., 10267 I-8
Willacoochee, 1480 M-8
Winder, 11654 E-6
Winterville, 1040 E-7
Woodbine, 1252 N-12
Woodbury, 1121 H-4
Woodland, 418 I-4
Woodstock, 14889 D-4
WORTH CO., 21849 M-6
Wrens, 2244 G-10
Wrightsville, 3003 I-9
Young Harris, 549 B-6
Zebulon, 1158 H-5

Hawaii

Map pp. 62-63

'Aiea, 9019 M-4
Anahola, 1932 I-2
Captain Cook, 3206 M-8
'Ewa Beach, 14650 N-3
'Ewa Villages, 4741 M-3
Hālawa Hts., 4000 M-4
Hale'iwa, 2225 I-4
Haliimaile, 895 I-9
Hanamaulu, 3272 I-2
Hanapepe, 2153 I-2
Hau'ula, 3651 K-4
HAWAII CO., 158423 L-10
Hawi, 938 L-8
Hilo, 40759 M-10
Holualoa, 6107 M-8
Hōnaunau M-8
Honoka'a, 2233 L-9
HONOLULU CO., 902704 I-5
Honolulu, 380149 J-5
Kaaawa, 1324 K-4
Kahalu'u, 2935 L-5
Kahuku, 2097 I-5
Kahului, 20146 K-7
Kailua, 36513 J-5
Kailua Kona, 9870 M-8
Kalaheo, 3913 I-2
Kāne'ohe, 34970 J-5
Kapaa, 9472 I-2
KAUAI CO., 60747 I-2
Kaunakakai, 2726 J-6
Kea'au, 2010 M-10
Kealakekua, 1645 M-8
Kekaha, 3175 I-2
Keokea K-8
Kihei, 16749 K-7
Kilauea, 2092 I-2
Koloa, 1942 I-2
Kurtistown, 1157 M-10
Lahaina, 9118 K-7
Lā'ie, 4585 J-4
Lāna'i City, 3164 K-7
Lihue, 5674 I-2
Lower Paia, 220 I-9
Mā'ili, 5943 M-2
Mākaha, 7753 L-1
Makakilo City, 13156 M-2
MAUI CO., 135605 J-7
Maunawili, 4869 M-5
Mililani Town, 28608 L-3
Nā'ālehu, 919 N-9
Nānākuli, 10814 J-4
Pa'auilo, 571 L-9
Pacific Palisades, 5600 M-3
Pāhala, 1378 N-9
Pāhoa, 962 M-10
Paia, 2499 I-9
Pāpa'ikou, 1414 M-10
Pearl City, 30976 J-5
Pukalani, 7380 K-8
Sunset Beach, 660 J-3
Volcano, 2231 M-9
Wahiawā, 16151 J-5
Waiakoa, 900 J-9
Waialua, 3761 K-2
Wai'anae, 10506 J-4
Wailua, 2083 I-2
Wailuku, 12296 K-7
Waimānalo, 3664 J-5
Waimānalo Beach, 4271 M-6
Waimea, 1787 I-2
Waimea, 7028 L-9
Waipahu, 33108 M-3
Waipi'o Acres, 5298 L-3
Whitmore Vil., 4057 L-3

Idaho

Map pp. 64-65

Aberdeen, 1839 L-6
ADA CO., 325151 K-2
ADAMS CO., 3515 H-2
Albion, 262 M-5
American Falls, 3958 L-6
Ammon, 8623 K-8
Arco, 1016 K-6
Arimo, 335 M-7
Ashton, 1129 J-8
Athol, 687 C-2
Bancroft, 366 L-8
BANNOCK CO., 75630 L-7
Basalt, 425 K-7
Bayview, 350 C-2
BEAR LAKE CO., 6306 N-9
Bellevue, 2115 K-5
BENEWAH CO., 9029 D-2
BINGHAM CO., 42926 L-6
Blackfoot, 10646 L-7
BLAINE CO., 20791 L-6
BOISE CO., 7236 J-3
Boise, 190117 K-2
BONNER CO., 39162 C-2
Bonners Ferry, 2647 B-2
BONNEVILLE CO., 87007 K-8
BOUNDARY CO., 10173 B-2
Bovill, 298 E-2
Buhl, 4019 M-4
Burley, 9313 M-5
BUTTE CO., 2873 K-6
Caldwell, 31041 K-1
CAMAS CO., 1049 K-4
Cambridge, 355 I-2
CANYON CO., 151508 K-1
Carey, 527 K-5
CARIBOU CO., 7152 L-8
Cascade, 975 I-2
CASSIA CO., 21610 M-5
Challis, 847 I-5
Chubbuck, 10151 L-7
CLARK CO., 904 I-7
Clark Fk., 566 C-2
CLEARWATER CO., 8401 E-3
Cobalt H-5
Coeur d'Alene, 37262 D-2
Cottonwood, 1008 F-2
Council, 765 I-2
Craigmont, 554 F-2
Culdesac, 375 F-2
CUSTER CO., 4090 J-5
Dalton Gardens, 2304 C-2
Dayton, 447 N-8
Deary, 534 E-2
Declo, 336 M-5
Downey, 599 M-7
Driggs, 1133 K-9
Dubois, 623 J-7
Eagle, 15253 K-2
Eden, 411 M-5
Elk City, 300 G-3
Elk River, 140 E-2
ELMORE CO., 28872 L-3
Emmett, 5933 J-2
Fairfield, 399 K-4
Fernwood, 425 E-2
Filer, 1690 M-4
Firth, 418 K-7
Ft. Hall, 1200 L-7
FRANKLIN CO., 11874 M-8
Franklin, 659 N-8
FREMONT CO., 12107 J-8
Fruitland, 4116 J-1
Garden City, 11083 B-5
GEM CO., 15795 J-2
Genesee, 915 F-1
Georgetown, 521 M-8
Glenns Ferry, 1514 L-3
GOODING CO., 14329 L-4
Gooding, 3323 L-4
Grace, 967 M-8
Grand View, 491 L-2
Grangeville, 3146 G-2
Greenleaf, 874 K-1
Hagerman, 685 L-4
Hailey, 7301 K-5
Hammett, 300 L-3
Hansen, 984 M-5
Harrison, 270 D-2
Hayden, 10421 C-2
Hayden Lake, 502 C-2
Hazelton, 703 M-5
Headquarters, 35 E-3
Heyburn, 2790 M-5
Homedale, 2590 K-1
Horseshoe Bend, 829 J-2
IDAHO CO., 15413 G-3
Idaho City, 494 K-3
Idaho Falls, 51507 K-7
Inkom, 722 L-7
Iona, 1219 K-8
JEFFERSON CO., 20194 J-7
JEROME CO., 18913 L-5
Jerome, 8039 M-4
Juliaetta, 591 F-2
Kamiah, 1160 F-2
Kellogg, 2236 D-2
Kendrick, 358 E-2
Ketchum, 3121 K-4
Kimberly, 2700 M-4
Kingston, 800 D-2
Kooskia, 666 F-2
KOOTENAI CO., 117481 C-2
Kootenai, 462 B-2
Kuna, 8839 K-2
Laclede, 400 C-2
Lapwai, 1126 F-1
LATAH CO., 35087 E-2
Lava Hot Sprs., 526 M-8
LEMHI CO., 7731 H-5
LEWIS CO., 3748 F-2
Lewiston, 30937 F-1
Lewisville, 481 K-7
LINCOLN CO., 4321 L-5
Lincoln, 500 K-8
Mackay, 531 J-5
MADISON CO., 29878 K-8
Malad City, 2108 M-7
Marsing, 986 K-1
Marysville, 180 J-8
McCall, 2207 I-2
McCammon, 800 M-7
Melba, 507 K-2
Menan, 718 K-8
Meridian, 41127 K-2
Middleton, 3651 K-2
MINIDOKA CO., 19349 L-5
Montpelier, 2636 M-8
Moreland, 500 L-7
Moscow, 21707 E-1
Mtn. Home, 11376 L-3
Moyie Sprs., 685 B-2
Mullan, 781 D-3
Nampa, 64269 K-2
Newdale, 364 J-8
New Meadows, 507 H-2
New Plymouth, 1390 J-1
NEZ PERCE CO., 37699 F-1
Nezperce, 515 F-2
Notus, 506 K-1
Oakley, 662 M-5
ONEIDA CO., 4132 M-6
Orofino, 3151 F-2
Osburn, 1459 D-2
OWYHEE CO., 11186 M-2
Paris, 544 M-8
Parker, 322 J-8
Parma, 1803 K-1
Paul, 963 M-5
PAYETTE CO., 21466 J-2
Payette, 7298 J-1
Pierce, 561 F-3
Pinehurst, 1590 D-2
Plummer, 974 D-1
Pocatello, 51009 L-7
Ponderay, 692 B-2
Post Falls, 19984 C-1
Potlatch, 759 E-1
POWER CO., 7373 M-7
Preston, 4845 N-8
Priest River, 1863 C-1
Rathdrum, 5296 C-1
Rexburg, 21862 J-8
Richfield, 429 L-5
Rigby, 3035 K-8
Riggins, 404 H-2
Ririe, 542 K-8
Roberts, 674 K-7
Rockland, 305 M-6
Rupert, 5351 M-5
St. Anthony, 3375 J-8
St. Maries, 2589 D-2
Salmon, 3038 H-5
Sandpoint, 7378 B-2
Shelley, 3885 K-7
SHOSHONE CO., 12993 D-3
Shoshone, 1488 L-4
Silverton, 300 D-3
Smelterville, 618 D-2
Soda Sprs., 3294 M-8
Spirit Lake, 1431 C-1
Star, 2178 K-2
Stites, 225 F-2
Sugar City, 1352 J-8
Sun Valley, 1446 K-4
TETON CO., 7058 K-8
Teton, 581 J-8
Troy, 774 E-2
TWIN FALLS CO., 67082 M-4
Twin Falls, 36742 M-4
Ucon, 966 K-8
VALLEY CO., 7743 I-3
Victor, 1103 K-9
Wallace, 887 D-3
WASHINGTON CO., 9995 I-1
Weippe, 386 F-3
Weiser, 5386 J-1
Wendell, 2335 L-4
Weston, 433 N-8
Wilder, 1465 K-1
Winchester, 307 F-2

Illinois

Map pp. 66-73

* City keyed to pp. 70-73
‡ City keyed to p. 120

Abingdon, 3469 G-6
ADAMS CO., 67582 J-4
Addison, 36767 *H-5
Albany, 898 C-6
Albers, 963 O-8
Albion, 1902 P-12
Aledo, 3582 E-5
ALEXANDER CO., 9327 T-8
Alexis, 847 F-5
Algonquin, 27569 B-11
Alorton, 2711 ‡F-8
Alpha, 714 E-6
Alsip, 19503 *K-8
Altamont, 2271 M-10
Alton, 29841 N-6
Amboy, 2572 C-8
Andalusia, 1052 D-5
Anna, 5073 S-9
Annawan, 900 E-7
Antioch, 10499 A-12
Arbury Hills, 1770 *M-7
Arcola, 2674 K-11
Argenta, 855 J-10
Arlington Hts., 75784 B-12
Aroma Park, 811 F-13
Arthur, 2177 K-11
Ashland, 1382 J-7
Ashton, 1196 C-9
Assumption, 1238 K-9
Astoria, 1164 I-6
Athens, 1781 J-7
Atkinson, 981 E-7
Atlanta, 1660 I-9
Atwood, 1267 J-11
Auburn, 4319 K-7
Aurora, 162184 C-11
Ava, 663 Q-8
Aviston, 1320 O-8
Avon, 886 G-5
Bannockburn, 1586 *D-7
Barrington, 10211 B-12
Barrington Hills, 4176 *E-3
Barry, 1324 K-4
Bartlett, 37558 *G-3
Bartonville, 6154 G-8
Batavia, 26328 C-11
Beach Park, 11126 A-12
Beardstown, 5767 J-5
Beckemeyer, 1081 O-8
Beecher, 2378 E-13

2000 Census populations or latest available estimate.
Index to Canada and Mexico cities and towns, pages 274-275.

ILLINOIS - IOWA 263

Belleville, 41209 ... O-7
Bellevue, 1830 ... *C-15
Bellwood, 20121 ... *H-7
Belvidere, 22927 ... A-10
Bement, 1747 ... J-11
Benld, 1512 ... M-7
Bensenville, 20668 ... *G-6
Benton, 6817 ... Q-10
Berkeley, 5148 ... *H-6
Berwyn, 52534 ... *I-8
Bethalto, 9649 ... N-6
Bethany, 1274 ... K-10
Bismarck, 547 ... I-13
Blandinsville, 754 ... H-4
Bloomingdale, 21801 ... C-12
Bloomington, 68507 ... H-9
Blue Island, 23175 ... *L-9
Blue Mound, 1061 ... K-9
Bluffs, 740 ... K-5
Bolingbrook, 66151 ... D-12
BOND CO., 17941 ... M-8
BOONE CO., 46477 ... A-10
Bourbonnais, 15840 ... E-12
Bradford, 767 ... E-8
Bradley, 13386 ... F-13
Braidwood, 5790 ... E-12
Brandywine, 3100 ... *I-6
Breese, 4196 ... O-8
Bridgeport, 2167 ... N-13
Bridgeview, 15274 ... *J-7
Brighton, 2313 ... M-6
Brimfield, 901 ... G-7
Broadview, 8093 ... *I-7
Brookfield, 18933 ... *I-7
Brookport, 1060 ... T-10
BROWN CO., 6879 ... J-5
Brownstown, 700 ... M-10
Buffalo Gr., 43237 ... *D-6
Bunker Hill, 1806 ... M-7
Burbank, 28049 ... *J-8
BUREAU CO., 35221 ... D-8
Burnham, 4141 ... *L-11
Burr Ridge, 10781 ... *J-6
Bushnell, 3150 ... H-5
Butterfield, 3750 ... *I-5
Byron, 3292 ... B-9
Cahokia, 16043 ... O-6
Cairo, 3462 ... T-9
CALHOUN CO., 5069 ... L-4
Calumet City, 38688 ... *L-10
Calumet Park, 8351 ... *L-9
Cambria, 1350 ... R-9
Cambridge, 2139 ... E-6
Camp Pt., 1209 ... I-4
Canton, 14970 ... H-7
Capron, 1126 ... A-10
Carbon Cliff, 1694 ... T-5
Carbondale, 24952 ... R-9
Carlinville, 5762 ... L-7
Carlyle, 3424 ... O-8
Carmi, 5341 ... Q-12
Carol Stream, 40114 ... *H-4
Carpentersville, 34815 ... B-11
Carrier Mills, 1864 ... R-10
CARROLL CO., 16242 ... B-7
Carrollton, 2552 ... L-5
Carterville, 4809 ... R-9
Carthage, 2585 ... H-3
Cary, 18121 ... B-11
Casey, 2943 ... L-12
Caseyville, 4385 ... O-6
CASS CO., 13841 ... J-6
Catlin, 2058 ... I-13
Cedarville, 709 ... A-8
Central City, 1366 ... O-9
Centralia, 13739 ... O-9
Centreville, 6008 ... ‡F-8
Cerro Gordo, 1397 ... J-10
CHAMPAIGN CO., 186800 ... I-11
Champaign, 71958 ... I-11
Chandlerville, 723 ... I-6
Channahon, 10065 ... D-12
Charleston, 20305 ... L-12
Chatham, 9330 ... K-7
Chatsworth, 1236 ... G-11
Chebanse, 1116 ... F-12
Chenoa, 1829 ... G-10
Cherry Valley, 2211 ... B-9
Chester, 7939 ... Q-7
Chicago, 2869121 ... C-13
Chicago Hts., 32297 ... D-13
Chicago Ridge, 13900 ... *K-8
Chillicothe, 5778 ... F-8
Chrisman, 1287 ... J-13
CHRISTIAN CO., 35127 ... L-8
Christopher, 2812 ... Q-9
Cicero, 83029 ... C-13
Cisne, 664 ... O-11
Cissna Park, 783 ... H-12
Clarendon Hills, 8235 ... *I-6
CLARK CO., 16998 ... L-13
CLAY CO., 14316 ... N-11
Clay City, 983 ... N-11
Clayton, 858 ... J-4
Clifton, 1284 ... F-12
CLINTON CO., 36135 ... N-8
Clinton, 7336 ... I-9
Coal City, 4910 ... E-11
Coal Valley, 3821 ... D-5
Cobden, 1094 ... S-9
Coffeen, 711 ... M-8
Colchester, 1458 ... H-4
COLES CO., 51880 ... K-11
Colfax, 996 ... H-10
Collinsville, 25218 ... N-7
Colona, 5217 ... T-6
Columbia, 8545 ... O-6
COOK CO., 5351552 ... D-12
Cottage Hills, 980 ... ‡A-8
Coulterville, 1202 ... P-8
Country Club Hills, 16339 ... *M-8
Countryside, 5938 ... *J-7
CRAWFORD CO., 19899 ... M-13
Creal Sprs., 714 ... R-10
Crest Hill, 15424 ... *M-4
Crestwood, 11323 ... *L-8
Crete, 8313 ... D-13
Creve Coeur, 5306 ... G-8
Crossville, 750 ... P-12
Crystal Lake, 40021 ... B-11
Crystal Lawns, 2933 ... *M-4
Cuba, 1385 ... H-6
CUMBERLAND CO., 11063 ... L-11
Dallas City, 1022 ... G-3
Danvers, 1150 ... H-9
Danville, 33106 ... I-13
Darien, 22871 ... *J-5
Decatur, 79285 ... J-10
Deer Cr., 647 ... G-8
Deerfield, 19232 ... *D-7
Deer Park, 3160 ... *D-4
DEKALB CO., 94041 ... C-10
De Kalb, 41348 ... C-10
Delavan, 1789 ... H-8
De Pue, 1796 ... E-9
De Soto, 1632 ... R-9
Des Plaines, 56450 ... B-12
DE WITT CO., 16679 ... I-9
Diamond, 1758 ... E-11
Diamond Lake, 1500 ... *C-5
Divernon, 1176 ... K-8
Dixmoor, 3934 ... *L-9
Dixon, 15429 ... C-8
Dolton, 25176 ... *L-10
Dongola, 803 ... S-9
DOUGLAS CO., 19923 ... K-11
Downers Gr., 49222 ... *I-5
Downs, 762 ... H-10
Dunlap, 898 ... G-8
DUPAGE CO., 925188 ... C-12
Dupo, 3899 ... O-6
Du Quoin, 6344 ... Q-9
Durand, 1081 ... A-8
Dwight, 4388 ... F-11
Earlville, 1788 ... D-10
E. Alton, 6725 ... N-6
E. Dubuque, 1945 ... A-5
E. Dundee, 3147 ... *E-2
E. Galesburg, 818 ... F-6
E. Hazel Crest, 1582 ... *M-9
E. Moline, 21211 ... D-6
E. Peoria, 22428 ... G-8
E. St. Louis, 30573 ... O-6
EDGAR CO., 19396 ... K-13
Edinburg, 1138 ... K-8
EDWARDS CO., 6850 ... O-12
Edwardsville, 23600 ... N-7
EFFINGHAM CO., 34529 ... M-10
Effingham, 12498 ... M-11
Elburn, 3323 ... C-11
Eldorado, 4434 ... R-11
Elgin, 97117 ... B-11
Elizabeth, 681 ... A-6
Elk Grove Vil., 34666 ... *F-5
Elkville, 966 ... Q-9
Elmhurst, 44054 ... C-12
Elmwood, 1868 ... G-7
Elmwood Pk., 24876 ... *H-7
El Paso, 2727 ... G-9
Elsah, 641 ... M-6
Elwood, 1985 ... E-12
Energy, 1175 ... R-9
Enfield, 616 ... Q-11
Equality, 695 ... R-11
Erie, 1561 ... D-6
Eureka, 4945 ... G-9
Evanston, 74360 ... B-13
Evansville, 705 ... Q-7
Evergreen Pk., 20464 ... *K-8
Fairbury, 3940 ... G-11
Fairfield, 5327 ... P-11
Fairmont, 2563 ... *M-4
Fairmont City, 2387 ... ‡E-8
Fairmount, 643 ... I-13
Fairview Hts., 15264 ... O-7
Farmer City, 2025 ... I-10
Farmingdale, 970 ... *J-6
Farmington, 2515 ... G-7
FAYETTE CO., 21539 ... M-9
Findlay, 683 ... K-10
Fisher, 1672 ... I-11
Flanagan, 1069 ... G-10
Flora, 4943 ... O-11
Flossmoor, 9438 ... *M-9
FORD CO., 14094 ... H-11
Ford Hts., 3382 ... *N-10
Forest Homes, 1700 ... ‡A-8
Forest Lake, 1530 ... *C-5
Forest Park, 15406 ... *I-7
Forest View, 763 ... *I-8
Forrest, 1210 ... G-11
Forreston, 1504 ... B-8
Fox Lake, 9937 ... A-12
Fox River Gr., 5059 ... B-11
Frankfort, 13381 ... D-12
FRANKLIN CO., 39117 ... Q-10
Franklin Gr., 1023 ... C-9
Franklin Pk., 19060 ... *G-7
Freeburg, 3946 ... O-7
Freeport, 25867 ... A-8
FULTON CO., 37658 ... H-6
Fulton, 3856 ... C-6
Gages Lake, 10415 ... *A-5
Galatia, 992 ... R-10
Galena, 3459 ... A-6
Galesburg, 32809 ... F-6
GALLATIN CO., 6220 ... R-12
Galva, 2714 ... E-7
Gardner, 1407 ... E-11
Geneseo, 6455 ... D-6
Geneva, 22236 ... C-11
Genoa, 4561 ... B-10
Georgetown, 3550 ... J-13
Germantown, 1124 ... O-8
Gibson City, 3284 ... H-11
Gifford, 942 ... I-12
Gilberts, 2784 ... *E-1
Gillespie, 3306 ... M-7
Gilman, 1791 ... G-12
Girard, 2247 ... L-7
Glasford, 1025 ... H-7
Glen Carbon, 11135 ... ‡C-9
Glencoe, 8869 ... B-13
Glendale Hts., 32848 ... *H-4
Glen Ellyn, 27210 ... *H-5
Glen Ellyn Countryside, 2500 ... *H-4
Glenview, 44818 ... *E-7
Glenview Countryside, 1950 ... *F-7
Glenwood, 8847 ... *M-10
Godfrey, 16571 ... M-6
Golconda, 681 ... S-11
Goreville, 965 ... S-9
Grafton, 650 ... M-5
Grand Tower, 609 ... R-8
Grandview, 1492 ... *F-17
Granite City, 31294 ... N-6
Grant Park, 1454 ... E-13
Granville, 1409 ... E-9
Grayslake, 21287 ... *B-5
Grayville, 1673 ... P-12
GREENE CO., 14708 ... L-5
Greenfield, 1166 ... L-6
Green Oaks, 3838 ... *B-6
Greenup, 1506 ... L-12
Green Valley, 705 ... H-8
Greenview, 832 ... J-7
Greenville, 7104 ... N-8
Gridley, 1411 ... G-10
Griggsville, 1215 ... K-5
GRUNDY CO., 39528 ... E-10
Gurnee, 30396 ... *A-6
HAMILTON CO., 8334 ... Q-11
Hamilton, 2895 ... H-3
Hampshire, 3093 ... B-11
Hampton, 1662 ... S-5
HANCOCK CO., 19393 ... I-3
Hanna City, 986 ... G-7
Hanover, 827 ... A-6
Hanover Pk., 37643 ... *G-4
HARDIN CO., 4711 ... S-11
Hardin, 951 ... M-5
Harrisburg, 9638 ... R-11
Harristown, 1271 ... J-9
Hartford, 1515 ... ‡B-8
Harvard, 8600 ... A-10
Harvey, 29367 ... D-13
Harwood Hts., 8315 ... *G-7
Havana, 3516 ... I-6
Hawthorn Woods, 6578 ... *C-5
Hazel Crest, 14745 ... *M-9
Hebron, 1099 ... A-11
HENDERSON CO., 8073 ... G-4
HENRY CO., 50644 ... E-6
Henry, 2513 ... F-8
Herrin, 11406 ... R-9
Herscher, 1565 ... F-12
Heyworth, 2478 ... I-9
Hickory Hills, 13752 ... *K-7
Highland, 8739 ... N-7
Highland Hills, 200 ... *I-5
Highland Pk., 30897 ... B-13
Highwood, 5478 ... B-13
Hillcrest, 1270 ... C-9
Hillsboro, 4253 ... M-8
Hillside, 8005 ... *H-6
Hinckley, 2048 ... C-10
Hinsdale, 17954 ... *I-6
Hodgkins, 2143 ... *J-7
Hoffman Estates, 50108 ... *F-5
Holiday Hills, 822 ... *B-3
Hollywood Hts., 1060 ... ‡E-9
Homer, 1190 ... I-12
Homer Glen, 23331 ... *L-6
Hometown, 4385 ... *K-8
Homewood, 19348 ... *M-9
Hoopeston, 5825 ... H-13
Hopedale, 914 ... H-8
Hudson, 1588 ... H-9
Huntley, 11769 ... B-11
Hurst, 790 ... R-9
Illiopolis, 892 ... J-9
Indian Head Park, 3737 ... *J-6
Ingalls Park, 3082 ... *N-5
Ingleside, 1700 ... *A-4
Inverness, 6971 ... *E-5
IROQUOIS CO., 30684 ... G-12
Island Lake, 8407 ... *B-3
Itasca, 8382 ... *G-5
JACKSON CO., 58976 ... Q-8
Jacksonville, 19603 ... K-6
JASPER CO., 9955 ... M-12
JEFFERSON CO., 40334 ... O-9
Jerome, 1373 ... *G-16
JERSEY CO., 22188 ... M-5
Jerseyville, 8051 ... M-6
JO DAVIESS CO., 22526 ... A-6
JOHNSON CO., 12951 ... S-10
Johnston City, 3487 ... R-10
Joliet, 123570 ... D-12
Jonesboro, 1838 ... S-9
Justice, 12453 ... *J-7
KANE CO., 457122 ... B-11
KANKAKEE CO., 105625 ... F-13
Kankakee, 26995 ... F-13
Kansas, 832 ... K-12
Keithsburg, 716 ... F-4
KENDALL CO., 66565 ... D-11
Kenilworth, 2451 ... *E-8
Kewanee, 12724 ... E-7
Kildeer, 3899 ... *D-5
Kincaid, 1446 ... K-8
Kinmundy, 881 ... N-10
Kirkland, 1218 ... B-10
Kirkwood, 762 ... F-5
Knollwood, 1500 ... *B-7
KNOX CO., 54491 ... F-6
Knoxville, 3081 ... F-6
Lacon, 1914 ... F-8
Ladd, 1307 ... E-9
La Grange, 15650 ... *I-7
La Grange Highlands, 3650 ... *J-6
La Grange Pk., 13062 ... *I-7
La Harpe, 1339 ... H-4
LAKE CO., 685019 ... B-12
Lake Barrington, 5020 ... *C-4
Lake Bluff, 6170 ... A-13
Lake Forest, 20762 ... B-13
Lake in the Hills, 26639 ... *D-2
Lakemoor, 4021 ... A-12
Lake Villa, 8089 ... A-12
Lakewood, 3144 ... *C-1
Lake Zurich, 19170 ... B-12
La Moille, 762 ... D-9
Lanark, 1517 ... B-7
Lansing, 27976 ... *M-10
LA SALLE CO., 112037 ... E-9
La Salle, 9596 ... E-9
LAWRENCE CO., 15287 ... O-13
Lawrenceville, 4597 ... N-13
Lebanon, 3566 ... O-7
LEE CO., 35537 ... C-8
Leland, 947 ... D-10
Leland Gr., 1538 ... *F-16
Lemont, 14319 ... *K-5
Lena, 2842 ... A-7
Le Roy, 3380 ... H-10
Lewistown, 2458 ... H-6
Lexington, 1902 ... G-10
Libertyville, 21113 ... A-12
Lincoln, 15039 ... I-8
Lincolnshire, 6398 ... *D-6
Lincolnwood, 12255 ... *F-8
Lindenhurst, 14247 ... A-12
Lisle, 21656 ... C-12
Litchfield, 6690 ... M-8
LIVINGSTON CO., 39208 ... F-10
Livingston, 809 ... M-7
Lockport, 19217 ... D-12
LOGAN CO., 30716 ... I-8
Lombard, 42971 ... *H-5
Long Gr., 7494 ... *D-5
Long Lake, 3356 ... *A-4
Louisville, 1231 ... N-11
Loves Park, 21660 ... A-9
Lovington, 1213 ... K-10
Lyndon, 550 ... C-7
Lynwood, 7599 ... *N-10
Lyons, 10514 ... *I-7
Machesney Pk., 21205 ... A-9
Mackinaw, 1467 ... H-8
Macomb, 18874 ... H-5
MACON CO., 111175 ... J-9
Macon, 1140 ... K-9
MACOUPIN CO., 49055 ... M-7
MADISON CO., 261689 ... N-7
Madison, 4445 ... ‡D-7
Mahomet, 5466 ... I-11
Malta, 971 ... C-10
Manhattan, 3818 ... E-12
Manito, 1724 ... H-7
Mansfield, 937 ... I-11
Manteno, 6906 ... E-13
Maple Park, 1014 ... C-10
Marengo, 6902 ... B-10
Marine, 934 ... N-7
MARION CO., 40751 ... O-10
Marion, 16624 ... R-10
Marissa, 2096 ... P-7
Markham, 12531 ... *L-9
Maroa, 1551 ... J-10
Marseilles, 4826 ... E-10
MARSHALL CO., 13039 ... F-8
Marshall, 3744 ... L-13
Martinsville, 1228 ... L-13
Maryville, 5043 ... ‡D-10
Mascoutah, 5687 ... O-7
MASON CO., 15884 ... I-7
Mason City, 2521 ... I-7
MASSAC CO., 15138 ... T-10
Matherville, 785 ... E-5
Matteson, 14278 ... *N-8
Mattoon, 17849 ... L-11
Maywood, 26398 ... *H-7
Mazon, 898 ... E-11
McClure, 600 ... S-8
McCullom Lake, 1028 ... *A-2
MCDONOUGH CO., 32852 ... H-4
MCHENRY CO., 286091 ... A-10
McHenry, 23119 ... A-11
MCLEAN CO., 156879 ... G-10
McLean, 781 ... I-9
McLeansboro, 2829 ... Q-11
Meadowbrook, 1000 ... ‡A-9
Melrose Park, 23057 ... *H-7
MENARD CO., 12593 ... I-7
Mendon, 883 ... I-3
Mendota, 7178 ... D-9
MERCER CO., 17003 ... E-5
Meredosia, 1008 ... J-5
Merrionette Park, 2058 ... *K-9
Metamora, 2789 ... G-8
Metropolis, 6368 ... T-10
Midlothian, 14253 ... *L-8
Milan, 5309 ... T-3
Milford, 1324 ... G-13
Milledgeville, 971 ... C-7
Millstadt, 2940 ... O-6
Minier, 1260 ... H-9
Minonk, 2146 ... F-9
Minooka, 4706 ... D-11
Mitchell, 1300 ... ‡C-8
Moecherville, 1320 ... *J-2
Mokena, 17172 ... *M-6
Moline, 43064 ... D-5
Momence, 3089 ... E-13
Monee, 4013 ... E-13
Monmouth, 9531 ... F-5
MONROE CO., 29723 ... P-6
MONTGOMERY CO., 30352 ... L-8
Montgomery, 8699 ... C-11
Monticello, 5184 ... J-11
MORGAN CO., 35990 ... J-6
Morris, 12352 ... E-11
Morrison, 4345 ... C-7
Morrisonville, 1051 ... L-8
Morton, 15365 ... G-8
Morton Gr., 22705 ... *F-8
MOULTRIE CO., 14469 ... K-10
Mound City, 673 ... T-9
Mounds, 1056 ... T-9
Mt. Carmel, 7772 ... O-13
Mt. Carroll, 1747 ... B-7
Mt. Morris, 3026 ... B-8
Mt. Olive, 2115 ... M-7
Mt. Prospect, 55784 ... *F-6
Mt. Pulaski, 1643 ... J-9
Mt. Sterling, 2037 ... J-4
Mt. Vernon, 16486 ... P-10
Mt. Zion, 4821 ... K-10
Moweaqua, 1860 ... K-9
Mulberry Gr., 676 ... N-9
Mundelein, 32251 ... *C-5
Murphysboro, 8509 ... R-8
Naperville, 137894 ... C-12
Nashville, 3130 ... P-8
Nauvoo, 1165 ... H-3
Neoga, 1809 ... L-11
Newark, 938 ... D-11
New Athens, 2002 ... P-7
New Baden, 3050 ... O-7
New Berlin, 1109 ... K-7
New Boston, 647 ... E-4
New Lenox, 21545 ... D-12
Newman, 941 ... J-12
Newton, 3021 ... M-12
New Windsor, 715 ... E-5
Niantic, 689 ... J-9
Niles, 29945 ... *F-7
Noble, 732 ... N-11
Nokomis, 2315 ... L-9
Normal, 48649 ... H-9
Norridge, 14362 ... *G-7
Norris City, 1043 ... Q-11
N. Aurora, 13091 ... C-11
N. Barrington, 3166 ... *C-4
N. Chicago, 36601 ... A-12
Northbrook, 34061 ... *E-7
Northfield, 5491 ... *E-8
N. Glen Ellyn, 1400 ... *H-5
Northlake, 11686 ... *H-6
N. Riverside, 6568 ... *I-7
Oak Brook, 8847 ... *I-6
Oakbrook Ter., 2270 ... *I-6
Oak Forest, 28229 ... *L-8
Oak Gr., 738 ... E-5
Oakland, 971 ... K-12
Oak Lawn, 55136 ... C-13
Oak Park, 50824 ... C-13
Oakwood, 1496 ... I-13
Oakwood Hills, 2292 ... *C-3
Oblong, 1559 ... M-13
Odell, 1010 ... F-11
Odin, 1114 ... O-9
O Fallon, 24006 ... O-7
Ogden, 745 ... I-12
OGLE CO., 52858 ... B-9
Oglesby, 3634 ... E-9
Okawville, 1347 ... O-8
Olney, 8575 ... N-12
Olympia Fields, 4738 ... *N-9
Onarga, 1400 ... G-12
Oneida, 733 ... F-6
Oquawka, 1504 ... F-4
Oreana, 912 ... J-10
Oregon, 4133 ... B-8
Orion, 1707 ... E-6
Orland Hills, 7144 ... *M-7
Orland Park, 54011 ... D-12
Oswego, 18521 ... D-11
Ottawa, 18635 ... E-10
Palatine, 66848 ... B-12
Palestine, 1344 ... M-13
Palmyra, 733 ... L-7
Palos Hts., 12255 ... *L-7
Palos Hills, 17619 ... *K-7
Palos Park, 4814 ... *K-7
Pana, 5543 ... L-9
Paris, 8987 ... K-13
Park City, 6849 ... *A-7
Park Forest, 23560 ... D-13
Park Ridge, 37460 ... *F-7
Pawnee, 2602 ... K-8
Paw Paw, 840 ... C-10
Paxton, 4486 ... H-12
Pecatonica, 2081 ... A-8
Pekin, 33190 ... H-8
PEORIA CO., 182335 ... F-7
Peoria, 112907 ... G-8
Peoria Hts., 6354 ... G-8
Peotone, 4354 ... E-13
Percy, 930 ... Q-8
PERRY CO., 22684 ... Q-8
Peru, 9817 ... E-9
Petersburg, 2223 ... J-7
Philo, 1466 ... J-12
Phoenix, 2121 ... *L-9
PIATT CO., 16426 ... I-10
PIKE CO., 16927 ... K-4
Pinckneyville, 5407 ... Q-8
Piper City, 756 ... G-12
Pittsfield, 4544 ... K-4
Plainfield, 20162 ... D-12
Plano, 5576 ... D-11
Pleasant Hill, 1012 ... L-4
Pleasant Plains, 758 ... J-7
Pocahontas, 721 ... N-8
Polo, 2485 ... B-8
Pontiac, 11463 ... G-10
Pontoon Beach, 6006 ... ‡D-8
POPE CO., 4261 ... S-11
Poplar Gr., 2182 ... A-10
Port Byron, 1575 ... D-6
Posen, 4869 ... *L-9
Potomac, 671 ... I-13
Prairie Du Rocher, 598 ... Q-6
Preston Hts., 2527 ... *N-4
Princeton, 7539 ... E-8
Princeville, 1551 ... F-7
Prophetstown, 1970 ... D-7
Prospect Hts., 16807 ... *E-6
PULASKI CO., 7077 ... T-9
PUTNAM CO., 6119 ... E-8
Quincy, 39922 ... J-3
Ramsey, 1052 ... M-9
RANDOLPH CO., 33244 ... P-7
Rankin, 604 ... H-12
Rantoul, 13009 ... I-12
Rapids City, 965 ... D-6
Raymond, 925 ... L-8
Red Bud, 3491 ... P-7
RICHLAND CO., 15997 ... O-12
Richmond, 1366 ... A-11
Richton Park, 12883 ... D-13
Ridge Farm, 891 ... J-13
Ridgway, 894 ... R-12
Riverdale, 14752 ... *L-9
River Forest, 11483 ... *H-7
River Gr., 10458 ... *H-7
Riverside, 8648 ... *I-7
Riverton, 3140 ... J-8
Riverwoods, 4051 ... *D-7
Roanoke, 1983 ... G-9
Robbins, 6560 ... *L-9
Robinson, 6558 ... M-13
Rochelle, 9556 ... C-9
Rochester, 2943 ... K-8
Rockdale, 1947 ... *N-4
Rock Falls, 9447 ... C-8
Rockford, 151725 ... A-9
ROCK ISLAND CO., 147912 ... E-4
Rock Island, 38857 ... D-5
Rockton, 5348 ... A-9
Rolling Meadows, 24334 ... *E-5
Rome, 1776 ... G-8
Romeoville, 32481 ... D-12
Roodhouse, 2229 ... L-6
Roscoe, 6337 ... A-9
Roselle, 23237 ... B-12
Rosemont, 4146 ... *G-7
Roseville, 1043 ... G-5
Rosewood Hts., 4262 ... ‡A-8
Rosiclare, 1180 ... S-11
Rossville, 1190 ... H-13
Round Lake, 9333 ... *A-4
Round Lake Beach, 28093 ... *A-4
Round Lake Hts., 2375 ... *A-4
Round Lake Park, 6203 ... *A-4
Roxana, 1524 ... N-6
Royalton, 1145 ... Q-9
Rushville, 3144 ... I-5
St. Anne, 1188 ... F-13
St. Charles, 32010 ... C-11
ST. CLAIR CO., 258606 ... O-6
St. David, 567 ... H-6
St. Elmo, 1408 ... M-10
St. Francisville, 756 ... O-13
St. Jacob, 897 ... N-7
St. Joseph, 3266 ... I-12
Salem, 7347 ... O-10
SALINE CO., 26158 ... Q-11
Sandoval, 1392 ... O-9
Sandwich, 6820 ... D-10
SANGAMON CO., 191875 ... K-7
Sauk Vil., 10550 ... *N-10
Savanna, 3542 ... B-6
Savoy, 4785 ... I-11
Saybrook, 744 ... H-10
Schaumburg, 74342 ... *F-4
Schiller Park, 11657 ... *G-7
Schram City, 630 ... M-8
SCHUYLER CO., 7021 ... I-4
SCOTT CO., 5505 ... K-5
Seneca, 2057 ... E-10
Sesser, 2122 ... Q-9
Shabbona, 927 ... C-10
Shannon, 813 ... B-7
Shawneetown, 1364 ... R-12
Sheffield, 946 ... E-7
SHELBY CO., 22407 ... K-10
Shelbyville, 4805 ... L-10
Sheldon, 1189 ... G-13
Sheridan, 2171 ... D-10
Sherman, 3261 ... J-8
Sherrard, 685 ... E-5
Shiloh, 9403 ... ‡F-10
Shorewood, 9814 ... D-12
Sidney, 1091 ... J-12
Signal Hill, 1160 ... ‡F-8
Silvis, 7341 ... S-5
Skokie, 63633 ... B-13
Sleepy Hollow, 3707 ... *E-2
Smithton, 2633 ... O-7
Somonauk, 1408 ... D-10
S. Barrington, 3914 ... *E-4
S. Beloit, 5435 ... A-9
S. Chicago Heights, 3960 ... *N-9
S. Elgin, 20229 ... *G-2
Southern View, 1647 ... *G-16
S. Holland, 22087 ... *M-10
S. Jacksonville, 3372 ... K-6
S. Roxana, 1860 ... ‡B-8
S. Streator, 500 ... F-10
S. Wilmington, 617 ... E-11
Sparta, 4434 ... Q-7
Springfield, 113586 ... J-8
Spring Valley, 5362 ... E-9
Stanford, 662 ... H-9
STARK CO., 6198 ... F-7
State Park Place, 2600 ... ‡E-9
Staunton, 5049 ... M-7
Steeleville, 2033 ... Q-7
Steger, 10035 ... D-13
STEPHENSON CO., 48151 ... A-7
Sterling, 15272 ... C-8
Stewardson, 736 ... L-10
Stickney, 6040 ... *I-8
Stillman Valley, 1072 ... B-9
Stockton, 1882 ... A-7
Stone Park, 5057 ... *H-7
Stonington, 933 ... K-9
Streamwood, 37477 ... *F-3
Streator, 14050 ... F-10
Stronghurst, 864 ... G-4
Sugar Gr., 6619 ... C-11
Sullivan, 4343 ... K-10
Summit, 10467 ... *J-7
Sumner, 1019 ... N-13
Swansea, 11589 ... O-7
Sycamore, 13230 ... B-10
Tallula, 630 ... J-7
Tamaroa, 726 ... P-9
Tamms, 1178 ... T-9
Tampico, 747 ... D-7
Taylor Sprs., 582 ... M-8
Taylorville, 11296 ... K-9
TAZEWELL CO., 128056 ... H-8
Teutopolis, 1600 ... M-11
Thayer, 720 ... K-8
Thomasboro, 1253 ... I-12
Thornton, 2525 ... *M-10
Tilden, 916 ... P-7
Tilton, 2909 ... I-13
Tinley Park, 53792 ... D-13
Tiskilwa, 765 ... E-8
Toledo, 1148 ... L-11
Tolono, 2741 ... J-11
Toluca, 1298 ... F-9
Tonica, 693 ... E-9
Toulon, 1372 ... F-7
Tower Hill, 602 ... L-9
Tower Lakes, 1330 ... *C-4
Tremont, 2009 ... H-8
Trenton, 2642 ... O-7
Tri-State Vil., 1200 ... *J-6
Troy, 9069 ... N-7
Tuscola, 4491 ... J-11
UNION CO., 18170 ... S-9
University Park, 7658 ... D-13
Urbana, 38725 ... I-12
Utica, 998 ... E-9
Valier, 649 ... Q-9
Valley View, 700 ... *G-2
Vandalia, 6790 ... M-9
Venice, 2482 ... ‡E-7
VERMILION CO., 82804 ... H-13
Vermont, 778 ... H-5
Vernon Hills, 22308 ... *C-6
Vienna, 1280 ... S-10
Villa Gr., 2501 ... J-12
Villa Hills, 1410 ... ‡G-8
Villa Park, 22891 ... *H-5
Viola, 954 ... E-5
Virden, 3493 ... K-7
Virginia, 1742 ... J-6
WABASH CO., 12680 ... O-13
Wadsworth, 3440 ... A-12
Walnut, 1432 ... D-8
Wamac, 1351 ... O-9
WARREN CO., 18246 ... G-5
Warren, 1468 ... A-7
Warrensburg, 1227 ... J-9
Warrenville, 13286 ... *I-4
Warsaw, 1689 ... H-3
Washburn, 1111 ... F-9
WASHINGTON CO., 15179 ... P-8
Washington, 12040 ... G-8
Washington Park, 5833 ... ‡E-8
Wataga, 830 ... F-6
Waterloo, 8749 ... P-6
Waterman, 1218 ... C-10
Watseka, 5572 ... G-13
Wauconda, 9991 ... A-12
Waukegan, 91452 ... A-13
Waverly, 1287 ... K-7
WAYNE CO., 16944 ... O-11
Wayne, 2288 ... *G-3
Wayne City, 1083 ... P-11
Wenona, 1060 ... F-9
Westchester, 16680 ... *I-6
W. Chicago, 25262 ... *H-3
W. City, 725 ... Q-10
W. Dundee, 6912 ... B-11
Western Sprs., 12512 ... *I-6
Westfield, 668 ... L-12
W. Frankfort, 8215 ... Q-10
Westmont, 24639 ... *I-5
W. Peoria, 4677 ... *C-16
W. Salem, 983 ... O-12
Westville, 3090 ... I-13
Wheaton, 55016 ... C-12
Wheeling, 35495 ... *E-6
WHITE CO., 15106 ... P-11
White Hall, 2622 ... L-5
WHITESIDE CO., 59886 ... C-7
Wildwood, 40 ... *A-5
WILL CO., 586706 ... D-12
WILLIAMSON CO., 62448 ... R-10
Williamsville, 1420 ... J-8
Willowbrook, 8983 ... *J-5
Willow Sprs., 6071 ... *K-7
Wilmette, 27266 ... B-13
Wilmington, 5604 ... E-12
Winchester, 1634 ... K-5
Windsor, 1087 ... L-10
Winfield, 9393 ... *H-4
WINNEBAGO CO., 284313 ... A-9
Winnebago, 2990 ... A-9
Winnetka, 12386 ... B-13
Winthrop Hbr., 6866 ... A-13
Witt, 990 ... L-8
Wonder Lake, 1675 ... A-11
Wood Dale, 13451 ... *G-6
WOODFORD CO., 36367 ... G-9
Woodhull, 813 ... E-6
Woodridge, 33695 ... *J-5
Wood River, 11121 ... N-6
Woodstock, 21103 ... A-11
Worden, 962 ... N-7
Worth, 10906 ... *K-8
Wyanet, 1010 ... E-8
Wyoming, 1395 ... F-7
Yates City, 706 ... G-7
York Cen., 4818 ... *I-5
Yorkfield, 1500 ... *I-6
Yorkville, 8116 ... D-11
Zeigler, 1657 ... Q-9
Zion, 23814 ... A-13

Indiana

Map pp. 72-77

* City keyed to pp. 72-73

ADAMS CO., 33592 ... F-13
Advance, 563 ... H-7
Akron, 1044 ... D-9
Albany, 2362 ... H-12
Albion, 2320 ... B-11
Alexandria, 6062 ... H-11
ALLEN CO., 340153 ... C-13
Anderson, 58394 ... I-10
Andrews, 1279 ... E-11
Angola, 7725 ... A-13
Arcadia, 1778 ... H-9
Ardmore, 2200 ... *B-18
Argos, 1826 ... C-8
Arlington, 500 ... K-11
Ashley, 997 ... B-13
Atlanta, 806 ... H-9
Attica, 3473 ... H-5
Auburn, 12497 ... B-13
Aurora, 3983 ... N-13
Austin, 4720 ... O-10
Avilla, 2240 ... B-12
Bainbridge, 753 ... J-6
Bargersville, 2279 ... L-9
BARTHOLOMEW CO., 72341 ... M-9
Bass Lake, 1249 ... C-7
Batesville, 6306 ... M-12
Battle Ground, 1344 ... G-6
Bedford, 13469 ... O-7
Beech Gr., 14457 ... K-9
BENTON CO., 9189 ... F-5
Berne, 4121 ... F-13
Beverly Shores, 699 ... A-6
Bicknell, 3288 ... O-4
Birdseye, 472 ... Q-7
BLACKFORD CO., 13876 ... G-12
Blackhawk, 80 ... M-4
Blanford, 300 ... K-3
Bloomfield, 2520 ... N-6
Bloomington, 70642 ... M-7
Bluffton, 9496 ... F-12
Boggstown, 400 ... K-10
BOONE CO., 49370 ... I-7
Boonville, 6930 ... S-4
Boswell, 801 ... G-4
Bourbon, 1740 ... C-9
Brazil, 8166 ... L-5
Bremen, 4593 ... B-9
Bristol, 1572 ... A-10
Brook, 1012 ... E-4
Brooklyn, 1519 ... K-8
Brookston, 1663 ... F-6
Brookville, 2932 ... L-13
BROWN CO., 15313 ... M-8
Brownsburg, 16956 ... J-8
Brownstown, 3025 ... O-9
Bruceville, 465 ... O-4
Bunker Hill, 1030 ... F-9
Burlington, 457 ... G-8
Burlington Beach, 900 ... B-5
Burns Hbr., 767 ... A-5
Butler, 2726 ... B-13
Cambridge City, 2059 ... J-12
Camden, 578 ... F-7
Campbellsburg, 579 ... P-8
Cannelton, 1174 ... S-6
Carlisle, 694 ... N-4
Carmel, 43083 ... I-9
CARROLL CO., 20499 ... F-7
Carthage, 901 ... K-11
CASS CO., 40415 ... E-8
Cayuga, 1114 ... I-4
Cedar Lake, 9509 ... B-4
Centerville, 2436 ... J-13
Chalmers, 494 ... F-6
Chandler, 3095 ... S-4
Charlestown, 5927 ... Q-11
Chesterton, 11139 ... A-5
Chrisney, 527 ... S-5
Churubusco, 1738 ... C-12
Cicero, 4347 ... I-9
CLARK CO., 99462 ... Q-10
Clarks Hill, 672 ... H-7
Clarksville, 21237 ... R-10
CLAY CO., 26772 ... L-5
Clay City, 1019 ... M-5
Clayton, 779 ... K-7
Clermont, 1475 ... *J-15
CLINTON CO., 33947 ... H-7
Clinton, 4951 ... K-4
Cloverdale, 2305 ... L-6
Coatesville, 548 ... K-7
Colfax, 774 ... H-7
Collegeville, 865 ... E-5
Columbia City, 7671 ... C-11
Columbus, 39058 ... M-9
Connersville, 14844 ... K-13
Converse, 1127 ... F-10
Corydon, 2720 ... R-9
Covington, 2522 ... H-4
CRAWFORD CO., 11146 ... R-8
Crawfordsville, 15201 ... I-6
Crothersville, 1541 ... O-10
Crown Pt., 20980 ... B-4
Culver, 1525 ... C-8
Cynthiana, 675 ... R-3
Dale, 1554 ... R-5
Daleville, 1629 ... I-11
Dana, 682 ... J-4
Danville, 6941 ... J-7
Darlington, 844 ... I-6
Darmstadt, 1392 ... S-3
DAVIESS CO., 30047 ... P-5
Dayton, 1139 ... G-6
DEARBORN CO., 47849 ... M-13
DECATUR CO., 24747 ... L-11
Decatur, 9459 ... E-13
DE KALB CO., 41129 ... B-13
DELAWARE CO., 117488 ... H-12
Delphi, 3000 ... F-7
Demotte, 3585 ... C-5
Denver, 530 ... E-9
Dillsboro, 1447 ... N-13
Dublin, 689 ... J-12
DUBOIS CO., 40200 ... Q-6
Dubois, 600 ... Q-6
Dugger, 965 ... N-4
Dunkirk, 2643 ... G-12
Dunlap, 5887 ... A-10
Dyer, 14670 ... B-4
E. Chicago, 31356 ... A-4
Eaton, 1576 ... H-12
Edgewood, 1940 ... I-10
Edinburgh, 4497 ... L-9
Elberfeld, 637 ... R-4
Elizabethtown, 406 ... M-10
ELKHART CO., 188779 ... A-10
Elkhart, 51682 ... A-9
Ellettsville, 5178 ... M-7
Elnora, 728 ... O-5
Elwood, 9324 ... H-10
English, 693 ... Q-7
Etna Green, 652 ... C-9
Evansville, 117881 ... S-3
Fairland, 1276 ... K-10
Fairmount, 2883 ... G-11
Fairview Park, 1497 ... K-4
Farmersburg, 1213 ... M-4
Farmland, 1410 ... H-13
FAYETTE CO., 24999 ... K-12
Ferdinand, 2254 ... R-6
Fillmore, 558 ... K-6
Fishers, 47790 ... I-9
Fish Lake, 1300 ... A-7
Flora, 2228 ... F-7
Florida, 100 ... D-1
FLOYD CO., 71148 ... Q-9
Floyds Knobs, 800 ... Q-10
Ft. Branch, 2334 ... R-3
Fortville, 3494 ... J-10
Ft. Wayne, 219495 ... D-13
FOUNTAIN CO., 17750 ... I-4
Fountain City, 722 ... I-13
Fowler, 2328 ... F-4
Francesville, 880 ... D-6
Francisco, 547 ... Q-4
Frankfort, 16478 ... H-7
FRANKLIN CO., 22773 ... L-13
Franklin, 20833 ... L-9
Frankton, 1901 ... H-10
Freelandville, 630 ... O-4
Freetown, 700 ... N-9
Fremont, 1691 ... A-13
French Lick, 1924 ... P-7
FULTON CO., 20508 ... D-8
Galena, 1831 ... Q-10
Galveston, 1472 ... F-9
Garrett, 5762 ... B-13
Gary, 99961 ... A-4
Gas City, 5910 ... G-11
Gaston, 992 ... H-11
Geneva, 1335 ... F-13
Georgetown, 2415 ... R-9
GIBSON CO., 32991 ... Q-3
Gilmer Park, 2100 ... *C-19
Goodland, 1094 ... E-4
Goshen, 29787 ... A-10
Gosport, 737 ... L-7
Grabill, 1147 ... C-13
Grandview, 692 ... S-5
Granger, 28284 ... A-9
GRANT CO., 71572 ... G-11
Greencastle, 9987 ... K-6
Greendale, 4335 ... M-14
GREENE CO., 33244 ... N-6
Greenfield, 15721 ... J-10
Greensburg, 10361 ... L-11
Greentown, 2494 ... G-9
Greenville, 586 ... Q-9
Greenwood, 39545 ... K-9
Griffith, 16961 ... B-4
Hagerstown, 1719 ... J-12
HAMILTON CO., 216826 ... H-9
Hamilton, 1224 ... B-13
Hamlet, 783 ... B-7
Hammond, 80547 ... A-4
HANCOCK CO., 59446 ... I-10
Hanna, 500 ... B-6
Hanover, 3868 ... O-11
Harlan, 1200 ... C-13
Harmony, 589 ... K-5
HARRISON CO., 35706 ... R-9
Hartford City, 6728 ... G-12
Hatfield, 700 ... S-4
Haubstadt, 1533 ... R-3
Hebron, 3541 ... C-5
Heltonville, 500 ... N-8
HENDRICKS CO., 118850 ... J-7
HENRY CO., 47699 ... I-11
Henryville, 1545 ... P-10
Highland, 4107 ... S-12
Highland, 23444 ... A-4
Hillsboro, 482 ... I-5
Hillsdale, 180 ... J-4
Hoagland, 675 ... D-13
Hobart, 26972 ... B-5
Holland, 698 ... R-5
Home Place, 1300 ... J-9
Hope, 2154 ... M-10
HOWARD CO., 84880 ... G-9
Howe, 900 ... A-11
Hudson Lake, 1300 ... A-7
Huntertown, 2335 ... C-12
Huntingburg, 5815 ... R-6
HUNTINGTON CO., 38143 ... E-11
Huntington, 17163 ... E-11
Hymera, 825 ... M-4
Idaville, 500 ... E-7
Indianapolis, 783438 ... J-9
Ingalls, 1203 ... I-10
JACKSON CO., 41639 ... N-9
Jamestown, 946 ... J-7
Jasonville, 2482 ... M-5
JASPER CO., 31078 ... D-5
Jasper, 13205 ... Q-6
JAY CO., 21732 ... G-13
JEFFERSON CO., 32250 ... O-11
Jeffersonville, 28025 ... R-10
JENNINGS CO., 28111 ... N-11
Jewell Vil., 700 ... M-10
JOHNSON CO., 123256 ... L-9
Jonesboro, 1810 ... G-11
Kendallville, 9682 ... B-12
Kentland, 1738 ... E-4
Kewanna, 612 ... D-8
Kingman, 538 ... I-4
Kingsford Hts., 1427 ... B-7
Kirklin, 773 ... H-8
Klondike ... B-1
Knightstown, 2042 ... J-11
Knightsville, 627 ... L-5
KNOX CO., 38745 ... O-4
Knox, 3649 ... C-7
Kokomo, 46154 ... G-9
Koontz Lake, 1554 ... B-7
KOSCIUSKO CO., 75301 ... C-10
Kouts, 1737 ... C-5
La Crosse, 554 ... C-6
Ladoga, 1036 ... J-6
Lafayette, 61229 ... G-6
La Fontaine, 872 ... F-10
LAGRANGE CO., 36026 ... A-11
Lagrange, 2949 ... A-11
Lagro, 446 ... E-10
LAKE CO., 487476 ... C-4
Lake Eliza, 600 ... B-5
Lake James, 800 ... A-13
Lake Sta., 13818 ... A-5
Laketon, 250 ... D-10
Lake Vil., 855 ... B-4
Lakeville, 555 ... B-8
Landess, 100 ... F-11
Lanesville, 618 ... R-9
Lapaz, 490 ... B-8
Lapel, 1862 ... I-10
LA PORTE CO., 109878 ... B-7
La Porte, 21067 ... A-7
Laurel, 581 ... L-12
LAWRENCE CO., 46201 ... O-8
Lawrence, 40795 ... J-9
Lawrenceburg, 4701 ... N-14
Lebanon, 14379 ... I-7
Leesburg, 615 ... C-10
Leo-Cedarville, 2874 ... C-13
Liberty, 1959 ... K-13
Ligonier, 4303 ... B-11
Linden, 697 ... H-6
Linton, 5778 ... N-5
Logansport, 19313 ... E-8
Long Beach, 1516 ... A-6
Loogootee, 2695 ... P-6
Lowell, 7759 ... C-4
Lydick, 800 ... A-8
Lynn, 1109 ... I-13
Lynnville, 804 ... R-4
Lyons, 747 ... N-5
MADISON CO., 131121 ... H-10
Madison, 12249 ... O-12
Maple Lane, 2100 ... *B-20
Marengo, 855 ... Q-8
MARION CO., 863251 ... J-8
Marion, 30609 ... F-11
Markle, 1090 ... E-12
MARSHALL CO., 46352 ... B-8
MARTIN CO., 10347 ... P-6
Martinsville, 11614 ... L-8
Maryland, 800 ... J-2
Marywood, 600 ... J-4
Matthews, 576 ... G-11
McCordsville, 1173 ... J-10
Medaryville, 555 ... D-6
Medora, 559 ... O-9
Melody Hill, 3066 ... S-13
Memphis, 400 ... Q-10
Mentone, 892 ... C-9
Merrillville, 30990 ... B-4
Mexico, 984 ... E-9
MIAMI CO., 36177 ... F-9
Michigan City, 32335 ... A-6
Michigantown, 413 ... H-8
Middlebury, 3035 ... A-10
Middletown, 2427 ... I-11
Middletown Park, 850 ... G-1
Milan, 1811 ... M-13
Milford, 1544 ... B-10
Millersburg, 877 ... B-10
Milltown, 932 ... Q-8
Milroy, 850 ... L-11
Milton, 616 ... J-12
Mishawaka, 48396 ... A-9
Mitchell, 4658 ... O-7
Monon, 1687 ... E-6
MONROE CO., 122903 ... M-7
Monroe, 732 ... E-13
Monroe City, 539 ... P-4
Monroeville, 1275 ... D-13
Monrovia, 625 ... K-7
Montezuma, 1166 ... J-4
MONTGOMERY CO., 37911 ... I-6
Monticello, 5548 ... F-6
Montpelier, 1879 ... F-12
Mooreland, 380 ... I-12
Moores Hill, 648 ... N-13
Mooresville, 10581 ... K-8
MORGAN CO., 68656 ... L-7
Morgantown, 954 ... L-8
Morocco, 1090 ... E-4
Morristown, 1174 ... K-10
Mt. Vernon, 7318 ... S-2
Mulberry, 1364 ... G-7
Muncie, 66521 ... H-12
Munster, 22135 ... A-4
Nappanee, 6762 ... B-9
Nashville, 816 ... M-8
New Albany, 36973 ... R-10
Newburgh, 3252 ... S-4
New Carlisle, 1615 ... A-7
New Castle, 18955 ... J-12
New Chicago, 2074 ... B-5
New Elliott, 800 ... *N-12
New Goshen, 500 ... K-4
New Harmony, 892 ... R-2
New Haven, 13592 ... D-13
New Market, 656 ... I-6
New Palestine, 1385 ... K-10
New Paris, 1006 ... B-10
Newport, 568 ... J-4
New Salisbury, 400 ... R-9
NEWTON CO., 14403 ... D-4
New Washington, 547 ... P-11
New Whiteland, 4484 ... K-9
NOBLE CO., 47039 ... C-12
Noblesville, 33046 ... I-9
N. Judson, 1884 ... C-6
N. Liberty, 1379 ... B-8
N. Manchester, 6064 ... D-10
N. Salem, 617 ... J-7
N. Terre Haute, 4606 ... L-4
N. Vernon, 6389 ... N-11
N. Webster, 1060 ... C-10
Norway, 437 ... E-6
Oakland City, 2587 ... Q-4
Oaktown, 626 ... O-4
Odon, 1393 ... O-5
Ogden Dunes, 1277 ... A-5
OHIO CO., 5732 ... N-13
Oldenburg, 644 ... L-12
Oolitic, 1127 ... O-7
ORANGE CO., 19616 ... P-8
Orestes, 328 ... H-10
Orleans, 2303 ... P-7
Osceola, 1826 ... A-9
Osgood, 1666 ... M-12
Ossian, 2917 ... E-12
Otterbein, 1272 ... G-5
Otwell, 400 ... Q-5
OWEN CO., 22827 ... M-6
Owensville, 1334 ... R-3
Oxford, 1232 ... G-5
Palmyra, 691 ... Q-9
Paoli, 3906 ... P-7
Paragon, 648 ... L-7
PARKE CO., 17329 ... J-5
Parker City, 1385 ... H-12
Patoka, 797 ... Q-3
Pendleton, 3790 ... I-10
Pennville, 709 ... G-12
PERRY CO., 18717 ... S-7
Peru, 12897 ... E-9
Petersburg, 2522 ... Q-4
Pierceton, 685 ... C-10
PIKE CO., 12931 ... Q-4
Pittsboro, 2123 ... J-7
Plainfield, 21386 ... K-8
Pleasant Lake, 500 ... A-13
Plymouth, 10607 ... C-8
Portage, 34915 ... A-5
PORTER CO., 152533 ... B-5
Porter, 5094 ... A-5
Portland, 6297 ... G-13
POSEY CO., 26876 ... S-2
Poseyville, 1161 ... R-2
Prince s Lakes, 1511 ... L-9
Princeton, 8512 ... Q-3
PULASKI CO., 13835 ... D-7
PUTNAM CO., 36692 ... K-6
RANDOLPH CO., 26833 ... H-13
Redkey, 1420 ... G-12
Reelsville, 150 ... K-6
Remington, 1265 ... E-5
Rensselaer, 6167 ... E-5
Reynolds, 535 ... F-6
Richland, 500 ... S-5
Richmond, 38201 ... J-13
Ridgeville, 817 ... H-13
RIPLEY CO., 27316 ... N-12
Rising Sun, 2441 ... N-14
Roachdale, 984 ... J-6
Roanoke, 1480 ... D-12
Rochester, 6407 ... D-8
Rockport, 2116 ... T-5
Rockville, 2722 ... J-5
Rolling Prairie, 500 ... A-7
Rome City, 1636 ... B-12
Rosedale, 754 ... K-4
Roseland, 637 ... A-8
Ross, 1100 ... B-4
Rossville, 1514 ... G-7
Royal Cen., 821 ... E-7
Royerton, 900 ... H-12
RUSH CO., 18016 ... K-11
Rushville, 5793 ... K-11
Russiaville, 1159 ... G-8
St. Bernice, 800 ... K-3
St. John, 9545 ... B-4
ST. JOSEPH CO., 266348 ... B-8
St. Leon, 496 ... M-13
St. Mary-of-the-Woods, 300 ... L-4
St. Meinrad, 500 ... R-6
St. Paul, 1022 ... L-11
St. Wendel, 500 ... R-3
Salem, 6325 ... P-9
Sandborn, 442 ... O-5
Santa Claus, 2164 ... S-6
Schererville, 26142 ... B-4
SCOTT CO., 23556 ... P-10
Scottsburg, 5912 ... P-10
Seelyville, 1181 ... L-4
Sellersburg, 6140 ... Q-10
Selma, 856 ... H-12
Seymour, 18500 ... N-10
Shadeland, 1648 ... G-6
Sharpsville, 621 ... G-9
Shelburn, 1287 ... M-4
SHELBY CO., 43717 ... K-10
Shelby, 750 ... C-4
Shelbyville, 17853 ... L-10
Sheridan, 2664 ... I-8
Shipshewana, 539 ... A-11
Shirley, 817 ... J-11
Shoals, 814 ... P-6
Silver Lake, 539 ... D-10
Simonton Lake, 4053 ... A-9
Smith Valley, 1800 ... K-8
S. Bend, 105540 ... A-8
Southport, 1776 ... K-9
S. Whitley, 1788 ... D-11
Speed, 300 ... Q-10
Speedway, 12793 ... J-8
Spelterville, 500 ... H-2
SPENCER CO., 20343 ... S-5
Spencer, 2548 ... M-6
Spiceland, 776 ... J-11
Star City, 377 ... D-7
STARKE CO., 23139 ... C-7
Staunton, 556 ... L-5
STEUBEN CO., 33706 ... A-12
Stockwell, 500 ... H-6
SULLIVAN CO., 21861 ... M-3
Sullivan, 4603 ... N-4
Summitville, 1077 ... H-11
Sunman, 807 ... M-13
Swayzee, 957 ... G-10
Sweetser, 865 ... F-10
SWITZERLAND CO., 9435 ... O-13
Syracuse, 3050 ... B-10
Taylorsville, 936 ... M-9
Tell City, 7684 ... S-6
Terre Haute, 58096 ... L-4
Thorntown, 1559 ... I-7
TIPPECANOE CO., 154848 ... H-6
TIPTON CO., 16422 ... H-9
Tipton, 5229 ... H-9
Topeka, 1173 ... B-11
Town of Pines, 792 ... A-6
Trafalgar, 895 ... L-9
Trail Creek, 2235 ... A-6
Troy, 391 ... S-6
UNION CO., 7238 ... K-13
Union City, 3502 ... H-14
Upland, 3717 ... G-11
Utica, 633 ... Q-11
Vallonia, 500 ... O-9
Valparaiso, 28365 ... B-5
Van Buren, 889 ... F-11
VANDERBURGH CO., 171889 ... R-3
Veedersburg, 2268 ... I-4
VERMILLION CO., 16572 ... J-4
Versailles, 1781 ... N-12
Vevay, 1670 ... O-13
VIGO CO., 104540 ... L-3
Vincennes, 18320 ... P-3
WABASH CO., 34339 ... E-10
Wabash, 11380 ... E-10
Wakarusa, 1619 ... B-9
Waldron, 800 ... L-10
Walkerton, 2205 ... B-7
Walton, 1042 ... F-8
Wanatah, 987 ... B-6
WARREN CO., 8703 ... G-4
Warren, 1258 ... F-11
WARRICK CO., 54744 ... R-4
Warsaw, 12688 ... C-10
WASHINGTON CO., 27618 ... P-9
Washington, 11292 ... P-5
Waterloo, 2209 ... B-13
Waveland, 410 ... J-5
WAYNE CO., 70235 ... J-13
Waynetown, 897 ... I-5
WELLS CO., 27912 ... F-12
W. Baden Sprs., 614 ... P-7
W. College Corner, 617 ... K-14
Westfield, 11182 ... I-9
W. Lafayette, 29835 ... G-6
W. Lebanon, 793 ... H-4
Westpoint, 250 ... G-5
Westport, 1491 ... M-11
W. Terre Haute, 2316 ... L-4
Westville, 5266 ... B-6
Wheatfield, 798 ... C-5
Wheeler, 500 ... B-5
WHITE CO., 24852 ... F-6
Whiteland, 4202 ... K-9
Whitestown, 583 ... I-8
Whiting, 4928 ... A-4
WHITLEY CO., 31651 ... D-11
Williamsburg, 360 ... I-13
Williamsport, 1935 ... H-4
Winamac, 2447 ... D-7
Winchester, 4889 ... H-13
Windfall, 701 ... G-9
Winona Lake, 4107 ... C-10
Winslow, 865 ... Q-5
Wolcott, 954 ... E-5
Wolcottville, 949 ... B-12
Woodburn, 1629 ... D-13
Woodland Park, 200 ... G-3
Woodridge, 700 ... J-2
Worthington, 1472 ... N-6
Yorktown, 4945 ... H-11
Zanesville, 602 ... E-12
Zionsville, 10336 ... I-8

Iowa

Map pp. 78-81

Ackley, 1781 ... E-11
ADAIR CO., 7922 ... J-7
Adair, 803 ... I-7
ADAMS CO., 4371 ... K-6
Adel, 3615 ... I-8
Afton, 877 ... K-8
Agency, 663 ... K-14
Akron, 1459 ... D-1
Albert City, 702 ... D-6
Albia, 3659 ... K-12
Albion, 582 ... G-11
Alden, 866 ... E-10
Algona, 5592 ... C-8
ALLAMAKEE CO., 14551 ... B-16

*, †, ‡, See explanation under state title in this index.
County/Parish names are listed in capital letters and in boldface type.

Allerton, 563 M-10
Allison, 988 E-12
Alta, 1857 E-5
Alton, 1106 D-3
Altoona, 11349 I-10
Amana, 420 H-15
Ames, 53284 G-10
Anamosa, 5570 G-16
Anita, 1023 I-6
Ankeny, 31144 I-10
Anthon, 644 F-3
Aplington, 1019 E-12
APPANOOSE CO., 13590 L-12
Armstrong, 918 B-7
Arnolds Park, 1164 B-5
Asbury, 2997 E-18
Atkins, 1107 H-15
Atlantic, 7110 J-5
AUDUBON CO., 6479 I-5
Audubon, 2274 H-6
Aurelia, 1013 E-4
Avoca, 1582 J-4
Badger, 584 E-8
Bancroft, 772 B-8
Batavia, 497 K-14
Battle Cr., 721 F-4
Baxter, 1073 H-11
Bayard, 533 H-7
Bedford, 1576 M-6
Belle Plaine, 2879 H-14
Bellevue, 2373 F-19
Belmond, 2495 D-10
BENTON CO., 26243 G-14
Bettendorf, 31456 I-19
BLACK HAWK CO., 126418 F-13
Blairstown, 701 H-14
Bloomfield, 2580 L-13
Blue Grass, 1223 I-18
Bondurant, 1991 I-10
BOONE CO., 26247 H-8
Boone, 12807 G-9
Boyden, 672 C-3
BREMER CO., 23368 E-13
Brighton, 694 K-15
Britt, 2019 C-9
Brooklyn, 1381 I-13
BUCHANAN CO., 20903 E-14
BUENA VISTA CO., 20205 D-5
Buffalo, 1283 J-18
Buffalo Cen., 925 B-9
Burlington, 25966 L-17
Burt, 530 C-8
BUTLER CO., 14968 E-12
CALHOUN CO., 10653 F-6
Calmar, 1083 C-15
Camanche, 4228 H-20
Cambridge, 813 H-10
Carlisle, 3485 J-10
CARROLL CO., 21086 G-6
Carroll, 9986 G-6
Carson, 696 K-4
Carter Lake, 3319 J-3
Cascade, 1975 F-17
CASS CO., 14314 J-6
CEDAR CO., 18264 H-17
Cedar Falls, 36429 E-13
Cedar Rapids, 122542 H-15
Center Pt., 2145 G-15
Centerville, 5814 M-12
Central City, 1161 G-16
CERRO GORDO CO., 45118 C-11
Chariton, 4590 K-11
Charles City, 7685 C-12
CHEROKEE CO., 12541 E-3
Cherokee, 5158 D-4
CHICKASAW CO., 12702 C-13
Clarence, 1008 H-17
Clarinda, 5540 L-5
Clarion, 2856 E-9
CLARKE CO., 9242 K-9
Clarksville, 1391 D-12
CLAY CO., 17073 C-5
CLAYTON CO., 18454 D-16
Clear Lake, 7977 C-10
Clermont, 714 C-15
CLINTON CO., 49804 H-19
Clinton, 27437 H-20
Clive, 13671 B-18
Coggon, 709 F-16
Colfax, 2220 I-11
Colo, 881 G-10
Columbus Jct., 1891 J-16
Conrad, 1036 G-12
Coon Rapids, 1308 H-6
Coralville, 16778 I-16
Corning, 1731 L-6
Correctionville, 858 F-3
Corydon, 1553 L-10
Council Bluffs, 58656 J-3
CRAWFORD CO., 16930 G-5
Cresco, 3840 B-14
Creston, 7359 K-7
Dakota City, 871 E-8
DALLAS CO., 46148 I-8
Dallas Cen., 1646 I-9
Danville, 905 L-16
Davenport, 97512 I-19
DAVIS CO., 8557 L-13
Dayton, 850 F-7
DECATUR CO., 8706 L-9
Decorah, 8120 B-15
DELAWARE CO., 18140 E-16
Delmar, 508 G-18
Denison, 7420 G-4
Denver, 1604 E-13
DES MOINES CO., 41247 L-17
Des Moines, 196093 I-10
De Soto, 1072 I-8
De Witt, 5128 H-19
Dexter, 718 I-8
DICKINSON CO., 16399 B-5
Dike, 1099 F-12
Donnellson, 924 M-16
Dows, 614 E-10
DUBUQUE CO., 90049 F-17
Dubuque, 57204 E-18
Dumont, 653 E-11
Dunkerton, 774 E-14
Dunlap, 1140 H-4
Durant, 1635 I-18
Dyersville, 4096 F-17
Dysart, 1295 G-13
Eagle Gr., 3563 E-9
Earlham, 1317 I-8
Earlville, 875 F-16
Early, 552 F-5
Eddyville, 1065 K-13
Edgewood, 912 E-16
Eldon, 987 L-14
Eldora, 2942 F-11
Eldridge, 4995 I-19
Elgin, 662 D-15
Elkader, 1409 D-16
Elk Horn, 629 I-5
Elk Run Hts., 1087 F-14
Elma, 586 C-13
EMMET CO., 10805 B-7
Emmetsburg, 3759 C-6
Epworth, 1567 F-17
Essex, 852 L-4
Estherville, 6566 B-6
Evansdale, 4460 F-14
Everly, 659 C-5
Exira, 783 I-6
Fairbank, 1043 E-14
Fairfax, 1280 H-15
Fairfield, 9486 K-15
Farley, 1347 F-17
Farmington, 740 M-15
FAYETTE CO., 21408 D-14
Fayette, 1275 D-15
FLOYD CO., 16608 C-12
Fonda, 615 E-6
Fontanelle, 683 J-7
Forest City, 4246 B-10
Ft. Dodge, 25917 F-8
Ft. Madison, 10949 M-17
FRANKLIN CO., 10693 E-10
Fredericksburg, 942 D-14
FREMONT CO., 7862 L-4
Fremont, 700 K-13
Garnavillo, 768 D-17
Garner, 2978 C-10
Garwin, 553 G-12
George, 1027 B-3
Gilbert, 1011 G-9
Gilbertville, 718 F-14
Gilman, 581 H-12
Gilmore City, 534 E-7
Gladbrook, 1018 G-12
Glenwood, 5418 K-3
Glidden, 1265 G-6
Goldfield, 648 E-9
Gowrie, 1073 F-8
Graettinger, 857 C-6
Grand Jct., 922 G-8
Grand Mound, 668 H-18
Granger, 638 H-9
GREENE CO., 10047 G-7
Greene, 1071 D-12
Greenfield, 2008 J-7
Greenfield Plaza D-20
Grimes, 5600 I-9
Grinnell, 9213 I-12
Griswold, 1005 K-5
GRUNDY CO., 12341 F-12
Grundy Cen., 2589 F-12
GUTHRIE CO., 11500 H-6
Guthrie Cen., 1654 I-7
Guttenberg, 1950 D-17
Hamburg, 1236 M-3
HAMILTON CO., 16316 F-9
Hampton, 4211 E-11
HANCOCK CO., 11945 C-9
HARDIN CO., 18297 F-10
Harlan, 5165 I-4
HARRISON CO., 15667 I-3
Hartford, 761 J-10
Hartley, 1562 C-4
Hawarden, 2428 C-1
Hazleton, 926 E-15
Hedrick, 851 K-13
HENRY CO., 20023 K-16
Hiawatha, 6506 G-15
Hills, 655 I-16
Hinton, 815 E-2
Holstein, 1431 F-4
Hopkinton, 667 F-17
Hospers, 677 C-3
HOWARD CO., 9784 B-13
Hubbard, 861 F-10
Hudson, 2133 F-13
Hull, 2041 C-2
HUMBOLDT CO., 10090 D-8
Humboldt, 4411 E-8
Humeston, 546 L-10
Huxley, 2475 H-10
IDA CO., 7512 F-4
Ida Gr., 2259 F-4
Independence, 5923 F-15
Indianola, 13205 J-10
Inwood, 871 B-1
IOWA CO., 15920 I-15
Iowa City, 63807 I-16
Iowa Falls, 5106 E-11
Ireton, 582 D-2
JACKSON CO., 20221 F-18
Janesville, 822 E-13
JASPER CO., 37708 I-11
JEFFERSON CO., 16022 K-15
Jefferson, 4440 G-7
Jesup, 2203 F-14
Jewell, 1227 F-9
JOHNSON CO., 115548 I-15
Johnston, 10842 I-9
JONES CO., 20299 G-17
Kalona, 2415 J-15
Kanawha, 708 D-9
Kellogg, 616 I-12
KEOKUK CO., 11352 J-14
Keokuk, 10918 N-16
Keosauqua, 1084 M-15
Keota, 987 J-14
Keystone, 671 H-14
Kingsley, 1234 E-3
Klemme, 572 D-10
Knoxville, 7536 J-11
KOSSUTH CO., 16443 C-8
Lake City, 1734 F-6
Lake Mills, 2101 B-10
Lake Park, 956 B-5
Lake View, 1315 F-5
Lamoni, 2424 M-9
Lansing, 993 B-16
La Porte City, 2324 F-14
Larchwood, 802 B-1
Laurens, 1409 D-6
Lawler, 442 C-14
Le Claire, 2873 I-19
LEE CO., 36714 M-16
Le Grand, 898 G-12
Lehigh, 488 F-8
Le Mars, 9241 D-2
Lenox, 1349 L-7
Leon, 1974 M-9
LINN CO., 196202 G-15
Lisbon, 1935 H-16
Logan, 1498 I-3
Lone Tree, 1171 J-16
LOUISA CO., 12201 K-16
Lovilia, 561 K-12
Lowden, 805 H-18
LUCAS CO., 9501 K-10
LYON CO., 11746 B-2
MADISON CO., 14510 J-8
Madrid, 2397 H-9
MAHASKA CO., 22303 J-12
Malvern, 1336 K-4
Manchester, 5139 F-16
Manilla, 827 H-5
Manly, 1341 B-11
Manning, 1453 H-5
Manson, 1799 F-7
Mapleton, 1277 G-3
Maquoketa, 6054 G-18
Marcus, 1084 D-3
Marengo, 2536 H-14
MARION CO., 32425 J-11
Marion, 28756 G-16
MARSHALL CO., 39103 G-11
Marshalltown, 25860 G-12
Mason City, 28274 C-11
Maxwell, 810 H-10
Maynard, 490 D-15
McGregor, 917 C-17
Mechanicsville, 1162 H-17
Mediapolis, 1584 K-17
Melbourne, 750 H-11
Melcher-Dallas, 1266 J-11
Merrill, 772 E-2
Milford, 2466 B-5
MILLS CO., 14909 K-4
Milo, 818 J-10
Milton, 503 M-14
Missouri Valley, 2894 I-3
MITCHELL CO., 10946 C-11
Mitchellville, 2095 I-10
MONONA CO., 9746 G-3
Monona, 1497 C-16
MONROE CO., 7796 L-12
Monroe, 1821 I-11
Montezuma, 1457 I-13
MONTGOMERY CO., 11289 K-5
Monticello, 3660 G-17
Montrose, 926 M-16
Moravia, 723 L-12
Morning Sun, 870 K-17
Moulton, 674 M-12
Mt. Ayr, 1803 M-8
Mt. Pleasant, 8518 L-16
Mt. Vernon, 3905 H-16
Moville, 1642 E-2
Murray, 761 K-9
MUSCATINE CO., 42093 I-16
Muscatine, 22614 J-17
Mystic, 612 L-12
Nashua, 1577 D-13
Neola, 820 J-4
Nevada, 6676 G-10
New Albin, 520 B-16
Newell, 880 E-5
Newhall, 972 H-14
New Hampton, 3569 C-13
New Hartford, 643 E-12
New London, 1887 L-16
New Sharon, 1268 J-12
Newton, 15794 I-11
Nora Sprs., 1504 C-11
N. English, 1010 I-14
N. Liberty, 6516 H-16
Northwood, 2012 B-11
Norwalk, 7794 J-9
Norway, 608 H-15
Norwoodville, 1200 B-20
Oakland, 1456 J-4
O'BRIEN CO., 14627 C-4
Ocheyedan, 519 B-4
Odebolt, 1060 F-5
Oelwein, 6498 E-15
Ogden, 2023 G-8
Okoboji, 813 B-5
Olin, 703 G-17
Onawa, 3011 G-2
Orange City, 5669 C-2
Osage, 3471 B-12
OSCEOLA CO., 6819 B-4
Osceola, 4730 K-9
Oskaloosa, 11037 J-12
Ossian, 856 C-15
Otho, 564 F-8
Ottumwa, 24697 K-13
Oxford, 679 I-15
Oxford Jct., 577 G-17
Pacific Jct., 517 K-3
PAGE CO., 16346 L-5
PALO ALTO CO., 9705 D-6
Panora, 1161 I-7
Parkersburg, 1872 E-12
Park View, 2169 I-19
Paullina, 1057 D-4
Pella, 10107 J-12
Perry, 8079 H-8
Pleasant Hill, 5752 C-20
Pleasantville, 1572 J-11
PLYMOUTH CO., 24719 E-2
POCAHONTAS CO., 8251 E-6
Pocahontas, 1907 E-6
POLK CO., 388606 I-10
Polk City, 2680 H-9
Pomeroy, 669 E-6
Postville, 2244 C-16
POTTAWATTAMIE CO., 88477 J-4
POWESHIEK CO., 19033 H-13
Prairie City, 1371 I-11
Preston, 935 G-19
Primghar, 855 C-4
Princeton, 937 I-19
Radcliffe, 582 F-10
Raymond, 598 F-14
Readlyn, 772 E-14
Redfield, 868 I-8
Red Oak, 5940 K-5
Reinbeck, 1690 F-13
Remsen, 1707 D-3
Riceville, 841 B-13
Richland, 587 K-14
RINGGOLD CO., 5421 L-7
Riverside, 968 I-15
Robins, 2068 G-15
Rockford, 898 C-12
Rock Rapids, 2661 B-2
Rock Valley, 2749 C-2
Rockwell, 978 D-11
Rockwell City, 2133 F-7
Roland, 1344 G-10
Rolfe, 640 D-7
Russell, 572 L-11
Ruthven, 706 C-6
Sabula, 674 G-20
SAC CO., 10872 F-5
Sac City, 2246 F-6
St. Ansgar, 1022 B-12
Sanborn, 1327 C-4
Saydel, 3500 A-20
Saylorville, 3238 A-20
Schaller, 732 E-5
Schleswig, 819 G-4
SCOTT CO., 159414 I-19
Scranton, 572 G-7
Sergeant Bluff, 3689 F-2
Seymour, 806 M-11
Sheffield, 954 D-11
SHELBY CO., 12717 I-4
Shelby, 677 I-4
Sheldon, 4927 C-3
Shell Rock, 1254 E-13
Shellsburg, 962 G-15
Shenandoah, 5290 L-4
Sibley, 2742 B-3
Sidney, 1221 L-3
Sigourney, 2210 J-14
SIOUX CO., 32104 C-2
Sioux Cen., 6527 C-2
Sioux City, 83876 E-1
Sioux Rapids, 709 D-5
Slater, 1386 H-9
Sloan, 1031 F-2
Solon, 1258 H-16
Spencer, 11219 C-5
Spirit Lake, 4444 B-5
Springville, 1036 G-16
Stanton, 700 L-5
Stanwood, 674 H-17
State Cen., 1318 G-11
Storm Lake, 9973 E-5
STORY CO., 83021 G-10
Story City, 3360 G-10
Stratford, 747 F-9
Strawberry Pt., 1335 E-16
Stuart, 1741 I-7
Sully, 895 J-12
Sumner, 2056 D-14
Sutherland, 677 D-4
Swea City, 611 B-8
Swisher, 838 H-15
Tabor, 995 L-3
TAMA CO., 17876 G-13
Tama, 2654 H-13
TAYLOR CO., 6793 L-6
Tipton, 3147 H-17
Titonka, 558 C-8
Toledo, 2501 H-13
Traer, 1599 G-13
Treynor, 946 J-4
Tripoli, 1288 D-14
UNION CO., 11932 L-7
University Park, 543 J-13
Urbana, 1229 G-15
Urbandale, 31868 B-19
VAN BUREN CO., 7777 L-14
Van Horne, 823 G-14
Van Meter, 907 I-9
Ventura, 663 C-10
Victor, 965 I-14
Villisca, 1286 L-5
Vinton, 5210 G-14
Walcott, 1516 I-18
Walker, 731 F-15
Wall Lake, 780 F-5
Walnut, 859 J-5
WAPELLO CO., 35885 K-13
Wapello, 2149 K-17
WARREN CO., 41997 K-9
Washburn, 1400 F-14
WASHINGTON CO., 21314 J-15
Washington, 7253 J-15
Waterloo, 67054 F-13
Waukee, 7287 I-9
Waukon, 4059 B-16
Waverly, 9075 E-13
Wayland, 948 K-15
WAYNE CO., 6669 L-10
WEBSTER CO., 39590 E-8
Webster City, 8106 F-9
Wellman, 1455 J-15
Wellsburg, 688 F-12
W. Bend, 827 D-7
W. Branch, 2297 I-16
W. Burlington, 3062 L-17
W. Des Moines, 51699 I-9
W. Liberty, 3462 I-17
W. Point, 966 M-16
W. Union, 2492 D-15
What Cheer, 671 J-13
Wheatland, 770 H-18
Whiting, 786 G-2
Whittemore, 510 C-7
Williamsburg, 2710 I-14
Wilton, 2837 I-17
Windsor Hts., 4692 B-18
Winfield, 1101 K-17
WINNEBAGO CO., 11445 B-9
WINNESHIEK CO., 21307 C-14
Winterset, 4738 J-8
Winthrop, 771 E-15
Woodbine, 1620 I-3
WOODBURY CO., 103220 F-2
Woodward, 1198 H-9
WORTH CO., 7773 B-11
WRIGHT CO., 13765 E-9
Wyoming, 579 G-17
Zearing, 580 G-11

Kansas

Map pp. 82-85

* City keyed to pp. 116-117

Abilene, 6456 E-13
ALLEN CO., 13907 H-17
Alma, 760 D-15
Almena, 460 B-7
Altamont, 1068 I-18
Alta Vista, 422 E-15
Altoona, 483 I-17
Americus, 944 F-15
Andale, 789 H-12
ANDERSON CO., 8208 G-17
Andover, 8222 H-13
Anthony, 2308 I-11
Argonia, 509 I-12
Arkansas City, 11788 I-13
Arlington, 444 H-11
Arma, 1508 I-19
Ashland, 951 J-7
Assaria, 446 F-12
ATCHISON CO., 16741 C-17
Atchison, 10111 C-18
Attica, 609 I-11
Atwood, 1218 B-4
Auburn, 1120 E-16
Augusta, 8486 H-14
Axtell, 433 B-15
Baldwin City, 3637 E-18
BARBER CO., 5034 I-9
BARTON CO., 27467 F-9
Basehor, 2715 D-18
Baxter Sprs., 4344 J-19
Bazine, 278 F-6
Bel Aire, 6522 K-9
Belle Plaine, 1654 I-13
Belleville, 2034 B-12
Beloit, 3869 C-11
Bennington, 622 D-12
Benton, 816 H-13
Bird City, 444 B-3
Blue Rapids, 1061 B-14
Bonner Sprs., 6782 D-18
BOURBON CO., 15086 H-18
BROWN CO., 10442 B-17
Bucklin, 719 I-7
Buhler, 1336 G-12
Burden, 557 I-14
Burlingame, 997 E-16
Burlington, 2764 G-16
Burrton, 921 H-12
BUTLER CO., 61127 H-14
Caldwell, 1224 K-12
Caney, 2004 J-16
Canton, 815 F-12
Carbondale, 1439 E-17
Cawker City, 504 C-10
Cedar Vale, 689 J-15
Centralia, 512 B-15
Chanute, 9053 H-17
Chapman, 1252 E-13
CHASE CO., 3107 G-14
Chase, 472 G-10
CHAUTAUQUA CO., 4185 J-15
Cheney, 1843 H-12
CHEROKEE CO., 21815 J-18
Cherokee, 723 I-19
Cherryvale, 2292 I-17
Chetopa, 1238 J-18
CHEYENNE CO., 2955 B-2
Cimarron, 2036 H-5
Claflin, 682 F-10
CLARK CO., 2333 J-6
CLAY CO., 8573 D-13
Clay Cen., 4405 C-13
Clearwater, 2202 I-12
Clifton, 520 C-13
CLOUD CO., 9859 C-11
Clyde, 721 C-12
COFFEY CO., 8815 G-16
Coffeyville, 10472 J-17
Colby, 5244 C-4
Coldwater, 771 J-8
Colony, 395 G-17
Columbus, 3286 J-19
Colwich, 1278 H-12
COMANCHE CO., 1915 J-8
Concordia, 5459 C-12
Conway Sprs., 1277 I-12
Cottonwood Falls, 977 F-15
Council Gr., 2275 F-15
COWLEY CO., 35860 J-14
CRAWFORD CO., 38398 I-18
Cunningham, 490 I-10
Dearing, 408 J-17
DECATUR CO., 3295 B-5
Deerfield, 900 H-4
Delphos, 459 D-12
Derby, 19200 I-13
De Soto, 4858 D-18
DICKINSON CO., 19255 E-13
Dighton, 1138 F-5
Dodge City, 25568 H-6
DONIPHAN CO., 8149 B-17
DOUGLAS CO., 102983 E-17
Douglass, 1797 I-13
Downs, 978 C-10
Eastborough, 810 M-9
Easton, 369 C-18
Edgerton, 1547 E-18
Edna, 420 J-18
EDWARDS CO., 3275 H-8
Edwardsville, 4460 D-19
Effingham, 585 C-17
El Dorado, 12686 H-14
ELK CO., 3167 I-15
Elkhart, 2120 J-2
Ellinwood, 2082 G-10
ELLIS CO., 27212 D-8
Ellis, 1827 E-7
ELLSWORTH CO., 6347 E-11
Ellsworth, 2887 E-10
Elwood, 1169 B-18
Emporia, 26666 F-15
Enterprise, 823 E-13
Erie, 1178 I-18
Eskridge, 572 E-16
Eudora, 4963 E-18
Eureka, 2816 H-15
Fairway, 3886 *J-3
FINNEY CO., 39176 G-4
Florence, 667 G-14
FORD CO., 33012 I-6
Ft. Scott, 8065 H-19
Fowler, 577 I-6
Frankfort, 817 B-15
FRANKLIN CO., 25540 F-17
Franklin, 350 I-19
Fredonia, 2520 I-16
Frontenac, 3103 I-19
Galena, 3168 J-19
Galva, 730 F-12
Garden City, 27216 H-4
Garden Plain, 807 I-12
Gardner, 11670 E-18
Garnett, 3388 G-18
Gas, 562 H-17
GEARY CO., 26313 E-14
Geneseo, 268 F-11
Girard, 2734 I-19
Glasco, 509 C-11
Glen Elder, 422 C-10
Goddard, 2932 I-12
Goessel, 557 G-13
Goodland, 4589 C-2
GOVE CO., 2910 E-5
GRAHAM CO., 2808 D-6
Grainfield, 313 D-5
Grandview Plaza, 1149 D-14
GRANT CO., 7745 I-3
GRAY CO., 6063 H-5
Great Bend, 14927 F-9
GREELEY CO., 1420 F-2
Greenleaf, 337 B-13
Greensburg, 1495 I-8
GREENWOOD CO., 7485 H-15
Gridley, 370 G-16
Gypsum, 401 E-12
Halstead, 1888 H-12
HAMILTON CO., 2666 G-2
Hanover, 605 B-14
HARPER CO., 6206 J-11
Harper, 1498 I-11
Hartford, 509 G-16
HARVEY CO., 33502 G-12
HASKELL CO., 4246 I-4
Haven, 1170 H-12
Haviland, 596 I-8
Hays, 19915 E-8
Haysville, 9545 I-13
Herington, 2492 F-14
Hesston, 3614 G-12
Hiawatha, 3331 B-17
Highland, 966 B-17
Hill City, 1511 C-7
Hillsboro, 2839 F-13
HODGEMAN CO., 2151 G-6
Hoisington, 2953 F-9
Holcomb, 1936 H-4
Holton, 3341 C-16
Holyrood, 449 F-10
Hope, 367 E-13
Horton, 1883 B-17
Howard, 786 I-15
Hoxie, 1180 C-5
Hoyt, 583 D-16
Humboldt, 1926 H-17
Hutchinson, 40783 G-11
Independence, 9393 J-17
Inman, 1194 G-12
Iola, 6033 H-17
JACKSON CO., 13017 C-16
JEFFERSON CO., 18798 D-17
Jetmore, 933 G-6
JEWELL CO., 3433 B-11
Jewell, 447 C-11
JOHNSON CO., 486515 E-18
Johnson, 1521 I-2
Jct. City, 17667 D-14
Kanopolis, 524 E-11
Kansas City, 145757 D-19
KEARNY CO., 4591 G-3
Kensington, 492 B-9
KINGMAN CO., 8382 I-11
Kingman, 3270 I-11
Kinsley, 1551 H-8
KIOWA CO., 3152 I-8
Kiowa, 989 K-10
Kismet, 511 J-5
LABETTE CO., 22259 J-18
La Crosse, 1319 F-8
La Cygne, 1123 F-19
La Harpe, 688 H-18
Lake Quivira, 923 *J-1
Lakin, 2343 H-3
LANE CO., 1946 F-5
Lansing, 10032 D-18
Larned, 3932 G-8
Lawrence, 82120 E-18
LEAVENWORTH CO., 71546 D-18
Leavenworth, 35211 C-18
Leawood, 28888 E-19
Lebanon, 279 B-10
Lebo, 966 F-16
Lecompton, 610 D-17
Lenexa, 41995 D-19
Leon, 646 I-14
Leonardville, 439 C-14
Leoti, 1538 F-3
Le Roy, 586 G-17
Lewis, 471 H-8
Liberal, 20067 J-4
LINCOLN CO., 3498 D-11
Lincoln, 1307 D-11
Lindsborg, 3290 F-12
LINN CO., 9722 G-18
Linn, 401 B-13
Little River, 523 F-11
LOGAN CO., 2855 E-3
Logan, 566 C-7
Longton, 382 I-16
Louisburg, 2889 F-19
Lucas, 416 D-10
Lyndon, 1028 F-17
LYON CO., 35805 G-15
Lyons, 3565 G-11
Macksville, 498 H-9
Madison, 822 G-16
Maize, 2042 H-12
Manhattan, 44733 D-14
Mankato, 880 B-10
Maple Hill, 477 D-16
MARION CO., 13299 G-13
Marion, 2058 G-13
Marquette, 567 F-11
MARSHALL CO., 10589 B-14
Marysville, 3133 B-14
McCune, 426 I-18
McLouth, 855 D-18
MCPHERSON CO., 29346 F-11
McPherson, 13731 F-12
MEADE CO., 4662 J-6
Meade, 1658 J-5
Medicine Lodge, 2067 J-10
Melvern, 426 F-17
Meriden, 691 D-17
Merriam, 10835 *J-2
MIAMI CO., 29187 F-18
Milford, 481 D-14
Miltonvale, 491 C-12
Minneapolis, 2044 D-12
Minneola, 702 I-6
Mission, 9559 *J-2
Mission Hills, 3552 *J-3
MITCHELL CO., 6707 D-11
Moline, 443 I-15
Montezuma, 974 I-5
MONTGOMERY CO., 34934 I-16
Moran, 550 H-18
MORRIS CO., 5995 E-14
MORTON CO., 3317 J-2
Mound City, 817 G-19
Moundridge, 1645 G-12
Mound Valley, 414 J-17
Mt. Hope, 843 H-12
Mulberry, 580 I-19
Mulvane, 5536 I-13
Natoma, 333 D-9
NEMAHA CO., 10500 B-16
Neodesha, 2734 I-17
NEOSHO CO., 16580 I-17
NESS CO., 3158 F-7
Ness City, 1403 F-7
Newton, 17977 G-13
Nickerson, 1183 G-11
N. Newton, 1563 G-13
NORTON CO., 5796 B-6
Norton, 2901 B-7
Nortonville, 605 C-17
Norwich, 535 I-11
Oaklawn, 3000 N-9
Oakley, 2030 D-4
Oberlin, 1884 B-5
Ogden, 1786 D-14
Olathe, 105274 E-19
Olpe, 513 G-15
Onaga, 687 C-15
OSAGE CO., 16784 F-16
Osage City, 2954 F-16
Osawatomie, 4595 F-18
OSBORNE CO., 4179 C-9
Osborne, 1497 C-9
Oskaloosa, 1157 D-17
Oswego, 1989 J-18
Otis, 316 F-9
OTTAWA CO., 6177 D-12
Ottawa, 12031 F-18
Overbrook, 960 E-17
Overland Park, 160368 D-19
Oxford, 1134 J-13
Ozawkie, 562 D-17
Paola, 5065 F-19
Park City, 6877 H-13
Parsons, 11296 I-18
PAWNEE CO., 6796 G-8
Pawnee Rock, 344 G-9
Peabody, 1354 G-13
Perry, 898 D-17
PHILLIPS CO., 5657 B-8
Phillipsburg, 2510 B-8
Pittsburg, 19276 I-19
Plains, 1180 J-5
Plainville, 1917 D-8
Pleasanton, 1381 G-19
Pomona, 952 F-17
POTTAWATOMIE CO., 18714 C-15
Potwin, 439 H-13
Prairie Vil., 21729 D-19
PRATT CO., 9437 H-9
Pratt, 6422 I-9
Pretty Prairie, 598 H-11
Protection, 540 J-7
Quenemo, 461 F-17
Quinter, 901 D-6
Ransom, 307 F-6
RAWLINS CO., 2843 B-3
RENO CO., 63832 H-11
REPUBLIC CO., 5307 B-12
RICE CO., 10412 F-10
Richmond, 518 F-18
RILEY CO., 62291 D-14
Riley, 884 D-14
Riverton, 600 J-19
Roeland Park, 7075 *J-3
Rolla, 456 J-2
ROOKS CO., 5417 D-8
Rose Hill, 3710 I-13
Rossville, 1001 D-16
RUSH CO., 3418 F-8
RUSSELL CO., 6907 D-9
Russell, 4404 E-9
Sabetha, 2559 B-16
St. Francis, 1390 B-2
St. John, 1249 H-9
St. Marys, 2253 D-16
St. Paul, 657 I-18
Salina, 45833 E-12
SALINE CO., 53737 E-11
Satanta, 1197 I-4
Scammon, 480 J-19
Scandia, 387 B-12
SCOTT CO., 4806 F-4
Scott City, 3640 F-4
Scranton, 711 E-16
Sedan, 1288 J-16
SEDGWICK CO., 462896 I-12
Sedgwick, 1637 H-12
Seneca, 2084 B-16
Severy, 358 I-15
SEWARD CO., 23091 J-4
Sharon Sprs., 762 E-2
SHAWNEE CO., 170902 E-16
Shawnee, 54093 D-19
SHERIDAN CO., 2662 D-5
SHERMAN CO., 6277 C-2
Silver Lake, 1340 D-16
SMITH CO., 4181 B-9
Smith Cen., 1773 B-9
Solomon, 1063 E-13
S. Haven, 379 J-13
S. Hutchinson, 2507 H-11
Spearville, 843 H-7
Spring Hill, 3745 E-19
STAFFORD CO., 4589 H-9
Stafford, 1097 H-10
STANTON CO., 2404 I-2
Sterling, 2568 G-11
STEVENS CO., 5389 J-3
Stockton, 1477 C-8
Strong City, 598 F-15
Sublette, 1576 I-4
SUMNER CO., 25256 J-12
Syracuse, 1848 H-2
Tecumseh, 650 M-17
Thayer, 499 I-17
THOMAS CO., 7933 D-3
Tonganoxie, 3317 D-18
Topeka, 122008 D-17
Towanda, 1338 H-13
TREGO CO., 3103 E-6
Tribune, 765 F-2
Troy, 1032 B-18
Turon, 432 H-10
Udall, 789 I-13
Ulysses, 5790 I-3
Valley Cen., 5167 H-13
Valley Falls, 1217 C-17
Victoria, 1181 E-8
WABAUNSEE CO., 6767 E-15
WaKeeney, 1800 D-7
Wakefield, 854 D-13
WALLACE CO., 1621 E-2
Wamego, 4237 D-15
WASHINGTON CO., 6131 B-13
Washington, 1168 B-13
Waterville, 646 B-14
Wathena, 1331 B-18
Waverly, 573 F-17
Weir, 768 I-19
Wellington, 8299 J-13
Wellsville, 1595 E-18
Westmoreland, 637 C-15
Westwood, 1504 *J-3
Westwood Hills, 369 *J-3
White City, 497 E-14
Whitewater, 636 H-13
WICHITA CO., 2447 F-3
Wichita, 354617 I-13
Wilroads Gardens, 400 I-6
WILSON CO., 10080 I-16
Wilson, 765 E-10
Winchester, 579 C-17
Winfield, 12016 J-14
WOODSON CO., 3631 H-16
WYANDOTTE CO., 157091 D-18
Yates Cen., 1520 H-17

Kentucky

Map pp. 86-89

ADAIR CO., 17458 L-10
Adairville, 917 N-5
Ages, 500 M-16
Airport Gardens, 700 K-17
Albany, 2255 M-10
Alexandria, 8206 D-13
ALLEN CO., 18262 N-7
Altro, 35 K-16
Anchorage, 2457 G-9
Anco, 360 K-17
ANDERSON CO., 19812 H-11
Argillite, 50 F-18
Arjay, 600 M-15
Arlington, 395 F-2
Artemus, 800 M-14
Ary, 60 K-17
Ashland, 21491 F-18
Auburn, 1468 M-5
Audubon Park, 1533 C-7
Augusta, 1222 E-14
Aurora, 200 M-1
Auxier, 900 I-18
Avawam, 250 K-16
BALLARD CO., 8193 E-2
Banner, 100 J-18
Barbourmeade, 1280 A-9
Barbourville, 3493 M-14
Bardstown, 10458 I-9
Bardwell, 796 F-2
Barlow, 705 E-2
BARREN CO., 39133 L-8
Baskett, 300 I-3
BATH CO., 11413 G-14
Baxter, 800 M-16
Beattyville, 1178 J-15
Beauty, 600 I-19
Beaver, 200 K-18
Beaver Dam, 3054 K-5
Bedford, 719 F-10
Beechmont, 600 K-4
Beechwood Vil., 1186 B-8
Belfry, 600 J-19
BELL CO., 29953 M-15
Bellefonte, 830 E-19
Bellemeade, 882 B-9
Bellevue, 6138 A-17
Benham, 560 L-17
Benton, 4165 F-4
Berea, 11259 J-13
Betsy Layne, 450 J-18
Bloomfield, 856 I-10
Bond, 90 K-14
Bonnieville, 357 K-8
BOONE CO., 97139 D-11
Boone Hts., 800 M-14
Boston, 300 I-9
BOURBON CO., 19598 H-13
Bowling Green, 50663 L-6
BOYD CO., 49554 G-18
BOYLE CO., 27837 J-11
BRACKEN CO., 8487 E-13
Brandenburg, 2158 H-7
BREATHITT CO., 15850 J-16
BRECKINRIDGE CO., 19011 I-6
Brodhead, 1185 K-13
Bromley, 800 B-16
Bronston, 400 L-12
Brooks, 2678 H-8
Brooksville, 601 E-14
Browder, 300 K-4
Brownsboro Farm, 686 A-9
Brownsboro Vil., 320 B-8
Brownsville, 933 K-7
Buckner, 4000 G-9
Buffalo, 400 J-9
Bulan, 600 K-17
BULLITT CO., 64909 H-9
Burgin, 880 I-11
Burkesville, 1765 M-10
Burlington, 10779 D-12
Burnside, 659 L-12
BUTLER CO., 13199 K-6
Butler, 626 E-13
Cadiz, 2443 M-2
CALDWELL CO., 12824 K-1
Calhoun, 812 J-4
CALLOWAY CO., 34671 N-1
Calvert City, 2723 E-4
Camargo, 952 H-14
CAMPBELL CO., 87970 E-13
Campbellsburg, 706 F-10
Campbellsville, 10689 K-10
Campton, 405 I-15
Canada, 400 J-19
Caneyville, 637 K-6
Cannel City, 250 I-16
Cannonsburg, 700 G-18
CARLISLE CO., 5384 F-2
Carlisle, 2002 G-14
CARROLL CO., 10230 E-10
Carrollton, 3802 F-10
CARTER CO., 27144 G-17
CASEY CO., 15977 K-11
Catlettsburg, 1908 F-18
Cave City, 1920 L-8
Cawood, 850 M-16
Cecilia, 750 J-8
Centertown, 413 K-4
Central City, 5787 K-4
Chaplin, 500 I-10
Cherrywood Vil., 327 B-8
Chloe, 150 J-19
CHRISTIAN CO., 69912 L-3
CLARK CO., 33958 H-13
Clarkson, 808 J-7
CLAY CO., 24346 K-15
Clay, 1166 J-2
Clay City, 1314 I-14
Clearfield, 1300 H-16
Cleaton, 500 K-4
CLINTON CO., 9605 M-11
Clinton, 1387 G-2
Cloverport, 1248 I-6
Cold Spring, 4772 C-17
Colonial Ter., 1000 B-9
Columbia, 4152 L-10
Combs, 900 K-16
Corbin, 7932 L-14
Corydon, 753 I-2
Covington, 42687 D-12
Crab Orchard, 860 J-12
Cranks, 120 M-17
Crescent Park C-15
Crescent Sprs., 3964 B-15
Crestview, 471 C-18
Crestview Hills, 3232 C-15
Crestwood, 2095 G-9
CRITTENDEN CO., 9092 J-1
Crittenden, 2506 E-12
Crofton, 794 L-3
Cromona, 400 K-18
Cub Run, 125 K-7
CUMBERLAND CO., 7159 M-9
Cumberland, 2380 L-17
Cunningham, 400 F-3
Custer, 125 I-7
Cynthiana, 6260 G-13
Danville, 15294 J-11
DAVIESS CO., 92540 J-4
Dawson Sprs., 2978 K-2
Dayton, 5677 A-17
Diablock, 200 K-17
Dixon, 604 J-2
Dorton, 250 K-18
Drakesboro, 622 K-4
Drift, 300 J-18
Dry Ridge, 2068 E-12
Dwarf, 100 K-17
Earlington, 1599 K-3
E. Bernstadt, 774 K-14
Eddyville, 2353 L-1
Edgewood, 9188 C-15
EDMONSON CO., 11869 K-7
Edmonton, 1578 L-9
Elizabethtown, 23239 I-8
Elkhorn City, 1038 K-19
Elkton, 1964 M-4
ELLIOTT CO., 6935 H-17
Elsmere, 8059 D-12
Eminence, 2242 G-10
Emlyn, 350 M-14
Eolia, 300 L-18
Erlanger, 16826 D-12
Ermine, 300 L-18
ESTILL CO., 15192 I-14
Evarts, 1068 M-17
Ezel, 300 I-16
Falmouth, 2103 E-13
Fancy Farm, 300 F-3
FAYETTE CO., 266798 H-13
Ferguson, 894 L-12
Flaherty, 250 I-7
Flat Lick, 700 M-15
Flatwoods, 7593 F-18
FLEMING CO., 14379 G-14
Fleming-Neon, 818 K-18
Flemingsburg, 3097 F-15
Florence, 24689 D-12
FLOYD CO., 42272 J-18
Fordsville, 535 J-5
Forest Hills, 508 C-9
Forest Hills, 300 J-19
Ft. Mitchell, 7822 D-12
Ft. Thomas, 16019 D-12
Ft. Wright, 5580 B-16
Fourmile, 450 M-15
Frankfort, 27408 G-11
FRANKLIN CO., 48051 G-11
Franklin, 8009 M-6
Fredonia, 411 K-1
Freeburn, 500 J-20
Frenchburg, 554 H-15
FULTON CO., 7419 G-1
Fulton, 2636 G-2
GALLATIN CO., 7995 E-11
Gamaliel, 435 N-8
Garner, 150 K-17
GARRARD CO., 15850 J-12
Garrett, 500 J-18
Garrison, 600 F-16
Georgetown, 19438 G-12
Ghent, 381 E-11
Gilbertsville, 800 E-4
Glasgow, 13614 L-8
Glendale, 350 J-8
Glenview Hills, 342 A-8
Goshen, 935 G-9
Graham, 700 K-3
Grahn, 550 G-17
Grand Rivers, 338 L-1
GRANT CO., 23983 F-12
GRAVES CO., 37252 F-3
Gray, 750 L-14
Graymoor-Devondale, 2957 B-9
Grays Knob, 300 M-16
GRAYSON CO., 24600 J-7
Grayson, 3980 G-17
GREEN CO., 11787 K-9
Greensburg, 2443 K-9
GREENUP CO., 36952 F-17
Greenup, 1173 F-18
Greenville, 4315 K-4
Guthrie, 1449 N-4
Hagerhill, 150 I-18
HANCOCK CO., 8433 I-5
Hanson, 622 J-3
HARDIN CO., 96052 J-7
Hardin, 567 M-1
Hardinsburg, 2393 I-6
Hardy, 650 J-20
HARLAN CO., 32095 L-17
Harlan, 1945 M-16
Harold, 400 J-18
HARRISON CO., 18227 F-12
Harrodsburg, 8085 I-11
HART CO., 17879 K-8
Hartford, 2603 J-5
Hawesville, 961 I-5
Hazard, 4745 K-17
Hazel, 439 G-4
Hebron, 3500 D-12
Heidrick, 700 M-14
Hellier, 400 K-19
HENDERSON CO., 45129 I-2
Henderson, 27468 I-3
HENRY CO., 15543 G-11
Herndon, 150 M-2
HICKMAN CO., 5165 G-2
Hickman, 2442 G-1
Highland Hts., 6472 C-17
Hillcrest, 300 I-13
Hillview, 7179 H-9
Hima, 250 L-15
Hindman, 771 K-17
Hitchins, 350 G-17
Hodgenville, 2787 J-8
Hollow Cr., 826 D-8
Hollyvilla, 494 H-8
HOPKINS CO., 46839 K-2
Hopkinsville, 28678 M-3
Horse Cave, 2272 L-8
Houston Acres, 497 C-9
Hulen, 300 M-16
Hurstbourne, 3959 B-9
Hustonville, 351 J-11
Hyden, 200 L-16
Independence, 17070 D-12
Indian Hills, 2967 B-8
Inez, 456 I-19
Ironville, 600 E-19
Irvine, 2748 I-14
Irvington, 1292 I-7
Island, 431 J-4
Jackhorn, 500 K-18
JACKSON CO., 13595 K-14
Jackson, 2407 J-16
Jamestown, 1666 L-11
Jeff, 400 K-17
JEFFERSON CO., 699017 H-9
Jeffersontown, 26331 G-9
Jeffersonville, 1867 H-14
Jenkins, 2321 K-18
JESSAMINE CO., 41508 I-12
JOHNSON CO., 23647 H-17
Jonancy, 125 K-18
Junction City, 2163 J-11
KENTON CO., 152287 E-12
Kenton, 175 E-12
Kenvir, 900 M-17
Kevil, 565 E-3
Kingsley, 426 C-8
KNOTT CO., 17614 K-17
Knottsville, 400 I-5
KNOX CO., 31708 L-15
Kuttawa, 613 L-1
La Center, 1026 E-2
La Grange, 5865 G-10
Lake City, 300 L-1
Lakeside Park, 2791 C-16
Lancaster, 4014 J-12
Langley, 400 J-18
LARUE CO., 13437 J-8
LAUREL CO., 55488 L-14
LAWRENCE CO., 15895 H-18
Lawrenceburg, 9246 H-11
Lebanon, 5821 J-10
Lebanon Jct., 1854 I-8
Leburn, 250 K-17
LEE CO., 7900 J-15
Leitchfield, 6263 J-7
Lejunior, 300 M-17
LESLIE CO., 12203 L-16
LETCHER CO., 24843 L-17
LEWIS CO., 13796 F-16
Lewisburg, 911 L-4
Lewisport, 1628 H-5
Lexington, 266798 H-12
Liberty, 1871 K-11
Lily, 500 L-14
LINCOLN CO., 24535 K-12
Lindseyville, 200 K-7
Livermore, 1467 J-4
LIVINGSTON CO., 9726 D-4
Lloyd, 900 F-17
LOGAN CO., 26841 L-5
London, 7653 L-14
Lone Oak, 445 E-3
Long View, 200 I-8
Lookout, 350 K-19
Loretto, 635 J-9
Louisa, 2007 H-18
Louisville, 248762 G-8
Lovely, 700 I-19
Loyall, 731 M-16
Ludlow, 4283 D-12
Lynch, 843 L-17
Lyndon, 10293 B-9
Lynnview, 974 C-7
LYON CO., 8078 L-1
Maceo, 500 I-4
MADISON CO., 74814 J-13
Madisonville, 19321 K-3
Magnolia, 800 J-8
MAGOFFIN CO., 13334 J-17
Majestic, 400 J-20
Manchester, 1668 L-15
MARION CO., 18533 J-10
Marion, 3087 K-1
MARSHALL CO., 30559 F-4
Marshes Siding, 700 M-12
MARTIN CO., 12521 I-19
Martin, 636 J-18
MASON CO., 16815 F-15
Masonville, 1075 I-4
Mayfield, 10228 F-3
Mays Lick, 350 F-14
Maysville, 8941 F-15
McAndrews, 450 J-19
MCCRACKEN CO., 64768 E-3
MCCREARY CO., 17190 N-12
McDaniels, 200 J-6
McDowell, 400 J-18
McHenry, 426 K-5
McKee, 856 J-14
MCLEAN CO., 9872 J-3
McRoberts, 921 K-18
McVeigh, 250 J-19
MEADE CO., 27619 H-7
Melbourne, 451 D-13
Melvin, 250 K-18
MENIFEE CO., 6618 H-15
MERCER CO., 21410 I-11
METCALFE CO., 10042 L-9
Middlesboro, 10266 N-15
Middletown, 6005 G-9
Midway, 1591 H-12
Millersburg, 833 G-13
Millstone, 300 K-18
Milton, 575 E-10
Minor Lane Hts., 1508 D-7
Mitchellsburg, 350 J-11
MONROE CO., 11740 M-9
MONTGOMERY CO., 23535 H-14
Monticello, 6053 M-11
Moorland, 469 B-9
Morehead, 7627 G-16
MORGAN CO., 14278 H-16
Morganfield, 3481 I-1
Morgantown, 2545 K-5
Mortons Gap, 954 K-3
Mt. Olivet, 294 F-14
Mt. Sterling, 6033 H-14
Mt. Vernon, 2589 K-13
Mt. Washington, 8605 H-9
Mousie, 400 J-18
MUHLENBERG CO., 31691 L-4
Muldraugh, 1346 H-8
Munfordville, 1581 K-8
Murray, 15311 G-4
Nazareth, 400 I-9
NELSON CO., 39635 I-9
New Castle, 919 F-10
New Haven, 854 J-9
New Hope, 200 J-9
Newport, 16243 D-12
NICHOLAS CO., 6937 G-14
Nicholasville, 22251 I-12
N. Corbin, 1662 L-14
Northfield, 987 B-8
N. Middletown, 558 H-14
Nortonville, 1259 K-3
Oakdale, 1900 E-4
Oak Grove, 7564 N-3
OHIO CO., 23165 J-5
Oil Sprs., 150 I-17
OLDHAM CO., 50517 G-10
Olive Hill, 1794 G-16
Oneida, 300 K-15
OWEN CO., 11092 F-11
Owensboro, 54312 I-4
Owenton, 1453 F-11
Owingsville, 1515 H-15
OWSLEY CO., 4755 J-15
Paducah, 25565 E-3
Paintsville, 4031 I-18
Paris, 9271 G-13
Park City, 527 L-7
Park Hills, 2880 B-16
Parkway Vil., 707 C-7
Pathfork, 400 M-16
Pembroke, 754 M-3
PENDLETON CO., 15090 F-13
PERRY CO., 29492 K-17
Perryville, 749 J-11
Petersburg, 400 D-11
Pewee Valley, 1490 A-10
Phelps, 1053 J-20
Philpot, 400 I-4
Phyllis, 350 J-19
PIKE CO., 67495 J-19
Pikeville, 6286 J-19
Pilgrim, 150 I-19
Pine Knot, 1680 N-13
Pine Ridge, 125 I-15
Pineville, 2060 M-15
Pioneer Village, 2569 H-9
Pittsburg, 600 L-14
Plantation, 914 B-9
Pleasant Ridge, 200 J-4
Pleasant View, 500 M-14
Pleasureville, 873 G-10
Poole, 400 J-2
Powderly, 851 K-4
POWELL CO., 13347 I-14
Premium, 150 L-17
Prestonsburg, 3677 I-18
Princeton, 6394 L-1
Prospect, 4824 G-9
Providence, 3544 K-2
PULASKI CO., 58013 L-12
Quicksand, 150 J-16
Quincy, 350 F-17
Raccoon, 400 J-19
Raceland, 2388 F-18
Radcliff, 21894 I-8
Ravenna, 672 I-14
Reed, 100 I-3
Reidland, 4353 E-4
Revelo, 700 M-12
Richlawn, 459 B-8
Richmond, 29080 I-13
Rineyville, 400 I-8
Riverwood, 479 A-8
Robards, 572 I-3

2000 Census populations or latest available estimate.
Index to Canada and Mexico cities and towns, pages 274-275.

KENTUCKY - MASSACHUSETTS 265

ROBERTSON CO., 2320 F-14
Robinson Cr., 400 K-19
ROCKCASTLE CO., 16644 K-13
Rockhouse, 200 K-19
Rockport, 337 K-4
Rolling Fields, 659 B-8
Rolling Hills, 916 A-9
Rosine, 200 J-5
ROWAN CO., 22397 H-16
Rowletts, 300 K-8
Royalton, 200 I-17
RUSSELL CO., 16586 M-10
Russell, 3574 F-18
Russell Sprs., 2464 L-10
Russellville, 7202 M-5
Sacramento, 510 K-3
St. Catharine, 500 I-10
St. Charles, 314 K-3
St. Dennis, 2400 C-5
St. Matthews, 17441 G-9
St. Regis Park, 1541 C-9
Salem, 753 K-1
Salt Lick, 346 H-15
Salvisa, 250 I-11
Salyersville, 1587 I-17
Sandgap, 300 J-14
Sandy Hook, 690 H-17
Sassafras, 950 K-17
Science Hill, 641 K-12
SCOTT CO., 36726 G-12
Scottsville, 4413 M-7
Sebree, 1566 J-3
Sedalia, 300 G-3
Seneca Gardens, 694 C-8
Sharpsburg, 299 G-14
Shelbiana, 350 J-19
SHELBY CO., 35900 G-10
Shelbyville, 10390 G-10
Shepherdsville, 8600 H-8
Shively, 15343 G-8
Sidney, 200 J-19
Silver Gr., 1181 D-13
SIMPSON CO., 16664 M-6
Simpsonville, 1329 G-10
Smith, 150 M-16
Smithland, 392 E-4
Smith Mills, 450 I-2
Smiths Gr., 762 L-7
Somerset, 11786 L-12
Southgate, 3444 B-17
S. Irvine, 400 I-14
S. Portsmouth, 900 E-17
S. Shore, 1225 E-17
S. Williamson, 1000 I-19
SPENCER CO., 14301 H-10
Spottsville, 350 I-3
Springfield, 2739 I-10
Springlee, 426 B-8
Staffordsville, 200 I-18
Stamping Ground, 612 G-12
Stanford, 3423 J-12
Stanley, 300 I-4
Stanton, 3026 I-14
Stanville, 125 J-18
Stearns, 1586 M-12
Strathmoor Vil., 621 C-8
Sturgis, 2027 J-1
Sublimity City, 800 L-14
Sullivan, 300 J-1
Summer Shade, 300 M-8
Summersville, 150 K-9
Summit, 900 F-18
Sunshine, 350 M-16
Symsonia, 500 F-4
Tateville, 500 L-12
TAYLOR CO., 23347 K-10
Taylor Mill, 6866 C-17
Taylorsville, 1107 H-10
Thealka, 400 I-18
Tinsley, 100 M-15
TODD CO., 12019 M-4
Tollesboro, 600 F-15
Tompkinsville, 2654 M-9
Topmost, 200 K-18
Trenton, 419 M-3
TRIGG CO., 12877 M-2
TRIMBLE CO., 8759 F-10
Ulysses, 30 H-18
UNION CO., 15751 J-2
Union, 3135 D-12
Uniontown, 1079 I-1
Upton, 638 J-8
Utica, 300 J-4
Vanceburg, 1680 F-16
Van Lear, 1050 I-18
Verda, 800 M-16
Verona, 600 E-12
Versailles, 7487 H-12
Villa Hills, 7919 B-15
Vine Gr., 4066 I-8
Viper, 100 K-17
Virgie, 300 K-18
Waco, 200 I-13
Walton, 2598 E-12
Warfield, 279 I-19
WARREN CO., 95778 L-7
Warsaw, 1808 E-11
WASHINGTON CO., 11260 I-10
Water Valley, 320 G-3
Watterson Park, 1039 C-8
Waverly, 295 I-2
Wayland, 290 J-18
WAYNE CO., 20277 M-11
WEBSTER CO., 14051 J-2
Weeksbury, 800 K-18
Wellington, 562 C-8
W. Buechel, 1332 C-8
W. Liberty, 3344 H-16
W. Point, 1062 H-8
Westport, 300 F-9
W. Van Lear, 600 I-18
Westwood, 4888 F-18
Westwood, 620 B-9
Wheelwright, 1025 K-18
White Plains, 817 K-3
Whitesburg, 1542 L-18
Whitesville, 599 I-5
WHITLEY CO., 37261 M-13
Whitley City, 1111 M-12
Wickliffe, 781 E-2
Wilder, 2766 B-17
Williamsburg, 5033 M-13
Williamstown, 3362 F-12
Wilmore, 5818 I-12
Winchester, 16378 H-13
Windy Hills, 2520 B-8
Wingo, 582 G-3
Wittensville, 200 I-18
WOLFE CO., 6939 I-15
Woodbine, 500 M-14
Woodburn, 327 M-6
WOODFORD CO., 23659 H-11
Woodlawn, 257 B-17
Woodlawn Park, 1046 B-8
Worthington, 1657 F-18
Wurtland, 1043 F-18
Zebulon, 200 J-19

Louisiana

Map pp. 90-91

Abbeville, 11698 H-5
Abita Sprs., 2112 G-9
ACADIA PAR., 59246 H-4
Addis, 2450 H-7
Albany, 956 G-8
Alexandria, 45649 E-4
ALLEN PAR., 25268 G-3
Amelia, 2423 I-7
Amite, 4064 G-8
Anacoco, 818 E-3
Anandale, 2000 E-4
Arabi, 8093 H-9
Arcadia, 2898 B-3
Arnaudville, 1393 G-5
ASCENSION PAR., 84424 H-7
ASSUMPTION PAR., 23269 I-7
Avondale, 5441 E-12
AVOYELLES PAR., 41791 E-5
Baker, 13552 G-7
Baldwin, 2682 I-6
Ball, 3682 E-4
Barataria, 1333 I-9
Basile, 2377 G-4
Bastrop, 12763 B-5
Baton Rouge, 225090 G-7
Bawcomville, 2300 C-5
Bayou Cane, 17046 I-8
Bayou Goula, 650 H-7
BEAUREGARD PAR., 33514 G-2
Belle Chasse, 9848 I-9
Belle Rose, 1944 H-7
Benton, 2922 B-2
Bernice, 1777 B-4
Berwick, 4350 I-7
BIENVILLE PAR., 15320 C-3
Bogalusa, 12949 F-10
Boothville, 900 J-11
BOSSIER PAR., 101999 B-2
Bossier City, 58111 B-2
Bourg, 2160 I-8
Boyce, 1192 E-4
Breaux Bridge, 7505 H-5
Bridge City, 8323 E-12
Broussard, 6314 H-5
Brusly, 2000 G-7
Bunkie, 4535 F-5
Buras, 1480 J-11
CADDO PAR., 250342 B-1
CALCASIEU PAR., 183889 H-2
CALDWELL PAR., 10599 C-5
CAMERON PAR., 9708 I-3
Cameron, 1965 I-3
Campti, 1058 D-3
Carencro, 6022 H-5
Carville H-7
CATAHOULA PAR., 10615 D-5
Catahoula, 700 H-6
Cecilia, 1505 H-6
Centerville, 700 I-6
Chalmette, 32069 H-10
Charenton, 1944 I-6
Chatham, 621 C-4
Chauvin, 3229 J-8
Cheneyville, 892 F-5
Choudrant, 578 B-4
Church Pt., 4704 G-5
CLAIBORNE PAR., 16534 B-3
Clarence, 496 D-3
Clarks, 1062 D-5
Clayton, 820 D-6
Clinton, 1958 F-7
Colfax, 1641 E-4
CONCORDIA PAR., 19730 E-6
Cottonport, 2274 F-5
Cotton Valley, 1166 B-2
Coushatta, 2228 D-3
Covington, 8769 G-9
Crowley, 13940 H-4
Cullen, 1254 A-2
Cut Off, 5635 I-9
Delcambre, 2155 H-5
Delhi, 3112 B-6
Denham Sprs., 9204 G-7
DeQuincy, 3310 G-2
DeRidder, 9758 F-3
Des Allemands, 2500 I-8
DE SOTO PAR., 25990 C-2
Donaldsonville, 7552 H-7
Doyline, 829 B-2
Dubach, 811 B-4
Duson, 1657 H-5
EAST BATON ROUGE PAR., 412447 G-7
EAST CARROLL PAR., 8997 B-7
EAST FELICIANA PAR., 21095 F-7
Elton, 1244 G-4
Empire, 2211 J-10
Epps, 1149 B-6
Erath, 2181 H-5
Estherwood, 814 H-4
Eunice, 11586 G-4
EVANGELINE PAR., 35149 G-4
Farmerville, 3776 B-4
Ferriday, 3615 D-6
Florien, 691 E-2
Fordoche, 962 G-6
Forest Oaks, 1500 B-14
FRANKLIN PAR., 20860 C-6
Franklin, 8059 I-6
Franklinton, 3641 F-9
French Settlement, 1009 H-8
Galliano, 7356 J-9
Garyville, 2775 H-8
Gibsland, 1091 B-3
Gilbert, 542 C-6
Glenmora, 1551 F-4
Golden Meadow, 2151 J-9
Gonzales, 8339 H-8
Grambling, 4371 B-4
Gramercy, 3120 H-8
Grand Coteau, 1036 G-5
Grand Isle, 1563 J-9
GRANT PAR., 18887 E-4
Gray, 4958 I-8
Grayson, 532 C-5
Greensburg, 604 F-8
Greenwood, 2485 C-1
Gretna, 17180 I-9
Grosse Tete, 640 G-6
Gueydan, 1594 H-4
Hackberry, 1699 H-2
Hahnville, 2792 H-9
Hammond, 17715 G-8
Harahan, 9797 H-9
Hardwood, 500 F-7
Harrisonburg, 734 D-6
Harvey, 22226 E-13
Haughton, 2802 B-2
Hayes, 880 H-3
Haynesville, 2561 A-3
Henderson, 1544 H-6
Hessmer, 647 F-5
Hodge, 483 C-4
Homer, 3604 B-3
Houma, 32025 I-8
IBERIA PAR., 74146 H-6
IBERVILLE PAR., 32811 H-6
Independence, 1711 G-8
Inniswold, 4944 C-13
Iota, 1388 H-4
Iowa, 2628 H-3
JACKSON PAR., 15259 C-4
Jackson, 3896 F-7
Jarreau, 520 G-6
Jeanerette, 5955 I-6
JEFFERSON PAR., 452459 I-9
Jefferson, 11843 E-12
JEFFERSON DAVIS PAR., 31113 H-3
Jena, 2925 D-5
Jennings, 10712 H-4
Jonesboro, 3808 C-4
Jonesville, 2369 D-6
Junction City, 650 A-4
Kaplan, 5104 H-5
Kenner, 70202 H-9
Kentwood, 2174 F-8
Killian, 1151 G-8
Kinder, 2129 G-3
Krotz Sprs., 1243 G-6
Labadieville, 1811 I-7
Lacombe, 7518 H-10
LAFAYETTE PAR., 194239 H-5
Lafayette, 111667 H-5
Lafitte, 1576 I-9
LAFOURCHE PAR., 91281 I-8
Lake Arthur, 2916 H-4
Lake Charles, 70735 H-3
Lake Providence, 4751 B-7
Lakeshore, 1400 B-5
Lakeview, 1200 A-8
La Place, 27684 H-8
Larose, 7306 I-9
LA SALLE PAR., 14179 D-5
Lawtell, 1000 G-5
Lecompte, 1340 F-4
Leesville, 6432 F-3
Leonville, 1013 G-5
LINCOLN PAR., 42413 B-4
Live Oak Manor, 1900 E-11
LIVINGSTON PAR., 102046 G-8
Livingston, 1432 G-8
Livonia, 1343 G-6
Lockport, 2611 I-8
Logansport, 1647 D-1
Loreauville, 955 H-6
Luling, 11512 H-9
Lutcher, 3632 H-8
Lydia, 1079 I-6
MADISON PAR., 13079 C-7
Madisonville, 709 G-9
Mamou, 3438 G-4
Mandeville, 11476 G-9
Mangham, 572 C-6
Mansfield, 5486 C-2
Mansura, 1574 F-5
Many, 2808 E-2
Maringouin, 1243 G-6
Marion, 808 A-5
Marksville, 5695 F-5
Marrero, 36165 E-13
Martin, 623 C-3
Melville, 1368 G-6
Meraux, 10192 H-10
Mermentau, 705 H-4
Mer Rouge, 695 B-6
Merryville, 1131 G-2
Metairie, 146136 H-9
Minden, 13313 B-3
Monroe, 52163 B-5
Montegut, 1803 J-8
Montgomery, 795 D-3
Mooringsport, 808 B-1
Moreauville, 931 F-5
MOREHOUSE PAR., 30671 B-5
Morgan City, 12282 I-7
Morganza, 635 G-6
Morse, 746 H-4
Moss Bluff, 10535 H-3
Nairn, 1000 J-10
Napoleonville, 699 H-7
NATCHITOCHES PAR., 39002 E-3
Natchitoches, 18113 D-3
Newellton, 1389 C-7
New Iberia, 32502 H-6
New Llano, 2273 F-3
New Orleans, 469032 H-9
New Roads, 4876 G-6
Norco, 3579 H-9
N. Merrydale, 4000 A-13
Oakdale, 7992 F-4
Oak Grove, 2126 B-6
Oak Manor, 1100 B-14
Oberlin, 1859 G-4
Oil City, 1188 B-1
Olla, 1375 D-5
Opelousas, 22753 G-5
ORLEANS PAR., 469032 H-9
OUACHITA PAR., 147898 C-5
Paincourtville, 884 H-7
Paradis, 1252 I-9
Patterson, 5156 I-7
Pearl River, 1932 G-10
Pierre Part, 3239 H-7
Pine Prairie, 1160 F-4
Pineville, 13858 E-4
Pitkin, 700 F-3
Plain Dealing, 1049 A-2
Plaquemine, 6894 H-7
PLAQUEMINES PAR., 28025 I-10
Pleasant Hill, 711 D-2
POINTE COUPEE PAR., 22564 G-6
Ponchatoula, 5450 G-9
Port Allen, 5150 G-7
Port Barre, 2290 G-5
Port Sulphur, 3115 J-10
Provencal, 705 D-3
Raceland, 10224 I-8
RAPIDES PAR., 127394 F-4
Rayne, 8537 H-5
Rayville, 4116 B-6
Red Oaks B-14
RED RIVER PAR., 9524 C-3
Reserve, 9111 H-8
RICHLAND PAR., 20623 C-6
Richwood, 2105 C-5
Ridgecrest, 760 E-6
Ringgold, 1592 C-3
River Ridge, 14588 E-11
Rosedale, 739 G-6
Roseland, 1233 G-8
Rosepine, 1386 F-3
Ruston, 20634 B-4
SABINE PAR., 23406 E-2
ST. BERNARD PAR., 66113 I-10
ST. CHARLES PAR., 49353 I-9
St. Francisville, 1672 F-7
ST. HELENA PAR., 10307 G-8
ST. JAMES PAR., 21118 I-8
ST. JOHN THE BAPTIST PAR., 44816 H-8
St. Joseph, 1222 D-7
ST. LANDRY PAR., 89041 G-5
ST. MARTIN PAR., 49911 H-6
St. Martinville, 6993 H-6
ST. MARY PAR., 52357 I-6
ST. TAMMANY PAR., 207743 G-9
Samtown, 3500 E-4
Sarepta, 914 A-2
Scotlandville G-7
Scott, 7885 H-5
Seymourville, 3000 H-7
Shreveport, 198364 B-2
Sibley, 1082 B-3
Simmesport, 2218 F-6
Simpson, 547 E-3
Simsboro, 686 B-4
Slaughter, 1002 G-7
Slidell, 26947 H-10
Sorrento, 1292 H-8
Springhill, 5246 A-2
Starks, 950 H-2
Sterlington, 1252 B-5
Stonewall, 1857 C-2
Sulphur, 19901 H-2
Sunnybrook, 800 A-13
Sunset, 2395 G-5
Tallulah, 8715 C-7
TANGIPAHOA PAR., 103591 G-8
Tangipahoa, 742 F-8
TENSAS PAR., 6247 C-6
TERREBONNE PAR., 106107 I-7
Terrytown, 25430 E-14
Thibodaux, 14463 I-8
Tickfaw, 624 G-8
Tioga, 1300 E-4
Triumph, 1080 J-11
Trout, 200 D-5
UNION PAR., 22966 A-4
Urania, 688 D-5
Vacherie, 2411 H-8
VERMILION PAR., 54222 I-4
VERNON PAR., 50669 F-3
Vidalia, 4349 E-6
Ville Platte, 8297 G-5
Vinton, 3215 H-2
Vivian, 3915 A-1
Waggaman, 9435 E-11
Walker, 5317 G-8
Wardville, 1200 E-4
WASHINGTON PAR., 43947 F-9
Washington, 1064 G-5
Waterproof, 775 D-7
WEBSTER PAR., 41404 B-2
Welsh, 3313 H-4
WEST BATON ROUGE PAR., 21717 G-7
WEST CARROLL PAR., 12236 B-6
WEST FELICIANA PAR., 15235 F-6
Westlake, 4603 H-3
Westminster, 2515 C-13
W. Monroe, 13018 B-5
Westwego, 10526 I-9
White Castle, 1887 H-7
Wilson, 659 F-7
WINN PAR., 16397 D-4
Winnfield, 5484 D-4
Winnsboro, 5149 C-6
Wisner, 1097 D-6
Wyandotte, 1200 I-7
Youngsville, 4717 H-5
Zachary, 11791 G-7
Zwolle, 1748 D-2

Maine

Map pp. 92-93

Alfred, 600 I-2
Andover, 600 E-2
ANDROSCOGGIN CO., 106115 G-3
Anson, 818 E-4
AROOSTOOK CO., 73428 B-12
Ashland, 750 B-13
Auburn, 23313 G-3
Augusta, 18618 F-4
Bailey Island, 650 H-3
Bangor, 31550 E-6
Bar Hbr., 2680 F-8
Bass Hbr., 500 F-7
Bath, 9322 H-4
Belfast, 6808 F-6
Berwick, 1993 J-1
Bethel, 1200 F-2
Biddeford, 21685 I-2
Bingham, 856 D-4
Blaine, 500 C-14
Blue Hill, 800 F-7
Boothbay, 450 H-4
Boothbay Hbr., 1237 H-4
Brewer, 9075 E-6
Bridgton, 2359 G-2
Brownville, 350 C-6
Brownville Jct., 800 C-6
Brunswick, 14816 H-3
Bucksport, 2970 E-6
Calais, 3363 C-10
Camden, 3934 G-6
Canton, 400 F-3
Cape Elizabeth, 8854 I-3
Cape Porpoise, 500 I-2
Caribou, 8308 B-14
Castine, 800 F-6
Chisholm, 1399 F-3
Clinton, 1305 E-5
Corinna, 1100 D-5
Cornish, 600 H-2
CUMBERLAND CO., 270923 G-2
Cumberland Cen., 2596 H-3
Damariscotta, 1100 G-5
Danforth, 500 B-8
Dexter, 2201 D-5
Dixfield, 1137 E-2
Dover-Foxcroft, 2592 C-5
Eagle Lake, 600 B-13
E. Corinth, 400 D-6
E. Hampden, 1200 I-6
E. Machias, 300 E-10
E. Millinocket, 1701 B-7
Eastport, 1594 D-10
Ellsworth, 6784 E-7
Fairfield, 2569 E-4
Falmouth, 7610 H-3
Falmouth Foreside, 1964 H-10
Farmingdale, 1935 F-4
Farmington, 4098 E-3
Ft. Fairfield, 1600 B-14
Ft. Kent, 1978 A-13
FRANKLIN CO., 29763 D-2
Freeport, 1813 H-3
Frenchville, 475 A-13
Friendship, 600 G-5
Fryeburg, 1549 G-1
Gardiner, 6209 F-4
Gorham, 4164 H-2
Grand Isle, 375 A-14
Gray, 1100 H-3
Greenville, 1319 B-4
Greenville Jct., 450 B-4
Guilford, 945 C-5
Hallowell, 2467 F-4
Hampden, 4126 E-6
Hampden Highlands, 800 E-6
HANCOCK CO., 52792 D-7
Harrison, 600 G-2
Hartland, 872 D-5
Houlton, 5270 C-14
Howland, 1210 C-7
Island Falls, 600 A-7
Jackman, 800 B-3
Jay, 600 F-3
Jonesport, 1100 E-9
KENNEBEC CO., 119683 F-4
Kennebunk, 4804 I-2
Kennebunkport, 1376 I-2
Kezar Falls, 900 H-1
Kingfield, 850 D-3
Kittery, 4884 J-2
Kittery Pt., 1135 J-2
KNOX CO., 40406 F-5
Lewiston, 35922 G-3
Limestone, 1453 B-14
LINCOLN CO., 34729 G-4
Lincoln, 2933 C-7
Lisbon, 1400 G-3
Lisbon Falls, 4420 G-3
Littleton, 200 C-14
Livermore Falls, 1626 F-3
Lubec, 800 D-10
Machias, 1376 E-9
Madawaska, 3326 A-13
Madison, 2733 E-4
Manchester, 650 F-4
Mapleton, 500 B-14
Mars Hill, 1200 C-14
Mattawamkeag, 650 B-7
Mechanic Falls, 2450 G-2
Medway, 900 B-7
Mexico, 1946 E-2
Milbridge, 600 E-8
Milford, 2197 D-7
Millinocket, 5190 B-6
Milo, 1898 C-6
Monmouth, 600 F-3
Monson, 500 C-5
Monticello, 400 C-14
Newcastle, 600 G-4
New Harbor, 500 H-5
Newport, 1754 D-5
Norridgewock, 1557 E-4
N. Anson, 750 D-4
N. Berwick, 1580 I-2
N. Bridgton, 500 G-2
Northeast Hbr., 650 F-8
N. Vassalboro, 900 F-4
N. Windham, 4568 H-2
Norway, 2623 G-2
Oakland, 2758 E-4
Ogunquit, 974 J-2
Old Orchard Beach, 8856 I-2
Old Town, 8127 D-7
Orono, 8253 D-7
OXFORD CO., 56151 F-2
Oxford, 1300 G-2
Patten, 1000 A-7
PENOBSCOT CO., 146982 B-7
Phillips, 750 E-3
Pine Pt., 200 I-3
PISCATAQUIS CO., 17394 B-5
Pittsfield, 3217 E-5
Port Clyde, 600 G-5
Portland, 63635 H-3
Presque Isle, 9449 B-14
Princeton, 750 C-9
Randolph, 1911 F-4
Rangeley, 700 D-2
Raymond, 600 H-2
Richmond, 1864 G-4
Rockland, 7613 G-6
Rockport, 1200 G-6
Rumford, 4795 E-2
Sabattus, 1300 G-3
Saco, 17876 I-2
SAGADAHOC CO., 36455 G-4
Sanford, 10133 I-2
Sangerville, 650 C-5
Scarborough, 3867 H-3
Searsport, 1102 F-6
Sebago Lake, 600 H-2
Sherman Mills, 450 A-7
Skowhegan, 6696 E-4
SOMERSET CO., 51154 C-3
S. Berwick, 3000 J-1
S. Bristol, 500 H-4
S. Eliot, 3445 J-1
S. Paris, 2237 F-2
S. Portland, 23553 H-3
S. Sanford, 4173 I-2
Southwest Hbr., 1200 F-7
S. Windham, 400 H-2
Springvale, 3488 I-2
Stonington, 800 G-7
Stratton, 400 C-2
Strong, 700 E-3
Thomaston, 2714 G-5
Topsham, 6271 G-3
Turner, 500 F-3
Union, 600 G-5
Unity, 486 E-5
Van Buren, 2369 A-14
Veazie, 1633 D-6
Vinalhaven, 800 G-6
WALDO CO., 38248 E-5
Waldoboro, 1291 G-5
Washburn, 1200 B-13
WASHINGTON CO., 33479 D-9
Waterboro, 750 I-2
Waterville, 15758 E-4
Wells, 1200 I-2
Westbrook, 16051 H-3
W. Enfield, 600 C-7
W. Kennebunk, 809 I-2
W. Paris, 550 F-2
W. Peru, 600 F-2
W. Scarborough, 900 I-2
Wilton, 2290 E-3
Winslow, 7743 E-4
Winter Hbr., 900 F-8
Winterport, 1307 E-6
Winthrop, 2893 F-3
Wiscasset, 1203 G-4
Woodland, 1044 C-9
Woolwich, 600 G-4
Yarmouth, 3560 H-3
YORK CO., 198026 I-1
York Beach, 900 J-2
York Hbr., 3321 J-2

Maryland

Map pp. 94-97

* City keyed to pp. 224-225
‡ Independent city: Not included in any county.

Aberdeen, 14184 B-15
Abingdon, 2000 C-15
Accokeek, 7349 G-12
Adelphi, 14998 *D-7
ALLEGANY CO., 73668 B-5
Annapolis, 36178 E-14
Annapolis Jct., 800 E-13
ANNE ARUNDEL CO., 506620 E-13
Arbutus, 20116 K-3
Arden-on-the-Severn, 1971 E-14
Ardmore, 1200 *F-9
Arnold, 23422 E-14
Arundel Gardens, 1250 L-5
Arundel Vil., 2700 L-5
Ashton, 1500 D-12
Aspen Hill, 50228 E-11
BALTIMORE CO., 777184 C-13
Baltimore, 628670 ‡C-13
Baltimore Highlands, 6700 K-4
Barnaby Vil., 5300 *H-7
Barton, 460 B-3
Bay Ridge, 2200 F-14
Bayside Beach, 950 D-14
Bel Air, 9948 B-15
Belcamp, 6128 B-15
Beltsville, 15690 E-12
Belvedere Hts., 5600 E-14
Bembe Beach, 110 M-20
Benedict, 600 H-13
Berlin, 3742 I-20
Berwyn Hts., 3049 *D-8
Bethesda, 55277 E-11
Bladensburg, 7911 *F-8
Boonsboro, 2841 B-9
Bowie, 53660 E-13
Bowling Green, 1800 B-4
Braddock Hts., 4627 C-9
Bradshaw, 500 C-14
Brandywine, 1410 G-12
Brentwood, 2915 *F-8
Bridgeport, 860 M-14
Brighton, 5100 H-3
Brinklow, 300 D-12
Brooklandville, 1700 G-4
Brooklyn Park, 10938 K-5
Brookmont, 3202 *E-5
Brookwood, 2200 *I-10
Brunswick, 5122 C-9
Bryans Road, 4912 G-11
Burtonsville, 7305 E-12
Cabin John, 1734 *E-4
California, 9300 I-14
CALVERT CO., 84110 G-13
Calverton, 12610 E-12
Cambridge, 10781 H-16
Camp Sprs., 17968 F-12
Cape Isle of Wight, 750 I-20
Cape St. Claire, 8022 E-14
Capitol Hts., 4274 F-12
Carney, 28264 G-7
CAROLINE CO., 30861 F-17
CARROLL CO., 163207 B-11
Carroll Highlands, 2000 C-12
Cascade, 1000 A-10
Catonsville, 39820 J-2
Catonsville Manor, 2600 J-2
Cavetown, 1486 A-9
Cearfoss, 300 L-13
CECIL CO., 92746 B-17
Cedar Hts., 1150 *F-8
Cedar Lawn, 400 M-13
Centreville, 2353 E-16
CHARLES CO., 133049 H-11
Charlestown, 1074 B-16
Charlotte Hall, 1214 H-13
Chase, 920 C-15
Chelsea Beach, 3300 E-14
Cheltenham, 950 G-12
Chesaco Park, 450 J-7
Chesapeake Beach, 3306 G-14
Chesapeake City, 783 B-17
Chesapeake Hts., 550 I-18
Chester, 3723 E-15
Chestertown, 4678 D-16
Cheverly, 6645 *F-8
Chevy Chase, 9381 *E-5
Chevy Chase View, 894 *D-5
Chillum, 34252 *E-7
Clarksburg, 1834 D-10
Clinton, 26064 G-12
Cockeysville, 19388 B-13
Colesville, 19810 E-12
College Park, 25329 E-12
Colmar Manor, 1299 *F-8
Colonial Park, 600 N-14
Columbia, 88254 D-12
Columbia Park, 1000 *F-9
Conowingo, 150 A-15
Coral Hills, 10720 *G-8
Corriganville, 930 A-4
Cottage City, 1165 *F-8
Cresaptown, 5884 B-4
Crisfield, 2780 K-17
Crofton, 20091 E-13
Crownsville, 1670 E-14
Cumberland, 20833 A-4
Damascus, 11430 D-11
Darlington, 800 B-15
Dayton, 800 D-12
Deale, 4796 F-14
Deal Island, 578 J-17
Defense Hts., 2250 *E-9
Delmar, 1933 H-18
Denton, 2996 F-17
Derwood, 2000 *B-4
District Hts., 6168 F-12
DORCHESTER CO., 30612 H-16
Dorsey, 1350 M-2
Drum Pt., 1600 I-14
Dundalk, 62306 D-14
Easton, 12503 F-16
Eastpines, 1250 *E-8
Eckhart Mines, 1500 A-3
Edgemere, 9248 D-14
Edgewater, 1400 N-19
Edgewood, 23378 C-15
Edmonston, 1378 *E-8
Eldersburg, 27741 C-12
Elkridge, 22042 D-13
Elkton, 13586 B-17
Ellerslie, 1400 A-4
Ellicott City, 56397 D-13
Elmwood, 1650 H-6
Emmitsburg, 2421 A-10
Emory Gr., 5300 *A-4
Essex, 39078 C-14
Fairland, 21738 E-12
Fairmount Hts., 1544 *F-8
Fallston, 8427 B-14
Feagaville, 220 N-16
Federalsburg, 2603 G-17
Fell's Point J-5
Ferndale, 16056 M-4
Fishing Cr., 700 I-15
Font Hill Manor, 2500 D-12
Forest Hts., 2682 F-12
Forest Hill, 900 B-14
Forestville, 12712 F-12
Ft. Howard, 890 D-14
Ft. Washington Forest, 1200 G-12
Fountain Green, 1400 B-15
Fountain Head, 1350 A-8
FREDERICK CO., 213662 B-10
Frederick, 56128 C-10
Friendly, 10938 *J-7
Friendsville, 529 A-1
Frostburg, 8107 A-3
Fruitland, 3774 I-18
Fullerton, 2400 J-4
Fulton, 1150 D-12
Funkstown, 968 B-9
Gaithersburg, 57365 D-11
Galesville, 1000 F-14
Gambrills, 1500 E-13
Garland, 1800 M-4
GARRETT CO., 30049 B-2
Garrett Park, 940 E-11
Garrison, 7969 G-2
Germantown, 55419 D-11
Glassmanor, 8800 *H-7
Glenarden, 6559 F-12
Glen Arm, 730 C-14
Glen Burnie, 38922 D-13
Glen Hills, 1400 *C-3
Glenn Dale, 12609 E-13
Glyndon, 900 B-13
Golden Beach, 2669 H-13
Granite, 950 C-12
Grantsville, 605 A-2
Grasonville, 2193 E-15
Greenbelt, 22096 E-12
Green Haven, 17415 D-14
Greensboro, 1697 E-17
Guilford, 1000 D-12
Hagerstown, 36953 A-8
Halfway, 10065 B-8
Hampstead, 5336 B-12
Hancock, 1699 A-6
Harewood Pk., 1100 C-14
HARFORD CO., 232175 B-14
Havre de Grace, 11398 B-16
Hebbville, 2500 I-2
Hebron, 880 H-18
Herald Hbr., 2313 E-14
Hereford, 700 B-13
Hernwood Hts., 960 H-1
Highland, 1700 D-12
High Pt., 3700 M-6
High Ridge, 2500 *B-9
Hillcrest Hts., 16359 F-12
Hillsmere Shores, 2977 F-14
Hollywood, 1000 I-14
HOWARD CO., 264265 D-12
Hughesville, 1537 H-13
Hurlock, 1865 G-17
Hyattsville, 15161 E-12
Indian Head, 3440 H-11
Jarrettsville, 2756 B-14
Jefferson Hts., 800 M-14
Jessup, 7865 M-2
Kemp Mill Estates, 3050 *C-6
Kensington, 1920 E-11
KENT CO., 19680 C-16
Kent Village, 2700 *F-9
Kenwood, 2500 I-7
Kettering, 11008 F-13
Kingstown, 1644 D-16
Kingsville, 4214 C-14
Knollwood, 1250 *D-7
Lake Shore, 13065 E-14
Landover, 640 *F-9
Landover Hills, 1589 *E-9
Langley Park, 16214 *E-7
Lanham, 5200 *E-9
Lansdowne, 8700 K-4
La Plata, 7590 H-12
Largo, 8408 *F-10
Laurel, 20653 E-12
La Vale, 4613 A-4
Lawsonia, 1326 K-17
Layhill, 1600 E-12
Leonardtown, 1965 I-13
Lewisdale, 3100 *E-7
Lexington Park, 11021 I-14
Liberty Manor, 920 H-1
Libertytown, 750 B-11
Linhigh, 2100 H-7
Linthicum, 7539 L-4
Lochearn, 25269 I-2
Lonaconing, 1164 B-3
Londontown, 4000 F-14
Long Beach, 1100 H-14
Long Green, 500 B-14
Love Point, 290 E-15
Lusby, 1666 I-14
Lutherville-Timonium, 15814 C-13
Luxmanor, 2500 *C-5
Lynne Acres, 6700 H-2
Manchester, 3490 A-12
Marbury, 1244 H-11
Margate, 1500 M-5
Marion Sta., 1050 K-17
Marley, 1500 M-5
Marlton, 7798 F-13
Maryland City, 6814 E-13
Maugansville, 2295 A-8
Meadowood, 1100 *C-7
Middle River, 23958 C-14
Middletown, 2805 C-9
Midland, 454 B-3
Milford, 690 H-2
Millersville, 950 E-13
Millwood, 1100 *G-9
MONTGOMERY CO., 918881 D-11
Montgomery Vil., 38051 D-11
Montpelier, 3600 *C-10
Montrose, 1800 *C-5
Morningside, 1351 F-12
Mtn. Lake Park, 2219 C-1
Mt. Airy, 7904 C-11
Mt. Hebron, 2000 C-12
Mt. Pleasant Beach, 2100 M-6
Mt. Rainier, 8731 *E-7
Mt. Savage, 1300 A-3
New Carrollton, 13043 E-12
New Windsor, 1331 B-11
N. Beach, 1829 G-14
N. East, 2753 B-16
N. Potomac, 23044 *C-2
Oakcrest, 780 *B-9
Oakland, 1936 C-1
Oakland, 2500 *G-8
Oakland, 2078 C-12
Oaklawn, 1600 *I-8
Oakmont *D-5
Oak View, 3400 *D-7
Ocean City, 7142 I-20
Odenton, 20534 E-13
Olney, 31438 D-11
Orchard Beach, 2200 M-6
Orchard Hills, 1250 L-14
Overlea, 12148 H-6
Owings Mills, 20193 G-2
Oxford, 748 G-15
Oxon Hill, 35355 F-12
Palmer Park, 7019 *F-9
Paradise Beach, 350 N-8
Paramount, 1450 L-14
Parkville, 31118 C-14
Parole, 14031 M-19
Parsonsburg, 680 I-19
Pasadena, 12093 E-14
Perry Hall, 28705 C-14
Perryman, 2461 B-15
Perryville, 3705 B-16
Pikesville, 29123 C-13
Pinefield, 8800 G-12
Pinehurst on the Bay, 570 E-14
Piney Glen Farms, 470 *C-3
Piney Pt., 1500 J-14
Pleasant Hills, 2851 B-14
Pocomoke City, 4147 K-18
Poolesville, 5423 D-10
Port Deposit, 672 B-16
Potomac, 44822 E-11
Potomac Park, 1600 B-4
Powhattan Mill, 2300 I-3
Prince Frederick, 1432 H-14
PRINCE GEORGE'S CO., 838716 G-13
Princess Anne, 2388 J-18
Providence, 1400 F-6
Pumphrey, 5317 L-4
QUEEN ANNE'S CO., 44108 E-16
Randallstown, 30870 C-13
Randolph Hills, 6150 *C-5
Reisterstown, 22438 C-12
Ridgely, 1346 E-17
Rippling Ridge, 2100 L-4
Rising Sun, 1766 A-16
Riva, 3966 E-14
Riverdale, 6564 *E-8
Riviera Beach, 12695 D-14
Rockdale, 6700 H-2
Rock Hall, 2321 D-15
Rock Hill Beach, 1350 M-7
Rockville, 55213 E-11
Rosedale, 19199 C-14
Rossville, 11515 I-7
St. Charles, 33379 H-12
ST. MARY'S CO., 92754 I-13
St. Marys City, 3300 J-14
St. Michaels, 1139 F-15
Salisbury, 25247 I-18
Sandy Spr., 1200 D-12
Sandyville, 650 B-12
Savage, 8000 D-13
Seabrook, 8000 *E-9
Seat Pleasant, 5044 F-12
Selby-on-the-Bay, 3674 F-14
Severn, 35076 D-13
Severna Park, 28507 E-14
Shady Side, 5559 F-14
Sharpsburg, 663 C-8
Sharptown, 622 H-18
Silver Hill, 1850 *H-8
Silver Spr., 76540 E-12
Smithsburg, 2594 A-9
Snow Hill, 2386 J-19
Solomons, 1536 I-14
SOMERSET CO., 25447 J-18
Somerset, 1152 *E-5
S. Gate, 28672 D-13
Spencerville, 2850 E-12
Springbrook, 1100 *C-7
Stevenson, 750 G-3
Stevensville, 5880 E-15
Suitland, 26750 F-12
Sunnybrook, 980 B-14
Sykesville, 4373 C-12
Takoma Park, 17717 *E-7
TALBOT CO., 34670 F-16
Taneytown, 5335 A-11
Temple Hills, 7792 *H-8
The Crest of Wickford, 900 *C-5
Thurmont, 5890 B-10
Tilghman, 1000 G-15
Towson, 51793 C-13
Union Bridge, 1018 B-11
University Park, 2384 *E-8
Upper Marlboro, 674 F-13
Van Lear Manor, 1050 N-13
Venice on the Bay, 300 M-7
Villa Nova, 940 H-2
Waldorf, 22312 G-12
Walkersville, 5517 B-10
WASHINGTON CO., 136796 A-7
W. Edmondale, 3450 J-3
Westernport, 2037 B-3
W. Friendship, 1200 C-12
Westminster, 17403 B-12
Westover, 800 J-18
Wheaton, 134800 E-11
White Marsh, 8485 C-14
White Oak, 20973 *C-7
White Plains, 3560 H-12
WICOMICO CO., 87375 I-18
Williamsport, 1914 B-8
Winchester on the Severn, 700 L-19
Woodlawn, 36079 C-13
Woodlawn Hts., 2400 L-4
Woodmoor, 8400 H-2
Woodstock, 850 C-12
WORCESTER CO., 49604 I-19
Worthington, 2350 K-1

Massachusetts

Map pp. 98-101

Abington, 14605 G-15
Acton, 2300 D-12
Acushnet, 3171 J-15
Adams, 5784 C-2
Agawam, 28528 G-5
Amesbury, 12327 A-15
Amherst, 17824 E-6
Andover, 7900 C-14
Arlington, 42389 E-14
Ashburnham, 1500 C-9
Ashland, 12066 F-12
Assinippi, 1400 G-15
Assonet, 1300 I-14
Athol, 8370 C-8
Attleboro, 43502 H-13
Auburn, 15005 F-10
Avon, 4558 G-14
Ayer, 2960 D-11
Baldwinville, 1852 C-8
Ballardvale, 1400 C-14
BARNSTABLE CO., 229545 J-17
Barnstable, 48907 J-19
Barre, 1150 E-8
Bedford, 12996 D-13
Belchertown, 2626 F-7
Bellingham, 4497 G-12
Belmont, 24194 E-13
BERKSHIRE CO., 133310 E-2
Beverly, 40255 D-15
Billerica, 6850 C-13
Blackstone, 5000 H-12
Bondsville, 1876 F-7
Boston, 581616 E-14
Bourne, 1443 J-17
Boxford, 2340 C-15
Braintree, 33698 F-14
Brant Rock, 1800 G-17
Brewster, 2212 J-20
Bridgewater, 6664 H-15
BRISTOL CO., 547008 I-13
Brockton, 95090 G-14
Brookfield, 1200 F-8
Brookline, 57107 E-14
Bryantville, 1800 G-15
Burlington, 22876 D-13
Buzzards Bay, 3549 J-17
Byfield, 1300 B-15
Cambridge, 101587 E-14
Canton, 18530 G-14
Carver, 1500 I-16
Chaffin, 4000 E-10
Charlton City, 1400 G-9
Chatham, 1667 J-20
Chelmsford, 34200 C-13
Chelsea, 34106 E-14
Cherry Valley, 1200 F-10
Cheshire, 1200 C-2
Chicopee, 54992 G-5
Clinton, 7884 E-11
Cochituate, 6768 E-12
Cohasset, 6000 F-16
Concord, 4700 D-13
Cordaville, 2515 F-12
Dalton, 7155 D-2
Danvers, 25212 C-15
Dedham, 23464 F-14
Dennis, 2798 J-19
Dennis Port, 3612 J-20
Dorothy Pond, 1700 F-10
Dover, 2216 F-13
Dracut, 25594 C-13
Dudley, 3700 G-9
DUKES CO., 15601 L-17
Duxbury, 1426 G-16
E. Billerica, 3850 C-13
E. Bridgewater, 3400 H-15
E. Brookfield, 1410 F-9
E. Dennis, 3299 J-19
E. Douglas, 2319 G-10
E. Falmouth, 6615 K-17
Eastham, 1250 I-20
Easthampton, 16340 F-5
E. Longmeadow, 13367 G-6
E. Millbury, 1000 F-10
E. Orleans, 1200 I-20
E. Pepperell, 2034 C-11
E. Templeton, 1350 C-9
E. Walpole, 3800 G-13
E. Wareham, 1500 J-16
Edgartown, 1500 L-17
Egypt, 900 F-16
ESSEX CO., 737848 C-14
Essex, 1426 C-16
Everett, 37540 E-14
Fairhaven, 16132 K-15
Fall River, 92760 J-14
Falmouth, 4115 K-17
Fayville, 1000 F-12
Feeding Hills G-5
Fiskdale, 2156 G-8
Fitchburg, 39948 C-10
Foxboro, 5509 G-13
Framingham, 66910 F-12
FRANKLIN CO., 72204 D-5
Franklin, 30175 G-12
Gardner, 21049 C-9
Georgetown, 2200 B-15
Gilbertville, 1050 E-8
Gloucester, 30730 C-16
Grafton, 1650 F-11
Granby, 1344 F-6
Graniteville, 1200 C-12
Great Barrington, 2459 F-1
Greenfield, 13716 C-5
Green Hbr., 1500 G-17
Groton, 1113 C-11
Groveland, 3800 B-14
Hamilton, 1000 C-15
HAMPDEN CO., 461190 G-7
HAMPSHIRE CO., 155101 E-4
Hanover, 2500 G-16
Hanover Cen., 1000 G-15
Hanson, 2044 G-15
Harvard, 1200 D-11
Harwich, 1832 J-20
Harwich Port, 1809 J-20
Hatfield, 1298 E-5
Haverhill, 60326 B-14
Hingham, 5352 F-15
Hinsdale, 1050 D-2
Holbrook, 10785 G-15
Holden, 4200 E-10
Holliston, 12926 F-12
Holyoke, 40015 F-5
Hopedale, 4158 G-11
Hopkinton, 2628 F-12
Housatonic, 1335 F-1
Hudson, 14388 E-11
Hull, 11050 E-15
Huntington, 1200 F-4
Hyannis J-19
Hyannis Port K-19
Ipswich, 4161 C-15
Islington, 4800 F-13
Kingston, 5380 H-16
Lakeville, 2233 I-15
Lanesboro, 1000 D-2
Lawrence, 72492 B-14
Lee, 2021 E-2
Leicester, 3200 F-9
Lenox, 1667 E-1
Leominster, 42000 D-10
Lexington, 30355 D-13
Lincoln, 2850 E-13
Littleton, 2816 D-12
Longmeadow, 15633 G-5
Lowell, 104351 C-13
Ludlow, 18820 G-6
Lunenburg, 1695 C-10
Lynn, 89571 D-15
Lynnfield, 11542 D-14
Malden, 55816 D-14
Manchaug, 800 G-10
Manchester, 5286 C-16
Manomet, 1600 H-17
Mansfield, 7320 H-13
Marblehead, 20377 D-15
Marion, 1202 J-16
Marlborough, 37980 E-11
Marshfield, 4246 G-16
Marshfield Hills, 2369 G-16
Mattapoisett, 2966 J-16
Maynard, 10433 D-12
Medfield, 6670 F-13
Medford, 54734 E-14
Medway, 4000 G-12
Melrose, 26784 D-14
Mendon, 1000 G-11
Merrimac, 2200 A-14
Methuen, 44850 B-13
Middleboro, 6913 I-15
MIDDLESEX CO., 1471724 D-12
Middleton, 4921 C-14
Mile Oak Center, 2050 G-6
Milford, 24230 G-12
Millbury, 5000 F-10
Millers Falls, 1072 C-6
Millis, 3800 F-12
Millville, 2236 H-11
Milton, 26062 F-14
Monson, 2103 G-7
Monument Beach, 2438 J-17
Morningdale, 1150 E-10
Nabnasset, 3600 C-12
Nahant, 3632 E-15
NANTUCKET CO., 10724 M-20
Nantucket, 3830 M-20
Natick, 32200 F-12
Needham, 28911 F-13
New Bedford, 94112 K-15
Newburyport, 17499 B-15
Newton, 84323 E-13
NORFOLK CO., 654331 F-13
N. Adams, 14334 B-2
N. Amherst, 6019 E-6
Northampton, 29287 E-5
N. Andover, 22792 B-14
N. Attleboro, 16796 H-13
N. Billerica, 5500 C-13
Northborough, 6257 E-11
Northbridge, 3600 G-11
N. Brookfield, 2527 F-8
N. Dighton, 1250 I-14
N. Eastham, 1915 I-20
N. Easton, 4500 G-14
N. Falmouth, 3355 J-17
Northfield, 1141 B-6
N. Grafton, 3150 F-10
N. Oxford, 1200 G-10
N. Pembroke, 2913 G-16
N. Reading, 12002 C-14
N. Scituate, 5065 F-16
N. Sudbury, 2600 E-12
N. Swansea, 900 J-13
N. Tewksbury, 1200 C-13
N. Uxbridge, 1800 G-11
Norton, 2618 H-13
Norton Gr., 2100 H-13
Norwell, 1200 G-16
Norwood, 28587 F-13
Nutting Lake, 3200 D-13
Oak Bluffs, 2000 L-17
Ocean Bluff, 2500 G-17
Ocean Gr., 3012 J-13
Onset, 1292 J-17
Orange, 3945 C-7
Orleans, 1716 I-20
Oxford, 5899 G-10
Palmer, 3900 G-7
Paxton, 1600 E-9
Peabody, 49759 D-15
Pembroke, 2100 G-16
Pepperell, 2517 C-11
Pigeon Cove, 1800 C-17
Pinehurst, 6941 D-13
Pittsfield, 44779 D-2
Plainville, 6871 H-13
PLYMOUTH CO., 487521 H-15
Plymouth, 7658 H-16
Pocasset, 2671 J-17
Provincetown, 3561 G-19
Quincy, 89059 F-14
Randolph, 30963 F-14
Raynham, 2100 H-14
Raynham Cen., 3633 H-14
Reading, 23708 D-14
Revere, 47002 E-14
River Pines, 3600 C-13
Rochdale, 1150 F-9
Rockland, 16123 G-15
Rockport, 5606 C-17
Rowley, 1434 B-15
Rutland, 2205 E-9
Sagamore, 3544 J-17
Salem, 42067 D-15
Salisbury, 4484 A-15
Sand Hill, 1800 F-16
Sandwich, 3058 J-18
Saugus, 26078 D-14
Scituate, 5069 F-16
Seekonk, 13046 I-13
Sharon, 5941 G-14
Shawsheen Vil., 2600 C-14
Sheffield, 1150 G-1
Shelburne Falls, 1951 C-5
Sherborn, 1400 F-12
Shirley, 1427 D-11
Shore Acres, 1200 F-16
Shrewsbury, 31600 F-10
Silver Lake, 2900 C-13
Smith Mills, 4432 K-15
Somerset, 18234 J-14
Somerville, 76296 E-14
S. Acton, 3200 D-12
S. Amherst, 5039 E-6
S. Ashburnham, 1013 C-9
Southborough, 1500 E-12
Southbridge, 12878 G-9
S. Deerfield, 1868 D-5
S. Dennis, 3679 J-19
S. Duxbury, 3062 H-16
S. Easton, 1500 G-14
S. Grafton, 2750 F-11
S. Hadley, 5500 F-6
S. Hadley Falls, 5100 F-5
S. Hamilton, 2800 C-15
S. Hanover, 1000 G-15
S. Hingham, 4000 F-15
S. Lancaster, 1742 D-11
S. Swansea, 1000 J-13
S. Walpole, 1300 G-13
S. Wellfleet, 600 H-20
Southwick, 1250 G-4
S. Yarmouth, 11603 J-19
Spencer, 6032 F-9
Springfield, 152157 G-5
Sterling, 1350 D-10
Stockbridge, 1100 F-1
Stoneham, 22219 D-14
Stoughton G-14

266 | MASSACHUSETTS – MISSISSIPPI

*, †, ‡, See explanation under state title in this index.
County names are listed in capital letters and in boldface type.

Stow, 1250 ... D-12
Sturbridge, 2047 ... G-8
Sudbury, 1950 ... E-12
Sudbury Cen., 2600 ... E-12
SUFFOLK CO., 680705 ... F-14
Swampscott, 14412 ... D-15
Taunton, 56781 ... I-14
Teaticket, 1907 ... K-17
Tewksbury, 11000 ... C-13
Thorndike, 1150 ... F-7
Three Rivers, 2939 ... F-7
Topsfield, 2826 ... C-15
Touisset, 1500 ... J-13
Townsend, 1043 ... C-10
Turners Falls, 4441 ... C-6
Upton, 1200 ... F-11
Uxbridge, 3500 ... G-11
Vineyard Haven, 2048 ... L-17
Wakefield, 24804 ... D-14
Walpole, 5867 ... G-13
Waltham, 58894 ... E-13
Wamesit, 2700 ... C-13
Ware, 6174 ... F-7
Wareham, 2874 ... J-16
Warren, 1452 ... F-8
Watertown, 32915 ... E-13
Wayland, 2500 ... E-12
Webster, 11600 ... G-9
Wellesley, 26613 ... F-13
Wellfleet, 1200 ... H-20
Wenham, 4212 ... C-15
W. Acton, 5200 ... D-12
W. Andover, 2000 ... C-14
Westborough, 3983 ... F-11
W. Boylston, 3300 ... E-10
W. Bridgewater, 2100 ... H-15
W. Brookfield, 1610 ... F-8
W. Chatham, 1446 ... J-20
W. Concord, 5632 ... D-12
W. Dennis, 2570 ... J-19
W. Falmouth, 1867 ... K-17
Westfield, 40560 ... G-4
Westford, 1400 ... C-12
W. Foxboro, 1100 ... G-13
W. Groton, 900 ... C-11
W. Hanover, 1700 ... G-15
W. Harwich, 1500 ... J-20
W. Medway, 2000 ... G-12
Westminster, 1100 ... D-9
W. Newbury, 1100 ... B-15
Weston, 10200 ... E-13
W. Springfield, 27953 ... G-5
W. Upton, 1100 ... F-11
W. Wareham, 1908 ... I-16
W. Warren, 1300 ... F-7
Westwood, 6500 ... F-13
W. Yarmouth, 6460 ... J-19
Weymouth, 53988 ... F-15
Whalom, 1400 ... C-10
White Island Shores, 2133 ... I-17
Whitinsville, 6340 ... G-11
Whitman, 13240 ... G-15
Wilbraham, 3544 ... G-6
Williamsburg, 1200 ... E-5
Williamstown, 4754 ... B-2
Wilmington, 21363 ... D-14
Winchendon, 4246 ... C-9
Winchester, 20810 ... D-14
Winthrop, 18303 ... E-15
Woburn, 37809 ... D-14
Woods Hole, 925 ... K-17
WORCESTER CO., 776610 ... D-8
Worcester, 175706 ... F-10
Wrentham, 2250 ... G-13
Yarmouth Port, 5395 ... J-19

Michigan

Map pp. 102-107

* City keyed to pp. 106-107

Ada, 2300 ... P-6
Addison, 619 ... S-9
Adrian, 22054 ... T-10
Albion, 9130 ... R-8
ALCONA CO., 11572 ... J-11
ALGER CO., 9767 ... E-3
Algonac, 4602 ... Q-14
ALLEGAN CO., 110331 ... Q-5
Allegan, 4909 ... R-5
Allendale, 11555 ... P-5
Allen Park, 28762 ... R-12
Alma, 9330 ... O-8
Almont, 2841 ... P-13
ALPENA CO., 30781 ... I-11
Alpena, 10951 ... I-11
Amasa, 400 ... C-13
Ann Arbor, 114498 ... R-11
ANTRIM CO., 24094 ... I-7
ARENAC CO., 17309 ... L-10
Argentine, 2285 ... Q-11
Armada, 1636 ... P-13
Athens, 1074 ... S-7
Atlanta, 757 ... I-10
Auburn, 1989 ... N-10
Auburn Hills, 20471 ... *F-5
Au Gres, 1001 ... L-11
Augusta, 873 ... R-7
Au Sable, 1533 ... K-12
Bad Axe, 3332 ... M-13
Baldwin, 1108 ... M-5
Bancroft, 604 ... P-10
Bangor, 1907 ... R-5
BARAGA CO., 8782 ... B-13
Baraga, 1268 ... B-13
Baroda, 874 ... S-4
Barron Lake, 1570 ... T-5
BARRY CO., 58774 ... Q-7
Bath, 730 ... Q-9
Battle Creek, 53827 ... R-7
BAY CO., 109452 ... M-10
Bay City, 35428 ... N-10
Beadle Lake, 1550 ... R-7
Beaverton, 1127 ... M-9
Beecher, 12793 ... *A-9
Beechwood, 2963 ... Q-5
Beechwood, 30 ... C-12
Belding, 5852 ... P-7
Bellaire, 1157 ... I-7
Belleville, 3944 ... S-11
Bellevue, 1357 ... R-8
Belmont, 730 ... P-6
Benton Hbr., 11010 ... S-4
Benton Heights, 5458 ... S-4
BENZIE CO., 17078 ... J-5
Bergland, 670 ... B-11
Berkley, 15239 ... *H-5
BERRIEN CO., 162766 ... S-4
Berrien Sprs., 1810 ... T-4
Bertrand, 5500 ... T-4
Bessemer, 2029 ... B-10
Beverly Hills, 10210 ... *H-5
Big Rapids, 10797 ... M-6
Birch Run, 1754 ... O-11
Birmingham, 19161 ... Q-12
Blissfield, 3258 ... T-11
Bloomfield, 42185 ... *G-4
Bloomfield Hills, 3880 ... *G-5
Boyne City, 3367 ... H-7
BRANCH CO., 46414 ... T-7
Breckenridge, 1330 ... N-9
Bridgeport, 7849 ... O-10
Bridgman, 2433 ... T-4
Brighton, 7029 ... Q-11
Britton, 685 ... S-11
Bronson, 2367 ... T-7
Brooklyn, 1220 ... S-10
Brown City, 1325 ... O-13
Brownlee Park, 2588 ... R-7
Brownstown, 26530 ... *M-4
Buchanan, 4579 ... T-4
Bullock Creek, 750 ... N-9
Burr Oak, 777 ... T-7
Burton, 30890 ... P-11
Burton, 30 ... P-9
Byron, 580 ... P-10
Byron Cen., 3777 ... Q-6
Cadillac, 10131 ... L-7
Caledonia, 1156 ... Q-6
CALHOUN CO., 138854 ... S-8
Calumet, 831 ... A-13
Canton, 76366 ... *J-2
Capac, 2193 ... P-13
Carleton, 2711 ... S-12
Caro, 4188 ... N-12
Carrollton, 6602 ... N-10
Carson City, 1190 ... O-8
Carsonville, 494 ... N-13
Cascade, 2300 ... P-6
Caseville, 895 ... M-12
Caspian, 960 ... C-12
CASS CO., 51385 ... S-5
Cass City, 2604 ... N-12
Cassopolis, 1831 ... T-5
Cedar Sprs., 3184 ... O-6
Center Line, 8370 ... *H-7
Central Lake, 998 ... I-7
Centreville, 1570 ... T-6
CHARLEVOIX CO., 26712 ... H-7
Charlevoix, 2851 ... H-7
Charlotte, 8795 ... Q-8
Chassell, 710 ... A-13
CHEBOYGAN CO., 27405 ... H-9
Cheboygan, 5290 ... G-9
Chelsea, 4586 ... R-10
Chesaning, 2482 ... O-10
Chesterfield, 41503 ... *E-10
CHIPPEWA CO., 38822 ... E-9
CLARE CO., 31589 ... M-8
Clare, 3219 ... M-8
Clarkston, 949 ... Q-12
Clawson, 12447 ... *H-6
Climax, 767 ... S-7
CLINTON CO., 67609 ... P-9
Clinton, 95648 ... *G-8
Clinton, 2373 ... S-10
Clio, 2638 ... O-11
Cloverville, 1950 ... O-5
Coldwater, 10731 ... T-8
Coleman, 1284 ... M-9
Coloma, 1554 ... S-4
Colon, 1196 ... S-7
Columbiaville, 802 ... O-12
Commerce, 5000 ... Q-11
Comstock, 5600 ... P-3
Comstock Park, 10674 ... P-6
Concord, 1114 ... S-8
Constantine, 2135 ... T-6
Coopersville, 4090 ... P-5
Corunna, 3389 ... P-10
Covert, 640 ... R-4
CRAWFORD CO., 14808 ... J-8
Croswell, 2439 ... O-14
Crystal Falls, 1726 ... C-13
Cutlerville, 15114 ... P-6
Davison, 5443 ... P-11
Dearborn, 96670 ... R-12
Dearborn Hts., 57373 ... *J-4
Decatur, 1882 ... S-5
Deckerville, 932 ... N-13
Deerfield, 979 ... T-11
DELTA CO., 38317 ... F-3
Delton, 500 ... R-7
Detroit, 911402 ... R-13
De Witt, 4499 ... P-9
Dexter, 2913 ... R-10
DICKINSON CO., 27186 ... C-14
Dimondale, 1340 ... Q-8
Dollar Bay, 1050 ... A-13
Dorr, 1600 ... Q-6
Douglas, 1197 ... Q-5
Dowagiac, 5857 ... S-5
Drayton Plains ... Q-12
Dryden, 814 ... P-12
Dundee, 3583 ... S-11
Durand, 3888 ... P-10
Eagle Lake, 1160 ... T-5
E. Grand Rapids, 10563 ... *B-3
E. Jordan, 2418 ... H-7
Eastlake, 579 ... L-4
E. Lansing, 47245 ... Q-9
Eastpointe, 33394 ... R-13
E. Tawas, 2864 ... K-11
EATON CO., 106197 ... R-8
Eaton Rapids, 5320 ... R-8
Ecorse, 11046 ... *L-6
Edmore, 1251 ... N-7
Edwardsburg, 1133 ... T-5
Elk Rapids, 1728 ... I-6
Elkton, 829 ... M-12
Elsie, 1016 ... P-9
EMMET CO., 32741 ... G-7
Erie, 690 ... T-11
Escanaba, 12778 ... F-2
Essexville, 3653 ... N-10
Evart, 1720 ... M-7
Fairgrove, 619 ... N-11
Farmington, 10168 ... *H-3
Farmington Hills, 80874 ... R-12
Farwell, 860 ... M-8
Fennville, 1471 ... Q-5
Ferndale, 21693 ... R-12
Ferrysburg, 3024 ... P-4
Flat Rock, 9056 ... S-12
Flint, 120292 ... P-11
Flushing, 8197 ... P-10
Forest Hills, 20942 ... *B-3
Fowler, 1092 ... P-8
Fowlerville, 3119 ... Q-10
Frankenmuth, 4804 ... O-11
Frankfort, 1502 ... J-4
Franklin, 2945 ... *H-4
Fraser, 15120 ... *G-8
Freeland, 5147 ... N-10
Fremont, 4252 ... N-5
Fruitport, 1094 ... O-5
Galesburg, 1982 ... R-7
Galien, 579 ... T-4
Garden City, 29547 ... R-12
Gaylord, 3741 ... I-8
GENESEE CO., 442250 ... P-11
Genesee, 1500 ... O-11
Gibraltar, 4704 ... S-12
Gladstone, 5290 ... F-2
GLADWIN CO., 26939 ... L-9
Gladwin, 3036 ... L-9
Gobles, 813 ... R-5
GOGEBIC CO., 17329 ... C-11
Goodrich, 1440 ... P-11
Grand Blanc, 8018 ... P-11
Grand Haven, 10842 ... P-4
Grand Ledge, 7816 ... Q-8
Grand Rapids, 195601 ... P-6
GRAND TRAVERSE CO., 82011 ... J-6
Grandville, 16622 ... P-6
Grant, 885 ... O-5
Grass Lake, 1106 ... R-10
GRATIOT CO., 42501 ... O-8
Grayling, 1960 ... J-8
Greenville, 8193 ... O-7
Grosse Ile, 10894 ... *M-6
Grosse Pointe, 5563 ... *J-8
Grosse Pointe Farms, 9557 ... *I-9
Grosse Pointe Park, 12189 ... *J-8
Grosse Pointe Shores, 2763 ... *I-9
Grosse Pointe Woods, 16713 ... R-13
Gwinn, 1965 ... E-1
Hagar Shores, 1509 ... S-4
Hamilton, 1170 ... Q-5
Hamtramck, 22437 ... R-13
Hancock, 4313 ... A-13
Harbert, 600 ... T-3
Harbor Beach, 1761 ... M-13
Harbor Sprs., 1573 ... G-7
Harper Woods, 13952 ... *I-8
Harrison, 2098 ... L-8
Hart, 1986 ... M-4
Hartford, 2472 ... S-5
Harvey, 1321 ... D-2
Haslett, 11292 ... Q-9
Hastings, 7122 ... Q-7
Hazel Park, 18549 ... *I-7
Hemlock, 1585 ... N-9
Hesperia, 980 ... N-5
Highland, 800 ... Q-11
Highland Park, 16044 ... R-12
HILLSDALE CO., 47230 ... T-8
Hillsdale, 8070 ... T-9
Holland, 34666 ... Q-5
Holly, 6233 ... P-11
Holt, 11315 ... Q-9
Homer, 1823 ... S-8
HOUGHTON CO., 36249 ... A-12
Houghton, 7134 ... A-13
Houghton Lake, 3749 ... K-8
Howard City, 1611 ... O-6
Howell, 9603 ... Q-10
Hubbell, 1105 ... A-13
Hudson, 2428 ... T-9
Hudsonville, 7175 ... P-5
Huntington Woods, 6015 ... *H-6
HURON CO., 35216 ... M-13
Ida, 1020 ... T-11
Imlay City, 3852 ... P-12
Indian Lake, 640 ... S-5
INGHAM CO., 282030 ... Q-9
Inkster, 29478 ... *K-4
IONIA CO., 63573 ... P-7
Ionia, 12124 ... P-7
IOSCO CO., 26888 ... K-11
IRON CO., 12787 ... C-12
Iron Mtn., 7973 ... D-13
Iron River, 3265 ... C-12
Ironwood, 5953 ... B-10
ISABELLA CO., 64663 ... N-8
Ishpeming, 6535 ... D-1
Ithaca, 3099 ... O-9
JACKSON CO., 162321 ... R-9
Jackson, 35152 ... R-9
Jenison, 17211 ... P-6
Jonesville, 2332 ... S-8
KALAMAZOO CO., 242110 ... S-6
Kalamazoo, 75312 ... R-6
KALKASKA CO., 17177 ... J-7
Kalkaska, 2250 ... J-7
Keego Hbr., 2736 ... *F-4
KENT CO., 590417 ... O-6
Kent City, 1057 ... O-6
Kentwood, 46487 ... P-6
KEWEENAW CO., 2227 ... A-13
Kingsford, 5435 ... D-13
Kingsley, 1522 ... J-6
Laingsburg, 1208 ... P-9
LAKE CO., 11795 ... M-5
Lake City, 937 ... K-7
Lake Fenton, 4876 ... P-11
Lake Linden, 1074 ... A-13
Lake Odessa, 2278 ... Q-7
Lake Orion, 2730 ... P-12
Lakeside, 1100 ... T-3
Lakeview, 1116 ... N-7
Lakewood Club, 1189 ... O-4
Lambertville, 9299 ... T-11
L'Anse, 2048 ... B-13
Lansing, 118379 ... Q-9
LAPEER CO., 91314 ... O-12
Lapeer, 9343 ... P-12
Lathrup Vil., 4220 ... *H-5
Laurium, 2095 ... A-13
Lawrence, 1046 ... S-5
Lawton, 1854 ... S-5
LEELANAU CO., 21860 ... I-5
LENAWEE CO., 100786 ... T-10
Leslie, 2009 ... R-9
Level Park, 3490 ... R-7
Lewiston, 990 ... I-9
Lexington, 1107 ... O-14
Lincoln Park, 39131 ... R-12
Linden, 3201 ... P-11
Litchfield, 1447 ... S-8
Little Lake, 800 ... D-2
LIVINGSTON CO., 172881 ... Q-10
Livonia, 99487 ... R-12
Lowell, 4121 ... P-7
LUCE CO., 6919 ... D-6
Ludington, 8303 ... M-4
Luna Pier, 1442 ... T-12
Lyons, 734 ... P-8
MACKINAC CO., 11470 ... E-7
Mackinaw City, 854 ... F-8
MACOMB CO., 813948 ... Q-13
Madison Hts., 30463 ... Q-12
Mancelona, 1401 ... I-7
Manchester, 2232 ... S-10
MANISTEE CO., 25317 ... K-5
Manistee, 6711 ... L-4
Manistique, 3481 ... F-4
Manitou Beach, 1400 ... S-9
Manton, 1224 ... K-6
Maple Rapids, 620 ... O-8
Marcellus, 1116 ... S-6
Marenisco, 700 ... C-11
Marine City, 4500 ... Q-14
Marion, 839 ... L-7
Marlette, 2086 ... O-12
MARQUETTE CO., 64616 ... D-1
Marquette, 20704 ... D-2
Marshall, 7295 ... R-8
Marysville, 9833 ... P-14
MASON CO., 28685 ... L-4
Mason, 7831 ... Q-9
Mattawan, 2755 ... S-6
Mayville, 1028 ... O-12
MECOSTA CO., 41728 ... N-7
Melvindale, 10601 ... *K-5
Memphis, 1127 ... P-13
Mendon, 925 ... S-6
MENOMINEE CO., 25084 ... G-1
Menominee, 8851 ... I-1
Merrill, 773 ... N-9
Michigan Cen., 4641 ... S-9
Middleville, 2802 ... Q-6
MIDLAND CO., 84492 ... N-9
Midland, 42175 ... N-9
Milan, 4977 ... S-11
Milford, 6319 ... Q-11
Millett, 770 ... Q-9
Millington, 1115 ... O-11
Mio, 2016 ... J-10
MISSAUKEE CO., 15189 ... K-7
Moline, 750 ... Q-6
MONROE CO., 150673 ... S-11
Monroe, 21630 ... T-12
Montague, 2347 ... N-4
MONTCALM CO., 62926 ... O-7
MONTMORENCY CO., 10492 ... I-9
Montrose, 1559 ... O-10
Morenci, 2352 ... T-10
Morrice, 887 ... P-10
Mt. Clemens, 17111 ... Q-13
Mt. Morris, 3351 ... O-11
Mt. Pleasant, 25687 ... N-8
Muir, 643 ... P-8
Munising, 2470 ... D-3
MUSKEGON CO., 173090 ... O-5
Muskegon, 39825 ... O-4
Muskegon Heights, 11817 ... O-4
Napoleon, 1254 ... S-10
Nashville, 1692 ... Q-7
Negaunee, 4483 ... D-1
NEWAYGO CO., 49271 ... N-5
Newaygo, 1688 ... N-6
New Baltimore, 9749 ... Q-13
Newberry, 1679 ... D-6
New Boston, 1300 ... *M-3
New Buffalo, 2201 ... T-3
New Haven, 4231 ... Q-13
New Hudson, 110 ... Q-11
New Lothrop, 597 ... O-10
Newport, 1070 ... S-12
Niles, 11906 ... T-4
N. Branch, 1008 ... O-12
N. Muskegon, 4023 ... O-4
Northport, 652 ... I-6
Northville, 6405 ... R-11
Norton Shores, 23193 ... O-4
Norway, 2896 ... D-14
Novi, 50786 ... R-11
Oak Hill, 920 ... L-4
OAKLAND CO., 1207869 ... P-12
Oak Park, 29146 ... R-12
OCEANA CO., 28074 ... N-4
OGEMAW CO., 21792 ... K-10
Okemos, 22805 ... Q-9
Olivet, 1714 ... R-8
Onaway, 974 ... H-9
ONTONAGON CO., 7571 ... B-11
Ontonagon, 1696 ... B-11
Orchard Lake, 2268 ... Q-12
Ortonville, 1526 ... P-11
OSCEOLA CO., 23509 ... M-7
OSCODA CO., 9461 ... J-9
Oscoda, 992 ... K-12
Oshtemo, 2000 ... R-6
Otisville, 867 ... O-11
OTSEGO CO., 24268 ... I-9
Otsego, 3944 ... R-6
OTTAWA CO., 249391 ... P-5
Ovid, 1455 ... P-9
Owosso, 15471 ... P-10
Oxford, 3568 ... P-12
Painesdale, 450 ... A-12
Palmer, 449 ... D-1
Parchment, 1881 ... O-2
Parkdale, 550 ... K-4
Parma, 890 ... R-9
Paw Paw, 3380 ... S-5
Paw Paw Lake, 3944 ... S-4
Pearl Beach, 3224 ... Q-14
Peck, 590 ... O-13
Pellston, 791 ... G-8
Pentwater, 966 ... M-4
Perry, 2044 ... P-10
Petersburg, 1146 ... T-11
Petoskey, 6154 ... H-7
Pigeon, 1160 ... M-12
Pinckney, 2409 ... R-10
Pinconning, 1354 ... M-10
Plainwell, 3986 ... R-6
Pleasant Ridge, 2528 ... *H-6
Plymouth, 8870 ... R-12
Pontiac, 67152 ... Q-12
Portage, 45679 ... S-6
Port Austin, 708 ... L-12
Port Huron, 31747 ... P-14
Portland, 3786 ... P-8
Port Sanilac, 644 ... N-14
Potterville, 2221 ... Q-8
PRESQUE ISLE CO., 14286 ... H-10
Quincy, 1655 ... S-8
Quinnesec, 1187 ... D-13
Ramsay, 1080 ... B-10
Rapid River, 800 ... F-3
Ravenna, 1231 ... O-5
Reading, 1118 ... T-8
Redford, 51622 ... R-12
Reed City, 2409 ... M-6
Reese, 1372 ... N-11
Republic, 614 ... C-13
Richmond, 5371 ... P-13
River Rouge, 9495 ... *K-6
Riverview, 13026 ... S-12
Rochester, 11021 ... Q-12
Rochester Hills, 68754 ... Q-12
Rockford, 4832 ... O-6
Rockwood, 3493 ... S-12
Rogers City, 3236 ... G-10
Romeo, 3791 ... P-13
Romulus, 23709 ... R-12
Roosevelt Park, 3841 ... O-4
ROSCOMMON CO., 26230 ... L-8
Roscommon, 1133 ... K-8
Rose City, 719 ... K-10
Roseville, 47925 ... Q-13
Royal Oak, 58650 ... Q-12
Rudyard, 1100 ... E-8
SAGINAW CO., 209327 ... O-10
Saginaw, 59235 ... N-10
St. Charles, 2169 ... O-10
ST. CLAIR CO., 169063 ... P-13
St. Clair, 5881 ... P-14
St. Clair Shores, 61896 ... Q-13
St. Ignace, 2535 ... F-8
St. Johns, 7513 ... P-9
ST. JOSEPH CO., 62864 ... T-6
St. Joseph, 8656 ... S-4
St. Louis, 5445 ... N-9
Saline, 8704 ... S-11
Sandusky, 2705 ... N-13
Sanford, 945 ... N-9
SANILAC CO., 44583 ... N-13
Saranac, 1321 ... P-7
Saugatuck, 1037 ... Q-5
Sault Ste. Marie, 14184 ... D-9
SCHOOLCRAFT CO., 8772 ... E-4
Schoolcraft, 1549 ... S-6
Scottville, 1262 ... M-4
Sebewaing, 1898 ... M-11
Shelby, 1971 ... N-4
Shepherd, 1427 ... N-8
Sheridan, 708 ... O-7
SHIAWASSEE CO., 72543 ... P-10
Shields, 6590 ... N-10
Shoreham, 858 ... S-4
Southfield, 77488 ... R-12
Southgate, 30064 ... S-12
S. Haven, 5075 ... R-4
S. Lyon, 10895 ... R-11
S. Range, 723 ... A-12
S. Rockwood, 1648 ... S-12
Sparta, 4102 ... O-6
Spring Arbor, 2188 ... S-9
Springfield, 5228 ... R-7
Spring Lake, 2427 ... P-5
Springport, 687 ... R-8
Stambaugh, 1243 ... C-12
Standish, 2072 ... L-10
Stanton, 1519 ... O-7
Stephenson, 848 ... H-1
Sterling Hts., 126182 ... Q-13
Stevensville, 1192 ... S-4
Stockbridge, 1292 ... R-10
Sturgis, 11127 ... T-7
Sunfield, 591 ... Q-8
Sunrise Heights, 1350 ... R-7
Swartz Creek, 5247 ... P-11
Sylvan Lake, 1700 ... Q-12
Tawas City, 1961 ... K-11
Taylor, 65589 ... *L-4
Tecumseh, 8751 ... S-10
Tekonsha, 699 ... S-8
Temperance, 7757 ... T-11
Three Oaks, 1791 ... T-3
Three Rivers, 7172 ... T-6
Traverse City, 14466 ... J-6
Trenton, 19619 ... S-12
Trowbridge Park, 2012 ... D-1
Troy, 81071 ... Q-12
TUSCOLA CO., 58382 ... N-11
Ubly, 843 ... M-13
Union City, 1767 ... S-7
Union Lake, 8500 ... *F-3
Union Pier, 1100 ... T-3
Unionville, 593 ... N-11
Utica, 4655 ... *F-7
VAN BUREN CO., 78210 ... R-5
Vandercook Lake, 4809 ... S-9
Vassar, 2774 ... N-11
Vermontville, 792 ... Q-8
Vernon, 826 ... P-10
Vicksburg, 2249 ... S-6
Wakefield, 2022 ... B-10
Waldron, 584 ... T-9
Walker, 23208 ... *B-1
Walled Lake, 6776 ... Q-11
Warren, 136016 ... Q-13
Washington, 1850 ... Q-13
WASHTENAW CO., 338562 ... R-10
Waterford, 71981 ... Q-12
Watervliet, 1802 ... S-4
Wayland, 3976 ... Q-6
WAYNE CO., 2028778 ... R-12
Wayne, 18934 ... *K-3
Webberville, 1531 ... Q-10
Wells, 1000 ... F-2
W. Bloomfield, 65452 ... *G-3
W. Branch, 1916 ... K-9
Westland, 85707 ... R-12
Westphalia, 842 ... P-8
WEXFORD CO., 31251 ... K-6
White Cloud, 1431 ... N-6
Whitehall, 2808 ... N-4
White Pigeon, 1619 ... T-6
White Pine, 910 ... B-11
Whitmore Lake, 6574 ... R-11
Williamston, 3784 ... Q-9
Wixom, 13548 ... Q-11
Wolf Lake, 4455 ... O-5
Woodhaven, 12802 ... *M-5
Wyandotte, 27432 ... S-12
Wyoming, 70205 ... P-6
Yale, 2005 ... O-13
Ypsilanti, 22492 ... R-11
Zeeland, 5645 ... Q-5
Zilwaukee, 1758 ... N-10

Minnesota

Map pp. 108-113

* City keyed to pp. 112-113

Ada, 1601 ... H-2
Adams, 787 ... T-11
Adrian, 1230 ... T-3
Afton, 2865 ... P-10
AITKIN CO., 15782 ... J-9
Aitkin, 2013 ... K-8
Albany, 1896 ... M-6
Albert Lea, 17886 ... T-9
Albertville, 5236 ... O-8
Alden, 638 ... T-9
Alexandria, 9746 ... M-5
Amboy, 555 ... S-7
Andover, 28938 ... O-9
Annandale, 2866 ... O-7
ANOKA CO., 314074 ... O-9
Anoka, 17858 ... O-9
Appleton, 2925 ... O-3
Apple Valley, 48938 ... P-9
Arden Hills, 9952 ... *D-6
Argyle, 637 ... E-2
Arlington, 2070 ... Q-8
Arnold, 3032 ... J-12
Atwater, 1060 ... O-6
Aurora, 1805 ... G-11
Austin, 23466 ... T-10
Avon, 1320 ... N-7
Babbitt, 1653 ... G-12
Bagley, 1218 ... G-5
Balaton, 614 ... R-3
Bald Eagle, 1800 ... *C-9
Barnesville, 2245 ... J-2
Battle Lake, 782 ... K-4
Baudette, 1044 ... D-6
Baxter, 6733 ... K-7
Bayport, 3172 ... O-10
BECKER CO., 31174 ... I-4
Becker, 3263 ... N-8
Belgrade, 743 ... N-5
Bellaire, 1900 ... *D-9
Belle Plaine, 4032 ... Q-8
BELTRAMI CO., 41797 ... E-6
Bemidji, 12724 ... H-6
Benson, 3279 ... N-4
BENTON CO., 36925 ... M-8
Bertha, 450 ... K-5
Big Lake, 7796 ... N-8
BIG STONE CO., 5653 ... N-2
Birchwood Vil., 959 ... *D-9
Bird Island, 1186 ... P-6
Biwabik, 922 ... G-11
Blackduck, 748 ... G-7
Blaine, 50425 ... O-9
Blooming Prairie, 1960 ... S-10
Bloomington, 83080 ... P-9
BLUE EARTH CO., 57306 ... S-7
Blue Earth, 3519 ... T-7
Bovey, 659 ... H-9
Braham, 1374 ... M-10
Brainerd, 13722 ... K-7
Breckenridge, 3458 ... K-2
Brewster, 496 ... T-4
Brooklyn Cen., 28362 ... *D-4
Brooklyn Park, 67781 ... *B-3
Brooten, 645 ... N-5
Browerville, 724 ... L-6
BROWN CO., 26505 ... R-6
Brownsdale, 723 ... S-10
Browns Valley, 647 ... M-1
Brownton, 804 ... P-7
Buffalo, 12486 ... O-8
Buffalo Lake, 764 ... P-6
Buhl, 989 ... H-10
Burnsville, 59805 ... *J-4
Butterfield, 549 ... S-6
Byron, 3531 ... R-11
Caledonia, 2967 ... T-13
Cambridge, 6382 ... N-9
Canby, 1838 ... P-3
Cannon Falls, 3881 ... Q-10
CARLTON CO., 33044 ... J-10
Carlton, 798 ... J-11
CARVER CO., 78960 ... P-8
Carver, 1857 ... P-8
CASS CO., 28205 ... J-7
Cass Lake, 842 ... H-6
Centerville, 3581 ... *B-8
Ceylon, 391 ... T-6
Champlin, 23003 ... *A-2
Chanhassen, 22124 ... P-9
Chaska, 20654 ... P-9
Chatfield, 2430 ... S-12
CHIPPEWA CO., 12808 ... O-4
CHISAGO CO., 46165 ... N-10
Chisago City, 2928 ... N-10
Chisholm, 4822 ... H-10
Chokio, 446 ... N-3
Circle Pines, 4774 ... *B-7
Clara City, 1359 ... P-5
Claremont, 615 ... R-10
Clarissa, 600 ... L-6
Clarkfield, 906 ... P-4
Clarks Gr., 730 ... S-9
CLAY CO., 51983 ... I-3
Clearbrook, 540 ... G-5
CLEARWATER CO., 8424 ... G-5
Cleveland, 710 ... R-8
Clinton, 438 ... N-2
Cloquet, 11407 ... J-11
Cohasset, 2487 ... H-8
Cokato, 2761 ... O-7
Cold Spr., 3301 ... N-7
Coleraine, 1062 ... H-9
Cologne, 1079 ... P-8
Columbia Hts., 18428 ... *D-5
COOK CO., 5282 ... A-11
Cook, 609 ... F-10
Coon Rapids, 62310 ... O-9
Corcoran, 5733 ... O-9
Cosmos, 588 ... P-6
Cottage Gr., 31800 ... P-10
COTTONWOOD CO., 12019 ... S-5
Cottonwood, 1132 ... Q-4
Crookston, 7939 ... G-2
Crosby, 2275 ... K-8
Crosslake, 1978 ... J-7
CROW WING CO., 58430 ... J-8
Crystal, 22258 ... *E-3
DAKOTA CO., 373311 ... P-9
Danube, 514 ... P-5
Dassel, 1260 ... O-7
Dawson, 1504 ... P-3
Dayton, 4684 ... O-9
Deephaven, 3797 ... *G-1
Deer River, 940 ... H-8
Delano, 4152 ... O-8
Dellwood, 1059 ... *C-9
Detroit Lakes, 7652 ... J-4
Dilworth, 3092 ... J-2
DODGE CO., 18931 ... S-10
Dodge Cen., 2372 ... R-10
DOUGLAS CO., 34117 ... L-4
Duluth, 85734 ... J-12
Eagan, 64006 ... *J-7
Eagle Bend, 591 ... L-5
Eagle Lake, 1944 ... R-8
E. Bethel, 11613 ... N-9
E. Grand Forks, 7562 ... F-1
Eden Prairie, 59470 ... *I-1
Eden Valley, 914 ... N-6
Edgerton, 1004 ... S-3
Edina, 46656 ... *H-3
Elbow Lake, 1264 ... L-3
Elgin, 872 ... R-12
Elk River, 18783 ... O-9
Ellendale, 589 ... S-9
Ellsworth, 528 ... T-3
Elmore, 712 ... T-7
Ely, 3714 ... F-12
Esko, 550 ... J-11
Evansville, 547 ... L-4
Eveleth, 3742 ... H-11
Excelsior, 2314 ... P-9
Eyota, 1660 ... S-12
Fairfax, 1293 ... Q-6
Fairmont, 10666 ... T-7
Falcon Hts., 5442 ... *F-6
FARIBAULT CO., 15737 ... T-8
Faribault, 21814 ... R-9
Farmington, 16060 ... Q-10
Fergus Falls, 14033 ... K-3
Fertile, 876 ... G-3
FILLMORE CO., 21314 ... T-12
Floodwood, 496 ... I-10
Foley, 2404 ... M-8
Forest Lake, 15942 ... O-10
Fosston, 1527 ... G-4
Frazee, 1393 ... J-4
FREEBORN CO., 31961 ... S-9
Freeport, 469 ... M-6
Fridley, 27169 ... *D-5
Fulda, 1251 ... S-4
Gaylord, 2237 ... Q-7
Gibbon, 788 ... Q-6
Gilbert, 1797 ... H-11
Glencoe, 5534 ... P-7
Glenville, 704 ... T-9
Glenwood, 2451 ... M-5
Glyndon, 1134 ... I-2
Golden Valley, 20505 ... *E-3
GOODHUE CO., 45167 ... Q-10
Goodhue, 874 ... Q-11
Good Thunder, 581 ... S-8
Goodview, 3401 ... R-13
Graceville, 585 ... N-2
Grand Marais, 1427 ... B-12
Grand Meadow, 947 ... S-11
Grand Rapids, 7764 ... H-9
Granite Falls, 2991 ... P-4
GRANT CO., 6243 ... M-3
Greenbush, 763 ... D-3
Grove City, 618 ... O-6
Hallock, 1125 ... C-2
Halstad, 597 ... H-2
Hancock, 700 ... N-4
Hanley Falls, 309 ... P-4
Harmony, 1136 ... T-12
Harris, 1201 ... N-10
Hastings, 19705 ... P-10
Hawley, 1855 ... J-3
Hayfield, 1383 ... S-10
Hector, 1143 ... P-6
Henderson, 925 ... Q-8
Hendricks, 689 ... Q-2
HENNEPIN CO., 1121035 ... O-8
Henning, 788 ... K-5
Herman, 441 ... M-3
Hermantown, 8367 ... J-11
Heron Lake, 766 ... S-5
Hibbing, 16851 ... H-10
Hills, 597 ... T-2
Hilltop, 787 ... *D-5
Hinckley, 1358 ... L-10
Hoffman, 666 ... M-4
Hokah, 604 ... S-14
Holdingford, 729 ... M-7
Hopkins, 17127 ... *G-2
HOUSTON CO., 19980 ... S-13
Houston, 1011 ... S-13
Howard Lake, 1922 ... O-8
Hoyt Lakes, 2069 ... G-12
HUBBARD CO., 18635 ... I-5
Hugo, 8758 ... *B-9
Hutchinson, 13451 ... P-7
Independence, 3504 ... O-8
International Falls, 6454 ... D-9
Inver Grove Hts., 31281 ... *J-9
Ironton, 536 ... K-8
ISANTI CO., 35372 ... N-9
Isanti, 4186 ... N-9
Isle, 807 ... L-9
ITASCA CO., 44265 ... G-9
Ivanhoe, 641 ... Q-3
JACKSON CO., 11170 ... T-5
Jackson, 3464 ... T-5
Janesville, 2111 ... R-8
Jasper, 584 ... S-2
Jordan, 4731 ... P-9
KANABEC CO., 15867 ... M-9
KANDIYOHI CO., 41148 ... O-5
Karlstad, 750 ... D-2
Kasota, 692 ... R-8
Kasson, 5030 ... R-10
Keewatin, 1135 ... H-10
Kenyon, 1657 ... R-10
Kerkhoven, 735 ... O-5
Kiester, 525 ... T-8
Kimball, 639 ... N-7
KITTSON CO., 4968 ... C-2
KOOCHICHING CO., 14018 ... E-8
LAC QUI PARLE CO., 7867 ... O-3
La Crescent, 5066 ... S-14
Lafayette, 532 ... Q-7
LAKE CO., 11160 ... G-13
Lake Benton, 687 ... R-3
Lake City, 5238 ... Q-12
Lake Crystal, 2490 ... R-7
Lake Elmo, 7714 ... O-10
Lakefield, 1701 ... T-5
Lakeland, 1899 ... P-10
LAKE OF THE WOODS CO., 4384 ... D-5
Lake Park, 821 ... I-3
Lakeville, 47805 ... Q-9
Lamberton, 819 ... R-5
Landfall, 737 ... *G-9
Lanesboro, 775 ... S-12
Lauderdale, 2296 ... *F-6
Le Center, 2306 ... Q-8
Le Roy, 919 ... T-11
Lester Prairie, 1431 ... P-8
LE SUEUR CO., 26763 ... Q-8
Le Sueur, 4220 ... Q-8
Lewiston, 1496 ... S-12
Lexington, 2134 ... *B-6
LINCOLN CO., 6159 ... Q-2
Lindstrom, 3519 ... N-10
Lino Lakes, 18795 ... O-10
Litchfield, 6685 ... O-7
Little Canada, 9738 ... *E-8
Little Falls, 7848 ... L-7
Littlefork, 690 ... E-9
Long Lake, 1838 ... P-9
Long Prairie, 2967 ... L-6
Lonsdale, 1912 ... Q-9
Luverne, 4531 ... T-3
Lyle, 570 ... T-10
LYON CO., 24819 ... R-4
Mabel, 755 ... T-13
Madelia, 2301 ... R-7
Madison, 1721 ... O-3
Madison Lake, 894 ... R-8
MAHNOMEN CO., 5113 ... H-4
Mahnomen, 1177 ... H-3
Mahtomedi, 8076 ... *D-10
Mankato, 33925 ... R-8
Mantorville, 1167 ... R-10
Maple Gr., 57172 ... O-9
Maple Lake, 1735 ... O-8
Maple Plain, 2033 ... O-8
Mapleton, 1670 ... S-8
Maplewood, 35945 ... *E-8
Marble, 692 ... H-9
Marine On St. Croix, 619 ... O-10
MARSHALL CO., 9997 ... E-3
Marshall, 12545 ... Q-4
MARTIN CO., 21221 ... S-6
Mazeppa, 791 ... R-11
McIntosh, 625 ... G-4
MCLEOD CO., 35864 ... P-7
Medford, 1078 ... R-9
MEEKER CO., 23205 ... O-6
Melrose, 3186 ... M-6
Menahga, 1212 ... J-5
Mendota Hts., 11343 ... *H-7
Milaca, 2820 ... M-8
MILLE LACS CO., 24317 ... L-8
Minneapolis, 373188 ... O-9
Minneota, 1396 ... Q-3
Minnesota Lake, 671 ... S-8
Minnetonka, 50690 ... *G-1
Montevideo, 5383 ... P-4
Montgomery, 2869 ... Q-9
Monticello, 9648 ... N-8
Moorhead, 32786 ... I-2
Moose Lake, 2371 ... K-10
Mora, 3457 ... M-9
Morgan, 863 ... Q-6
Morris, 5161 ... N-3
MORRISON CO., 32589 ... M-8
Morristown, 1013 ... R-9
Mound, 9376 ... P-8
Mounds View, 12696 ... *C-6
Mtn. Iron, 2976 ... G-11
Mtn. Lake, 2048 ... S-6
MOWER CO., 38823 ... T-11
MURRAY CO., 8981 ... R-4
Nashwauk, 912 ... H-9
New Brighton, 21751 ... *D-6
New Hope, 20317 ... *D-3
New London, 1102 ... O-6
Newport, 3677 ... *I-9
New Prague, 5391 ... Q-9
New Richland, 1168 ... S-9
New Ulm, 13401 ... R-7
New York Mills, 1189 ... K-5
NICOLLET CO., 30733 ... Q-7
Nicollet, 972 ... R-7
Nisswa, 2012 ... K-7
NOBLES CO., 20621 ... T-3
NORMAN CO., 7191 ... H-2
N. Branch, 9457 ... N-10
Northfield, 18187 ... Q-10
N. Mankato, 12248 ... R-8
N. Oaks, 4181 ... *D-7
N. St. Paul, 11839 ... *E-9
Norwood Young America, 3176 ... P-8
Oakdale, 27673 ... *F-10
Ogilvie, 483 ... M-9
Olivia, 2524 ... P-5
OLMSTED CO., 131384 ... R-11
Onamia, 888 ... L-8
Oronoco, 891 ... R-11
Ortonville, 2096 ... N-2
Osakis, 1570 ... M-5
Osseo, 2517 ... *C-2
OTTER TAIL CO., 58847 ... K-3
Owatonna, 23333 ... R-9
Parkers Prairie, 1024 ... L-5
Park Rapids, 3392 ... I-5
Paynesville, 2301 ... N-6
Pelican Rapids, 2443 ... J-3
Pengilly, 850 ... H-9
PENNINGTON CO., 13636 ... F-3
Pequot Lakes, 974 ... J-7
Perham, 2718 ... J-4
Pierz, 1296 ... L-7
PINE CO., 27746 ... K-11
Pine City, 3212 ... M-10
Pine Island, 2943 ... R-11
Pine River, 954 ... J-7
PIPESTONE CO., 9681 ... R-2
Pipestone, 4297 ... S-2
Plainview, 3245 ... R-12
Plymouth, 69164 ... *E-1
POLK CO., 30905 ... F-2
POPE CO., 11252 ... N-4
Preston, 1402 ... T-12
Princeton, 4437 ... N-9
Prior Lake, 20038 ... P-9
Proctor, 2776 ... J-12
RAMSEY CO., 506355 ... O-10
Ramsey, 19524 ... O-9
Randall, 616 ... L-7
Raymond, 781 ... O-5
RED LAKE CO., 4319 ... F-3
Redlake, 1430 ... F-6
Red Lake Falls, 1594 ... F-3
Red Wing, 16020 ... Q-11
REDWOOD CO., 16231 ... Q-5
Redwood Falls, 5339 ... Q-5
RENVILLE CO., 16851 ... Q-6
Renville, 1288 ... P-5
RICE CO., 59667 ... Q-9
Rice, 889 ... M-7
Richfield, 34079 ... *H-4
Richmond, 1291 ... N-7
Robbinsdale, 13668 ... *E-3
Rochester, 92507 ... S-11
ROCK CO., 9614 ... S-2
Rockford, 3880 ... O-8
Rogers, 5934 ... O-9
Rollingstone, 664 ... R-13
ROSEAU CO., 16318 ... D-4
Roseau, 2740 ... C-4
Rosemount, 16974 ... P-10
Roseville, 33105 ... *E-7
Round Lake, 416 ... T-4
Royalton, 868 ... M-7
Rush City, 2469 ... M-10
Rushford, 1754 ... S-13
Sacred Heart, 530 ... P-5
St. Anthony, 7830 ... *E-5
St. Bonifacius, 2310 ... P-8
St. Charles, 3393 ... S-12
St. Clair, 813 ... R-8
St. Cloud, 59458 ... N-7
St. Francis, 6449 ... N-9
St. James, 4592 ... S-6
St. Joseph, 5089 ... N-7
ST. LOUIS CO., 198799 ... H-10
St. Louis Park, 44114 ... *G-3
St. Michael, 12850 ... O-8
St. Paul, 280404 ... P-10
St. Paul Park, 5028 ... P-10
St. Peter, 10162 ... R-8
Sandstone, 2481 ... L-10
Sartell, 11854 ... M-7
Sauk Ctr., 4001 ... M-6
Sauk Rapids, 11620 ... N-7
Savage, 25202 ... P-9
Scanlon, 827 ... J-11
SCOTT CO., 108578 ... Q-9
Sebeka, 693 ... J-5
Shakopee, 26681 ... P-9
Sherburn, 1065 ... T-6
SHERBURNE CO., 74667 ... N-8
Shoreview, 27105 ... *D-7
Shorewood, 7522 ... P-9
SIBLEY CO., 15277 ... Q-7
Silver Bay, 2037 ... H-14
Silver Lake, 774 ... P-7
Slayton, 2015 ... S-4
Sleepy Eye, 3416 ... R-6
Soudan, 900 ... G-11
S. St. Paul, 19699 ... *H-8
Spicer, 1123 ... O-6
Springfield, 2177 ... R-5
Spr. Grove, 1296 ... T-13
Spr. Lake Park, 6806 ... *C-5
Spr. Valley, 2527 ... T-11
Staples, 3042 ... K-6
Starbuck, 1244 ... N-4
STEARNS CO., 137149 ... N-6
STEELE CO., 34753 ... S-9
Stephen, 684 ... D-2
STEVENS CO., 9888 ... N-3
Stewart, 559 ... P-7
Stewartville, 5522 ... S-11
Stillwater, 16734 ... O-10
SWIFT CO., 11656 ... O-4
Taylors Falls, 981 ... N-11
Thief River Falls, 8427 ... F-3
TODD CO., 24309 ... L-6
Tower, 469 ... G-11
Tracy, 2145 ... R-4
TRAVERSE CO., 3911 ... M-2
Trimont, 727 ... S-6
Truman, 1217 ... S-7
Twin Valley, 834 ... H-3
Two Harbors, 3561 ... I-13
Tyler, 1154 ... R-3
Ulen, 536 ... I-3
Vadnais Hts., 13104 ... *D-8
Verndale, 569 ... K-6
Victoria, 5176 ... P-8
Virginia, 8888 ... G-11
WABASHA CO., 22144 ... Q-12
Wabasha, 2597 ... Q-12
Wabasso, 666 ... Q-5
Waconia, 7986 ... P-8
WADENA CO., 13603 ... K-6
Wadena, 4175 ... K-5
Waite Park, 6864 ... N-7
Walker, 1125 ... I-6
Walnut Gr., 568 ... R-4
Wanamingo, 1029 ... R-10
Warren, 1650 ... E-2
Warroad, 1684 ... C-5
WASECA CO., 19435 ... S-8
Waseca, 9576 ... R-9
WASHINGTON CO., 213564 ... O-10
Watertown, 3608 ... P-8
Waterville, 1882 ... R-9
Watkins, 896 ... N-7
WATONWAN CO., 11621 ... S-6
Waverly, 784 ... O-8
Wayzata, 4032 ... *F-1
Welcome, 696 ... T-6
Wells, 2434 ... S-8
Westbrook, 780 ... R-4
W. Concord, 822 ... R-10
W. St. Paul, 19468 ... *H-7
Wheaton, 1531 ... M-2
White Bear Lake, 24388 ... O-10
WILKIN CO., 6945 ... K-2
Willernie, 547 ... *D-10
Willmar, 18303 ... O-5
Windom, 4499 ... S-5
Winnebago, 1446 ... S-7
WINONA CO., 49482 ... S-12
Winona, 26641 ... R-13
Winsted, 2279 ... P-8
Winthrop, 1323 ... Q-7
Woodbury, 49415 ... *G-10
Woodland, 471 ... *G-1
Worthington, 11192 ... T-4
WRIGHT CO., 102529 ... O-7
Wykoff, 453 ... S-12
Wyoming, 3683 ... N-10
YELLOW MEDICINE CO., 10677 ... P-3
Zimmerman, 3679 ... N-9
Zumbrota, 2941 ... R-11

Mississippi

Map pp. 114-115

Abbeville, 429 ... C-7
Aberdeen, 6278 ... D-9
Ackerman, 1655 ... F-8
ADAMS CO., 33233 ... J-3
ALCORN CO., 34930 ... B-9
AMITE CO., 13594 ... K-4
Amory, 6800 ... D-9
Anguilla, 859 ... F-4
Arcola, 540 ... F-4
Artesia, 495 ... E-9
Ashland, 559 ... B-8
ATTALA CO., 19673 ... F-7
Baldwyn, 3332 ... B-9
Batesville, 7598 ... C-6
Bay St. Louis, 8150 ... M-8
Bay Sprs., 2178 ... I-8
Bear Town, 1300 ... K-5
Beaumont, 974 ... K-9
Belmont, 1945 ... C-10
Belzoni, 2568 ... F-5
Benoit, 599 ... E-4
BENTON CO., 7774 ... B-8
Bentonia, 495 ... G-5
Beulah, 465 ... D-4
Biloxi, 48972 ... M-9
Blue Mtn., 673 ... B-8
Bogue Chitto, 700 ... J-5
BOLIVAR CO., 39235 ... D-4
Bolton, 618 ... H-5
Bond, 500 ... L-8
Booneville, 8619 ... B-9
Boyle, 691 ... E-5
Brandon, 18065 ... H-6
Brookhaven, 9810 ... J-5
Brooklyn, 900 ... K-8
Brooksville, 1164 ... F-9
Bruce, 2055 ... D-8
Buckatunna, 600 ... J-9
Bude, 1018 ... J-4
Burnsville, 1028 ... B-10
Byhalia, 717 ... B-7
Caledonia, 998 ... E-10
CALHOUN CO., 14827 ... D-7
Calhoun City, 1835 ... D-8
Canton, 12856 ... G-6
Carriere, 880 ... L-7
CARROLL CO., 10462 ... E-6
Carson, 500 ... J-7
Carthage, 4642 ... G-7
Cary, 405 ... G-4
Centreville, 1614 ... K-4
Charleston, 2102 ... D-6
CHICKASAW CO., 19204 ... D-8
CHOCTAW CO., 9661 ... E-8
CLAIBORNE CO., 11502 ... I-4
CLARKE CO., 17746 ... I-9
Clarksdale, 19833 ... C-5
CLAY CO., 21625 ... E-9
Cleveland, 13184 ... D-5
Clinton, 24207 ... H-5
COAHOMA CO., 29546 ... C-5
Coffeeville, 935 ... D-7
Coldwater, 1632 ... B-6
Collins, 2743 ... J-7
Columbia, 6344 ... K-7
Columbus, 24959 ... E-9
Como, 1311 ... C-6
COPIAH CO., 28928 ... I-5
Corinth, 14083 ... A-9
Courtland, 472 ... C-6
COVINGTON CO., 20177 ... J-7
Crawford, 650 ... F-9
Crenshaw, 932 ... C-6
Crosby, 354 ... K-4
Crowder, 769 ... C-6
Cruger, 445 ... E-6
Crystal Sprs., 5841 ... I-5
Decatur, 1432 ... H-8
De Kalb, 945 ... G-9
De Lisle, 680 ... M-8
Derma, 985 ... D-8
DESOTO CO., 124378 ... B-6
D Iberville, 7539 ... M-9
D Lo, 384 ... I-6
Drew, 2287 ... D-5
Duck Hill, 1215 ... E-7
Dumas, 452 ... B-9
Duncan, 560 ... D-5
Durant, 2886 ... F-7
Ecru, 989 ... C-8
Edwards, 1322 ... H-5
Elliott, 1100 ... E-7
Ellisville, 3442 ... J-8
Enterprise, 457 ... H-9
Escatawpa, 3566 ... M-9
Ethel, 448 ... F-7
Eupora, 2261 ... E-8
Fayette, 2169 ... J-4
Fernwood, 400 ... K-5
Flora, 1527 ... G-6
Florence, 2718 ... H-6
Flowood, 6260 ... C-3
Forest, 5970 ... H-7
FORREST CO., 74386 ... K-8
Foxworth, 600 ... K-6
FRANKLIN CO., 8340 ... J-4
French Camp, 389 ... F-7
Friars Pt., 1429 ... C-5
Fulton, 3935 ... C-10
Gautier, 16753 ... M-9
GEORGE CO., 20407 ... L-9
Georgetown, 344 ... I-6
Glen Allan, 500 ... F-4
Glendale, 1300 ... J-8
Gloster, 1050 ... K-4
Goodman, 1201 ... F-6
GREENE CO., 13169 ... K-9
Greenville, 39521 ... E-4
Greenwood, 17594 ... E-6
GRENADA CO., 22809 ... E-6
Grenada, 14649 ... D-7
Gulfport, 71810 ... M-8
Gunnison, 615 ... D-4
Guntown, 1205 ... C-9
HANCOCK CO., 45145 ... M-7
HARRISON CO., 189614 ... L-8
Hatley, 472 ... D-10
Hattiesburg, 46664 ... K-8
Hazlehurst, 4373 ... I-5
Heidelberg, 823 ... I-8
Hernando, 8344 ... B-6
Hickory, 500 ... H-8
Hickory Flat, 540 ... B-8
HINDS CO., 249087 ... H-5
Hollandale, 3248 ... F-4
Holly Sprs., 7924 ... B-7
HOLMES CO., 21347 ... F-6
Horn Lake, 15146 ... A-6
Houlka, 702 ... D-8
Houston, 3982 ... D-8
HUMPHREYS CO., 10722 ... F-5
Hurley, 985 ... L-9
Indianola, 11562 ... E-5
Inverness, 1085 ... E-5
Isola, 734 ... F-5
ISSAQUENA CO., 2016 ... G-4
ITAWAMBA CO., 22964 ... C-9
Itta Bena, 2085 ... E-6
Iuka, 2977 ... B-10
JACKSON CO., 133928 ... L-9
Jackson, 179599 ... H-6
JASPER CO., 18280 ... I-8
JEFFERSON CO., 9533 ... I-4
JEFFERSON DAVIS CO., 13399 ... J-6
JONES CO., 65168 ... J-8
Jonestown, 1676 ... C-5
Jonestown, 350 ... G-5
Jumpertown, 406 ... B-9
KEMPER CO., 10435 ... G-9
Kilmichael, 765 ... E-7
Kiln, 2040 ... M-7
Kosciusko, 7351 ... F-7
LAFAYETTE CO., 40188 ... C-7
Lake, 404 ... H-8
LAMAR CO., 41957 ... K-7
Lamar Park, 570 ... F-1
Lambert, 1867 ... C-6
LAUDERDALE CO., 77706 ... H-9
Lauderdale, 650 ... G-9
Laurel, 18044 ... J-8
LAWRENCE CO., 13520 ... J-6
LEAKE CO., 21820 ... G-7
Leakesville, 1011 ... K-9
LEE CO., 77690 ... C-9
LEFLORE CO., 36470 ... E-5
Leland, 5234 ... E-4
Le Tourneau, 200 ... H-4
Lexington, 1963 ... F-6
Liberty, 675 ... K-4
LINCOLN CO., 33549 ... J-5
Long Beach, 16938 ... M-8
Lorman, 560 ... I-4
Louin, 338 ... I-8
Louise, 303 ... F-5
Louisville, 6831 ... F-8
LOWNDES CO., 60658 ... E-9
Lucedale, 2750 ... L-9
Lumberton, 2345 ... K-7
Lyon, 399 ... C-5
Macon, 2373 ... F-9
MADISON CO., 79758 ... G-6
Madison, 15869 ... H-6
Magee, 4169 ... I-7
Magnolia, 2047 ... K-5
Mantachie, 1120 ... C-9
MARION CO., 25090 ... K-6
Marion, 1335 ... H-9
Marks, 1940 ... C-6
MARSHALL CO., 35442 ... B-7
Mathiston, 713 ... E-8
Mayersville, 689 ... G-4
McComb, 13127 ... K-5
McLain, 591 ... K-9
McNeill, 1050 ... L-7
Meadville, 507 ... J-4
Mendenhall, 2526 ... I-6
Meridian, 39559 ... H-9
Merigold, 632 ... D-5
Metcalfe, 1178 ... E-4
Mississippi State, 15680 ... E-9
Mize, 278 ... I-7
MONROE CO., 37842 ... D-9
MONTGOMERY CO., 11935 ... E-7
Monticello, 1726 ... J-6
Moorhead, 2429 ... E-5
Morgantown, 2900 ... J-3
Morton, 3426 ... H-7
Moselle, 700 ... J-8
Moss Pt., 15327 ... M-9
Mound Bayou, 2055 ... D-5
Mt. Olive, 899 ... I-7
Myrtle, 420 ... B-8
Natchez, 17621 ... J-3
Nellieburg, 1354 ... G-1
NESHOBA CO., 29134 ... G-8
Nettleton, 1942 ... D-9
New Albany, 7796 ... C-8
New Augusta, 703 ... K-8
New Hebron, 446 ... I-6
NEWTON CO., 22044 ... H-8
Newton, 3665 ... H-8
N. Carrollton, 482 ... E-6
N. Gulfport ... M-1
N. Tunica, 1450 ... B-5
Noxapater, 418 ... F-8
NOXUBEE CO., 12318 ... F-9
Oakland, 596 ... D-6
Ocean Sprs., 17443 ... M-9
Okolona, 2949 ... D-9

2000 Census populations or latest available estimate.
Index to Canada and Mexico cities and towns, pages 274-275.

MISSISSIPPI - NEW JERSEY 267

OKTIBBEHA CO., 42573 E-8
Olive Branch, 24938 A-7
Osyka, 483 K-5
Ovett, 630 J-8
Oxford, 12761 C-7
Pace, 352 D-4
Palmer, 2800 K-8
PANOLA CO., 35243 C-6
Pascagoula, 25865 M-9
Pass Christian, 6599 M-8
Pearl, 22824 H-6
Pearlington, 1684 M-7
PEARL RIVER CO., 50894 K-7
Pelahatchie, 1477 H-7
Perkinston, 100 L-8
PERRY CO., 12288 K-8
Petal, 7687 J-8
Philadelphia, 7277 G-8
Philipp, 350 D-6
Picayune, 10641 M-7
Pickens, 1276 G-6
PIKE CO., 38935 K-5
Piney Woods, 100 I-6
Plantersville, 1173 C-9
PONTOTOC CO., 27575 C-8
Pontotoc, 5636 C-8
Poplarville, 2664 L-7
Port Gibson, 1748 I-4
Potts Camp, 510 B-8
PRENTISS CO., 25581 B-9
Prentiss, 1074 J-6
Purvis, 2308 K-7
QUITMAN CO., 9740 D-5
Quitman, 2407 I-9
Raleigh, 1223 I-7
RANKIN CO., 124695 H-6
Raymond, 1758 H-5
Red Banks, 580 B-7
Richton, 1037 J-8
Ridgeland, 21435 H-6
Rienzi, 324 B-9
Ripley, 5509 B-8
Rolling Fk., 2343 F-4
Rosedale, 2427 D-4
Rose Hill, 250 I-8
Roxie, 559 J-4
Ruleville, 3030 D-5
Saltillo, 3426 C-9
Sandersville, 793 I-8
Sardis, 2045 C-6
Schlater, 381 E-5
Scooba, 608 G-9
SCOTT CO., 28450 H-7
Senatobia, 6667 B-6
Shannon, 1697 C-9
SHARKEY CO., 6224 G-4
Shaw, 2288 E-5
Shelby, 2802 D-5
Sherman, 588 C-9
Shubuta, 645 I-9
Shuqualak, 543 F-9
Sidon, 654 E-6
Silver City, 320 F-5
SIMPSON CO., 27592 I-6
Sledge, 505 C-6
SMITH CO., 15834 I-7
Smithville, 878 D-10
Soso, 378 I-8
Southaven, 34760 A-6
Star, 550 I-6
Starkville, 22419 E-9
State Line, 551 J-9
STONE CO., 14206 L-8
Stonewall, 1108 H-9
Stringer, 430 I-8
Summit, 1400 K-5
Sumner, 380 D-5
Sumrall, 1085 J-7
SUNFLOWER CO., 33374 E-5
Sunflower, 662 E-5
TALLAHATCHIE CO., 14394 D-6
TATE CO., 25794 B-6
Taylorsville, 1281 I-7
Tchula, 2291 F-6
Terry, 672 I-6
Thaxton, 526 C-8
Tie Plant, 300 D-7
TIPPAH CO., 20920 B-8
TISHOMINGO CO., 18966 B-10
Tishomingo, 310 B-10
Tremont, 393 C-10
TUNICA CO., 9917 B-5
Tunica, 1067 B-5
Tupelo, 35297 C-9
Tutwiler, 1320 D-5
Tylertown, 1873 K-6
UNION CO., 26113 B-8
Union, 2058 G-8
University C-7
Utica, 932 I-5
Vaiden, 776 E-7
Vancleave, 4910 L-9
Vardaman, 1038 D-8
Verona, 3371 C-9
Vicksburg, 26005 H-4
Walnut, 750 A-8
Walnut Gr., 1011 G-7
Waltersville, 350 H-4
WALTHALL CO., 15191 K-6
WARREN CO., 48993 H-5
WASHINGTON CO., 60345 E-4
Washington, 750 J-3
Water Valley, 3763 C-7
Waveland, 6820 M-8
WAYNE CO., 21149 I-9
Waynesboro, 5133 J-9
Webb, 551 D-6
WEBSTER CO., 10159 E-7
Weir, 546 F-8
Wesson, 1696 J-5
W. Point, 11858 E-9
Wheeler, 600 B-9
WILKINSON CO., 10241 K-3
Winona, 5086 E-7
WINSTON CO., 19911 F-8
Woodville, 1170 K-3
YALOBUSHA CO., 13347 D-7
YAZOO CO., 28272 G-6
Yazoo City, 12098 G-5

Missouri

Map pp. 116-121

* City keyed to pp. 120-121
‡ Independent city: Not included in any county.

ADAIR CO., 24790 C-13
Adrian, 1819 G-9
Advance, 1217 K-19
Affton, 20535 *G-5
Agency, 599 D-8
Albany, 1846 B-9
Alton, 647 L-16
Anderson, 1835 L-9
ANDREW CO., 16813 C-8
Appleton City, 1309 H-10
Arbyrd, 509 N-18
Arcadia, 530 J-17
Archie, 899 G-9
Arnold, 20070 G-18
Ash Gr., 1446 J-11
Ashland, 2234 F-14
ATCHISON CO., 6286 B-7
AUDRAIN CO., 25716 E-14
Aurora, 7121 K-10
Auxvasse, 923 F-15
Ava, 3037 K-13
Avondale, 530 H-4
Ballwin, 31006 G-17
Barnhart, 6108 G-18
BARRY CO., 34629 L-10
BARTON CO., 12999 J-9
BATES CO., 16937 H-9
Battlefield, 2738 K-11
Bella Villa, 671 *G-6
Belle, 1329 H-15
Bellefontaine Neighbors, 10865 *C-6
Bel-Nor, 1550 *D-5
Bel-Ridge, 3011 *D-5
Belton, 23575 F-9
BENTON CO., 18076 G-11
Benton, 730 K-20
Berkeley, 9867 *C-5
Bernie, 1801 L-19
Bertrand, 721 K-20
Bethany, 3065 B-10
Beverly Hills, 587 *D-6
Bevier, 724 D-13
Billings, 1137 K-11
Birch Tree, 615 K-15
Bismarck, 1516 J-17
Black Jack, 6941 *C-6
Bland, 570 H-15
Bloomfield, 1898 K-19
Blue Sprs., 49398 F-9
Blue Summit, 1200 I-5
Bolivar, 9598 I-11
BOLLINGER CO., 12318 J-18
Bonne Terre, 4696 I-17
BOONE CO., 141122 E-13
Boonville, 8399 F-13
Bourbon, 1380 H-16
Bowling Green, 5228 E-16
Branson, 6231 L-12
Braymer, 951 D-10
Breckenridge Hills, 4706 *D-5
Brentwood, 7519 *F-5
Bridgeton, 15515 *C-4
Brookfield, 4633 C-12
Brunswick, 907 D-12
BUCHANAN CO., 84909 D-8
Bucklin, 505 C-12
Buckner, 2702 E-10
Buffalo, 2851 I-12
Burlington Jct., 622 B-8
BUTLER CO., 40854 L-18
Butler, 4214 H-9
Cabool, 2120 K-14
CALDWELL CO., 9159 D-10
California, 4054 G-13
CALLAWAY CO., 42225 F-14
Calverton Park, 1318 *C-5
CAMDEN CO., 38302 I-13
Camdenton, 2949 H-13
Cameron, 9908 D-9
Campbell, 1863 L-19
Canton, 2495 B-15
CAPE GIRARDEAU CO., 69876 J-19
Cape Girardeau, 35741 J-20
Cardwell, 761 N-18
Carl Jct., 5860 K-9
CARROLL CO., 10149 D-11
Carrollton, 4010 E-11
Carsonville, 2000 *D-5
CARTER CO., 5974 K-17
Carterville, 1895 *L-3
Carthage, 12892 K-9
Caruthersville, 6564 M-20
CASS CO., 88834 F-9
Cassville, 3012 L-10
CEDAR CO., 13838 I-10
Cedar Hill, 1703 G-17
Center, 636 D-15
Centralia, 3768 E-14
Chaffee, 3000 K-19
CHARITON CO., 8251 D-12
Charlack, 1393 *D-5
Charleston, 5855 K-20
Chesterfield, 47067 G-17
Chillicothe, 8791 C-11
CHRISTIAN CO., 61571 K-12
Clarence, 900 D-14
CLARK CO., 7420 B-15
Clarkson Valley, 2638 *F-2
Clarkton, 1293 M-19
CLAY CO., 194247 E-9
Claycomo, 1272 G-4
Clayton, 15974 G-18
CLINTON CO., 20140 D-9
Clinton, 9349 G-10
COLE CO., 72454 G-13
Cole Camp, 1045 G-12
Columbia, 88534 F-14
Concord, 16689 *G-5
Concordia, 2384 F-11
Conway, 748 J-12
Cool Valley, 1054 *D-6
COOPER CO., 17009 F-12
Corder, 425 E-11
Country Club Hills, 1351 *D-6
Country Club Village, 1892 C-8
Crane, 1418 K-11
CRAWFORD CO., 23513 I-16
Crestwood, 11831 *F-5
Creve Coeur, 16718 F-18
Crocker, 1042 I-14
Crystal City, 4421 H-18
Cuba, 3351 H-16
DADE CO., 7845 J-10
DALLAS CO., 16113 I-12
DAVIESS CO., 8004 C-10
Dearborn, 541 D-8
DEKALB CO., 13063 C-9
Dellwood, 5144 *C-6
DENT CO., 14921 I-15
Desloge, 4938 I-17
De Soto, 6501 H-17
Des Peres, 8628 *F-4
Dexter, 7374 L-19
Diamond, 825 K-9
Dixon, 1610 H-14
Doe Run, 300 I-18
Doniphan, 1909 L-17
Doolittle, 672 I-14
DOUGLAS CO., 13363 K-13
Drexel, 1098 G-9
DUNKLIN CO., 32654 N-19
Duquesne, 1693 *M-3
E. Prairie, 3134 L-20
Edgerton, 548 D-9
Edina, 1207 B-14
Edmundson, 821 *D-5
Eldon, 4892 G-13
El Dorado Sprs., 3761 I-10
Ellington, 1022 J-17
Ellisville, 9255 *F-2
Elsberry, 2253 E-17
Eminence, 542 K-16
Essex, 529 L-19
Eureka, 8575 G-17
Excelsior Sprs., 11226 E-9
Fairfax, 631 B-7
Fair Grove, 1260 J-12
Farmington, 14335 I-18
Fayette, 2724 E-13
Fenton, 4340 *G-4
Ferguson, 21907 *D-5
Festus, 9938 H-18
Flordell Hills, 908 *D-6
Florissant, 51018 *C-5
Forsyth, 1659 L-12
FRANKLIN CO., 96905 G-16
Fredericktown, 3854 J-18
Frontenac, 3502 *E-4
Fulton, 12315 F-14
Gainesville, 610 L-13
Gallatin, 1754 C-10
Garden City, 1627 G-9
GASCONADE CO., 15542 G-15
GENTRY CO., 6566 B-9
Gerald, 1218 G-16
Gideon, 1059 M-19
Gladstone, 27089 E-9
Glasgow, 1212 E-12
Glenaire, 584 G-5
Glendale, 5674 *F-5
Golden City, 915 J-10
Goodman, 1190 L-9
Gower, 1431 D-9
Granby, 2164 K-9
Grandview, 25210 F-9
Grant City, 871 B-9
Grantwood Vil., 891 *G-5
Gray Summit, 2640 G-17
Green City, 668 B-12
GREENE CO., 245765 J-11
Greenfield, 1319 J-10
Greenwood, 4401 F-9
GRUNDY CO., 10311 B-11
Hale, 471 D-11
Hallsville, 988 E-14
Hamilton, 1820 D-10
Hanley Hills, 2112 *E-5
Hannibal, 17577 D-16
Hardin, 602 E-10
HARRISON CO., 8828 B-10
Harrisonville, 9418 G-9
Hartville, 602 J-13
Hayti, 3130 M-19
Hazelwood, 25848 *C-5
HENRY CO., 22419 G-11
Herculaneum, 3162 H-18
Hermann, 2698 F-15
HICKORY CO., 9005 H-12
Higbee, 642 E-13
Higginsville, 4655 E-11
High Ridge, 4236 G-17
Hillsboro, 1680 H-17
Hillsdale, 1436 *D-6
Holcomb, 693 M-19
Holden, 2555 F-10
Hollister, 3884 L-12
HOLT CO., 5145 B-7
Holts Summit, 3196 G-14
Hopkins, 568 A-8
Horine, 923 H-18
Hornersville, 675 N-19
House Springs, 300 G-17
Houston, 1969 J-14
HOWARD CO., 10007 E-13
HOWELL CO., 37499 L-14
Humansville, 970 I-11
Huntsville, 1599 D-13
Iberia, 661 H-14
Independence, 112079 E-9
IRON CO., 10306 I-16
Ironton, 1377 I-17
JACKSON CO., 659723 F-9
Jackson, 12477 J-19
Jamesport, 507 C-10
JASPER CO., 108112 J-9
Jasper, 1034 J-9
JEFFERSON CO., 206786 H-17
Jefferson City, 37550 G-14
Jennings, 15160 *D-6
JOHNSON CO., 50262 G-10
Jonesburg, 680 F-16
Joplin, 46373 K-9
Kahoka, 2218 B-15
Kansas City, 442768 E-9
Kearney, 6573 E-9
Kennett, 11072 M-19
Keytesville, 523 D-12
Kimberling City, 2370 L-11
King City, 950 C-9
Kirksville, 17157 B-13
Kirkwood, 27294 *F-4
Knob Noster, 2652 F-11
KNOX CO., 4311 C-14
La Belle, 662 C-14
LACLEDE CO., 33326 I-13
Laddonia, 599 E-15
Ladue, 8359 *E-5
LAFAYETTE CO., 32951 F-10
La Grange, 965 C-15
Lake Lotawana, 2065 F-9
Lake Ozark, 1725 H-13
Lakeshire, 1347 *G-5
Lake Tapawingo, 824 J-7
Lake Waukomis, 917 G-3
Lake Winnebago, 999 M-6
Lamar, 4538 J-9
La Monte, 1042 F-11
Lancaster, 733 A-13
La Plata, 1447 C-13
Lathrop, 2216 D-9
LAWRENCE CO., 36426 K-10
Lawson, 2387 D-10
Leadwood, 1145 I-17
Lebanon, 12628 I-13
Lees Summit, 77052 L-6
Lemay, 17215 *G-6
LEWIS CO., 10226 B-15
Lexington, 4667 E-10
Liberal, 808 J-9
Liberty, 27982 E-9
Licking, 2572 J-15
Lilbourn, 1275 L-20
LINCOLN CO., 44207 F-16
Lincoln, 1064 G-11
LINN CO., 13460 C-12
Linn, 1399 G-15
LIVINGSTON CO., 14387 C-11
Lockwood, 969 J-10
Louisiana, 3808 D-16
Lowry City, 726 H-11
MACON CO., 15577 C-13
Macon, 5438 D-13
MADISON CO., 11804 J-18
Madison, 570 D-14
Malden, 4659 L-19
Manchester, 19106 *F-3
Mansfield, 1342 K-13
Maplewood, 8972 *F-5
Marble Hill, 1505 J-19
Marceline, 2466 D-12
MARIES CO., 8841 H-14
MARION CO., 28289 C-15
Marionville, 2140 K-11
Marlborough, 2219 *F-5
Marshall, 12017 E-12
Marshfield, 6291 J-12
Marston, 593 L-20
Maryland Hts., 25583 *D-4
Maryville, 10622 B-8
Mattese, 2500 *H-5
Matthews, 571 L-20
Maysville, 1160 C-9
MCDONALD CO., 21973 L-9
Mehlville, 28822 *G-5
Memphis, 2004 B-14
MERCER CO., 3596 B-11
Mexico, 10956 E-14
Milan, 1902 B-12
MILLER CO., 24255 H-13
Miller, 778 K-10
Miner, 1209 K-20
MISSISSIPPI CO., 14386 K-20
Moberly, 13733 D-13
Moline Acres, 2606 *C-6
Monett, 7735 K-10
MONITEAU CO., 14965 G-13
MONROE CO., 9396 D-14
Monroe City, 2602 D-15
MONTGOMERY CO., 12068 F-15
Montgomery City, 2483 F-15
Morehouse, 990 L-19
MORGAN CO., 20000 G-12
Morley, 806 K-20
Mound City, 1131 B-7
Mtn. Grove, 4563 K-14
Mtn. View, 2451 K-15
Mt. Vernon, 4227 K-10
Murphy, 9048 *H-3
Naylor, 608 L-17
Neosho, 10714 K-9
Nevada, 8411 I-9
Newburg, 481 I-14
New Florence, 783 F-15
New Franklin, 1104 F-13
New Haven, 1895 G-16
New London, 986 D-16
NEW MADRID CO., 19187 L-19
New Madrid, 3223 L-20
NEWTON CO., 54033 K-9
Nixa, 13906 K-11
NODAWAY CO., 21743 B-8
Noel, 1452 L-9
Norborne, 795 E-11
Normandy, 5139 *D-6
N. Kansas City, 4728 H-3
Northwoods, 4542 *D-6
Novinger, 526 B-13
Oak Grove, 391 H-16
Oak Grove, 6552 F-10
Oakland, 1537 *F-5
Oakville, 35309 *H-6
Odessa, 4846 F-10
O Fallon, 63677 F-17
Olivette, 7508 *E-5
Olympian Vil., 687 H-18
Oran, 1247 K-19
OREGON CO., 10301 L-16
Oregon, 908 C-8
Orrick, 875 E-10
OSAGE CO., 13134 G-14
Osage Beach, 3949 H-13
Osceola, 822 H-11
Overland, 16438 *D-4
Owensville, 2519 G-15
OZARK CO., 9498 L-13
Ozark, 13070 K-12
Pacific, 5702 G-17
Pagedale, 3502 *E-5
Palmyra, 3476 C-15
Paris, 1494 D-14
Park Hills, 8322 I-17
Parkville, 4892 E-8
Parma, 828 L-19
Pasadena Hills, 1134 *D-6
Peculiar, 3331 F-9
PEMISCOT CO., 19729 M-19
PERRY CO., 18225 I-19
Perry, 651 D-15
Perryville, 7777 I-19
PETTIS CO., 39344 F-11
Pevely, 4036 H-18
PHELPS CO., 41668 I-15
Piedmont, 1956 K-17
Pierce City, 1401 K-10
PIKE CO., 18519 D-16
Pilot Gr., 735 F-12
Pilot Knob, 672 I-17
Pine Lawn, 4143 *D-6
Pineville, 770 L-9
PLATTE CO., 79390 D-8
Platte City, 4836 E-8
Plattsburg, 2448 D-9
Pleasant Hill, 6176 F-9
Pleasant Valley, 3390 G-5
Point Lookout, 1200 *J-9
POLK CO., 28081 I-11
Poplar Bluff, 16583 L-18
Portage Des Sioux, 349 *A-5
Portageville, 3186 M-19
Potosi, 2687 I-17
Princeton, 979 B-11
PULASKI CO., 45254 I-14
Purdy, 1110 L-10
PUTNAM CO., 5148 A-12
Puxico, 1142 K-18
Queen City, 638 B-13
RALLS CO., 9653 D-15
RANDOLPH CO., 25045 D-13
RAY CO., 23926 E-10
Raymore, 13221 F-9
Raytown, 29747 F-9
Republic, 9680 K-11
REYNOLDS CO., 6581 J-16
Rich Hill, 1494 H-9
Richland, 1831 I-13
Richmond, 6078 E-10
Richmond Hts., 9438 *E-5
RIPLEY CO., 13781 L-17
Riverside, 2962 G-3
Riverview, 3064 *C-7
Rock Hill, 4765 *F-5
Rock Port, 1359 B-7
Rogersville, 1744 K-12
Rolla, 17266 I-15
Russellville, 737 G-13
St. Ann, 13408 *D-5
ST. CHARLES CO., 311531 F-17
St. Charles, 61253 F-18
ST. CLAIR CO., 9679 H-10
St. Clair, 4420 G-16
STE. GENEVIEVE CO., 18094 I-18
Ste. Genevieve, 4463 H-19
ST. FRANCOIS CO., 57929 I-17
St. George, 1260 *G-5
St. James, 3941 H-15
St. John, 6704 *D-5
St. Joseph, 72663 D-8
ST. LOUIS CO., 1013123 G-17
St. Louis, 332223 ‡G-18
St. Peters, 53397 F-17
St. Robert, 3037 I-14
Salem, 4743 I-15
SALINE CO., 22887 E-12
Salisbury, 1663 D-13
Sappington, 7287 *G-5
Sarcoxie, 1347 K-10
Savannah, 4887 C-8
SCHUYLER CO., 4209 B-13
SCOTLAND CO., 4905 B-14
SCOTT CO., 40779 K-20
Scott City, 4570 J-20
Sedalia, 20048 F-12
Senath, 1632 M-18
Seneca, 2161 L-9
Seymour, 1905 K-13
SHANNON CO., 8293 K-15
Shelbina, 1891 D-14
SHELBY CO., 6702 C-14
Shelbyville, 681 C-14
Shrewsbury, 6509 *F-5
Sikeston, 16960 K-20
Slater, 1950 E-12
Smithton, 495 G-12
Smithville, 6206 E-9
S. West City, 868 L-8
Spanish Lake, 21337 *C-7
Sparta, 1207 K-12
Springfield, 150867 K-11
Stanberry, 1199 B-9
Steele, 2197 N-19
Steelville, 1445 H-16
Stewartsville, 746 D-9
Stockton, 1954 I-10
STODDARD CO., 29626 L-19
STONE CO., 29941 L-11
Stover, 1000 G-12
Strafford, 1884 J-12
Sturgeon, 941 E-14
Sugar Cr., 3706 I-5
SULLIVAN CO., 7080 B-12
Sullivan, 6486 H-16
Sunset Hills, 8367 *G-4
Sweet Sprs., 1546 F-11
Sycamore Hills, 711 *D-5
TANEY CO., 41403 L-12
Taos, 850 G-14
Tarkio, 1883 B-7
TEXAS CO., 24142 J-14
Thayer, 2133 L-15
Tipton, 3197 G-13
Trenton, 6123 C-11
Troy, 8317 F-16
Union, 8421 G-16
Unionville, 1984 B-12
University City, 37757 *E-5
Valley Park, 6382 *G-3
Van Buren, 833 K-16
Vandalia, 4097 E-15
Velda City, 1576 *D-6
Velda Vil. Hills, 1078 *D-6
VERNON CO., 20283 I-9
Verona, 722 K-10
Versailles, 2631 G-12
Viburnum, 812 I-16
Vienna, 620 H-14
Vinita Park, 1871 *D-5
Wardsville, 953 G-14
WARREN CO., 26862 F-16
Warrensburg, 17075 F-10
Warrenton, 6016 F-16
Warsaw, 2139 H-11
Warson Woods, 1942 *F-4
WASHINGTON CO., 23884 H-16
Washington, 13608 G-16
Waverly, 809 E-11
WAYNE CO., 13090 K-18
Waynesville, 3572 I-14
Weatherby Lake, 1882 G-2
Webb City, 10251 K-9
WEBSTER CO., 33124 J-12
Webster Groves, 23164 *F-5
Wellington, 784 E-10
Wellston, 2389 *E-6
Wellsville, 1401 E-15
Wentzville, 12253 F-17
Weston, 1649 D-8
W. Plains, 10930 L-15
Wilbur Park, 474 *F-6
Wildwood, 34145 *F-1
Willard, 3253 J-11
Willow Sprs., 2080 K-14
Winchester, 1620 *F-3
Windsor, 3258 G-11
Winfield, 800 F-17
Winona, 1298 K-16
Woods Heights, 774 E-10
Woodson Ter., 4175 *D-5
WORTH CO., 2270 B-9
WRIGHT CO., 18186 J-13
Wright City, 1941 F-16

Montana

Map pp. 122-125

Absarokee, 1234 I-11
Alberton, 393 F-3
Anaconda, 8953 H-6
Ashland, 464 I-16
Augusta, 284 E-6
Baker, 1647 G-20
BEAVERHEAD CO., 8919 K-6
Belfry, 219 J-12
Belgrade, 6816 I-8
Belt, 615 E-9
Bigfork, 1421 C-4
BIG HORN CO., 12894 J-13
Big Sandy, 658 C-10
Big Sky, 1221 J-8
Big Timber, 1695 I-10
Billings, 95220 I-13
Billings Heights, 6000 M-19
Black Eagle, 914 E-8
BLAINE CO., 6729 C-12
Boulder, 1363 H-7
Box Elder, 794 C-10
Bozeman, 30753 I-9
Bridger, 759 J-12
Broadus, 446 I-18
BROADWATER CO., 4430 G-8
Brockton, 241 C-18
Browning, 1066 B-6
Busby, 695 I-15
Butte, 32519 H-6
CARBON CO., 9770 J-12
CARTER CO., 1333 I-19
CASCADE CO., 79561 F-8
Cascade, 800 E-8
Charlo, 439 E-4
Chester, 833 B-9
Chinook, 1325 B-11
Choteau, 1776 D-7
CHOUTEAU CO., 5576 C-8
Circle, 593 E-17
Clyde Park, 333 I-9
Colstrip, 2382 H-16
Columbia Falls, 3963 C-4
Columbus, 1890 I-12
Conrad, 2657 C-7
Coram, 337 C-4
Corvallis, 443 G-4
Crow Agency, 1552 I-14
Culbertson, 708 C-19
CUSTER CO., 11369 H-17
Custer, 145 H-14
Cut Bank, 3096 B-7
DANIELS CO., 1940 A-17
Darby, 785 H-4
DAWSON CO., 8776 E-18
DEER LODGE CO., 8953 H-5
Deer Lodge, 3324 G-6
Denton, 293 E-10
Dillon, 4035 J-6
Drummond, 327 G-5
Dutton, 385 D-8
E. Glacier Park, 396 C-5
E. Helena, 1682 G-7
Ekalaka, 401 H-19
Ennis, 884 J-7
Eureka, 1009 A-2
Evergreen, 6215 C-4
Fairfield, 652 E-7
Fairview, 671 D-20
FALLON CO., 2752 H-19
Fallon, 138 F-18
FERGUS CO., 11695 E-12
FLATHEAD CO., 79485 D-5
Forest Park, 1000 F-19
Forsyth, 1914 H-16
Ft. Belknap Agency, 1262 C-12
Ft. Benton, 1502 D-9
Ft. Peck, 229 C-16
Frazer, 452 C-17
Fromberg, 498 J-12
GALLATIN CO., 73243 J-8
Gardiner, 851 K-9
GARFIELD CO., 1233 F-15
Geraldine, 266 E-10
Gildford, 185 B-10
GLACIER CO., 13250 A-6
Glasgow, 3122 C-16
Glendive, 4717 F-19
GOLDEN VALLEY CO., 1047 G-11
GRANITE CO., 2894 G-5
Great Falls, 56155 E-8
Hamilton, 4163 H-4
Hardin, 3448 I-14
Harlem, 828 B-12
Harlowton, 977 G-11
Havre, 9448 B-11
Havre North, 973 B-11
Hays, 702 D-12
Helena, 26718 G-7
HILL CO., 16350 C-10
Hobson, 231 F-11
Hot Sprs., 531 D-3
Hungry Horse, 934 C-4
Hysham, 281 H-15
JEFFERSON CO., 10499 H-7
Joliet, 586 J-12
Jordan, 353 E-15
JUDITH BASIN CO., 2192 F-9
Kalispell, 16391 C-4
LAKE CO., 27197 D-3
Lakeside, 1679 C-4
Lame Deer, 2018 I-16
Laurel, 6292 I-12
LEWIS AND CLARK CO., 57137 E-6
Lewistown, 5923 F-11
Libby, 2606 B-2
LIBERTY CO., 2055 B-9
Lima, 231 K-6
LINCOLN CO., 18835 B-2
Lincoln, 1100 F-6
Livingston, 7073 I-9
Lockwood, 4306 I-13
Lodge Grass, 518 J-15
Lolo, 3388 F-4
MADISON CO., 6967 J-7
Malta, 1974 C-14
Manhattan, 1447 I-8
Martin City, 331 C-4
MCCONE CO., 1818 D-17
MEAGHER CO., 1967 F-8
Medicine Lake, 239 B-19
Miles City, 8242 G-17
Milltown, 175 F-4
MINERAL CO., 3884 F-3
MISSOULA CO., 98616 F-4
Missoula, 60722 F-4
MUSSELSHELL CO., 4464 G-13
Nashua, 312 C-16
Noxon, 230 C-1
Orchard Homes, 5199 M-12
Paradise, 184 E-3
PARK CO., 15840 I-9
Park City, 870 I-12
PETROLEUM CO., 491 E-13
Philipsburg, 939 G-5
PHILLIPS CO., 4271 B-13
Pinesdale, 823 G-3
Plains, 1169 E-3
Plentywood, 1855 B-19
Polson, 4497 D-4
PONDERA CO., 6166 C-7
Poplar, 899 C-18
POWDER RIVER CO., 1834 J-17
POWELL CO., 7006 G-6
PRAIRIE CO., 1154 F-17
RAVALLI CO., 38662 H-4
Red Lodge, 2273 J-12
Richey, 180 D-18
RICHLAND CO., 9155 D-19
Roberts, 320 J-12
Ronan, 1900 E-4
ROOSEVELT CO., 10451 C-18
ROSEBUD CO., 9303 G-16
Roundup, 1910 G-13
Rudyard, 275 B-9
Ryegate, 271 H-12
Saco, 206 C-14
St. Ignatius, 796 E-4
St. Regis, 315 E-2
Sand Coulee, 250 E-8
SANDERS CO., 10455 D-2
Savage, 300 E-19
Scobey, 1047 B-17
Seeley Lake, 1436 E-5
Shelby, 3306 B-7
SHERIDAN CO., 3668 A-19
Sheridan, 670 J-7
Sidney, 4512 D-20
SILVER BOW CO., 33208 I-6
Somers, 556 C-4
Stanford, 429 F-10
Stevensville, 1784 G-4
STILLWATER CO., 8459 H-12
Sunburst, 413 B-7
Superior, 886 E-3
SWEET GRASS CO., 3604 H-11
Terry, 589 F-18
TETON CO., 6369 D-6
Thompson Falls, 1323 D-2
Three Forks, 1823 I-8
TOOLE CO., 5337 B-8
Townsend, 1914 H-8
TREASURE CO., 735 H-15
Troy, 963 B-1
Twin Bridges, 405 I-6
Ulm, 750 E-8
Valier, 476 C-7
VALLEY CO., 7349 B-15
Vaughn, 701 E-8
Victor, 859 G-4
Walkerville, 689 H-6
Westby, 153 A-20
W. Glacier, 425 B-4
W. Yellowstone, 1213 K-8
WHEATLAND CO., 2106 H-11
Whitefish, 5784 C-4
Whitehall, 1100 I-7
White Sulphur Sprs., 1010 G-9
WIBAUX CO., 977 F-19
Wibaux, 520 F-20
Wolf Pt., 2619 C-17
Worden, 506 H-13
YELLOWSTONE CO., 133191 H-13

Nebraska

Map pp. 126-129

ADAMS CO., 30890 L-13
Ainsworth, 1817 F-10
Albion, 1711 H-14
Alda, 659 K-13
Alliance, 8579 G-3
Alma, 1174 M-11
Ansley, 500 J-11
ANTELOPE CO., 7211 G-14
Arapahoe, 995 M-10
Arlington, 1222 I-18
Arnold, 624 I-9
ARTHUR CO., 398 I-5
Ashland, 2380 J-18
Atkinson, 1188 F-12
Auburn, 3125 L-19
Aurora, 4247 K-14
Axtell, 721 L-12
BANNER CO., 774 I-1
Bassett, 681 F-11
Battle Cr., 1168 H-15
Bayard, 1193 H-2
Beatrice, 12945 M-17
Beaver City, 620 M-10
Beemer, 736 H-17
Bellevue, 46734 J-19
Benkelman, 962 M-6
Bennet, 651 K-18
Bennington, 916 I-18
Bertrand, 814 L-11
BLAINE CO., 533 H-9
Blair, 7798 I-18
Bloomfield, 1075 F-15
Blue Hill, 829 M-13
BOONE CO., 5923 H-14
BOX BUTTE CO., 11669 G-2
BOYD CO., 2330 E-12
Boys Town, 869 J-18
Bridgeport, 1536 H-3
Broken Bow, 3385 I-10
BROWN CO., 3490 F-10
BUFFALO CO., 43043 K-12
BURT CO., 7562 H-18
Burwell, 1082 H-12
BUTLER CO., 8899 J-16
Butte, 353 E-12
Cairo, 786 K-13
Callaway, 630 J-10
Cambridge, 1014 M-9
CASS CO., 25242 K-18
CEDAR CO., 9242 F-16
Cedar Bluffs, 612 I-17
Central City, 2946 J-14
Ceresco, 893 J-17
Chadron, 5598 E-3
Chappell, 959 J-4
CHASE CO., 4041 L-5
CHERRY CO., 6053 F-7
CHEYENNE CO., 9940 J-2
Clarkson, 681 H-16
CLAY CO., 6896 L-14
Clay Cen., 839 L-14
Coleridge, 510 F-16
COLFAX CO., 10497 I-16
Columbus, 20880 I-16
Cozad, 4229 K-10
Crawford, 1071 E-2
Creighton, 1219 F-14
Crete, 6321 L-17
Crofton, 723 E-15
Culbertson, 573 M-8
CUMING CO., 9863 H-17
Curtis, 770 L-8
CUSTER CO., 11542 J-10
DAKOTA CO., 20492 F-17
Dakota City, 1883 F-18
David City, 2618 J-16
DAWES CO., 8985 E-3
DAWSON CO., 24598 K-10
Decatur, 598 G-18
Deshler, 817 M-15
DEUEL CO., 2053 J-5
De Witt, 577 L-17
DIXON CO., 6121 F-17
DODGE CO., 35961 I-17
Dodge, 682 H-17
Doniphan, 764 K-13
Dorchester, 626 L-16
DOUGLAS CO., 476703 J-18
DUNDY CO., 2225 M-6
Eagle, 1134 K-18
Edgar, 522 L-14
Elgin, 706 H-14
Elkhorn, 7869 J-18
Elm Cr., 884 K-11
Elmwood, 711 K-18
Elwood, 739 L-10
Emerson, 817 G-17
Exeter, 685 L-16
Fairbury, 4112 M-16
Fairmont, 667 L-15
Falls City, 4375 M-20
FILLMORE CO., 6425 L-15
Ft. Calhoun, 906 I-19
FRANKLIN CO., 3442 M-12
Franklin, 990 M-12
Fremont, 25198 I-18
Friend, 1176 L-16
FRONTIER CO., 2904 L-8
Fullerton, 1287 I-14
FURNAS CO., 5196 M-9
GAGE CO., 23363 L-17
GARDEN CO., 2193 I-5
GARFIELD CO., 1841 H-12
Geneva, 2164 L-15
Genoa, 905 I-15
Gering, 7832 H-1
Gibbon, 1792 K-12
Gordon, 1630 E-5
GOSPER CO., 2089 L-10
Gothenburg, 3631 K-9
Grand Island, 43771 K-13
GRANT CO., 695 H-5
Grant, 1158 K-6
GREELEY CO., 2603 I-13
Greeley, 501 I-13
Gretna, 3924 J-18
HALL CO., 54293 K-13
HAMILTON CO., 9478 K-14
HARLAN CO., 3664 M-11
Hartington, 1606 F-16
Harvard, 969 L-14
Hastings, 23536 L-13
HAYES CO., 1104 L-7
Hay Sprs., 602 E-4
Hebron, 1469 M-15
Hemingford, 946 G-3
Henderson, 999 K-15
Hershey, 561 J-7
Hickman, 1229 L-17
HITCHCOCK CO., 3031 M-7
Holdrege, 5521 L-11
HOLT CO., 11078 G-12
Homer, 603 F-18
HOOKER CO., 737 H-7
Hooper, 799 I-17
HOWARD CO., 6632 J-13
Howells, 631 H-16
Humboldt, 885 M-19
Humphrey, 761 H-15
Imperial, 1969 L-6
Indianola, 622 M-9
JEFFERSON CO., 8082 M-16
JOHNSON CO., 4429 L-18
KEARNEY CO., 6862 L-12
Kearney, 28211 K-12
KEITH CO., 8472 J-6
Kenesaw, 853 L-13
KEYA PAHA CO., 953 E-10
KIMBALL CO., 3853 J-1
Kimball, 2396 J-1
KNOX CO., 9054 F-15
LANCASTER CO., 260995 K-17
Laurel, 939 F-16
La Vista, 13895 D-17
Lexington, 10113 K-10
LINCOLN CO., 34802 K-7
Lincoln, 235594 K-17
LOGAN CO., 710 I-9
Louisville, 1061 J-18
LOUP CO., 744 H-11
Loup City, 929 J-12
Lyons, 923 H-18
Macy, 956 G-18
MADISON CO., 35777 H-15
Madison, 2344 H-15
McCook, 7847 M-8
MCPHERSON CO., 542 I-7
MERRICK CO., 8134 J-14
Milford, 2067 K-16
Minatare, 792 H-2
Minden, 2952 L-12
Mitchell, 1804 H-1
MORRILL CO., 5284 H-3
Morrill, 936 G-1
Mullen, 456 G-7
NANCE CO., 3741 I-14
Nebraska City, 7113 K-19
Neligh, 1591 G-14
Nelson, 557 M-14
NEMAHA CO., 7136 L-19
Newman Gr., 788 H-15
Norfolk, 24061 G-15
N. Bend, 1199 I-17
N. Platte, 23924 J-8
NUCKOLLS CO., 4841 M-14
Oakland, 1310 H-18
Ogallala, 4773 J-6
Omaha, 404267 J-19
O Neill, 3596 F-13
Ord, 2220 I-12
Osceola, 915 J-15
Oshkosh, 839 I-4
Osmond, 769 F-15
OTOE CO., 15504 K-18
Overton, 654 K-11
Oxford, 849 M-10
Papillion, 17829 J-19
PAWNEE CO., 2918 N-18
Pawnee City, 966 M-19
Paxton, 561 J-7
Pender, 1135 G-17
PERKINS CO., 3057 K-6
Peru, 846 L-19
PHELPS CO., 9630 L-11
PIERCE CO., 7713 G-15
Pierce, 1750 G-15
Plainview, 1314 F-15
PLATTE CO., 31197 I-15
Plattsmouth, 7031 J-19
POLK CO., 5478 J-15
Ponca, 1033 F-17
Ralston, 6241 C-17
Randolph, 908 F-16
Ravenna, 1308 J-12
Red Cloud, 1062 M-13
RED WILLOW CO., 11252 M-8
RICHARDSON CO., 9008 M-19
ROCK CO., 1613 G-11
Rushville, 926 E-4
St. Edward, 757 I-14
St. Paul, 2257 J-13
SALINE CO., 14189 L-16
Sargent, 624 I-11
SARPY CO., 132476 J-18
SAUNDERS CO., 20008 J-17
Schuyler, 5381 I-16
SCOTTS BLUFF CO., 36954 H-1
Scottsbluff, 14774 H-1
SEWARD CO., 16671 K-16
Seward, 6752 K-16
Shelby, 662 J-15
Shelton, 1142 K-13
SHERIDAN CO., 5808 F-4
SHERMAN CO., 3127 J-12
Sidney, 6443 J-3
SIOUX CO., 1491 F-1
S. Sioux City, 12030 F-18
Spalding, 520 H-13
Spencer, 518 E-13
Springfield, 1482 J-18
STANTON CO., 6582 H-16
Stanton, 1645 H-16
Stromsburg, 1179 J-15
Stuart, 597 F-12
Superior, 1946 M-14
Sutherland, 1189 J-7
Sutton, 1429 L-15
Syracuse, 1812 K-18
Tecumseh, 1707 L-18
Tekamah, 1842 H-18
Terrytown, 669 H-1
THAYER CO., 5662 M-15
THOMAS CO., 669 H-8
THURSTON CO., 7142 G-17
Tilden, 1083 G-15
Trenton, 488 M-7
Utica, 835 K-16
Valentine, 2784 E-8
VALLEY CO., 4572 I-12
Valley, 1823 I-18
Verdigre, 501 F-14
Wahoo, 4010 J-17
Wakefield, 1336 G-17
Walthill, 893 G-18
WASHINGTON CO., 19690 I-18
Wauneta, 608 L-7
Waverly, 2598 K-18
WAYNE CO., 9474 G-16
Wayne, 5391 G-16
WEBSTER CO., 3867 M-13
Weeping Water, 1130 K-18
W. Point, 3545 H-17
WHEELER CO., 821 H-13
Wilber, 1790 L-17
Winnebago, 779 G-18
Wisner, 1222 H-17
Wood River, 1202 K-13
Wymore, 1629 M-17
YORK CO., 14363 K-15
York, 7873 K-15
Yutan, 1199 J-18

Nevada

Map pp. 130-131

* City keyed to p. 28
† City keyed to p. 133
‡ Independent city: Not included in any county.

Alamo, 400 J-8
Austin, 350 F-5
Battle Mtn., 2871 D-6
Beatty, 1154 K-6
Blue Diamond, 282 L-8
Boulder City, 15314 L-9
Caliente, 1131 I-9
Carlin, 2060 D-7
Carson City, 55311 ‡F-2
CHURCHILL CO., 24773 F-4
CLARK CO., 1576541 K-8
Crystal Bay, 1500 F-1
Dayton, 5907 F-2
DOUGLAS CO., 44110 G-2
East Las Vegas, 11087 L-4
ELKO CO., 44094 C-7
Elko, 16075 C-7
Ely, 3691 F-9
ESMERALDA CO., 858 I-5
EUREKA CO., 1513 E-6
Eureka, 600 F-7
Fallon, 7748 F-3
Fernley, 10047 F-2
Gabbs, 318 G-4
Gardnerville, 3357 G-2
Hawthorne, 3311 H-3
Henderson, 214852 L-9
HUMBOLDT CO., 14709 C-4
Incline Village, 5500 *A-2
Indian Sprs., 1302 K-8
Jackpot, 600 A-9
LANDER CO., 5049 E-6
Las Vegas, 517017 L-8
Laughlin, 7076 N-9
LINCOLN CO., 4264 I-9
Logandale, 1000 K-9
Lovelock, 1898 E-3
Lund, 200 G-8
LYON CO., 40126 F-2
Mason, 400 G-2
McGill, 1054 F-9
Mesquite, 11780 K-10
Mina, 350 H-4
Minden, 2836 G-2
MINERAL CO., 4791 H-3
N. Las Vegas, 144502 L-8
NYE CO., 35717 H-6
Overton, 1200 K-9
Owyhee, 1017 A-7
Pahrump, 24631 L-7
Panaca, 600 I-9
PERSHING CO., 6444 D-3
Pioche, 800 I-9
Reno, 193882 F-2
Ruth, 500 F-8
Schurz, 721 G-3
Silver Sprs., 4708 F-2
South Hills, 1100 †J-2
Sparks, 77295 F-2
Spring Creek, 10548 D-8
Spring Valley, 117390 L-2
Stateline, 1215 G-1
STOREY CO., 3511 F-2
Summit Village, 1000 *C-3
Sunrise Manor, 156120 K-4
Sun Valley, 19461 †G-2
Tonopah, 2627 H-5
Verdi, 1500 F-1
Virginia City, 930 F-2
Wadsworth, 881 F-2
Walker Lake, 400 G-3
WASHOE CO., 370853 D-2
Wells, 1281 C-8
West Wendover, 4857 D-10
WHITE PINE CO., 8490 F-8
Winnemucca, 6570 C-5
Yerington, 3127 G-3
Zephyr Cove, 1000 G-1

New Hampshire

Map pp. 132-133

Alstead, 500 L-4
Alton, 1000 J-8
Alton Bay, 900 J-8
Amherst, 900 M-7
Antrim, 1389 L-6
Ashland, 1500 I-7
Atkinson, 900 M-9
Bartlett, 900 G-8
Bedford, 1800 M-7
BELKNAP CO., 60356 J-8
Belmont, 1200 J-7
Bennington, 850 L-6
Berlin, 10122 E-8
Bethlehem, 800 F-7
Bow, 700 L-7
Bradford, 600 K-6
Bristol, 1670 I-7
Campton, 700 H-7
Canaan, 700 I-6
Canobie Lake, 700 M-8
CARROLL CO., 46134 G-9
Center Hbr., 650 I-8
Cen. Ossipee, 600 I-9
Charlestown, 1145 K-4
CHESHIRE CO., 75965 L-4
Chester, 600 M-8
Claremont, 13355 K-4
Colebrook, 1100 C-7
Concord, 41823 K-7
Contoocook, 1444 K-7
Conway, 1692 H-9
COOS CO., 33019 D-8
Danville, 700 M-9
Derry, 22661 M-8
Dover, 28216 K-10
Dublin, 650 M-5
Durham, 9024 L-9
E. Derry, 850 M-8
E. Hampstead, 1400 M-9
Enfield, 1698 I-5
Epping, 1673 L-9
Exeter, 9759 L-9
Farmington, 3468 J-9
Fitzwilliam, 650 M-5
Franconia, 600 F-7
Franklin, 8613 J-7
Fremont, 900 L-9
Gilmanton, 700 J-8
Gilsum, 400 L-5
Goffstown, 3200 L-7
Gorham, 1773 F-8
GRAFTON CO., 84038 H-6
Greenfield, 900 M-6
Greenland, 1400 L-10
Greenville, 1131 M-6
Groveton, 1197 E-7
Hampstead, 900 M-9
Hampton, 9126 M-10
Hampton Beach, 600 M-10
Hampton Falls, 550 M-10
Hanover, 8162 I-5
Henniker, 1627 K-6
HILLSBOROUGH CO., 394663 M-6
Hillsborough, 1842 L-6
Hinsdale, 1713 M-4
Hooksett, 3609 L-8
Hudson, 7814 M-8
Jaffrey, 2802 M-6
Keene, 22780 M-5
Kingston, 1400 M-9
Laconia, 17134 J-7
Lancaster, 1695 E-7
Lebanon, 12792 I-5
Lincoln, 900 G-7
Lisbon, 1070 G-6
Little Boars Head, 120 L-10
Littleton, 4431 F-6
Londonderry, 11417 M-8
Manchester, 108871 L-8
Marlborough, 1089 M-5
Meredith, 1739 I-7
MERRIMACK CO., 143622 K-6
Merrimack, 2400 M-7
Milford, 8293 M-7
Milton, 1100 J-9
Nashua, 87285 M-7
Newfields, 700 L-9
New Ipswich, 800 N-6
New London, 1400 J-6
Newmarket, 5124 L-9
Newport, 4008 K-5
Newton, 650 M-9
N. Branch, 150 L-6
N. Conway, 2069 G-9
Northfield, 1500 J-7
N. Hampton, 500 L-10
N. Salem, 300 M-8
N. Stratford, 400 D-7
N. Walpole, 800 L-4
N. Woodstock, 600 G-7
Peterborough, 2944 M-6
Pinardville, 5779 B-4
Pittsfield, 1669 K-8
Plaistow, 2200 M-9
Plymouth, 3528 I-7
Portsmouth, 21002 L-10
Raymond, 2839 L-8
Rochester, 29654 K-9
ROCKINGHAM CO., 290102 L-8
Rollinsford, 1500 K-10
Rye, 850 L-10
Rye Beach, 450 L-10
Salem, 12000 M-8
Sanbornville, 1200 J-9
Seabrook, 900 M-10
Somersworth, 11786 K-10
S. Hooksett, 5282 L-8
STRAFFORD CO., 117740 K-9
Stratham, 800 L-9
SULLIVAN CO., 42048 K-4
Sunapee, 1000 J-5
Suncook, 5362 L-8
Tamworth, 600 H-8
Tilton, 1300 J-7
Troy, 1200 M-5
Twin Mtn., 300 F-7
Walpole, 800 L-4
Warner, 750 K-6
Warren, 550 H-6
W. Chesterfield, 550 M-4
Westport, 500 M-4
W. Swanzey, 1118 M-4
Westville, 400 M-9
Whitefield, 1089 F-7
Wilton, 1236 M-7
Winchester, 1832 M-4
Winnisquam, 650 J-7
Wolfeboro, 2979 J-8
Wolfeboro Falls, 600 I-8
Woodsville, 1081 G-6

New Jersey

Map pp. 134-137

* City keyed to pp. 146-148
‡ City keyed to p. 182

Aberdeen, 18723 H-12
Absecon, 7835 P-10
Allendale, 6775 D-12
Allentown, 1859 J-10
Alpha, 2488 G-6
Alpine, 2303 D-14
Asbury Park, 16693 J-13
Atco, 3500 N-8
ATLANTIC CO., 263410 P-8
Atlantic City, 40385 Q-10
Atlantic Highlands, 4644 H-13
Audubon, 9118 M-7
Avalon, 2155 S-9
Avenel, 17552 G-11
Avon-By-The-Sea, 2233 J-13
Barrington, 7072 M-7
Basking Ridge, 4000 F-10
Bayonne, 60905 F-12
Beachwood, 10712 L-12
Belford, 1340 H-13

Belleville, 35928 .... E-12
Bellmawr, 11261 .... M-6
Belmar, 5975 .... J-13
Belvidere, 2777 .... E-7
BERGEN CO., 897569 .... C-12
Bergenfield, 26181 .... D-13
Berkeley Hts., 13407 .... F-10
Berlin, 6819 .... M-7
Bernardsville, 7559 .... F-10
Beverly, 2680 .... K-7
Blackwood, 4692 .... M-7
Bloomfield, 47683 .... E-12
Bloomingdale, 7693 .... D-11
Bogota, 8181 .... A-5
Boonton, 8427 .... E-11
Bordentown, 4013 .... K-9
Bound Brook, 10151 .... G-10
Bradley Beach, 4770 .... J-13
Bridgeton, 22785 .... P-6
Bridgewater, 7000 .... G-9
Brielle, 4994 .... K-13
Brigantine, 12631 .... P-11
Brooklawn, 2336 .... ‡G-5
Brookwood, 4000 .... K-11
Browns Mills, 11257 .... L-10
Browntown, 2400 .... I-11
Budd Lake, 8100 .... E-9
Buena, 3832 .... P-7
BURLINGTON CO., 444381 .... M-9
Burlington, 9809 .... K-8
Butler, 8099 .... D-11
Caldwell, 7620 .... E-11
CAMDEN CO., 513909 .... N-8
Camden, 80089 .... L-6
Candlewood, 4000 .... K-12
CAPE MAY CO., 101845 .... R-8
Cape May, 3923 .... T-7
Cape May Court House, 4704 .... S-8
Carlstadt, 5994 .... B-4
Carneys Pt., 6914 .... N-4
Carteret, 21653 .... G-12
Cedar Gr., 12300 .... E-12
Centre City, 1800 .... M-6
Chatham, 8440 .... F-11
Cheesequake, 300 .... H-11
Cherry Hill, 69319 .... L-7
Chesilhurst, 1756 .... N-8
Cinnaminson, 14583 .... L-7
Clark, 14597 .... G-11
Clayton, 7157 .... N-6
Clementon, 4975 .... M-7
Cliffside Park, 22892 .... E-13
Cliffwood Beach, 3538 .... H-12
Clifton, 79823 .... E-12
Clinton, 2649 .... G-8
Closter, 8541 .... D-13
Collingswood, 14220 .... L-7
Colonia, 17811 .... G-11
Cranford, 22578 .... G-11
Cresskill, 7896 .... D-13
Crestwood Vil., 8392 .... L-11
CUMBERLAND CO., 149306 .... Q-6
Deal, 1071 .... J-13
Delanco, 3316 .... K-7
Delran, 13178 .... L-7
Demarest, 4910 .... *B-11
Denville, 13812 .... E-10
Dover, 18372 .... E-10
Dumont, 17523 .... D-13
Dunellen, 7008 .... G-10
E. Brunswick, 46756 .... H-11
E. Hanover, 9926 .... E-11
E. Newark, 2333 .... D-3
E. Orange, 69212 .... F-12
E. Rutherford, 8697 .... B-4
E. Windsor, 4000 .... J-10
Eatontown, 14124 .... I-13
Edgewater, 9277 .... B-6
Edgewater Park, 2000 .... K-8
Edison, 97597 .... H-11
Egg Hbr. City, 4486 .... O-9
Elizabeth, 123215 .... F-12
Elmer, 1370 .... O-6
Elmwood Park, 18964 .... A-3
Emerson, 7284 .... D-13
Englewood, 26106 .... E-13
Englewood Cliffs, 5564 .... E-13
Espanong, 3000 .... D-9
ESSEX CO., 796313 .... E-12
Ewing, 35707 .... J-8
Fairfield, 7063 .... E-11
Fair Haven, 5949 .... I-13
Fair Lawn, 31585 .... D-12
Fairview, 13379 .... C-6
Fairview, 125 .... M-8
Fairview M-6
Fanwood, 7257 .... G-11
Finderne, 3000 .... G-10
Flemington, 4234 .... H-8
Florence, 5500 .... K-8
Florence N-7
Florham Park, 12508 .... F-11
Folsom, 1977 .... O-8
Fords, 15032 .... H-11
Forked River, 4914 .... M-12
Ft. Lee, 37139 .... E-13
Franklin, 5249 .... C-10
Franklin Lakes, 11142 .... D-12
Freehold, 11465 .... J-11
Frenchtown, 1520 .... H-7
Garfield, 29701 .... E-12
Garwood, 4165 .... *J-3
Gibbsboro, 2481 .... M-7
Gibbstown, 3758 .... M-5
Gilford Park, 8668 .... L-12
Glassboro, 19094 .... N-6
Glendola, 2400 .... J-13
Glen Gardner, 1991 .... F-7
Glen Ridge, 7166 .... C-2
Glen Rock, 11502 .... D-12
GLOUCESTER CO., 266962 .... O-7
Gloucester City, 11435 .... M-6
Green Brook, 2400 .... G-10
Groveville, 2500 .... J-9
Guttenberg, 11038 .... C-5
Hackensack, 43493 .... E-13
Hackettstown, 9366 .... E-8
Haddonfield, 11616 .... M-7
Haledon, 8408 .... D-12
Hamburg, 3495 .... C-10
Hamilton Square, 11000 .... J-9
Hammonton, 12994 .... O-8
Hampton, 1591 .... F-7
Harrington Park, 4830 .... *A-10
Harrison, 14262 .... F-12
Hasbrouck Hts., 11636 .... E-13
Haworth, 3407 .... *B-10
Hawthorne, 18363 .... D-12
Hazlet, 12000 .... H-12
High Bridge, 3816 .... F-8
Highland Park, 14221 .... H-11
Highlands, 5367 .... I-13
Hightstown, 5311 .... J-10
Hillsdale, 10090 .... D-13
Hillside, 21747 .... F-12
Hoboken, 39482 .... F-13
Hopatcong, 16097 .... D-9
Hopewell, 2044 .... I-8
HUDSON CO., 607419 .... F-13
HUNTERDON CO., 128265 .... G-7
Irvington, 60695 .... F-12
Iselin, 16698 .... G-11
Jamesburg, 6477 .... I-10
Jersey City, 239097 .... F-13
Keansburg, 10746 .... H-12
Kearny, 39853 .... F-12
Kendall Park, 9006 .... H-10
Kenilworth, 7736 .... *I-4
Kenvil, 2500 .... E-9
Keyport, 7504 .... H-12
Kinnelon, 9475 .... D-11
Lakehurst, 2582 .... L-11
Lakewood, 36065 .... K-12
Lambertville, 3880 .... I-7
Laurence Hbr., 6227 .... H-12
Lavallette, 2716 .... L-13
Lawrenceville, 4081 .... I-9
Leonardo, 3975 .... H-13
Leonia, 8888 .... B-6
Lincoln Park, 10870 .... D-11
Lincroft, 6255 .... I-12
Linden, 39877 .... G-12
Lindenwold, 17377 .... M-7
Linwood, 7370 .... Q-10
Little Falls, 11793 .... E-12
Little Ferry, 10799 .... B-5
Little Silver, 6123 .... I-13
Livingston, 27391 .... E-11
Lodi, 24182 .... E-13
Long Branch, 31523 .... I-13
Long Valley, 1818 .... F-8
Loveladies, 200 .... N-12
Lyndhurst, 19383 .... E-12
Madison, 15352 .... F-11
Magnolia, 4409 .... M-7
Mahwah, 12000 .... C-12
Manahawkin, 2004 .... N-12
Manasquan, 6413 .... K-13
Manville, 10401 .... G-10
Maple Shade, 18700 .... L-7
Maplewood, 23868 .... *H-4
Margate City, 8328 .... Q-10
Marlton, 10260 .... M-8
Matawan, 8873 .... I-12
Mays Ldg., 2321 .... P-9
Maywood, 9494 .... A-4
Medford, 2400 .... L-8
Medford Lakes, 4205 .... M-8
Mendham, 5130 .... F-9
MERCER CO., 361981 .... I-8
Mercerville, 15000 .... J-9
Merchantville, 3815 .... L-7
Metuchen, 13293 .... G-11
MIDDLESEX CO., 780995 .... I-11
Middlesex, 13992 .... G-10
Middletown, 24000 .... I-12
Midland Park, 6927 .... D-12
Millburn, 19765 .... F-11
Millington, 2500 .... F-10
Milltown, 7175 .... H-10
Millville, 27119 .... P-7
Mine Hill, 2800 .... E-9
MONMOUTH CO., 632274 .... I-12
Monmouth Beach, 3619 .... I-13
Montclair, 38658 .... E-12
Montvale, 7289 .... D-13
Montville, 2600 .... D-11
Moonachie, 2835 .... B-5
Moorestown, 19000 .... L-7
MORRIS CO., 483150 .... E-10
Morris Plains, 5513 .... E-10
Morristown, 18816 .... E-10
Mtn. Lakes, 4307 .... E-11
Mountainside, 6659 .... F-11
Mt. Arlington, 5017 .... D-9
Mt. Ephraim, 4497 .... ‡G-6
Mt. Freedom, 1900 .... E-10
Mt. Holly, 10639 .... L-8
National Park, 3199 .... M-6
Neptune, 19000 .... J-13
Neptune City, 5196 .... J-13
Netcong, 3283 .... E-9
Newark, 277911 .... F-12
New Brunswick, 49803 .... H-10
New Egypt, 2519 .... K-10
Newfield, 1628 .... O-7
New Milford, 16367 .... *B-10
New Providence, 11983 .... F-11
Newton, 8389 .... C-9
N. Arlington, 15209 .... C-3
N. Bergen, 48414 .... E-13
N. Branch, 1300 .... G-9
N. Brunswick, 36287 .... H-10
N. Caldwell, 7380 .... E-12
N. Cape May, 3618 .... T-7
Northfield, 7954 .... Q-10
N. Haledon, 8340 .... D-12
N. Middletown, 3165 .... H-12
N. Plainfield, 21091 .... G-10
Northvale, 4536 .... D-13
N. Wildwood, 4854 .... T-8
Norwood, 6149 .... *A-11
Nutley, 27362 .... E-12
Oakland, 13616 .... D-12
Oaklyn, 4156 .... ‡F-6
OCEAN CO., 546081 .... L-11
Ocean City, 15558 .... Q-10
Oceanport, 5952 .... I-13
Ogdensburg, 2654 .... C-9
Old Bridge, 22833 .... H-11
Old Tappan, 5798 .... D-13
Oradell, 8025 .... D-13
Orange, 32868 .... F-12
Oxford, 2283 .... E-7
Palisades Park, 18007 .... E-13
Palmyra, 7653 .... L-7
Paramus, 26503 .... D-13
PASSAIC CO., 498357 .... C-11
Passaic, 68528 .... E-12
Paterson, 150782 .... D-12
Paulsboro, 6116 .... M-6
Pennington, 2706 .... I-8
Pennsauken, 35737 .... L-7
Penns Gr., 4840 .... N-4
Pennsville, 11657 .... N-4
Pequannock D-11
Perth Amboy, 48447 .... H-11
Phillipsburg, 15177 .... F-6
Pine Beach, 2005 .... L-12
Pine Hill, 11092 .... M-7
Piscataway, 50500 .... G-10
Pitman, 9274 .... N-6
Plainfield, 48025 .... G-11
Plainsboro, 2000 .... I-9
Pleasantville, 19016 .... Q-10
Pompton Lakes, 11085 .... D-11
Port Monmouth, 3742 .... H-12
Port Norris, 1507 .... R-7
Pt. Pleasant, 19835 .... K-13
Pt. Pleasant Beach, 5403 .... K-13
Port Reading, 3829 .... G-12
Princeton, 13577 .... I-9
Princeton Jct., 2382 .... I-9
Rahway, 26779 .... G-11
Ramblewood, 6003 .... L-7
Ramsey, 14490 .... C-12
Raritan, 6357 .... G-9
Red Bank, 11792 .... I-13
Red Bank, 1100 .... ‡G-4
Ridgefield, 10919 .... E-13
Ridgefield Park, 12781 .... B-5
Ridgewood, 24831 .... D-12
Ringwood, 12704 .... C-11
Rio Grande, 2444 .... T-8
Riverdale, 2606 .... D-11
River Edge, 10978 .... D-13
Riverside, 7974 .... K-7
Riverton, 2756 .... L-7
River Vale, 9449 .... D-13
Robertsville, 2500 .... I-11
Rochelle Park, 5528 .... A-4
Rockaway, 6427 .... E-10
Roebling, 3000 .... K-8
Roselle, 21423 .... G-11
Roselle Park, 13310 .... *J-4
Rumson, 7312 .... I-13
Runnemede, 8541 .... M-7
Rutherford, 18020 .... E-12
Saddle Brook, 13155 .... A-4
SALEM CO., 64854 .... O-5
Salem, 5793 .... O-4
Sayreville, 42064 .... H-11
Sayre Woods S., 10000 .... I-11
Scotch Plains, 22732 .... F-11
Sea Bright, 1792 .... I-13
Sea Girt, 2197 .... K-13
Sea Isle City, 2957 .... R-9
Seaside Hts., 3180 .... L-13
Seaside Park, 2292 .... L-13
Secaucus, 15735 .... E-13
Sewaren, 2780 .... *M-4
Sewell, 2000 .... N-6
Shrewsbury, 3726 .... I-13
Silverton, 4800 .... L-12
Slackwoods, 6000 .... J-9
Somerdale, 5185 .... M-7
SOMERSET CO., 311600 .... H-9
Somerset, 23040 .... H-10
Somers Pt., 11618 .... Q-9
Somerville, 12391 .... G-9
S. Amboy, 8032 .... H-11
S. Bound Brook, 4496 .... G-10
S. Hackensack, 2106 .... A-5
S. Orange, 16964 .... F-12
S. Plainfield, 22965 .... G-11
S. River, 16041 .... H-11
S. Toms River, 3703 .... L-12
Sparta, 9755 .... D-9
Spotswood, 8236 .... I-11
Springfield, 14429 .... F-11
Spring Lake, 3679 .... J-13
Spring Lake Hts., 5248 .... J-13
Stanhope, 3688 .... D-9
Stirling, 1800 .... F-10
Stratford, 7246 .... M-7
Succasunna, 4000 .... E-9
Summit, 21262 .... F-11
SUSSEX CO., 151146 .... C-9
Sussex, 2180 .... B-9
Swedesboro, 2049 .... N-5
Teaneck, 39260 .... E-13
Tenafly, 14101 .... D-13
Thorofare, 1700 .... M-6
Tinton Falls, 15975 .... J-13
Toms River, 86327 .... L-12
Totowa, 10030 .... E-12
Trenton, 85314 .... J-8
Tuckerton, 3612 .... O-11
Twin Rivers, 7422 .... J-10
UNION CO., 529360 .... F-11
Union, 54405 .... F-11
Union Beach, 6745 .... H-12
Union City, 66573 .... F-13
Upper Saddle River, 8237 .... C-12
Ventnor City, 12778 .... Q-10
Verona, 13533 .... E-12
Villas, 9064 .... S-7
Vineland, 57057 .... P-7
Waldwick, 9628 .... D-12
Wallington, 11522 .... B-4
Wanaque, 10419 .... C-11
WARREN CO., 109219 .... F-7
Washington, 6829 .... F-7
Watchung, 5738 .... G-10
Wayne, 54069 .... D-12
Weehawken, 12385 .... D-5
Wenonah, 2313 .... M-6
W. Berlin, 3000 .... M-7
Westfield, 29951 .... G-11
W. Long Branch, 8216 .... I-13
W. Milford, 26410 .... C-11
W. New York, 46348 .... E-13
W. Orange, 44943 .... F-12
W. Paterson, 11255 .... A-2
Westville, 4473 .... M-6
Westville Gr., 1500 .... ‡G-5
Westwood, 11010 .... D-13
Wharton, 6223 .... E-10
White Horse, 9373 .... J-9
Whitman Square, 3500 .... N-7
Wildwood, 5260 .... T-8
Wildwood Crest, 3884 .... T-8
Williamstown, 11812 .... N-7
Willingboro, 36291 .... K-8
Woodbine, 2677 .... R-8
Woodbridge, 18309 .... G-11
Woodbury, 10439 .... M-6
Woodbury Hts., 3001 .... M-6
Woodlynne, 2776 .... ‡F-5
Wood-Ridge, 7622 .... B-4
Woodstown, 3260 .... N-5
Wrightstown, 749 .... K-9
Wyckoff, 16508 .... D-12
Yardville, 3500 .... J-9

New Mexico

Map pp. 138-139

Acomita, 800 .... E-3
Adobe Acres, 2500 .... N-7
Agua Fria, 2051 .... M-4
Alameda, 6000 .... E-5
Alamogordo, 35551 .... I-6
Albuquerque, 471856 .... E-5
Alcalde, 377 .... C-5
Alto, 800 .... H-6
Anthony, 7904 .... J-5
Arenas Valley, 500 .... I-2
Arroyo Seco, 500 .... B-6
Artesia, 10518 .... I-8
Aztec, 6818 .... B-3
Bayard, 2419 .... I-2
Belen, 6961 .... F-4
BERNALILLO CO., 581442 .... E-4
Bernalillo, 6986 .... D-5
Black Rock, 1252 .... E-1
Bloomfield, 7210 .... B-3
Bluewater, 500 .... E-3
Bosque Farms, 3898 .... E-5
Capitan, 1500 .... H-6
Carlsbad, 25303 .... J-8
Carrizozo, 1048 .... G-6
Casa Blanca, 669 .... E-3
CATRON CO., 3415 .... G-2
Cedar Crest, 1060 .... E-5
Chama, 1175 .... B-5
Chamisal, 301 .... C-6
Chaparral, 6117 .... J-5
CHAVES CO., 60591 .... H-9
Chimayo, 2924 .... C-6
CIBOLA CO., 26453 .... E-3
Cimarron, 909 .... B-7
Clayton, 2225 .... B-10
Cloudcroft, 724 .... I-6
Clovis, 32815 .... F-10
Cochiti Pueblo, 507 .... D-5
COLFAX CO., 14051 .... B-7
Columbus, 1818 .... K-3
Cordova, 700 .... C-6
Crownpoint, 2630 .... D-2
Cuba, 619 .... C-4
Cubero, 500 .... E-3
CURRY CO., 45440 .... F-10
Datil, 300 .... G-3
DE BACA CO., 2091 .... F-8
Deming, 14381 .... J-3
Dexter, 1216 .... H-8
Dixon, 850 .... C-6
DONA ANA CO., 182165 .... I-4
Dona Ana, 1379 .... J-4
Dulce, 2623 .... B-4
EDDY CO., 51470 .... J-8
Edgewood, 1797 .... E-5
Espanola, 9762 .... C-5
Estancia, 1559 .... E-5
Eunice, 2561 .... J-10
Farmington, 41420 .... B-2
Five Points, 4200 .... M-8
Flora Vista, 1383 .... B-2
Ft. Stanton, 100 .... H-6
Ft. Sumner, 1124 .... F-8
Fruitland, 800 .... B-2
Gallina, 430 .... C-4
Gallup, 19868 .... D-1
Gamerco, 400 .... D-1
Garfield, 200 .... I-4
Gila, 350 .... I-2
GRANT CO., 29818 .... I-1
Grants, 8972 .... E-3
GUADALUPE CO., 4574 .... F-7
Hacienda Acres, 600 .... J-4
Hagerman, 1153 .... H-8
Hanover, 450 .... I-2
HARDING CO., 747 .... C-9
Hatch, 1668 .... I-4
HIDALGO CO., 5234 .... K-1
High Rolls, 450 .... I-6
Hobbs, 28311 .... I-10
Hurley, 1379 .... I-2
Isleta, 1703 .... E-5
Jal, 1980 .... J-10
Jemez Pueblo, 1953 .... D-4
Jemez Sprs., 386 .... D-4
Kirtland, 6190 .... B-2
Laguna, 423 .... E-3
Lake Arthur, 431 .... I-8
Lake Valley, 300 .... C-2
La Luz, 1615 .... I-6
La Mesa, 1000 .... J-4
La Mesilla, 2149 .... J-4
Las Cruces, 76990 .... J-4
Las Vegas, 14194 .... D-7
La Union, 700 .... K-5
LEA CO., 55504 .... H-9
Lemitar, 450 .... G-4
LINCOLN CO., 20322 .... G-6
Logan, 1046 .... D-9
Lordsburg, 2904 .... J-1
LOS ALAMOS CO., 18802 .... C-5
Los Alamos, 11909 .... C-5
Los Lunas, 11265 .... E-4
Los Padillas, 2500 .... E-4
Los Ranchos de Albuquerque, 5156 .... L-8
Loving, 1320 .... J-8
Lovington, 9456 .... I-10
LUNA CO., 25732 .... J-2
Magdalena, 883 .... G-4
McCartys, 300 .... E-3
MCKINLEY CO., 72555 .... D-3
Melrose, 739 .... F-9
Mescalero, 1233 .... H-6
Mesquite, 948 .... J-4
Milan, 1974 .... E-3
MORA CO., 5216 .... C-7
Mora, 1200 .... C-6
Moriarty, 1813 .... E-5
Mountainair, 1078 .... F-5
Nambe, 1246 .... C-6
Navajo, 2097 .... C-1
Ojo Caliente, 350 .... C-5
Organ, 500 .... J-5
OTERO CO., 62371 .... I-6
Paguate, 474 .... E-3
Pajarito, 1500 .... E-4
Pecos, 1424 .... D-6
Pena Blanca, 661 .... D-5
Penasco, 572 .... C-6
Peralta, 3750 .... E-5
Placitas, 3452 .... D-5
Playas, 700 .... J-2
Pojoaque, 1261 .... C-5
Portales, 11078 .... F-10
Prewitt, 460 .... D-3
Pueblo Pintado, 247 .... C-3
QUAY CO., 9605 .... E-9
Questa, 1927 .... B-6
Ramah, 407 .... E-2
Ranchos de Taos, 2390 .... C-6
Raton, 7186 .... B-8
Red River, 489 .... B-6
Reserve, 353 .... G-1
RIO ARRIBA CO., 40731 .... B-4
Rio Rancho, 58981 .... E-5
ROOSEVELT CO., 18107 .... G-9
Roswell, 44228 .... H-8
Roy, 256 .... C-8
Ruidoso, 8270 .... H-6
Ruidoso Downs, 1888 .... H-6
San Antonio, 450 .... G-4
Sandia Park, 700 .... E-5
SANDOVAL CO., 98786 .... D-4
San Felipe Pueblo, 2080 .... D-5
San Jon, 288 .... E-9
SAN JUAN CO., 122272 .... B-2
San Juan Pueblo, 800 .... C-5
SAN MIGUEL CO., 29670 .... D-7
San Rafael, 600 .... E-3
Santa Clara, 1867 .... I-2
Santa Cruz, 423 .... C-5
SANTA FE CO., 136423 .... E-5
Santa Fe, 66476 .... D-6
Santa Rosa, 2637 .... E-7
Santo Domingo Pueblo, 2550 .... D-5
Shiprock, 8156 .... B-2
SIERRA CO., 13125 .... I-4
Silver City, 10052 .... I-2
SOCORRO CO., 18178 .... G-5
Socorro, 8708 .... G-4
Springer, 1265 .... C-8
Sunland Park, 13815 .... K-5
Talpa, 450 .... C-6
TAOS CO., 31269 .... B-6
Taos, 5008 .... C-6
Taos Pueblo, 1264 .... B-6
Tatum, 685 .... H-10
Texico, 1080 .... F-10
Thoreau, 1863 .... D-2
Tierra Amarilla, 700 .... B-5
Tijeras, 468 .... E-5
Tohatchi, 1037 .... C-1
Tome, 600 .... F-4
TORRANCE CO., 16802 .... F-6
Truchas, 500 .... C-6
Truth or Consequences, 7116 .... H-4
Tucumcari, 5564 .... E-9
Tularosa, 2861 .... I-5
Tyrone, 950 .... I-2
UNION CO., 3814 .... B-9
University Park, 3460 .... J-4
Vado, 3003 .... J-4
VALENCIA CO., 67839 .... F-4
Vanderwagen, 300 .... E-1
Vaughn, 508 .... F-7
Velarde, 450 .... C-6
Villanueva, 280 .... E-6
Wagon Mound, 359 .... C-7
Waterflow, 320 .... B-2
Williamsburg, 517 .... H-4
Zuni, 6367 .... E-1

New York

Map pp. 140-149

Index keys SA to SJ refer to Southern NY, pp. 140-141, NA to NN refer to Northern NY, pp. 142-145
* City keyed to pp. 146-149

Adams, 1631 .... NF-12
Adams Center, 1500 .... NF-12
Addison, 1778 .... NM-8
Akron, 3048 .... NI-5
ALBANY CO., 297845 .... NK-18
Albany, 93919 .... NK-19
Albertson, 5200 .... SF-8
Albion, 5839 .... NH-6
Alden, 2674 .... NJ-5
Alexandria Bay, 1093 .... ND-12
Alfred, 4530 .... NL-7
ALLEGANY CO., 50562 .... NL-6
Allegany, 1839 .... NM-5
Altamont, 1721 .... NJ-18
Altona, 1056 .... NA-19
Amagansett, 1067 .... SE-13
Amawalk, 1390 .... SD-7
Amenia, 1115 .... NN-20
Amherst, 45800 .... NI-4
Amityville, 9551 .... SF-8
Amsterdam, 17974 .... NI-18
Andover, 1050 .... NM-7
Angelica, 892 .... NL-6
Angola, 2227 .... NK-3
Angola on the Lake, 1771 .... NK-3
Apalachin, 1126 .... NM-12
Arcade, 1974 .... NK-5
Arlington, 12481 .... SB-7
Armonk, 3461 .... SD-7
Armor, 1550 .... NJ-4
Athens, 1713 .... NL-19
Atlantic Beach, 1981 .... SG-7
Attica, 2525 .... NJ-5
Auburn, 28121 .... NJ-10
Au Sable Forks, 670 .... NC-19
Averill Park, 1517 .... NK-19
Avoca, 991 .... NL-8
Avon, 2977 .... NJ-7
Babylon, 12759 .... SF-9
Bainbridge, 1349 .... NL-14
Baldwin, 23455 .... SG-8
Baldwinsville, 7190 .... NI-11
Ballston Spa, 5565 .... NI-19
Balmville, 3339 .... SB-6
Batavia, 15939 .... NI-6
Bath, 5574 .... NL-8
Baxter Estates, 1002 .... *E-16
Bayberry, 6200 .... ND-7
Bayport, 8662 .... SI-14
Bay Shore, 23852 .... SF-9
Bayville, 7139 .... SE-8
Beacon, 16059 .... SC-6
Bedford, 1724 .... SD-8
Bedford Hills, 3200 .... SD-7
Belfast, 1100 .... NL-6
Bellerose, 1161 .... *H-16
Bellerose Ter., 2157 .... *H-16
Bellport, 2379 .... SF-10
Belmont, 912 .... NL-6
Bergen, 1215 .... NI-6
Berlin, 1200 .... NJ-20
Bethpage, 16543 .... SF-8
Big Flats, 2482 .... NM-9
Big Tree, 1000 .... NJ-4
Binghamton, 46310 .... NM-12
Black River, 1293 .... NE-13
Blasdell, 2638 .... NJ-4
Blauvelt, 5200 .... SE-6
Blooming Gr., 500 .... SC-6
Bloomington, 800 .... NN-18
Blue Pt., 4407 .... SI-14
Boght Corners, 1150 .... SG-5
Bohemia, 9871 .... SI-13
Bolivar, 1154 .... NM-6
Bolton Ldg., 1600 .... NG-19
Boonville, 2102 .... NG-14
Brasher Falls, 750 .... NB-16
Brentwood, 53917 .... SF-9
Brewerton, 3453 .... NH-12
Brewster, 2178 .... SC-8
Briarcliff Manor, 7906 .... SD-7
Bridgehampton, 1381 .... SE-13
Brighton, 35584 .... NC-9
Brightwaters, 3282 .... SF-9
Broadacres, 1280 .... SA-11
Broadalbin, 1401 .... NI-18
Brockport, 8097 .... NH-6
Brocton, 1516 .... NL-2
BRONX CO., 1363198 .... *E-13
Bronxville, 6515 .... *B-13
Brookville, 3395 .... *F-19
BROOME CO., 199360 .... NM-14
Brownville, 1026 .... NE-12
Buchanan, 2224 .... SD-6
Buffalo, 285018 .... NJ-3
Bullville, 900 .... SB-5
Burnt Hills, 1620 .... NI-18
Cadyville, 900 .... NB-19
Cairo, 1390 .... NL-18
Caledonia, 2256 .... NI-7
Calverton, 5704 .... SE-11
Cambridge, 1913 .... NI-20
Camden, 2300 .... NH-13
Camillus, 1233 .... NI-11
Canajoharie, 2212 .... NJ-16
Canandaigua, 11449 .... NJ-8
Canastota, 4445 .... NI-13
Canisteo, 2297 .... NL-7
Canton, 5961 .... NC-15
Carmel, 5650 .... SC-7
Carthage, 3734 .... NE-13
Castile, 1026 .... NK-6
Castleton on Hudson, 1600 .... NK-19
Catskill, 4360 .... NL-19
CATTARAUGUS CO., 83354 .... NL-4
Cattaraugus, 1044 .... NL-3
CAYUGA CO., 81726 .... NJ-11
Cayuga Hts., 3776 .... NK-11
Cazenovia, 2710 .... NJ-13
Cedarhurst, 6121 .... *K-16
Celoron, 1258 .... NM-2
Centereach, 27285 .... SE-10
Cen. Moriches, 6655 .... SF-11
Centerport, 5446 .... SE-9
Central Islip, 31950 .... SF-9
Central Square, 1651 .... NH-12
Central Valley, 1857 .... SC-6
Chadwicks, 2100 .... NI-14
Champlain, 1163 .... NA-20
Champlain Park, 1200 .... NB-20
Chappaqua, 9468 .... SD-7
Chatham, 1787 .... NL-19
CHAUTAUQUA CO., 137645 .... NL-2
Chazy, 1000 .... NA-20
Cheektowaga, 79988 .... NE-5
CHEMUNG CO., 90413 .... NM-10
CHENANGO CO., 51659 .... NK-13
Chenango Bridge, 2890 .... NM-12
Chester, 3521 .... SC-5
Chili Cen., 4350 .... NI-7
Chittenango, 4876 .... NI-13
Churchville, 1908 .... NI-6
Cicero, 1100 .... NI-12
Circleville, 1350 .... SB-5
Clarence, 2100 .... NI-4
Clarence Cen., 1747 .... NI-4
Claverack, 1000 .... NL-19
Clayton, 1830 .... ND-12
Clifton Park, 1200 .... NJ-19
Clifton Sprs., 2196 .... NI-9
CLINTON CO., 81366 .... NB-18
Clinton, 1922 .... NI-14
Clintondale, 1424 .... SB-6
Clinton Park, 880 .... SJ-5
Clyde, 2222 .... NI-10
Cobleskill, 4533 .... NK-17
Coeymans, 835 .... NK-19
Cohoes, 15303 .... NJ-19
Coldenham, 330 .... SB-6
Cold Spr., 1998 .... SC-6
Cold Spring Hbr., 4975 .... SH-10
Colonie, 8080 .... NJ-19
COLUMBIA CO., 63405 .... NL-20
Commack, 36367 .... SF-9
Congers, 8303 .... SD-7
Conklin, 1800 .... NM-13
Constantia, 1107 .... NH-12
Coopers Plains, 750 .... NM-9
Cooperstown, 1936 .... NJ-15
Copake, 1200 .... NM-20
Coram, 34923 .... SE-10
Corinth, 2483 .... NH-19
Corning, 10625 .... NM-9
Cornwall On Hudson, 3110 .... SC-6
CORTLAND CO., 48691 .... NK-12
Cortland, 18462 .... NK-12
Coxsackie, 2876 .... NL-19
Cross River, 980 .... SD-8
Croton Falls, 970 .... SC-8
Croton-on-Hudson, 7801 .... SD-7
Crown Pt., 1000 .... NE-20
Crugers, 1752 .... SD-7
Cuba, 1605 .... NL-5
Cuddebackville, 1100 .... SC-4
Cutchogue, 2849 .... SE-12
Dannemora, 4154 .... NB-19
Dansville, 4705 .... NK-7
Deer Park, 28316 .... SF-9
Defreestville, 960 .... NK-19
DELAWARE CO., 47226 .... NL-15
Delevan, 1064 .... NK-5
Delhi, 2551 .... NL-15
Delmar, 8292 .... NK-19
Depew, 16194 .... NJ-4
Deposit, 1657 .... NM-14
Derby, 1200 .... NJ-3
De Witt, 8244 .... NI-12
Dexter, 1123 .... NE-12
Dix Hills, 26024 .... SH-11
Dobbs Ferry, 11041 .... SE-7
Dolgeville, 2105 .... NI-16
Dover Plains, 1996 .... SA-8
Downsville, 1100 .... NM-15
Dryden, 1867 .... NK-11
Dundee, 1689 .... NK-9
Dunkirk, 12715 .... NK-2
DUTCHESS CO., 290885 .... SA-8
Earlville, 782 .... NJ-13
E. Atlantic Beach, 2257 .... *L-16
E. Aurora, 6493 .... NJ-4
Eastchester, 18564 .... *B-14
E. Glenville, 6064 .... NJ-18
E. Greenbush, 4085 .... NK-19
E. Hampton, 1354 .... SE-13
E. Hills, 6818 .... SF-8
E. Islip, 14078 .... SI-12
E. Marion, 756 .... SD-12
E. Meadow, 37461 .... SF-8
E. Middletown, 6061 .... SC-5
E. Northport, 20845 .... SE-9
E. Norwich, 2675 .... *E-19
Eastport, 1486 .... SF-11
E. Rochester, 6510 .... NI-8
E. Rockaway, 10341 .... *J-17
E. Syracuse, 3118 .... NF-9
Eden, 3579 .... NK-3
Elbridge, 1090 .... NI-11
Elizabethtown, 950 .... ND-19
Ellenville, 4106 .... SA-5
Elma, 2491 .... NJ-4
Elmira, 30336 .... NM-10
Elmira Hts., 4072 .... NM-10
Elmont, 32657 .... SF-7
Elmsford, 4723 .... SH-7
Elsmere, 4200 .... NK-19
Endicott, 12876 .... NM-12
Endwell, 11706 .... NM-12
ERIE CO., 941293 .... NK-3
Escarpment, 1200 .... NA-2
ESSEX CO., 38992 .... NE-19
Fair Haven, 873 .... NH-10
Fairmount, 10795 .... NI-11
Fairport, 5690 .... NI-8
Fairview, 2887 .... SI-7
Falconer, 2470 .... NM-2
Falconwood, 1500 .... ND-2
Farmingdale, 8665 .... SJ-10
Farmingville, 16458 .... SF-10
Fayetteville, 4164 .... NI-12
Ferndale, 850 .... NN-16
Fishkill, 1754 .... SB-7
Flanders, 3643 .... SE-11
Floral Park, 15862 .... *H-16
Florida, 2769 .... SC-5
Flower Hill, 4523 .... *F-16
Fluvanna, 900 .... NM-2
Fonda, 791 .... NI-17
Forestport, 900 .... NG-14
Ft. Covington, 1200 .... NA-16
Ft. Edward, 3115 .... NH-19
Ft. Montgomery, 1418 .... SC-6
Ft. Plain, 2243 .... NJ-16
Ft. Salonga, 9634 .... SG-11
Frankfort, 2462 .... NI-15
FRANKLIN CO., 51056 .... NC-17
Franklin Park, 2600 .... NE-9
Franklin Square, 29342 .... *H-17
Franklinville, 1804 .... NL-5
Fredonia, 10569 .... NK-2
Freeport, 43726 .... SG-8
Frewsburg, 1965 .... NM-3
Friendship, 1176 .... NL-6
FULTON CO., 55206 .... NI-17
Fulton, 11639 .... NH-11
Galeville, 4476 .... NE-8
Gang Mills, 3304 .... NM-9
Garden City, 21787 .... *H-18
Gardiner, 856 .... SB-6
Gardnertown, 4533 .... SB-6
Gasport, 1248 .... NH-4
Gates, 29300 .... NI-7
GENESEE CO., 60020 .... NJ-6
Geneseo, 7916 .... NJ-7
Geneva, 13517 .... NJ-9
Germantown, 862 .... NM-19
Getzville, 2300 .... NI-4
Glasco, 1692 .... NM-18
Glen Cove, 26781 .... SF-8
Glenham, 2000 .... SB-7
Glenmont, 1200 .... NK-19
Glens Falls, 14212 .... NH-19
Glenwood Ldg., 3541 .... *E-17
Gloversville, 15227 .... NI-17
Goldens Bridge, 1578 .... SC-7
Gorham, 950 .... NJ-9
Goshen, 5370 .... SC-5
Gouverneur, 4167 .... ND-14
Gowanda, 2766 .... NK-3
Grand Gorge, 1000 .... NL-17
Grand Island, 800 .... NI-3
Granville, 2620 .... NG-20
Great Neck, 9623 .... SF-7
Great Neck Estates, 2746 .... *F-15
Greece, 65000 .... NH-7
GREENE CO., 48865 .... NL-17
Greene, 1684 .... NL-13
Green Island, 2612 .... NJ-19
Greenlawn, 13286 .... SH-11
Greenport, 2066 .... SD-12
Greenville, 8648 .... SI-7
Greenville, 493 .... NL-18
Greenwich, 1880 .... NI-20
Greenwood Lake, 3454 .... SD-5
Groton, 2497 .... NK-11
Guilderland, 1900 .... SI-2
Hagaman, 1334 .... NI-18
Halesite, 2582 .... SH-10
Half Hollow Hills, 4950 .... SI-11
Hamburg, 9841 .... NJ-4
HAMILTON CO., 5278 .... NF-16
Hamilton, 3556 .... NJ-13
Hammondsport, 712 .... NL-8
Hampton Bays, 12240 .... SE-12
Hancock, 1147 .... NN-14
Hbr. Hills, 563 .... *F-15
Harriman, 2288 .... SC-6
Harris Hill, 4881 .... NI-4
Harrison, 25150 .... SE-7
Hartsdale, 9830 .... SI-7
Hastings-on-Hudson, 7771 .... SE-7
Hauppauge, 20100 .... SH-12
Haverstraw, 10133 .... SD-6
Head of the Hbr., 1503 .... SG-13
Hempstead, 53162 .... SF-8
Henrietta, 1200 .... NI-7
HERKIMER CO., 63704 .... NG-15
Herkimer, 7298 .... NI-15
Hewlett, 7060 .... *J-16
Hicksville, 41260 .... SF-8
Highland, 5060 .... SA-6
Highland Falls, 3766 .... SC-6
Highland Mills, 3468 .... SC-6
Highland-on-the-Lake, 1800 .... NJ-3
Hillcrest, 7106 .... SD-6
Hilton, 5962 .... NH-7
Hinsdale, 900 .... NM-5
Holbrook, 27512 .... SH-13
Holland, 1261 .... NK-4
Holley, 1762 .... NH-6
Holtsville, 17006 .... SH-14
Homer, 3333 .... NK-12
Honeoye Falls, 2602 .... NI-7
Hoosick Falls, 3383 .... NJ-20
Hopewell Jct., 2610 .... SB-7
Hornell, 8817 .... NL-7
Horseheads, 6363 .... NM-10
Houghton, 1748 .... NL-6
Hudson, 7296 .... NL-19
Hudson Falls, 6857 .... NH-19
Hughsonville, 1400 .... SB-7
Huguenot, 800 .... SC-4
Huguenot *M-6
Huntington, 18403 .... SF-8
Huntington, 18403 .... SE-9
Huntington Bay, 1499 .... SG-10
Huntington Sta., 29910 .... SF-9
Hurley, 3561 .... NN-18
Hyde Park, 100 .... NK-15
Hyde Park, 2650 .... NN-18
Ilion, 8370 .... NI-15
Indian Vil., 700 .... NI-12
Inwood, 9325 .... SG-7
Irondequoit, 52354 .... NH-7
Islip, 20575 .... SF-9
Islip Ter., 5641 .... SI-12
Ithaca, 30343 .... NK-11
Jamesport, 1526 .... SE-12
Jamestown, 30726 .... NM-2
JEFFERSON CO., 114651 .... NE-13
Jefferson Valley, 6700 .... SC-7
Jericho, 13045 .... SF-8
Jericho, 100 .... NB-19
Johnson City, 15230 .... NM-12
Johnstown, 8516 .... NI-17
Jordan, 1367 .... NI-11
Katonah, 2400 .... SD-7
Keeseville, 1828 .... NC-19
Kenmore, 15933 .... NI-4
Kensington, 1203 .... *F-15
Kensington *J-11
Kerhonkson, 1732 .... NN-17
Keuka Park, 1200 .... NK-9
Kinderhook, 1292 .... NL-19
KINGS CO., 2472523 .... SG-7
Kings Park, 15976 .... SE-9
Kings Pt., 5175 .... SF-7
Kingston, 23294 .... NN-18
Lackawanna, 18622 .... NJ-4
Lake Carmel, 8663 .... SC-7
Lake Delta, 2020 .... NH-14
Lake Erie Beach, 4499 .... NK-3
Lake George, 987 .... NG-19
Lake Gr., 10602 .... SF-10
Lake Katrine, 2396 .... NM-18
Lakeland, 2852 .... NE-7
Lake Luzerne, 1150 .... NH-19
Lake Peekskill, 2150 .... SC-7
Lake Placid, 2733 .... ND-18
Lake Ronkonkoma, 19701 .... SH-13
Lake Success, 2832 .... *G-16
Lake View, 150 .... NJ-3
Lakeville, 1200 .... NJ-7
Lakewood, 3175 .... NM-2
Lancaster, 11381 .... NJ-4
Lansing, 3474 .... NK-11
Larchmont, 6523 .... SE-7
Lattingtown, 1865 .... SE-8
Lawrence, 6546 .... SG-7
Le Roy, 4373 .... NI-6
Levittown, 53067 .... SF-8
LEWIS CO., 26636 .... NF-13
Lewiston, 2719 .... NH-3
Liberty, 3970 .... NN-16
Lido Beach, 2825 .... SG-8
Lima, 2450 .... NJ-7
Lindenhurst, 28469 .... SF-9
Little Falls, 5049 .... NI-16
Little Valley, 1100 .... NL-4
Liverpool, 2457 .... NE-7
LIVINGSTON CO., 64658 .... NK-7
Livingston Manor, 1355 .... NN-16
Livonia, 1357 .... NJ-7
Lloyd Hbr., 3738 .... SE-8
Loch Sheldrake, 1050 .... NN-16
Lockport, 21600 .... NI-4
Locust Gr., 9700 .... *F-20
Locust Valley, 3521 .... SF-8
Long Beach, 35415 .... SG-8
Loudonville, 10822 .... SI-5
Lowville, 3340 .... NF-14
Lynbrook, 19803 .... SG-8
Lyndon, 4593 .... NI-12
Lyndonville, 854 .... NH-5
Lyon Mtn., 458 .... NB-18
Lyons, 3589 .... NI-9
Macedon, 1533 .... NI-8
MADISON CO., 70182 .... NJ-13
Mahopac, 8478 .... SC-7
Mahopac Falls, 1200 .... SC-7
Maine, 1110 .... NM-12
Malone, 5998 .... NB-17
Mamaroneck, 18493 .... SE-7
Manchester, 1479 .... NI-8
Manhasset, 8362 .... *F-16
Manlius, 4759 .... NI-12
Manorhaven, 6272 .... *E-16
Manorville, 11131 .... SE-11
Maplewood, 800 .... SH-5
Marathon, 1050 .... NL-12
Marcellus, 1820 .... NI-11
Marion, 1100 .... NI-9
Marlboro, 2339 .... SB-6
Massapequa, 22652 .... SF-8
Massapequa Park, 17453 .... SJ-10
Massena, 10982 .... NA-15
Mastic, 15436 .... SF-11
Mastic Beach, 11543 .... SF-11
Mattituck, 4198 .... SE-12
Mattydale, 6367 .... NI-12
Maybrook, 4003 .... SC-5
Mayville, 1744 .... NL-1
Maywood, 3400 .... NJ-19
McGraw, 990 .... NK-12
McKownville, 4850 .... SI-3
Mechanicville, 5001 .... NJ-19
Medford, 21985 .... SF-10
Medina, 6308 .... NH-5
Menands, 3880 .... NJ-19
Mendon, 1000 .... NI-8
Merrick, 22764 .... SG-8
Mexico, 1567 .... NG-11
Middleburgh, 1469 .... NK-17
Middle Hope, 3000 .... SB-6
Middle Island, 9702 .... SE-10
Middleport, 1860 .... NH-5
Middletown, 25863 .... SC-5
Middleville, 544 .... NI-15
Middleville, 1400 .... SG-11
Millbrook, 1544 .... NN-19
Millerton, 935 .... NM-20
Millwood, 1000 .... SD-7
Milton, 1251 .... SB-6
Mineola, 19164 .... SF-8
Minetto, 1086 .... NH-11
Mineville, 950 .... NE-19
Minoa, 3303 .... NI-12
Modena, 900 .... SB-6
Mohawk, 2588 .... NI-15
Mohegan Lake, 3600 .... SC-7
Mongaup Valley, 750 .... SB-3
MONROE CO., 736738 .... NH-7
Monroe, 8052 .... SC-6
Monsey, 14504 .... SD-6
Montauk, 3851 .... SD-14
MONTGOMERY CO., 49371 .... NJ-16
Montgomery, 3989 .... SB-5
Monticello, 6493 .... SB-4
Montour Falls, 1798 .... NL-10
Montrose, 2250 .... SD-7
Moravia, 1349 .... NJ-11
Morrisonville, 1702 .... NB-19
Morrisville, 2102 .... NJ-13
Mountain Lodge, 1000 .... SC-6
Mt. Ivy, 6536 .... SD-6
Mt. Kisco, 10035 .... SD-7
Mt. Morris, 3198 .... NJ-6
Mt. Vernon, 68404 .... SE-7
Mt. Vernon, 2800 .... NJ-3
Munsey Park, 2618 .... *F-16
Muttontown, 3499 .... *E-19
Nanuet, 16707 .... SD-6
Napanoch, 1168 .... SA-5
Naples, 1058 .... NK-8
NASSAU CO., 1339463 .... SF-8
Nassau, 1146 .... NK-19
Nedrow, 2265 .... NI-12
Nesconset, 11992 .... SH-13
Newark, 9507 .... NI-9
Newark Valley, 1046 .... NL-12
New Baltimore, 960 .... NK-19
New Berlin, 1121 .... NK-14
Newburgh, 28412 .... SB-6
New City, 34038 .... SD-6
New Falconwood, 1200 .... ND-2
Newfane, 3129 .... NH-4
New Hamburg, 1080 .... SB-6
New Hampton, 1200 .... SC-5
New Hartford, 1853 .... NI-14
New Hyde Park, 9526 .... *H-16
New Lebanon, 950 .... NK-20
New Paltz, 6428 .... SA-6
New Rochelle, 72582 .... SE-7
New Suffolk, 337 .... SE-12
Newtonville, 2300 .... SH-4
New Windsor, 9077 .... SC-6
NEW YORK CO., 1564798 .... *G-10
New York, 8085742 .... SG-6
New York Mills, 3157 .... NI-14
NIAGARA CO., 218150 .... NH-4
Niagara Falls, 53989 .... NI-3
Nimmonsburg, 900 .... NM-12
Niskayuna, 4892 .... NJ-19
Nissequogue, 1577 .... SE-9
Niverville, 1737 .... NK-19
Norfolk, 1334 .... NB-15
N. Bellmore, 20079 .... *I-19
N. Bloomfield, 2260 .... NI-7
N. Boston, 2680 .... NJ-4
N. Chili, 2300 .... NI-7
N. Collins, 1048 .... NK-3
N. Creek, 700 .... NF-18
N. Hornell, 836 .... NL-7
N. New Hyde Park, 14542 .... *G-16
Northport, 7671 .... SE-9
N. Salem, 930 .... SC-8
N. Sea, 4493 .... SE-12
N. Syracuse, 6863 .... NI-12
N. Tonawanda, 32359 .... NI-3
N. Valley Stream, 15789 .... *I-16
Northville, 1138 .... NH-18
Norwich, 7251 .... NK-14
Norwood, 1645 .... NB-15
Noyack, 2696 .... SE-12
Nunda, 1297 .... NK-6
Nyack, 6749 .... SD-7
Oakdale, 8075 .... SI-13
Oakfield, 1759 .... NI-5
Oceanside, 32733 .... SG-8
Odessa, 617 .... NL-10
Ogdensburg, 11832 .... NB-14
Olcott, 1156 .... NH-4
Old Brookville, 2202 .... *E-18
Old Forge, 1450 .... NF-15
Olean, 14989 .... NM-5
ONEIDA CO., 234373 .... NH-13
Oneida, 10956 .... NI-13
Oneonta, 12799 .... NK-15
ONONDAGA CO., 460517 .... NI-12
ONTARIO CO., 102445 .... NJ-8
Ontario, 1000 .... NH-8
ORANGE CO., 363153 .... SD-5
Orange Lake, 6085 .... SB-6
Orchard Park, 3218 .... NJ-4
Orient, 709 .... SD-13
Oriskany, 1438 .... NI-14
ORLEANS CO., 43629 .... NH-6
Ossining, 24229 .... SD-7
OSWEGO CO., 123495 .... NG-12
Oswego, 18223 .... NG-11
Otego, 998 .... NL-15
Otisville, 1035 .... SC-4
OTSEGO CO., 62196 .... NK-15
Owego, 3809 .... NM-11
Oxford, 1565 .... NL-13
Oxford, 250 .... SC-5
Oyster Bay, 6826 .... SF-8
Painted Post, 1804 .... NM-9
Palenville, 1120 .... NM-18
Palmyra, 3440 .... NI-8
Patchogue, 12016 .... SF-10
Patterson, 1200 .... SB-8
Pawling, 2259 .... SB-8
Pearl River, 15553 .... SE-6
Peconic, 1081 .... SD-12
Peekskill, 23436 .... SC-7
Pelham, 6399 .... *C-14
Pelham Manor, 5450 .... *C-14
Penfield, 6300 .... NI-8
Penn Yan, 5123 .... NK-9
Perry, 3876 .... NJ-6
Peru, 1514 .... NC-19
Phelps, 1934 .... NI-9
Philadelphia, 1533 .... ND-13
Philmont, 1447 .... NL-19
Phoenicia, 381 .... NM-17
Phoenix, 2211 .... NH-11
Pine Bush, 1539 .... SB-5
Pine Island, 1500 .... SD-5
Pine Plains, 1412 .... NM-19
Pitcher Hill, 5000 .... NE-8
Pittsford, 1384 .... NI-8
Plainview, 25637 .... SF-8
Plandome Hts., 964 .... *F-16
Plattekill, 1050 .... SB-6
Plattsburgh, 19163 .... NB-20
Plattsburgh West, 1289 .... NB-19
Pleasant Valley, 1839 .... SA-7
Pleasantville, 7178 .... SD-7
Poestenkill, 1024 .... NJ-19
Pomona, 2873 .... SD-6
Port Byron, 1285 .... NI-10
Port Chester, 27955 .... SE-8
Port Dickinson, 1658 .... NM-12
Port Ewen, 3650 .... NN-18
Port Henry, 1122 .... NE-20
Port Jefferson, 7948 .... SE-10
Port Jervis, 9100 .... SC-4
Portland, 950 .... NL-2
Portville, 1007 .... NM-5
Port Washington, 15215 .... SF-8
Port Washington N., 2700 .... *E-16
Potsdam, 9555 .... NB-15
Poughkeepsie, 30174 .... SB-7
Pound Ridge, 1000 .... SD-8
Prattsburgh, 950 .... NK-8
Pulaski, 2358 .... NG-12
Purdys, 970 .... SC-8
PUTNAM CO., 99550 .... SC-8
Putnam Lake, 3855 .... SC-8
QUEENS CO., 2225486 .... SF-8
Quogue, 1071 .... SF-11
Randolph, 1282 .... NM-3
Ransomville, 1488 .... NH-3
Ravena, 3356 .... NK-19
Red Hook, 1833 .... NM-19
Red Oaks Mill, 4930 .... SB-7
RENSSELAER CO., 154007 .... NJ-20
Rensselaer, 7743 .... NK-19
Rhinebeck, 3114 .... NN-18
Richfield Sprs., 1197 .... NJ-15
RICHMOND CO., 459737 .... SG-6
Richmondville, 785 .... NK-16
Ridge, 13380 .... SE-10
Ripley, 1030 .... NL-1
Riverhead, 10513 .... SE-11
Rochester, 215093 .... NI-7
Rock City Falls, 700 .... NI-18
Rock Hill, 1056 .... SB-4
ROCKLAND CO., 292989 .... SD-6
Rockville Ctr., 24397 .... SG-8
Rocky Pt., 10185 .... SE-10
Roessleville, 10753 .... SI-4
Rome, 34512 .... NH-14
Ronkonkoma, 20029 .... SH-13
Roscoe, 597 .... NN-15
Rosendale, 1374 .... NN-18
Roslyn, 2587 .... *F-17
Rotterdam, 20536 .... NJ-18
Rotterdam Jct., 1000 .... NJ-18
Rouses Pt., 2363 .... NA-20
Russell Gardens, 1067 .... *G-16
Rye, 15066 .... SE-7
Rye Brook, 9234 .... SI-9
Sackets Hbr., 1394 .... NE-12
Sagaponack, 587 .... SE-13
Sag Hbr., 2367 .... SE-13
St. James, 13268 .... SG-13
St. Johnsville, 1650 .... NI-16
ST. LAWRENCE CO., 111655 .... ND-15
St. Regis Falls, 950 .... NB-16
Salamanca, 5942 .... NM-4
Salem, 961 .... NH-20
Sands Pt., 2838 .... SF-7
Sandy Beach, 2350 .... NI-3
San Remo, 8550 .... SH-12
Saranac Lake, 4974 .... ND-18
SARATOGA CO., 209818 .... NH-18
Saratoga Sprs., 27332 .... NI-19
Saugerties, 3903 .... NM-18
Sauquoit, 930 .... NI-14
Savona, 809 .... NL-8
Sayville, 16735 .... SF-10
Scarsdale, 17929 .... SE-7
SCHENECTADY CO., 147289 .... NJ-18
Schenectady, 61016 .... NJ-18
SCHOHARIE CO., 31685 .... NK-16
Schoharie, 1026 .... NK-17
Schroon Lake, 1100 .... NF-19
SCHUYLER CO., 19455 .... NL-9
Schuylerville, 1303 .... NI-19
Scotia, 7856 .... NJ-18
Scottsville, 2089 .... NI-7
Sea Cliff, 5034 .... *E-17
Seaford, 15791 .... *I-20
Selden, 21861 .... SE-10
SENECA CO., 35183 .... NJ-10
Seneca Falls, 6901 .... NJ-10
Shelter Island, 1234 .... SD-12
Shelter Island Hts., 981 .... SD-12
Sherburne, 1444 .... NK-14
Sherrill, 3109 .... NI-13
Shinnecock Hills, 1749 .... SE-12
Shortsville, 1306 .... NI-8
Shrub Oak, 1812 .... SC-7
Sidney, 3936 .... NL-14
Silver Cr., 2857 .... NK-3
Silver Sprs., 826 .... NK-6
Skaneateles, 2596 .... NI-11
Skaneateles Falls, 850 .... NI-11
Sleepy Hollow, 9275 .... SD-7
Slingerlands, 2100 .... SJ-3
Sloan, 3670 .... NE-4
Sloatsburg, 3134 .... SD-6
Smithtown, 26901 .... SH-12
Sodus, 1686 .... NH-9
Sodus Pt., 1162 .... NH-9
Solvay, 6734 .... NI-11
Sound Beach, 9807 .... SE-10
Southampton, 4075 .... SE-12
S. Cairo, 950 .... NL-18
S. Corning, 1142 .... NM-9
S. Fallsburg, 2061 .... SB-4
S. Floral Park, 1573 .... *H-16
S. Glens Falls, 3417 .... NH-19
S. Lockport, 8552 .... NI-4
Southold, 5465 .... SD-12
Southport, 7396 .... NM-10
S. Salem, 12300 .... SD-8
S. Valley Stream, 5638 .... *J-16
Southwood, 900 .... NG-9
Sparrow Bush, 1200 .... SC-4
Speigletown, 1200 .... NJ-19
Spencerport, 3560 .... NH-7
Springs, 4950 .... SE-13
Spr. Valley, 25509 .... SD-6
Springville, 4367 .... NK-4
Staatsburg, 911 .... NN-18
Stamford, 1223 .... NL-16
Stanford Hts., 1050 .... NJ-18
Stannards, 868 .... NM-6
Star Lake, 860 .... ND-15
Steamburg, 900 .... NM-3
STEUBEN CO., 99012 .... NL-8
Stillwater, 1670 .... NI-19
Stone Ridge, 1173 .... NN-18
Stony Brook, 13727 .... SE-10
Stony Pt., 11744 .... SD-6
Stottville, 1355 .... NL-19
Suffern, 11014 .... SD-6
SUFFOLK CO., 1468037 .... SE-11
SULLIVAN CO., 74948 .... SA-3
Swan Lake, 1200 .... SA-3
Sycaway, 1950 .... SH-6
Sylvan Beach, 1066 .... NH-13
Syosset, 18544 .... SF-8
Syracuse, 144001 .... NI-12
Tappan, 6757 .... SE-6
Tarrytown, 11411 .... SE-7
Taunton, 1050 .... NF-7
Terryville, 10589 .... SG-14
Theresa, 812 .... ND-13
Thomaston, 2595 .... *F-16
Ticonderoga, 2700 .... NF-20
Tillson, 1709 .... NN-18
TIOGA CO., 51746 .... NM-11
Tivoli, 1175 .... NM-18
TOMPKINS CO., 101411 .... NL-10
Tonawanda, 15700 .... NI-3
Town Line, 2521 .... NJ-4
Troy, 48649 .... NJ-19
Trumansburg, 1615 .... NK-10
Tuckahoe, 1741 .... SE-12
Tuckahoe, 6243 .... SE-12
Tully, 907 .... NJ-12
Tupper Lake, 3900 .... ND-17
Twin Orchards, 1600 .... SB-10
ULSTER CO., 181111 .... SA-6
Unadilla, 1074 .... NL-14
Union Cen., 1500 .... NM-12
Uniondale, 23011 .... *H-18
Union Sprs., 1072 .... NJ-10
University Gardens, 4138 .... *G-16
Utica, 59485 .... NI-14
Vails Gate, 3319 .... SC-6
Valatie, 1818 .... NL-19
Valhalla, 5379 .... SE-7
Valley Cottage, 9269 .... SD-7
Valley Stream, 36214 .... SG-7
Verdoy, 1000 .... SG-4
Vernon, 1175 .... NI-13
Verona, 600 .... NI-13
Verona Beach, 700 .... NH-13
Verplanck, 777 .... SD-6
Vestal, 5000 .... NM-12
Vestal Cen., 800 .... NM-12
Victor, 2526 .... NI-8
Vil. of the Branch, 1970 .... SH-12
Voorheesville, 2810 .... NK-18
Waddington, 941 .... NB-14
Walden, 6608 .... SB-6
Walker Valley, 758 .... SB-5
Wallkill, 2143 .... SB-6
Walton, 2953 .... NM-15
Wanakah, 1600 .... NJ-3
Wantagh, 18971 .... *I-20
Wappingers Falls, 4991 .... SB-7
WARREN CO., 64715 .... NG-18
Warrensburg, 3208 .... NG-19

2000 Census populations or latest available estimate.
Index to Canada and Mexico cities and towns, pages 274-275.

NEW YORK - OHIO 269

Warsaw, 3737 NJ-6
Warwick, 6548 SD-5
WASHINGTON CO., 61872 NH-20
Washington Mills, 1700 SC-12
Washingtonville, 6243 SC-6
Waterloo, 5132 NJ-10
Water Mill, 1724 SE-12
Watertown, 26782 NE-12
Waterville, 1690 NJ-14
Watervliet, 10052 NJ-19
Watkins Glen, 2114 NL-9
Waverly, 4515 NM-11
Wawarsing, 800 SA-5
Wayland, 1851 NK-7
WAYNE CO., 93728 NI-9
Webster, 5175 NH-8
Weedsport, 1985 NI-10
Wellsville, 4833 NM-6
W. Babylon, 43452 SF-9
Westbury, 14283 SF-8
Westbury, 1550 NH-10
W. Carthage, 2116 NE-13
WESTCHESTER CO., 940302 SD-8
W. Corners, 1000 NM-12
W. Elmira, 5136 NM-10
Westfield, 3480 NL-1
W. Glens Falls, 6721 NH-19
Westhampton, 2864 SF-11
Westhampton Beach, 1949 SF-11
W. Hurley, 2105 NM-18
Westmere, 7188 NJ-18
Westmoreland, 950 NI-14
Westons Mills, 1608 NM-5
W. Point, 7138 SC-6
W. Sand Lake, 2439 NK-19
W. Sayville, 5003 SJ-13
W. Seneca, 45943 NJ-4
Westvale, 5166 NI-11
W. Webster, 8700 NH-8
W. Winfield, 843 NJ-15
Whitehall, 2644 NG-20
White Plains, 55900 SE-7
Whitesboro, 3875 SA-12
Whitney Pt., 957 NL-12
Willard, 600 NK-10
Williamson, 1850 NH-9
Williamsville, 5427 ND-5
Williston Park, 7193 *G-17
Willow Pt., 1700 SB-10
Willsboro, 950 ND-20
Wilson, 1186 NH-4
Windsor, 885 NM-13
Witherbee, 750 NE-19
Wolcott, 1694 NH-10
Woodbourne, 1200 NN-16
Woodbury, 9010 SH-10
Woodlawn Beach, 1000 NG-4
Woodmere, 16447 *J-16
Woodsburgh, 822 *K-16
Woodstock, 2187 NM-18
Worcester, 900 NK-16
Wurtsboro, 1239 SB-4
Wyandanch, 10546 SI-11
Wynantskill, 3018 SI-6
WYOMING CO., 42932 NJ-5
Yaphank, 5025 SF-10
YATES CO., 24720 NK-8
Yonkers, 197388 SE-7
Yorkshire, 1403 NK-5
Yorktown Hts., 7972 SD-7
Yorkville, 2624 NI-14
Youngstown, 1920 NH-3
Youngsville, 850 NN-16

North Carolina

Map pp. 150-155

* City keyed to pp. 154-155

Aberdeen, 4110 G-9
Ahoskie, 4314 C-16
ALAMANCE CO., 136773 D-9
Albemarle, 15408 F-7
ALEXANDER CO., 34784 D-4
Alexander Mills F-2
ALLEGHANY CO., 10874 B-4
Andrews, 1591 M-2
Angier, 3880 F-11
ANSON CO., 25168 G-8
Ansonville, 630 G-7
Apex, 26588 E-11
Archdale, 9241 D-8
Arlington, 795 C-5
ASHE CO., 25071 B-4
Asheboro, 22839 E-8
Asheville, 69045 E-1
Atlantic, 1150 H-18
Atlantic Beach, 1744 H-17
Aulander, 862 C-16
Aurora, 580 F-17
AVERY CO., 17700 D-2
Ayden, 4570 F-15
Badin, 1107 F-7
Banner Elk, 885 C-3
Bannertown, 1000 B-6
Bayboro, 730 G-17
BEAUFORT CO., 45407 E-17
Beaufort, 3854 H-17
Belhaven, 1929 E-17
Belmont, 8793 F-5
Belwood, 997 F-3
Benson, 3031 F-12
BERTIE CO., 19544 D-16
Bessemer City, 5100 F-4
Bethel, 1682 D-15
Bethesda, 30 *B-4
Beulaville, 1080 H-14
Biltmore Forest, 1448 E-1
Biscoe, 1721 F-8
Black Mtn., 7551 E-1
BLADEN CO., 32723 I-12
Bladenboro, 1711 I-11
Blowing Rock, 1434 C-3
Boger City, 554 F-4
Boiling Spr. Lakes, 3659 K-13
Boiling Sprs., 3857 F-3
Boone, 13127 C-3
Boonville, 1107 C-6
Brevard, 6693 M-5
Broadway, 984 F-10
BRUNSWICK CO., 81592 J-13
Bryson City, 1392 L-3
Buies Cr., 2215 F-11
BUNCOMBE CO., 212672 E-1
Burgaw, 3613 I-14
BURKE CO., 89657 D-3
Burlington, 46271 D-9
Burnsville, 1636 D-1
Butner, 5792 C-11
Buxton, 1480 F-20
CABARRUS CO., 142740 F-6
CALDWELL CO., 78728 D-3
CAMDEN CO., 7863 B-18
Candor, 827 F-8
Canton, 3957 L-5
Cape Carteret, 1399 H-16
Carolina Beach, 5118 K-14
Carrboro, 16747 D-10
CARTERET CO., 60865 H-16
Carthage, 1913 F-9
Cary, 99824 E-11
Castle Hayne, 1116 J-14
CASWELL CO., 23632 C-9
CATAWBA CO., 146971 E-4
Cedar Point, 929 H-16
Chadbourn, 2080 J-11
Chapel Hill, 49301 D-10
Charlotte, 584658 F-5
CHATHAM CO., 55238 E-10
CHEROKEE CO., 25048 M-1
Cherryville, 5422 F-4
China Gr., 3696 E-6
Chocowinity, 724 E-16
CHOWAN CO., 14433 C-17
Claremont, 1068 E-4
Clarkton, 696 I-12
CLAY CO., 9288 M-2
Clayton, 11293 E-12
Clemmons, 16118 D-7
CLEVELAND CO., 98249 F-3
Cleveland, 814 E-6
Clinton, 8636 G-13
Clyde, 1336 L-4
Coats, 1948 F-11
Colfax, 1050 *G-11
Columbia, 801 D-18
COLUMBUS CO., 54518 I-11
Columbus, 994 F-1
Concord, 58943 F-6
Connelly Springs, 1825 E-4
Conover, 6772 E-4
Conway, 710 B-15
Cooleemee, 907 E-6
Cornelius, 16827 F-5
Cramerton, 2935 G-5
CRAVEN CO., 91754 F-16
Creedmoor, 2924 C-11
Crouse, 900 F-4
Cullowhee, 3579 L-4
CUMBERLAND CO., 303953 H-11
Cumberland, 730 G-11
CURRITUCK CO., 20834 B-19
Dallas, 3382 F-4
DARE CO., 33116 E-20
DAVIDSON CO., 152178 E-7
Davidson, 8142 F-5
DAVIE CO., 37151 D-6
Denton, 1458 E-7
Dobson, 1454 C-6
Drexel, 1906 E-3
Dunn, 9722 F-12
DUPLIN CO., 51181 G-14
DURHAM CO., 236781 D-11
Durham, 198376 D-11
E. Bend, 659 C-6
E. Flat Rock, 4122 F-1
Eastover, 1376 G-11
E. Spencer, 1757 E-7
Eden, 15622 B-8
Edenton, 4981 C-17
EDGECOMBE CO., 54895 D-14
Elizabeth City, 17570 C-18
Elizabethtown, 3675 I-12
Elkin, 4089 C-5
Ellerbe, 1002 G-8
Elm City, 1374 D-14
Enfield, 2332 C-14
Enka, 5000 L-5
Erwin, 4697 F-11
Fair Bluff, 1169 J-10
Fairmont, 2569 I-10
Fairplains, 2051 C-4
Faison, 759 G-13
Farmville, 4557 E-15
Fayetteville, 124372 G-11
Fearrington Village, 903 *D-1
Fletcher, 4342 F-1
Forest City, 7373 F-2
FORSYTH CO., 317810 C-7
Four Oaks, 1631 F-12
FRANKLIN CO., 52006 C-12
Franklin, 3573 M-3
Franklinton, 1848 C-12
Fremont, 1428 E-13
Fuquay-Varina, 10089 E-11
Gamewell, 3754 D-3
Garland, 826 H-12
Garner, 20537 E-12
Garysburg, 1228 B-15
GASTON CO., 193097 F-4
Gaston, 953 B-14
Gastonia, 67781 F-4
GATES CO., 10754 B-17
Gibsonville, 4447 C-9
Glen Alpine, 1097 E-3
Goldsboro, 38484 F-13
Gorman, 1002 D-11
GRAHAM CO., 7994 M-2
Graham, 13282 D-9
Grandy, 950 C-19
Granite Falls, 4572 E-4
Granite Quarry, 2221 E-6
Granthams, 950 G-16
GRANVILLE CO., 51852 B-11
GREENE CO., 19990 E-14
Greensboro, 229110 D-8
Greenville, 67190 E-15
Grifton, 2056 F-15
GUILFORD CO., 433789 D-9
HALIFAX CO., 56491 C-15
Hamlet, 5866 H-9
Harkers Island, 1525 H-18
HARNETT CO., 99407 F-11
Harrisburg, 4849 F-6
Hatteras, 1150 F-20
Havelock, 22499 H-16
Haw River, 1945 D-10
Hays, 1731 C-5
HAYWOOD CO., 55442 K-4
Hazelwood L-4
HENDERSON CO., 93817 F-1
Henderson, 16231 C-12
Hendersonville, 11123 F-1
Henrietta, 1000 F-3
HERTFORD CO., 22310 C-16
Hertford, 2070 C-18
Hickory, 39476 E-4
Hiddenite, 880 D-5
Highlands, 906 M-4
High Pt., 91543 D-8
High Shoals, 733 F-4
Hildebran, 1855 E-4
Hillsborough, 5361 D-10
HOKE CO., 37643 G-10
Holly Sprs., 12694 E-11
Hope Mills, 11966 G-11
Hudson, 3064 D-3
Huntersville, 32323 F-5
HYDE CO., 5567 E-19
Indian Trail, 14173 G-6
IREDELL CO., 133387 D-5
JACKSON CO., 34304 M-4
Jackson, 674 B-15
Jacksonville, 67386 H-15
Jamestown, 3041 D-8
Jamesville, 488 D-16
Jefferson, 1424 B-4
JOHNSTON CO., 136802 F-12
JONES CO., 10197 G-15
Jonesville, 2259 C-5
Kannapolis, 38178 F-6
Kenansville, 875 G-14
Kenly, 1652 E-13
Kernersville, 20053 C-8
Kill Devil Hills, 6287 C-20
King, 6187 C-7
Kings Mtn., 10537 F-4
Kinston, 22978 F-15
Kitty Hawk, 3242 C-20
Kure Beach, 1858 K-14
La Grange, 2813 F-14
Lake Waccamaw, 1420 J-12
Landis, 2997 E-6
Laurel Hill, 2400 H-9
Laurinburg, 15552 H-9
LEE CO., 49138 E-10
LENOIR CO., 58549 G-14
Lenoir, 17952 D-3
Lewiston, 603 C-16
Lewisville, 9332 D-7
Lexington, 20385 D-7
Liberty, 2663 D-9
Lillington, 3106 F-11
LINCOLN CO., 67275 F-4
Lincolnton, 10114 F-4
Littleton, 666 B-14
Locust, 2418 F-6
Long View, 4745 E-4
Louisburg, 3103 C-13
Lowell, 2644 F-5
Lucama, 867 E-13
Lumberton, 21161 I-11
MACON CO., 31175 M-3
MADISON CO., 19858 K-5
Madison, 2241 C-8
Magnolia, 954 H-13
Maiden, 3191 E-4
Manteo, 1208 D-20
Marble, 830 M-2
Marion, 4854 E-2
Marshall, 832 K-5
Marshallberg, 700 H-18
Mars Hill, 1720 D-1
Marshville, 2601 G-7
MARTIN CO., 25070 D-16
Matthews, 23436 G-6
Maxton, 2520 H-10
Mayodan, 2382 B-8
Maysville, 981 H-16
McAdenville, 616 *B-8
MCDOWELL CO., 42867 E-2
Mebane, 8464 D-10
MECKLENBURG CO., 752366 G-5
Middlesex, 846 E-13
Midland, 2582 G-6
Mint Hill, 16477 G-6
MITCHELL CO., 15831 D-1
Mocksville, 4291 D-6
Monroe, 28222 G-6
MONTGOMERY CO., 27306 F-8
Montreat, 657 E-1
MOORE CO., 79267 F-9
Mooresville, 19606 E-5
Moravian Falls, 1440 D-4
Morehead City, 8064 H-17
Morganton, 17261 E-3
Morgantown, 2180 C-9
Morven, 571 H-8
Mt. Airy, 8394 B-6
Mt. Gilead, 1388 G-8
Mt. Holly, 9591 F-5
Mt. Olive, 4488 G-13
Mt. Pleasant, 1307 F-6
Mulberry, 2269 C-4
Murfreesboro, 2347 B-16
Murphy, 1562 M-1
Nags Head, 2993 D-20
NASH CO., 89732 D-13
Nashville, 4375 D-13
Nebo, 840 E-2
New Bern, 23308 G-16
Newell, 1050 *A-13
NEW HANOVER CO., 168088 J-14
Newland, 706 D-2
Newport, 3672 H-17
Newton, 12682 E-4
Norlina, 1072 B-13
NORTHAMPTON CO., 21782 B-15
N. Wilkesboro, 4122 C-4
Norwood, 2178 G-7
Oakboro, 1194 G-7
Oak Island, 6965 K-13
Oak Ridge, 4056 C-8
Ocracoke, 769 G-19
Old Ft., 972 E-2
ONSLOW CO., 147524 H-15
ORANGE CO., 118183 C-10
Oteen, 1650 E-1
Oxford, 8495 C-12
PAMLICO CO., 12783 G-17
PASQUOTANK CO., 36071 B-18
Pembroke, 2702 H-10
PENDER CO., 43527 I-13
PERQUIMANS CO., 11644 C-18
PERSON CO., 36864 C-11
Pfafftown, 1050 C-7
Pikeville, 701 F-13
Pilot Mtn., 1268 C-6
Pinebluff, 1153 G-9
Pinehurst, 10774 G-9
Pine Level, 1395 F-13
Pinetops, 1357 D-14
Pineville, 3656 G-5
Pisgah Forest, 2150 M-5
PITT CO., 138690 F-15
Pittsboro, 2379 E-10
Pleasant Garden, 4800 D-8
Plymouth, 3994 D-17
POLK CO., 18824 F-2
Polkton, 1894 G-7
Princeton, 1146 F-13
Princeville, 1712 D-15
Raeford, 3484 G-10
Raleigh, 316802 E-12
Ramseur, 1585 E-9
Randleman, 3559 E-8
RANDOLPH CO., 135151 E-8
Ranlo, 2175 F-4
Red Sprs., 3429 H-10
Reidsville, 14777 C-9
Richlands, 854 H-15
RICHMOND CO., 46643 G-8
Rich Square, 1029 C-15
Riegelwood, 1200 J-13
River Bend, 2851 G-16
Roanoke Rapids, 16512 B-14
Robbins, 1213 F-9
Robbinsville, 743 L-2
Robersonville, 1666 D-15
ROBESON CO., 125756 I-10
ROCKINGHAM CO., 92590 C-8
Rockingham, 9301 H-8
Rockwell, 1973 E-7
Rocky Mt., 55984 D-14
Roper, 593 D-17
Roseboro, 1276 G-12
Rose Hill, 1360 H-13
Rosewood, 4300 F-13
Rowland, 1128 I-10
Roxboro, 8794 C-11
Rural Hall, 2532 C-7
RUTHERFORD CO., 63540 F-2
Rutherford College, 1292 E-3
Rutherfordton, 4066 F-2
St. Pauls, 2235 H-11
Salisbury, 26548 E-6
SAMPSON CO., 62037 G-12
Sanford, 23346 F-10
Sawmills, 4949 D-3
SCOTLAND CO., 35757 H-9
Scotland Neck, 2281 C-15
Seaboard, 673 B-15
Seagate, 4590 M-20
Sedgefield, 1000 *H-13
Selma, 6333 E-13
Shallotte, 1490 K-12
Sharpsburg, 2431 D-14
Shelby, 21215 F-3
Siler City, 7603 E-9
Silver City, 1146 G-10
Skyland, 2000 F-1
Smithfield, 11462 F-12
Snow Hill, 1427 F-14
Southern Pines, 11446 G-9
South Gastonia, 5433 K-19
Southport, 2605 K-13
Sparta, 1818 B-5
Spencer, 3321 E-6
Spindale, 3917 F-2
Spr. Hope, 1255 D-13
Spr. Lake, 8163 G-11
Spruce Pine, 2013 D-2
Stallings, 3552 G-6
Stanley, 3086 F-5
Stanleyville, 4779 C-7
STANLY CO., 58846 F-7
Stantonsburg, 706 E-14
Star, 807 F-8
Statesville, 24129 E-5
Stedman, 655 G-11
STOKES CO., 45168 C-7
Stokesdale, 3367 C-8
Stoneville, 989 B-8
Stony Pt., 1380 D-5
Summerfield, 7144 C-8
Surf City, 1523 I-15
SURRY CO., 72278 B-6
SWAIN CO., 13126 L-3
Swannanoa, 4132 E-1
Swansboro, 1334 H-16
Swepsonville, 939 D-10
Sylva, 2426 L-4
Tabor City, 2602 J-11
Tarboro, 10701 D-15
Taylorsville, 1846 D-4
Thomasville, 25466 D-7
Toast, 1922 B-6
TRANSYLVANIA CO., 29406 M-5
Triangle, 850 F-5
Trinity, 6818 D-8
Troutman, 1651 E-5
Troy, 3465 F-8
Tryon, 1740 G-1
Tuxedo, 1100 F-1
TYRRELL CO., 4156 D-18
UNION CO., 145986 H-6
Valdese, 4549 E-3
VANCE CO., 43736 C-12
Vanceboro, 875 F-16
Vander, 1204 G-11
Vass, 763 F-10
Wadesboro, 3463 G-7
WAKE CO., 695681 D-12
Wake Forest, 16029 D-12
Walkertown, 4148 C-7
Wallace, 3483 H-13
Walnut Cove, 1467 C-7
Walnut Creek, 842 F-14
Wanchese, 1527 D-20
WARREN CO., 19812 C-13
Warrenton, 774 B-13
Warsaw, 3044 G-13
WASHINGTON CO., 13399 D-17
Washington, 9677 E-16
WATAUGA CO., 42808 C-3
Waxhaw, 2937 H-6
WAYNE CO., 113104 F-14
Waynesville, 9347 L-4
Weaverville, 2423 E-1
Weddington, 7666 G-6
Welcome, 3538 D-7
Weldon, 1328 B-14
Wendell, 4322 E-12
W. Jefferson, 1076 B-4
Whispering Pines, 2131 F-10
Whitakers, 778 C-14
Whiteville, 5099 J-11
WILKES CO., 67055 C-4
Wilkesboro, 3206 C-4
Williamston, 5749 D-16
Wilmington, 91137 J-14
WILSON CO., 75338 E-14
Wilson, 45921 E-14
Windsor, 2243 D-16
Wingate, 2665 G-6
Winston-Salem, 190299 D-7
Winterville, 4660 E-15
Winton, 918 B-16
Woodfin, 3222 K-5
Woodland, 805 C-16
Wrightsville, 750 M-20
Wrightsville Beach, 2510 J-14
YADKIN CO., 37421 C-6
Yadkinville, 2842 C-6
YANCEY CO., 18069 D-1
Yanceyville, 2108 B-10
Zebulon, 4133 D-12

North Dakota

Map pp. 156-157

Abercrombie, 293 G-13
ADAMS CO., 2505 H-4
Adams, 190 B-11
Anamoose, 271 D-8
Aneta, 264 D-11
Arthur, 388 E-12
Ashley, 822 H-9
BARNES CO., 11083 F-11
Beach, 1054 F-2
Belcourt, 2440 A-8
Belfield, 833 F-3
BENSON CO., 6881 C-9
Berthold, 447 C-5
Beulah, 3073 E-5
BILLINGS CO., 850 E-3
Binford, 185 D-11
Bismarck, 56344 F-7
BOTTINEAU CO., 6820 A-7
Bottineau, 2223 A-7
Bowbells, 378 A-5
BOWMAN CO., 3045 H-2
Bowman, 1509 G-3
BURKE CO., 2098 A-4
BURLEIGH CO., 71693 F-7
Burlington, 1044 C-6
Buxton, 347 D-12
Cando, 1235 B-9
Cannon Ball, 864 G-7
Carrington, 2106 E-9
Carson, 293 G-6
CASS CO., 127138 E-12
Casselton, 1885 F-12
CAVALIER CO., 4484 B-10
Cavalier, 1479 A-12
Center, 624 E-6
Cooperstown, 985 D-11
Crosby, 1067 A-3
Devils Lake, 6971 C-10
DICKEY CO., 5492 H-10
Dickinson, 15683 F-4
DIVIDE CO., 2247 A-3
Drake, 299 C-7
Drayton, 870 B-12
DUNN CO., 3539 E-4
Dunseith, 738 A-8
EDDY CO., 2598 D-9
Edgeley, 598 G-10
Edmore, 244 B-10
Elgin, 615 G-5
Ellendale, 1500 H-10
Emerado, 504 C-12
EMMONS CO., 4005 G-8
Enderlin, 1070 F-12
Fairmount, 389 H-13
Fargo, 91484 F-13
Fessenden, 568 D-9
Finley, 470 D-11
Flasher, 275 G-6
Fordville, 248 C-11
Forman, 487 H-12
Ft. Totten, 952 C-10
FOSTER CO., 3495 D-10
Gackle, 313 F-9
Garrison, 1272 D-6
Gilby, 238 C-12
Glenburn, 349 B-6
Glen Ullin, 839 F-5
GOLDEN VALLEY CO., 1828 E-2
Golden Valley, 176 E-5
Grafton, 4299 B-12
GRAND FORKS CO., 64736 D-12
Grand Forks, 48618 C-13
GRANT CO., 2665 G-5
Granville, 266 C-7
Grenora, 195 B-2
GRIGGS CO., 2578 D-11
Gwinner, 715 G-12
Halliday, 220 E-4
Hankinson, 1015 H-13
Harvey, 1826 D-8
Harwood, 642 F-13
Hatton, 682 D-12
Hazelton, 219 G-8
Hazen, 2392 E-5
Hebron, 759 F-5
HETTINGER CO., 2548 G-4
Hettinger, 1272 H-4
Hillsboro, 1523 E-13
Hoople, 274 B-12
Hope, 275 E-12
Horace, 969 F-13
Hunter, 311 E-12
Jamestown, 15158 F-10
Kenmare, 1119 B-5
KIDDER CO., 2577 E-8
Killdeer, 700 E-4
Kindred, 591 F-13
Kulm, 404 G-10
Lakota, 761 C-11
LAMOURE CO., 4512 G-10
Lamoure, 924 G-11
Langdon, 1934 A-10
Lansford, 244 B-6
Larimore, 1371 C-12
Leeds, 445 C-9
Leonard, 244 F-12
Lidgerwood, 754 H-12
Lignite, 166 A-4
Lincoln, 1990 F-7
Linton, 1209 G-8
Lisbon, 2259 G-12
LOGAN CO., 2157 G-9
Maddock, 480 C-9
Mandan, 16781 F-7
Mandaree, 558 D-4
Manvel, 356 C-12
Mapleton, 587 F-13
Max, 270 D-6
Mayville, 1914 D-12
McClusky, 369 D-7
MCHENRY CO., 5722 C-7
MCINTOSH CO., 3178 H-9
MCKENZIE CO., 5615 D-2
MCLEAN CO., 8935 D-6
McVille, 436 D-11
Medina, 317 F-9
MERCER CO., 8449 E-5
Michigan, 322 C-11
Milnor, 695 G-12
Minnewaukan, 308 C-9
Minot, 35424 C-6
Minto, 627 C-12
Mohall, 771 A-6
MORTON CO., 25135 F-6
Mott, 757 G-4
MOUNTRAIL CO., 6480 C-4
Munich, 246 B-10
Napoleon, 794 G-8
Neche, 432 A-12
NELSON CO., 3454 C-11
New England, 513 G-3
New Leipzig, 254 G-5
New Rockford, 1370 D-9
New Salem, 897 F-6
New Town, 1339 C-4
Noonan, 154 A-3
Northwood, 915 D-12
Oakes, 1864 G-11
OLIVER CO., 1905 E-6
Page, 213 E-12
Park River, 1457 B-11
Parshall, 1009 C-5
PEMBINA CO., 8201 B-11
Pembina, 610 A-12
PIERCE CO., 4480 C-8
Portland, 585 D-12
Powers Lake, 284 B-4
RAMSEY CO., 11616 B-10
RANSOM CO., 5838 G-12
Ray, 522 B-3
Reeder, 173 H-3
Regent, 195 G-4
RENVILLE CO., 2473 A-5
Reynolds, 342 D-12
Richardton, 589 F-4
RICHLAND CO., 17598 G-12
Riverdale, 267 D-6
ROLETTE CO., 13732 B-8
Rolette, 535 B-8
Rolla, 1423 A-9
Rugby, 2808 B-8
St. John, 357 A-8
St. Thomas, 424 B-12
SARGENT CO., 4225 G-12
Sawyer, 357 C-6
Scranton, 284 G-3
Selfridge, 219 H-7
SHERIDAN CO., 1540 D-7
Sherwood, 238 A-6
Sheyenne, 301 D-9
SIOUX CO., 4070 H-6
SLOPE CO., 746 G-2
S. Heart, 294 F-3
Stanley, 1236 B-4
Stanton, 333 E-6
STARK CO., 22131 F-4
STEELE CO., 2081 D-11
Steele, 720 F-8
Strasburg, 509 H-8
STUTSMAN CO., 21255 E-9
Surrey, 889 C-6
Tappen, 198 F-9
Thompson, 985 D-12
Tioga, 1100 B-3
Tolna, 190 D-10
Tower City, 244 F-12
TOWNER CO., 2667 B-9
Towner, 541 B-7
TRAILL CO., 8278 D-12
Turtle Lake, 550 D-7
Underwood, 773 D-6
Valley City, 6420 F-11
Velva, 1005 C-7
Wahpeton, 8443 G-13
Walhalla, 1008 A-11
WALSH CO., 11720 C-11
WARD CO., 56721 C-6
Washburn, 1328 E-6
Watford City, 1376 D-3
WELLS CO., 4702 D-8
W. Fargo, 16431 F-13
Westhope, 503 A-6
WILLIAMS CO., 19316 B-3
Williston, 12224 C-2
Willow City, 212 B-8
Wilton, 769 E-7
Wimbledon, 220 E-10
Wishek, 1063 G-9
Wyndmere, 513 G-12
Zap, 221 E-5

Ohio

Map pp. 158-165

Index keys NA to NN refer to Northern OH, pp. 158-161, SA to SN refer to Southern OH, pp. 162-165

Aberdeen, 1673 SI-6
Ada, 5583 NJ-5
ADAMS CO., 28026 SH-8
Addyston, 986 SG-1
Adena, 785 NM-19
Akron, 212215 NH-16
Albany, 839 SF-13
Alger, 880 NK-5
ALLEN CO., 108241 NJ-4
Alliance, 22892 NI-17
Amanda, 717 SC-10
Amberley, 3342 SK-4
Amberly, 900 SI-20
Amelia, 3314 SG-3
Amherst, 11738 NF-12
Amsterdam, 559 NL-18
Andover, 1249 NE-20
Anna, 1392 NL-3
Ansonia, 1123 NM-1
Antwerp, 1659 NG-1
Apple Cr., 988 NJ-14
Arcanum, 2043 SA-2
Archbold, 4443 NE-3
Arlington, 1344 NI-6
Arlington Hts., 853 SK-3
ASHLAND CO., 53749 NH-12
Ashland, 21449 NI-12
Ashley, 1235 NL-9
ASHTABULA CO., 103120 ND-19
Ashtabula, 20355 NC-19
Ashville, 3201 SC-9
ATHENS CO., 64380 SF-14
Athens, 22220 SE-13
Attica, 926 NH-9
Atwater, 850 NH-17
AUGLAIZE CO., 46740 NK-4
Aurora, 14270 NG-16
Austintown, 31627 NH-19
Avon, 13877 NF-13
Avondale, 3050 NI-16
Avondale SC-4
Avon Lake, 19782 NE-13
Bainbridge, 1022 SF-8
Ballville, 3255 NG-8
Baltimore, 2901 SB-11
Barberton, 27462 NH-15
Barnesville, 4196 SA-18
Barton, 465 NM-19
Batavia, 1649 SG-4
Bay View, 673 NF-10
Bay Vil., 15731 NF-14
Beach City, 1120 NK-15
Beachwood, 11906 NF-16
Beavercreek, 39196 SC-4
Bedford, 13790 NF-16
Bedford Hts., 11189 NF-16
Bellaire, 4766 NN-19
Bellbrook, 6966 SC-3
Belle Cen., 795 NK-5
Bellefontaine, 12980 NL-5
Bellevue, 8111 NG-10
Bellville, 1743 NK-11
BELMONT CO., 69636 NN-17
Beloit, 1007 NI-18
Belpre, 6570 SE-16
Berea, 18505 NF-14
Bergholz, 753 NK-19
Berlin, 1000 NK-14
Berlin Hts., 664 NG-11
Bethel, 2570 SH-4
Bethesda, 1399 SA-18
Bettsville, 765 NG-8
Beverly, 1257 SD-16
Bevis, 1100 SF-2
Bexley, 12632 SB-9
Black Horse, 500 NG-17
Blacklick Estates, 9518 SB-10
Blanchester, 4308 SF-5
Bloomdale, 711 NG-6
Bloomingburg, 862 SD-7
Bloomville, 1016 NH-9
Blue Ash, 12108 SF-3
Bluffton, 3963 NI-5
Boardman, 37215 NH-19
Bolivar, 902 NJ-16
Boston Hts., 1172 NG-16
Botkins, 1192 NL-3
Bowerston, 421 NL-17
Bowling Green, 29382 NF-6
Bradford, 1832 NN-2
Bradner, 1149 NF-7
Bratenahl, 1333 SK-18
Brecksville, 13474 NG-15
Bremen, 1244 SC-12
Brentwood, 5500 SF-2
Brentwood Lake, 650 NG-13
Brewster, 2306 NJ-15
Briarwood Beach NH-14
Bridgeport, 2125 NN-19
Bridgetown, 12569 SF-2
Brilliant, 1600 NM-20
Brimfield, 3248 NH-16
Broadview Hts., 16721 NG-15
Brookfield, 1288 NG-20
Brooklyn, 11276 NF-15
Brooklyn Hts., 1549 SM-17
Brook Park, 20679 NF-14
Brookside Estates, 670 SF-18
Brookville, 5279 SB-3
BROWN CO., 43807 SI-5
Brunswick, 34788 NG-14
Bryan, 8241 NF-2
Buckeye Lake, 3100 SB-12
Bucyrus, 12945 NJ-9
Buffalo, 200 SB-16
Burlington, 2794 SK-11
Burton, 1444 NF-17
BUTLER CO., 343207 SE-1
Butler, 905 NK-11
Byesville, 2611 SB-16
Cadiz, 3373 NM-18
Calcutta, 3491 NJ-20
Caldwell, 1760 SC-16
Caledonia, 565 NK-9
Cambridge, 11596 SA-16
Camden, 2291 SD-1
Campbell, 9020 NH-20
Camp Dennison, 600 SK-5
Canal Fulton, 5017 NI-15
Canal Winchester, 5193 SB-10
Canfield, 7188 NH-19
Canton, 79255 NI-16
Cardington, 1979 NK-9
Carey, 3864 NI-7
Carlisle, 5522 SD-3
CARROLL CO., 29599 NJ-18
Carrollton, 3306 NK-18
Castalia, 925 NF-10
Cedarville, 4085 SC-5
Celina, 10275 NK-2
Centerburg, 1469 NM-10
Centerville, 23133 SD-4
Chagrin Falls, 3912 NF-16
CHAMPAIGN CO., 39544 NN-4
Champion, 4727 NG-19
Chardon, 5270 NE-17
Chauncey, 1118 SE-13
Cherry Gr., 4555 SG-3
Chesapeake, 856 SK-12
Chesterland, 2646 NE-16
Cheviot, 8543 SF-2
Chillicothe, 22170 SE-9
Churchill, 2601 NG-19
Cincinnati, 317361 SG-2
Circleville, 13400 SD-9
CLARK CO., 143351 SB-6
Clayton, 13268 SB-3
Clearview, 750 NF-13
CLERMONT CO., 185799 SH-3
Cleveland, 461324 NF-15
Cleveland Hts., 49016 NE-15
Cleves, 2641 SF-1
CLINTON CO., 41756 SD-6
Clinton, 1391 NI-15
Clyde, 6047 NG-9
Coal Gr., 2056 SJ-11
Coldwater, 4457 NL-1
Colerain Hts., 2600 SF-2
COLUMBIANA CO., 111523 NI-18
Columbiana, 5703 NI-19
Columbus, 728432 SB-9
Columbus Gr., 2169 NI-4
Conneaut, 12666 NC-20
Continental, 1170 NH-3
Convoy, 1083 NI-1
Coolville, 552 SF-15
Copley, 750 NH-15
Corning, 611 SD-13
Cortland, 6703 NF-19
COSHOCTON CO., 37132 NM-13
Coshocton, 11630 NM-14
Covedale, 6360 SM-1
Covington, 2555 NN-3
Craig Beach, 1217 NH-18
CRAWFORD CO., 46091 NI-9
Crestline, 4974 NJ-10
Creston, 2149 NI-14
Cridersville, 1800 NK-4
Crooksville, 2530 SC-13
Crystal Lakes, 1411 SB-4
Curtice, 800 NF-7
CUYAHOGA CO., 1363888 NG-15
Cuyahoga Falls, 50375 NH-16
Cuyahoga Hts., 578 SM-18
Dalton, 1588 NJ-15
Damascus, 950 NI-18
Danville, 1100 NL-12
Darbydale, 600 SB-8
DARKE CO., 52960 NM-1
Dayton, 161696 SC-4
Deer Park, 5800 SF-3
DEFIANCE CO., 39054 NF-1
Defiance, 16163 NG-3
DeForest, 1150 NB-12
De Graff, 1189 NM-5
DELAWARE CO., 132797 NM-10
Delaware, 28358 NM-8
Delhi Hills, 20000 SM-2
Delphos, 6872 NI-3
Delta, 2921 NE-4
Dennison, 2941 NL-17
Deshler, 1849 NG-5
Devola, 2771 SE-16
Dillonvale, 767 NM-19
Dover, 12345 NK-16
Doylestown, 2819 NI-15
Dresden, 1423 NN-13
Drexel, 2057 SC-3
Dry Run, 750 SI-9
Dublin, 33606 NN-8
Duncan Falls, 600 SB-14
Dunkirk, 949 NJ-6
E. Alliance, 1175 NI-18
E. Canton, 1611 NJ-17
E. Cleveland, 26255 NE-15
Eastlake, 19990 ND-16
E. Liverpool, 12611 NK-20
E. Palestine, 4835 NI-20
E. Sparta, 789 NJ-16
Eastview SL-9
Eaton, 8170 SC-2
Eaton Estates, 1409 NG-13
Eden Park, 430 SI-9
Edgerton, 2050 NF-1
Edon, 872 NE-1
Elida, 1901 NJ-3
Elmore, 1401 NF-8
Elmwood Place, 2524 SL-3
Elyria, 56096 NF-13
Englewood, 12460 SB-3
Enon, 2573 SB-5
ERIE CO., 78709 NF-10
Euclid, 51260 NE-16
Evendale, 2989 SK-4
Excello, 50 SD-3
Fairborn, 32474 SB-4
Fairfax, 1857 SL-4
FAIRFIELD CO., 132549 SB-11
Fairfield, 42544 SE-2
Fairhope, 1720 NJ-17
Fairlawn, 7287 NH-15
Fairport Hbr., 3192 ND-17
Fairview Park, 17087 NF-14
Farmersville, 968 SC-3
FAYETTE CO., 28158 SD-8
Fayette, 1323 ND-3
Felicity, 912 SH-4
Findlay, 39797 NH-6
Finneytown, 13492 SK-3
Flushing, 909 NN-18
Forest, 1467 NJ-7
Forest Hills, 200 SM-11
Forest Park, 18738 SF-2
Forestville, 10978 SG-3
Ft. Loramie, 1432 NL-3
Ft. Recovery, 1305 NL-1
Ft. Shawnee, 3881 NJ-4
Fostoria, 13720 NH-7
Frankfort, 1012 SE-8
FRANKLIN CO., 1088944 SB-8
Franklin, 12065 SD-3
Franklin Furnace, 1537 SJ-10
Frazeysburg, 1278 NN-13
Fredericktown, 2552 NL-11
Freeport, 403 NM-17
Fremont, 17236 NF-8
Fruit Hill, 3945 SG-3
FULTON CO., 42446 NE-4
Gahanna, 33224 SA-10
Galion, 11491 NJ-10
GALLIA CO., 31398 SH-13
Gallipolis, 4176 SI-13
Gambier, 1986 NL-12
Garfield Hts., 29881 NF-15
Garrettsville, 2223 NG-17
Gates Mills, 2432 NE-16
GEAUGA CO., 93941 NE-17
Geneva, 6511 ND-18
Geneva-on-the-Lake, 1545 NC-18
Genoa, 2346 NE-7
Georgetown, 3786 SH-5
Germantown, 5043 SD-3
Ghent, 1600 NG-15
Gibsonburg, 2454 NF-7
Girard, 10654 NG-19
Glandorf, 943 NH-4
Glendale, 2179 SJ-3
Glenmoor, 2192 NJ-20
Glouster, 2041 SD-13
Gnadenhutten, 1287 NL-16
Golf Manor, 3819 SL-3
Goshen, 730 SF-4
Grafton, 6105 NG-13
Grand Rapids, 990 NF-5
Grandview Hts., 6452 SB-9
Granville, 5125 NN-11
Gratis, 912 SC-2
Green, 23378 NI-16
GREENE CO., 151257 SC-4
Greenfield, 4939 SE-7
Greenhills, 3910 SJ-3
Greensburg NI-16
Green Sprs., 1237 NG-9
Greentown, 3154 NI-16
Greenview, 600 SK-7
Greenville, 13234 NN-1
Greenwich, 1547 NH-11
Groesbeck, 7202 SF-2
Grove City, 29165 SB-9
Groveport, 4367 SB-10
GUERNSEY CO., 41362 NM-16
Hamden, 911 SF-11
HAMILTON CO., 823472 SF-1
Hamilton, 60763 SE-2
Hamilton Meadows, 2100 SB-9
Hamler, 693 NG-4
HANCOCK CO., 73133 NI-5
Hanover, 967 NN-12
HARDIN CO., 31608 NJ-6
HARRISON CO., 15967 NM-18
Harrison, 7478 SF-1
Harrisville, 262 NM-19
Hartville, 2236 NI-16
Heath, 8704 SA-12
Hebron, 2067 SB-12
HENRY CO., 29318 NG-4
Hicksville, 3565 NG-1
HIGHLAND CO., 41963 SF-7
Highland Hts., 8512 SK-20
Highland Hills, 1605 SM-19
Highland Park, 700 NI-16
Hilliard, 25808 SA-8
Hillsboro, 6632 SF-6
Hiram, 1231 NG-17
HOCKING CO., 28644 SE-11
Holgate, 1181 NG-4
Holland, 1319 NE-6
HOLMES CO., 40681 NK-14
Hopedale, 986 NM-18
Hubbard, 8105 NG-20
Huber Hts., 38240 SB-4
Hudson, 23053 NG-16
HURON CO., 60231 NG-11
Huron, 7718 NF-11
Independence, 7096 NF-15
Ironton, 11230 SJ-11
JACKSON CO., 33074 SH-11
Jackson, 6159 SG-11
Jackson Cen., 1461 NL-4
Jamestown, 1881 SC-6
JEFFERSON CO., 71888 NK-19
Jefferson, 3534 ND-19
Jeffersonville, 1257 SD-7
Jewett, 788 NL-18
Johnstown, 3650 NN-10
Junction City, 857 SC-12
Kalida, 1093 NI-3
Kendall Hts., 850 NB-8
Kent, 28082 NH-16
Kenton, 8181 NK-6
Kenwood, 7423 SK-4
Kettering, 56494 SC-4
Killbuck, 884 NK-14
Kingston, 1010 SE-10
Kingsville, 650 NC-19
Kinsman, 600 NF-20
Kirtland, 6970 NE-16
KNOX CO., 56930 NM-12
Lagrange, 1813 NG-13
LAKE CO., 228878 ND-17
Lake Cable, 2500 NB-8
Lake Milton, 1100 NH-18
Lakemore, 2488 NH-16
Lakeside, 950 NE-10
Lakeview, 1106 NL-5
Lakewood, 54378 NF-14
Lancaster, 35914 SC-11
Lansing, 400 NN-19
La Rue, 754 NK-7
Laurel Ridge, 2350 NI-17
LAWRENCE CO., 62550 SK-11
Leavittsburg, 2200 NG-18
Lebanon, 18766 SE-4
Leesburg, 1304 SE-7
Leetonia, 2009 NI-19
Leipsic, 2231 NH-4
Lewisburg, 1788 SB-2
Lexington, 4117 NJ-11
Liberty Cen., 1118 NF-4
LICKING CO., 150634 NN-11
Lima, 40549 NJ-4
Lincoln Hts., 3947 SK-3
Lincoln Vil., 9482 SB-9
Lisbon, 2872 NJ-19
Little Farms SI-17
Lockland, 3505 SK-3
Lodi, 3239 NH-13
LOGAN CO., 46411 NL-5
Logan, 6870 SD-12
London, 9087 SB-7
LORAIN CO., 291164 NG-13
Lorain, 67955 NF-13
Lordstown, 3661 NG-19
Loudonville, 2997 NK-12
Louisville, 9138 NI-17
Loveland, 11302 SF-3
Loveland Park, 1799 SJ-6
Lowell, 607 SD-16
Lowellville, 1202 NH-20
LUCAS CO., 454216 NE-5
Lucas, 609 NJ-12
Lucasville, 1588 SH-9
Luckey, 980 NF-7
Lynchburg, 1402 SF-5
Lyndhurst, 14875 NE-16
Macedonia, 10087 NG-16
Mack, 2000 SL-1
Madeira, 8608 SF-3
MADISON CO., 40624 SC-7
Madison, 2990 ND-18
Magnolia, 926 NK-17
MAHONING CO., 251660 NH-19
Malta, 684 SC-14
Malvern, 1233 NJ-17
Manchester, 2051 SI-6
Manchester, 4000 NI-15
Mansfield, 50688 NJ-11
Mantua, 1025 NG-17
Maple Hts., 25490 NF-15
Marble Cliff, 624 SH-18
Marblehead, 854 NE-10
Mariemont, 3239 SG-3
Marietta, 14035 SE-16
MARION CO., 66396 NK-9
Marion, 37300 NK-8
Marshallville, 822 NI-15
Martins Ferry, 7021 NN-19
Marysville, 16245 NM-7
Mason, 27308 SE-3
Massillon, 31542 NJ-16
Masury, 2618 NG-20
Maumee, 14705 NE-6
Mayfield, 3351 SK-20
Mayfield Hts., 18922 NE-16
McArthur, 1977 SF-12
McClure, 754 NF-5
McComb, 1706 NH-5
McConnelsville, 1783 SC-15
McDonald, 3409 NB-13
McKinley Hts., 700 NG-19
Mechanicsburg, 1731 NN-6
MEDINA CO., 161641 NH-14
Medina, 26487 NH-14
Medway, 2000 SB-4
MEIGS CO., 23242 SG-14
Mendon, 696 NJ-2
Mentor, 50004 ND-16
Mentor-on-the-Lake, 8209 ND-16
MERCER CO., 40933 NK-1
MIAMI CO., 100230 NN-3
Miamisburg, 19857 SD-3
Miamitown, 730 SF-1
Middleburg Hts., 15680 NF-14
Middlefield, 2396 NF-18
Middle Pt., 589 NI-2
Middleport, 2505 SG-14
Middletown, 51941 SD-3
Milan, 1407 NG-11
Milford, 6404 SF-3
Milford Cen., 669 NM-7
Millbury, 1148 NE-7
Millersburg, 3500 NK-14
Millersport, 961 SB-11
Millville, 862 SE-1
Mineral City, 856 NK-16
Mineral Ridge, 3900 NH-19
Minerva, 3966 NJ-17
Minerva Park, 1242 NN-9
Mingo Jct., 3472 NL-20
Minster, 2787 NL-3
Mogadore, 3954 NH-16
MONROE CO., 14927 SB-17
Monroe, 8821 SE-3
Monroeville, 1412 NG-10
MONTGOMERY CO., 552187 SC-2
Montgomery, 9777 SF-3
Montpelier, 4182 NE-2
Moraine, 6862 SC-4
Moreland Hills, 3264 SM-20
MORGAN CO., 14843 SD-14
MORROW CO., 33568 NK-9
Morrow, 1422 SE-4
Mt. Carmel, 4308 SG-3
Mt. Carmel Hts., 1200 SM-5
Mt. Gilead, 3470 NK-10
Mt. Healthy, 6835 SF-2
Mt. Orab, 2701 SG-5
Mt. Repose, 4102 SF-3
Mt. Sterling, 1841 SC-8
Mt. Vernon, 15826 NL-11
Mulberry, 3139 SF-3
Munroe Falls, 5320 NA-6
MUSKINGUM CO., 85423 SB-15
Napoleon, 9279 NF-4
Navarre, 1440 NJ-16
Nefts, 1138 NN-19
Negley, 900 NJ-20
Nelsonville, 5483 SE-13
Nevada, 799 NJ-8
Newark, 46601 NN-12
New Athens, 350 NM-18
New Boston, 2230 SI-9
New Bremen, 2965 NL-3
Newburgh Hts., 2289 SM-18
New Carlisle, 5655 SB-4
Newcomerstown, 3973 NM-15
New Concord, 2744 SA-15
New Holland, 777 SD-8
New Knoxville, 901 NK-3
New Lebanon, 4242 SC-3
New Lexington, 4712 SC-13
New London, 2693 NH-12
New Madison, 788 SB-1
New Matamoras, 930 SD-18
New Miami, 2588 SE-2
New Middletown, 1644 NI-20
New Paris, 1562 SB-1
New Philadelphia, 17363 NL-16
Newport, 700 SE-17
New Richmond, 2356 SH-3
New Springfield, 600 NI-20
New Straitsville, 801 SD-13
Newton Falls, 4892 NG-18
Newtown, 2336 SG-3
New Vienna, 1358 SE-6
New Washington, 965 NI-10
New Waterford, 1383 NI-20
Niles, 20337 NG-19
NOBLE CO., 14054 SC-16
N. Baltimore, 3330 NG-6
Northbrook, 11076 SF-2
N. Canton, 16722 NI-16
N. College Hill, 9685 SF-2
Northfield, 3771 NF-16
Northfield Cen., 2570 NG-16
N. Industry, 2700 NJ-16
N. Jackson, 900 NH-19
N. Kingsville, 2647 NC-19
N. Lawrence, 800 NI-15
N. Lewisburg, 1605 NM-6
N. Lima, 900 NI-20
N. Olmsted, 33481 NF-14
N. Perry, 897 ND-17
N. Randall, 886 SM-19
Northridge, 8487 SB-4
Northridge, 6853 SA-6
N. Ridgeville, 24294 NF-13
N. Royalton, 29598 NG-15
Northwood, 5484 NE-7
Norton, 11648 NH-15
Norwalk, 16353 NG-11
Norwood, 20781 SF-2
Oak Hbr., 2819 NE-8
Oak Hill, 1662 SH-11
Oakwood, 3643 SN-20
Oakwood, 8902 SC-4
Oakwood, 571 NH-3
Oberlin, 8139 NG-12
Obetz, 4115 SB-9
Ohio City, 763 NJ-1
Olmsted Falls, 8445 SN-14
Oneida SE-3
Ontario, 5271 NJ-10
Orange, 3366 SM-20
Oregon, 19419 NE-7
Orrville, 8506 NI-14
Orwell, 1532 NE-18
OTTAWA CO., 41192 NE-7
Ottawa, 4491 NH-4
Ottawa Hills, 4608 ND-6
Ottoville, 855 NI-3
Overlook SL-9
Owensville, 823 SG-4
Oxford, 22283 SD-1
Page Manor SC-4
Painesville, 17428 ND-17
Painesville on the Lake, 850 ND-17
Pandora, 1214 NI-5
Parkman, 600 NF-18
Parma, 83861 NF-15
Parma Hts., 21209 NF-14
Pataskala, 11850 SA-11
PAULDING CO., 19665 NG-1
Paulding, 3442 NH-2
Payne, 1149 NH-1
Peebles, 1793 SH-7
Pemberville, 1339 NF-7
Pepper Pike, 5959 NF-16
PERRY CO., 35074 SC-13
Perry, 1225 ND-17
Perry Hts., 8900 NC-8
Perrysburg, 16840 NE-6
Perrysville, 830 NK-12
Petersburg, 950 NI-20
Pettisville, 500 NE-3
Phillipsburg, 620 SB-3
Philo, 765 SB-14
PICKAWAY CO., 51723 SD-9
Pickerington, 12627 SB-10
PIKE CO., 28194 SG-9
Piketon, 1962 SG-9
Pioneer, 1431 ND-2
Piqua, 20728 NN-3
Pisgah, 1000 SE-3
Plain City, 3167 NN-8
Pleasant Hill, 1131 NN-3
Pleasant Run Farms, 4731 SJ-2
Pleasant Valley, 500 SE-9
Pleasantville, 861 SC-11
Plymouth, 1866 NI-10
Poast Town, 150 SD-3
Poland, 2780 NH-20
Pomeroy, 1997 SG-14
PORTAGE CO., 154870 NG-17
Portage Lakes, 9870 NH-16
Port Clinton, 6316 NE-9
Portsmouth, 19913 SI-9
Powhatan Pt., 1719 SB-19
PREBLE CO., 42417 SC-1
Proctorville, 615 SK-12
Prospect, 1157 NL-8
PUTNAM CO., 34754 NI-4
Queen Acres, 650 SE-2
Quincy, 710 NM-4
Racine, 769 SH-14
Randolph, 750 NH-17
Ravenna, 11506 NG-17
Reading, 10747 SF-2
Reedurban, 4400 NJ-16
Reminderville, 2377 NF-16
Reno, 850 SE-17

*, †, ‡, See explanation under state title in this index.
County names are listed in capital letters and in boldface type.

Rensselaer Park, 850 ....SK-3
Republic, 597 ....NH-9
Reynoldsburg, 32878 ....SB-10
Richfield, 3517 ....NG-15
RICHLAND CO., 128267 ....NI-11
Richmond Dale, 700 ....SF-10
Richmond Hts., 10855 ....NE-16
Richville, 1600 ....NJ-16
Richwood, 2177 ....NL-7
Rio Grande, 916 ....SH-12
Ripley, 1791 ....SI-5
Risingsun, 602 ....NG-7
Rittman, 6272 ....NI-14
Riverside, 23071 ....SL-9
Rockford, 1111 ....NJ-1
Rocky River, 20188 ....NF-14
Rosemount, 2043 ....SI-9
Roseville, 1933 ....SC-13
ROSS CO., 74424 ....SE-8
Ross, 1971 ....SF-1
Rossford, 6357 ....NE-6
Russells Pt., 1580 ....NL-5
Sabina, 2819 ....SD-6
Sagamore Hills, 1930 ....NG-15
Sahara Sands, 650 ....NB-8
St. Bernard, 4640 ....SF-2
St. Clairsville, 5025 ....NN-19
St. Henry, 2301 ....NL-1
St. Marys, 8276 ....NK-2
St. Paris, 1984 ....NN-4
Salem, 12101 ....NI-19
Salineville, 1357 ....NK-19
SANDUSKY CO., 61753 ....NF-8
Sandusky, 27030 ....NF-10
Sardinia, 890 ....SG-5
Sawyerwood, 1730 ....NC-6
Schoenbrunn, 700 ....NL-16
Scio, 786 ....NL-18
SCIOTO CO., 77453 ....SI-8
Sciotodale, 982 ....SI-10
Seaman, 1060 ....SH-6
Sebring, 4744 ....NI-18
SENECA CO., 57734 ....NH-8
Seven Hills, 12098 ....NF-15
Seven Hills, 2000 ....SJ-2
Seven Mile, 713 ....SE-2
Seville, 2259 ....NH-14
Shadyside, 3608 ....SA-20
Shaker Hts., 28459 ....NF-15
Sharonville, 13505 ....SF-3
Shawnee, 656 ....SD-13
Sheffield, 3287 ....NF-13
Sheffield Lake, 9222 ....NF-13
SHELBY CO., 48566 ....NL-4
Shelby, 9579 ....NI-10
Sherwood, 792 ....NG-2
Shiloh, 11272 ....SB-3
Shiloh, 711 ....NI-11
Shreve, 1537 ....NJ-13
Sidney, 20254 ....NM-4
Silver Lake, 3189 ....NH-16
Silverton, 4935 ....SL-4
Singing Hills SD-4
Smithfield, 839 ....NM-19
Smithville, 1319 ....NI-14
Solon, 22248 ....NF-16
Somerset, 1599 ....SC-12
S. Amherst, 1817 ....NF-12
S. Bloomfield, 1310 ....SC-9
S. Charleston, 1813 ....SB-6
S. Euclid, 22860 ....NE-16
S. Lebanon, 2928 ....SE-4
S. Point, 3831 ....SK-11
S. Russell, 4013 ....NF-16
S. Webster, 744 ....SI-10
S. West Hubbard, 1200 ....NC-14
S. Zanesville, 1986 ....SB-14
Spencer, 788 ....NH-13
Spencerville, 2230 ....NJ-3
Springboro, 15051 ....SD-3
Springdale, 10129 ....SF-2
Springfield, 64483 ....SB-5
STARK CO., 377519 ....NI-17
Steubenville, 19568 ....NL-20
Stow, 34290 ....NH-16
Strasburg, 2453 ....NK-16
Streetsboro, 13822 ....NG-16
Strongsville, 44560 ....NG-14
Struthers, 11334 ....NH-20
Stryker, 1398 ....NE-2
Sugarcreek, 2159 ....NK-15
Summerside, 5523 ....SM-5
Summerside Estates, 1700 ....SM-5
SUMMIT CO., 546773 ....NH-15
Summit, 700 ....NC-13
Sunbury, 3051 ....NM-9
Sunnyland, 250 ....SN-11
Surrey Hill, 700 ....NB-12
Swanton, 3331 ....NE-5
Sycamore, 896 ....NI-8
Sylvania, 19027 ....ND-6
Syracuse, 874 ....SG-14
Tallmadge, 17165 ....NH-16
Terrace Pk., 2197 ....SL-5
The Plains, 2931 ....SE-13
The Vil. of Indian Hill, 5711 ....SK-5
Thornville, 794 ....SB-12
Tiffin, 17497 ....NH-8
Tiltonsville, 1267 ....NM-19
Timberlake, 758 ....ND-16
Tipp City, 9285 ....SB-4
Toledo, 308973 ....NE-6
Toronto, 5537 ....NL-20
Trenton, 9953 ....SD-2
Trotwood, 27070 ....SC-3
Troy, 22169 ....NN-3
TRUMBULL CO., 221785 ....NF-19
Turpin Hills, 4960 ....SM-4
TUSCARAWAS CO., 91706 ....NM-16
Tuscarawas, 958 ....NL-16
Twinsburg, 17236 ....NG-16
Uhrichsville, 5696 ....NL-16
UNION CO., 43750 ....NM-7
Union, 5536 ....SB-3
Union City, 1711 ....NM-1
Uniontown, 2802 ....NI-16
University Hts., 13723 ....NF-16
Upper Arlington, 32406 ....SA-9
Upper Sandusky, 6458 ....NJ-8
Urbana, 11597 ....NN-5
Urbancrest, 870 ....SB-9
Utica, 2074 ....NM-11
Valley View, 2157 ....SN-18
Valleyview, 577 ....SH-17
Vandalia, 14495 ....SB-4
VAN WERT CO., 29277 ....NJ-2
Van Wert, 10599 ....NI-2
Venice Hts., 1300 ....NA-12
Vermilion, 10940 ....NF-12
Versailles, 2546 ....NM-2
Viking Vil., 1230 ....SM-5
Villa Nova, 800 ....NK-2
VINTON CO., 13231 ....SF-11
Wadsworth, 19462 ....NH-15
Wakeman, 972 ....NG-12
Walbridge, 3117 ....NE-7
Walton Hills, 2391 ....SN-19
Wapakoneta, 9518 ....NK-3
WARREN CO., 181743 ....SE-4
Warren, 46608 ....NG-19
Warrensville Hts., 14719 ....NF-15
Warsaw, 782 ....NL-13
WASHINGTON CO., 62505 ....SD-16
Washington Court House, 13317 ....SD-7
Washingtonville, 769 ....NI-19
Waterford, 600 ....SD-15
Waterville, 5137 ....NE-6
Wauseon, 7183 ....NE-4
Waverly, 4448 ....SG-9
WAYNE CO., 113121 ....NI-14
Wayne, 832 ....NG-7
Wayne Lakes, 672 ....SA-1
Waynesburg, 983 ....NJ-17
Waynesfield, 808 ....NK-4
Waynesville, 2833 ....SD-4
Wellington, 4560 ....NG-12
Wellston, 5994 ....SG-11
Wellsville, 4089 ....NK-20
W. Alexandria, 1359 ....SC-2
W. Carrollton, 13487 ....SC-3
W. Chester, 800 ....SE-3
Westerville, 34922 ....NN-9
Westfield Cen., 1113 ....NH-14
W. Jefferson, 4266 ....SB-8
W. Lafayette, 2330 ....NM-15
Westlake, 32024 ....NF-14
W. Liberty, 1790 ....NM-5
W. Mansfield, 696 ....NL-6
W. Milton, 4663 ....SB-3
Weston, 1653 ....NF-5
W. Portsmouth, 3458 ....SI-9
W. Salem, 1503 ....NI-13
W. Union, 3033 ....SI-7
W. Unity, 1738 ....NE-2
Westview, 530 ....NF-14
Wheelersburg, 6471 ....SI-10
Whitehall, 18611 ....SB-10
Whitehouse, 2961 ....NE-5
White Oak, 13277 ....SF-2
Wickliffe, 13299 ....NE-16
Wilberforce, 1579 ....SC-5
Wildbrook Acres, 1500 ....SK-3
Willard, 6869 ....NH-10
WILLIAMS CO., 38802 ....NE-1
Williamsburg, 2316 ....SG-4
Williamsdale, 600 ....SE-2
Williamsport, 994 ....SD-9
Williston, 600 ....NE-7
Willoughby, 22488 ....NE-16
Willoughby Hills, 8476 ....NE-16
Willowick, 14072 ....NE-16
Wilmington, 12187 ....SE-5
Winchester, 1049 ....SH-6
Windham, 2766 ....NG-18
Wintersville, 3824 ....NL-19
Withamsville, 3145 ....SG-3
WOOD CO., 123020 ....NG-6
Woodlawn, 2684 ....SK-3
Woodmere, 813 ....SL-20
Woodsfield, 2535 ....SC-18
Woodville, 1990 ....NF-7
Woodworth, 700 ....NI-20
Wooster, 25322 ....NJ-14
Wooster Hts., 850 ....NJ-11
Worthington, 13602 ....NN-9
WYANDOT CO., 22826 ....NJ-7
Wyoming, 7987 ....SK-3
Xenia, 23822 ....SC-5
Yellow Sprs., 3702 ....SC-5
Yorkville, 1196 ....NM-19
Youngstown, 79271 ....NH-20
Zanesville, 25277 ....SB-14

Oklahoma

Map pp. 166-169

Ada, 16008 ....H-15
ADAIR CO., 21614 ....E-20
Adair, 699 ....C-18
Afton, 1100 ....C-19
Alex, 642 ....H-12
ALFALFA CO., 5910 ....C-11
Allen, 948 ....H-16
Altus, 20559 ....I-9
Alva, 5034 ....C-10
Anadarko, 6539 ....G-11
Antlers, 2534 ....J-18
Apache, 1598 ....H-11
Arapaho, 713 ....F-10
Ardmore, 23928 ....J-14
Arkoma, 2185 ....F-20
Arnett, 505 ....D-8
Asher, 430 ....H-14
ATOKA CO., 14142 ....J-16
Atoka, 2983 ....I-16
Barnsdall, 1289 ....C-16
Bartlesville, 34708 ....C-17
BEAVER CO., 5582 ....C-7
Beaver, 1478 ....B-6
BECKHAM CO., 19894 ....G-8
Beggs, 1378 ....E-16
Bethany, 20009 ....F-13
Bethel Acres, 2852 ....G-14
Billings, 560 ....C-13
Binger, 709 ....G-11
Bixby, 16611 ....E-17
Blackwell, 7423 ....B-14
BLAINE CO., 11678 ....E-11
Blair, 850 ....H-9
Blanchard, 3178 ....G-13
Boise City, 1384 ....B-2
Bokchito, 567 ....J-16
Bokoshe, 457 ....G-19
Boley, 1110 ....F-15
Boswell, 709 ....J-17
Bristow, 4307 ....E-16
Broken Arrow, 83607 ....E-17
Broken Bow, 4132 ....J-20
BRYAN CO., 37306 ....J-16
Buffalo, 1139 ....B-8
Burns Flat, 1725 ....G-9
Cache, 2397 ....I-10
CADDO CO., 30070 ....G-11
Caddo, 950 ....J-16
Calera, 1767 ....K-16
CANADIAN CO., 92904 ....F-12
Canton, 597 ....E-11
Canute, 514 ....F-9
Carmen, 386 ....C-11
Carnegie, 1593 ....G-11
CARTER CO., 46396 ....J-13
Catoosa, 5838 ....D-17
Cement, 522 ....H-12
Chandler, 2824 ....F-15
Checotah, 3484 ....F-18
Chelsea, 2213 ....C-18
CHEROKEE CO., 43783 ....E-19
Cherokee, 1559 ....C-11
Cheyenne, 714 ....F-8
Chickasha, 16345 ....G-12
CHOCTAW CO., 15431 ....J-17
Choctaw, 10156 ....F-14
Chouteau, 1958 ....D-18
CIMARRON CO., 2961 ....B-2
Claremore, 16773 ....D-17
Clayton, 728 ....I-18
CLEVELAND CO., 219966 ....G-13
Cleveland, 3241 ....D-15
Clinton, 8364 ....F-10
COAL CO., 5946 ....I-16
Coalgate, 1956 ....I-16
Colbert, 1085 ....K-15
Colcord, 857 ....D-19
Collinsville, 4263 ....D-17
COMANCHE CO., 113890 ....I-11
Comanche, 1502 ....I-12
Commerce, 2581 ....B-19
Copan, 805 ....B-17
Cordell, 2861 ....G-10
Corn, 571 ....G-10
COTTON CO., 6582 ....J-11
Countyline, 300 ....I-13
Covington, 545 ....D-13
Coweta, 7781 ....E-17
Cowlington, 135 ....G-19
CRAIG CO., 14880 ....C-18
CREEK CO., 68794 ....E-15
Crescent, 1293 ....E-13
Cushing, 8510 ....E-15
CUSTER CO., 24962 ....F-9
Cyril, 1165 ....H-11
Davenport, 878 ....F-15
Davidson, 361 ....J-9
Davis, 2609 ....I-14
DELAWARE CO., 38709 ....C-19
Delaware, 468 ....B-17
Del City, 22171 ....F-13
Depew, 568 ....E-15
Dewar, 913 ....F-17
DEWEY CO., 4549 ....E-9
Dewey, 3296 ....B-17
Dickson, 1167 ....J-14
Dill City, 516 ....G-9
Drumright, 2886 ....E-15
Duncan, 22031 ....I-12
Durant, 14565 ....J-16
Dustin, 448 ....G-16
Edmond, 71643 ....F-13
Eldorado, 504 ....I-8
Elgin, 1217 ....H-11
Elk City, 10511 ....F-9
ELLIS CO., 3996 ....D-8
Elmore City, 762 ....I-13
El Reno, 15938 ....F-12
Enid, 46436 ....D-12
Erick, 1010 ....G-8
Eufaula, 2723 ....G-18
Fairfax, 1518 ....C-15
Fairland, 1010 ....C-19
Fairview, 2662 ....D-11
Fletcher, 1027 ....H-11
Forest Park, 1138 ....K-3
Forgan, 511 ....B-6
Ft. Cobb, 655 ....G-11
Ft. Gibson, 4170 ....E-18
Ft. Towson, 613 ....J-18
Frederick, 4378 ....I-10
Garber, 818 ....D-13
GARFIELD CO., 57105 ....C-12
GARVIN CO., 27218 ....H-13
Geary, 1223 ....F-11
Geronimo, 962 ....I-11
Glencoe, 592 ....D-14
Glenpool, 8407 ....E-17
Goodwell, 1175 ....C-4
Gore, 887 ....F-19
GRADY CO., 47439 ....H-12
Grandfield, 1047 ....J-10
Granite, 1897 ....H-9
GRANT CO., 4973 ....B-12
GREER CO., 5888 ....H-8
Grove, 5574 ....C-19
Guthrie, 10110 ....E-13
Guymon, 10565 ....C-4
Haileyville, 890 ....H-18
Hammon, 439 ....F-9
HARMON CO., 3053 ....H-8
HARPER CO., 3398 ....C-8
Harrah, 4912 ....F-14
Hartshorne, 2069 ....H-18
HASKELL CO., 12044 ....G-19
Haskell, 1791 ....E-17
Healdton, 2775 ....J-13
Heavener, 3199 ....H-20
Helena, 1412 ....C-11
Hennessey, 2024 ....D-12
Henryetta, 6042 ....F-17
Hinton, 2172 ....F-11
Hobart, 3878 ....H-9
Holdenville, 5575 ....G-16
Hollis, 2108 ....H-7
Hominy, 3766 ....D-16
Hooker, 1704 ....B-5
Howe, 708 ....H-20
HUGHES CO., 13898 ....G-16
Hugo, 5569 ....J-18
Hulbert, 534 ....E-19
Hydro, 1037 ....F-11
Idabel, 6946 ....K-19
Inola, 1677 ....D-18
JACKSON CO., 27338 ....I-8
Jay, 2713 ....C-19
JEFFERSON CO., 6535 ....J-12
Jenks, 11560 ....E-17
JOHNSTON CO., 10522 ....I-15
Jones, 2607 ....J-6
KAY CO., 47260 ....B-14
Kellyville, 919 ....E-16
Keota, 526 ....G-19
Keyes, 386 ....B-2
Kiefer, 1090 ....E-16
KINGFISHER CO., 14072 ....E-12
Kingfisher, 4452 ....E-12
Kingston, 1444 ....J-15
KIOWA CO., 9977 ....H-10
Kiowa, 694 ....H-17
Konawa, 1429 ....H-15
Krebs, 2093 ....H-17
Lamont, 450 ....C-13
Langley, 671 ....C-19
Langston, 1678 ....E-14
LATIMER CO., 10575 ....H-18
Laverne, 1046 ....C-8
Lawton, 91730 ....I-11
Leedey, 333 ....E-9
LE FLORE CO., 48896 ....I-19
Lexington, 2120 ....H-13
LINCOLN CO., 32262 ....E-14
Lindsay, 2886 ....H-13
Locust Gr., 1405 ....D-18
LOGAN CO., 35420 ....E-13
Lone Gr., 4868 ....J-14
Lone Wolf, 481 ....H-9
LOVE CO., 8905 ....J-13
Luther, 496 ....F-14
Madill, 3519 ....J-15
MAJOR CO., 7422 ....D-10
Mangum, 2753 ....H-8
Mannford, 2217 ....D-16
Marietta, 2431 ....K-14
Marlow, 4486 ....I-12
MARSHALL CO., 13652 ....J-15
Maud, 1148 ....G-15
MAYES CO., 38870 ....C-18
Maysville, 1294 ....H-13
McAlester, 17870 ....H-17
MCCLAIN CO., 28595 ....H-13
MCCURTAIN CO., 34006 ....I-19
McCurtain, 469 ....G-19
MCINTOSH CO., 19735 ....G-17
McLoud, 3698 ....F-14
Medford, 1133 ....B-13
Meeker, 976 ....F-14
Miami, 13485 ....B-19
Midwest City, 54662 ....F-13
Minco, 1713 ....G-12
Moore, 44987 ....G-13
Mooreland, 1206 ....C-9
Morris, 1327 ....F-17
Morrison, 629 ....D-14
Mounds, 1158 ....E-16
Mtn. Park, 383 ....H-10
Mtn. View, 849 ....G-10
Muldrow, 3136 ....F-20
MURRAY CO., 12718 ....I-14
MUSKOGEE CO., 70255 ....F-18
Muskogee, 38635 ....E-18
Mustang, 14551 ....F-13
Newcastle, 5814 ....G-13
Newkirk, 2188 ....B-14
Nichols Hills, 4032 ....J-2
Nicoma Park, 2424 ....K-5
Ninnekah, 1036 ....H-12
NOBLE CO., 11251 ....C-14
Noble, 5402 ....G-13
Norman, 99197 ....G-13
N. Enid, 827 ....D-12
NOWATA CO., 10836 ....B-17
Nowata, 4035 ....C-17
Oakhurst, 2731 ....D-16
Oilton, 1109 ....D-15
Okarche, 1143 ....F-12
Okay, 603 ....E-18
Okeene, 1213 ....D-11
Okemah, 3003 ....F-16
OKFUSKEE CO., 11679 ....F-15
OKLAHOMA CO., 676066 ....F-13
Oklahoma City, 523303 ....F-13
OKMULGEE CO., 39681 ....E-17
Okmulgee, 12727 ....F-17
Olustee, 657 ....I-9
Oologah, 1026 ....C-17
OSAGE CO., 45249 ....C-15
OTTAWA CO., 32761 ....B-19
Owasso, 21634 ....D-17
Paden, 444 ....F-15
Panama, 1383 ....G-20
Paoli, 653 ....H-14
Pauls Valley, 6179 ....H-14
Pawhuska, 3571 ....C-16
PAWNEE CO., 16789 ....D-14
Pawnee, 2200 ....D-15
PAYNE CO., 71059 ....E-14
Perkins, 2316 ....E-14
Perry, 5138 ....D-14
Picher, 1617 ....B-19
Piedmont, 4088 ....F-13
Pink, 1213 ....G-14
PITTSBURG CO., 44168 ....H-17
Pocola, 4255 ....G-20
Ponca City, 25596 ....C-14
Pond Cr., 862 ....C-12
PONTOTOC CO., 35174 ....I-15
Porter, 576 ....E-18
Porum, 732 ....F-18
Poteau, 7990 ....G-20
POTTAWATOMIE CO., 67348 ....G-14
Prague, 2110 ....F-15
Pryor, 9098 ....D-18
Purcell, 5627 ....H-13
PUSHMATAHA CO., 11750 ....I-18
Quapaw, 975 ....B-19
Quinton, 1075 ....G-18
Ralston, 354 ....C-15
Ramona, 568 ....C-17
Red Oak, 572 ....H-19
Ringling, 1093 ....J-13
Roff, 722 ....I-15
ROGER MILLS CO., 3201 ....E-8
ROGERS CO., 77193 ....D-17
Roland, 2977 ....F-20
Rush Sprs., 1283 ....H-12
Ryan, 858 ....J-12
Salina, 1434 ....D-18
Sallisaw, 8383 ....F-19
Sand Sprs., 17695 ....D-16
Sapulpa, 19759 ....E-16
Savanna, 743 ....H-17
Sayre, 4221 ....G-8
Seiling, 826 ....D-10
SEMINOLE CO., 24489 ....G-15
Seminole, 6756 ....G-15
Sentinel, 834 ....G-9
SEQUOYAH CO., 39979 ....F-20
Shattuck, 1254 ....D-8
Shawnee, 29446 ....G-14
Shidler, 523 ....C-15
Skiatook, 5879 ....D-17
Slaughterville, 3856 ....G-13
Snyder, 1475 ....I-10
S. Coffeyville, 804 ....B-17
Spavinaw, 561 ....D-19
Spencer, 3770 ....J-4
Sperry, 1038 ....D-17
Spiro, 2253 ....G-20
STEPHENS CO., 42474 ....I-13
Sterling, 761 ....H-12
Stigler, 2777 ....G-19
Stillwater, 41320 ....D-14
Stilwell, 3419 ....E-20
Stonewall, 465 ....I-15
Stratford, 1482 ....H-14
Stroud, 2747 ....E-15
Sulphur, 4810 ....I-14
Tahlequah, 15405 ....E-19
Talihina, 1216 ....H-19
Tecumseh, 6264 ....G-14
Temple, 1146 ....J-11
Terral, 364 ....K-12
TEXAS CO., 19935 ....B-4
Texhoma, 906 ....C-3
The Village, 10067 ....F-13
Thomas, 1160 ....E-10
TILLMAN CO., 8835 ....I-10
Tipton, 866 ....I-9
Tishomingo, 3186 ....J-15
Tonkawa, 3160 ....C-14
TULSA CO., 570313 ....E-17
Tulsa, 387807 ....D-17
Turley, 3231 ....D-17
Tuttle, 4852 ....G-12
Tyrone, 853 ....B-5
Valley Brook, 805 ....L-3
Valliant, 760 ....J-19
Velma, 660 ....I-13
Verden, 664 ....G-12
Vian, 1375 ....F-19
Vici, 645 ....D-9
Vinita, 5969 ....C-18
WAGONER CO., 61827 ....E-18
Wagoner, 7818 ....E-18
Wakita, 411 ....B-12
Walters, 2614 ....I-11
Wapanucka, 443 ....I-16
Warner, 1446 ....F-18
Warr Acres, 9658 ....K-1
WASHINGTON CO., 49121 ....C-17
WASHITA CO., 11247 ....G-9
Watonga, 4457 ....E-11
Waukomis, 1228 ....D-12
Waurika, 1891 ....J-12
Wayne, 712 ....H-14
Waynoka, 930 ....C-10
Weatherford, 9510 ....F-10
Webbers Falls, 733 ....F-19
Welch, 597 ....B-19
Weleetka, 983 ....G-16
Wellston, 824 ....F-14
Westville, 1612 ....E-20
Wetumka, 1421 ....G-16
Wewoka, 3417 ....G-15
Wilburton, 2932 ....H-18
Wilson, 1605 ....J-13
Wister, 1014 ....H-20
WOODS CO., 8670 ....C-10
WOODWARD CO., 18461 ....C-9
Woodward, 11789 ....D-9
Wright City, 816 ....J-19
Wynnewood, 2322 ....I-14
Wynona, 540 ....C-16
Yale, 1328 ....D-15
Yukon, 21152 ....F-13

Oregon

Map pp. 170-173

Albany, 43091 ....F-4
Aloha, 41741 ....C-4
Amity, 1469 ....D-4
Applegate, 100 ....M-3
Ashland, 20406 ....M-4
Astoria, 9660 ....A-2
Athena, 1215 ....B-13
Aumsville, 3104 ....E-4
Aurora, 657 ....D-5
BAKER CO., 16375 ....E-15
Baker City, 9671 ....E-15
Bandon, 2827 ....J-1
Barview, 1872 ....J-1
Bay City, 1152 ....C-2
Beaverton, 80520 ....C-4
Bend, 59779 ....H-8
BENTON CO., 79335 ....F-3
Bly, 700 ....L-8
Boardman, 3028 ....B-11
Brookings, 5878 ....M-1
Brownsville, 1480 ....G-4
Bunker Hill, 1462 ....J-1
Burns, 2880 ....I-12
Canby, 14238 ....D-5
Cannon Beach, 1608 ....B-2
Canyon City, 611 ....G-12
Canyonville, 1382 ....K-3
Carlton, 1484 ....D-4
Cascade Locks, 1112 ....C-6
Cave Jct., 1395 ....M-2
Central Pt., 14630 ....M-4
Charleston, 700 ....J-1
Chenoweth, 3412 ....C-8
Chiloquin, 719 ....L-6
CLACKAMAS CO., 357435 ....E-5
Clackamas, 5177 ....M-20
Clatskanie, 1608 ....B-4
CLATSOP CO., 35820 ....B-3
Coburg, 984 ....G-4
COLUMBIA CO., 46261 ....B-4
Columbia City, 1644 ....B-4
Condon, 703 ....D-10
COOS CO., 63019 ....J-2
Coos Bay, 15345 ....J-1
Coquille, 4144 ....J-1
Cornelius, 10165 ....C-4
Corvallis, 50126 ....F-3
Cottage Gr., 8514 ....H-4
Crater Lake K-6
Creswell, 4024 ....H-4
CROOK CO., 20600 ....G-9
Culver, 805 ....F-8
CURRY CO., 21813 ....L-1
Dallas, 13221 ....E-3
Dayton, 2175 ....D-4
Depoe Bay, 1303 ....E-2
DESCHUTES CO., 129492 ....H-7
Dillard, 350 ....J-3
DOUGLAS CO., 102332 ....J-3
Drain, 1028 ....I-3
Dufur, 584 ....D-8
Durham, 1405 ....M-18
Eagle Pt., 6306 ....L-4
Elgin, 1647 ....C-15
Enterprise, 1835 ....C-16
Estacada, 2395 ....D-5
Eugene, 142185 ....H-4
Fairview, 8749 ....C-5
Falcon Hts., 800 ....M-6
Falls City, 995 ....E-3
Florence, 7583 ....H-2
Forest Gr., 18880 ....C-4
Four Corners, 13922 ....B-20
Garden Home, 4900 ....L-18
Gardiner, 540 ....H-2
Garibaldi, 911 ....C-2
Gearhart, 985 ....B-2
Gervais, 2161 ....D-4
Gilchrist, 500 ....I-7
GILLIAM CO., 1778 ....D-10
Gladstone, 11978 ....D-5
Glendale, 886 ....K-3
Gleneden Beach, 900 ....E-2
Glenwood, 80 ....C-3
Glide, 1690 ....J-4
Gold Beach, 1911 ....L-1
Gold Hill, 1072 ....L-4
GRANT CO., 7454 ....F-12
Grants Pass, 25700 ....L-3
Green, 6174 ....J-3
Gresham, 95816 ....C-5
Halsey, 728 ....G-4
Happy Valley, 6475 ....M-20
Harbor, 2622 ....M-1
HARNEY CO., 7184 ....J-12
Harrisburg, 2908 ....G-4
Hayesville, 18222 ....A-20
Heppner, 1435 ....D-11
Hermiston, 14086 ....B-12
Hillsboro, 77709 ....C-4
Hines, 1560 ....I-12
HOOD RIVER CO., 20760 ....C-7
Hood River, 6139 ....C-7
Hubbard, 2505 ....D-4
Huntington, 494 ....G-16
Independence, 6974 ....E-4
JACKSON CO., 190077 ....L-4
Jacksonville, 2238 ....M-4
JEFFERSON CO., 19667 ....F-7
Jefferson, 2594 ....F-4
John Day, 1657 ....G-12
Joseph, 1021 ....D-16
JOSEPHINE CO., 79030 ....L-2
Junction City, 5237 ....G-3
Keizer, 34154 ....E-4
King City, 1954 ....M-18
KLAMATH CO., 64769 ....L-6
Klamath Falls, 19286 ....M-6
Lafayette, 2777 ....D-4
La Grande, 12282 ....D-14
LAKE CO., 7440 ....J-9
Lake Oswego, 36085 ....D-5
Lakeside, 1445 ....I-1
Lakeview, 2446 ....M-10
LANE CO., 330527 ....H-4
La Pine, 5799 ....I-7
Lebanon, 13271 ....F-4
LINCOLN CO., 44667 ....F-2
Lincoln Beach, 2078 ....E-2
Lincoln City, 7399 ....E-2
LINN CO., 106121 ....F-5
Lowell, 905 ....H-4
Lyons, 1054 ....E-5
Madras, 5128 ....F-8
MALHEUR CO., 31239 ....J-15
Mapleton, 900 ....H-2
MARION CO., 296995 ....E-5
Maywood Park, 780 ....K-20
McMinnville, 28514 ....D-4
Medford, 66638 ....M-4
Merrill, 894 ....N-7
Metzger, 3354 ....M-18
Mill City, 1563 ....F-5
Milton-Freewater, 6457 ....B-14
Milwaukie, 20638 ....M-19
Molalla, 6075 ....D-5
Monmouth, 8109 ....E-3
MORROW CO., 11627 ....D-11
Mt. Angel, 3319 ....E-4
MULTNOMAH CO., 677813 ....C-6
Myrtle Cr., 3479 ....K-3
Myrtle Pt., 2453 ....J-1
Newberg, 19732 ....D-4
Newport, 9548 ....F-2
N. Bend, 9565 ....I-1
N. Plains, 1763 ....C-4
Nyssa, 3080 ....H-17
Oak Grove, 12808 ....M-19
Oakland, 960 ....I-3
Oakridge, 3167 ....I-5
Ontario, 10964 ....H-17
Oregon City, 28407 ....D-5
Pendleton, 16458 ....C-13
Philomath, 4198 ....F-3
Phoenix, 4385 ....M-4
Pilot Rock, 1530 ....C-13
POLK CO., 65995 ....E-3
Portland, 538544 ....C-5
Port Orford, 1153 ....K-1
Powers, 736 ....K-2
Prairie City, 990 ....F-13
Prineville, 8115 ....G-8
Rainier, 1787 ....B-4
Raleigh Hills, 5865 ....L-18
Redmond, 16822 ....G-8
Reedsport, 4348 ....I-2
Riddle, 1011 ....K-3
Rockaway Beach, 1261 ....C-2
Rogue River, 1890 ....L-3
Roseburg, 20162 ....J-3
St. Helens, 11209 ....B-4
Salem, 142914 ....E-4
Sandy, 7186 ....D-6
Santa Clara, 12834 ....C-19
Scappoose, 5506 ....C-4
Scio, 698 ....F-4
Seaside, 5916 ....B-2
Shady Cove, 2336 ....L-4
Sheridan, 5515 ....D-3
SHERMAN CO., 1754 ....D-9
Sherwood, 13901 ....D-4
Siletz, 1132 ....F-2
Silverton, 7781 ....E-4
Sisters, 1156 ....G-7
Springfield, 54773 ....H-4
Stanfield, 1980 ....B-12
Stayton, 7060 ....E-4
Sublimity, 2282 ....E-4
Sunnyside, 6791 ....M-20
Sutherlin, 7178 ....J-3
Svensen, 550 ....A-3
Sweet Home, 8238 ....G-4
Talent, 5623 ....M-4
The Dalles, 11873 ....C-8
Tigard, 45538 ....D-4
TILLAMOOK CO., 24590 ....C-2
Tillamook, 4487 ....C-2
Toledo, 3409 ....F-2
Tri-City, 3519 ....K-3
Troutdale, 14851 ....C-5
Tualatin, 24790 ....D-4
Turner, 1508 ....E-4
UMATILLA CO., 72008 ....C-13
Umatilla, 5154 ....B-12
UNION CO., 24561 ....D-14
Union, 1949 ....D-15
Vale, 1940 ....H-16
Veneta, 2958 ....H-3
Vernonia, 2244 ....B-4
Waldport, 2043 ....F-2
WALLOWA CO., 7082 ....C-16
Wallowa, 841 ....C-15
Warren, 970 ....B-4
Warrenton, 4205 ....A-2
WASCO CO., 23591 ....E-8
WASHINGTON CO., 479496 ....C-3
W. Linn, 24696 ....D-5
Weston, 713 ....B-13
Westport, 280 ....A-3
W. Slope, 6442 ....L-18
WHEELER CO., 1505 ....E-10
White City, 6199 ....L-4
Willamina, 1849 ....E-3
Wilsonville, 15211 ....D-4
Winchester, 2700 ....J-3
Winchester Bay, 488 ....I-1
Winston, 4732 ....J-3
Woodburn, 21747 ....D-4
Yachats, 633 ....G-2
YAMHILL CO., 89384 ....D-3
Yamhill, 794 ....D-4
Yoncalla, 1048 ....I-3

Pennsylvania

Map pp. 174-183

Index keys WA to WT refer to Western PA, pp. 174-177, EA to ET refer to Eastern PA, pp. 178-181.
* City keyed to pp. 182-183

Abington, 10000 ....*A-5
Acmetonia, 1500 ....*H-9
ADAMS CO., 96456 ....EP-2
Adamstown, 1251 ....EN-8
Akron, 4037 ....EO-7
Albion, 1573 ....WE-2
Alburtis, 2100 ....EM-10
Aldan, 4322 ....*F-2
Aliquippa, 11324 ....WL-2
ALLEGHENY CO., 1261303 ....WM-4
Allentown, 105958 ....EL-11
Allison, 850 ....WP-4
Allison Park, 6000 ....WM-4
Almedia, 1056 ....EJ-6
Altoona, 47980 ....WM-11
Ambler, 6426 ....EO-12
Ambridge, 7460 ....WL-3
Ancient Oaks, 3161 ....EM-10
Andalusia, 3500 ....*B-8
Annville, 4518 ....EN-6
Apollo, 1712 ....WL-6
Archbald, 6213 ....EG-10
ARMSTRONG CO., 71659 ....WK-6
Arnold, 5485 ....WL-5
Ashland, 3184 ....EK-7
Ashley, 2780 ....EI-9
Ashtola, 150 ....WO-9
Aspinwall, 2869 ....*I-7
Atglen, 1302 ....EP-8
Athens, 3328 ....ED-6
Atlas, 1200 ....EK-6
Atlasburg, 500 ....WN-2
Auburn, 821 ....EL-8
Audubon, 6549 ....EO-11
Avalon, 5114 ....WM-3
Avella, 500 ....WN-1
Avis, 1469 ....EI-2
Avoca, 2755 ....EB-10
Avon, 2856 ....EN-7
Avondale, 1099 ....EQ-9
Avonia, 1331 ....WD-3
Avonmore, 801 ....WM-6
Baden, 4240 ....WL-3
Bainbridge, 900 ....EO-5
Bairdford, 800 ....WL-4
Bakerstown, 1000 ....WL-4
Baldwin, 19420 ....*L-6
Bally, 1093 ....EN-10
Bangor, 5275 ....EK-12
Baresville, 800 ....EQ-4
Bareville, 1250 ....EO-8
Bath, 2745 ....EL-11
Bausman, 300 ....ET-8
BEAVER CO., 178697 ....WL-2
Beaver, 4603 ....WL-2
Beaverdale, 800 ....WN-9
Beaver Falls, 9632 ....WK-2
Beaver Meadows, 961 ....EJ-9
Beaver Sprs., 634 ....EL-3
Beavertown, 879 ....EL-3
Bechtelsville, 927 ....EN-10
BEDFORD CO., 49941 ....WO-10
Bedford, 3057 ....WP-10
Beech Cr., 702 ....EJ-1
Belfast, 1301 ....EK-12
Bell Acres, 1399 ....WL-3
Bellefonte, 6352 ....WK-14
Belle Vernon, 1176 ....WO-4
Belleville, 1386 ....WL-14
Bellevue, 8479 ....WM-3
Bellwood, 1942 ....WL-11
Belmont, 2846 ....WT-2
Ben Avon, 1850 ....*I-4
Bensalem, 58639 ....*A-8
Bentleyville, 2459 ....WO-3
Benton, 935 ....EI-7
BERKS CO., 385307 ....EM-8
Berlin, 2153 ....WP-8
Bernville, 865 ....EM-8
Berwick, 10500 ....EJ-7
Berwyn, 3000 ....EP-11
Bessemer, 1138 ....WJ-1
Bethel Park, 32915 ....WN-3
Bethlehem, 72570 ....EL-11
Big Beaver, 2185 ....WK-2
Biglerville, 1129 ....EP-3
Birdsboro, 5161 ....EN-9
Bishop, 800 ....WN-3
Black Lick, 1438 ....WM-7
Blaine Hill, 1100 ....WN-4
BLAIR CO., 127175 ....WN-11
Blairsville, 3489 ....WM-7
Blakely, 6884 ....EG-10
Blanchard, 621 ....EJ-1
Blandburg, 550 ....WL-11
Blandon, 1200 ....EM-9
Blawnox, 1511 ....*I-8
Bloomingdale, 2100 ....ES-9
Bloomsburg, 12652 ....EJ-6
Blossburg, 1470 ....EF-3
Blue Ball, 800 ....EO-8
Blue Bell, 6395 ....EO-12
Blue Ridge Summit, 1500 ....ER-2
Boalsburg, 3578 ....WK-14
Bobtown, 1100 ....WQ-3
Boiling Sprs., 2769 ....EO-3
Bonneauville, 1420 ....EQ-3
Boston, 1300 ....*N-9
Boswell, 1316 ....WO-8
Bovard, 700 ....WN-6
Bowmanstown, 899 ....EK-10
Boyertown, 3912 ....EN-10
Brackenridge, 3420 ....WL-5
Braddock, 2835 ....*K-8
Braddock Hills, 1936 ....*K-8
Bradenville, 1300 ....WN-6
BRADFORD CO., 62643 ....EE-6
Bradford, 8826 ....WD-10
Branch Dale, 436 ....EL-7
Brentwood, 10114 ....WN-4
Bridgeport, 4405 ....EO-11
Bridgeville, 5160 ....WN-3
Bridgewater, 820 ....WL-2
Bristol, 9947 ....EO-13
Brockway, 2137 ....WI-9
Brodheadsville, 1637 ....EJ-11
Brookhaven, 7893 ....EQ-11
Brookside, 2200 ....WC-4
Brookville, 4151 ....WI-8
Broomall, 11046 ....EP-11
Broughton, 3000 ....*M-6
Brownstown, 851 ....WN-8
Brownstown, 1000 ....EO-7
Brownsville, 2715 ....WP-4
Browntown, 900 ....EB-9
Bryn Athyn, 1367 ....EO-13
Buck Hill Falls, 950 ....EI-11
Buckingham, 2000 ....EN-13
BUCKS CO., 613110 ....EM-12
Burgettstown, 1536 ....WN-2
Burnham, 2097 ....EL-1
Bushkill, 1200 ....EI-13
BUTLER CO., 180040 ....WJ-4
Butler, 14766 ....WK-4
Butztown, 1500 ....EA-5
Cairnbrook, 1000 ....WO-9
California, 5472 ....WO-4
Caln, 850 ....EP-9
CAMBRIA CO., 149453 ....WM-10
Cambridge Sprs., 2309 ....WE-3
CAMERON CO., 5777 ....WG-11
Campbelltown, 2415 ....EN-6
Camp Hill, 7533 ....EO-4
Canadensis, 1200 ....EI-12
Canadohta Lake, 572 ....WE-5
Canonsburg, 8716 ....WN-3
Canton, 1755 ....EF-4
CARBON CO., 60131 ....EJ-9
Carbondale, 9487 ....EG-10
Carlisle, 18110 ....EO-3
Carnegie, 8265 ....*K-4
Carnot, 4500 ....WM-3
Carrolltown, 1023 ....WL-9
Carroll Valley, 3402 ....EQ-2
Castanea, 1189 ....EI-2
Castle Shannon, 8521 ....WN-3
Catasauqua, 6506 ....EL-11
Catawissa, 1555 ....EJ-6
Cecil, 900 ....WN-3
Cementon, 1100 ....EL-10
Cen. Square, 700 ....EO-12
Cen. Valley, 900 ....EM-11
Centerville, 3326 ....WP-4
Centerville, 1700 ....ES-7
Central City, 1218 ....WO-9
CENTRE CO., 141636 ....WJ-13
Centre Hall, 1101 ....WK-14
Cetronia, 1000 ....EB-2
Chadds Ford, 1200 ....EQ-10
Chalfant, 839 ....*K-8
Chalfont, 4061 ....EN-12
Chalkhill, 400 ....WQ-5
Chambersburg, 17864 ....WP-14
Charleroi, 4738 ....WO-4
Chatwood, 1000 ....EP-10
Cheltenham, 34923 ....*B-5
CHESTER CO., 457393 ....EP-9
Chester, 37017 ....EQ-11
Chester Hts., 2469 ....EQ-11
Chester Hill, 896 ....WK-12
Cheswick, 1846 ....*H-9
Chevy Chase Hts., 1511 ....WL-7
Chicora, 1018 ....WJ-5
Chinchilla, 1300 ....EA-13
Christiana, 1104 ....EP-8
Churchill, 3454 ....*J-8
Churchville, 4469 ....EO-13
Clairton, 8204 ....*N-8
Claridge, 1200 ....WN-5
CLARION CO., 41208 ....WI-6
Clarion, 5953 ....WI-6
Clarks Green, 1594 ....EA-13
Clarks Summit, 5044 ....EG-10
Claysburg, 1503 ....WN-10
Claysville, 703 ....WO-2
CLEARFIELD CO., 82874 ....WJ-11
Clearfield, 6413 ....WJ-11
Cleona, 2110 ....EN-6
Clifton Hts., 6680 ....*E-2
CLINTON CO., 37435 ....EI-1
Clymer, 1489 ....WL-8
Coaltown, 1200 ....WJ-2
Coatesville, 11221 ....EP-9
Cochranton, 1114 ....WG-3
Cokeburg, 687 ....WO-3
Collegeville, 4564 ....EO-11
Collingdale, 8545 ....*F-2
Colmar, 800 ....EN-12
Colonial Park, 13259 ....EN-5
COLUMBIA CO., 64605 ....EJ-6
Columbia, 10201 ....EP-6
Columbus, 1200 ....WD-6
Colver, 1035 ....WM-9
Colwyn, 2412 ....*F-3
Conewago Heights, 900 ....EO-5
Confluence, 810 ....WQ-6
Conneaut Lake, 687 ....WF-2
Conneautville, 820 ....WE-2
Connellsville, 8765 ....WP-5
Conshohocken, 7768 ....EO-11
Conway, 2224 ....WL-2
Conyngham, 1891 ....EJ-8
Coopersburg, 2554 ....EM-11
Coplay, 3349 ....EL-10
Coral, 400 ....WM-7
Coraopolis, 5914 ....WM-3
Cornwall, 3449 ....EN-6
Corry, 6685 ....WE-5
Coudersport, 2641 ....WE-12
Courtdale, 764 ....EA-8
Crabtree, 320 ....WN-6
Crafton, 6473 ....WM-3
CRAWFORD CO., 89846 ....WF-3
Creighton, 1500 ....WL-5
Cresson, 1567 ....WM-10
Cressona, 1573 ....EL-7
Crucible, 600 ....WP-4
Cuddy, 1200 ....WN-3
CUMBERLAND CO., 219892 ....EO-2
Curtisville, 1173 ....WL-4
Curwensville, 2578 ....WJ-10
Daisytown, 1100 ....WP-4
Dale, 1445 ....WN-8
Dallas, 2504 ....EH-8
Dallastown, 4067 ....EQ-5
Dalton, 1251 ....EG-9
Danboro, 500 ....EN-12
Danielsville, 750 ....EK-10
Danville, 4711 ....EJ-5
Darby, 10136 ....EP-12
DAUPHIN CO., 253388 ....EM-5
Dauphin, 774 ....EN-4
Davidsville, 1119 ....WO-8
Dawson Ridge, 1200 ....WL-2
Deemston, 799 ....WP-3
DELAWARE CO., 554432 ....EP-11
Delaware Water Gap, 788 ....EJ-12
Delmont, 2520 ....WM-5
Delta, 726 ....ER-7
Denver, 3461 ....EO-8
Derrick City, 1000 ....WD-10
Derry, 2905 ....WN-7
Devon, 2000 ....EP-11
Dickerson Run, 400 ....WP-5
Dickson City, 6036 ....EG-10
Dillsburg, 2187 ....EO-4
Dingmans Ferry, 1000 ....EI-13
Distant, 750 ....WJ-6
Dixonville, 600 ....WL-8
Donora, 5470 ....WO-4
Dormont, 8957 ....WN-3
Dorneyville, 1450 ....EC-2
Douglassville, 1200 ....EN-10
Dover, 1915 ....EP-4
Downingtown, 7849 ....EP-10
Doylestown, 8185 ....EN-12
Dravosburg, 1947 ....*M-7
Drifton, 800 ....EJ-9
Dry Tavern, 500 ....WP-3
Dublin, 2202 ....EN-12
Du Bois, 7879 ....WI-9
Duboistown, 1242 ....EI-4
Duke Cen., 850 ....WD-10
Dunbar, 1189 ....WP-5
Duncannon, 1476 ....EN-4
Duncansville, 1214 ....WM-11
Dunlo, 750 ....WN-9
Dunmore, 13715 ....EC-13
Dunnstown, 1365 ....EI-2
Dupont, 2648 ....EB-10
Duquesne, 7116 ....WN-4
Duryea, 4466 ....EH-9
Dushore, 632 ....EG-6
Eagleville, 4458 ....EO-11
E. Bangor, 988 ....EK-12
E. Berlin, 1400 ....EP-4
E. Berwick, 1998 ....EJ-7
E. Brady, 1019 ....WJ-5
E. Butler, 674 ....WK-4
E. Conemaugh, 1238 ....WN-9
E. Faxon, 3000 ....EI-4
E. Greenville, 3104 ....EM-11
E. Lansdowne, 2538 ....*E-2
E. McKeesport, 2271 ....*L-9
Easton, 26189 ....EL-12
E. Petersburg, 4402 ....EO-7
E. Pittsburgh, 1953 ....*L-8
E. Springfield, 400 ....WD-2
E. Stroudsburg, 10385 ....EJ-12
E. Uniontown, 2760 ....WP-5
E. Vandergrift, 717 ....WL-5
E. Washington, 1866 ....WO-2
E. York, 8782 ....WS-10
Ebensburg, 2989 ....WM-9
Economy, 9331 ....WL-3
Eddystone, 2402 ....EQ-11
Edgemont, 900 ....ES-3
Edgewood, 2619 ....EK-6
Edgewood, 3191 ....*K-8
Edgeworth, 1670 ....WM-3
Edinboro, 7073 ....WE-3
Edwardsville, 4808 ....EH-9
Effort, 1000 ....EJ-11
Egypt, 1300 ....EA-2
Eighty Four, 800 ....WO-3
Eldred, 839 ....WD-11
Elizabeth, 1559 ....WN-4
Elizabethtown, 11898 ....EO-6
Elizabethville, 1313 ....EM-5
ELK CO., 34310 ....WG-10
Elkland, 1739 ....ED-2
Ellport, 1133 ....WK-2
Ellsworth, 1052 ....WO-3
Ellwood City, 8386 ....WK-2
Elmhurst, 834 ....EH-10
Elrama, 600 ....WN-4
Elysburg, 2067 ....EK-6
Emigsville, 2467 ....EP-5
Emlenton, 759 ....WI-5
Emmaus, 11243 ....EM-11
Emporium, 2419 ....WG-11
Emsworth, 2510 ....WM-3
Enhaut, 950 ....ET-4
Enola, 5627 ....EN-4
Ephrata, 13158 ....EO-7
ERIE CO., 279966 ....WD-4
Erie, 101373 ....WC-3
Espy, 1428 ....EJ-6
Estherton, 1200 ....ES-3
Etna, 3779 ....WM-4
Evansburg, 1536 ....EO-11
Evans City, 1986 ....WK-3
Everett, 1912 ....WP-11
Everson, 814 ....WO-5
Exeter, 6023 ....EB-9
Export, 866 ....WM-5
Exton, 4267 ....EP-10
Factoryville, 1160 ....EG-9
Fairchance, 2130 ....WQ-5
Fairdale, 1955 ....WQ-4
Fairfield, 499 ....EQ-2
Fairfield, 1100 ....WC-4
Fairhope, 1800 ....WO-4
Fairview, 1998 ....WD-3
Falling Spring, 200 ....EQ-1
Falls Cr., 963 ....WI-9
Farmington, 250 ....WQ-5
Farmington, 800 ....EB-4
Farrell, 5959 ....WI-1
Faxon, 1500 ....EI-4
FAYETTE CO., 146121 ....WP-5
Fayette City, 695 ....WO-4
Fayetteville, 2774 ....EP-1
Fellsburg, 1000 ....WO-4
Ferndale, 1759 ....WN-8
Fernway, 12188 ....WL-3
Fleetwood, 3971 ....EM-9
Flemington, 1268 ....EI-2
Fogelsville, 950 ....EL-10
Folcroft, 6933 ....*F-2
Ford City, 3340 ....WK-6
FOREST CO., 4989 ....WG-7
Forest City, 1795 ....EF-11
Forest Gr., 2600 ....*I-3
Forest Hills, 6610 ....*K-8
Ft. Loudon, 1200 ....WP-13
Ft. Washington, 3680 ....EO-12
Forty Ft., 4399 ....EH-9
Foster Brook, 800 ....WD-10
Fountain Hill, 4556 ....EL-11
Fox Chapel, 5352 ....*I-8
Frackville, 4235 ....EK-7
FRANKLIN CO., 133155 ....WP-13
Franklin, 6991 ....WH-4
Franklin Park, 11596 ....WL-3
Frazer, 2000 ....EP-10
Fredericksburg, 987 ....EM-6
Fredericksburg, 1140 ....WF-3
Fredericktown, 200 ....WP-3
Freedom, 1695 ....WL-2
Freeland, 3507 ....EJ-9
Freeport, 1899 ....WL-5
Friedens, 1673 ....WP-8
Frisco, 850 ....WK-2
FULTON CO., 14534 ....WP-12
Gabby Hts., 1200 ....WO-2
Galeton, 1345 ....WF-14
Gallitzin, 1697 ....WM-10
Gap, 1611 ....EP-8
Garden View, 2679 ....EI-4
Gastonville, 3002 ....WN-4
Geistown, 2473 ....WN-9
Gettysburg, 7825 ....EQ-3
Ghennes Hts., 900 ....WO-4
Gibsonia, 3500 ....WL-4
Gilberton, 846 ....EK-7
Gilbertsville, 4242 ....EN-10
Girard, 3082 ....WD-2
Girardville, 1690 ....EK-7
Glassport, 4822 ....WN-4
Glenburn, 1212 ....EG-9
Glen Lyon, 1881 ....EI-8
Glen Moore, 1000 ....ES-9
Glenmoore, 900 ....EO-9
Glenolden, 7369 ....*F-2
Glen Rock, 1809 ....EQ-5
Glenwood, 3000 ....ES-3
Gordon, 759 ....EL-7
Grassflat, 700 ....WJ-12
Graterford, 900 ....EO-11
Great Bend, 688 ....ED-9
Greeley, 1000 ....EG-13
Greenawalds, 1200 ....EA-2
Greencastle, 3736 ....WQ-14
GREENE CO., 40398 ....WQ-2
Greenock, 2400 ....*N-9
Greensburg, 15525 ....WN-6
Greentown, 1000 ....EH-11
Green Tree, 4587 ....*K-5
Green Tree, 1350 ....EP-11
Greenville, 6434 ....WG-2
Greenwood, 1600 ....WM-11
Grill, 750 ....ET-12
Grindstone, 600 ....WP-4
Grove City, 7801 ....WI-3
Halifax, 857 ....EM-4
Hallam, 2140 ....EP-6
Hallstead, 1176 ....ED-9
Hamburg, 4112 ....EM-8
Hamilton Park, 3500 ....ET-8
Hamlin, 1100 ....EH-11
Hanover, 14835 ....EQ-4
Hanover, 800 ....EA-4
Harborcreek, 1500 ....WC-4
Harleysville, 8795 ....EN-11
Harmarville, 1100 ....*H-8
Harmony, 916 ....WK-3
Harrisburg, 48322 ....EN-4
Harrison City, 155 ....WN-5
Harrisville, 919 ....WI-4
Harveys Lake, 2812 ....EH-8
Harwick, 1100 ....*H-9
Hastings, 1361 ....WL-9
Hatboro, 7381 ....EO-12
Hatfield, 2880 ....EN-11
Hawk Run, 900 ....WJ-12
Hawley, 1304 ....EG-12
Hayti, 950 ....EP-9
Hazleton, 22492 ....EJ-8
Hecktown, 1200 ....EL-11
Hegins, 1200 ....EL-6
Heidelberg, 1183 ....WN-3
Heilwood, 786 ....WL-8
Hellertown, 5580 ....EL-11
Hereford, 850 ....EM-10
Herminie, 856 ....WN-5
Hermitage, 16521 ....WH-2
Hershey, 12771 ....EN-5
Hesston, 175 ....WM-12
Hibbs, 200 ....WP-4
Hickory, 850 ....WN-2
Highland Park, 1446 ....EL-1
Highland Park, 1900 ....ET-2
Highspire, 2671 ....EO-5
Hilldale, 600 ....EB-9
Hiller, 1234 ....WP-4
Hillsville, 600 ....WJ-1
Hilltown, 800 ....EN-12
Hokendauqua, 3411 ....EL-11
Holland, 5300 ....EO-13
Hollidaysburg, 5312 ....WM-11
Hollywood, 800 ....*B-5
Homer City, 1787 ....WM-7
Homestead, 3626 ....*K-7
Hometown, 1399 ....EK-8
Honesdale, 4900 ....EG-12
Honey Brook, 1341 ....EO-9
Hooversville, 754 ....WO-8
Hopwood, 2006 ....WQ-5
Horsham, 14779 ....EO-12
Hostetter, 460 ....WN-6
Houserville, 1809 ....WK-13
Houston, 1284 ....WN-3
Houtzdale, 914 ....WK-11
Howard, 691 ....WJ-14
Hudson, 1150 ....EB-8
Hughestown, 1487 ....EB-10
Hughesville, 2133 ....EI-5
Hulmeville, 885 ....EO-13
Hummelstown, 4365 ....EN-5
Hummels Wharf, 641 ....EK-4
HUNTINGDON CO., 45865 ....WN-12
Huntingdon, 6864 ....WM-12
Hyde, 1491 ....WJ-10
Hyde Park, 2200 ....ES-13
Hyndman, 981 ....WQ-9
Imperial, 2200 ....WM-2
INDIANA CO., 89054 ....WL-8
Indiana, 14636 ....WL-7
Indianola, 900 ....WM-4
Industry, 1877 ....WL-2
Ingram, 3588 ....*J-4
Inkerman, 735 ....EB-9
Intercourse, 1200 ....EP-8
Iona, 800 ....EN-7
Irwin, 4237 ....WN-5
Jacksonwald, 1100 ....ET-14
Jacobus, 1194 ....EQ-5
Jamestown, 615 ....WG-2
Jamison, 850 ....EN-12
Jeannette, 10369 ....WN-5
JEFFERSON CO., 45945 ....WH-8
Jefferson Hills, 9685 ....WN-4
Jenkintown, 4459 ....EO-12
Jenners, 250 ....WO-8
Jermyn, 2265 ....EG-10
Jerome, 1068 ....WO-8
Jersey Shore, 4479 ....EI-3
Jessup, 4630 ....EG-10
Jim Thorpe, 4827 ....EK-9
Johnsonburg, 2891 ....WG-10
Johnstown, 22957 ....WN-8
Jonestown, 1009 ....EN-6
JUNIATA CO., 23065 ....EM-2
Juniata Gap, 1100 ....WA-13
Kane, 3972 ....WF-9
Kelayres, 600 ....EK-8
Kenhorst, 2644 ....EN-9
Kenilworth, 1576 ....EO-10
Kennett Square, 5271 ....EQ-10
Kersey, 700 ....WH-10
King of Prussia, 18511 ....EO-11
Kingston, 13368 ....EH-9
Kissel Hill, 750 ....EO-7
Kittanning, 4556 ....WK-6
Knox, 1137 ....WI-6
Koppel, 823 ....WK-2
Korn Krest, 850 ....EA-6
Kulpmont, 2895 ....EK-6
Kulpsville, 8005 ....EN-11
Kutztown, 5067 ....EM-9
La Belle, 350 ....WP-4
Laboratory, 850 ....WO-3
LACKAWANNA CO., 210458 ....EG-9
Laflin, 1513 ....EB-9
Lake Ariel, 1250 ....EG-11
Lake City, 2967 ....WD-2
Lake Harmony, 850 ....EJ-10
Lamar, 900 ....EJ-1
Lampeter, 800 ....EP-7
LANCASTER CO., 482775 ....EP-7
Lancaster, 55351 ....EP-7
Landisville, 1400 ....EO-6
Langeloth, 1500 ....WN-2
Langhorne, 1987 ....EO-13
Lansdale, 16115 ....EN-12
Lansdowne, 10861 ....EP-12
Lansford, 4198 ....EK-9
Larimer, 750 ....WN-5
Larksville, 4571 ....EI-8
Latrobe, 8747 ....WN-6
Lattimer Mines, 600 ....EJ-8
Laughlintown, 950 ....WO-7
Laureldale, 3729 ....EN-9
Laurel Run, 720 ....EI-9
Laurys Sta., 1100 ....EL-10
Lavelle, 600 ....EK-7
LAWRENCE CO., 93408 ....WI-2
Lawrence, 1100 ....WN-3
Lawrence Park, 4048 ....WC-4
Leaders Hts., 1200 ....WT-10
LEBANON CO., 122652 ....EN-6
Lebanon, 23894 ....EN-6

PENNSYLVANIA - TENNESSEE 271

2000 Census populations or latest available estimate.
Index to Canada and Mexico cities and towns, pages 274-275.

Leechburg, 2324 ... WL-5
Lee Park, 3600 ... EI-9
Leesport, 1845 ... EM-8
Leetsdale, 1188 ... WL-3
LEHIGH CO., 320517 ... EL-10
Lehighton, 5513 ... EK-10
Leisenring, 600 ... WP-5
Leith, 900 ... WQ-5
Lemont, 2116 ... WK-13
Lemoyne, 3969 ... ET-3
Leola, 1100 ... EO-7
Level Green, 2500 ... WN-5
Levittown, 53966 ... EO-14
Lewisburg, 5499 ... EJ-4
Lewistown, 8752 ... EL-1
Liberty, 2585 ... *M-8
Library, 6000 ... WN-3
Light Street, 881 ... EJ-6
Ligonier, 1646 ... WN-7
Lilly, 911 ... WM-10
Limerick, 800 ... EO-10
Lime Ridge, 951 ... EJ-7
Lincoln, 1185 ... *N-8
Lincoln Hts., 300 ... WN-5
Lincoln Park, 1800 ... ET-11
Linesville, 1139 ... WF-2
Linglestown, 6414 ... EN-5
Linntown, 1542 ... EJ-4
Linwood, 3374 ... EQ-11
Listie, 700 ... WP-8
Lititz, 8957 ... EO-7
Littlestown, 4036 ... EQ-3
Liverpool, 878 ... EM-4
Llewellyn, 800 ... EL-7
Lock Haven, 8957 ... EI-2
Loganville, 971 ... EQ-5
Long Pond, 900 ... EJ-11
Lorain, 719 ... WN-9
Lorane, 2994 ... EN-9
Loretto, 1143 ... WM-10
Lost Cr., 500 ... EK-7
Lower Burrell, 12531 ... WL-5
Lucernemines, 951 ... WM-7
Ludlow, 500 ... WF-8
Luxor, 750 ... WN-6
LUZERNE CO., 313528 ... EI-7
Luzerne, 2842 ... EH-9
LYCOMING CO., 118438 ... EH-3
Lykens, 1888 ... EM-5
Lyndon, 750 ... EP-7
Lyndora, 1300 ... WK-4
Lynnwood, 1300 ... EA-7
Lynnwood, 1200 ... WO-4
Macungie, 3078 ... EM-10
Madera, 1000 ... WK-11
Mahanoy City, 4499 ... EK-8
Mainland, 2000 ... EN-11
Malvern, 3083 ... EP-11
Manchester, 2417 ... EP-5
Manheim, 4721 ... EO-7
Manor, 2720 ... WN-5
Manor Ridge, 1000 ... ET-8
Mansfield, 3412 ... EE-3
Marcus Hook, 2278 ... EQ-11
Marienville, 1325 ... WG-8
Marietta, 2639 ... EP-6
Marion, 800 ... WQ-14
Marion Hts., 714 ... EK-6
Mars, 1721 ... WL-3
Marshallton, 1437 ... EK-6
Martinsburg, 2193 ... WN-11
Martins Cr., 1200 ... EK-12
Marysville, 2367 ... EN-4
Masontown, 3511 ... WQ-4
Matamoras, 2487 ... EH-14
Mather, 1000 ... WP-3
Mayfield, 1734 ... EG-10
Maytown, 2604 ... EO-6
McAdoo, 2182 ... EK-8
McAlisterville, 765 ... EL-3
McCandless, 29022 ... WL-3
McClure, 959 ... EL-2
McConnellsburg, 1049 ... WP-13
McDonald, 2211 ... WN-2
McGovern, 2538 ... WN-2
MCKEAN CO., 45236 ... WE-11
McKeesport, 23324 ... WN-4
McKees Rocks, 6384 ... WM-3
McMurray, 4726 ... WN-3
McSherrystown, 2749 ... EQ-4
Meadow Lands, 900 ... WO-2
Meadville, 13410 ... WF-3
Mechanicsburg, 8901 ... EO-4
Media, 5472 ... EP-11
MERCER CO., 119895 ... WH-2
Mercer, 2313 ... WI-3
Mercersburg, 1542 ... WQ-13
Meridian, 3794 ... WK-4
Merrittstown, 200 ... WP-4
Meyersdale, 2387 ... WQ-8
Middleburg, 1369 ... EK-4
Middletown, 9105 ... EO-5
Midland, 3018 ... WL-2
Midway, 956 ... WN-2
MIFFLIN CO., 46335 ... WM-14
Mifflinburg, 3567 ... EK-4
Mifflintown, 844 ... EM-2
Mifflinville, 1213 ... EJ-7
Milesburg, 1179 ... WJ-14
Milford, 1176 ... EH-14
Millcreek, 52596 ... WD-3
Millersburg, 2510 ... EM-4
Millersville, 7573 ... EP-7
Mill Hall, 1503 ... EI-2
Millheim, 750 ... EK-2
Mill Run, 400 ... WP-6
Millvale, 3878 ... WM-4
Millville, 969 ... EI-6
Milroy, 1386 ... EL-1
Milton, 6539 ... EJ-4
Minersville, 4416 ... EL-7
Mocanaqua, 1000 ... EI-8
Mohnton, 3018 ... EN-8
Mohrsville, 700 ... EM-8
Monaca, 6077 ... WL-2
Monessen, 8467 ... WO-4
Monongahela, 4613 ... WO-4
MONROE CO., 154495 ... EJ-11
Monroeville, 28707 ... WM-5
Mont Alto, 1369 ... EQ-1
Mont Clare, 1800 ... EO-11
MONTGOMERY CO., 770747 ... EN-11
Montgomery, 1635 ... EI-4
Montgomeryville, 12031 ... EN-12
MONTOUR CO., 18083 ... EJ-5
Montoursville, 4617 ... EI-4
Montrose, 1617 ... EE-9
Moon, 1000 ... WM-2
Moon Run, 400 ... WM-3
Moosic, 5679 ... EH-9
Morgan, 800 ... WN-3
Morgantown, 700 ... EO-9
Morrisdale, 600 ... WJ-12
Morrisville, 1443 ... WP-3
Morrisville, 9955 ... EO-14
Morton, 2688 ... *F-1
Moscow, 1890 ... EH-10
Mountainhome, 1169 ... EI-12
Mtn. Top, 15269 ... EI-9
Mt. Allen, 2000 ... EO-4
Mt. Carmel, 6161 ... EK-6
Mt. Cobb, 2140 ... EH-10
Mt. Holly Springs, 1927 ... EO-3
Mt. Jewett, 1046 ... WF-10
Mt. Joy, 6865 ... EO-6
Mt. Lebanon, 33017 ... *L-4
Mt. Morris, 1300 ... WQ-3
Mt. Oliver, 3883 ... *K-6
Mt. Penn, 2970 ... EN-9
Mt. Pleasant, 4584 ... WO-6
Mt. Pocono, 2924 ... EI-11
Mt. Union, 2432 ... WN-13
Mt. Vernon, 2200 ... *N-9
Mountville, 2662 ... EP-6
Mt. Wolf, 1349 ... EP-5
Muncy, 2564 ... EI-5
Munhall, 11854 ... WM-4
Murrysville, 19192 ... WM-5
Muse, 1000 ... WN-3
Myerstown, 3111 ... EN-7
Nanticoke, 10533 ... EI-8
Nanty-Glo, 2960 ... WM-9
Narberth, 4213 ... EP-12
Natrona Hts., 10934 ... WL-5
Nazareth, 6009 ... EL-11
Neffsville, 1000 ... EO-7
Nemacolin, 1034 ... WQ-4
Nescopeck, 1476 ... EJ-7
Nesquehoning, 3320 ... EK-9
New Beaver, 1660 ... WK-2
New Bedford, 800 ... WI-1
New Berlin, 829 ... EK-4
New Berlinville, 800 ... EN-10
New Bethlehem, 1017 ... WJ-7
New Bloomfield, 1089 ... EN-3
New Brighton, 6384 ... WK-2
New Britain, 3105 ... EN-12
New Castle, 25338 ... WJ-2
New Cumberland, 7230 ... EO-4
New Derry, 800 ... WN-7
New Eagle, 2315 ... WO-4
New Florence, 764 ... WN-8
New Freedom, 3672 ... ER-5
New Holland, 5197 ... EO-8
New Hope, 2263 ... EN-13
New Kensington, 14279 ... WM-5
Newmanstown, 1536 ... EN-7
New Milford, 848 ... EE-9
New Oxford, 1736 ... EQ-4
New Philadelphia, 1118 ... EL-8
Newport, 1465 ... EM-3
New Salem, 850 ... WP-4
New Sheffield, 2000 ... WL-2
New Stanton, 2003 ... WO-5
Newtown, 2285 ... EO-13
Newtown, 1400 ... EB-7
Newtown Square, 11300 ... EP-11
Newville, 1339 ... EO-2
New Wilmington, 2515 ... WI-2
Nicholson, 690 ... EF-9
Norristown, 31069 ... EO-11
NORTHAMPTON CO., 278169 ... EK-11
Northampton, 9599 ... EL-11
N. Apollo, 1389 ... WL-6
N. Belle Vernon, 2043 ... WO-4
N. Bend, 800 ... WH-14
N. Braddock, 6176 ... *K-8
N. Cambria, 4080 ... WL-9
N. Catasauqua, 2835 ... EA-3
N. Charleroi, 1367 ... WO-4
N. East, 4469 ... WC-5
NORTHUMBERLAND CO., 93323 ... EK-5
Northumberland, 3638 ... EK-5
N. Wales, 3341 ... EO-12
N. Warren, 2400 ... WE-7
N. Washington, 500 ... WM-5
N. Weissport, 900 ... EK-10
N. York, 1655 ... EP-5
Norvelt, 1100 ... WO-6
Norwood, 5903 ... *F-2
Nuangola, 659 ... EI-8
Nuremberg, 231 ... EJ-8
Oakdale, 1502 ... WM-3
Oakland, 1516 ... WJ-2
Oakmont, 6727 ... WM-4
Oak Park, 700 ... EO-12
Oaks, 850 ... EO-11
Ohioville, 3689 ... WL-1
Oil City, 11132 ... WG-5
Oklahoma, 888 ... WL-5
Old Forge, 8603 ... EH-9
Oley, 900 ... EN-9
Oliver, 2925 ... WP-5
Olyphant, 4918 ... EG-10
Orchard Hills, 2152 ... WL-6
Orwigsburg, 3020 ... EL-8
Osceola Mills, 1208 ... WK-11
Oxford, 4636 ... EQ-8
Paint, 1075 ... WO-9
Palmer Hts., 3612 ... EL-12
Palmerton, 5248 ... EK-10
Palmyra, 6977 ... EN-6
Palo Alto, 1026 ... EL-7
Paoli, 5425 ... EP-11
Paradise, 1028 ... EP-8
Paris, 200 ... WM-1
Parker, 781 ... WI-5
Parker Ford, 800 ... EO-10
Parkesburg, 3408 ... EP-9
Parkhill, 300 ... WS-2
Parkside, 2231 ... EQ-11
Parkville, 6593 ... EQ-4
Patton, 1948 ... WL-10
Paxtang, 1531 ... ET-4
Paxtonia, 5254 ... ER-4
Pen Argyl, 3620 ... EK-12
Penbrook, 2975 ... ES-3
Penndel, 2377 ... EO-13
Penn Hills, 46809 ... WM-4
Pennsburg, 3208 ... EN-11
Penns Creek, 668 ... EK-4
Pennside, 3000 ... ET-13
Perkasie, 8806 ... EN-11
PERRY CO., 44188 ... EN-3
Perryopolis, 1737 ... WO-5
PHILADELPHIA CO., 1479339 ... EP-12
Philadelphia, 1479339 ... EP-12
Philipsburg, 3049 ... WK-12
Phoenixville, 14739 ... EO-10
PIKE CO., 52163 ... EH-13
Pilgrim Gardens, 1650 ... *E-1
Pine Gr., 2098 ... EM-7
Pine Gr. Mills, 1141 ... WL-13
Pineville, 950 ... EN-13
Pitcairn, 3550 ... *K-9
Pittsburgh, 325337 ... WM-4
Pittston, 7807 ... EB-10
Plains, 4694 ... EH-9
Pleasant Gap, 1611 ... WK-14
Pleasant Hills, 8178 ... WN-4
Pleasant Hills, 1650 ... ER-4
Pleasant Unity, 600 ... WN-6
Pleasureville, 1200 ... WR-10
Plum, 26797 ... WM-5
Plumsteadville, 1300 ... EN-12
Plymouth, 6250 ... EI-8
Plymouth Meeting, 6034 ... *A-2
Plymptonville, 1040 ... WJ-11
Pocono Pines, 1013 ... EI-11
Pocono Summit, 1500 ... EI-11
Polk, 1017 ... WH-4
Pomeroy, 750 ... EP-9
Portage, 2738 ... WN-10
Port Allegany, 2309 ... WE-11
Port Carbon, 1938 ... EL-8
Pt. Marion, 1289 ... WQ-4
Pt. Pleasant, 800 ... EM-12
Port Royal, 971 ... EM-2
Port Vue, 4093 ... *M-8
POTTER CO., 18141 ... WF-13
Pottstown, 21793 ... EN-10
Pottsville, 14990 ... EL-7
Primrose, 600 ... EL-7
Pringle, 956 ... EA-8
Progress, 9647 ... ES-3
Prospect, 1279 ... WJ-3
Prospect Park, 6494 ... EQ-11
Punxsutawney, 6150 ... WJ-8
Quakertown, 8816 ... EM-11
Quarryville, 2079 ... EQ-8
Rahns, 700 ... EO-11
Rankin, 2245 ... *K-8
Reading, 80305 ... EN-9
Reamstown, 3498 ... EO-8
Red Hill, 2391 ... EN-11
Red Lion, 6093 ... EQ-6
Reedsville, 858 ... EL-1
Rehrersburg, 600 ... EM-7
Reiffton, 2888 ... ET-13
Reightown, 350 ... WL-11
Renovo, 1255 ... WH-14
Republic, 1396 ... WP-4
Reynoldsville, 2658 ... WI-9
Rheems, 1557 ... EO-6
Richboro, 6678 ... EO-13
Richland, 1481 ... EN-7
Richlandtown, 1355 ... EM-11
Ridgeview, 800 ... ES-4
Ridgway, 4419 ... WH-9
Ridley Park, 7103 ... *G-1
Riegelsville, 852 ... EL-12
Rillton, 900 ... WN-5
Rimersburg, 1014 ... WJ-6
Ringtown, 795 ... EK-7
Riverside, 1838 ... EJ-5
Roaring Spr., 2335 ... WN-11
Robertsdale, 240 ... WO-12
Robesonia, 2027 ... EN-8
Robinson, 650 ... WN-7
Rochester, 3868 ... WL-2
Rockledge, 2568 ... *B-5
Rockwood, 947 ... WP-7
Rohrerstown, 1200 ... ES-8
Roscoe, 825 ... WO-4
Roseto, 1660 ... EK-12
Rose Valley, 935 ... EP-11
Rossiter, 790 ... WK-8
Rossmoyne, 1100 ... ET-2
Rothsville, 3017 ... EO-7
Roulette, 1000 ... WE-12
Rouzerville, 862 ... ER-1
Rowes Run, 400 ... WP-4
Royalton, 947 ... EO-5
Royersford, 4321 ... EO-10
Ruffs Dale, 800 ... WO-5
Rural Ridge, 1000 ... WL-4
Rural Valley, 896 ... WK-7
Russell, 1200 ... WD-8
Russellton, 1530 ... WL-4
Rutledge, 844 ... *F-1
Sadsburyville, 700 ... EP-9
Saegertown, 1070 ... WF-3
Sagamore, 450 ... WK-7
St. Clair, 3123 ... EL-7
St. Lawrence, 1791 ... EN-9
St. Marys, 14182 ... WG-10
St. Michael, 850 ... WN-9
St. Thomas, 900 ... WP-13
Salisbury, 847 ... WQ-8
Saltsburg, 923 ... WM-6
Salunga, 950 ... EO-6
Sanatoga, 7734 ... EN-10
Sand Hill, 2345 ... EN-6
Sandy, 1687 ... WI-9
Sandy Lake, 722 ... WH-3
Sankertown, 656 ... WM-10
Saxonburg, 1640 ... WK-4
Saxton, 781 ... WO-11
Saylorsburg, 500 ... EK-11
Sayre, 5659 ... ED-6
Scalp Level, 822 ... WN-9
Schaefferstown, 984 ... EN-7
Schnecksville, 1989 ... EL-10
School Lane Hills, 1840 ... ES-8
SCHUYLKILL CO., 147944 ... EL-7
Schuylkill Haven, 5377 ... EL-7
Schwenksville, 1730 ... EN-11
Sciota, 700 ... EJ-11
Scotland, 650 ... EP-1
Scotrun, 650 ... EJ-11
Scottdale, 4631 ... WO-5
Scranton, 74320 ... EH-10
Selinsgrove, 5436 ... EK-4
Sellersville, 4516 ... EN-11
Seneca, 966 ... WH-5
Sewickley, 3769 ... WM-3
Sewickley Heights, 960 ... *H-3
Shamokin, 7732 ... EK-5
Shamokin Dam, 1479 ... EK-5
Sharon, 15735 ... WH-1
Sharon Hill, 5386 ... *F-2
Sharpsburg, 3463 ... WM-4
Sharpsville, 4338 ... WH-2
Shavertown, 2000 ... EA-8
Sheffield, 1268 ... WF-8
Shenandoah, 5387 ... EK-7
Shenandoah Hts., 1298 ... EK-7
Shickshinny, 921 ... EI-8
Shillington, 5009 ... EN-8
Shiloh, 10192 ... EP-5
Shinglehouse, 1228 ... WD-12
Shippensburg, 5620 ... EP-1
Shiremanstown, 1499 ... EO-4
Shoemakersville, 2115 ... EM-8
Shrewsbury, 3393 ... EQ-5
Silverdale, 985 ... EN-12
Simpson, 1500 ... EF-10
Sinking Spr., 3153 ... EN-8
Skippack, 2889 ... EO-11
Slatedale, 600 ... EL-10
Slateford, 250 ... EJ-12
Slatington, 4373 ... EL-10
Slickville, 372 ... WM-6
Sligo, 707 ... WI-6
Slippery Rock, 3028 ... WJ-3
Slovan, 1100 ... WN-2
Smethport, 1654 ... WE-11
Smithfield, 834 ... WQ-4
Smithfield, 4181 ... WM-12
Smock, 600 ... WP-4
Snow Shoe, 785 ... WJ-13
SNYDER CO., 38015 ... EK-3
SOMERSET CO., 79365 ... WQ-7
Somerset, 6617 ... WP-8
Souderton, 6768 ... EN-11
S. Coatesville, 999 ... EP-9
S. Connellsville, 2227 ... WP-5
S. Fork, 1090 ... WN-9
S. Greensburg, 2267 ... WN-6
S. Lakemont, 1100 ... WB-13
Southmont, 2189 ... WN-8
S. Mountain, 600 ... EQ-2
S. New Castle, 783 ... WJ-2
S. Pottstown, 2135 ... EO-10
S. Temple, 1400 ... ER-13
S. Uniontown, 3500 ... WQ-5
S. Waverly, 979 ... ED-6
Southwest Greensburg, 2322 ... WN-6
S. Williamsport, 6240 ... EI-4
Speers, 1212 ... WO-4
Spring City, 3281 ... EO-10
Springdale, 3718 ... WM-4
Springfield, 23677 ... *E-1
Spr. Garden, 11207 ... WT-10
Spr. Grove, 2168 ... EQ-4
Spr. House, 3290 ... EO-12
Springhouse Farms, 750 ... EB-2
Spr. Mount, 2205 ... EN-11
Springtown, 750 ... EM-12
Spry, 4903 ... WT-10
Stafore Estates, 1200 ... EA-4
Star Brick, 800 ... WE-7
Star Jct., 500 ... WO-5
State College, 39728 ... WK-13
State Line, 1100 ... WR-14
Steelton, 5781 ... EO-5
Stewartstown, 1992 ... EQ-6
Stewartsville, 700 ... *M-10
Stiles, 800 ... EA-2
Stoneboro, 1076 ... WH-3
Stonybrook, 1500 ... EP-5
Stony Cr. Mills, 2500 ... ET-13
Stowe, 3585 ... EN-10
Strabane, 1100 ... WN-3
Strafford, 4500 ... EP-11
Strasburg, 2763 ... EP-7
Strongstown, 400 ... WM-8
Stroudsburg, 6127 ... EJ-12
Sturgeon, 1000 ... WN-3
Sugarcreek, 5213 ... WG-4
Sugar Notch, 985 ... EI-9
SULLIVAN CO., 6427 ... EH-6
Summerdale, 800 ... ES-2
Summit Hill, 2968 ... EK-9
Sunbury, 10277 ... EK-5
Sunset Valley, 2700 ... *N-10
SUSQUEHANNA CO., 41812 ... EE-9
Susquehanna, 1630 ... ED-10
Sutersville, 618 ... WN-4
Swarthmore, 6154 ... *F-1
Swiftwater, 600 ... EI-11
Swissvale, 9313 ... *K-8
Swoyersville, 5002 ... EH-9
Sykesville, 1222 ... WJ-9
Sylvan Hills, 1000 ... WB-13
Tamaqua, 6878 ... EK-8
Tannersville, 1200 ... EJ-11
Tarentum, 4809 ... WL-5
Tarrs, 600 ... WO-5
Tatamy, 1010 ... EL-12
Taylor, 6325 ... EH-9
Telford, 4665 ... EN-11
Temple, 1491 ... EN-9
Templeton, 400 ... WJ-6
Terre Hill, 1258 ... EO-8
Thorndale, 3561 ... EP-9
Throop, 3945 ... EB-13
Tidioute, 764 ... WF-6
TIOGA CO., 41557 ... EF-3
Tionesta, 597 ... WG-6
Tipton, 1225 ... WL-11
Tire Hill, 900 ... WN-8
Titusville, 5890 ... WF-5
Tobyhanna, 1200 ... EI-11
Topton, 1943 ... EM-10
Toughkenamon, 1375 ... EQ-9
Towanda, 2946 ... EF-6
Tower City, 1355 ... EM-6
Trafford, 3147 ... WN-5
Trainer, 1881 ... EQ-11
Trappe, 3352 ... EO-11
Tremont, 1742 ... EL-7
Tresckow, 964 ... EK-8
Trevorton, 2010 ... EK-5
Trexlertown, 1000 ... EM-10
Trooper, 6061 ... EO-11
Troy, 1471 ... EE-5
Trucksville, 1650 ... EA-8
Trumbauersville, 1080 ... EM-11
Tullytown, 2019 ... EO-14
Tunkhannock, 1847 ... EG-8
Turtle Cr., 5868 ... *K-9
Tuscarora, 939 ... EK-8
Tyrone, 5398 ... WL-11
UNION CO., 42552 ... EJ-3
Union City, 3407 ... WE-4
Union Deposit, 700 ... EN-5
Uniontown, 12096 ... WP-5
Unionville, 900 ... EQ-9
Upland, 2931 ... EQ-11
Upper Darby, 80556 ... EP-12
Upper St. Clair, 20053 ... WN-3
Valley Forge, 1500 ... EO-11
Valley View, 1677 ... EL-6
Vandergrift, 5267 ... WL-5
Vanport, 1406 ... WL-2
VENANGO CO., 56600 ... WG-4
Verona, 3017 ... WM-4
Versailles, 1664 ... WN-4
Vestaburg, 975 ... WP-4
Wall, 702 ... *L-9
Walmo, 900 ... WJ-2
Walnutport, 2065 ... EK-10
Warminster, 31592 ... EO-12
WARREN CO., 42820 ... WF-6
Warren, 9835 ... WE-7
Warrington, 7000 ... EN-12
WASHINGTON CO., 204286 ... WO-3
Washington, 14858 ... WO-2
Washington Crossing, 850 ... EN-13
Waterford, 1457 ... WD-4
Watsontown, 2190 ... EJ-4
Waverly, 1000 ... EG-10
Waymart, 1442 ... EG-11
WAYNE CO., 49092 ... EE-11
Wayne Hts., 1805 ... EQ-1
Waynesboro, 9628 ... EQ-1
Waynesburg, 4038 ... WP-3
Weatherly, 2613 ... EJ-9
Webster, 400 ... WO-4
Weedville, 950 ... WH-10
Weigelstown, 10117 ... WS-8
Wellsboro, 3323 ... EF-2
Wernersville, 2192 ... EN-8
Wescosville, 1250 ... EC-2
Wesleyville, 3549 ... WC-4
W. Brownsville, 1062 ... WP-4
W. Catasauqua, 700 ... EA-3
W. Chester, 17722 ... EP-10
W. Conshohocken, 1461 ... *B-1
W. Enola, 800 ... ES-2
W. Fairview, 1403 ... ES-2
Westfield, 1166 ... EE-1
Westgate Hills, 110 ... EL-11
W. Grove, 2634 ... EQ-9
W. Hazleton, 3400 ... EJ-8
W. Homestead, 2122 ... *K-7
W. Kittanning, 1446 ... WK-6
W. Lancaster, 800 ... ET-8
W. Lawn, 1572 ... EN-8
W. Leechburg, 1268 ... WL-5
W. Leisenring, 600 ... WP-5
W. Mayfield, 1149 ... WK-2
W. Middlesex, 897 ... WI-2
W. Mifflin, 21892 ... *L-8
W. Milton, 850 ... EJ-4
Westmont, 5330 ... WN-8
WESTMORELAND CO., 368224 ... WM-5
Westmoreland City, 1400 ... WN-5
W. Nanticoke, 1200 ... EI-8
W. Newton, 2986 ... WO-5
W. Pittsburg, 1100 ... WJ-2
W. Pittston, 4873 ... EH-9
W. Reading, 3995 ... ET-12
W. View, 7051 ... WM-3
W. Wyoming, 2752 ... EA-9
W. Wyomissing, 3016 ... ET-12
W. York, 4237 ... EP-5
Wexford, 1100 ... WL-3
Wheatland, 733 ... WI-1
Whitaker, 1292 ... *K-7
Whitehall, 14268 ... EL-11
Whitehall, 14100 ... *L-6
White Haven, 1166 ... EJ-9
White Oak, 8388 ... WN-4
Wiconisco, 1300 ... EM-5
Wilcox, 1000 ... WG-10
Wilkes-Barre, 41630 ... EI-9
Wilkinsburg, 18518 ... WM-4
Williamsburg, 1297 ... WM-12
Williamsport, 29871 ... EI-4
Williamstown, 1394 ... EM-5
Willow Grove, 16234 ... EO-12
Willow Street, 7258 ... EP-7
Wilmerding, 2066 ... *L-9
Wilson, 7608 ... EL-12
Winburne, 550 ... WJ-12
Windber, 4197 ... WO-9
Wind Gap, 2818 ... EK-11
Windsor, 1312 ... EP-6
Windsor Park, 1100 ... ET-1
Wolfdale, 2873 ... WO-2
Womelsdorf, 2636 ... EN-7
Woodland, 400 ... WJ-11
Woodland Park, 950 ... EH-4
Woodlawn, 1850 ... EL-10
Woodside, 100 ... EJ-9
Woolrich, 800 ... EI-2
Worcester, 900 ... EO-11
Wormleysburg, 2683 ... EN-4
Worthington, 758 ... WK-5
Wrightsville, 2187 ... EP-6
Wyalusing, 549 ... EF-7
Wyano, 750 ... WO-5
WYOMING CO., 28153 ... EG-7
Wyoming, 3103 ... EH-9
Wyomissing, 11079 ... EN-8
Yardley, 2529 ... EN-14
Yeadon, 11587 ... EP-12
Yeagertown, 1035 ... EL-1
Yoe, 1012 ... EP-5
YORK CO., 394915 ... EP-5
York, 40081 ... EP-5
York Haven, 801 ... EO-5
Yorkshire, 1700 ... WS-11
Youngsville, 1769 ... WE-7
Youngwood, 3210 ... WN-5
Yukon, 1200 ... WO-5
Zelienople, 4056 ... WK-3
Zieglerville, 900 ... EN-11
Zion, 2054 ... WK-14

Rhode Island

Map pp. 184-185

Abbott Run Valley, 1800 ... B-7
Albion, 170 ... B-6
Allenton, 650 ... G-6
Anthony, 3400 ... E-5
Arnold Mills, 640 ... B-7
Ashaway, 1537 ... I-3
Ashton, 910 ... B-6
Barrington, 16819 ... E-7
Berkeley, 910 ... B-6
Block Island, 836 ... L-5
Bradford, 1497 ... I-3
BRISTOL CO., 50989 ... E-8
Bristol, 22469 ... F-8
Carolina, 880 ... H-4
Central Falls, 19287 ... C-7
Charlestown, 2000 ... I-4
Chepachet, 1100 ... C-4
Common Fence Pt., 900 ... F-8
Coventry, 8600 ... E-5
Cranston, 81679 ... D-6
Cumberland Hill, 7738 ... B-6
Davisville, 550 ... F-6
Diamond Hill, 910 ... B-6
E. Greenwich, 11865 ... F-6
E. Providence, 49906 ... D-7
Esmond, 5000 ... C-6
Forestdale, 550 ... B-5
Glendale, 860 ... B-4
Greenville, 8626 ... C-5
Harmony, 1050 ... C-5
Harris, 1250 ... E-5
Harrisville, 1561 ... B-4
Hope Valley, 1649 ... H-4
Island Park, 1550 ... F-8
Jamestown, 4999 ... H-7
Johnston, 29283 ... D-6
KENT CO., 171297 ... F-4
Kingston, 5446 ... H-5
Lonsdale, 4200 ... C-7
Manville, 3200 ... B-6
Mapleville, 1600 ... B-4
Matunuck, 580 ... I-5
Middletown, 3800 ... G-8
Mt.View, 700 ... F-6
Narragansett, 3671 ... I-6
NEWPORT CO., 85934 ... G-8
Newport, 26136 ... H-7
N. Kingstown, 3000 ... G-6
N. Providence, 32411 ... C-6
Oakland, 600 ... B-4
Pascoag, 4742 ... B-4
Pawtucket, 74330 ... C-7
Peacedale, 3400 ... H-6
Portsmouth, 4200 ... F-8
PROVIDENCE CO., 639442 ... C-4
Providence, 176365 ... D-7
Quidnessett, 2000 ... F-6
Quidnick, 2700 ... E-5
Quonochontaug, 2000 ... J-4
Saylesville, 3800 ... C-6
Shannock, 1100 ... H-4
Slatersville, 2400 ... A-5
S. Hopkinton, 500 ... I-3
Tiverton, 7282 ... F-8
Union Vil., 2300 ... B-5
Valley Falls, 11599 ... C-7
Wakefield, 300 ... H-6
Warren, 11385 ... E-8
Warwick, 87365 ... E-7
WASHINGTON CO., 128502 ... G-5
Watch Hill, 580 ... J-2
Westerly, 17682 ... I-3
W. Kingston, 1400 ... H-5
W. Warwick, 29581 ... E-5
Woonsocket, 44654 ... A-6
Wyoming, 1100 ... H-4

South Carolina

Map pp. 186-187

ABBEVILLE CO., 26381 ... D-4
Abbeville, 5786 ... D-4
AIKEN CO., 146736 ... E-6
Aiken, 26456 ... F-6
Alcolu, 600 ... E-9
ALLENDALE CO., 10934 ... H-6
Allendale, 3910 ... G-7
ANDERSON CO., 171510 ... C-3
Anderson, 25563 ... C-3
Andrews, 3053 ... F-11
Arcadia, 2000 ... G-1
Arcadia Lakes, 866 ... I-3
Arial, 2607 ... B-3
Arkwright, 680 ... G-2
BAMBERG CO., 16040 ... G-8
Bamberg, 3568 ... F-7
BARNWELL CO., 23369 ... G-6
Barnwell, 4958 ... G-7
Batesburg-Leesville, 5536 ... E-6
BEAUFORT CO., 132889 ... I-8
Beaufort, 12376 ... I-8
Beech Island, 1500 ... F-5
Belton, 4490 ... C-4
Bennettsville, 9296 ... C-11
Berea, 14158 ... I-4
BERKELEY CO., 146449 ... G-10
Bishopville, 3688 ... D-9
Blacksburg, 1890 ... A-6
Blackville, 2951 ... F-7
Bluffton, 1778 ... J-8
Boiling Springs, 4544 ... A-5
Bowling Green, 500 ... A-7
Bowman, 1178 ... F-8
Branchville, 1059 ... G-8
Brunson, 581 ... H-7
Bucksport, 1117 ... E-12
Buffalo, 1426 ... B-6
Burton, 7180 ... I-8
CALHOUN CO., 15367 ... E-8
Calhoun Falls, 2294 ... D-3
Camden, 6861 ... D-8
Capitol View, 4000 ... D-8
Cayce, 12388 ... J-2
Central, 3516 ... B-3
CHARLESTON CO., 321014 ... H-10
Charleston, 101024 ... H-10
Cheraw, 5416 ... B-10
CHEROKEE CO., 53555 ... A-6
Chesnee, 1010 ... A-5
CHESTER CO., 33906 ... C-7
Chester, 6326 ... B-7
CHESTERFIELD CO., 43251 ... B-9
Chesterfield, 1342 ... B-10
City View, 1254 ... I-4
CLARENDON CO., 32871 ... E-9
Clemson, 11936 ... B-3
Clinton, 9010 ... C-5
Clio, 756 ... C-11
Clover, 3933 ... A-7
COLLETON CO., 39173 ... H-9
Columbia, 117357 ... D-7
Conestee, 580 ... B-4
Converse, 1200 ... A-5
Conway, 12538 ... E-12
Cowpens, 2306 ... A-5
DARLINGTON CO., 67956 ... C-10
Darlington, 6582 ... C-10
Denmark, 3168 ... F-7
Denny Ter., 1750 ... D-7
Dentsville, 13049 ... H-3
DILLON CO., 31027 ... C-11
Dillon, 6362 ... C-11
DORCHESTER CO., 104168 ... G-9
Drayton, 1400 ... G-3
Due West, 1295 ... C-4
Duncan, 2900 ... B-5
Dunean, 4158 ... J-4
Easley, 18479 ... B-4
East Gaffney, 3349 ... A-6
Eastover, 808 ... E-8
EDGEFIELD CO., 24703 ... E-5
Edgefield, 4501 ... E-5
Elloree, 710 ... F-8
Enoree, 1100 ... B-5
Estill, 2410 ... H-7
Eureka Mill, 1737 ... B-7
Fairfax, 3179 ... G-7
FAIRFIELD CO., 23840 ... C-7
Fairforest, 800 ... G-1
FLORENCE CO., 128335 ... D-11
Florence, 30267 ... D-10
Folly Beach, 2197 ... H-10
Forest Acres, 10343 ... I-3
Forestbrook, 3391 ... J-12
Ft. Mill, 7879 ... A-8
Fountain Inn, 6440 ... B-5
Gaffney, 12877 ... A-6
Gantt, 13962 ... J-4
Gaston, 1390 ... E-7
GEORGETOWN CO., 58924 ... F-11
Georgetown, 8951 ... F-12
Glendale, 1000 ... B-5
Gloverville, 2805 ... F-5
Golden Grove, 2348 ... B-4
Goose Cr., 30574 ... G-10
Graniteville, 1100 ... F-5
Gray Court, 1008 ... C-5
Great Falls, 2122 ... C-8
GREENVILLE CO., 395357 ... B-4
Greenville, 55926 ... B-4
GREENWOOD CO., 67503 ... D-5
Greenwood, 22252 ... D-5
Greer, 19333 ... B-4
HAMPTON CO., 21391 ... H-7
Hampton, 2822 ... H-7
Hanahan, 12971 ... H-10
Hardeeville, 1813 ... I-7
Harleyville, 690 ... G-9
Hartsville, 7435 ... C-10
Heath Sprs., 854 ... C-8
Hemingway, 538 ... E-11
Hilton Head Island, 34407 ... J-8
Holly Hill, 1377 ... F-9
Hollywood, 4223 ... H-9
Honea Path, 3540 ... C-4
HORRY CO., 210757 ... D-12
Inman, 1882 ... A-5
Inman Mills, 1151 ... A-5
Irmo, 11170 ... D-7
Isle of Palms, 4496 ... H-10
Iva, 1165 ... C-3
Jackson, 1635 ... F-5
James Island, 4400 ... H-10
JASPER CO., 20998 ... I-7
Jefferson, 696 ... B-9
Joanna, 1609 ... C-5
Johnsonville, 1428 ... E-11
Johnston, 2323 ... E-5
Jonesville, 943 ... B-6
Judson, 2456 ... J-4
Kensington, 600 ... F-12
KERSHAW CO., 54481 ... C-9
Kershaw, 1619 ... C-8
Kingstree, 3308 ... E-10
Ladson, 13264 ... G-10
La France, 900 ... C-3
Lake City, 6536 ... E-10
Lake Forest, 1000 ... I-5
Lake View, 788 ... C-12
Lamar, 1007 ... D-10
LANCASTER CO., 62520 ... B-8
Lancaster, 8354 ... B-8
Lando, 300 ... B-7
Landrum, 2490 ... A-5
Lane, 562 ... F-10
Latta, 1416 ... C-11
Laurel Bay, 6625 ... I-8
LAURENS CO., 70269 ... C-5
Laurens, 9819 ... C-5
LEE CO., 20331 ... D-9
Lesslie, 2268 ... B-8
LEXINGTON CO., 226528 ... E-6
Lexington, 11746 ... D-7
Liberty, 3002 ... B-3
Livingston, 146 ... F-7
Loris, 2192 ... D-13
Lugoff, 6278 ... D-8
Lyman, 2681 ... B-5
Manning, 3978 ... E-9
Marietta, 1200 ... A-4
MARION CO., 35113 ... D-11
Marion, 7008 ... D-11
MARLBORO CO., 28411 ... C-10
Mauldin, 17716 ... B-4
Mayesville, 1067 ... D-9
McBee, 711 ... C-9
McColl, 2441 ... B-11
MCCORMICK CO., 10233 ... D-4
McCormick, 2684 ... E-4
Monarch Mills, 1930 ... B-6
Moncks Corner, 6019 ... G-10
Montmorenci, 900 ... F-6
Mt. Pleasant, 54788 ... H-10
Mullins, 4854 ... D-12
Murrells Inlet, 5519 ... F-12
Myrtle Beach, 24691 ... E-13
NEWBERRY CO., 36840 ... D-5
Newberry, 10608 ... D-6
New Ellenton, 2276 ... F-6
Nichols, 397 ... D-12
Ninety Six, 1917 ... D-5
Norris, 860 ... B-3
North, 796 ... F-7
N. Augusta, 18413 ... F-5
N. Charleston, 81577 ... H-10
N. Myrtle Beach, 12442 ... E-13
Oak Grove, 8183 ... E-7
OCONEE CO., 68523 ... B-2
Olanta, 614 ... E-10
ORANGEBURG CO., 91028 ... F-8
Orangeburg, 12758 ... F-8
Pacolet, 2754 ... B-6
Pacolet Mills ... B-6
Pageland, 2522 ... B-9
Pamplico, 1133 ... D-11
Paris, 1950 ... B-4
Park Place, 1500 ... I-4
Pendleton, 2994 ... B-3
PICKENS CO., 112859 ... B-3
Pickens, 3015 ... B-3
Piedmont, 4684 ... B-4
Pinewood, 510 ... E-9
Port Royal, 4424 ... I-8
Prosperity, 1082 ... D-6
Quinby, 849 ... D-11
Ravenel, 2336 ... H-9
Reidville, 499 ... B-5
RICHLAND CO., 332104 ... E-8
Ridgeland, 2591 ... I-7
Ridge Spr., 807 ... E-6
Ridgeville, 1790 ... G-9
Riverside, 2350 ... I-4
Rock Hill, 56114 ... B-7
Roebuck, 1725 ... B-5
St. Andrews, 21814 ... H-1
St. Andrews, 10000 ... B-12
St. George, 2097 ... G-8
St. Matthews, 2093 ... E-8
St. Stephen, 1749 ... F-10
SALUDA CO., 19087 ... D-6
Saluda, 3007 ... D-6
Sans Souci, 7836 ... I-4
Scranton, 983 ... E-11
Seneca, 7674 ... B-3
Shannontown, 1500 ... E-9
Simpsonville, 14781 ... B-4
Socastee, 14295 ... E-12
Society Hill, 706 ... C-10
S. Congaree, 2318 ... E-7
SPARTANBURG CO., 261281 ... B-5
Spartanburg, 38718 ... B-5
Springdale, 2878 ... E-7
Springfield, 488 ... F-7
Sullivans Island, 1854 ... H-10
Summerton, 1033 ... F-9
Summerville, 31734 ... G-9
SUMTER CO., 105957 ... E-9
Sumter, 39790 ... E-9
Surfside Beach, 4515 ... E-12
Swansea, 528 ... E-7
Taylors, 20125 ... B-4
Tega Cay, 4178 ... A-7
Timmonsville, 2335 ... D-10
Travelers Rest, 3948 ... A-4
Turbeville, 718 ... E-10
UNION CO., 29105 ... B-6
Union, 8431 ... B-6
Utica, 1322 ... B-3
Varnville, 2057 ... H-7
Wagener, 866 ... E-7
Walhalla, 3810 ... B-2
Walterboro, 5356 ... H-8
Ware Shoals, 2352 ... C-4
Warrenville, 1000 ... F-5
Watts Mills, 1479 ... C-5
Welcome, 6390 ... J-4
Wellford, 2049 ... B-5
W. Columbia, 12920 ... J-2
Westminster, 2759 ... B-2
W. Pelzer, 888 ... B-4
Westview, 2000 ... G-1
Westville, 2200 ... I-4
Whitehall, 3600 ... D-7
Whitmire, 1505 ... C-6
Whitney, 1500 ... F-2
WILLIAMSBURG CO., 36008 ... E-11
Williamston, 3817 ... C-4
Williston, 3267 ... F-6
Winnsboro, 3583 ... C-7
Winnsboro Mills, 2263 ... C-7
Woodruff, 4162 ... B-5
Yemassee, 828 ... H-8
YORK CO., 178070 ... B-7
York, 6960 ... A-7

South Dakota

Map pp. 188-189

Aberdeen, 24086 ... B-10
Alcester, 887 ... G-13
Alexandria, 630 ... F-11
Alpena, 254 ... E-10
Arlington, 962 ... D-12
Armour, 741 ... F-10
AURORA CO., 2926 ... F-10
Aurora, 476 ... D-13
Avon, 548 ... G-11
Baltic, 899 ... E-13
BEADLE CO., 16269 ... D-10
Belle Fourche, 4577 ... D-2
BENNETT CO., 3530 ... G-5
Beresford, 1956 ... G-13
Big Stone City, 591 ... B-13
Bison, 360 ... B-4
Black Hawk, 2432 ... E-3
Blunt, 362 ... D-8
Bonesteel, 281 ... G-9
BON HOMME CO., 7104 ... G-11
Bowdle, 542 ... B-8
Box Elder, 2884 ... E-3
Brandon, 6522 ... F-13
Bridgewater, 592 ... F-11
Bristol, 352 ... B-11
Britton, 1245 ... A-11
BROOKINGS CO., 28265 ... D-13
Brookings, 18464 ... D-12
BROWN CO., 34666 ... B-10
Bruce, 266 ... D-12
BRULE CO., 5205 ... F-9
Bryant, 391 ... D-11
BUFFALO CO., 1994 ... E-9
Buffalo, 364 ... B-3
Burke, 640 ... G-9
BUTTE CO., 9212 ... C-3
CAMPBELL CO., 1679 ... A-8
Canistota, 704 ... F-12
Canton, 2955 ... F-13
Castlewood, 685 ... C-12
Centerville, 876 ... G-12
Chamberlain, 2279 ... E-9
Chancellor, 315 ... F-12
CHARLES MIX CO., 9178 ... F-10
Cherry Cr., 300 ... D-5
CLARK CO., 3915 ... C-11
Clark, 1215 ... C-11
CLAY CO., 13191 ... G-12
Clear Lake, 1291 ... C-13
CODINGTON CO., 25929 ... C-12
Colman, 561 ... E-12
Colome, 322 ... G-8
Colton, 664 ... E-12
Corsica, 625 ... F-10
CORSON CO., 4288 ... A-6
Crooks, 953 ... F-12
CUSTER CO., 7585 ... F-3
Custer, 1860 ... E-2
DAVISON CO., 18744 ... F-11
DAY CO., 5891 ... B-12
Deadwood, 1307 ... D-2
Dell Rapids, 3115 ... E-13
Delmont, 244 ... G-10
De Smet, 1100 ... D-11
DEUEL CO., 4364 ... C-13
DEWEY CO., 6133 ... C-6
Doland, 274 ... C-10
DOUGLAS CO., 3310 ... F-10
Dupree, 438 ... C-5
Eagle Butte, 665 ... C-6
Edgemont, 823 ... F-2
EDMUNDS CO., 4221 ... B-9
Elk Pt., 1795 ... H-13
Elkton, 633 ... D-13
Emery, 490 ... F-11
Estelline, 687 ... D-12
Ethan, 320 ... F-11
Eureka, 1025 ... A-8
Faith, 499 ... C-5
FALL RIVER CO., 7305 ... G-3
FAULK CO., 2469 ... C-9
Faulkton, 739 ... C-9
Flandreau, 2323 ... E-13
Ft. Pierre, 1998 ... D-7
Ft. Thompson, 1375 ... E-9
Frederick, 244 ... A-10
Freeman, 1265 ... F-12
Garretson, 1148 ... E-13
Gary, 219 ... C-13
Gayville, 399 ... G-12
Geddes, 247 ... G-10
Gettysburg, 1257 ... C-8
GRANT CO., 7625 ... C-12
GREGORY CO., 4500 ... F-9
Gregory, 1246 ... G-9
Groton, 1338 ... B-10
HAAKON CO., 2007 ... D-6
HAMLIN CO., 5615 ... C-12
HAND CO., 3520 ... D-9
HANSON CO., 3510 ... E-11
HARDING CO., 1288 ... B-3
Harrisburg, 1031 ... F-13
Hartford, 1968 ... F-12
Hayti, 368 ... D-12
Hecla, 299 ... A-10
Hermosa, 323 ... E-3
Herreid, 449 ... A-8
Highmore, 790 ... D-9
Hill City, 820 ... E-2
Hosmer, 270 ... B-8
Hot Sprs., 4038 ... F-2
Hoven, 464 ... B-8
Howard, 1000 ... E-11
Hudson, 369 ... G-13
HUGHES CO., 16684 ... D-8
Humboldt, 555 ... F-12
Hurley, 408 ... F-12
Huron, 11377 ... D-10
HUTCHINSON CO., 7731 ... F-11
HYDE CO., 1573 ... D-9
Ipswich, 913 ... B-9
Irene, 421 ... G-12
Iroquois, 267 ... D-11
Isabel, 237 ... B-6
JACKSON CO., 2853 ... F-5
Jefferson, 585 ... H-13
JERAULD CO., 2180 ... E-10
JONES CO., 1087 ... E-7
Kadoka, 675 ... E-5
Kennebec, 284 ... E-8
Keystone, 317 ... E-3
Kimball, 705 ... F-9
KINGSBURY CO., 5555 ... D-11
LAKE CO., 11040 ... E-12
Lake Andes, 790 ... G-10
Lake Norden, 431 ... D-12
Lake Preston, 687 ... D-12
Langford, 270 ... B-11
LAWRENCE CO., 21880 ... D-2
Lead, 2939 ... D-2
Lemmon, 1302 ... A-5
Lennox, 1929 ... F-12
Leola, 429 ... A-9
LINCOLN CO., 29302 ... G-13
Little Eagle, 370 ... B-7
Lower Brule, 599 ... E-8
LYMAN CO., 3916 ... E-8
Madison, 6303 ... E-12
Marion, 853 ... F-12
MARSHALL CO., 4272 ... A-11
Martin, 1049 ... G-5
MCCOOK CO., 5864 ... E-12
McIntosh, 215 ... A-6
McLaughlin, 780 ... A-7
MCPHERSON CO., 2723 ... A-9
MEADE CO., 24715 ... D-4
MELLETTE CO., 2118 ... F-7
Menno, 706 ... G-11
Midland, 165 ... E-6
Milbank, 3495 ... B-13
Miller, 1435 ... D-9
MINER CO., 2717 ... E-11
MINNEHAHA CO., 154617 ... E-12
Mission, 926 ... F-7
Mitchell, 14677 ... F-11
Mobridge, 3309 ... B-7
Montrose, 473 ... F-12
MOODY CO., 6511 ... E-13
Mt. Vernon, 465 ... F-10
Murdo, 562 ... E-7
Newell, 639 ... C-3
New Underwood, 625 ... E-3
N. Sioux City, 2398 ... H-13
Oacoma, 398 ... E-9
Onida, 687 ... D-8
Parker, 1005 ... F-12
Parkston, 1594 ... F-11
Parmelee, 650 ... F-6
PENNINGTON CO., 91881 ... E-4
PERKINS CO., 3187 ... B-4
Philip, 799 ... E-5
Piedmont, 350 ... D-3
Pierre, 13939 ... D-7
Pine Ridge, 3171 ... G-4
Plankinton, 567 ... F-10
Platte, 1329 ... F-9
Pollock, 316 ... A-7
POTTER CO., 2508 ... C-8
Presho, 614 ... E-8
Pringle, 124 ... F-2
Pukwana, 283 ... E-9
Rapid City, 60876 ... E-3
Redfield, 2345 ... C-10
ROBERTS CO., 10128 ... B-12
Roscoe, 310 ... B-9
Rosebud, 1557 ... G-6
Rosholt, 434 ... A-12
Roslyn, 211 ... B-11
St. Francis, 705 ... G-6
St. Lawrence, 195 ... D-9
Salem, 1389 ... F-12
SANBORN CO., 2612 ... E-11
Scotland, 846 ... G-11
Selby, 701 ... B-8
SHANNON CO., 13209 ... F-4
Sioux Falls, 133834 ... F-13
Sisseton, 2594 ... A-12
S. Shore, 266 ... C-12
Spearfish, 8870 ... D-2
Spencer, 156 ... F-11
SPINK CO., 6972 ... C-10
Springfield, 773 ... G-11
STANLEY CO., 2752 ... D-7
Stickney, 316 ... F-10
Sturgis, 6389 ... D-2
SULLY CO., 1456 ... C-8
Summit, 279 ... B-12
Tabor, 394 ... G-11
Tea, 1987 ... F-12
Timber Lake, 440 ... B-6
TODD CO., 9468 ... G-7
TRIPP CO., 6177 ... G-8
Tripp, 684 ... G-11
Tulare, 206 ... C-10
TURNER CO., 8594 ... F-12
Tyndall, 1181 ... G-11
UNION CO., 13024 ... G-13
Valley Sprs., 825 ... F-13
Veblen, 255 ... A-12
Vermillion, 10070 ... G-12
Viborg, 815 ... G-12
Volga, 1435 ... D-12
Wagner, 1619 ... G-10
Wakonda, 359 ... G-12
Wakpala, 200 ... B-7
Wall, 820 ... E-4
WALWORTH CO., 5562 ... B-8
Wanblee, 641 ... F-5
Warner, 426 ... B-10
Watertown, 20191 ... C-12
Waubay, 625 ... B-12
Webster, 1821 ... B-11
Wessington, 233 ... D-10
Wessington Sprs., 953 ... E-10
White, 507 ... D-13
White Lake, 390 ... F-10
White River, 598 ... F-7
Whitewood, 844 ... D-2
Willow Lake, 277 ... D-11
Wilmot, 542 ... B-12
Winner, 3001 ... F-8
Wolsey, 399 ... D-10
Woonsocket, 698 ... E-10
Worthing, 640 ... F-13
YANKTON CO., 21452 ... G-12
Yankton, 13440 ... G-12
ZIEBACH CO., 2551 ... C-6

Tennessee

Map pp. 190-193

* City keyed to p. 195

Adams, 575 ... B-10
Adamsville, 2019 ... F-6
Alamo, 2385 ... D-4
Alcoa, 8174 ... D-19
Alexandria, 837 ... C-13
Algood, 3006 ... C-15
Allardt, 646 ... B-16
Altamont, 1149 ... F-14
ANDERSON CO., 71904 ... C-18
Apison, 500 ... G-16
Ardmore, 1097 ... G-11
Arlington, 3195 ... F-2
Asbury, 300 ... J-8
Ashland City, 4193 ... C-10
Ashwood, 500 ... E-10
Athens, 13625 ... F-17
Atoka, 4522 ... E-2
Atwood, 995 ... D-5
Bartlett, 42245 ... F-2
Baxter, 1329 ... C-14
Bean Sta., 2669 ... K-16
BEDFORD CO., 40253 ... E-12
Beersheba Sprs., 546 ... F-14
Belle Meade, 3006 ... C-11
Bells, 2294 ... E-4
BENTON CO., 16500 ... C-7
Benton, 1137 ... G-17
Berry Hill, 681 ... L-8
Berrys Chapel, 3000 ... D-11
Bethel Sprs., 763 ... F-6
Bethpage, 300 ... B-12
Big Sandy, 521 ... C-7
Birchwood, 480 ... F-16
Blaine, 1653 ... C-20
BLEDSOE CO., 12556 ... E-15
Bloomingdale, 10350 ... J-18
BLOUNT CO., 111510 ... E-19
Blountville, 2959 ... J-18
Bluff City, 1576 ... J-18
Bolivar, 5689 ... F-4
Boones Creek, 2000 ... *M-3
Bradford, 1085 ... C-5
BRADLEY CO., 90264 ... G-17
Brentwood, 28960 ... D-11
Briarwood, 590 ... B-9
Briceville, 800 ... C-19
Brighton, 2068 ... E-2
Bristol, 25021 ... J-19
Brownsville, 10725 ... E-4
Bruceton, 1508 ... C-7
Bulls Gap, 700 ... K-16
Burlison, 449 ... E-2
Burns, 1407 ... C-9
Butler, 500 ... K-19
Byrdstown, 910 ... B-16
Calhoun, 506 ... F-17
Camden, 3764 ... C-7
Campaign, 500 ... D-14
CAMPBELL CO., 40125 ... B-19
CANNON CO., 13204 ... D-13
Capleville, 580 ... G-2
CARROLL CO., 29342 ... D-6
Carson Spr., 700 ... L-16
CARTER CO., 58394 ... K-19
Carter, 500 ... J-19
Carthage, 2246 ... C-13
Caryville, 2342 ... C-18
Celina, 1364 ... B-15
Centerville, 3940 ... D-9
Chapel Hill, 939 ... E-11
Charleston, 638 ... F-17
Charlotte, 1155 ... C-9
Chattanooga, 154887 ... G-15
CHEATHAM CO., 37364 ... B-10
CHESTER CO., 15842 ... E-5
Church Hill, 6119 ... J-17
CLAIBORNE CO., 30415 ... B-20
Clarksville, 107953 ... B-9
CLAY CO., 7947 ... B-14
Cleveland, 37368 ... G-17
Clifton, 2673 ... F-7
Clinton, 9328 ... C-19
Coalmont, 958 ... F-14
COCKE CO., 34329 ... L-16
COFFEE CO., 49643 ... F-13
Collegedale, 7129 ... G-16
Collierville, 35445 ... G-2
Collinwood, 1011 ... G-8
Colonial Hts., 7067 ... K-9
Columbia, 33305 ... E-10
Cookeville, 27052 ... C-15
Copperhill, 498 ... G-18
Cornersville, 933 ... F-11
Counce, 700 ... G-6
Covington, 9001 ... E-2
Cowan, 1757 ... G-13
Crab Orchard, 868 ... D-17
CROCKETT CO., 14491 ... D-4
Cross Plains, 1450 ... B-11
Crossville, 9725 ... D-16
CUMBERLAND CO., 49391 ... D-16
Cumberland Furnace, 300 ... C-9
Dandridge, 2205 ... C-20
DAVIDSON CO., 569842 ... C-11
Dayton, 6371 ... E-16
DECATUR CO., 11610 ... E-7
Decatur, 1437 ... E-17
Decaturville, 842 ... E-7
Decherd, 2206 ... F-13
DEKALB CO., 18037 ... D-14
DICKSON CO., 44935 ... C-9
Dickson, 12688 ... C-9
Dover, 1471 ... B-8
Dresden, 2755 ... B-5
Drummonds, 500 ... E-2
Ducktown, 419 ... G-18
Dunlap, 4414 ... F-15
DYER CO., 37308 ... C-3
Dyer, 2415 ... C-4
Dyersburg, 17301 ... C-3
Eagleville, 448 ... E-11
E. Ridge, 20003 ... G-16
Eastview, 618 ... G-6
Edgemont, 500 ... L-16
Elizabethton, 14015 ... K-19
Ellendale ... F-2
Englewood, 1647 ... F-18
Erin, 1456 ... B-8
Erwin, 5764 ... L-18
Estill Sprs., 2165 ... F-13
Ethridge, 548 ... F-9
Etowah, 3665 ... F-18
Fairview, 6548 ... D-10
Fall Branch, 1313 ... K-17
Farragut, 18669 ... D-19
FAYETTE CO., 32289 ... F-3
Fayetteville, 6955 ... G-12
FENTRESS CO., 16935 ... B-16
Finley, 1000 ... C-3
Forest Hills, 4948 ... L-7
FRANKLIN CO., 40512 ... G-13
Franklin, 46528 ... D-11
Friendship, 607 ... D-4
Friendsville, 919 ... D-19
Gadsden, 555 ... D-4
Gainesboro, 867 ... B-14
Gallatin, 25107 ... B-12
Gallaway, 719 ... F-3
Gates, 883 ... D-3
Gatlinburg, 3870 ... E-20
Germantown, 37520 ... G-2
GIBSON CO., 47922 ... C-4
GILES CO., 29390 ... F-10
Gilt Edge, 489 ... E-2
Gleason, 1452 ... C-6
Goodlettsville, 14229 ... B-11
Gordonsville, 1107 ... C-13
GRAINGER CO., 21445 ... C-20
Grand Jct., 315 ... G-4
Gray, 1273 ... K-18
Graysville, 1423 ... F-16
GREENE CO., 63991 ... K-17
Greeneville, 15204 ... L-17
Greenfield, 2133 ... C-5

Green Hill, 7068 C-12
Grimsley, 700 C-16
Gruetli-Laager, 1883 F-14
GRUNDY CO., 14389 F-14
Halls, 2291 D-3
Halls Crossroads, 1250 C-19
HAMBLEN CO., 58851 K-16
HAMILTON CO., 309510 F-16
Hampton, 2000 K-19
HANCOCK CO., 6702 J-16
HARDEMAN CO., 28174 G-4
HARDIN CO., 25927 G-7
Harriman, 6663 D-18
Harrison, 7630 I-14
Harrogate, 3974 B-20
Hartsville, 7447 B-13
HAWKINS CO., 55037 J-17
HAYWOOD CO., 19626 E-3
HENDERSON CO., 25900 E-6
Henderson, 6148 F-5
Hendersonville, 43027 C-11
Henning, 1278 E-3
HENRY CO., 31185 C-7
HICKMAN CO., 23352 E-9
Hohenwald, 3808 E-9
Hollow Rock, 961 C-7
Hornbeak, 428 B-4
HOUSTON CO., 8085 C-8
Humboldt, 9339 D-5
HUMPHREYS CO., 18123 C-8
Huntingdon, 4251 D-6
Huntland, 897 G-12
Huntsville, 988 B-18
Iron City, 373 G-9
Jacksboro, 1959 B-19
JACKSON CO., 11208 C-14
Jackson, 61110 E-5
Jakestown, 500 D-12
Jamestown, 1844 B-16
Jasper, 3118 G-14
JEFFERSON CO., 46919 C-20
Jefferson City, 7850 C-20
Jellico, 2472 A-19
JOHNSON CO., 17948 K-20
Johnson City, 57394 K-18
Jonesborough, 4391 K-18
Karns, 1458 D-19
Kenton, 1302 C-4
Kimball, 1346 G-14
Kimberlin Hts., 680 D-20
Kingsport, 44231 J-18
Kingston, 5327 D-18
Kingston Sprs., 2848 C-10
KNOX CO., 392995 C-20
Knoxville, 173278 D-19
Lafayette, 4009 B-13
La Follette, 8052 B-19
LAKE CO., 7824 B-3
Lake City, 1856 C-19
Lakeland, 7210 F-2
Lake Tansi Vil., 2621 D-16
Lakewood, 2363 C-11
LAUDERDALE CO., 27077 D-2
La Vergne, 23052 D-12
LAWRENCE CO., 40704 F-9
Lawrenceburg, 10864 F-9
Lebanon, 21406 C-12
Leipers Fork, 510 D-10
Lenoir City, 7271 D-18
LEWIS CO., 11438 E-9
Lewisburg, 10698 F-11
Lexington, 7472 E-6
Limestone, 550 K-17
LINCOLN CO., 31773 G-11
Linden, 996 E-8
Livingston, 3431 B-15
Lobelville, 921 D-8
Lookout Mtn., 1921 K-11
Loretto, 1691 G-9
LOUDON CO., 41624 E-18
Loudon, 4633 E-18
Luttrell, 957 C-20
Lynchburg, 5911 F-12
Lynn Garden, 4000 J-8
Lynnville, 340 F-10
MACON CO., 21023 A-13
MADISON CO., 93873 E-5
Madisonville, 4110 E-18
Manchester, 8929 F-13
Maple Hill, 410 *J-4
MARION CO., 27880 G-14
MARSHALL CO., 27537 F-11
Martin, 10237 B-5
Maryville, 25062 D-19
Mascot, 2119 C-20
MAURY CO., 73198 E-10
Maury City, 713 D-4
Maynardville, 1877 C-20
McEwen, 1676 C-8
McKenzie, 5357 C-6
MCMINN CO., 50632 F-17
McMinnville, 12981 E-14
MCNAIRY CO., 24938 F-6
Medina, 952 D-5
MEIGS CO., 11430 E-17
Memphis, 645978 F-1
Michie, 655 G-6
Middleton, 623 G-5
Middle Valley, 11854 G-16
Midtown, 1338 D-18
Milan, 7818 D-5
Millersville, 6039 B-11
Millington, 10229 F-2
MONROE CO., 41051 E-18
Monteagle, 1220 F-14
Monterey, 2771 C-15
MONTGOMERY CO., 141064 B-9
MOORE CO., 5911 F-12
MORGAN CO., 20080 C-17
Morgantown, 600 E-16
Morrison, 693 E-13
Morrison City, 1900 J-8
Morristown, 25144 K-16
Moscow, 518 G-3
Mosheim, 1761 K-17
Mtn. City, 2445 J-20
Mt. Carmel, 5103 J-17
Mt. Juliet, 16495 C-12
Mt. Pleasant, 4503 E-10
Munford, 5249 E-2
Murfreesboro, 78074 D-12
Nashville, 544765 C-11
Newbern, 2996 C-4
New Hope, 1023 G-14
New Johnsonville, 1958 D-7
New Market, 1264 C-20
Newport, 7203 L-16
New Tazewell, 2857 B-20
Niota, 786 E-18
Nolensville, 2520 D-11
Norris, 1408 C-19
Oak Hill, 4629 L-8
Oakland, 1385 F-3
Oak Ridge, 27338 D-18
OBION CO., 32386 B-4
Obion, 1117 C-4
Oliver Sprs., 3284 C-18
Oneida, 3659 B-18
Ooltewah, 5681 G-16
Orebank, 1300 J-9
OVERTON CO., 20151 B-15
Palmer, 724 F-15
Paris, 9650 B-6
Parsons, 2428 E-7
Pegram, 2159 C-10
PERRY CO., 7627 E-8
Petersburg, 582 F-11
Petros, 1350 C-18
Philadelphia, 559 E-18
PICKETT CO., 5006 A-16
Pigeon Forge, 5456 D-20
Pikeville, 1798 E-16
Piperton, 742 G-3
POLK CO., 16171 G-19
Portland, 9786 B-12
Powell, 7534 C-19
Powells Crossroads, 1240 G-15
Prospect, 600 G-16
Pulaski, 7947 F-10
Puryear, 669 B-6
PUTNAM CO., 64973 C-15
Ramsey, 700 M-14
Red Bank, 12013 I-12
Red Boiling Sprs., 1039 B-14
RHEA CO., 29286 E-16
Riceville, 700 F-17
Rickman, 750 C-15
Ridgely, 1649 C-3
Ridgeside, 382 G-15
Ridgetop, 1652 B-11
Ripley, 7745 D-3
ROANE CO., 52424 D-17
Roan Mtn., 1160 K-19
Robbins, 500 B-17
ROBERTSON CO., 58181 B-11
Rockford, 816 D-19
Rockwood, 5389 D-17
Rogersville, 4233 K-16
Russellville, 1200 K-16
RUTHERFORD CO., 202310 D-12
Rutherford, 1247 C-5
Ruthton, 900 J-19
Rutledge, 1215 C-20
St. Joseph, 847 G-9
Sale Cr., 1200 F-16
Saltillo, 346 F-7
Samburg, 261 B-3
Savannah, 7135 F-7
SCOTT CO., 21675 B-18
Scotts Hill, 901 E-7
Selmer, 4558 G-6
SEQUATCHIE CO., 11958 F-15
Sequatchie, 600 G-14
SEVIER CO., 75503 D-20
Sevierville, 14167 D-20
Sewanee, 2361 G-13
Seymour, 8850 D-20
Sharon, 955 C-5
SHELBY CO., 906178 G-2
Shelbyville, 17538 F-12
Sherwood, 500 G-13
Signal Mtn., 7265 G-15
SMITH CO., 18225 B-13
Smithville, 4109 D-14
Smyrna, 30172 D-12
Sneedville, 1328 J-16
Soddy-Daisy, 11967 F-16
Somerville, 2861 F-3
S. Carthage, 1304 C-13
S. Fulton, 2480 B-5
S. Pittsburg, 3164 G-14
Sparta, 4661 D-15
Spencer, 1697 E-15
Spr. City, 2011 E-17
Springfield, 15117 B-11
Spr. Hill, 12205 E-10
Stanton, 599 E-3
STEWART CO., 12847 B-8
Strawberry Plains, 700 C-20
SULLIVAN CO., 153050 J-19
Sullivan Gardens, 100 J-18
Summertown, 900 F-9
Summitville, 450 E-13
SUMNER CO., 138752 B-12
Sunbright, 587 C-17
Surgoinsville, 1691 J-17
Sweetwater, 5784 E-18
Talbott, 550 C-20
Tazewell, 2128 B-20
Tellico Plains, 887 F-18
Tennessee Ridge, 1328 C-8
TIPTON CO., 54184 E-2
Tiptonville, 4180 B-3
Tracy City, 1666 F-14
Trenton, 4594 D-5
Trezevant, 906 C-6
Trimble, 716 C-4
TROUSDALE CO., 7447 B-13
Troy, 1265 B-4
Tullahoma, 18434 F-13
Tusculum, 2096 K-17
UNICOI CO., 17709 L-18
Unicoi, 3530 K-18
UNION CO., 18830 B-19
Union City, 10769 B-4
Valley Forge, 2200 *N-5
VAN BUREN CO., 5478 E-15
Vonore, 1263 E-18
Walden, 1969 G-15
Walland, 500 E-20
Walnut Hill, 2756 *J-4
WARREN CO., 39129 E-14
Wartburg, 918 C-17
Wartrace, 562 E-12
WASHINGTON CO., 110078 K-18
Watauga, 435 K-18
Watertown, 1388 C-13
Waverly, 4073 C-8
WAYNE CO., 16947 F-8
Waynesboro, 2166 F-8
WEAKLEY CO., 34314 B-5
Westmoreland, 2124 B-13
Westover, 600 E-5
Westwood F-10
WHITE CO., 23584 D-14
White Bluff, 2257 C-10
White House, 8256 B-11
White Pine, 2049 L-16
Whiteside, 600 G-15
Whiteville, 4465 F-4
Whitwell, 1631 F-15
Wildwood, 530 D-19
WILLIAMSON CO., 141301 D-10
WILSON CO., 95366 C-12
Winchester, 7602 G-13
Woodbury, 2498 D-13
Woodland Mills, 291 B-4
Wrigley, 450 D-9

Texas

Map pp. 194-205

Index keys WA to WT refer to Western TX, pp. 198-201, EA to ET refer to Eastern TX, pp. 202-205.
* City keyed to pp. 194-195
† City keyed to pp. 196-197

Abernathy, 2772 WG-10
Abilene, 114889 WJ-14
Addison, 13886 †E-10
Agua Dulce, 734 EO-6
Alamo, 15731 ES-5
Alamo Hts., 7250 EL-4
Alba, 462 ED-10
Albany, 1922 EE-3
Aldine, 13979 EK-10
Aledo, 2257 EE-6
Algoa, 400 EL-11
Alice, 19310 EP-5
Allen, 62400 ED-8
Alpine, 6103 WO-7
Alto, 1125 EG-11
Alton, 6339 WO-1
Alvarado, 3770 EE-7
Alvin, 21978 EL-11
Alvord, 1184 EC-6
Amarillo, 178612 WD-10
Ames, 1141 EJ-12
Amherst, 779 WG-9
Anahuac, 2173 EK-12
ANDERSON CO., 54790 EG-10
ANDREWS CO., 12868 WJ-8
Andrews, 9509 WJ-9
ANGELINA CO., 80935 EH-11
Angleton, 18625 EL-10
Anna, 1486 EC-8
Anson, 2412 WJ-14
Anthony WK-1
Anton, 1169 WG-10
ARANSAS CO., 23574 EO-7
Aransas Pass, 8612 EO-7
ARCHER CO., 9189 EC-4
Archer City, 1893 EC-4
Arcola, 1167 EL-10
Argyle, 2681 ED-7
Arlington, 355007 EE-7
ARMSTRONG CO., 2056 WD-11
Arp, 911 EE-11
Asherton, 1336 WS-14
Aspermont, 879 WI-13
ATASCOSA CO., 41867 EM-4
Athens, 11962 EF-9
Atlanta, 5606 EC-12
Aubrey, 1880 EC-7
AUSTIN CO., 25057 EK-8
Austin, 672011 EJ-6
Avinger, 452 ED-12
Azle, 10149 ED-6
Bacliff, 6962 EK-11
BAILEY CO., 6660 WF-8
Baird, 1625 EE-3
Balch Sprs., 19455 EE-8
Balcones Hts., 3019 ER-11
Ballinger, 4002 WL-14
Balmorhea, 494 WM-7
BANDERA CO., 19347 EK-3
Bandera, 1097 EK-3
Bangs, 1625 EG-3
Banquete, 600 EO-6
Barrett, 2872 *C-8
Barstow, 381 WL-7
Bartlett, 1685 EI-6
Bartonville, 1283 ED-7
BASTROP CO., 67077 EK-6
Bastrop, 6682 EJ-7
Batesville, 1298 EM-2
Batson, 200 EJ-12
Bay City, 18573 EM-9
BAYLOR CO., 3909 EB-3
Bayou Vista, 1656 EL-11
Baytown, 67251 EK-11
Beach City, 1763 EK-11
Beasley, 646 EL-9
Beaumont, 112434 EJ-13
Beaumont Place, 8000 *C-7
Beckville, 748 EE-12
Bedford, 48572 †F-6
BEE CO., 32431 EN-6
Beeville, 13007 EN-6
BELL CO., 248727 EH-6
Bellaire, 16891 EK-10
Bellmead, 9583 EG-7
Bells, 1238 EC-8
Bellville, 4157 EK-9
Belton, 14883 EH-6
Benavides, 1603 EP-5
Benbrook, 21000 EE-6
Ben Wheeler, 500 EE-9
Bertram, 1258 EI-5
Beverly Hills, 2099 WF-6
Bevil Oaks, 1297 EJ-12
BEXAR CO., 1471644 EK-4
Big Lake, 2649 WM-11
Big Sandy, 1322 EE-10
Big Spr., 24556 WK-11
Big Wells, 749 EN-2
Bishop, 3236 EP-6
BLANCO CO., 8809 EI-4
Blanco, 1583 EJ-4
Blessing, 861 EM-9
Blooming Gr., 870 EF-8
Bloomington, 2562 EN-8
Blossom, 1463 EB-10
Blue Mound, 2400 †F-4
Blue Ridge, 817 EC-8
Boerne, 6849 EK-4
Bogata, 1345 EC-10
Boling, 1000 EL-9
Bonham, 10336 EC-8
Booker, 1339 WA-13
BORDEN CO., 682 WI-11
Borger, 13638 WC-11
BOSQUE CO., 17696 EF-6
Bosqueville WE-5
Bovina, 1855 WF-8
BOWIE CO., 89699 EB-11
Bowie, 5450 EC-5
Boyd, 1247 ED-6
Brackettville, 1836 WQ-13
Brady, 5331 EH-3
BRAZORIA CO., 263149 EL-10
Brazoria, 2842 EM-10
BRAZOS CO., 159830 EI-8
Breckenridge, 5676 EE-3
Bremond, 861 EH-8
Brenham, 13999 EJ-8
BREWSTER CO., 9247 WO-8
Bridge City, 8660 EJ-13
Bridgeport, 5258 EC-6
BRISCOE CO., 1663 WE-11
Bronte, 1027 WK-13
BROOKS CO., 7720 EQ-5
Brookshire, 3533 EK-9
BROWN CO., 38103 EF-3
Brownfield, 9237 WI-9
Brownsboro, 833 EE-10
Brownsville, 156178 ET-7
Brownwood, 19320 EG-3
Bruceville-Eddy, 1538 EH-7
Bryan, 67774 EI-8
Bryson, 531 ED-4
Buchanan Dam, 1688 EI-4
Buda, 3745 EJ-6
Buffalo, 1884 EG-9
Buffalo Gap, 446 WK-14
Bullard, 1356 EF-10
Buna, 2269 EI-13
Bunker Hill Vil., 3732 *D-3
Burkburnett, 10732 EB-4
BURLESON CO., 16941 EI-8
Burleson, 25334 EE-6
BURNET CO., 38809 EI-5
Burnet, 5156 EI-5
Byers, 526 EB-5
Cactus, 2642 WB-10
Caddo Mills, 1193 ED-8
CALDWELL CO., 35572 EK-6
Caldwell, 3647 EI-8
CALHOUN CO., 20454 EN-8
CALLAHAN CO., 13110 EF-2
Calvert, 1376 EH-8
Camelot, 4000 ER-13
CAMERON CO., 363092 ES-7
Cameron, 5896 EI-7
CAMP CO., 11756 ED-11
Campbell, 771 EC-9
Camp Wood, 808 WP-14
Canadian, 2212 WC-13
Canton, 3427 EE-9
Canutillo, 5129 WK-1
Canyon, 12987 WE-10
Carrizo Sprs., 5635 WS-14
Carrollton, 116714 ED-7
CARSON CO., 6507 WC-11
Carthage, 6493 EF-12
CASS CO., 29995 EC-11
Castle Hills, 4197 ER-11
CASTRO CO., 7900 WE-9
Castroville, 2839 EL-4
Cedar Hill, 39260 †J-8
Cedar Park, 41482 EI-6
Celeste, 842 EC-8
Celina, 2304 EC-7
Center, 5716 EF-12
Center Pt., 750 EK-3
Centerville, 942 EH-9
CHAMBERS CO., 27581 EK-12
Chandler, 2262 EE-10
Channelview, 29685 *D-8
Charlotte, 1754 EM-4
CHEROKEE CO., 47568 EF-10
Chico, 1032 EC-5
CHILDRESS CO., 7563 WE-13
Childress, 6632 WF-13
Chillicothe, 750 EA-2
China, 1080 EJ-12
China Grove, 1278 ES-13
Christoval, 422 WM-13
Cibolo, 4685 EP-14
Cisco, 3779 EE-3
Clarendon, 1970 WE-12
Clarksville, 3699 EB-10
Claude, 1262 WD-11
CLAY CO., 11207 EC-5
Cleburne, 27928 EE-6
Cleveland, 7828 EJ-11
Clifton, 3609 EG-6
Clint, 981 WL-2
Cloverleaf, 23508 *D-7
Clute, 10704 EM-10
Clyde, 3444 EE-2
Coahoma, 920 WJ-11
COCHRAN CO., 3486 WG-8
Cockrell Hill, 4314 †H-9
COKE CO., 3725 WK-13
Coldspring, 734 EI-11
COLEMAN CO., 8777 EG-2
Coleman, 4927 EG-3
College Sta., 73536 EI-8
Colleyville, 21389 †F-6
COLLIN CO., 597147 EC-7
COLLINGSWORTH CO., 3023 WE-13
Collinsville, 1368 EC-7
Colmesneil, 633 EH-12
COLORADO CO., 20643 EK-8
Colorado City, 4007 WJ-12
Columbus, 3905 EK-8
COMAL CO., 87785 EK-5
COMANCHE CO., 13541 EF-4
Comanche, 4275 EF-4
Combes, 2830 ES-6
Comfort, 2358 EK-3
Commerce, 8782 EC-9
Como, 636 ED-10
CONCHO CO., 3774 EH-1
Conroe, 39896 EJ-10
Converse, 11967 EL-5
COOKE CO., 37996 EB-6
Coolidge, 872 EG-8
Cooper, 2175 EC-9
Coppell, 38938 †E-8
Copperas Cove, 29988 EH-5
Corinth, 16338 ED-7
Corpus Christi, 279208 EO-7
Corrigan, 1891 EH-11
Corsicana, 25466 EF-8
CORYELL CO., 75195 EH-5
COTTLE CO., 1752 WF-13
Cotulla, 3593 EN-3
Crandall, 3184 EE-8
CRANE CO., 3885 WL-9
Crane, 3093 WL-9
Crawford, 767 EG-6
CROCKETT CO., 3934 WM-11
Crockett, 7065 EH-10
CROSBY CO., 6742 WH-11
Crosby, 1714 EK-11
Crosbyton, 1777 WH-11
Cross Plains, 1078 EF-3
Crowell, 1080 WG-14
Crowley, 8831 EE-6
Crystal City, 7131 WR-14
Cuero, 6659 EM-7
CULBERSON CO., 2760 WK-5
Cumby, 627 EC-9
Cushing, 639 EF-11
Cut and Shoot, 1239 EJ-10
Daingerfield, 2527 ED-11
Daisetta, 1081 EJ-12
Dalhart, 7153 WB-9
DALLAM CO., 6100 WA-9
DALLAS CO., 2284096 EE-8
Dallas, 1208318 ED-7
Dalworthington Gardens, 2339 †H-6
Danbury, 1646 EL-10
DAWSON CO., 14411 WI-10
Dawson, 878 EF-8
Dayton, 6363 EJ-11
DEAF SMITH CO., 18415 WD-9
Decatur, 5743 EC-6
Deer Park, 28844 EK-11
De Kalb, 1781 EC-11
De Leon, 2346 EF-4
Dell City, 397 WK-4
Del Rio, 35136 WQ-12
DELTA CO., 5451 EC-9
Del Valle, 1300 EJ-6
Denison, 23335 EB-8
DENTON CO., 510795 EC-7
Denton, 93435 EC-7
Denver City, 3923 WI-8
Deport, 710 EC-10
De Soto, 41703 †J-10
Detroit, 752 EB-10
Devine, 4324 EM-4
Deweyville, 1190 EJ-13
DEWITT CO., 20100 EM-6
D Hanis, 600 EL-3
Diboll, 5439 EH-11
DICKENS CO., 2705 WG-12
Dickinson, 17847 EL-11
Dilley, 4203 EN-3
DIMMIT CO., 10341 EN-2
Dimmitt, 4142 WF-9
DONLEY CO., 3877 WD-12
Donna, 15562 ES-5
Doucette, 250 EI-12
Dripping Springs, 1645 EJ-5
Driscoll, 820 EP-6
Dublin, 3672 EF-5
Dumas, 13724 WC-10
Duncanville, 35670 EE-7
DUVAL CO., 12616 EO-5
Eagle Lake, 3696 EK-9
Eagle Pass, 24462 WR-13
Early, 2704 EG-3
Earth, 1096 WF-9
E. Bernard, 1729 EL-9
EASTLAND CO., 18300 EE-4
Eastland, 3799 EE-4
E. Tawakoni, 909 ED-9
ECTOR CO., 122692 WK-9
Ector, 618 EC-8
Edcouch, 4165 ES-6
Eden, 2471 WM-14
Edgecliff, 2561 †I-4
Edgewood, 1404 EE-9
Edinburg, 55302 ES-5
Edna, 5838 EM-8
Edroy, 420 EO-6
EDWARDS CO., 2031 WO-13
El Campo, 10842 EL-9
Eldorado, 1871 WN-12
Electra, 3055 EB-3
Elgin, 7218 EJ-6
Elkhart, 1246 EG-10
El Lago, 3043 *G-9
ELLIS CO., 124411 EE-7
Elmendorf, 702 EL-5
Elm Mott, 950 EG-7
EL PASO CO., 705436 WK-2
El Paso, 584113 WK-2
Elsa, 6174 ES-5
Emory, 1213 ED-9
Encinal, 637 EO-3
Encino, 177 EQ-5
Ennis, 18319 EE-8
ERATH CO., 33370 EE-4
Escobares, 1954 ES-4
Euless, 50118 ED-7
Eustace, 841 EE-9
Evadale, 1430 EI-13
Everman, 5849 †I-4
Fabens, 8043 WL-2
Fairfield, 3398 EG-9
Falfurrias, 5100 EQ-5
FALLS CO., 17860 EH-7
Falls City, 589 EM-5
FANNIN CO., 32276 EB-9
Farmers Branch, 27025 ED-7
Farmersville, 3252 EC-8
Farwell, 1331 WF-8
FAYETTE CO., 22370 EK-7
Ferris, 2275 EE-8
FISHER CO., 4142 WI-13
Flatonia, 1421 EK-7
Flint, 700 EE-10
Florence, 1110 EI-6
Floresville, 6475 EL-5
Flower Mound, 60621 †D-7
FLOYD CO., 7446 WF-11
Floydada, 3433 WG-11
FOARD CO., 1541 EB-2
Forest Hill, 13265 †I-5
FORT BEND CO., 419772 EL-9
Ft. Davis, 1050 WN-6
Ft. Gates, 300 EG-6
Ft. Hancock, 1713 WL-3
Ft. Stockton, 7387 WN-8
Ft. Worth, 585122 EE-6
FRANKLIN CO., 9906 EC-10
Franklin, 1450 EH-8
Frankston, 1215 EF-10
Fredericksburg, 9955 EJ-4
Freeport, 12715 EM-10
Freer, 3129 EO-4
FREESTONE CO., 18605 EG-9
Fresno, 6603 EK-10
Friendswood, 32460 EK-11
FRIO CO., 16345 EM-4
Friona, 3807 WE-9
Frisco, 55126 ED-7
Fritch, 2148 WC-11
Frost, 679 EF-7
Fulshear, 896 EK-9
Fulton, 1634 EO-7
GAINES CO., 14438 WI-8
Gainesville, 16040 EC-7
Galena Park, 10443 *E-6
GALVESTON CO., 266775 EL-12
Galveston, 56667 EL-12
Ganado, 1874 EM-8
Gardendale, 1197 WK-9
Garden Ridge, 2161 EP-14
Garfield, 1660 EJ-6
Garland, 218027 ED-8
Garrison, 832 EF-12
Garwood, 850 EL-8
GARZA CO., 5011 WH-11
Gatesville, 15373 EG-6
Gause, 500 EI-8
Georgetown, 34815 EI-6
George W., 2416 EN-5
Gholson, 948 EG-7
Giddings, 5386 EJ-7
GILLESPIE CO., 22226 EJ-3
Gilmer, 5025 ED-11
GLASSCOCK CO., 1355 WK-11
Glenn Heights, 8100 †J-10
Glen Rose, 2373 EF-6
Godley, 944 EE-6
Goldthwaite, 1760 EG-4
GOLIAD CO., 7116 EM-7
Goliad, 2015 EN-7
GONZALES CO., 19057 EL-6
Gonzales, 7320 EL-6
Gordon, 455 EE-4
Gorman, 1258 EF-4
Graford, 598 ED-5
Graham, 8651 ED-4
Granbury, 6403 EE-6
Grandfalls, 368 WM-8
Grand Prairie, 136671 ED-7
Grand Saline, 3125 EE-9
Grandview, 1492 EF-7
Granger, 1307 EI-6
Grapeland, 1434 EG-10
Grapevine, 46891 ED-7
GRAY CO., 21496 WC-12
GRAYSON CO., 115153 EC-7
Greenville, 24838 ED-9
GREGG CO., 113941 EE-11
Gregory, 2275 EO-7
GRIMES CO., 24963 EI-9
Groesbeck, 4348 EG-8
Groom, 582 WD-12
Groves, 15333 EJ-13
Groveton, 1124 EH-11
Grulla, 1707 ES-4
Gruver, 1123 WB-11
GUADALUPE CO., 97101 EL-5
Gun Barrel City, 5570 EE-9
Gunter, 1487 EC-7
HALE CO., 35874 WF-10
Hale Cen., 2161 WG-10
HALL CO., 3833 WF-12
Hallettsville, 2527 EL-7
Hallsburg, 533 EG-7
Hallsville, 2813 EE-12
Haltom City, 40475 ED-6
HAMILTON CO., 8118 EG-5
Hamilton, 2938 EG-5
Hamlin, 2096 WI-13
Hamshire, 600 EK-12
Hankamer, 600 EK-12
HANSFORD CO., 5210 WA-11
Happy, 629 WE-10
HARDEMAN CO., 4440 EA-2
HARDIN CO., 49634 EI-13
Hardin, 796 EJ-12
Hargill, 950 ER-5
Harker Hts., 18365 EH-6
Harlingen, 60769 ES-6
HARRIS CO., 3596086 EK-10
HARRISON CO., 62708 ED-11
Hart, 1149 WF-10
HARTLEY CO., 5223 WB-9
HASKELL CO., 5739 EC-2
Haskell, 2909 WI-14
Haslet, 1338 ED-6
Hawkins, 1424 EE-10
Hawley, 624 WJ-14
HAYS CO., 114193 EJ-5
Hearne, 4657 EI-8
Hebbronville, 4498 EQ-4
Hebron, 157 ED-7
Hedwig Vil., 2341 *D-3
Helotes, 5239 EK-4
HEMPHILL CO., 3333 WB-13
Hemphill, 1076 EG-13
Hempstead, 6051 EJ-9
HENDERSON CO., 77277 EF-9
Henderson, 11069 EF-11
Henrietta, 3321 EB-5
Hereford, 14428 WE-9
Hewitt, 12261 EG-7
Hickory Creek, 2656 †B-7
Hico, 1345 EF-5
HIDALGO CO., 635540 ES-5
Hidalgo, 9110 ES-5
Higgins, 434 WB-14
Highland Park, 8819 †F-10
Highlands, 7089 EK-11
Highland Village, 14080 †C-7
HILL CO., 34444 EF-7
Hill Country Village, 1066 EQ-12
Hillister, 300 EI-12
Hillsboro, 8705 EF-7
Hilshire Vil., 734 *D-4
Hitchcock, 7176 EL-11
HOCKLEY CO., 22807 WG-9
Holland, 1101 EI-6
Holliday, 1710 EB-4
Hollywood Park, 3107 EQ-12
Hondo, 8208 EL-3
Honey Gr., 1788 EC-9
HOOD CO., 45046 EE-5
Hooks, 2935 EC-12
HOPKINS CO., 32681 EC-10
Horizon City, 7432 WK-2
Houmont Park, 2500 *C-7
HOUSTON CO., 23109 EG-10
Houston, 2009690 EK-10
HOWARD CO., 32849 WJ-11
Howe, 2670 EC-8
Hubbard, 1653 EF-7
Hudson, 3949 EH-11
HUDSPETH CO., 3193 WL-3
Huffman, 3000 EJ-11
Hughes Sprs., 1849 ED-11
Hull, 1400 EJ-12
Humble, 14753 EJ-11
Hungerford, 645 EL-9
HUNT CO., 81024 EC-9
Hunters Creek Vil., 4502 *D-3
Huntington, 2088 EH-12
Huntsville, 35567 EI-10
Hurst, 37141 ED-7
Hutchins, 2805 †I-11
HUTCHINSON CO., 22959 WB-11
Hutto, 4036 EI-6
Idalou, 2138 WG-11
Imperial, 428 WM-9
Inez, 1787 EM-8
Ingleside, 9203 EO-7
Ingram, 1813 EJ-3
Iowa Park, 6318 EB-4
Iraan, 1184 WM-10
IRION CO., 1742 WL-12
Irving, 194455 ED-7
Italy, 2057 EF-7
Itasca, 1585 EF-7
Jacinto City, 10258 *D-6
JACK CO., 8949 EC-5
Jacksboro, 4575 EC-5
JACKSON CO., 14247 EM-8
Jacksonville, 13974 EF-10
Jamaica Beach, 1077 EL-11
JASPER CO., 35509 EH-13
Jasper, 7541 EH-13
Jayton, 462 WH-13
JEFF DAVIS CO., 2236 WM-5
JEFFERSON CO., 248605 EK-13
Jefferson, 1994 ED-12
Jersey Vil., 7195 *C-3
Jewett, 905 EG-9
JIM HOGG CO., 5024 EQ-4
JIM WELLS CO., 40469 EO-5
Joaquin, 930 EF-13
JOHNSON CO., 139068 EF-6
Johnson City, 1274 EJ-4
JONES CO., 20039 EE-1
Jones Cr., 2158 EM-10
Jonestown, 1748 EJ-5
Joshua, 5161 EE-6
Jourdanton, 4052 EM-4
Junction, 2649 WN-14
Justin, 2409 ED-6
Karnack, 300 ED-12
KARNES CO., 15276 EM-5
Karnes City, 3397 EM-6
Katy, 12726 EK-9
KAUFMAN CO., 81955 EE-8
Kaufman, 7502 EE-8
Keene, 5514 EE-6
Keller, 33951 †E-5
Kemah, 2345 EK-11
Kemp, 1221 EE-8
KENDALL CO., 26178 EJ-4
Kendleton, 505 EL-9
KENEDY CO., 408 EQ-6
Kenedy, 3413 EM-6
Kennedale, 6399 †I-5
KENT CO., 770 WH-12
Kerens, 1747 EF-8
Kermit, 5367 WK-8
KERR CO., 45311 EK-2
Kerrville, 21343 EJ-3
Kilgore, 11472 EE-11
Killeen, 96159 EH-6
KIMBLE CO., 4535 EI-2
KING CO., 319 WG-13
Kingsland, 4584 EI-4
Kingsville, 25270 EP-6
Kingwood, 42000 EJ-11
KINNEY CO., 3311 WP-13
Kirby, 8712 EL-5
Kirbyville, 2037 EI-13
KLEBERG CO., 31308 EP-6
KNOX CO., 3928 EC-2
Knox City, 1131 WH-14
Kosse, 511 EH-8
Kountze, 2128 EI-12
Kress, 802 WF-10
Krum, 2632 EC-7
Kyle, 11248 EK-5
LaCoste, 1339 EL-4
Lacy-Lakeview, 5805 WD-6
Ladonia, 678 EC-9
La Feria, 6436 ES-6
Lago Vista, 5167 EI-5
La Grange, 4581 EK-7
Laguna Vista, 2166 ES-7
Laird Hill, 400 EE-11
La Joya, 4235 ES-4
Lake Brownwood, 1694 EG-3
Lake Dallas, 6779 ED-7
Lakehills, 4668 EL-3
Lake Jackson, 26950 EM-10
Lakeport, 897 EE-11
Lakeside, 1131 †G-2
Lakeside City, 1035 EB-4
Lake Tanglewood, 834 WD-10
Lakeway, 8190 EJ-5
Lake Worth, 4676 †G-3
LAMAR CO., 49464 EB-10
La Marque, 13788 EL-11
LAMB CO., 14637 WF-9
Lamesa, 9462 WI-10
LAMPASAS CO., 19407 EH-5
Lampasas, 7426 EH-5
Lancaster, 27814 †J-11
La Porte, 33263 EK-11
La Pryor, 1491 WR-14
Laredo, 197488 EP-2
LA SALLE CO., 5822 EN-3
LAVACA CO., 19063 EL-7
La Vernia, 1005 EL-5
La Villa, 1412 ES-6
League City, 54775 EK-11
Leander, 13846 EI-6
LEE CO., 16530 EJ-7
Lefors, 537 WD-12
Leming, 600 EM-4
LEON CO., 16017 EG-9
Leonard, 1953 EC-8
Leon Valley, 9358 ER-10
Levelland, 12904 WH-9
Lewisville, 87127 ED-7
Lexington, 1262 EJ-7
LIBERTY CO., 74117 EJ-11
Liberty, 8261 EJ-11
Liberty Hill, 1485 EI-5
LIMESTONE CO., 22621 EG-8
Lindale, 3592 EE-10
Linden, 2198 ED-12
Lindsay, 881 EC-7
LIPSCOMB CO., 3092 WB-13
Little Elm, 12003 †B-9
Littlefield, 6432 WG-9
Little River, 1625 EH-6
LIVE OAK CO., 11902 EO-5
Live Oak, 9786 EL-5
Livingston, 6317 EI-11
LLANO CO., 18034 EI-4
Llano, 3464 EI-4
Lockhart, 13064 EK-6
Lockney, 1960 WG-11
Loeb, 200 EJ-13
Lolita, 548 EM-8
Lometa, 837 EH-4
Lone Oak, 546 ED-9
Lone Star, 1625 ED-11
Longview, 74902 EE-11
Lopezville, 4476 WO-3
Loraine, 616 WJ-12
Lorena, 1503 EH-7
Lorenzo, 1304 WG-11
Los Fresnos, 4960 ES-7
Lott, 686 EH-7
Louise, 977 EL-8
LOVING CO., 62 WK-7
Lowry Crossing, 1567 ED-8
LUBBOCK CO., 250446 WG-10
Lubbock, 206481 WH-10
Lucas, 3501 ED-8
Lufkin, 33162 EG-11
Luling, 5291 EK-6
Lumberton, 9122 EJ-13
Lyford, 1962 ES-6
LYNN CO., 6182 WH-10
Lytle, 2576 EL-4
Mabank, 2426 EE-9
MADISON CO., 12821 EH-9
Madisonville, 4192 EH-9
Magnolia, 1214 EJ-10
Malakoff, 2319 EF-9
Manchaca, 1500 EJ-6
Manor, 1169 EJ-6
Mansfield, 33123 EE-7
Manvel, 3234 EL-10
Marathon, 455 WO-7
Marble Falls, 5503 EI-5
Marfa, 2029 WO-6
MARION CO., 11028 ED-12
Marion, 1128 EL-5
Markham, 1138 EM-9
Marlin, 6340 EH-7
Marshall, 23938 EE-12
Mart, 2233 EG-7
MARTIN CO., 4600 WJ-10
Martindale, 999 EK-6
MASON CO., 3777 EI-3
Mason, 2168 EI-3
Matador, 679 WG-12
MATAGORDA CO., 38290 EM-10
Matagorda, 850 EM-9
Mathis, 5159 EO-6
Maud, 1018 EC-12
Mauriceville, 2743 EJ-13
MAVERICK CO., 50178 WQ-13
Maypearl, 828 EE-7
McAllen, 116501 ES-5
McCamey, 1656 WM-9
MCCULLOCH CO., 7896 EH-2
McGregor, 4795 EG-6
McKinney, 79958 EC-8
McLean, 782 WD-13
MCLENNAN CO., 219807 EG-7
MCMULLEN CO., 868 EN-4
McQueeney, 2527 EK-5
Meadow, 636 WH-10
Meadowood Acres, 500 ET-9
Meadows, 5281 EK-10
MEDINA CO., 41553 EL-3
Melissa, 1884 EC-8
Memphis, 2502 WE-13
MENARD CO., 2354 EI-2
Menard, 1652 WN-14
Mercedes, 14128 ES-6
Meridian, 1503 EF-6
Merkel, 2599 WJ-14
Mertzon, 828 WM-12
Mesquite, 129270 ED-8
Mexia, 6710 EG-8
Miami, 545 WC-12
MIDLAND CO., 118624 WK-10
Midland, 96573 WK-10
Midlothian, 10942 EE-7
MILAM CO., 25103 EI-7
Miles, 819 WL-13
Milford, 705 EF-7
MILLS CO., 5038 EG-4
Millsap, 375 EE-5
Mineola, 4840 EE-10
Mineral Wells, 16970 ED-5
Mission, 54619 ES-5
Mission Bend, 30831 *E-2
Missouri City, 62570 EK-10
MITCHELL CO., 9316 WJ-12
Monahans, 6397 WL-8
MONTAGUE CO., 19416 EB-5
Mont Belvieu, 2472 EK-11
Monte Alto, 1611 ES-5
MONTGOMERY CO., 344700 EJ-10
Moody, 1399 EH-6
MOORE CO., 20234 WB-10
MORRIS CO., 13167 EC-11
Morton, 2088 WG-9
MOTLEY CO., 1304 WF-12
Moulton, 940 EK-7
Mt. Pleasant, 14266 EC-11
Mt. Vernon, 2366 EC-10
Muenster, 1645 EC-6
Muleshoe, 4556 WF-9
Munday, 1410 EC-2
Murchison, 617 EE-9
Murphy, 7991 †D-13
NACOGDOCHES CO., 59584 EF-11
Nacogdoches, 30441 EG-11
Naples, 1426 EC-11
Nash, 2180 EC-12
Nassau Bay, 4130 EK-11
Natalia, 1764 EL-4
NAVARRO CO., 47331 EF-8
Navasota, 7235 EJ-9
Nederland, 16928 EJ-13
Needville, 2987 EL-9
Nevada, 598 ED-8
New Boston, 4633 EC-12
New Braunfels, 42693 EK-5
New Caney, 3000 EJ-11
Newcastle, 572 ED-4
Newgulf EL-9
New Hope, 701 †A-13
New London, 992 EE-11
NEWTON CO., 14869 EI-13
Newton, 2437 EH-13
New Waverly, 942 EI-10
Nixon, 2215 EL-6
Nocona, 3228 EB-6
NOLAN CO., 15110 WJ-13
Nolanville, 2152 EH-6
Nome, 508 EJ-12
Normangee, 750 EH-9
N. Houston, 2000 EK-10
N. Richland Hills, 60238 ED-7
N. Zulch, 550 EH-9
NUECES CO., 315206 EP-6
Oak Point, 2225 †A-8
Oak Ridge North, 3122 EJ-10
Oakwood, 489 EG-9
OCHILTREE CO., 8986 WA-12
Odem, 2457 EO-6
Odessa, 91113 WK-9
O Donnell, 963 WI-10
Olden, 500 EE-4
OLDHAM CO., 2159 WC-9
Old Ocean, 950 EL-10
Old River-Winfree, 1839 EJ-11
Olmito, 1198 ES-6
Olmos Park, 2304 ER-11
Olney, 3340 EC-4
Olton, 2305 WF-10
Omaha, 981 EC-11
ORANGE CO., 84390 EJ-13
Orange, 18073 EJ-13
Orangefield, 900 EJ-13
Orange Gr., 1356 EO-6
Ore City, 1154 ED-11
Overton, 2301 EE-11
Oyster Cr., 1240 EM-11
Ozona, 3436 WN-11
Paducah, 1372 WG-13
Palacios, 5270 EM-9
Palestine, 17808 EG-10
Palmer, 1950 EE-8
PALO PINTO CO., 27325 EE-4
Palo Pinto, 425 ED-5
Pampa, 16897 WC-12
Panhandle, 2574 WD-11
PANOLA CO., 22606 EE-12
Pantego, 2348 †H-6
Paris, 26523 EB-10
PARKER CO., 97480 ED-5
Parker, 1816 †C-13
PARMER CO., 9896 WE-8
Pasadena, 144413 EK-11
Pearland, 47903 EK-11
Pearsall, 7132 EM-3
PECOS CO., 16039 WN-9
Pecos, 8752 WL-7
Pelican Bay, 1611 †E-2
Penitas, 1177 ES-5
Perryton, 7775 WB-12
Petersburg, 1233 WG-11
Petrolia, 802 EB-5
Pettus, 608 EN-6
Pflugerville, 24661 EJ-6
Pharr, 54452 ES-5
Phillips, 900 WC-11
Pilot Pt., 3859 EC-7
Pine Forest, 629 EJ-13
Pinehurst, 2240 EJ-13
Pineland, 925 EG-13
Piney Point Vil., 3457 *D-3
Pittsburg, 4370 ED-11
Placedo, 700 EM-8
Plains, 1431 WH-8
Plainview, 21889 WF-11
Plano, 241991 ED-8
Pleak, 1051 EL-10
Pleasanton, 8999 EM-4
POLK CO., 45323 EI-11
Port Aransas, 3534 EO-7
Port Arthur, 57042 EK-13
Port Bolivar, 1300 EL-12
Pt. Comfort, 755 EM-8
Porter, 7000 EJ-11
Port Isabel, 5199 ES-7
Portland, 15489 EO-7
Port Lavaca, 11865 EN-8
Port Neches, 13269 EJ-13
Port O Connor, 1200 EN-8
Post, 3817 WI-11
Poteet, 3528 EM-4
Poth, 2002 EM-5
POTTER CO., 117335 WC-10
Pottsboro, 1715 EB-8
Prairie View, 4540 EJ-9
Premont, 2825 EP-5
PRESIDIO CO., 7591 WN-5
Presidio, 4575 WP-5
Preston, 450 EB-8
Price, 650 EF-11
Princeton, 3789 EC-8
Progreso, 5043 ES-6
Prosper, 2920 EC-7
Quanah, 2826 WF-14
Queen City, 1586 EC-12
Quinlan, 1437 ED-9
Quitaque, 400 WF-12
Quitman, 2126 ED-10
RAINS CO., 10857 ED-9
Ralls, 2144 WG-11
RANDALL CO., 107333 WE-10
Ranger, 2544 EE-4
Rankin, 747 WM-10
Raymondville, 9512 ER-6
REAGAN CO., 3054 WL-11
REAL CO., 3020 EK-2
Red Oak, 5871 EE-7
RED RIVER CO., 13812 EB-10
Redwater, 882 EC-12
Reese Vil., 42 WG-10
REEVES CO., 12238 WL-7
REFUGIO CO., 7625 EN-7
Refugio, 2793 EN-7
Rendon, 9022 †J-5
Reno, 2677 ED-6
Reno, 2867 EB-10
Richardson, 99536 ED-7
Richland Hills, 8184 †G-5
Richmond, 12752 EK-10
Riesel, 991 EG-7
Rio Grande City, 12985 ES-4
Rio Hondo, 2057 ES-6
Rising Star, 845 EF-3
River Oaks, 7024 †G-3
Roanoke, 3441 ED-7
Robert Lee, 1115 WK-13
ROBERTS CO., 820 WC-12
ROBERTSON CO., 15832 EH-8
Robinson, 8392 EG-7
Robstown, 12637 EO-6
Roby, 645 WJ-13
Rochester, 359 WH-14
Rockdale, 6024 EI-7
Rockport, 8469 EO-7
Rocksprings, 1216 WP-13
ROCKWALL CO., 54630 ED-8
Rockwall, 24624 ED-8
Rogers, 1081 EH-7
Rollingwood, 1366 EJ-6
Roma, 10315 ES-3
Ropesville, 522 WH-10
Roscoe, 1301 WJ-13
Rosebud, 1430 EH-7
Rose City, 519 EA-14
Rosenberg, 27808 EK-10
Rotan, 1515 WI-13
Round Rock, 77946 EI-6
Rowlett, 51102 †E-13
Roxton, 700 EC-9
Royse City, 4129 ED-8
Rule, 656 WI-14
Runaway Bay, 1261 ED-5
Runge, 1070 EM-6
RUNNELS CO., 10911 EF-1
RUSK CO., 47255 EF-11
Rusk, 5212 EF-11
Sabinal, 1637 EL-2
SABINE CO., 10379 EG-13
Sabine Pass EK-13
Sachse, 14550 †D-13
Saginaw, 16127 †F-3
St. Francis Vil., 500 †I-2
St. Jo, 969 EB-6
San Angelo, 87922 WL-13
San Antonio, 1214725 EL-4
SAN AUGUSTINE CO., 8913 EG-12
San Augustine, 2475 EG-13
San Benito, 24208 ES-6
Sanderson, 861 WO-9
San Diego, 4633 EP-5
Sand Sprs., 600 WJ-11
San Elizario, 11046 WL-2
Sanger, 5122 EC-7
San Isidro, 270 ER-5
SAN JACINTO CO., 23917 EI-10
San Juan, 28894 ES-5
San Leon, 4365 *H-10
San Marcos, 43007 EK-5
SAN PATRICIO CO., 68050 EO-7
SAN SABA CO., 6053 EH-3
San Saba, 2635 EH-4
Sansom Park, 4199 †G-3
Santa Anna, 1029 EG-3
Santa Fe, 10259 EL-11
Santa Rosa, 2910 ES-6
San Ygnacio, 1000 EQ-3
Saratoga, 1200 EJ-12
Savoy, 878 EC-8
Schertz, 23690 EL-5
SCHLEICHER CO., 2816 WM-12
Schulenburg, 2752 EK-7
SCURRY CO., 16081 WI-12
Seabrook, 10822 EK-11
Seadrift, 1367 EN-8
Seagoville, 11019 EE-8
Seagraves, 2296 WI-9
Sealy, 5771 EK-9
Sebastian, 1864 ES-6
Seguin, 23186 EL-5
Seminole, 5839 WJ-9
Seth Ward, 1926 WF-11
Seymour, 2773 EC-3
SHACKELFORD CO., 3305 ED-2
Shady Shores, 1803 †B-7
Shallowater, 2187 WG-10
Shamrock, 1828 WD-13
SHELBY CO., 25882 EF-12
Sheldon, 1831 EK-11
Shenandoah, 1554 EJ-10
Shepherd, 2186 EI-11
SHERMAN CO., 3158 WB-10
Sherman, 36261 EC-8
Shiner, 2044 EL-7
Shoreacres, 1575 EK-11
Sierra Blanca, 533 WM-4
Silsbee, 6498 EJ-13
Silverton, 718 WF-11
Sinton, 5549 EO-6
Skellytown, 610 WC-12
Skidmore, 1013 EN-6
Slaton, 6022 WH-11
Smiley, 470 EL-6
SMITH CO., 184015 EE-11
Smithville, 4391 EK-7
Snyder, 10536 WJ-12
Socorro, 28140 WK-2
Somerset, 1721 EL-4
SOMERVELL CO., 7331 EE-5
Somerville, 1741 EJ-8
Sonora, 2953 WN-12
Sour Lake, 1693 EJ-12
S. Houston, 16058 *F-7
Southlake, 24192 †E-6
S. Padre Island, 2475 ES-7
Southside Place, 1607 *E-4
Spearman, 2928 WB-12
Spring, 36385 EJ-10
Springtown, 2451 ED-6
Spr. Valley, 3662 *D-3
Spur, 1060 WH-12
Stafford, 18295 EK-10
Stamford, 3374 WI-14
Stanton, 2428 WK-10
STARR CO., 57678 ER-4
STEPHENS CO., 9449 ED-4
Stephenville, 15216 EF-5
STERLING CO., 1342 WK-12
Sterling City, 1044 WK-12
Stinnett, 1884 WC-11
Stockdale, 1489 EL-5
STONEWALL CO., 1448 WH-13
Stowell, 1572 EK-12
Stratford, 2003 WB-10
Strawn, 743 EE-4
Sudan, 1040 WG-9
Sugar Land, 70815 EK-10
Sullivan City, 4203 ES-4
Sulphur Sprs., 14787 EC-10
Sundown, 1539 WH-9
Sunnyvale, 3598 †G-13
Sunray, 1944 WB-10
Sunset, 350 EC-6
SUTTON CO., 4110 WN-13
Sweeny, 3658 EM-10
Sweetwater, 10892 WJ-13
SWISHER CO., 8015 WE-11
Taft, 3423 EO-7
Tahoka, 2723 WI-10
Talco, 575 EC-10
TARRANT CO., 1559148 ED-7
Tatum, 1175 EE-12
TAYLOR CO., 125339 EF-1
Taylor, 14204 EI-6
Taylor Lake Vil., 3640 *G-9
Teague, 4638 EG-8
Telferner, 700 EM-7
Temple, 54975 EH-6
Tenaha, 1081 EF-12
TERRELL CO., 1034 WN-9
Terrell, 15771 ED-8
Terrell Hills, 5049 ER-12
TERRY CO., 12453 WH-10
Texarkana, 35199 EC-12
Texas City, 43233 EL-11
The Colony, 35189 ED-7
The Woodlands, 55649 EJ-10
Thorndale, 1309 EI-7
Thrall, 813 EI-7
Three Rivers, 1782 EN-5
THROCKMORTON CO., 1697 ED-3
Throckmorton, 827 ED-3
Tiki Island, 1126 EO-10
Tilden, 450 EN-4
Timpson, 1118 EF-12
Tioga, 842 EC-7
TITUS CO., 28603 EC-11
Tivoli, 700 EN-8
Tomball, 9784 EJ-10
Tom Bean, 976 EC-8
TOM GREEN CO., 103528 WL-13
Tornillo, 1609 WL-2
Town West, 6166 *F-2
TRAVIS CO., 857204 EJ-5
Trenton, 673 EC-8
Trinidad, 1116 EF-9
TRINITY CO., 14151 EH-11
Trinity, 2750 EH-10
Trophy Club, 7194 †D-5
Troup, 2007 EF-11
Troy, 1365 EH-7
Tulia, 4869 WF-10
Turkey, 507 WF-12
Tuscola, 720 WK-14
Tye, 1161 WJ-14
TYLER CO., 20651 EI-12
Tyler, 88316 EE-10
Universal City, 15428 EL-5
University Park, 23745 †F-11
UPSHUR CO., 36959 ED-11
UPTON CO., 3153 WL-10
UVALDE CO., 26787 EL-2
Uvalde, 16391 WQ-14

2000 Census populations or latest available estimate.
Index to Canada and Mexico cities and towns, pages 274-275.

TEXAS – WEST VIRGINIA 273

Valley Mills, 1136 ... EG-6
Valley View, 788 ... EC-7
VAL VERDE CO., 46569 ... WO-12
Van, 2488 ... EE-10
Van Alstyne, 2605 ... EC-8
Vanderbilt, 411 ... EM-8
Van Horn, 2271 ... WM-5
Van Vleck, 1411 ... EM-9
VAN ZANDT CO., 50664 ... EE-9
Vega, 921 ... WD-9
Vernon, 10902 ... EA-3
VICTORIA CO., 85395 ... EM-7
Victoria, 61410 ... EM-7
Vidor, 11283 ... EJ-13
Von Ormy, 800 ... EL-4
Waco, 116887 ... EG-7
Waelder, 978 ... EK-7
Wake Vil., 5181 ... EC-12
WALKER CO., 62038 ... EH-10
WALLER CO., 34579 ... EK-9
Waller, 2061 ... EJ-9
Wallis, 1232 ... EK-9
Walnut Sprs., 786 ... EF-6
WARD CO., 10293 ... WL-7
WASHINGTON CO., 30950 ... EJ-8
Waskom, 2104 ... EE-13
Watauga, 23593 ... †F-5
Waxahachie, 23915 ... EE-7
Weatherford, 21420 ... EE-6
WEBB CO., 213615 ... EP-3
Webster, 9074 ... EK-11
Weimar, 1995 ... EK-8
Wellington, 2129 ... WE-13
Wells, 784 ... EG-11
Weslaco, 30416 ... ES-6
West, 2699 ... EG-7
W. Columbia, 4284 ... EL-10
Westfield, 800 ... EJ-10
W. Lake Hills, 3029 ... EJ-6
W. Odessa, 17799 ... WH-1
W. Orange, 4028 ... EJ-13
Westover Hills, 680 ... †H-3
W. Tawakoni, 1632 ... ED-9
W. University Place, 14904 ... *E-4
Westworth, 2104 ... †G-3
WHARTON CO., 41144 ... EL-9
Wharton, 9337 ... EL-9
WHEELER CO., 4809 ... WC-13
Wheeler, 1247 ... WD-13
White Deer, 1060 ... WD-12
Whitehouse, 6582 ... EE-10
White Oak, 5858 ... EE-11
Whitesboro, 3961 ... EC-7
White Settlement, 15553 ... ED-6
Whitewright, 1768 ... EC-8
Whitney, 1987 ... EF-6
WICHITA CO., 129257 ... EB-4
Wichita Falls, 102340 ... EB-4
Wickett, 426 ... WL-8
WILBARGER CO., 13858 ... EB-3
WILLACY CO., 20094 ... ER-6
WILLIAMSON CO., 303587 ... EI-6
Willis, 4225 ... EI-10
Wills Pt., 3661 ... EE-9
Wilmer, 3604 ... †J-12
WILSON CO., 35244 ... EL-5
Wimberley, 2710 ... EK-5
Windcrest, 5111 ... ER-13
Wink, 885 ... WK-8
WINKLER CO., 6780 ... WK-8
Winnie, 2914 ... EK-12
Winnsboro, 3745 ... ED-10
Winters, 2739 ... WK-14
WISE CO., 54465 ... EC-6
Wolfe City, 1631 ... EC-9
Wolfforth, 2725 ... WH-10
WOOD CO., 39286 ... ED-10
Woodsboro, 1631 ... EN-7
Woodville, 2329 ... EI-12
Woodway, 8747 ... EG-7
Wortham, 1084 ... EG-8
Wylie, 21720 ... ED-8
YOAKUM CO., 7249 ... WH-9
Yoakum, 5734 ... EL-7
Yorktown, 2238 ... EM-6
YOUNG CO., 17901 ... ED-4
ZAPATA CO., 12905 ... EQ-3
Zapata, 4856 ... EQ-3
ZAVALA CO., 11593 ... EM-2
Zavalla, 653 ... EH-12

Utah

Map pp. 206-209

Alta, 365 ... E-9
American Fk., 22876 ... E-8
Aurora, 939 ... I-8
Ballard, 590 ... E-12
Bear River City, 791 ... B-8
BEAVER CO., 6105 ... J-5
Beaver, 2511 ... K-6
Beaver River City, 791 ... B-8
Bicknell, 337 ... J-9
Blanding, 3035 ... L-13
Bluffdale, 5672 ... E-8
Bountiful, 41401 ... D-8
BOX ELDER CO., 44504 ... C-4
Brigham City, 17334 ... B-8
CACHE CO., 95664 ... B-8
CARBON CO., 19764 ... G-11
Castle Dale, 1618 ... H-10
Cedar City, 21946 ... L-6
Centerfield, 1068 ... H-8
Centerville, 14748 ... D-8
Charleston, 404 ... E-9
Circleville, 484 ... K-7
Clarkston, 686 ... A-8
Clearfield, 27146 ... C-8
Cleveland, 510 ... H-10
Clinton, 15281 ... D-1
Coalville, 1426 ... D-9
Copperton, 800 ... E-8
Corinne, 650 ... B-8
Cottonwood, 5800 ... H-20
Cottonwood Hts., 27569 ... I-20
DAGGETT CO., 889 ... D-12
DAVIS CO., 255597 ... D-7
Delta, 3186 ... H-7
Draper, 31020 ... E-8
DUCHESNE CO., 14846 ... F-11
Duchesne, 1447 ... F-11
E. Carbon, 1313 ... G-11
Elsinore, 724 ... J-7
EMERY CO., 10651 ... I-10
Enoch, 3876 ... L-6
Enterprise, 1298 ... L-4
Ephraim, 4962 ... H-9
Erda, 2473 ... E-7
Escalante, 771 ... L-9
Eureka, 772 ... F-8
Fairview, 1170 ... G-9
Farmington, 13407 ... D-8
Ferron, 1576 ... I-9
Fillmore, 2220 ... I-7
Ft. Duchesne, 621 ... E-12
Fountain Green, 952 ... G-9
GARFIELD CO., 4542 ... L-9
Garland, 1964 ... B-8
Goshen, 846 ... F-8
GRAND CO., 8759 ... H-12
Granite, 1989 ... J-20
Grantsville, 6824 ... E-7
Green River, 958 ... I-11
Gunnison, 2484 ... H-8
Harrisville, 4452 ... A-2
Heber City, 8605 ... E-9
Helper, 1911 ... G-10
Henefer, 723 ... D-9
Herriman, 5632 ... K-17
Hildale, 1938 ... N-6
Hinckley, 755 ... H-6
Holden, 393 ... H-7
Holladay, 19667 ... D-8
Honeyville, 1276 ... B-8
Huntington, 2087 ... H-10
Huntsville, 650 ... C-8
Hurricane, 9465 ... M-5
Hyde Park, 2978 ... L-17
Hyrum, 6305 ... B-8
IRON CO., 35741 ... J-5
Ivins, 6049 ... M-4
JUAB CO., 8792 ... G-6
Kamas, 1429 ... E-9
Kanab, 3490 ... N-7
KANE CO., 6039 ... M-8
Kanosh, 476 ... I-7
Kaysville, 21386 ... C-8
Kearns, 33659 ... H-17
La Verkin, 3731 ... M-5
Layton, 60769 ... C-8
Lehi, 23266 ... E-8
Levan, 782 ... G-8
Lewiston, 1847 ... A-8
Lindon, 8680 ... F-1
Loa, 504 ... J-8
Logan, 43675 ... B-8
Maeser, 2855 ... E-13
Magna, 22770 ... G-16
Manti, 3070 ... H-8
Mantua, 796 ... B-8
Mapleton, 6180 ... F-9
Mendon, 993 ... B-8
Midvale, 27166 ... I-19
Midway, 2387 ... E-9
Milford, 1438 ... J-6
MILLARD CO., 12455 ... I-6
Minersville, 829 ... K-6
Moab, 4845 ... J-13
Mona, 993 ... G-8
Monroe, 1819 ... J-7
Montezuma Cr., 507 ... M-13
Monticello, 1900 ... L-13
MORGAN CO., 7518 ... C-8
Morgan, 2711 ... D-8
Moroni, 1296 ... G-9
Mt. Pleasant, 2735 ... G-9
Murray, 43617 ... D-8
Myton, 552 ... F-12
Naples, 1411 ... E-13
Neola, 533 ... E-12
Nephi, 4962 ... G-8
Newton, 717 ... A-8
N. Logan, 6872 ... M-18
N. Ogden, 16084 ... C-8
N. Salt Lake, 9321 ... E-19
Ogden, 78293 ... C-8
Orangeville, 1349 ... H-10
Orderville, 593 ... M-6
Orem, 87599 ... E-8
Panguitch, 1525 ... L-7
Paradise, 753 ... B-8
Park City, 7854 ... D-9
Parowan, 2518 ... L-6
Payson, 14761 ... F-8
Perry, 2832 ... B-8
PIUTE CO., 1380 ... J-8
Plain City, 3932 ... C-8
Pleasant Gr., 23901 ... E-8
Price, 8229 ... G-10
Providence, 5186 ... B-8
Provo, 105410 ... F-8
Randolph, 478 ... B-9
Redmond, 778 ... I-8
RICH CO., 2019 ... B-9
Richfield, 6936 ... I-8
Richmond, 2045 ... A-8
Riverdale, 7791 ... C-2
River Heights, 1484 ... N-17
Riverton, 29244 ... E-8
Roosevelt, 4404 ... E-12
Roy, 35249 ... C-8
St. George, 56382 ... N-4
Salem, 4926 ... F-8
Salina, 2378 ... I-8
SALT LAKE CO., 924247 ... D-7
Salt Lake City, 179894 ... D-8
Sandy, 89319 ... E-8
SAN JUAN CO., 13901 ... L-12
SANPETE CO., 23689 ... H-9
Santa Clara, 5360 ... N-4
Santaquin, 5751 ... F-8
SEVIER CO., 19103 ... I-9
Smithfield, 7877 ... A-8
South Jordan, 33589 ... J-18
S. Ogden, 15003 ... C-8
S. Salt Lake, 21719 ... G-19
S. Weber, 5384 ... D-3
Spanish Fk., 23000 ... F-9
Spring City, 965 ... H-9
Spring Glen, 900 ... G-10
Springville, 21929 ... F-9
Stansbury Park, 2385 ... D-7
Stockton, 555 ... E-7
SUMMIT CO., 33020 ... D-9
Sunnyside, 388 ... G-11
Sunset, 5068 ... C-8
Syracuse, 14159 ... C-8
Taylorsville, 58701 ... H-18
TOOELE CO., 47965 ... E-6
Tooele, 27052 ... E-7
Tremonton, 6083 ... B-7
Tropic, 479 ... L-8
UINTAH CO., 26296 ... F-12
Uintah, 1205 ... C-8
Union, 10500 ... I-19
UTAH CO., 398059 ... F-9
Vernal, 7892 ... E-13
WASATCH CO., 17509 ... E-10
WASHINGTON CO., 104132 ... M-5
Washington, 10496 ... N-5
Washington Ter., 8455 ... C-2
WAYNE CO., 2454 ... K-10
WEBER CO., 205827 ... C-8
Wellington, 1592 ... G-10
Wellsville, 2729 ... B-8
Wendover, 1620 ... D-4
W. Haven, 4991 ... B-1
W. Jordan, 84701 ... E-8
W. Point, 6472 ... D-1
W. Valley City, 111687 ... D-8
Willard, 1647 ... C-8
Woods Cross, 7466 ... D-8

Vermont

Map pp. 210-211

ADDISON CO., 36835 ... F-3
Alburg, 514 ... A-2
Arlington, 1199 ... K-3
Bakersfield, 370 ... B-4
Barre, 9166 ... E-5
Barton, 755 ... C-6
Beecher Falls, 350 ... A-9
Bellows Falls, 3086 ... K-5
BENNINGTON CO., 37178 ... K-3
Bennington, 9168 ... L-3
Berlin Corners, 360 ... E-5
Bethel, 970 ... G-5
Bomoseen, 250 ... H-3
Bradford, 824 ... F-7
Brandon, 1684 ... G-3
Brattleboro, 8289 ... L-5
Bridgewater, 300 ... H-5
Bristol ... F-3
Burlington, 39148 ... D-3
CALEDONIA CO., 29940 ... D-6
Canaan, 360 ... A-9
Castleton, 650 ... H-3
Cen. Rutland, 500 ... H-3
Charlotte, 350 ... E-2
Chelsea, 500 ... F-5
Chester, 550 ... J-5
Chester Depot, 500 ... J-5
CHITTENDEN CO., 148990 ... D-3
Colchester, 450 ... D-3
Concord, 350 ... D-7
Danby, 350 ... J-3
Danville, 360 ... D-6
Derby, 688 ... B-7
Derby Line, 792 ... A-7
Dorset, 600 ... J-3
E. Arlington, 620 ... K-3
E. Barre, 700 ... F-5
E. Dorset, 350 ... J-3
E. Middlebury, 500 ... G-3
E. Montpelier, 600 ... E-5
E. Poultney, 500 ... I-3
Enosburg Falls, 1492 ... B-4
ESSEX CO., 6569 ... C-8
Essex Cen., 850 ... D-3
Essex Jct., 8717 ... D-3
Fairfax, 350 ... C-3
Fair Haven, 2435 ... H-2
Fairlee, 400 ... G-6
Forest Dale, 350 ... G-3
FRANKLIN CO., 47023 ... C-4
Gilman, 500 ... D-8
Grafton, 300 ... K-5
GRAND ISLE CO., 7490 ... B-2
Graniteville, 500 ... F-5
Groton, 400 ... E-6
Hardwick, 1400 ... D-6
Hartford, 500 ... H-6
Hartland, 500 ... I-5
Highgate Cen., 350 ... B-3
Hinesburg, 400 ... E-3
Hyde Park, 430 ... C-5
Hydeville, 450 ... H-2
Island Pond, 849 ... B-7
Jeffersonville, 568 ... C-4
Jericho, 1457 ... D-3
Johnson, 1427 ... C-5
Jonesville, 330 ... D-4
LAMOILLE CO., 24284 ... C-5
Lower Vil., 300 ... D-4
Ludlow, 939 ... I-4
Lyndon, 450 ... D-7
Lyndon Cen., 300 ... D-7
Lyndonville, 1213 ... D-7
Manchester, 669 ... K-3
Manchester Cen., 2069 ... K-3
Middlebury, 6252 ... F-3
Milton, 1557 ... C-3
Montgomery Cen., 380 ... B-5
Montpelier, 7945 ... E-5
Morrisville, 2063 ... D-5
Moscow, 260 ... D-4
Newbury, 413 ... F-7
Newport, 5092 ... B-6
N. Bennington, 1399 ... L-2
N. Clarendon, 550 ... I-3
Northfield, 3178 ... F-5
N. Hyde Park, 380 ... C-5
N. Pownal, 350 ... L-2
N. Springfield, 750 ... J-5
N. Troy, 609 ... A-6
Norwich, 1000 ... H-6
ORANGE CO., 29081 ... F-6
ORLEANS CO., 27103 ... B-6
Orleans, 845 ... B-6
Pittsford, 650 ... H-3
Plainfield, 600 ... E-5
Poultney, 1558 ... I-2
Pownal, 320 ... M-2
Proctor, 1979 ... H-3
Proctorsville, 480 ... I-5
Putney, 1150 ... L-5
Quechee, 600 ... H-5
Randolph, 2200 ... G-5
Readsboro, 400 ... M-3
Richford, 970 ... A-5
Richmond, 700 ... D-3
Rochester, 500 ... G-4
Roxbury, 300 ... F-4
RUTLAND CO., 63504 ... I-3
Rutland, 17103 ... H-3
St. Albans, 7565 ... B-3
St. Albans Bay, 500 ... B-3
St. Johnsbury, 6319 ... D-7
St. Johnsbury Cen., 450 ... D-7
Saxtons River, 515 ... K-5
Shaftsbury, 772 ... K-3
Shelburne, 400 ... D-3
S. Barre, 1242 ... E-5
S. Burlington, 16285 ... D-3
S. Hero, 350 ... C-2
S. Londonderry, 400 ... J-4
S. Royalton, 750 ... G-5
S. Ryegate, 450 ... E-6
Springfield, 3938 ... J-5
Stowe ... D-5
Swanton, 2578 ... B-3
Troy, 300 ... B-6
Underhill, 400 ... D-4
Vergennes, 2789 ... F-2
Waitsfield, 320 ... E-4
Wallingford, 948 ... I-3
Warren, 370 ... F-4
WASHINGTON CO., 58836 ... E-5
Washington, 320 ... F-5
Waterbury, 1701 ... E-4
Waterbury Cen., 500 ... D-4
Websterville, 450 ... F-5
Wells, 400 ... I-3
Wells River, 329 ... F-7
W. Branch, 250 ... D-4
W. Burke, 362 ... C-7
Westminster, 273 ... K-5
Weston, 300 ... J-4
W. Pawlet, 300 ... J-2
W. Rupert, 180 ... J-2
W. Rutland, 2263 ... H-3
White River Jct., 2569 ... H-6
Whitingham, 330 ... L-4
Wilder, 1636 ... H-6
Williamstown, 700 ... F-5
Williston, 450 ... D-3
Wilmington, 600 ... L-4
WINDHAM CO., 44379 ... K-4
WINDSOR CO., 57895 ... I-5
Windsor, 3714 ... I-6
Winooski, 6387 ... D-3
Winooski Park, 400 ... L-9
Woodstock, 960 ... H-5

Virginia

Map pp. 212-217

* City keyed to pp. 216-217
† City keyed to pp. 224-225
‡ Independent city: Not included in any county.

Abingdon, 7750 ... D-6
Accomac, 543 ... I-19
ACCOMACK CO., 39025 ... I-20
Achilles, 650 ... K-17
Adwolf, 1457 ... M-1
ALBEMARLE CO., 87670 ... G-10
Alexandria, 128923 ... ‡E-15
ALLEGHANY CO., 16816 ... I-6
Allison Gap, 700 ... D-7
Altavista, 3339 ... L-8
AMELIA CO., 11742 ... K-12
Amelia Court House, 900 ... K-12
AMHERST CO., 31891 ... J-8
Amherst, 2220 ... J-9
Amonate, 400 ... K-1
Annalee Hts., 1800 ... †G-4
Annandale, 54994 ... E-14
Appalachia, 1756 ... C-3
APPOMATTOX CO., 13710 ... J-9
Appomattox, 1725 ... K-9
ARLINGTON CO., 187873 ... D-14
Arlington, 187873 ... D-15
Arvonia, 750 ... J-11
Ashland, 6876 ... I-14
Atkins, 1138 ... L-1
AUGUSTA CO., 67427 ... G-8
Austinville, 850 ... M-3
Baileys Crossroads, 23166 ... †G-5
Banners Corner, 300 ... D-5
Bassett, 1338 ... M-6
Bastian, 420 ... K-2
BATH CO., 5013 ... H-7
Bay View, 180 ... K-19
BEDFORD CO., 62661 ... K-7
Bedford, 6339 ... ‡K-7
Bel Air, 1500 ... †G-4
Belle Haven, 6269 ... †I-6
Belle Haven, 480 ... I-19
Belle View, 2300 ... †E-3
Belvedere, 2200 ... †H-4
Bensley, 5435 ... *E-8
Berryville, 3030 ... C-12
Big Rock, 650 ... B-5
Big Stone Gap, 5839 ... D-3
Blacksburg, 40066 ... K-4
Blackstone, 3593 ... L-12
BLAND CO., 6965 ... K-2
Bland, 600 ... L-2
Bluefield, 4996 ... K-2
Blue Ridge, 3188 ... J-6
Boissevain, 900 ... K-1
Bon Air, 16213 ... *C-6
BOTETOURT CO., 31448 ... J-6
Bowling Green, 946 ... H-14
Boyce, 437 ... D-12
Boydton, 469 ... M-11
Boykins, 596 ... M-15
Bridgewater, 5273 ... F-9
Bristol, 17206 ... ‡E-5
Broadway, 2415 ... F-9
Brodnax, 304 ... M-12
Brookneal, 1237 ... L-9
Broyhill Park, 3700 ... †G-3
BRUNSWICK CO., 18199 ... M-13
BUCHANAN CO., 25598 ... C-6
Buchanan, 1237 ... J-7
BUCKINGHAM CO., 15839 ... I-10
Buckingham, 350 ... J-10
Bucknell Manor, 2350 ... †I-6
Buena Vista, 6320 ... ‡I-8
Burke, 57737 ... †I-2
Burkeville, 480 ... K-11
Callao, 550 ... H-16
CAMPBELL CO., 51322 ... K-9
Cape Charles, 1108 ... K-18
CAROLINE CO., 23190 ... H-14
CARROLL CO., 29336 ... M-3
Carrsbrook, 950 ... H-11
Carver Gardens, 500 ... *F-3
Castlewood, 2036 ... D-5
Cave Spr., 24941 ... H-1
Cedar Bluff, 1071 ... L-1
Cedarville, 450 ... D-11
Centreville, 48661 ... E-14
Chantilly, 41041 ... D-14
Chapel Acres, 1200 ... †J-3
CHARLES CITY CO., 7118 ... J-15
CHARLOTTE CO., 12452 ... L-10
Charlotte Court House, 453 ... L-10
Charlottesville, 39162 ... ‡H-10
Chase City, 2414 ... M-11
Chatham, 1297 ... M-8
Cheriton, 490 ... K-19
Chesapeake, 210834 ... ‡M-18
Chester, 17890 ... J-14
Chesterbrook, 1600 ... †F-4
CHESTERFIELD CO., 276840 ... K-13
Chesterfield, 3558 ... J-14
Chester Gap, 400 ... E-11
Chilhowie, 1796 ... M-1
Chincoteague, 4358 ... H-20
Christiansburg, 17756 ... K-4
Churchville, 400 ... G-8
Claremont, 338 ... K-15
CLARKE CO., 13364 ... D-12
Clarksville, 1305 ... M-10
Claypool Hill, 1719 ... L-1
Clearbrook, 550 ... K-6
Clear Brook, 190 ... C-12
Clifton Forge, 4716 ... I-6
Clinchco, 411 ... C-5
Clintwood, 1514 ... C-4
Cloverdale, 2986 ... J-6
Coeburn, 1967 ... C-4
Collinsville, 7777 ... M-6
Colonial Beach, 3241 ... G-15
Colonial Heights, 17286 ... ‡K-14
Concord, 500 ... K-9
Courtland, 1240 ... M-15
Covington, 6284 ... ‡I-6
CRAIG CO., 5159 ... J-5
Craigsville, 998 ... H-8
Crewe, 2309 ... K-12
Crozet, 2820 ... H-10
Culmore, 5200 ... †G-4
CULPEPER CO., 38555 ... F-12
Culpeper, 10442 ... F-12
CUMBERLAND CO., 9189 ... J-11
Dahlgren, 997 ... G-15
Dale City, 55971 ... E-14
Daleville, 1454 ... J-6
Damascus, 1091 ... E-6
Dante, 700 ... C-5
Danville, 46988 ... ‡N-8
Dayton, 1333 ... F-9
Deltaville, 1000 ... J-17
DICKENSON CO., 16119 ... C-5
Dillwyn, 444 ... J-11
DINWIDDIE CO., 24853 ... L-14
Disputanta, 550 ... K-15
Dooms, 1282 ... H-9
Drakes Branch, 490 ... L-10
Dryden, 1253 ... D-3
Dublin, 2232 ... L-4
Dumfries, 4934 ... F-14
Dunn Loring, 7861 ... †F-3
E. Stone Gap, 500 ... D-3
Edinburg, 835 ... E-10
Elkton, 2027 ... F-10
Elliston, 950 ... K-5
Emory, 1300 ... D-6
Emporia, 5656 ... ‡M-14
Engleside, 28582 ... †J-5
Esserville, 300 ... C-4
ESSEX CO., 10260 ... H-15
Ettrick, 5627 ... K-14
Ewing, 436 ... D-1
Exmore, 1434 ... J-19
FAIRFAX CO., 1000405 ... E-14
Fairfax, 22031 ... ‡E-14
Fairlawn, 2211 ... K-4
Fair Port, 450 ... H-17
Falls Church, 10485 ... ‡D-14
Falmouth, 3624 ... G-14
Farmville, 6959 ... K-11
FAUQUIER CO., 61137 ... E-12
Ferrum, 1313 ... L-6
Ferry Farms, 4000 ... G-14
Fieldale, 929 ... M-6
Fishers Hill, 200 ... D-11
Fishersville, 4998 ... H-9
Five Mile Fk., 700 ... G-13
FLOYD CO., 14350 ... L-4
Floyd, 428 ... L-5
FLUVANNA CO., 23078 ... I-11
Fork Union, 400 ... I-11
Franconia, 31907 ... †I-4
FRANKLIN CO., 49095 ... L-5
Franklin, 8254 ... ‡M-16
FREDERICK CO., 64565 ... C-11
Fredericksburg, 20189 ... ‡G-14
Fries, 575 ... M-3
Front Royal, 14160 ... D-11
Gainesville, 4382 ... E-13
Galax, 6655 ... ‡M-3
Gate City, 2090 ... E-4
GILES CO., 16956 ... K-3
Glade Spr., 1547 ... M-1
Glasgow, 1024 ... I-8
Glen Allen, 12562 ... *A-7
Glenwood ... N-8
GLOUCESTER CO., 36698 ... J-16
Gloucester, 150 ... J-17
Gloucester Pt., 9429 ... K-17
GOOCHLAND CO., 18138 ... I-12
Goochland, 600 ... I-12
Gordonsville, 1557 ... G-11
Goshen, 394 ... H-7
Grafton, 1050 ... *H-4
GRAYSON CO., 16557 ... M-1
Great Falls, 8549 ... †D-2
GREENE CO., 16779 ... G-11
GREENSVILLE CO., 11581 ... M-13
Gretna, 1226 ... L-8
Grottoes, 2102 ... G-9
Grove, 680 ... *G-3
Groveton, 21296 ... †I-5
Grundy, 1030 ... B-5
HALIFAX CO., 36632 ... M-9
Halifax, 1321 ... M-9
Hamilton, 654 ... C-13
Hampden Sydney, 1264 ... K-11
Hampton, 146878 ... ‡L-17
HANOVER CO., 94081 ... I-13
Hanover, 500 ... I-14
Harman, 600 ... B-5
Harris Grove, 170 ... *G-5
Harrisonburg, 41170 ... ‡F-9
Hayes, 1000 ... *F-5
Hayfield, 2350 ... †J-4
Haymarket, 960 ... E-13
HENRICO CO., 271083 ... J-14
HENRY CO., 57090 ... M-6
Herndon, 21721 ... D-14
HIGHLAND CO., 2504 ... G-7
Highland Sprs., 15137 ... *C-9
Hilander Park, 400 ... D-5
Hillsville, 2760 ... M-3
Hillwood, 1650 ... †G-4
Hollins, 14309 ... F-3
Holmes Run Acres, 1400 ... †G-3
Honaker, 922 ... C-6
Hopewell, 22391 ... ‡K-14
Horse Pasture, 2255 ... M-6
Hot Springs, 300 ... H-6
Hunterdale, 600 ... M-15
Huntington, 8325 ... †I-6
Hurley, 600 ... B-6
Hurt, 1252 ... L-8
Hybla Valley, 16721 ... †J-5
Independence, 936 ... M-2
Iron Gate, 387 ... I-6
Irvington, 661 ... I-17
ISLE OF WIGHT CO., 31925 ... L-16
Ivanhoe, 550 ... M-3
JAMES CITY CO., 53487 ... K-16
Jarratt, 568 ... M-14
Jefferson Vil., 2500 ... †G-4
Jewell Ridge, 350 ... B-6
Jolivue, 1037 ... H-9
Jonesville, 987 ... D-2
Keezletown, 400 ... F-10
Kenbridge, 1328 ... L-12
Keokee, 316 ... D-3
Keysville, 790 ... L-11
Kilmarnock, 1235 ... I-17
KING AND QUEEN CO., 6588 ... I-15
KING GEORGE CO., 18213 ... G-15
King George, 550 ... G-15
Kings Park, 6500 ... †H-3
Kings Park W., 6300 ... †H-2
Kings Point, 500 ... *F-2
KING WILLIAM CO., 14131 ... I-15
Lackey, 500 ... *G-4
La Crosse, 612 ... M-12
Ladd, 410 ... H-9
Lakeside, 11157 ... *B-7
LANCASTER CO., 12074 ... I-17
Langley, 1450 ... †E-4
Laurel, 14875 ... *A-7
Lawrenceville, 1231 ... M-13
Lebanon, 3218 ... D-5
LEE CO., 23734 ... D-2
Leesburg, 33319 ... D-13
Lexington, 7076 ... ‡I-7
Lightfoot, 400 ... J-16
Lincolnia, 15788 ... †H-4
Lincolnia Hts., 1800 ... †H-4
Lorton, 17786 ... E-14
LOUDOUN CO., 221746 ... D-13
LOUISA CO., 28031 ... H-12
Louisa, 1469 ... H-12
Lovettsville, 1050 ... C-13
Lovingston, 600 ... I-9
Lowmoor, 367 ... I-6
LUNENBURG CO., 13167 ... L-11
Luray, 4892 ... E-11
Lynchburg, 65113 ... ‡J-8
Lynch Sta., 500 ... K-8
MADISON CO., 13036 ... F-11
Madison Hts., 11584 ... J-8
Manassas, 37166 ... ‡E-14
Manassas Park, 10990 ... ‡E-14
Mappsville, 400 ... H-20
Marion, 6208 ... M-1
Marshall, 900 ... E-12
Martinsville, 15121 ... ‡M-6
MATHEWS CO., 9216 ... J-17
Mathews, 700 ... J-17
Matoaca, 2273 ... *H-7
Max Meadows, 512 ... L-3
McClure, 350 ... C-5
McGaheysville, 550 ... G-10
McKenney, 479 ... L-13
McLean, 38929 ... †F-4
Meadowview, 900 ... D-6
Mechanicsville, 30464 ... *B-9
MECKLENBURG CO., 32551 ... M-11
Melfa, 446 ... I-19
Merrifield, 11170 ... †G-3
Middleburg, 760 ... D-13
MIDDLESEX CO., 10211 ... I-17
Middletown, 1058 ... D-11
Midlothian, 450 ... J-13
Milford, 500 ... H-14
Mineral, 445 ... H-12
Monroe, 400 ... I-8
MONTGOMERY CO., 85614 ... L-4
Montross, 313 ... G-16
Montvale, 550 ... J-7
Mt. Jackson, 1720 ... E-10
Mt. Sidney, 500 ... G-9
Narrows, 2151 ... K-3
Nassawadox, 616 ... J-19
NELSON CO., 14942 ... I-9
New Alexandria, 950 ... †I-6
New Baltimore, 550 ... E-13
Newington, 19784 ... †J-4
NEW KENT CO., 14843 ... J-15
New Market, 1782 ... E-10
Newport News, 181647 ... ‡L-17
Nickelsville, 440 ... D-4
Norfolk, 241727 ... ‡L-18
Norge, 1000 ... J-16
NORTHAMPTON CO., 13285 ... J-19
N. Springfield, 9173 ... †H-3
NORTHUMBERLAND CO., 12742 ... H-17
Norton, 3909 ... ‡C-4
NOTTOWAY CO., 15603 ... K-12
Oakton, 29348 ... †G-2
Oakwood, 500 ... B-6
Occoquan, 765 ... E-14
Onancock, 1494 ... I-19
Onley, 495 ... I-19
ORANGE CO., 28018 ... G-12
Orange, 4258 ... G-12
PAGE CO., 23589 ... F-10
Parklawn, 2400 ... †H-4
Parksley, 830 ... I-19
Parrott, 590 ... K-4
PATRICK CO., 19182 ... M-4
Pearisburg, 2793 ... K-3
Pembroke, 1164 ... K-4
Pender, 500 ... †G-1
Pennington Gap, 1769 ... D-3
Petersburg, 33091 ... ‡K-14
Pimmit Hills, 6152 ... †F-3
PITTSYLVANIA CO., 61640 ... L-8
Plasterco, 300 ... D-6
Pocahontas, 420 ... K-2
Poquoson, 11844 ... ‡K-17
Portsmouth, 99617 ... ‡L-17
Pound, 1085 ... C-4
POWHATAN CO., 24649 ... J-12
PRINCE EDWARD CO., 20180 ... K-10
PRINCE GEORGE CO., 34305 ... K-15
PRINCE WILLIAM CO., 325324 ... E-14
PULASKI CO., 35030 ... L-3
Pulaski, 9173 ... L-3
Purcellville, 4244 ... C-13
Quantico, 603 ... F-14
Queens Lake, 1400 ... *E-3
Quinby, 350 ... I-19
Radford, 15006 ... ‡K-4
RAPPAHANNOCK CO., 7110 ... E-11
Raven, 2593 ... C-6
Ravensworth, 3000 ... †H-3
Ravenwood, 2550 ... †G-4
Remington, 658 ... F-13
Rescue, 400 ... L-17
Reston, 56407 ... D-14
Rich Cr., 680 ... J-3
Richlands, 4095 ... C-6
RICHMOND CO., 9006 ... H-16
Richmond, 194729 ... ‡J-14
Ridgeway, 807 ... N-6
Ripplemead, 550 ... K-4
Riverdale, 630 ... M-9
ROANOKE CO., 87329 ... K-5
Roanoke, 92863 ... ‡K-6
ROCKBRIDGE CO., 20973 ... H-7
ROCKINGHAM CO., 69365 ... E-9
Rocky Mt., 4542 ... L-6
Rose Hill, 15058 ... †I-5
Rose Hill, 714 ... D-1
Round Hill, 582 ... C-13
Roxbury ... J-15
Rural Retreat, 1339 ... L-2
RUSSELL CO., 28861 ... C-6
Rustburg, 1271 ... K-9
St. Paul, 969 ... D-5
Salem, 24603 ... ‡K-6
Saltville, 2268 ... L-1
Sandston, 4200 ... *C-10
Saxis, 337 ... H-19
SCOTT CO., 23005 ... D-4
Seaford, 2700 ... K-17
Sedley, 560 ... M-15
Selma, 485 ... I-6
Shawsville, 1029 ... K-5
SHENANDOAH CO., 37199 ... E-10
Shenandoah, 1874 ... F-10
Sleepy Hollow, 640 ... †G-4
Smithfield, 6703 ... L-16
SMYTH CO., 32700 ... L-1
SOUTHAMPTON CO., 17453 ... M-15
S. Boston, 8222 ... M-9
S. Hill, 4628 ... M-12
SPOTSYLVANIA CO., 107838 ... H-13
Spotsylvania, 600 ... G-13
Springfield, 30417 ... †I-4
STAFFORD CO., 111021 ... F-13
Stafford, 1600 ... F-14
Stanley, 1341 ... F-10
Stanleytown, 1515 ... M-6
Staunton, 23848 ... ‡G-9
Stephens City, 1195 ... D-11
Stephenson, 560 ... C-12
Sterling, 20512 ... D-14
Strasburg, 4153 ... D-11
Stuart, 930 ... M-5
Stuarts Draft, 8367 ... H-9
Suffolk, 73515 ... ‡M-17
Sugar Gr., 741 ... M-1
Sugar Loaf, 2500 ... H-1
SURRY CO., 7009 ... K-15
SUSSEX CO., 11956 ... L-14
Tabb, 950 ... K-17
Tangier, 692 ... H-18
Tappahannock, 2155 ... H-16
TAZEWELL CO., 44362 ... L-1
Tazewell, 4115 ... K-1
Temperanceville, 750 ... H-20
Timberlake, 10683 ... K-8
Timberville, 1704 ... E-10
Toano, 1200 ... J-16
Tookland, 500 ... B-5
Trammel, 400 ... C-5
Triangle, 5500 ... F-14
Troutville, 432 ... J-6
Tyler Park, 1250 ... †G-4
Tysons Corner, 18540 ... †F-3
Urbanna, 542 ... I-16
Vansant, 989 ... B-5
Varina, 3000 ... *E-9
Verona, 3638 ... G-9
Victoria, 1783 ... L-11
Vienna, 14868 ... D-14
Vinton, 7749 ... K-6
Virginia Beach, 439467 ... ‡L-18
Virginia Hills, 2840 ... †I-5
Wakefield, 984 ... L-15
WARREN CO., 33871 ... D-12
Warrenton, 7840 ... E-13
Warsaw, 1379 ... H-16
WASHINGTON CO., 51405 ... D-6
Waverly, 2211 ... L-15
Waynesboro, 20388 ... ‡H-9
Waynewood, 3450 ... †J-6
Weber City, 1299 ... E-4
Wellington, 1750 ... †J-6
WESTMORELAND CO., 16946 ... G-15
W. Point, 2974 ... J-16
W. Springfield, 28378 ... †I-3
Weyanoke, 1500 ... †H-4
White Stone, 354 ... I-17
Wicomico, 1350 ... K-17
Williamsburg, 11605 ... ‡K-16
Willis Wharf, 250 ... J-19
Wilton Woods, 1400 ... †I-5
Winchester, 24434 ... ‡C-11
Windsor, 2375 ... M-16
WISE CO., 41803 ... C-4
Wise, 3240 ... C-4
Woodbridge, 31941 ... E-14
Woodlawn, 2249 ... M-3
Woodstock, 4071 ... E-10
WYTHE CO., 27941 ... L-2
Wytheville, 7865 ... L-2
YORK CO., 60948 ... K-16
York Ter., 800 ... *F-2
Yorktown, 203 ... K-17

Washington

Map pp. 218-223

* City keyed to pp. 222-223

Aberdeen, 16207 ... H-3
ADAMS CO., 16602 ... H-17
Airway Hts., 4583 ... F-19
Alderwood Manor, 15329 ... E-7
Algona, 2583 ... *K-9
Allyn, 850 ... G-6
Anacortes, 15474 ... C-6
Arlington, 13911 ... D-8
ASOTIN CO., 20625 ... K-20
Asotin, 1098 ... J-20
Auburn, 44655 ... G-7
Bainbridge Island (Winslow), 21701 ... F-7
Battle Ground, 12731 ... L-7
Beaver, 600 ... D-2
Bellevue, 112344 ... F-7
Bellingham, 71289 ... B-7
BENTON CO., 153660 ... J-13
Benton City, 2879 ... K-14
Bingen, 675 ... M-9
Black Diamond, 3925 ... G-8
Blaine, 4003 ... A-6
Bonney Lake, 13215 ... *N-10
Bothell, 30568 ... F-7
Bremerton, 39597 ... F-6
Brewster, 2154 ... D-13
Bridgeport, 2051 ... E-13
Brier, 6361 ... *A-8
Browns Pt., 1950 ... *K-6
Bryn Mawr, 1500 ... *G-9
Buckley, 4502 ... H-8
Buena, 800 ... J-12
Burbank, 3303 ... K-15
Burien, 31116 ... G-7
Burlington, 7710 ... C-7
Camas, 14976 ... M-7
Carnation, 1843 ... F-8
Carson, 1000 ... M-8
Carthcart, 3015 ... E-8
Cashmere, 2960 ... F-12
Castle Rock, 2093 ... K-6
Centralia, 14981 ... I-6
Central Park, 2558 ... H-4
Chehalis, 7105 ... I-6
CHELAN CO., 67973 ... E-11
Chelan, 3563 ... E-13
Cheney, 9743 ... F-19
Chewelah, 2199 ... D-18
CLALLAM CO., 66892 ... E-4
Clallam Bay, 900 ... D-3
CLARK CO., 379577 ... M-7
Clarkston, 7211 ... J-20
Clearlake, 942 ... C-7
Cle Elum, 1792 ... H-11
Clinton, 868 ... E-7
Clyde Hill, 2921 ... *D-9
Colchester, 200 ... *F-5
Colfax, 2793 ... H-19
College Place, 8446 ... L-17
COLUMBIA CO., 4093 ... K-18
Colville, 4960 ... C-18
Concrete, 789 ... C-9
Connell, 3178 ... I-16
Cosmopolis, 1607 ... H-4
Coulee City, 612 ... F-14
Coulee Dam, 1080 ... E-15
Country Homes, 5203 ... *A-2
Coupeville, 1797 ... D-6
COWLITZ CO., 95146 ... K-6
Darrington, 1324 ... D-9
Davenport, 1710 ... F-17
Dayton, 2690 ... J-18
Deer Park, 3066 ... E-19
Desert Aire, 1124 ... I-13
Des Moines, 29039 ... G-7
Dishman, 10031 ... F-19
DOUGLAS CO., 33753 ... F-14
Duvall, 5568 ... F-8
Eagledale, 650 ... *D-5
Eastgate, 4558 ... *E-10
E. Wenatchee, 8590 ... G-12
Eatonville, 2207 ... I-7
Edgewood, 9526 ... *L-8
Edmonds, 39882 ... E-7
Electric City, 970 ... E-15
Ellensburg, 16257 ... H-11
Elma, 3131 ... H-4
Enumclaw, 10941 ... G-8
Ephrata, 7069 ... G-14
Everett, 96643 ... E-7
Everson, 2072 ... A-7
Fairwood, 2000 ... *H-10
Fall City, 1638 ... F-8
Federal Way, 81711 ... G-7
Ferndale, 9591 ... B-7
FERRY CO., 7417 ... C-16
Fife, 4966 ... *L-7
Fircrest, 5993 ... *L-5
Fords Prairie, 1961 ... I-5
Forks, 3176 ... E-2
FRANKLIN CO., 56126 ... J-15
Freeland, 1313 ... E-7
Friday Hbr., 2003 ... C-6
GARFIELD CO., 2371 ... J-19
Garfield, 629 ... H-20
Gig Hbr., 6616 ... G-7
Gold Bar, 2181 ... E-9
Goldendale, 3736 ... L-11
Grand Coulee, 907 ... E-15
Grandview, 8515 ... K-13
Granger, 2727 ... K-12
Granite Falls, 2645 ... D-8
GRANT CO., 78691 ... G-14
Grayland, 1002 ... I-3
GRAYS HARBOR CO., 69406 ... G-4
Greenacres, 5158 ... F-20
Hansville, 1700 ... E-7
Hazelwood, 700 ... *F-10
Hollywood, 800 ... *B-10
Hoquiam, 8925 ... H-3
Hunts Point, 455 ... *D-9
Ilwaco, 944 ... J-3
Inglewood, 6500 ... F-8
ISLAND CO., 76384 ... C-7
Issaquah, 14662 ... F-8
JEFFERSON CO., 27716 ... F-4
Kalama, 1893 ... L-6
Kelso, 11744 ... K-6
Kenmore, 19032 ... *A-9
Kennewick, 59334 ... K-15
Kent, 81567 ... G-7
Kettle Falls, 1545 ... B-17
KING CO., 1761411 ... F-9
Kirkland, 45573 ... F-7
KITSAP CO., 240719 ... F-6
KITTITAS CO., 35206 ... H-11
Kittitas, 1098 ... H-12
KLICKITAT CO., 19547 ... L-11
Klickitat, 417 ... L-10
Lacey, 32781 ... H-6
La Conner, 769 ... C-7
Lake Forest Park, 12578 ... *B-8
Lake Stevens, 7015 ... E-8
Lakewood, 58789 ... D-7
Langley, 1011 ... D-7
La Push, 500 ... E-2
Leavenworth, 2120 ... F-11
LEWIS CO., 70404 ... I-6
Lexington, 800 ... K-6
LINCOLN CO., 10201 ... F-16
Long Beach, 1350 ... J-3
Longview, 35741 ... K-6
Lynden, 10039 ... A-7
Lynnwood, 33704 ... E-7
Lynwood Cen., 700 ... *E-5
Mabton, 2038 ... K-13
Maltby, 8267 ... E-8
Manchester, 4958 ... *F-5
Maplewood Heights, 3300 ... G-8
Marysville, 28260 ... D-8
MASON CO., 52129 ... G-5
McCleary, 1439 ... H-5
Mead, 2150 ... E-19
Medical Lake, 4003 ... F-18
Medina, 3025 ... *D-9
Mercer Island, 22351 ... *E-9
Meridian Heights, 600 ... *I-10
Midland, 7414 ... *N-7
Mill Creek, 12832 ... E-7
Millwood, 1640 ... *B-4
Milton, 6028 ... *L-8
Monroe, 14798 ... E-8
Montesano, 3318 ... H-4
Morgan Acres, 1500 ... *B-3
Morton, 1062 ... J-7
Moses Lake, 16147 ... H-14
Mountlake Ter., 20606 ... E-7
Mt. Vernon, 27935 ... C-7
Moxee, 882 ... J-12
Mukilteo, 19169 ... E-7
Naches, 669 ... I-11
Napavine, 1419 ... J-6
Neah Bay, 794 ... C-2
Newcastle, 8786 ... *F-10
Newport, 2105 ... D-20
Normandy Park, 6250 ... *H-8
N. Bend, 4608 ... F-8
N. Puyallup, 2886 ... *M-8
Oak Hbr., 21071 ... D-6
Ocean Park, 1459 ... J-3
Ocean Shores, 4125 ... H-3
Odessa, 940 ... G-16
OKANOGAN CO., 39134 ... B-13
Okanogan, 2389 ... C-14
Olalla, 600 ... *H-5
Olympia, 43963 ... H-6
Omak, 4730 ... C-14
Opportunity, 25065 ... F-19
Orchards, 17852 ... M-6
Oroville, 1591 ... A-14
Orting, 4387 ... H-7
Othello, 6003 ... I-15
Otis Orchards, 3200 ... F-20
PACIFIC CO., 21103 ... J-4
Pacific, 5626 ... *L-9
Pacific Beach, 1200 ... G-3
Packwood, 1050 ... J-9
Palouse, 986 ... H-20
Parkland, 24053 ... H-7
Parkwater ... *B-4
Pasadena Park, 1700 ... *B-4
Pasco, 38233 ... K-15
Pe Ell, 669 ... J-5
PEND OREILLE CO., 12254 ... B-19
Peshastin, 900 ... F-11
PIERCE CO., 740957 ... H-8
Pomeroy, 1502 ... J-19
Port Angeles, 18516 ... D-5
Port Hadlock, 3476 ... D-6
Port Orchard, 7903 ... F-6
Pt. Roberts, 800 ... A-5
Port Townsend, 8685 ... D-6
Poulsbo, 7336 ... F-6
Prosser, 5053 ... K-14
Pullman, 25237 ... I-20
Puyallup, 35641 ... H-7
Quilcene, 591 ... E-6
Quincy, 5325 ... G-13
Rainier, 1634 ... I-6
Raymond, 2961 ... I-4
Redmond, 46391 ... F-8
Renton, 54028 ... F-7
Republic, 985 ... B-16
Richland, 42537 ... K-15
Ridgefield, 2230 ... L-6
Ritzville, 1709 ... H-17
Riverton Hts., 11188 ... *G-8
Rosalia, 631 ... G-19
Roslyn, 983 ... G-10
Royal City, 1895 ... I-14
Ruston, 746 ... G-7
Salmon Cr., 16767 ... M-6
Sammamish, 33916 ... F-8
SAN JUAN CO., 14761 ... C-5
SeaTac, 25014 ... *H-8
Seattle, 569101 ... F-7
Sedro-Woolley, 9660 ... C-7
Selah, 6573 ... I-11
Sequim, 4704 ... D-5
Shelton, 8789 ... G-5
Sheridan Beach, 6518 ... *B-8
Shoreline, 52380 ... F-7
Silverdale, 15816 ... F-6
SKAGIT CO., 109234 ... C-8
SKAMANIA CO., 10292 ... L-8
Skyway, 8500 ... *G-9
SNOHOMISH CO., 639409 ... E-9
Snohomish, 8620 ... E-8
Snoqualmie, 4742 ... F-8
Soap Lake, 1777 ... G-14
S. Bend, 1804 ... I-3
S. Hill, 31623 ... *N-8
S. Wenatchee, 1991 ... G-12
Spanaway, 21588 ... H-7
SPOKANE CO., 431027 ... F-19
Spokane, 196624 ... F-19
Spokane Valley, 82005 ... F-19
Stanwood, 4515 ... D-7
Steilacoom, 6165 ... H-6
STEVENS CO., 40776 ... D-18
Stevenson, 1233 ... M-8
Sultan, 3684 ... E-8
Sumas, 1003 ... A-7
Summit, 8041 ... *N-7
Sumner, 9026 ... G-7
Sunnyside, 14080 ... K-13
Tacoma, 196790 ... G-7
Tekoa, 807 ... G-20
Tenino, 1541 ... I-6
THURSTON CO., 221950 ... I-7
Toledo, 664 ... J-6
Tonasket, 962 ... B-14
Toppenish, 9108 ... J-12
Trentwood, 4388 ... *B-5
Tukwila, 17081 ... *G-9
Tumwater, 13162 ... H-6
Twisp, 904 ... C-12
Union Gap, 5710 ... J-12
University Place, 30638 ... *L-5
Vancouver, 151654 ... M-6
Vashon, 10123 ... G-7
Vashon Hts., 700 ... *G-6
Veradale, 9387 ... *C-5
WAHKIAKUM CO., 3748 ... J-5
Waitsburg, 1227 ... K-17
WALLA WALLA CO., 56751 ... J-17
Walla Walla, 30134 ... K-17
Wapato, 4575 ... J-12
Warden, 2611 ... H-15
Washougal, 9541 ... M-7
Waterville, 1147 ... F-13
Wenatchee, 28636 ... G-12
Westport, 2188 ... H-3
W. Richland, 9290 ... K-14
WHATCOM CO., 176571 ... B-8
White Cen., 20975 ... *F-7
White Salmon, 2244 ... M-9
WHITMAN CO., 40702 ... H-18
Wilbur, 898 ... E-16
Winlock, 1183 ... J-6
Wishram, 324 ... M-10
Wollochet, 300 ... *L-4
Woodinville, 9632 ... *B-10
Woodland, 4007 ... L-6
Woodmont Beach, 3550 ... *J-8
Woodway, 1135 ... *A-7
YAKIMA CO., 226727 ... J-11
Yakima, 80223 ... J-12
Yarrow Pt., 1004 ... *D-9
Yelm, 4085 ... H-6
Zenith ... *I-8
Zillah, 2505 ... J-12

West Virginia

Map pp. 226-227

Alderson, 1086 ... I-6
Amherstdale, 1100 ... H-3
Ansted, 1590 ... G-5
Arthurdale, 1500 ... C-9
Athens, 1083 ... J-5
BARBOUR CO., 15653 ... D-8
Barboursville, 3186 ... F-2
Barrackville, 1288 ... B-8
Barrett, 200 ... H-4
Beaver, 1378 ... H-5
Beckley, 16994 ... H-5
Belington, 1816 ... D-8
Belle, 1201 ... G-4
Belmont, 1028 ... C-5
Benwood, 1508 ... A-6
BERKELEY CO., 85272 ... B-13
Berkeley Sprs., 711 ... B-13
Bethany, 977 ... B-2
Bethlehem, 2606 ... A-6
Big Chimney, 650 ... F-4
Blair, 500 ... H-3
Blennerhassett, 3225 ... C-4
Bluefield, 11124 ... J-5
Bolivar, 1074 ... C-14
Boomer, 600 ... G-5
BOONE CO., 25785 ... H-4
Bradley, 2371 ... H-5
Bramwell, 408 ... J-5
BRAXTON CO., 14771 ... E-6
Brenton, 700 ... I-4
Bridgeport, 7470 ... C-7
BROOKE CO., 24939 ... B-2
Buckhannon, 5753 ... D-7
Buffalo, 1188 ... E-3
CABELL CO., 95043 ... F-2
CALHOUN CO., 7294 ... E-5
Cameron, 1161 ... A-7
Caretta, 600 ... J-4
Cedar Gr., 833 ... G-4
Cedar Gr., 350 ... C-4
Ceredo, 1637 ... G-12
Chapmanville, 1168 ... H-3
Charleston, 51394 ... F-4
Charles Town, 3180 ... C-14
Charmco, 150 ... H-6
Chattaroy, 1136 ... I-2
Chesapeake, 1584 ... G-4
Chester, 2454 ... A-2
Clarksburg, 16425 ... C-7
CLAY CO., 10352 ... F-5
Clay, 584 ... F-5
Clearview, 578 ... C-2
Clendenin, 1067 ... F-4
Clothier, 270 ... H-3
Coalwood, 700 ... J-4
Colliers, 600 ... B-2
Cowen, 511 ... F-7
Crab Orchard, 2761 ... H-5
Craigsville, 2204 ... F-6
Cross Lanes, 10353 ... F-3
Culloden, 2940 ... F-3
Daniels, 1846 ... I-5
Danville, 548 ... G-3
Davis, 595 ... D-9
Delbarton, 451 ... I-2
Despard, 1039 ... C-7
DODDRIDGE CO., 7491 ... C-6
Dunbar, 7868 ... F-3
E. Bank, 896 ... G-4
Eccles, 900 ... H-5
Eleanor, 1426 ... F-3
Elizabeth, 971 ... D-4
Elk Forest, 600 ... I-14
Elkins, 6976 ... D-8
Elkview, 1182 ... F-4
Elm Gr. ... J-11
Enterprise, 939 ... C-7
Fairmont, 18984 ... C-8
Fairview, 435 ... B-7
FAYETTE CO., 47270 ... H-5
Fayetteville, 2706 ... G-5
Follansbee, 2992 ... B-2
Ft. Ashby, 1354 ... B-11
Ft. Gay, 820 ... G-1
Franklin, 837 ... E-10
Gary, 822 ... J-4
Gassaway, 876 ... E-6
Gauley Bridge, 72C ... G-5
GILMER CO., 7037 ... D-6
Glasgow, 755 ... G-4
Glen Dale, 1505 ... A-6
Glen Fk., 450 ... I-4
Glen Jean, 400 ... H-5
Glenville, 1501 ... D-6
Grafton, 5351 ... C-8
GRANT CO., 11434 ... D-10
Grantsville, 537 ... D-5
Grant Town, 640 ... B-8
GREENBRIER CO., 34656 ... G-7
Guthrie, 600 ... H-13
Hamlin, 1096 ... G-2
HAMPSHIRE CO., 21247 ... C-11
HANCOCK CO., 31742 ... A-2
HARDY CO., 12990 ... D-11
HARRISON CO., 68032 ... C-7
Harrisville, 1868 ... C-5
Henderson, 320 ... E-2
Henlawson, 500 ... H-3
Hico, 900 ... G-5
Hinton, 2746 ... I-6
Holden, 1105 ... H-3
Hometown, 350 ... F-3
Huntington, 49533 ... F-2
Hurricane, 5623 ... F-3
Iaeger, 330 ... I-3
Institute, 1800 ... F-3
Inwood, 2084 ... C-13
JACKSON CO., 28285 ... E-4
JEFFERSON CO., 46270 ... C-14
Jeffrey, 500 ... H-3
Jolo, 500 ... J-3
Julian, 200 ... G-3
Junior, 443 ... D-8
KANAWHA CO., 195413 ... F-4
Kenova, 3358 ... F-1
Keyser, 5515 ... C-11
Keystone, 412 ... J-4
Kimball, 372 ... J-4
Kimberly, 500 ... G-5
Kincaid, 450 ... G-5
Kingwood, 2928 ... C-9
Kistler, 700 ... H-3
Lavalette, 1100 ... F-2
Lesage, 250 ... F-2
LEWIS CO., 17148 ... E-7
Lewisburg, 3577 ... H-7
LINCOLN CO., 22251 ... G-2
LOGAN CO., 36745 ... H-2
Logan, 1551 ... H-3
Lubeck, 1303 ... C-4
Lumberport, 943 ... C-7
Mabscott, 137 ... H-5
Madison, 2671 ... G-3
Malden, 850 ... G-4
Mallory, 1143 ... H-3
Man, 734 ... H-3
Mannington, 2085 ... B-7
MARION CO., 56484 ... B-7
Marlinton, 1226 ... G-8
Marlowe, 700 ... B-14
Marmet, 1645 ... G-4
MARSHALL CO., 34897 ... A-6
Martinsburg, 15309 ... C-13
MASON CO., 26079 ... E-3
Mason, 1065 ... D-3
Masontown, 642 ... B-9
Matewan, 512 ... I-2
Maybeury, 300 ... J-4

*, †, ‡, See explanation under state title in this index.
County names are listed in capital letters and in boldface type.

MCDOWELL CO., 25348 ... J-4
McMechen, 1859 ... A-6
MERCER CO., 62113 ... I-5
Middlebourne, 862 ... C-6
Mill Cr., 660 ... E-8
Milton, 2273 ... F-2
Minden, 1000 ... H-5
MINERAL CO., 27147 ... C-11
Mineral Wells, 200 ... C-4
MINGO CO., 27585 ... H-2
Monongah, 912 ... C-7
MONONGALIA CO., 84370 ... B-8
MONROE CO., 13503 ... I-6
Montcalm, 885 ... J-5
Montgomery, 1981 ... G-5
Moorefield, 2409 ... D-11
MORGAN CO., 15514 ... B-12
Morgantown, 27969 ... B-8
Moundsville, 9745 ... A-6
Mt. Gay, 700 ... H-3
Mt. Hope, 1428 ... H-5
Mullens, 1674 ... I-4
Nettie, 600 ... G-6
New Cumberland, 1049 ... A-2
Newell, 1602 ... A-2
New Haven, 1541 ... D-3
New Manchester, 700 ... A-2
New Martinsville, 5823 ... B-6
NICHOLAS CO., 26243 ... F-6
Nitro, 6708 ... F-3
Northfork, 468 ... J-4
Nutter Ft., 1647 ... C-7
Oak Hill, 7486 ... H-5
Oceana, 1500 ... I-4
Odd, 200 ... I-5
OHIO CO., 45828 ... B-2
Omar, 600 ... H-3
Paden City, 2771 ... B-6
Parkersburg, 32100 ... C-4
Parsons, 1451 ... D-9
Paw Paw, 513 ... B-12
PENDLETON CO., 7896 ... E-10
Pennsboro, 1201 ... C-6
Petersburg, 2585 ... D-10
Peterstown, 501 ... J-6
Philippi, 2822 ... D-8
Piedmont, 956 ... C-11
Pinch, 2811 ... F-4
Pine Grove, 542 ... B-6
Pineville, 684 ... I-4
PLEASANTS CO., 7521 ... C-5
Pleasant Valley, 3154 ... C-8
Poca, 1009 ... F-3
POCAHONTAS CO., 8944 ... F-8
Pocatalico, 1500 ... F-4
Pt. Pleasant, 4572 ... E-2
Powellton, 1796 ... G-5
Pratt, 531 ... G-4
PRESTON CO., 29705 ... B-9
Princeton, 6201 ... J-5
Prosperity, 1310 ... H-5
PUTNAM CO., 53035 ... F-3
Racine, 450 ... G-4
Rainelle, 1513 ... H-6
RALEIGH CO., 79254 ... H-5
Ramage, 200 ... H-3
Rand, 2200 ... G-4
RANDOLPH CO., 28254 ... E-8
Ranson, 3282 ... C-14
Ravenswood, 4007 ... D-3
Reader, 500 ... B-6
Red Jacket, 728 ... I-2
Richwood, 2361 ... G-7
Ridgeley, 713 ... B-11
Ripley, 3263 ... E-4
RITCHIE CO., 10515 ... D-5
ROANE CO., 15362 ... E-4
Rock Cr., 200 ... H-4
Roderfield, 1000 ... I-3
Romney, 1969 ... C-11
Ronceverte, 1536 ... H-7
Rowlesburg, 611 ... C-9
Rupert, 948 ... H-6
Ruth, 175 ... F-4
Ruthdale, 65 ... J-12
St. Albans, 11167 ... F-3
St. Marys, 1979 ... C-5
Salem, 1779 ... C-7
Seth, 750 ... G-4
Shady Spr., 2078 ... I-5
Shepherdstown, 1140 ... C-14
Shinnston, 2233 ... C-7
Sissonville, 4399 ... F-4
Sistersville, 1533 ... B-5
Smithers, 869 ... G-5
Sophia, 1281 ... I-5
S. Charleston, 12933 ... F-4
Spencer, 2283 ... E-4
Spring Valley, 900 ... G-12
Squire, 450 ... J-4
Star City, 1383 ... B-8
Stonewood, 1830 ... C-7
SUMMERS CO., 13917 ... I-6
Summersville, 3300 ... G-6
Sutton, 993 ... E-6
Switzer, 1138 ... H-3
TAYLOR CO., 16127 ... C-8
Terra Alta, 1474 ... C-9
Thomas, 427 ... D-9
Tornado, 1111 ... F-3
Triadelphia, 789 ... C-2
TUCKER CO., 7162 ... D-9
TYLER CO., 9439 ... C-6
Union, 551 ... I-7
UPSHUR CO., 23668 ... E-7
Valley Gr., 415 ... C-2
Verdunville, 500 ... H-3
Vienna, 10884 ... C-4
War, 719 ... J-4
WAYNE CO., 42418 ... G-2
Wayne, 1154 ... G-2
WEBSTER CO., 9790 ... F-7
Webster Sprs., 796 ... F-7
Weirton, 19838 ... B-2
Welch, 2485 ... J-4
Wellsburg, 2840 ... B-2
W. Liberty, 1204 ... B-2
W. Logan, 400 ... H-3
Weston, 4239 ... D-7
Westover, 3963 ... B-8
W. Pea Ridge, 2500 ... G-14
W. Union, 807 ... C-6
WETZEL CO., 17160 ... B-6
Wheeling, 30096 ... A-6
White Sulphur Sprs., 2373 ... H-7
Whitman, 450 ... H-3
Williamson, 3217 ... I-2
Williamstown, 2928 ... C-4
Winfield, 1930 ... F-3
WIRT CO., 5790 ... D-4
WOOD CO., 87336 ... D-4
WYOMING CO., 24830 ... I-4

Wisconsin

Map pp. 228-233

* City keyed to pp. 232-233

Abbotsford, 1944 ... H-7
ADAMS CO., 20567 ... L-9
Adams, 1840 ... K-8
Albany, 1148 ... P-9
Algoma, 3231 ... I-14
Allouez, 15181 ... S-3
Alma, 906 ... J-4
Altoona, 6545 ... I-5
Amery, 2865 ... G-2
Amherst, 971 ... J-10
Antigo, 8340 ... G-10
Appleton, 70354 ... J-12
Arcadia, 2332 ... J-4
Argyle, 810 ... P-8
ASHLAND CO., 16651 ... D-6
Ashland, 8397 ... C-6
Ashwaubenon, 17168 ... S-2
Athens, 1072 ... H-8
Augusta, 1406 ... I-5
Baldwin, 3089 ... H-2
Balsam Lake, 977 ... F-2
Bangor, 1395 ... L-6
Baraboo, 10768 ... M-9
BARRON CO., 45514 ... F-4
Barron, 3308 ... G-4
BAYFIELD CO., 15114 ... C-5
Bayfield, 608 ... B-6
Bayside, 4483 ... *B-6
Beaver Dam, 14949 ... M-11
Belgium, 1920 ... M-13
Belleville, 2011 ... O-9
Bellevue, 200 ... J-13
Belmont, 905 ... O-7
Beloit, 35505 ... P-10
Benton, 992 ... P-7
Berlin, 5303 ... K-11
Big Bend, 1276 ... O-12
Birnamwood, 782 ... H-10
Biron, 875 ... J-9
Black Cr., 1197 ... J-12
Black Earth, 1297 ... N-9
Black River Falls, 3578 ... J-6
Blair, 1271 ... J-5
Blanchardville, 796 ... O-8
Bloomer, 3284 ... H-5
Bloomington, 683 ... O-6
Bonduel, 1404 ... I-12
Boscobel, 3191 ... N-6
Boyceville, 1048 ... H-3
Boyd, 654 ... H-6
Brandon, 887 ... L-11
Brillion, 2940 ... K-13
Brodhead, 3095 ... P-10
Brookfield, 39637 ... N-13
BROWN CO., 233888 ... J-13
Brown Deer, 12031 ... *B-5
Bruce, 752 ... F-5
BUFFALO CO., 13814 ... J-4
Buffalo, 1058 ... J-4
Burlington, 10836 ... P-12
BURNETT CO., 16242 ... E-2
Butler, 1857 ... *D-4
Caddy Vista, 900 ... *J-6
Cadott, 1308 ... H-5
CALUMET CO., 43383 ... K-12
Cambria, 782 ... M-10
Cambridge, 1172 ... O-10
Cameron, 1609 ... G-4
Campbellsport, 1914 ... M-12
Cascade, 674 ... L-13
Cashton, 1019 ... L-6
Cassville, 1053 ... P-6
Cedarburg, 11169 ... N-13
Cedar Gr., 1928 ... M-13
Centuria, 963 ... F-2
Chetek, 2157 ... G-4
Chilton, 3646 ... K-12
CHIPPEWA CO., 56773 ... H-5
Chippewa Falls, 12708 ... H-5
CLARK CO., 33969 ... I-7
Clear Lake, 1079 ... G-3
Cleveland, 1399 ... K-13
Clinton, 2755 ... P-11
Clintonville, 4568 ... I-11
Colby, 1666 ... H-7
Coleman, 716 ... H-13
Colfax, 1097 ... H-4
COLUMBIA CO., 54076 ... M-10
Columbus, 4844 ... M-10
Combined Locks, 2744 ... O-4
Coon Valley, 735 ... L-6
Cornell, 1417 ... G-5
Crandon, 1874 ... F-11
CRAWFORD CO., 16949 ... N-6
Crivitz, 1037 ... G-13
Cross Plains, 3295 ... N-9
Cuba City, 2131 ... P-7
Cudahy, 18300 ... O-13
Cumberland, 2302 ... F-3
DANE CO., 449378 ... N-9
Darien, 1629 ... P-11
Darlington, 2391 ... P-8
Deerfield, 1989 ... N-10
De Forest, 8088 ... N-10
Delafield, 6705 ... N-12
Delavan, 8304 ... P-11
Denmark, 2002 ... J-13
De Pere, 22229 ... J-13
Dickeyville, 1055 ... P-7
DODGE CO., 87115 ... M-11
Dodgeville, 4625 ... O-8
DOOR CO., 28402 ... I-14
DOUGLAS CO., 44093 ... C-3
Dousman, 1819 ... N-12
Dresser, 770 ... G-2
DUNN CO., 41114 ... H-4
Durand, 1936 ... I-3
Eagle, 1721 ... O-12
Eagle River, 1565 ... E-10
E. Troy, 4046 ... O-12
EAU CLAIRE CO., 94186 ... I-5
Eau Claire, 62496 ... I-4
Edgar, 1354 ... H-8
Edgerton, 4926 ... O-10
Elkhart Lake, 1034 ... L-13
Elkhorn, 8245 ... P-12
Ellsworth, 3013 ... I-2
Elm Gr., 6290 ... *E-3
Elmwood, 812 ... I-3
Elroy, 1535 ... L-7
Evansville, 4289 ... O-10
Fairchild, 546 ... I-6
Fall Cr., 1235 ... I-5
Fall River, 1133 ... M-10
Fennimore, 2349 ... O-6
Fitchburg, 21736 ... T-7
FLORENCE CO., 5081 ... E-12
Florence, 750 ... E-12
FOND DU LAC CO., 97833 ... L-12
Fond du Lac, 42095 ... L-12
Fontana, 1884 ... P-12
Footville, 764 ... P-10
FOREST CO., 9938 ... F-11
Ft. Atkinson, 11781 ... O-11
Fountain City, 940 ... K-4
Fox Lake, 1461 ... M-11
Fox Pt., 6922 ... N-13
Franklin, 31994 ... O-13
Frederic, 1253 ... F-2
Fredonia, 2102 ... M-13
French Island, 4410 ... L-5
Friendship, 772 ... K-8
Galesville, 1408 ... K-5
Gays Mills, 611 ... M-6
Genoa City, 2394 ... P-12
Germantown, 18973 ... N-13
Gillett, 1222 ... H-12
Glendale, 13181 ... N-13
Glenwood City, 1200 ... H-3
Grafton, 11356 ... M-13
GRANT CO., 49368 ... O-6
Grantsburg, 1410 ... E-2
GREEN CO., 34280 ... P-9
Green Bay, 101467 ... J-13
Greendale, 14183 ... *G-5
Greenfield, 36101 ... O-13
GREEN LAKE CO., 19204 ... L-10
Green Lake, 1115 ... L-11
Greenwood, 1092 ... I-7
Hales Corners, 7688 ... O-13
Hammond, 1643 ... H-2
Hartford, 11852 ... M-12
Hartland, 8558 ... N-12
Hayward, 2245 ... E-5
Hazel Green, 1188 ... P-7
Highland, 834 ... N-7
Hilbert, 1096 ... K-12
Hillsboro, 1304 ... L-7
Holmen, 6976 ... K-5
Horicon, 3690 ... M-11
Hortonville, 2470 ... J-11
Howard, 15277 ... I-13
Howards Grove, 2880 ... L-13
Hudson, 10240 ... H-2
Hurley, 1734 ... C-8
Hustisford, 1119 ... M-11
Independence, 1249 ... J-5
Iola, 1262 ... J-10
IOWA CO., 23288 ... N-7
IRON CO., 6727 ... D-7
Iron Ridge, 994 ... M-12
Iron River, 900 ... C-5
JACKSON CO., 19538 ... J-7
Jackson, 5676 ... M-12
Janesville, 61145 ... P-10
JEFFERSON CO., 77421 ... N-11
Jefferson, 7388 ... O-11
Johnson Cr., 1761 ... N-11
JUNEAU CO., 25029 ... K-8
Juneau, 2472 ... M-11
Kaukauna, 14121 ... J-12
KENOSHA CO., 156209 ... P-14
Kenosha, 92871 ... P-13
Kewaskum, 3436 ... M-12
KEWAUNEE CO., 20455 ... J-14
Kewaunee, 2863 ... J-14
Kiel, 3480 ... K-13
Kimberly, 6237 ... J-12
King, 750 ... J-10
Kohler, 1945 ... L-13
Lac du Flambeau, 1646 ... E-8
LA CROSSE CO., 108612 ... L-5
La Crosse, 51001 ... L-5
Ladysmith, 3835 ... F-5
La Farge, 773 ... M-6
LAFAYETTE CO., 16341 ... P-8
Lake Delton, 2775 ... M-9
Lake Geneva, 7369 ... P-12
Lake Mills, 4875 ... N-11
Lake Nebagamon, 1057 ... C-4
Lancaster, 3981 ... O-6
LANGLADE CO., 20788 ... G-10
Lannon, 1024 ... *C-2
Laona, 750 ... F-11
Lena, 516 ... H-13
LINCOLN CO., 30076 ... G-8
Little Chute, 10737 ... J-12
Lodi, 2957 ... N-9
Lomira, 2373 ... M-12
Loyal, 1301 ... I-7
Luck, 1223 ... F-2
Luxemburg, 2078 ... I-13
Madison, 218432 ... N-10
Manawa, 1356 ... J-11
MANITOWOC CO., 82065 ... K-13
Manitowoc, 34080 ... K-14
Maple Bluff, 1332 ... R-8
MARATHON CO., 127168 ... H-8
Marathon, 1577 ... H-8
MARINETTE CO., 43237 ... G-12
Marinette, 11420 ... H-14
Marion, 1272 ... I-11
Markesan, 1376 ... L-10
MARQUETTE CO., 14853 ... L-9
Marshall, 3569 ... N-10
Marshfield, 18670 ... I-8
Mauston, 4017 ... L-8
Mayville, 4979 ... M-12
Mazomanie, 1479 ... N-8
McFarland, 7076 ... N-10
Medford, 4215 ... G-7
Mellen, 828 ... D-6
Menasha, 16259 ... K-12
MENOMINEE CO., 4623 ... H-11
Menomonee Falls, 33727 ... N-13
Menomonie, 15155 ... H-3
Mequon, 23449 ... N-13
Mercer, 1300 ... D-8
Merrill, 10164 ... G-9
Merrillan, 593 ... J-6
Merton, 2216 ... N-12
Middleton, 16189 ... N-9
Milltown, 905 ... F-2
Milton, 5335 ... O-11
MILWAUKEE CO., 933221 ... N-13
Milwaukee, 586941 ... N-13
Mineral Pt., 2510 ... O-8
Minocqua, 1280 ... E-9
Mishicot, 1408 ... J-14
Mondovi, 2640 ... I-4
Monona, 7987 ... N-10
MONROE CO., 41796 ... L-7
Monroe, 10676 ... P-9
Montello, 1442 ... L-10
Monticello, 1130 ... O-9
Montreal, 797 ... C-7
Mosinee, 4062 ... I-9
Mt. Calvary, 936 ... L-12
Mt. Horeb, 6074 ... O-9
Mukwonago, 6562 ... O-12
Muscoda, 1425 ... N-7
Muskego, 22314 ... O-13
Necedah, 869 ... K-8
Neenah, 24629 ... K-12
Neillsville, 2693 ... I-7
Nekoosa, 2631 ... J-8
Neopit, 839 ... H-11
New Berlin, 38627 ... *F-3
Newburg, 1128 ... M-13
New Glarus, 2054 ... O-9
New Holstein, 3270 ... K-13
New Lisbon, 1417 ... L-8
New London, 7063 ... J-11
New Richmond, 7058 ... G-2
Niagara, 1813 ... F-13
N. Fond du Lac, 4870 ... L-12
N. Freedom, 634 ... M-8
N. Hudson, 3665 ... H-2
N. Prairie, 1797 ... O-12
Oak Cr., 31983 ... O-13
Oakfield, 1009 ... L-12
Oconomowoc, 13189 ... N-12
OCONTO CO., 36904 ... H-12
Oconto, 4656 ... H-13
Oconto Falls, 2813 ... H-12
Okauchee, 1500 ... N-12
Omro, 3270 ... K-11
Onalaska, 15474 ... L-5
ONEIDA CO., 37187 ... F-10
Oneida, 1070 ... J-12
Oostburg, 2679 ... L-13
Oregon, 8037 ... O-9
Orfordville, 1302 ... P-10
Osceola, 2641 ... G-2
Oshkosh, 63237 ... K-11
Osseo, 1655 ... I-5
OUTAGAMIE CO., 167411 ... J-12
Owen, 929 ... H-7
OZAUKEE CO., 84772 ... M-13
Paddock Lake, 3131 ... P-13
Palmyra, 1762 ... O-11
Pardeeville, 2043 ... M-10
Park Falls, 2579 ... E-7
Pell Lake, 2988 ... P-12
PEPIN CO., 7383 ... I-3
Pepin, 930 ... J-3
Peshtigo, 3375 ... H-13
Pewaukee, 8648 ... N-12
Phillips, 1573 ... F-7
PIERCE CO., 37872 ... I-3
Pittsville, 852 ... J-8
Plain, 767 ... N-8
Plainfield, 902 ... K-9
Platteville, 9846 ... O-7
Pleasant Prairie, 18091 ... P-13
Plover, 11033 ... J-9
Plymouth, 8132 ... L-13
POLK CO., 43270 ... F-2
PORTAGE CO., 67386 ... J-9
Portage, 9959 ... M-9
Port Edwards, 1857 ... J-8
Port Washington, 10730 ... M-13
Potosi, 726 ... P-6
Poynette, 2445 ... M-9
Prairie du Chien, 5803 ... N-5
Prairie du Sac, 3390 ... N-9
Prentice, 590 ... F-7
Prescott, 3783 ... I-1
PRICE CO., 15401 ... F-7
Princeton, 1486 ... L-10
Pulaski, 3430 ... I-12
RACINE CO., 192284 ... O-13
Racine, 80266 ... O-13
Randolph, 1839 ... M-10
Random Lake, 1561 ... M-13
Redgranite, 1247 ... K-10
Reedsburg, 8227 ... M-8
Reedsville, 1170 ... K-13
Reeseville, 700 ... N-11
Rhinelander, 7813 ... F-9
Rib Lake, 857 ... G-8
Rice Lake, 8270 ... F-4
RICHLAND CO., 18193 ... M-7
Richland Cen., 5173 ... M-7
Rio, 966 ... M-10
Ripon, 7274 ... L-11
River Falls, 12967 ... H-2
River Hills, 1633 ... *B-5
Roberts, 1322 ... H-2
ROCK CO., 154794 ... O-10
Rothschild, 4837 ... H-9
RUSK CO., 15268 ... F-5
ST. CROIX CO., 71155 ... H-2
St. Croix Falls, 2052 ... F-2
St. Francis, 8809 ... O-13
St. Nazianz, 813 ... K-13
Salem, 1150 ... P-13
SAUK CO., 56432 ... M-8
Sauk City, 3025 ... N-9
Saukville, 4154 ... M-13
SAWYER CO., 16713 ... E-5
Schofield, 2234 ... H-9
Seymour, 3294 ... J-12
Sharon, 1564 ... P-11
SHAWANO CO., 41050 ... I-11
Shawano, 8351 ... I-11
SHEBOYGAN CO., 113376 ... L-13
Sheboygan, 49263 ... L-14
Sheboygan Falls, 6995 ... L-13
Shell Lake, 1346 ... E-4
Sherwood, 2054 ... K-12
Shiocton, 933 ... J-11
Shorewood, 13424 ... N-13
Shorewood Hills, 1697 ... S-6
Shullsburg, 1229 ... P-7
Silver Lake, 2422 ... P-12
Siren, 1015 ... E-2
Sister Bay, 864 ... A-13
Slinger, 4142 ... M-12
Solon Sprs., 575 ... C-4
Somerset, 2264 ... G-2
S. Milwaukee, 21258 ... O-13
Sparta, 8708 ... K-6
Spencer, 1886 ... I-7
Spooner, 2700 ... E-4
Spring Green, 1417 ... N-8
Spring Valley, 1206 ... H-3
Stanley, 1857 ... H-6
Stevens Pt., 24412 ... J-9
Stockbridge, 672 ... K-12
Stoddard, 802 ... L-5
Stoughton, 12611 ... O-10
Stratford, 1552 ... I-8
Strum, 977 ... I-5
Sturgeon Bay, 9484 ... H-14
Sturtevant, 5225 ... O-13
Sun Prairie, 23484 ... N-10
Superior, 27206 ... B-3
Sussex, 9561 ... N-12
TAYLOR CO., 19539 ... G-7
Theresa, 1270 ... M-12
Thiensville, 3176 ... N-13
Thorp, 1571 ... H-6
Tigerton, 749 ... I-10
Tomah, 8525 ... K-7
Tomahawk, 3807 ... F-9
TREMPEALEAU CO., 27306 ... J-5
Trempealeau, 1435 ... K-5
Turtle Lake, 1016 ... G-3
Twin Lakes, 5323 ... P-12
Two Rivers, 12239 ... K-14
Union Gr., 4498 ... P-13
Valders, 992 ... K-13
VERNON CO., 28496 ... M-6
Verona, 9371 ... O-9
VILAS CO., 22041 ... D-9
Viola, 656 ... M-6
Viroqua, 4351 ... M-6
Wabeno, 960 ... F-11
Wales, 2604 ... O-12
WALWORTH CO., 96812 ... O-11
Walworth, 2511 ... P-11
WASHBURN CO., 16466 ... E-4
Washburn, 2299 ... B-6
WASHINGTON CO., 122241 ... M-12
Waterford, 4483 ... O-12
Waterloo, 3268 ... N-10
Watertown, 22675 ... N-11
WAUKESHA CO., 374079 ... O-12
Waukesha, 66840 ... N-12
Waunakee, 9803 ... N-9
WAUPACA CO., 52564 ... J-10
Waupaca, 5812 ... J-10
Waupun, 10451 ... L-11
Wausau, 37430 ... H-9
Wausaukee, 552 ... G-13
WAUSHARA CO., 23623 ... K-10
Wautoma, 2134 ... K-10
Wauwatosa, 46260 ... *E-4
W. Allis, 60192 ... *F-4
W. Baraboo, 1363 ... M-9
W. Bend, 28932 ... M-12
Westby, 2116 ... L-6
Westfield, 1222 ... L-9
W. Milwaukee, 4093 ... *F-5
W. Salem, 4810 ... L-5
Weyauwega, 1821 ... J-11
Whitefish Bay, 13848 ... N-13
Whitehall, 1622 ... J-5
Whitelaw, 729 ... K-13
Whitewater, 14120 ... O-11
Whiting, 1746 ... J-9
Wild Rose, 756 ... K-10
Williams Bay, 2572 ... P-12
Wind Lake, 5202 ... O-13
Wind Pt., 1845 ... O-13
WINNEBAGO CO., 158500 ... K-11
Winneconne, 2418 ... K-11
Wisconsin Dells, 2444 ... M-9
Wisconsin Rapids, 18041 ... J-8
Wittenberg, 1148 ... I-10
Wonewoc, 811 ... L-7
WOOD CO., 75402 ... I-8
Woodruff, 1500 ... E-9
Woodville, 1207 ... H-3
Wrightstown, 2105 ... J-12
Wyocena, 720 ... M-10

Wyoming

Map pp. 234-235

Afton, 1781 ... E-4
ALBANY CO., 31887 ... G-11
Baggs, 358 ... H-9
Bairoil, 95 ... F-9
Bar Nunn, 985 ... E-10
Basin, 1203 ... B-8
BIG HORN CO., 11199 ... B-8
Big Horn, 198 ... B-10
Big Piney, 436 ... F-5
Buffalo, 4220 ... B-10
Byron, 546 ... B-8
CAMPBELL CO., 36240 ... C-11
CARBON CO., 15302 ... G-9
Casper, 50632 ... E-10
Cheyenne, 54374 ... H-13
Cody, 8973 ... B-7
Cokeville, 492 ... F-4
CONVERSE CO., 12330 ... E-11
Cowley, 571 ... A-8
CROOK CO., 5928 ... B-12
Dayton, 703 ... A-9
Diamondville, 702 ... G-5
Douglas, 5398 ... E-12
Dubois, 975 ... D-6
E. Thermopolis, 262 ... D-8
Eden, 388 ... G-6
Edgerton, 171 ... D-11
Encampment, 441 ... H-10
Etna, 123 ... E-4
Evanston, 11375 ... H-4
Evansville, 2324 ... E-11
Ft. Laramie, 234 ... F-13
Ft. Washakie, 1477 ... E-7
FREMONT CO., 35914 ... E-8
Gillette, 21840 ... B-12
Glenrock, 2274 ... E-11
GOSHEN CO., 12219 ... G-13
Green River, 11541 ... H-6
Greybull, 1749 ... B-8
Guernsey, 1115 ... F-13
Hanna, 874 ... G-10
HOT SPRINGS CO., 4665 ... C-7
Hudson, 408 ... E-8
Hulett, 410 ... B-13
Jackson, 8825 ... D-5
Jeffrey City, 106 ... F-9
JOHNSON CO., 7543 ... C-10
Kaycee, 266 ... D-10
Kemmerer, 2554 ... G-5
La Barge, 422 ... F-5
Lander, 6864 ... E-7
LARAMIE CO., 84083 ... H-13
Laramie, 26956 ... H-12
LINCOLN CO., 15208 ... F-4
Lingle, 491 ... F-13
Lovell, 2283 ... B-8
Lusk, 1320 ... E-13
Lyman, 1924 ... H-5
Marbleton, 780 ... F-5
Medicine Bow, 269 ... G-11
Meeteetse, 351 ... C-7
Midwest, 412 ... D-11
Mills, 2894 ... G-2
Moorcroft, 819 ... C-12
Mtn. View, 103 ... G-1
Mtn. View, 1154 ... H-5
NATRONA CO., 68211 ... E-9
Newcastle, 3234 ... C-13
NIOBRARA CO., 2237 ... E-13
Orchard Valley, 1800 ... H-13
Osage, 215 ... C-13
PARK CO., 26284 ... C-7
Pine Bluffs, 1177 ... H-14
Pinedale, 1501 ... E-6
PLATTE CO., 8628 ... G-12
Powell, 5253 ... B-7
Ranchester, 719 ... A-9
Rawlins, 8665 ... G-9
Reliance, 665 ... G-7
Riverton, 9314 ... E-8
Rock Sprs., 18400 ... G-7
Rolling Hills, 462 ... E-11
Saratoga, 1714 ... H-10
SHERIDAN CO., 27111 ... A-10
Sheridan, 16016 ... B-10
Shoshoni, 661 ... D-8
Sinclair, 408 ... G-10
Story, 887 ... B-10
SUBLETTE CO., 6368 ... F-6
Sundance, 1160 ... B-13
Superior, 235 ... G-7
SWEETWATER CO., 37018 ... H-8
Ten Sleep, 310 ... C-9
TETON CO., 18625 ... C-5
Thermopolis, 3030 ... D-8
Torrington, 5581 ... F-13
UINTA CO., 19700 ... H-4
Upton, 871 ... C-13
Wamsutter, 262 ... G-8
WASHAKIE CO., 7883 ... C-8
WESTON CO., 6659 ... C-13
Wheatland, 3476 ... G-12
Wilson, 1294 ... D-5
Worland, 4944 ... C-8

CANADA Cities and Towns

Alberta

Map pp. 238-241

* City keyed to p. 236

Airdrie, 20382 ... H-16
Alix, 825 ... G-17
Athabasca, 2415 ... C-16
Banff, 7135 ... I-15
Barrhead, 4213 ... D-15
Bashaw, 825 ... F-17
Bassano, 1320 ... I-18
Beaverlodge, 2110 ... B-11
Bentley, 1035 ... G-16
Berwyn, 546 ... A-12
Black Diamond, 1866 ... I-16
Blackfalds, 3042 ... G-16
Bon Accord, 1532 ... D-16
Bonnyville, 5709 ... D-19
Bow Island, 1704 ... J-19
Bowden, 1174 ... G-16
Boyle, 836 ... C-17
Brooks, 11604 ... I-18
Bruderheim, 1202 ... D-17
Calgary, 878866 ... I-16
Calmar, 1902 ... E-16
Camrose, 14854 ... F-17
Canmore, 10792 ... I-15
Cardston, 3475 ... L-17
Carstairs, 2254 ... H-16
Castor, 935 ... G-18
Claresholm, 3622 ... J-17
Coaldale, 6008 ... K-18
Cochrane, 11798 ... I-16
Cold Lake, 11520 ... C-19
Consort, 634 ... G-19
Coronation, 902 ... G-19
Crossfield, 2389 ... H-16
Crowsnest Pass, 6262 ... K-16
Daysland, 779 ... F-18
Delburne, 719 ... G-17
Devon, 4969 ... E-16
Didsbury, 3932 ... H-16
Drayton Valley, 5801 ... E-15
Drumheller, 7785 ... H-17
Eckville, 1019 ... G-16
Edmonton, 666104 ... E-17
Edson, 7585 ... E-14
Elk Pt., 1440 ... D-19
Evansburg ... E-15
Fairview, 3150 ... A-12
Falher, 1109 ... B-13
Foremost, 531 ... K-19
Forestburg, 870 ... F-18
Ft. Macleod, 2990 ... K-17
Ft. McMurray ... *F-4
Ft. Saskatchewan, 13121 ... E-17
Fox Cr., 2337 ... D-13
Gibbons, 2654 ... D-17
Grand Centre ... C-19
Grande Cache, 3828 ... E-11
Grande Prairie, 36983 ... C-12
Grimshaw, 2435 ... A-13
Hanna, 2986 ... H-18
Hardisty, 743 ... F-19
High Prairie, 2737 ... B-13
High River, 9345 ... J-16
Hinton, 9405 ... E-13
Hythe, 582 ... B-11
Innisfail, 6928 ... G-16
Jasper, 4180 ... F-12
Killam, 1004 ... F-18
Kitscoty, 671 ... E-19
Lac La Biche, 2776 ... C-18
Lacombe, 9384 ... G-16
Lake Louise ... H-14
Lamont, 1692 ... D-17
Leduc, 15032 ... E-16
Legal, 1058 ... D-16
Lethbridge, 67374 ... K-17
Lloydminster, 13148 ... E-20
Magrath, 1993 ... K-17
Mannville, 722 ... E-19
Mayerthorpe, 1570 ... D-15
McLennan, 804 ... B-13
Medicine Hat, 51249 ... J-20
Milk River, 879 ... L-18
Millet, 2037 ... F-16
Morinville, 6540 ... E-21
Mundare, 653 ... E-17
Nanton, 1841 ... J-17
Okotoks, 11664 ... I-16
Olds, 6607 ... H-16
Onoway, 847 ... E-16
Oyen, 1020 ... H-20
Peace River, 6240 ... A-13
Penhold, 1729 ... G-16
Picture Butte, 1701 ... J-17
Pincher Cr., 3666 ... K-16
Ponoka, 6330 ... F-16
Provost, 1980 ... F-19
Raymond, 3200 ... K-18
Red Deer, 67707 ... G-16
Redcliff, 4372 ... J-19
Redwater, 2172 ... D-17
Rimbey, 2118 ... F-16
Rocky Mtn. House, 13121 ... E-17
Rycroft, 609 ... B-12
St. Albert, 53081 ... E-16
St. Paul, 5061 ... D-18
Sedgewick, 865 ... F-18
Sexsmith, 1653 ... B-11
Sherwood Park ... E-17
Slave Lake, 6600 ... B-15
Smoky Lake, 1011 ... D-17
Spirit River, 1100 ... B-11
Spruce Gr., 15983 ... E-16
Stettler, 5215 ... G-17
Stirling, 877 ... K-18
Stony Plain, 9589 ... E-16
Strathmore, 7621 ... I-17
Sundre, 2267 ... H-15
Swan Hills, 1807 ... C-15
Sylvan Lake, 7493 ... G-16
Taber, 7671 ... K-18
Thorsby, 799 ... E-16
Three Hills, 2902 ... H-17
Tofield, 1818 ... E-17
Trochu, 1033 ... H-17
Turner Valley, 1608 ... I-16
Two Hills, 1091 ... E-18
Valleyview, 1856 ... C-13
Vauxhall, 1112 ... J-18
Vegreville, 5376 ... E-18
Vermilion, 3948 ... E-19
Viking, 1052 ... E-18
Vulcan, 1762 ... J-17
Wabamun, 601 ... E-15
Wabasca-Desmarais ... A-16
Wainwright, 5117 ... F-19
Wembley, 1497 ... C-11
Westlock, 4819 ... D-16
Wetaskiwin, 11154 ... F-17
Whitecourt, 8334 ... D-14

British Columbia

Map pp. 238-241

* City keyed to p. 236

Abbotsford, 115463 ... L-8
Armstrong, 4256 ... J-11
Ashcroft, 1788 ... J-9
Barrière ... I-10
Black Cr. ... G-9
Burnaby, 193954 ... L-7
Burns Lake, 1942 ... D-5
Cache Cr., 1056 ... I-9
Campbell River, 28456 ... J-5
Castlegar, 7002 ... L-13
Chase, 2460 ... I-11
Chemainus ... L-6
Chetwynd, 2591 ... B-9
Chilliwack, 62927 ... L-8
Clearwater ... H-10
Coldstream, 9106 ... J-11
Comox, 11172 ... K-5
Courtenay, 18304 ... K-5
Cranbrook, 18476 ... K-15
Creston, 4795 ... L-14
Crofton ... L-7
Cumberland, 2618 ... K-5
Dawson Cr., 10754 ... B-10
Duncan, 4699 ... L-6
Elkford, 2589 ... J-15
Enderby, 2818 ... J-11
Esquimalt, 16127 ... M-7
Fernie, 4611 ... K-15
Fort Nelson, 4188 ... *E-3
Fort St. James, 1927 ... D-6
Fort St. John, 16034 ... A-10
Fraser Lake, 1268 ... D-6
Fruitvale, 2025 ... L-13
Gold River, 1359 ... K-4
Golden, 4020 ... I-13
Grand Forks, 4054 ... L-12
Greenwood, 666 ... L-12
Hope, 6184 ... L-9
Houston, 3577 ... C-4
Hudson's Hope, 1039 ... A-9
Invermere, 2858 ... J-14
Kamloops, 77281 ... J-10
Kelowna, 96288 ... K-11
Kimberley, 6484 ... K-14
Kitimat, 10285 ... D-2
Ladysmith, 6587 ... L-6
Lake Cowichan, 2827 ... L-6
Langley, 23643 ... L-8
Lillooet, 2741 ... I-8
Lions Bay, 1379 ... K-7
Logan Lake, 2185 ... J-10
Lumby, 1618 ... J-11
Mackenzie, 5206 ... B-8
Maple Ridge, 63169 ... C-6
Merritt, 7088 ... J-9
Mission, 31272 ... L-8
Montrose, 1067 ... L-13
Nakusp, 1698 ... J-13
Nanaimo, 73000 ... L-6
Nelson, 9298 ... K-13
New Westminster, 54656 ... N-3
N. Vancouver, 44303 ... L-7
Oak Bay, 17798 ... M-7
Ocean Falls ... F-3
Okanagan Falls ... L-11
Oliver, 4224 ... L-11
One Hundred Mile House, 1739 ... H-9
Osoyoos, 4295 ... L-11
Oyama ... J-11
Parksville, 10323 ... L-6
Peachland, 4654 ... K-11
Penticton, 30985 ... K-11
Port Alberni, 17743 ... L-5
Port Alice, 1126 ... J-3
Port Coquitlam, 51257 ... L-7
Port Hardy, 4574 ... I-3
Port McNeill, 2821 ... I-3
Port Moody, 23816 ... L-7
Powell River, 12983 ... K-6
Prince George, 72406 ... D-8
Prince Rupert, 14643 ... C-1
Princeton, 2610 ... K-10
Qualicum Beach, 6921 ... K-6
Quesnel, 10044 ... F-8
Revelstoke, 7500 ... I-12
Richmond, 164345 ... L-7
Robson ... L-13
Rossland, 3646 ... L-12
Royston ... K-5
Salmo, 1120 ... L-13
Salmon Arm, 15210 ... J-11
Sechelt, 7775 ... K-7
Sicamous, 2720 ... I-11
Sidney, 10929 ... M-7
Smithers, 5414 ... C-4
Sparwood, 3812 ... K-15
Squamish, 14247 ... K-7
Summerland, 10713 ... K-11
Surrey, 347825 ... L-7
Tahsis, 600 ... J-4
Terrace ... C-3
Trail, 7575 ... L-13
Tumbler Ridge, 1851 ... C-10
Ucluelet, 1559 ... L-5
Valemount, 1195 ... F-11
Vancouver, 545671 ... L-7
Vanderhoof, 4390 ... D-7
Vernon, 33494 ... J-11
Victoria, 74125 ... M-7
Westbank ... K-11
Whistler, 8896 ... J-7
White Rock, 18250 ... L-7
Williams Lake, 11153 ... G-8
Youbou ... L-6

Manitoba

Map pp. 244-245

* City keyed to p. 236

Altona, 3434 ... M-17
Arborg, 959 ... J-17
Ashern ... I-15
Austin ... L-15
Baldur ... M-14
Beausejour, 2772 ... K-18
Benito, 415 ... H-12
Binscarth, 445 ... J-12
Birch River ... G-12
Birtle, 715 ... K-12
Boissevain, 1495 ... M-13
Bowsman, 320 ... G-12
Brandon, 39716 ... L-14
Camperville ... H-13
Carberry, 1513 ... L-14
Carman, 2831 ... L-16
Cormorant ... C-13
Cranberry Portage ... C-12
Crystal City, 414 ... M-15
Cypress River ... L-15
Dauphin, 8085 ... I-13
Deloraine, 1026 ... M-13
Dominion City ... M-17
Duck Bay ... G-13
E. Selkirk ... K-17
Easterville ... E-14
Elkhorn, 470 ... L-12
Elm Creek ... L-16
Elphinstone ... J-13
Emerson, 655 ... M-17
Erickson, 448 ... K-14
Ethelbert, 335 ... I-13
Fisher Branch ... I-16
Flin Flon, 6000 ... B-11
Gilbert Plains, 757 ... I-13
Gimli, 1657 ... J-17
Gladstone, 848 ... K-15
Glenboro, 656 ... L-14
Grand Rapids, 355 ... E-14
Grandview, 814 ... I-13
Gretna, 563 ... M-17
Grunthal ... L-18
Hamiota, 858 ... K-13
Hartney, 446 ... M-13
Holland ... L-15
Killarney, 2221 ... M-14
La Broquerie, 2894 ... L-18
Lac du Bonnet, 1089 ... K-18
Lorette ... L-18
Lundar ... J-16
Lynn Lake, 699 ... *F-6
MacGregor, 882 ... L-15
Manitou, 775 ... M-15
McCreary, 522 ... J-14
Melita, 1111 ... M-12
Miami ... M-16
Minitonas, 538 ... G-12
Minnedosa, 2426 ... K-14
Moose Lake ... D-13
Morden, 6142 ... M-16
Morris, 1673 ... M-17
Neepawa, 3325 ... K-14
Niverville, 1921 ... L-17
Norway House ... D-16
Notre Dame de Lourdes, 619 ... L-15
Oak Lake, 359 ... L-13
Oakville ... L-16
Onanole ... J-14
Pilot Mound, 676 ... M-15
Pinawa, 1500 ... K-19
Pine Falls, 650 ... J-18
Plum Coulee, 725 ... M-16
Portage la Prairie, 12976 ... K-16
Powerview, 750 ... J-18
Rapid City, 424 ... K-13
Reston ... L-12
Rivers, 1119 ... K-13
Riverton, 594 ... I-17
Roblin, 1818 ... I-12
Rossburn, 568 ... J-12
Russell, 1587 ... J-12
St. Adolphe ... L-17
St. Claude, 558 ... L-16
St. Georges ... J-18
St. Jean Baptiste ... M-17
St. Laurent ... K-16
St. Malo ... M-17
Ste. Anne, 1513 ... L-18
Ste. Rose du Lac, 1047 ... I-14
Sandy Lake ... J-13
Selkirk, 9752 ... K-17
Shoal Lake, 801 ... K-13
Snow Lake, 1207 ... B-13
Somerset, 459 ... M-15
Souris, 1683 ... L-13
Steinbach, 9227 ... L-18
Stonewall, 4012 ... K-17
St-Pierre-Jolys, 893 ... L-17
Swan River, 4032 ... G-12
Teulon, 1058 ... K-17
The Pas, 5795 ... D-12
Thompson, 13256 ... *F-6
Treherne, 644 ... L-15
Tyndall ... K-18
Virden, 3109 ... L-12
Wabowden ... B-15
Warren ... K-17
Wawanesa, 516 ... L-14
Winkler, 7943 ... M-16
Winnipeg, 619544 ... L-17
Winnipeg Beach, 801 ... J-17
Winnipegosis, 621 ... H-14

New Brunswick

Map pp. 254-255

Alma, 290 ... I-8
Aroostook, 380 ... F-3
Atholville, 1381 ... D-5
Balmoral, 1836 ... D-6
Bas-Caraquet, 1689 ... D-8
Bath, 592 ... G-4
Bathurst, 12924 ... E-7
Belledune, 1923 ... D-6
Beresford, 4414 ... D-7
Bertrand, 1269 ... D-8
Blacks Harbour, 1082 ... J-5
Blackville, 1015 ... G-6
Bouctouche, 2426 ... G-8
Campbellton, 7798 ... D-5
Canterbury, 399 ... H-4
Cap-Pele, 2266 ... H-9
Caraquet, 4442 ... D-8
Charlo, 1449 ... D-6
Chipman, 1432 ... H-6
Clair, 863 ... E-2
Dalhousie, 3975 ... D-6
Debec ... H-3
Dieppe, 14951 ... H-8
Doaktown, 955 ... G-6
Dorchester, 954 ... H-9
Edmundston, 17373 ... E-3
Eel River Crossing, 1335 ... D-6
Elgin ... J-8
Fairvale ... J-6
Florenceville, 762 ... G-4
Fredericton, 47560 ... H-5
Gagetown, 682 ... I-6
Geary ... I-5
Grand Bay ... J-6
Grand Falls/Grand Sault, 5858 ... F-3
Grande-Anse, 853 ... D-7
Hampton, 3997 ... I-6
Hartland, 902 ... G-4
Havelock ... H-7
Hillsborough, 1288 ... H-8
Juniper ... G-4
Kedgwick, 1184 ... D-4
Lac-Baker, 226 ... E-2
Laméque, 1580 ... D-8
Lawrence Sta. ... I-4
Lorne ... D-6
Maugerville ... H-6
McAdam, 1513 ... I-4
Memramcook, 4719 ... H-8
Millville, 319 ... H-4
Minto, 2776 ... H-6
Miramichi, 18508 ... F-7
Moncton, 61046 ... H-8
Nackawic, 1042 ... H-4
Neguac, 1697 ... E-8
New Maryland, 4284 ... I-5
Nigadoo, 983 ... D-7
N. Head ... K-5
Norton, 1370 ... I-7
Oromocto, 8843 ... I-5
Penniac ... H-5
Perth-Andover, 1908 ... F-4
Petit Rocher, 1966 ... D-7
Petitcodiac, 1444 ... H-7
Plaster Rock, 1219 ... F-4
Pointe-Verte, 1041 ... D-7
Port Elgin, 436 ... H-9
Quispamsis, 13757 ... J-6
Renforth ... K-17
Rexton, 810 ... G-8
Richibucto, 1341 ... G-8
Riverview, 17010 ... H-8
Riviére-Verte, 856 ... E-3
Robertville ... D-7
Rogersville, 1248 ... G-7
Rothesay, 11505 ... J-6
Sackville, 5361 ... H-9
St. Andrews, 1869 ... J-4
St. George ... J-5
St. John, 69661 ... J-6
St. Martins, 374 ... J-7
St. Stephen, 4667 ... J-4
Salisbury, 1954 ... H-8
Seal Cove ... K-5
Shediac, 4892 ... H-8
Shemogue ... H-9
Shippagan, 2872 ... D-8
St-Antoine, 1472 ... G-8
St-Basile ... E-3
Ste-Anne-de-Madawaska, 1168 ... E-3
St-Isidore, 877 ... E-8
St-Jacques ... E-2
St-Léonard ... E-3
St-Louis de Kent, 991 ... G-8
St-Quentin, 2280 ... E-4
Sussex, 4182 ... I-7
Sussex Corner, 1321 ... I-7
Taymouth ... H-5
Tide Head, 1149 ... D-5
Tracadie-Sheila, 4724 ... E-8
Tracy, 601 ... I-5
Upper Kent ... G-4
Welsford ... I-6
Westfield ... J-6
Wilsons Beach ... K-5
Woodstock, 5198 ... H-4

Newfoundland and Labrador

Map pp. 256-257

Arnold's Cove, 1024 ... E-19
Badger, 906 ... D-18
Baie Verte, 1492 ... C-18
Bay Roberts, 5237 ... E-20
Bishop's Falls, 3688 ... D-18
Bonavista, 4021 ... D-20
Botwood, 3221 ... D-18
Buchans, 877 ... D-17
Burgeo, 1782 ... E-17
Burin, 2470 ... F-19
Carbonear, 4759 ... E-20
Catalina, 995 ... D-20
Channel-Port aux Basques, 4637 ... E-16
Clarenville, 5104 ... E-19
Corner Brook, 20103 ... D-17
Deer Lake, 4769 ... D-17
Dunville ... F-19
Durrell ... C-19
Englee, 694 ... B-18
Fogo, 803 ... C-19
Fortune, 1615 ... F-18
Gambo, 2084 ... D-19
Gander, 9651 ... D-19
Glenwood, 845 ... D-19
Glovertown, 2163 ... D-19
Goulds ... E-20
Grand Bank, 2841 ... F-18
Grand Falls-Windsor, 13340 ... D-18
Happy Valley-Goose Bay, 7969 ... B-20
Harbour Breton, 2079 ... E-18
Harbour Grace, 3380 ... E-20
Hare Bay, 1065 ... D-19
Isle aux Morts, 813 ... E-16
Joe Batt's Arm ... C-19
La Scie, 1063 ... C-18
Labrador City, 7744 ... B-19
Lawn, 779 ... F-18
Lewisporte, 3312 ... D-19
Marystown, 5908 ... F-18
Mt. Pearl, 24964 ... E-20
Musgrave Harbour, 1294 ... D-19
Nain, 1159 ... A-20
Norris Pt., 786 ... C-17
Pasadena, 3133 ... D-17
Peterview, 811 ... D-18
Placentia, 4426 ... F-19
Pouch Cove, 1669 ... E-20
Rocky Harbour, 1002 ... C-17
Roddickton, 1003 ... B-18
St. Alban's, 1372 ... E-18
St. Anthony, 2730 ... B-18
St. George's, 1354 ... E-16
St. John's, 99182 ... E-20
St. Lawrence, 1558 ... F-18
Shoal Harbour ... E-19
Springdale, 3045 ... D-18
Stephenville, 7109 ... D-16
Stephenville Crossing, 1993 ... D-16
Torbay, 5474 ... E-20
Wabana, 2679 ... E-20
Wabush, 1894 ... B-19
Wesleyville ... D-19
Whitbourne, 930 ... F-20
Witless Bay, 1056 ... F-20

Northwest Territories

Map p. 236

Ft. McPherson, 761 ... B-3
Ft. Providence, 753 ... D-4
Ft. Simpson, 1163 ... D-4
Ft. Smith, 2185 ... E-4
Hay River, 3510 ... D-4
Inuvik, 2894 ... B-3
Tuktoyaktuk, 930 ... A-3
Yellowknife, 16541 ... D-4

Nova Scotia

Map pp. 255-257

Advocate Harbour ... J-8
Amherst, 9470 ... I-9
Annapolis Royal, 550 ... K-7
Antigonish, 4754 ... I-13
Arichat ... I-14
Aylesford ... J-8
Baddeck ... H-14
Barrington ... N-7

Barrington Passage N-7
Bear River K-7
Berwick, 2282 ..... J-8
Bridgetown, 1035 ..... K-7
Bridgewater, 7621 ..... L-9
Brighton I-6
Brookfield J-10
Brooklyn M-8
Canning J-9
Canso, 992 ..... J-14
Chester K-9
Chéticamp G-14
Cheverie J-9
Church Pt. L-6
Clark's Harbour, 944 ..... N-7
Clementsport K-7
Clementsvale K-7
Dartmouth K-10
Debert I-10
Deep Brook K-7
Digby, 2111 ..... K-6
Dingwall F-15
Dominion H-16
Elmsdale K-10
Enfield K-10
Falmouth J-9
Five Islands J-9
Freeport L-6
Glace Bay H-16
Grand-Étang G-14
Granville Ferry K-7
Great Vil. J-10
Guysborough I-13
Halifax, 359111 ..... K-10
Hantsport, 1202 ..... J-9
Havre Boucher I-13
Hebron M-6
Hilden J-10
Hopewell I-11
Hubbards K-9
Ingonish F-15
Ingonish Beach G-15
Inverness H-14
Joggins I-9
Kentville, 5610 ..... J-9
Kingston K-8
L'Ardoise I-14
Larrys River J-14
Lawrencetown K-7
Little Brook L-6
Liverpool M-8
Lockeport, 701 ..... M-8
Louisbourg H-16
Louisdale I-14
Lunenburg, 2568 ..... L-9
Mabou H-13
Maccan I-9
Mahone Bay, 991 ..... L-9
Maitland J-10
Meteghan L-6
Meteghan River L-6
Middle Musquodoboit J-11
Middleton, 1744 ..... K-8
Milford Sta. J-10
Milton M-8
Mulgrave, 904 ..... I-13
Musquodoboit Harbour K-11
New Germany L-8
New Glasgow, 9432 ..... I-12
New Minas J-9
New Ross K-9
New Waterford G-15
N. Sydney H-15
Oxford, 1332 ..... I-10
Parrsboro, 1529 ..... J-9
Petite Riviére L-9
Pictou, 3875 ..... I-11
Pleasant Bay F-14
Port Hastings I-13
Port Hawkesbury, 3701 ..... I-14
Port Hood H-13
Port Maitland M-6
Port Medway L-8
Port Morien H-16
Pugwash I-10
River Hebert I-9
River John I-11
St. Peters I-14
Sheet Harbour K-12
Shelburne, 2013 ..... M-7
Sherbrooke J-13
Ship Harbour K-11
Shubenacadie J-10
Springhill, 4091 ..... I-9
Stellarton, 4809 ..... I-11
Stewiacke, 1388 ..... J-10
Sydney H-15
Sydney Mines G-15
Tatamagouche I-10
Three Mile Plains K-9
Tiverton L-6
Trenton, 2798 ..... I-12
Truro, 11457 ..... J-10
Tusket M-6
Upper Musquodoboit J-11
Valley J-11
Waterville J-8
Waverley K-10
Wedgeport M-6
W. Arichat I-14
Western Shore L-9
Westport L-6
Westville, 3879 ..... I-11
Weymouth L-6
Whycocomagh H-14
Windsor, 3778 ..... K-9
Wolfville, 3658 ..... J-9
Yarmouth, 7561 ..... M-6

Nunavut

Map pp. 236-237

Ikaluktutiak C-6
Iqaluit, 5236 ..... D-10
Kugluktuk, 1212 ..... C-5
Pangnirtung, 1276 ..... C-10
Sachs Harbour A-4

Ontario

Map pp. 246-249

Acton J-9
Ailsa Craig K-6
Ajax, 73753 ..... I-11
Aldershot J-20
Alexandria E-19
Alfred D-18
Alliston H-9
Almonte E-16
Alvinston L-5
Amherstburg, 20339 ..... M-3
Amherstview H-15
Angus H-9
Arnprior, 7192 ..... E-16
Arthur I-8
Athens, 3053 ..... G-17
Atikokan, 3632 ..... L-14
Atwood I-7
Aurora, 40167 ..... I-10
Aylmer, 7126 ..... L-7
Ayr J-8
Baden J-8
Bancroft, 4089 ..... F-13
Barrie, 103710 ..... H-10
Barriefield H-15
Barry's Bay E-13
Bath H-15
Bayfield J-6
Beachburg D-16
Beachville D-15
Beamsville K-10
Beaverton H-11
Belle River M-4
Belleville, 45986 ..... H-14
Belmont K-7
Blackburn Hamlet D-19
Blenheim M-5
Blind River, 3969 ..... C-4
Bloomfield I-14
Blyth I-6
Bobcaygeon G-12
Bolton I-9
Bonfield, 2064 ..... C-11
Bothwell L-5
Bourget E-18
Bowmanville I-11
Bracebridge, 13751 ..... F-10
Bradford H-10
Brampton, 325428 ..... I-9
Brantford, 86417 ..... K-8
Bridgenorth H-12
Brighton, 9449 ..... H-13
Brights Grove K-5
Brockville, 21375 ..... G-17
Bruce Mines, 627 ..... C-2
Brussels I-7
Burford K-8
Burk's Falls, 940 ..... D-10
Burlington, 150836 ..... J-9
Cache Bay C-9
Calabogie E-15
Caledon, 50595 ..... I-9
Caledonia K-9
Callander C-10
Cambridge, 110372 ..... J-8
Campbellford H-13
Cannington H-11
Capreol B-7
Cardinal F-17
Carleton Place, 9083 ..... F-16
Casselman, 2910 ..... E-18
Cayuga K-9
Chalk River C-14
Chapleau M-19
Chatham M-5
Chesley H-7
Chesterville F-18
Clarington, 69834 ..... I-12
Clifford I-7
Clinton J-6
Cobalt, 1229 ..... M-20
Cobden D-15
Cobourg, 17172 ..... I-12
Cochrane, 5690 ..... L-20
Colborne I-13
Colchester N-3
Coldwater G-10
Collingwood, 16039 ..... G-9
Collins Bay H-15
Comber M-4
Coniston N-20
Cookstown H-10
Cornwall, 45640 ..... F-19
Corunna K-4
Courtland L-8
Craigleith G-9
Creemore H-9
Crystal Beach K-11
Deep River, 4135 ..... C-13
Delhi L-9
Deseronto, 1796 ..... H-14
Dorchester K-7
Drayton I-8
Dresden L-5
Dryden, 8198 ..... K-14
Dundalk H-8
Dunnville K-10
Durham H-7
Dutton L-6
Eganville E-14
Elliot Lake, 11956 ..... B-4
Elmira J-8
Elmvale G-9
Elora I-8
Embro K-8
Embrun E-17
Emo, 1331 ..... L-13
Englehart, 1595 ..... M-20
Erin, 11052 ..... I-9
Espanola, 5449 ..... C-6
Essex, 20085 ..... M-4
Exeter J-6
Fenelon Falls G-11
Fergus I-8
Fonthill K-10
Forest K-5
Ft. Erie, 28143 ..... K-11
Ft. Frances, 8315 ..... L-13
Frankford H-13
Gananoque, 5167 ..... H-16
Georgetown J-9
Geraldton K-17
Glencoe L-6
Gloucester E-17
Goderich, 7604 ..... I-6
Gore Bay, 898 ..... D-5
Grand Bend J-6
Grand Valley I-8
Gravenhurst, 10899 ..... F-10
Grimsby, 21297 ..... K-10
Guelph, 106170 ..... J-9
Haileybury, 4543 ..... M-20
Haliburton F-12
Hamilton, 490268 ..... K-9
Hanover, 6869 ..... H-7
Harriston I-7
Harrow N-4
Harrowsmith G-15
Hastings H-13
Havelock G-13
Hawkesbury, 10314 ..... D-19
Hearst, 5825 ..... K-18
Hensall J-6
Hillsburgh I-9
Hornepayne, 1362 ..... L-18
Huntsville, 17338 ..... E-10
Ingersoll, 10977 ..... K-7
Ingleside F-18
Iroquois F-17
Iroquois Falls, 5217 ..... L-20
Kanata E-16
Kapuskasing, 9238 ..... L-19
Keewatin K-13
Kemptville F-17
Kenora, 15838 ..... K-13
Keswick H-10
Kettle Pt. K-5
Killaloe E-14
Kincardine, 11029 ..... H-6
Kingston, 114195 ..... H-15
Kingsville, 19619 ..... N-4
Kirkland Lake, 8616 ..... L-20
Kitchener, 190399 ..... J-8
L'Orignal D-18
Lakefield H-12
Lanark F-16
Lancaster E-19
Lansdowne G-16
LaSalle, 25285 ..... M-3
Leamington, 27138 ..... N-4
Limoges E-18
Lindsay H-11
Listowel I-7
Little Current D-6
London, 336539 ..... K-7
Long Sault F-18
Longlac K-17
Lucan K-6
Lucknow I-6
Madoc, 2044 ..... G-14
Malton G-1
Manitouwadge, 2949 ..... L-17
Manotick E-17
Marathon, 4416 ..... L-17
Markdale H-8
Markham, 208615 ..... I-10
Marmora, 3985 ..... G-13
Massey C-5
Mattawa, 2270 ..... C-11
Maxville E-18
Meaford G-8
Merlin M-5
Merrickville F-17
Metcalfe E-17
Midland, 16214 ..... G-9
Mildmay H-7
Millbrook H-12
Milton, 31471 ..... J-9
Milverton J-7
Minden F-11
Mississauga, 612925 ..... J-10
Mitchell J-7
Morrisburg F-18
Mt. Albert H-10
Mt. Brydges K-6
Mt. Forest I-8
Mt.Pleasant K-8
Nanticoke L-9
Napanee, 15132 ..... H-15
Nepean E-17
New Dundee J-9
New Hamburg J-8
New Liskeard, 4906 ..... M-20
Newburgh G-16
Newmarket, 65788 ..... H-10
Niagara Falls, 78815 ..... K-11
Niagara-on-the-Lake, 13839 ..... K-11
Nipigon, 1964 ..... L-16
Nobleton I-10
N. Bay, 52771 ..... C-10
N. Gower F-17
Norwich, 10478 ..... K-9
Norwood H-13
Oakville, 144738 ..... J-10
Odessa H-15
Oil Sprs., 758 ..... L-5
Omemee H-12
Orangeville, 25248 ..... I-9
Orillia, 29121 ..... G-10
Orléans D-19
Osgoode E-18
Oshawa, 139051 ..... I-11
Ottawa, 774072 ..... E-17
Otterville K-9
Owen Sound, 21431 ..... G-7
Paisley H-7
Palmerston I-7
Paris K-8
Parkhill K-6
Parry Sound, 6124 ..... E-8
Pembroke, 13490 ..... D-14
Penetanguishene, 8316 ..... G-9
Perth, 6003 ..... F-16
Petawawa, 14398 ..... D-14
Peterborough, 71446 ..... H-12
Petrolia, 4849 ..... K-5
Pickering, 87139 ..... I-11
Picton I-14
Plantagenet E-18
Pt. Edward K-5
Port Burwell L-7
Port Carling E-11
Port Colborne, 18450 ..... K-10
Port Credit J-10
Port Elgin G-6
Port Hope I-12
Port McNicoll G-9
Port Perry H-11
Port Rowan L-8
Port Stanley L-7
Powassan, 3252 ..... C-10
Prescott, 4228 ..... G-17
Preston J-8
Rainy River, 981 ..... L-13
Renfrew, 7942 ..... E-15
Richmond E-17
Richmond Hill, 132030 ..... I-10
Ridgetown M-5
Ripley H-6
Rockland E-17
Rockwood J-9
Rodney L-6
Russell, 12412 ..... E-17
St. Catharines, 129170 ..... K-10
St. Clements J-8
St. George K-9
St. Jacobs J-8
St. Mary's, 6293 ..... J-7
St. Thomas, 33236 ..... L-7
Sarnia, 70876 ..... K-5
Sauble Beach G-7
Sault Ste. Marie, 74566 ..... B-1
Schreiber, 1448 ..... L-16
Seaforth J-6
Shakespeare J-8
Sharon H-10
Shelburne, 4122 ..... H-9
Simcoe L-8
Smiths Falls, 9140 ..... F-16
Smithville K-11
Smooth Rock Falls, 1830 ..... L-19
South River, 1040 ..... D-10
Southampton G-6
Spanish C-5
Stayner H-9
Stirling H-15
Stoney Cr. K-9
Stoney Pt. M-4
Stratford, 29676 ..... J-7
Strathroy K-6
Streetsville J-9
Sturgeon Falls C-9
Sudbury, 155219 ..... B-7
Sunderland H-11
Sundridge, 983 ..... D-10
Sutton H-10
Sydenham G-15
Tara G-7
Tavistock J-7
Tecumseh, 25105 ..... M-4
Teeswater I-7
Terrace Bay, 1950 ..... L-17
Thamesford K-7
Thamesville L-5
Thedford K-5
Thessalon, 1386 ..... C-3
Thornbury G-8
Thorold, 18048 ..... K-10
Thunder Bay, 109016 ..... L-15
Tilbury M-4
Tillsonburg, 14052 ..... L-8
Timmins, 43686 ..... L-20
Toronto, 2481494 ..... I-10
Trenton H-13
Tweed, 5612 ..... G-14
Uxbridge, 17377 ..... H-10
Vankleek Hill D-19
Verner B-9
Walkerton H-7
Wallaceburg L-4
Wasaga Beach, 12419 ..... G-9
Waterdown I-19
Waterloo, 86543 ..... J-8
Watford K-5
Waubaushene F-10
Wawa M-18
Welland, 48402 ..... K-10
Wellesley, 9365 ..... J-8
Wellington I-14
W. Lorne L-6
Westport, 647 ..... G-15
Wheatley M-4
Whitby, 87413 ..... I-11
Whitechurch-Stouffville, 22008 ..... I-10
Whitney E-12
Wiarton G-7
Williamstown E-20
Winchester F-17
Windsor, 208402 ..... M-3
Wingham I-7
Winona K-11
Woodstock, 33061 ..... K-8
Woodville H-11
Wyoming K-5
Zurich J-6

Prince Edward Island

Map pp. 254-257

Alberton, 1115 ..... F-9
Borden H-10
Charlottetown, 32245 ..... H-11
Georgetown, 721 ..... H-12
Kensington, 1385 ..... G-10
Montague, 1945 ..... H-11
Mt. Stewart, 312 ..... G-11
Murray Harbour, 357 ..... H-12
Murray River, 435 ..... H-12
O'Leary, 860 ..... G-9
Souris, 1248 ..... G-12
Summerside, 14654 ..... G-10
Tignish, 831 ..... F-9

Québec

Map pp. 250-253

Acton Vale, 7299 ..... L-9
Alma, 25918 ..... G-11
Amos, 13044 ..... F-2
Amqui, 6473 ..... G-16
Asbestos, 6580 ..... L-10
Ayer's Cliff, 1102 ..... N-18
Baie-Comeau, 23079 ..... F-15
Baie-St-Paul, 7290 ..... I-12
Barraute, 2010 ..... G-3
Beauceville, 6261 ..... K-12
Beauharnois, 11464 ..... M-14
Beaupré, 2761 ..... J-12
Bécancour, 11051 ..... K-10
Bedford, 2667 ..... M-9
Bégin, 924 ..... G-11
Berthierville, 3939 ..... K-16
Bic G-15
Black Lake, 4109 ..... L-11
Blainville, 36029 ..... L-8
Bonaventure, 2756 ..... H-19
Brome, 286 ..... M-9
Bromptonville, 5571 ..... M-18
Brownsburg L-13
Cabano, 3213 ..... I-14
Cacouna H-14
Campbell's Bay, 766 ..... L-4
Candiac, 12675 ..... F-13
Cap-Chat, 2913 ..... F-17
Cap-de-la-Madeleine J-17
Cap-St-Ignace, 3204 ..... I-20
Carleton H-18
Causapscal, 2634 ..... G-17
Chandler, 3004 ..... G-20
Charlemagne, 5662 ..... A-14
Charny I-19
Châteauguay, 41003 ..... M-8
Château-Richer, 3442 ..... I-20
Chicoutimi G-12
Chute-aux-Outardes, 1968 ..... F-15
Clermont, 3078 ..... I-13
Coaticook, 8988 ..... N-10
Compton, 3047 ..... M-18
Contrecoeur, 5222 ..... L-9
Cookshire, 1543 ..... M-11
Coteau-du-Lac, 5573 ..... M-14
Cowansville, 12032 ..... M-9
Danville, 4301 ..... L-18
Delisle, 4208 ..... G-11
Desbiens, 1128 ..... G-10
Deschambault, 1263 ..... J-18
Disraëli, 2635 ..... L-11
Donnacona, 5479 ..... J-11
Drummondville, 46599 ..... L-10
Dunham, 3215 ..... N-9
E. Angus, 3570 ..... M-11
E. Broughton, 2367 ..... K-12
Ferme-Neuve, 2947 ..... J-6
Forestville, 3748 ..... F-14
Fort-Coulonge, 1661 ..... L-4
Gaspé, 14932 ..... F-20
Gatineau, 226696 ..... M-5
Girardville, 1285 ..... F-10
Granby, 44121 ..... M-9
Grand-Mére K-9
Grenville, 1315 ..... L-7
Hébertville, 2425 ..... G-11
Hudson, 4796 ..... M-14
Huntingdon, 2666 ..... M-7
Iberville, 9424 ..... M-8
Joliette, 17837 ..... L-8
Jonquiére, 54842 ..... G-11
Kingsey Falls, 2023 ..... L-18
L'Annonciation, 1984 ..... K-6
L'Assomption, 15615 ..... L-8
L'Avenir, 1277 ..... L-17
L'Épiphanie, 4208 ..... L-15
L'Île-Perrot, 9375 ..... M-14
L'Islet, 3866 ..... J-12
L'Isle-Verte, 1519 ..... H-14
La Baie, 19940 ..... G-12
La Doré, 1553 ..... F-9
La Guadeloupe, 1716 ..... L-12
La Malbaie-Pointe-au-Pic I-13
La Pérade J-17
La Pocatiére, 4518 ..... I-13
La Prairie, 18896 ..... F-14
La Sarre, 7728 ..... F-1
La Tuque, 11298 ..... I-9
Lac-à-la-Croix G-11
Lac-au-Saumon, 1539 ..... G-16
Lac-Bouchette, 1370 ..... G-10
Lac-Etchemin, 2276 ..... K-12
Lachute, 11628 ..... L-7
Lac-Mégantic, 5897 ..... M-12
Lacolle, 1503 ..... N-15
Lanoraie K-15
Laurier-Sta., 2376 ..... J-19
Laurierville, 1528 ..... K-18
Laval, 343005 ..... C-12
Lavaltrie, 5967 ..... L-15
Lebel-sur-Quévillon, 3236 ..... E-4
Les Escoumins, 2106 ..... G-14
Les Méchins, 1220 ..... F-17
Lévis, 121999 ..... J-11
Longueuil, 371934 ..... D-14
Louiseville, 7622 ..... K-9
Luceville, 1351 ..... G-15
Lyster, 1685 ..... K-11
Macamic, 1519 ..... F-1
Magog, 14283 ..... M-10
Malartic, 3704 ..... G-2
Maniwaki, 3571 ..... K-5
Mansonville N-17
Marieville, 7240 ..... M-16
Mascouche, 29556 ..... A-13
Maskinongé, 1087 ..... K-16
Matagami, 1939 ..... D-3
Matane, 11635 ..... F-16
Métabetchouan G-11
Mistassini F-10
Montebello, 1039 ..... L-6
Mont-Joli, 5886 ..... G-15
Mont-Laurier, 7365 ..... J-6
Montmagny, 11654 ..... J-12
Mont-Rolland K-14
Montréal, 1812723 ..... M-8
Mont-Tremblant K-7
Morin-Hts., 2575 ..... L-7
Murdochville, 1171 ..... F-19
N. Hatley, 746 ..... M-18
Napierville, 3073 ..... M-15
New Richmond, 3760 ..... G-18
Nicolet, 7928 ..... K-9
Normandin, 3524 ..... F-10
Normétal, 1019 ..... E-1
Notre-Dame-du-Lac, 2152 ..... I-15
Oka, 3194 ..... M-14
Ormstown, 3647 ..... N-14
Outremont D-12
Papineauville, 2247 ..... L-6
Pierrefonds M-14
Pierreville, 950 ..... L-9
Plessisville, 6756 ..... K-11
Pointe-du-Lac K-17
Pont-Rouge, 7146 ..... I-18
Port-Cartier, 6412 ..... D-17
Portneuf, 1436 ..... J-10
Price, 1800 ..... G-15
Princeville, 5703 ..... K-10
Québec, 507986 ..... J-11
Rawdon, 8648 ..... K-15
Repentigny, 54550 ..... L-8
Richmond, 3424 ..... L-10
Rigaud, 6095 ..... M-13
Rimouski, 41549 ..... G-15
Riviére-Bleue, 1477 ..... I-14
Riviére-du-Loup, 17772 ..... H-14
Robertsonville, 1705 ..... K-19
Roberval, 10906 ..... G-10
Rock Island N-18
Rougemont, 2583 ..... M-16
Rouyn-Noranda, 39611 ..... G-1
Roxton Falls, 1300 ..... L-17
Roxton Pond, 3527 ..... M-17
Saguenay, 60008 ..... G-12
Saint-Ambroise, 3463 ..... G-11
Saint-Anselme, 3224 ..... K-12
Saint-Apollinaire, 3930 ..... J-19
Saint-Aubert, 1365 ..... J-13
Saint-Basile [-Sud], 2575 ..... I-18
Saint-Boniface-de Shawinigan, 3998 ..... J-16
Saint-Bruno, 2384 ..... G-11
Saint-Camille-de-Lellis, 907 ..... K-13
Saint-Casimir, 1582 ..... K-10
Saint-Charles-de-Bellechasse, 2237 ..... I-20
Saint-Chrysostome, 2590 ..... N-14
Saint-Constant, 22577 ..... M-15
Saint-Damase, 1327 ..... M-16
Saint-Denis-sur-Richelieu, ... L-16
Saint-Dominique, 2231 ..... L-16
Sainte-Adéle, 9215 ..... L-7
Sainte-Agathe-des-Monts, 7116 ..... L-7
Sainte-Anne-de-Beaupré, 2752 ..... J-12
Sainte-Anne-des-Monts, 6835 ..... F-17
Sainte-Blandine G-15
Sainte-Croix, 1533 ..... K-11
Sainte-Julie, 26580 ..... L-15
Saint-Elzéar, 1769 ..... J-20
Saint-Eustache, 40378 ..... M-8
Saint-Félicien, 10622 ..... G-10
Saint-Félix-de-Valois, 5465 ..... K-15
Saint-Ferréol-les-Neiges, 2014 ..... J-12
Saint-Flavien, 1492 ..... J-19
Saint-Franćois-du-Lac, 1976 ..... K-16
Saint-Gabriel, 2775 ..... G-15
Saint-Gédéon-de-Beauce, 1829 ..... L-12
Saint-Georges J-17
Saint-Georges, 20787 ..... L-12
Saint-Germaine-de-Grantham, 3661 ..... L-17
Saint-Gervais, 1910 ..... J-12
Saint-Gilles, 1803 ..... J-19
Saint-Guillaume Nord J-7
Saint-Honoré-de-Shenley L-20
Saint-Honoré-de-Témiscouata, 804 ..... I-14
Saint-Hubert M-15
Saint-Hyacinthe, 38739 ..... L-9
Saint-Jean-sur-Richelieu, 37386 ..... M-8
Saint-Jérôme, 59614 ..... L-7
Saint-Joseph-de-Beauce, 4487 ..... K-12
Saint-Léonard [-d'Aston], 2231 ..... K-17
Saint-Lin-Laurentides L-14
Saint-Louis-du-Ha! Ha!, 1427 ..... I-14
Saint-Michel-de-Bellechasse, 1633 ..... I-20
Saint-Nicéphore L-10
Saint-Nicolas I-19
Saint-Pacôme, 1706 ..... I-13
Saint-Pamphile, 2847 ..... J-13
Saint-Pascal, 3643 ..... I-13
Saint-Paul-de-Montminy, 853 ..... J-12
Saint-Prime, 2702 ..... G-10
Saint-Raphaël, 2231 ..... J-12
Saint-Raymond, 8836 ..... J-10
Saint-Rémi, 5736 ..... M-8
Saint-Sauveur-des-Monts, 3316 ..... L-14
Saint-Siméon, 984 ..... H-13
Saint-Tite, 3845 ..... J-10
Saint-Victor, 2460 ..... L-12
Saint-Zacharie, 2100 ..... K-20
Saint-Zotique, 4158 ..... M-13
Sainte-Madeleine, 2011 ..... L-16
Sainte-Marie, 11320 ..... K-12
Sainte-Marthe, 1094 ..... M-13
Sainte-Pétronille, 1038 ..... B-3
Sainte-Thécle, 2513 ..... I-17
Sainte-Thérése, 24269 ..... L-14
Sainte-Véronique, 1050 ..... K-6
Salaberry-de-Valleyfield, 26170 ..... M-7
Sawyerville, 836 ..... M-11
Sayabec, 1999 ..... G-16
Senneterre, 3275 ..... G-4
Sept-Îles, 23791 ..... D-17
Shawinigan, 52040 ..... K-9
Shawinigan-Sud J-16
Shawville, 1582 ..... L-4
Sherbrooke, 75916 ..... M-10
Sorel-Tracy L-9
Squatec H-15
Stanstead, 2995 ..... N-10
Sutton, 1631 ..... N-17
Tadoussac, 870 ..... H-13
Terrebonne, 43149 ..... L-15
Thetford Mines, 16628 ..... L-11
Thurso, 2436 ..... L-6
Tracy L-9
Tring-Jonction, 1333 ..... K-20
Trois-Pistoles, 3635 ..... H-14
Trois-Riviéres, 122395 ..... K-9
Valcourt, 2411 ..... M-17
Val-David, 3819 ..... K-14
Val-d'Or, 31430 ..... G-3
Vallée-Jonction, 1882 ..... K-12
Varennes, 19653 ..... L-8
Vaudreuil-Dorion, 19920 ..... M-14
Verchéres, 4782 ..... L-15
Victoriaville, 38841 ..... L-10
Ville-Marie, 2770 ..... H-1
Warwick, 4874 ..... L-10
Waterloo, 3993 ..... M-9
Waterville, 1824 ..... M-18
Weedon, 2646 ..... L-11
Windsor, 5321 ..... M-10
Yamachiche, 2631 ..... K-16

Saskatchewan

Map pp. 242-245

* City keyed to p. 236

Aberdeen, 534 ..... G-6
Allan, 679 ..... H-6
Alsask, 178 ..... H-1
Arborfield, 411 ..... E-9
Arcola, 532 ..... L-10
Asquith, 574 ..... G-5
Assiniboia, 2483 ..... L-6
Avonlea, 412 ..... K-7
Balcarres, 622 ..... J-9
Balgonie, 1239 ..... J-8
Battleford, 3820 ..... F-4
Beauval, 843 ..... A-5
Bengough, 401 ..... M-7
Bienfait, 786 ..... M-10
Big River, 741 ..... D-5
Biggar, 2243 ..... G-4
Birch Hills, 957 ..... F-7
Blaine Lake, 508 ..... F-5
Bredenbury, 354 ..... J-11
Broadview, 669 ..... K-10
Bruno, 571 ..... G-7
Burstall, 388 ..... J-1
Cabri, 483 ..... J-3
Canora, 2200 ..... H-11
Carlyle, 1260 ..... L-11
Carnduff, 1017 ..... M-11
Carrot River, 1017 ..... E-9
Central Butte, 439 ..... J-5
Choiceland, 370 ..... E-8
Churchbridge, 796 ..... J-11
Coleville, 313 ..... H-2
Colonsay, 426 ..... H-6
Coronach, 822 ..... M-6
Craik, 418 ..... I-6
Creighton, 1556 ..... B-11
Cudworth, 766 ..... G-7
Cumberland House, 632 ..... D-11
Cupar, 602 ..... J-8
Cut Knife, 556 ..... F-3
Dalmeny, 1610 ..... G-5
Davidson, 1035 ..... I-6
Delisle, 884 ..... G-5
Denare Beach, 784 ..... B-11
Duck Lake, 624 ..... F-6
Dundurn, 596 ..... H-6
Eastend, 576 ..... L-2
Eatonia, 474 ..... I-2
Edam, 429 ..... E-3
Elrose, 517 ..... I-4
Esterhazy, 2348 ..... J-11
Estevan, 10242 ..... M-10
Eston, 1048 ..... I-3
Foam Lake, 1218 ..... H-9
Ft. Qu'Appelle, 1940 ..... J-9
Frontier, 302 ..... M-3
Glaslyn, 375 ..... E-4
Gravelbourg, 1187 ..... L-5
Green Lake, 498 ..... C-4
Grenfell, 1067 ..... K-10
Gull Lake, 1016 ..... K-3
Hafford, 401 ..... F-5
Hague, 711 ..... F-6
Hanley, 495 ..... H-6
Hepburn, 475 ..... F-5
Herbert, 812 ..... J-5
Hudson Bay, 1783 ..... F-11
Humboldt, 5161 ..... G-7
Indian Head, 1758 ..... J-9
Ituna, 709 ..... I-9
Kamsack, 2009 ..... H-11
Kelvington, 1007 ..... G-9
Kerrobert, 1111 ..... G-2
Kindersley, 4548 ..... H-2
Kinistino, 702 ..... F-8
Kipling, 1037 ..... K-10
Kyle, 478 ..... J-4
La Loche, 2136 ..... *F-5
La Ronge, 2727 ..... A-7
Lafleche, 446 ..... L-5
Lampman, 650 ..... M-10
Langenburg, 1107 ..... J-11
Langham, 1145 ..... G-5
Lanigan, 1289 ..... H-7
Lashburn, 783 ..... E-2
Leader, 914 ..... I-2
Leask, 447 ..... E-6
Lemberg, 306 ..... J-10
Leroy, 413 ..... H-8
Lloydminster, 7840 ..... E-2
Lumsden, 1581 ..... J-7
Luseland, 602 ..... G-2
Macklin, 1330 ..... F-2
Maidstone, 995 ..... E-3
Maple Cr., 2270 ..... K-2
Marshall, 633 ..... E-2
Martensville, 4365 ..... G-5
Meadow Lake, 4582 ..... C-4
Melfort, 5559 ..... F-8
Melville, 4453 ..... J-10
Midale, 496 ..... M-9
Milestone, 542 ..... K-8
Montmartre, 465 ..... K-9
Moose Jaw, 32131 ..... K-7
Moosomin, 2361 ..... K-11
Mossbank, 379 ..... K-6
Naicam, 761 ..... G-8
Nipawin, 4275 ..... E-9
Nokomis, 436 ..... H-7
Norquay, 485 ..... H-11
N. Battleford, 13692 ..... F-4
Osler, 823 ..... G-6
Outlook, 2129 ..... H-5
Oxbow, 1132 ..... M-11
Paradise Hill, 486 ..... D-3
Pelican Narrows, 690 ..... A-10
Pense, 533 ..... K-7
Pierceland, 449 ..... B-2
Pilot Butte, 1850 ..... J-8
Ponteix, 550 ..... L-4
Porcupine Plain, 820 ..... F-10
Preeceville, 1074 ..... H-10
Prince Albert, 34291 ..... E-7
Qu'Appelle, 648 ..... J-9
Quill Lake, 439 ..... G-8
Radisson, 401 ..... F-5
Radville, 735 ..... M-8
Raymore, 625 ..... I-8
Redvers, 917 ..... L-11
Regina, 178225 ..... K-8
Regina Beach, 1039 ..... J-7
Rocanville, 887 ..... K-11
Rockglen, 450 ..... M-6
Rose Valley, 395 ..... G-9
Rosetown, 2471 ..... H-4
Rosthern, 1504 ..... F-6
Rouleau, 434 ..... K-7
St. Louis, 474 ..... F-7
St. Walburg, 672 ..... D-3
Saltcoats, 494 ..... I-11
Saskatoon, 196811 ..... G-5
Shaunavon, 1775 ..... L-3
Shellbrook, 1276 ..... E-6
Southey, 693 ..... J-8
Spiritwood, 907 ..... E-5
Springside, 525 ..... I-10
Star City, 482 ..... F-8
Stoughton, 720 ..... L-10
Strasbourg, 760 ..... I-7
Sturgis, 627 ..... H-10
Swift Current, 14821 ..... K-4
Theodore, 381 ..... I-10
Tisdale, 3063 ..... F-9
Turtleford, 465 ..... D-3
Unity, 2243 ..... F-3
Wadena, 1412 ..... H-9
Wakaw, 884 ..... F-7
Waldheim, 889 ..... F-6
Wapella, 354 ..... K-11
Warman, 3481 ..... G-6
Watrous, 1808 ..... H-7
Watson, 794 ..... G-8
Wawota, 538 ..... L-11
Weyburn, 9534 ..... L-9
White Fox, 436 ..... E-9
Whitewood, 947 ..... K-11
Wilkie, 1282 ..... F-3
Willow Bunch, 395 ..... M-6
Wolseley, 766 ..... K-9
Wynyard, 1919 ..... H-8
Yellow Grass, 422 ..... L-8
Yorkton, 15107 ..... I-10

Yukon Territory

Map p. 236

Dawson, 1251 ..... B-2
Haines Jct., 531 ..... C-2
Ross River, 337 ..... C-2
Watson Lake, 912 ..... D-2
Whitehorse, 19058 ..... C-2

MEXICO Cities and Towns

Mexico

Map pp. 258-259

Acámbaro, 55516 ..... G-8
Acaponeta, 18145 ..... F-5
Acapulco, 620656 ..... I-8
Acatlán, 14976 ..... H-9
Acayucan, 47826 ..... H-10
Agua Prieta, 60420 ..... B-4
Aguascalientes, 594092 ..... G-7
Aguililla, 9179 ..... H-7
Álamos, 8034 ..... D-4
Aldama, 15481 ..... C-5
Allende, 18679 ..... D-7
Alvarado, 22608 ..... H-10
Ameca, 34703 ..... G-6
Amecameca, 29949 ..... H-8
Apan, 25119 ..... H-9
Apatzingán de la Constitución, 93756 ..... H-7
Arandas, 39478 ..... G-7
Arcelia, 16114 ..... H-8
Ario de Rosales, 14209 ..... H-7
Arriaga, 23154 ..... I-11
Atlixco, 82838 ..... H-9
Atoyac, 19514 ..... I-8
Autlán de Navarro, 39310 ..... H-6
Becal, 6401 ..... G-12
Buenaventura, 5678 ..... C-5
Cárdenas San Luis Potosí, 14738 ..... F-8
Cárdenas Tabasco, 78637 ..... H-11
Caborca, 49917 ..... B-3
Cadereyta, 55468 ..... E-8
Campeche, 190813 ..... G-12
Cananea, 30515 ..... B-4
Cancún, 397191 ..... G-14
Castaños, 19794 ..... D-7
Celaya, 277750 ..... G-8
Cerralvo, 8173 ..... E-8
Cerritos, 12932 ..... F-8
Champotón, 23035 ..... H-12
Chetumal, 121602 ..... H-13
Chiapa de Corzo, 29341 ..... I-11
Chihuahua, 657876 ..... C-5
Chilapa de Alvarez, 22511 ..... I-8
Chilpancingo de los Bravos, 142746 ..... I-8
China, 8918 ..... E-8
Cholula, 70715 ..... H-9
Cihuatlán, 15697 ..... H-6
Cintalapa, 32745 ..... I-11
Ciudad Acuña, 108159 ..... C-7
Ciudad Altamirano, 23336 ..... H-8
Ciudad Anáhuac, 15976 ..... D-8
Ciudad Camargo, 37456 ..... D-6
Ciudad del Carmen, 126024 ..... H-12
Ciudad de México, 8605239 ..... H-8
Ciudad Guzmán, 85118 ..... H-6
Ciudad Hidalgo, 54854 ..... H-8
Ciudad Juárez, 1187275 ..... B-5
Ciudad Lerdo, 58862 ..... E-6
Ciudad Madero, 182325 ..... F-9
Ciudad Mante, 80533 ..... F-8
Ciudad Netzahualcóyotl, 1225083 ..... I-3
Ciudad Obregón, 250790 ..... D-4
Ciudad Valles, 105721 ..... G-8
Ciudad Victoria, 249029 ..... F-8
Coatzacoalcos, 225973 ..... H-10
Cocula, 13715 ..... G-6
Colima, 119639 ..... H-6
Comitán de Domínguez, 70311 ..... I-12
Compostela, 15797 ..... G-6
Concepción del Oro, 6475 ..... E-7
Córdoba, 133807 ..... H-9
Cosamaloapan, 28496 ..... H-10
Cozumel, 59225 ..... G-14
Cuatrociénegas, 8907 ..... D-7
Cuauhtémoc, 85387 ..... C-5
Cuautla, 136932 ..... H-8
Cuernavaca, 327162 ..... H-8
Culiacán, 540823 ..... E-5
Delicias, 98615 ..... D-6
Durango, 427135 ..... F-6
Ebano, 22133 ..... F-9
Ejutla, 7699 ..... I-9
El Dorado, 13575 ..... E-5
El Fuerte, 10728 ..... D-4
El Salto, 19210 ..... F-6
Emiliano Zapata, 17246 ..... H-12
Empalme, 38533 ..... D-3
Ensenada, 223492 ..... A-1
Escárcega, 25911 ..... H-12
Escuinapa de Hidalgo, 27914 ..... F-5
Felipe Carrillo Puerto, 18545 ..... G-13
Fresnillo, 97023 ..... F-7
Frontera, 20965 ..... H-11
Gomez Palacio, 210113 ..... E-6
Guadalajara, 1646183 ..... G-6
Guadalupe, 78879 ..... F-7
Guamúchil, 57547 ..... E-4
Guanajuato, 74874 ..... G-7
Guasave, 62801 ..... E-4
Guaymas, 97593 ..... D-3
Hecelchakán, 9427 ..... G-12
Hermosillo, 545928 ..... C-3
Hidalgo del Parral, 98876 ..... D-5
Huajuapan de León, 43073 ..... H-9
Huatabampo, 29789 ..... D-4
Huauchinango, 46671 ..... G-9
Huetamo, 21335 ..... H-7
Huixtla, 26990 ..... J-11
Iguala, 104759 ..... H-8
Irapuato, 319148 ..... G-7
Isla, 24036 ..... H-10
Ixtlán del Río, 21157 ..... G-6
Izúcar de Matamoros, 39693 ..... H-9
Jalpa, 13586 ..... G-7
Jerez, 37558 ..... F-7
Jiménez, 31195 ..... D-6
Juan Aldama, 14058 ..... E-6
Juchitán, 64642 ..... I-10
La Paz, 162954 ..... E-3
La Piedad Cavadas, 70703 ..... G-7
Lagos de Moreno, 79592 ..... G-7
León, 1020818 ..... G-7
Linares, 53681 ..... E-8
Los Mochis, 200906 ..... E-4
Los Reyes de Salgado, 36095 ..... H-7
Madera, 14810 ..... C-4
Magdalena, 22023 ..... B-3
Manzanillo, 94893 ..... H-6
Mapastepec, 14836 ..... J-11
Martínez de la Torre, 49565 ..... G-9
Matamoros Coahuila, 44053 ..... E-6
Matamoros Tamaulipas, 376279 ..... E-9
Matehuala, 64206 ..... F-8
Matías Romero, 19979 ..... I-10
Mazatlán, 327989 ..... F-5
Melchor Muzquiz, 32094 ..... D-7
Meoqui, 19498 ..... D-5
Mérida, 662530 ..... G-13
Mexicali, 549873 ..... A-2
Mexico City, 8605239 ..... H-8
Miahuatlán, 16724 ..... I-9
Miguel Auza, 12592 ..... E-6
Minatitlán, 109193 ..... H-10
Mocorito, 5093 ..... E-4
Monclova, 192554 ..... D-7
Montemorelos, 37713 ..... E-8
Monterrey, 1110909 ..... E-8
Morelia, 549996 ..... H-7
Moroleón, 40512 ..... G-7
Motul, 19868 ..... G-13
Nacozari de García, 11193 ..... B-4
Nava, 17730 ..... C-8
Navojoa, 98187 ..... D-4
Navolato, 26095 ..... E-4
Nogales, 156854 ..... B-3
Nueva Rosita, 36974 ..... D-7
Nuevo Casas Grandes, 50378 ..... B-5
Nuevo Laredo, 308828 ..... D-8
Oaxaca, 251846 ..... I-9
Ocotlán Jalisco, 75942 ..... G-7
Ocotlán Oaxaca, 12583 ..... I-9
Ojinaga, 20371 ..... C-6
Ometepec, 16933 ..... I-9
Orizaba, 118552 ..... H-9
Pachuca, 231602 ..... G-8
Papantla de Olarte, 48804 ..... G-9
Paraíso, 22085 ..... H-11
Parras, 31032 ..... E-7
Pátzcuaro, 47993 ..... H-7
Pénjamo, 32035 ..... G-7
Perote, 30848 ..... H-9
Petatlán, 20012 ..... I-7
Peto, 16572 ..... G-13
Piedras Negras, 126386 ..... C-8
Pijijiapan, 13931 ..... I-11
Poza Rica, 151441 ..... G-9
Progreso, 44354 ..... G-13
Puebla, 1271673 ..... H-9
Puerto Peñasco, 30466 ..... B-2
Puerto Vallarta, 151432 ..... G-6
Querétaro, 536463 ..... G-8
Reynosa, 403718 ..... E-9
Rincón de Romos, 22570 ..... F-7
Ríoverde, 46691 ..... G-8
Río Grande, 29214 ..... F-7
Rosario, 13998 ..... F-5
Sabinas, 47578 ..... D-7
Sabinas Hidalgo, 30910 ..... D-8
Sahuayo de Morelos, 57827 ..... G-7
Salamanca, 137000 ..... G-7
Salina Cruz, 72218 ..... I-10
Saltillo, 562587 ..... E-7
Salvatierra, 34066 ..... G-7
San Andrés Tuxtla, 54853 ..... H-10
San Blas, 8812 ..... G-5
San Buenaventura, 17904 ..... D-7
San Cristóbal, 112442 ..... I-11
San Felipe, 24935 ..... G-7
San Fernando, 27053 ..... E-9
San Francisco del Oro, 5175 ..... D-5
San Juan del Río, 99483 ..... G-8
San Luis Potosí, 629208 ..... F-7
San Luis Río Colorado, 126645 ..... A-2
San Pedro Pochutla, 12404 ..... I-10
Santa Ana, 9689 ..... B-3
Santa Bárbara, 9943 ..... D-5
Santa Rosalía, 10609 ..... D-3
Santiago Ixcuintla, 17950 ..... G-6
Santiago Papasquiaro, 22571 ..... E-5
Santiago Pinotepa Nacional, 24347 ..... I-9
Santo Domingo Tehuantepec, 37068 ..... I-10
Saucillo, 9754 ..... D-6
Sayula, 24051 ..... H-6
Silao, 61661 ..... G-7
Sombrerete, 18668 ..... F-6
Tacámbaro, 20517 ..... H-7
Tamazunchale, 20699 ..... G-9
Tamiahua, 5153 ..... G-9
Tampico, 295442 ..... F-9
Tantoyuca, 25492 ..... G-9
Tapachula, 179839 ..... J-11
Taxco, 50488 ..... H-8
Tecalitlán, 12828 ..... H-6
Tecate, 52394 ..... A-1
Tecolotlán, 8174 ..... G-6
Tecomán, 74106 ..... H-6
Tecpan de Galeana, 13924 ..... I-8
Tecuala, 14584 ..... F-5
Tehuacán, 204598 ..... H-9
Tempoal, 12291 ..... G-9
Teocaltiche, 21518 ..... G-7
Tepatitlán, 74262 ..... G-7
Tepic, 265817 ..... G-6
Tequila, 24024 ..... G-6
Teziutlán, 56029 ..... H-9
Tiacolula de Matamoros, 11087 ..... I-10
Ticul, 28502 ..... G-13
Tierra Blanca, 44565 ..... H-10
Tihuatlán, 11791 ..... G-9
Tijuana, 1148681 ..... A-1
Tizimín, 39525 ..... G-13
Tlalnepantla, 714735 ..... G-2
Toluca, 435125 ..... H-8
Tonalá, 31212 ..... I-11
Torreón, 502964 ..... E-6
Tulancingo, 94637 ..... G-9
Tuxpan Nayarit, 22248 ..... G-5
Tuxpan Veracruz, 74527 ..... G-9
Tuxtepec, 84199 ..... H-10
Tuxtla Gutiérrez, 424579 ..... I-11
Uruapan del Progreso, 225816 ..... H-7
Valladolid, 37332 ..... G-13
Valle Hermoso, 43018 ..... E-9
Valparaíso, 10468 ..... F-6
Venustiano Carranza, 13906 ..... I-11
Veracruz, 411582 ..... H-10
Villa Unión, 13140 ..... F-5
Villahermosa, 330846 ..... H-11
Villanueva, 11057 ..... F-7
Xalapa, 373076 ..... H-9
Zacapu, 49086 ..... H-7
Zacatecas, 113947 ..... F-7
Zacoalco, 15648 ..... G-6
Zacualtipán, 16216 ..... G-8
Zamora, 122881 ..... H-7
Zihuatanejo, 56853 ..... I-7

	Acapulco, GR	Albany, NY	Albuquerque, NM	Amarillo, TX	Anchorage, AK	Atlanta, GA	Baltimore, MD	Bangor, ME	Billings, MT	Birmingham, AL	Bismarck, ND	Boise, ID	Boston, MA	Brownsville, TX	Buffalo, NY	Cabo San Lucas, BS	Cairo, IL	Calgary, AB	Cancún, QR	Casper, WY	Charleston, SC	Charleston, WV	Charlotte, NC	Cheyenne, WY	Chicago, IL	Chihuahua, CI	Cincinnati, OH	Cleveland, OH	Columbus, OH	Concord, NH	Dallas, TX	Davenport, IA	Daytona Beach, FL	Denver, CO	Des Moines, IA
Acapulco, GR		2944	1589	1500	5192	1980	2636	3299	2470	1854	2520	2529	3036	828	2740	2926	1967	3021	1254	2195	2296	2415	2224	2015	2297	1083	2302	2554	2413	3114	1364	2238	2146	1930	2047
Albany, NY	2944		2081	1796	4492	1006	337	399	2075	1091	1662	2507	164	2116	295	3862	1088	2460	3592	1910	896	664	768	1773	820	2391	727	478	617	149	1674	969	1162	1816	1138
Albuquerque, NM	1589	2081		285	3716	1404	1926	2480	994	1256	1140	944	2245	993	1792	1781	1098	1545	2405	719	1725	1555	1630	539	1343	506	1399	1606	1465	2225	647	1146	1736	439	977
Amarillo, TX	1500	1796	285		3692	1119	1641	2195	970	971	948	1245	1960	790	1507	2066	813	1521	2244	695	1440	1270	1345	515	1058	621	1114	1321	1180	1940	362	967	1451	430	798
Anchorage, AK	5192	4492	3716	3692		4389	4377	4545	2722	4337	2834	2805	4656	4482	4203	4599	4021	2171	5936	2997	4581	4156	4441	3177	3663	4222	3963	4013	4020	4497	4150	3614	4823	3277	3499
Atlanta, GA	1980	1006	1404	1119	4389		674	1361	1831	149	1559	2179	1098	1152	896	3122	418	2357	2628	1582	321	503	244	1445	713	1513	464	716	575	1176	794	786	434	1419	899
Baltimore, MD	2636	337	1926	1641	4377	674		639	1960	783	1547	2392	404	1808	378	3707	843	2345	3284	1795	563	369	436	1658	705	2083	523	380	416	454	1366	854	829	1696	1023
Bangor, ME	3299	399	2480	2195	4545	1361	639		2474	1446	2061	2906	249	2471	694	4261	1493	2565	3947	2309	1198	1019	1071	2172	1219	2746	1126	877	1016	228	2029	1368	1464	2215	1537
Billings, MT	2470	2075	994	970	2722	1831	1960	2474		1779	417	620	2239	1760	1786	2315	1426	551	3214	275	2136	1739	1996	455	1246	1500	1546	1596	1603	2219	1428	1112	2265	555	943
Birmingham, AL	1854	1091	1256	971	4337	149	783	1446	1779		1507	2127	1183	1026	905	2977	366	2305	2502	1530	470	570	393	1393	661	1368	467	719	578	1261	649	734	556	1339	847
Bismarck, ND	2520	1662	1140	948	2834	1559	1547	2061	417	1507		1039	1826	1703	1373	2734	1191	802	3157	522	1751	1326	1611	601	833	1646	1133	1183	1190	1806	1168	784	1993	701	669
Boise, ID	2529	2507	944	1245	2805	2179	2392	2906	620	2127	1039		2671	2035	2218	1980	1774	755	3345	703	2484	2134	2344	735	1702	1446	1958	2028	2024	2651	1703	1536	2613	830	1367
Boston, MA	3036	164	2245	1960	4656	1098	404	249	2239	1183	1826	2671		2208	459	4026	1230	2624	3684	2074	963	756	836	1937	984	2483	891	642	781	73	1766	1133	1229	1980	1302
Brownsville, TX	828	2116	993	790	4482	1152	1808	2471	1760	1026	1703	2035	2208		1849	2529	1076	2311	1476	1485	1468	1524	1396	1305	1480	681	1411	1663	1522	2286	547	1421	1318	1220	1230
Buffalo, NY	2740	295	1792	1507	4203	896	378	694	1786	905	1373	2218	459	1849		3573	799	2171	3325	1621	864	439	658	1484	531	2093	438	189	328	439	1376	680	1130	1527	849
Cabo San Lucas, BS	2926	3862	1781	2066	4599	3122	3707	4261	2315	2977	2734	1980	4026	2529	3573		2879	2632	3726	2145	3443	3336	3366	2177	3106	1859	3180	3387	3246	4006	2326	2940	3405	2097	2771
Cairo, IL	1967	1088	1098	813	4021	418	843	1493	1426	366	1191	1774	1230	1076	799	2879		1977	2552	1177	723	474	583	1040	375	1320	361	613	472	1308	603	407	852	1014	494
Calgary, AB	3021	2460	1545	1521	2171	2357	2345	2565	551	2305	802	755	2624	2311	2171	2632	1977		3765	826	2549	2124	2409	1006	1631	2051	1931	1981	1988	2517	1979	1582	2791	1106	1467
Cancún, QR	1254	3592	2405	2244	5936	2628	3284	3947	3214	2502	3157	3345	3684	1476	3325	3726	2552	3765		2939	2944	3000	2872	2759	2934	1899	2887	3139	2998	3762	2001	2875	2794	2674	2684
Casper, WY	2195	1910	719	695	2997	1582	1795	2309	275	1530	522	703	2074	1485	1621	2145	1177	826	2939		1887	1537	1747	180	1105	1225	1361	1431	1427	2054	1153	939	2016	280	770
Charleston, SC	2296	896	1725	1440	4581	321	563	1198	2136	470	1751	2484	963	1468	864	3443	723	2549	2944	1887		471	208	1750	911	1834	619	721	638	1013	1115	1038	329	1724	1207
Charleston, WV	2415	664	1555	1270	4156	503	369	1019	1739	570	1326	2134	756	1524	439	3336	474	2124	3000	1537	471		265	1400	486	1768	193	250	167	834	1051	613	737	1374	782
Charlotte, NC	2224	768	1630	1345	4441	244	436	1071	1996	393	1611	2344	836	1396	658	3366	583	2409	2872	1747	208	265		1610	771	1757	479	515	432	886	1038	898	474	1584	1067
Cheyenne, WY	2015	1773	539	515	3177	1445	1658	2172	455	1393	601	735	1937	1305	1484	2177	1040	1006	2759	180	1750	1400	1610		968	1045	1224	1294	1290	1917	973	802	1879	100	633
Chicago, IL	2297	820	1343	1058	3663	713	705	1219	1246	661	833	1702	984	1480	531	3106	375	1631	2934	1105	911	486	771	968		1594	293	341	350	964	933	175	1147	1011	333
Chihuahua, CI	1083	2391	506	621	4222	1513	2083	2746	1500	1368	1646	1446	2483	681	2093	1859	1320	2051	1899	1225	1834	1768	1757	1045	1594		1655	1907	1766	2561	717	1503	1763	945	1334
Cincinnati, OH	2302	727	1399	1114	3963	464	523	1126	1546	467	1133	1958	891	1411	438	3180	361	1931	2887	1361	619	193	479	1224	293	1655		252	111	871	938	420	885	1211	589
Cleveland, OH	2554	478	1606	1321	4013	716	380	877	1596	719	1183	2028	642	1663	189	3387	613	1981	3139	1431	721	250	515	1294	341	1907	252		142	622	1190	490	987	1337	659
Columbus, OH	2413	617	1465	1180	4020	575	416	1016	1603	578	1190	2024	781	1522	328	3246	472	1988	2998	1427	638	167	432	1290	350	1766	111	142		761	1049	486	904	1277	655
Concord, NH	3114	149	2225	1940	4497	1176	454	228	2219	1261	1806	2651	73	2286	439	4006	1308	2517	3762	2054	1013	834	886	1917	964	2561	871	622	761		1844	1113	1279	1960	1282
Dallas, TX	1364	1674	647	362	4150	794	1366	2029	1428	649	1168	1703	1766	547	1376	2326	603	1979	2001	1153	1115	1051	1038	973	933	717	938	1190	1049	1844		852	1089	882	683
Davenport, IA	2238	969	1146	967	3614	786	854	1368	1112	734	784	1536	1133	1421	680	2940	407	1582	2875	939	1038	613	898	802	175	1503	420	490	486	1113	852		1220	845	167
Daytona Beach, FL	2146	1162	1736	1451	4823	434	829	1464	2265	556	1993	2613	1229	1318	1130	3405	852	2791	2794	2016	329	737	474	1879	1147	1763	885	987	904	1279	1089	1220		1853	1333
Denver, CO	1930	1816	439	430	3277	1419	1696	2215	555	1339	701	830	1980	1220	1527	2097	1014	1106	2674	280	1724	1374	1584	100	1011	945	1211	1337	1277	1960	882	845	1853		676
Des Moines, IA	2047	1138	977	798	3499	899	1023	1537	943	847	669	1367	1302	1230	849	2771	494	1467	2684	770	1207	782	1067	633	333	1334	589	659	655	1282	683	167	1333	676	
Detroit, MI	2564	648	1586	1301	3950	726	533	1047	1533	729	1120	1965	812	1673	359	3369	623	1918	3149	1368	839	368	633	1231	278	1837	262	169	202	792	1200	427	1105	1274	596
Dodge City, KS	1685	1629	463	246	3654	1120	1432	2028	932	972	752	1207	1793	997	1340	2244	677	1483	2451	657	1441	1110	1258	477	873	867	947	1154	1013	1773	462	707	1526	386	538
Duluth, MN	2446	1293	1376	1197	3201	1190	1178	1692	861	1138	448	1483	1457	1629	1004	3170	811	1169	3083	1002	1382	957	1242	1032	464	1733	764	814	821	1437	1082	420	1624	1075	397
Durango, CO	1801	2194	212	497	3434	1616	1989	2593	828	1468	1080	734	2358	1205	1905	1812	1310	1263	2617	553	1937	1667	1842	479	1389	718	1504	1715	1570	2338	859	1223	1948	379	1054
Edmonton, AB	3194	2495	1718	1694	1998	2392	2380	2548	724	2340	837	928	2659	2484	2206	2805	2024	173	3938	999	2584	2159	2444	1179	1666	2224	1966	2016	2023	2500	2152	1617	2826	1279	1502
El Paso, TX	1322	2307	267	432	3983	1429	1999	2662	1261	1284	1407	1207	2399	836	1939	1693	1236	1812	2138	986	1750	1684	1673	806	1490	239	1571	1753	1612	2477	633	1293	1712	706	1124
Ely, NV	2181	2450	821	1106	3186	2122	2335	2849	758	2017	1177	386	2614	1807	2161	1593	1717	1075	2997	646	2427	2077	2287	678	1645	1098	1901	1971	1967	2594	1468	1479	2556	678	1310
Eureka, CA	2670	3079	1370	1655	2904	2751	2964	3478	1305	2626	1724	677	3243	2296	2790	1796	2346	1209	3486	1275	3056	2706	2916	1307	2274	1587	2530	2600	2596	3223	2017	2108	3106	1402	1939
Fargo, ND	2437	1472	1314	1011	3024	1369	1357	1871	607	1317	194	1229	1636	1620	1183	2924	1003	992	3074	712	1561	1136	1421	791	643	1673	943	993	1000	1616	1085	594	1803	876	479
Flagstaff, AZ	1782	2408	327	612	3559	1731	2253	2807	1071	1583	1467	859	2572	1320	2119	1454	1425	1388	2598	822	2052	1882	1957	866	1670	699	1726	1933	1792	2552	974	1473	2063	766	1304
Fresno, CA	2231	2959	922	1207	3238	2326	2848	3358	1258	2178	1677	723	3123	1857	2670	1357	2020	1575	3047	1193	2647	2477	2552	1225	2154	1148	2321	2480	2387	3103	1569	1988	2658	1145	1819
Gallup, NM	1703	2220	139	424	3526	1543	2065	2619	1133	1395	1279	826	2384	1132	1931	1642	1237	1355	2519	858	1864	1694	1769	678	1482	620	1538	1745	1604	2364	786	1285	1875	578	1116
Gaspé, QC	3696	783	2718	2433	4810	1789	1119	514	2666	1874	2253	3098	761	2805	969	4502	1755	2830	4281	2501	1678	1402	1551	2364	1411	2969	1394	1152	1291	739	2332	1560	1944	2407	1729
Grand Junction, CO	1971	2060	382	674	3325	1665	1942	2459	664	1585	945	625	2224	1375	1771	1853	1260	1154	2787	389	1970	1620	1830	344	1255	888	1457	1581	1523	2204	1128	1089	2099	246	920
Grants Pass, OR	2738	2976	1352	1637	2736	2648	2861	3375	1137	2608	1556	509	3140	2364	2687	1864	2243	1041	3554	1172	2953	2603	2813	1204	2171	1655	2427	2497	2493	3120	1999	2005	3082	1299	1836
Great Falls, MT	2692	2207	1216	1192	2499	2053	2092	2606	222	2001	549	581	2371	1982	1918	2337	1648	328	3436	497	2296	1871	2156	677	1378	1722	1678	1728	1735	2351	1650	1329	2487	777	1165
Green Bay, WI	2497	1038	1448	1258	3544	929	923	1437	1127	877	714	1749	1202	1680	749	3242	582	1512	3134	1074	1127	702	987	1104	209	1794	509	559	566	1182	1133	331	1363	1147	469
Guadalajara, JA	518	2710	1197	1167	4913	1746	2402	3065	2191	1620	2187	2137	2802	628	2407	2366	1634	2742	1358	1916	2062	2082	1990	1736	1964	691	1969	2221	2080	2880	1031	1883	1912	1636	1714
Halifax, NS	3763	863	2944	2659	5023	1825	1103	466	2879	1910	2466	3311	713	2935	1158	4725	1957	3043	4411	2714	1662	1483	1535	2577	1624	3210	1590	1341	1480	692	2493	1773	1928	2620	1942
Houston, TX	1183	1761	890	605	4397	797	1453	2116	1675	671	1415	1950	1853	355	1495	2446	722	2226	1831	1400	1113	1170	1041	1220	1089	804	1057	1309	1168	1931	247	1117	963	1035	948
Idaho Falls, ID	2403	2290	818	1028	2826	1962	2175	2689	338	1910	757	282	2454	1818	2001	1977	1557	655	3219	377	2267	1917	2127	518	1485	1320	1741	1811	1807	2434	1486	1319	2396	613	1150
Indianapolis, IN	2246	789	1292	1007	3851	528	592	1188	1434	476	1021	1851	953	1379	500	3073	311	1819	2883	1254	728	303	588	1117	181	1543	110	314	173	933	882	313	962	1104	482
International Falls, MN	2588	1457	1518	1339	3075	1354	1342	1856	863	1302	450	1485	1621	1771	1168	3180	975	1095	3225	968	1546	1121	1406	1047	628	1875	928	978	985	1601	1224	654	1788	1132	539
Jackson, MS	1625	1331	1055	770	4283	386	1023	1686	1688	241	1453	2047	1423	797	1130	2736	380	2239	2273	1497	707	810	630	1317	747	1127	692	944	803	1501	408	760	681	1226	828
Jacksonville, FL	2058	1072	1648	1363	4735	346	739	1374	2177	468	1905	2525	1139	1230	1040	3317	764	2703	2706	1928	239	647	384	1791	1059	1675	795	897	814	1189	1001	1132	90	1765	1245
Juneau, AK	4614	3914	3138	3114	865	3811	3799	3967	2144	3759	2256	2227	4078	3904	3625	4021	3443	1593	5358	2419	4003	3578	3863	2599	3085	3644	3385	3435	3442	3919	3572	3036	4245	2699	2921
Kansas City, MO	1853	1285	783	604	3619	811	1088	1684	1024	759	789	1372	1449	1036	996	2564	406	1575	2490	775	1116	766	976	638	529	1140	603	810	669	1429	489	363	1245	608	194
Knoxville, TN	2110	834	1400	1115	4212	216	526	1189	1766	257	1382	2114	926	1282	706	3181	353	2180	2758	1517	370	313	230	1380	542	1557	250	502	361	1004	840	669	636	1354	838
La Crosse, WI	2342	1107	1250	1071	3422	1004	992	1506	954	952	592	1576	1271	1525	818	3044	625	1390	2979	876	1196	771	1056	906	278	1607	578	628	635	1251	956	196	1438	949	271
Laredo, TX	937	2106	776	660	4352	1142	1798	2461	1630	1016	1583	1720	2198	203	1803	2295	1030	2181	1640	1355	1458	1478	1386	1175	1360	608	1365	1617	1476	2276	427	1279	1308	1090	1110
Las Vegas, NV	1936	2563	576	861	3455	1980	2445	2962	967	1832	1386	632	2727	1562	2274	1350	1674	1284	2752	797	2301	2123	2206	829	1758	853	1960	2084	2026	2707	1223	1592	2312	749	1423
Lexington, KY	2238	807	1378	1093	4042	387	546	1196	1609	403	1212	1957	933	1347	518	3159	297	2010	2823	1360	542	177	402	1223	372	1591	80	332	191	1011	874	496	808	1197	665
Lincoln, NE	1993	1332	814	597	3494	1002	1217	1731	856	950	664	1178	1496	1176	1043	2582	597	1407	2630	581	1307	957	1167	444	527	1229	783	853	849	1476	641	361	1436	487	192
Little Rock, AR	1679	1359	881	596	4002	529	1051	1714	1407	381	1172	1785	1451	788	1061	2641	288	1958	2264	1235	850	736	755	1055	655	1032	623	875	734	1529	315	611	935	964	576
Los Angeles, CA	2016	2836	799	1084	3457	2203	2725	3235	1240	2055	1659	846	3000	1642	2547	1142	1897	1557	2832	1070	2524	2354	2429	1102	2031	933	2198	2357	2264	2980	1439	1865	2518	1022	1696

	Detroit, MI	Dodge City, KS	Duluth, MN	Durango, CO	Edmonton, AB	El Paso, TX	Ely, NV	Eureka, CA	Fargo, ND	Flagstaff, AZ	Fresno, CA	Gallup, NM	Gaspé, QC	Grand Junction, CO	Grants Pass, OR	Great Falls, MT	Green Bay, WI	Guadalajara, JA	Halifax, NS	Houston, TX	Idaho Falls, ID	Indianapolis, IN	International Falls, MN	Jackson, MS	Jacksonville, FL	Juneau, AK	Kansas City, MO	Knoxville, TN	La Crosse, WI	Laredo, TX	Las Vegas, NV	Lexington, KY	Lincoln, NE	Little Rock, AR	Los Angeles, CA
Acapulco, GR	2564	1685	2446	1801	3194	1322	2181	2670	2437	1782	2231	1703	3696	1971	2738	2692	2497	518	3763	1183	2403	2246	2588	1625	2058	4614	1853	2110	2342	937	1936	2238	1993	1679	2016
Albany, NY	648	1629	1293	2194	2495	2307	2450	3079	1472	2408	2959	2220	783	2060	2976	2207	1038	2710	863	1761	2290	789	1457	1331	1072	3914	1285	834	1107	2106	2563	807	1332	1359	2836
Albuquerque, NM	1586	463	1376	212	1718	267	821	1370	1314	327	922	139	2718	382	1352	1216	1448	1197	2944	890	818	1292	1518	1055	1648	3138	783	1400	1250	776	576	1378	814	881	799
Amarillo, TX	1301	246	1197	497	1694	432	1106	1655	1011	612	1207	424	2433	674	1637	1192	1258	1167	2659	605	1028	1007	1339	770	1363	3114	604	1115	1071	660	861	1093	597	596	1084
Anchorage, AK	3950	3654	3201	3434	1998	3983	3186	2904	3024	3559	3238	3526	4810	3325	2736	2499	3544	4913	5023	4397	2826	3851	3075	4283	4735	865	3619	4212	3422	4352	3455	4042	3494	4002	3457
Atlanta, GA	726	1120	1190	1616	2392	1429	2122	2751	1369	1731	2326	1543	1789	1665	2648	2053	929	1746	1825	797	1962	528	1354	386	346	3811	811	216	1004	1142	1980	387	1002	529	2203
Baltimore, MD	533	1432	1178	1989	2380	1999	2335	2964	1357	2253	2848	2065	1119	1942	2861	2092	923	2402	1103	1453	2175	592	1342	1023	739	3799	1088	526	992	1798	2445	546	1217	1051	2725
Bangor, ME	1047	2028	1692	2593	2548	2662	2849	3478	1871	2807	3358	2619	514	2459	3375	2606	1437	3065	466	2116	2689	1188	1856	1686	1374	3967	1684	1189	1506	2461	2962	1196	1731	1714	3235
Billings, MT	1533	932	861	828	724	1261	758	1305	607	1071	1258	1133	2666	664	1137	222	1127	2191	2879	1675	338	1434	863	1688	2177	2144	1024	1766	954	1630	967	1609	856	1407	1240
Birmingham, AL	729	972	1138	1468	2340	1284	2017	2626	1317	1583	2178	1395	1874	1585	2608	2001	877	1620	1910	671	1910	476	1302	241	468	3759	759	257	952	1016	1832	403	950	381	2055
Bismarck, ND	1120	752	448	1080	837	1407	1177	1724	194	1467	1677	1279	2253	945	1556	549	714	2187	2466	1415	757	1021	450	1453	1905	2256	789	1382	592	1583	1386	1212	664	1172	1659
Boise, ID	1965	1207	1483	734	928	1207	386	677	1229	859	723	826	3098	625	509	581	1749	2137	3311	1950	282	1851	1485	2047	2525	2227	1372	2114	1576	1720	632	1957	1178	1785	846
Boston, MA	812	1793	1457	2358	2659	2399	2614	3243	1636	2572	3123	2384	761	2224	3140	2371	1202	2802	713	1853	2454	953	1621	1423	1139	4078	1449	926	1271	2198	2727	933	1496	1451	3000
Brownsville, TX	1673	997	1629	1205	2484	836	1807	2296	1620	1320	1857	1132	2805	1375	2364	1982	1680	628	2935	355	1818	1379	1771	797	1230	3904	1036	1282	1525	203	1562	1347	1176	788	1642
Buffalo, NY	359	1340	1004	1905	2206	1939	2161	2790	1183	2119	2670	1931	969	1771	2687	1918	749	2407	1158	1495	2001	500	1168	1130	1040	3625	996	706	818	1803	2274	518	1043	1061	2547
Cabo San Lucas, BS	3369	2244	3170	1812	2805	1693	1593	1796	2924	1454	1357	1642	4502	1853	1864	2337	3242	2366	4725	2446	1977	3073	3180	2736	3317	4021	2564	3181	3044	2295	1350	3159	2582	2641	1142
Cairo, IL	623	677	811	1310	2024	1236	1717	2346	1003	1425	2020	1237	1755	1260	2243	1648	582	1634	1957	722	1557	311	975	380	764	3443	406	353	625	1030	1674	297	597	288	1897
Calgary, AB	1918	1483	1169	1263	173	1812	1075	1209	992	1388	1575	1355	2830	1154	1041	328	1512	2742	3043	2226	655	1819	1095	2239	2703	1593	1575	2180	1390	2181	1284	2010	1407	1958	1557
Cancún, QR	3149	2451	3083	2617	3938	2138	2997	3486	3074	2598	3047	2519	4281	2787	3554	3436	3134	1358	4411	1831	3219	2883	3225	2273	2706	5358	2490	2758	2979	1640	2752	2823	2630	2264	2832
Casper, WY	1368	657	1002	553	999	986	646	1275	712	822	1193	858	2501	389	1172	497	1074	1916	2714	1400	377	1254	968	1497	1928	2419	775	1517	876	1355	797	1360	581	1235	1070
Charleston, SC	839	1441	1382	1937	2584	1750	2427	3056	1561	2052	2647	1864	1678	1970	2953	2296	1127	2062	1662	1113	2267	728	1546	707	239	4003	1116	370	1196	1458	2301	542	1307	850	2524
Charleston, WV	368	1110	957	1667	2159	1684	2077	2706	1136	1882	2477	1694	1402	1620	2603	1871	702	2082	1483	1170	1917	303	1121	810	647	3578	766	313	771	1478	2123	177	957	736	2354
Charlotte, NC	633	1258	1242	1842	2444	1673	2287	2916	1421	1957	2552	1769	1551	1830	2813	2156	987	1990	1535	1041	2127	588	1406	630	384	3863	976	230	1056	1386	2206	402	1167	755	2429
Cheyenne, WY	1231	477	1032	479	1179	806	678	1307	791	866	1225	678	2364	344	1204	677	1104	1736	2577	1220	518	1117	1047	1317	1791	2599	638	1380	906	1175	829	1223	444	1055	1102
Chicago, IL	278	873	464	1389	1666	1490	1645	2274	643	1670	2154	1482	1411	1255	2171	1378	209	1964	1624	1089	1485	181	628	747	1059	3085	529	542	278	1360	1758	372	527	655	2031
Chihuahua, CI	1837	867	1733	718	2224	239	1098	1587	1673	699	1148	620	2969	888	1655	1722	1794	691	3210	804	1320	1543	1875	1127	1675	3644	1140	1557	1607	608	853	1591	1229	1032	933
Cincinnati, OH	262	947	764	1504	1966	1571	1901	2530	943	1726	2321	1538	1394	1457	2427	1678	509	1969	1590	1057	1741	110	928	692	795	3385	603	250	578	1365	1960	80	783	623	2198
Cleveland, OH	169	1154	814	1715	2016	1753	1971	2600	993	1933	2480	1745	1152	1581	2497	1728	559	2221	1341	1309	1811	314	978	944	897	3435	810	502	628	1617	2084	332	853	875	2357
Columbus, OH	202	1013	821	1570	2023	1612	1967	2596	1000	1792	2387	1604	1291	1523	2493	1735	566	2080	1480	1168	1807	173	985	803	814	3442	669	361	635	1476	2026	191	849	734	2264
Concord, NH	792	1773	1437	2338	2500	2477	2594	3223	1616	2552	3103	2364	739	2204	3120	2351	1182	2880	692	1931	2434	933	1601	1501	1189	3919	1429	1004	1251	2276	2707	1011	1476	1529	2980
Dallas, TX	1200	462	1082	859	2152	633	1468	2017	1085	974	1569	786	2332	1128	1999	1650	1133	1031	2493	247	1486	882	1224	408	1001	3572	489	840	956	427	1223	874	641	315	1439
Davenport, IA	427	707	420	1223	1617	1293	1479	2108	594	1473	1988	1285	1560	1089	2005	1329	331	1883	1773	1117	1319	313	654	760	1132	3036	363	669	196	1279	1592	496	361	611	1865
Daytona Beach, FL	1105	1526	1624	1948	2826	1712	2556	3106	1803	2063	2658	1875	1944	2099	3082	2487	1363	1912	1928	963	2396	962	1788	681	90	4245	1245	636	1438	1308	2312	808	1436	935	2518
Denver, CO	1274	386	1075	379	1279	706	678	1402	876	766	1145	578	2407	246	1299	777	1147	1636	2620	1035	613	1104	1132	1226	1765	2699	608	1354	949	1090	749	1197	487	964	1022
Des Moines, IA	596	538	397	1054	1502	1124	1310	1939	479	1304	1819	1116	1729	920	1836	1165	469	1714	1942	948	1150	482	539	828	1245	2921	194	838	271	1110	1423	665	192	576	1696
Detroit, MI		1109	751	1652	1953	1733	1908	2537	930	1913	2417	1725	1136	1518	2434	1665	496	2231	1349	1319	1748	294	915	954	1015	3372	765	512	565	1627	2021	342	790	885	2294
Dodge City, KS	1109		937	505	1656	610	1064	1779	761	790	1385	602	2242	632	1676	1154	1009	1352	2492	709	990	840	1079	869	1438	3076	344	1028	811	821	1039	933	350	597	1262
Duluth, MN	751	937		1453	1204	1523	1709	2168	258	1703	2218	1515	1614	1319	2000	993	329	2113	1827	1347	1201	652	164	1176	1536	2623	593	1013	239	1509	1822	843	591	975	2095
Durango, CO	1652	505	1453		1436	479	543	1262	1254	358	953	170	2785	170	1159	968	1525	1409	2998	1102	608	1397	1510	1267	1860	2856	901	1612	1327	988	614	1490	865	1093	830
Edmonton, AB	1953	1656	1204	1436		1985	1248	1382	1027	1561	1748	1528	2813	1327	1214	501	1547	2915	3026	2399	828	1854	1078	2286	2738	1420	1622	2215	1425	2354	1457	2045	1497	2005	1730
El Paso, TX	1733	610	1523	479	1985		971	1460	1375	572	1021	381	2865	649	1528	1483	1595	930	3126	753	1081	1439	1665	1043	1624	3405	930	1473	1397	602	726	1507	961	948	806
Ely, NV	1908	1064	1709	543	1248	971		667	1367	494	457	682	3041	434	648	780	1781	1744	3254	1711	420	1794	1623	1876	2468	2608	1315	2057	1583	1573	245	1900	1121	1642	518
Eureka, CA	2537	1779	2168	1262	1382	1460	667		1914	1043	456	1231	3670	1153	168	1132	2410	2233	3883	2213	971	2423	2170	2425	3018	2326	1944	2686	2212	2062	795	2529	1750	2251	654
Fargo, ND	930	761	258	1254	1027	1375	1367	1914		1641	1867	1453	2063	1120	1746	739	524	2104	2276	1332	947	831	260	1265	1715	2446	601	1192	402	1500	1576	1022	476	984	1849
Flagstaff, AZ	1913	790	1703	358	1561	572	494	1043	1641		595	188	3045	435	1025	1093	1775	1345	3271	1217	733	1619	1845	1382	1975	2981	1110	1727	1577	1174	249	1705	1141	1208	472
Fresno, CA	2417	1385	2218	953	1748	1021	457	456	1867	595		783	3550	901	503	1280	2290	1794	3763	1774	920	2214	2123	1977	2570	2660	1753	2322	2092	1623	398	2300	1630	1803	215
Gallup, NM	1725	602	1515	170	1528	381	682	1231	1453	188	783		2857	361	1213	1060	1587	1311	3083	1029	700	1431	1657	1194	1787	2948	922	1539	1389	915	437	1517	953	1020	660
Gaspé, QC	1136	2242	1614	2785	2813	2865	3041	3670	2063	3045	3550	2857		2651	3567	2798	1477	3363	592	2451	2881	1426	1787	2114	1854	4232	1898	1617	1698	2759	3154	1474	1923	2017	3427
Grand Junction, CO	1518	632	1319	170	1327	649	434	1153	1120	435	901	361	2651		1050	859	1391	1579	2864	1279	499	1350	1376	1472	2011	2747	854	1600	1193	1158	505	1443	731	1210	778
Grants Pass, OR	2434	1676	2000	1159	1214	1528	648	168	1746	1025	503	1213	3567	1050		964	2266	2301	3780	2242	786	2320	2002	2407	2994	2158	1841	2583	2093	2130	776	2426	1647	2233	722
Great Falls, MT	1665	1154	993	968	501	1483	780	1132	739	1093	1280	1060	2798	859	964		1259	2413	3011	1897	360	1566	995	1910	2399	1921	1246	1927	1137	1852	989	1757	1078	1629	1262
Green Bay, WI	496	1009	329	1525	1547	1595	1781	2410	524	1775	2290	1587	1477	1391	2266	1259		2164	1690	1280	1467	397	493	954	1275	2966	665	758	204	1560	1894	588	663	846	2167
Guadalajara, JA	2231	1352	2113	1409	2915	930	1746	2235	2104	1345	1794	1311	3363	1579	2303	2413	2164		3529	953	2011	1913	2255	1391	1824	4335	1520	1876	1987	604	1501	1905	1660	1346	1579
Halifax, NS	1349	2492	1827	2998	3026	3126	3254	3883	2276	3271	3763	3083	592	2864	3780	3011	1690	3529		2580	3094	1652	2000	2150	1838	4445	2148	1653	1911	2925	3367	1660	2136	2178	3640
Houston, TX	1319	709	1347	1102	2399	753	1711	2213	1332	1217	1774	1029	2451	1279	2242	1897	1280	953	2580		1733	1025	1489	442	875	3819	732	927	1221	349	1466	993	888	434	1559
Idaho Falls, ID	1748	990	1201	608	828	1081	420	971	947	733	920	700	2881	499	786	360	1467	2011	3094	1733		1634	1203	1830	2308	2248	1155	1897	1294	1688	629	1740	961	1568	902
Indianapolis, IN	294	840	652	1397	1854	1439	1794	2423	831	1619	2214	1431	1426	1350	2320	1566	397	1913	1652	1025	1634		816	683	874	3273	496	359	466	1309	1853	186	676	591	2091
International Falls, MN	915	1079	164	1510	1078	1665	1623	2170	260	1845	2123	1657	1787	1376	2002	995	493	2255	2000	1489	1203	816		1340	1700	2497	735	1177	403	1651	1832	1007	733	1117	2105
Jackson, MS	954	869	1176	1267	2286	1043	1876	2425	1265	1382	1977	1194	2114	1472	2407	1910	954	1391	2150	442	1830	683	1340		593	3705	664	497	990	787	1631	628	859	262	1849
Jacksonville, FL	1015	1438	1536	1860	2738	1624	2468	3018	1715	1975	2570	1787	1854	2011	2994	2399	1275	1824	1838	875	2308	874	1700	593		4157	1157	546	1350	1220	2224	718	1348	847	2430
Juneau, AK	3372	3076	2623	2856	1420	3405	2608	2326	2446	2981	2660	2948	4232	2747	2158	1921	2966	4335	4445	3819	2248	3273	2497	3705	4157		3041	3634	2844	3774	2877	3464	2916	3424	2879
Kansas City, MO	765	344	593	901	1622	930	1315	1944	601	1110	1753	922	1898	854	1841	1246	665	1520	2148	732	1155	496	735	664	1157	3041		746	467	916	1357	589	195	383	1630
Knoxville, TN	512	1028	1013	1612	2215	1473	2057	2686	1192	1727	2322	1539	1617	1600	2583	1927	758	1876	1653	927	1897	359	1177	497	546	3634	746		827	1272	1976	173	937	525	2199
La Crosse, WI	565	811	239	1327	1425	1397	1583	2212	402	1577	2092	1389	1698	1193	2093	1137	204	1987	1911	1221	1294	466	403	990	1350	2844	467	827		1383	1696	657	465	849	1969
Laredo, TX	1627	821	1509	988	2354	602	1573	2062	1500	1174	1623	915	2759	1158	2130	1852	1560	604	2925	349	1688	1309	1651	787	1220	3774	916	1272	1383		1328	1301	1056	742	1408
Las Vegas, NV	2021	1039	1822	614	1457	726	245	795	1576	249	398	437	3154	505	776	989	1894	1499	3367	1466	629	1853	1832	1631	2224	2877	1357	1976	1696	1328		1946	1234	1457	275
Lexington, KY	342	933	843	1490	2045	1507	1900	2529	1022	1705	2300	1517	1474	1443	2426	1757	588	1905	1660	993	1740	186	1007	628	718	3464	589	173	657	1301	1946		780	559	2177
Lincoln, NE	790	350	591	865	1497	961	1121	1750	476	1141	1630	953	1923	731	1647	1078	663	1660	2136	888	961	676	733	859	1348	2916	195	937	465	1056	1234	780		578	1507
Little Rock, AR	885	597	975	1093	2005	948	1642	2251	984	1208	1803	1020	2017	1210	2233	1629	846	1346	2178	434	1568	591	1117	262	847	3424	383	525	849	742	1457	559	578		1680
Los Angeles, CA	2294	1262	2095	830	1730	806	518	654	1849	472	215	660	3427	778	722	1262	2167	1579	3640	1559	902	2091	2105	1849	2430	2879	1630	2199	1969	1408	275	2177	1507	1680	

	Louisville, KY	Mackinaw City, MI	Memphis, TN	Mexico City, DF	Miami, FL	Milwaukee, WI	Minneapolis, MN	Minot, ND	Missoula, MT	Mobile, AL	Monterrey, NL	Montgomery, AL	Montréal, QC	Nashville, TN	Needles, CA	New Orleans, LA	New York, NY	Norfolk, VA	North Platte, NE	Odessa, TX	Oklahoma City, OK	Omaha, NE	Ottawa, ON	Page, AZ	Pendleton, OR	Philadelphia, PA	Phoenix, AZ	Pierre, SD	Pittsburgh, PA	Portland, ME	Portland, OR	Pueblo, CO	Québec, QC	Raleigh, NC	Redding, CA
Acapulco, GR	2201	2680	1818	219	2373	2380	2292	2627	2713	1655	791	1820	3129	2027	1872	1534	2835	2538	1937	1304	1560	2024	3041	1919	2742	2738	1646	2309	2592	3167	2949	1821	3286	2387	2564
Albany, NY	830	926	1222	2725	1415	921	1235	1769	2417	1335	2252	1166	226	1012	2616	1432	159	509	1556	2028	1536	1278	310	2439	2720	243	2544	1615	474	267	2927	1924	373	628	2925
Albuquerque, NM	1306	1726	1014	1376	1963	1351	1222	1224	1128	1245	961	1302	2151	1223	535	1173	2022	1910	702	399	544	869	2063	452	1157	1941	463	966	1651	2348	1364	330	2308	1759	1217
Amarillo, TX	1021	1441	729	1287	1678	1141	1043	1055	1312	960	806	1017	1866	938	820	888	1737	1625	473	258	259	652	1778	737	1458	1656	748	737	1366	2063	1665	321	2023	1474	1502
Anchorage, AK	3969	3741	4072	4979	5050	3592	3260	2725	2554	4469	4498	4427	4244	4148	3567	4463	4483	4564	3355	3950	3942	3436	4160	3422	2587	4434	3695	3041	4133	4507	2490	3386	4398	4481	2911
Atlanta, GA	418	992	391	1761	661	812	1132	1666	2173	329	1288	160	1222	243	1939	468	873	558	1228	1150	860	995	1161	1856	2392	772	1867	1391	686	1229	2599	1442	1379	407	2597
Baltimore, MD	618	811	914	2417	1082	806	1120	1654	2302	1003	1944	834	562	704	2461	1124	203	234	1441	1720	1382	1163	531	2378	2605	102	2389	1500	251	507	2812	1719	709	295	2810
Bangor, ME	1229	1325	1577	3080	1717	1320	1634	2168	2816	1690	2607	1521	300	1367	3015	1787	443	811	1955	2383	1935	1677	425	2838	3119	545	2943	2014	821	132	3326	2323	229	930	3324
Billings, MT	1537	1361	1477	2257	2492	1175	843	444	340	1874	1776	1869	2099	1590	1079	1868	2066	2147	633	1228	1220	841	1777	934	744	2017	1207	491	1716	2342	891	664	2256	2064	1155
Birmingham, AL	366	952	243	1635	783	760	1080	1614	2121	261	1162	92	1307	189	1791	342	982	707	1176	1005	712	943	1246	1708	2340	885	1719	1339	753	1314	2547	1270	1464	556	2473
Bismarck, ND	1139	948	1242	2307	2220	762	430	111	759	1639	1729	1597	1686	1318	1498	1633	1653	1734	475	1206	960	606	1364	1353	1163	1604	1603	211	1303	1929	1310	810	1843	1651	1574
Boise, ID	1885	1983	1825	2316	2840	1741	1465	1066	370	2237	1901	2217	2531	1938	744	2228	2498	2544	955	1343	1495	1233	2443	722	218	2449	922	1113	2148	2774	425	939	2688	2473	525
Boston, MA	994	1090	1314	2817	1482	1085	1399	1933	2581	1427	2344	1258	324	1104	2780	1524	208	576	1720	2120	1700	1442	449	2603	2884	310	2708	1779	586	117	3091	2088	403	695	3089
Brownsville, TX	1310	1863	927	609	1545	1563	1475	1810	2102	827	186	992	2238	1136	1498	706	2007	1710	1203	632	743	1207	2150	1445	2248	1910	1272	1492	1701	2339	2455	1111	2395	1559	2190
Buffalo, NY	541	637	924	2527	1383	632	946	1480	2128	1164	1949	995	402	716	2327	1243	399	576	1267	1730	1247	989	341	2150	2431	388	2255	1326	216	562	2638	1635	559	637	2636
Cabo San Lucas, BS	3087	3502	2795	2697	3632	3145	3016	2761	2287	2914	2354	2983	3935	3004	1339	2793	3803	3691	2359	1974	2325	2637	3847	1591	2117	3722	1318	2623	3432	4129	2109	2111	4092	3540	1690
Cairo, IL	260	755	169	1754	1079	465	753	1298	1768	566	1176	456	1188	177	1633	560	1029	863	823	957	553	590	1100	1550	1987	950	1561	986	651	1361	2194	1037	1345	712	2192
Calgary, AB	1937	1589	2028	2808	3018	1560	1228	693	388	2425	2327	2395	2264	2116	1396	2419	2451	2532	1184	1779	1771	1392	2180	1251	648	2402	1524	1009	2101	2527	795	1215	2418	2449	1113
Cancún, QR	2786	3317	2403	1029	3021	3017	2929	3264	3556	2303	1496	2468	3714	2612	2688	2182	3483	3186	2657	2086	2197	2661	3626	2735	3558	3386	2462	2946	3177	3815	3765	2565	3871	3035	3380
Casper, WY	1288	1330	1228	1982	2243	1077	848	591	617	1687	1501	1620	1934	1341	909	1678	1901	1947	358	953	945	636	1846	764	916	1852	958	413	1551	2177	1123	389	2091	1876	1121
Charleston, SC	614	1105	712	2077	582	1010	1324	1858	2478	645	1604	476	1121	548	2260	784	762	431	1533	1471	1181	1300	1092	2177	2697	661	2188	1696	654	1066	2904	1747	1268	280	2902
Charleston, WV	249	634	599	2202	990	585	899	1433	2081	826	1624	657	835	391	2090	911	555	410	1183	1405	1010	950	774	2007	2347	476	2018	1287	229	887	2554	1397	992	325	2552
Charlotte, NC	474	899	618	2005	727	870	1184	1718	2338	573	1532	404	984	408	2165	712	635	320	1393	1394	1086	1160	923	2082	2557	534	2093	1556	448	939	2764	1607	1141	169	2762
Cheyenne, WY	1151	1364	1091	1802	2106	1007	878	685	797	1507	1321	1483	1797	1204	941	1498	1764	1810	221	773	765	499	1709	723	948	1715	1002	436	1414	2040	1155	209	1954	1739	1153
Chicago, IL	299	411	536	2084	1374	92	406	940	1588	920	1506	751	844	472	1870	927	811	892	751	1231	798	473	756	1634	1915	762	1806	786	461	1087	2122	1119	1001	811	2120
Chihuahua, CI	1554	1977	1171	870	1990	1677	1579	1730	1630	1272	495	1374	2402	1380	789	1151	2282	2067	1208	365	795	1260	2314	836	1659	2185	563	1472	1945	2614	1866	836	2559	1916	1481
Cincinnati, OH	103	528	486	2089	1125	392	706	1240	1888	726	1511	557	827	278	1934	805	661	603	1007	1292	854	729	739	1851	2171	580	1862	1094	290	994	2378	1234	984	518	2376
Cleveland, OH	355	447	738	2341	1240	442	756	1290	1938	978	1763	809	585	530	2141	1057	486	567	1077	1544	1061	799	524	1960	2241	437	2069	1136	136	745	2448	1445	742	575	2446
Columbus, OH	214	468	597	2200	1157	449	763	1297	1945	837	1622	668	724	389	2000	916	554	577	1073	1403	920	795	663	1917	2237	473	1928	1143	183	884	2444	1300	881	492	2442
Concord, NH	974	1070	1392	2895	1532	1065	1379	1913	2561	1505	2422	1336	252	1182	2760	1602	258	626	1700	2198	1680	1422	377	2583	2864	360	2688	1759	636	96	3071	2068	329	745	3069
Dallas, TX	837	1316	454	1151	1316	1016	928	1275	1770	598	573	655	1765	663	1182	526	1565	1350	756	354	208	672	1677	1099	1916	1468	1069	957	1228	1897	2123	683	1922	1199	1864
Davenport, IA	424	560	549	2025	1447	214	358	891	1454	946	1425	824	993	545	1704	940	960	1023	585	1140	707	307	905	1468	1749	911	1609	672	610	1236	1956	953	1150	938	1954
Daytona Beach, FL	852	1371	797	1927	255	1246	1566	2100	2607	491	1454	464	1387	677	2271	634	1028	697	1662	1445	1266	1429	1358	2188	2826	927	2148	1825	920	1332	3033	1772	1534	546	3031
Denver, CO	1125	1407	1097	1717	2080	1050	921	785	897	1416	1236	1429	1840	1178	861	1407	1807	1784	264	689	674	542	1752	625	1043	1753	902	528	1457	2083	1250	109	1997	1713	1248
Des Moines, IA	593	729	617	1834	1560	372	243	776	1285	1014	1256	937	1162	658	1535	1008	1129	1192	416	971	538	138	1074	1299	1580	1080	1440	503	779	1405	1787	784	1319	1107	1785
Detroit, MI	365	292	748	2351	1387	379	693	1227	1875	988	1773	819	569	540	2121	1067	639	720	1014	1474	1041	736	481	1897	2178	590	2049	1073	289	915	2385	1382	726	693	2383
Dodge City, KS	861	1242	730	1472	1753	912	783	859	1274	1059	967	1062	1675	852	998	987	1570	1520	277	504	254	405	1587	915	1420	1489	926	541	1199	1896	1627	274	1832	1387	1625
Duluth, MN	770	423	965	2233	1851	393	157	474	1203	1362	1655	1228	1047	949	1934	1356	1284	1365	815	1370	937	537	919	1698	1607	1235	1839	640	934	1560	1754	1183	1204	1282	2018
Durango, CO	1418	1785	1226	1588	2175	1428	1299	1164	918	1457	1173	1514	2218	1435	566	1385	2127	2122	642	611	756	920	2130	262	947	2046	494	906	1756	2461	1154	270	2375	1971	1108
Edmonton, AB	1972	1744	2075	2981	3053	1595	1263	728	561	2472	2500	2430	2247	2151	1569	2466	2486	2567	1357	1952	1944	1439	2163	1424	821	2437	1697	1044	2136	2510	968	1388	2401	2484	1286
El Paso, TX	1470	1873	1087	1109	1939	1498	1369	1491	1391	1221	694	1290	2298	1296	662	1100	2198	1983	969	281	691	1016	2210	694	1420	2101	436	1233	1861	2530	1627	597	2455	1832	1354
Ely, NV	1828	2041	1775	1968	2783	1684	1555	1204	645	2066	1593	2107	2474	1881	357	1994	2441	2487	898	1252	1352	1176	2386	368	599	2392	535	1059	2091	2717	806	785	2631	2416	513
Eureka, CA	2457	2670	2384	2457	3333	2313	2150	1680	965	2615	2082	2672	3103	2510	835	2543	3070	3116	1527	1741	1914	1805	3015	1069	621	3021	1024	1688	2720	3346	414	1511	3260	3045	154
Fargo, ND	949	758	1054	2224	2030	572	240	284	949	1451	1646	1407	1496	1128	1688	1445	1463	1544	612	1310	877	418	1174	1543	1353	1414	1777	333	1113	1739	1500	984	1653	1461	1764
Flagstaff, AZ	1633	2053	1341	1569	2290	1678	1549	1517	1043	1572	1194	1629	2478	1550	208	1500	2349	2237	1029	726	871	1196	2390	137	1072	2268	136	1293	1978	2675	1279	657	2635	2086	890
Fresno, CA	2228	2550	1936	2018	2885	2193	2064	1704	1068	2167	1643	2224	2983	2145	387	2095	2950	2832	1407	1302	1466	1685	2895	672	887	2863	585	1671	2573	3226	748	1252	3140	2681	329
Gallup, NM	1445	1865	1153	1490	2102	1490	1361	1363	1010	1384	1075	1441	2290	1362	396	1312	2161	2049	841	538	683	1008	2202	313	1039	2080	324	1105	1790	2487	1246	469	2447	1898	1078
Gaspé, QC	1497	1248	1880	3483	2197	1512	1826	2085	3008	2118	2905	1949	568	1672	3253	2215	941	1291	2147	2606	2173	1869	695	3030	3311	1025	3181	2206	1179	644	3518	2515	430	1410	3516
Grand Junction, CO	1371	1651	1343	1758	2326	1294	1165	1029	809	1662	1343	1675	2084	1424	617	1653	2051	2030	508	781	920	786	1996	381	838	1999	571	772	1701	2327	1045	353	2241	1959	999
Grants Pass, OR	2354	2500	2366	2525	3309	2314	1982	1512	797	2597	2150	2654	3000	2407	890	2525	2967	3013	1424	1809	1896	1702	2912	1050	453	2918	1092	1630	2617	3243	246	1408	3157	2942	176
Great Falls, MT	1684	1493	1699	2479	2714	1307	975	548	167	2096	1998	2091	2231	1812	1101	2090	2198	2279	855	1450	1442	1063	1909	956	571	2149	1229	713	1848	2474	718	886	2388	2196	1036
Green Bay, WI	515	258	743	2284	1590	117	287	821	1469	1136	1706	967	910	688	2006	1134	1029	1110	887	1431	998	609	782	1770	1873	980	1911	712	679	1305	2020	1255	1067	1027	2256
Guadalajara, JA	1868	2347	1485	329	2139	2047	1959	2294	2321	1421	458	1586	2796	1694	1435	1300	2601	2304	1604	971	1227	1691	2708	1484	2350	2504	1209	1976	2259	2933	2548	1527	2953	2153	2129
Halifax, NS	1693	1461	2041	3544	2181	1725	2039	2298	3221	2154	3071	1985	781	1831	3479	2251	907	1275	2360	2847	2399	2082	908	3243	3524	1009	3407	2419	1285	596	3731	2728	643	1394	3729
Houston, TX	956	1469	573	964	1190	1163	1171	1522	2017	472	495	637	1884	782	1425	351	1652	1355	1003	549	455	919	1796	1342	2163	1555	1189	1204	1347	1984	2370	926	2041	1204	2107
Idaho Falls, ID	1668	1701	1608	2190	2623	1515	1183	784	310	2020	1834	2000	2314	1721	741	2011	2281	2327	738	1286	1278	1016	2226	596	495	2232	869	831	1931	2557	702	722	2471	2256	817
Indianapolis, IN	114	480	472	2033	1189	280	594	1128	1776	735	1455	566	859	287	1827	814	730	713	900	1180	747	622	771	1744	2064	649	1755	987	359	1056	2271	1127	1016	628	2269
International Falls, MN	934	587	1129	2375	2015	557	299	433	1205	1526	1797	1392	1221	1113	1944	1520	1448	1529	868	1512	1079	679	1137	1799	1609	1399	1981	589	1098	1724	1756	1240	1375	1446	2020
Jackson, MS	591	1127	212	1406	908	837	1062	1560	2030	190	933	247	1547	417	1590	180	1222	944	1085	764	615	852	1486	1507	2260	1125	1479	1248	993	1554	2467	1091	1704	793	2272
Jacksonville, FL	764	1281	709	1839	343	1158	1478	2012	2519	403	1366	376	1297	589	2183	546	938	607	1574	1357	1178	1341	1268	2100	2738	837	2060	1737	830	1242	2945	1684	1444	456	2943
Juneau, AK	3391	3163	3494	4401	4472	3014	2682	2147	1976	3891	3920	3849	3666	3570	2989	3885	3905	3986	2777	3372	3364	2858	3582	2844	2009	3856	3117	2463	3555	3929	1912	2808	3820	3903	2333
Kansas City, MO	517	898	453	1640	1472	568	439	896	1366	850	1062	849	1331	570	1318	844	1226	1176	421	777	344	188	1243	1233	1585	1145	1246	584	855	1552	1792	631	1488	1105	1790
Knoxville, TN	245	778	388	1891	877	641	955	1489	2108	513	1418	344	1050	178	1935	598	725	510	1163	1194	856	930	989	1852	2327	628	1863	1326	496	1057	2534	1377	1207	359	2532
La Crosse, WI	584	460	779	2129	1665	207	163	699	1296	1176	1529	1042	1131	763	1808	1170	1098	1179	689	1244	811	411	1043	1572	1700	1049	1713	514	748	1374	1847	1057	1288	1096	2058
Laredo, TX	1264	1743	881	724	1535	1443	1355	1690	1972	817	146	982	2192	1090	1264	696	1997	1700	1073	431	623	1087	2104	1228	1933	1900	1038	1372	1655	2329	2140	981	2349	1549	1956
Las Vegas, NV	1874	2154	1590	1723	2539	1797	1668	1413	939	1821	1348	1878	2587	1799	112	1749	2554	2486	1011	1007	1120	1289	2499	276	845	2502	290	1275	2204	2830	1021	856	2744	2335	641
Lexington, KY	72	608	422	2025	1048	471	785	1319	1951	662	1447	493	907	214	1913	741	732	587	1006	1228	833	773	819	1830	2170	653	1841	1169	406	1064	2377	1220	1064	502	2375
Lincoln, NE	708	923	648	1780	1663	566	437	771	1198	1045	1202	1040	1356	761	1346	1039	1323	1367	227	866	433	58	1268	1110	1391	1274	1277	459	973	1599	1598	595	1513	1296	1596
Little Rock, AR	522	1035	139	1466	1162	729	821	1279	1749	452	888	471	1450	348	1416	423	1250	1035	838	669	337	571	1362	1333	1998	1153	1344	967	913	1582	2205	895	1607	884	2098
Los Angeles, CA	2105	2427	1813	1803	2745	2070	1941	1686	1212	2027	1428	2096	2860	2022	264	1906	2827	2709	1284	1087	1343	1562	2772	549	1010	2740	370	1548	2450	3103	967	1129	3017	2558	548

	Regina, SK	Reno, NV	Roanoke, VA	Robbinsville, NC	Roswell, NM	Saginaw, MI	St. George, UT	St. Louis, MO	Salt Lake City, UT	San Antonio, TX	San Diego, CA	San Francisco, CA	Sault Ste. Marie, ON	Savannah, GA	Seattle, WA	Shreveport, LA	Sioux City, IA	Sioux Falls, SD	Spokane, WA	Springfield, MO	Sturgis, SD	Sudbury, ON	Tallahassee, FL	Tampa, FL	Thunder Bay, ON	Toronto, ON	Tulsa, OK	Twin Falls, ID	Vancouver, BC	Washington, DC	Whitehorse, YT	Wichita, KS	Winnemucca, NV	Winnipeg, MB	Yuma, AZ
Acapulco, GR	2758	2381	2368	2126	1445	2572	2057	1997	2190	1087	1938	2397	2738	2155	3019	1421	2114	2199	2912	1787	2249	2922	1895	2170	2634	2796	1626	2411	3157	2596	4469	1717	2402	2656	1766
Albany, NY	2014	2729	584	897	2010	735	2443	1038	2206	1956	2896	2953	809	938	2897	1553	1337	1398	2616	1250	1762	631	1231	1270	1189	400	1433	2389	3035	371	3769	1475	2565	1693	2725
Albuquerque, NM	1282	1021	1658	1463	198	1618	608	1043	605	715	816	1097	1784	1656	1434	833	964	1096	1327	833	840	1968	1485	1760	1564	1818	650	826	1572	1886	2993	593	958	1533	644
Amarillo, TX	1258	1306	1373	1178	214	1333	893	758	944	512	1101	1382	1499	1371	1735	548	747	794	1511	548	749	1683	1200	1475	1385	1533	365	1127	1873	1601	2969	417	1303	1230	929
Anchorage, AK	2482	3068	4335	4286	3774	3975	3335	3871	3040	4204	3581	3126	3683	4641	2315	4162	3341	3259	2413	3787	3015	3865	4640	4847	3242	4104	3868	2930	2241	4378	723	3785	3011	2806	3751
Atlanta, GA	1911	2401	430	149	1296	801	2048	557	1878	992	2157	2501	1050	252	2653	608	1085	1170	2372	685	1538	1188	265	458	1378	958	796	2061	2791	636	3666	970	2237	1590	1985
Baltimore, MD	1899	2614	276	589	1855	620	2325	841	2091	1648	2742	2838	869	605	2782	1245	1222	1283	2501	1053	1647	721	898	937	1310	490	1236	2274	2920	38	3654	1278	2450	1578	2570
Bangor, ME	2096	3128	939	1252	2409	1134	2842	1437	2605	2311	3295	3352	920	1240	3296	1908	1736	1797	3015	1649	2161	733	1533	1572	1303	630	1832	2788	3434	673	3822	1874	2964	1739	3124
Billings, MT	475	959	1918	1829	1052	1558	847	1276	552	1482	1300	1183	1282	2083	820	1613	746	664	539	1192	293	1466	2082	2289	1049	1766	1237	502	958	1961	1999	1063	795	723	1263
Birmingham, AL	1859	2277	515	270	1151	804	1864	505	1826	866	2012	2353	1010	401	2601	463	1033	1118	2320	527	1486	1191	305	580	1326	961	648	2009	2739	743	3614	822	2185	1538	1840
Bismarck, ND	356	1378	1505	1456	1198	1145	1266	1041	971	1433	1719	1602	869	1811	1239	1332	511	429	958	957	278	1053	1810	2017	636	1353	1038	921	1377	1548	2111	803	1214	413	1682
Boise, ID	1097	424	2313	2177	1142	1990	635	1624	340	1757	965	648	1904	2431	495	1888	1328	1286	423	1540	915	2088	2430	2637	1671	2198	1512	130	633	2393	2082	1338	260	1345	928
Boston, MA	2178	2893	676	989	2174	899	2607	1202	2370	2048	3060	3117	944	1005	3061	1645	1501	1562	2780	1414	1926	757	1298	1337	1327	564	1597	2553	3199	438	3933	1639	2729	1763	2889
Brownsville, TX	2055	2007	1540	1298	813	1755	1683	1180	1598	278	1564	2023	1921	1327	2525	593	1297	1382	2301	970	1628	2105	1067	1342	1817	1905	809	1917	2663	1768	3759	900	2028	1839	1392
Buffalo, NY	1725	2440	502	769	1721	446	2154	749	1917	1653	2607	2664	519	906	2608	1257	1048	1109	2327	961	1473	341	1122	1238	958	110	1144	2100	2746	389	3480	1186	2276	1404	2436
Cabo San Lucas, BS	2792	1580	3439	3244	1836	3394	1469	2824	1764	2251	1059	1523	3560	3318	2284	2514	2732	2753	2486	2614	2385	3744	3154	3429	3358	3602	2431	1850	2427	3667	3876	2374	1693	3040	1177
Cairo, IL	1543	1996	611	416	1027	647	1643	161	1473	880	1914	2220	813	670	2248	484	680	765	1967	269	1133	997	669	876	999	855	450	1656	2386	839	3298	523	1832	1222	1742
Calgary, AB	471	1276	2303	2254	1603	1943	1164	1827	869	2033	1617	1500	1703	2609	675	2164	1297	1215	443	1743	844	1885	2608	2815	1262	2124	1788	819	601	2346	1448	1614	1112	826	1580
Cancún, QR	3509	3197	3016	2774	2267	3209	2873	2634	3006	1732	2754	3213	3375	2803	3835	2069	2751	2836	3755	2424	3082	3559	2543	2818	3271	3381	2263	3227	3973	3244	5213	2354	3218	3293	2582
Casper, WY	622	925	1716	1580	777	1393	677	1027	402	1207	1130	1149	1359	1834	1097	1338	558	586	816	943	240	1543	1833	2040	1190	1601	962	585	1235	1796	2274	788	761	931	1093
Charleston, SC	2103	2706	398	348	1617	914	2353	862	2183	1308	2478	2822	1163	105	2958	929	1390	1475	2677	990	1843	1205	398	437	1570	974	1117	2366	3096	525	3858	1291	2542	1782	2306
Charleston, WV	1678	2356	179	376	1484	443	2003	512	1833	1328	2371	2580	692	513	2561	932	981	1066	2280	724	1434	780	729	845	1133	549	907	2016	2699	366	3433	956	2192	1357	2199
Charlotte, NC	1963	2566	192	208	1559	708	2213	722	2043	1236	2401	2727	957	250	2818	852	1250	1335	2537	850	1703	999	466	582	1398	768	1022	2226	2956	398	3718	1104	2402	1642	2229
Cheyenne, WY	743	957	1579	1443	597	1256	709	890	434	1027	1162	1181	1422	1697	1225	1158	594	615	996	806	301	1606	1696	1903	1220	1464	782	617	1363	1659	2454	608	793	1010	1183
Chicago, IL	1185	1924	665	616	1272	303	1638	300	1401	1210	2091	2148	469	953	2068	851	532	569	1787	512	933	653	964	1171	652	511	695	1584	2206	706	2940	719	1760	864	1987
Chihuahua, CI	1788	1298	1815	1620	442	1869	974	1294	1107	609	855	1314	2035	1709	1936	905	1350	1435	1829	1084	1346	2219	1512	1787	1921	2069	901	1328	2074	2043	3499	953	1319	1892	683
Cincinnati, OH	1485	2180	372	324	1328	337	1840	356	1657	1215	2215	2404	586	661	2368	819	788	873	2087	568	1241	724	729	922	952	494	751	1840	2506	524	3240	793	2016	1164	2043
Cleveland, OH	1535	2250	429	576	1535	256	1964	563	1727	1467	2417	2474	505	763	2418	1071	858	919	2137	775	1283	530	981	1095	946	299	958	1910	2556	381	3290	1000	2086	1214	2250
Columbus, OH	1542	2246	346	435	1394	277	1906	422	1723	1326	2281	2470	526	680	2425	930	854	926	2144	634	1290	669	840	1033	967	438	817	1906	2563	417	3297	859	2082	1221	2109
Concord, NH	2048	2873	754	1067	2154	879	2587	1182	2350	2126	3040	3097	872	1055	3041	1723	1481	1542	2760	1394	1906	685	1348	1387	1255	582	1577	2533	3179	488	3774	1619	2709	1691	2869
Dallas, TX	1520	1668	1098	903	500	1208	1255	633	1402	277	1361	1744	1374	990	2193	186	762	847	1969	423	1093	1558	838	1113	1270	1432	262	1585	2331	1326	3427	365	1761	1304	1189
Davenport, IA	1136	1758	792	743	1181	452	1472	265	1235	1129	1925	1982	618	1038	1934	807	366	451	1653	402	819	802	1037	1244	608	660	614	1418	2072	855	2891	553	1594	815	1790
Daytona Beach, FL	2345	2835	664	583	1591	1180	2344	991	2312	1158	2440	2833	1429	230	3087	903	1519	1604	2806	1119	1972	1471	251	139	1812	1240	1202	2495	3225	791	4100	1376	2671	2024	2268
Denver, CO	843	1052	1553	1417	497	1299	629	864	529	942	1082	1276	1465	1671	1320	1067	637	658	1096	761	401	1649	1642	1877	1263	1507	691	712	1458	1697	2554	517	888	1095	1083
Des Moines, IA	1021	1589	961	912	1012	621	1303	344	1066	960	1756	1813	787	1151	1765	736	197	282	1484	361	650	971	1150	1357	585	829	445	1249	1903	1024	2776	384	1425	700	1621
Detroit, MI	1472	2187	547	586	1515	101	1901	543	1664	1477	2354	2411	350	881	2355	1081	795	856	2074	755	1220	466	991	1184	791	236	938	1847	2493	534	3227	955	2023	1151	2230
Dodge City, KS	1104	1429	1289	1091	471	1134	1015	600	906	727	1279	1560	1300	1372	1697	647	500	544	1473	412	648	1484	1275	1550	1125	1342	324	1089	1835	1433	2931	154	1265	980	1107
Duluth, MN	723	1822	1136	1087	1411	615	1702	681	1465	1359	2155	2046	424	1442	1683	1135	454	423	1402	760	787	608	1441	1648	188	847	844	1365	1821	1179	2478	783	1658	380	2020
Durango, CO	1222	912	1870	1675	410	1677	494	1157	395	927	847	1136	1843	1868	1224	1045	1015	1036	1117	1045	780	2027	1697	1972	1641	1885	862	616	1362	2098	2711	659	748	1473	675
Edmonton, AB	485	1449	2338	2289	1776	1978	1337	1874	1042	2206	1790	1673	1686	2644	807	2165	1344	1262	616	1790	1017	1868	2643	2850	1245	2107	1871	992	733	2381	1275	1787	1285	809	1753
El Paso, TX	1549	1171	1731	1536	203	1765	847	1190	868	558	728	1187	1931	1625	1697	821	1111	1158	1590	980	1107	2115	1461	1736	1711	1965	797	1089	1835	1959	3260	740	1192	1594	556
Ely, NV	1235	317	2256	2120	1019	1933	213	1567	244	1529	578	541	2099	2374	876	1654	1271	1232	804	1439	886	2283	2320	2580	1897	2141	1369	256	1014	2336	2463	1195	271	1483	541
Eureka, CA	1547	352	2885	2749	1568	2562	914	2196	873	2018	778	281	2728	3003	589	2203	1900	1861	766	2112	1515	2912	2855	3130	2356	2770	2020	807	732	2965	2181	1910	514	1902	945
Fargo, ND	546	1568	1315	1266	1236	955	1456	853	1161	1350	1909	1792	679	1621	1429	1144	323	241	1148	769	470	863	1620	1827	446	1163	850	1111	1567	1358	2301	687	1404	221	1872
Flagstaff, AZ	1548	694	1985	1790	525	1945	293	1370	520	1042	489	770	2111	1983	1349	1160	1291	1423	1242	1160	1167	2295	1812	2087	1891	2145	977	741	1487	2213	2836	920	715	1860	317
Fresno, CA	1735	299	2580	2385	1120	2442	517	1965	812	1579	339	183	2608	2578	923	1755	1780	1801	997	1755	1433	2792	2407	2682	2406	2650	1572	756	1066	2808	2515	1515	463	1983	506
Gallup, NM	1421	882	1797	1602	337	1757	469	1182	487	854	677	958	1923	1795	1316	972	1103	1235	1209	972	979	2107	1624	1899	1703	1957	789	708	1454	2025	2803	732	840	1672	505
Gaspé, QC	2361	3320	1367	1680	2647	1192	3034	1675	2797	2609	3487	3544	1190	1720	3488	2213	1928	1989	3207	1887	2353	1003	2013	2052	1568	900	2070	2980	3431	1153	4087	2088	3156	2004	3362
Grand Junction, CO	1087	803	1799	1663	580	1543	385	1110	286	1097	838	1027	1709	1917	1115	1313	881	902	1008	1007	645	1893	1888	2123	1507	1751	937	507	1253	1943	2602	763	639	1339	752
Grants Pass, OR	1379	333	2782	2646	1550	2459	895	2093	770	2086	846	391	2421	2900	421	2185	1797	1803	598	2009	1432	2605	2837	3106	2188	2667	1981	634	564	2862	2013	1807	411	1734	1013
Great Falls, MT	473	981	2050	2001	1274	1690	869	1498	574	1704	1322	1205	1414	2305	647	1835	968	886	366	1414	515	1598	2304	2511	1181	1898	1459	524	785	2093	1776	1285	817	820	1285
Green Bay, WI	1066	2060	881	832	1472	241	1774	500	1537	1410	2227	2284	287	1169	1949	1042	526	495	1668	712	859	471	1180	1387	517	532	895	1631	2087	924	2821	855	1896	745	2092
Guadalajara, JA	2479	1946	2134	1892	1112	2239	1622	1664	1798	754	1413	1960	2405	1921	2627	1163	1781	1866	2520	1454	2037	2589	1661	1936	2301	2463	1293	2003	2765	2362	4190	1384	1967	2323	1268
Halifax, NS	2574	3533	1403	1716	2873	1405	3247	1901	3010	2775	3700	3757	1403	1704	3701	2372	2141	2202	3420	2113	2566	1216	1997	2036	1781	1113	2296	3193	3644	1137	4300	2338	3369	2217	3588
Houston, TX	1767	1911	1185	943	730	1361	1498	780	1649	199	1481	1940	1527	972	2440	239	1009	1094	2216	666	1340	1711	712	987	1513	1551	505	1832	2578	1413	3674	612	2008	1551	1309
Idaho Falls, ID	815	621	2096	1960	1016	1773	509	1407	214	1540	962	845	1622	2214	790	1671	1086	1004	509	1323	633	1806	2213	2420	1389	1981	1295	164	928	2176	2103	1121	457	1063	925
Indianapolis, IN	1373	2073	482	433	1221	345	1733	249	1550	1159	2108	2297	538	770	2256	787	681	766	1975	461	1134	722	779	986	840	526	644	1733	2394	593	3128	686	1909	1052	1936
International Falls, MN	626	1824	1300	1251	1553	779	1712	845	1417	1501	2165	2048	660	1606	1685	1277	579	497	1404	902	726	842	1605	1812	219	1081	986	1367	1696	1343	2352	925	1660	269	2162
Jackson, MS	1805	2076	755	510	910	1029	1663	495	1746	637	1771	2152	1185	582	2537	222	942	1027	2229	496	1395	1416	430	705	1364	1186	535	1929	2675	983	3560	709	2105	1484	1599
Jacksonville, FL	2257	2747	574	495	1503	1090	2256	903	2224	1070	2352	2745	1339	140	2999	815	1431	1516	2718	1031	1884	1381	163	202	1724	1150	1114	2407	3137	701	4012	1288	2583	1936	2180
Juneau, AK	1904	2490	3757	3708	3196	3397	2757	3293	2462	3626	3003	2548	3105	4063	1737	3584	2763	2681	1835	3209	2437	3287	4062	4269	2664	3526	3290	2352	1663	3800	211	3207	2433	2228	3173
Kansas City, MO	1141	1594	945	809	818	790	1237	256	1071	766	1599	1818	956	1063	1846	543	278	363	1565	168	731	1140	1062	1269	781	998	251	1254	1984	1089	2896	190	1430	820	1427
Knoxville, TN	1734	2336	258	74	1329	587	1983	492	1813	1122	2216	2497	836	412	2588	719	1020	1105	2307	620	1473	974	481	674	1201	744	792	1996	2726	486	3489	874	2172	1413	2044
La Crosse, WI	944	1862	950	901	1285	590	1576	495	1339	1233	2029	2086	489	1256	1776	1009	328	297	1495	634	661	673	1255	1462	427	798	718	1458	1914	993	2699	657	1698	623	1894
Laredo, TX	1935	1773	1530	1288	579	1635	1449	1060	1381	150	1330	1789	1801	1317	2210	559	1177	1262	2171	850	1508	1985	1057	1332	1697	1859	689	1602	2348	1758	3629	780	1794	1719	1158
Las Vegas, NV	1444	445	2234	2039	774	2046	121	1613	416	1284	335	573	2212	2232	1122	1409	1384	1405	1138	1409	1037	2396	2061	2336	2010	2254	1226	502	1260	2462	2732	1169	466	1692	296
Lexington, KY	1564	2179	356	247	1307	417	1826	335	1656	1151	2194	2403	666	584	2431	755	863	948	2150	547	1316	804	652	845	1031	574	730	1839	2569	543	3319	779	2015	1243	2022
Lincoln, NE	1016	1400	1136	1000	822	815	1114	447	877	906	1567	1624	981	1254	1668	738	153	238	1397	363	546	1165	1253	1460	779	1023	450	1060	1806	1218	2771	276	1236	695	1458
Little Rock, AR	1524	1902	783	588	810	927	1489	346	1484	592	1676	1978	1093	781	2275	196	661	746	1948	215	1114	1277	684	959	1163	1117	273	1667	2413	1011	3279	447	1843	1203	1504
Los Angeles, CA	1717	473	2457	2262	949	2319	394	1842	689	1364	124	381	2485	2455	1142	1627	1657	1678	1215	1632	1310	2669	2267	2542	2283	2527	1449	775	1285	2685	2734	1392	586	1965	291

	Acapulco, GR	Albany, NY	Albuquerque, NM	Amarillo, TX	Anchorage, AK	Atlanta, GA	Baltimore, MD	Bangor, ME	Billings, MT	Birmingham, AL	Bismarck, ND	Boise, ID	Boston, MA	Brownsville, TX	Buffalo, NY	Cabo San Lucas, BS	Cairo, IL	Calgary, AB	Cancún, QR	Casper, WY	Charleston, SC	Charleston, WV	Charlotte, NC	Cheyenne, WY	Chicago, IL	Chihuahua, CI	Cincinnati, OH	Cleveland, OH	Columbus, OH	Concord, NH	Dallas, TX	Davenport, IA	Daytona Beach, FL	Denver, CO	Des Moines, IA
Louisville, KY	2201	830	1306	1021	3969	418	618	1229	1537	366	1139	1885	994	1310	541	3087	260	1937	2786	1288	614	249	474	1151	299	1554	103	355	214	974	837	424	852	1125	593
Mackinaw City, MI	2680	926	1726	1441	3741	992	811	1325	1361	952	948	1983	1090	1863	637	3502	755	1589	3317	1330	1105	634	899	1364	411	1977	528	447	468	1070	1316	560	1371	1407	729
Memphis, TN	1818	1222	1014	729	4072	391	914	1577	1477	243	1242	1825	1314	927	924	2795	169	2028	2403	1228	712	599	618	1091	536	1171	486	738	597	1392	454	549	797	1097	617
Mexico City, DF	219	2725	1376	1287	4979	1761	2417	3080	2257	1635	2307	2316	2817	609	2527	2697	1754	2808	1029	1982	2077	2202	2005	1802	2084	870	2089	2341	2200	2895	1151	2025	1927	1717	1834
Miami, FL	2373	1415	1963	1678	5050	661	1082	1717	2492	783	2220	2840	1482	1545	1383	3632	1079	3018	3021	2243	582	990	727	2106	1374	1990	1125	1240	1157	1532	1316	1447	255	2080	1560
Milwaukee, WI	2380	921	1351	1141	3592	812	806	1320	1175	760	762	1741	1085	1563	632	3145	465	1560	3017	1077	1010	585	870	1007	92	1677	392	442	449	1065	1016	214	1246	1050	372
Minneapolis, MN	2292	1235	1222	1043	3260	1132	1120	1634	843	1080	430	1465	1399	1475	946	3016	753	1228	2929	848	1324	899	1184	878	406	1579	706	756	763	1379	928	358	1566	921	243
Minot, ND	2627	1769	1224	1055	2725	1666	1654	2168	444	1614	111	1066	1933	1810	1480	2761	1298	693	3264	591	1858	1433	1718	685	940	1730	1240	1290	1297	1913	1275	891	2100	785	776
Missoula, MT	2713	2417	1128	1312	2554	2173	2302	2816	340	2121	759	370	2581	2102	2128	2287	1768	388	3556	617	2478	2081	2338	797	1588	1630	1888	1938	1945	2561	1770	1454	2607	897	1285
Mobile, AL	1655	1335	1245	960	4469	329	1003	1690	1874	261	1639	2237	1427	827	1164	2914	566	2425	2303	1687	645	826	573	1507	920	1272	726	978	837	1505	598	946	491	1416	1014
Monterrey, NL	791	2252	961	806	4498	1288	1944	2607	1776	1162	1729	1901	2344	186	1949	2354	1176	2327	1496	1501	1604	1624	1532	1321	1506	495	1511	1763	1622	2422	573	1425	1454	1236	1256
Montgomery, AL	1820	1166	1302	1017	4427	160	834	1521	1869	92	1597	2217	1258	992	995	2983	456	2395	2468	1620	476	657	404	1483	751	1374	557	809	668	1336	655	824	464	1429	937
Montréal, QC	3129	226	2151	1866	4244	1222	562	300	2099	1307	1686	2531	324	2238	402	3935	1188	2264	3714	1934	1121	835	984	1797	844	2402	827	585	724	252	1765	993	1387	1840	1162
Nashville, TN	2027	1012	1223	938	4148	243	704	1367	1590	189	1318	1938	1104	1136	716	3004	177	2116	2612	1341	548	391	408	1204	472	1380	278	530	389	1182	663	545	677	1178	658
Needles, CA	1872	2616	535	820	3567	1939	2461	3015	1079	1791	1498	744	2780	1498	2327	1339	1633	1396	2688	909	2260	2090	2165	941	1870	789	1934	2141	2000	2760	1182	1704	2271	861	1535
New Orleans, LA	1534	1432	1173	888	4463	468	1124	1787	1868	342	1633	2228	1524	706	1243	2793	560	2419	2182	1678	784	911	712	1498	927	1151	805	1057	916	1602	526	940	634	1407	1008
New York, NY	2835	159	2022	1737	4483	873	203	443	2066	982	1653	2498	208	2007	399	3803	1029	2451	3483	1901	762	555	635	1764	811	2282	661	486	554	258	1565	960	1028	1807	1129
Norfolk, VA	2538	509	1910	1625	4564	558	234	811	2147	707	1734	2544	576	1710	575	3691	863	2532	3186	1947	431	410	320	1810	892	2067	603	567	577	626	1350	1023	697	1784	1192
North Platte, NE	1937	1556	702	473	3355	1228	1441	1955	633	1176	475	955	1720	1203	1267	2359	823	1184	2657	358	1533	1183	1393	221	751	1208	1007	1077	1073	1700	756	585	1662	264	416
Odessa, TX	1304	2028	399	258	3950	1150	1720	2383	1228	1005	1206	1343	2120	632	1730	1974	957	1779	2086	953	1471	1405	1394	773	1231	365	1292	1544	1403	2198	354	1140	1445	689	971
Oklahoma City, OK	1560	1536	544	259	3942	860	1382	1935	1220	712	960	1495	1700	743	1247	2325	553	1771	2197	945	1181	1010	1086	765	798	795	854	1061	920	1680	208	707	1266	674	538
Omaha, NE	2024	1278	869	652	3436	995	1163	1677	841	943	606	1233	1442	1207	989	2637	590	1392	2661	636	1300	950	1160	499	473	1260	729	799	795	1422	672	307	1429	542	138
Ottawa, ON	3041	310	2063	1778	4160	1161	531	425	1777	1246	1364	2443	449	2150	341	3847	1100	2180	3626	1846	1092	774	923	1709	756	2314	739	524	663	377	1677	905	1358	1752	1074
Page, AZ	1919	2439	452	737	3422	1856	2378	2838	934	1708	1353	722	2603	1445	2150	1591	1550	1251	2735	764	2177	2007	2082	723	1634	836	1851	1960	1917	2583	1099	1468	2188	625	1299
Pendleton, OR	2742	2720	1157	1458	2587	2392	2605	3119	744	2340	1163	218	2884	2248	2431	2117	1987	648	3558	916	2697	2347	2557	948	1915	1659	2171	2241	2237	2864	1916	1749	2826	1043	1580
Philadelphia, PA	2738	243	1941	1656	4434	772	102	545	2017	885	1604	2449	310	1910	388	3722	950	2402	3386	1852	661	476	534	1715	762	2185	580	437	473	360	1468	911	927	1753	1080
Phoenix, AZ	1646	2544	463	748	3695	1867	2389	2943	1207	1719	1603	922	2708	1272	2255	1318	1561	1524	2462	958	2188	2018	2093	1002	1806	563	1862	2069	1928	2688	1069	1609	2148	902	1440
Pierre, SD	2309	1615	966	737	3041	1391	1500	2014	491	1339	211	1113	1779	1492	1326	2623	986	1009	2946	413	1696	1287	1556	436	786	1472	1094	1136	1143	1759	957	672	1825	528	503
Pittsburgh, PA	2592	474	1651	1366	4133	686	251	821	1716	753	1303	2148	586	1701	216	3432	651	2101	3177	1551	654	229	448	1414	461	1945	290	136	183	636	1228	610	920	1457	779
Portland, ME	3167	267	2348	2063	4507	1229	507	132	2342	1314	1929	2774	117	2339	562	4129	1361	2527	3815	2177	1066	887	939	2040	1087	2614	994	745	884	96	1897	1236	1332	2083	1405
Portland, OR	2949	2927	1364	1665	2490	2599	2812	3326	891	2547	1310	425	3091	2455	2638	2109	2194	795	3765	1123	2904	2554	2764	1155	2122	1866	2378	2448	2444	3071	2123	1956	3033	1250	1787
Pueblo, CO	1821	1924	330	321	3386	1442	1719	2323	664	1270	810	939	2088	1111	1635	2111	1037	1215	2565	389	1747	1397	1607	209	1119	836	1234	1445	1300	2068	683	953	1772	109	784
Québec, QC	3286	373	2308	2023	4398	1379	709	229	2256	1464	1843	2688	403	2395	559	4092	1345	2418	3871	2091	1268	992	1141	1954	1001	2559	984	742	881	329	1922	1150	1534	1997	1319
Raleigh, NC	2387	628	1759	1474	4481	407	295	930	2064	556	1651	2473	695	1559	637	3540	712	2449	3035	1876	280	325	169	1739	811	1916	518	575	492	745	1199	938	546	1713	1107
Redding, CA	2564	2925	1217	1502	2911	2597	2810	3324	1155	2473	1574	525	3089	2190	2636	1690	2192	1113	3380	1121	2902	2552	2762	1153	2120	1481	2376	2446	2442	3069	1864	1954	3031	1248	1785
Regina, SK	2758	2014	1282	1258	2482	1911	1899	2096	475	1859	356	1097	2178	2055	1725	2792	1543	471	3509	622	2103	1678	1963	743	1185	1788	1485	1535	1542	2048	1520	1136	2345	843	1021
Reno, NV	2381	2729	1021	1306	3068	2401	2614	3128	959	2277	1378	424	2893	2007	2440	1580	1996	1276	3197	925	2706	2356	2566	957	1924	1298	2180	2250	2246	2873	1668	1758	2835	1052	1589
Roanoke, VA	2368	584	1658	1373	4335	430	276	939	1918	515	1505	2313	676	1540	502	3439	611	2303	3016	1716	398	179	192	1579	665	1815	372	429	346	754	1098	792	664	1553	961
Robbinsville, NC	2126	897	1463	1178	4286	149	589	1252	1829	270	1456	2177	989	1298	769	3244	416	2254	2774	1580	348	376	208	1443	616	1620	324	576	435	1067	903	743	583	1417	912
Roswell, NM	1445	2010	198	214	3774	1296	1855	2409	1052	1151	1198	1142	2174	813	1721	1836	1027	1603	2267	777	1617	1484	1559	597	1272	442	1328	1535	1394	2154	500	1181	1591	497	1012
Saginaw, MI	2572	735	1618	1333	3975	801	620	1134	1558	804	1145	1990	899	1755	446	3394	647	1943	3209	1393	914	443	708	1256	303	1869	337	256	277	879	1208	452	1180	1299	621
St. George, UT	2057	2443	608	893	3335	2048	2325	2842	847	1864	1266	635	2607	1683	2154	1469	1643	1164	2873	677	2353	2003	2213	709	1638	974	1840	1964	1906	2587	1255	1472	2344	629	1303
St. Louis, MO	1997	1038	1043	758	3871	557	841	1437	1276	505	1041	1624	1202	1180	749	2824	161	1827	2634	1027	862	512	722	890	300	1294	356	563	422	1182	633	265	991	864	344
Salt Lake City, UT	2190	2206	605	944	3040	1878	2091	2605	552	1826	971	340	2370	1598	1917	1764	1473	869	3006	402	2183	1833	2043	434	1401	1107	1657	1727	1723	2350	1402	1235	2312	529	1066
San Antonio, TX	1087	1956	715	512	4204	992	1648	2311	1482	866	1433	1757	2048	278	1653	2251	880	2033	1732	1207	1308	1328	1236	1027	1210	609	1215	1467	1326	2126	277	1129	1158	942	960
San Diego, CA	1938	2896	816	1101	3581	2157	2742	3295	1300	2012	1719	965	3060	1564	2607	1059	1914	1617	2754	1130	2478	2371	2401	1162	2091	855	2215	2417	2281	3040	1361	1925	2440	1082	1756
San Francisco, CA	2397	2953	1097	1382	3126	2501	2838	3352	1183	2353	1602	648	3117	2023	2664	1523	2220	1500	3213	1149	2822	2580	2727	1181	2148	1314	2404	2474	2470	3097	1744	1982	2833	1276	1813
Sault Ste. Marie, ON	2738	809	1784	1499	3683	1050	869	920	1282	1010	869	1904	944	1921	519	3560	813	1703	3375	1359	1163	692	957	1422	469	2035	586	505	526	872	1374	618	1429	1465	787
Savannah, GA	2155	938	1656	1371	4641	252	605	1240	2083	401	1811	2431	1005	1327	906	3318	670	2609	2803	1834	105	513	250	1697	953	1709	661	763	680	1055	990	1038	230	1671	1151
Seattle, WA	3019	2897	1434	1735	2315	2653	2782	3296	820	2601	1239	495	3061	2525	2608	2284	2248	675	3835	1097	2958	2561	2818	1225	2068	1936	2368	2418	2425	3041	2193	1934	3087	1320	1765
Shreveport, LA	1421	1553	833	548	4162	608	1245	1908	1613	463	1332	1888	1645	593	1257	2514	484	2164	2069	1338	929	932	852	1158	851	905	819	1071	930	1723	186	807	903	1067	736
Sioux City, IA	2114	1337	964	747	3341	1085	1222	1736	746	1033	511	1328	1501	1297	1048	2732	680	1297	2751	558	1390	981	1250	594	532	1350	788	858	854	1481	762	366	1519	637	197
Sioux Falls, SD	2199	1398	1096	794	3259	1170	1283	1797	664	1118	429	1286	1562	1382	1109	2753	765	1215	2836	586	1475	1066	1335	615	569	1435	873	919	926	1542	847	451	1604	658	282
Spokane, WA	2912	2616	1327	1511	2413	2372	2501	3015	539	2320	958	423	2780	2301	2327	2486	1967	443	3755	816	2677	2280	2537	996	1787	1829	2087	2137	2144	2760	1969	1653	2806	1096	1484
Springfield, MO	1787	1250	833	548	3787	685	1053	1649	1192	527	957	1540	1414	970	961	2614	269	1743	2424	943	990	724	850	806	512	1084	568	775	634	1394	423	402	1119	761	361
Sturgis, SD	2249	1762	840	749	3015	1538	1647	2161	293	1486	278	915	1926	1628	1473	2385	1133	844	3082	240	1843	1434	1703	301	933	1346	1241	1283	1290	1906	1093	819	1972	401	650
Sudbury, ON	2922	631	1968	1683	3865	1188	721	733	1466	1191	1053	2088	757	2105	341	3744	997	1885	3559	1543	1205	780	999	1606	653	2219	724	530	669	685	1558	802	1471	1649	971
Tallahassee, FL	1895	1231	1485	1200	4640	265	898	1533	2082	305	1810	2430	1298	1067	1122	3154	669	2608	2543	1833	398	729	466	1696	964	1512	729	981	840	1348	838	1037	251	1642	1150
Tampa, FL	2170	1270	1760	1475	4847	458	937	1572	2289	580	2017	2637	1337	1342	1238	3429	876	2815	2818	2040	437	845	582	1903	1171	1787	922	1095	1033	1387	1113	1244	139	1877	1357
Thunder Bay, ON	2634	1189	1564	1385	3242	1378	1310	1303	1049	1326	636	1671	1327	1817	958	3358	999	1262	3271	1190	1570	1133	1398	1220	652	1921	952	946	967	1255	1270	608	1812	1263	585
Toronto, ON	2796	400	1818	1533	4104	958	490	630	1766	961	1353	2198	564	1905	110	3602	855	2124	3381	1601	974	549	768	1464	511	2069	494	299	438	582	1432	660	1240	1507	829
Tulsa, OK	1626	1433	650	365	3868	796	1236	1832	1237	648	1038	1512	1597	809	1144	2431	450	1788	2263	962	1117	907	1022	782	695	901	751	958	817	1577	262	614	1202	691	445
Twin Falls, ID	2411	2389	826	1127	2930	2061	2274	2788	502	2009	921	130	2553	1917	2100	1850	1656	819	3227	585	2366	2016	2226	617	1584	1328	1840	1910	1906	2533	1585	1418	2495	712	1249
Vancouver, BC	3157	3035	1572	1873	2241	2791	2920	3434	958	2739	1377	633	3199	2663	2746	2427	2386	601	3973	1235	3096	2699	2956	1363	2206	2074	2506	2556	2563	3179	2331	2072	3225	1458	1903
Washington, DC	2596	371	1886	1601	4378	636	38	673	1961	743	1548	2393	438	1768	389	3667	839	2346	3244	1796	525	366	398	1659	706	2043	524	381	417	488	1326	855	791	1697	1024
Whitehorse, YT	4469	3769	2993	2969	723	3666	3654	3822	1999	3614	2111	2082	3933	3759	3480	3876	3298	1448	5213	2274	3858	3433	3718	2454	2940	3499	3240	3290	3297	3774	3427	2891	4100	2554	2776
Wichita, KS	1717	1475	593	417	3785	970	1278	1874	1063	822	803	1338	1639	900	1186	2374	523	1614	2354	788	1291	956	1104	608	719	953	793	1000	859	1619	365	553	1376	517	384
Winnemucca, NV	2402	2565	958	1303	3011	2237	2450	2964	795	2185	1214	260	2729	2028	2276	1693	1832	1112	3218	761	2542	2192	2402	793	1760	1319	2016	2086	2082	2709	1761	1594	2671	888	1425
Winnipeg, MB	2656	1693	1533	1230	2806	1590	1578	1739	723	1538	413	1345	1763	1839	1404	3040	1222	826	3293	931	1782	1357	1642	1010	864	1892	1164	1214	1221	1691	1304	815	2024	1095	700
Yuma, AZ	1766	2725	644	929	3751	1985	2570	3124	1263	1840	1682	928	2889	1392	2436	1177	1742	1580	2582	1093	2306	2199	2229	1183	1987	683	2043	2250	2109	2869	1189	1790	2268	1083	1621

Detroit, MI	Dodge City, KS	Duluth, MN	Durango, CO	Edmonton, AB	El Paso, TX	Ely, NV	Eureka, CA	Fargo, ND	Flagstaff, AZ	Fresno, CA	Gallup, NM	Gaspé, QC	Grand Junction, CO	Grants Pass, OR	Great Falls, MT	Green Bay, WI	Guadalajara, JA	Halifax, NS	Houston, TX	Idaho Falls, ID	Indianapolis, IN	International Falls, MN	Jackson, MS	Jacksonville, FL	Juneau, AK	Kansas City, MO	Knoxville, TN	La Crosse, WI	Laredo, TX	Las Vegas, NV	Lexington, KY	Lincoln, NE	Little Rock, AR	Los Angeles, CA	
365	861	770	1418	1972	1470	1828	2457	949	1633	2228	1445	1497	1371	2354	1684	515	1868	1693	956	1668	114	934	591	764	3391	517	245	584	1264	1874	72	708	522	2105	Louisville, KY
292	1242	423	1785	1744	1873	2041	2670	758	2053	2550	1865	1248	1651	2500	1493	258	2347	1461	1469	1701	480	587	1127	1281	3163	898	778	460	1743	2154	608	923	1035	2427	Mackinaw City, MI
748	730	965	1226	2075	1087	1775	2384	1054	1341	1936	1153	1880	1343	2366	1699	743	1485	2041	573	1608	472	1129	212	709	3494	453	388	779	881	1590	422	648	139	1813	Memphis, TN
2351	1472	2233	1588	2981	1109	1968	2457	2224	1569	2018	1490	3483	1758	2525	2479	2284	329	3544	964	2190	2033	2375	1406	1839	4401	1640	1891	2129	724	1723	2025	1780	1466	1803	Mexico City, DF
1387	1753	1851	2175	3053	1939	2783	3333	2030	2290	2885	2102	2197	2326	3309	2714	1590	2139	2181	1190	2623	1189	2015	908	343	4472	1472	877	1665	1535	2539	1048	1663	1162	2745	Miami, FL
379	912	393	1428	1595	1498	1684	2313	572	1678	2193	1490	1512	1294	2314	1307	117	2047	1725	1163	1515	280	557	837	1158	3014	568	641	207	1443	1797	471	566	729	2070	Milwaukee, WI
693	783	157	1299	1263	1369	1555	2150	240	1549	2064	1361	1826	1165	1982	975	287	1959	2039	1171	1183	594	299	1062	1478	2682	439	955	163	1355	1668	785	437	821	1941	Minneapolis, MN
1227	859	474	1164	728	1491	1204	1680	284	1517	1704	1363	2085	1029	1512	548	821	2294	2298	1522	784	1128	433	1560	2012	2147	896	1489	699	1690	1413	1319	771	1279	1686	Minot, ND
1875	1274	1203	918	561	1391	645	965	949	1043	1068	1010	3008	809	797	167	1469	2321	3221	2017	310	1776	1205	2030	2519	1976	1366	2108	1296	1972	939	1951	1198	1749	1212	Missoula, MT
988	1059	1362	1457	2472	1221	2066	2615	1451	1572	2167	1384	2118	1662	2597	2096	1136	1421	2154	472	2020	735	1526	190	403	3891	850	513	1176	817	1821	662	1045	452	2027	Mobile, AL
1773	967	1655	1173	2500	694	1593	2082	1646	1194	1643	1075	2905	1343	2150	1998	1706	458	3071	495	1834	1455	1797	933	1366	3920	1062	1418	1529	146	1348	1447	1202	888	1428	Monterrey, NL
819	1062	1228	1514	2430	1290	2107	2672	1407	1629	2224	1441	1949	1675	2654	2091	967	1586	1985	637	2000	566	1392	247	376	3849	849	344	1042	982	1878	493	1040	471	2096	Montgomery, AL
569	1675	1047	2218	2247	2298	2474	3103	1496	2478	2983	2290	568	2084	3000	2231	910	2796	781	1884	2314	859	1221	1547	1297	3666	1331	1050	1131	2192	2587	907	1356	1450	2860	Montréal, QC
540	852	949	1435	2151	1296	1881	2510	1128	1550	2145	1362	1672	1424	2407	1812	688	1694	1831	782	1721	287	1113	417	589	3570	570	178	763	1090	1799	214	761	348	2022	Nashville, TN
2121	998	1934	566	1569	662	357	835	1688	208	387	396	3253	617	890	1101	2006	1435	3479	1425	741	1827	1944	1590	2183	2989	1318	1935	1808	1264	112	1913	1346	1416	264	Needles, CA
1067	987	1356	1385	2466	1100	1994	2543	1445	1500	2095	1312	2215	1653	2525	2090	1134	1300	2251	351	2011	814	1520	180	546	3885	844	598	1170	696	1749	741	1039	423	1906	New Orleans, LA
639	1570	1284	2127	2486	2198	2441	3070	1463	2349	2950	2161	941	2051	2967	2198	1029	2601	907	1652	2281	730	1448	1222	938	3905	1226	725	1098	1997	2554	732	1323	1250	2827	New York, NY
720	1520	1365	2122	2567	1983	2487	3116	1544	2237	2832	2049	1291	2030	3013	2279	1110	2304	1275	1355	2327	713	1529	944	607	3986	1176	510	1179	1700	2486	587	1367	1035	2709	Norfolk, VA
1014	277	815	642	1357	969	898	1527	612	1029	1407	841	2147	508	1424	855	887	1604	2360	1003	738	900	868	1085	1574	2777	421	1163	689	1073	1011	1006	227	838	1284	North Platte, NE
1474	504	1370	611	1952	281	1252	1741	1310	726	1302	538	2606	781	1809	1450	1431	971	2847	549	1286	1180	1512	764	1357	3372	777	1194	1244	431	1007	1228	866	669	1087	Odessa, TX
1041	254	937	756	1944	691	1352	1914	877	871	1466	683	2173	920	1896	1442	998	1227	2399	455	1278	747	1079	615	1178	3364	344	856	811	623	1120	833	433	337	1343	Oklahoma City, OK
736	405	537	920	1439	1016	1176	1805	418	1196	1685	1008	1869	786	1702	1063	609	1691	2082	919	1016	622	679	852	1341	2858	188	930	411	1087	1289	773	58	571	1562	Omaha, NE
481	1587	919	2130	2163	2210	2386	3015	1174	2390	2895	2202	695	1996	2912	1909	782	2708	908	1796	2226	771	1137	1486	1268	3582	1243	989	1043	2104	2499	819	1268	1362	2772	Ottawa, ON
1897	915	1698	262	1424	694	368	1069	1543	137	672	313	3030	381	1050	956	1770	1482	3243	1342	596	1744	1799	1507	2100	2844	1233	1852	1572	1228	276	1830	1110	1333	549	Page, AZ
2178	1420	1607	947	821	1420	599	621	1353	1072	887	1039	3311	838	453	571	1873	2350	3524	2163	495	2064	1609	2260	2738	2009	1585	2327	1700	1933	845	2170	1391	1998	1010	Pendleton, OR
590	1489	1235	2046	2437	2101	2392	3021	1414	2268	2863	2080	1025	1999	2918	2149	980	2504	1009	1555	2232	649	1399	1125	837	3856	1145	628	1049	1900	2502	653	1274	1153	2740	Philadelphia, PA
2049	926	1839	494	1697	436	535	1024	1777	136	585	324	3181	571	1092	1229	1911	1209	3407	1189	869	1755	1981	1479	2060	3117	1246	1863	1713	1038	290	1841	1277	1344	370	Phoenix, AZ
1073	541	640	906	1044	1233	1059	1688	333	1293	1671	1105	2206	772	1630	713	712	1976	2419	1204	831	987	589	1248	1737	2463	584	1326	514	1372	1275	1169	459	967	1548	Pierre, SD
289	1199	934	1756	2136	1861	2091	2720	1113	1978	2573	1790	1179	1701	2617	1848	679	2259	1285	1347	1931	359	1098	993	830	3555	855	496	748	1655	2204	406	973	913	2450	Pittsburgh, PA
915	1896	1560	2461	2510	2530	2717	3346	1739	2675	3226	2487	644	2327	3243	2474	1305	2933	596	1984	2557	1056	1724	1554	1242	3929	1552	1057	1374	2329	2830	1064	1599	1582	3103	Portland, ME
2385	1627	1754	1154	968	1627	806	414	1500	1279	748	1246	3518	1045	246	718	2020	2546	3731	2370	702	2271	1756	2467	2945	1912	1792	2534	1847	2140	1021	2377	1598	2205	967	Portland, OR
1382	274	1183	270	1388	597	785	1511	984	657	1252	469	2515	353	1408	886	1255	1527	2728	926	722	1127	1240	1091	1684	2808	631	1377	1057	981	856	1220	595	895	1129	Pueblo, CO
726	1832	1204	2375	2401	2455	2631	3260	1653	2635	3140	2447	430	2241	3157	2388	1067	2953	643	2041	2471	1016	1375	1704	1444	3820	1488	1207	1288	2349	2744	1064	1513	1607	3017	Québec, QC
693	1387	1282	1971	2484	1832	2416	3045	1461	2086	2681	1898	1410	1959	2942	2196	1027	2153	1394	1204	2256	628	1446	793	456	3903	1105	359	1096	1549	2335	502	1296	884	2558	Raleigh, NC
2383	1625	2018	1108	1286	1354	513	154	1764	890	329	1078	3516	999	176	1036	2256	2127	3729	2107	817	2269	2020	2272	2943	2333	1790	2532	2058	1956	641	2375	1596	2098	548	Redding, CA
1472	1104	723	1222	485	1549	1235	1547	546	1548	1735	1421	2361	1087	1379	473	1066	2479	2574	1767	815	1373	626	1805	2257	1904	1141	1734	944	1935	1444	1564	1016	1524	1717	Regina, SK
2187	1429	1822	912	1449	1171	317	352	1568	694	299	882	3320	803	333	981	2060	1944	3533	1911	621	2073	1824	2076	2747	2490	1594	2336	1862	1773	445	2179	1400	1902	473	Reno, NV
547	1289	1136	1870	2338	1731	2256	2885	1315	1985	2580	1797	1367	1799	2782	2050	881	2134	1403	1185	2096	482	1300	755	574	3757	945	258	950	1530	2234	356	1136	783	2457	Roanoke, VA
586	1091	1087	1675	2289	1536	2120	2749	1266	1790	2385	1602	1680	1663	2646	2001	832	1892	1716	943	1960	433	1251	510	495	3708	809	74	901	1288	2039	247	1000	588	2262	Robbinsville, NC
1515	471	1411	410	1776	203	1019	1568	1236	525	1120	337	2647	580	1550	1274	1472	1112	2873	730	1016	1221	1553	910	1503	3196	818	1329	1285	579	774	1307	822	810	949	Roswell, NM
101	1134	615	1677	1978	1765	1933	2562	955	1945	2442	1757	1192	1543	2459	1690	241	2239	1405	1361	1773	345	779	1029	1090	3397	790	587	590	1635	2046	417	815	927	2319	Saginaw, MI
1901	1015	1702	494	1337	847	213	914	1456	293	517	469	3034	385	895	869	1774	1620	3247	1498	509	1733	1712	1663	2256	2757	1237	1983	1576	1449	121	1826	1114	1489	394	St. George, UT
543	600	681	1157	1874	1190	1567	2196	853	1370	1965	1182	1675	1110	2093	1498	500	1664	1901	780	1407	249	845	495	903	3293	256	492	495	1060	1613	335	447	346	1842	St. Louis, MO
1664	906	1465	395	1042	868	244	873	1161	520	812	487	2797	286	770	574	1537	1798	3010	1649	214	1550	1417	1746	2224	2462	1071	1813	1339	1381	416	1656	877	1484	689	Salt Lake City, UT
1477	727	1359	927	2206	558	1529	2018	1350	1042	1579	854	2609	1097	2086	1704	1410	754	2775	199	1540	1159	1501	637	1070	3626	766	1122	1233	150	1284	1151	906	592	1364	San Antonio, TX
2354	1279	2155	847	1790	728	578	778	1909	489	339	677	3487	838	846	1322	2227	1413	3700	1481	962	2108	2165	1771	2352	3003	1599	2216	2029	1330	335	2194	1567	1676	124	San Diego, CA
2411	1560	2046	1136	1673	1187	541	281	1792	770	183	958	3544	1027	391	1205	2284	1960	3757	1940	845	2297	2048	2152	2745	2548	1818	2497	2086	1789	573	2403	1624	1978	381	San Francisco, CA
350	1300	424	1843	1686	1931	2099	2728	679	2111	2608	1923	1190	1709	2421	1414	287	2405	1403	1527	1622	538	660	1185	1339	3105	956	836	489	1801	2212	666	981	1093	2485	Sault Ste. Marie, ON
881	1372	1442	1868	2644	1625	2374	3003	1621	1983	2578	1795	1720	1917	2900	2305	1169	1921	1704	972	2214	770	1606	582	140	4063	1063	412	1256	1317	2232	584	1254	781	2455	Savannah, GA
2355	1697	1683	1224	807	1697	876	589	1429	1349	923	1316	3488	1115	421	647	1949	2627	3701	2440	790	2256	1685	2537	2999	1737	1846	2588	1776	2210	1122	2431	1668	2275	1142	Seattle, WA
1081	647	1135	1045	2165	821	1654	2203	1144	1160	1755	972	2213	1313	2185	1835	1042	1163	2372	239	1671	787	1277	222	815	3584	543	719	1009	559	1409	755	738	196	1627	Shreveport, LA
795	500	454	1015	1344	1111	1271	1900	323	1291	1780	1103	1928	881	1797	968	526	1781	2141	1009	1086	681	579	942	1431	2763	278	1020	328	1177	1384	863	153	661	1657	Sioux City, IA
856	544	423	1036	1262	1158	1232	1861	241	1423	1801	1235	1989	902	1803	886	495	1866	2202	1094	1004	766	497	1027	1516	2681	363	1105	297	1262	1405	948	238	746	1678	Sioux Falls, SD
2074	1473	1402	1117	616	1590	804	766	1148	1242	997	1209	3207	1008	598	366	1668	2520	3420	2216	509	1975	1404	2229	2718	1835	1565	2307	1495	2171	1138	2150	1397	1948	1215	Spokane, WA
755	412	760	1045	1790	980	1439	2112	769	1160	1755	972	1887	1007	2009	1414	712	1454	2113	666	1323	461	902	496	1031	3209	168	620	634	850	1409	547	363	215	1632	Springfield, MO
1220	648	787	780	1017	1107	886	1515	470	1167	1433	979	2353	645	1432	515	859	2037	2566	1340	633	1134	726	1395	1884	2437	731	1473	661	1508	1037	1316	546	1114	1310	Sturgis, SD
466	1484	608	2027	1868	2115	2283	2912	863	2295	2792	2107	1003	1893	2605	1598	471	2589	1216	1711	1806	722	842	1416	1381	3287	1140	974	673	1985	2396	804	1165	1277	2669	Sudbury, ON
991	1275	1441	1697	2643	1461	2320	2855	1620	1812	2407	1624	2013	1888	2837	2304	1180	1661	1997	712	2213	779	1605	430	163	4062	1062	481	1255	1057	2061	652	1253	684	2267	Tallahassee, FL
1184	1550	1648	1972	2850	1736	2580	3130	1827	2087	2682	1899	2052	2123	3106	2511	1387	1936	2036	987	2420	986	1812	705	202	4269	1269	674	1462	1332	2336	845	1460	959	2542	Tampa, FL
791	1125	188	1641	1245	1711	1897	2356	446	1891	2406	1703	1568	1507	2188	1181	517	2301	1781	1513	1389	840	219	1364	1724	2664	781	1201	427	1697	2010	1031	779	1163	2283	Thunder Bay, ON
236	1342	847	1885	2107	1965	2141	2770	1163	2145	2650	1957	900	1751	2667	1898	532	2463	1113	1551	1981	526	1081	1186	1150	3526	998	744	798	1859	2254	574	1023	1117	2527	Toronto, ON
938	324	844	862	1871	797	1369	2020	850	977	1572	789	2070	937	1981	1459	895	1293	2296	505	1295	644	986	535	1114	3290	251	792	718	689	1226	730	450	273	1449	Tulsa, OK
1847	1089	1365	616	992	1089	256	807	1111	741	756	708	2980	507	634	524	1631	2001	3193	1832	164	1733	1367	1929	2407	2352	1254	1996	1458	1602	502	1839	1060	1667	775	Twin Falls, ID
2493	1835	1821	1362	733	1835	1014	732	1567	1487	1066	1454	3431	1253	564	785	2087	2765	3644	2578	928	2394	1696	2675	3137	1663	1984	2726	1914	2348	1260	2569	1806	2413	1285	Vancouver, BC
534	1433	1179	2098	2381	1959	2336	2965	1358	2213	2808	2025	1153	1943	2862	2093	924	2362	1137	1413	2176	593	1343	983	701	3800	1089	486	993	1758	2462	543	1218	1011	2685	Washington, DC
3227	2931	2478	2711	1275	3260	2463	2181	2301	2836	2515	2803	4087	2602	2013	1776	2821	4190	4300	3674	2103	3128	2352	3560	4012	211	2896	3489	2699	3629	2732	3319	2771	3279	2734	Whitehorse, YT
955	154	783	659	1787	740	1195	1910	687	920	1515	732	2088	763	1807	1285	855	1384	2338	612	1121	686	925	709	1288	3207	190	874	657	780	1169	779	276	447	1392	Wichita, KS
2023	1265	1658	748	1285	1192	271	514	1404	715	463	840	3156	639	411	817	1896	1965	3369	2008	457	1909	1660	2105	2583	2433	1430	2172	1698	1794	466	2015	1236	1843	586	Winnemucca, NV
1151	980	380	1473	809	1594	1483	1902	221	1860	1983	1672	2004	1339	1734	820	745	2323	2217	1551	1063	1052	269	1484	1936	2228	820	1413	623	1719	1692	1243	695	1203	1965	Winnipeg, MB
2230	1107	2020	675	1753	556	541	945	1872	317	506	505	3362	752	1013	1285	2092	1268	3588	1309	925	1936	2162	1599	2180	3173	1427	2044	1894	1158	296	2022	1458	1504	291	Yuma, AZ

	Louisville, KY	Mackinaw City, MI	Memphis, TN	Mexico City, DF	Miami, FL	Milwaukee, WI	Minneapolis, MN	Minot, ND	Missoula, MT	Mobile, AL	Monterrey, NL	Montgomery, AL	Montréal, QC	Nashville, TN	Needles, CA	New Orleans, LA	New York, NY	Norfolk, VA	North Platte, NE	Odessa, TX	Oklahoma City, OK	Omaha, NE	Ottawa, ON	Page, AZ	Pendleton, OR	Philadelphia, PA	Phoenix, AZ	Pierre, SD	Pittsburgh, PA	Portland, ME	Portland, OR	Pueblo, CO	Québec, QC	Raleigh, NC	Redding, CA
Louisville, KY		590	385	1988	1079	398	712	1246	1879	625	1410	456	930	177	1841	704	764	659	934	1191	761	701	842	1758	2098	683	1769	1097	393	1097	2305	1148	1087	574	2303
Mackinaw City, MI	590		916	2467	1653	375	521	894	1703	1211	1889	1042	681	763	2261	1290	917	998	1147	1614	1181	869	553	2030	2107	868	2189	968	567	1193	2254	1515	838	959	2516
Memphis, TN	385	916		1605	1024	626	851	1349	1819	398	1027	333	1313	211	1549	392	1113	898	874	808	470	641	1225	1466	2038	1016	1477	1037	776	1445	2245	1028	1470	747	2231
Mexico City, DF	1988	2467	1605		2154	2167	2079	2414	2500	1436	578	1601	2916	1814	1659	1315	2616	2319	1724	1091	1347	1811	2828	1706	2529	2519	1433	2096	2379	2948	2736	1608	3073	2168	2351
Miami, FL	1079	1653	1024	2154		1473	1793	2327	2834	718	1681	691	1640	904	2498	861	1281	950	1889	1672	1493	1656	1611	2415	3053	1180	2375	2052	1173	1585	3260	1999	1787	799	3258
Milwaukee, WI	398	375	626	2167	1473		335	869	1517	1019	1589	850	945	571	1909	1017	912	993	790	1314	881	512	857	1673	1921	863	1814	715	562	1188	2068	1158	1102	910	2159
Minneapolis, MN	712	521	851	2079	1793	335		537	1185	1248	1501	1170	1259	891	1780	1242	1226	1307	661	1216	783	383	1045	1544	1589	1177	1685	486	876	1502	1736	1029	1416	1224	2030
Minot, ND	1246	894	1349	2414	2327	869	537		715	1746	1836	1704	1518	1425	1525	1740	1760	1841	582	1313	1067	713	1390	1380	1119	1711	1653	318	1410	2036	1266	894	1675	1758	1601
Missoula, MT	1879	1703	1819	2500	2834	1517	1185	715		2216	2118	2211	2441	1932	1051	2210	2408	2489	975	1570	1562	1183	2119	906	404	2359	1179	833	2058	2684	551	1006	2598	2406	869
Mobile, AL	625	1211	398	1436	718	1019	1248	1746	2216		963	169	1551	448	1780	143	1202	887	1271	954	805	1038	1490	1697	2450	1101	1657	1434	1009	1558	2657	1281	1708	736	2462
Monterrey, NL	1410	1889	1027	578	1681	1589	1501	1836	2118	963		1128	2338	1236	1284	842	2143	1846	1219	568	769	1233	2250	1331	2114	2046	1058	1518	1801	2475	2321	1127	2495	1695	1976
Montgomery, AL	456	1042	333	1601	691	850	1170	1704	2211	169	1128		1382	279	1837	308	1033	718	1266	1011	802	1033	1321	1754	2430	932	1726	1429	840	1389	2637	1360	1539	567	2519
Montréal, QC	930	681	1313	2916	1640	945	1259	1518	2441	1551	2338	1382		1105	2686	1648	384	734	1580	2039	1606	1302	128	2463	2744	468	2614	1639	612	262	2951	1948	158	853	2949
Nashville, TN	177	763	211	1814	904	571	891	1425	1932	448	1236	279	1105		1758	527	903	688	987	1017	679	754	1017	1675	2151	806	1686	1150	568	1235	2358	1201	1262	537	2356
Needles, CA	1841	2261	1549	1659	2498	1909	1780	1525	1051	1780	1284	1837	2686	1758		1708	2557	2445	1123	943	1079	1401	2598	343	957	2476	226	1387	2186	2883	1135	865	2843	2294	716
New Orleans, LA	704	1290	392	1315	861	1017	1242	1740	2210	143	842	308	1648	527	1708		1323	1026	1281	882	733	1032	1587	1625	2441	1226	1536	1428	1094	1655	2648	1209	1805	875	2390
New York, NY	764	917	1113	2616	1281	912	1226	1760	2408	1202	2143	1033	384	903	2557	1323		375	1547	1919	1477	1269	464	2430	2711	109	2485	1606	389	311	2918	1857	531	494	2916
Norfolk, VA	659	998	898	2319	950	993	1307	1841	2489	887	1846	718	734	688	2445	1026	375		1593	1704	1366	1360	713	2362	2757	278	2373	1687	438	679	2964	1807	881	177	2962
North Platte, NE	934	1147	874	1724	1889	790	661	582	975	1271	1219	1266	1580	987	1123	1281	1547	1593		731	548	282	1492	887	1168	1498	1165	264	1197	1823	1375	372	1737	1522	1373
Odessa, TX	1191	1614	808	1091	1672	1314	1216	1313	1570	954	568	1011	2039	1017	943	882	1919	1704	731		432	897	1951	851	1556	1822	717	995	1582	2251	1763	580	2196	1553	1635
Oklahoma City, OK	761	1181	470	1347	1493	881	783	1067	1562	805	769	802	1606	679	1079	733	1477	1366	548	432		464	1518	996	1708	1396	1007	749	1106	1803	1915	558	1763	1215	1761
Omaha, NE	701	869	641	1811	1656	512	383	713	1183	1038	1233	1033	1302	754	1401	1032	1269	1360	282	897	464		1214	1165	1446	1220	1332	401	919	1545	1653	650	1459	1289	1651
Ottawa, ON	842	553	1225	2828	1611	857	1045	1390	2119	1490	2250	1321	128	1017	2598	1587	464	713	1492	1951	1518	1214		2375	2656	453	2526	1551	551	387	2670	1860	285	824	2861
Page, AZ	1758	2030	1466	1706	2415	1673	1544	1380	906	1697	1331	1754	2463	1675	343	1625	2430	2362	887	851	996	1165	2375		935	2393	273	1151	2103	2706	1142	531	2620	2211	915
Pendleton, OR	2098	2107	2038	2529	3053	1921	1589	1119	404	2450	2114	2430	2744	2151	957	2441	2711	2757	1168	1556	1708	1446	2656	935		2662	1135	1237	2361	2987	207	1152	2901	2686	525
Philadelphia, PA	683	868	1016	2519	1180	863	1177	1711	2359	1101	2046	932	468	806	2476	1226	109	278	1498	1822	1396	1220	453	2393	2662		2404	1557	308	413	2869	1776	615	393	2867
Phoenix, AZ	1769	2189	1477	1433	2375	1814	1685	1653	1179	1657	1058	1726	2614	1686	226	1536	2485	2373	1165	717	1007	1332	2526	273	1135	2404		1429	2114	2811	1337	793	2771	2222	918
Pierre, SD	1097	968	1037	2096	2052	715	486	318	833	1434	1518	1429	1639	1150	1387	1428	1606	1687	264	995	749	401	1551	1151	1237	1557	1429		1256	1882	1384	636	1796	1612	1534
Pittsburgh, PA	393	567	776	2379	1173	562	876	1410	2058	1009	1801	840	612	568	2186	1094	389	438	1197	1582	1106	919	551	2103	2361	308	2114	1256		689	2568	1486	769	499	2566
Portland, ME	1097	1193	1445	2948	1585	1188	1502	2036	2684	1558	2475	1389	262	1235	2883	1655	311	679	1823	2251	1803	1545	387	2706	2987	413	2811	1882	689		3194	2191	276	798	3192
Portland, OR	2305	2254	2245	2736	3260	2068	1736	1266	551	2657	2321	2637	2951	2358	1135	2648	2918	2964	1375	1763	1915	1653	2670	1142	207	2869	1337	1384	2568	3194		1359	3108	2893	421
Pueblo, CO	1148	1515	1028	1608	1999	1158	1029	894	1006	1281	1127	1360	1948	1201	865	1209	1857	1807	372	580	558	650	1860	531	1152	1776	793	636	1486	2191	1359		2105	1736	1357
Québec, QC	1087	838	1470	3073	1787	1102	1416	1675	2598	1708	2495	1539	158	1262	2843	1805	531	881	1737	2196	1763	1459	285	2620	2901	615	2771	1796	769	276	3108	2105		1000	3106
Raleigh, NC	574	959	747	2168	799	910	1224	1758	2406	736	1695	567	853	537	2294	875	494	177	1522	1553	1215	1289	824	2211	2686	393	2222	1612	499	798	2893	1736	1000		2891
Redding, CA	2303	2516	2231	2351	3258	2159	2030	1601	869	2462	1976	2519	2949	2356	716	2390	2916	2962	1373	1635	1761	1651	2861	915	525	2867	918	1534	2566	3192	421	1357	3106	2891	
Regina, SK	1491	1292	1594	2545	2572	1114	782	247	640	1991	2081	1949	1795	1670	1556	1985	2005	2086	827	1516	1312	958	1711	1411	986	1956	1684	563	1655	2058	1133	952	1949	2003	1451
Reno, NV	2107	2320	2035	2168	3062	1963	1834	1405	769	2266	1793	2323	2753	2160	557	2194	2720	2766	1177	1452	1565	1455	2665	719	588	2671	735	1338	2370	2996	578	1161	2910	2695	198
Roanoke, VA	428	813	646	2149	917	764	1078	1612	2260	759	1676	590	800	436	2193	856	475	280	1362	1452	1114	1129	739	2110	2526	378	2121	1466	365	807	2733	1576	957	169	2731
Robbinsville, NC	319	852	451	1907	810	715	1029	1563	2171	475	1434	306	1113	241	1998	614	788	488	1226	1257	919	993	1052	1915	2390	691	1926	1389	559	1120	2597	1440	1270	337	2595
Roswell, NM	1235	1655	943	1232	1818	1355	1257	1282	1394	1100	712	1157	2080	1152	733	1028	1951	1839	698	201	473	877	1992	650	1355	1870	579	962	1580	2277	1562	388	2237	1688	1415
Saginaw, MI	440	192	823	2359	1462	404	718	1252	1900	1063	1781	894	625	615	2153	1142	726	807	1039	1506	1073	761	537	1922	2203	677	2081	1098	376	1002	2410	1407	782	768	2408
St. George, UT	1754	2034	1622	1844	2571	1677	1548	1293	819	1853	1469	1910	2467	1807	233	1781	2434	2413	891	1007	1152	1169	2379	156	848	2382	411	1155	2084	2710	1055	736	2624	2342	760
St. Louis, MO	263	683	284	1784	1218	383	578	1148	1618	681	1206	595	1108	316	1578	675	979	922	673	931	498	440	1020	1495	1837	898	1506	836	608	1305	2044	887	1265	851	2042
Salt Lake City, UT	1584	1797	1524	1977	2539	1440	1311	998	524	1936	1562	1916	2230	1637	528	1927	2197	2243	654	1004	1194	932	2142	383	553	2148	656	815	1847	2473	760	638	2387	2172	719
San Antonio, TX	1114	1593	731	874	1385	1293	1205	1540	1824	667	296	832	2042	940	1220	546	1847	1550	925	354	473	937	1954	1167	1970	1750	994	1222	1505	2179	2177	833	2199	1399	1912
San Diego, CA	2122	2487	1830	1725	2667	2130	2001	1746	1272	1949	1350	2018	2920	2039	324	1828	2838	2726	1344	1009	1360	1622	2832	609	1102	2757	353	1608	2467	3163	1091	1146	3077	2575	672
San Francisco, CA	2331	2544	2111	2184	3060	2187	2058	1629	993	2342	1809	2399	2977	2320	562	2270	2944	2990	1401	1468	1641	1679	2889	847	812	2895	751	1562	2594	3220	636	1385	3134	2856	217
Sault Ste. Marie, ON	648	58	974	2525	1711	404	550	895	1624	1269	1947	1100	623	821	2319	1348	937	1056	1205	1672	1239	927	495	2088	2028	926	2247	997	625	882	2175	1573	780	1017	2574
Savannah, GA	656	1147	643	1936	483	1052	1384	1918	2425	539	1463	335	1163	495	2191	643	804	473	1480	1346	1112	1247	1134	2108	2644	703	2119	1643	696	1108	2851	1694	1310	322	2849
Seattle, WA	2359	2183	2299	2806	3314	1997	1665	1195	480	2727	2391	2691	2921	2412	1234	2718	2888	2969	1445	1833	1985	1663	2599	1212	277	2839	1412	1313	2538	3164	175	1429	3078	2886	596
Shreveport, LA	718	1231	335	1202	1130	925	981	1439	1955	412	705	469	1646	544	1368	344	1444	1166	941	542	393	731	1558	1285	2101	1347	1257	1127	1109	1776	2308	869	1803	1015	2050
Sioux City, IA	791	782	731	1901	1746	529	300	618	1088	1128	1323	1123	1361	844	1496	1122	1328	1391	377	987	554	95	1273	1260	1492	1279	1427	306	978	1604	1639	745	1518	1306	1746
Sioux Falls, SD	876	751	816	1986	1831	498	269	536	1006	1213	1408	1208	1422	929	1517	1207	1389	1470	398	1072	639	180	1334	1281	1410	1340	1559	224	1039	1665	1557	766	1579	1391	1707
Spokane, WA	2078	1902	2018	2699	3033	1716	1384	914	199	2415	2317	2410	2640	2131	1250	2409	2607	2688	1174	1769	1761	1382	2318	1105	205	2558	1378	1032	2257	2883	352	1205	2797	2605	670
Springfield, MO	475	895	285	1574	1346	595	606	1064	1534	682	996	617	1320	444	1368	676	1191	1134	589	721	288	356	1232	1285	1753	1110	1296	752	820	1517	1960	784	1477	979	1958
Sturgis, SD	1244	1115	1184	2036	2199	862	633	381	635	1581	1654	1576	1786	1297	1149	1575	1753	1834	371	1007	885	548	1698	1004	1039	1704	1303	176	1403	2029	1186	510	1943	1759	1361
Sudbury, ON	827	242	1158	2709	1724	588	734	1079	1808	1450	2131	1281	436	1002	2503	1529	759	917	1389	1856	1423	1111	308	2272	2212	748	2431	1181	557	695	2359	1757	593	978	2758
Tallahassee, FL	669	1255	546	1676	478	1063	1383	1917	2424	240	1203	213	1456	492	2020	383	1097	766	1479	1194	1015	1246	1427	1937	2643	996	1897	1642	912	1401	2850	1521	1603	615	2702
Tampa, FL	876	1450	821	1951	254	1270	1590	2124	2631	515	1478	488	1495	701	2295	658	1136	805	1686	1469	1290	1453	1466	2212	2850	1035	2172	1849	1028	1440	3057	1796	1642	654	3055
Thunder Bay, ON	958	499	1153	2421	2039	581	345	652	1391	1550	1843	1416	1002	1137	2122	1544	1343	1497	1003	1558	1125	725	918	1886	1795	1332	2027	828	1066	1265	1942	1371	1156	1458	2206
Toronto, ON	597	483	980	2583	1493	612	926	1460	2108	1220	2005	1051	333	772	2353	1299	528	685	1247	1706	1273	969	245	2130	2411	517	2281	1306	326	592	2618	1615	490	747	2616
Tulsa, OK	658	1078	406	1413	1429	778	690	1145	1579	725	835	738	1503	615	1185	692	1374	1302	565	538	105	437	1415	1102	1725	1293	1113	766	1003	1700	1932	622	1660	1151	1930
Twin Falls, ID	1767	1865	1707	2198	2722	1623	1347	948	389	2119	1783	2099	2413	1820	614	2110	2380	2426	837	1225	1377	1115	2325	604	343	2331	792	995	2030	2656	550	821	2570	2355	653
Vancouver, BC	2497	2321	2437	2944	3452	2135	1803	1294	618	2865	2529	2829	2865	2550	1372	2856	3026	3107	1583	1971	2123	1801	2781	1350	415	2977	1550	1451	2676	3302	318	1567	3019	3024	739
Washington, DC	615	812	874	2377	1044	807	1121	1655	2303	965	1904	796	596	664	2421	1084	237	196	1442	1680	1342	1164	569	2338	2606	136	2349	1501	252	541	2813	1720	743	257	2811
Whitehorse, YT	3246	3018	3349	4256	4327	2869	2537	2002	1831	3746	3775	3704	3521	3425	2844	3740	3760	3841	2632	3227	3219	2713	3437	2699	1864	3711	2972	2318	3410	3784	1767	2663	3675	3758	2188
Wichita, KS	707	1088	580	1504	1603	758	629	910	1405	899	926	912	1521	698	1128	890	1416	1366	391	590	157	310	1433	1045	1551	1335	1056	592	1045	1742	1758	428	1678	1233	1756
Winnemucca, NV	1943	2156	1883	2189	2898	1799	1670	1241	605	2295	1814	2275	2589	1996	578	2286	2556	2602	1013	1357	1553	1291	2501	639	424	2507	756	1174	2206	2832	512	997	2746	2531	360
Winnipeg, MB	1170	935	1273	2443	2251	793	461	297	987	1670	1865	1628	1438	1349	1804	1664	1684	1765	831	1529	1096	637	1354	1659	1341	1635	1996	552	1334	1701	1488	1203	1592	1682	1880
Yuma, AZ	1950	2370	1658	1553	2495	1995	1866	1709	1235	1777	1178	1846	2795	1867	184	1656	2666	2554	1346	837	1188	1513	2707	454	1141	2585	181	1610	2295	2992	1258	974	2952	2403	839

Regina, SK	Reno, NV	Roanoke, VA	Robbinsville, NC	Roswell, NM	Saginaw, MI	St. George, UT	St. Louis, MO	Salt Lake City, UT	San Antonio, TX	San Diego, CA	San Francisco, CA	Sault Ste. Marie, ON	Savannah, GA	Seattle, WA	Shreveport, LA	Sioux City, IA	Sioux Falls, SD	Spokane, WA	Springfield, MO	Sturgis, SD	Sudbury, ON	Tallahassee, FL	Tampa, FL	Thunder Bay, ON	Toronto, ON	Tulsa, OK	Twin Falls, ID	Vancouver, BC	Washington, DC	Whitehorse, YT	Wichita, KS	Winnemucca, NV	Winnipeg, MB	Yuma, AZ	
1491	2107	428	319	1235	440	1754	263	1584	1114	2122	2331	648	656	2359	718	791	876	2078	475	1244	827	669	876	958	597	658	1767	2497	615	3246	707	1943	1170	1950	Louisville, KY
1292	2320	813	852	1655	192	2034	683	1797	1593	2487	2544	58	1147	2183	1231	782	751	1902	895	1115	242	1255	1450	499	483	1078	1865	2321	812	3018	1088	2156	935	2370	Mackinaw City, MI
1594	2035	646	451	943	823	1622	284	1524	731	1830	2111	974	643	2299	335	731	816	2018	285	1184	1158	546	821	1153	980	406	1707	2437	874	3349	580	1883	1273	1658	Memphis, TN
2545	2168	2149	1907	1232	2359	1844	1784	1977	874	1725	2184	2525	1936	2806	1202	1901	1986	2699	1574	2036	2709	1676	1951	2421	2583	1413	2198	2944	2377	4256	1504	2189	2443	1553	Mexico City, DF
2572	3062	917	810	1818	1462	2571	1218	2539	1385	2667	3060	1711	483	3314	1130	1746	1831	3033	1346	2199	1724	478	254	2039	1493	1429	2722	3452	1044	4327	1603	2898	2251	2495	Miami, FL
1114	1963	764	715	1355	404	1677	383	1440	1293	2130	2187	404	1052	1997	925	529	498	1716	595	862	588	1063	1270	581	612	778	1623	2135	807	2869	758	1799	793	1995	Milwaukee, WI
782	1834	1078	1029	1257	718	1548	578	1311	1205	2001	2058	550	1384	1665	981	300	269	1384	606	633	734	1383	1590	345	926	690	1347	1803	1121	2537	629	1670	461	1866	Minneapolis, MN
247	1405	1612	1563	1282	1252	1293	1148	998	1540	1746	1629	895	1918	1195	1439	618	536	914	1064	381	1079	1917	2124	652	1460	1145	948	1294	1655	2002	910	1241	297	1709	Minot, ND
640	769	2260	2171	1394	1900	819	1618	524	1824	1272	993	1624	2425	480	1955	1088	1006	199	1534	635	1808	2424	2631	1391	2108	1579	389	618	2303	1831	1405	605	987	1235	Missoula, MT
1991	2266	759	475	1100	1063	1853	681	1936	667	1949	2342	1269	539	2727	412	1128	1213	2415	682	1581	1450	240	515	1550	1220	725	2119	2865	965	3746	899	2295	1670	1777	Mobile, AL
2081	1793	1676	1434	712	1781	1469	1206	1562	296	1350	1809	1947	1463	2391	705	1323	1408	2317	996	1654	2131	1203	1478	1843	2005	835	1783	2529	1904	3775	926	1814	1865	1178	Monterrey, NL
1949	2323	590	306	1157	894	1910	595	1916	832	2018	2399	1100	335	2691	469	1123	1208	2410	617	1576	1281	213	488	1416	1051	738	2099	2829	796	3704	912	2275	1628	1846	Montgomery, AL
1795	2753	800	1113	2080	625	2467	1108	2230	2042	2920	2977	623	1163	2921	1646	1361	1422	2640	1320	1786	436	1456	1495	1002	333	1503	2413	2865	596	3521	1521	2589	1438	2795	Montréal, QC
1670	2160	436	241	1152	615	1807	316	1637	940	2039	2320	821	495	2412	544	844	929	2131	444	1297	1002	492	701	1137	772	615	1820	2550	664	3425	698	1996	1349	1867	Nashville, TN
1556	557	2193	1998	733	2153	233	1578	528	1220	324	562	2319	2191	1234	1368	1496	1517	1250	1368	1149	2503	2020	2295	2122	2353	1185	614	1372	2421	2844	1128	578	1804	184	Needles, CA
1985	2194	856	614	1028	1142	1781	675	1927	546	1828	2270	1348	643	2718	344	1122	1207	2409	676	1575	1529	383	658	1544	1299	692	2110	2856	1084	3740	890	2286	1664	1656	New Orleans, LA
2005	2720	475	788	1951	726	2434	979	2197	1847	2838	2944	937	804	2888	1444	1328	1389	2607	1191	1753	759	1097	1136	1343	528	1374	2380	3026	237	3760	1416	2556	1684	2666	New York, NY
2086	2766	280	488	1839	807	2413	922	2243	1550	2726	2990	1056	473	2969	1166	1391	1470	2688	1134	1834	917	766	805	1497	685	1302	2426	3107	196	3841	1366	2602	1765	2554	Norfolk, VA
827	1177	1362	1226	698	1039	891	673	654	925	1344	1401	1205	1480	1445	941	377	398	1174	589	371	1389	1479	1686	1003	1247	565	837	1583	1442	2632	391	1013	831	1346	North Platte, NE
1516	1452	1452	1257	201	1506	1007	931	1004	354	1009	1468	1672	1346	1833	542	987	1072	1769	721	1007	1856	1194	1469	1558	1706	538	1225	1971	1680	3227	590	1357	1529	837	Odessa, TX
1312	1565	1114	919	473	1073	1152	498	1194	473	1360	1641	1239	1112	1985	393	554	639	1761	288	885	1423	1015	1290	1125	1273	105	1377	2123	1342	3219	157	1553	1096	1188	Oklahoma City, OK
958	1455	1129	993	877	761	1169	440	932	937	1622	1679	927	1247	1663	731	95	180	1382	356	548	1111	1246	1453	725	969	437	1115	1801	1164	2713	310	1291	637	1513	Omaha, NE
1711	2665	739	1052	1992	537	2379	1020	2142	1954	2832	2889	495	1134	2599	1558	1273	1334	2318	1232	1698	308	1427	1466	918	245	1415	2325	2781	569	3437	1433	2501	1354	2707	Ottawa, ON
1411	719	2110	1915	650	1922	156	1495	383	1167	609	847	2088	2108	1212	1285	1260	1281	1105	1285	1004	2272	1937	2212	1886	2130	1102	604	1350	2338	2699	1045	639	1659	454	Page, AZ
986	588	2526	2390	1355	2203	848	1837	553	1970	1102	812	2028	2644	277	2101	1492	1410	205	1753	1039	2212	2643	2850	1795	2411	1725	343	415	2606	1864	1551	424	1341	1141	Pendleton, OR
1956	2671	378	691	1870	677	2382	898	2148	1750	2757	2895	926	703	2839	1347	1279	1340	2558	1110	1704	748	996	1035	1332	517	1293	2331	2977	136	3711	1335	2507	1635	2585	Philadelphia, PA
1684	735	2121	1926	579	2081	411	1506	656	994	353	751	2247	2119	1412	1257	1427	1559	1378	1296	1303	2431	1897	2172	2027	2281	1113	792	1550	2349	2972	1056	756	1996	181	Phoenix, AZ
563	1338	1466	1389	962	1098	1155	836	815	1222	1608	1562	997	1643	1313	1127	306	224	1032	752	176	1181	1642	1849	828	1306	766	995	1451	1501	2318	592	1174	552	1610	Pierre, SD
1655	2370	365	559	1580	376	2084	608	1847	1505	2467	2594	625	696	2538	1109	978	1039	2257	820	1403	557	912	1028	1066	326	1003	2030	2676	252	3410	1045	2206	1334	2295	Pittsburgh, PA
2058	2996	807	1120	2277	1002	2710	1305	2473	2179	3163	3220	882	1108	3164	1776	1604	1665	2883	1517	2029	695	1401	1440	1265	592	1700	2656	3302	541	3784	1742	2832	1701	2992	Portland, ME
1133	578	2733	2597	1562	2410	1055	2044	760	2177	1091	636	2175	2851	175	2308	1639	1557	352	1960	1186	2359	2850	3057	1942	2618	1932	550	318	2813	1767	1758	512	1488	1258	Portland, OR
952	1161	1576	1440	388	1407	736	887	638	833	1146	1385	1573	1694	1429	869	745	766	1205	784	510	1757	1521	1796	1371	1615	622	821	1567	1720	2663	428	997	1203	974	Pueblo, CO
1949	2910	957	1270	2237	782	2624	1265	2387	2199	3077	3134	780	1310	3078	1803	1518	1579	2797	1477	1943	593	1603	1642	1156	490	1660	2570	3019	743	3675	1678	2746	1592	2952	Québec, QC
2003	2695	169	337	1688	768	2342	851	2172	1399	2575	2856	1017	322	2886	1015	1306	1391	2605	979	1759	978	615	654	1458	747	1151	2355	3024	257	3758	1233	2531	1682	2403	Raleigh, NC
1451	198	2731	2595	1415	2408	760	2042	719	1912	672	217	2574	2849	596	2050	1746	1707	670	1958	1361	2758	2702	3055	2206	2616	1930	653	739	2811	2188	1756	360	1880	839	Redding, CA
	1436	1857	1808	1340	1497	1324	1393	1029	1785	1777	1660	1234	2163	1062	1684	863	781	781	1309	508	1416	2162	2369	793	1655	1390	979	1072	1900	1759	1155	1272	357	1740	Regina, SK
1436		2535	2399	1219	2212	564	1846	523	1729	565	224	2378	2653	753	1854	1550	1511	793	1762	1165	2562	2506	2859	2010	2420	1734	457	896	2615	2345	1560	164	1684	684	Reno, NV
1857	2535		321	1587	622	2182	691	2012	1380	2474	2755	871	440	2740	977	1160	1245	2459	878	1613	844	656	772	1312	612	1050	2195	2878	236	3612	1135	2371	1536	2302	Roanoke, VA
1808	2399	321		1392	661	2046	555	1876	1138	2279	2560	910	390	2651	732	1083	1168	2370	683	1536	1048	414	607	1275	818	855	2059	2789	549	3563	937	2235	1487	2107	Robbinsville, NC
1340	1219	1587	1392		1547	806	972	803	535	871	1295	1713	1492	1632	688	972	1019	1593	762	898	1897	1340	1615	1599	1747	579	1024	1770	1815	3051	631	1156	1455	699	Roswell, NM
1497	2212	622	661	1547		1926	575	1689	1485	2379	2436	250	956	2380	1123	820	881	2099	787	1245	434	1066	1259	691	292	970	1872	2518	621	3252	980	2048	1127	2262	Saginaw, MI
1324	564	2182	2046	806	1926		1493	296	1405	454	692	2092	2300	1125	1441	1264	1285	1018	1390	917	2276	2093	2368	1890	2134	1320	517	1263	2326	2612	1146	484	1572	417	St. George, UT
1393	1846	691	555	972	575	1493		1323	910	1859	2070	741	809	2098	542	530	615	1817	212	983	925	808	1015	869	775	395	1506	2236	878	3148	446	1682	1072	1687	St. Louis, MO
1029	523	2012	1876	803	1689	296	1323		1320	749	747	1855	2130	830	1587	1027	988	723	1239	642	2039	2129	2336	1653	1897	1211	222	968	2092	2317	1037	359	1277	712	Salt Lake City, UT
1785	1729	1380	1138	535	1485	1405	910	1320		1286	1745	1651	1167	2247	409	1027	1112	2023	700	1358	1835	907	1182	1547	1709	539	1639	2385	1608	3481	630	1750	1569	1114	San Antonio, TX
1777	565	2474	2279	871	2379	454	1859	749	1286		505	2545	2353	1266	1549	1717	1738	1471	1649	1370	2729	2189	2464	2343	2587	1466	835	1409	2702	2858	1409	678	2025	172	San Diego, CA
1660	224	2755	2560	1295	2436	692	2070	747	1745	505		2602	2753	811	1930	1774	1735	885	1930	1389	2786	2582	2857	2234	2644	1747	681	954	2839	2403	1784	388	1908	672	San Francisco, CA
1234	2378	871	910	1713	250	2092	741	1855	1651	2545	2602		1205	2104	1289	811	780	1823	953	1144	184	1313	1508	441	423	1136	1786	2304	870	2960	1146	2214	877	2428	Sault Ste. Marie, ON
2163	2653	440	390	1492	956	2300	809	2130	1167	2353	2753	1205		2905	804	1337	1422	2624	937	1790	1247	299	338	1630	1016	1048	2313	3043	567	3918	1222	2489	1842	2181	Savannah, GA
1062	753	2740	2651	1632	2380	1125	2098	830	2247	1266	811	2104	2905		2378	1568	1486	281	2014	1115	2288	2904	3111	1871	2588	2002	620	143	2783	1592	1828	701	1417	1433	Seattle, WA
1684	1854	977	732	688	1123	1441	542	1587	409	1549	1930	1289	804	2378		821	906	2154	405	1274	1473	652	927	1323	1313	352	1770	2516	1205	3439	550	1946	1363	1377	Shreveport, LA
863	1550	1160	1083	972	820	1264	530	1027	1027	1717	1774	811	1337	1568	821		85	1287	446	453	995	1336	1543	642	1028	527	1210	1706	1223	2618	400	1386	542	1608	Sioux City, IA
781	1511	1245	1168	1019	881	1285	615	988	1112	1738	1735	780	1422	1486	906	85		1205	531	371	964	1421	1628	611	1089	612	1168	1624	1284	2536	485	1347	460	1740	Sioux Falls, SD
781	793	2459	2370	1593	2099	1018	1817	723	2023	1471	885	1823	2624	281	2154	1287	1205		1733	834	2007	2623	2830	1590	2307	1778	548	419	2502	1690	1604	629	1136	1434	Spokane, WA
1309	1762	878	683	762	787	1390	212	1239	700	1649	1930	953	937	2014	405	446	531	1733		899	1137	830	1143	948	987	185	1422	2152	1090	3064	258	1598	988	1477	Springfield, MO
508	1165	1613	1536	898	1245	917	983	642	1358	1370	1389	1144	1790	1115	1274	453	371	834	899		1328	1789	1996	975	1453	902	797	1253	1648	2292	728	1001	689	1333	Sturgis, SD
1416	2562	844	1048	1897	434	2276	925	2039	1835	2729	2786	184	1247	2288	1473	995	964	2007	1137	1328		1453	1579	623	245	1320	1970	2486	731	3142	1330	2398	1059	2612	Sudbury, ON
2162	2506	656	414	1340	1066	2093	808	2129	907	2189	2582	1313	299	2904	652	1336	1421	2623	830	1789	1453		275	1629	1223	951	2312	3042	860	3917	1125	2488	1841	2017	Tallahassee, FL
2369	2859	772	607	1615	1259	2368	1015	2336	1182	2464	2857	1508	338	3111	927	1543	1628	2830	1143	1996	1579	275		1836	1348	1226	2519	3249	899	4124	1400	2695	2048	2292	Tampa, FL
793	2010	1312	1275	1599	691	1890	869	1653	1547	2343	2234	441	1630	1871	1323	642	611	1590	948	975	623	1629	1836		862	1032	1553	1863	1311	2519	971	1846	436	2208	Thunder Bay, ON
1655	2420	612	818	1747	292	2134	775	1897	1709	2587	2644	423	1016	2588	1313	1028	1089	2307	987	1453	245	1223	1348	862		1170	2080	2725	499	3381	1188	2256	1298	2462	Toronto, ON
1390	1734	1050	855	579	970	1320	395	1211	539	1466	1747	1136	1048	2002	352	527	612	1778	185	902	1320	951	1226	1032	1170		1394	2140	1278	3145	174	1570	1069	1294	Tulsa, OK
979	457	2195	2059	1024	1872	517	1506	222	1639	835	681	1786	2313	620	1770	1210	1168	548	1422	797	1970	2312	2519	1553	2080	1394		758	2275	2207	1220	293	1227	798	Twin Falls, ID
1072	896	2878	2789	1770	2518	1263	2236	968	2385	1409	954	2304	3043	143	2516	1706	1624	419	2152	1253	2486	3042	3249	1863	2725	2140	758		2921	1518	1966	839	1427	1576	Vancouver, BC
1900	2615	236	549	1815	621	2326	878	2092	1608	2702	2839	870	567	2783	1205	1223	1284	2502	1090	1648	731	860	899	1311	499	1278	2275	2921		3655	1279	2451	1579	2530	Washington, DC
1759	2345	3612	3563	3051	3252	2612	3148	2317	3481	2858	2403	2960	3918	1592	3439	2618	2536	1690	3064	2292	3142	3917	4124	2519	3381	3145	2207	1518	3655		3062	2288	2083	3028	Whitehorse, YT
1155	1560	1135	937	631	980	1146	446	1037	630	1409	1784	1146	1222	1828	550	400	485	1604	258	728	1330	1125	1400	971	1188	174	1220	1966	1279	3062		1396	906	1237	Wichita, KS
1272	164	2371	2235	1156	2048	484	1682	359	1750	678	388	2214	2489	701	1946	1386	1347	629	1598	1001	2398	2488	2695	1846	2256	1570	293	839	2451	2288	1396		1520	762	Winnemucca, NV
357	1684	1536	1487	1455	1127	1572	1072	1277	1569	2025	1908	877	1842	1417	1363	542	460	1136	988	689	1059	1841	2048	436	1298	1069	1227	1427	1579	2083	906	1520		1988	Winnipeg, MB
1740	684	2302	2107	699	2262	417	1687	712	1114	172	672	2428	2181	1433	1377	1608	1740	1434	1477	1333	2612	2017	2292	2208	2462	1294	798	1576	2530	3028	1237	762	1988		Yuma, AZ

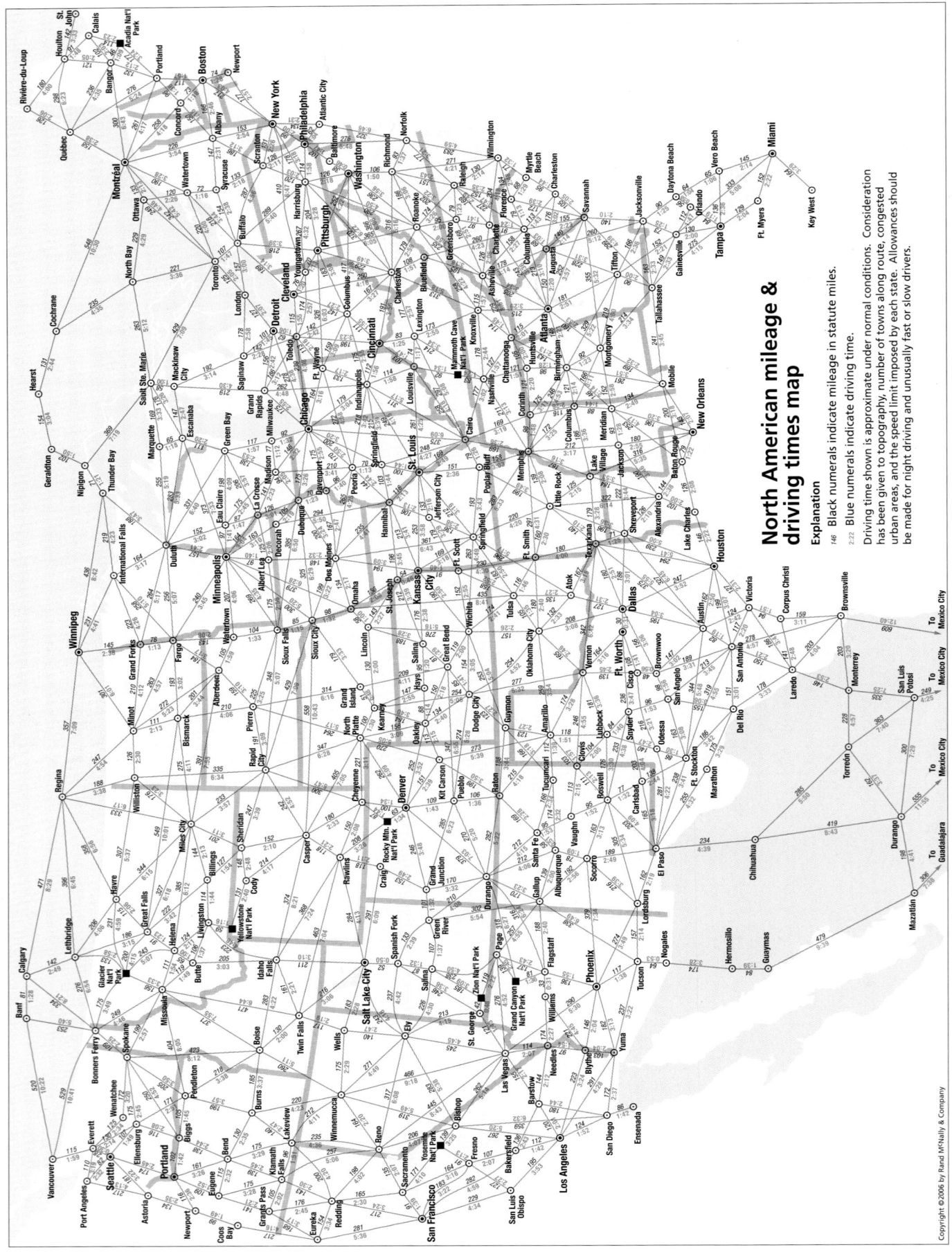

North American mileage & driving times map

Explanation

146 Black numerals indicate mileage in statute miles.

2:22 Blue numerals indicate driving time.

Driving time shown is approximate under normal conditions. Consideration has been given to topography, number of towns along route, congested urban areas, and the speed limit imposed by each state. Allowances should be made for night driving and unusually fast or slow drivers.

5. Olympic National Park

Near Port Angeles, Washington
(P. 218, E-4)

Established: 1938
Visitors in 2004: 3,073,722
Website: www.nps.gov/olym
Visitor Information: 360-565-3130

Ride: Washington Highway 101 from Sequim skirts the northern edge of the park, past falls and forest en route to the Pacific.

In northwest Washington, 60-plus miles of Pacific Ocean coastline, inland temperate rainforest, and glacier-capped mountains combine to offer incredible ecological diversity in nearly one million acres. Watch huge banana slugs slime over rainforest paths and hike or drive to high mountain vistas.

Don't miss: Wading in the Hole in the Wall tidal pools; nature walks through the Hoh Rain Forest; rafting on the Elwha River; gazing at the glaciers from Hurricane Ridge.

6. Yellowstone National Park

Northwestern Wyoming & parts of Montana and Idaho
(P. 234, B-5)

Established: 1872
Visitors in 2004: 2,868,317
Website: www.nps.gov/yell
Visitor Information: 307-344-7381

Ride: Take the park loop (US 89) and pull over to watch bison, check out Yellowstone Lake, and smell and see the bubbling sulphurous thermal pools.

Dotted by more than 10,000 thermal features like mudpots, hot springs, and geysers (including Old Faithful), Yellowstone's landscape is at once eerie and serene. Wildlife to watch for includes wolves, grizzly bears, elk, bison, and osprey. Backcountry trails thread through the more than 2.2 million acres.

Don't miss: Old Faithful Geyser erupting every 80 minutes; massive white travertine terraces at Mammoth Hot Springs; colorful vistas at Grand Canyon of the Yellowstone; winter snowcoach tour of the park for wildlife viewing.

7. Rocky Mountain National Park

Near Estes Park and Grand Lake, Colorado
(P. 42, C-12)

Established: 1915
Visitors in 2004: 2,781,899
Website: www.nps.gov/romo
Visitor Information: 970-586-1206

Ride: Trail Ridge Road (US 34) hugs the edge of Arapaho National Forest before climbing the lofty heights past several of the Rockies signature 10,000-plus-foot peaks.

Colorado is known for its 54 "Fourteeners" mountain peaks that rise 14,000 feet or higher. This park claims more than 60 peaks at more than 12,000 feet and the northernmost Fourteener, Longs Peak. Hike some of the 359 miles of trails, fly fish, or spot some of the amazing wildlife: Rocky Mountain bighorn sheep, mule deer, elk, moose, and eagles.

Don't miss: Longs Peak trail to Chasm Lake and the boulder field; snowshoeing in the Kawuneeche Valley; wildflower walks in the meadows in spring and summer; spectacular mountain vistas from Trail Ridge Road, the highest continuous paved road in the U.S.

8. Zion National Park

Near Springdale, Utah
(P. 207, M-5)

Established: 1919
Visitors in 2004: 2,677,342
Website: www.nps.gov/zion
Visitor Information: 435-772-3256

Ride: Take the Zion Canyon Scenic Drive from the south entrance, winding up the switchbacks along the Zion-Mt. Carmel Highway. The mountain views are spectacular.

From the majestic 6,700-plus foot white peak of Great White Throne to the 21 switchbacks of Walter's Wiggles that climb up nearly 1,500 feet to Angel's Landing, this is a hiker's and rock climber's paradise. The 229 square miles of park preserve an amazing array of flora and fauna, including 290 species of birds.

Don't miss: The 10-mile scenic drive through tunnels and switchbacks on the Zion-Mt. Carmel highway; hiking in summer through the Narrows, a slot canyon that the icy-cold Virgin River flows through; narration from the witty, wise drivers of the park's shuttle bus system.

9. Grand Teton National Park

Northwestern Wyoming
(P. 234, C-5)

Established: 1929
Visitors in 2004: 2,360,373
Website: www.nps.gov/grte
Visitor Information: 307-739-3300

Ride: Take US 89 through the flathead valley, pausing to look west at the Tetons and the Snake River flowing through the valley.

Sandwiched between the swanky town of Jackson Hole and Yellowstone National Park, Grand Teton holds its own. The Snake River cuts through the flatlands and meadows, with eight 12,000-plus foot peaks of the Tetons rising to the west. Hikers, rafters, and paddlers enjoy exploring the trails, lakes, and streams.

Don't miss: Rafting on the Snake River; searching for moose near Willow Flats; watching the sunset from Signal Mountain summit; snowshoeing with a park ranger in winter; wildflower walks in the valley in late spring.

10. Acadia National Park

Bar Harbor, Maine
(P. 92, F-7)

Established: 1919
Visitors in 2004: 2,207,847
Website: www.nps.gov/acad
Visitor Information: 207-288-3338

Ride: Follow Maine Highway 3 as it loops around the northern section of Mount Desert Island, past Otter Cliffs and Thunder Hole and overlooking the Atlantic Ocean.

Originally Lafayette National Park, Acadia is the first national park established east of the Mississippi River. It perches on the Maine coast and was once a playground for the wealthy. Today, its 47,000 acres harbor tidepools, woods, and mountain peaks. Hikers like to climb Cadillac Mountain to watch the rays of the sun first touch the U.S.

Don't miss: Shore walk at Sand Beach; horsedrawn carriage rides at Wildwood Stable; biking along the 44 miles of carriage trails built by John D. Rockefeller; high cliffs and rocky coastline along the 27-mile Park Loop Road; fall foliage hikes in October.